IMĀM AL-BUKHĀRĪ

Al-Adab al-Mufrad

WITH FULL COMMENTARY

A Perfect Code of
Manners and Morality

ADIL SALAHI

Imām al-Bukhārī Al-Adab al-Mufrad with full commentary
A Perfect Code of Manners and Morality

First published in England by

The Islamic Foundation
Markfield Conference Centre
Ratby lane, Markfield
Leicestershire LE67 9SY
United Kingdom
Website: www.Islamic-foundation.com
Email: publications@islamic-foundation.com

Quran House, Po Box 30611, Nairobi, Kenya
P.M.B 3193, Kano, Nigeria

Distributed by
Kube Publishing Ltd
Tel: +44 (0) 1530 249230
Fax: +44 (0) 1530 249656
Email: info@kubepublishing.com

With special thank you for the immense contribution of ICMG Youth Australia.

Cataloguing-in-Publication Data is available from the British library
ISBN 978-0-86037-614-9 casebound
ISBN 978-0-86037-609-5 paperback
ISBN 978-0-86037-619-4 ebook

Cover Design & Typesetting: Nasir Cadir

Printed by: Elma Basim, Turkey

About the Publishers

THE ISLAMIC FOUNDATION was established in 1973 to promote scholarly research and publication, as well as building bridges between Muslims and non-Muslims through respectful and informed dialogue. Since its inception, the Foundation has developed its national and international standing through the character, variety and scope of its activities. Its publishing imprint, now managed by Kube Publishing Ltd, currently has over 300 published titles. The Foundation is based in Markfield in the United Kingdom.

ISLAMIC COMMUNITY MILLI GORUS (ICMG) AUSTRALIA is an Islamic organization that caters for the social-religious and cultural needs of Muslims on a global platform. ICMG Australia emphasizes the moral and spiritual strength of Islam and endeavours to improve and protect the fundamental rights of Muslims through its multi-dimensional structure.

It has been successful in establishing educational institutions as well as providing social interactive services such as youth programs, community management and humanitarian aid. With its primary objective of teaching Islam and conveying it to subsequent generations, ICMG Australia is at the forefront of developing tomorrow's leaders today. ICMG also acknowledges the great support by ICMG Youth Australia.

Dedication

To Hayfa, my wife, who has always given me
encouragement and valued support,
without which I could not have produced this work.

To Abd al-Rahman and Sundus, my grandchildren.
They will do well to observe Islamic manners and morality.

Contents

Foreword

PROPHET MUHAMMAD (PEACE BE UPON HIM) always used concise language, preferring to impart his meaning in fewer words. He was recognised as the most eloquent of people at a time when the Arabs greatly valued fine speech and celebrated poets and poetry. When translating the text of his statements it is necessary sometimes to add some explanatory words. I have indicated such additions by placing them within square brackets. I have used ordinary brackets for any addition or explanatory phrases already used in the Arabic text, either by Imam al-Bukhari himself or a narrator of the *ḥadīth* in question.

Imam al-Bukhari divided this anthology into 644 chapters, giving each chapter a title. Whilst hardly any chapter included more than four *ḥadīths*, some chapters included only one. Moreover, his titles often highlight a point in the *ḥadīth*, or draw attention to the reason he enters the *ḥadīth* at a particular point. As such matters are fully apparent in the commentary, I have dispensed with these titles.

A problem that I had to wrestle with is how to divide the book into chapters dealing with main subjects. This is due to the fact that the way Imam al-Bukhari divided his chapters enabled him to include some chapters on one topic, then move to another, and then come back to a different aspect of the earlier topic. To treat each main topic in an integrated chapter would necessitate a rearrangement of the *ḥadīths* included in the anthology. I felt that this would cause more problems than it would solve. I have, therefore, opted to retain the arrangement of the anthology, using subtitles to indicate change to a fresh point. I realise that such division is not particularly accurate, and indeed I have had to use the heading 'miscellaneous' more than once. I hope that my readers will overlook any shortcoming in my work.

Imam al-Bukhari enters certain *ḥadīths* more than once in his anthology, often under different headings. When he repeats a *ḥadīth* under the same heading, his reason is either to give a different chain of transmission or to give a slightly different version that highlights a different point. I give the new number of the *ḥadīth* and mention the earlier number for reference to text and commentary. However, sometimes I have given the new text in full, when there is difference in text, and may add some explanation on the relevance of the *ḥadīth* to the chapter in which it occurs a second or third time.

When a *ḥadīth* refers to several points and Imam al-Bukhari enters it under a topic relating to the main point of the *ḥadīth*, my commentary is not limited to that point. I explain the other points as necessary. On the other hand, I may list several *ḥadīths* and explain them together when they are closely interlinked. Readers will note that some *ḥadīths* are given long commentary while others have short explanations. This is simply due to the issues addressed.

A considerable portion of this work was written in the form of articles published in the Saudi daily newspaper *Arab News*, in a series under the heading of, 'Guidance from the Prophet'. This was published in my twice-weekly column 'Islam in Perspective' which I wrote and edited during the period between 1980 to 2011. I am indebted to *Arab News*, its publishers and Chief Editors for giving me the opportunity to make this contribution. I look back with fond memories on my association with the *Arab News*.

In writing this commentary I relied heavily on the scholarly work of Fadlullah al-Jaylani, *Fadl Allah al-Samad fi Sharh al-Adab al-Mufrad*, and I referred to the commentaries on the major *Ḥadīth* anthologies. In translating the text of the *ḥadīths,* I referred to, and benefited by, the translation of *Al-Adab al-Mufrad* published by the UK Islamic Academy; but I did not restrict myself to it, preferring to rely mainly on my earlier translation and to amend it where the Academy's translation provided improvement.

Adil Salahi
London, 2 May 2017

Introduction

Ḥadīth: Verification and Acceptability

Although at the time of the Prophet, few Arabs were able to read and write – indeed, the overwhelming majority, including the Prophet himself, were unlettered – nevertheless, a number of his companions were literate and it was they who were entrusted with the task of writing down the Qur'an. Whenever the Prophet received Qur'anic revelations, he ordered one of them to commit it to writing. Thus, after the Prophet passed away, his companions were able to collate a complete copy of the Qur'an, and this copy was kept by Abu Bakr, the first to succeed the Prophet as ruler of the Muslim state. Some of the Prophet's companions also wrote down the Prophet's pronouncements, which came to be known as *ḥadīth*, (plural: *aḥādīth* or *ḥadīths*). He had, however, issued an order to all his companions to erase whatever they had written down of his own statements, for fear that such might come to be confused with the Qur'an. Yet those who had accepted

Islam and who had not had the opportunity to meet the Prophet, as well as new generations of Muslims, were understandably eager to learn what the Prophet had said, since it is clear from the Qur'an and Islamic practices that all this was meant to remain as guidance to all Muslims across all generations. So much so, in fact, that a considerable part of Islam cannot be learnt from any source other than the Prophet's Sunnah (i.e. his statements and actions).

Muslims have been aware of this since the very early days of Islam. Even the Prophet's companions realised it, some even taking shifts to attend him. The one who had so attended a certain shift would report to others what he had heard the Prophet saying, and they, in turn, would make a similar report when they attended him. In this way, *ḥadīths* were transmitted by word of mouth, with the Prophet's companions keen to ensure totally accurate memorisation. They were even cautioned by him in these terms: 'He who deliberately and knowingly attributes to me something which I have not said will certainly take his place in hell'. With such a warning, it is not surprising that the Prophet's companions and their successors, as well as scholars throughout subsequent generations, exercised a great measure of diligence in order to report the Prophet's *ḥadīths* in his own words.

In those early days, when people's commitment to Islam was at its highest, no-one entertained the slightest idea of attributing to the Prophet something which he was not certain the Prophet had actually said. However, a quarter of a century after the Prophet had passed away, civil war erupted in the Muslim state. Essentially, there were those who whilst assuming an Islamic mantle were nonetheless working day and night in order to create division, hostility and conflict among the Muslim ranks. So successful were their efforts, that fighting erupted between the two Muslim camps. It is not surprising, therefore, that such elements were prepared to fabricate any story to serve their purposes. Furthermore, to give credence to their stories, they attributed them to no lesser authority than the Prophet. Thus started the fabrication of *ḥadīth*.

Faced with this situation, Muslim scholars started to enquire about the reporters of any *ḥadīth*. This was the beginning of an area of scholarship which is unique to Islamic civilisation. It included several disciplines, among the most important of which is that of classifying these reporters or transmitters of *ḥadīth* as to the degree of their reliability. This is the discipline known in Arabic as *'Ilm al-Jarḥ wal-Ta'dīl.* It is a finely regulated discipline, one that requires studying the case of every *ḥadīth* reporter individually. As years went by, with one generation following another, every *ḥadīth* had to be reported by a chain of such reporters or transmitters. Every single one had to be studied and classified. This was by no means an easy task. Scholars too realised the great importance of their work, since their efforts made the difference between reliability and confusion with regard to the Prophet's *ḥadīth* heritage.

Islamic scholarship began to flourish in the very early days of Islam. Once the Muslim state was well established, people gathered around the companions of the Prophet in order to learn from them and acquire insight into the teachings and principles of Islam. Since Islam encourages learning and puts it on a par with worship, people realised that the more careful they are with their studies, the greater their reward from God. Hence, it is not surprising that from its very early days, Islamic scholarship was renowned for the dedication, accuracy and attention to detail of its scholars.

We cannot emphasise strongly enough the element of accuracy in the study of *ḥadīth*. It is sufficient to say that leading scholars devoted much of their attention to the study of and confirmation of the authenticity of each *ḥadīth* before they made their judgement on it. We note that the founders of three of the four major schools of Islamic law, i.e. *Fiqh*, namely, Mālik, al-Shāfi'i and Ahmad ibn Ḥanbal, each compiled a major work containing the authentic *ḥadīths* known to him. Indeed, Imam Ahmad ibn Ḥanbal devoted much of his time to this study and his work *al-Musnad* ranks among the leading anthologies of the Prophet's *ḥadīths*.

There were other learned scholars, in various parts of the Muslim state, who also devoted much of their time and effort to the sifting of statements attributed to the Prophet and establishing the authenticity of what was really said by him. Succeeding scholars built on the work done by their teachers, and the study of *Ḥadīth* attracted the attention of every new scholar who wanted to serve Islam and benefit from his study.

The study of the chain of transmission, i.e. *sanad* or *isnād*, gathered great momentum as the proper way to establish the authenticity of any *ḥadīth*. In order to appreciate how this developed into a great discipline, we have to remember that five or six generations after the Prophet, there was a huge number of transmitters of *ḥadīth* who had to be studied carefully in order to establish the reliability of each one of them. Professor Muhammad Mustafa Azami explains how *isnād* flourished:

> It is the common phenomenon of the *isnād* system that as we go further, the number of transmitters increases. Sometimes a tradition transmitted by one companion of the Prophet acquires ten students in the next generation, in the class of Successors, and in turn these ten students have in some cases twenty or thirty students belonging to different countries and provinces.[1]

He then gives the example of a *ḥadīth* reported by Abu Hurairah in which the Prophet said: 'When anyone amongst you wakes up from sleep, he must not put his hand in his plate till he has washed it three times, for he does not know where his hand was during his sleep'. Professor Azami explains that at least thirteen students of Abu Hurairah transmitted this *ḥadīth* from him. Eight of them were from Madinah, two from Basrah and one each from Kufah, Yemen and Syria. Sixteen scholars also transmitted this tradition on the authority of Abu Hurairah's thirteen students. Six of these were from Madinah, four from Basrah, two from Kufah and one each from Makkah, Yemen, Khurasan and Syria.

Professor Azami then explains why the *isnād* gives us a clear idea of the reliability and authenticity of a certain *ḥadīth*. The common feature of a good many traditions in the early part of the second century AH is the great number of transmitters who belonged to different provinces and countries, as we have seen (in the previous example). It was hardly possible for all these people to consult each other so as to give a similar form and sense in transmitting a particular tradition. So, if a particular tradition is transmitted by so many people with a

---

1. M.M. Azami, *Ḥadīth Methodology and Literature*, Indianapolis, 1977, pp. 33-34.

similar form and sense, then its genuineness cannot be questioned, while the trustworthiness of the individuals is confirmed by their contemporaries. It is general practice that if a man's honesty is proved by his dealings with people, then his words are accepted as a true statement unless proved otherwise by facts. For any past generation with whom personal contact is impossible, one needs to rely, to a large extent, on the testimony of contemporary sources. The standard fixed by scholars of *Ḥadīth* from the very early days was that if someone had told a lie in his personal life, though he was deemed honest in his transmitting of *ḥadīth*, nonetheless, his *ḥadīth* would not be accepted. In this way, people even criticised their fathers, brothers, friends and close relatives. Perhaps it was the highest possible standard that could be set for the documentation of any source. Therefore, there is no good reason to reject the testimony of contemporaries.

Furthermore, *ḥadīth* literature offers additional opportunities to satisfy us. In this respect, another method to test people's trustworthiness and honesty in certain cases is by cross-reference to the scholars' statements. This method was also employed by *ḥadīth* scholars from the very early days.

Professor Azami outlines the conditions for the acceptance of any *ḥadīth* attributed to the Prophet as follows:

I. Conditions for the acceptance of ḥadīth.

A *ḥadīth* must meet the following criteria in order to be accepted in Islamic law as a source of legal ordinance:

1. Continuity of the chain of transmitters [*ittiṣāl al-sanad*]: This chain of transmitters has to be unbroken in order for the *ḥadīth* to be acceptable. That is, none of the transmitters must be missing from the chain of narrators. Furthermore, each transmitter must also have heard the *ḥadīth* in question directly from the transmitter before him. Knowledge of this is verified with the help of the biographical science of *ḥadīth*.
2. The integrity [*ʿadālah*] of the transmitters: This is established in terms of their outward observance of Islam. In other words,

it is ascertained that they practice what is required of them by Islam and they are not known to engage in the doing of things which are forbidden. Again, this precondition is verified through the biographical science of *ḥadīth*

3. The soundness of transmitters' memory: It must be verified through the biographical science of *ḥadīth* that each transmitter had a sound memory or that his books were accurate and that the process of his transmission was to read out from his books.
4. Conformity of the *ḥadīth*: It is important that the *ḥadīth* conforms with similar *ḥadīths* on the same topic which are stronger than it. This conformity should be both in the chain of transmitters and the text. Non-conformity in the chain of transmitters for example, might be if one of the transmitters in the chain is different than in a stronger version of the same *ḥadīth*. Non-conformity in text would imply divergence in the meaning of the *ḥadīth* with one which is stronger.
5. The absence of defects [*ʿillah*] in the *ḥadīth*. A defect in this context is defined as a hidden shortcoming in the *ḥadīth* which takes away from its authenticity. A *ḥadīth* which has such a defect is one which appears to be free from defects at first, but after investigation the presence of a defect is discovered. The defect can be in the chain of transmitters, or in the text, or in both.

II. Classification of ḥadīth.

There are two distinct types of *ḥadīth*:

1. The recurrent *ḥadīth* [*al-ḥadith al-mutawātir*]: This type of *ḥadīth* is decisive in its certainty [*qatʿi al-thubūt*]. There is no doubt that it actually came down from the Prophet (peace be upon him). There are four conditions which must be met for a *ḥadīth* to be of this category:
    - 1.1. At least four different persons must have narrated the *ḥadīth*.
    - 1.2. It must have been impossible for these four or more persons to have agreed on a lie.

1.3. They must have narrated the *ḥadīth* from similar people [the first two conditions being applicable] from the beginning of the chain of transmitters until the end of it.

1.4. Their narration of *ḥadīth* must rely on the mind and the senses not the mind only because the mind might be mistaken [as imagining something to have happened].

2. The non-recurrent *ḥadīth* [*ḥadīth al-āḥād*]: Any *ḥadīth* which is not reoccurring [i.e. *mutawātir*] is called non-recurrent [*āḥād*]. This category is divided into three sub-groupings according to the number of narrators of the *ḥadīth*:

2.1. The well-known *ḥadīth* [*al-ḥadīth al-mashhūr*]. This is a *ḥadīth* which has been narrated by three or more people in the chain of transmission but did not arrive at the rank of the recurrent *ḥadīth*.

2.2. The strong *ḥadīth* [*al-ḥadīth al-ʿazīz*]. This is a *ḥadīth* in which there are no less than two narrators in each part of the chain.

2.3. The rare *ḥadīth* [*al-ḥadīth al-gharīb*]. This is a *ḥadīth* which is narrated by a single person at one point in the chain of transmitters.

The non-recurrent *ḥadīth* is subdivided into three more classifications regarding the beginning of the chain of transmission:

2.4. The elevated *ḥadīth* [*al-ḥadīth al-marfūʿ*.] This is a *ḥadīth* whereby the chain of transmitters begins with the Prophet Muhammad (peace be upon him).

2.5. The suspended *ḥadīth* [*al-ḥadīth al-mawqūf*]. This is a *ḥadīth* the chain of transmitters of which does not trace back to the Prophet (peace be on him) but traces back instead to a companion of the Prophet.

2.6. The cut-off *ḥadīth* [*al-ḥadīth al-maqṭūʿ*]. This is a *ḥadīth* the chain of narrators of which traces back only to a successor of the companions of the Prophet (peace be upon him).

The non-recurrent *ḥadīth* is broken down into three classifications regarding its acceptance as a source of Islamic law:

2.7. The authentic *ḥadīth* [*ṣaḥīḥ*]. This is a *ḥadīth* which satisfies the five criteria for accepting a *ḥadīth*.

2.8. The good *ḥadīth* [*ḥasan*]. This is a *ḥadīth* which, like the authentic *ḥadīth*, also satisfies these five criteria except that the third criterion of the soundness of memory of transmitters is only slightly satisfied.

2.9. The weak *ḥadīth* [*ḍaʿīf*]. This is a *hadith* which does not satisfy all the five criteria for accepting *ḥadīth*. The weak *ḥadīth* is classified in different categories regarding which of these five criteria of acceptance is not met:

a. Weakness in the *ḥadīth* due to lack of continuity in the chain of transmitters:
   i. If the continuity is missing at the end of the chain of transmitters, the *ḥadīth* is called 'hanging', [*muʿallaq*].
   ii. If the continuity is missing in the middle of the chain of transmitters, the *ḥadīth* is known as 'interrupted', [*munqaṭiʿ*].
   iii. If two successive transmitters or more are missing in the middle of the chain of transmitters, the *ḥadīth* is called 'problematic', [*muʿḍal*].
   iv. If the first transmitter, a companion of the Prophet (peace be upon him), is missing from the chain of transmitters, the *ḥadīth* is called 'incompletely transmitted', [*mursal*].

b. Weakness in the *ḥadīth* due to lack of integrity [*ʿadālah*] in the narrators:
   i. A *ḥadīth* which has been fabricated is known as [*mawḍūʿ*], [fabricated].
   ii. If the *matn*, i.e. text, of a *ḥadīth* came down through one channel of transmission only and the transmitter of that *ḥadīth* does not satisfy the criteria of integrity, or his memory is not good, then the *ḥadīth* is said to be 'rejected', [*munkar*].
   iii. If a *ḥadīth* is transmitted by somebody who is charged with lying and that *ḥadīth* is known only through this transmission then the *ḥadīth* is said to be 'abandoned', or [*matrūk*].
   iv. Three subgroupings of weak *ḥadīth* are classified as:

- *Mudallas* is the chain of 'forged'[2] transmitters. This is a *ḥadīth* which the transmitter reports from some other transmitter whom he has met, but under whom he did not study, yet regarding whom he transmitted the *ḥadīth* in a way implying that he heard it from him.
- Forged regarding teachers [*mudallas al-shuyūkh*]. This is a *ḥadīth* in which the transmitter calls his teacher [*shaykh*] by nicknames other than the names by which he is well known.
- Forged regarding the naming of transmitters [*mudallas at-tasmiyah*]. This is the *ḥadīth* which is transmitted by a weak reporter, between two trustworthy transmitters who met each other with the weak transmitter between them having been deleted, so as not to be detected.
- If one of the transmitters of the *ḥadīth* is not named, then the *ḥadīth* is called 'obscure' [*mubham*].

v. If something has been added to a *ḥadīth*, then that *ḥadīth* is known as 'interpolated', [*mudraj*]. Such interpolation might be in the chain of narrators or in the *matn*.[3]

c. Weakness due to the inaccuracy of the memories of the transmitters:

i. If a *ḥadīth* has been transmitted by different weak channels, none of them being stronger than the others, then the *ḥadīth* is called 'shaky', [*muḍṭarib*].

ii. If there is a change in the wording of the *ḥadīth* then it is called either 'distorted' [*muṣaḥḥaf*] or 'interpolated', [*muḥarraf*].

iii. If there is inversion in the words of the chain of narrators [*sanad*] or text [*matn*] of the *ḥadīth*, then the *ḥadīth* is called 'inverted', [*maqlūb*].

---

2. I think that translating *mudallas* as 'forged' is problematic, because it connotes deliberate action. Perhaps a better translation is 'confused'.
3. Such insertions are often explanatory comments by one of the narrators. Alternatively, they cases of a narrator mixing up the text of the *ḥadīth* with a comment by an intermediary narrator from whom he received the *ḥadīth*.

iv. If the weakness is due to non-conformity of a *ḥadīth*, then it is called 'odd', [*shādhdh*].

v. Weakness in a *ḥadīth* because of a defect [*'illah*]. In this case the *ḥadīth* is called 'defective', [*mu'all*]. It has to be stressed that in Islamic law only authentic and good *ḥadīths* are used in deriving ordinances.

Only the best

Professor Azami's outline of the conditions that must be met for the acceptance of any *ḥadīth* attributed to the Prophet shows the extent of importance scholars have attached to the chain of transmitters and reporters. Scholars made sure that no *ḥadīth* should be classified as authentic unless there was no doubt whatsoever of its being correctly attributed to the Prophet. Indeed, perfectionism has always pervaded this branch of Islamic scholarship. *Ḥadīth* study, however, branched into several areas and disciplines that required a great deal of attention from scholars of the highest standing in Islamic civilisation. As noted earlier, perhaps the most important of these is the one known as *al-Jarḥ wal-Ta'dīl.*

This discipline is concerned with the study of the biography, character and knowledge of every reporter of *ḥadīth*, throughout every generation and in every city, from the time when a scholar of *ḥadīth* made his own classification to the time of the Prophet. The standards set for the acceptance or rejection of any particular report were absolutely stringent. Indeed, scholars of *Ḥadīth* might reject a certain reporter even though they knew him to be a man of great piety and integrity. The reason for their judgement would be something like his memory being relatively weak, or that he might transmit a report without making absolutely certain that it was authentic. In such a scenario, they classified the man as good and honourable, but also pointed out that his *ḥadīth* was 'weak', or sub-standard.

If a transmitter was known to have made even a slight mistake, his reports would be unacceptable. For example, we have stories telling us that a certain transmitter was rejected because he was seen driving his mule too fast. In another instance, a scholar of *ḥadīth* went to Basrah to meet its renowned scholars. He went to one of them, hoping to learn of the *ḥadīths* he had compiled. On arrival, he found the scholar playing chess. He left without sitting to hear from him. It should be explained here that there is nothing wrong with playing chess or driving a mule quickly. Neither is forbidden or discouraged. However, according to the strict standards of *Ḥadīth* scholars, such activities are unbecoming of one who devotes himself to the study of *Ḥadīth*.

There were several thousands of statements, actions and approvals attributed to the Prophet, but there were many more that were falsely or fraudulently attributed to him. Therefore, the study of transmitters and reporters suggests that there was a huge mass of biographical data that came under this discipline of *al-Jarḥ wal-Taʿdīl*. The very name of this discipline indicates its formal boundaries. *Al-Jarḥ* means, in the context of *ḥadīth* and its reporters, to fault or reject a certain transmitter. *Al-Taʿdīl*, on the other hand, means to classify a certain person as acceptable.

In order to appreciate the conscientiousness demonstrated by the scholars of this discipline we need only to state that if a transmitter or reporter was classified as acceptable, no specific reason was required for such classification. In order for anyone to earn such classification, he or she would have to have met the highest and most stringent of standards. When someone was rejected, however, a specific reason for so doing was required. In this respect, it is the duty of the scholar to state whether he rejected the transmitter because he knew him to tell lies, or to indulge in practices that were unacceptable from the Islamic point of view, or because he was a person who could be easily influenced by others who may not have the interests of Islam at heart.

We make a grave mistake if we think that such a great volume of biographical study consisted merely of millions of notes about the reporters of *ḥadīth* which may have been properly classified. Some people make an even more serious mistake when they imagine that the fact that no computers or printing machines being available to the scholars of *Ḥadīth* could only make their work imperfect. In fact, what that meant was that scholars needed to exert more effort and rely extensively on their excellent memories, hand written books and hard work. Today, with the result of centuries of *Ḥadīth* study becoming available to a much greater number of people as a result of technological advancement, we realise that the standard of perfection achieved by scholars of olden days is far more admirable than has ever been thought. The following well-documented story gives us an insight as to what level of scholarship they strove to achieve.

When al-Bukhari was still a young man, he visited Basrah in Iraq. One day, people in Basrah's great mosque heard someone making a loud announcement: 'Scholars, Muhammad ibn Ismā ʿīl al-Bukhari has arrived'. They hurried to meet him. When he finished his prayers, they asked him to arrange for a dictation session for them. That was the commonly accepted way scholars circulated their books. He accepted and the caller again announced in the mosque: 'Scholars, Muhammad ibn Ismā ʿīl al-Bukhari has arrived. We have requested him to dictate to us and he will be sitting tomorrow at this particular spot for dictation'.

The following day, thousands of scholars, students, men of learning and ordinary people attended at the time specified. Al-Bukhari sat down for dictation. He introduced that session as follows: 'People of Basrah, I am only a young man and you have asked me to speak to you about *Ḥadīth*. I will relate to you a number of *ḥadīths* transmitted by people from your own city which will form a contribution to what you have. I mean, you do not have these *ḥadīths* now'. People inevitably wondered how he could do such a thing. He began by saying: 'It has been related to me by ʿAbdullāh ibn ʿUthmān al-ʿAtāki in your city, when he said that he was told by his father on the authority of Shu ʿbah, on the authority of Manṣūr and others, quoting Sālim who quotes Anas ibn Mālik that a bedouin came to the Prophet and asked him...'. Al-Bukhari related to them the *ḥadīth* and concluded by saying to his audience: 'You have this *ḥadīth* with a chain of transmitters that does not include Mansur, but includes someone else in his stead. Now you have it with another chain of reporters'. He went on with this line of giving them new chains of reporters for *ḥadīth* texts they already had. In turn, they were much gratified, benefiting a great deal from that session.[4]

We thus realise that when a *ḥadīth* text has different chains of reporters, this adds to its authenticity, provided that all reporters in

---

4. A. Alqaḍah, *Madrasat al-Ḥadīth fi al-Baṣrah*, Amman, 1989, p. 443, quoting Al-Khatīb al-Baghdādi, *Tarīkh Baghdad*, vol. 2, p. 15.

such chains are reliable and acceptable. The story shows that the study of *Ḥadīth* and the various disciplines branching from it were carried out with a standard of perfectionism that is rare in human scholarship. It also tells us how the Prophet's *ḥadīths* were meticulously served by dedicated scholars.

Every discipline of study, in every branch of knowledge, develops over time until it reaches its maturity and becomes well established. As we have noted, scholars started to request information about the reporters of *ḥadīths* when they realised that some statements were being falsely attributed to the Prophet, in order to support some political or sectarian leaning. The inquiry into *ḥadīths* reporters started in the second half of the first century of Islam. Over time, the discipline of *al-Jarḥ wal-Ta'dīl* developed until it reached its perfection with Yaḥya ibn Ma'īn (158–233 AH, 775–849 CE) and Ahmad ibn Ḥanbal (164–241 AH, 781–856 CE).

Scholars of *Ḥadīth* did not just confine themselves to the study of reporters and transmitters. They also paid great attention to the text of *ḥadīths*, or what is termed in Arabic *matn*. Indeed, their concern with reporters of *ḥadīth* was not confined to their honesty, integrity and good character. These were important, no doubt; but scholars of *Ḥadīth* were also concerned with their accurate reporting. Hence, they would reject reporters who were otherwise known to be honest, truthful and pious just because their reporting was suspect. Imam Mālik said that among his teachers were seventy of great piety. Anyone of them could be trusted with a state treasury, but he did not transmit a single *ḥadīth* they reported 'because they did not belong to this area of scholarship'.[5]

A reporter is classified as 'accurate' after comparing the texts of the *ḥadīths* he reports with the same *ḥadīths* reported by others who are already known to be highly accurate. If his reports agree with theirs, he is classified as 'accurate' or 'reliable'. If not, his reports are abandoned. One reason for rejecting a *ḥadīth* is that a reliable reporter states it in

---

5. R.F. Abd al-Muttalib, *Tawthiq al-Sunnah fi al-Qarn al-Thāni al-Hijri*, Maktabat al-Khanji, Cairo, 1981, p. 160, quoted from Justice 'Iyāḍ, *Tartīb al-Madārik*, Morocco, vol. 1, p. 123.

a way that is at variance with the one stated by another reporter who is more reliable.

Ḥadīth scholars established five conditions for the acceptability of *ḥadīth*, two of which apply to the chain of reporters, two to the text, and one that applies to both. Moreover, *ḥadīth* study branched into several disciplines with three concerned only with the chain of transmission and three concerned with the texts themselves.

What is an athar

Readers will note that some *ḥadīths* are preceded by the word *athar*, and these are given a second number. According to scholars of *Ḥadīth* an *athar* is a text that is stated by a companion of the Prophet who does not state that he heard it from the Prophet. They consider that no companion of the Prophet ever made a statement of a religious nature unless he heard it directly from the Prophet or from another companion who attended the Prophet when he said it. However, they were very cautious with what they attributed to the Prophet, fearing that they might not have remembered accurately what he actually said. In order not to misquote the Prophet, they did not attribute the statement to him. *Ḥadīth* scholars have always treated an *athar* as a *ḥadīth* stated by the Prophet, even though the Prophet's companion does not attribute it to him, for the reasons I have mentioned.

An *athar* will also have a chain of transmission going from the Prophet's companion who reported it down to the one who narrated it to the *Ḥadīth* scholar who entered it in his anthology. Therefore, we should treat it in the same way as scholars have done, i.e. as a *ḥadīth*. Thus, when we use the term *ḥadīth* it includes what is described as *athar*.

Imam al-Bukhari

ABU 'ABDULLĀH MUHAMMAD ibn Ismā'īl was born on Friday 13 Shawwal 194 A.H, 810 CE at Bukhara. His father, Ismā'īl, was a scholar of *Ḥadīth* who studied this subject under a number of very famous scholars, such as Mālik ibn Anas, Ḥammād ibn Zayd and Ibn al-Mubārak. His father died when al-Bukhari was a very young boy. He inherited a good fortune which he entrusted to someone else to invest on a partnership basis, and this kept him well off. He was also very generous, spending much of his earnings on schools, the fortification of state boundaries, outposts and border-guard places as well as scholarly activities.

He actually lived by the guidance he learnt from the Prophet's *ḥadīths*, conscientiously implementing all this in his own lifestyle. One day a trade caravan which belonged to him arrived in town, perhaps at a time of scarcity. A group of merchants came straight to him seeking to buy the whole consignment and offering him a net profit of five thousand gold pieces. He told them he would give them his answer in due course. Another group came a short while later, offering to double his profit and give him ten thousand gold pieces. He said to them: 'I have intended to sell it to the other group, and I do not like to go back on my intention'. He then sent for the first group and sold the merchandise to them at the price they had initially offered. He was certainly aware that had he opted for the higher profit, he would have violated no Islamic rule, because he had not promised the first group anything. He had only formulated an intention known only to God and himself, without committing himself to anything. This intention was by no means a binding commitment. Nonetheless, his attitude was one of making absolutely certain that his action was in line with his intention.

Al-Bukhari enjoyed a position of honour and high respect throughout the Muslim world. Wherever he travelled, he was received well. Indeed the governor, leaders and people of any town he visited would go out to receive him at a distance from their locale. Nobles, scholars and the general public would sit to learn from him. Yet despite all this, he preferred a simple living, aspiring to no luxuries or comforts. He hastened to do whatever good action was needed. He once saw someone throwing dirt in the mosque, without being seen by others. He left the person alone, saying nothing of his action. Then, when no one was around, he picked up the dirt himself so as to throw it out of the mosque. He also had a slave girl who once did something that made him angry. She refused to apologise to him so that he could pardon her. When he realised, he said: if she is unwilling to make peace with me, then I will have my own wish. He set her free.

Al-Bukhari began his study of *Ḥadīth* at a very young age, perhaps when he was ten. By the age of sixteen, he had memorised many books by prominent scholars such as Ibn Al-Mubārak and Wakīʿ. He was not content, however, to memorise the *ḥadīths* and books of early scholars; he also learnt the history of all narrators who took part in the transmission of any *ḥadīth* including every one's date and place of birth and death.

He stayed in Hijaz for six years learning *Ḥadīth* and travelled to Baghdad eight times. In the course of one of his journeys to study under the renowned scholar Adam ibn Abu Iyās, he spent all his money and was left with nothing. Penniless, he lived for a time eating only the leaves of wild plants. He was an excellent marksman and he continued to practise his military skills so that he might be ready to join the Muslim army at any time.

In his critical assessment of early scholars and narrators of *Ḥadīth*, al-Bukhari used very moderate and mild language. He was unwilling to bear the responsibility for describing anyone in bad terms, which could be constituted as backbiting. Scholars, however, know very well what those mild words of al-Bukhari signify. He was very kind and generous to his students. His scribe, Muhammad ibn Abu Ḥātim says: 'Al-Bukhari used to wake up in the night dozens of times, light the lamp by flint, make some remarks on certain *ḥadīths* before going back to sleep. I asked him once why he did not wake me up. He answered: "You are young and I do not wish to disturb your sleep".'

When al-Bukhari arrived in Baghdad, scholars wanted to test his famous memory. They appointed ten men and told them to ask al-Bukhari about ten *ḥadīths* each, substituting for each statement by the Prophet a chain of reporters which belonged to another *ḥadīth*. One by one, they began to read their *ḥadīths*, asking whether he knew them. He always replied: 'This is unknown to me'. Those who knew that it was an examination of al-Bukhari said he understood the situation, while the general impression other people gathered was that al-Bukhari's knowledge was very meagre and his memory suspect. After the questions had ended, he repeated all hundred *ḥadīths*, stating them in the same ordered and with the same wrong chain of transmission, giving the correct version of each one of them with its proper transmission chain. What is most amazing here is his ability to repeat the wrong information word by word, after having heard it only once.[6]

Al-Bukhari wrote and compiled no less than twenty-two books, mostly on *Ḥadīth*. Some of them have been published several times, while others have been lost. His most famous work is the one which is widely known as *Ṣaḥīḥ*. Its proper title means that it is an anthology containing all types of authentic *ḥadīths* concerning the Prophet, his

---

6. Al-Husaini Hashim, *Al-Imam al-Bukhari: Muhaddithan wa Faqihan*, Cairo (n.d.) p. 54. The story is quoted in numerous works including Ibn Hajar, *Fath al-Bari*.

traditions and military campaigns. He spent sixteen years compiling it. Before including any *ḥadīth* in his *Ṣaḥīḥ*, al-Bukhari used to take a shower, pray two *rak'ahs* in voluntary worship and pray to God for guidance as to whether to include it or not. He only included *ḥadīths* which he was satisfied were authentic. He habitually used a portion of a *ḥadīth* as the heading of its chapter. He also repeated *ḥadīths* several times according to their relevance to different chapters and subjects. The number of *ḥadīths* in his *Ṣaḥīḥ* anthology is 7,563, but if we omit the repetition, the number reduces to 2,761. *Al-Bukhari's Ṣaḥīḥ anthology is divided into ninety-seven 'books' and each of these is sub-divided into sections which themselves total in number to 3,450.*

Authors usually make changes to their works and bring out new editions improving on earlier efforts. Al-Bukhari did likewise. He stated that he composed his work three times. We know for certain that his work, *At-Tārīkh Al-Kabīr* was written three times and every edition differed a little, and that the last edition was the most accurate. He did the same with his *Ṣaḥīḥ*. Even after this final draft, he continually made changes, adding some *ḥadīths* and discarding others.

Al-Bukhari laid down the most strict conditions for the inclusion of any *ḥadīth* in his *Ṣaḥīḥ*. These included that every narrator of *ḥadīth* must be of a very high standard of personal character and must have attained a high literary and academic standard. Moreover, there must be positive information about narrators whereby they had met one another and that the student had actually learnt from the teacher.

It is very difficult to obtain complete data about every scholar. In fact, we do not have complete information about any scholar's list of students. On this count, there was a difference of opinion between al-Bukhari and Muslim. In Muslim's opinion, if two scholars were contemporaries of each other and lived where it was possible for them to learn from each other, then even if we have no positive information that they met, we should accept their *ḥadīths* and regard the chain of reporters unbroken, provided that they did not mix up their teachers. Al-Bukhari did not agree with this position. He insisted on positive evidence of learning and teaching. He did not consider even this condition sufficient and required further scrutiny in selecting authorities.

Al-Bukhari's *Ṣaḥīḥ* has been translated, in full or in part, into many languages. Hundreds of commentaries have been written on it, some of them exceeding twenty-five volumes. The best known commentary is that by Imam Ibn Ḥajar, who died in 852 AH, 1449 CE. His *Fatḥ al-Bāri* is published in fourteen large volumes.

Al-Bukhari himself recognized the need to relax certain conditions slightly. This is apparent in his other works, most notably *Al-Adab al-Mufrad.* He devoted this work to highlighting Islamic moral values and good manners. Although these topics are included in his *Ṣaḥīḥ*, they are specifically emphasised in *Al-Adab al-Mufrad.* This book is divided into 644 sections and includes 1,329 *ḥadīths.* They are all concerned with the sort of behaviour a Muslim should adopt in different situations.

When we speak of the relaxation of conditions for acceptance, this does not mean that al-Bukhari included in this book any *ḥadīth* which he had any slight doubt that the Prophet might not have said. Indeed, half of the *ḥadīths* in this book are included in his *Ṣaḥīḥ*. Hence, they are highly authentic. The other half meets the necessary conditions to earn the classification of 'good'. It is well known that a 'good' *ḥadīth* should be acted upon. It cannot be easily dismissed by any Muslim who wishes to follow the Sunnah of the Prophet. The present book is devoted to an explanation of these *ḥadīths* and their relevance to daily conduct and behaviour. Every Muslim, indeed every person, benefits much by understanding these *ḥadīths* and acting upon them. May God reward al-Bukhari richly for his great effort in putting this book together and including in it all that people need to know about Islamic behaviour.

Al-Bukhari died on Saturday, the last day of Ramadan in the year 256 AH, 870 CE.

1

Dutifulness to Parents

ALL PEOPLE AGREE that to be kind and dutiful to one's parents is the proper attitude. All societies, including those where family ties have become very loose, agree that sons and daughters must always be kind to their parents. Parents sacrifice a great deal to bring up their children. They take pains to provide the happiest life they can for them. Yet, it cannot be denied that not all parents provide their children with the same standards of care and love. Some children are more fortunate than others in this respect. In most cases, however, parents do care for their children and look after them well. In doing so, they have to work hard and sacrifice much of their time, effort, money as well as physical and mental rest.

From time to time we hear about parents who are cruel to their children. Cases are reported of parents who kill their children, or cause them to die. These cases are exceptions that do not invalidate the rule. When we examine any such scenario, we find that the perpetrators are far from normal people. The healthier and more virtuous a society is, the less frequent and more far between such cases of perversion become. The closer a society moves towards Islamic life, the more likely such instances disappear and become largely non-existent.

Because parents sacrifice much to bring up their children, all religions tend to emphasise the virtue of kindness to parents. Islam makes such kindness to parents a personal duty of every son and daughter, allowing no exception whatsoever. A number of Qur'anic verses make dutifulness to parents a universal requirement, second only to believing in God's oneness. God says in the Qur'an: '*Say: Come, let me tell you what your Lord has forbidden to you: Do not associate partners with Him; [do not offend against but, rather,] be kind to your parents; do not kill your children because of your poverty – We provide for you and for them; do not commit any shameful deed, whether open or secret; do not take any human being's life – which God has made sacred, except in the course of justice. This He has enjoined upon you so that you may use your reason*'. (6: 151)

We also have a large number of *ḥadīths* that encourage in all manners of emphasis treating parents with a devoted kindness, and which further stress the importance of overlooking their faults. Al-Bukhari opens this book with a section on dutifulness to parents, showing it to be the most important of Islamic moral values. Each section comprises a number of chapters, with a small number of *ḥadīths* in each and which is given a significant heading. The first chapter in this section is headed with a Qur'anic verse that says: '*We have enjoined man to be kind to his parents*'. (29: 8)

1. 'Abdullāh ibn Mas'ūd reports: I asked God's Messenger: 'Which action does God love best?' He answered: 'Prayer at its proper time'. I asked: 'What comes next?' He said: 'Dutifulness to parents'. I asked: 'What comes next?' He said: 'Next comes jihad for God's cause'.

Ibn Mas'ūd adds: 'He told me of these, but he would have added more, had I asked him to do so'.[7]

---

7. This *ḥadīth* is also related by al-Bukhari in his *Ṣaḥīḥ*, Muslim, al-Nasā'ī, Abū Dāwūd, al-Tirmidhi, al-Dāraquṭni, al-Ḥākim, Ibn Khuzaymah and Ibn Ḥibbān.

Many people may be surprised at this order of priority. Were we to ask people where they would place jihad, i.e. striving for God's cause, in the list of deeds earning great reward from God, most of them would give it first priority. Jihad requires a person to believe that Islam is the religion of the truth, accept it, hold firmly to it and present it to others. In doing so, a person may have to sacrifice his wealth and his life. Jihad means willingly accepting such risks. Although most people understand jihad to mean fighting the enemies of Islam so that it may achieve supremacy over all other religions, creeds and philosophies, its significance is much wider than its erroneous translation as 'holy war'. Indeed, there is no such concept as a 'holy war' in Islam. War is either legitimate, when it is for a just cause, or else it is unacceptable aggression. Every action that serves the dual purpose of establishing Islam firmly in its own land and delivering its message to others so that they can make their own choice about it is part of jihad.

However, the Prophet places as our first priority a simple act of worship; this also falls within the ambit of one's personal relationship with God. Prayer at its proper time is the action God loves best. It is followed by a deed that concerns family relations. Both come ahead of jihad which has more to do with public life and with the common welfare of the Muslim community. Needless to say, prayer and dutifulness to parents require much less effort and sacrifice than jihad.

This *ḥadīth* shows that the Prophet had a keen insight into what motivates people to work and to sacrifice. We know that prayer is the most important Islamic duty, but it does not impose a heavy burden on the individual. It is an easy and pleasant duty which makes man constantly aware of what God requires of him and which keeps him on guard against falling into sin. It is only logical that the fulfilment of the top and most frequent duty should earn the greatest reward from God. What the *ḥadīth* tells us is that prayer should be offered on time in order to earn its great reward and be most pleasing to God. In other words, punctuality is of the essence for prayer to be highly rewarded.

Dutifulness to parents is placed second in importance. There is no doubt that our parents have the greatest claim on our love and kindness. Nothing that we may do for them in their old age, when they grow weaker and more dependent on us, is enough to pay them back for the care, kindness and love they gave us when we were young and totally dependent on them. It is sufficient to observe a mother taking care of a young child to appreciate her sacrifice and to realise that there is little a child can do in return.

Few people will argue about parents' claims on their children's kindness. Islam, however, makes such kindness a duty which earns God's reward. He rewards us for our good actions even though we may do them only by way of duty. However, the emphasis Islam places on kindness and dutifulness to parents is due to two different considerations. First, it is easy for children just reaching adulthood to be preoccupied with their own affairs, looking after their own interests and being proud of their strength, youth, position, etc. This may easily lead them to be negligent of their duty to their parents. Some people find it very difficult to part with their money even when it is needed by their own parents. They may have more than enough for their own needs, and their parents may be poor, but they still find it extremely difficult to help their parents financially. It is not uncommon to hear about cases of unkind treatment of parents by their own sons or daughters. Hence, the reminder is needed and the Prophet does so in the most effective way.

Secondly, with such a great claim on our kindness and love, negligence of this duty towards parents may lead to negligence of other duties Islam requires of us. For example, we will definitely be less inclined to be kind towards others who are not related to us. We will be hesitant to extend our help and support to those who need it and have no immediate claim on us. Such an attitude is totally alien to Islamic behaviour. Hence, the Prophet stresses the importance of dutifulness to parents in a variety of ways. The second *ḥadīth* listed in this section runs as follows:

> 2. (*Athar* 1) 'Abdullāh ibn 'Umar said: 'God's pleasure lies in the parents' pleasure and His displeasure is caused by the parents' displeasure'.[8]

In this *ḥadīth* the Prophet shows that the surest way to earn God's pleasure is to be dutiful to one's parents. If one is unkind to them, to

---

8. Related by al-Ḥākim and al-Tirmidhi.

the extent that their love is replaced by displeasure, anger or bitterness, then this is the surest way to incur God's displeasure. There can be no gloomier prospect than this.

Questions that may arise here are: what constitutes kind treatment of parents and whether both parents have the same claim to their children's kindness. A *ḥadīth* that defines kindness to parents will be discussed presently, but we may say now in brief that it includes everything that tends to please parents and makes them happy, without involving any disobedience of God. It also includes looking after them and supporting them financially if they are so in need. As for whether either parent has a greater claim, the Prophet gives us a clear answer:

3. Mu'āwiyah ibn Ḥaydah reports: 'I said: Messenger of God, to whom should I be most kind? He said: "Your mother". I asked: to whom should I be most kind? He said: "Your mother". I again asked: to whom should I be most kind? He said: "Your mother". I asked once more: to whom should I be most kind? He said: "Your father. Then the nearest of kin then the next nearest".'[9]

4. (*Athar* 2) 'Aṭā' ibn Yasār said: 'A man came to Ibn 'Abbās and said: "I asked a woman to marry me but she refused. Another man proposed to her and she accepted him. I was so jealous, I killed her. Will my repentance be accepted by God?" Ibn 'Abbās asked him: "Is your mother alive?" The man said: "No". Ibn 'Abbās said to him: "Then repent sincerely to God, the Mighty, the Exalted, and try as hard as you can to draw closer to Him". 'Aṭā' said: I went back to Ibn 'Abbās and asked him why he had enquired from the man if his mother was alive. He said: "I know nothing which earns God's pleasure more than dutifulness to one's mother".'[10]

5. Abu Hurayrah said: 'Someone said: "Messenger of God, to whom should I be dutiful?" He said: "Your mother". The questioner asked: "Who comes next?" The Prophet said: "Your

9. Related by Abū Dāwūd, al-Tirmidhi and al-Ḥākim.
10. Related by al-Bayhaqi.

mother". The man asked again: "And who next?" The Prophet said: "Your mother". The man said: "Who next?" The Prophet said: "Your father".'[11]

6. Abu Hurayrah reported: 'A man came to the Prophet and said: "What do you command me [to do]?" He replied: "Be dutiful to your mother". The man asked him again and he replied: "Be dutiful to your mother". The man repeated the question yet again, and the Prophet said: "Be dutiful to your mother". He asked the same question for the fourth time and the Prophet said: "Be dutiful to your mother". When he repeated the question for the fifth time, the Prophet said: "Be dutiful to your father".'

Three of these four *ḥadīths* mention a question put to the Prophet asking him who of all people deserves our kind treatment. Whether these *ḥadīths* refer to the same occasion or to different ones, it appears that the enquirer wanted to learn an order of preference. Hence the repeated question when he gets the same answer three or four times.

Muslim scholars have spoken at length on this point and we can conclude from their discussion that the mother takes precedence over the father in her claim to her children's dutifulness. This does not mean that the father has a lesser claim. Indeed, some scholars consider that the father has even greater rights to his children's dutifulness. However, this does not contradict her right to precedence. This is, however, a fine point that needs some elaboration.

The Prophet emphasises the mother's right to be the recipient of kindly and dutiful treatment from her children for a number of reasons. There is firstly the fact that people tend to take the mother's rights lightly; they are more negligent of their duties towards her. The relationship between a mother and her children, including her sons, is normally confined within the family home. A son, or a daughter, may be unkind, disobedient and even insulting without anyone outside the home knowing anything about it. He or she may even continue to enjoy the respect and friendliness of other people. If, on the other hand, a son is unkind to his father, the likelihood of people in the

11. Related by Aḥmad, al-Bukhari, Muslim and Ibn Mājah.

neighbourhood getting to know about it is much greater. Social embarrassment is an inevitable result. Hence, there is a definite social inhibition against showing disrespect towards one's father.

Sometimes parents disagree with each other. Each one of them may ask their son or daughter to do something that displeases the other. So how does a child behave in such a scenario? Some Muslim scholars say that he should give priority to his father's right to be honoured and respected, because he adopts his name. At the same time, he should give priority to the mother's right to be served and supported. For example, if both of them enter his home or room, he stands up to show his respect for his father. With his mother, he may need to show love rather than respect. If both ask him to give them something, he begins by giving his mother. If they need to be financially supported and he can support only one of them, he gives priority to his mother, because in Muslim society women are normally supported by their male relatives. The other reason is that one's mother takes more trouble looking after her child, from pregnancy to birth, to breastfeeding and upbringing. In short, Islam takes a practical, reasonable and balanced attitude in looking after both parents.

There is secondly the element of physical strength. A father's strength may deter his undutiful child from going too far in his unkindness. There is no such deterrent in the case of the mother. Hence, the emphasis by the Prophet on the mother's first claim to her children's kind treatment. What normally happens if a child abuses his mother is that the mother, aware that she cannot match her son's physical strength, prays to God to punish him for his unkindness. Such a prayer will always be answered. In order to avoid this, the Prophet stresses the mother's right so emphatically in order to create in every Muslim's consciousness an awareness that under no circumstances should abuse or unkindness be directed at one's mother. Once this awareness is present, its effect is beneficial to both mother and child. It spares the child his mother's anger which is bound to be detrimental to him since it incurs God's displeasure with him. It also ensures that even the most ungrateful of people hesitate before displaying undutifulness towards their mothers.

Islam takes all factors into consideration when it puts a stronger emphasis on a certain element. We know that both parents sacrifice a great deal in order to give their children a proper upbringing. They spare no effort or expense in order to see their children successful. The least they are entitled to in return is kindly and dutiful treatment. Human beings, however, tend to think of their own interests first. Some children go so far as to actually abuse their parents when they feel that the parents' claims on them stand between them and what they want. In order to protect the rights of the parents and to provide the incentive for children to be kind to them, God promises great reward for those who are very kind to their parents. This is a unique aspect of God's Grace. When we are kind to our parents, we are only repaying a debt. They have been kind to us when we were helpless. When they are old and in need of our help, we are simply paying them back. Indeed, we cannot pay them back in full no matter how obedient, dutiful and kind we are to them. Yet for our good treatment of our parents, God promises us great reward.

The above quoted *ḥadīth* of the man who killed the woman who refused to marry him states this very clearly. The man committed an unprovoked murder, but he regretted his action and wanted to be sure of how he could obtain God's forgiveness. The first thing Ibn ʿAbbās considered to ensure such forgiveness was kindness towards his mother. He stated clearly that nothing could earn God's pleasure better than kindness to one's mother.

What pleases parents is normally very small and easy for every child to accomplish. Consider the following *ḥadīth* stated by the Prophet's learned cousin, ʿAbdullāh ibn ʿAbbās:

7. (*Athar* 3) For every Muslim who has two Muslim parents and who greets them every morning showing his dutifulness, God opens two gates of heaven. If he has only one parent, then one gate is opened. If he displeases either of them, God will not be pleased with him until that parent is pleased with him.

Ibn ʿAbbās was asked: Even when they are unjust to him? He said: Even if they are unjust.[12]

12. Related by al-Bayhaqi in *Shuʿab al-Īmān*.

This is another of the many ways by which the Prophet explains to us that one of the surest ways to be admitted into heaven is to be dutiful to one's parents. In this *ḥadīth* we are told that we must even tolerate injustice by our parents. There are occasions when a parent may be unjust. If we can tolerate such injustice, we should do so. However, we must not obey them when their injustice affects someone else. We should, in such a case, counsel them against it. This is because injustice is forbidden. If we help anyone in doing what is forbidden, we are partners in guilt. It is more dutiful to try to dissuade our parents from committing injustice.

Where we must not obey our parents is when they order us to do something unlawful. If a parent commands one of his children to do something forbidden, that parent must not be obeyed. The Prophet says: 'No creature may be obeyed in what constitutes disobedience of the Creator'.[13]

Dutifulness to parents is sometimes highlighted within a different context, and normally as one of the things a person may do to earn rich reward from God, and to facilitate one's entry into heaven on the Day of Judgement. Consider, for example, the following *ḥadīth* which speaks about the most serious sins:

> **8.** (*Athar* 4) Ṭaysalah ibn Mayyās said: 'I was with the Najdites[14] when I committed wrong actions which I supposed to be major sins. I mentioned this to ['Abdullāh] ibn 'Umar. He asked me about them and I mentioned them to him. He said: "These are not grave sins. There are nine grave sins: associating partners with God; murder; desertion from the Muslim army on the day of battle; false accusation of a chaste woman; usury; taking away an orphan's property; heresy in the sacred mosque [of Makkah]; ridiculing others; and causing one's parents to weep through undutifulness".
>
> 'Ibn 'Umar then said to me: "Do you fear hell? Do you love to be in heaven?" I said: "By God, I do". He asked: "Are your parents alive?" I replied: "My mother is with me". He said: "By

---

13. Related by Aḥmad.
14. These were the followers of Najdah ibn 'Āmir, a group of al-Khawarij.

God, if you speak kindly to her and feed her well, then you will certainly be in heaven, provided that you avoid grave sins".'[15]

This *ḥadīth* contrasts kind treatment of parents and the reward it earns with the gravity of bringing tears to one's parents' eyes through the sin of undutiful conduct. Ibn 'Umar who was one of the leading scholars among the Prophet's companions ranks such conduct as one of the nine gravest sins. By contrast, he asserts that by a kind word and looking after one's parents, one is certain to be in heaven, provided that one refrains from grave sins. Such great rewards then for something that is so easy for everyone to achieve.

When we hear about the great reward God grants for kindness and dutifulness towards parents we may wonder what it involves. We may think that it requires strenuous and sustained effort. Nothing of the kind. Explaining this, 'Urwah ibn al-Zubayr, a highly renowned scholar of the second generation of Muslims, said:

9. (*Athar* 5) God says: 'Spread over them [i.e. your parents] humbly the wings of your tenderness'. This means that you should not refrain from doing whatever pleases them.

As mentioned earlier, dutifulness to one's parents simply repays a debt we owe them. They looked after us when we were young and helpless. We must repay their kindness by ensuring that they are happy. A question that arises here is: does anyone repay his parents fully? The Prophet gives us the answer:

10. No child repays his father [or mother] fully unless he finds him a slave and buys him and sets him free.[16]

It is not difficult to appreciate the reason the Prophet considers this as full repayment of a parent's kindness. A slave is committed to obey his master in whatever he orders of him. He cannot choose how or where he lives, or what job to do. He simply does what he is told.

---

15. Related by al-Ṭabari in his commentary on the Qur'an.
16. Related by Muslim, Abū Dāwūd, al-Tirmidhi and Ibn Mājah.

If he gains something as a result of his work, his gains go to his master. By setting him free, his son gives him his freedom back, and a feeling of being re-born. Nowadays we can hardly imagine what it is like to be a slave, considering that slavery is virtually non-existent. We can, however, imagine what it means to be committed to obey someone else every day of one's life, to the extent that one is told when to eat, sleep or wake up.

It is important to note here that when a child buys his father or mother who have been slaves, the moment they come into his possession they are set free. He does not need to grant them their freedom, as it were. According to Islam, even in the black days of slavery, the mere fact that a parent comes to be owned by his son or daughter means gaining complete freedom. No slave can be owned by his own child. This is most clearly apparent in the case of a slave woman who gives birth to a child by her master. Once the child is born, she gains the status of 'mother of child' (or *umm walad*) and she can no longer be sold to anyone. However, she remains her master's slave. When he dies, she is technically inherited by her child. This sets her free. This was one of the many ways through which Islam reduced world slavery.

Nowadays when slavery has been almost totally eradicated, by God's Grace, sons and daughters cannot repay their parents fully, no matter how much they love and serve them. Even when care for a parent is excessively demanding and the children still actually take care of them, the parents' rights are greater. It is rare that a parent is so ill and handicapped that he or she needs to be looked after in the same way as a baby is looked after by his parents.

11. (*Athar* 6) 'Abdullāh ibn 'Umar saw a man from Yemen carrying his mother on his back and going around the Ka'bah performing the ṭawāf. The man was chanting: "I am her humble camel... If other mounts are frightened, I am not". The man asked Ibn 'Umar: "Do you think I have repaid her?" He replied: "No, not even for a single pang of pain [during labour]". Ibn 'Umar then performed the ṭawāf and offered two rak'ahs at

Maqam Ibraheem. He said [to his companion]: "Ibn Abi Mūsa, every two rak'ahs expiate what was done before them".[17]

This is not an exaggeration by Ibn 'Umar. The man was certainly dutiful to his mother and he showed no displeasure at having to serve her in this way. Yet this is not repayment for what she did in looking after him and bringing him up. The point is that a mother goes to every trouble in looking after her child and she does it with much pleasure, while carers of elderly people always consider them a burden and look forward to the time when the burden is gone.

As Islam stresses the great importance of dutifulness to parents, it wants sons and daughters to always remember that they could not have survived without the care and love shown them when they were young. The Qur'an often places the importance of dutifulness to parents as second only to belief in God's oneness. God says: '*Your Lord has ordained that you shall worship none but Him, and that you must be kind to your parents. Should one of them, or both, attain to old age in your care, never say 'Ugh' to them or chide them, but always speak gently and kindly to them, and spread over them humbly the wings of your tenderness, and say, "My Lord, bestow on them Your Grace, even as they reared and nurtured me when I was a child".*' (17: 23-24)

We are recommended to say this supplication at all times, when our parents are alive and after they die. It highlights the loving care parents take of their young children, and it appeals to God to treat our parents with abundant compassion and erase their sins. When they hear us say this supplication, they are filled with pleasure as they realise that we appreciate what they have done for us; and when we say it after they die, God increases their reward because this is one of the ways that dead people can earn more reward. The Prophet says: 'When a person dies, all his action comes to an end except in one of three ways: a continuous act of charity, a useful contribution to knowledge and a dutiful child praying for him'. Al-Bukhari includes here two *ḥadīths* (Numbers 12 and 14) in very similar wording, speaking of Abu Hurayrah frequently saying this supplication:

---

17. Related by al-Bayhaqi in *Shu'ab al-Īmān*.

12. (*Athar* 7) Marwān [ibn al-Ḥakam, the Governor of Madinah][18] used to appoint Abu Hurayrah as his deputy when he travelled. Abu Hurayrah used to live at Dhul-Ḥulayfah, while his mother used to be in a different house. When he went out, he stopped at her door and said: 'Peace be on you, mother, together with God's mercy and blessings'. She replied: 'And peace be to you, my son, together with God's mercy and blessings'. He then said: 'May God grant you mercy as you reared and nurtured me when I was a child'. She answered: 'May God grant you mercy as you are dutiful to me as a man'. He did the same if he wanted to go in.

One question we might well ask is: how does dutifulness to parents compare with other Islamic duties? Can it be given greater priority than other important duties? During the Prophet's lifetime, when he and his companions migrated to Madinah, migration to join the Muslim community was the mark of being fully committed to Islam. It signified that a Muslim who migrated totally disregarded all his past loyalties, including tribal, which would have been the most important bond in his life. His migration constituted a declaration that his commitment to Islam was final, absolute and could not be superseded by any other bond or commitment.

13. 'Abdullāh ibn 'Amr reported: 'A man came to the Prophet to make a pledge to him to migrate. He had left his parents weeping. The Prophet said to him: "Go back to your parents and make them laugh as you made them weep".'[19]

14. (*Athar* 8) The same as *ḥadīth* No. 12

The Prophet thus made it very clear to the man that if his parents were so miserable as to weep because he was leaving them to join the Prophet, it was better for him to stay with them and make them happy. The Prophet did not wish that sadness should be felt by parents as

---

18. And later Caliph.

19. Related by al-Bukhari, Muslim, Abū Dāwūd, al-Tirmidhi and al-Nasā'ī.

a result of a duty Islam required of its followers. This should tell us that being undutiful and unkind to parents is a very serious sin. The Prophet makes this very clear in the following *ḥadīth*:

15. Abu Bakrah quotes the Prophet as saying: 'Shall I tell you which are the gravest of the most serious sins?' He repeated this three times. [His audience] said: 'Yes, Messenger of God'. He said: 'To associate partners with God and to be undutiful to one's parents'. As he said this, he was reclining but he then sat up and said: 'And to knowingly say what is false'.

Abu Bakrah added: 'He continued to repeat this until I wished that he would stop'.[20]

That the Prophet considered undutifulness to parents one of the most serious of sins confirms what the Qur'an tells us as it ranks it second to denying God's oneness in the list of prohibitions. A Muslim is required to do everything to ensure that his parents are happy and respected. Hence, it is not permissible to say anything that might cause others to abuse them.

When people quarrel, they often start to hurl verbal abuse on each other. Sometimes this is carried further with abuse of each other's parents. The Prophet warns against this in clear terms.

16. Warrād, al-Mughīrah ibn Shu'bah's scribe said: Mu'āwiyah [the Caliph] wrote to al-Mughīrah: 'Write for me something you heard from God's Messenger (peace be upon him)'. Warrad said: 'Al-Mughīrah dictated and I wrote with my own hand: "God's Messenger used to forbid asking too many questions, wasting property and idle talk".'[21]

This *ḥadīth* is very important and precise. It will be repeated in a longer version in *ḥadīth* Number 298. We will discuss it then in full, but for the present we may say that all three things the Prophet prohibited are wasteful and give little return for what one expends on them.

---

20. Related by al-Bukhari, Muslim and al-Tirmidhi.
21. Related by al-Bukhari, Muslim and Abū Dāwūd.

17. 'Ali was asked: 'Did the Prophet teach you anything special which he did not teach to all people?' He replied: 'God's Messenger did not teach us anything special other than what I have in my scabbard'. He took out a scroll on which was written: 'God curses anyone who sacrifices an animal to other than God; God curses anyone who steals a landmark; God curses anyone who curses his parents; God curses anyone who gives shelter to one who is guilty of a serious crime'.

This *ḥadīth* makes clear that the Prophet never favoured anyone with anything special related to the Islamic faith. He taught all people the same principles and gave them the same advice. When 'Ali said that he only gave him what was in that scroll, all that it contained was known to other people through various injunctions in the Qur'an and other *ḥadīths*. Sacrificing an animal for the sake of any person or idol is a mark of associating partners with God, and this is the first thing Islam prohibits. Stealing a landmark is an act of taking away other people's property, or blurring the borders between people's plots. This leads to infringing people's rights. Giving shelter to a person guilty of a serious crime is to help the criminal to escape justice. No Muslim may perpetrate any of these offences.

The other one who is mentioned in this *ḥadīth* as deserving God's curse is the one who curses his parents. The Prophet was addressing an audience in a society which valued family and tribal relations as higher and more important than any other relations. Although Islam replaced tribal loyalty with loyalty to the Muslim community, Islam endorsed every virtue in any society. In the case of kindness and dutifulness towards parents, Islam elevates this to a higher degree than in any other society.

The Prophet stressed the gravity of the offence of cursing one's parents on other occasions. In a highly authentic *ḥadīth*, 'Abdullāh ibn 'Amr quotes the Prophet as saying: 'One of the most serious of grave sins is for a person to curse his own parents'. People asked: 'Messenger of God, how does a person curse his own parents?' He answered: 'He curses a man's father and the man retaliates by cursing his father, and he curses a man's mother and the other curses back'.[22]

---

22. Related by al-Bukhari, *ḥadīth* No. 5973.

Those who heard this *ḥadīth* directly from the Prophet were obviously surprised at the way it was phrased. They expressed their surprise by asking whether anyone would even contemplate cursing his own parents. The Prophet's answer suggests that it is highly unlikely that a person directly curses his own parents. Even when family relations are far from healthy, there always remains that lingering feeling of respect to one's parents which prevents a person from verbally abusing them. Some children may be very unkind to their parents, but there is an intrinsic inhibition which makes verbal abuse of one's parents come at a later stage in a family where relations between parents and children are exceptionally bad. Hence the Prophet's companions' surprise was only to be expected.

The Prophet's answer shows that kindness towards parents must include a positive attempt to guard them against abuse by others, even as a result of one's own actions. In other words, one must avoid any action and refrain from using any words which are likely to cause another person to abuse one's parents. By cursing another person, we only invite that person to retaliate by cursing us or our parents.

We know that the Prophet employed this indirect manner in order to bring home to his audience the need to refrain from abusing others. On this occasion, he does not simply counsel them against retaliation when abused, he tells them that abusing others will only invite their retaliation. In other words, they bring on themselves and on their own parents the curses of others. This method is highly effective, as it makes everyone in the audience keen to understand how other people may curse their own parents. The explanation given by the Prophet is very simple to understand. Moreover, it is very logical. The Prophet's method thus achieves the dual purpose of showing the need to refrain from abusing others since such abuse will only lead to more abuse and certain retaliation. When we refrain from verbally abusing others, we actually promote good relations in society. Moreover, we do a kindness to ourselves since we avoid other people's abuse of our parents.

The Prophet describes inviting other people's curses of our parents as one of the gravest sins. Perhaps no other religion describes cruelty to parents in these terms and no other religion places kindness to parents as second only to its main article of faith.

Some *ḥadīths* mention several points, such as the following *ḥadīth*:

18. Abu al-Dardā' said: 'God's Messenger instructed me to observe nine things: Do not associate partners with God, even if you are cut to pieces or burnt [for refusing to do so]. Do not deliberately neglect an obligatory prayer: anyone who deliberately neglects an obligatory prayer dissociates himself from the Muslim community. Do not drink wine for it is the key to every evil. Obey your parents: if they order you to give them your worldly possession, give it all to them. Do not contend with those in power, even if you believe you have a stronger claim. Do not desert the army when it is engaged in battle, even if you may be killed and your comrades have run away. Support your wife according to your means. Do not raise a stick against your wife. Warn your family against disobeying God'.[23]

This *ḥadīth* mentions nine matters that must be heeded. The first is the main article of faith, which is God's oneness. A Muslim may not associate partners with God, not even under compulsion. The unbelievers in Makkah used to inflict great torture on the early companions of the Prophet to force them to revert to idolatry but these noble companions endured all the hardship without giving way. Secondly, the Prophet makes clear that deliberate neglect of even a single obligatory prayer places a Muslim outside the Muslim community. The Prophet describes intoxicating drinks as the key to all evil, and therefore, a Muslim may not drink. The Prophet also warns against contention for power, because this leads to strife and may even go as far as to start a conflict that may involve the loss of life of innocent people. Even if one feels that one is more entitled to be the ruler, giving up one's right to safeguard the community is a better option. The Prophet also warns against deserting the army in battle, even if a defeat is inevitable and others abandon the army. He impresses on his companions the need to enjoin a peaceful atmosphere at home. Therefore, a man should not resort to beating his wife or other members of his family, and he must look after them as best he can, ensuring too that they remain obedient to God, steering away from sin.

---

23. Related in part by Aḥmad and Ibn Mājah.

The other matter the Prophet identifies in this *ḥadīth* is dutifulness to parents. He thus brings it within our current ambit. The Prophet commands all Muslims to obey their parents. He stresses this in a clear and precise way, stating that if the parents require their son or daughter to give them all that they possess, they should so give everything to their parents. Thus parents are placed in a position to order anything, and their children must obey. This requires some explanation.

Dutifulness to parents is expressed in the Qur'an and *Ḥadīth* by the Arabic word *birr* which connotes kindness, compassion, benevolence and almost every aspect of good and generous treatment of others. One of God's own attributes is derived from this root. God is the '*Barr*' which means that His Kindness, Compassion, Grace and Generosity never fail. Scholars say that this term includes everything that is good.

Muslim scholars divide *birr* into two main themes: financial and non-financial. In respect of the child/parent relationship, if either or both parents are poor, a child must support them according to his means. This is not a matter of choice. Islam makes it a duty incumbent on sons and daughters to look after their parents, providing them with the same standard of living as they provide for their own children. If a son is well off, he should go beyond the mere provision of what is necessary for a decent living so as to allow his parents to share in the comforts and luxury which he can afford. When he does so, he actually makes an investment for the Hereafter. Nothing goes amiss with God. He is so pleased with any son or daughter who pleases their parents. Looking for God's reward, some people make their parents feel that whatever they own is theirs as well. They can use it in the way they please. Although some people are careless how they spend their money, most parents are more careful when it comes to spending their children's money than spending their own.

Hence, to make parents feel that they do not live on their offspring's charity is to give them that little extra, making the difference between them feeling themselves to be a burden and feeling perfectly at home. The more a parent feels happy and contented with his child, the more God is pleased with that child. Moreover, a parent pays his child back immediately. This takes the form of praying to God for him. Such a prayer by parents for their children, which, for Muslims, normally takes the form of 'May God be pleased with you', is certain to be answered. When God is pleased with someone, He helps him or her overcome their difficulties, eases their hardships and guides them to success in life.

The duty required of children with respect to the financial support of their parents is to provide them with what is reasonable according to their means. A son of moderate means cannot be expected to provide his parents with the same standard of living as a much wealthier son. Although we speak of this as kind treatment by children, it is indeed a repayment of a debt. Parents look after their children when they are young and helpless. They provide them with all they need according to their means. Moreover, they do it willingly. A child takes what he or she is given unaware of how much effort his father puts in to earn his money. When the child grows up and his parents are in need of his support, that support must come naturally, without letting the parents feel themselves to be a burden. In order to emphasise this, the Prophet uses a special formula in this *ḥadīth*, telling us that if the parents ask their child to relinquish all his possessions, he should do so. Needless to say, parents normally want their children to do well and lead a comfortable life. They will not require them to give up all their possessions, but the Prophet says that obedience is required even in such extremity.

Apart from financial support, a child must respect and honour his parents and extend to them the sort of treatment which befits their position as parents. In any social situation, and even when they go out together on the street, a son must not precede his father or take a higher or more favourable position than his. He should always allow him to take precedence. In Muslim society, such treatment always earns the child more respect. Muslim society looks down on anyone who does not extend to his parents the standard of honourable treatment expected from children.

Moreover, a child is expected to do as his parents tell him. From the Islamic point of view, this does not apply only when a child is young. As long as a son or a daughter is able to grant the wishes of their parents, and by doing so they neither incur any sin, nor jeopardise any greater interest, then they should do so just as if the wishes of their parents were commands. There is nothing excessive in this. It does not impose a great, heavy burden. Normally, a parent is easy to please. Even when parents ask for something which is difficult to obtain, a child can manoeuvre his way to please his parents without undertaking any great difficulty.

Some parents, however, may be unreasonable in their demands, especially when they live with their son in his home. Relations between his wife and his mother may occasionally be strained. A mother may feel that her daughter-in-law takes her son away from her. This may lead to friction between the two. A wise son tries his best to reconcile his mother's rights with those of his wife. He must not be unfair to either. Should his mother ask him to divorce his wife, he must not do so if his wife fulfils her duties towards him and his mother. All that a daughter-in-law is required to do towards her mother-in-law is to respect her and to look after her in a reasonable manner. If a wife takes care of her family, fulfilling her duties, showing respect to her husband's parents and looking after them reasonably, her husband must look after her and protect her against injustice. She has her rights and fulfillment of these by her husband is absolutely necessary.

The other condition that restricts the obedience of parents is a scenario whereby parents want their son or daughter to do something that God forbids. In such a case, parents must not be obeyed. Indeed, all the *ḥadīths* included in this section are subject to the rule that 'no creature may be obeyed in what constitutes disobedience of the Creator'.

Dutifulness v. other duties

Al-Bukhari's method involves the repetition of some *ḥadīths* under different headings. Such repetition is always for valid reason, such as a slight variation of wording that places emphasis on different aspects of the *ḥadīth*, or a different chain of transmission. The next *ḥadīth* is the same as the above-quoted *ḥadīth* Number 13, but it is taken here in conjunction with the one that comes after it.

19. 'Abdullāh ibn 'Amr reported: 'A man came to the Prophet to make a pledge to him to migrate. He had left his parents

weeping. The Prophet said to him: "Go back to your parents and make them laugh as you made them weep".'[24]

20. ʿAbdullāh ibn ʿAmr reported: 'A man came to the Prophet wanting to join jihad. The Prophet asked him: "Are your parents alive?" The man said: "Yes". The Prophet said: "Then focus your jihad on exerting yourself in serving them".'[25]

Together, the two *ḥadīths* put dutifulness to parents in the proper perspective as actions that earn rich reward from God. At the Prophet's time, migration to join the Muslim community in Madinah was most important, because the Muslim community was threatened from all quarters and the state established by the Prophet was in a precarious position. At any time enemies of all sorts could muster large forces to attack it. Moreover, a migrant was required to join the Muslim army in any emergency situation. All Muslims placed themselves at the Prophet's command, and anyone might have been required to undertake any task. Yet the Prophet told the man who wanted to pledge to migrate to go back and make sure that his parents were pleased to have him back.

In the second *ḥadīth* the man made it clear that he wanted to join a jihad campaign, which might have involved fighting enemies, with all the risks attendant in such a battle. It is well known that to take part in jihad, or struggle for God's cause, is one of the most highly rewarded actions a Muslim can do. Everyone in the Muslim army is prepared to sacrifice his life for God's cause. God is certain to reward him amply. However, linguistically speaking, jihad means to exert one's best efforts. In this ḥadīth, the Prophet gives clear instructions to this man to go and try as hard as he can to please his parents; the more kindness he shows them the better for him. What is more is that to do so is equivalent in reward to fighting the enemies of Islam.

One may ask: how can kindness to parents compensate for fighting the enemy when God states in the Qur'an, warning the believers against sitting back when it is time to fight the unbelievers: 'If you do not go

24. Related by al-Bukhari, Muslim, Abū Dāwūd, al-Tirmidhi and al-Nasā'ī.
25. Related by al-Bukhari, Muslim, Abū Dāwūd, al-Tirmidhi and al-Nasā'ī.

forth to fight [in God's cause], He will punish you severely and replace you by other people'? (9: 39) There is certainly no contradiction in the teachings of Islam. Jihad is a community duty. As we said earlier, if a sufficient number of Muslims go on jihad, the others are not deemed to have absconded. Jihad becomes a personal duty only when the ruler of a Muslim country makes it so by declaring full mobilisation. To be dutiful to one's parents is a personal duty.

Reward for dutifulness

It has been mentioned more than once that dutifulness to parents is richly rewarded by God. People may wonder about this rich reward. It is clearly stated by the Prophet:

> 21. Abu Hurayrah reported that the Prophet said: 'Disgraced is he! Disgraced is he! Disgraced is he!' People asked: 'Who is that, Messenger of God?' He said: 'The one whose parents, or one of them, attain to old age in his care and he still goes to hell'.[26]

The *ḥadīth* makes clear that anyone whose parents, or either one of them, are elderly and under his care, has a sure path to heaven if he takes good care of them. They are at a period of their life when they need to be looked after. Everything their children do for them is credited into their account with God who multiplies the reward of every good action at least by ten times its value. Elderly parents need comforting and looking after every day; which means that their children have a continuous opportunity to earn reward that is certain to be multiplied exponentially. This is certain to outweigh any sin they may commit. Therefore, their account with God will be in credit, full of good deeds, and they should be in heaven. A person who is in such a situation and yet still manages to be in hell must be a great sinner, or one who has wasted this opportunity by being unkind and undutiful towards his parents.

God's reward for dutifulness to parents is granted even in this life.

---

26. Related by Aḥmad, Muslim and al-Tirmidhi.

22. Mu'ādh ibn Anas al-Juhani reported that the Prophet said: 'Blessed is the one who is dutiful to his parents. God, the Mighty, the Exalted, will prolong his life'.[27]

This is an aspect of the reward God grants to those who are dutiful to their parents. Some people are surprised when they read this *ḥadīth* because everyone knows that a person's life is fixed, even before he is born. How come then that the Prophet speaks about prolonging one's life as a result of what one does? Scholars interpret this differently. Some say that God bestows blessings on such a person, so that their day is full of achievement. Others say that God grants them greater provision. I am more inclined to the view that says when God fixes a person's age, He may ordain that such a person will live for such a number of years, but if he is dutiful to his parents, that number is increased by a specific period He determines. The angel of death will act on these instructions.

Unbeliever parents

As is well known, Islam makes the bond of faith more important than any other bond. Hence, the question arises about parents who are non-Muslims: should a Muslim child be dutiful to them? The first point in this regard is that a Muslim may not pray to God to forgive an unbeliever.

23. (*Athar* 9) 'Ikrimah related that Ibn 'Abbās explained the Qur'anic verses that say: 'Your Lord has ordained that you shall worship none but Him, and that you must be kind to your parents. Should one of them, or both, attain to old age in your care, never say 'Ugh' to them or chide them, but always speak gently and kindly to them, and spread over them humbly the wings of your tenderness, and say, 'My Lord, bestow on them Your Grace, even as they reared and nurtured me when I was a child', (17: 23-24) He said that this was abrogated by the

27. Related by Abu Ya'la and al-Ṭabārani.

> subsequently related verse that says: '*It is not for the Prophet and the believers to pray for the forgiveness of those who associate partners with God, even though they may be their close relatives, after it has become clear that they are destined for the blazing fire*'. (9: 113)

These Qur'anic verses are very clear. God may forgive any sin, minor or very serious, and His forgiveness is complete. However, the only sin that He does not forgive is that of associating partners with Him. He says: '*For a certainty, God does not forgive that partners are associated with Him. He forgives any lesser sin to whomever He wills. He who associates partners with God contrives an awesome sin indeed*'. (4: 48) In the same *Surah*, He says: '*For a certainty, God does not forgive that partners should be associated with Him, but He forgives any lesser sin to whomever He wills. He who associates partners with God has indeed gone far astray*'. (4: 116)

The question of forgiveness concerns the relation between God and man. As for the relation between parents and children, Islam is clear that dutifulness and kind treatment must be extended by all children to their parents. It may be hard for a Muslim child to be unable to pray for the forgiveness of his non-Muslim parents. Let us remember that the Prophet's own parents were non-Muslims. He tells us that he asked for God's permission to pray to Him to forgive his mother. His request was declined. We know that God granted every prayer the Prophet made either for himself or his companions or, indeed, Muslims generally. The fact that God did not permit the Prophet to pray for the forgiveness of his own mother suggests that this is not a trifling matter at all. It is indeed far more beneficial to one's non-Muslim parents who are alive that one prays to God to guide them to Islam.

Kindness to non-Muslim parents does not depend on what religion they follow. Even if they worship idols, we are supposed to be kind to them. Although such kindness may help win them over to Islam, this is not the only reason. The parent/child relationship transcends matters of personal inclination, desire, habit, creed and faith. It is well known that a parent tries hard to overcome his prejudice against something if he feels that his son or daughter likes it. Islam does not like to stir up trouble in every family where the parents are not

Muslims. It recognises that the parent/child tie need not be broken on account of faith. It, therefore, instructs its followers to be kind to their non-Muslim parents.

Only when such parents try to persuade their Muslim son or daughter to turn away from Islam does God command us not to listen to or obey them. God states in the Qur'an: '*We have enjoined upon man goodness to his parents: his mother bore him going from weakness to weakness, and his weaning takes place within two years. Be grateful to Me and to your parents. With Me is the end of all journeys. Yet should they endeavour to make you associate as partner with Me something of which you have no knowledge, do not obey them, but [even then] bear them company in this world's life with kindness, and follow the path of those who turn towards Me*'. (31: 14–15)

24. Sa'd ibn Abi Waqqāṣ said: 'Four verses of God's Book [i.e. the Qur'an] were revealed about me. My mother had sworn that she would neither eat nor drink until I left Muhammad (peace be upon him). God, the Mighty, the Exalted, revealed: "Should they endeavour to make you associate as partner with Me something of which you have no knowledge, do not obey them, but [even then] bear them company in this world's life with kindness, and follow the path of those who turn towards Me".'[28]

Sa'd's mother tried hard to persuade him to revert to his old faith. Realising that he was determined to follow the Prophet, she tried to increase the pressure on him. She knew that he was a most dutiful son

---

28. Related by Aḥmad, Muslim and Abū Dāwūd. The rest of the *ḥadīth* says: 'The second was when I took [from the booty gained in the Battle of Badr] a sword that I liked and said: "Messenger of God, give me this". God revealed the verse that says: "*They ask you about war gains*". (8: 1). The third was when I was ill and God's Messenger visited me. I said: "Messenger of God, I would like to bequeath my property. May I give away half of it by will?" He said: "No". I asked: "A third, then?" He remained silent. After that, giving away one third of one's property by will was permissible. The fourth was when I had been drinking with a group of the Anṣār. One of them hit me on my nose with the jaw bone of a camel. I went to the Prophet and God, the Mighty, the Exalted, revealed the verse prohibiting intoxicating drinks'.

and that he loved her dearly. She thought that if she brought hardship on herself, he would feel sorry for her and he might listen to her. In this way she swore that she would not taste any food or drink until he had left the Prophet. The judgement in his case was given by God in the above verses. Sa'd did not listen to his mother and continued to be one of the Prophet's best companions. He was later given the happy news by the Prophet that he was certain to be admitted into heaven.

It is clear from this story and the verses revealed by God concerning it that when it comes to matters of faith, a non-Muslim parent may not be obeyed. This does not, however, mean that one can be unkind to such a parent. We are still required to be kind to him or her, hoping always that they may recognise the truth of Islam.

25. Asmā' bint Abu Bakr said: 'After the Prophet had concluded the [al-Ḥudaybiyah] treaty [with the Quraysh], my mother came to me hoping [for something]. I asked the Prophet if I should be dutiful to her. He said: "Yes".'[29]

Ibn 'Uyaynah said: 'Then God revealed about her the verse: "*God does not forbid you to deal kindly and with full equity with those who do not fight you on account of your faith, nor drive you out of your homes. God loves those who behave equitably*".' (60: 8)

The phraseology of this *ḥadīth* suggests that Asmā's mother had not yet become a Muslim when she went to see her daughter. Another version of this *ḥadīth* suggests that the mother was hostile to Islam. Had she shown any inclination to become a Muslim, Asmā' would not have needed to ask the Prophet's permission to be kind to her. Many Muslims at that time were very kind to their parents and relatives who were not Muslims, hoping to win them over to Islam. This *ḥadīth* makes clear that even when a parent is determined to reject Islam, we should still treat him or her kindly. God later revealed in the Qur'an: '*God does not forbid you to deal kindly and with full equity with those who do not fight you on account of your faith, nor drive you out of your homes. God loves those who behave equitably*'. (60: 8)

---

29. Related by al-Bukhari and Muslim.

It is clear both from this Qur'anic verse and *ḥadīth* that to show kindness to parents who are non-Muslims is also a duty on children, provided that such parents do not fight against Muslims and do not drive them out of their land. This is further supported by the following *ḥadīth*:

26. Ibn ʿUmar reported: 'ʿUmar saw a silk suit being sold in the market place. He said: "Messenger of God, would you like to buy this suit to wear on Fridays and when you receive delegations". The Prophet said: "Only the one who has no portion in the life to come wears such a suit". Later, the Prophet received a few suits of the same material. He sent one of these to ʿUmar. ʿUmar said to him: "How can I wear it when you said what you have about it?" The Prophet replied: "I have not given it to you so that you wear it, but to sell it or give it to someone as a gift". ʿUmar sent it to a relative of his in Makkah before the latter embraced Islam.[30]

This *ḥadīth* suggests that kindness to, and friendliness with unbelievers are recommended if they do not take an attitude of active hostility towards Islam or the Muslim community.

Inviting abuse

The next two *ḥadīths* in this section confirm Number 17, which we have already discussed. The fact that all three speak about the same point confirms its seriousness:

27. ʿAbdullāh ibn ʿAmr said: 'The Prophet said: "Reviling one's own parents is one of the most serious sins". People asked: "How does anyone revile his own parents?" He said: "He reviles a man who then responds by reviling the other's father and mother".'[31]

30. Related by al-Bukhari, Muslim, Abū Dāwūd and al-Nasā'ī.
31. Related by al-Bukhari, Muslim, Abu Dawud and al-Tirmidhi

28. (*Athar* 10) 'Abdullāh ibn 'Amr said: 'One of the most serious sins is that one should provoke someone else to revile his own parents'.

A punishable offence

With all this emphasis on dutifulness to parents, people may wonder whether undutifulness is a punishable offence. The answer is that it is an offence which God places second only to rejecting His oneness and is definitely punishable. Such punishment may occur both in this present life and in the life to come.

29. Abu Bakrah reported that the Prophet said: 'No sin is more likely to be swiftly punished in this world, in addition to what awaits the offender in the Hereafter, than rebellion [against a legitimate and just ruler] and severing ties of kinship'.[32]

The *ḥadīth* speaks about severing ties of kinship, which applies to all relatives. It certainly applies, in greater measure, to undutifulness towards parents. As we have noted, the Prophet clearly stated that this is one of the more serious of grievous sins:

30. 'Imran ibn Ḥuṣayn reported that the Prophet asked us: 'What do you say about fornication, drinking intoxicants and theft?' We said: 'God and His Messenger know best'. He said: 'These are outrageous sins and carry mandatory punishment. Shall I tell you which the worst of grievous sins are? Associating partners with God, the Mighty, the Exalted; undutifulness to parents'. He was reclining as he said this, but then he sat up and said, 'and lying [in testimony]'.[33]

---

32. Related by Aḥmad, Abū Dāwūd, al-Tirmidhi, Ibn Mājah, Ibn Ḥibbān, al-Ḥākim.
33. Related by al-Ṭabārani and al-Bayhaqi.

Although no specific punishment is mentioned in any of these *ḥadīths* as mandatory for undutifulness towards parents, they nonetheless make it clear that its punishment is very severe. One reason for not specifying a punishment is that it is exceedingly difficult to prove undutifulness beyond doubt. Moreover, such undutifulness may vary considerably, according to the situation pertaining in each family. Therefore, its punishment is left to God who knows all situations and all circumstances.

Aggrieved parents

Some people do not appreciate the importance of dutifulness towards parents. Some are careless, and even worse. The Prophet warned against this, making it clear that this is a grievous offence. Al-Bukhari repeats here a portion of *ḥadīth* Number 8:

> 31. (*Athar* 11) Ṭaysalah mentions that he heard 'Abdullāh ibn 'Umar saying: 'Parents' weeping as a result of undutifulness is a grievous sin'.

When parents are unhappy with the behaviour of their children, they counsel them. They try hard to ensure that the atmosphere in the family home is right and everyone in the family is fulfilling their responsibilities. If a son or a daughter is consistently disobedient and unkind, they look into their own conduct to determine whether the fault lies with them. If they cannot mend the situation, they resort to every possible way or seek advice or intervention by some close relative. If every attempt fails and the situation worsens, they may resort to the ultimate in their power, which is to appeal to God for help. This could eventually lead to praying to God against their own child. Perhaps this is the worst situation parents may find themselves in. This means that the one who has forced his parents to resort to this is in serious trouble, because God answers such a prayer:

32. Abu Hurayrah reports that the Prophet said: 'Three prayers are certain to be answered, without a doubt: a prayer by a person suffering injustice; a prayer by a believer on travel; and a prayer by parents against their own child'.[34]

This is so because parents do not reach a situation in which they earnestly pray to God against their own child unless he or she has caused them much grief. They normally overlook mistakes and errors, they try to justify their children's failings and help them to mend them. It is only when they reach a point of despair regarding an amicable resolution and when their children give them much grief that they pray against them. Everyone should beware of such a prayer because it is definitely answered, as the Prophet clearly states.

We may link such a prayer by parents with the first of these three prayers, which is a prayer by a person suffering injustice, because parents do not pray against their children unless they feel that those children have been clearly unjust towards them. God does not approve of injustice. He forbids it in whatever form it takes. He says in a sacred, or *qudsi*, *ḥadīth*: 'My servants, I have forbidden injustice for Myself and have made it forbidden among you. So, do not be unjust to one another'.[35] God will certainly support the sufferer of injustice until He compensates him fully and punishes the perpetrator of injustice. As for the traveller, his prayers are answered because he is away from his relatives and friends. He feels his estrangement and realises that the only certain source of help he has is God. So he prays to Him earnestly, and God is certain to respond.

The Prophet tells us a very significant story, showing that God responds to a prayer by parents, even though the fault on the part of the child is a minor one:

33. Abu Hurayrah reports that the Prophet said: 'No human child ever spoke in the cradle except Jesus, son of Mary, and Jurayj's friend'. People asked: 'What about Jurayj's friend?' He said: 'Jurayj was a monk devoted to worship in his hermitage.

---

34. Related by Aḥmad, Abū Dāwūd, al-Tirmidhi and Ibn Mājah.

35 Related by Muslim, al-Tirmidhi and Ibn Mājah.

There was a cow-herd who took shelter below his hermitage. A woman from the village nearby used to come to the cow-herd.

'One day his mother came over and called to him, "Jurayj" while he was praying. He thought: "My mother or my prayer?" He felt he should continue with his prayer. His mother called out to him a second time. Again he thought: "My mother or my prayer?" He felt he should continue with his prayer. She then called out to him a third time. Once more he asked himself: "My mother or my prayer?" He felt he should continue with his prayer. As he did not answer her, she said: "May God not let you die until you have looked prostitutes in the face". She then went away.

'Some time later, the woman [who frequented the cow-herd] was brought before the king after she had given birth to a child. The King asked her who the father was. She said: "Jurayj." The King asked her: "Do you mean the monk in that hermitage?" She said: "Yes". The king ordered: "Destroy his hermitage and bring him to me". They hacked his hermitage with axes until it collapsed. They bound his hand to his neck with a rope and took him along. They passed by the prostitutes with him. When he saw them, he smiled. They were staring at him along with other people.

'The king asked him: "What do you say to that which this woman claims?" He said: "What does she claim?" He said: "She claims that you are the father of her child". He asked her, "Do you claim that?" She answered: "Yes". He asked, "Where is the little one?" They replied that it was in her lap. He turned to the child and said: "Who is your father?" The child answered: "The cow-herd". The king said to him: "Shall we rebuild your hermitage with gold?" He replied, "No". He said, "With silver, then?" He answered, "No". The king asked, "Then of what shall we make it?" He answered, "Put it back as it was". The king asked him, "What made you smile?" He answered, "Something which I recognised. My mother's supplication has been fulfilled. He told them the story".'

In this *ḥadīth*, the Prophet teaches us that even a man who has dedicated himself to prayer cannot escape the consequences of his mother's supplication against him, if she has a genuine grievance. Jurayj did not make any mistake by continuing with his prayer. His mother might have been unaware that he was in the middle of his prayer, but she was genuinely annoyed when he did not answer her after she had called him three times. Her supplication was not extremely serious. She felt a little humiliated and she prayed that her son would be humiliated in return. God granted her prayer in the terms she wished. We should, then, be careful how we treat our parents. Whatever we do, we must not let them feel offended by our attitude towards them. We should guard against them feeling hurt by us such that they turn to God for justice.

As explained earlier, God grants a parent's supplication against their child without delay. He also answers the supplication of parents for their children. This, however, may be deferred. A dutiful child, however, will certainly feel that his parent's supplication on his behalf brings him immeasurable benefit. He will undoubtedly be successful in life.

It should be noted that Jurayj's mother expected him to answer her call straightaway. She knew that he might be engaged in prayer, but perhaps it was permissible for them to speak during prayer. In our worship, ordinary talk invalidates prayer. As one begins a prayer, one needs to continue it until it is finished; it must not be interrupted.

One of the best acts of dutifulness towards parents is that of introducing Islam to one's non-Muslim parents and inviting them to adopt Islam. Abu Hurayrah, the Prophet's companion, was very devoted to his mother, but when he accepted Islam, his mother refused to follow his suit, time after time. He reports:

34. Anyone who hears of me would love me, even a Jew or a Christian. I tried to persuade my mother to accept Islam, but she refused. I told her about it but she still refused. I went to the Prophet and said: 'Please pray to God for her'. He did and I went to her. She was behind a closed door. She said: 'Abu Hurayrah, I accept Islam'. I informed the Prophet and requested that he pray

for me and my mother. He said: 'My Lord, let people love Your servant, Abu Hurayrah, and his mother'.[36]

A believer who has a relative or a close friend who is not a Muslim will always hope that their bond will be strengthened by that person's acceptance of Islam. The believer realises that Islam makes life easier, happier and more caring for others. He wants all people to share in the blessings that Islam imparts to life. Hence, a believer will always try to persuade his close relatives and friends to look at Islam and understand its message so that they can make an informed decision about it. If that relative is a parent, then the believer will be more eager to bring him or her into the Islamic fold.

---

36. Related by Aḥmad and Muslim. Muslim's version is much more detailed, quoting Abu Hurayrah as follows: 'I used to persuade my mother to accept Islam as she was an unbeliever. One day I appealed to her to accept the faith, but she abused the Prophet. I went to God's Messenger weeping, and I said to him: "Messenger of God I have been trying to get my mother to accept Islam and she refused. I tried again today but she said something about you which I hated to hear. Pray to God to guide my mother to the truth". The Prophet said: "My Lord, guide Abu Hurayrah's mother to the truth". I left him, full of hope because of this supplication. When I reached home and was by the door, it was locked. My mother heard my footsteps, and said to me: "Abu Hurayrah, do not enter". I heard water being poured. She had her bath and put on her clothes, but not her scarf. She opened the door then said: "Abu Hurayrah, I bear witness that there is no deity other than God, and I bear witness that Muhammad is God's servant and Messenger". I went back to the Prophet, and I arrived weeping with delight. I said: "Messenger of God, rejoice, as God has answered your prayer and guided Abu Hurayrah's mother to the truth". He praised God and glorified Him and said some good words. I said: "Messenger of God, pray to God to make His believer servants love me and my mother, and to make us love them". The Prophet said: "My Lord, make your believer servants love this servant of Yours and his mother, and make these two love all believers". Every believer God creates who hears of me without seeing me will love me".

Dutifulness after parents' death

Does a child's supplication and prayer for his parents benefit them? The answer is definitively in the affirmative. God orders us in the Qur'an to pray for our parents, in these terms: '*My Lord, have mercy on them (my parents) as they have brought me up when I was young*'. (17: 24) He would not have told us to pray to Him for our parents if our prayers were not beneficial for them. Our supplication on their behalf, however, benefits us as well. It is a mark of being dutiful, and God rewards a dutiful child. In other words, when we pray to God to be kind to our parents, to have mercy on them and to forgive them, He credits us with a good deed for being dutiful and He answers our prayer with having mercy on our parents. Indeed, thinking of one's parents and remembering their kindness and love to us when we were young becomes intertwined with worship.

When one's parents are alive, their presence may be a great motivator for one to be dutiful. When they die, we tend to think that we discharge our duty fully towards them by praying for them. The Prophet teaches us that there are also other ways in which we demonstrate our dutifulness. The emphasis the Prophet put on kindness to parents motivated his companions to be exemplary in their treatment of their parents. They always came to him with questions exploring every way they might earn them greater reward.

35. Abu Usayd reported: 'We were with God's Messenger when a man said: "Messenger of God, now that my parents are dead, is there any act of dutifulness left for me to do so as to be dutiful to them?" The Prophet answered: "Yes. There are four things: supplicating for them and praying that God grants them forgiveness; fulfilment of their wills; being kind to their friends and maintaining good relations with those of your relatives with whom your kinship is established only through them".'[37]

It goes without saying that the Prophet considered supplication for parents and praying for their forgiveness as one, because, when we

---

37. Related by Abu Dawud, Ibn Majah, al-Hakim and Ibn Hibban.

supplicate on behalf of anyone the first thing we ask for is their forgiveness. It may be useful to point out that family relations may be established through breast feeding, marriage and birth. If a child is breast fed by a woman who is a stranger to him, he becomes related to her in the same way as he is related to his own mother. In this *ḥadīth*, the Prophet lays emphasis on the need to be kind to our relations with whom our tie of kinship is established through birth.

These *ḥadīths* mean that we can help our parents to a higher position with God by praying for them every time we stand in prayer, whether obligatory or voluntary, when they are alive and after they die:

> 36. (*Athar* 12) Abu Hurairah reported: 'The rank of a dead person may be raised after his death. He asks: My Lord, how does this come about? He is then told: Your child has prayed for your forgiveness'.[38]

Muslim scholars understand this *ḥadīth* as stating that prayer for any deceased person is useful and benefits the deceased. Even a prayer someone said during his lifetime for people who do a certain action will benefit those who do it long after his own death. Muhammad ibn Sīrīn, an eminent scholar of the generation that followed the Prophet's companions relates:

> 37. (*Athar* 13) We were at Abu Hurayrah's one night when he said: 'My Lord, forgive Abu Hurayrah and his mother and whoever prays for forgiveness for both of them'. Ibn Sīrīn added: 'We, therefore, pray for their forgiveness so that we may be included in Abu Hurayrah's prayer'.

Abu Hurayrah would not have said this supplication unless he was certain that it would apply to everyone who acted on it. Ibn Sīrīn was also certain of this and he acted on it, praying to God to forgive Abu Hurayrah and his mother so that Abu Hurayrah's supplication would apply to him. It applies even more in the case of children praying for their deceased parents:

---

38. Related by Mālik and Ibn Mājah.

38. Abu Hurayrah reported that the Prophet said: 'When a person dies, his actions come to an end, except in one of three ways: a continuing act of charity (or *ṣadaqah*), or a useful contribution to knowledge, or a righteous child who prays for him'.[39]

This *ḥadīth* and the one numbered 36 need no comment. A child who does not pray to God for his parents, particularly after their death, when he knows that his supplication on their behalf benefits them and him is either undutiful or lacking in faith.

Again in this respect the whole question is one of debt repayment. When our children notice that we, their parents, supplicate for our own parents and ask Him to have mercy on them, they will supplicate on our behalf when we are dead. In the same way, if they see us treat our parents when they are alive as a dutiful child should treat their parents, it is more than likely that they will treat us in the same way. If they realise that we are undutiful to our parents, the likelihood of them being undutiful to us is very high indeed. If we care for our children, then we would like them to be dutiful because of the reward a dutiful child earns from God. In short, to be a dutiful child is to walk along the path which brings benefit to oneself, one's parents and one's children. In view of this, an undutiful person can only be a real loser.

Furthermore, performing good deeds on one's deceased parents' behalf is a sure way of increasing their reward on the Day of Judgement:

39. Ibn 'Abbās reported: 'A man addressed the Prophet saying: "Messenger of God, my mother has passed away, and she did not make a will. Would it benefit her if I give to charity on her behalf"? The Prophet said: "Yes".'[40]

This *ḥadīth* delivers the same message as earlier ones, asserting that a deceased person will benefit by good actions undertaken on his or her behalf. The most important of these are performing the pilgrimage

39. Related by Muslim, al-Nasā'ī, Abū Dāwūd and al-Tirmidhi.
40. Related by al-Bukhari, al-Tirmidhi, al-Nasā'ī and Abū Dāwūd.

and the umrah, giving charitable donations, praying to God to forgive them their sins and bestow mercy on them. In *ḥadīth* Number 35, the Prophet mentions four acts of dutifulness to parents that may be done after they have passed away. The last two of these are 'being kind to their friends and maintaining good relations with those of your relatives with whom your kinship is established only through them'. These may not be so easily appreciated. Someone may say: 'What claim does my father's friend have on me when our ways hardly meet? I may have nothing to do with him. His way of thinking may be very different from mine'. The Prophet is stressing this point as a mark of good upbringing, good personality and dutifulness. We lose nothing by treating our parents' friends with respect and kindness. Indeed, we gain a great deal as our reputation in society is greatly enhanced. The same applies, perhaps in greater measure, to our relatives who belong to the families of either of our parents. We should do like the companions of the Prophet who learnt this lesson from him and acted on it.

40. 'Abdullāh ibn Dinār reported: 'As 'Abdullāh ibn 'Umar was on a journey, he passed by a bedouin whose father was a friend of 'Umar's. The bedouin asked him: "Are you not 'Umar's son?" He said: "Yes, indeed". Ibn 'Umar then gave instructions that the bedouin be given his own donkey which he occasionally rode [when he was tired of camel riding]. He also took his turban off his head and gave it to the man. Some of his companions wondered: Would not a couple of *dirhams* have been sufficient? Ibn 'Umar replied that the Prophet said: "Maintain your father's friendly ties. Do not sever them lest God puts out your light".'[41]

A different version of the same *ḥadīth* is also attributed to Ibn 'Umar without the introductory account of his meeting with the bedouin.

41. The Prophet said: 'The highest form of dutifulness is when a man maintains good relations with the people his father loved'.

---

41. Related by Aḥmad and Muslim.

It goes without saying that whatever applies to fathers in the Prophet's *ḥadīths* concerning being dutiful applies, in no lesser degree, to mothers.

Apparently, the Prophet mentioned this on several occasions, as we have several reports of different companions acting on it. ʿAbdullāh ibn Salām was an eminent rabbi. When the Prophet migrated to Madinah, he ascertained that he was truly God's Messenger and he accepted Islam. The Prophet gave him the name of ʿAbdullāh instead of his former name, al-Ḥuṣayn. ʿAbdullāh was a friend of ʿUthmān ibn ʿAffān.

42. (*Athar* 14) ʿUbādah al-Anṣāri reported: 'I was sitting with ʿAmr ibn ʿUthmān in the mosque in Madinah when ʿAbdullāh ibn Salām passed by us. He was leaning on his nephew. He walked along passing our group, then he turned and said: "Do as you like, ʿAmr ibn ʿUthmān [repeating this twice or three times]. By Him Who sent Muhammad with the message of the truth, it is in the book of God, the Mighty [i.e. the Torah, and he repeated this twice]: Do not cut relations with those who had ties with your father; otherwise, your light will be put out".'

This confirms that all Divine religions agree that to maintain good relations with one's parents' friends, after they have passed away, is an important aspect of dutifulness. The Prophet expressed this on several occasions, and ʿAbdullāh ibn Salām confirms that this was clearly stated in the Torah. This means that sound and good relations can be passed on to one's children:

43. A Companion of the Prophet said: 'It is enough that I tell that God's Messenger said: "Love may be inherited".'[42]

With all these *ḥadīths* urging complete dutifulness to parents, as well as such dutifulness as is given in the Qur'an, it may be asked what things we should avoid in our treatment of our parents. This is clear in the following *ḥadīth*:

42. Related by al-Ḥākim and al-Bayhaqi.

44. (*Athar* 15) Abu Hurayrah saw two men. He asked one of them: 'Who is this man in relation to you?' The man answered: 'He is my father'. Abu Hurayrah said: 'Do not call him by his name, nor walk ahead of him, nor sit down before he is seated'.[43]

It is a tradition of the Arabs that has continued to be observed over many centuries that they show respect by calling a person by the name of his or her eldest son, saying Abu [for father of] or Umm [for mother of]. Since a son may not call his father or mother by their own names, can he call them by the name of their eldest son, even if he himself is the eldest son? A couple of *ḥadīths* indicate that this is perfectly appropriate:

45. (*Athar* 16) Shahr ibn Ḥawshab said: 'We went out with 'Abdullāh ibn 'Umar and [his son] Sālim. Sālim said to him: "It is time for prayer, Abu 'Abd al-Raḥmān".'

46. (*Athar* 17) 'Abdullāh ibn 'Umar said: '...But Abu Ḥafṣ [i.e. 'Umar] ruled...'

43. Related by 'Abd al-Razzāq and al-Bayhaqi.

2

Kindness to Relatives

CERTAIN VIRTUES ARE universally acclaimed. You will not find a person who will not praise truthfulness, sincerity or kind treatment of others. Their universal acceptance, however, does not seem sufficient to make all people commit themselves to their observance in all situations. In societies where religion has lost much of its influence on people's attitudes and behaviour we find that, although all people do accept that telling the truth in all situations is a matter of great importance, yet still the occasional lie is not met with reproach. Lies are divided into 'white' lies which are met with a smile, and ones that are not so white, or, let us say, 'coloured'. These are viewed more seriously.

This obviously represents a deviation from the universal virtue of telling the truth in all situations. This virtue represents an idea which seems to people a little impractical sometimes. When one's interests are served by the occasional lie, this seems to be acceptable. When you speak to people about this, they immediately try to justify this attitude by adding a proviso that an acceptable lie is one which does not hurt anyone. Needless to say, this line is too vague to serve as a boundary dividing what is acceptable and what is unacceptable.

Religion, however, tells us that if something is universally accepted as virtuous, it must be observed in all situations. We cannot impose artificial divisions in order to make the violation of a universal virtue more respectable. What Islam says is that when one's interests are served by telling a lie which may not hurt anyone, to lie is still unacceptable. It is forbidden. To tell the truth is more virtuous and earns more respect. Hence, this great emphasis on maintaining virtue, even when a slight deviation here or there may be very tempting.

It is universally accepted that fostering ties of kinship through kindness to relatives is bound to benefit not only the person concerned and one's relatives, but also benefits society as a whole. It strengthens the unity of the community and establishes its structure on very solid foundations. Moreover, it is something which comes naturally. There is something within us which draws us close to our relatives. We feel that we belong to the same branch of a large tree. There is much to unite and keep us close together. Together, we go through a great deal of what life has to offer.

A question arises about what is meant by one's relatives in this context. Is every relative entitled to the same sort of good treatment the Prophet is emphasising in numerous *ḥadīths*? This very question was put to the Prophet by Bakr ibn al-Ḥārith al-Anmāri.

47. Kulayb ibn Manfaʿah said: 'My grandfather asked: "Messenger of God, to whom should I extend my kindness?" He answered: "To your mother and father; to your sister and brother; and to your relative that comes next. This is an obligatory duty and those ties of kinship must be maintained".'[44]

This *ḥadīth* provides us with a definite order of relatives who have the strongest claims on us. Commentators on the Sunnah point out here that although the Prophet uses the conjunction 'and', this signifies an order of priority. A mother's claim takes precedence over that of the father, which in turn comes ahead of the claims of sisters and brothers.

44. Related by Muslim, Abū Dāwūd and al-Tirmidhi.

We have already spoken at length about the claims of parents to receive the kindest of treatments from their children. It is only logical that they also would have the strongest claim from the point of view of fostering one's ties of kinship. None is closer to a person than one's parents. This *ḥadīth* and others which speak of the ties of kinship make it clear that other relatives also have a strong claim on one's affection and material help. It is only to be expected that sisters and brothers will take precedence over other relatives. They are, therefore, specifically mentioned by the Prophet as having the next strongest claim. Other relatives come next according to their degree of relation.

We note here that the Prophet mentions the mother ahead of the father and the sister ahead of the brother. This is in line with the Islamic view that women must be looked after by their male relatives. In the normal state of affairs, a sister is likely to need help more than a brother. Moreover, she is less likely to be able to repay her brother's kindness. Hence, the Prophet gives sisters precedence over their brothers. This applies throughout this sort of relationship. Women relatives always take precedence over their male counterparts in having a stronger claim to one's help and kindness.

The Prophet applied this to himself in all his actions. Prior to prophethood, he was very kind to his relatives, particularly to those who looked after him as an orphan. When Makkah suffered famine, he suggested to his uncle, al-ʿAbbās that both of them should take one child of his other uncle's, Abu Ṭālib, who was poor and had a large family. They did so. After prophethood he maintained his kind treatment to all, including those of his relatives who vigorously opposed him and his message. There was no greater kindness he could offer them than helping them achieve a better result on the Day of Judgement, through accepting Islam, the message of truth.

48. Abu Hurayrah said: 'When the following verse was revealed: "*Warn your nearest relatives*" (26: 214), the Prophet stood up and called out [to his closest clans]: "Bani Kaʿb ibn Lu'ayy! Save yourselves from the Fire. Bani ʿAbd Manāf! Save yourselves from the Fire. Bani Hāshim! Save yourselves from the Fire. Bani ʿAbd al-Muṭṭālib! Save yourselves from the Fire. Fāṭimah bint Muhammad! Save yourself from the Fire. I cannot save you if

God determines otherwise. However, you have ties of kinship with me and I shall maintain these".'[45]

The Prophet immediately carried out every order he received from God. In this verse, God commands him to warn his closest relatives. According to the traditions of Arabian tribal society, the whole tribe is related to each individual in that tribe. Therefore, the Prophet immediately stood up and called out to his tribe, mentioning its different clans and starting with the furthest relationship and ending with his own youngest daughter. He tells them all that everyone is judged by God as an individual and according to their own deeds. He cannot alter God's decision regarding any one of them. However, he promises to maintain his good ties with them all as his relatives.

On every occasion the Prophet impressed on his companions the importance of kindness to relatives. He mentions this as one of the best deeds to ensure one's salvation in the life to come.

49. Abu Ayyūb al-Anṣāri said: 'A bedouin came to the Prophet when he was travelling and said: "Tell me what will bring me closer to Heaven and keep me away from the Fire". The Prophet answered: "Worship God, associating no partners with Him, attend regularly to prayers, pay the zakat and foster ties of kinship".'[46]

The first three are the most essential aspects of Islam and all Divine religions. Anyone who associates partners with God is barred from heaven. Prayer and zakat are the next most important acts of worship. The Prophet mentions all three and adds fostering ties of kinship as the next in importance.

Does fostering ties of kinship rank so highly among Islamic duties? In response, we say that this is part of the heritage of all Divine messages. It is also part of the universal values that all societies accept, but they give it different degrees of importance. Needless to say, in societies that stress individualism, ties of kinship get weaker with every

45. Related by Muslim, al-Nasā'ī, al-Tirmidhi, al-Dārimi and Ibn Ḥibbān.
46. Related by al-Bukhari, Muslim and al-Nasā'ī.

new generation. Yet cohesion in society is enhanced when they are maintained and strengthened. Hence, the Divine faith, right from the start of human life until the final message of Prophet Muhammad (peace be upon him), stresses its importance.

50. Abu Hurayrah reported that the Prophet said: 'God, the Mighty, the Exalted, created His creation. When He finished, kinship stood up. God said: "What is it?" She answered: "This I do as I seek refuge with You from being severed". God said: "Will you be content that I bestow My favour on the one who fosters you and cut off the one who cuts you off?" She said: "I will indeed, my Lord". He said: "I grant you that". Abu Hurayrah then added: 'Recite, if you will: "*If you turn away now, is it to be expected of you that you will spread corruption in the land and break your ties of kinship?*"'[47] (47: 22)

The Prophet describes kinship here as a living creature. She can be nurtured and fostered, and on the other hand, she can be adversely affected when she is ignored and severed. She cannot motivate people into fostering her unless such motivation comes from God Himself. She realises her inability to persuade people to give her the right sort of treatment and she, therefore, appeals to God for help. God's response is most gratifying to her. He promises to bestow His Grace on people who foster their ties of kinship and deprive those who sever such ties of His own Grace.

The Prophet's description of kinship as a living creature is especially effective. As we read it, the first thought in our minds is that it is a figurative description. The Prophet uses this metaphor to emphasise the importance of kinship and the honour gained by any person who fosters his ties with his relatives and the deprivation which is sure to befall the one who severs such ties. We can take this description, however, at its face value. Any abstract idea can, by God's will, take shape and be embodied in physical form. This presents no difficulty for God. It is not difficult for us to imagine that kinship was given a form in this particular instance and that she spoke to God directly.

---

47. Related by al-Bukhari, Muslim and al-Nasā'ī.

However, the *ḥadīth* in its Arabic form admits a third explanation. An angel may have stood up to speak for kinship. The answer would have been given to him in order to be conveyed by the Prophet to mankind. Whichever one of the three explanations we prefer, the message of the *ḥadīth* is clear. God is pleased with anyone who fosters His ties of kinship and bestows His Grace on him.

The Prophet stresses the importance of fostering ties of kinship on many occasions. In doing so, he is only echoing the Qur'an. The next *ḥadīth* al-Bukhari enters here consists of commentary on the following verses: "*Give to the near of kin their due, and also to the needy and the traveller in need. Do not squander your substance wastefully, for the wasteful squanderers are Satan's brothers, and Satan has always been ungrateful to His Lord. But if you must turn aside from them in pursuit of an act of kindness you hope to receive from your Lord, then at least speak to them kindly. Do not be miserly, allowing your hand to remain shackled to your neck, nor stretch it out fully to the utmost limit, lest you find yourself being blamed or reduced to destitution*". (17: 26-29) Ibn 'Abbās was the Prophet's cousin and well versed in Islamic knowledge, particularly the meanings of the Qur'an.

51. (*Athar* 18) Ibn 'Abbās said: '[God] begins by stating the most important of the obligatory dues and directs man to the best of deeds when one has some [money], saying "*Give to the near of kin their due, and also to the needy and the traveller in need*". He then teaches man how to excuse himself if he has nothing to give: "*If you must turn aside from them in pursuit of an act of kindness you hope to receive from your Lord, then at least speak to them kindly*" in the form of a good promise, saying that God has given and will give, if He so wills. "*Do not be miserly, allowing your hand to remain shackled to your neck*", giving nothing to anyone. "*Nor stretch it out fully to the utmost limit*", giving all that you have. "*Lest you find yourself blamed*" by some other needy person who seeks your help but discovers that you have nothing. "*Or reduced to destitution.*" The one to whom you gave what you had would have reduced you to destitution'.

Al-Bukhari enters Ibn ʿAbbās's commentary on these verses in this section as they begin by stipulating that the near of kin has the first claim when it comes to helping those in need. A needy relative should always have priority over everyone else.

Rebuffed kindness

In spite of all this, some people do not give ties of kinship their true value. Some even go further than this. They meet kindness by their relatives with ingratitude. This is bound to hurt those who are at the receiving end of such treatment. Nothing is more painful than lack of appreciation by those to whom we are attached. When a person finds his kindness so badly received, his immediate reaction is to deal back measure for measure. This is bound to weaken the community and sow division in its ranks. It is not surprising, therefore, that Islam, which wants the Muslim community always to be united and closely knit, places great emphasis on the need to foster ties of kinship. As part of this emphasis, it counsels those whose kindness is not properly appreciated not to react in the same way.

> 52. Abu Hurayrah reports: 'A man came to the Prophet and said: "Messenger of God, I have some relatives whose relationship I foster but they cut me off. I am kind to them but they are unkind to me. They treat me harshly and I forebear". The Prophet said: "If things are as you describe, it is as if you are making them eat burning ashes. You will continue to have God's support against them as long as you maintain your attitude towards them".'[48]

We note in this *ḥadīth* that the man puts his case to the Prophet in a way which suggests that he is deeply hurt. He does everything that may be expected from a relative who is keen to foster his ties with his kinsfolk, but everything he does is met with hostility. No one can blame him when he wonders how long he is expected to continue with this sort of relationship, one which most of us would consider

48. Related by Aḥmad and Muslim.

untenable. How long can one continue to show kindness to someone who not only continues to be ungrateful but who also rebuffs you? We have all heard of people who behave in this way. Although their attitude fills us with disgust, it remains a fact of life. So how should one treat such relatives?

It is clear from this *ḥadīth* that the Prophet counsels his questioner to continue being kind to his relatives in spite of their hostility. First, he tells him that they are like a person who eats burning ashes. This is a very vivid image of a hungry person who finds nothing to eat except something which badly burns his stomach in addition to its being absolutely distasteful. While no one would eat anything of the like if he could help it, the image describes the condition of a person experiencing deep and genuine regret. When they realise how God will reward their kind relative and punish them for the bad deal they have given him, and they also realise that it is all their own fault. It is not difficult to return kindness. A genuinely kind person, like the Prophet's questioner, is happy with even the slightest expression of appreciation.

Some people, however, are unkind to their relatives for a variety of reasons which are simply unacceptable to Islam. A relative may be in a low social position which causes his more privileged relatives to look down upon him. Someone who may have managed to acquire wealth over a short period of time may consider that his poorer relatives want to try to trick him out of a portion of his wealth. Some people find their relatives not very intelligent, or they consider their company not very pleasant. Whatever the reason, being unkind to relatives cannot be considered acceptable. Indeed, such reasons should encourage us to be even more kind to them. If we can help them, then our help should be forthcoming. The more unfortunate they seem to be, the more they are in need of our kindness and the easier it is for us to be kind to them. Our duty towards them acquires even greater urgency. Moreover, it earns us more reward from God. The less we expect for our kindness, the more genuine it is. God rewards us not only for the kindness we do, but also for the motive behind it. If our motive is pure from any self interest, our reward is always greater.

Yet it is difficult to continue to be kind when the recipients of our kindness are hostile towards us. For this reason, the Prophet reassures his questioner that he will always enjoy God's support as long as he maintains his highly commendable attitude. To a Muslim, this reassurance is very real indeed. It is not merely moral support. It strengthens us in our daily life. It gives us what we need so that we can do what Islam expects of us. It encourages us to be even more kind to those who are unkind to us. What is more, it gives us reassurance that when God supports us, we are in no need of support from anyone else.

A name to be proud of

It is well known that the message of Islam is given in Arabic. The Qur'an and the Prophet's statements and traditions are all in Arabic, which is a derivative language. A root word may generate several verbs, nouns, adjectives and adverbs, with no maximum limit to derivation. All derived words have connotations of the root word. In Arabic, the root word *raḥama* means mercy, grace, compassion. It is from this root that God's two names *Raḥmān* and *Raḥīm* are derived. They are translated as 'the Lord of Grace' and 'the Ever Merciful', respectively. The first is a proper noun used only to refer to God. Like His other Arabic name, Allah, it cannot be applied to anyone else. 'Kinship' in Arabic means *raḥim* and relatives are referred to in the general term as *al-arḥām*. *Raḥim* also denotes the uterus. It is not difficult to see the connection between the two usages of the word as family relations are established through being born into the same family. What is relevant to our subject is the fact that God's name *al-Raḥmān* and *raḥim* are derived from the same root and, as a result, have some connotations in common. Bearing this in mind, we are better able to understand the next *ḥadīth*:

53. 'Abd al-Raḥmān ibn 'Awf reports that the Prophet said: 'God, the Mighty, the Exalted, says: "I am the Lord of Grace (*al-Raḥmān*). I have created kinship (*raḥim*) and derived for it a name from My name. I will maintain ties with anyone who maintains ties of kinship and will cut off anyone who cuts ties of kinship".'[49]

---

49. Related by Aḥmad, 'Abd al-Razzāq and al-Ḥākim.

This is a sacred, i.e. *qudsi ḥadīth*, which means that it is God's statement expressed in the Prophet's words. That the name of kinship is derived from God's own name gives us a clear idea of the importance He attaches to fostering ties of kinship and looking after one's relatives. The *ḥadīth* promises good reward to those who do this and warns those who sever their ties of kinship. This idea is expressed in largely similar words in the next two *ḥadīths*:

54. 'Abdullāh ibn 'Amr said: 'The Prophet pointed his finger towards us and said: "Kinship (*raḥim*) is derived from the Lord of Grace [i.e. God's name *al-Raḥmān*]. Whoever fosters it will have his ties with God maintained and whoever cuts it off will cut off his ties with Him. It will have a highly eloquent, expressive tongue on the Day of Resurrection".'[50]

55. 'Ā'ishah reported that the Prophet said: 'Kinship (*raḥim*) is derived from the Lord of Grace [i.e. God's name *al-Raḥmān*]. Whoever fosters it will have his ties with God maintained and whoever cuts it off will cut off his ties with Him'.[51]

We note that the two *ḥadīths* have the same wording, although they are reported by different companions of the Prophet, and with one having more text. This suggests that the Prophet said this *ḥadīth* more than once, in different situations. The addition in the first *ḥadīth* means that kinship will argue for or against people, according to what attitude they take of it in this life. Her argument will be highly effective considering its great eloquence and power of expression. It will not be given this power by God on the Day of Resurrection if He does not consider its case to be important. This *ḥadīth*, then, serves as a warning to people that the sort of relationship they choose to maintain with their kinsfolk is bound to affect their destiny in the Hereafter. Their reward will be much increased if they have fostered their ties of kinship in this life.

---

50. Related by al-Ḥākim.
51. Related by al-Bukhari.

Advanced reward

The reward promised in the above *ḥadīths* for fostering ties of kinship, in terms of having maintained ties with God Himself, is especially appealing to a believer. With such ties maintained a believer will lack for nothing. However, there is an expedient reward that all people love to have, as it relates to this present life. It is expressed in several *ḥadīths*:

56. Anas ibn Mālik reports that the Prophet said: 'Whoever loves to have his provisions increased and his term of life prolonged should foster his ties of kinship'.[52]

57. Abu Hurayrah reports that the Prophet said: 'Whoever is pleased to have his provisions increased and his term of life extended should foster his ties of kinship'.[53]

58. (*Athar* 19) Ibn 'Umar said: 'Whoever fears his Lord and fosters his ties of kinship will have his term of life extended, his property increased and will be loved by his people'.

59. (*Athar* 20) The same as 58 above, but with a different chain of transmission.

In these four *ḥadīths* we have an immediate reward for fostering ties of kinship, which is expressed in the same terms. The reward is spelled out and it is in terms of what all people love most: longer life and better provisions. This makes life more comfortable and happier.

People may say that they understand the aspect of increased provisions, but what about longer life? Is it not true that God has determined every person's term of life? Indeed, every creature's? The answer is that He certainly has. What this means is that the increase is stated in the instructions given to the angel who gathers people's souls when their life on earth comes to an end. God will say, for example: 'This man lives for 60 years if he does not foster his ties of kinship,

---

52. Related by al-Bukhari, Muslim and Abū Dāwūd.
53. Related by al-Bukhari.

but if he fosters such ties, then he lives for 70 years'. Thus the increase is real, depending on man's actions, but God knows from the start whether the man will foster his ties of kinship or not, and He knows how long he will live.

Scholars give an alternative meaning to this increase in life term. They say that God may bless him and his mind and time, so that he can accomplish more and achieve great results that are unlikely to be achieved by one who does not foster ties of kinship. Moreover, he spends his time of life in what is bound to bring him good results and so increases his reward in the life to come.

Order of priority

The Prophet gives us clear instructions concerning our relatives who are entitled to receive our kindness:

> 60. Al-Miqdām ibn Ma'd Yakrib reports that the Prophet said: 'God enjoins you to be kind and dutiful to your mothers; then He enjoins you to be kind and dutiful to your mothers; then He enjoins you to be kind and dutiful to your fathers; then he enjoins you to be kind to your relatives: the nearest then the ones next to them'.[54]

What is worth noting in this *ḥadīth* is that the Prophet mentions mothers twice as having the strongest claim to our kindness. We have talked about this when we discussed dutifulness to one's parents. It is easier to be dutiful to one's father because the father's position commands more respect. In addition, children fear to incur their fathers' anger more than their mothers'. Hence, the Prophet places much greater emphasis on our duty towards our mothers.

The *ḥadīth* makes clear that relatives come next to parents, according to their degree of relationship. The Prophet does not put a limit here. He only says that the nearest in relation has priority. It is a question of closeness. When we contemplate this, we realise that in Islamic society

---

54. Related by Aḥmad, Ibn Majah and al-Ḥākim.

no one is left out. Everyone receives the kindness of their next of kin and reciprocates this treatment to the relatives next in line.

The Prophet's companions implemented his instructions with diligence. They realised that he gave them sound advice that was sure to bring them much benefit in this life and earn them reward in the life to come. This applies to everyone who follows the Prophet's teachings because he only recommended what is certain to earn God's pleasure. We would do well to follow the Prophet's companions' examples.

61. Abu Ayyūb Sulaymān, 'Uthmān ibn 'Affān's servant, said: 'Abu Hurayrah came to us on a Thursday evening. As he sat down, he said: "I most seriously ask anyone who severed his ties of kinship to leave us". No one left until he had repeated this three times. Then a young man went to his parental aunts with whom he had severed ties for two years. When he entered her house, she asked him: "Nephew, what has brought you?" He said that he had heard Abu Hurayrah's words. She said: "Go back to him and ask him why he said that". Abu Hurayrah answered: "I heard the Prophet say that the actions of human beings are presented to God on Thursday evening, the night before Friday, but He does not accept the actions of anyone who has severed his ties of kinship".'[55]

This *ḥadīth* tells us that severing ties of kinship outweighs any good action we may do. Therefore, it is necessary for us to foster our ties with our relatives to ensure that God accepts our good deeds and rewards us for them. When we do this we ensure that our reward will be ample. We have the reward of our good deeds and we have the reward of fostering our ties of kinship, which is a rich reward indeed.

God gives us numerous ways to earn His reward. Some of these ways come as a surprise when we learn of them. We work to earn money so that we may buy what we need to live our life. Few people may imagine that as we attend to our essential needs, we earn reward, but the Prophet makes this clear:

---

55. Related by Aḥmad.

62. (Athar 21) Ibn 'Umar said: 'Whatever a man spends on himself and his family, dedicating this to God, will not fail to be rewarded by God (exalted be He). One should begin with one's [immediate] dependents. If one has something to spare, then one should spend it on one's nearest relatives, then the next nearest. If there is still something left, one may give it away'.

Although Islam considers that one's wife, children and dependants are one's partners in whatever one earns, God rewards us for spending our earnings in legitimate ways, starting with looking after our families and dependants. People tend to think that only charitable donations earn reward, but the Prophet makes clear that even looking after one's family earns reward. This is most generous, because it is giving reward for doing what is a binding duty.

Wider repercussions of negligence

With all this emphasis on the importance of maintaining and fostering ties of kinship, a question arises about the punishment that may be in store for a person who severs ties with his kinsfolk. Generally speaking, Islam does not specify punishment or make it mandatory except in very few cases. It is enough for a believer to realise that a certain action displeases God to steer away from it, because incurring God's displeasure is a very serious matter and makes the person concerned liable to severe punishment, unless he repents and seeks His forgiveness. However, the Prophet warns against punishment that may befall a person who severs his ties of kinship or is unkind to his relatives:

63. 'Abdullāh ibn Abu Awfa reports that the Prophet said: 'God's mercy is not conferred on people when there is among them one who severs ties of kinship'.[56]

This *ḥadīth* makes the immediate punishment for severing ties of kinship shared by the people close to the perpetrator. It thus makes

56. Related by al-Bayhaqi.

them share in the responsibility for this offence. The punishment is not directed only at the individual who commits this sin. He certainly has the greater share of it, but why are others made to suffer for his offence? We must remember that Divine justice is absolute. God does not punish anyone who does not deserve punishment. How can we explain this *ḥadīth* which tends to suggest, when taken at face value, that a sin committed by an individual makes the community liable to punishment? Commentators on *Ḥadīth* give two explanations. They say that the word 'people' used in the *ḥadīth* refers specifically to those who assist the individual concerned in severing his ties of kinship, or at least they do not reproach him for doing so. This makes them partners in his sin, and as such they deserve punishment.

The other explanation picks up a different meaning for the *ḥadīth* so as to make it imply that 'rain does not fall on people...'. It is common usage in Arabic to refer to rain by the word *raḥmah*, which means 'mercy'. Such usage refers to the fact that rain causes plants and vegetation to grow, which in turn provides food for man and animals. Without rain famine becomes widespread and people die of starvation. Rain is indeed the most tangible aspect of God's mercy to mankind. Hence, the word *raḥmah*, or mercy, is used as a synonym for rain. When severance of ties of kinship becomes common practice in society, God punishes it by withholding rain.

It is to be noted that this does not apply to a person who severs his ties with a relative whom God has bidden us to boycott because he takes a hostile attitude towards Islam. Yet Islam encourages us to treat such a person with the sort of kindness that is allowed, like giving him a present or showing some thoughtfulness. As we have noted, the Prophet encouraged Asmā', his sister-in-law, and 'Umar to be kind to their relatives who were unbelievers. The Prophet himself treated the people of Makkah with compassion when they surrendered to him. Prior to that, when they were fighting him on every occasion, he prayed to God to make them suffer famine. They knew that his prayers were always answered. They came hastily to him and begged him to overlook their misdeeds and appealed to him by his ties of kinship with them. That touched a soft spot with the Prophet and he prayed to God to lift the famine. It was soon ended.

Varied punishment

As we have seen, Islam promises rich reward, both in this life and in the life to come, for people who foster their ties of kinship. By contrast, those who are unkind to their relatives and sever their ties with them may receive terrible punishment. God promises to cut off the person who severs his ties of kinship, so that he does not receive His mercy and He promises to be kind to the one who is kind to his kinsfolk. A more specific *ḥadīth* explains the punishment that awaits those guilty of severing their ties of kinship in the life to come.

64. Jubayr ibn Muṭʿim reports that the Prophet said: 'A person who severs his ties of kinship will not be admitted into heaven'.[57]

This is a very serious threat. When we remember that a Muslim strives throughout his life for the attainment of a simple goal, which is admission into heaven, then all his striving and efforts seem to be futile if he is negligent of his duty towards his relatives, treats them badly and severs his ties with them. This is the punishment of a person who is extremely hostile to his relatives. However, it is a fitting punishment. In this present life, he deprives his relatives of his kindness. Therefore, God deprives him of His kindness in the life to come.

This is not surprising, considering *ḥadīth* Numbers 50, 53 and 54 in which God promises kinship itself, to cut off whoever cuts it off. Al-Bukhari includes here a shorter version of *ḥadīth* Number 50.

65. Abu Hurayrah reports that the Prophet said: 'Kinship (*raḥim*) is derived from the Lord of Grace [i.e. God's name *al-Raḥmān*]. She says: "My Lord, I have been wronged! My Lord, I have been severed! My Lord, I have...! I have...!" He answers her: "Will you be content that I cut off anyone who cuts you off and I foster ties with anyone who fosters ties with you".'[58]

57. Related by al-Bukhari, Muslim and al-Tirmidhi.
58. Related by Ibn Hibban, al-Hakim and Abu ʿAwanah

This *ḥadīth* does not need explanation. It makes kinship something close to God Who is certain to richly reward those who foster their ties of kinship and punish those who sever it. When we hear this promise every one of us should make sure that we maintain and nurture our ties of kinship, looking for no reciprocation. We should always look forward to God's reward.

Ḥadīths on this subject are numerous, which tells us that the Prophet was keen to impress its importance on his companions and Muslims generally. His *ḥadīths* give us an idea that a society which allows ties of kinship to falter and weaken is one where corruption spreads and people's vision becomes blurred.

66. (*Athar* 22) Sa'd ibn Sam'ān said: 'I heard Abu Hurayrah supplicating, seeking refuge from the rule of the young and the foolish. Ibn Ḥasanah al-Juhani told me that he asked Abu Hurayrah "What is the token of such rule?" Abu Hurayrah said: "Ties of kinship will be severed. People who misguide others will be obeyed and those who provide sound guidance will be disobeyed".'

It is in a society that allows power to fall into the hands of fools and people of immature judgement that such social illnesses spread. Perhaps there is no greater punishment than power being in the hands of fools and youths who are immature. We can imagine how such a society will be run.

This is a punishment for society as a whole, which is bound to take place when society allows such events to take place. However, kinship is fostered or severed by individuals and everyone is either rewarded or punished according to their deeds. We have mentioned the punishment awaiting the one who severs ties of kinship in the life to come. However, this is not the only punishment:

67. Abu Bakrah reports that the Prophet said: 'No sinful action merits a swifter punishment by God in this world, in addition to what He has in store for the wrongdoer in the life to come, than

the severing of ties of kinship and rebellion [against legitimate rulers]'.[59]

This *ḥadīth* is the same as Number 29, which is cited earlier in connection with undutifulness to parents, as parents are the nearest relatives a person should treat with kindness and care. The two sinful actions the *ḥadīth* highlights share in common the fact that they weaken the structure of society and undermine its very existence. The *ḥadīth* definitely confirms that punishment in this world will be forthcoming for severing ties of kinship. However, no specific punishment is mentioned here.

True kindness

The Prophet teaches us that kindness to relatives must not be viewed on a strictly reciprocal basis. We must not adopt the attitude of being kind only to those of our relatives who are kind to us. This is a very narrow view. When we set our aim correctly, hoping for reward from God only for whatever we do to our relatives, we must not attach any importance to whether our kindness is reciprocated. As human beings, we naturally feel hurt when a good turn we do to some of our relatives remains unappreciated. However, if we remember that we are certain to earn God's reward, our resolve to be kind to others is strengthened. This is why the Prophet emphasises that a narrow view based on strict reciprocation of kindess is not the proper Islamic view.

68. 'Abdullāh ibn 'Amr quotes the Prophet as saying: 'The one who truly fosters ties of kinship is not the one who simply reciprocates kindness. The one who truly fosters ties of kinship is the one who, when his relatives cut him off, still maintains his ties of kinship'.[60]

---

59. Related by Aḥmad, Abū Dāwūd, al-Tirmidhi, Ibn Mājah, Ibn Ḥibbān and al-Ḥākim.
60. Related by Aḥmad, al-Bukhari, Abū Dāwūd, al-Tirmidhi and Ibn Ḥibbān.

The *ḥadīth* gives us a clear concept of fostering ties of kinship which does not wait to receive kind treatment in order to reciprocate it. It is important to be the one who initiates such a seemly relationship, being kind to all. Most importantly, however, is that one should foster one's ties with even those of one's relatives who are not keen on maintaining these ties. This is the person who reacts to severance by mending relations and showing kindness to the very ones who severed him.

The Prophet emphasised the importance of maintaining strong ties with relatives on every occasion. When someone asked him for advice regarding highly rewarded actions, he did not fail to point out fostering ties of kinship as one such action.

69. Al-Barā' ibn 'Āzib said: 'A bedouin came and said: "Prophet, teach me an action that will ensure my admittance into heaven". The Prophet said: "You might have stated your question briefly, but what you are asking about is broad indeed. Set someone free and free a slave". [The bedouin] said: "Are these two not the same?" He said: "No. To set someone free is to do it on your own, while freeing a slave is to help in ensuring the slave's freedom. Lend an animal with much milk for milking, and give generously to your relatives. If you cannot do that, then enjoin what is right and forbid what is wrong. If you cannot do that, then restrain your tongue from everything except what is good".'[61]

It is clear that al-Bukhari enters this *ḥadīth* here because it refers to fostering ties of kinship as one of the actions that help a person to follow the path that leads to heaven. We note that all the actions that the Prophet identifies in this *ḥadīth* have a social dimension. He begins by freeing a slave from bondage, or at least contributing to this. Islam tolerated slavery as it was a universal system, but it put in place legislation that was certain to quickly end it.[62] Here, the Prophet says that freeing a slave brings the one who does so closer to

61. Related by Aḥmad, Ibn Ḥibbān and al-Bayhaqi.

62. Islam put in place various laws requiring the freeing of slaves and it outlawed all methods of enslaving people. A full discussion of these is beyond the scope of this book.

heaven. Another action of equal importance is to be very generous to neighbours and the needy. If one cannot do any of these, then one can enjoin what is right and forbid what is wrong. Some people may find this too hard as they cannot speak out in the face of strong opposition. In this case, the Prophet gives an alternative that has no difficulty. Everyone can make sure that they say only what is good. Everyone knows how to restrain themselves from telling lies and saying words of abuse about others. This is a sure measure to put one on the way to heaven.

Because Islam places such high importance on fostering ties of kinship, a person who embraces Islam will be credited with reward for any kindness he did towards his relatives prior to embracing Islam. This is particularly significant since kindness to relatives earns reward both in this life and in the life to come. Unbelievers are rewarded for their good actions in this life only. Therefore, the person who embraces Islam reserves for himself another reward in the life to come. It is important for any good action to be linked to faith so as to earn God's reward.

70. Ḥakīm ibn Ḥizām reported that he asked the Prophet: 'Do you think that the good deeds I used to do in my pre-Islamic days to keep on a good course, such as maintaining ties of kinship, freeing slaves and charitable donation will earn me reward?' The Prophet answered: 'When you become a Muslim you keep the good actions you have already done'.[63]

Ḥakīm ibn Ḥizām was a nephew of Khadījah, the Prophet's first wife. He was held in high regard by the people of Quraysh because he was very generous and kind, before and after he became a Muslim. He lived a long life, with some reports suggesting that he lived more than 100 years. He owned Dar al-Nadwah in Makkah, the building the Quraysh used as a sort of parliament. Their chiefs assembled there to discuss any grave matter that needed their full collaboration. Mu'āwiyah, the first Umayyad Caliph, bought it from him for 100,000 dirhams. People said to him that the Caliph gave him a raw deal. Ḥakīm said:

63. Related by al-Bukhari and Muslim.

'By God, I bought it in pre-Islamic days for a barrel of wine. Now I am donating its price for God's cause. So, who has had a raw deal?'[64]

Kindness to non-Muslim relatives

Questions are often asked, especially by people who have non-Muslim relatives, whether they should still foster their relations with them. As we noted earlier, Asmā' bint Abu Bakr asked the Prophet whether she should be kind to her mother who was an unbeliever. The Prophet told Asmā' to treat her mother kindly. But what about other non-Muslim relatives? What if they are atheists or polytheists? The following *ḥadīth* tells us what the Prophet initially said as he walked with 'Umar in the market place, and what he said to him subsequently.

> **71.** Ibn 'Umar said: ''Umar saw a silk suit and said: "Messenger of God, may I suggest that you buy this suit to wear on Fridays and when you receive delegations". The Prophet replied: "'Umar! Only the one who has no portion in the life to come may wear such a suit". Later, the Prophet received a gift consisting of a number of similar suits and he sent one to 'Umar as a gift. 'Umar went to see God's Messenger and said: "Messenger of God, you sent me this suit and I heard what you said about it!" The Prophet said: "I have not gifted it to you so that you may wear it. I gifted it to you so that you may sell it or give it to someone else". 'Umar sent it as a present to his half brother who was an idolater'.

This *ḥadīth* is the same as Number 26, but it is given here in slightly different wording. It is more relevant to the present topic as it tells of maintaining ties of kinship. The Prophet tells 'Umar that it is not permissible for Muslim men to wear a silk garment. He expresses this very effectively, stating that wearing such a garment shows that the wearer will receive no reward from God on the Day of Judgement. Yet the Prophet sends one such suit to 'Umar. No doubt he considered that 'Umar would not wear it after having heard what he had to say

64. Al-Dahabi, *Siyar A'lām al-Nubalā'*, vol. 3, p. 44.

about it. However, 'Umar was confused when he received the garment as a gift from the Prophet. Hence, he hurried to see him and make sure. The Prophet told him that it was permissible for him to either sell it or give it to someone else who may wear it. 'Umar realised that he could only do so to someone who was not Muslim. Hence, he sent it to his non-Muslim half brother.

The Prophet's companions were keenly aware of the importance of maintaining good relations with their relatives, since they heard the Prophet stressing this virtue time after time. They also tried to impart what they learnt from the Prophet to others, as Islam stresses the importance of spreading knowledge, particularly the knowledge that helps a person to become a better Muslim.

72. (*Athar* 23) Jubayr ibn Muṭ'im said: ''Umar ibn al-Khaṭṭāb said once in a speech he delivered in the mosque: "Learn your lineage so that you can maintain and foster your ties of kinship. By God, it may happen that bad feelings may exist between one person and his [Muslim] brother. Had he been aware that kinship exists between them, such knowledge would prevent him from breaking up with him".'[65]

This *ḥadīth* gives us an additional duty of learning our lineage. This is particularly important in modern societies where families have tended to shrink into small units, especially in large towns and cities. According to Islam, it is not enough to keep in touch with one's relatives; it is also necessary to foster one's ties with them. This can only be done through the cultivation of close relationships.

Another *ḥadīth* also urges the need to learn one's lineage.

73. (*Athar* 24) Ibn 'Abbās said: 'Remember your line of descent so that you can maintain your ties of kinship. Close relatives cannot be made distant, even though they may live far away, and distant relatives cannot be made close, even though they may live nearby. On the Day of Resurrection every kinship will come

---

65. Related by al-Tirmidhi, adding the following: 'Fostering ties of kinship engenders love in families, increases one's money and prolongs life'.

before its holder to testify on his behalf, stating whether he had fostered or severed it'.[66]

This *ḥadīth* states an important fact, that one cannot alter the ties of kinship that exist between one and one's relatives, no matter whether they live nearby or at a great distance. It is important, however, to foster relations with them according to their degree of nearness to one. The *ḥadīth* also warns against severing relations because the tie itself will testify for or against everyone of us, according to our conduct in maintaining and fostering relations or severing them.

In Arabian tribal society, individuals might attach themselves to a certain tribe, because they lived with them and they needed the protection that tribal affiliation provides. Also, freed slaves attached themselves to the tribes of their former masters for the same purpose. Such attachment was a weaker bond than belonging to the tribe by descent, and a person who entered into such an attachment was called an 'ally' if he was a free man or a *mawla* if he was a freed slave. A question may arise here: should a person who attached himself to a tribe say that he belongs to it, or should he declare the degree of belonging when asked? The following two *ḥadīths* give different answers.

74. (*Athar* 25) ʿAbd al-Raḥmān ibn Ḥabīb said: 'ʿAbdullāh ibn ʿUmar asked me: "To whom do you belong?" I said: "To Taym of Tamīm". He said: "Are you one of themselves or one of their mawlās?" I said: "I am one of their mawlās". He said: "Should you have not, then, said that you are one of their mawlās?"

75. Rifāʿah ibn Rafiʿ said: 'The Prophet said to ʿUmar: "Call your people [i.e. the Muhājirīn] to assemble". He did so. When they were at the Prophet's door, ʿUmar went in to see him and said: "I have assembled my people for you". The Anṣār heard this and said: "Some revelation might have been brought [to the Prophet] about the Quraysh". Some of them came over to listen and watch what would take place. The Prophet came out

---

66. Related by al-Ḥākim.

and stood among them. He asked them: "Are there among you some who do not belong to you?" They said: "Yes, there are among us our allies, and our nephews [born to our sisters] and our mawlās". The Prophet said: "Our ally belongs to us, and our nephew belongs to us and our mawla belongs to us. You listen to me: my friends among you are the God-fearing. If you are among them, then that is good. If not, await the results of your actions. Let not other people come on the Day of Resurrection with their good actions and you come with your heavy burdens, for then you will be shunned". Then he called out saying: "People!" He raised his hands and put them on the heads of the Quraysh: "People! The Quraysh are trustworthy people. Whoever tries to lure them into pitfalls, God will let him fall over his own head". He repeated this three times.'

We can reconcile the two *ḥadīths* without difficulty. In the first *ḥadīth*, Ibn ʿUmar wanted to establish the identity of the person to whom he was talking. Therefore, a full statement of his status should have been given. In the second *ḥadīth* the Prophet wanted the Quraysh to maintain their bonds together. Therefore, he stated that their allies and freed slaves as well as those born to their women who married into other tribes belonged to them. They are all attached together and they should maintain their relationships and foster their ties of kinship. Furthermore, the *ḥadīth* places kinship on a much wider scale than we tend to think. This is to stress that kindness is due to all people in a Muslim society. When viewed in this light, it is bound to cement relations within society and keep the Muslims strong and united.

3

Looking after Young Girls

IN PRE-ISLAMIC DAYS, women in Arabia were very badly treated. The birth of a girl was considered a personal catastrophe for her father. The practice of burying one's daughter alive in her early years was not uncommon. This is clearly stated in the Qur'an:

> *And when any of them is given the happy news of the birth of a girl, his face darkens and he is filled with gloom. He tries to avoid all people on account of the [allegedly] bad news he has received, [debating within himself:] shall he keep the child despite the shame he feels, or shall he bury it in the dust? Evil indeed is their judgement.* (16: 58-59)

If a girl was allowed to live, marriage was the only prospect to which she could look forward. Her husband looked on her as an article he bought. If the marriage did not produce children, she took the full blame for this. If her husband died, she was considered as part of the estate he left behind. The family chief could claim her as his own, paying no attention whatsoever to her feelings in the matter. It is true that some women escaped such bad treatment, yet most women experienced misery in their lives.

However, the pre-Islamic Arabian society was not unique in its ill-treatment of women. Most societies, regardless of their degree of progress, treated women with nothing of the respect and honour their human status required. Notable exceptions were those societies where Divine religions brought about the sort of social change that elevated both men and women to the standard God wanted for them. Even in Europe, women's lot in the Middle Ages did not give them much to boast about; a woman was always treated as inferior. When she married, her possessions were practically transferred to her husband. Her ties with her own family were no longer of any value. She even lost her family name and adopted that of her husband.

Women's emancipation in the nineteenth and twentieth centuries in Europe brought about a process of real change. Over time, women were able to claim equal status to men. Legal reforms endorsed the idea of equality. Yet women continued to be exploited, and they were often treated as sex objects. Commercial advertising for a great variety of goods shows women in a way that is bound to excite men's sexual desire. Moreover, the social setup requires women to go to work, neglecting their homes and children during the day and having to compress their household duties into a few hours in the evenings and at weekends. In Muslim countries where the hold of Islam has weakened, women also suffer. Strangely enough, the blame for their suffering is laid at Islam's doorstep.

Islam is the religion of justice. It is also a religion for both men and women. It does not countenance the ill-treatment of a single person, let alone half of society. Prophet Muhammad (peace be upon him) always emphasised the importance of man's duty to be kind to his womenfolk. Indeed his last words included a strong recommendation and clear advice to treat women with much kindness. When we look at what the Prophet said on different occasions concerning women, we find that his guidance makes it clear that it is the duty of every man to look after his female relatives: his wife, mother, sisters and daughters.

76. 'Uqbah ibn 'Āmir said: 'I heard God's Messenger as he said: "He who has three daughters and is patient with them and clothes them according to his means, they will be to him a shield from the Fire".'[67]

77. Ibn 'Abbās reports that the Prophet said: 'Any Muslim who has two daughters and takes good care of them, they will be his pass into heaven'.[68]

In both these *ḥadīths*, the Prophet stresses the need to be kind to one's daughters. The main point is the need to change people's basic attitude to the birth of girls. The above Qur'anic verses tell us how the birth of a girl was received with dismay in the society which was the first to be addressed by the Qur'an. It may not be difficult for a family to tolerate the birth of one girl, but people normally expect the second child to be a boy. When another girl is born and a third one follows, a cloud of gloom settles over the household. It was often the case that the woman was blamed for bringing 'bad luck' into the family. The Prophet here tells his companions, and all Muslims, that girls should be more than welcome into any family. He does not express this notion directly. He chooses to tell fathers of the great blessings their daughters bring them. In the second *ḥadīth*, we are told that people have only to take good care of their daughters in order to book their places in heaven. In the first *ḥadīth* patience with the girls is emphasised, because people often feel at least downhearted when the third girl is born. Yet it is the opposite feeling, the acceptance of three, or even more, daughters which brings the parents something they cannot afford to lose. They only have to be patient with their daughters, willingly accept the responsibility they bring and care for them well, according to their own means and what they can afford. When they do this, their daughters become like a shield protecting them from the fire of hell. What this means is that God will reward them amply for being patient with their daughters and looking after them. This is sufficient to wipe away their sins.

67. Related by Aḥmad and Ibn Mājah.

68. Related by Ibn Mājah.

We might well ask if the same reward is given to a father who looks after three or more sons? If not, then why not? In answer we may say that the *ḥadīth* is meant to emphasise the rights of daughters, because they are often thought of as a burden to the family, and in many societies they cannot look after themselves. Moreover, people have a natural tendency to look after their sons well because they look at them as the children who carry on the family name and maintain its place in society. In most societies, boys become able to look after themselves very early in life, which is not the case with girls in general.

The phraseology of these two *ḥadīths* makes clear that in order to gain this great reward, a father must continue to look after his daughters until they no longer need his care, such as happens when they are married. It is also important to point out that earning this sort of reward requires a father to do more than his essential duty. People may do their duty in order not to be liable for punishment, but when kindness is voluntarily offered, it is much more genuine. It is this sort of genuine kindness that wins God's pleasure.

Some people may think, when reading these *ḥadīths* and similar ones, that they are at a disadvantage because they do not have two or three daughters. To them we say that God has given us many ways to earn great reward. Moreover, the following *ḥadīth* suggests that even one daughter can win for her parents an easy way to heaven:

78. Jābir ibn 'Abdullāh reports that the Prophet said: 'Whoever has three daughters whom he looks after them at home and is compassionate to them will definitely enter heaven by right'. A man in the audience asked: 'Messenger of God, what if he has two daughters?' The Prophet said: 'Even two'.

This *ḥadīth* is also related by Aḥmad ibn Ḥanbal in his anthology *Al-Musnad*, but Aḥmad's version adds: 'A number of people who were present felt that had the man asked 'Even if one?' the Prophet would have said: 'Yes, even one'. We will be discussing this *ḥadīth* again later on.

It may be suggested that it is easy for people to be kind to their own daughters. There is, after all, the natural tendency for a father to love his own daughter, no matter how unwelcome she may be socially. What about women who find themselves in need of support but cannot claim it by right? An adult woman may be unable to earn her living, for a variety of reasons. She may have lost her father and she may have no income of her own. Who looks after her? In such a situation, Islam makes it a duty of her brothers to support her. Once more, the Prophet explains the great reward such a brother can expect from God for taking good care of his sister.

79. Abu Sa'id al-Khudri reports that the Prophet said: 'Anyone who has three daughters or three sisters and is kind to them will certainly be admitted into heaven'.[69]

The Prophet thus clarifies that it is the same whether a person looks after three daughters or three sisters. When he is kind to them and takes good care of them he puts himself firmly on the road to heaven. This is the ultimate prize that should be sought every minute of one's life.

The kinder a person is to his female dependents, the greater his reward from God. However, kindness is not measured in quantity. A person with restricted means who supports his sisters or daughters as best as he can may be, in God's sight, kinder to them than a rich man who pampers them with luxuries. What is important is to do one's duty according to one's means.

When the Prophet specifies daughters and sisters, he actually puts all female dependants in one class. They are in need of our care and we should provide it willingly. By doing so, we are doing ourselves a very good turn. Our kindness is credited to our account with God. With Him, it earns great returns. Islam does not like to see a woman neglected by her relatives. If she is, she may feel broken hearted and her disappointment may weigh very heavily on her.

Perhaps no woman feels more in need of good care than a divorced woman when she goes back to her parents' home. Her family may not be very understanding. They may underestimate her plight. When a girl is married, her family help her set up her new home. They give her gifts and try to give her an honourable start with her husband. In many societies, the marriage of a daughter places a heavy financial burden on her family. The family is only willing to pay the expense

---

69. Related by Aḥmad, Abū Dāwūd and Ibn Ḥibbān.

because they hope it will ensure their daughter a comfortable future. When things do not turn out well and their daughter is divorced and comes back home sad, helpless and maybe with children of her own, there is a great feeling of anti-climax that pervades the family. Her father who might have given her all that he could may be very angry at her return. Yet she may have come back through no fault of her own. Things might simply not have turned out as well as expected. What becomes of a woman in this situation?

If she is to feel that she is unwelcome in her own father's home, her grief is multiplied. She feels let down by a person in whom she has had the greatest trust. Who will look after her if he does not? The Prophet highlights this situation and stresses the importance of a father's duty:

80. 'Ulayy ibn Rabāḥ reports that the Prophet said to Surāqah ibn Ju'shum: 'Shall I point out to you the greatest act of charity [i.e. *ṣadaqah*], or one of the greatest acts of charity?' He said: 'Yes indeed, Messenger of God'. The Prophet said: 'To provide for your daughter when she is returned to you and you are her sole source of support'.[70]

81. The same *ḥadīth* is entered here with a different chain of transmission.

When a woman returns to her father's home after she is divorced, she has the same right to be looked after by her father as she had prior to her marriage. When her father takes good care of her, he is only doing his duty, although we know that God richly rewards everyone who fulfils this duty. In these two *ḥadīths* the Prophet says that looking after such a daughter is the greatest, or at least one of the greatest acts of charity. How can we though describe one thing as both a duty and a charity?

Charity is something we do voluntarily as is the case when we donate money to a good cause or give to a poor person, after we have paid our zakat to those who are entitled to receive it. There are numerous Qur'anic verses and *ḥadīths* that urge believers to give such charity. Hence, nothing which is incumbent on us as a duty may be

---

70. Related by Aḥmad, al-Nasā'ī and Ibn Majah.

described as charity. When we do our duty we are not charitable; we are only doing what we are bound to do. These two *ḥadīths* should be understood as saying that although a father is only doing his duty when he is kind to his divorced daughter, God rewards him as if he is giving the greatest charity. God rewards us for fulfilling the duties He has assigned to us, but He rewards us even more when, having done our duty, we go on to voluntarily add to it. In this case, the fulfilment of one's duty earns us a much greater reward.

We see clearly that the Prophet was aiming to change attitudes. These two *ḥadīths* provide a very good example of how he set about achieving this. When a father feels that his divorced daughter constitutes an unwarranted burden on him, the Prophet tells him that that very burden should be more than welcome to him because it earns him a great reward.

Duty counting as charity

Islam opens many ways for people to earn God's reward. It shows them how many of the actions they do in the normal course of life can bring them much benefit and without them exerting any effort. The Prophet identified many such ways of earning reward, and some of these may well come to us as a surprise:

82. Al-Miqdām ibn Ma'd Yakrib reports that he heard the Prophet as he said: 'Whatever you feed yourself counts as a charity [*ṣadaqah*] for you; and whatever you feed your children counts as a charity for you; and whatever you feed your wife counts as a charity for you; and whatever you feed your servant counts as a charity for you'.[71]

The Prophet states four things that are credited as acts of charity, but these we do naturally. We eat to survive. Unless we do, we are bound to die. In fact, much of human effort is a struggle for survival, and food is the one thing that man cannot survive without. Yet the Prophet tells us that when we obtain food to eat and feed our dependents – spouses,

---

71. Related by Aḥmad.

children and servants – we earn God's reward for charitable actions. How can eating be a charity? The Islamic view is that when a believer does what is permissible or acceptable, thanking God for making it so, he is rewarded for it. Eating is permissible, and when we eat and thank God for making it so, we are doing two good things and we are rewarded for this. The same applies when we refrain from what is prohibited, realising that it is unacceptable to God. The same applies when we feed our children, or our other dependents, intending to fulfil our duty that God has assigned to us. The reward is not merely for the fulfilment of our duty, but God credits us with an act of charity for doing so. This is immensely generous, and who is more generous than God?

What is important is that we should do this, realising that our children and dependents are our partners in what we own. God gives us whatever we have and we cannot shirk our responsibilities. A believer should feel that having a wife and children to look after is a blessing, and a means to earn reward from God. Therefore, he should not feel burdened with having to look after them.

83. (*Athar* 26) Abu al-Rawwāʿ ʿUthmān ibn al-Ḥārith said: 'A man who had daughters was with Ibn ʿUmar when [because of his poverty] he said he wished them dead. Ibn ʿUmar was very angry and said to him: "Are you the one who gives them their provisions?"'

What is important is to remember that our present life is a test. We are all tested in a variety of ways, and we have to prove ourselves so that we earn our reward in the life to come. If one is tested by having restricted provisions and a large family, one should not wish death upon one's dependents, particularly if they are young girls and circumstances are such that do not enable them to be earners. One should try one's best to fulfil one's responsibilities, hoping to receive God's reward for this.

Sometimes, a person with stinted means feels the burden of having children to be very heavy. He may be a loving and caring father and he wants to give his children a comfortable life, but his means do not help him to fulfil his desire. There is nothing wrong with this if he continues to do his best and prays to God to give him better provisions. Islam recognises the importance of the parent–child relationship.

84. (*Athar* 27) 'Ā'ishah reports that one day Abu Bakr said: 'By God, no man on the face of the earth I love better than 'Umar'. When he returned after having gone out, he said: 'How did I take the oath, daughter?' I told him what he said. [Correcting himself], he said: 'He is the dearest to me, but one's child is closer'.

85. Ibn Abu Nu'm said: 'I was with Ibn 'Umar when a man asked him about the blood of a gnat. Ibn 'Umar asked him: "To whom do you belong?" The man said: "To the people of Iraq". Ibn 'Umar said: "Look at this man asking me about the blood of a gnat when they have killed the Prophet's grandson. I heard the Prophet say [about his two grandsons]: 'They are my sweet flowers in this world'."[72]

These two *ḥadīths* stress the fact that the strongest bond is that of parent and child or grandchild. Abu Bakr corrects himself because he said that 'Umar was the person he loved most. He realised that love is strongest for one's children. The Prophet described his two grandchildren, al-Ḥasan and al-Ḥusayn, as the dearest of all people to him.

The reference to the blood of a gnat is a reference to asking about killing a gnat when a person is in a state of consecration, or *iḥrām.* It may also be to ask whether it is considered an impurity that may affect one's ablution.

Ibn 'Umar's reference to the Prophet's love of his grandchildren is based on good authority. Many of the Prophet's companions recorded this. To give an example:

86. Al-Barā' said: 'I saw the Prophet carrying al-Hasan on his shoulder. He said: "My Lord, I do love him, and I pray that You love him".'[73]

Needless to say, the Prophet could not have wished for his grandson a greater prize than God's love. Hence, he prayed to God to love him.

---

72. Related by Aḥmad, al-Bukhari, al-Tirmidhi and Ibn Ḥibbān.

73. Related by al-Bukhari, Muslim, al-Nasā'ī and al-Tirmidhi.

4

Wishing for What We Missed

SOMETIMES WHEN WE read about events in Islamic history we wish we were present. We think that we would have done at least as well as those whose greatness we admire. This is not a vain wish. It is normally motivated by a desire to have been able to serve Islam during the great days of its history. It is also natural that this wish is present with us when we read about events that took place during the Prophet's time. Indeed, it is quite pertinent to ask whether it is appropriate for a Muslim to wish that he was around at the time of the Battle of Badr or the Encounter of the Moat so that he could have made a real contribution to the cause of Islam. One of the Prophet's companions gives us a clear answer:

87. Jubayr ibn Nufayr said: 'One day we were with al-Miqdād ibn al-Aswad when a man who was passing by said to him: "Blessed be these two eyes which saw God's Messenger. By God, we wish that we had seen what you have seen and witnessed what you

have witnessed". His words made al-Miqdād very angry. I was surprised, considering that the man had only said what was good. Al-Miqdād turned to the man and said: "Why should anyone wish to have been present on an occasion from which God has kept him away, when he does not know what his attitude would have been had he then been present? By God certain people saw God's Messenger (peace be upon him) but God has thrown them on their faces in hell because they neither responded to him nor did they believe him. Why do you not thank God, the Mighty and Exalted, for having brought you forth knowing only your Lord, so that you can easily accept what your Prophet brought? You have been spared going through a hard trial like others have had to go through. By God, the Prophet was sent in the most difficult situation with which any prophet had to contend, at a time of no revelation and when ignorance was widespread. People thought that there was no religion better than the worship of idols. He came with a Criterion that distinguished truth from falsehood and separated father from son. A man for whom God had unlocked his heart when he accepted the faith would see his father or his son or his brother hardened in disbelief, and he knew that if that person died in that state he would definitely be in hell. He would experience no happiness, knowing that his loved one was in the Fire. It is to this that God refers when He says [of the believers]: *They pray: Our Lord! Grant us spouses and offspring who will be a joy to our eyes, and cause us to be foremost among the God-fearing*".'[74] (25: 74)

Al-Miqdād was one of the very early companions of the Prophet, and he was the only one in the Muslim army to be on horseback in the Battle of Badr. He was married to the Prophet's cousin, Ḍubāʿah bint al-Zubayr. The *ḥadīth* needs no comment from us. Al-Miqdād's explanation is very clear. Those of us who have been brought up in Muslim families and within a Muslim community can easily overlook al-Miqdād's point. A person can judge himself only in his present circumstances. He cannot tell what attitude he would have taken

74. Related by Aḥmad.

had he found himself in totally different circumstances. People are influenced by a great variety of motives, pressures and feelings. When a person migrates to another country, he is influenced by his new surroundings. When he goes back home, those who had known him well in the past will detect change in him. On the other hand, he looks at the traditions and customs of his own home society in a totally different light. When a new situation comes up, his reaction may be very different from that of his closest relatives. Indeed, it may be different from his own reaction had he not been influenced by another society. How then can a man know what he would have done had he seen the Prophet and lived in the early days of Islam when the overwhelming majority of people rejected the Prophet's call? Does he think that his intelligence would have been enough to guide him aright? Among the unbelievers and those who staunchly opposed the Prophet were people who would have been classified as very intelligent in any society. Nevertheless, they were hardened in their rejection of the truth of Islam. How can any person tell that he would have acted differently from them?

Al-Miqdād also tells us something that only newcomers to Islam can experience. Those of us who have been brought up in Muslim families should thank God for having been spared the feeling of knowing that people we dearly love persist in disbelief and their erring ways that are certain to lead them to hell. We may feel that we can go to any length and give every sacrifice in order to open their eyes to the truth and unlock their hearts so that they can accept the true faith. If our efforts to guide them come to nothing a deep sorrow will continue to trouble our hearts. We will be grateful to God for having enabled us to recognise the truth and follow it, but we can never be happy at failing to make the truth equally recognisable and similarly followed by our loved ones.

What al-Miqdād said is echoed by Hudhayfah ibn al-Yamān, a prominent figure among the Anṣār. A man said to him: 'We complain to God that you were companions of the Prophet and we have missed out on his company. You were with him and you saw him but we have not'. Hudhayfah said: 'And we complain to God that you believed in God's Messenger although you have not seen him. By God, you, my nephew, do not know what attitude you would have taken had you seen him'. Hudhayfah then recounted at length an incident that took place towards the end of the Expedition of the Moat when the Prophet wanted a volunteer to go into the unbelievers' camp and find out what was taking place. None of the Prophet's companions volunteered because the night was very cold and windy. The Prophet ordered Hudhayfah to go and he went into their camp. He cited this event to show the man that even the Prophet's companions might have found a certain task too difficult, being reluctant to volunteer for it.

5

Parents and Children

THE PROPHET WAS very kind to children, showering them with his love. This was important in a society that considered showing love to children a sign of weakness. People brought him their children, especially when they were newly born, to bless and pray for them. He also blessed and prayed for children of all ages.

88. Anas reports that he went into the Prophet's home one day. 'I was with my mother, Umm Sulaym, and my aunt, Umm Ḥarām. When he came to us, he said: "Shall I pray with you?" It was not the time for an obligatory prayer. One man in the audience asked: "Where did he have Anas stand in relation to him?" Anas answered: "He put him to his right. He then prayed with us and said supplication for us, the people of the house, praying that we may have the best of blessing in this life and in the life to come". My mother said: "Messenger of God, add some supplication for your young servant". He prayed to God to grant

me of every good thing. At the end of his supplication, he said: "My Lord, grant him plenty of wealth and children, and bless him".'[75]

As reported here, the *ḥadīth* suggests that it tells of two different situations, one with Anas going into the Prophet's home and the other the Prophet visiting Anas's mother. Anas was the Prophet's servant for ten years and he entered the Prophet's home at all times. Perhaps he meant that on this occasion, he went to the Prophet with a request to visit his mother and the Prophet did so straightaway. The version al-Bukhari enters in his *Ṣaḥīḥ* anthology speaks only of the Prophet's visit to Umm Sulaym, which he did on many occasions.

We note that Anas was interrupted by someone in the audience to ask him about his own position in relation to the Prophet when they organised this prayer. He was the only male with the Prophet, so he had to stand to the Prophet's right. The two ladies stood in a row behind them.

Umm Sulaym was keen that the Prophet should come and pray in her house. She and her sister were related to the Prophet through his mother. She realised that his prayer in her home was a great blessing, but the Prophet added a supplication praying to God to grant the people of that house of all good things in both this life and the life to come.

The *ḥadīth* clearly shows that a prayer for wealth and children is not contrary to seeking the Hereafter and what it may offer. To have plenty in this life and to use it in legitimate ways, including what serves God's cause, is indeed a blessing. It is only when one uses one's wealth in what constitutes disobedience of God that money becomes a liability.

In none of the reports about this event, in any *Ḥadīth* anthology, is it suggested that Abu Ṭalḥah, Anas's stepfather, was present. Therefore, scholars express the view that it is permissible for a man to enter someone else's home when the head of the house is absent, provided that he is certain that the man would be pleased with his visit to his family.

---

75. Related by al-Bukhari, Muslim and al-Tirmidhi.

The *ḥadīth* is entered here because of the fact that Umm Sulaym could not forget her motherly instinct and requested the Prophet to add a special prayer for her son, Anas. She realised that a prayer by the Prophet is certain to be answered in the best and most comprehensive way. The Prophet obliged and prayed for Anas to have of every good thing. He then added a supplication to be granted wealth and many children. That supplication by the Prophet was certainly answered and Anas was well off and had many children and grandchildren.

The motherly instinct is always present and can be expressed in the most telling ways. The expression may be a casual or small gesture, but its significance may be great, as we see in the following *ḥadīth*:

89. Anas ibn Mālik said: 'A woman came to 'Ā'ishah and 'Ā'ishah gave her three dates. The woman gave each of her two boys a date and kept one for herself. The boys ate the two dates and looked at their mother. She took the date and split it in half. She gave each boy half a date. When the Prophet came in, 'Ā'ishah told him. He said: "Why do you wonder at that? God has bestowed grace on her because of her compassion for her sons".'[76]

It is clear that the Prophet's household was mostly in a situation of poverty. In this *ḥadīth* we realise that 'Ā'ishah had nothing to give to the woman, who was apparently poor, except three dates. As the woman had her two young boys with her, she gave a date to each of them, but both were hoping to receive more. The woman had only the date she wanted to eat herself but when she saw her boys looking at her holding the date in her hand, she gave one half of it to each of them. 'Ā'ishah was amazed at this, but it is something mothers often do. Poor mothers often go hungry in order to feed their children. The Prophet tells 'Ā'ishah, and all Muslims, that the mother's action was certain to bring her God's Mercy.

The Arabian society at the advent of Islam was of two types: there were cities and towns like Makkah and Madinah, where social ties were strong and manners were refined, and there were desert tribes

---

76. Related by al-Bukhari, al-Tirmidhi and Ibn Mājah.

with rough manners and blind tribal loyalty. The roughness of the bedouins reflected itself clearly in the way they treated their children.

90. 'Ā'ishah reports: 'A bedouin came to the Prophet. He asked: "Do you kiss your children? We do not kiss ours". The Prophet said: "How can I help you if God has removed mercy from your heart?"'

91. Abu Hurayrah reports: 'The Prophet kissed Ḥasan ibn 'Ali [his grandson] when al-Aqra' ibn Ḥābis al-Tamīmi was visiting him. Al-Aqra' said: "I have ten children and I never kissed any of them". The Prophet looked at him and said: "A person who is not merciful will not be shown mercy".'

These two *ḥadīths* show us the Prophet in his normal and natural way. He kisses his young grandson in front of his visitor, whom he knew to be a bedouin. Most probably the Prophet did it to show him that taking loving care of young children does not take away anything from a man's character. On the contrary, it shows him to be compassionate to the young who definitely benefit from such.

Such love and compassion go hand in hand with proper upbringing and education. It is the parents' responsibility to educate their children and teach them good manners and proper moral values. Children are entitled by right to such instruction.

92. (*Athar* 28) Al-Walīd ibn Numayr ibn Aws said that he heard his father say: 'People used to say that righteousness is from God but proper conduct is from parents'.

This *ḥadīth* is not directly attributed to the Prophet, but as the reporter was a companion of the Prophet, scholars are unanimous that the Prophet's companions did not mention anything relating to religion unless they had heard it from the Prophet. At any rate, this statement defines parents' roles and it says that without proper instruction by parents, children will neither learn good manners nor acquire proper values.

One of the most important values that children learn from their parents is fairness in their treatment of their children. Islam requires parents to treat all their children equally. Children must not be made to feel that they are favoured over their siblings. The Prophet made this absolutely clear.

93. Al-Nuʿmān ibn Bashīr said that his father took him to God's Messenger and said: 'Messenger of God, I request you to witness that I have gifted such-and-such to this son of mine'. The Prophet asked him: 'Have you given the same to all your children?' He said: 'No'. The Prophet said: 'Then seek someone else for witness'. The Prophet then asked him: 'Would it not please you that all your children should be equally dutiful to you?' He said: 'Yes, indeed'. The Prophet said: 'Then do not do this'.[77]

This *ḥadīth* is highly authentic and reported in several ways. In one, the Prophet is quoted to have said to the father: 'I do not witness injustice'. In another, it is reported that it was the child's mother that requested her husband go to the Prophet and request him to be a witness to the gift. Perhaps the father had other children by another wife and this son of his was much younger, as it is stated that the father carried him on the way.

Be that as it may, the Prophet teaches us a very important Islamic value, which is the need to maintain fairness among one's children. Parents must not show favouritism so that their children feel aggrieved or unloved. Fair treatment, coupled with love and compassion, is bound to make them equally dutiful.

Some people may imagine that fairness means giving a daughter half of what is given to a son. They rely on the fact that the inheritance system gives a daughter half the share of her brother when a parent dies. The inheritance system takes the responsibilities and liabilities of men and women into account. In the case of voluntary gifts by parents, sons and daughters must be treated on an equal basis, because

---

77. Related by al-Bukhari, Muslim, al-Nasāʾī, Abū Dāwūd, al-Tirmidhi, Ibn Mājah and al-Dāraquṭni.

they are entitled to the same treatment, education, health care and general upbringing. Therefore, we cannot differentiate between them in treatment and kindness.

Certain situations, however, may necessitate giving a son or a daughter something without giving one's other children similar gifts. A child may need help during a serious illness, or to repay a debt that was legitimately incurred. Providing such help is given to enable one's child to overcome a difficulty, it need not be extended to other children who do not need similar help.

Dutifulness is highly regarded in Islam, and dutifulness is broader in meaning than showing respect and obedience to those who are entitled to these. In Arabic, dutifulness is called *birr*, and dutiful people are *al-abrār*.

94. (*Athar* 29) Ibn ʿUmar explained the meaning of the word al-abrār, used in the Qur'an: 'God has called them "the dutiful" [i.e. abrār] because they fulfil their duties to their parents and their children. Just as you have a duty which you owe to your parents, so you have a duty which you owe to your child'.[78]

When parents fulfil their duties in bringing up their children, the children are more likely to be dutiful when they grow up. The first duty of parents is to be compassionate to their children, particularly when they are young. A young child needs to be shown endless care and compassion so that it will grow up physically and mentally healthy. A well loved child will reciprocate love in both childhood and adulthood. This will benefit both parents and children. Parents will feel that the care and effort they put into bringing up their children gave its proper results and children earn God's pleasure and His reward. Compassion is absolutely essential in the upbringing of children. Hence, the Prophet stresses its importance in several *ḥadīths*:

95. Abu Saʿīd al-Khudri reports that the Prophet said: 'A person who is not merciful will not be shown mercy'.

78. Related by al-Ṭabarāni.

96. Jarīr ibn ʿAbdullāh reports that God's Messenger said: 'God will not show mercy to one who shows no mercy to people'.

97. Jarīr ibn ʿAbdullāh reports that the Prophet said: 'A person who does not treat people with compassion will not be treated by God with compassion'.

98. ʿĀ'ishah reports that some bedouin Arabs came to the Prophet. One of them said to him: 'Messenger of God, do you kiss your children? By God, we do not kiss ours'. The Prophet said: 'How can I help you if God has removed mercy from your heart?'

99. (*Athar* 30) Abu ʿUthmān reports that ʿUmar decided to assign certain public duties to a certain person. The man said to him: 'I have a number of children and I never kissed any of them'. ʿUmar said: 'God, the Mighty and Exalted, will only be compassionate to the most dutiful of His servants'.

These *ḥadīths* stress the same point. Some of them are in the same wording as others we have mentioned. Some differ slightly. When al-Bukhari repeats a *ḥadīth* or gives a similar version to it, he does so in order to give a different chain of transmission or to highlight a particular point. Anyway, a *ḥadīth* that is reported by different transmitters or in different wording is more likely to be authentic. The fact that these *ḥadīths*, speaking of compassion, are given in different versions, emphasises its importance. In fact, compassion is characteristic of Islamic society, because Muslims always pray for God's Mercy. He is the Lord of Grace, the Ever Merciful:

100. Abu Hurayrah said: 'I heard God's Messenger (peace be upon him) say: "God, the Mighty and Exalted, has divided mercy into one hundred parts. He retained ninety-nine parts and placed one single part on earth. It is through this single part that

creatures are merciful to one another, to the extent that a mare may lift its hoof so that she does not kick her foal".'[79]

This *ḥadīth* gives us great hope for the Hereafter. The fact that God will exercise all these ninety-nine parts of His Mercy on the Day of Judgement means that His compassion and forgiveness will be far ahead of His punishment. When we consider that all the mercy that all creatures show, including animals and what they do by instinct, derive from this one per cent of God's mercy, then His mercy on the Day of Judgement will encompass a great deal. However, this should not make us complacent, permitting ourselves to indulge in what displeases God and relying on His mercy. We should always maintain a balanced attitude, steering away, as much as we can, from what He has prohibited and doing whatever we can of what He has bidden us. Only in this way can we hope to have our sins erased and our good deeds well rewarded.

---

79. Related by al-Bukhari, Muslim, Ibn Mājah, al-Dārimi, Abu 'Awānah, Ibn Ḥibbān and al-Ḥākim.

6

Good Neighbourliness

Recommendation from on High

PROPHET MUHAMMAD (PEACE BE ON HIM) did not leave aside a single area of human life without providing us with the necessary guidance for right conduct. Every aspect was given its due importance, and the course of action which we should follow to improve life and benefit both individual and community was outlined. In so doing, he identified how we earn reward; reward which brings us nearer to heaven.

An important area in which the Prophet's guidance is both emphatic in style and broad in scope is the relationship between neighbours. While human beings are social by nature, always forming communities, they also need to make their social ties stronger. Tribal society forms a very close community, the tribe. However, relations between different tribes may be very hostile. Arabian tribal society at the advent of Islam was characterised by endless wars between neighbouring and rival families. On the other hand, the human instinct of self preservation often leads to selfishness, causing relations between people to be cold and superficial. In large cities, community feeling is often limited. People work together only when they have common interests and, inevitably, intimacy between people is rare. Friendship is often based on personal interests, and these develop around mutuality and longevity. This is hardly the sort of relationship which Islam promotes for its community.

Everyone knows that Islam establishes a bond of brotherhood between its followers. But it also seeks to strengthen this bond in a variety of ways. It wants the Muslim community to be coherent, united by very solid ties. Hence, good neighbourliness is emphasised as a duty of every Muslim. The Prophet provides extensive guidance on the sort of relationship which must be nurtured between neighbours:

> **101.** 'Ā'ishah reports that the Prophet said: 'Gabriel continued to enjoin me to be good to my neighbour until I thought that he would include him among my heirs'.[80]

The first thing to point out in discussing this *ḥadīth* is that it is worded in a surprising way. The Prophet attributes the strong recommendation about good neighbourliness to Gabriel, the angel who brings him Divine revelations. This emphasises the fact that it is a recommendation from God. It is He who commands Gabriel to impart His revelations to His prophets and messengers. The very fact that the Prophet mentions the source of this recommendation as Gabriel means that it is an order from God.

Secondly, the Prophet points out that this recommendation was frequently repeated, showing that it is given special importance by God Who sends Gabriel with it; the angel carries it, and its recipient, the Prophet conveys it to his followers. So important is this that the Prophet begins to think that a neighbour could be given a share of inheritance, along with one's family and close relatives. Islam has an elaborate system of inheritance with a direct line that goes upwards to include parents and grandparents, and downwards to include children and grandchildren. It includes spouses but does not give siblings a

80. Related by Malik, al-Bukhari, Muslim, Abū Dāwūd, al-Tirmidhi and Ibn Mājah.

share in the inheritance unless the deceased has no surviving father or sons of his own. For a neighbour to be an heir means that he is placed on the same level as close relatives. That the Prophet begins to think that a neighbour could be an heir suggests how emphatic and wide in scope the recommendation to be kindly to neighbours is. The fact that neighbours have not in the final analysis been included among heirs does not, however, detract from their entitlement to our kindness.

Thirdly, the recommendation speaks of a 'neighbour' without any qualification. This means that it applies to any neighbour, and it is earned by virtue of proximity of location. This means that a neighbour who is entitled to our kindly treatment is every neighbour we have, whether he is a Muslim or non-Muslim, pious or transgressor, friendly or hostile, belonging to our community or a stranger, good to us or causing trouble, close or distant in location. As long as he is a neighbour, he is entitled to be treated well by his Muslim neighbours. The right of a neighbour is applicable to all. A *ḥadīth* emphasising the virtue of good neighbourliness highlighting three types of actions which are likely to strengthen ties within the Muslim community:

> 102. Abu Shurayḥ al-Khuzāʿī reports that the Prophet said: 'Whoever believes in God and the Last Day should be good to his neighbour. Whoever believes in God and the Last Day should be hospitable to his guest. Whoever believes in God and the Last Day should say what is good or remain silent'.[81]

The phraseology of this *ḥadīth* lays very strong emphasis on each one of the three aspects of kind relations within the Muslim community. It links each one of them separately to the basic rule of faith: believing in God and in the Day of Judgement. This suggests that without each one of them our belief in God is suspect. Linking them to believing in the Day of Judgement is also highly significant, because the Day of Judgement is the time when we stand accountable for our deeds in this life. It means that we are definitely going to be questioned about the sort of treatment we give to our neighbours, hospitality to our guests and about the type of things we say.

---

81. Related by al-Bukhari, Muslim, al-Nasā'ī, Abū Dāwūd and al-Tirmidhi.

The first point in the *ḥadīth*, 'should be good to his neighbour', is reported in different versions by different transmitters. This suggests that the Prophet said this *ḥadīth* more than once in different forms to emphasise its importance.

We may wonder why the Prophet chose to group together neighbours and guests, and to add to them the need to watch what we say, and to say only what is of benefit. The common factor between neighbours and guests is that they are not relatives with whom we have a blood relationship. Nor are they friends we choose because of common interests. They happen to be with us and our actions are bound to affect them and touch their feelings. Hence, the Prophet insists that we treat them with thorough kindness. Such behaviour is bound to be mutually beneficial to both parties, and also provide benefit to the community as a whole.

The Prophet adds a third point: 'Whoever believes in God and the Last Day should say what is good or remain silent'. This is an all embracing statement. If we look at what people say, we find that it is either good or bad, or leading to one way or the other. Hence, the need to emphasise that whatever we say should be good in itself or lead to something good. We should examine what we say, and if we find that it will lead to no good then we had better not say it. When we say something good we earn reward from God, but when we say something bad we incur God's displeasure and we encourage what is bad. This is discouraged in a Muslim community.

Who is a good neighbour?

In both *hadiths*, kindness to neighbours is very strongly emphasised. It is, however, expressed in general terms. The question is: what constitutes good neighbourliness?

We do not need to think a great deal about this before we realise the answer. Everything which tends to strengthen friendly ties within the local community is automatically included in good neighbourliness, provided that it does not contravene, or lead to the contravention of Islamic teachings. Good neighbourliness begins with showing pleasure when neighbours meet and includes every action which suggests that neighbours care for one another. When you meet your neighbours you should greet them and enquire after them. If they need help, you should be ready to give it. You should speak to them kindly and invite them occasionally to have food with you. If they need to borrow some money, then you should be willing to lend them such, if you can. You should visit them and enquire after their health when they are ill. If a neighbour suffers a loss of a relative or someone who is dear to them, you should offer your condolences. On happy occasions, you should congratulate them. If anyone of your neighbours or any member of their families dies, you should attend his or her funeral. On the other hand, you should remove any cause of complaint which is in your power to remove, whether physically or otherwise. Moreover, you should not build your house high above theirs, depriving them of fresh air and sunlight. It is well known in all Muslim communities that neighbours frequently exchange gifts. These may be as modest and informal as sending them some food on a plate, or as formal and valuable as any present people wish to exchange on social occasions.

Islam teaches us to accept presents from our neighbours whether they are of the first, informal type, or highly valuable. It also teaches us to extend a helping hand to our neighbours in whatever way we can, either to do what they want, or to remove what causes them irritation or hardship. Needless to say, when neighbours extend such treatment to one another, their neighbourhood will benefit a great deal. There will be no poor family suffering the hardship of poverty when other families in the neighbourhood are well off. There will be no widow or old age pensioner spending days on end without having a chance to talk to someone, as happens in materialistic societies. This is indeed the sort of community Islam wants to establish in every village and in every district of every town and city. It is for this reason that the Prophet associates kind treatment of neighbours with faith in God and in the Day of Judgement.

Offence against neighbours

Yet not all people are ready to accept such good counsel and maintain such high standards. Indeed, people are sometimes ready to be absolutely unfaithful to their neighbours. What encourages them to do so is the fact that it is easier to have access to their neighbours' homes or their property. Neighbours overlook one another, and they are likely to learn much about their neighbours and their affairs. A person with no moral scruples may be aware that a family quarrel has erupted in his neighbour's home, and he immediately tries to approach his neighbour's wife offering help and good counsel which may soon become merely a means to achieve a dishonourable end. For this reason, the Prophet emphasises that an offence against one's neighbour is far worse than the same offence committed against someone else.

103. Al-Miqdād ibn al-Aswad said: 'God's Messenger (peace be upon him) asked his companions about adultery. They answered: "It is prohibited. God and His Messenger have made it absolutely forbidden". The Prophet said: "For a man to commit adultery with ten women is less serious than to commit adultery with his neighbour's wife". He then asked them about stealing. They said: "It is prohibited. God and His Messenger have absolutely forbidden it". The Prophet said: "For a man to steal from ten houses is a lesser crime than to steal from his neighbour's home".'[82]

The Prophet makes it clear that an offence of immorality or dishonesty committed against one's neighbour is worse than the same offence when committed against ten other people who are not one's neighbours. A neighbour is supposed to protect his neighbours against anything untoward. When that wrong comes from him, after deliberation and planning, it is much more serious and merits greater punishment. Other versions of this *ḥadīth* also mention the preliminaries of adultery. This refers to a determined attempt to seduce one's neighbour's wife with sweet words, presents and all sorts of promises. Such a person may try to persuade her that he loves her and that he cannot live without her using words similar to those lovers use. When a person does so with his neighbour's wife, he is guilty of a very wicked and serious crime which is even worse than adultery committed when a chance presents

82. Related by Aḥad.

itself, without premeditation. This is a scenario which may have lasting effects on the whole community of neighbours.

Similar is the case of stealing from one's neighbour's house. A neighbour knows what valuables his neighbour has and where they are kept. Moreover, no-one suspects him when he enters his neighbour's house, because neighbours often visit and invite one another. Because of his knowledge, a neighbour is supposed to protect his neighbour's property. When he steals it, making use of what he has learnt through social and neighbourly contact, his crime becomes that much worse.

These two examples apply in other cases. In the first example, adultery or fornication with a girl or a woman who is placed in one's care is a far worse crime than adultery with someone with whom one has no such relationship. In the other case, theft by a servant, a doorkeeper, a relative or a friend is much worse than theft committed by a stranger. What the Prophet tells us in this *ḥadīth* is that when we are in a position of trust, or when we have a special relationship with someone, to make use of this relationship for illegitimate gain is viewed very seriously by God. Its punishment is much greater than what the same crime earns in the absence of such a relationship.

Neighbourly treatment

The Prophet's companions who were directly addressed by the message of Islam used to ask the Prophet about its every detail. They realised that he was among them to provide guidance. The more they learnt from him, the better they were able to understand the message of Islam and to act on its teachings. They knew that there was no other authority to explain to them what they needed, and their attitude was of great benefit to all future Muslim generations. Without such an approach from the Prophet's companions we would have been left with no guidance on many details of different aspects of our religion. We should be grateful to them for their endeavours which have ensured that we have the information we need in order to approach everything we want to do in such a way as to earn reward from God.

Some people may suggest that seeking guidance on every detail may restrict us to a certain pattern of behaviour and deprive life of what they term as its rich variety. This is a totally mistaken idea. The Prophet provides us with certain principles and opens for us certain gates. It is we who can act on these principles, decide how to approach these gates and determine what to do after we have entered. His guidance tells us how not to slip. Moreover, much of what he teaches us is voluntary. It provides a certain approach to the implementation of a principle God has laid down. Taken as a whole, his recommendations provide a perfect approach to life in general. If we act on them, we attain a very high standard. If we seek to implement a principle laid down by the Prophet in a way that differs with his guidance, we soon discover that our approach lacks something or other in its details. It is for this reason that we should always try to follow the Sunnah of the Prophet. By doing so, we are not only certain of our footsteps, but we also earn reward from God. Within the Prophet's guidance there is plenty of room for variety that adds a very rich colour to Islamic life.

Moreover, the Prophet's companions were able to understand his guidance fully. When they heard a particular statement made by the Prophet, they knew to which area it applied.

104. Ibn 'Umar reports that the Prophet said: 'Gabriel continued to enjoin me to be good to my neighbour until I thought that he would include him among my heirs'.

This is the same *ḥadīth* as Number 101, but it has a different chain of transmission. It sets a general principle. It is important to know which of our neighbours have a greater claim to our kindness. The practice of the Prophet's companions provides very important guidance in this regard, as we see in the following *ḥadīth*:

105. Mujāhid said that a sheep was slaughtered for 'Abdullāh ibn 'Amr. He repeatedly asked his servant: 'Have you sent some meat as a present to our Jewish neighbour? I heard God's Messenger say: "Gabriel continued to enjoin me to be good to my neighbour until I thought that he would include him among my heirs".'

106. The same as *ḥadīth* Number 101 with yet a different chain of transmission.

From this report we learn that the companions of the Prophet were certain that every neighbour, regardless of his religion, is entitled to our kindness. Everyone knows that the Jews have always been hostile to Muslims, throughout the history of Islam, although they enjoyed good and kindly treatment by Muslims, the like of which they rarely experienced anywhere outside the Muslim world. We note in this report that ʿAbdullāh ibn ʿAmr considered his Jewish neighbour as being as entitled to his kind treatment as any other neighbour he might have had. A different version of this *ḥadīth* adds that someone questioned about mentioning him too often. In reply he did not say that the Jew was a good neighbour or that he had been very hospitable to him, but his only reason for his kindness to that Jewish neighbour was the *ḥadīth* he heard from the Prophet. This tells us that the application of this *ḥadīth* is general, and that every neighbour is entitled to be treated well by his Muslim neighbour, regardless of religious differences.

One may have many neighbours, and if one is expected to give each a present, then this may be very difficult. It is, therefore, important to know who is a neighbour and who of our neighbours should have priority.

107. ʿĀ'ishah reports that she said to the Prophet: 'Messenger of God, I have two neighbours. To whom shall I direct my present?' He answered: 'To the one whose door is closer to yours'.

108. The same as 107, with a different chain of transmission.

These two *ḥadīths* are self explanatory. They hardly need any comment from us. But we note, however, that kindness to neighbours is taken for granted. However, it may be asked who is a neighbour?

109. (*Athar* 31) Al-Ḥasan al-Baṣri was asked: 'Who is a neighbour?' He answered: 'One's neighbours are forty houses ahead of one, forty houses to one's back, forty houses to one's right and forty houses to one's left'.

When we consider that all these people are our neighbours, and we note how strongly the Prophet recommends us to be kind to our neighbours, we realise what sort of community Islam creates in every locality. When we want to give something to a neighbour, as a gesture of goodwill, we should start with the nearest ones:

110. (*Athar* 32) Abu Hurayrah said: 'Do not begin with your distant neighbour ahead of the one closer to you. Rather, give priority to your nearer neighbour ahead of your more distant one'.

Having established these priorities, we need to realise that we should always be ready to help our neighbours. In modern urban societies, neighbours hardly speak to each other. There are cases, especially in materialistic societies, where people do not know even the names of their next door neighbours. Islam teaches us that our doors must always be open for our neighbours, and we must always be ready to do them a good turn:

111. Ibn 'Umar said: 'There was a time when a person felt that he had no greater claim to his own money than his Muslim brother. Now people love their money more than their Muslim brother. I heard the Prophet say: "Many a neighbour will hold his neighbour on the Day of Judgement and say: 'My Lord, this one closed his door to me and denied me neighbourly kindness'".'

In this *ḥadīth* 'Abdullāh ibn 'Umar laments the fact that attitudes have changed within the Muslim community and deteriorated below the standard known at the time of the Prophet, when his companions would willingly give their money to their neighbours and Muslim brothers without any hesitation. Ibn 'Umar quotes this *ḥadīth* in support of his view that Muslims should always be ready to show kindness to their neighbours. The *ḥadīth* shows that a neighbour's claim is very real indeed, so much so that a person who has been denied it in this life may claim justice from God on the Day of Resurrection. He would not have been able to do so, if his claim was not very serious. If we deny our neighbours kind treatment, we will be made to answer for it. We need to remember that God forgives faults and sins that are within the sphere of His relationship with His servants, but He does not forgive those committed against other people until they have forfeited their rights. This applies to neighbours who will be complaining to God for being unkindly treated by their neighbours.

There must be something which tells us what is the minimum degree of kindness to neighbours. The following *ḥadīth* gives us an idea:

112. ʿAbdullāh ibn ʿAbbās states that he heard the Prophet say: 'He is not a [true] believer who eats his fill when his neighbour is hungry'.[83]

This is a very significant statement by the Prophet. It speaks of mutual care by neighbours. They must know how their neighbours live, and if they are poor, then they must send them food. Indeed, this has been a tradition in Muslim societies which has survived for centuries. The Prophet even gives us a hint of how we can share our food with our neighbours without increasing our expenses a great deal.

113. Abu Dharr reports: 'My close friend (peace be upon him) enjoined three things upon me: 1) Listen and obey, even if [the ruler] is a slave with cut off limbs; 2) If you cook a broth, give it plenty of water, then choose some of your neighbours and give them a share; and 3) Offer your prayers at the best time. Then if you find that the imam has finished his prayer, you will have secured your prayer. If not, [you join him and] it will count as voluntary prayer for you'.

114. Abu Dharr reports that the Prophet said to him: 'Abu Dharr, if you cook a broth, give it plenty of water and give a portion to your neighbours, or share it among your neighbours'.

---

83. Related by al-Ḥākim and al-Bayhaqi.

These two *ḥadīths* mention in similar words an important principle, which is not to think too little of anything which we can give to our neighbours. Even a person who is not rich can give his neighbours some food which may not be the best they can have, but will be more than useful in a neighbourhood where poverty is common. The first *ḥadīth* adds two more qualities. The first is to be law-abiding, even though the ruler may be a person who is normally looked down upon. This is important in order to keep law and order in Muslim society. As long as the ruler does not order us to do what God prohibits, we should listen and obey.

The other quality is to attend to one's prayer at the best time, which is as early as possible in its time range. If one is away from the mosque and a prayer falls due, one should offer it to make sure that one has fulfilled one's duty. If one then proceeds to the mosque and finds congregation about to start, one should join the congregation, repeating one's prayer. It is not right to stand away, showing that one does not belong to the congregation. This second prayer counts as a voluntary prayer, or *nafl*, and is rewarded accordingly.

The best of neighbours

The Prophet was keen to establish the kind treatment of neighbours as an intrinsic value which is true of every Muslim society. In this, the Prophet was so successful that good neighbourliness continued to be characteristic of Muslim societies even when these societies moved far away from true Islam. This was when illiteracy spread across the Muslim world and much of it fell under colonial rule. Indeed, Muslims always aspire to maintain this characteristic to a very high level.

Furthermore, the Prophet viewed a bad neighbour as one of the worst things a person may have to endure in this life. He did not want any of his companions to be a bad neighbour. He, therefore, emphasised to us that God views a person in the light of his treatment of friends and neighbours:

115. ‘Abdullāh ibn ‘Amr quotes the Prophet as saying: ‘The best of companions in God’s sight is the one who is best to his companion, and the best of neighbours in God’s sight is the one who is best towards his neighbour’.[84]

This *ḥadīth* shows that a person can enhance his standing with God by being kind and hospitable to his friends and neighbours. This is something every person should be keen to achieve, because it not only earns him a better reward from God, but it also makes him loved by his friends and neighbours. Kindness is never wasted. A person who is kind to others will at least be praised for such kindness. Hence, if he aims at pleasing God by being kind to his neighbours, he earns a dual reward, one in this life and the other in the life to come.

Because of the importance of good neighbourliness, people make enquiries about their neighbours before they move into a certain area. This is only reasonable, because one has to come into contact with neighbours, and if they are of the wrong type, they can make life miserable. Indeed, the Prophet mentions a good neighbour as one of the sources of happiness for any Muslim:

116. Nāfi‘ ibn ‘Abd al-Ḥārith reports that the Prophet said: ‘Among the things that contribute to the happiness of a Muslim are a spacious dwelling, a good neighbour and a comfortable means of transport’.[85]

People readily agree that all these three are essential for a comfortable life. A spacious home provides the amenities that people require. No one can appreciate the comfort that a spacious home gives more than one who has lived in a small overcrowded place and then circumstances change to give him a much larger one. Similarly, when people need to use transport, comfort is essential. When people have to take an overcrowded bus, they are far from pleased.

A good neighbour is a blessing that adds to man’s happiness. People used to say: ‘Look for your neighbour before you choose your

---

84. Related by Aḥmad, al-Tirmidhi, al-Ḥākim, Ibn Khuzaymah and al-Dārimi.
85. Related by Aḥmad and al-Ḥākim.

residence'. On the other hand, the Prophet used to pray for shelter with God from bad neighbours:

117. Abu Hurayrah reports 'The Prophet used to say in his supplication: "My Lord, I seek refuge with you from a bad neighbour in my place of abode. For a temporary neighbour is bound to depart".'[86]

Had it not been for the fact that a bad neighbour causes a great deal of harm and unhappiness, the Prophet would not have sought refuge with God from having such a difficulty.

The Prophet warned against bad neighbourliness, further telling that when relations become very bad between neighbours, then this is a sign of the Day of Judgement's approach.

118. Abu Mūsa al-Ash'ari reports that the Prophet said: 'The Last Hour will not be due until a man kills his neighbour, his brother and his father'.

The Prophet is not referring here to a particular person who might commit such crimes. He refers to a state of things that makes such crime quite common. It should be noted that the Prophet places the killing of one's neighbour on the same footing as killing one's brother or father. Needless to say, these are the most horrific of crimes.

Indeed, when neighbourly ties decline so badly, good actions become of little use. Acts of worship do not earn enough reward to compensate for bad neighbourliness.

119. Abu Hurayrah mentions that people said to the Prophet: 'Messenger of God, a certain woman stands up for prayer at night and fasts during the day, and does many a good thing and gives money for charity but she offends her neighbours with what she says'. He said: 'She is devoid of goodness. She is one of the people of the Fire'. They said: 'A certain woman prays only obligatory prayers and gives little for charity, but she does not

86. Related by al-Nasā'ī, al-Ḥākim and Ibn Ḥibbān.

offend anyone'. The Prophet said: 'She is one of the people of heaven'.[87]

What the first woman did was to offer a variety of voluntary worship, such as standing up for prayer at night and fasting during the day. Nevertheless, all of this was of no avail to her because of her offensive remarks against her neighbours. This was apparently a habit with her. The woman who simply offered obligatory worship merited heaven because she did not offend anyone. This stresses beyond any doubt the importance of good neighbourliness and good social behaviour.

Caring for a neighbour's feelings

Some *ḥadīths* give us details of a particular situation or incident. As such, they may touch on a host of issues and a scholar like al-Bukhari will enter the same *ḥadīth* under different headings. If he has different versions of the *ḥadīth*, or if the *ḥadīth* has more than one chain of transmission, he uses these versions, entering each one under its most suitable heading. The following *ḥadīth* is entered by al-Bukhari under the prohibition of offending neighbours.

120. 'Umārah ibn Ghurāb reported that his paternal aunt related to him that she asked 'Ā'ishah: 'If a woman's husband desires her and she refuses him because she is angry or tired, is she to blame?' 'Ā'ishah replied: 'Yes. It is his right that if he desires you and you are on a pack-saddle, you must not refuse him'.

She said: I asked her: 'If a woman is in her period and she shares the same bed with her husband or they have only one quilt, what should she do?' 'Ā'ishah answered: 'She should wrap herself properly and go to bed with him. What is above that he may have. However, I will tell you what the Prophet did. On one of my nights with him, I had ground some barley and made a loaf for him. He came in, closed the door and then went into the mosque. Whenever he wanted to go to sleep, he would shut

87. Related by Aḥmad, al-Ḥākim, al-Bazzār and Ibn Ḥibbān.

the door, tie up the waterskin, turn the cup over and put out the light. I waited for him to finish [his night worship] so that I might serve him the loaf, but he took too long. I fell asleep and he felt very cold. He came over to me and woke me up, saying: "Warm me, warm me". I said: "I am in my period". He said: "Even though. Uncover your thighs". I uncovered my thighs for him and he put his cheek and his head on my thigh, until he felt the warmth. Then a pet sheep belonging to our neighbour came in and took away the loaf. I was very upset and caught up with her at the door. The Prophet woke up and said: "Take what you have left of your loaf and do not hurt your neighbour because of his sheep".'[88]

We need not wonder that al-Bukhari enters this *ḥadīth* under the overall heading of kindness to neighbours. The Prophet instructs 'Ā'ishah to let the sheep get away with whatever it had of the loaf she had baked for him, but she must not show displeasure with the sheep, because it was a neighbour's pet. If she ate the loaf, good for her, and if 'Ā'ishah managed to get back some of it, all well and good. The important thing is that the neighbour should not feel upset.

The *ḥadīth* includes other important points relating to marital relations. A woman may not refuse her husband if he desires her because both man and wife should help each other maintain their chastity. When a husband is refused, he feels very hurt and may be tempted to seek satisfaction elsewhere. This may lead him to what is forbidden. Therefore, his wife should not refuse him.

We also learn from this *ḥadīth*, and others on the subject, that when a woman has her period, her husband may not have intercourse with her. However, he may enjoy foreplay with her. As 'Ā'ishah, the Prophet's wife, tells us in this *ḥadīth*, what is forbidden during the period is sexual intercourse, but everything else is permissible as usual. The Prophet asked her to uncover her thighs for him and she did. He put his head and cheek on her thigh to warm himself. We know that the Prophet was always in full control of his sexual desire, but he showed us by his practice what is permissible in certain situations.

---

88. Related by Abū Dāwūd.

In this instance, he demonstrated that nothing is forbidden between a man and wife during her period except intercourse.

Unkind neighbours

As we have seen, Islam lays much emphasis on the need to be good to one's neighbours. There is no shortage of *ḥadīths* that require Muslims to be kind to their neighbours. At the same time, the Prophet warned against unkind behaviour towards one's neighbours. However, some people scheme against their neighbours and try to gain advantage of them, even by resorting to unacceptable or illegitimate means. The Prophet warns most emphatically against such behaviour:

121. Abu Hurayrah reports that the Prophet said: 'A person whose neighbours are unsafe from his evil schemes shall not be admitted into heaven'.

This is a very grim prospect for a person who does not hesitate to devise a wicked scheme against his neighbours to achieve some selfish objective. The *ḥadīth* makes maintaining goodwill and friendly relations with one's neighbours a condition for admittance into heaven.

We will have more to say about this type of neighbour, but al-Bukhari enters at this point a couple of *ḥadīths* that encourage Muslims not to belittle or underestimate any small kindness they may do to their neighbours.

122. Ḥawwā' bint Yazīd ibn al-Sakan reports: 'God's Messenger said to me: "Believing women! Do not let any of you women disdain to give her neighbour [a small gift], even if it is only a burnt sheep's hoof".'

123. Abu Hurayrah reports that the Prophet said: 'Muslim women! Muslim women! A woman should not disdain to give her neighbour a gift as small as a sheep's hoof'.[89]

---

89. Related by al-Bukhari.

These two *ḥadīths* admit the two possibilities of the address being to the women giving the gifts or to the women receiving the gifts. A person may hesitate to give a small gift, even though he cannot give a better one, for fear of being criticised. The Prophet tells Muslim women not to disdain giving such a gift because its the thought that matters. If a woman can give her neighbour only a very small gift, she should not hesitate to give it because giving a gift strengthens relations. At the same time, the one who receives such a small gift should not look at it with contempt. She should appreciate the fact that her neighbour has been thoughtful and has given her a gift as per her own means. If neither woman belittles even a small gift, relations between them will be better. Moreover, with repeated small gifts, what is given becomes plentiful.

In these two *ḥadīths*, the Prophet addresses women in particular, but the meaning equally applies to men and women. The women are mentioned in particular because they are more sensitive to appearances. Hence, they are more likely either to hesitate to give a small gift or to belittle one when they receive it.

With all this emphasis on goodly treatment of neighbours, Muslim society values good neighbourliness among its top qualities. Thus, a bad neighbour is shown in very bad light. When it is established that a particular person is unkind to his neighbours or hurts them, the entire community shuns his behaviour. Therefore, in a Muslim society, the best thing to stop anyone from behaving badly towards his neighbours is to publicise his unkind actions:

124. Abu Hurayrah reports that a man said to the Prophet: 'Messenger of God, I have a neighbour who does me harm'. The Prophet said: 'Go and take your things out into the road'. The man did what the Prophet suggested. People gathered around him, asking him what the matter was. He said: 'I have a neighbour who harms me. I mentioned this to the Prophet (peace be upon him) and he told me to take my things out into the road'. People cursed him [the bad neighbor] and prayed to God to visit him with disgrace. The man was informed of what

happened. He came directly and said to his neighbour: 'Go back to your house. By God, I will do you no harm'.[90]

125. Abu Juḥayfah said: 'A man complained to the Prophet about his neighbour. The Prophet said: "Take your things out and put them on the road. Whoever passes will curse him". Everyone who passed began to curse that neighbour. So he went to the Prophet and complained of the treatment he received from people. The Prophet said: "God's curse is on top of their curses". He then said to the one who had complained: "You have had redress", or something to this effect.'[91]

In Muslim society, no one likes to be known as a bad neighbour. This is because Islam stresses the virtue of good neighbourliness. When a person is known to be bad to his neighbours, his reputation suffers a great deal. People will have no respect for him. Indeed, they curse him because he violates an important principle of Islamic social behaviour. It is important, however, that when one publicises the fact that his neighbour does not treat him well, he must not indulge in backbiting that neighbour or exaggerating his bad treatment. What the Prophet advised was to show that the complainant's neighbour's attitude towards him had caused him to leave his home. He did not say more than this. This was sufficient for people to recognise that the matter was serious. For this reason, they were willing to lend their moral support, and this was enough for the neighbour to change his attitude.

This topic of good neighbourliness includes three more *ḥadīths* which mostly repeat what has already been stated:

126. Jābir said: 'A man came to the Prophet (peace be upon him) to complain about his neighbour's hostility towards him. As he sat [close to the Ka'bah] between the corner [of the Black Stone] and the Maqam [i.e. Abraham's place], the Prophet came over. He was accompanied by a man wearing white garments.

90. Related by Abū Dāwūd, al-Ḥākim and Ibn Ḥibbān.
91. Related by al-Ḥākim and al-Ṭabarāni.

They were close to the Maqam where they used to offer the prayer for the deceased. The Prophet then came to him, and the man asked him: "Both my parents be your ransom, Messenger of God! Who was the man I saw with you wearing white garments?" The Prophet asked: "Did you really see him?" The man said: "Yes". The Prophet said: 'Then you have seen much good. That was Gabriel, my Lord's messenger. He repeatedly urged me to be good to neighbours until I thought that he would give a neighbour a share of inheritance".'

People rarely see angels, and only on particular occasions. In this case, the man's sight of the angel was to comfort him after he had been badly treated by his neighbour. The Prophet told him that he had thus seen much good, i.e. the angel.

127. (*Athar* 33) Thawbān said: 'If two men break off with each other for longer than three days and one of them dies [which means that] both will die with their relations severed, both of them are ruined. And anyone who wrongs his neighbour to the extent that he finds no option but to leave his home is ruined'.

128. Mujāhid said: 'I was at 'Abdullāh ibn 'Amr when his servant was skinning a sheep. He said: "Young lad! When you finish, start [its distribution] with our Jewish neighbour". A man who was present said [in surprise]: "The Jew! May God give you good guidance". 'Abdullāh replied: "I heard the Prophet (peace be upon him) urging good treatment of neighbours to the point that we feared, or we thought, that he would make a neighbour an heir".'[92]

This *ḥadīth* has been entered several times in this chapter. This is yet another version of it, attributing the thought that a neighbour might become an heir to the Prophet's companions rather than to the Prophet himself.

---

92. Related by Abū Dāwūd and al-Tirmidhi.

7

The Most Noble of People

THE IDEA OF nobility is recognised by all societies. Everywhere in the world we find people who are distinguished and hold special positions in society. These positions need not be official. Many achieve good reputation through their personal good qualities such as courage, generosity, kindness or sagacity. Many build on what their fathers and grandfathers have achieved of distinction. This is how the noble class develops and manages to hold sway in society. When hereditary distinction is combined with affluence, the family which enjoys both is recognised as one of the most noble. Social orders may differ in their outlook and the systems they establish, but the idea of distinction imposes itself on all societies regardless of how the factors which bring distinction about differ.

In a tribal society like the one that existed in Arabia at the time the Prophet was given his message, social distinction was very much present in people's minds. Everyone wanted to achieve high honour in his own tribe, and every tribe worked hard to elevate its position vis-à-vis other tribes. There were several areas of distinction over which people vied with one another. There were also rigid constraints which made some people lag behind, although they possessed all the qualities which make for the achievement of a highly distinguished position. For example, a man from a mediocre clan in a middle-of-the-road tribe who might have a great personality could never aspire to come close to the position enjoyed by an average person from one of the top clans of the Quraysh, Arabia's most celebrated tribe.

Islam preached equality among all people, and this was by no means easy for the Arabs to accept. Those who accepted Islam, however, were soon to learn that the proper standards of distinction among people were their degree of faith and their observance of Islamic duties. This did not, however, preclude the idea of nobility being achieved by some people. Hence, they were keen to ask the Prophet about all this.

129. Abu Hurayrah reports that God's Messenger was asked: 'Who are the most noble of people?' He said: 'The most noble in God's view are the most God-fearing among them'. They said: 'We are not asking you about that'. He then replied: 'The most noble among them, then, was Joseph, a prophet and son of a prophet who was the grandson of God's friend'. They again said: 'It is not that either that we are asking you about'. He enquired of them: 'Are you then asking me about the metals of the Arabs?' They said: 'Yes'. He said: 'The best of you in the days of ignorance are the best in Islam, provided that they acquire a deep insight into it'.[93]

This is a *ḥadīth* of great significance. The first answer the Prophet gave to his questioners points out a basic Islamic principle: nobility is based on faith and adherence to its requirements. This is a field open to all of us in equal measure. None is impeded or handicapped by any external factor. It is our own free choice which sets us on the road to nobility and it is our own desire to achieve nobility and readiness to work for it which ensure what grade of distinction we acquire. The Prophet tells us that it is through strong faith and abidance by its

93. Related by al-Bukhari and Muslim.

teaching, fulfilment of its duties and willingness to exceed duty in order to do voluntary works which earn reward from God that give people honour, distinction and nobility. The Prophet says that the most noble among us in God's sight is the most God-fearing. Family lineage or hereditary position is not enough to give any one a single degree higher than the rest. A strong faith, knowledge of the principles of Islam and its teachings, good actions and readiness to always do one's Islamic duty, even when it imposes a heavy burden, ensure for us the sort of distinction and honour which does not end with the termination of our life in this world.

The Prophet's questioners had, however, something else in mind. They were aware of the Islamic view of true honour and distinction, because the Prophet's first answer is stated in the Qur'an. Then the Prophet gave them a different answer combining truly noble lineage with distinguished personal qualities such as profound knowledge, high moral standards, great position in society, good manners and handsome appearance. These qualities were not all combined together in one person as they were in the case of Joseph who himself was a prophet. His father, Jacob, was also a prophet and his grandfather Isaac, was one as well. Abraham, his great grandfather was not only one of the greatest messengers God has sent to mankind, but he was also a friend of God's. Joseph was the man for whom the title of the most noble among mankind could be claimed.

The Prophet's questioners still had something different in mind. They mentioned this to the Prophet and he made sure, before giving another answer, that he understood what sort of information they sought. They confirmed that they were asking about the tribal ancestry in which the Arabs took so much pride.

We note here that the Prophet's question is expressed in a metaphor: 'Are you asking me about the metals of the Arabs?' Tribes are likened to metals and it is a very apt metaphor. Metals differ in many aspects: value, weight, strength, purity, solidity, etc. Moreover, metals can be shaped and put to many uses in the same way as people are shaped by their environment, upbringing, education and faith. Differences among people are caused by many factors, some are internal while others are external. Their acceptance of Islam is a positive step to earn them distinction, but they still differ in how they are influenced by it, how much knowledge of it they acquire and how much they allow it to shape their thinking. All this makes for a very wide range of distinction, in the same way as metals differ. Metals are not only different from one another, but samples of the same metal differ in quality, colour and weight.

The Prophet's answer to this specific point tells of his profound insight into human nature and how Islam affects people and makes of them better human beings. He recognises that there are people who achieve distinction of character, wisdom and position in all societies, Islamic or otherwise. Even in the most ignorant of societies, such as the Arabian pagan society in the days which preceded the advent of Islam, there were good people of noble character. They could only have achieved that through adopting certain values and abiding by certain principles. In every social order there are good values and those who abide by them are distinctly better than those who observe no value when it comes into conflict with personal interests. When people who are prepared to abide by high values and principles are also endowed with a good measure of intelligence and wisdom, they are bound to distinguish themselves in their societies. The Prophet's answer tells us that if people of this sort accept Islam, understand it well and exert their efforts to implement it in their lives and abide by its rules, they become the most noble among Muslims. This means in effect that they become the most noble of all mankind. Islam is the most complete of religions and its teachings have been devised by God to make of every man or woman a person of high morality, good manners and a likeable character. When Islamic teachings have a chance to do their work on a person who combines good personality with knowledge, intelligence and wisdom, they achieve the best results. A seed which is planted in rich soil is bound to produce the best fruit. Islam which makes of all people good men and women also achieves its best results with people who are essentially good, intelligent and wise.

Most importantly, however, the Prophet's answer tells us that distinction is not something that people have by luck. They have to work for it and achieve it through determined effort. What is more is that people can squander what distinction they may happen to have, or increase it manifold, depending on whether or not they accept and implement Islam.

8

Caring for the Weak

KINDNESS TO OTHERS is not the preserve of any particular group of people. In all communities there are kind-hearted people who are always willing to extend a helping hand to whoever needs it. Islam makes clear that every good action is well rewarded by God.

130. (*Athar* 34) Commenting on the Qur'anic verse that says: '*Shall the reward of good be anything but good?*' (55:60) Muhammad ibn 'Ali (ibn al-Ḥanafiyyah) said: 'It applies to both the dutiful and the errant'.

Al-Bukhari said that Abu 'Ubayd[94] explained that the equal application is unrestricted.

---

94. Abu 'Ubayd al-Qāsim ibn Sallām (157-224 AH 774-838 CE) was a highly eminent scholar of *Fiqh*, *Ḥadīth* and the Qur'an. He is considered to be of the same rank as the founders of the four Islamic schools of *Fiqh*.

This means that everyone who looks after a vulnerable or weak person, including widows and orphans, will have their reward. There can be no stinting of reward. It is often stated that Islam builds a closely-knit community, in which the individual cares for the whole community and the community looks after every individual. As a general statement, this sounds great. The important thing is to know how far it is implemented in real life. Moreover, there may be good reasons for the community to look after its adult, able-bodied and productive individuals. For one thing, the task does not present much trouble since they can look after themselves. For another, if their rights are threatened, they can cause problems to the community as a whole. The community might find itself in a position where looking after individuals and ensuring that they get what is rightfully theirs is a more productive and cost-effective course.

But what about the weak in society: an orphaned child[95] who lost their father in their early years and the father was poor leaving his children little money to see them through life; a widow who is left without support and does not have any immediate family from whom to seek help. Can such people be guaranteed their rights?

The answer that offers itself immediately to such questions is that the state, or the community, must establish a system of social security which provides all citizens who cannot look after themselves with the means to guarantee their rights to a decent living. In advanced societies, we find that the social security system is so elaborate that it takes good care of almost all cases which need help. But no social security system can work without people to take upon themselves responsibilities for individual cases. No two cases are the same while legislation is normally oriented to take care of average or common cases. Moreover, in the two examples we have given, i.e. those of orphans and widows, personal care is needed and this cannot be legislated for.

An orphan may be entitled, under the social security legislation, to receive an allowance which may be sufficient to meet all their needs. They may, on the other hand, be entitled to receive payments from the

95. From the Islamic point of view, an orphan is a child who lost his father, because it is the father who is responsible to provide for his children. In this, Islam differs with the Western concept that makes an 'orphan' only that child who lost both parents.

pension fund of which their late father was a member. But an orphan needs much more than money in order to grow up and learn how to deal with life's challenges. The education system may offer an orphan the chance to go to a good school, but he also needs to learn things which no school can teach. On the other hand, many orphans find themselves in orphanages where life is not too pleasant.

What is recognised by all societies is that the best way to look after orphans is to ensure that they have good homes with proper and happy families where they may be well looked after. Such a home and a family allow them a chance to lead a proper life and live through all the experiences a child normally has. Moreover, they may be provided with the love and care of which the death of their parents has deprived them.

The other case we have mentioned is that of a poor widow. Her husband might have left her with very little to live on. Her own family may be totally unable to look after her. Her own parents may have died and her brothers may have heavy responsibilities towards their own families. If, on top of that, she has had little education and did not have, in her younger years, to work for her living, there is little chance that she can find a job. Some widows cannot work even if jobs are available. They may have some sort of illness or handicap to prevent them from working. Or they may have young children to look after. What happens to such widows? It is certainly the responsibility of society to look after them. So what has been said about orphans may also be applicable, to a large extent, to widows. They need good homes and security so that they do not suffer poverty and exploitation.

In Islam, which provides a perfect social system, orphans, widows and other 'weak' members are well looked after. There are obligations which Islam imposes on its followers to look after those who need help. These are not given in general terms. They are highly specific and they define the order of priority and the strength of claims which an orphan or a widow has against their relatives. In a Muslim society, you will not find a child going to a foster family if it has relatives. Its relatives know that everyone in society expects them to take charge of their orphans and widows. If they try to dodge their responsibilities, they will find themselves in an untenable position in society.

But it is not merely social pressure which ensures that orphans and widows are looked after by their relatives. Islam provides a motive which is very hard to resist. Consider this *ḥadīth* which enjoys a high degree of authenticity.

131. Abu Hurayrah reports that the Prophet said: 'A person who looks after a widow and needy individuals is like those who join jihad for God's cause, and like the one who fasts in the day and stands up in prayer during the night'.[96]

The Prophet gives two examples which earn very high reward from God. When a person goes on jihad, he puts his life at risk and declares that he is ready to sacrifice his life in support of God's cause. If he is killed, he is a martyr, certain to be admitted to heaven. Similarly, a person who offers voluntary worship indicates that he has very strong faith. He seeks God's pleasure and demonstrates the fact by not limiting himself only to obligatory worship. He also fasts voluntarily and stays up at night praying despite having offered his obligatory prayers. We know that fasting is rewarded most generously by God Who tells us that He considers fasting as something dedicated especially to Him, and He rewards it accordingly. It is for this reason that proper fasting through the month of Ramadan ensures the forgiveness of all past sins. When fasting is done voluntarily, in days other than Ramadan, the reward is very great.

Again, night worship is rewarded more generously. A person who offers it demonstrates that he prefers God's pleasure to his own rest. He does not do so to show off, for nobody sees him when he is engaged in night worship except his Lord. When worship is dedicated so sincerely to God, His reward is not limited to the basic ten times the value of the thing offered. Instead, He increases the reward manifold.

What this *ḥadīth* means is that when a person looks after an orphan, a needy person or a widow, working hard during the day in order to earn enough money to support them properly and meet their needs, he is doing something similar to that done by a person who goes on jihad. In jihad, one risks one's life, and in looking after orphans and widows, people know that there can be little by way of material return on the investment. Such investment must be placed with God in order

---

96. Related by al-Bukhari, Muslim, al-Nasā'ī, al-Tirmidhi and Ibn Mājah.

that people can come forward to benefit by it. Hence, Islam provides this motivation. The reward is of the most generous type because it ensures admittance into heaven.

Legislation and responsibility

As we have already noted, Islam puts in place legislation to ensure that the weaker elements of society, including orphans and helpless widows, are well looked after. However, legislation is not sufficient on its own to ensure that everyone fulfils their responsibilities, especially when the recipients are unaware of what is due to them. An orphan, for example, does not know what they are entitled to from their guardian. Even if they knew, they cannot demand it. A guardian may remind the orphan in his care of their weakness every day, making the orphan feel that whatever little they receive is due to their guardian's charity, rather than their own right. Some people consider that having an orphan to look after is not much different from a calamity befalling them. Moreover, they make their feelings clear to the orphan and, sometimes, treat the child as if were responsible for the death of their father. Therefore, something more than the fulfilment of responsibility is needed to ensure that orphans receive good treatment from their guardians.

Islam provides such motivation with the reward God promises guardians for the trouble they take looking after their orphan relatives. As noted above, the Prophet defines this reward as equal to that of jihad or to fasting during the day and standing up in prayer during the night. These are great rewards, for the one who goes on jihad, risking his life and for the one who is engaged in voluntary worship at such a level that demonstrates very strong faith. The one who looks after an orphan incurs expenses to provide for someone who is not his own child and from whom he expects little in return. Needless to say, looking after an orphan is a hard job.

When the Prophet wanted to impress on his companions, and Muslims in general, the great importance Islam attaches to something, he took every opportunity to remind them of the great reward from God it is bound to earn them. The Prophet was very compassionate and he always felt for the weak, trying to make sure that they received the care they needed. He wanted orphans in the Muslim community to always find the help and care they deserved. This could only be achieved by providing adequate motivation so that people would come forward and undertake the responsibility. To a Muslim, the reward of the Hereafter is something very real and a good reward is always something to strive for. So, what does an orphan's guardian who takes good care of his charge expect to receive?

> 132. 'Ā'ishah, the Prophet's wife, said: 'A woman came to me with her two daughters. She asked me for something, but I could find nothing except a single date, which I gave to her. She divided it between her two daughters and then got up and left. When the Prophet came in, I told him what happened. He said: "For whoever looks after such girls and is good to them, they will be for him a shield from the Fire".'[97]

The Prophet makes this comment about a woman who split a single date between her two daughters. The woman did this on the promptings of motherly instinct. Mothers do everything for their young children and favour them over themselves. The woman might have been hungry herself, but she would not think of eating before her daughters, when she had nothing to give them. Her action makes the Prophet's statement applicable to her.

If these girls were orphans, then their mother would also benefit from another *ḥadīth*:

> 133. Murrah al-Fihri reports that the Prophet said: 'I and the orphan's guardian will be in heaven like these two,' or 'like this one to this one'.

The Prophet pointed with his two fingers, and the reporter was unsure whether these were the forefinger and the middle one, but they were two fingers of the same hand and the Prophet separated them. In this *ḥadīth* the Prophet declares that there is perhaps no one in a better position in heaven than an orphan's guardian, provided that he takes

97. Related by al-Bukhari.

good care of his charge. Needless to say, the Prophet is in the highest position in heaven. No one will have greater reward from God. It is God Who chose him to deliver His final message to mankind. He did his best to make people understand it and respond to God's call to them to believe in His oneness. He spared no effort to deliver his mission complete, clear and easy to implement. He was the best of teachers. He thus earned his top position.

134. (*Athar* 35) Al-Ḥasan al-Baṣri said: 'An orphan used to attend Ibn 'Umar when he had his meals. One day he called for food and looked for the orphan but could not find him. The orphan arrived after Ibn 'Umar had finished eating. Ibn 'Umar called for more food to be brought for the orphan, but there was none. So he fetched *sawīq* and honey, and said to the orphan: "Eat this. By God, you are not a loser".' Al-Ḥasan commented: 'Nor was Ibn 'Umar a loser'.

135. Sahl ibn Sa'd reports that the Prophet said: 'I and the orphan's guardian are in heaven like this', pointing with his forefinger and middle finger.

136. (*Athar* 36) Abu Bakr ibn Ḥafṣ said that 'Abdullāh [ibn 'Umar] would not have a meal unless an orphan joined in the eating with him.

The first and the last of these three *ḥadīths* refer to the same condition in different wordings and chains of transmission, while the middle one is the same as *ḥadīth* Number 133. Ibn 'Umar was a model of a Muslim who wanted to follow the Prophet's guidance in every respect. He heard what the Prophet said about caring for orphans and he wanted to implement it. He, therefore, sought to have an orphan eating with him every time he had a meal. When the orphan was late, he gave him a better meal than he himself had partaken of.

Ḥadīth Numbers 133 and 135 make clear that an orphan's guardian will be close to the Prophet in heaven like one finger is close to the next finger. This proximity is the prize for which every believer will work very hard to achieve. We strive through life and do whatever we can in the hope of being included among those who are forgiven their sins by God. Here is something that not only brings about forgiveness, but also ensures a very high position in heaven, alongside the Prophet. There is nothing better in the Hereafter.

Commentators on *Ḥadīth* mention that this proximity to the Prophet is the result of the similarity of the task of an orphan's guardian to that of a prophet. God sends a prophet to a nation when ignorance spreads and few would know the truth about God and faith. To them, the prophet is a guardian who teaches them and guides them along their lives. He points out to them the way which ensures happiness in this present life and in the life to come. An orphan's guardian also takes upon himself the charge of someone who understands very little about faith, and even about anything. He educates them and instils in them proper values so that they grow up as a good person who is useful to their community. Hence, he deserves a special reward.

A fuller version of this *ḥadīth*, which enjoys an excellent degree of authenticity, includes not only the orphan's guardian but all members of the family looking after an orphan. If such a family, parents and children, learn to be kind to the orphan, they achieve a high degree of excellence.

137. Abu Hurayrah reports that the Prophet said: 'The best home in a Muslim society is a home where an orphan is well treated. The worst home in a Muslim society is one in which an orphan suffers ill-treatment. I and the guardian of an orphan will be in heaven like these two', pointing with his two fingers.[98]

Sometimes, the head of the family takes on an orphan who is a close relative. He himself is kind to that orphan and treats them like his own child. However, his wife may not be so good to the orphan, feeling that it is a burden on her. Furthermore, his children may not like the orphan child, and regard them as one who competes with them for their father's kindness. If the father takes extra care of the orphan child trying to compensate for the loss they must keenly feel, then his own children may feel jealous and, sensing that their own mother does not

98. Related by Muslim and Ibn Mājah.

like the orphan child, they could be very brutal to them. In order to guard against such possibility, which is bound to badly affect the child, the Prophet makes sure that all members of the family understand that they will be highly rewarded if they are kind to the orphan in their charge. They can earn that great degree of being the best home or the best family in a society. That is a very great honour.

This emphasis Islam gives to the care of orphans is inherent in all Divine religions. Right from the time of Adam, prophets urged their followers to treat orphan children with the maximum of care and compassion.

> 138. (*Athar* 37) 'Abd al-Raḥmān ibn Abza said: '[Prophet] David said: "Be to the orphan child like a compassionate father. Know that you will only reap what you sow. How miserable poverty is after wealth! Worse still is the pursuit of error after having had guidance. When you give your friend a promise, keep it. If you do not, it will bring about enmity between you. Seek refuge with God against a companion who, when you remember something, does not help you and when you forget does not remind you".'

These are part of the teachings of Prophet David. Islam endorses them all, and they are entered in *Ḥadīth* anthologies because Islam accepts all that remains unaltered of the heritage of earlier prophets (peace be upon them all). This *ḥadīth* is entered here because it starts with the recommendation of being like a compassionate father to an orphan child. The rest of the *ḥadīth* is self explanatory. Everyone reaps what they sow. If they work well, then they receive the reward of their actions. When a wealthy person squanders his wealth and is reduced to poverty, he feels it worse than one who has always been poor. Likewise, a person who has followed Divine faith, but then disbelieved is more miserable with his new status than one who has never known the faith. The *ḥadīth* urges everyone to fulfil their promises and concludes with showing that a good friend is one that reminds his friend of his duties when he forgets and offers a helping hand when such help is needed.

When religious values are prominent in a community, people urge one another to fulfil their duties, particularly those that do not offer immediate returns. When such values weaken, no such reminders are forthcoming:

139. (*Athar* 38) Al-Ḥasan al-Baṣri said: 'I remember a time when anyone in the Muslim community would loudly address his family: "My household, my household! [Look after] your orphan! [Be kind to] your orphan! My household, my household! [Look after] your poor one, [be kind to] your poor one! My household, my household! [Look after] your neighbour, [be kind to] your neighbour!" But the best among you were swiftly taken away and you get worse every day'.

Al-Ḥasan also said: 'If you wish, you can see a sinful person go 30,000 times deeper into the Fire. What is wrong with him? Confound him! He has sold his portion from God for a paltry price. If you wish, you can see him lost, wretched, following Satan's path. He takes warning neither from himself nor from anyone else'.

Al-Ḥasan, a scholar of high standing who belonged to the generation of *tabiʿīn* who followed the Prophet's companions, lamented the deterioration of values in the Muslim community during that very early period in the history of Islam. People used to urge their families to take care of orphans, needy people and neighbours, while in his time, he saw more and more people pursuing material comforts and worldly riches. He gives a graphic image of a person who does not mind committing violations of Islamic values and standards in such a pursuit.

Orphan's treatment

Some people ask whether a guardian may reprimand an orphan child in his care if the child misbehaves.

140. (*Athar* 39) 'Ubayd said: I said to Ibn Sīrīn: 'I have an orphan boy in my care'. He said: 'Treat him as you would treat your own child. Discipline him as you would discipline your child'.

This makes clear that kindness to an orphan child does not mean that he must not be disciplined for misbehaving. We will discuss this point in more detail presently.

Orphans with double loss

An orphan may sometimes suffer a double loss. A father may die leaving behind a young child. The mother, who may be young or may be in need of someone to support her, remarries. Thus, she has more duties to fulfil than merely looking after her young fatherless child. Her new husband may only suffer the presence of her child, but expects her to give her duties towards him first priority. If they have children, he assumes that they automatically have higher priority over her orphan child. It is he who supports her and her orphan, so her first duty is towards him and his children, or so he argues. Practical life shows that when such a woman marries again, her child comes to suffer a measure of hardship which they otherwise would have been spared, had she chosen the option of devoting herself to them.

141. 'Awf ibn Mālik reports that the Prophet said: 'I and a woman with a careworn face, having been widowed devoted herself to her children, are like these two in heaven'.[99]

The Prophet pointed out with his two fingers to indicate the proximity of such a woman's position to him in heaven.

This *ḥadīth* does not order every woman whose husband dies not to marry again. If she remarries, she commits no sin. The *ḥadīth* simply shows that a position adopted by free choice is far more praiseworthy and rewarding to the widow who adopts it. Needless to say, no one

99. Related by Abū Dāwūd.

can take better care of an orphan than their own mother. When she devotes her love and kindness to her orphaned children, she is certain to compensate them best for their loss. However, it takes courage and determination for a young woman to decide to dedicate her future to her orphaned children. Such courage and determination is rewarded by a high position in heaven.

Misbehaving orphans

Apart from *ḥadīth* Number 140, we have been speaking about extending kindness to orphans and taking good care of them. No doubt, to be unkind to an orphan is an immoral act which deserves stern punishment. This does however lead us to the question of what to do with an orphan who misbehaves. Are we supposed to be extra kind to him even when he deserves to be disciplined? Does that not make of him a spoilt child?

Every child needs to learn good manners and needs to be taught how to behave well. Children may often try to discover how far they can push the limits of behaviour without being reprimanded. In such cases, if no action is taken, the child will go on misbehaving. When this is repeated, the child tries to get away with their every whim. That is the makings of a spoilt child.

'Ā'ishah, the Prophet's wife who had profound insight into the Islamic faith, gives us guidance on how to manage such a situation:

> 142. (*Athar* 40) Shumaysah al-'Atakiyyah said: 'The subject of disciplining an orphan child was mentioned in the presence of 'Ā'ishah, and she said: "I would discipline an orphan even though he would lie on the floor".'[100]

She said that she might have to discipline an orphan child even though the child resorted to lying on the floor. She meant that the child might be stubbornly rebellious, and might show his anger by lying on the floor, obstinately refusing to stand up. This means that the

---

100. Related by al-Bayhaqi in Al-Sunan al-Kubra.

situation was serious. She would not have mentioned this if she had any qualms of conscience about reprimanding the orphans she looked after, who were, in any case, the children of her deceased brother. There is no doubt that she dearly loved them. As their aunt, she undertook their upbringing as a duty and in the hope of God's reward. This does not preclude having to discipline them when they misbehaved. Indeed, every father feels the need to discipline his child at times. Contemporary educators definitely object to corporal punishment, but it was certainly practised in most societies.

From this *ḥadīth* we learn that to discipline an orphan, when needed, is acceptable. Scholars say that a person who undertakes the guardianship of an orphan must question himself when he subjects the orphan in his charge to any corrective or disiciplinary measure. If he is certain that he loves the child and cares for him, and he is certainly kind to him, then he should not worry about disciplining the child, as and when necessary, provided that his measures are not too strong. Many a father finds it necessary to discipline his children although there is no question about his great love for them. Furthermore, there are many ways of instilling good behaviour and manners into children.

Islam is a practical religion and looks at all problems in life in a very practical way. It does not tell us to be extra kind to orphans when such extra kindness may have an undesirable effect. It is true kindness which ensures that an orphan grows up a balanced, unspoilt person who knows how to balance duty against desire and is always ready to fulfil his duties, is the benchmark. In fact, an orphan who grows up like this is bound to appreciate their guardian's kindness and care, even any corrective measure that was administered to them. They realise that without discipline, their education and upbringing would have lacked certain important elements.

9

On the Loss of One's Children

PERHAPS NO CALAMITY that can befall anyone is greater than the loss of one's child, this because parents' love of their children is greater than any other love. Human beings feel for their young as they do not feel for anyone else. Every smile on the face of a child sends a feeling of happiness into the hearts of their parents. To them, a child represents fulfilment and hope for the future. The birth of a child ensures continuity of the family and gives a new meaning to life. When we care for our children, we have a sense of happiness which is pure, even though the care we take of our children may represent a heavy burden for us. Moreover, our love of our children grows with them. With every day that passes our relationship with our children acquires new strength. When a father sits down to relax or reflect on his life, his first thoughts turn to his children. He feels that without them, his life might appear meaningless. The same applies in equal measure to mothers.

Because of this, the loss of a child creates a great void in the lives of parents. The hope which was represented by their departed child is no longer there. The sense of fulfilment given them by the presence of their child is turned into a feeling of great frustration. Moreover, parents feel that they are helpless. They cannot prevent death, yet ever since the birth of their child, they view their role as that of taking care of them and protecting them against every harm and evil. But they nonetheless cannot protect the child against the one calamity that takes it away from them. Such frustration is felt most keenly by both parents. When we talk to parents who have lost a child, they tell us that their sense of loss is always present in their minds. One woman told me that no day passes without her remembering every minute of the life of her 18 year old who was drowned in a river close to their home. Her feeling is by no means unique.

In the light of the Prophet's statement that there is something good for a Muslim in any development which takes place throughout one's life, how does Islam view the situation of losing a child? The Prophet's statement explains that when something good happens to a Muslim, he or she praises and thanks God for it and this gives them good reward. When something evil happens to them, they bear it with patience and this again earns them good reward. How does this work in the case of losing one child or more? We have a number of *ḥadīths* which speak about this particular point in largely similar fashion. They may appear repetitive, but they were said on different occasions or they were reported by different companions of the Prophet.

143. Abu Hurayrah reports that the Prophet said: 'Any Muslim who loses three of his children would not be touched by the Fire except for the fulfilment of God's oath'.[101]

The *ḥadīth* uses an Arabic expression that literally translates as 'for the bare fulfilment of an oath', the connotation being 'something very slight'. The oath referred to by the *ḥadīth* is stated in the Qur'anic verse that refers to hell: '*There is not one among you who shall not pass over it: this is, for your Lord, a decree that must be fulfilled*'. (19: 71)

101. Related by al-Bukhari, Muslim, al-Nasā'ī, al-Tirmidhi and Ibn Mājah.

This means that anyone suffering this loss will pass very speedily over hell, without suffering any punishment.

144. Abu Hurayrah said: 'A woman came to the Prophet (peace be upon him) carrying a young boy. She said to him: "Pray for him, for I have already buried three children". The Prophet said to her: "You have placed a very heavy shield protecting you from the Fire".'

145. Khalid al-'Absi said: 'A son of mine died and my grief for him was very keen indeed. I said to Abu Hurayrah: "Have you heard anything from the Prophet to console us for the loss of our dead?" He said: "I heard the Prophet say, 'Your children are the ever present young ones in heaven'."'[102]

A fuller version of this *ḥadīth* is related by Muslim and adds: 'Each one of them will meet their parents on the Day of Judgement, hold their hands or their clothes, and they will not let go of them until they have entered heaven'.

146. Jabir ibn 'Abdullah reports that the Prophet said: 'Anyone who loses three of his children and accepts their loss with resignation will be admitted into heaven'. We said: 'Messenger of God, how about two? He said: 'Even two'. Mahmud ibn Labid [the narrator from Jabir] said: 'I said to Jabir: "By God, I think that had you said that about one, he would have given a similar answer". Jabir said: "By God, I think so too".'

147. The same as Number 143, with a different chain of transmission.

148. Abu Hurayrah reports: 'A woman came to the Prophet and said: "Messenger of God, we cannot come to sit with you, so set aside a day for us when we can come to you".' He said: "Your appointment is at the house of so-and so". He came to meet

---

102. Related by Aḥmad, Muslim and Abu 'Awānah.

them at the appointed time. Included in what he said to them was: "Any woman among you who loses three children, and she accepts her loss with resignation, will certainly be admitted into heaven". A woman asked: "How about two?" He said: "Even two".'[103]

149. Umm Sulaym said: 'I was at the Prophet's when he said to me: "Umm Sulaym! Any Muslim couple who lose three children shall certainly be admitted by God into heaven by virtue of His Grace to them". I said: "How about two?" He said: "Even two".'[104]

150. Sa'sa'ah ibn Mu'awiyah reported that he met Abu Dharr who was carrying a waterskin. He asked him: 'How many children do you have, Abu Dharr?' He said: 'Shall I tell you a *ḥadīth*?' Sa'sa'ah replied: 'Yes, please'. Abu Dharr said: 'I heard the Prophet say: "Any Muslim who loses three children before they attain puberty will be admitted into heaven, by virtue of His grace to them. Anyone who frees a Muslim will have every one of his organs freed [from hell] in return for every organ of the freed person".'[105]

151. Anas ibn Malik reports that the Prophet said: 'Anyone who loses three children before they attain puberty will be admitted, together with them, into heaven'.[106]

All these *ḥadīths* express the same idea, with great similarity in their wording. Obviously, they were said by the Prophet to different people on different occasions. We note that the Prophet always mentions the loss of three children to start with. This is because parents who lose three children suffer this terrible calamity three times. If they, nevertheless, accept the calamity with resignation, submitting to God's will, they actually demonstrate their strong faith and merit admittance

103. Related by al-Bukhari and Muslim.
104. Related by Aḥmad and al-Ṭabarāni.
105. Related by Aḥmad, Abu 'Awānah, Ibn Ḥibbān and al-Ṭabarāni.
106. Related by al-Bukhari, al-Nasā'ī and Ibn Mājah.

into heaven. We note that the idea of resigned acceptance of God's will is stressed in more than one *ḥadīth*. Needless to say, a parent who complains and expresses dissatisfaction with God's will cannot expect to be admitted into heaven. Indeed, a person of faith always accepts what happens to him, without questioning God's will. He resigns himself to whatever befalls him without entertaining any thought that he has been unfairly treated by God. No Muslim would doubt for the briefest moment that God is always just.

In two of these *ḥadīths* the Prophet describes the deceased children as below the age of puberty. This does not mean that if the children were adults the parents' reward will be any less. In fact, the loss of an adult son or daughter may be greater than the loss of a young one. A parent expects much of his grown up children. If they are dutiful children then his life will be much more easy and comfortable. Moreover, there are so many memories and associations which a father or a mother will always have of their grown up children. It is certainly a greater loss to the parents if the dead child is an adult on whom they rely for help. So if heaven is assured to a parent who loses three young children, it is also certain for a parent who loses three adult children.

While no one would ever wish to lose one of his children, a person who has suffered such a loss may be consoled when reading these *ḥadīths* by the Prophet. Muslims who learn this resign themselves to such happenings and bear their calamities with fortitude and patience. They realise that such an attitude earns them generous reward from God.

We also learn that this does not apply only to the death of one's children; it also applies to the loss of an embryo. Even before a child is born, the parents look forward to the birth and entertain high hopes. When a pregnant woman suffers a miscarriage, she experiences a profound sense of loss. The same is felt by her husband. Acceptance of God's will in such a situation is indicative of strong faith. Hence, the reward is great. The Prophet's companions were aware of the fact that God rewards generously any parent who loses a child, even before they were born, and accepts such loss, with resignation.

152. (*Athar* 41) Sahl ibn al-Ḥanẓaliyyah, a companion of the Prophet who did not have any children, said: 'If I were to lose a

child before he is born and to accept this loss with patience, it is far more preferable to me than possessing the whole world with all that it contains'.

Sahl was a devout companion of the Prophet who spent much time in worship. He took part in the Battle of Uḥud and all the subsequent expeditions with the Prophet. He also took part in the pledge the Muslims gave to the Prophet to fight to the end when the Quraysh prevented them from entering Makkah. He understood perfectly what it meant to lose one's child and this is the reason for his statement.

The Prophet was keen to bring about a total change of outlook on life and its values among his community and future Muslim generations. Therefore, he might at times ask an obvious question. When his companions gave him the expected answer, he would speak about something totally different. He realised that in this way, his idea would be perfectly understood and well remembered.

153. 'Abdullāh ibn Mas'ūd reports that the Prophet said: 'Who of you holds his heirs' property dearer to him than his own property?' They answered: 'Messenger of God, everyone of us loves his own property more than that of his heirs'. The Prophet said: 'You should know that every one of you loves his heirs' property more than his own. Your own property is that which you put forward and your heirs' property is what you hold'.[107]

In an Islamic context, 'to put forward' or 'to send forward' means to do something purely for God's sake in the hope of receiving reward from Him in the life to come.

All people love money and are willing to work hard to obtain it. The more they have of it the more they want. Wealth is associated with comfort, luxury and happiness. Hence, it is very dear to man. The Prophet, however, tells us that we love our heirs' property more than we love our own. This is a very apt description which is explained by the last part of this *ḥadīth*. When we spend money for God's cause, either giving it in charity to poor people, or putting it in the service

107. Related by al-Bukhari and al-Nasā'ī.

of God's cause, we have 'put it forward'. This means that we receive a reward for it from God. It is an investment with assured returns. It remains ours until the Day of Judgement when we enjoy it like we never enjoy wealth in this life. What remains with us, however, whether kept in a safe or deposited with a bank, does not actually belong to us. We do not benefit by it in this life and we do not have reward for it in the Hereafter. When we die it is taken by our heirs. Hence it belongs to them. Yet we love it more than the money we spend on our needs. When we look at our bank accounts and find that we have a healthy balance, we feel very happy. It gives us a sense of safety and power. But unless we spend it, we do not benefit by it. If we spend it on buying some luxury articles, we get that benefit. If we spend it in a better way, either to further God's cause or to help a poor person, we benefit by its reward. Hence, it is our money. What we hold on to throughout our life and then leave behind belongs to our heirs.

Changing concepts

The Prophet went about the fulfilment of his task with patience. He was always prepared to give whatever it took to change people's feelings, attitudes, concepts and ideals. He seized every opportunity to teach his followers Islamic values and to instil in them a sense of Islamic awareness which enabled them to judge all matters in the light of Islam. What that meant in effect was that the Prophet made use of every situation and event to strengthen and consolidate the Islamic viewpoint in the minds of his followers. As we have noted, he might ask a question in order to provide a new outlook:

154. 'Abdullāh ibn Mas'ūd reports that the Prophet asked: 'Who among you do you consider as childless?' They answered: 'He is the one who has no children'. The Prophet said: 'No. The childless is the one who has not sent forward any of his children'.[108]

---

108. Related by al-Bukhari and Muslim.

Within the context of this *ḥadīth*, the Prophet describes as childless a person who has not lost any of his children. When a parent loses a child and accepts his loss with resignation, submitting himself to the will of God, he is certain to have great reward for his attitude.

There is something special about the loss of children. People normally associate death with old age. When a person dies after a long life, his death is accepted as natural. When a child dies, people are at a loss to explain the wisdom behind such a death. The only thing that enables them to accept such loss is to attribute it, as it should rightly be attributed, to God's will. When they do this, they rightly declare themselves to be believers. Their reward is commensurate with their faith.

What the Prophet says in this *ḥadīth* is that proper acceptance of the loss of a child ensures for the parent a high position with God on the Day of Judgement. Hence, the loss is an assured gain. The one who does not lose a child does not have a similar certainty of reward. Hence, he is the one who is childless when it comes to considering reward in the Hereafter.

Another example of this method of teaching the Prophet used on a different occasions is the following *ḥadīth*:

> 155. ʿAbdullāh ibn Masʿūd reports that the Prophet asked: 'Whom do you consider the strongest of men?' They said: 'The one who is never overcome by strong men?' He said: 'No. The strongest of people is the one who is in good self control when angry'.[109]

The misconception to which this *ḥadīth* refers is that of strength being associated with physical power. An overwhelming majority of people consider the person endowed with abundant physical power to be the strongest of men. Contests are organised everywhere in the world in wrestling, boxing and similarly brutal games. Their object is to find title holders at national, continental and world levels. The Prophet teaches us that there is something which requires greater power to defeat: anger which makes a person blind. In a fit of temper many

109. Related by al-Bukhari, Muslim and Abū Dāwūd.

a person says or does things which they will later regret. At the time when a person says or does such things he is not aware of what he is actually saying or doing. We have only to remember how many people divorce their wives during a quarrel in which tempers become extremely heated. To overcome anger, and to hold oneself in check is something that requires great willpower and the ability to keep one's sense of proportion foremost in one's mind. Because this is very difficult to achieve, so much so that only a few individuals in any community can aspire to attain to it, the Prophet describes the one who can hold his anger in check as the strongest of all people.

10

Best Manners

REPORTS AND COMMENTS about the last few days of the Prophet's life and what he said during his illness are numerous. The importance of the Prophet's final words derives from the fact that he was so keen that his followers should maintain their implementation of Islam as best as they could. He wanted people to be good Muslims, because he cared for every human being. He knew that by being a good Muslim, a human being opens up his way to heaven. Nothing would have pleased the Prophet more than for every human being to accept Islam and submit himself willingly to God. His final words are, in this light, indicative of the most important duties of Islam.

156. 'Ali said: 'When illness weighed down heavily on the Prophet, he said to me: "'Ali, bring me a sheet and write down on it what makes sure that my community will never go astray". I feared that he might die before I could do that. I said that I will be certain to remember [what he wanted to be written].

> His head was in between his forearm and my upper arm. He urged us to attend to our prayers and pay our zakat and to be kind to those in our possession. He repeated those words until his soul departed. He also commanded us to declare that there is no deity other than God and that Muhammad is His servant and Messenger. He said that whoever believes in this is immune from the Fire.'[110]

The first thing to be noted in this *ḥadīth* is that the Prophet wanted to have something written down which would ensure that his community would never go astray. However, what he subsequently stated was merely reminders of the basic teachings of Islam. This is not surprising, because, the faith of Islam had reached its stage of completeness beyond which nothing could be added to it. It reached that stage with the revelation of the third verse in Surah five which states: '*This day I have perfected your religion for you and have bestowed on you the full measure of My blessings and have chosen Islam as a religion for you*' (5: 3). This verse was revealed more than ten weeks before the Prophet's departure from this life. No legal injunction was revealed after it. This is only logical, because if Islam was made perfect by God, then nothing more could be added to it.

This has prompted some scholars to suggest that the Prophet wanted to nominate Abu Bakr as his successor in the leadership of the Muslim state. It might have been so, but we cannot say for certain.

That the Prophet should urge us to attend regularly to our prayers and pay our zakat without fail is understandable. These are the two pillars of Islam, and all Divine religions, which ensure the proper wellbeing of the individual and the community. Moreover, they are the source of every good thing in Islamic society. A person who neglects his prayers will find it easier to neglect the lesser duties of Islam. Similarly, a person who fails to pay his zakat deprives its beneficiaries of their dues. He is, then, guilty of injustice.

Moreover, the Prophet continued to recommend that we be kind to the weakest group in society, namely, servants who are in our possession, i.e. those who are referred to as 'slaves' in other societies.

---

110. Related by Aḥmad in a shorter version.

This recommendation applies to every weak section in society. To comment on the Islamic attitude towards slavery is beyond the scope of this account. Suffice it to say here that Islam *took every possible measure to ensure that slavery would soon disappear from human society.* Pending its disappearance, the Prophet took care to ensure that slaves were well treated in Muslim society.

The last part of this *ḥadīth* stresses the importance of the declaration which, when consciously pronounced, brings any person into the fold of Islam. That is the declaration of belief in God's oneness and in the message of Muhammad as being the last message to be revealed by God. Whoever believes in the two parts of this declaration is a Muslim, and whoever denies either of them is not. It was, therefore, important that the Prophet should remind his community of this declaration. Moreover, this reminder brings together the first day and the last day of the Prophet's mission which lasted for twenty-three years. The first thing the Prophet did after receiving his first revelation was to call on people to believe that there is no deity other than God and that Muhammad is His Messenger. The last thing he said before his soul departed was to remind us of the need to make this declaration in order to be on the right track. His, then, was a clear message which underwent no change whatsoever. It will remain the same for the rest of time.

The Prophet says in his final statement that whoever makes this declaration is immune from the Fire of hell. God has made this declaration, when consciously and sincerely made, a reason for forgiving all sins. Some scholars argue that this was at the beginning of Islam when emphasis was placed solely on believing in God's oneness. When duties were detailed and punishments for the contravention of some of them were outlined, things changed and it was no longer enough to believe in God's oneness to ensure immunity from the Fire of hell. This argument, however, cannot be supported by any evidence. In matters of faith, personal argument counts for little.

That certain punishments have been decreed for certain sins does not contradict this rule. Unless these punishments are enforced in this life, anyone who has committed a sin for which a punishment is prescribed may be punished for it in the Hereafter, although he may be a believer. If he is sincere in his belief, it is very likely that God will forgive him his sins.

There are other arguments which suggest that it is most essential for any person to do his Islamic duties and refrain from what is forbidden in order to ensure admission into heaven. There is no denying that it is extremely important to fulfil one's Islamic duties and refrain from all forbidden things, but we cannot make this an argument which detracts from the general nature of this *ḥadīth* which states that the declaration of believing in God's oneness and in the message of Muhammad is the reason for being immune from suffering in hell. The two are not mutually exclusive. No one says that a believer does not need to do his duties or refrain from all forbidden practices. What we say is that this declaration of the oneness of God ensures admission into heaven if it is the final statement by anyone and he says it consciously and sincerely until he dies. If he does, all sins he might have committed during his life will be forgiven by the grace of God. Muslim relates that the Prophet said: 'Any servant of God who says it and dies will be admitted into heaven'. By saying it at his time of death, a person makes sure of his place in heaven. This is because even at the time of death, his thoughts turn towards God declaring his belief in His oneness. He goes towards Him with an open heart, associating with Him no partners. God has made it clear in numerous verses in the Qur'an'an that He will never turn back anyone who comes towards Him, believing in Him, consciously and sincerely. Even at the last minute of one's life, full forgiveness is possible. This is due to God's limitless grace. Anyone who wants to impose limits and conditions on God's grace is wrong and ill-advised.

It should be added that it is not advisable for people to think that they can always utter this declaration at the point of death. No one can guarantee that they will remember it. We may die suddenly, without having enough time to make the declaration. When we look around us and see how people die, we realise that we must always be prepared for death and that we should not leave anything to chance. That realisation should be enough to prompt us to do our duties, so that when the hour comes, we are prepared to meet with God. A person who neglects his duties and commits what is forbidden, then dies suddenly loses everything. It is this situation of utter loss that we should guard against.

Moreover, when people nurture their belief in God's oneness through doing their duties and doing the utmost good work, the declaration that they believe in God as the only deity in the universe and that Muhammad is His final messenger comes naturally to them. They do not need to think about it. When they realise that death is on its way, they look forward to meeting with God because they know that what He has in store for them is better than what they leave behind in this world. They make this declaration to ensure their place in heaven.

Simple and important

The Prophet lays great emphasis on the strengthening of social ties within the Muslim community. This does not come as a surprise to anyone who knows something about the community Islam builds. The first characteristic of this community is the brotherhood of all its members. This brotherhood imposes obligations on everyone. The Prophet took good care to point out these obligations, making some of them binding on everyone, while leaving others at the encouragement level. When the Prophet highlighted any such obligation, expressing it in the imperative form, then that obligation merits careful consideration and proper implementation. We find a good example of such obligations in the following *ḥadīth*:

> 157. 'Abdullāh ibn Mas'ūd reports that the Prophet said: 'Accept invitations. Do not refuse gifts. Do not beat up Muslims'.[111]

Sometimes the imperative form is used to express what is only recommended. Hence, it is important to know when we read a *ḥadīth* like this whether it is meant as a binding duty or not. All scholars agree that accepting an invitation to the banquet given by a bridegroom on the occasion of his marriage is obligatory. The reason for this is obvious: Islam takes special care to encourage community participation in the important events in the life of every one of its

111. Related by Aḥmad and Ibn Ḥibbān.

members. The community shares in the happiness of everyone who gets married or who has a child. The community also shares in the sorrow of anyone who loses a close relative. In fact, the marriage dinner party is recommended for this particular purpose. While serving such a dinner party itself is not obligatory on the bridegroom, yet when he organises one, those who are invited must accept the invitation unless they have a valid reason for excusing themselves.

Scholars, however, differ as to other invitations. Imam Mālik and the majority of scholars are of the opinion that accepting other invitations is not obligatory. It is only recommended. Imam Ibn Ḥazm and his school of thought, which relies heavily on taking religious statements at their face value, argue that the expression used by the Prophet is in the imperative which signifies an obligation. Hence, acceptance of invitations is obligatory. This view is further supported by earlier scholars.

One important reason for considering the acceptance of invitations a binding duty is the fact that the host normally provides much more food than what is sufficient for his guests. When only a small number of those invited turn up, the purpose of the invitation is not achieved, but the host has incurred a great deal of expense. Moreover, close relatives who have had grievances against the bridegroom may try to get some amends from him. As he is certain to invite them, they realise that if they do not turn up, he will appear in very bad light in front of his guests who will wonder why his close relatives are absent on this particular social occasion. Such a state of affairs tends to harden attitudes and make differences more permanent. Islam tries to settle such differences the easy way. By merely inviting his relatives, the host takes steps towards reconciliation. By accepting it, his relatives take a similar step and the atmosphere is automatically more suitable to the achievement of a proper settlement.

It goes without saying that Islam impresses on its followers the need to be truthful in whatever they do. Hence, if a person invites others to a meal, that invitation must be sincere, aiming to cement relations and giving evidence to the fact that the host values highly his relationship with his guests. The best way to reciprocate such feelings is to accept the invitation, even when the host has only very little to offer his guests.

There are reasons, however, which justify declining an invitation. These are detailed by Imam Al-Nawawi, a prominent figure in the al-Shāfiʿi school of thought. These include a well grounded suspicion by the guest that the money his host spends on the invitation has not been earned in a legitimate manner, or that the host invites only rich people, or the potentiality for the presence of someone with whom it is socially unacceptable to associate, or knowledge that the host merely invites him in order to make use of his position or influence, or to gain through him something unlawful. Other reasons which justify declining an invitation include knowledge that there will be something forbidden on that occasion such as wine or using a table cover and napkins made of silk or cutlery made of gold and silver. On the other hand, if the person invited apologises in time to his host, making it clear that other commitments prevent him from accepting, he does not disobey the Prophet's instruction by not accepting.

All the arguments which we have mentioned in favour of accepting invitations apply to the second instruction in this *ḥadīth*, namely that gifts should not be rejected. This instruction is understood by the overwhelming majority of scholars as a very strong recommendation. It is, however, forbidden for a judge to accept gifts. The reason for a such prohibition is clear. Islam is keen that justice should prevail in every Islamic society. People do not normally give gifts to judges unless they are looking forward to a favourable return. This may mean a miscarriage of justice if the person who gives such a present knows that he has a case coming up before that particular judge. Even when the judge knows that he will not be influenced in his judgement by accepting the gift, his consciousness that he must appear to maintain absolute justice may cause him to err on the other side, thus doing injustice to the person who has given him that present. Rather than putting himself in such an untenable position, a judge must not accept a gift in the first place.

It may be said that judges are human beings who have relatives and friends. Are they forbidden to accept from them what all people accept from their own relatives? The answer is that Islam does not impose on Muslim judges a position of total detachment or isolation from society. A judge may maintain good relations with his family and close relatives whom he is certain would not entertain any thought of exploiting his position. Should any of them have a case to be heard, the judge should decline to hear it himself. He should refer it to one of his colleagues who does not have any close relationship with either party.

The last instruction in this *ḥadīth* is: '*Do not beat up Muslims*'. The Prophet uses this mode because it gives a jolt to the listener when he hears it. The normal relationship between Muslims is one of courtesy and good manners. *The thought of beating up others should not arise in the first place.* However, it may happen that a person may try to make use of his physical strength either to settle a dispute with another or to usurp something to which he has no claim. Hence, the instruction that *such an action is forbidden.*

This instruction does not override inflicting any punishment which Islam prescribes for certain offences, or the authority of a judge to make a judgement inflicting *corporal punishment* on an offender. These are proper justifications for such an action. Apart from these, however, to beat up a Muslim is a grave sin. The very usage of the word 'Muslims' in this instruction serves as a reminder that Islam forbids beating up people without justification. Scholars agree that the prohibition also includes non-Muslims.

The case of the Christian Egyptian who complained to 'Umar ibn al-Khaṭṭāb, the second caliph, about the son of the Muslim governor of Egypt for having unjustifiably beaten him up is well known. 'Umar ordered that the governor and his son should attend him without delay. He then allowed the Egyptian to beat up the governor's son in public to restore justice.

11

On the Treatment of the Weak

AT THE ADVENT of Islam, slavery was a universal system, practised everywhere in the world. Inevitably, there were also somewhat different routes to enslavement. An insolvent debtor might find himself a slave because of his inability to repay what he had borrowed. Some offences were punished by depriving the offender of his freedom and making him a slave. The children of slaves were also slaves.

Islam abhorred slavery, quickly seeking to eradicate all its sources, with the exception of prisoners of war. The latter was a universal practice and Islam could not unilaterally abolish it. So, if the enemy took some Muslim captives in a battle and put them into slavery, the Muslims could not then set their own prisoners of war free. In essence, the same treatment should apply. However, when this practice was stopped, Islam reverted to its standard principle which is to set prisoners of war free either against ransom or as an act of grace. This is the principle set out in the Qur'an: '*Now when you meet the unbelievers in battle, smite their necks. Then when you have thoroughly subdued them, bind them firmly. Thereafter, set them free either by an act of grace or against ransom, until war shall lay down its burden*'. (47: 4)

This meant that the early generations of Muslims continued to have slaves. However, Islamic teachings and the Prophet's instructions ensured that the treatment of slaves in Muslim communities was totally different from the grim picture that prevailed elsewhere. In fact, the Prophet described slaves as brothers of their masters. As we go through the *ḥadīths* included on this subject we realise how Islam put the treatment of slaves and servants onto a different level.

The Prophet always cared for the weaker members of society. He continued to urge his community to show the maximum care for their subordinates. In fact, his last words urged Muslims to be kind to their slaves:

158. 'Ali reports: 'The Prophet's last words were: "[Attend to your] prayers! Prayers! Fear God in [your treatment of] those your hands possess [i.e. your slaves]".'[112]

This *ḥadīth* is an abridged version of *ḥadīth* Number 156. We note here that the Prophet does not mention zakat, but prayers are mentioned because it is the most essential part of Islamic worship. Without attending to prayer, people reduce their religion to an insignificance.

The Prophet urged Muslims to always remain God-fearing, particularly in their treatment of slaves, because when slaves are subjected to abuse, they are often helpless and have no recourse to proper justice. Therefore, their best guarantee of good treatment is that their masters should be people who fear God. A God-fearing person realises that God will hold him to account for any abuse of other people's rights.

159. (*Athar* 42) Abu al-Dardā' used to say to people: 'We know you better than the veterinarians know animals. We are able to distinguish the good ones among you from the bad ones. The good person is one whose good turn is hoped for and from

---

112. Related by Abū Dāwūd and Ibn Mājah.

whom none fear any evil, while the bad is one from whom you hope for no good, feel unsafe and whose slave will not be freed'.

160. (*Athar* 43) Abu Umāmah said: 'A truly ingrate person is one who is stingy, stands aloof and beats up his slave'.

161. (*Athar* 44) Al-Ḥasan said: 'A man ordered a slave of his to draw water using a camel of his, but the slave was overtaken by sleep. The man took a torch and threw it at his face which caused the slave to tumble into the well. In the morning, the slave went to 'Umar ibn al-Khaṭṭāb [the second Caliph]. When 'Umar saw what happened to his face, he ordered that he be set free'.

These three *ḥadīths* give us a good idea of how Islam changed people's attitude so that the freeing of a slave became a social virtue. The first *ḥadīth* gives a set of values that distinguish good people from bad. These are exact opposites, but the bad person has an additional quality, which is that he never grants a slave his or her freedom. The second *ḥadīth* outlines the qualities by which one is known to be absolutely ungrateful of God's favours. Such a person is tight-fisted and remains aloof so that he receives neither visitors nor guests. Moreover, he ill-treats his slave or those who fall under his authority.

The third *ḥadīth* tells of a slave being badly treated by his master for having gone to sleep instead of fulfilling a task assigned to him. His master punishes him by burning his face. As a result, the Caliph sets him free. We will presently see that this is an important principle Islam lays down with regard to the treatment of slaves.

However, sometimes a slave was guilty of a serious offence, but even then, under Islam, they were still treated fairly. They did not face the sort of punishment slaves in other societies endured, such as torture, mutilation and death.

162. (*Athar* 45) 'Amrah said: ''Ā'ishah arranged for a slave girl of hers to be set free after her own death. Soon after, 'Ā'ishah became ill. Her nephews consulted a [travelling] African or Indian doctor. He said to them: "You are reporting to me the case of a woman who is under a magic spell. A slave girl has cast

a spell on her". 'Ā'ishah was informed and she interrogated her: "Have you cast a spell on me?" The girl said: "Yes." 'Ā'ishah said: "Why? You will never be free". 'Ā'ishah then gave instructions: "Sell her to the worst masters among the Arabs".'[113]

This is a case of a truly ungrateful slave girl. She was with the best mistress she could ever have had, none other than 'Ā'ishah, the Prophet's wife. Furthermore, 'Ā'ishah had arranged that she would be automatically freed from slavery upon her death. Instead of being grateful, this girl cast a magic spell on 'Ā'ishah causing her ill health in the hope that she would soon die. In Mālik's version of this *ḥadīth*, 'Ā'ishah's nephews only consulted the doctor after her illness continued for a long time. Al-Ḥākim's version adds that when the girl was interrogated about the reason for her action, she said that she wanted to regain her freedom. Therefore, 'Ā'ishah decided to ensure that her purpose would never be achieved, selling her to someone who would never set his slaves free.

The Prophet was keenly aware of his companions' characters, particularly those who attended him frequently. He might say something to one of them because he knew that others would learn from them. Alternatively, he might give someone a hint, realising that he would understand and act on it in the best manner:

163. Abu Umāmah said: 'The Prophet came with two slaves. He gave one to 'Ali and said: "Do not beat him. I have been forbidden to beat people who attend to their prayer. I have seen him praying on our return". He gave the other to Abu Dharr and said: "Take good care of him". Abu Dharr set the slave free. The Prophet [later] asked him: "How is he?" Abu Dharr said: "You instructed me to take good care of him, so I set him free".'[114]

We note that the Prophet gave different instructions to two of his companions concerning the treatment of these two slaves. 'Ali gained profound Islamic insight through his long association with the

113. Related by Mālik, Aḥmad and al-Ḥākim.

114. Related by Aḥmad.

Prophet, and he was later to be a great judge and one of the four rightly guided Caliphs. Therefore, the Prophet told him a principle of Islamic treatment, which is that corporal punishment must not be administered to anyone who is regular in his prayer. To Abu Dharr the Prophet gave a simple instruction to take good care of the slave he was given. Abu Dharr, an idealist, always implemented the Prophet's instructions in the simplest and broadest way. Therefore, he set the slave free, hoping to receive good reward from God for his action.

The Prophet gave the perfect example of the treatment deserved by the weaker members in society, including servants and slaves.

164. Anas reported: 'When the Prophet came to Madinah, he had no servant. Abu Ṭalḥah [Anas's stepfather] took me by the hand to the Prophet and said: "Prophet, Anas is a clever, intelligent boy. Let him serve you". I served him when he was at home and on his travels, from the time he came to Madinah until he passed away. He never said to me about anything I did, "Why have you done this?" nor did he say about anything I omitted to do, "Shouldn't you have done this in such a way?"'[115]

There is nothing that could be more exemplary in the treatment of servants. When Anas came to the Prophet, he was a young lad, perhaps no more than thirteen years of age, although some reports put his age at ten, but this cannot be supported as he attended the Battle of Uḥud, and the Prophet did not allow boys younger than fifteen to be in the army at that time. The Battle took place less than three years after the Prophet's arrival in Madinah.

The Prophet set an example that is perhaps too ideal to emulate, yet we must still try as hard as possible to follow this. It is difficult to imagine that a servant, no matter how intelligent he may be, would not need correction over a period of ten years. It is very probable that Anas did certain things which were not according to what the Prophet had in mind, or he might have omitted certain things which the Prophet wanted to be done. Nevertheless, the Prophet never rebuked him for doing anything in a particular fashion, nor did he tell him that he

115. Related by Aḥmad, al-Bukhari, Muslim and al-Tirmidhi.

should have done certain things differently. He preferred that Anas should learn through practical example.

Misbehaviour by servants

Servants may misbehave and may need to be disciplined. Today, this may take different forms, according to the type of misbehaviour. Serious misbehaviour may result in sacking the servant. A criminal offence may put the servant in prison. Slaves, however, could not be sacked. So what sort of disciplinary measures were open to people?

165. Abu Hurayrah reports that the Prophet said: 'If a slave steals, sell him, even for a *nash* [i.e. a trifling price]'.[116]

The *nash* was a currency unit equal to twenty *dirhams*, and the *dirham* was the silver issue of the time. A slave could sell at a much higher price, but a thieving slave should not be kept because he may be tempted to steal again when he realises that the first offence did not land him in any great trouble.

The Prophet took every opportunity to teach his companions the manners that Islam encourages. His teachings were short and direct. Sometimes he put together two or three diverse instructions so as not to overly dwell on a point that was more suitably kept short. If he was with some of his companions for any length of time, as when waiting for a dinner to be served, he might give several instructions during the conversation, as in the following *ḥadīth* which speaks about very different matters. It is entered by al-Bukhari here because of its reference to the punishment of an offending slave girl:

166. Laqīṭ ibn Ṣabirah said: 'I went to the Prophet. The shepherd drove a newborn sheep into their night shed. The Prophet said [to me]: "Do not suppose [that we are slaughtering a sheep especially for you]. We have a hundred sheep and we do not want them to increase. When the shepherd brings a newborn

---

116. Related by Aḥmad, al-Nasā'ī, Abū Dāwūd and Ibn Mājah.

sheep, we slaughter one". Part of what he said to me was, "Do not beat your wife like you would beat your slave girl. When you wash your nose, snuff up water freely unless you are fasting".'[117]

This version is an abridged one, while Abū Dāwūd gives a much longer one. From Abū Dāwūd's version we learn that the narrator was the leader of a tribal delegation. As the Prophet was not at home when they arrived, 'Ā'ishah ordered some fruit to be served. When the Prophet entered, he welcomed them and ordered a sheep to be slaughtered for their dinner, but he told them that it was in place of the newborn sheep, so that they did not feel that they had put him to unnecessary expense.

Abu Dāwūd's version mentions that the Prophet spoke about various things, including the best method to perform ablution, and divorce a wife *who is verbally abusive.* The *ḥadīth* is entered here by al-Bukhari because it includes a reference to the disciplining of a slave and that a man should never beat his wife for an offence she commits.

167. (*Athar* 46) Abu al-'Āliyah said: 'We were instructed to seal things we entrust to our servants, and to weigh and count things so that they should not get into habits of bad behaviour and we do not unfairly suspect them'.

This *ḥadīth* mentions a recommended practice of making sure that when a servant is entrusted with a task that is open to cheating, measures should be taken to prevent it. This is not contrary to the kind treatment that is required of all Muslims when dealing with weaker members, including slaves and servants. Abu Hurayrah used to count what his servant returned with after sending him to do the day's shopping. Yet when Abu Hurayrah took his meals, he instructed the same servant to sit and eat with him. He was questioned about this and he said that counting the shopping made things clear; in other words, there was then no suspicion of pilfering.

This was the practice of a number of the Prophet's companions, because they felt that suspecting their servants or slaves was a much worse option:

117. Related by Aḥmad and Abū Dāwūd.

168. (*Athar* 47) Salmān said: 'I count pieces of bone [in front of] my servants for fear of unfairly suspecting him'.

169. (*Athar* 48) The same as Number 168 but with a different chain of transmission.

While the Prophet's companions were keen not to unfairly suspect their servants, they did not allow them to do anything Islam did not permit, particularly when they were running errands for their masters. If any committed such an offence, they would not hesitate to punish them, and the punishment was commensurate with the offence.

170. (*Athar* 49) Yazīd ibn 'Abdullāh ibn Qusayṭ said: ''Abdullāh ibn 'Umar sent a slave of his with some gold or silver. The slave changed it, deferring the exchange. When he returned, Ibn 'Umar gave him a painful thrashing and said: 'Go back and take what is mine. Do not agree to a deferred exchange'.

The slave was acting on behalf of Ibn 'Umar when he committed a serious offence that Islam very strictly prohibits, namely making a deferred exchange for a better price. This is a form of usury. Therefore, it is not surprising that Ibn 'Umar was extremely upset, teaching the slave a good lesson, so that he would not do the same thing again. He also explained the reason behind the punishment when he ordered the slave to go back and get the normal price for an immediate exchange.

We note that this was a physical punishment, but it was earned. When there is no good reason for such a punishment, then it is forbidden. The Prophet was keen to instil this in the minds of his companions and the Muslim community in general:

171. Abu Mas'ūd reports: 'I was beating a slave of mine when I heard someone behind me saying: "Know, Abu Mas'ūd, that most certainly God has greater power over you than you have over him". I turned around and there was God's Messenger (peace be upon him). I said: "Messenger of God, he is free for God's sake". He said: "Had you not done so, the Fire would

have touched you", or he might have said "the Fire would have scorched you".'[118]

Here, the Prophet delivers Abu Mas'ūd 'Uqbah ibn 'Āmir with a very strong warning, stating that had he not set the slave free, he would have been scorched by the fire of hell. This means that the Prophet saw something that was definitely unwarranted, such as a severe beating, or a painful slapping of the slave's face.

We note that the Prophet's companion took immediate action once he realised the Prophet's disapproval. The Prophet had issued him with a warning, stating the fact that God's power over everyone is much greater than man's power over his subordinates, regardless of their relative positions. This mere reminder was sufficient for the Prophet's companion and the realisation that he was so in the wrong was sufficient for him to set the slave free. He, thus, gave the slave the best amends for the wrong he had suffered.

Sometimes a word of insult hurts more than a beating. Islam recognises this and the Prophet teaches us that verbal abuse is unacceptable. Just as slapping is disallowed, so is an insult directed at someone's face.

172. Abu Hurayrah reports that the Prophet said: 'Do not say [to anyone]: may God make his face ugly'.[119]

173. Abu Hurayrah reports that the Prophet said: 'Do not say [to anyone]: may God make your face and every face like yours ugly. God, the Mighty and Exalted, created Adam in his form'.[120]

The face is what gives every person his or her unique image. To direct verbal abuse at it is to choose what hurts most. This form of abuse is, therefore, prohibited in Islam. Some people compound it by directing insults at others who may have a similar face, even though they have nothing to do with the problem that has caused the insult. Therefore,

---

118. Related by Muslim, Abū Dāwūd and al-Tirmidhi.

119. Related by Ibn Khuzaymah and Ibn Ḥibbān.

120. Related by Muslim, Abū Dāwūd and al-Tirmidhi.

the Prophet explains that when one uses such a compounded form, he is insulting his own ancestors, up to Adam, the first man on earth. He created Adam in this form and made man in the best form, as He clearly states in the Qur'an: '*We indeed have created man in the finest form*'. (95: 4)

If a verbal insult directed at a servant's face is prohibited, then a slap on the face is even more so. It is certainly forbidden to slap someone, even a servant or a slave [in the days of slavery], on the face.

174. Abu Hurayrah reports that the Prophet said: 'If any of you strikes his servant, he must avoid the face'.[121]

The Prophet never punished anyone physically. However, he realised that some people might exceed their limits and sometimes mere advice or verbal rebuke might not bring about the required result. There are times when only physical punishment is effective. Therefore, if a master found it necessary to strike his servant, the Prophet advised him not to slap him on the face. He must avoid this, because the face is a person's appearance, and if it shows the mark of a strike or a beating, this could overly hurt the punished person. As such, it could be counterproductive.

In fact, the Prophet wanted that a Muslim must not hurt an animal, least of all on its face:

175. Jābir said: 'The Prophet passed by an animal which had been branded [with a hot iron] and smoke was coming out of its nostrils. The Prophet said: "May God curse the person who did this. No one should ever brand or strike the face".'[122]

Perhaps nothing could express the Prophet's displeasure more than his curse of the person who had so branded an animal on its face; this is certainly unacceptable.

The Prophet took every possible measure to ensure that slaves were well treated in the Muslim community. If they needed to be punished for misbehaviour, the punishment was to be commensurate to the

---

121. Related by Aḥmad, al-Bukhari, Muslim, Abū Dāwūd and al-Tirmidhi.
122. Related by Aḥmad, Muslim, Abū Dāwūd and al-Tirmidhi.

offence. The punishment should be corrective, not insulting or causing severe psychological damage. Although slavery is no longer practised in the world, the Prophet's guidance with respect to the treatment of slaves is still relevant, because it applies to the treatment of all vulnerable groups, particularly servants. In this context, it is pertinent to ask: what measure was applicable if a slave was slapped on the face?

176. Hilāl ibn Yasāf said: 'We were selling linen in the house of Suwayd ibn Muqarrin when a slave girl came out and said something to one of the men. The man slapped her. Suwayd ibn Muqarrin said to him: "Have you slapped her on the face? We were seven brothers and we had only one servant. One of us slapped her and the Prophet commanded him to set her free".'[123]

177. Ibn 'Umar reports that the Prophet said: 'Anyone who slaps his slave or beats him up for an offence he has not committed must set him free in compensation.'[124]

178. Mu'āwiyah ibn Suwayd ibn Muqarrin said: 'I slapped a slave of ours and he escaped. Then my father called me and said [to the slave]: "Avenge yourself". We, the sons of Muqarrin, were seven and we had one servant. When one of us slapped her, this was mentioned to the Prophet (peace be upon him). He said [to the one who informed him]: "Tell them to set her free". The Prophet was told: "She is their only servant". He said: "Then they may engage her and when they can spare her, let her go free".' [125]

179. Abu Shu'bah said: 'When Suwayd ibn Muqarrin al-Muzani saw a man slapping a slave of his, he said to him: "Are you not aware that [slapping on] the face is forbidden? During the Prophet's lifetime, we were seven brothers and we had onlyl one servant. One of us slapped him and the Prophet commanded us to set him free".'[126]

---

123. Related by Muslim and al-Tirmidhi.

124. Related by Aḥmad, Abu 'Awānah and Ibn Ḥibbān.

125. Related by Muslim and Abū Dāwūd.

126. Related by Muslim and Abū Dāwūd and al-Tirmidhi.

180. Abu ʿUmar Zādhān said: ʿWe were at Ibn ʿUmar's when he summoned a slave of his he had beaten. He uncovered the slave's back and asked him: "Does it hurt?" He said: "No." Ibn ʿUmar set him free. He then picked up a small wooden stick from the ground and said: "I do not have a reward [for setting him free] that is equal to the weight of this stick". I asked him: "Why do you say this, Abu ʿAbd al-Raḥmān?" He said: "The Prophet said: ʿAnyone who beats his slave up for an offence he has not committed or slaps him must set him free in compensation".ʾ[127]

These five *ḥadīths* speak about the compensation a slave should be given for being slapped on the face by his master. They do not refer to the offence the slave might have committed, which could be serious. *Ḥadīth* Numbers 177 and 180 refer to the same incident involving ʿAbdullāh ibn ʿUmar and his slave. It is important to point out here that Ibn ʿUmar always did his best to follow the Prophet's example and obey his orders. Whenever he learnt something from the Prophet, he implemented it without hesitation. He was a man who realised that following the Prophet's example in every sense, taking his orders at face value and implementing them to the best of his ability, was the surest way to heaven. It is not surprising, therefore, that he was exemplary in his conduct and that many people valued his company because he was a living example of how Islam should be practised.

In order to understand the significance of this story, it should be pointed out that Ibn ʿUmar could never have beaten up his slave by way of revenge or in a fit of rage. He was not a hot-tempered person, flying off the handle at every provocation. Indeed, he was the opposite. He was a very conscientious person who considered his actions carefully. Nor is it to be imagined that he might have beaten up his slave for no reason. He could only have punished him for a clear fault he must have committed. It may also be understood from the story that ʿAbdullāh ibn ʿUmar learned later that the slave might not have been at fault, or he might have thought that the punishment was much more severe than the slave's fault deserved. Hence, he wanted to make amends and so set that slave free.

---

127. Related by Muslim and Abū Dāwūd.

Another point of significance is that ʿAbdullāh ibn ʿUmar did not want his attendants to give him more credit for his action than he deserved. Hence, he made it clear how much reward he expected for setting that slave free. To him, there could not be any more reward than the little weight of a wooden stick, which he had picked up from the ground. His argument being that since the Prophet had specified freedom for a slave as compensation for beating him up unjustly or slapping him on the face, then the compensation merited no reward. It simply wipes off the effects of the earlier action which was not allowed in Islam. We know that setting a slave free was a benevolent action that earned rich reward. We also know that it was prescribed as compensation for a number of grave sins. This shows the seriousness with which Islam viewed the improper action of beating a slave who had committed no grave sin or of slapping him on the face.

The question arises here whether it was obligatory to set a slave free once he or she had been slapped on the face by his or her master or mistress. The other three *ḥadīths* give us an answer. These *ḥadīths* are authentic as they are related by Muslim, and as they have different reporters they are considered even more authentic. *Ḥadīth* Number 178 is given more fully by Muslim. It quotes Muʿāwiyah, its reporter, as saying that he was the one who fled after slapping the slave. He came back before noon and offered the midday prayer, Ẓuhr, in congregation with his father. When the prayer had finished, his father, Suwayd ibn Muqarrin called in the slave and told him to avenge himself against his own son, adding the reason for this by reporting what the Prophet told him and his brothers when one of them slapped their maid.

Scholars agree that these *ḥadīths* set the desired compensation for slapping a slave or beating him up for no reason. That compensation was setting the slave free. They also agree that it was not compulsory to do so. This opinion is based on the fact that when it was pointed out to the Prophet that those seven brothers had no servant other than this one whom they kept from pre-Islamic days, he allowed them to continue to benefit by the service of their slave woman until such a time when they were able to let her go. We also note that the Prophet's reaction left a very strong impression on the minds of those brothers. Suwayd ibn Muqarrin related this story every time an occasion arose. Moreover, when his own son was guilty of the same practice, he called in the slave who had been slapped by his son and gave him a chance to avenge himself. No one would have acted in this way unless he viewed the matter very seriously. Suwayd wanted his son not to commit an offence without having to pay the proper compensation. Hence, his willingness to allow the slave to slap him back. Needless to say, his son could not be asked to free the slave as he did not belong to him.

Reflection on this *ḥadīth* makes it abundantly clear that a person must never slap anyone on the face, simply because that person is in a vulnerable position which makes them unable to retaliate. If a slave must not be slapped on the face for any reason, this applies in a much stronger measure to an ordinary servant. While a servant may be reproached for improper conduct, a slap on the face is too severe a punishment for any such misdemeanour. There are other effective methods of discipline which Islam approves of. A Muslim must not exceed these and commit what is forbidden.

Unjust treatment of weaker members

Islam makes clear that justice must always be maintained. On the Day of Judgement, God makes sure that everyone who has committed injustice will suffer the consequences of what he has done. Thus, no one who manages to escape punishment for some injustice he committed in this world will be able to escape it in the life to come. Those who suffer injustice in this life, on the other hand, will be able to claim their dues from those who have wronged them. Islamic abhorrence of injustice applies even more clearly to those who are vulnerable to other people's abuse of power or authority. Perhaps no category of people were more susceptible than slaves. Although slavery is no longer practised in human society, there are still weak and vulnerable people who must be protected. If we establish that something is viewed by Islam as intolerable when it is practised against slaves, it is even more so when it is practised against free people, no matter what position in society they occupy.

Under Islam a person who suffers injustice is entitled to claim his right in full measure against the one who has been unjust to him. It also asserts that all people are equal in front of the law.

181. (*Athar* 50) ʿAmmār ibn Yāsir said: 'Anyone among you who beats up a slave of his unjustly shall have to repay him fully on the Day of Judgement'.

ʿAmmār was one of the earliest people to embrace Islam. The Prophet described him as a person who is full of faith to the top of his head. It is also authentically reported that the Prophet had impressed upon Muslims that they follow ʿAmmār's example. He also said: 'Whoever is inimical to ʿAmmār will suffer God's enmity, and he who is hostile to ʿAmmār will suffer God's hostility'. What the Prophet tells us in this statement is that a master who beats his slave unjustly will have to pay him back on the Day of Judgement. Although he belonged to the weaker class of citizens in pre-Islamic days, ʿAmmār was later appointed by ʿUmar as governor of the Province of Kufah.

This principle is further supported by another of the Prophet's companions who acquired high standing.

182. (*Athar* 51) Abu Layla said: 'Salmān came out and saw the fodder falling from the manger. He said to his servant: "Had it not been for fearing retaliation on the Day of Judgement, I would have beaten you hard".'

These two statements are perfect examples of how Islam influenced the behaviour of its followers. They acquired a sense of propriety which is unparalleled in the history of any nation. This is not surprising, for those people were taught by the best educator in human history, Prophet Muhammad (peace be upon him). He cultivated in them a sense of justice which made them consider every action before doing it. If there was the slightest suspicion of injustice in it, he would not do it. How could he, when he knew that he would inevitably face retaliation?

183. Abu Hurayrah reports that the Prophet said: 'You shall most certainly pay back every rightful claim. Even a hornless sheep shall have retaliation against a horned one'.

Perhaps this *ḥadīth* should not be taken literally. For animals do not enjoy freedom of choice in their actions like humans. Moreover, they are not accountable for what they do in the same way as we are. The image the Prophet gives in this *ḥadīth* is very powerful. It strikes fear in the hearts of believers. That fear has a positive effect, making everyone aware that God will question him about even the slightest claim other people have against him. Hence, it is far better for him to give them their dues in this life than to incur God's displeasure and pay them back in the Hereafter out of his own reward for good deeds.

The Prophet goes even further than this:

> 184. Umm Salamah [the Prophet's wife] reports that the Prophet was in her house. 'He called in a slave girl of his [or hers], but she was slow. Anger was seen in his face. Umm Salamah went to look behind the curtain and she saw the girl playing. The Prophet had a tooth stick in his hand. He said: 'Had it not been for fearing retaliation on the Day of Judgement, I would have hurt you with this tooth stick'.
>
> Muhammad ibn al-Haytham adds: 'She was playing with an animal'. He also adds that 'on bringing the slave girl back, Umm Salamah said: Messenger of God, she swears that she did not hear you'.

We need only to remember one or two of the stories which abound in history books about the treatment of slaves in all cultures to realise that they were subjected to that which was worse than animals or even inanimate objects. They were killed at will, with no one being able to lift a finger against such a master. People watched passively when a master made some of his slaves torture others. Yet, in Islam we find the Prophet expressing his own fear of punishment on the Day of Judgement for hitting a maid, who had not responded to his call, with a toothbrush. It is enough to be aware of this *ḥadīth* in order to have a genuine fear of wronging servants.

185. Abu Hurayrah reports that the Prophet said: 'He who beats up someone unjustly will have to make amends to him on the Day of Judgement'.[128]

186. The same as Number 185 with a different chain of transmission.

Now what we need to understand is that punishment on the Day of Judgement is something very real in the minds of all Muslims. It is never taken lightly. In all generations, Muslims with a keen sense of Islam, have expressed their fear of having to make amends for their bad deeds on the Day of Judgement. This is because the punishment of the Hereafter is much worse than any punishment in this life. When one develops such a fear of this punishment, one acquires a keen sense of having to do what is right in this life. The *ḥadīths* and reports which we have quoted make it clear that one such important aspect of a Muslim's behaviour is to be just to those who are vulnerable to injustice. This applies equally to servants, employees and other weak groups over whom one may have power. When such a sense of justice prevails in society, little can go wrong with it.

The way to treat servants

Our discussion so far has largely centred on what a person must not do when treating servants and weaker members of society. We also provided the best example of acceptable treatment in how the Prophet treated those who served him. There are, however, certain aspects of Islamic treatment which we have not as yet discussed.

187. 'Ubādah ibn al-Walīd ibn 'Ubādah ibn al-Ṣāmit said: 'My father and I went out to seek knowledge from the Anṣār while their people of knowledge were still alive. The first one we met was Abu al-Yasar, the Prophet's companion who was accompanied by a slave of his. Abu al-Yasar was wearing one

128. Related by al-Bayhaqi, al-Bazzār and al-Ṭabarāni.

striped robe and a Yemeni robe [called *maʿāfiri*], and his slave was likewise wearing a striped robe and a Yemeni robe. I said to him: "Uncle, if you take your servant's striped robe and give him your Yemeni robe, or if you take his Yemeni robe and give him your striped robe, you would be wearing a suit and he a suit". Abu al-Yasar wiped his [ʿUbādah's] head and said: "My Lord, bless him. Nephew, these two eyes of mine have seen, and my two ears heard, and my heart learnt [pointing to his heart] what the Prophet said: 'Feed them from the food you eat and clothe them from what you wear'. It is easier for me to give him of the goods of this world than that he should take away some of my good actions on the Day of Judgement".'[129]

188. Jābir ibn ʿAbdullāh said: 'The Prophet used to urge good treatment of slaves and used to say: "Feed them from the food you eat and clothe them from what you wear. Do not be hard on God's creatures".'

The Prophet's words are reported in the same way by several companions, as we will presently see in another *ḥadīth*. This suggests that the Prophet gave the same advice on several occasions, attended by different people. Kind treatment of servants and slaves can hardly be expressed in a more effective way: giving them of the food we eat and the clothes we wear. This stresses equality in the true sense of the word. The Prophet went even further than this:

189. Al-Maʿrūr ibn Suwayd said: 'I saw Abu Dharr wearing a suit and accompanied by a slave who was wearing a similar suit. We questioned him about that. He said: "I once exchanged verbal abuse with someone and he complained to the Prophet who said to me: 'Have you insulted him on account of his mother?' I said that I did. The Prophet then said: 'Your servants are your brothers. God has placed them under you. He of you who has a brother of his under him should feed him of the food he eats

---

129. Related by Muslim and Ibn Mājah.

and dress him of the same clothes he wears. Do not charge them with what is beyond their ability. If you do, then help them'.'"[130]

This incident and the Prophet's directives which follow it had a very strong impression on Abu Dharr's mind. We learn from this *ḥadīth* that he implemented the Prophet's directives to the letter. He gave his slave the same type of dress he himself wore, which surprised other people who questioned him about it, perhaps suggesting to him that he should wear clothes of a better quality than those of his slave's. Abu Dharr was a highly sensitive person. Having made a mistake, he wanted to remove its traces completely, correcting his future behaviour so that he did not make the same mistake twice.

The incident Abu Dharr refers to in this *ḥadīth* is given in a fuller version in other books. The person with whom he exchanged verbal abuse was Bilāl, a companion of the Prophet of Abyssinian origin. Bilāl was a former slave and was tortured very badly by his master after embracing Islam. The torture was increased following Bilāl's resolute refusal to denounce Islam and the Prophet. He insisted on declaring his belief in God's oneness. Abu Bakr bought Bilāl and set him free.

It is reported that when Abu Dharr abused Bilāl, he said to him: 'You, son of a black woman'. These were the words to which the Prophet strongly objected, expressing his objection in the terms quoted in the *ḥadīth* above. Abu Dharr was very angry with himself for committing this mistake.

Let us now consider how the Prophet states his instruction. The first sentence is highly significant. The Prophet uses the mode of inversion in order to stress the brotherhood between master and slave. To retain the inversion, we would translate it as: 'Your brothers your servants are'. Brotherhood comes first because it is the original state on two counts: humanity and Islam. All human beings come from the same origin, hence they are brothers and sisters. On the other hand, Islam establishes a bond of brotherhood between all its followers. The bondage of slavery is an incidental aspect which is bound to disappear.

---

130. Related by al-Bukhari, Muslim, Abū Dāwūd, al-Tirmidhi and Ibn Mājah. In al-Bukhari's Ṣaḥīḥ version the Prophet is quoted as having said to Abu Dharr: 'Have you insulted him on account of his mother? You still have traces of ignorance about you'.

Hence, it cannot be given precedence over the original relationship. Moreover, the Prophet does not use the term, 'slaves'. He prefers to describe them as servants. This is a mark of the Prophet's manners and it indicates that the same rules apply to servants, employees and others whom a person may hire for a particular job. He describes all these as being placed 'under you'. He then defines the sort of treatment which Islam wants to be extended to slaves. They must be fed of the same food of the family and dressed with the same type of clothes. Moreover, they should be helped when they are charged with a task beyond their ability.

The same directives were repeated by the Prophet on several occasions:

190. Sallām ibn ʿAmr quotes a companion of the Prophet: 'The Prophet said: "Your slaves are your brothers, so be kind to them. Ask their help with what is too hard for you and help them with what is too hard for them".'[131]

191. (*Athar* 52) Abu Hurayrah said: 'Help the worker in his work. He that works for God will not be disappointed'.[132]

192. Abu Hurayrah reports that the Prophet said: 'A slave is entitled to be fed and dressed and not to be charged with something which exceeds his ability".'[133]

193. Abu Hurayrah reports that the Prophet said: 'A slave is entitled to be fed and dressed and not to be charged except with what he is able to do'.[134]

194. Maʿrur said: 'We passed by Abu Dharr and he was wearing a robe while his slave was wearing a suit. We suggested: "If you would take this and give this man something else, you would have a suit". He told us that the Prophet said: "These are your

---

131. Related by Aḥmad.
132. Related by Aḥmad.
133. Related by Aḥmad, Mālik and Muslim.
134. Related by Aḥmad, Mālik and Muslim.

brothers and God has placed them under you. He of you who has a brother of his under him should feed him of the food he eats and dress him of the same clothes he wears. You must not charge them with what is beyond their ability. If you do, then help them with it".'[135]

These *ḥadīths* state some very important principles. To start with, the right of a slave to be fed and clothed is established beyond doubt. It is not left to the master to decide whether to feed a slave or not. He is further entitled to be given appropriate clothes which do not leave him cold in winter and suffering extreme heat in summer. The second principle is that his tasks must be within his ability. This is extremely important. We have only to remember how slaves were treated in other cultures and societies. They were no more than labourers who toiled all day and night, given very little rest and charged with tasks which defeated any man's ability. Islam did not approve of this at all. If there was something to be done and a slave could not do it by himself he was to be given help, even by his master. This is not surprising. Indeed it is only to be expected from a religion which considers all its followers brothers, regardless of their social status. It is indeed a supreme standard to which Islam has lifted its followers, in pressing on their minds that the weaker groups in society are not to be looked upon with contempt.

In order to ensure that servants receive what they are entitled to, particularly concerning food and clothing, the Prophet made it clear that people are richly rewarded by God for the expenses they incur in doing so:

195. Al-Miqdām reports that he heard the Prophet say: 'What you feed yourself counts as *ṣadaqah* (i.e. charity), and what you feed your children, wife and servant counts as *ṣadaqah*'.[136]

A *ṣadaqah* is the sort of charity that a Muslim gives voluntarily, without obligation. It is always well rewarded by God. Here, the Prophet tells

135. Related by Abu 'Awānah and Ibn Ḥibbān.
136. Related by Aḥmad and al-Nasā'ī.

us that even the food we eat or feed our families with counts as *ṣadaqah*. People may be surprised at this because we eat in order to live. So how come what we do in order to ensure our own survival counts as an act of charity? This is an aspect of the grace God bestows on His servants when they benefit from what He has provided for them and put it to good use, acknowledging His favour and thanking Him for what He gives them.

The Prophet makes clear that charity begins with oneself, and the proper thing is to give away of what one has in excess of one's immediate and essential needs:

196. Abu Hurayrah reports that the Prophet said: 'The best *ṣadaqah* (i.e. charity) is what keeps you free of need. The hand that gives is better than the one that takes. Start with your dependents, lest that your wife should say to you: "Provide for me or divorce me", or your slave should say: "Provide for me or sell me", or your children say: "Who will look after us?"'[137]

The Prophet stressed the importance of looking after one's immediate family before helping others. He said this on several occasions so that the point should be understood by all:

197. Abu Hurayrah said: 'The Prophet commanded [that Muslims should give] *ṣadaqah*. A man said to him: "I have a *dinār* [the gold currency]". The Prophet said: "Spend it on your own needs". The man said: "I have another". The Prophet said: "Spend it on your wife." The man said: "I have another". The Prophet said: "Spend it on your servants, and then you know best whom to help".'[138]

When scholars comment on this *ḥadīth* they point out that the right of one's children is the same as that of one's wife. However, another version of this *ḥadīth* includes the Prophet's advice: 'Spend it on your children', before the instruction to spend on one's wife.

---

137. Related by al-Bukhari and Abu 'Awānah.
138. Related by Aḥmad, al-Nasā'ī, Abū Dāwūd, al-Ḥākim and Ibn Ḥibbān.

As we have noted, in these *ḥadīths* the words 'slave' and 'servant' are used interchangeably. Other words used in the same context are *ghulām* and *mawla*, which mean 'young man' and 'associate' respectively. This makes clear that the instructions given by the Prophet do not apply to slaves only, but to all people who are in a weaker position. Indeed, if slaves are entitled to the sort of treatment outlined in these *ḥadīths,* the claims of servants and subordinates are even stronger. The following *ḥadīths* give us an even clearer picture of the treatment Islam requires of such people:

198. Abu al-Zubayr reports: 'A man asked Jābir about one's servant who has spared one the trouble of preparing food and the heat [of cooking]: did the Prophet order that the servant be invited? Jabir said: "Yes. However, if any of you dislikes to have his servant eating with him, he should give him some of the food to eat".'[139]

199. Jābir ibn 'Abdullāh said: 'The Prophet used to urge good treatment of slaves and used to say: "Feed them from the food you eat and clothe them from what you wear. Do not be hard on God's creatures".'

200. Abu Hurayrah reports that the Prophet said: 'When a servant of yours brings you your food, let him sit with you. If he is unwilling to do so, give him some of it'.[140]

The second of these three *ḥadīths* is the same as *ḥadīth* Number 188, but with a different chain of transmission. The other two speak of the servant, or the slave being invited to sit and eat. The question is whether this is obligatory.

Taking all these *ḥadīths* together, it may be asked whether it is absolutely compulsory or simply strongly recommended to give servants

---

139. Related by Aḥmad and Ibn Ḥibbān.
140. Related by Aḥmad, al-Bukhari, Muslim, Abū Dāwūd, al-Tirmidhi, Ibn Mājah, al-Dārimi and Ibn Ḥibbān.

the same food we eat and the same clothes we wear. Furthermore, is it obligatory to ask them to sit with us at the table when we eat?

Many scholars are of the opinion that what a slave is entitled to is to have good food and proper clothing. The guide here is what is socially acceptable as good food and clothing. It is not proper that a master gives his slave food and clothing which are far inferior to what he eats and dresses in. Only if the master is accustomed to luxurious living, always having the finest of food and clothing need he not give the same to servants, provided however that he gives them what is considered to be good and reasonable in society. Some scholars say that the equality between master and servant in food and dress was specially addressed to the Arabs whose food and clothing were of a simple nature. If they were to give their slaves what was greatly inferior to what they themselves had, then that would have been completely unacceptable. What is required by way of obligation, according to these scholars, is to give a slave or servant reasonable and nourishing food and clothing which keep him warm in winter and cool in summer.

In considering the second question of the servant sitting with the family at the table, al-Shāfiʿi explains in commenting on the third *ḥadīth* that if the master orders his servant to sit with him at table, then this is far better. If he does not do so, he does not, however, fail to fulfil a duty. It is open to him to ask his servant to sit with him or to give him some of the same food. Alternatively, this directive may be understood as a recommendation. Other scholars express a different opinion, considering the *ḥadīth* as giving a clear order which must be acted upon. They, however, make an exception in two cases: when the food is barely enough for those sitting to eat and when the servant abstains of his own accord, as a gesture of respect to his employer. In these cases, it is not obligatory to make the servant sit at the table, although it is obligatory to give him something of the food. Similar cases may be treated in the same way.

It seems to me that al-Shāfiʿi's opinion is weightier. The first of the three *ḥadīths* suggests the alternative of giving the servant some of the food to eat alone or with his own family as a matter of choice. This means that the obligation is limited to giving the servant something to eat of the same food he prepared. To add further requirement of commanding him to sit with his employer is not supported by clear evidence.

Scholars understand this *ḥadīth* as constituting a servant's right. The fact that he has worked to prepare and cook the food gives him a share in it. This is unlike what some people think suggesting that it is better to give a servant of the food that he or she prepares to avoid the effects of his or her evil eye. It is not for this reason that the Prophet gave us this directive. If we feel that we are giving a servant something to avoid evil, it means that the servant does not deserve it or is not entitled to it. According to these *ḥadīths*, he is entitled to have something of the food he prepares. So, it is his right.

The companions of the Prophet understood his instructions well and practised them:

> 201. (*Athar* 53) Abu Maḥdhūrah reports: 'I was sitting at 'Umar's when Ṣafwān ibn Umayyah brought in a tray of food, carried in a cloth by some people. They placed it in front of 'Umar. 'Umar invited some poor people and some slaves belonging to other people and they ate with him. He then said: "May God punish people who are too proud to allow their slaves to eat with them". Ṣafwān said: "By God, we are not too proud but we prefer ourselves. By God, we do not have enough of the good food to eat and feed them".'

This report tells us that 'Umar felt strongly about Ṣafwān's servants not sharing in the food. He himself called in some slaves to partake of it. Hence his reproach to Ṣafwān. When Ṣafwān explained that it was the expense which prevented him from calling in his servants, 'Umar did not object to this.

Double reward for slaves

When slavery was practised in most societies, slaves had no rights. In most cultures, they were treated like any other possession. Slaves could be killed or mutilated by their masters without anyone raising even an objection, let alone defend them or speak of their rights. The case was totally different in Islamic society. As we have explained, Islam put in place various measures to reduce slavery and help its ultimate abolition. It could not abolish it straightaway because it was a universal practice. Therefore, it ensured that slaves received kind treatment. Most Islamic rules concerning slaves apply to servants and other weaker elements in society.

Under Islam, however, a slave was considered a human being who enjoyed his rights and had his own choice with regard to faith. Thus, he was required to believe in God and the message of Muhammad (peace be on him) like everyone else. If a slave did not accept Islam only to follow his master's lead, he was an unbeliever in his own right and he faced his destiny as such on the Day of Judgement. On the other hand, if a slave accepted Islam when his master did not, he earned great reward. Indeed, he would receive greater reward than a free man for his proper fulfilment of his Islamic duties.

202. 'Abdullāh ibn 'Umar reports that the Prophet said: 'A slave who is sincere to his master and worships God well earns double reward'.[141]

The thought of a slave's accountability for his deeds and his receiving reward from God which may be doubled up in certain cases is an indication of the great divide which separates the Islamic view of slaves and that of other cultures. According to Islam, a slave is a human being who is responsible like everyone else. His bondage is incidental and does not detract in any way from his humanity. Moreover, he is responsible as an individual. He does not follow his master blindly in matters of faith. A slave may be one of those who will be admitted into Heaven on the Day of Judgement while his master will be doomed to Hell. What separates them is their actions. If the slave is a God-fearing person while his master is a hardened sinner, they will have different destinies in the Hereafter.

When we consider this statement by the Prophet carefully, we find that a slave can double his reward by fulfilling two conditions: serving his master with sincerity and being conscientious in his worship.

141. Related by al-Bukhari, Muslim and Abū Dāwūd.

A slave's duty towards his master is to seek what is good for him. He should obey him and look after him. As far as his duty towards God is concerned, it is the same as everyone else. A slave must do what God has ordered us to do and refrain from what He has forbidden us. He, nevertheless, earns a double reward because slavery imposes a burden on him. Hence, it is harder for a slave to fulfil his duties. Does this mean that a slave's reward is always double that of his master? The answer is that when a slave does something which constitutes obedience of God and obedience of his master, then his reward is doubled. This is something special for slaves. This does not mean that slavery is better than freedom. There may be other ways by which a free person can gain more reward than a slave for the same action. What is important to realise is that God's treatment of slaves is not influenced by their bondage. God treats them as a group of His servants who are required to do His bidding. When they do, they are rewarded. When they disobey Him, they are punished.

The idea of doubling or multiplying reward is a well-known concept in Islam. God's generosity knows no limit. He multiplies reward to whomever He wills. A verse in the Qur'an speaks of charity being rewarded by seven hundred times its value, or even more. When the Prophet specifies certain actions as earning a double reward, his statement serves as encouragement to his followers to do these actions without any hesitation. Needless to say, such actions normally require harder effort. Otherwise, they would not have merited a double reward.

203. Ṣāliḥ ibn Ḥayy reports: 'A man said to ʿĀmir al-Shaʿbi: "Abu ʿAmr, we say that if a man sets free a slave woman who has given him a child, then marries her, it is like one who rides his own camel". Al-Shaʿbi said: "Abu Burdah told me, quoting his father, that God's Messenger said to them: 'Three people will earn double reward: one from the followers of earlier Divine religions who believed in his prophet then believed in Muslim earns double reward; a slave in bondage who fulfils his duties towards God and his masters; and a man who has a bondswoman with whom he has intercourse: he teaches her fine manners and educates her well, then he sets her free and marries her earns double reward".'

'Āmir [al-Sha'bi] said [to his questioner]: "We have given you this free of charge while people used to travel to Madinah for something less significant".'[142]

This *ḥadīth* specifies three groups of people as having double reward for their actions. It is particularly relevant to our topic, since two of the three actions are relevant to slavery. It is difficult for a person to change his religion especially when he follows a well-established religion that has been followed by people for centuries. Divine religions have special appeal for people. It may be easy for a person who worships idols to realise that his faith is baseless. If he is called upon to believe in Islam and if the message of Islam is explained well to him, its strong logic will appeal to him. A person who follows a Divine religion such as Christianity or Judaism has much stronger motives to adhere to his faith. If he is wise enough to consider Islam carefully and accept it when he recognises its truthfulness, he deserves a double reward. The second type of person mentioned in this *ḥadīth* is the same as the one mentioned in the earlier one. The last type is that of a free person who has no motive whatsoever to set his slave woman free and marry her. Indeed, he has all the reasons not to do so. There may be social objections to contend with. People will say that her social class is far below his own. He earns a double reward for setting her free and marrying her. Can there be a better motive to set slaves free? This is one indication of how Islam has mobilised all efforts to reduce slavery and eradicate it altogether.

The idea of double reward is repeated in several *ḥadīths*, which may have very similar wording, but have different chains of transmission. Scholars of *Ḥadīth* classified each such narration as a different *ḥadīth*, even if the difference is only one reporter in the chain. Therefore, we add these here without further explanation.

204. Abu Mūsa reports that the Prophet said: 'A slave who worships his Lord well and fulfils his duties of obedience and sincerity which he owes to his master will have a double reward'.

---

142. Rleated by al-Bukhari, Muslim, al-Tirmidhi, al-Nasā'i and Ibn Majah.

205. Abu Mūsa reports that the Prophet said: 'A slave has dual reward if he fulfils his duty of worship (or perhaps he said 'of proper worship') and his duty which he owes to his owner'.

When we talk about a slave's duty towards his master, we should remember that he is in a position of trust, and Islam makes clear that everyone in such a position must fulfil his trust and will be accountable for it.

206. Ibn 'Umar reports that the Prophet said: 'All of you are shepherds and all of you are accountable for whatever is under your charge. A ruler who is in power is a shepherd and is accountable for his flock. A man is a shepherd of his household and is accountable for his flock. A man's slave is a shepherd of his master's property and is accountable for his trust. Everyone of you is a shepherd and everyone is accountable for their trust'.[143]

This *ḥadīth* will come up again (Number 212) in slightly different wording and a different chain of transmission. In its present version, it mentions a slave being a shepherd of his master's property. It gives a totally different concept of the role of a slave, making him or her a person of trust with accountability. The Prophet uses the same word in all these cases, making the ruler, the head of the family and the slave all shepherds.

It is also important to realise that the Islamic view of the relationship between master and slave is also different. In other cultures, a slave was required to show blind obedience to his master, in whatever he ordered. In Islam, no one may order a subordinate to disobey God in any way. It is in this light and within this principle that we should understand the following *ḥadīth*:

207. (*Athar* 54) Abu Hurayrah said: 'If a slave obeys his master, he has obeyed God, the Mighty and Exalted, and if he disobeys his master, he has disobeyed Him'.

143. Related by al-Bukhari, Muslim and Abū Dāwūd.

Needless to say, if a master orders a slave to do what constitutes disobedience of God, the slave must not obey him. Under Islamic rule, the state would support him against his master.

In view of all that we have said about the treatment of slaves and servants in Muslim society, and the double reward a slave might hope to have, it is not surprising that some highly respected people thought that they would have hoped for a higher position on the Day of Judgement if they were slaves:

208. Abu Hurayrah reports that the Prophet said: 'A Muslim slave who fulfils what is due to God and what is due to his master will receive double reward'.

Abu Hurayrah added: 'By Him who holds Abu Hurayrah's soul in His hand, were it not for jihad for God's cause, offering the pilgrimage and being dutiful to my mother, I would have wished to die a slave'.[144]

We have already spoken about a slave's double reward. Abu Hurayrah's added statement needs no comment, as he himself points out some of the areas where a free man is far better placed.

When people find themselves in a position of strength, they tend to try to impress their strength on others. They may sometimes do this unintentionally. In many cases, they enjoy telling people about their strength and indulge in showing-off. One way of doing this is to speak about those who are in one's employment or under one's charge in a condescending manner. At the time of slavery, slaves were spoken of as insignificant. The Prophet teaches the Muslim community that this is not allowed in Islam.

209. Abu Hurayrah reports that the Prophet said: 'Let none of you say [in reference to those he possesses]: "My slave; my slave-girl". All of you are God's slaves and all your women are God's slaves. You should rather say: "My boy, my girl; or my lad, my maid".'[145]

---

144. Related by Aḥmad, al-Bukhari, Muslim and Abu 'Awānah.
145. Related by al-Bukhari, Muslim, al-Nasā'ī and Ibn Ḥibbān.

210. Abu Hurayrah reports that the Prophet said: 'Let none of you say: "My slave, my slave-girl". Nor may the salve say [in reference to his master]: "My Lord, my Lady". Let them say: "My lad, my servant and my master, my mistress". All of you are slaves and the Lord is God, the Mighty and Exalted'.[146]

In its two versions, this *ḥadīth* gives very clear instructions that *people must not address their slaves* or refer to them in their conversation with others *as slaves*. Nor are slaves allowed to address their masters as their lords. Both master and slave are required to show their humility before God. Conceit is a vice which Islam forbids. Anything that leads a person to be conceited or arrogant is not allowed in Islam. We must not underestimate this directive by the Prophet. The way one speaks about those who are under one subconsciously influences one's attitude towards them. Using the more polite form helps a master to be kinder and helps those under him to be more aware of their humanity.

146. Related by Abū Dāwūd and al-Nasā'ī.

12

Humility and Responsibility

CERTAIN WORDS CARRY different shades of meaning. Hence, they may be unsuitable in certain contexts while being appropriate in others. One such word is *sayyid* in Arabic, which means: 'master, respected person, chief, etc'. However, in certain contexts it means 'sovereign'. We noted towards the end of the last chapter that the Prophet prohibited the reference by slaves or servants to their master as 'my lord'. He instructed them instead to use the word 'master' or its Arabic equivalent, *sayyid*. However, in a different situation, the Prophet objected to the use of the same word in addressing anyone:

211. 'Abdullāh ibn al-Shakhkhīr reports: 'I travelled with the delegation of the 'Āmir tribe to meet the Prophet (peace be upon him). They said: "You are our master". He said: "God is the Master". They said: "And you are the best of us in your grace

and the most generous". He responded: "State your purpose and do not let Satan lead you to exaggeration".'[147]

As we noted, the Prophet suggested that the use of '*sayyid*', meaning 'master' is appropriate in certain situations. Here, he is addressed by the same word, but objects to it, stating that 'God is the Master'. The difference is that the delegation used the word in the sense of 'an overall master' or 'sovereign'. He always made sure that people understood his position and did not give him more than what was due to him. Therefore, when they continued to praise him, he stopped them and asked them to state the purpose for which they had come. He further told them that going into such exaggeration may be a way Satan could lead them astray. The Prophet's attitude is one example of his characteristic humility. He always objected to being given more than his status as God's Messenger.

In defining responsibility, the Prophet made clear that everyone has his or her responsibility and we will all be accountable to God for the way we discharge it.

212. Ibn ʿUmar reports that the Prophet said: 'All of you are shepherds and all of you are accountable for whatever is under your charge. A ruler is a shepherd and is accountable. A man is a shepherd of his household and is accountable. A woman is a shepherd in charge of her husband's home and she is accountable. Every one of you is a shepherd and everyone is accountable for their trust'.[148]

213. Mālik ibn al-Ḥuwayrith said: 'We came to the Prophet (peace be upon him) and we all were young men of similar age. We stayed twenty nights with him. He felt that we were homesick. He asked us whom we had left in charge of our families and we told him. He was caring and compassionate. He said: "Go back to your people to teach them and give them instructions. Pray as you have seen me pray. When it is time for prayer, let one of you

---

147. Related by Aḥmad, al-Nasāʾī and Abū Dāwūd.
148. Related by al-Bukhari, Muslim and Abū Dāwūd.

say the *adhān* [i.e. the normal call to prayer] and let your eldest lead the prayer".'[149]

214. Ibn 'Umar reports that the Prophet said: 'All of you are shepherds and all of you are accountable for whatever is under your charge. A ruler who is in power is a shepherd and is accountable for his flock. A man is a shepherd of his household. A woman is a shepherd in her husband's home, and a servant is a shepherd of his master's property'.

Ibn 'Umar adds: 'I heard these words from the Prophet (peace be upon him) and I reckon that he also said: 'And a man is a shepherd responsible for his father's property'.

These three *ḥadīths* are grouped together here because the first and the third are the same, as also *ḥadīth* Number 206, with slightly different wording and a different chain of transmission each time. In all versions, the ruler is mentioned first and this is understandable because the ruler is in charge of the community. The metaphor the Prophet uses in this *ḥadīth* stresses the aspect of care Islam expects of every ruler. He is a shepherd tending his flock in order to guard them against any trouble or threat.

Highly significant in this *ḥadīth* is the mutual responsibility of man and wife. The Prophet puts this mutuality of responsibility in the clearest of terms. They are both responsible for their family. Their responsibility is total and includes all affairs. They discharge it by doing their best to provide their household with a comfortable living. Yet it is not merely the material aspect of life that is meant here. It is the general welfare of the family and its place in society. When parents work for the welfare of their family, they do not do it as a charity. It is their responsibility, for which they are accountable.

When he explains the woman's responsibility, the Prophet adds further that a woman is a shepherd over her husband's children. This is an indication of the woman's most important responsibility. Had the Prophet not added these words, it would be understood that both

---

149. Related by al-Bukhari, Muslim, al-Nasā'ī, Abū Dāwūd, al-Tirmidhi and Ibn Mājah.

man and wife have the same duties. However, their responsibilities differ in accordance with their capabilities and the tasks assigned to each. The care a father provides to his children differs from that of their mother. Her role in the family is much more important because it has more to do with the future of the family, while a man's role has much more to do with the present. In any human situation, the future is normally more important than the present. The special care Islam takes of women is an indication of the importance it attaches to their role in looking after the future generation of Muslims. The *ḥadīth* may also be construed as placing special emphasis on the complementarity between the roles of husband and wife.

The second of these *ḥadīths* shows us an aspect of the Prophet's character. He was keenly aware of the concerns of his visiting delegation. Realising that those young men must have left behind people who were close to them, he asked them about their families and friends. As they told him, he must have shown the sort of care that merits the reporter's description that 'he was caring and compassionate'. The Prophet did not wish to detain them further, although any young Muslim would have greatly benefited by remaining close to the Prophet. He let them return home, instructing them on how to instruct their people and give them the knowledge of Islam they had gathered during their stay in Madinah.

The Prophet gave instructions to this delegation to pray in the same manner which he himself followed in his prayers. When the Prophet gives such religious instruction to certain people, the instructions apply universally to all his followers, unless it is combined with a clear indication that it is meant to have limited application. In other words, this instruction that prayers must always be offered as the Prophet offered his prayers applies to all Muslims throughout all generations. It is for this reason that Muslims pray in the fashion they do. The Qur'an gives us instructions to attend to our prayers regularly. It does not specify a mode of prayer which we should follow. Had we not received any instruction from the Prophet with regard to how to pray, any method of prayer would have been adequate in fulfilment of God's commandment that we pray. The Prophet, however, gave us further clarification as to how to obey God's order; he demonstrated the way of prayer and made clear that we must follow his method. Hence, we cannot pray in any other fashion. If we do, our prayers are not accepted, because we would not be following the Prophet. By not following him, we disobey God's clear commandment.

This *ḥadīth* is a clear answer to all those who try to belittle the importance of the Sunnah. They claim that they will follow only the Qur'an, yet the Qur'an tells them to follow the Prophet. In some *ḥadīths* we find clear instructions on how to conduct even the most important aspect of worship. A *ḥadīth* of similar importance is the one which tells us to follow the Prophet's footsteps in our pilgrimage. He said: 'Learn from me your pilgrimage rituals'. When we study how the Prophet conducted his pilgrimage, we realise that he was following a set pattern which could only have been taught by God. He went to Mina, Arafat and Muzdalifah and indicated that these were the duties of pilgrimage. Had he not taught us this, we would have thought that pilgrimage only consisted of going to the Ka'bah. The Qur'anic verse that specifies the pilgrimage duty only mentions '*pilgrimage to the House*', (3: 97) which is a reference to the Ka'bah. The Prophet, however, demonstrated otherwise and we follow in his footsteps, knowing that he only provided us with guidance which he received from God. If we want to win God's pleasure we must follow the Prophet's example.

This *ḥadīth* mentions two further points about prayer. The call to prayer, i.e. the *adhān*, which announces that a certain prayer has fallen due, could be done by anyone, regardless of his age or knowledge. Obviously, anyone who makes it will earn a reward for so doing.

Leading the prayer, on the other hand, is something more important for which certain criteria have been laid down. Here, the Prophet mentions the criterion of age. However, this is not the only or the overriding criterion. Other *ḥadīths*, in conjunction with which this *ḥadīth* must be taken, specify that the one who recites the Qur'an best is the one to be chosen to lead the prayer. If two or more recite the Qur'an equally well, then the one with more knowledge about Islam is preferred. When we have two or more of equal knowledge, then we apply the criterion of age. The elder is preferred to the younger. It is not the absolute number of years of people's age which counts, but how long have they been Muslims. An old man who has spent much of his life committing sins of all sorts and only recently mended his ways and repented of his sins is not to be preferred to a younger person who has been following Islam conscientiously for a much longer period. We only need to consider these criteria for a moment in order to appreciate their wisdom.

It may be that the Prophet mentioned the criterion of age in this particular context because the delegation was composed of young men of similar age. We may assume that they adopted Islam at more or less the same period and their knowledge of Islam was perhaps of the same standard. Hence, the Prophet draws their attention to the other criterion which becomes applicable in cases of such equality.

Returning favours

The Prophet often emphasised the need to establish strong ties within the Muslim community. He chose certain aspects for special emphasis on different occasions:

> 215. Jābir ibn 'Abdullāh reports that the Prophet said: 'Whoever is done a favour should repay it. If he has no means to do so, he should praise the person who has done it. By praising him, he gives due thanks. If he conceals it, he is ungrateful. A person who wears an ornament which he has not been given is like one who wears a false suit'.[150]

The Prophet makes it clear that a favour should be rewarded. This includes gifts of all sorts. Indeed, any action of kindness should be rewarded by something similar, according to what the recipient can afford. The Prophet gave us a good practical example, as 'Ā'ishah reports: 'God's Messenger (peace be upon him) used to accept gifts and reward them'.[151] The statement indicates that it was the Prophet's habit to do so. He always rewarded gifts with something much better in value. This is only to be expected from the Prophet who was keen to further social ties and to look after people's feelings. Indeed, he

---

150. Related by Aḥmad, Abū Dāwūd and al-Tirmidhi.
151. Related by al-Bukhari.

made a point of telling us that gifts and favours should be returned and rewarded because this helps cement social ties. When a gift is merely accepted and not returned when the occasion arises, the giver may start to think ill of the recipient, especially if this omission to reward a gift is repeated.

The Prophet takes care to indicate one way of returning favours to which people of limited means may resort. Yet, not everyone who receives a favour or a gift is able to return it with something of similar or higher value, as the Prophet used to do. The Prophet tells such people of limited means that they can reward favours with thanking the person who has done that favour. Such an expression of gratitude is to be done in the absence of that person; this is how real gratitude is expressed. People take praise of a person as genuine when such praise is made in that person's absence. In the overwhelming majority of cases, it is then seen as free from ulterior motives. Indeed praising anyone in their presence is not acceptable in Islam; it is viewed, rather, as an aspect of hypocrisy.

The Prophet says that by praising the giver in his absence, the recipient duly expresses his thanks to him. This puts a special colour on thanking someone or expressing gratitude to him. No words of thanks addressed to the person directly are equal to one word of thanks expressed in his absence. Moreover, a Muslim must not praise someone straight to his face. If he has something good to say about him, he says it in his absence. Then, it is genuine, free from exaggeration and easily accepted by other people, because they do not suspect that the praise is made in order to win favour with the person so praised.

On the other hand, concealment of a favour done by someone to us is a mark of ingratitude. A Muslim is never ungrateful for any kindness shown to him. Hence, to conceal a favour is repugnant.

The last part of this *ḥadīth* touches on something different. It speaks of a deliberate action that aims at giving a false impression. This is expressed in the context of gifts being given. The example the Prophet gives is that of wearing some type of ornament which one was not given, in order to create a wrong impression in the minds of others. One common example of this sort is done by women who are married to the same husband. One wife wears an article of jewellery in front of the other wife in order to give the latter the impression that it was their husband that has given it to her. She thus makes her feel unjustly treated by her husband or feel that he favours his other wife. Jealousy is thus enhanced.

Another example is that of a person who wears emblems distinctive of a certain group of people, such as a tribe or a society in order to give an impression that he belongs to that group; he is thus able to deceive people. All such actions are forbidden and the prohibition is expressed in a unique way. The Prophet describes such an action as similar to wearing 'a false suit'. The metaphor serves to indicate that a person who performs an such action is one who is full of forgery from head to foot.

216. 'Abdullāh ibn 'Umar reports that the Prophet said: 'Give refuge to one who seeks it with you, appealing to you by God. Grant the one who asks you something, appealing to you by God, his wish. Whoever does you a favour, repay him. If you find nothing to repay him with, pray for him until it is known that you have rewarded his favour'.[152]

In this *ḥadīth*, the Prophet stresses that if someone asks us to do something, appealing to us by God, then we should give him what he asks, whether it is something or some service he requests, or security that he seeks. This applies to everyone, regardless of faith. If a person appeals to us by God to give him protection so that he feels secure, then we grant him this. We do so because of his appeal to us by God. What we do, then, is for God's sake. The Prophet also stresses the importance of returning a gift or a favour. Should we be unable to reward it, then we pray for the person who has done it for us. By praying to God to reward him and to grant him his wishes, we repay him, because a prayer which we make in favour of a brother or sister of ours is certainly answered. The last phrase in the *ḥadīth* indicates that such prayers should be repeated time after time, until we are satisfied that we have repaid the favour.

When a person prays for someone in his absence, his prayer is bound to have a beneficial effect on him. It is true that his prayer

152. Related by Aḥmad, Abū Dāwūd and al-Nasā'ī.

is known only to himself and to God. Nevertheless, when he prays for him, he feels that he is indebted to him and that he is asking for a reward for him which is far better than whatever he could give in return. Even the smallest reward given by God to someone is better than the greatest reward any human being can give. When a person prays to God for other people, their kindness is present in his mind. He truly loves them and learns from their example to be kind to others who may stand in need of help and kindness.

217. Anas ibn Mālik reports: 'The Muhājirīn said [to the Prophet]: "Messenger of God, the Anṣār have taken up all the reward". He said: "No, not as long as you pray for them and praise them for [their kindness to you]".'[153]

What the Muhājirīn among the Prophet's companions were worried about was that they stood no chance of receiving a reward equal to that of the Anṣār who shared with them every sacrifice that was needed for the cause of Islam. They were quick to render every service the message of Islam required. Moreover, they opened their homes and their hearts to their brothers who came to settle among them in their city. They accommodated them in their homes, shared their income with them, allowed them to marry their women and treated them as equal partners in everything they had. Many of them willingly relinquished to their migrant brothers half their wealth. This was an act of hospitality that has remained without equal in history. The Muhājirīn themselves could not equal them in this, although they could match them in their sacrifice for the cause of Islam. Hence, their anxiety that the Anṣār were far ahead of them. The Prophet, however, reassured them by showing the way to earn an equal reward. All they had to do was pray to God for their Anṣār brothers and praise them for their kindness and hospitality.

This concept of being grateful for other people's kindness is re-emphasised in the following *ḥadīth*:

153. Related by Abū Dāwūd and al-Nasā'ī.

218. Abu Hurayrah reports that the Prophet said: 'A person who does not thank people is ungrateful to God'.

219. Abu Hurayrah reports that the Prophet said: 'God the Exalted said to the soul: "Come out". It said: "I only come out under duress".'[154]

This *ḥadīth* relates thanking people to being grateful to God, which may not be readily apparent. Yet the *ḥadīth* states a simple fact. Everyone knows that people are gratified when they are thanked for a kind gesture. Indeed, most people feel hurt if they have done a favour for someone but receive no thanks. The more expressive the recipient is of his gratitude to them, the more ready they are to repeat their kindness. This is human nature. Not everyone knows, however, that God wants us to thank Him for the favours He has bestowed on us. Indeed, many people take His favours for granted and think of them as something they have by right. If you tell people that they should thank God for giving them their eyesight or their hearing or their other faculties, many of them wonder at what you are saying. They think they are entitled to have all these. Hence, they think they owe nothing for what they have and enjoy. Only if they happen to have something exceptionally fortunate, may they think that they ought to thank God for it. Many of them, however, do not even entertain the idea of thanking God for it. Yet God would like us to thank Him for His kindness and for all the favours which He has bestowed on us. He benefits nothing by our thanks and expressions of gratitude. He simply likes to see us appreciate His bounty. If people turn a blind eye to God's favours and do not thank Him for them, God is not affected in any way. Their attitude only reflects on them.

What the Prophet tells us in this *ḥadīth* is that a person who is not used to thanking people for the favours they do him will not thank

---

154. Related by Aḥmad, Abū Dāwūd, al-Tirmidhi, Ibn Mājah and Ibn Ḥibbān. In some copies of Al-Adab al-Mufrad, these two *ḥadīths* are entered as one. Only the first is related to the topic under discussion. Perhaps this is the reason why al-Bukhari included them both here. He most probably felt that they were the same, particularly because they have the same chain of transmission.

God for what He has given him. This is merely a logical progression of the same attitude. If we do not thank our fellow human beings for a kindness they do not owe us, we are less likely to thank God for what He has given us. On the other hand, when we thank people for their favours, we are by implication thanking God for providing the means for these favours to be done to us. This is the proper attitude which is expected from every Muslim.

The best of actions

The Prophet's companions were always keen to understand what actions would bring them closer to God and His reward in the life to come:

> 220. Abu Dharr reports that the Prophet was asked: 'Which actions are best?' He replied: 'Belief in God and jihad in His cause'. He was asked: 'Which slaves are best to free?' He said: 'The highest in price and the most precious in their owner's view'. His questioner said: 'Suppose that I am unable to do certain deeds?' The Prophet answered: 'Help a poor person who has a family, or do something for an unskilled person'. He said: 'Suppose that I lack the strength [to do this]'. The Prophet said: 'Refrain from doing harm to people. This is an act of charity [i.e. *ṣadaqah*] you do to yourself'.[155]

The most interesting thing in this conversation is that the Prophet's interlocutor starts by seeking knowledge about the best actions, before he goes down the scale to ask what an almost helpless person can do to earn reward from God. The Prophet states first that the best action is to have faith. This is not surprising because without faith no action is of value. People who are good in themselves and observe high moral values may do many good things. If they do not have faith, their actions do not bring them any reward. God's reward is given only to those who believe in Him. It is repeatedly emphasised in the Qur'an that good deeds must be motivated by faith in order to merit God's

---

155. Related by Aḥmad, al-Bukhari, Muslim, al-Nasāʾī, al-Dārimi and Ibn Ḥibbān.

reward. Needless to say, faith which does not have a practical effect on what a person does in his daily life remains theoretical and devoid of reality.

The Prophet's answer combines this with fighting for God's cause. In fact, the Prophet uses the term jihad, which is erroneously translated as 'holy war'. Jihad has a much wider meaning than war. It means 'to strive hard for a clear objective'. A war is the ultimate form of jihad or struggle in the service of God's cause. It is this aspect which is stressed more often because going to war for a certain cause means that the person concerned is prepared to sacrifice his life for it.

It is worth noting that the next question put to the Prophet concerns the freeing of slaves. Slavery was practised on a very wide scale at that time. As we have said, Islam took every possible measure to ensure that slavery would be quickly abolished. To free a slave was one of the best actions a person might do to earn reward from God, or to atone for a grave sin which he might have committed. The Prophet's companion wanted to know whether granting certain slaves their freedom would earn more reward. The Prophet's answer is clear and logical. The one which costs more to buy or is viewed by its master as the most precious is the one who brings more reward from God when freed for His sake. This is a rule which applies to everything in life. The action which requires more effort is valued more than the one which comes very easily. When one has to pay more for a slave to be free, it stands to reason that he will earn more reward. There is, however, one exception to this rule. If one buys two slaves for the price of one, who is considered the better person to free? In this situation, it is more rewarding from an Islamic point of view to free the two lesser slaves; by freeing them, two are free instead of one.

The man then asks what he should do if he cannot perform some of these or other actions which bring high reward. His question means that he is still keen to know how to earn reward from God, but he may not have the power or the means to do the actions already mentioned, because of what they require of effort or money. He wants an easy and readily available way of earning reward. The Prophet's answer directs his interlocutor to helping other people. A person in need, who may be poor and with a large family, always welcomes help. Helping the poor always brings high reward from God. It should perhaps be mentioned here that because of the way Arabic was written in the early periods of Islam, the Prophet's answer could be translated differently. Our preferred translation is, 'help a poor person who has a family, or do something for an unskilled person'. However, it may also be translated as: 'help someone in what he does for a living'. This answer points to a person who is facing difficulty in earning enough to meet his family's needs. He may stand in need of help, and helping him will earn great reward. This reading of the *ḥadīth* fits perfectly with the next part of the Prophet's answer, 'or do something for an unskilled person'. The Prophet's answer is, therefore, a directive to help anyone who is in need.

In the last resort, the Prophet's interlocutor wants to know how to earn reward from God even when he lacks the strength or the determination to do any of the foregoing. The Prophet's answer directs him not to cause harm to anyone. By sparing other people any harm, one is charitable to oneself. This may seem to be a negative way of earning reward. In fact, it is not. Many people find themselves in a position where they will benefit by causing harm to others. If they restrain themselves from causing harm to those who are weaker than them, they are sure to earn reward from God. We note how the Prophet describes this as an act of charity one does to oneself. It is certainly an apt description because by inflicting harm on others, a person wrongs himself, and incurs God's displeasure. When he restrains himself from doing so, he spares himself God's displeasure and consequent punishment. This, then, is a net gain.

13

Promotion of Goodness

WITH REGARD TO their effect on the quality of human life, all Islamic teachings meet at one point, namely, the promotion of goodness. Everything that sound human nature approves of as good and right is encouraged by Islam. There are certain basic values that all people, regardless of their beliefs, social environment or stage of civilisation accept: sincerity, telling the truth, faithfulness, helping the poor and the weak are only a few examples. Islam requires its followers to observe these values all the time. Moreover, it ensures that such values are essential characteristics of Islamic society.

While it recognises that other people share these values, it taps these qualities most fully within Islamic society. The basic component in this process is belief in the Day of Judgement and in a second life. All will have to account for what they do in this present life, they end either in a life of everlasting bliss or one of total misery. This belief makes every Muslim conscious of the need to get the right result. Every single deed, no matter how small, and every word, however trifling, are taken into account. Good deeds are weighed against bad ones and the result determines people's destiny. The seriousness of the whole affair cannot be over-emphasised. Hence, preparing for this awesome test is central to a believer's thinking.

It is the combination of this need to prepare for the Hereafter, to make sure that one's good deeds are weighty, and the natural human tendency to do what is good that Islam seeks to strengthen within every Muslim. Islam thus imparts its own colour to its followers, making of them men and women who are always prepared to do what is good and to sacrifice for it their time, wealth and comfort. Islam achieves all this very easily, through a method which makes Muslims aware that when they do good they get the benefit of their deeds both in this life and in the life to come. Thus, they combine immediate worldly benefit with future reward from God.

The Prophet emphasised this combination on every occasion. He always tried to instil in his followers this double motivation to observe Islamic norms, which are indeed the highest of moral values:

> 221. Qabīṣah ibn Burmah said: 'I was with the Prophet and I heard him as he said: "The people of goodness in this world are the people of goodness in the life to come, and the people of evil in this world are the people of evil in the life to come".'

This statement by the Prophet has more or less become a proverb in the Arabic language. Its message is very clear. The person who is accustomed to doing good turns to other people in this life will be given a much better reward in the life to come. Ibn 'Abbās, the Prophet's cousin, explains this *ḥadīth* as follows: 'When those who have always done good in this life are resurrected on the Day of Judgement, they are forgiven their sins by virtue of what they have done in this present life. Their own good deeds which they have done for themselves remain intact. They are allowed to pass them on to others whose bad deeds are found to be in excess of their good ones. Thus they help them to avoid punishment in hell. They are, thus, made charitable in this life and in the next'.

Needless to say, the people of evil are those who do all things that God has forbidden. They will find their bad deeds too much of a burden in the Hereafter. They will have to face their inevitable destiny.

222. Ḥarmalah ibn ʿAbdullāh said: 'I went to the Prophet and stayed with him until he recognised me. When he was about to leave, I thought I should better go to him and learn more. I walked until I caught up with him and was close to him. I asked: "What do you command me to do?" He said: "Ḥarmalah, do what is right and avoid evil". I went back to my she-camel. But then I went up to him again until I was very close to him. I asked again: "What do you command me to do?" He said: "Ḥarmalah, do what is right and avoid evil. Consider what you like people to say about you when you leave them and do it. Consider also what you dislike people saying about you when you leave them and avoid it". When I returned, I reflected on these two points and realised that they had left out nothing'.

The Prophet's statements in this *ḥadīth* and the preceding one do not require any explanation or comment. It is sufficient to say that they are examples of how the Prophet always tried to cultivate a sense of doing good in his followers so that they were prepared for the reckoning on the Day of Judgement. His method of cultivation is definitely strengthened by the combination of immediate benefit in this world with reward in the Hereafter. This is a consistent Islamic method which tries to relate this life to the future one so that it all becomes a continuous process. Therefore, everything we do counts on the Day of Judgement.

223. (*Athar* 55) Salmān said: 'The people of goodness in this world are the people of goodness in the life to come'.

This is the same as the first part of *ḥadīth* Number 221, but it is attributed here to a different companion of the Prophet and has a different chain of transmission.

To enhance the motivation to do good among Muslims, the Prophet broadened the concept of charity, or *ṣadaqah*. In its narrow sense, *ṣadaqah* refers to what is given to the poor to relieve their poverty, even in a very small way. In effect, it means a charitable donation to a poor person. Islam encourages its followers to pay *ṣadaqah* promising good reward even for a small amount. As noted earlier, God rewards good actions by at least ten times their value. However, God may multiply the reward for a charity given with kindness and benevolence up to seven hundred times its value. This makes it an investment with assured returns that may be as much as 70,000 per cent. Yet God's reward may be even greater than this. When a Muslim realises the importance given by Islam to *ṣadaqah*, he is always ready to do what he can to help others.

> 224. Jābir ibn 'Abdullāh reports that the Prophet said: 'Every good action is a *ṣadaqah*'.[156]

This *ḥadīth* provides a maxim which should influence a Muslim's actions everyday of his life. However, the Prophet used to explain his meaning in a variety of ways. At times, he might make a statement that could be construed to impose a hard task. This was to invite his companions to seek clarification.

> 225. Abu Mūsa reports that the Prophet said: 'It is a duty of every Muslim to give a *ṣadaqah*'. People asked: 'What if he has nothing [to give]?' The Prophet said: 'He does something with his hands, and thus he benefits himself and gives a *ṣadaqah*'. They asked: 'What if he cannot, or does not, do that?' He said: 'He assists someone with a pressing need'. They still asked: 'What if he does not do that?' He said: 'He enjoins the doing of what is good, or what is right'. They asked: 'And what if he does not do that?' He said: 'He refrains from doing evil. That counts as a ṣadaqah for him'.[157]

The first statement in this *ḥadīth* imposes an act of charity on every Muslim. Considering that the Muslims were not well off during the

---

156. Related by al-Bukhari, Muslim, al-Ḥākim and al-Dāraquṭni.
157. Related by al-Bukhari, Muslim and al-Nasā'ī.

Prophet's lifetime, it is not surprising that his companions should immediately react by asking about a person who does not have enough to give to the poor. The question includes those who are themselves poor. The Prophet's explanation makes it clear that the concept of *ṣadaqah* is much wider than giving the poor some money. He says that any good action a person does with his own hands ensures beneficial returns for the doer and counts as a charity. Even this, however, may not come easily to a person. Different circumstances may make him unable or unwilling to do something that counts as a charity. The Prophet's answer points out one way of doing good which has great benefits for the community as a whole. He suggests that one may help a person with a pressing need. This is expressed by the Prophet in the most general terms. Any matter which has a sense of urgency, provided that it involves nothing that displeases God, is worth helping. It is not merely help rendered to one who is suffering injustice, or struggling to obtain something he needs, that is included here. It is good to give help to anyone with an urgent legitimate business. This counts as a charitable donation.

Even if this is not available to someone, or if he is prevented from doing it, encouraging what is good and right fulfils his duty of giving *ṣadaqah*. Even if someone fails to do this, they may still earn the reward of *ṣadaqah* by refraining from evil. Although this could be considered as a negative way of doing good, it nonetheless discharges the duty of giving *ṣadaqah*.

226. Abu Dharr reports that he asked the Prophet: 'Which actions are best?' He replied: 'Belief in God and jihad in His cause'. He was asked: 'Which slaves are best to free?' He said: 'The highest in price and the most precious in their owner's view'. His questioner said: 'Suppose that I am unable to do certain deeds?' The Prophet answered: 'Help a poor person who has a family, or do something for an unskilled person'. He said: 'Suppose that I lack the strength [to do this]'. The Prophet said: 'Refrain from doing harm to people. This is an act of charity [i.e. *ṣadaqah*] you do to yourself'.

This *ḥadīth* is the same as *ḥadīth* Number 220, but it is given in a different chain of transmission. This version makes clear that the Prophet's questioner was Abu Dharr himself.

227. Abu Dharr reports that someone said to the Prophet: 'Messenger of God, the wealthy have taken all the rewards: they pray like we pray, and fast like we fast, but they give *ṣadaqah* [i.e. charity] out of their surplus'. The Prophet said: 'Has God not given you something to give as ṣadaqah? Every glorification and every praise of God you say is a ṣadaqah. Even in sexual intercourse, there is *ṣadaqah*'. He was asked: 'Is there a *ṣadaqah* in satisfying one's sexual desire?' He said: 'Is it not true that if one satisfies it in a prohibited manner, he incurs a grave sin? Likewise, if he does it in a lawful manner, he earns a reward'.[158]

Abu Dharr was one of the poor among the Prophet's companions, but he was always keen to seek ways of earning reward. His initial question shows his concern at not being able to match rich people who could donate generously. The Prophet points out to him other ways of earning such reward. His answer reveals the broad scope of earning reward through voluntary worship and abiding by what God requires of people.

The first aspect the Prophet mentions is to glorify God and praise Him. This a Muslim does frequently, after prayers and whenever he encounters something in which he appreciates God's grace and blessings. However, the Prophet adds to this the satisfaction of natural sexual desire. His companions wonder at this: how come one indulges in such pleasure and earns reward for it? The Prophet's answer makes it clear that since any unlawful satisfaction of sexual desire is sinful and liable to punishment, the lawful opposite earns reward. This is an aspect of God's grace that knows no limit. People do not expect to be rewarded for doing what is permissible or lawful, but God rewards them for remaining within what is lawful and refraining from what is unlawful.

---

158. Related by Muslim, Abū Dāwūd and Ibn Khuzaymah.

At times, the Prophet was very specific, singling out a very simple, ordinary action and describing it as a charitable act or even something that leads to heaven:

> 228. Abu Barzah al-Aslami reports: 'I said: "Messenger of God, indicate to me an action which will admit me to heaven". He said: "Remove offensive objects from people's path".'[159]

The Arabic word *adha*, translated as 'offensive objects', includes anything which causes harm or disgust. No one would imagine that the removal of such objects from people's pathway was an action that earns very high reward. The Prophet's statement shows that it does. It is a commendable, social deed which reflects genuine concern about the welfare of the community. Hence, its reward is high in relation to the simplicity of the action itself. However, it should be pointed out that, by itself, such an action is not enough to take any person into heaven. Its reward is high when the doer is a good believer who does not hesitate to undertake any action which serves the cause of Islam when he is required to do so. Abu Barzah, who put the question to the Prophet, was a man who fought with the Prophet on seven occasions, a fact that reflects his readiness to sacrifice his life for the cause of Islam. Hence, the Prophet's answer indicated an action which might be classified under the finer manners of Muslims.

The Prophet praised the same action on more than one occasion:

> 229. Abu Hurayrah reports that the Prophet said: 'A man found a branch of a thorny tree in a lane. He said: "I will remove this thorny branch, lest it should harm a Muslim". [For this action] he was granted forgiveness of his sins'.[160]

The Prophet's statement and the incident itself stress the social aspect in this simple action of removing an offensive object from people's pathways. When such an action comes to a person naturally, they reflect a keen sense of social responsibility. It is this sense that makes

---

159. Related by Aḥmad, Muslim, Ibn Mājah, Ibn Ḥibbān and Abu ʿAwānah.
160. Related by al-Bukhari, Muslim, al-Tirmidhi and Abu ʿAwānah.

a person undertake the trouble of removing dirt and other offensive objects when it is not his duty to do so. This is further emphasised in the following *ḥadīth*:

230. Abu Dharr reports that the Prophet said: 'I was shown the actions of my community, both good and bad. Among the good ones I found the action of removing offensive objects from people's pathway, and among the bad ones I found a drop of phlegm which had fallen on the floor of the mosque and been left unburied'.[161]

It should be noted that the Prophet's mosque did not have a carpet. Hence, dirt found in it was normally buried. In our mosques, any dirt on the floor of the mosque should be removed in the normal way, so that a mosque always remains clean and free of any harmful or offensive object.

Do every good thing

The Prophet encouraged every good thing, and his companions learnt good practices and implemented them. They realised that he provided guidance in every good way. He showed them that there is no limit to goodness:

231. 'Abdullāh ibn Yazīd al-Khaṭmi reports that the Prophet said: 'Every good action is a *ṣadaqah*'.[162]

232. Anas said: 'When the Prophet was given a present, he would say: "Take it to so-and-so: he was a friend of Khadījah; or take it to the house of so-and-so: she loved Khadījah".'[163]

---

161. Related by Aḥmad, al-Bukhari, Muslim, Ibn Mājah, Ibn Khuzaymah, Ibn Ḥibbān and Abu 'Awānah.

162. Related by Aḥmad.

163 Related by al-Ḥākim, Ibn Ḥibbān and al-Bazzār.

233. Hudhayfah said: 'Your Prophet used to say: "Every good action is a *ṣadaqah*".'

The first and last of these three *ḥadīths* are the same as *ḥadīth* Number 224, and we have already explained it. They are entered here with different reporters.

The second *ḥadīth* tells us about an aspect of the Prophet's character. He was most caring and retained loving memories of his first wife, Khadījah. He always remembered her and was kind to her friends and those who loved her. The very fact that they had been friendly with her was enough reason for him to show that they had a special position with him. People used to give him presents of the best things they had, and he would immediately think of Khadījah's friends and send such presents over to them.

234. 'Amr ibn Abu Qurrah al-Kindi said: 'My father offered his sister in marriage to Salmān [the Prophet's companion], but he refused. He later married a servant of his, called Buqayrah'.

'Abu Qurrah later heard that there was some bad feeling between Hudhayfah and Salmān. So he went to see Salmān, and he was told that he was in his vegetable garden. He went there to meet him. He saw him with a sack of vegetables, and he had put his stick into the knot of the sack and lifted it onto his shoulder. Abu Qurrah asked him: "Abu 'Abdullāh, what was the matter between you and Hudhayfah?" Salmān read [the verse that says] "*Man is ever hasty*" (17: 11), [indicating that he should be patient].

'They went to Salmān's home, and Salmān entered and said "Peace be to you", then let Abu Qurrah in. There was a fibre mat placed at the doorway and there were some bricks at the top, and also a saddle. He said [to Abu Qurrah]: "Sit on the rug of your servant which she has put out for herself".

'He then started to speak to Abu Qurrah and said: "Hudhayfah used to relate certain things the Prophet had said to some people when he was angry. People came to ask me about these. I said to them: 'Hudhayfah knows what he says', as I disliked that there should be rancour between people. People went to Hudhayfah and told him: 'Salmān neither confirms nor denies what you say'. He came over to me and said: 'Salmān, son of Salmān's mother!' I said: 'Hudhayfah, son of Hudhayfah's mother. You must stop this or else I will write to 'Umar about you'. When I threatened him with [writing to] 'Umar, he left me.

'God's Messenger said: "I am one of Adam's children. If I ever curse or abuse anyone of my community when he does not deserve it, may God make it a blessing for him."'[164]

This long *ḥadīth* shows the refined manners of the Prophet's companions, and the respect they showed for each other. Salmān did not say a word against Hudhayfah, although he objected to the way the latter quoted the Prophet without putting his words into context. When they met and expressed their disagreement, they did no more than show their displeasure, and just put the matter at that. They did not carry their dispute to further lengths.

The *ḥadīth* also shows that Salmān was willing to marry a former slave and to undertake his work by himself. He worked on his vegetable garden and carried the produce on his shoulder.

We note also that Abu Qurrah, who belonged to the generation that followed the Prophet's companions, was willing to offer his sister in marriage to Salmān. She could have no better than a companion of the Prophet who was very close to him.

235. (*Athar* 56) Ibn 'Abbās reported: ''Umar said: "Let us go together to our people's plot". Ubay ibn Ka'b and I were right at the end. A cloud gathered and Ubay said: "My Lord, spare us its harm". We caught up with the others and their saddles were wet. They said: "How come that you have not suffered what we have". I said: "He prayed to God, the Mighty and Exalted, to spare us its harm". 'Umar said: "Should you not have included us in your supplication?"'

236. Abu Salamah said: 'I went to Abu Sa'īd al-Khudri – who was a friend of mine – and said: "Would you like to come with us

164. Related by Aḥmad and Abū Dāwūd.

to the palm date farm?" He came out wearing a black-bordered cloak'.

The *ḥadīth* shows how supplication may be immediately answered in exactly the terms the supplicant specifies. Ubay ibn Kaʿb was a young companion of the Prophet who learnt the Qur'an and excelled in it. In fact, the Prophet once went to him and said: 'God has commanded me to recite to you this surah'. Ubay said: 'And my Lord has named me, Messenger of God?' The Prophet confirmed that He had. Ubay was in tears and said to the Prophet: 'Then, recite it, Messenger of God'. The Prophet recited it to him. This shows how the Prophet immediately complied with God's order and showed the high honour conferred on Ubay by the fact that God mentioned him by name in a context related to his excellence in memorising and reciting the Qur'an.

Brotherhood in faith

The Qur'an makes clear that all believers have a bond of brotherhood that unites them all. The Prophet took care to emphasise that every single believer must be well respected in Muslim society. No one may be ridiculed or treated as a source of laughter as a result of any defect he or she may have. The Prophet gave the best example of treating every one of his companions with the respect they deserved:

237. ʿAli said: 'The Prophet ordered ʿAbdullāh ibn Masʿūd to climb a tree and bring him something from it. His companions looked at ʿAbdullāh's shin and laughed at the thinness of his legs. The Prophet said: "Why are you lauging? ʿAbdullāh's leg is heavier in [God's] balance than Mount Uhud".' [165]

We see how the Prophet was keen that every one of his companions, and indeed every Muslim, must be treated with the respect they deserve. ʿAbdullāh was a devoted servant of Islam. He never hesitated to render any sacrifice required of him. When battle flared up against unbelievers,

165. Related by Aḥmad and al-Ṭayālisi.

he was at the forefront of the Muslim army. Hence, he earned high esteem. The size of his legs was immaterial. It was his actions that counted. Through action, he achieved a very high position as a devoted servant of Islam. Hence, he was not one to be made fun of in any situation. The Prophet made this very clear by stating that, in God's measure, either one of his two small legs was heavier than a mountain.

The brotherhood of believers is clearly stated in the Qur'an: "*Believers are but brothers*". (49: 10) This is a general statement which applies to every believer regardless of race, nationality, colour or station in society. It further applies to all believers in past and future generations, as well as contemporary believers. This bond of brotherhood is even felt with those who lived before the advent of Islam and followed earlier prophets who conveyed God's message to them. Thus, a Muslim living today feels a strong bond with an Israelite who joined Prophet Moses against the Pharaoh of Egypt and with a Christian follower of Jesus who tried to put an end to the corruption that prevailed in his society. He feels they all belong to the same camp, united in their faith in God's oneness and determined to stand against disbelief.

This brotherhood is not confined to the realms of feelings and ideals. It must have practical effects. By its nature, Islam cultivates a community feeling among its followers. They pray in congregation, standing side by side, shoulder to shoulder, with no distinction made favouring rank, position or class. What applies to prayer also applies to all other acts of worship which Islam requires of its followers. Moreover, a Muslim must look after his neighbours and make sure that they have what they need. Such a sense of good neighbourliness is strongly emphasised by the Prophet, as we have already noted.

This brotherhood of believers also imposes certain duties:

238. (*Athar* 58) Abu Hurayrah said: 'A believer is a mirror to his brother: if he sees a fault with him, he will correct it'.

239. Abu Hurayrah reports that the Prophet said: 'A believer is a mirror to his brother. A believer is a brother of a believer: he protects him against danger and guards him from behind'.[166]

166. Related by Abū Dāwūd.

By stating that a believer is a mirror to his brother, the Prophet points out the way for the Muslim community to get rid of any shortcomings which affect its individual members or indeed the whole community. A mirror shows a person exactly as he is: when we stand in front of a mirror, we want to know that we are well dressed or we look in good shape. The mirror tells us about any defect in our appearance. Moreover, we are not angry with the mirror for showing us as we are. A believer acts like a mirror to his brother. This means that if he notices that his brother is doing something wrong or making a certain mistake, he gives him a kind warning. He tells him that such an action may not be good for his wellbeing, either in this life or in the life to come. He must do this in a very kind manner, giving sound advice without giving the impression of being a fault finder. He speaks about it to his brother because he cares that his brother should do only what serves his own interest. He does not have any ulterior motive. He is only after what brings benefit to his brother.

The way the second *ḥadīth* is phrased means that the brotherhood in faith applies to all Muslims. Thus, the duty to give advice is not limited to a certain group. It applies to all, since every one of them is a brother to all. The Prophet leaves us in no doubt as to what this brotherhood entails. He gives it its proper direction. Thus, a believer protects his brother believer 'against danger'. Anything which may threaten the life or the welfare of a believer comes under this statement. Moreover, it applies to anything that endangers a believer's wellbeing in the life to come. In other words, if you find your Muslim brother doing something that is bound to incur God's displeasure, you warn him against it in a kindly manner. You should not give such admonition in public, because a mirror does not reveal defects in public. You should speak to him privately and kindly. When he feels that you are looking after his interests, it is easier for him to accept your advice.

A believer also guards his brother 'from behind'. This means that he is always ready to come to his aid against outside danger. He does not stand idle when his brother is exposed to any kind of danger of which he might be unaware, without rushing to his defence. When we consider these details, we are bound to conclude that the brotherhood of the believers is very real indeed.

These two *ḥadīths* stress the positive aspects of the brotherhood of believers. On other occasions, the Prophet emphasised what we may term as 'negative' aspects which spoil the relationship between people, identifying that a Muslim may never take advantage of another Muslim or try to secure personal gain at his expense.

240. Al-Mustawrid reports that the Prophet said: 'Whoever eats a meal at the expense of a Muslim, God will make him have a similar meal of the fire of hell; and whoever is clothed with a garment at the expense of a Muslim, God, the Mighty and Exalted, will give him a garment from hell. Whoever takes up a position through hypocrisy at the expense of a Muslim, God will put him in a position of hypocrisy on the Day of Judgement'.[167]

First of all the Prophet denounces a person who is given a meal at the expense of another Muslim. Needless to say, the Prophet is not referring here to one who is invited to a meal by a friend or a neighbour. He is speaking of one who tries to secure a meal through foul means such as speaking ill of a Muslim. Commentators on *Ḥadīth* give the example of a man who goes to a person who may be hostile to one of his friends and speaks ill of that friend, backbiting him and magnifying his faults in order to please his interlocutor, who is hostile to the one being spoken of. His effort is rewarded by giving him a meal or a gift. The speaker thus makes a gain out of speaking ill of his friend. Such a gain is foul. God does not bless it. Indeed, it is a source of suffering for the recipient. God will give him a similar gain on the Day of Judgement, but one made of the fire of hell. His punishment is of the same type as the gain he made, but this time it is made from fire.

The last part of the *ḥadīth* includes every possible way of speaking falsely about someone else, or trying to give someone a false impression of oneself. This includes the case of a person speaking very highly of another, describing him in terms of integrity, piety, generosity and kindness to others so that he is held in high esteem by other people. Thus he can make material gain at their expense. At the end of the day, the two share their ill-gotten gains. God takes it upon Himself to show

---

167. Related by Aḥmad and Abū Dāwūd.

that this speaker is a liar. He will appear in that light in front of all on the Day of Judgement. It also includes the person who tries to show himself as a man of piety and integrity. He thus goes through every action that enhances this impression in the minds of other people, without seeking God's pleasure. His only aim is to win favour with people and to profit by it. He is, in effect, a hypocrite who deliberately appears in a false light. Again, God promises this man that He will reveal his reality to all mankind on the Day of Judgement.

The Prophet's statement is perhaps more related to a person who speaks ill of another in order that he himself appears before others in a false light. To give an example: a man finds himself in the company of a group of people belonging to a particular party or organisation, but he has no views concerning that party or organisation. Nevertheless, he begins to speak ill of their opponents who may be very good people. By doing so, he does not express an honest opinion, but simply tries to win favour with those people he happens to be with. He hopes for some reward. This is a common form of hypocrisy. The Prophet warns that indulging in such hypocrisy will raise the terrible prospect of the truth being revealed before all mankind on the Day of Judgement.

The Prophet also warns against taking away any material object from another, in seriousness or in jest:

241. Yazīd ibn Saʿīd reports that the Prophet said: 'Let none of you take an article belonging to his friend in jest or seriously. If any of you takes away his friend's stick, let him return it to him'.[168]

This is a very clear statement that to take away something belonging to another person, even a close friend, in earnest or in jest, is not permissible. Some commentators give the example of a person who falls asleep and a friend may play a trick on him by hiding some important article of his. When the sleeper wakes up and discovers his loss, he is terribly annoyed. His friend may laugh at him or tease him about it. Others may join in to have a bit of fun at the man's expense.

168. Related by Abū Dāwūd, al-Tirmidhi and al-Ṭaḥāwi.

All this is forbidden. The article may well have been taken away in jest, but the intention to tease the sleeper and poke fun is serious.

The Prophet's statement perhaps has wider connotations which forbid taking away something that belongs to others despite the intention of giving it back. The Prophet makes his message absolutely clear by giving the example of a stick which is worth very little. Even if one takes it away against its owner's will, one must return it without hesitation.

As we have often said, the Prophet never lost an opportunity to strengthen ties between his community. To this end, he took care to bring people into closer contact with one another and emphasised that when they help one another, both the giver and the recipient will benefit:

242. Abu Mas'ūd al-Anṣāri reports: 'A man came to the Prophet and said: "I am in a dire situation and I request you to give me a mount". The Prophet said: "I have none, but go to so-and-so. He will perhaps give you one". He went to that man who gave him a mount. The man went back to the Prophet and told him of this. The Prophet said: "Whoever points out a way of doing good receives a reward similar to that of the person who does it".'[169]

We note here that the Prophet's companions asked his help in every situation. In this story, the man's words suggest that he had never found himself in a situation where he had to travel and so had no means of transport. It was a new experience for him and he needed a camel or a horse to make his journey. The Prophet recognised that this was a legitimate claim but he did not have a mount to give the man. He nonetheless told him of someone else who might help. Thus, the Prophet tells us that it is very important that we should always try to help others by at least pointing out to them where and how they can get the help they need, when we ourselves cannot provide the needed help. The Prophet describes this as pointing out a way of doing a good deed. The person who provided the mount realised that he was not approached for help by coincidence. He must have been a very generous man; otherwise the Prophet would not have named

169. Related by Muslim, Abū Dāwūd and al-Tirmidhi.

him. Most probably the person who approached him told him that the Prophet had given him his name as a possible source for the help he needed. He then acted so as not to disappoint the man seeking help and also to follow the Prophet's guidance. Thus, by naming him, the Prophet had encouraged him to do a good deed. This encouragement earned the Prophet a similar reward to that of the man giving the assistance. This applies to everyone who points out a way of doing good. When we fully realise the import of this story we will not fail to recognise that the Muslim community is one in which good action is always highly valued.

To win hearts

To follow the Prophet's example in any matter is to choose the right course of action. This applies, in perhaps greater measure, to social behaviour and relations between people. It is, therefore, important to study how the Prophet treated other people in a comprehensive range of situations in order to understand the Islamic approach to social relations. One characteristic that stands out in the Prophet's own social behaviour is his forgiveness of his enemies.

Perhaps the description 'personal enemy' cannot be attached more appropriately than to one who tries to kill someone. When the attempt is made after contemplation and careful plotting, the hostility is obviously deeply rooted. During his life, the Prophet had several enemies who plotted against his life. One such plot took place soon after the Battle of Khaibar which ended in destroying Jewish military power in Arabia. In short, Khaibar fell to the Prophet after a long siege and a fierce battle.

243. Anas reports: 'A Jewish woman brought the Prophet a poisoned lamb, and he ate of it. When she was brought in to him, people suggested: "Shall we kill her". The Prophet said: "No". I have recognised the effects of that [poisoning] in the Prophet's throat ever since'.[170]

---

170. Related by Aḥmad, al-Bukhari, Muslim and Abū Dāwūd.

This was an attempt on the Prophet's life. He was also the head of the Islamic state. In any country, an attempt on the life of the head of state is viewed very seriously. Anyone caught making such an attempt, or preparing for it, is normally charged with high treason, or launching an aggression against the state and its people. Such a person hardly ever escapes the death penalty. Yet the Prophet's immediate reaction was that the woman must not be killed. Moreover, there was no question about the identity of the perpetrator. The woman herself brought the lamb and told the Prophet that she was giving him a gift. It was a premeditated assassination attempt. The woman did not deny having poisoned the lamb. When questioned, she said: 'I thought that if you were truly a Prophet, you would not be harmed. If you were a king [meaning that if his claim to prophethood was false], I would have rid people of you'.

When the woman contemplated her attempt, she must have realised that if she were to be successful, she would have avenged the defeat of her people. She was certain that the Prophet accepted people's gifts and always tried to please whoever gave him one. He would eat from it if it was food, or use it if it was something to be used. She also realised that the Prophet would not be the only one to eat of that lamb. Any of his companions who were present would be invited to join him. A good number of them, probably some leading figures, might also die with him. Such could have been the outcome of her scheme. Indeed, the Prophet invited those who were attending him to join in this meal. One of them, Bishr ibn al-Barā' was the first to eat, and the Prophet himself ate one or two bites. He then signaled to his companions to stop. He said to them: 'Do not touch it. One of its limbs tells me that it is poisoned'. Bishr ibn al-Barā' soon died as there was no antidote available to treat him. The Prophet himself complained of the effects of the poison for the rest of his blessed life. Anas, who continued in the Prophet's service for ten years until he passed away, recognised the change that affected the Prophet as a result of this poisoning. The woman must have used a very powerful poison to produce such a lasting effect. It is reported that he said during his final illness that he continued to complain of the poisoned food he had eaten at Khaibar. A number of scholars argue that the Prophet was also a martyr.

The Prophet's tendency to forgive his opponents, manifested in his immediate rejection of his companions' suggestion that the woman should be put to death, is highly significant. He always forgave even the most hardened of his enemies. In this case, it was his own life that was the immediate target. God foiled the woman's attempt and the Prophet was inclined to forgive her. Few heads of state, if any, would have taken the same approach.

Some scholars mention that the Prophet later ordered that the woman should be executed. There is no contradiction between his earlier forgiveness and her subsequent punishment. The Prophet first pardoned her for making an attempt on his life. Her attempt failed and he survived. It was his prerogative to forgive her. Her subsequent punishment was for killing Bishr, his companion who ate of the poisoned lamb.

244. (*Athar* 59) Wahb ibn Kaysān said: 'During his speech, 'Abdullāh ibn al-Zubayr quoted [the Qur'anic verse]: "*Make due allowance for man's nature, and enjoin the doing of what is right; and turn away from those who choose to remain ignorant*". (7: 199) He then said: "By God, He has ordered that these [values reflected in] people's manners are to be upheld and I will uphold them as long as I live".'[171]

Scholars comment that the quoted verse sums up the best of good manners. They say that there are three forces that influence man's behaviour: reason, desire and anger. The rational force gives man wisdom, and this includes enjoining what is right. The 'desire' force is countered by restraint, which includes forgiveness and giving people due allowance. The 'anger' force is manifested in courage and this includes turning away from people who choose to remain ignorant.

The Prophet strove hard to give the Muslim community refined manners in every respect. He also defined its role as a teacher of mankind. Muslims must educate the world in the Divine message, in its final form which is Islam. When he assigned this role to his Muslim

171. Related by al-Bukhari and Abū Dāwūd.

community, the Prophet did not forget to highlight an essential quality to make education effective:

> 245. Ibn ʿAbbās reports that the Prophet said: 'Teach others and make things easy, not difficult. When any of you is in a state of anger, let him keep silent'.[172]

The first instruction in this *ḥadīth* is that Muslims should teach others. The most important thing to teach is Islam, God's final message to mankind which provides guidance for them on how to conduct their lives in a way which brings them peace and happiness in this world and eternal bliss in the life to come. They have to teach them that Divine guidance is provided for their own sake. God does not benefit by people's adherence to His guidance. It is they who benefit. They learn the method which spares them the need to go through the process of trial and error in running their affairs. They have to teach them how to submit themselves to God and associate no partners with Him. It is this submission which brings their lives in harmony with the life of everything in the universe. All creatures submit to God's will. Man only has been given the ability to rebel. It is to balance that element of rebellion in man's nature that Divine guidance has been provided. When the Muslim community teach people how to follow Divine guidance, it has only one purpose in mind: to bring happiness to mankind.

It is important through this process of teaching that things should appear, as they truly are, easy to follow. This involves no deception. Islam is made easy to practise. People need only to understand the wisdom behind its legislation in order to implement it with a keenness for excellence. Past generations have benefited by the implementation of Islam. Future generations may reap the same benefit and even more, if they try to implement Islam with a proper understanding of its message, one which confirms that God has made this religion easy for people to follow.

Certain people have the habit of portraying everything that is relevant to faith in a very rigid light. This is bound to make people

---

172. Related by Aḥmad.

feel that the implementation of Islam is very difficult. Yet if we study carefully the life of the Prophet and the life of the first Muslim generation that learnt directly from him, we find that their approach to the implementation of Islam was an easy one. Why should we portray it in any other light? It is indeed against the teachings of the Prophet to make things appear difficult. God wants to make them easy for us and we, or at least some of us, try our best to make them difficult. For this reason, the Prophet instructs us not to follow such an approach.

The final part of the *ḥadīth* speaks of the need to exercise self control in the case of anger. A teacher must never allow his anger to get the better of him. If he does, he is bound to regret whatever he does. The most important characteristic of man is the ability to exercise choice between alternatives whenever he has to make an important decision. If he allows his anger to impair his judgement, then he actually foregoes the privilege of free choice. Moreover, allowing anger to get the better of oneself is most unbecoming of a teacher. If it does not suit a school teacher, it certainly does not suit a teacher of mankind, whose subject is Divine guidance.

Here, the Prophet teaches us one way of exercising self-control and allowing our anger no chance of impairing our judgement. He tells us to remain silent when we are angry. If we do so, we are certain not to say anything that we may later regret. People may say all sorts of things when they are possessed by anger. In order not to allow ourselves to be in such a position, the safest approach is not to say anything.

14

Reliance on God, Ease and Simplicity

THE CONCEPT OF reliance on God and trusting to His wisdom is central to the Islamic faith. This is what makes hardship easy to accept. The Prophet gives us the perfect example of total reliance on God:

> 246. ʿAṭāʾ ibn Yasār said: ʿI met ʿAbdullāh ibn ʿAmr ibn al-ʿĀṣ and said to him: "Tell me how God's Messenger is described in the Torah". He said: "Yes. By God, he is described in the Torah by some of his qualities mentioned in the Qurʾan: ʿ*Prophet! We have sent you as a witness, a bearer of good news and a warner*ʾ, (33: 45) and a guardian for the unlettered. You are My servant and My Messenger. I have named you Al-Mutawkkil [one who totally relies on God]; who is neither rude nor unkind, nor quarrelsome in the markets; who does not repel a bad deed by a bad one, but forgives and pardons. God, the Exalted, will not cause him to die until He has, through him, straightened the faith that has become crooked so that [its followers] will say: ʿThere is no deity

other than God', opening with this statement blind eyes, deaf ears and sealed hearts".'[173]

247. (*Athar* 60) 'Abdullāh ibn 'Amr said: 'This Qur'anic verse, "*Prophet! We have sent you as a witness, a bearer of good news and a warner,*" (33: 45) is also in the Torah, in similar phraseology'.

'Abdullāh ibn 'Amr, a learned companion of the Prophet, begins by saying that the Prophet's description in the Qur'an is more detailed than in the Torah, but what is in the Torah is also in the Qur'an. He then quotes a verse from the Qur'an which describes the Prophet as a witness, a herald and a warner. What is meant by a witness is that he testifies to earlier messengers stating that they had conveyed God's messages to people. It could also mean that he was the leader of his own nation who would give his testimony either for or against them. It is in the essence of a message from God to mankind that it contains both happy news and a warning of painful doom. This dual purpose seeks to persuade those who receive the message that it is a true one, revealed by God, who may inflict punishment on those who do not respond but who will bestow mercy on those who accept His message.

This is followed by a description of the Prophet as a 'guardian for the unlettered'. 'The unlettered' refers to the Arabs, the overwhelming majority of whom could not, at the time, read or write. The Prophet himself did not. This is an indication of the truthfulness of his message. A person who never held a pen in his hand could have never fabricated a message so detailed and elaborate like that of Islam. It must have been revealed to him from on High. The same Arabic term, *al-ummiyyīn*, rendered as 'the unlettered', is also used in the Qur'an as an equivalent for 'the gentiles'. What is meant by the Prophet being their guardian is that those among them who respond to his message will be guarded from the fire of Hell.

Arabic admits a sudden change from one form of speech to another. Having used the third person singular in the earlier part of this *ḥadīth*, it now uses the second person, quoting God directly as saying to the Prophet: 'You are my servant and Messenger'. This clearly identifies

173. Related by al-Bukhari.

the Prophet as a human being and a servant of God. He has no divine nature, for only God Himself has such nature. He chooses whom He wills to entrust with His message giving him prophethood.

This is followed by giving the Prophet a name which is unfamiliar to most people. 'Al-Mutawakkil' means the one who depends or relies on God. The precise meaning of this reliance is to genuinely and deeply believe in what God says in the Qur'an: '*There is no living creature on earth but depends for its sustenance on God*'. (11: 6) Its means of sustenance is thus apportioned to it by God. This does not mean that people need not work for their living. What it means is that the provisions are there to be taken, but a person must work in order to obtain them. Imam Aḥmad ibn Ḥanbal was asked about a man who stayed in his home or at the mosque, declaring that he would not do any work until he received his provisions apportioned to him by God. He answered: This is a man totally devoid of knowledge. The Prophet (peace be upon him) says: 'God has placed my provisions under the shade of my spear'.[174] This signifies that he has to work in order to secure his provisions. He also says: 'If you genuinely rely on God as He should be relied on, He will give you your provisions in the same way as he gives birds their provisions: they go out hungry in the morning and return in the evening, having had their fill'.[175] It is especially significant that the Prophet mentions that the birds have to go out and come back seeking their provisions. His companions understood this fact very well and they were all busy in their jobs, whether they were merchants, self-employed or employed by others.

Certain figures among the Sufis maintain that true reliance on God means that one should fear nothing and need not go out to work. All scholars agree that this view is totally mistaken. The Prophet mentions very clearly in an authentic *ḥadīth*: 'The best thing a person eats is that which he has earned through working. Prophet David used to eat only of his own earnings'.[176] There is, then, no fatality in the emphasis Islam places on the need to rely totally on God.

---

174. Related by al-Bukhari and Aḥmad.
175. Related by Aḥmad, al-Tirmidhi and Ibn Mājah.
176. Related by al-Bukhari.

The next qualities of the Prophet mentioned in this *ḥadīth* are that he was neither rude nor unkind. These two qualities mean that in both word and deed unkindness was alien to the Prophet. He would not say a word to hurt anyone. Nor would he ever do anything to cause pain or distress to anyone. Both these qualities are mentioned in the Qur'an in terms which clearly indicate that rudeness and unkindness were sufficient to make people turn away from an advocate of any cause. Therefore, an advocate of God's cause must steer away from using offensive language or doing anything which smacks of unkindness.

In line with these two qualities, Prophet Muhammad is described as 'not quarrelsome in markets'. It is in the market place that most quarrels occur because people try to obtain the best bargain for themselves. Hence, interests clash. Selfishness may easily lead to quarrels. The Prophet would do nothing of the kind. If he went to the market place, he would be very generous, giving the other party more than his due. In fact, this was one of his lifetime characteristics. He is reported to have often bought something and then left what he bought to the shopkeeper together with the price he paid for it; this was unparalleled generosity.

Another quality of the Prophet the *ḥadīth* highlights is that he did not repel one bad deed by another. By nature people think of retaliation when they are exposed to injury or bad treatment, reacting in the same manner as the aggressor. Hence, the person who has suffered unkind treatment is likely to try to avenge himself. The Prophet did nothing of the sort. Indeed, he was instructed by God to return a bad deed with a good one, so as to erase its effect. He is also described as one who 'forgives and pardons'. The two words are almost identical in meaning. Both are used in order to emphasise the Prophet's readiness to forgive his enemies and those who tried to hurt him. Indeed, his forgiveness knew no limits.

The next description given in the Torah relates to the length of the Prophet's mission. He would achieve the ultimate goal of correcting the Divine faith that had been distorted, with erroneous and mistaken beliefs creeping into it. 'God will not cause him to die until He has, through him, straightened the faith that has become crooked'. The faith mentioned here is that of Abraham who was the first to call those who followed the Divine faith Muslims, meaning those who submit themselves totally to God. His faith is, then, to maintain the essential attributes of God's oneness and His control of the universe. The Prophet's mission, then was to see to it that this faith was finally rectified.

This must not be a passive acceptance. Those who believe in God's oneness have a mission to fulfil, namely, to open the eyes, ears and hearts of people to this essential fact. This was exactly what the Prophet's companions did during his lifetime and afterwards. They understood their task and they went about fulfilling it with unparalleled dedication. As a result of their efforts, eyes, ears and hearts became open and attentive. People accepted the new faith and Islam moved from strength to strength.

As is mentioned in this *ḥadīth*, the Qur'an refers to more of the Prophet's qualities than those which occur here. Combined together, these qualities produce the perfect example of a true Muslim. It is for this reason that God has made the Prophet's character an example for us to follow.

One of the Prophet's important qualities mentioned in this *ḥadīth* is his forgiveness. A related aspect of people's relations is that they overlook their own mistakes and do not expose or publicise their faults and negative aspects.

248. Muʿāwiyah reports: 'I heard the Prophet say some words by which God has given me clear benefit. I heard him say: "If you delve into people's secret faults, you will corrupt them". Therefore, I do not go into people's secrets so that I will not corrupt them'.[177]

Every one may have faults, or do some wrong in private, and people do not like these to be publicised. Islam prefers that such matters be kept private. A person who commits a sin in private may regret it and may repent and seek God's forgiveness. God will forgive any sin when a person genuinely repents and resolves not to do it again. The availability of this way of erasing past errors and sins provides a ready and appealing opportunity for mending one's ways and maintaining

177. Related by Ibn Ḥibbān and al-Bayhaqi in Shuʿab al-Īmān.

proper conduct. Therefore, we should help people to choose this way of mending their ways. Should we learn of any faults and weaknesses they might have in private, we respect their privacy and overlook their faults. We should always remember that God gives all people a cover of privacy, and we must not take it away.

When people's faults are made public, they may be encouraged to persist in these. This is what the Prophet refers to when he says that delving into people's suspicious areas may corrupt them. Perhaps the Prophet said this to Muʿāwiyah as a hint to his future role. Muʿāwiyah was a governor of Syria for twenty years before he became caliph and ruled the Muslim state for another twenty years. A ruler has greater opportunities to delve into people's secrets and pursue his suspicions about them. Therefore, the Prophet's words were of particular significance to Muʿāwiyah for he later was able to unite the Muslim community after they had experienced serious division.

Love and compassion

The Prophet was a loving and caring man. It is only natural that these characteristics should be more visible in his treatment of children, particularly his own children and grandchildren:

> 249. Abu Hurayrah reports: 'These two ears of mine have heard, and these two eyes of mine have seen God's Messenger as he held al-Ḥasan – or perhaps al-Ḥusayn – by his two hands, and placed [the child's] two feet on his own feet. He then said to him: "Climb up". The boy climbed until his feet were on God's Messenger's chest. Then the Prophet said to him: "Open your mouth". He then kissed him and said: "My Lord, love him, for I love him".'[178]

Some of us may question the propriety of this action being done by a grandfather in public. We need to remember that the Arabs were hard people who did not show their children any manifestation of love. The

178. Related by al-Tabarāni.

Prophet wanted to correct this attitude, showing them that treating children with compassion is perfectly appropriate. When he kissed one of his grandchildren in public some Arabs were taken aback. One of them even questioned him about it, saying that he had many children and never kissed any of them once. The Prophet said to him: 'How can I help it if God has taken mercy away from you'.

The Prophet's care and kindness did not stop with his grandchildren or immediate family.

250. Jarīr said: 'Ever since I became a Muslim, God's Messenger met me with a smile every time he saw me'.

The Prophet said: 'A man from among the best people of Yemen and who has the look of an angel will enter through this door'. Then Jarīr came in.[179]

This *ḥadīth* shows that the Prophet was always happy to meet his companions, especially those whom he knew to be very good people. When he smiled at them, they were very happy. Indeed, it is their pleasant and happy reaction to the Prophet smiling at them that moved them to note his smiling and to tell us about it. This confirms the description of the Prophet in the Qur'an, when God reminds the Arabs of the nature of the messenger He sent them: '*Indeed there has come to you a Messenger from among yourselves: one who grieves much that you should suffer; one who is full of concern for you; and who is tender and full of compassion towards the believers*'. (9: 128) This last quality of love and mercy towards the believers expressed itself in his smiling whenever he saw one whom he knew to be a true believer. Jarīr was such a believer and he tells us how the Prophet smiled at him whenever he saw him. He was delighted to see his smile and felt that he was close to him. Who could need anything else?

The Prophet's care for his people manifested itself in various ways. When he feared that something unpleasant might happen, he was anxious, hoping that nothing would befall them:

179. Related by Aḥmad, al-Bukhari, Muslim, al-Tirmidhi, Abū Dāwūd and Ibn Mājah.

251. 'Ā'ishah said: 'I have never seen God's Messenger laugh in such a way that enabled me to see the back of his mouth. Rather, he used only to smile. When he saw clouds gathering, or noticed wind blowing, this could be seen [in the change] in his face. I said to him: "Messenger of God, when people see clouds gathering, they are pleased, hoping that they bring rain. Yet, when you see clouds, unease is clearly visible in your face". He said: "'Ā'ishah, how can I be certain that it does not bring punishment? Certain people were punished by storm winds, and people saw such punishment but they thought: 'This cloud will bring us rain'."'[180]

What we understand from this *ḥadīth* is that the Prophet was highly sensitive towards what might befall his people. He was so compassionate to them that the thought of what God might do to them was always present in his mind. The Quraysh and the majority of the Arabs not only rejected his message, but they fought tooth and nail to suppress it altogether, exposing the believers to extreme torture and turning people away from Islam by spreading rumours about the faith and its great advocate,. The Prophet was also very much aware of what had befallen other nations, when they opposed the messengers and prophets who called on them to believe in God alone. The people of 'Ād, who were giants enjoying great physical strength, rejected the message brought to them by their prophet, Hūd. They lived in Arabia itself, where rain was always welcome because of the nature of its climate. Any rainfall was certain to make life easier for them, allowing vegetation to grow and giving them water to drink. However, when God decided to punish them for their rejection of His message and their sinful ways, He sent them clouds and very strong winds. When they first saw the clouds, they were so pleased thinking that they were bringing welcome rain. Soon they realised that it was a different sort of cloud. It brought in tempestuous winds which overturned everything and everyone. All died except Hūd, their prophet, and those who followed him.

---

180. Related by al-Bukhari, Muslim and Abū Dāwūd.

Prophet Muhammad (peace be upon him) was aware of this fact and of the opposition he received from his own people. Hence, he was always afraid that God might decide to punish them in one way or another. Since punishment had once been administered through rain and clouds, he naturally felt concerned when he saw clouds approaching. This feeling was so present in his mind that it could be seen in his face to the extent that his wife, ʿĀ'ishah spoke to him about it. His explanation clearly explains his worry that he could never be sure that such did not foretell doom for the Arabs who opposed God's message and messenger.

This does not mean that the Prophet looked gloomy at any time. Indeed, he used to smile on every pleasant occasion. Yet he did not laugh loudly, as some people do, because he considered this unbecoming. This is what his wife meant when she said that his laughter was never of the type which could be heard at a distance; i.e. implying she could never see the inside of the Prophet's mouth when he laughed. He only smiled. In other words, he never lost his presence of mind by being totally absorbed in laughter, as is the case with some people, when they are aware of nothing but the thought which causes that laughter.

It is important to note that it was not the Prophet's wife's intention to give an impression that he was always reserved, or slow to express his happiness. She simply wanted to show that the Prophet always conducted himself in a highly respectable manner, expressing his feelings in a balanced way, not ever appearing to be self-indulgent. The question arises whether there is any guidance from him to suggest a particular approach to laughter?

It is universally agreed by scholars that to follow the Prophet's example is the proper way in every respect. His example is perfect, whether it relates to matters of religion or to ordinary, simple, day-to-day affairs. When we state that Islam is a way of life, then it touches upon all affairs. Hence, to do in any matter what the Prophet did is to seek good example. Moreover, it is highly rewarding, since God rewards us for our intention to follow the Prophet's example. As for the question of laughter and smiling, the Prophet gave us clear guidance in addition to what his wife relayed about how he behaved.

252. Abu Hurayrah reports that the Prophet said: 'Laugh a little, for too much laughter leaves one's heart dead'.[181]

253. Abu Hurayrah reports that the Prophet said: 'Do not laugh too much, for too much laughter leaves one's heart dead'.[182]

There is nothing in the Qur'an or *Ḥadīth* to stop anyone laughing. There is no suggestion that laughter is unacceptable from an Islamic point of view. Indeed, the Prophet himself responded to jokes and funny situations. What he is advising us of in these two *ḥadīths* is that we should not indulge ourselves too much in laughter, in the way some people do when they cannot control themselves. There may be a funny situation which causes people to laugh, then they develop that situation and add more funny remarks which could invite further funny thoughts and ideas, to the extent that they can no longer control themselves. We have often seen people laughing and laughing to the extent that they cannot sit or stand. They may bend with laughter and generate more laughter by the way they behave and look in such a situation. It is in the light of such a situation that we should understand the Prophet's recommendation.

The other point concerns the need to keep one's heart alive and responsive. A believer looks at things in the light of his faith, trying always to strengthen his commitment to faith, by appreciating every sign which tells of God's perfect design in His creation. He appreciates God's favours as he bestows them on people and feels that God is present with us all the time. A person who does not appreciate God's signs and does not relate events and happenings to God's creation is described as having a dead heart. If one frequently indulges in uncontrollable laughter, one does not leave oneself enough time to reflect on God's creation. Instead, one is always thinking of something new to laugh at. One even laughs at people, which is something Islam censures. The Prophet always points out to us what draws us nearer to God and to admission into Heaven and warns us against what checks

181. Related by Ibn Mājah.
182. Related by Aḥmad and Ibn Mājah.

our approach to it. While laughter is not a sin, too much of it does not fit with the proper manner of a serious believer.

It is important to remember that the Prophet was keenly aware of the truth of the Day of Judgement and the great suffering that awaits those who merit God's punishment. Perhaps this awareness affected his attitude to laughter.

254. Abu Hurayrah reports: 'The Prophet passed by a group of his companions who were talking and laughing. He said to them: "By Him Who holds my soul in His hand, had you known what I know, you would have laughed little and wept much". When he left, the people were in tears. God, the Mighty and Exalted, revealed to him: "Muhammd, why do you make My servants lose hope?" The Prophet returned and said to his companions: "Rejoice, and do what you can and try to maintain a middle of the road stance".'[183]

This *ḥadīth* provides us with the proper explanation of the Prophet's attitude. He would have done everything to get people to do what it takes to avoid punishment on the Day of Judgement. However, it is in the nature of things that some people will continue to disobey God and thus merit punishment. He grieved for such people. In this instance, he did not tell his companions not to laugh, but simply reminded them that it was not proper to be always laughing. In fact, it behoves a believer to always remember the Day of Judgement.

However, the Prophet's statement may make some people lose hope. The rest of Abu Hurayrah's report tells us that God intervened in this particular situation to provide the right balance. What the Prophet's final words mean is that God accepts from us what little good we can do and rewards us highly for it. Therefore, we must never lose hope, or despise a little good action. If we think that our situation is hopeless because we can do only little that will be of benefit on the Day of Judgement, then we are taking the wrong attitude.

---

183. Related by Aḥmad and Ibn Ḥibbān, and related in part by al-Bukhari.

The Prophet's description

People who did not see the Prophet often asked his companions to describe him. Some of them could not because they rarely looked directly at him. Others provided detailed descriptions:

> 255. Abu Hurayrah sometimes described the Prophet as he reported *ḥadīths* he heard from him, saying: 'I have been told this by the one who had long eyelashes and fair-complexioned flanks. When he came along, he faced fully, and when he turned away, he turned away fully. No human eye has ever seen the like of him, nor will ever see'.

This *ḥadīth* appears to be included in this section because of the way the Prophet faced when coming forward and the way he turned to go away. No description is fully adequate to give us a picture of such movement. However, it appears that this reflected his honest and straightforward character. Even his gait and his turning looked straight, without any sideways leaning.

15

Consultation and Advice

256. Abu Hurayrah said: 'The Prophet asked Abu al-Haytham [ibn al-Tayyihān]: "Do you have a servant?" He answered: "No". The Prophet said: "When we receive some captives, come to us". [Some time later] the Prophet was brought two slaves only. Abu al-Haytham went to him and the Prophet said to him: "Choose one of these". He said: "You choose for me, Messenger of God." The Prophet said: "A person who is consulted is in a position of trust. Take this one, as I have seen him praying. Treat him well". Abu al-Haytham's wife said to him: "You will not be able to fulfil what the Prophet said to you unless you set him free." He said: "Then I set him free". The Prophet said: "Every Prophet sent by God and every Caliph has two sets of advisers: one that urges him to do good and forbids what is wrong and the other

does its best to corrupt him. Whoever is spared the evil adviser is truly protected".'[184]

This *ḥadīth* gives us very important aspects of the sort of care, values and manners a Muslim needs to acquire and enhance so that he or she always remain a good follower of Prophet Muhammad (peace be upon him). The first point to note is the Prophet's awareness of the circumstances of his followers. This is a quality a good leader must have. It is the Prophet who asks his companion, Abu al-Haytham, whether he had a servant. He realised his hardship and saved him the need to express it. Then he assured him that he would give him a servant when he received some captives.

Abu al-Haytham was one of the very early Muslims from the Anṣār, and he attended the two pledges the Anṣār gave to the Prophet when he was still in Makkah. It was the second pledge that sealed the agreement that the Prophet and the Muslims from Makkah would migrate to Madinah and settle there. Abu al-Haytham took part in the Battle of Badr and all subsequent expeditions with the Prophet.

When the Prophet received two slaves he went to him and the Prophet honoured his promise, giving him preference of choice, but he wanted the Prophet to choose for him, accepting his choice. The Prophet's choice was based on the fact that the one he recommended was seen praying. He recommended him to Abu al-Haytham and advised him to treat him well. Here we see an example of the total devotion of the Prophet's companions. When Abu al-Haytham's wife heard of the Prophet's recommendation, she advised her husband that a full implementation of the Prophet's recommendation meant that he should set the slave free. This was the best treatment they could do, and they certainly did so. Abu al-Haytham recognised the validity of her advice and set the man free.

The Prophet provides a principle that applies at all times. When someone is asked for advice, he must give the advice he is certain to be true and of benefit to the one seeking advice. In this *ḥadīth* the Prophet says: 'A person who is consulted is in a position of trust'.

---

184. Related by Aḥmad, Abū Dāwūd, al-Tirmidhi, Ibn Majah and Ibn Ḥibbān.

Therefore, his advice must be honest, uncoloured by any consideration other then the best interests of the person seeking the advice. The Prophet based his advice on the fact that the slave he chose was a believer who could be trusted.

The Prophet then mentions a situation that we encounter all the time. Every ruler, and indeed prophet, is surrounded by two sets of advisers: one that gives sound advice that is good for the ruler and his community and the other who aims to corrupt him. The first realises that when the ruler adheres to the right path and maintains justice and uses his power well, he will be loved and the country he rules will achieve prosperity. The other advisers are motivated by self interest. They want to corrupt the ruler so that they can go ahead with their own corrupt ways, using the wealth of the country for their own ends, as we see in almost all dictatorial governments.

257. (*Athar* 61) 'Amr ibn Dīnār said: 'Ibn 'Abbās recited [and commented]: "Consult with them on the conduct of some affairs".'

This refers to the verse that says: '*Consult with them on the conduct of public affairs*'. (3: 159) His comment makes clear that a ruler need not hold consultations on every matter that requires a decision. Public affairs of importance must be subjected to consultation, but where the choices are clear and the interests of the community are served by a particular line of action, consultation need not be carried out. However, this must not be an excuse for a ruler to become dictatorial. Islam is fundamentally opposed to dictatorship.

258. (*Athar* 62) Al-Ḥasan said: 'People never seek advice without being guided to the best option available to them. He then recited: "*They conduct their affairs by mutual consultation*".' (42: 38)

Consultation must be the criterion by which public or community affairs are decided. This does not need to be restricted to national matters or affairs that affect the majority of the population in a country.

Indeed, any group that needs to take a decision on a serious matter that affects them all should make their decision based on consultation. This is the best way to arrive at the best option. In this *ḥadīth*, al-Ḥasan confirms that when consultation is adhered to, the group or the community is guided to the best option available to them.

259. Abu Hurayrah reports that the Prophet said: 'Whoever attributes to me something that I have not said shall take his place in the Fire. Whoever is consulted by his Muslim brother and gives him a flawed advice has betrayed him. Whoever gives a ruling [i.e. fatwa] that is not based on clear evidence, the sin thereof shall rest with the one giving the ruling'.[185]

This *ḥadīth* gives us three very important principles. The first is concerned with what is attributed to the Prophet. This is because what the Prophet said relates to the faith. If people attribute to him something he did not say, they are introducing into Islam what does not belong to it. This is a fabrication against God and His Messenger, and it merits no lesser punishment than hell.

The Prophet's companions were very diligent in reporting only what they heard directly from the Prophet or what they heard from other reliable companions. If they were in doubt about a word or a part of the *ḥadīth* they would indicate this without hesitation. Later, when political groups needed to give their creeds some authority, they invented statements and attributed them to the Prophet. By so doing, they sought to perpetuate their doctrines. Scholars of *Ḥadīth* undertook a meticulous exercise of research and verification to establish which statements were authentic *ḥadīths* and which were not. To do so, they studied the history of every single reporter and verified that he attended the scholar he claimed to have heard it from. If they found any flaw in the reporting of a single reporter in the chain, such as his being known to have told even one lie, or that he mixed up his teachers, attributing to some what he heard from others,

185. Related by Aḥmad and Ibn Mājah without the first sentence. Also, Abū Dāwūd and Ibn Mājah relate the last sentence only with a different chain of transmission.

they classified him as unreliable, or a liar, as the case might be. The *ḥadīth* in question is then classified as unacceptable, weak or false, etc. Thus, only the most authentic *ḥadīths* are accepted and acted upon.

The second principle warns against giving advice that is not based on sound judgement. When consulted, a Muslim must give advice only when he is certain of its wisdom. To take a casual attitude in advising others is to betray them. They may rely on one's advice and come to regret it. Therefore, if a person is unsure of his grounds, he should make this clear to the person seeking his advice.

The third principle takes the matter of advice further, speaking about rulings on some religious matters. Again, the person giving such a ruling must be sure of his basis. He should rely only on what is definitive and applicable to the case in question. If he gives a wrong ruling, because he is unaware of the statements or the principles that govern the case, he is giving a baseless ruling and he bears the consequences of his ill advised action. He will bear the sin of anyone who acts upon his advice.

16

Love and Friendliness

THE PROPHET WAS keen that the Muslim community should always be characterised by its strong bond and the love that Muslims feel towards one another. He encouraged this in every way.

260. Abu Hurayrah reports that the Prophet said: 'By Him Who holds my soul in His hand, you shall not be admitted into heaven until you are truly Muslims, and you shall not be true Muslims until you love one another. Spread the greeting of peace and you will love one another. Guard against hatred, for it is the razor. I do not say to you that it shaves hair; rather it shaves the faith altogether'.[186]

The first thing to note about this *ḥadīth* is that it is preceded by the oath the Prophet used to start a statement to which he attached

---

186. Related by Muslim, Abū Dāwūd and Ibn Mājah.

much importance. When he said this oath, his companions listened attentively so as to fully understand the message he wished to give them. On this occasion, the Prophet starts by telling them admittance into heaven depended on the accomplishment of certain duties. The first of these was to be true Muslims. They were well aware of this and they adopted Islam hoping to save themselves from hell. However, the Prophet tells them that they are not truly Muslims until they have met certain conditions. The surprise is that the Prophet does not tell them that they become true Muslims if they pray more often or fast more frequently or give so much of their property in charity. Rather, he tells them that they are not true Muslims unless they genuinely love one another.

Perhaps it is surprising even to us today that mutual love within the Muslim community should be given such high priority. However, our surprise disappears when we consider the Islamic values and teachings relevant to what sort of feelings should characterise the life of the Muslim community. A religion that establishes a bond of brotherhood between all its followers cannot fail to cement this bond with genuine love. Indeed, the first Muslim community witnessed the most effective and practical demonstration of such love when the Muslims of Makkah migrated to Madinah, where they were received with open arms and heart-felt love by their brethren of Madinah. The latter shared with their migrant brothers their homes, incomes and provisions. The Prophet was keen to make future generations of Muslims well aware of the need to have such love towards one another. He also tells them how to strengthen such mutual feelings of love.

The Prophet tells us that if we spread the greetings of peace between us, we are certain to enhance and strengthen our mutual love. This is certainly true. The Islamic greeting is *al-salām 'alaikum*, which means 'peace be to you'. In its complete version, the greeting means 'peace be to you, together with God's mercy and blessings'. We are also advised to greet all those whom we meet, whether we know them or not. It is common practice in Muslim communities that people exchange such greetings whenever they meet, in houses, business places or in the street. The greeting itself is significant because it helps to spread an atmosphere of peace within the community. Moreover, '*salam*', or 'peace', is one of the blessed names or attributes of God. So, when we offer this greeting to people, we are in effect telling them that we are extending to them the peace sanctioned by God. This is sure to generate feelings of amity, friendship and love. Moreover, while Islam recommends that its followers take the initiative and offer greetings to others when they meet them, it is deemed obligatory to return the greeting. God says: '*When a greeting is offered you, answer it with an even better greeting, or [at least] with its like*'. (4: 86)

The Prophet goes further than this, warning us against hatred. He wants us to stay away from hatred at any cost. He describes it as the 'razor' which removes everything in its way. To heighten the effect of his words, he borrows the connotations associated with hair shaving, but makes his meaning absolutely clear, stating that it shaves faith altogether. This means that when hatred spreads within the Muslim community, it leads that community to abandon faith. Hatred prompts people to cause harm to those whom they hate. To achieve their purpose, they resort to foul means. When they have such priorities, they cannot maintain the path of faith. Every time they contemplate harming others, or take actual steps to do so, they remove themselves from faith. If hatred is allowed to take roots, it certainly causes the Islamic faith to be divorced from community life. Hence, the Prophet's description is most appropriate.

Love: the mark of the Muslim community

Whenever Islamic society exists, its distinctive mark is the love which its individual members feel towards one another. There is a basic quality of love, companionship and trust between people of the Muslim community. Other communities may speak of a tie of brotherhood, citizenship or tribal bond which unites them. None has real substance as compared with the brotherhood and companionship that exist between Muslims. This is not surprising because it is a quality which God has planted within the Muslim community. Indeed, God Himself points to this in the Qur'an, when He addresses the Prophet mentioning the love and companionship He has established in the hearts of believers as one of the favours He has granted the Prophet. '*He it is Who has strengthened you with His help and rallied the believers round you, uniting their hearts. If you were to spend all that is on earth you could not have so united their hearts, but God has united them. He is Mighty and Wise.* (8: 62-63)

This unity and feeling of love and companionship are, then, the work of God Himself. They are substantive, not abstract. It brings Muslim's hearts and souls together. This is what the Prophet points out:

261. 'Abdullāh ibn 'Amr reports that the Prophet said: 'The souls of two believers meet when they are a full day's travel apart, even though they have never seen each other'.[187]

This *ḥadīth* speaks of an actual meeting of souls despite the fact that the two believers are physically wide apart. Their souls meet, although they themselves do not know each other. The love that exists between them is generated by their common belief in God and in Islam. This is certainly a strong tie which cannot be easily overlooked. How souls meet is something which we cannot tell, since knowledge of the world of souls and spirits is the preserve of God. That they meet, however, is something we know for certain, because the Prophet speaks about it. He tells us: 'Souls are like soldiers: those who have common grounds are united, and those who have no common grounds between them are in conflict'.[188]

This is something that the Prophet's companions have always confirmed:

262. (*Athar* 63) Ibn 'Abbās said: 'Favours may be met with ingratitude; kinship may be severed; but we have seen nothing stronger than hearts drawing close to one another'.[189]

263. (*Athar* 63) 'Umayr ibn Isḥāq said: 'We used to say that the first thing to be removed from people would be mutual affection'.

---

187. Related by Aḥmad.

188. Related by al-Bukhari and Muslim.

189. Related by Aḥmad and Ibn Ḥibbān.

In practical terms, this love, unity and feeling of companionship demonstrate themselves in a variety of ways. Perhaps the most vivid of these is seen in the way the Muslim community looks after the weak, the poor, widows, the elderly and the very young. Every one of these is viewed as a member of the community who must enjoy all the rights and privileges and fulfil whatever duties are assigned to him or her. It is also demonstrated in the way Muslims hurry to help one another in every situation which so requires it. The absence of this love foretells a weakness of the bond of faith and, indeed, a weakness in faith itself. Scholars of the early period of Islam, when love and companionship were very strong in the Muslim community, used to say that the first tie to disappear is the bond of unity and love between believers. This means that its loss signals weakness of faith which leads to a total change in people's behaviour.

Some humour

The Prophet used to enjoin a pleasant atmosphere, condusive to speaking at ease, adding some humour, but he never deviated from saying what is right or true.

264. Anas ibn Mālik reports: 'The Prophet joined some of his wives, and Umm Sulaym was with them. He said: "Anjashah! Take it easy as you are driving gentle creatures".' [Literally: Slow down a bit as you are driving glass vessels.]

Abu Qilābah said: 'The Prophet said a word which you would have criticised if said by any of you. He said: "as you are driving glass vessels".'[190]

This *ḥadīth* refers to an occasion when the Prophet and his companions were on their way back to Madinah after a trip. He had some of his wives and other women with him. Anjashah was a servant of the Prophet who had a melodious voice. They were travelling at night and Anjashah was chanting. Camels go faster when their driver chants. The

190. Related by al-Bukhari, Muslim, al-Nasā'ī and al-Ṭayālisi.

Prophet did not want the camels to go too fast so as not to trouble the women. Hence, his remark in which he used a metaphor, comparing women to glass vessels that should be handled with care.

This *ḥadīth* is entered by al-Bukhari under a subheading referring to the Prophet's occasional use of jest.

265. Abu Hurayrah said that the Prophet's companions said to him: 'Messenger of God, at times you joke with us'. He said: 'But I only say what is true'.[191]

It was a characteristic of the Prophet that even in jest he would say nothing but what is true. He never said something untrue, not even in jest. People do not think much of telling a lie when they speak in jest, but the Prophet's guidance is clearly against this. Lying is forbidden in Islam, even when it is in jest.

266. (*Athar* 65) Bakr ibn 'Abdullāh said: 'The Prophet's companions used to throw pieces of melons at one another [in jest], but when real effort was needed, they were the men [to rely upon]'.

This *ḥadīth* gives us a glimpse of the life of the Prophet's companions and Islamic society during his lifetime. It was a normal society with people joking and playing with one another. Here, we see them throwing water melons at each other. However, when a serious situation needed to be addressed, they were quick to respond and make every effort. They were truly reliable.

Jesting also took place in the Prophet's own home:

267. Ibn Abu Mulaykah said: ''Ā'ishah jested in the presence of God's Messenger. Her mother said: "Messenger of God, these are some of the jokes of our clan from Kinānah". The Prophet said: "Rather, some of our own".'

268. Anas ibn Mālik reports that a man came to the Prophet requesting a mount. The Prophet said: 'I will give you a she-

191. Related by Aḥmad and al-Tirmidhi.

camel's offspring to ride'. The man said: 'Messenger of God, what benefit will a colt be to me?' The Prophet said: 'Are camels born to any female other than a she-camel?'[192]

'Ā'ishah's mother might have thought that for her daughter to be jesting in the Prophet's presence was unbecoming. Hence, her explanation that 'Ā'ishah only said some jokes that were circulated in her own community. The Prophet reassured her by saying that these were also jokes of his own community.

In the second *ḥadīth*, the Prophet wanted to give an air of relaxation, saying to the man that he was giving him a colt born to a she-camel. In his sense of urgency, the man thought that the Prophet would give him only a recently born colt, which would not be fit to ride. The Prophet explained that every camel was born to a she-camel; as such it is an offspring of its own mother.

The Prophet cared for children and talked to them about their concerns and what they played with.

269. Anas ibn Mālik said: 'The Prophet used to be one of us. He would even say to my young brother: "Abu 'Umayr, what have you done with your little sparrow".'[193]

270. Abu Hurayrah said: 'The Prophet held al-Ḥasan – or perhaps al-Ḥusayn – by his two hands, and placed [the child's] two feet on his own feet. He then said to him: "Climb up".'

The boy used to play with his little sparrow, but the sparrow died and the child was upset. The Prophet sought to divert his attention by asking him to recall some of the things he used to do with his little bird. His preoccupation with the welfare of his community and the schemes of his enemies did not stop him from taking care of a young boy who keenly felt the loss of his pet.

The second of these two *ḥadīths* has been discussed in its longer version, entered at Number 249.

---

192. Related by Aḥmad, Abū Dāwūd and al-Tirmidhi.
193. Related by al-Bukhari, Muslim, Abū Dāwūd, al-Tirmidhi, al-Nasā'ī and Ibn Mājah.

17

Refined Manners

SINCE ISLAM, by definition, promotes every good, it encourages the adoption of all universally agreed values that come under the heading of 'good manners', and promises reward for them. The Prophet speaks about good manners in no ambiguous terms. Indeed, he takes every opportunity to stress the fact that good manners earn high reward.

> 271. Abu al-Dardā' reports that the Prophet said: 'Nothing is weightier in [God's] scales than good manners'.[194]

Under the term 'good manners' we may include all the characteristics and attitudes that are highly praised by all religions, philosophies and societies. In whichever society you live, courage is admired, cowardice despised; generosity is endearing; self-restraint is commendable, losing one's temper criticised; humility respected, conceit contemptible;

194. Related by Aḥmad, Abū Dāwūd, al-Tirmidhi and Ibn Ḥibbān.

taking care of others rewarding; selfishness repugnant. The list of these virtues and their opposite vices is much longer. The attitude towards each of them is universal. This because such virtues are indicative of good upbringing, noble character and a generous heart. They help to set relationships within the community on a sound basis. They strengthen the community feeling and promote wellbeing in society. Hence, Islam promotes them all.

272. ʿAbdullāh ibn ʿAmr said: 'The Prophet never uttered or did an indecency, neither casually nor deliberately. He used to say: "The best among you are the best mannered".'[195]

Good manners are not confined to action, but what people may say reflects their manners. Needless to say the Prophet was the best mannered of all people. It is enough to remember God's description of him: '*Most certainly, you have a sublime character*'. (68: 4) In this *ḥadīth* ʿAbdullāh ibn ʿAmr describes the Prophet's speech. It is what one expects from the person with the most sublime character. He never uttered an indecent word. We would do well to follow his example.

273. ʿAbdullāh ibn ʿAmr reports that the Prophet said: 'Shall I tell you who of you is dearest to me and will be seated closest to me on the Day of Resurrection?' His audience remained silent. He repeated the question twice or three times and the people said: 'Please do, Messenger of God'. He said: 'They are the best mannered among you'.[196]

All Muslims agree that the highest place in heaven belongs to the Prophet himself. What we should strive for is to gain as near a position to him as possible. This can only be earned through hard work. The Prophet, however, tells us that good manners, when refined and at a high standard, are the surest way to gain such advantage. This is not surprising, since his mission is all to do with good morality and the best of manners:

---

195. Related by al-Bukhari, Muslim and al-Tirmidhi.
196. Related by Aḥmad and Ibn Ḥibbān.

274. Abu Hurayrah reports that the Prophet said: 'I have been sent to bring good manners to perfection'.[197]

This *ḥadīth* again confirms that good manners are generally welcomed by all communities and all societies. However, the message of Islam puts these at a higher level as it provides the link between human virtues and God's acceptance and reward. Thus, it creates strong motivation to put them into practice.

The Prophet disliked hard attitudes and hardness of character. He believed that it was always better to make things easier for people.

275. 'Ā'ishah said: 'God's Messenger was never offered a choice between two alternatives [over matters of this world] without choosing the easier one, unless it was sinful. If it was, he kept furthest away from it. God's Messenger never sought revenge for himself. Only if God's sanctity was violated would he take revenge for God, the Mighty and Exalted.'

The Prophet realised that the easier alternative was kinder to his followers. He, thus, taught his companions and followers throughout all generations to prefer the easier course in all matters. Whatever would please people and ensure their comfort and happiness was always preferable to the Prophet. The only proviso being that this easier option must be legitimate. If it was sinful, he would steer away from it. This was only to be expected from the Prophet who had been sent as mercy for mankind. A sinful practice is indeed the more difficult choice, although it may appear easy or more enjoyable. Such ease and enjoyment, however, can only be momentary, for they are attended by God's displeasure, which puts people in a very difficult position.

Moreover, the Prophet never sought vengeance for himself. Seeking vengeance is characteristic of a hard person who finds it difficult to forgive. The Prophet was willing to forego any personal injury he might have suffered, but he was unwilling to forgive the violation of God's strict bounds. We can easily see the distinction between the two.

---

197. Related by Aḥmad and al-Ḥākim.

When it was a matter of principle, relevant to what God has made lawful or forbidden, then the Prophet was unwilling to sacrifice even a minor principle.

> 276. (*Athar* 66) 'Abdullāh ibn Mas'ūd said: 'God, the Exalted, has apportioned character among you in the same way as He has apportioned your provisions. God, the Exalted, gives wealth to those He loves and those He does not love, but He does not grant faith except to those whom He loves. He who holds money too dearly to spend it [for God's cause], fears to fight the enemy and is too weary to stand up at night in worship should often repeat: '*La ilāha illa Allah* [i.e. There is no deity except God]', and '*Subḥān Allah* [i.e. Limitless is God in His glory]' and '*Al-ḥamd lillāh* [i.e. All praise be to God]' and 'Allah akbar [i.e. God is supreme]'.[198]

The first sentence in this *ḥadīth* tells us that our characters are given to us by God. This means that by nature we have the aptitude to follow a certain course, or adopt a certain line. It does not mean that some of us are created liars while others are, by their nature, truthful. We can certainly develop our characters, taking free decisions to be, for example, generous, forgiving, reasonable, etc. This is no different from the apportioning of our provisions by God. It does not mean that we will get our money whether we work for it or not. God certainly does not shower money or provisions on us from the clouds. He facilitates our work for us and makes our efforts successful. The more we do, the greater our earnings. People sometimes suggest that it is better to spend time in worship than to work for one's living. They argue that what God has apportioned for us we will receive. Such a fatalistic attitude is not Islamic. God tells us to work in order to earn our living. If we do not work, we earn nothing. The Prophet once saw a man spending all his time in the mosque. He asked who supported him. When he was told that it was his brother, the Prophet said that his brother was the better of the two in worship.

---

198. Related by Aḥmad and al-Ḥākim.

The second sentence tells us that wealth is not that important from an Islamic perspective. God gives wealth to believers and non-believers, to those He loves and those He does not love. So, when we see a man who is very wealthy, his wealth does not signify that he is dearer to God. Nor is a poor person less favoured by God. The Prophet tells us: 'Had this world [and all its riches] been worth even the span of one wing of a mosquito in God's sight, not a glass of water would He have allowed of it to any unbeliever'.[199] If this world and all its riches so worthless in God's view, then being wealthy does not mean that one is favoured or loved by God. It is faith with which God favours those whom He loves. Faith gives a person a good character. He earns respect in his community even by those who do not share his faith. This is due to the fact that when one has faith, one behaves well with others, improves one's manners and adheres to noble moral values. This is bound to earn one the love and respect of others. This is true wealth indicative of God's favour.

Faith places certain requirements on people. They are supposed to sacrifice their money and their lives for God's cause. Yet such sacrifice does not come so easy to all people. Man is sometimes governed by his narrow view of this world. He finds it difficult to part with his money, even for a good cause. He may slacken when he is called upon to join jihad. He may prefer to rest at night and find it difficult to wake up in the middle of the night for voluntary worship. None of this takes a person out of the realm of faith altogether. He is still a believer, but his faith does not seem to dictate his choices. Therefore, he is advised to repeat praises and glorifications of God. By doing so, he reminds himself of his position in this world and that he is totally dependent on God. He remembers that God has given him so much of His Grace and he should always be thankful. He may then remember that when he fulfils his duty, sacrifices his wealth and shows his readiness to sacrifice his life, God will give him more. This may come in this world or in the next life.

Repeating such praises of God is important, even if it does not bring about such a change of attitude. God rewards us generously for praising and glorifying Him. Moreover, we feel our relationship

---

199. Related by al-Tirmidhi, Ibn Mājah and al-Ḥākim.

with God to be more intimate. We know that we depend on Him for everything in our lives. We know that His Grace and bounty is so great that we cannot thank Him enough for it, even if we were to spend all our time in worship. After all, our worship does not benefit God; it benefits only us. We also gain a better character for it, and so should not hold it as a favour which we do for God.

Definition of wealth

Everyone loves to be rich. Even those who place their principles and values above wealth do not object to being wealthy provided that they do not have to compromise their values or principles. People feel that wealth allows them to enjoy what they want in this world. Moreover, a wealthy person normally enjoys respect by his community. Position, respect and independence, which are enjoyed by a wealthy person, make wealth a universally desirable asset. However, the Prophet gives us a different definition of wealth:

> 277. Abu Hurayrah reports that the Prophet said: 'Wealth does not mean the possession of too many things. True wealth is to be content'.[200]

The *ḥadīth* begins with a negative statement which dispels the notion that only through owning property, and much of it at that, can one be rich. Having plenty of property and material comfort gives the proprietor an air of being rich. This is, however, a narrow view. It is only through being content that true wealth is achieved. This is the message of the second, positive part of the Prophet's statement. When we examine it carefully, we find that it is absolutely correct.

To start with, a person who is content does not look to other people for the accomplishment of what he wants. Nor does he humble himself at any time to request their assistance, whether financial or otherwise. He only seeks God's help. He may be of limited means, but he is satisfied with what he has. He knows that it is sufficient for his own

200. Related by Aḥmad, al-Bukhari, Muslim and al-Tirmidhi.

and his family's basic needs. He may have only a little, but that little goes a long way when one is content. Moreover, he can always pray to God for more. To pray to God to increase one's means is in no way contrary to being content. We praise God for what He has given us and ask Him for more, because what He gives us does not decrease His kingdom by even the smallest amount. It is authentically reported that God says in a sacred, or *qudsi*, *ḥadīth* that if all human beings and jinn prayed to God for whatever they desired and He granted every one of them his request, that does not decrease His kingdom except by as much as a needle decreases the water of the ocean when it is dipped once in it. Moreover, praying to God strengthens one's feeling of contentment. We know that God answers prayers in His good time. So, when we pray to Him, we trust that He will grant us our wishes. We also know that He does not hold it as a favour against us when He grants our requests.

All this gives a contented person all the good effects of being wealthy. He feels himself to be strong, since he does not have to go to any human being with a humble request for assistance. He is assured of God's help, so he is independent of all human beings. Moreover, the fact that he does not begrudge anyone what God has given them earns him great respect within his community. Thus, he combines self-sufficiency with independence and respect from his fellow human beings. If these are compared with their counterparts which are generated by owning much property, they will definitely be found to be more precious. This is why the Prophet defines true wealth as a state of contentment.

The Prophet himself was exemplary in his contentedness. He was not only content with what property he owned, but was content with whatever help or service he received. Anas ibn Mālik was probably twelve years of age when his stepfather brought him to the Prophet and said that he was a bright lad. He requested the Prophet to allow Anas to serve him.

278. Anas ibn Mālik reports: 'I have served the Prophet (peace be on him) for ten years. He never said to me the word "Ugh", nor did he ever say about something which I had omitted, "Would

it not have been better if you had done it", or to anything I did, "Why have you done that?"'[201]

We discussed this *ḥadīth* under Number 164, but we may add that it speaks of a very rare quality of contentedness in addition to an exemplary degree of forbearance. It is only to be expected that a servant in his teens should make mistakes, omitting certain things and doing some others incorrectly. It is true that Anas was a highly dedicated servant who loved the Prophet dearly. He was also a bright lad, as his mother and stepfather rightly described him. Yet, perfection is not a human quality. It cannot be expected from an adolescent. The Prophet, however, was extremely kind-hearted. He never showed his servant that he was dissatisfied with what he did. He did not express this in gestures, nor in words. He never questioned Anas why he had done one thing or omitted another. While this speaks much of Anas's eagerness to please the Prophet and do what he liked, it also speaks more of the Prophet's forbearance and that he would tolerate what other people cannot tolerate from their servants.

This was only to be expected from the Prophet who was granted this inclination to be forbearing and tolerant with people by God's grace. This is what God states in the Qur'an: '*It is by God's grace that you deal gently with them. Had you been harsh and hard-hearted, they would surely have broken away from you. Therefore, pardon them and pray for them to be forgiven and consult with them in the conduct of public affairs*'. (3: 159)

Exemplary generosity

The Prophet was very generous. He cared little for material comfort and gave away whatever was available to him:

279. Anas ibn Mālik said: 'The Prophet was very compassionate. Whoever came to him was promised help, and the Prophet fulfilled that promise, if he had [the means. One day] prayers

201. Related by al-Bukhari, Muslim and al-Tirmidhi.

were called [with iqāmah] when a bedouin came up to him and took hold of his garment and said: "I have only very little left of my request and I fear that I may forget it". The Prophet attended to him until he finished what he wanted. The Prophet then returned and prayed'.[202]

This *ḥadīth* starts with a statement by Anas that the Prophet was very compassionate. This is how he is described in the Qur'an. Therefore, on the face of it, Anas's description does not add anything, unless we take it to mean that the Prophet's compassion was exceptional, which indeed it was. It is most likely that Anas intended this very meaning.

Anas elaborates on this by saying that the Prophet would promise well anyone who came to him with a request; he reassured the person that he would do what he wanted. This applied when the Prophet did not have at hand the means to grant that person's request immediately. We understand this from Anas's further statement that the Prophet would have fulfilled the wishes of anyone who came to him, if he was able to do so.

Anas then mentions a situation when a man went to the Prophet and held him by his garment at a time when the Prophet and his companions were just about to start their obligatory prayer after its announcement. This is a time when anyone else would have delayed his request in order to allow the congregation the chance to complete their prayers. The bedouin excused himself by saying that what was left of his request was only a little and he feared that he might forget what he wanted to ask the Prophet. It may be surprising to many people that the Prophet attended to him at that particular time. Perhaps no one leading prayers would have done so. He would have told the man to wait until the prayer was over. The Prophet, however, recognised that whatever the bedouin wanted was of great importance to him. Whichever way we understand the statement, it is indicative of the Prophet's care of his followers and his compassion towards them. When he finished with the man, he immediately started the prayer.

---

202. Related by al-Bukhari, Muslim, al-Nasā'ī, Abū Dāwūd, al-Tirmidhi and Ibn Mājah.

This *ḥadīth* tells us that it is permissible to wait a short while after the congregational prayer is announced, if something happens to delay it. It is true that some schools of thought, especially the Ḥanafi, speak against separating the announcement of prayer and actually starting it, except for an emergency. However, if the separation is to conduct something of the affairs of religion or its practices, then there is no harm in delaying prayer. The normal practice, however, is to start prayer when the announcement is made. If there is a long delay, then it is preferable that the announcement be repeated.

This particular incident of delaying prayer in order to attend to a request by a bedouin is in keeping with the Prophet's attitude to any request put to him.

280. Jābir ibn 'Abdullāh said: 'The Prophet (peace be upon him) never said, "No", to any request put to him'.[203]

It was very hard for the Prophet to turn away anyone who might have requested something or other. He would either grant him his request immediately or promise to fulfil his request once he was able to do so. Otherwise, he would have kept quiet. It is true that the Prophet apologised at times, giving his reasons for not granting a certain request. A case in mind is that mentioned in the Qur'an with reference to the mobilisation of the Muslim army for the Tabuk Expedition. This was when the Prophet gave instructions to his companions to prepare for a march to fight the Byzantine Empire. Because of the very long distance which the army had to traverse, and the fact that this came in midsummer, when temperatures in Arabia were very high, anyone who wanted to join the army had to find his own transport. Some of the poorer companions of the Prophet wanted to join the army but could not find any means of transport of their own. They came to the Prophet, requesting him to arrange for their transport. He apologised saying, 'I have nothing to give you to ride'. This is certainly different from turning them away empty handed. The Prophet simply made it clear to them that

203. Related by al-Bukhari, Muslim, al-Tirmidhi, Abu 'Awānah, Ibn Ḥibbān and al-Dārimi.

he did not have what they needed. Otherwise it was very hard for him to turn anyone away.

Those who were close to the Prophet learnt from him and emulated his attitude:

281. (*Athar* 67) 'Abdullāh ibn al-Zubayr said: 'I never saw two women more generous than 'Ā'ishah and Asmā', even though their generosity was of different types. 'Ā'ishah used to collect things and when she had [something worthwhile] she distributed it. Asmā' never held anything to the following day'.

This *report* is by a companion of the Prophet, describing the generosity of his mother, Asmā', and his aunt, 'Ā'ishah, the daughters of Abu Bakr who once donated all his possessions for God's cause. It is not surprising then that they too were exemplary in their generosity. Yet their methods were different. 'Ā'ishah preferred to have something worth distributing among a number of people. If she had very little, she would delay giving it away, for she felt that it neither satisfied a certain need, nor could it be distributed among people. Hence, she preferred to wait until she had enough. Asmā', on the other hand, acted on the Prophet's advice to her when he said: 'Spend and never calculate, lest God may calculate things against you. Nor reckon, so that God will not reckon things against you'.[204] Asmā' felt that keeping something till tomorrow might be included in calculation and reckoning which the Prophet had advised her against.

Bearing in mind that they differed in this respect, they were nonetheless perfect examples of generosity. 'Urwah ibn al-Zubayr, describes his aunt 'Ā'ishah's generosity in these words: 'I saw 'Ā'ishah distributing 70,000 *dirhams*, [the silver currency at the time], while mending her dress'. Mu'āwiyah, the fifth Caliph, sent her a gold necklace with diamonds which was valued at 100,000 *dirhams* and she distributed this among the needy. On another occasion, her nephew, 'Abdullāh ibn al-Zubayr, sent her money in two sacks, which amounted to 180,000 *dirhams*. She asked for a large plate and began distributing all the money; when it was time to break her fast at sunset, she had not

204. Related by al-Bukhari and Muslim.

a single *dirham* of it left. Then it was time to eat, and she called her servant, asking her to bring the food. She could bring only some bread and some oil. A woman called Umm Dharr was present and said to her: 'Could you not have spared one *dirham* of all that you distributed today so that we both might have some meat for our fast breaking meal?' She said: 'Do not reproach me. Had you reminded me of it, I would have done so'. In other words, she distributed all the money, overlooking the fact that she was fasting and needed some food to eat in the evening. She did not spare for herself or her household a single *dirham* for their basic needs, including food. Such generosity does not come easy. It comes only through cultivation by a great master. That master was none other than the Prophet, the most generous man ever to walk our planet.

To be a miser

Both Asmā' and 'Ā'ishah were very kind and generous women. And this tells us that both were very firm believers. To be able to part with one's possessions for charity, motivated only by a desire to earn reward from God, is indicative of faith having established itself firmly in a person's heart.

It may be asked why we make generosity so strongly associated with faith. Is it not true that a person may be a good believer in God and yet he loves his property so much that he does not wish to part with it, preferring to use it only for that which he and his family may need? This is something which cannot be subject to personal opinion. God Himself has coupled the two together. He says in the Qur'an: '*Believe in God and His Messenger, and give [in charity] of that of which He has made you trustees. Those of you who believe and give [in charity] will have a great reward*'. (57: 7) As we see, generosity and spending in charity are mentioned together with faith. Muslim scholars consider this to be highly significant, both from the point of view of the reward God gives for generosity and the fact that one quality is an expression of the other.

Generosity is a practical quality, i.e. it involves action. One cannot be generous by making emphatic claims to be so. One practical gesture may be a far more powerful expression of this trait than the strongest of verbal claims. Faith, on the other hand, is something which establishes its roots in the heart. It manifests itself through action. There is, however, a well defined set of requirements, the fulfilment of which earns a person the title of believer. There are certain qualities which may take various manifestations and the aggregation of which proves that the person concerned is a firm believer. In the above Qur'anic verse, God makes clear that readiness to part with one's money and property for God's cause is one of the most important manifestations of faith.

Perhaps we should point out that when we speak about generosity and spending within an Islamic context, we are only referring to something being spent for no motive other than earning God's pleasure. It is something given for God's sake and with no expectation of immediate financial return. You give away your money or your property, recognising that you will get nothing in return, either financially or morally, except what God chooses to give you. In other words, you give it away hoping for God's reward and nothing else.

In human life, money is so important that in all societies which do not conduct their affairs on the basis of a Divine religion, people enjoy high esteem if they are wealthy. Wealth is equated with success and good character. To be wealthy is to have the one virtue which covers up most of a person's faults. This love of money is a universal human trait. It is, however, moderated by faith which imparts to a believer certain motives which can overcome personal feelings and desires.

To be generous is to demonstrate one's trust in God. As believers, we know that we gain only what God gives us. Moreover, we know that God provides all His creatures with their sustenance. He has placed in our planet enough resources and potential to ensure that every human being and every creature will have what they need to survive and lead a comfortable life. Moreover, He has apportioned for us our provisions. Nevertheless, people always tend to forget this and they are keen to preserve what they have. They tend to think that if they keep what they have in hand and work to get more, then that is the proper, indeed the only, way to climb the social ladder and be among the rich. A believer has different ideas. He knows that he can only get what God gives him. When he parts with his money for God's sake, God is sure to reward him. He also knows that God's reward is better for him than anything he owns. It is for this reason that the Prophet says:

282. Abu Hurayrah reports that the Prophet said: 'Dust raised [in a campaign of jihad] for God's cause and the smoke of hell can never be together inside the body of a servant of God. Avarice and faith cannot exist side by side in the heart of any person'.[205]

283. Abu Sa'īd al-Khudri reports that the Prophet said: 'Two traits cannot exist together in a believer's heart, namely, miserliness and bad manners'.[206]

In these two statements from the Prophet, we are told of the qualities and traits which pull a man in opposite directions. Hence, they cannot exist side by side. First, the Prophet tells us that when a person inhales dust raised for God's cause, he will not inhale the smoke of hell. When we read this, a picture of a battle in which the believers engage in the defence of Islam is drawn in our minds with horses raising dust as they run, or, in our modern times, military vehicles raising a trail of dust as they traverse rough ground. People engaged in fighting have to breathe and they are bound to inhale part of that dust. The fact that they are present in the battle, ready to sacrifice their lives for God's cause, tells us a great deal about the strength of their faith. When they have shown such readiness and when that is an essential part of their characters, they protect themselves against hell. They are forgiven their sins and slip ups. They are not thrown into hell as punishment for sins they may have done. Since they have a firm belief in God and the Day of Judgement, their errors are overlooked. The blazing fire of hell will not touch them and they will not inhale its smoke.

Similarly two mutually exclusive traits are avarice and faith. Avarice, which indicates greed and an eager desire to hold on to what one may have, suggests that one does not have enough trust in God. This leads one to think that to hold on to one's belongings is the best insurance for the future. A believer, on the other hand, thinks that giving away

---

205. Related by al-Nasā'ī.
206. Related by al-Tirmidhi.

one's property for God's sake is the surest way of getting something better in return.

These are not theoretical principles; rather, they have great practical value. I say without hesitation that no one who wishes to take up the challenge, parting with one's money for God's cause, will ever be disappointed. What is more is that the reward is not only in the Hereafter. Part of it is paid immediately in this life. When a human being demonstrates that he has total trust in God, God will certainly respond to him and show that his trust is well placed. People have only to try and they will never regret trying.

284. (*Athar* 68) ʿAbdullāh ibn Rabīʿah said: 'We were sitting with ʿAbdullāh [ibn Masʿūd] and some people mentioned a certain person and his manners. ʿAbdullāh said: "Suppose that you have his head cut off, can you put it back?" They said: "No". He said: "What about his hand?" They said: "No". He said: "And his leg?" They said: "No". He said: "Learn, then, that you cannot change his character unless you can change his physical form. The drop of sperm stays in the [woman's] womb for forty nights, then it becomes like congealed blood, and then it becomes a clinging mass and then a lump of flesh. God then sends an angel who writes down its means of livelihood and character, and whether happy or unhappy'.

In this *ḥadīth*, ʿAbdullāh ibn Masʿūd, one of the best scholars among the Prophet's companions, makes clear that it is not possible to change any person's character. However, it is possible to direct the different aspects of one's character so as they work for what is good and beneficial to the person himself and to his community. A person may get angry very easily. If he trains himself to direct his anger away from personal matters, then he is only angry when there is some violation of Islamic values or rules. In this way, he may contribute to improving social values.

As we have noted, the Prophet often stressed the importance of good manners and moral values. In some communities, devotion is emphasised so strongly that worship seems to be an end in itself. In Islam, worship has a dual purpose: to maintain the faith purely and to improve the character of the worshipper. Hence, Islam encourages voluntary worship, especially in the depth of the night, when a person is alone, standing up to worship in preference to sleep and rest. Such worship has a profound influence on the character of the worshipper. Because of this influence, the Prophet and his companions were commanded in the early days of Islam to stand up in worship at night, to help them mould their new characters and to give them additional strength of faith. The Prophet and his companions fulfilled this order, spending several hours during the night in prayer and worship. They did so for a whole year devoting a portion of one to two thirds of each night to worship. This directive was later relaxed to make night worship voluntary, but strongly recommended.

However, good manners are given similar importance with regard to character building:

> 285. Abu Hurayrah quotes the Prophet as saying: 'Through good manners, a man may attain the high standard of one who stands up at night in worship'.[207]

The Prophet is obviously referring here to a person who consciously implements what good manners and high moral values require of him in all his dealings with other people. The Prophet is not referring here only to a small set of universal virtues. He is referring to a high standard of good manners and a refined sense of virtues and morality. According to one scholar, the lowest degree of good manners is to react to ill-treatment by relatives and friends with forbearance, to forgo what one may earn of compensation for injury, to show compassion to those who may transgress and to pray to God to forgive them. If this is the lowest standard of good manners, we can imagine what a high standard means.

The Prophet emphasised that good manners are very broad in scope. Hence, they are related to faith and to a good understanding of Islam:

---

207. Related by Abū Dāwūd and al-Ḥākim.

286. Abu Hurayrah reports that he heard the Prophet say: 'The best of you in regard to faith are the best in manners, provided that they have sound knowledge [of their faith]'.[208]

What the Prophet tells us in this *ḥadīth* is that people who have good manners need only to acquire a good understanding of Islamic teachings in order to be the best of the faithful. At first glance, this equation may seem to need some justification. A little reflection, however, will show that it is absolutely correct. Every commandment, directive, or instruction from God, requiring us to do certain things or to refrain from doing others, recommending us to adopt a certain attitude or restraining us from reacting in a particular way has our best interest in mind. The aim which is served by these teachings, taken individually or as a whole, is to make of us better people. Needless to say, a person who has a thorough understanding of these teachings, knowing which of them is compulsory and which is recommended, which must be observed at all times and which may be relaxed according to the situation, develops a good sense of the Islamic ideal of human character. If such an understanding is coupled with a natural aptitude for observing good manners, then all the requirements for making a virtuous person are fulfilled.

There is, however, another element which is needed to make the mixture complete. This element is to believe in Islam. This means believing in God's oneness and that Muhammad is God's Messenger. The point is that every virtue acquires a rich increase in real value when it is tied to faith. In the absence of faith, it remains shaky and cannot establish its roots in people's hearts. There is no denying that among non-believers there are people of good character. They may abide by a strict standard of morality. If such people believe in God and the Day of Judgement, they become infinitely better.

At this point, al-Bukhari enters a *ḥadīth* that refers to the character of one of the most distinguished of the Prophet's companions:

208. Related by Aḥmad.

287. (*Athar* 69) Thābit ibn 'Ubayd said: 'I have never seen anyone who is more respectable when he sits with people, or more relaxed at home than Zayd ibn Thābit'.

Zayd ibn Thābit was a young companion of the Prophet who was given the task of collating the Qur'an, so that nothing of it was lost. He did this during the reign of Abu Bakr, the first Caliph who ruled the Muslim state for less than two years. He subsequently headed the committee that made copies of the Qur'an which were sent to the main centres of the Muslim state to be their reference copies. Thus, the preservation of the Qur'an was ensured. He was a man who looked very serious and respectable when with people, but was relaxed and jocular at home when he was with his family.

288. Ibn 'Abbās reports: 'The Prophet (peace be upon him) was asked: "Which religion does God, the Mighty and Exalted, love best?" He answered: "The pure and simple faith".'[209]

This *ḥadīth* tells us how the Prophet's companions were eager to know how close to God they were. Hence, their question which indicates that they wanted to be sure of their grounds. Yet, the question is in a way redundant. The Prophet was among them and he received revelations from on High. His message was clearly stated to be the final one from God. Hence, it should be the most perfect and the one God loves best. However, the Prophet does not answer his companions giving the name of the religion so highly valued. Instead, he gives them two qualities that distinguish this religion: purity and simplicity. This is the faith of Prophet Abraham and all subsequent prophets. It takes its final form in the message of Prophet Muhammad (peace be upon him). It is easy to understand and to implement.

---

209. Related by Aḥmad.

Four qualities

Four qualities are highlighted as being the most important to have:

> 289. (*Athar* 70) 'Abdullāh ibn 'Amr said: 'If you have these four qualities, you need not bother about what you have been denied of in this world: good manners, integrity with regard to food, maintaining the truth in what you say and being faithful to your trust'.[210]

This *ḥadīth* speaks of good manners generally, but expresses this in such a way as to give us the impression of the need to maintain an essentially good character, always trying to get on with people. Thus, a Muslim is supposed to show generosity of attitude and character, forbearance, forgiveness, courage, easy dealings, etc. Whenever he is in a position to determine his course of action, he chooses what is virtuous. All this is included under the heading of 'good manners'.

The *ḥadīth* then gives us three aspects of good character. The first is to maintain integrity with regard to what we eat. I must admit that I found it extremely difficult to translate the Arabic phrase which expresses this characteristic. It is true that food is specifically mentioned, but this is merely an example. It applies to everything one may take, receive, earn or acquire, in addition to what one eats. Therefore, the values of integrity which must be observed apply here to everything that a person may wish to have. Thus, the *ḥadīth* makes clear that it is all right to have something which is permissible, provided that one observes the rules of integrity. This means that we must never do something forbidden in order to acquire something we desire, even our food. We may not see or take something in a fraudulent manner and we may not cheat or deny people their rights. All this is very obvious. However, the word 'integrity' is used here in order to indicate that a good Muslim should also not take what is permissible if taking it will subject him to valid criticism. In other words, he must not use any unbecoming manner in obtaining it. With regard to food, he should not overeat, although eating gives him pleasure. It is unbecoming of a

210. Related by Aḥmad.

Muslim to overeat, whether he is eating at home, alone, with friends or at a party.

The next quality is to maintain truthfulness in what we say. A Muslim must never tell a lie. In fact the Prophet stresses this point in numerous *ḥadīths* and speaks of lying as one of the characteristics of hypocrites. Needless to say, hypocrisy is strongly condemned by Islam. To understand the importance Islam attaches to telling the truth, we may refer to the *ḥadīth* in which the Prophet answers questions by his companions who enquired whether a Muslim may commit certain sins. They enumerated all cardinal sins and the Prophet answered that a Muslim may exhibit the weakness of character that leads him to committing such sins. When they enquired whether a Muslim may lie, the Prophet answered that he may not. According to the present *ḥadīth*, telling the truth is one of the characteristics which we should be so pleased to have that we do not feel sorry to have missed any other thing.

The fourth and final characteristic is to be faithful to our trust. This is indeed a correlative of being truthful. One cannot always maintain the truth in what one says without being faithful to one's trust.

We have always stressed the importance of taking our values and principles into the practical world. We should 'live' what we believe in. Therefore, if we give high importance to being faithful to one's trust, we should give a practical example of what that means. If at any time neglecting our trust gives us a particular gain, then we should show that that gain is unimportant. We should value being faithful to our trust as immeasurably more important. This not only gains praise for us among people, but also ensures God's reward.

The Prophet himself gave the best example of a man being faithful to his trust. When he was preaching his message in Makkah, he was met with fierce opposition. His people inflicted untold torture on his followers. He himself was exposed to derision, humiliation and physical abuse. Nevertheless, the very people who opposed him so determinedly recognised that he never told a lie and that he was always faithful to his trust. They always gave him their valuables for safekeeping, realising that with him they were safe. When the Prophet finally decided to migrate, having been directed by God to do so, the pagan Arabs of Makkah worked out an elaborate plan to assassinate him outside his own home. God helped him to escape and he left everything behind. In such a situation, someone might think that if he could take something belonging to those people, it would only be partly in compensation for what he left behind. The Prophet never thought of doing so. Instead, he charged his cousin, 'Ali, with returning all things deposited with him for safekeeping to their owners.

When we realise this, we appreciate better his valuable instruction that truthfulness in what we say and faithfulness to our trust are two of the four characteristics which, if we have them, should make us unconcerned about what we may miss of this world.

At times the Prophet himself raised a certain question in order to alert his companions to the need to maintain certain values or exert certain efforts in order to emphasise certain aspects of human behaviour which should be followed or avoided.

> 290. Abu Hurayrah reports that the Prophet asked: 'Do you know which are the top causes of throwing people in hell?' They said: 'God and His messenger know better'. He said: 'The two hollow organs: the genitals and the mouth. Do you also know the means by which most people are admitted to heaven? To fear God and maintain good manners'.[211]

This *ḥadīth* hardly needs any comment or interpretation. It speaks of the two strongest desires as being the two major causes for people being thrown into hell. This is perfectly natural because if people try to satisfy these desires through illegitimate means they will inevitably commit all sorts of sin.

Islam does not speak contemptuously of man's desires. Indeed, it deals with man as a complete individual, recognising that he has needs and desires which should be satisfied. It provides legitimate means for fulfilling these needs and tells man that he will be rewarded for having this satisfaction in only a legitimate manner. Sexual desire is fulfilled through marriage and the Prophet tells us that we are rewarded when we confine our sexual desire within the bounds of marriage. Similarly, if we eat only what we can buy by our legitimate earnings and do not

211. Related by Aḥmad, al-Tirmidhi and Ibn Mājah.

accept any money from illegitimate sources, we have a reward which God keeps in store for us. It should be noted here that what applies to food applies to all our earnings and material needs such as clothing, housing, etc. When we try to satisfy these needs, paying no regard to what God has forbidden us, we are liable to commit a great variety of sins, including adultery, telling lies, embezzlement of funds which we may have in our trust and even theft, injustice to others, etc. On the other hand, confining ourselves to what God has allowed us in the satisfaction of these two most important desires will enable us to lead a clean life which earns for us respect by other people and God's pleasure which admits us into heaven in the Hereafter.

To be conscious of one's duty to avoid all these sins and to guard oneself against committing them is called, in Islamic terminology, *taqwa*, or 'fearing God'. A person who has this fear tries hard to do what God has commanded us to do and refrains from what He has forbidden us. It is for this reason that the Prophet describes fearing God as one of the two most important ways of gaining admission into heaven. The other is that we have good manners. The two complement each other, since good manners, in its wider Islamic sense, means committing oneself to a totally virtuous lifestyle. If we acquire both aspects, we have the motivation to do good and to translate into practice what we are taught of good Islamic behaviour.

Abu al-Dardā' was a scholar companion of the Prophet who was renowned for his piety and great devotion. His wife gives us the following story.

291. (*Athar* 71) 'Abu al-Dardā' stood up at night to pray and he wept as he supplicated: 'My Lord, You have created me in a fine shape, so make my manners also fine'. He continued to do so until the morning. I said to him: 'Abu al-Dardā'! You have confined your supplication all night to asking God to give you good manners!' He said: 'A Muslim servant of God may have good manners and he maintains these until his fine manners cause him to be admitted to heaven. Or he may adopt bad manners until his bad manners take him into hell as a result. Yet, a Muslim servant of God may be forgiven his sins while he is asleep'. I asked: 'How is he forgiven while he is asleep?' He said:

'A brother of his may wake up for night worship and he prays to God, the Mighty and Exalted, for all things and his prayers are answered. If he prays for his brother, God answers his prayer'.

This story is self explanatory. Abu al-Dardā's comments are put in very clear terms. He has recognised the importance of good manners and devoted all his supplication during night worship to be granted improvement of his already good manners. He also emphasises what may be the decisive factor in the destiny of any person whether he behaves well or badly. If he maintains good behaviour and good manners, then God is bound to look favourably on him and instruct His angels to admit that person into heaven. If his behaviour and manners are bad in this life, then the angels guarding hell will lead him straight to it.

Abu al-Dardā', however, highlights one aspect of fine Islamic manners, namely, to remember our brethren in our supplication, when we worship in the depth of the night. Night worship, when alone, is a mark of pure dedication to God. It is a time when we address Him directly and He answers us. So, when we remember our brethren, He answers our prayers and forgives them their sins. He also rewards us for praying for them. This is one way of consolidating the ties of brotherhood and mutual love within the Muslim community.

292. Usāmah ibn Sharīk said: 'I was with the Prophet when some bedouins came. There were many other people from various places. Most people remained silent, but the bedouins spoke. They asked: "Messenger of God, is there any restriction on us in this or that?" They were asking about various ordinary, permissible matters. The Prophet said: "Servants of God! Know that God has removed restrictions, except in the case where a man slanders another unjustly. It is such a person that condemns himself to ruin". They asked: "Messenger of God, should we seek medical treatment?" The Prophet said: "Yes, servants of God. Seek medical treatment because God, the Mighty and Exalted, has not created an illness without creating a cure for it, except for one illness". They asked: "Which is that, Messenger of God?" He

said: "Old age". They asked: "Messenger of God, what is the best thing a human being is given?" He said: "Good manners".'[212]

The first thing to note about this *ḥadīth* is that people who were attending the Prophet kept quiet when they saw the bedouins come to speak to him. They recognised that these people did not have many chances to speak to the Prophet directly and learn from him first hand. However, the questions they asked were of an ordinary, simple nature. People should know these without questioning the Prophet. Hence, he himself drew their attention to something of importance, telling them of one grave sin, namely, unjust backbiting. This is a sin which people always commit. It is very easy to fall into the trap of backbiting. People tend to make fun of others when they are absent. When this happens and other people laugh, there is always the temptation to make further fun of the same person and this may lead to exaggeration, false claims and lies. Thus, insult is added to injury and injustice to backbiting. It is, then, a double offence which puts the person who commits it in a very difficult position. The Prophet expresses the difficulty by saying that that person sends himself to perdition. That is a very wise method of teaching. It goes without saying that there are other sins and some of them are more serious than backbiting. However, the Prophet did not want to burden those people with making a long list of sins. He merely pointed to something which takes place very frequently when people sit and chat together.

The bedouins continued with their obvious questions and asked whether they should seek medical treatment for illnesses. Here, the Prophet draws their attention to the fact that both illness and cure have been created by God. He has made one the cause to eradicate the other. Both illness and cure work by His will, and it is His will that made the rule of cause and effect. Moreover, the Prophet's answer serves as an encouragement to Muslim doctors to try to find a cure for every illness. They should conduct every possible test and undertake any research in the hope of discovering cures for illnesses which have so

---

212. Related by Aḥmad, Abū Dāwūd, al-Tirmidhi, Ibn Mājah, Ibn Khuzaymah, al-Ḥākim, Ibn Abi Shaybah and others.

far remained incurable. We should not, however, wonder that people ask such a question. People of different religions sometimes think that they need not, indeed should not, take any medicine, for medicine is, in their view, a challenge to God's will. This notion is alien to Islam which views both illness and cure as aspects of God's creation. When one abolishes the other, it can only work by God's will.

The Prophet's answer, however, makes one exception and names an illness which is incurable. Here again we note the Prophet's unique method of teaching. He seizes the opportunity to remind his questioners of the Hereafter. For the incurable illness is nothing but old age. We should not be surprised at the fact that the Prophet calls it an illness. After all, what does illness do to man if not to weaken him and sap his strength. Old age does exactly that, although it is caused by no germ or virus. When the Prophet says that old age is incurable, he means that it is a terminal illness which ends in death. When one dies, one has to face the reckoning. If the person has done well in life, he is a winner. If he has not, he is an absolute loser. The Prophet's answer, therefore, serves as a reminder to people to do well before they are overtaken by this incurable illness. If the victim of old age acts on this reminder, he can save himself the punishment of the Hereafter. If not, he is doomed.

The final question given in this *ḥadīth* asks the Prophet about the best quality given to man. This quality, according to the Prophet, is good manners. It is a quality which affects every aspect of life, especially dealings with fellow human beings. We are not surprised at the Prophet's answer because in another *ḥadīth* he states that the essence of faith is proper dealings with fellow human beings. Proper and good dealings with other people can only be achieved when one is endowed with good manners. Hence, we pray that God enables us to improve our manners all the time.

No limit to generosity

As generosity is an important aspect of moral values and good manners, al-Bukhari enters here a *ḥadīth* describing the Prophet's generosity:

293. Ibn ʿAbbās said: 'God's Messenger was the most generous of people. He was even at his most generous during Ramadan when the Angel Gabriel would meet him. Gabriel came to him every night when God's Messenger would recite the Qur'an to him. When Gabriel met him, God's Messenger was more generous than unrestrained wind'.[213]

This *ḥadīth* describes the Prophet's generosity in terms that are rarely applicable to human action. The Prophet never refused to give away anything he had. He never retained money for any unforeseen emergency. He would give away even what he needed for his own use. But he excelled himself during Ramadan. We need only to think of a blowing wind when there is nothing to obstruct its flow. This is how the Prophet's generosity is described.

The *ḥadīth* also tells us that the Prophet met the Angel Gabriel every night during Ramadan when the Prophet recited the Qur'an and Gabriel listened. It was a study of God's Words between the archangel and the last messenger of God. This was certainly a most blessed session. When we offer night worship during Ramadan and listen to the Qur'an being recited, we carry on this tradition that will continue, God willing, for the rest of human life.

Islam stresses the fact that we all have to account for our deeds, and it is the balance between our good and bad deeds that determines our fate on the Day of Judgement. However, God deals with us in mercy and He rewards us generously for our good deeds. A good deed which is pure of pride and self interest may be so generously rewarded that it may wipe off a long catalogue of bad deeds:

294. Abu Masʿūd al-Anṣāri reports that the Prophet said: 'A man who lived before your time was brought to account. Nothing good was found to be credited to him except for the fact that he used to mix socially with people and had business transactions. He was rich and he used to give instructions to his employees to write off the debts of those who were insolvent.

213. Related by al-Bukhari, Muslim and al-Nasā'ī.

God, the Mighty and Exalted, said: "We are better placed than him to do that. Write off whatever is recorded against him".'[214]

This *ḥadīth* describes the case of a man who had nothing of good actions credited to his account. Therefore he was certain of an awful doom. He could not hope for forgiveness, because he had nothing to show of good deeds or good intentions. He apparently had his bit of fun in this life and he enjoyed it to the brim. The only thing which could work to his advantage in the Hereafter was the fact that he wrote off any outstanding loans which he had given to people, and his debtors were insolvent at the time when repayment was due. By our human standards, this is merely a trivial thing compared with the good deeds which may be done by people who are dedicated to every good cause. Moreover, his action was addressed to other people, and was not meant to please God. He might even have had a soft spot for those who could not pay their debts.

We note that this *ḥadīth* speaks of what will happen to this man on the Day of Judgement. It speaks of the reckoning, the results of which are presented to God. Nevertheless, it is given in the past tense. That reckoning has not taken place when the Prophet said this *ḥadīth*. The Prophet often employed this formula in order to enhance the effect of the message he wanted to give. It shows that the reckoning is so real that it has actually happened and the results were actually known. The Qur'an also employs this form of expression so that its message is clearly understood. What is important to remember here is that when a situation like the one the *ḥadīth* mentions is expressed in the past tense, it means that this will happen exactly as related by the Prophet.

In this *ḥadīth* the man is brought to account. He has nothing to show to his credit except for the writing off of debts when the debtor was insolvent. When the matter is submitted to God, He looks at the man's situation. He knows that a person who lends money or other things to people is kind-hearted. To give money as a loan is to relieve the difficulty faced by the debtor for no particular gain accruing to oneself. This man, however, wrote off the debts if he found out that the debtor could not pay him back. God treats this man as a debtor.

---

214. Related by Muslim and al-Tirmidhi.

He had received all sorts of favours from Him. He should have shown his gratitude and praised God for His Grace. However, He did not do this throughout his life, and his negligence could be treated as an outstanding debt. On the Day of Judgement, it is still owed by him. In return for his generosity to other people, however, God writes off this debt, saying that He is in a better position to do this than the man towards his insolvent debtors. What is highly significant is that the man did not do so to please God. Had it been so, it would have been credited to him as such and he would have earned reward for it. But when the angels reckoned his actions, they found nothing in his favour. This indicates that his action was done for some other purpose. Nevertheless, God accepts his good action as something to be rewarded. The reward was of the same kind and the man's sins were forgiven as a reward for his good action.

295. Abu Hurayrah reports that the Prophet was asked: 'What is the main cause for admittance into heaven?' He said: 'To fear God and maintain good manners'. He was then asked: 'What are the top causes to throw people in hell?' He said: 'The two hollow organs: the genitals and the mouth'.[215]

This *ḥadīth* is the same as *ḥadīth* Number 290, except that the questions here are put by the Prophet's companions, while in Number 290 it was the Prophet who initiated the questions. Moreover, here it is the question about the cause that takes people to heaven that is mentioned first.

296. Nawwās ibn Sam'ān said that he asked God's Messenger about righteousness and sin. He said: 'Righteousness is good manners, and sin is what irritates you at heart and what you dislike that people should be aware of'.[216]

---

215. Related by al-Tirmidhi, Ibn Mājah, Ibn Ḥibbān and al-Ḥākim.

216. Related by Aḥmad, Muslim, al-Tirmidhi, Ibn Ḥibbān, al-Ḥākim, al-Dārimi and Abu 'Awānah.

This *ḥadīth* confirms that human nature dislikes what is contrary to the universal values that people have generally accepted. What a person does in private, feeling it to be wrong, and he, therefore, dislikes that people should know about it, because it is certain to bring him criticism and blame, is undoubtedly sinful. When people in a religious community view something as highly reprehensible, it must be a sin. By contrast, righteousness includes all good qualities, values and manners.

The Prophet was always keen to instil Islamic values in the hearts of his followers. He took every opportunity to drive certain points home to people. At times, he raised a question in order to draw the attention of his interlocutor away from the obvious answer so as to stress a different point.

297. Jābir ibn 'Abdullāh said that the Prophet asked a clan of the Anṣār: 'Who is your master, Bani Salamah?' They said: 'Jadd ibn Qays, although he is rather miserly'. He said: 'What vice is worse than miserliness? Your master is 'Amr ibn Al-Jamūḥ'.

'Amr was in charge of their idols in their pre-Islamic days. He organised the dinner party for the Prophet when he got married.[217]

This *ḥadīth* describes miserliness as the worst of all vices making it akin to a serious disease. Since the Prophet's question to those tribesmen was simply to name their master, the *ḥadīth* tells us that a miser simply cannot be the master of any group of people. The Prophet also goes so far as naming a different person as their master.

Perhaps one does not need to say any more about this trait which ruins the character of any human being who allows his love of money and property to overshadow his view of life. It is sufficient to remember that avarice and greed indicate lack of trust in God.

It is useful to look at the characters of the two people named in this *ḥadīth*. Jadd ibn Qays was a very rich person yet, his miserliness was very apparent to his own people. He belonged to a high class family and owed his distinguished position to his birth and wealth. He was,

217. Related by al-Ḥākim and al-Ṭabārani on the authority of different reporters.

however, suspected of being a hypocrite. This *ḥadīth* goes back to the Prophet's early days in Madinah, since ʿAmr ibn Al-Jamūḥ was among the Muslim martyrs in the Battle of Uḥud which took place in the third year of the Islamic calendar. At that time, the hypocrites were not clearly identified. The Prophet may have suspected something or another in Judd's character or behaviour, but he did not tell his people or indeed anyone else of his hypocrisy. It was sufficient for the Prophet to learn of his miserliness in order to suggest that he was not qualified to be the master of his clan.

ʿAmr ibn Al-Jamūḥ, on the other hand, was generous and a man of very firm faith. Indeed his attitude at the time of the Battle of Uḥud shows the sort of person he was. Shortly before the Muslim army was ready to proceed to Uḥud, ʿAmr came to the Prophet complaining about his four sons. He was lame and, as such, he was exempt from taking part in any fighting. Nevertheless, he was keen to fight, hoping to achieve martyrdom. His four sons tried to dissuade him from joining the army, reminding him all the time that he was exempt from fighting. He said to the Prophet: 'Messenger of God, my sons are preventing me from joining you and it is my dearest wish to step with this deformed leg of mine into heaven'. His sons told the Prophet that they were telling their father that they would fight on his behalf. The Prophet said: 'As far as you are concerned, ʿAmr, God has relieved you of the duty of fighting'. He then turned to ʿAmr's sons and said: 'Why do you not let him do what he wants. God may grant him martyrdom'.[218] Thus, ʿAmr ibn Al-Jamūḥ, was granted his chance to join the battle and he fought most courageously until he was killed and earned his place among the martyrs who sacrificed their lives for the cause of Islam in its early days. It was such great qualities which the Prophet recognised in ʿAmr that qualified him to be the master of his clan. In Islam, it is considerations of faith which distinguish a person. Birth and wealth are far inferior in importance.

As already noted, Jadd ibn Qays was suspected of hypocrisy. However, certain reports suggest that he later repented for his misbehaviour and that he became a good believer. That is something God knows best. We very much hope that such reports are correct,

---

218. Ibn Hisham, Al-Sīrah al-Nabawiyyah, vol. 3, p. 40.

because we feel that good faith gives the believer happiness both in this life and in the life to come.

Few words, broad meanings

The Prophet often used very few words to express great ideas. He was given this talent by God. This quality enabled his audience to understand his immediate meaning, because he often referred to what was taking place before them. It has also enabled future generations to improve on their understanding of the Divine message of Islam. While the understanding of past generations serves as a guide for us, we are not bound to limit our understanding to theirs. We can uncover further meanings as they may apply to human life as it develops.

> 298. Muʿāwiyah wrote to al-Mughīrah ibn Shuʿbah: 'Write for me something you heard from God's Messenger (peace be upon him)'. Al-Mughīrah wrote back: 'God's Messenger used to forbid idle talk, wasting property, asking too many questions, being close fisted and ready to take, undutifulness to mothers and burying young girls alive'.[219]

If we look briefly at each of the points the Prophet criticises in this *ḥadīth*, we will come out with a fine picture of what Islam dislikes of words and deeds. The first thing the Prophet prohibits is idle talk, but he expresses his meaning by saying that we should not repeat 'he said' and 'it is said'. In other words, he tells us not to quote people in an idle way. For one thing, we may not be able to ascertain whether their statements are true or false. Besides, we will then be telling people about things which belong to others and it is not up to us to divulge such things. Such an attitude tends to create problems for both us and for others. A Muslim should always be certain of what he says, as to its correctness so that he may not be accused of lying, and with due regard to the advisability of saying what he wants to say. Hence, the Prophet's discouragement of repeating everything one hears or comes to one's mind.

---

219. Related by al-Bukhari, Muslim and Abū Dāwūd.

Next the Prophet warns against wasting one's property. This implies a warning against using one's money in what constitutes disobedience to God's teachings and commandments as well as any use of money that serves no good purpose. Money should not be given to a person who does not value its importance so as to prevent him spend it according to his whims. Nor is it appropriate to spend one's money on things which do not benefit oneself or one's family or community. That does not mean to deny oneself the luxuries of life, if one can afford them. It means that once a person has paid out his due zakat, he may enjoy what God has given him provided that he spends his money on what is only legitimate. However, he will do well to spend more in charity and on what serves the community.

The next thing the Prophet speaks against is 'asking too many questions'. In fact the Arabic phrase may be rendered into English in more than one way. It may be understood as a discouragement from begging. This would mean a prohibition against begging without real need, or a prohibition against imploring people to give one a part of their money, and to be so persistent as to cause real annoyance to them by such begging. Thus, the Prophet's statement may be understood as meaning that if one asks another for something, he should put his request gently, without persistence. However, it is more appropriate to understand the Prophet's statements in their broadest context so that we do not miss out on any part of their meaning. In this particular instance, the Prophet discourages not only persistence by beggars, but also asking too many questions about people's affairs, and trying to find out what they prefer to keep to themselves. In other words, one should not be too nosy.

In the same vein, we can understand this statement as a discouragement from trying to imagine certain unlikely situations or problems and asking what view Islam takes of them. Since they are highly unlikely, then it does not concern anyone to find a solution for them and to make that solution part of Islamic scholarship. Should they happen, certainly scholars of the day will give a verdict on them. In short, too much questioning and asking is not appreciated.

The Prophet also discourages us from being close fisted while at the same time trying to get from others what belongs to them. He refers to this in the shortest of expressions. Al-Mughīrah states that the Prophet has prohibited 'rejection and demand'. The Prophet here prohibits stinginess. When a person is asked to give what he owes to others or to fulfil his duties, he refuses to do so. That is what is meant by 'rejection'. Nevertheless he always demands that others should give him that to which he has no rightful claim. Thus, he is eager to gain but refuses to give what he owes to others.

The Prophet also speaks against undutifulness to mothers. The Arabic term also includes grandmothers. We have spoken at length about being undutiful to one's parents. It is sufficient for us to state here that God has mentioned undutifulness to parents in the Qur'an as one of the cardinal sins. Indeed, on more than one occasion in the Qur'an, it occurs next to associating partners with God on the list of the worst sins. That mothers are singled out here is only a question of emphasis. It is easier for children to be undutiful to their mothers because the relationship between a son or a daughter and their mother is a very private one. It is easier for people outside the family to know about the type of relationship a son has with his father. Therefore, children are more reluctant to show their disobedience of their fathers because they fear being censured by their community.

The last thing mentioned in this *ḥadīth* is the burial of young girls when they are alive. This used to be practised in Arabian society prior to Islam. The main reason for killing one's daughter was poverty. God tells people in the Qur'an that they must not kill their children out of poverty or out of fear of poverty. God provides for every living soul. Normally girls were buried alive because boys were thought to be bread winners. They could earn their own living while a girl remained dependent on her father and family. Hence, when a girl was born to a poor family, she was buried alive. Another reason for choosing girls was that they might have brought shame on their families if they were to commit a gross indecency. Boys were not thought of in this light at all. Whatever the reason, Islam prohibits this crime in the clearest of terms.

299. Jābir ibn 'Abdullāh said: 'The Prophet (peace be upon him) never said, "No," to any request put to him'.[220]

---

220. Related by al-Bukhari, Muslim, al-Tirmidhi, Abu 'Awānah, Ibn Ḥibbān and al-Dārimi.

This is the same as *ḥadīth* Number 280, but it is given here with a different chain of transmission.

It is not uncommon for people to think that a religious person should not be wealthy. Somehow, the thought that being rich is incompatible with being religious has forced itself on the minds of many people. This may be due to the fact that when a rich person is not religious, his lack of faith becomes easily apparent. He indulges himself in many activities which cannot be sanctioned by Islam. He makes use of his wealth to do all this. Hence, his disobedience to God is not merely apparent, but also his being rich gives an impression that he enjoys being disobedient to God, and that his wealth adds to such enjoyment.

300. ʿAmr ibn al-ʿĀṣ reports: 'The Prophet (peace be upon him) sent for me, ordering me to be fully dressed, carrying my armour and to go to him. I did and went to him. I found him doing his ablutions. He looked up at me, then he looked at the ground. He said: "ʿAmr, I want to send you with an army under your command, and God may give you victory and spoils of war. I will give you a good sum of money". I said: "I have not embraced Islam in order to get money. I have accepted Islam because I realise that it is the true religion and I want to be with God's Messenger (peace be upon him)". He said: "ʿAmr, blessed be the good money for a person who is good".'[221]

It should be pointed out that ʿAmr was sent on this mission, commanding an army, when he was still a newcomer to Islam. This shows that the Prophet recognised his leadership qualities and the fact that he was a firm believer. When the Prophet put the case to him in the way he did, ʿAmr must have felt that he was being given money to strengthen his belief in Islam. Therefore, his answer to the Prophet stressed that he was a true believer who embraced Islam because he recognised its value and that it is the faith of truth. The Prophet reassured him that there was nothing wrong with having good money if the person concerned is a true believer. That is the decisive point. It is

221. Related by Aḥmad, Ibn Ḥibbān, al-Ḥākim and Abu ʿAwānah.

the person, not the money which counts. For the rest of his life, 'Amr showed that he was a good servant of Islam. As a governor of Egypt, he set a good example for rulers. He was instrumental in establishing Islam in Egypt and helped give Egypt its Islamic character, which it was never to lose. This speaks a great deal for 'Amr ibn Al-'Āṣ, the Prophet's companion, for whom wealth did not mean much. It was being with the Prophet that was his only motive for joining the ranks of Muslims.

301. 'Ubaydullāh ibn Miḥṣān reports from his father that the Prophet said: 'Whoever wakes up in the the morning feeling secure in his dwelling place, enjoying good personal health, having enough food for the day is like one who has the world at his disposal'.[222]

This *ḥadīth* underlines the most essential requirements for a life of happiness and contentment. The first element of these is a sense of security. When a person feels that he and his family are secure, then he has acquired the most essential element of contented life. Perhaps nothing is more detrimental to human life than to live under a shadow of fear. This is why dictatorship casts a sense of fear throughout society, allowing no one to feel really secure, not even the dictator's closest associates. Under all dictatorships, it is a familiar practice that close associates are made scapegoats for the regime's failure. Alternatively, they are victimised for the dictator's own sense of security. When he feels that they are looked upon as alternatives to him, he deprives his people of any obvious alternative by getting rid of associates through imprisonment, assassination, humiliation or disgrace.

For this reason Islam makes it one of the most important duties of a Muslim ruler to spread a sense of security among all people by establishing justice and the rule of Islamic law. Nothing is more abhorrent to God than injustice. He says in a *qudsi* or sacred *ḥadīth*: 'My servants, I have forbidden Myself injustice and made it forbidden

222. Related by Ibn Majah, Ibn Ḥibbān and al-Tirmidhi. The last one adds: '...is like one who has the whole world with all its riches at his disposal'.

among you. Therefore, do not be unjust to one another'.[223] Needless to say, injustice and insecurity are closely linked. Similarly, justice is closely linked with security. To feel secure and to feel that one's position, wealth and members of one's household, as well as oneself, are safe and have nothing to fear is the prime factor which brings happiness.

Secondly, the Prophet stresses the importance of good health. Illness wears people down and drives away any feeling of happiness. A person may have the money to buy everything he wants, but he may not be able to enjoy it because it may aggravate his illness. Many wealthy people have complicated illnesses which compel them to observe a very strict diet, depriving them of the chance to enjoy much of what they may fancy. Illness may sometimes leave them bed-ridden, unable to move about or enjoy fresh air or a pleasant scene. On the other hand, an able-bodied, healthy person can go where he likes and occupy his time with doing what he wants. This may bring him a sense of happiness for which a rich but ill person will always be ready to barter away all his wealth.

The third factor is having enough food for the day. Some people may be surprised by this statement. They may ask: Is a man supposed to look only to the present day's needs. What about tomorrow? Universal wisdom says that we have to think of tomorrow and the following year and to the future generally. Now, you want us to limit our outlook to the present day. In fact, there is no contradiction between what the Prophet states here and saving for the future. This statement emphasises that we should not worry about tomorrow because it has not arrived yet and its needs are not yet pressing. This does not mean that we must not think about it. When things became plentiful in Madinah, the Prophet allowed his wives to store provisions for a whole year. It is the balance between keeping the future in mind by not spending everything we have on buying immediate needs and momentary luxuries and keeping ourselves free of worry about the future that the Prophet is stressing. We know that God provides his servants with all they need for their living. If we believe in this, then we must not worry about what we will be eating tomorrow. He who

223. Related by Muslim, al-Tirmidhi and Ibn Mājah.

provides for animals and insects, will not forget to provide for human beings, whom He describes as the most honoured of His creation.

The Prophet stresses that he who has acquired all these three qualities is like one who finds the world at his disposal. Indeed, it is so because he enjoys the best elements of life. All three are essential for contentedness and happiness. When any of them is absent, then worry starts and misery is prolonged. If anyone of us looks at his children at home, knowing that they do not have enough to eat for lunch and he has no money to buy them anything, this will weigh heavily on him. If he has enough to feed them, he is free of such anxiety. The same applies to health and a sense of security. All three are essential for happiness. When anyone has them all together at the same time, he need not worry about anything else in the world.

302. ʿUbayd ibn Muʿādh reports: 'God's Messenger (peace be upon him) came out to us, appearing to have just had a bath, and he looked fresh and relaxed. We thought that he might have been with [one of] his wives. We said: 'Messenger of God, you look fresh'. He said: 'Indeed, praise be to God'. The subject of wealth was then raised, and God's Messenger said: 'Wealth is a good thing for a God-fearing person, but good health is better than wealth to a God-fearing person. To be and feel good is an aspect of God's Grace'.[224]

It should be noted that the Prophet did not open the subject of money and wealth on this occasion. He came upon a group of his companions and the subject was raised by them. Presumably they went on with their conversation when the Prophet joined them. Perhaps the Prophet said his words when there was perhaps some disagreement among them on that subject. We understand this from the version reported by Ibn Mājah, which differs slightly from the above report. It goes as follows: 'Those people spoke extensively about the subject of wealth and the Prophet said, ... Therefore, the Prophet put the whole subject in the proper perspective.

224. Related by Ibn Mājah.

It is clear from this statement that Islam does not find anything wrong with having plenty of money or being very rich, provided that the rich person is God-fearing. When he fears God, he is reluctant to use his money in any way which Islam does not sanction. Indeed, a God-fearing wealthy person is keen to use his wealth for generating more reward. There were a number of the Prophet's companions who acquired much wealth either during the Prophet's lifetime or after he had passed away. Perhaps the most famous among them was 'Uthmān ibn 'Affān. They provided good examples for every Muslim who is favoured with much money. They used their wealth in ways which were certain to earn them God's pleasure. In short, no one should be criticised for being wealthy; it is how he uses his wealth which earns him either praise or criticism.

The Prophet then points out another aspect which is superior to wealth for a God-fearing person, namely, good health. Since both poor and rich people may be healthy or ill, the Prophet's statement means that a poor person who enjoys good health is more fortunate than a rich person who suffers ill health. Perhaps nobody can disagree with this statement.

303. Nawwās ibn Sam'ān said that he asked God's Messenger about righteousness and sin. He said: 'Righteousness is good manners, and sin is what irritates you at heart and what you dislike people should be aware of'.[225]

This is the same as *ḥadīth* Number 296.

The Prophet took exemplary care of individuals among his companions in addition to his community as a whole.

304. Anas said: 'The Prophet [peace be on him] was the best of people [in looks and behaviour], the most generous and most courageous. One night the people of Madinah were frightened, [having heard some terrible noise]. People rushed towards the source of the noise. They were soon met by the Prophet coming

---

225. Related by Aḥmad, Muslim, al-Tirmidhi, Ibn Ḥibbān, al-Ḥākim, al-Dārimi and Abu 'Awānah.

back, having been ahead of all people to the source of the noise. He said to the people: "Do not be alarmed. Do not be alarmed". He was riding an unsaddled horse which belonged to Abu Ṭalḥah. His sword was hanging around his neck. He said: "I have found it [i.e. the horse] a good runner", or, "It is certainly a good runner".'[226]

This is an example of how the Prophet looked after his community. When there was some disturbance, he was the first to determine its source and what action needed to be taken. He was always keen to reassure his followers. At that time the people of Madinah were exposed to many dangers. They were not only facing the opposition of the rest of Arabia; they had enemies within Madinah itself, including the Jews and hypocrites. Their position in Madinah was indeed very vulnerable. Therefore, any source of danger could have started them worrying. That explains why many people went out that night to find out what fearful noise they were hearing and to deal with it. When they found that the Prophet had already accomplished this, they were not merely reassured about their safety, but were also happy to find him taking such care of them.

We note that the Prophet did not forget to take his sword with him in case he needed it. However, he did not bother to saddle the horse, but rode it unsaddled. The horse belonged to one of his companions, Abu Ṭalḥah. Some reports indicate that Abu Ṭalḥah later gave the Prophet that horse. Apparently, the Prophet realised that Abu Ṭalḥah would not mind him using his horse. Indeed, Abu Ṭalḥah was one of the Prophet's most devoted companions. On the other hand, in circumstances like these, the ruler, or the chief of the Muslim community, may borrow something which belongs to a member in order to use it for what serves the interests of the community. It is just like the chief or the mayor of a village borrowing a car without obtaining consent, in order to take someone in urgent need of medical help to hospital rather than wait for an ambulance.

This sort of report shows us that the Prophet lived with his companions as one of them, affected by any factor which affected

226. Related in all six authentic *Ḥadīth* anthologies.

them and taking every care he could to ensure their safety and security. These were some of the reasons why the companions of the Prophet loved him more than they loved their own parents, children and even themselves. He made use of this love to instil in them feelings of love for one another, making the tie of brotherhood which united them all a very real one. He never failed to emphasise the importance of this tie, making it a practical one, not something to which we merely pay lip service. Let us consider, for example, the following *ḥadīth*:

305. Jābir reports that the Prophet said: 'Every kind action is an act of charity [i.e. *ṣadaqah*]. It is an act of kindness to look cheerful when you meet your brother and to pour water out of your pail into your brother's water vessel'.

When the Prophet describes something as *ṣadaqah*, this description means that this kind of action is rewarded by God. The reward is at least ten times its value. In this *ḥadīth*, the Prophet includes every kind action, no matter how small. He clarifies this by mentioning that appearing cheerful when we meet each other is a kindness and, by implication, it is a *ṣadaqah* which is rewarded by God. The Prophet even encourages simple and easy actions which are conducive to strengthening the ties between us. On this occasion, he mentions pouring water from our containers into those of our brothers. This is a symbolic action which shows that we care for them. It is also bound to be reciprocated by a similar action. But more importantly, it encourages mutual care and love, which the Prophet was keen to foster. He was very successful in this because he moulded out of his followers, belonging as they did to several tribes, a coherent community in which everyone cared for the rest.

At this point, al-Bukhari again enters two *ḥadīths* giving examples of good actions that count as *ṣadaqah*, or acts of charity:

306. Abu Dharr reports that the Prophet was asked: 'Which actions are best?' He replied: 'Belief in God and jihad in His cause'. He was asked: 'Which slaves are best to free?' He said: 'The highest in price and the most precious in their owner's view'. His questioner said: 'Suppose that I am unable to do certain deeds?'

The Prophet answered: 'Help a poor person who has a family, or do something for an unskilled person'. He said: 'Suppose that I lack the strength [to do this].' The Prophet said: 'Refrain from doing harm to people. This is an act of charity [i.e. *ṣadaqah*] you do to yourself'.[227]

This *ḥadīth* is the same as *ḥadīth* Number 220, with the same chain of transmission. It is repeated because it clearly fits with al-Bukhari's subject matter and chapter heading.

307. Abu Mūsa reports that the Prophet said: 'It is a duty of every Muslim to give *ṣadaqah*'. People asked: 'What if he has nothing [to give]? The Prophet said: 'He does something with his hands, and thus he benefits himself and gives *ṣadaqah*'. They asked: 'What if he cannot, or does not, do that?' He said: 'He assists someone with a pressing need'. They still asked: 'What if he does not do that?' He said: 'He enjoins the doing of what is good, or what is right'. They asked: 'And what if he does not do that?' He said: 'He refrains from doing evil. That counts as *ṣadaqah* for him'.[228]

This *ḥadīth* is the same as Number 225, but with slightly different wording although the meaning does not change as a result.

---

227. Related by Aḥmad, al-Bukhari, Muslim, al-Nasā'ī, al-Dārimi and Ibn Ḥibbān.
228. Related by al-Bukhari, Muslim and al-Nasā'ī.

18

The Prophet's Supplication

ALL BELIEVERS TURN to God and pray to Him for all sorts of things, relating to this present life or to the life to come. The Prophet describes supplication as 'the essence of worship'. So what did he pray for?

> 308. 'Abdullāh ibn 'Amr reports that God's Messenger frequently used the following form in his supplication: 'My Lord, I beseech you to grant me health, rectitude, trustworthiness, good manners and satisfaction with whatever You decree'.[229]

A brief look at each of these qualities is sufficient to make us realise their importance and why the Prophet frequently included them in his supplication.

---

229. Related by al-Bayhaqi and al-Bazzār.

Health is perhaps the most important quality and gives a human being what he wishes for. In all societies, regardless of their prevailing faith or philosophy, standard of civilisation, and all other considerations, when you ask a pregnant woman to express her desire for her unborn child, most often you will hear that she asks for nothing other than that her child should be healthy. This is due to the fact that with health, human beings can do something about their lot. If they are unhealthy, especially if that is a continuous condition from childhood, they suffer a great deal.

The Arabic term, *'iffah*, which is translated here as 'rectitude', stresses in the first instance the importance of being virtuous. It is closely associated with fidelity in marriage, but it certainly has much wider significance. It actually refers to excellence acquired through obedience to the Islamic moral code. Self-discipline is clearly implied here. What the Prophet is praying for, then, is to have the motivation to always choose what is right and legitimate and to stop short of committing any sinful action.

Trustworthiness refers to the quality of being honest with oneself and in one's dealings with others. It should be remembered that the Prophet was always trustworthy. In fact, long before he received Divine revelations and before the beginning of his prophethood, he demonstrated a degree of honesty which was, to his compatriots and indeed by all standards, exemplary. This earned him the title 'trustworthy'. The fact that he included trustworthiness in his prayer shows the great importance he attached to it.

In a strictly Islamic sense, however, the term has an added significance of being faithful to the trust that God has assigned to us, namely, the task of building the earth and establishing a system of living worthy of man. This means a system that upholds all the proper values and provides the motivation to observe them all the time. This only comes through the implementation of God's law. Indeed, we are entrusted with its implementation and being worthy of, and true to, this trust means to do our best to implement it properly.

We have spoken extensively about what 'good manners' mean in the Islamic sense. We do not need to repeat this again here. The fact that the Prophet did not omit this in a supplication he used very frequently tells of its importance.

The last thing included in the Prophet's supplication is to be satisfied with one's lot, or what God has decreed for him. This is a superior level to that of being patient in adversity. Patience means restraining oneself from expressing dissatisfaction and asking the removal of what causes such dissatisfaction. What the Prophet is praying for here is to be content with our fortune, even when that is much to our dislike. It is to actually feel that whatever we receive from God is eventually to our benefit. This is a concept of interest in Islamic literature. The Prophet says: 'I wonder at the case of a true believer: if he happens to suffer a misfortune, he shows patience and that is good for him; and if he receives good fortune, he expresses his gratitude to God for having given it to him, and that is good for him'.[230] But as we say, to be satisfied with one's fortunes and content with one's lot is of an even higher degree. It ensures happiness in all situations, and it is such happiness that earns reward from God. Ultimately, this leads to happiness in the Hereafter.

309. Yazīd ibn Bābanūs said: 'We went to 'Ā'ishah and said to her: "Mother of the believers! What were God's Messenger's manners like?" She answered: "His manners were [a practical translation of] the Qur'an. Do you read the surah entitled 'The Believers'? Read this surah which begins with, 'Successful are the believers'."

Yazīd said: 'So I recited: "*Truly, successful shall be the believers, who humble themselves in their prayer, who turn away from all that is frivolous, who are active in deeds of charity, who refrain from sex except with those joined to them in marriage*". (23: 1-6) She said: "Such were the manners of God's Messenger [peace be on him]".'[231]

'Ā'ishah's description of the Prophet's manners is both concise and expressive. What it means is that the Prophet observed everything that the Qur'an ordered and refrained from everything it described as improper or unbecoming of believers. Every quality, attitude or

230. Related by Muslim.
231. Related by al-Nasā'ī and al-Ḥākim.

behaviour the Qur'an encourages, recommends or praises, whether directly or in the context of describing other prophets, or relating their stories with their communities, was followed or observed by the Prophet. Conversely, everything the Qur'an criticises, directly or indirectly, the Prophet avoided. This is by no means easy. It requires a fine sense of distinction and a mind that is always alert to what is becoming or unbecoming of a man whom God has chosen to convey His message. But diligence in such a pursuit is bound to develop and enhance a sense of priority which seeks to win God's pleasure in this life and happiness in the life to come. Such a quality was acquired by the Prophet's companions as well as countless others in subsequent generations. It is not difficult to acquire by the person who sets his objectives clearly and works hard to win God's pleasure.

This is, however, a very general description of the Prophet's manner. We have a large number of *ḥadīths* which describe one aspect or another of the Prophet's manners or the moral values he observed. When we read these, we are bound to come to the conclusion that in action and in words, the Prophet was exemplary; his manners were faultless and his moral values were of the highest standard. Take, for example, the proper way of talking to people:

310. Sālim ibn 'Abdullāh said: 'I never heard 'Abdullāh curse anyone'.

Sālim used to say that 'Abdullāh ibn 'Umar reported: 'God's Messenger said: "It is unfitting for a believer to be one who curses [others]".'[232]

The emphasis in this *ḥadīth* is on a person's language. A believer does not curse others. What is meant by cursing is an earnest request that the one who is so cursed should be rejected by God and denied His mercy. This is not acceptable from the Islamic point of view. A believer always prays to God to have mercy on others, even those with whom he may disagree or quarrel. Even in these cases, a believer should conduct himself according to the best manners of propriety, always

---

232. Related by al-Tirmidhi and al-Ḥākim.

using proper language and refraining from using obscenities. This is what the Prophet says about a believer's language:

> 311. Jābir ibn 'Abdullāh reports that the Prophet said: 'God does not love the one who is quick with obscenities and coarse language, nor one who yells in the marketplace'.

This *ḥadīth* refers to types of bad language so as to emphasise that a believer always watches his words and selects proper language. Backbiting is cowardly and unbecoming of a believer. If a person has something to say against another, it should only be said within a proper context, such as when he is asked to testify about that person's character, either in court or when his advice is sought by others who may have important business to do with that person. For example, if you are asked about the character of a person by the family of a woman to whom he has proposed marriage, or by a person who wants to enter into a commercial partnership with him, you have to state your opinion truthfully, pointing out any defects in a fair manner and without exaggeration. Nor should you forget to mention the person's good points.

Moreover, a believer does not use abusive or obscene language. Obscenity may come naturally to many people but a believer always refrains from it because it is unbecoming; it cannot be sanctioned by good taste. We have the perfect example of how the Prophet watched his words.

'Ā'ishah reports that a group of Jews see the Prophet and instead of using the Islamic greeting of *al-salam 'alaykum*, which means 'peace be to you', they said, *assām 'alaykum*, substituting a word that means death for that which means peace. In other words, these Jews twisted their tongues in order to distort the word of peace, turning the greeting into a death wish.

> 312. 'Ā'ishah reports: 'Some Jews came to the Prophet (peace be upon him) and said: "assām 'alaykum". 'Ā'ishah said to them, "and to you. May God curse you and may He be angry with you". The Prophet said: "Take it easy, 'Ā'ishah. You should be gentle and refrain from violent and aggressive language". She

said to him: "Have you not heard what they said?" He answered: "And have you not heard what I said? I returned their word to them. My request will be answered while theirs remains unanswered".'[233]

This *ḥadīth* gives us an example of the Prophet's forbearance and his unwillingness to answer a bad word with another. These Jews who went to him pretended to greet him while in fact expressing a wish that he should die. Hence 'Ā'ishah's angry reply. As a loving wife and a believer, she must have felt that the Jews' attitude was sly, wicked and ill-mannered. Therefore, she replied in kind. The Prophet restrained her, emphasising that it was far better to restrain oneself and keep one's reaction to reasonable limits. He had noticed what the Jews had said and replied to their wish by saying: 'And the same to you' (*wa 'alaykum*). His good manners did not allow him to make a reply like the natural reaction expressed by his wife. He was simply returning the wish, knowing that God would answer his wish and reject that of the Jews. It was they who had started with such unkindness. God does not answer a prayer that wishes something bad should befall another person unless it is made by a parent or someone who is unjustly treated. The Prophet's return wish would certainly be answered, not merely because he was the Prophet and his prayers are answered, but also because he was, in this particular situation, the aggrieved party. The Jews treated him unfairly and that is enough reason for his prayer to be answered.

313. 'Abdullāh ibn Mas'ūd reports that the Prophet said: 'A believer is not a person who defames, curses, uses abusive language or obscenities'.[234]

This *ḥadīth* is similar to Number 311, but stresses, in addition, the defamation of others, particularly in backbiting. This is totally unacceptable in Islam.

---

233. Related by al-Bukhari, Muslim, al-Nasā'ī, al-Tirmidhi and Ibn Mājah.

234. Related by Aḥmad, al-Tirmidhi, Ibn Ḥibbān and al-Ḥākim.

When we remember that good manners are a social exercise, we can easily appreciate that words are as important as deeds. A kind word is always welcome. In fact, what people say to one another is of great importance in strengthening social ties and building a united community. It is only natural, therefore, that Islam should take care to direct its followers to select their words well and to say only what is useful, truthful and conducive to strengthening community feeling.

314. Abu Hurayrah reports that the Prophet said: 'A double faced person should never be trusted'.[235]

One quality which Islam condemns is speaking differently about people in different situations. We have all come across those who speak ill of someone in their absence, identifying defects, exaggerating them and portraying them in a generally bad light. Should that same person appear on the scene, they immediately switch tone and speak in a very friendly manner to them, praise them and try to persuade anyone who is present that they love and hold them in very high regard. They may try to explain away their first attitude with certain excuses that cannot reasonably be accepted.

There are others who are a little more careful than to allow themselves to say one thing and its opposite in the same place or to the same person. However, they will not hesitate to do so in different situations. When they meet you, they express their friendship and are prepared to do any service for you. When they are with others and you are absent, they do not hesitate to use any critical remarks against you, disparage your character and try to discredit you in front of others. They may go as far as doing this deliberately in order to harm you or foil your projects or make your efforts fruitless.

Moreover, people of this type go around speaking ill of others to their opponents, while extolling the praises of their interlocutors. However, as soon as they meet the first group, they lavish their praises on them while criticising the others.

All such behaviour is repugnant to Islam. But the matter may not stop at that. People of this type may fabricate stories, spreading them

---

235. Related by Aḥmad and al-Tirmidhi.

around in order to create an atmosphere of hostility between people. They do not care if that hostility brings in its wake trouble, quarrels or fights. They only want to enhance their own position with each group or to serve their own selfish ends. If this means that they should create trouble, then trouble they will create. Islam shuns such behaviour.

315. (*Athar* 72) 'Abdullāh ibn Mas'ūd said: 'The characteristic which is most blameworthy for a believer to have is the use of shameless language'.[236]

316. (*Athar* 73) 'Ali ibn Abu Ṭālib said: 'Cursed will be those who are given to cursing others'.

This is another example of how Islam refines the character of a Muslim and impresses on him the need to use only proper language, avoiding any obscenity or foul language. The unscrupulous use of vulgar and shameless language is blameworthy because it is indicative of loose character, selfishness and greed. All these qualities deserve blame.

Some people, however, do not hesitate to use foul, shameless language in any situation. They even boast of it. Islam certainly does not approve of their behaviour, because it teaches its followers to watch their language. The Prophet specifically employed various ways to drive the point home to his followers that a believer must give credence to his claim to believe in God and the message of Muhammad (peace be on him) in both word and deed. His companions understood this very well and tried to impress the same on others. Hence the second *ḥadīth* attributed to 'Ali ibn Abu Ṭālib, the Prophet's cousin and son-in-law.

317. Abu al-Dardā' reports that the Prophet said: 'Cursers will be neither witnesses nor intercessors on the Day of Judgement'.[237]

When we speak of a characteristic or a moral value which Islam tries to instil in its followers, we need to look at how Islam relates this

---

236. Related by Ibn Ḥibbān.

237. Related by Aḥmad, Muslim, Abū Dāwūd, al-Ḥākim, Ibn Ḥibbān and Abu 'Awānah.

to its overall message and fundamental principles. One of the most essential principles in Islam is belief in the Day of Judgement and that people will be resurrected on that day, when their deeds and everything they have said or done in this life will be reckoned either for or against them. They will then be given their reward or punishment according to the results of the test they have undergone in this life. An important aspect of this is the fact that the Muslim nation will be called upon to testify against other nations to the effect that God has sent a clear message to mankind and required them to believe in it. This is a position of honour. The Muslim community will be given this position as a complement to its role in this life as a conveyor of that message. Therefore, every Muslim is keen to be included among those who testify against other nations. The Prophet tells us that those who are given to cursing others will be denied that position. They will also be denied any chance to pray to God to show kindness to their relatives, parents or children. When we realise that this is denied them only because of their cursing, we can appreciate how seriously Islam views such unbecoming behaviour.

It has been pointed out that the Arabic term *shuhadā'* used in the *ḥadīth* and rendered in the translation as 'witnesses', also means 'martyrs'. Therefore, the *ḥadīth* may be understood as meaning that such people who are given to cursing others will never qualify as martyrs, nor will they be allowed to intercede on behalf of their immediate relatives. However, if we take it to mean only 'witnesses', we can add another aspect to its meaning. That is, that their testimony will not be accepted because they disqualify themselves as reliable witnesses due to their foul language.

The other point in this *ḥadīth* is that they will not be intercessors. We know that the Prophet is the only one who is granted the honour of intercession, but his is a general intercession on behalf of mankind, and another on behalf of his community. Moreover, he may intercede on behalf of anyone else. The Qur'an makes clear that intercession on the Day of Judgement is only by God's permission. He may grant such permission to whomever He wills. For example, those who die in childhood intercede on behalf of their parents and God accepts their intercession allowing them to go into heaven with their parents.

318. Abu Hurayrah reports that the Prophet said: 'A ṣiddīq cannot be a curser'.[238]

The Prophet is speaking here of a *ṣiddīq*, a term derived from a root that indicates truthfulness. A *ṣiddīq* is truthful and believes that whatever the Prophet said is the truth. He entertains no doubt whatsoever about the truthfulness of Islam and that it is the right faith. It was the title the Prophet gave to his closest companion, Abu Bakr. He later explained that Abu Bakr never allowed any doubt to pass through his mind with regard to the truthfulness of the Islamic message.

As the Prophet contrasts the term with cursing others, this implies that cursing is incompatible with truthfulness. In other words, there is an element of untruth about cursing.

319. (*Athar* 74) Ḥudhayfah said 'When people exchange curses, the curse will certainly befall them'.

Islam tries to relate results to causes. In this context of refraining from using foul or shameless language, it teaches its followers that when people exchange curses, they bring about that curse on themselves. This is what Ḥudhayfah, a prominent Anṣāri companion of the Prophet emphasised. This *ḥadīth* is similar to one which forbids a Muslim to call another Muslim an unbeliever. It states that if one person calls another an unbeliever, then that description will certainly be true of one of them. It means that either the person so described or the one who attributed the description is truly an unbeliever.

Cursing is one way of expressing anger. A quick tempered person is likely to curse those who cause him fury. It is well known that anger causes a person to behave irrationally, without thinking. Most people instinctively curse those who infuriate them. A believer should try to check his anger and not allow himself to abuse or curse others. As mentioned in *ḥadīth* Number 315 above, a believer could curse others without it taking him beyond the pale of Islam. However, it is something that is very strongly discouraged. There is perhaps no more expressive way of discouraging it than that used by the Prophet:

---

238. Related by al-Ḥākim and Abu 'Awānah.

320. 'Ā'ishah reports that Abu Bakr cursed some of his slaves. The Prophet said to him: 'Abu Bakr! To curse and to be truthful [i.e. *ṣidddīq*]! No, by the Lord of the Ka'bah!' He repeated this twice or three times. So on the same day Abu Bakr set some of his slaves free. He then came to the Prophet and said: 'I will not do it again [meaning the cursing]'.[239]

This story, reported by 'Ā'ishah, the Prophet's wife and Abu Bakr's daughter, is highly expressive. The Prophet indicated in the most emphatic way that to be an adherent to the truth and to curse are two incompatible qualities. Abu Bakr was a believer in the truth, a *ṣiddīq*. The Prophet gave him that title which testified to his truthfulness and to his firm belief in Islam. Abu Bakr, however, was a human being who could be infuriated by the actions of his subordinates. Although Abu Bakr was generally very kind to his slaves, he could be put into a rage by some of them if they did something unpardonable. In this particular case, some of them did so and Abu Bakr was infuriated. Hence, he cursed them.

However, the Prophet was close at hand and he heard him. He wanted to give Abu Bakr a lesson which he could never forget. The Prophet was certainly very kind to Abu Bakr and he wanted him to live up to his title and to set an example for all Muslims across all generations. He, therefore, reminded him of that quality which must have been dearest to Abu Bakr, namely, dedication to the truth, emphasising that this cannot be compatible with cursing others. Abu Bakr realised his mistake and thought of a way of doing justice to these slaves he had so cursed. In essence, he could think of no better way than to set them free, which he did. Yet still he was not satisfied, and so pledged his word to the Prophet that he would not do so again under any circumstances.

All cursing is unacceptable to Islam. However, people are given to invoke God's curse on others, by saying to them, 'May God curse you, or may God be angry with you, etc'. The Prophet took great care to point out that this is completely unacceptable.

---

239. Related by al-Bayhaqi in Shu'ab al-Īmān.

321. Samurah ibn Jundub reports that the Prophet said: 'Do not invoke God's curse on one another, nor invoke God's wrath, nor [invoke the curse of] the Fire'.[240]

This is a particularly severe form of cursing and the Prophet made sure of singling it out to emphasise its unacceptability. If God wants to curse someone and deny him mercy and grace, He will do so without the need to be invoked by human beings. For any person to so curse is to use the most emphatic expression of extreme anger. This can only aggravate matters between him and the person he is cursing. Islam is keen to teach its followers to always leave room for reconciliation. When they take their quarrels to extremes, that room for reconciliation becomes insignificant or non-existent. The nature of the Muslim community does not allow this. Hence, the Prophet draws our attention to it by instructing us not to use such language. He himself did not curse anyone, not even unbelievers.

322. Abu Hurayrah reports: 'Some people said: "Messenger of God, pray to God to punish the unbelievers". He said: "I was not sent to be a curser; I was sent as a mercy".'[241]

This shows that cursing and kindness or mercy are incompatible. God describes the Prophet as having been sent as a manifestation of His mercy to mankind. How can he, then, invoke His curse on anyone?

323. Hammām ibn al-Ḥārith said: 'We were with Ḥudhayfah when he was told that a certain person slanders people before 'Uthmān. He said: I heard the Prophet say: "A slanderer will not enter heaven".'

This *ḥadīth* is self explanatory. A person who speaks ill of others in front of the Caliph either aims to undermine their position or to enhance his own. He is motivated by selfishness, greed and bad intention. Therefore, he has no place in heaven.

240. Related by Abū Dāwūd and al-Tirmidhi.
241. Related by Muslim.

While all communities and philosophies try to maintain strong social relations, Islam makes it a duty upon the individual. It works to that end through the establishment of a host of values that complement one another and give the individual a sense of responsibility to maintain close and sound relations with the rest of the community. This means that everyone will be pulling in the same direction.

When something or someone works against this set-up and tries to undermine it, such action incurs very strong censure. The perpetrator is viewed in a very bad light and is warned against very heavy punishment. For example, backbiting is considered repugnant by all human societies. However, Islam describes it in terms which make it appear extremely repugnant to the person who contemplates backbiting and much more so to those who listen or are forced to listen to him. Backbiting is defined as 'mentioning your brother in his absence in a way which he dislikes'. Muslims are warned against this in the Qur'an: '*Do not backbite one another. Would any one of you like to eat the flesh of his dead brother? Surely you would loathe it*'. (49: 11)

There is another sort of backbiting which is even more hateful and repugnant. That is to go about in society spreading tales which are certain to spoil relations. If a man comes to you with a tale about one of your friends which suggests that he does not respect your friendship and that he speaks ill of you in your absence, you are bound to be upset. You may decide to have as little dealings with that person as possible. You may take such a decision when you realise that you have no means of proving whether what you have been told is true or false. Now, assume that this very person goes to that particular friend of yours and tells him that you have been telling tales about him, do not respect his friendship, and that you speak ill of him in his absence. He is bound to have the same attitude towards you. The net result is that your friendship is spoilt, broken and replaced by a hostile attitude towards each other. This sort of telling false tales and spoiling social relations is viewed very seriously by Islam.

324. Asmā' bint Yazīd reports that the Prophet said: 'Shall I tell you who are the best among you?' They said: 'Yes, please'. He said: 'They are those who, when people see them, they remember God. Shall I tell you who the evil ones among you are?' They

said: 'Yes, please'. He said: 'Those who go about telling tales about people, spoil relations between intimate friends and seek to bring affliction to innocent people'.[242]

This *ḥadīth* tells us that those who go about telling tales about others are certainly evil. Indeed, this is an apt description because such tales are bound to bring hostility within a Muslim community instead of close relations. By so doing, they replace unity within the community with division. People become weary of one another and they are unwilling to trust even those who are close to them. Thus, the very fabric of society is weakened. They may feel that they stand to gain as a result of spoiling certain relations. If this is the case, then they are exhibiting a degree of selfishness which cannot be tolerated by any community. They are placing their own interests above those of their community. While individual and communal interests should be accommodated as far as possible, without either encroaching on the other, for a person to try to spoil relations between people in order to ensure their own personal gain is most unacceptable. When this means that close friendship is replaced by hostility, their sinful action appears in a light that is extremely repugnant.

The last action of those evil people is described by the Prophet as bringing about affliction to innocent people. It is their aim that others, innocent as they may be, will be afflicted. Scholars have explained this as trying to facilitate sinful action for those who would otherwise have refrained from it. Fornication and adultery are particularly mentioned in this context, when a person makes it easier for another to commit such. This can only bring about affliction. On the other hand, the person who is persuaded or led to commit such a grossly indecent act may otherwise have refrained from it.

By contrast, the best people are described as those whose very presence reminds us of God. This is either a reference to the fact that they are very pious, much praised for their conscientious implementation of Islamic rules and abidance by Islamic moral values, or to the fact that when they talk to people, their discussion always encourages them to implement Islam and conduct their lives according to Islamic

242. Related by Aḥmad and al-Bayhaqi.

principles. So, it is either because of the example they provide of how a Muslim should live or because of the advice and counsel they give to people that their very presence becomes associated with remembrance of God. This means that they are indeed people who bring goodness with them wherever they go. They are certainly the best of people, as the Prophet describes. The contrast between such people and the other evil ones is complete. It is perhaps useful to mention here that the first type of people, i.e. the good ones, help maintain community ties at the strongest level. That is what Islam wants of its followers. Moreover, when people remember God they remember their obligations towards one another. When they try to fulfil these obligations as best as they can, their efforts are certainly conducive to improving social ties.

Publicising sinful actions

It is well known that Islam is a religion of serious morality. All acts of indecency are forbidden in Islam. To commit an indecency in totally private surroundings, whether it goes as far as adultery or not, is forbidden. To commit it in public is a far greater sin because it involves not only the violation of Islamic regulations on decency, but it becomes a public defiance of God's orders and encourages others to violate social moral standards.

One aspect of such encouragement is to speak about one's own violation of Islamic moral standards. If a person commits fornication, he has committed a gross indecency. If he is a Muslim, his religion tells him to keep quiet about this, repent having done it and pray to God sincerely for forgiveness. But if he goes to his friends and tells them about his 'adventure', describing it in terms which makes it appealing or interesting to them, then he is certainly encouraging others to do likewise. To start with, when he boasts about what he has done, he reduces the sense of guilt which should be associated with such a violation of Islamic morality. When his friends laugh at what he has done, they go a little closer to committing similar offences themselves. Therefore, talking about indecency is also forbidden. It is indeed viewed very seriously by Islam.

325. (*Athar* 75) ʿAli ibn Abu Ṭālib said: 'The one who says an indecency and the one who spreads it commit equal offences'.[243]

326. (*Athar* 76) Shubayl ibn ʿAwf said: 'It is said: "Whoever broadcasts an indecency after having heard of it is party to it in the same way as the one who started it".'

327. (*Athar* 77) Ibn Jurayj said: 'ʿAṭā's view was that an exemplary punishment should be inflicted on the one who publicises adultery'.

328. (*Athar* 78) Ḥukaym ibn Saʿd said: 'I heard ʿAli ibn Abu Ṭālib say: "Do not be hasty, spreading and divulging secrets. Facing you is a severe, distressing affliction that leaves people badly shaken, as well as long oppressive conflicts".'[244]

All these statements speak about discouraging indecency and violating Islamic morality by word of mouth. It may be suggested that words are harmless. If people joke about indecency, it does not mean to say that they will commit it the next day. Islam, however, does not take that view. It strongly objects to anything which is conducive to making the committal of indecency a little easier. If people refrain from speaking and joking about immorality, it will remain repugnant to them. They will not lose that sense of abhorrence which makes immorality exceedingly hateful. Moreover, if we refrain from joking about it, we do not run the risk of undermining anyone's reputation, especially Muslim women. To undermine such reputation is to commit a very serious offence. Therefore, it is far better to refrain from speaking about immorality or boasting about one's spoils in that direction.

When a person who has slipped into immorality, committing fornication or adultery, refrains from speaking about it, he is more likely to feel his guilt quicker and pray to God for forgiveness. When he does, his forgiveness may be more quickly forthcoming, for he will

243. Related by al-Bayhaqi in Shuʿab al-Īmān.
244. Related by al-Dārimi.

have committed only one offence which needs to be forgiven in order to wipe his slate clean.

God's forgiveness is always forthcoming when one of His servants turns to Him in genuine repentance. However, when a person commits one sin on top of another, he is less likely to repent and seek forgiveness. Sometimes, people think that they have committed too many violations of Islamic principles and that God will never forgive them. This notion is unacceptable from the Islamic point of view. God forgives all sins without hesitation. The thought that one's sins are too numerous to be forgiven should never be entertained by a Muslim. God's forgiveness encompasses everything when repentance is genuine and sincere. In a *qudsi ḥadīth* the Prophet quotes God as saying: 'My servants, you sin by night and day, and I forgive all sins. So seek forgiveness of Me and I shall forgive you'.[245]

In another *qudsi ḥadīth* the Prophet says: 'God the Almighty has said: Son of Adam, so long as you call upon Me and ask of Me, I shall forgive you what you have done, and I shall not mind. Son of Adam, were your sins to reach the clouds in the sky and were you then to ask forgiveness of Me, I would forgive you. Son of Adam, were you to come to Me with sins nearly as great as the earth and were you then to face Me, ascribing no partner to Me, I would bring you forgiveness nearly as great as it [i.e. the earth]'.[246]

Islam establishes a bond of brotherhood between its followers. It tells them that the believers are brothers and that everyone should be conscious of what may adversely affect his brother in order to avoid it. It then goes further to stamp out those common practices that could very easily erode any sense of brotherhood or communal feeling, namely, publicising one's friend's or brother's shortcomings.

329. (*Athar* 79) Ibn 'Abbās said: 'If you are about to mention your friend's faults, remember your own faults'.

245. Related by Muslim.
246. Related by al-Tirmidhi.

Needless to say, none of us is free of shortcomings. Nevertheless, it is always tempting to speak of other people's faults. When this is done, in the presence of others, it becomes a matter for laughter and derision. People tend to make fun of others when they find encouragement to do so by their audience who may participate with a contribution of their own. If this becomes known to the person so abused, it is bound to create ill feelings and probably hatred within the community. At least, it will encourage that person to retaliate by making fun in his own circle of those who had abused him. While such a retaliatory measure comes naturally to people, it is certainly not conducive to the improvement of social relations. The Prophet suggests the best remedy for this by instructing every one of us to remember his own faults. Since none of us is without fault, everyone may be made a source of laughter. Therefore, when we remember our own faults, we are less inclined to highlight or laugh at the faults of others.

330. (*Athar* 80) Ibn 'Abbās said commenting on the verse that says, '*Do not defame yourselves*': 'It means: let none of you take a stab at another'.

In fact, Islam views very seriously the practice of making fun of others; making it forbidden. Its prohibition comes in the Qur'an: '*Do not defame yourselves, nor insult one another by [opprobrious] epithet*'. (49: 11) What this verse forbids is to try to deliberately find fault with someone else. It is indeed the opposite attitude that Islam encourages, namely, to overlook the faults of others and to pardon them. It should be noted that the verse says: 'Do not defame yourselves', but we all know that no one defames himself. The Qur'an describes the Muslims as a single community and, therefore, they should look at each other as one entity. When we find fault with others, we are actually finding these faults within ourselves.

Abusing others by giving them nicknames is also forbidden. It is definitely un-Islamic to give someone a funny name and to repeat it so that he is so known when he himself does not like it. The appropriate practice which Islam encourages is to call a person by the name he likes best.

331. Abu Jubayrah ibn al-Ḍaḥḥāk said: '[The order,] "Do not insult one another by opprobrious epithets" was revealed in reference to us, the Salamah clan. God's Messenger came to us and every one of us had two names. The Prophet would address anyone, saying: "You, so-and-so". People would tell him: "Messenger of God, this name makes him angry".'[247]

However, if the nickname given to someone is acceptable to him and is not meant as flattery, which is also unacceptable, then it is permissible to use. If he dislikes it, then it is either strongly discouraged or forbidden, depending on the nickname itself and how hateful it is to the person concerned. We are, then, differentiating between a nickname which is acceptable to the person and one which is not. The instruction given in this verse of the Qur'an is not to use unacceptable nicknames; they create ill feeling and weaken community relations.

Islam teaches us to watch our words. We should be very careful in how we address other people. When we abuse someone, we give them a privilege which they may use against us. They can claim their right under such privilege. Even a single word may give him the authority to impose on us a very severe punishment.

332. (*Athar* 81) 'Ikrimah said: 'I am not sure which of the two, Ibn 'Abbās or Ibn 'Umar, gave his friend a dinner. A slave-girl was serving them when one of them said to her, "You adulteress!" The other said: "Watch your word! If she does not get you punished in this life [for slander], then she may seek to put you to punishment in the Hereafter". The other asked him: "What do you say if it [i.e. what I have said] is true?" He answered: "God does not love the one who abuses others or exceeds the limits of decency".'

Clearly, one of these two eminent scholars and devoted companions of the Prophet warned the other that by calling the girl an adulteress, he had given her the right to ask that he be punished. If she did not

247. Related by Aḥmad, Abū Dāwūd, al-Nasā'ī, Ibn Mājah and al-Ḥākim.

exercise her right in this life, she may do so in the life to come, when the punishment would be much more severe.

In the last sentence of the *ḥadīth* we have a clear example of how to be careful with what we say. Even when we know someone has committed some indecency, we do not go around and spread that information everywhere. We would be saying something indecent and God does not like such behaviour. This is in harmony with Islamic manners and moral values. Even when such indecency has been committed and what we say is true, Islam still discourages it, because by speaking about it we help it to spread.

333. ʿAbdullāh ibn Masʿūd reports that the Prophet said: 'A believer is not a person who defames, curses, uses abusive language or obscenities'.

This *ḥadīth* is the same as Number 313, but it is given here via a completely different chain of transmission.

Sometimes even good words are censurable:

334. Abu Bakrah said: 'A man was mentioned in the Prophet's presence. Someone [lavishly] praised the man and the Prophet said: "Hold it. You have cut your friend's throat". He said this repeatedly. [He then added]: "If any of you must praise someone, he should say: 'I trust that this person is such and such', if he really thinks him to be so. God takes account of what he says. No one may appropriate God's right to judge anyone as a good person".'[248]

335. Abu Mūsa reports: 'The Prophet heard someone praising another man in lavish terms. He said: "You have broken – or cut – the man's back".'[249]

---

248. Related by Aḥmad, al-Bukhari, Muslim, Abū Dāwūd, al-Tirmidhi, Ibn Ḥibbān and Abu ʿAwānah.

249. Related by al-Bukhari and Muslim.

336. (*Athar* 82) Ibrāhīm al-Taymi reports that his father said: 'We were sitting at 'Umar's when a man praised another to his face. 'Umar said: "You have stabbed the man! May God stab you".'

337. (*Athar* 83) Aslam said: 'I heard 'Umar say: "Praise is slaughter". Muhammad [ibn Salām] said: "He meant that it is so if the praised person accepts it".'

All these *ḥadīths* focus on a practice that many people are guilty of. That is, they praise someone to their face. This is wrong when the two are alone, because it gives the praised person a sense of self gratification. A feeling of arrogance may creep into him as he thinks that people admire him. It is even worse when such praise is given in public and the praised person is present. It involves an element of hypocrisy, particularly if the praised person enjoys a position of power or influence. Such praise becomes even worse if it aims to gain something as a result. It is then insincere and motivated by self interest.

However, these *ḥadīths* are more concerned with the effect such admiration has on the praised person. If it makes him proud or conceited, it certainly works to his disadvantage. Hence, the Prophet's warning.

Yet the Prophet himself praised certain people by name and criticised others:

338. Abu Hurayrah reports that the Prophet said: 'Truly good is Abu Bakr; truly good is 'Umar; truly good is Abu 'Ubaydah; truly good is Usayd ibn Ḥuḍayr; truly good is Thābit ibn Qays ibn Shammās; truly good is Mu'ādh ibn 'Amr ibn al-Jamūḥ; truly good is Mu'ādh ibn Jabal'. He also said: 'A bad man is so-and-so; a bad man is so-and-so'. He named seven.[250]

This *ḥadīth* tells us that the Prophet praised eight of his companions by name. The first three belonged to the Muhājirīn and the last five to the Anṣār. The *ḥadīth* does not mention if any of these were present when the Prophet said this. Most probably they were not.

250. Related by al-Nasā'ī, al-Tirmidhi, al-Ḥākim and Ibn Ḥibbān.

The criterion that al-Bukhari mentions in his subheading under which he enters this *ḥadīth* is that the one saying the praise should be certain that the praise does not adversely affect the praised person. Moreover, when the praise is confined to what is known of the character of the praised person, it is appropriate, provided that one is confident that the praise does not make the one so praised too proud. If this is feared, then to praise that person becomes highly reprehensible or even forbidden. It is also important to make sure that such praise does not tend to exaggerate a person's good points.

Kind treatment was the trait the Prophet always showed when he dealt with people, even though they did not deserve his kindness. Yet at times the Prophet's attitude towards some people could not be readily explained. Hence, he was asked by those who were close to him and he always provided the reason that was paramount in his mind to explain his attitude to such people.

339. 'Ā'ishah reports: 'A man sought permission to see God's Messenger, and [when the Prophet heard his name], he said, "This is a bad son of his tribe". But when the man came in, the Prophet welcomed him well and was cheerful with him. After he left, another man sought permission to see him, and [on hearing his name] the Prophet said, "This is a good son of his tribe". Yet when he came in, the Prophet was not as friendly with him as he was with the other man, nor did he welcome him as well. When he left, I said, "Messenger of God, you said what you said about the first man but welcomed him well, and said something [different] about the other but did not do the same!" He said, "'Ā'ishah, the worst of people is one who is warded off for being abusive".'

The first thing we need to explain about this *ḥadīth* is the Prophet's remarks in the two cases when people sought to see him. In neither case did the Prophet's remark constitute backbiting. He was making a simple statement about the status of the person concerned to alert those present to his situation. He did not go into any detail of what he knew about him, because giving such detail may involve backbiting. He simply gave a statement, like that of a witness. It was merely to warn those who were present that the character of the first man was suspect, while the other person was a good man. Needless to say, giving an unsolicited opinion praising a certain person *in his absence* is always acceptable.

The next question to be asked is whether the Prophet's welcome to each person was in line with his character. We note that the Prophet was more friendly with the person he had just described as bad. His explanation was that people may be given friendly treatment only to guard against the development of an unsavoury situation that may arise by treating them as they deserve. In other words, the Prophet wanted to win over that man by the kindness he had shown him and the warmth of his reception. He might in this way reduce the effects of his ill manners, or keep his relationship with him on a friendly basis. Needless to say, this was a great kindness by the Prophet because if that man had been given a less warm welcome and, as a result, he expressed displeasure with the Prophet, it would have led to an even worse situation. He would then make the Prophet displeased, and that could incur God's displeasure for that person. By being friendly to him, the Prophet sought to reduce his bad side, give him no reason to adopt any negativity towards the Prophet and provide him with a motive to mend his ways.

On the other hand, the Prophet might have had a reason for being less friendly with the other man whom he described as a good person. It may be that the Prophet was aware of a certain trait in his character which might have led to a misinterpretation of a very friendly attitude by the Prophet. This might have led him to think too highly of his own importance, which, in turn, might allow arrogance to creep into his character. Besides, the Prophet was friendly with all his companions. 'Ā'ishah would probably not have noticed anything wrong with his attitude to him except for the contrast with the first person whom he did not consider to deserve any praise.

Clear order

What should we do when someone starts praising another to his face?

340. Abu Maʿmar said: 'A man began to praise a ruler, and [on hearing him] al-Miqdād began to throw dust in that man's face. He said: "God's Messenger (peace be upon him) ordered us to throw dust at the faces of those who praise people [in their presence]".'[251]

341. 'Aṭā' ibn Abu Rabāḥ said: 'A man was praising another in the presence of Ibn 'Umar. Ibn 'Umar began to throw dust towards his mouth and said: "God's Messenger said: 'When you see those who praise people, throw dust at their faces'."'[252]

The first of these *ḥadīths* gives us a clear idea of the practice the Prophet censured in such clear terms. The man started to praise a ruler to his face. Needless to say, rulers love to be praised. People often praise them to exaggeration, hoping to be rewarded or at least to be looked upon with favour. Therefore, such praise is not genuine, and is often hyperbolic. It is, therefore, insincere. Moreover, it tends to make the ruler lean towards dictatorship, particularly when such praises come from different people. He gets used to this praise, begins to think it is all true, and becomes very arrogant. The Prophet wanted to put an end to such a practice in the Muslim community. Hence, his order to throw dust at the faces of such people to silence them.

342. Rajā' said: 'I accompanied Miḥjan to the mosque of the people of Basra. Buraydah al-Aslami was sitting there at one of the gates of the mosque. In the mosque there was a man called Sakbah who used to offer his prayers long, and he was clad in a cloak. When we were at the mosque gate, Buraydah, who liked to joke, said: "Miḥjan, do you pray like Sakbah prays?" Miḥjan did not answer him and went back.

---

251. Related by Muslim, Abū Dāwūd, al-Tirmidhi, Ibn Mājah and Abu 'Awānah.
252. Related by Ibn Ḥibbān.

Rajā' said: 'Miḥjan said: "God's Messenger (peace be upon him) took me by the hand and we walked on until we went up Mount Uḥud. As he overlooked Madinah, he said: 'Woe to this village: its people leave it even though it will be very prosperous. The Impostor (al-Dajjāl) will come to it and find an angel at each one of its gates, so he will not enter'."

'The Prophet then went down [and we walked] until we reached the mosque. The Prophet saw a man praying, prostrating himself and bowing down. God's Messenger asked me: "Who is this?" I began to praise him, saying he is this and he is that. The Prophet said: "Hold it. Do not let him hear or you will ruin him".

Miḥjan said: 'The Prophet walked on until he reached his rooms. He shook [the dust off] his hands, then said: "The best of your faith is its easiest". He repeated this three times'.[253]

This *ḥadīth* is entered at this point in this anthology because it includes the Prophet's order to Miḥjan not to lavish his praise on the man the Prophet saw praying in the mosque. Related to this is the fact that Miḥjan did not answer Buraydah when he said to him: 'Do you pray like Sakbah prays?' He considered the question as praise of Sakbah and he did not want to take part in it, because of what the Prophet had told him earlier. He related to his companion his walk with the Prophet in detail, highlighting the Prophet's words about praising someone to his face.

The Prophet also told Miḥjan something about Madinah, which became very prosperous after the Prophet had passed away. A large number of the Prophet's companions travelled to the areas that joined the Muslim state, and they settled there teaching the new Muslims their faith. He also told him that Madinah will always be protected by God, and even the Impostor (*al-Dajjāl*) will not be able to enter it, guarded as it is by angels.

It is also significant that the Prophet concluded by repeating three times that the best of faith is the easiest. This is contrary to all trends that seek to make it hard and rigid. Even these days we see many groups

---

253. Related by Aḥmad, al-Ṭayālisi, Abū Dāwūd, al-Nasā'ī and Ibn Khuzaymah.

that learn certain aspects of detail, in which there are different views, and they take a particular view and try to impose it on others, treating it as one of the essentials of faith. Such rigidity goes to extremes at times, making Islam appear too rigid, when rather it is easy and gives people options and alternatives.

Muslim poets have also devoted much of their poetry to God's praises and to pointing out the fine character of the Prophet.

343. Al-Aswad ibn Surayʿ said: 'I went to the Prophet (peace be upon him) and I said to him: "Messenger of God, I have praised God in some poems and I have praised you". He said: "Your Lord loves to be praised". I went on and recited some poetry. A tall, bald man sought permission to see the Prophet, and he said to me to stop. The man came in and spoke to the Prophet for a while before leaving. I then resumed reciting my poems, but the man came again and the Prophet told me to stop. Then he left. This was repeated two or three times. I asked the Prophet: "Who is this man for whose sake you told me to stop". He said, "This is a man that hates falsehood".'[254]

We all know that glorifying and praising God is one of the acts of worship Islam recommends. The Prophet also clarified that God gains nothing by our glorification or worship. It is we who benefit by it, because such praise gives us a clear sense that whatever blessings we have and enjoy was granted to us by God. It is not the result of our own endeavour. It is what God bestows on us of His Grace. God has also promised us that He will give us an increase of His blessings if we show gratitude to Him for what He has given us.

We need to point out here that the Prophet's last statement explaining why he told the poet to stop does not imply that what the poet was reciting might have included some falsehood. The Prophet would not have allowed him to continue if this had been the case. He simply informed the poet that to use poetry as a means to earn money by praising some people or discrediting others is to engage in falsehood. The Prophet merely pointed out a quality of the man

---

254. Related by Aḥmad, al-Nasāʾī, al-Ḥākim and Ibn Ḥibbān.

which highlighted why the Prophet was keen to attend to his purpose as soon as he came in. If a man takes such an attitude to falsehood, he is worthy of being honoured. Some reports mention that the man was ʿUmar ibn al-Khaṭṭāb. ʿUmar was tall and bald, and he certainly hated falsehood.

344. (*Athar* 84) Yūsuf ibn Nujayd said: 'My father, Nujayd, told me that a poet came to ʿImrān ibn Ḥuṣayn and ʿImrān gave him a gift. He was asked: "Do you give a gift to a poet?" He said: "Yes, to preserve my honour".'

345. (*Athar* 85) Ibn ʿAwn quotes Muhammad as saying: 'They used to say: "Do not give to your friend of your generosity what will be burdensome to him".'

ʿImrān ibn Ḥuṣayn was a companion of the Prophet and he was well known for his devotion. He was ill for thirty years but never complained or slackened his worship. When his visitors showed their grief for his suffering, he used to say to them: 'Do not be sorry for my condition; if God loves it for me, I love it'.

With such devotion, people wondered why he had given the poet a gift. Poets were given generous gifts by rulers and wealthy people in return for some lines of praise. They were like journalists in dictatorial regimes: they use their talent in applauding the dictator in return for well-paid media jobs. Needless to say, ʿImrān did not want a poet to sing his praises, but he gave this poet a gift in order to keep him quiet, so that he neither praised nor criticised him. This is what he meant by saying that he only wanted to preserve his honour.

The second *ḥadīth* tells us not to lavish one's generosity or hospitality on one's friend so that he becomes embarrassed by it and finds it a burden. Normally, a good friend likes to return his friend's generosity. If he cannot match what his friend has done for him, he feels that he is burdened by his friend's kindness. If this is repeated, it may lead to the break up of the friendship, because the one who is on the receiving end feels that he cannot match the level of his friend. Therefore, he stays away from him. Islam prefers that relations between Muslims should be preserved and strengthened.

The Prophet encouraged all Muslims to visit their friends and brothers in faith. When such a visit is made for no purpose other than the social aspect for which most visits are exchanged, it earns the visitor a reward from God and it earns the host also a reward if he receives his visitors well.

346. Abu Hurayrah reports that the Prophet said: 'When a man visits his brother [because he is ill or just socially], God says to him: "You are good and your walk is good. You deserve a home in heaven".'[255]

This *ḥadīth* provides very strong encouragement for us to visit one another. More important is to visit people who are ill, to enquire after their health and to show them that we care for them. Needless to say, when a person is ill, he finds visits by his relatives and friends most encouraging. It helps him to pass his time and bear his illness with patience. But also visits to friends who are not ill, i.e. social visits, are a means to earn reward from God. The reward which this *ḥadīth* outlines is inevitably felt to be far greater than the action merits. People normally visit their friends because they like them and enjoy their company. So why should they receive a reward for this? There is indeed no reason except for the fact that their community becomes more coherent and united. Islam is keen to achieve this goal because the Muslim community faces much opposition from different quarters. Unless it is well united and closely knit together, it cannot face up to the many challenges it may encounter. The best thing to ensure its continued strength is for its members to be well united. The *ḥadīth* shows that God Himself promises this reward, which includes the blessing on the life of the visitor, his journey, and also promises him a house in heaven.

Since God rewards us for visiting our friends and brethren for no purpose other than to maintain our ties with them, do we need to do any particular thing on such visits?

---

255. Related by Aḥmad, al-Tirmidhi, Ibn Mājah and Ibn Ḥibbān.

347. (*Athar* 86) Umm al-Dardā' said: 'Salmān visited us coming on foot from al-Madā'in [in Iraq] to Syria. He was wearing a garment and an *andarward* [i.e. short trousers covering the knees]'. Ibn Shawdhab said: 'Salmān was seen wearing a garment, with shaved head and dropped ears. He was told: "You have given yourself the wrong appearance". He said: "The real good is that of the life to come".'

Abu al-Dardā' and Salmān were made brothers by the Prophet when, shortly after his migration to Madinah, he told his companions that they should be bound by a tie of brotherhood. In compliance, each one of the Muhājirīn, who came from Makkah, became a brother of one of the Anṣār. This tie continued for the rest of their lives. Hence, Salmān and Abu al-Dardā' exchanged visits, even when they were living far apart.

Did Salmān undertake this long journey on foot? This is how the *ḥadīth* is reported, but some scholars suggest that perhaps the Arabic word *māshi* which means 'walking' was a distortion of *māḍi* which would make the *ḥadīth* indicate that he paid them a short visit on his way to somewhere else. If this was the correct word, then the suggestion that he travelled walking is not intended and he was probably riding.

Salmān's appearance is highlighted on this occasion. We cannot say much about what he was wearing, or why he shaved his head. However, his answer indicates that he cared little for appearances. Yet it is important that both host and visitor should show their pleasure to see each other, offering what may be pleasant or useful to their friends.

348. Anas ibn Mālik reports that 'God's Messenger (peace be upon him) visited a family of the Anṣār and he had some food at their place. When he wanted to leave, he pointed to a place in their house where water was sprinkled on a rug which was put out for him. He offered his prayers on it and made his supplication, praying for the family'.

The Prophet's guidance shows us the best course of action that cements friendship and strengthens social ties. As we have noted, the establishment of brotherly relations between all members of the Muslim community is given high priority in the Islamic social set-up. From this *ḥadīth* we learn that it is recommended that we visit one another and that it is also proper for a person in a high position to visit his subordinates if he is invited by them. Needless to say, the invitation should have no aim other than the strengthening of social ties and the demonstration of brotherly feeling. If the invitation has ulterior motives, such as gaining unfair advantage over others, then it should not be accepted.

We also learn from this *ḥadīth* that it is recommended for a host to offer his guests whatever he has available of food, drink or fruit. This helps strengthen friendly ties. Jābir ibn ʿAbdullāh, a companion of the Prophet who has reported numerous *ḥadīths*, was visited by a number of the Prophet's companions. He offered them bread and vinegar, and said: 'Please have something to eat. I heard God's Messenger (peace be upon him) say: "Vinegar is good food to eat with bread".' It ruins a person who has friends visiting him and he feels that the food he has at home is too humble to offer to guests, and it is equally ruinous for them to disdain what is offered to them.

Apparently, this incident happened when the Muslim community in Madinah was still very poor. Jābir was a young man whose father was killed in battle and he was left to support several sisters. It is very likely that he had nothing at home at that time other than bread and vinegar. Nevertheless, he presented this to his guests and requested them to eat, quoting the Prophet's *ḥadīth* in which the Prophet describes vinegar as something good to eat with bread.

The *ḥadīth* tells us about the Prophet's visit to an Anṣāri family and his praying at their home. A similar *ḥadīth* tells us that one of his companions, ʿItbān ibn Mālik of the Anṣār, requested the Prophet to come to his house and pray there. He told him that as an old man, sometimes he found it difficult to go to the mosque. He wanted the Prophet to pray in his home so that the place would be blessed. The Prophet obliged and when he arrived at ʿItbān's home, he asked him before sitting down where he would like him to pray in his home.

'Itbān pointed to a place and the Prophet prayed there. He then continued the visit.

349. (*Athar* 87) Abu Khaldah said: 'Abu Umayyah 'Abd al-Karīm visited Abu al-'Āliyah wearing a woollen garment. Abu al-'Āliyah said: "Such are the garments of monks. When Muslims visit each other, they dress well".'

The objection expressed by Abu al-'Āliyah focuses on wearing uncomfortable garments. It is not the fact that his visitor was wearing a woollen garment that was inappropriate, because in cold weather we wear woollen articles to keep warm. The objection compared his visitor's clothes to those of monks who wear rough clothes. Abu al-'Āliyah tells his friend that the practice of Muslims is to wear fine clothes when they visit their friends.

350. 'Abdullāh [ibn Kaysān], Asmā's servant, said: 'Asmā' [bint Abu Bakr] brought me a long black woollen shirt with a brocade border, with its sleeves having a similar span-wide border. She said: "This was God's Messenger's long shirt which he used to wear when he received delegations and on Fridays".'[256]

351. Ibn 'Umar said: ''Umar saw a silk suit and brought it to the Prophet. He said: "[You may wish to] buy this suit to wear on Fridays and when you receive delegations." The Prophet replied: "Only the one who has no portion in the life to come may wear such a suit".

Later, the Prophet received a gift consisting of a number of similar suits and he sent one to 'Umar as a gift, and one to Usāmah and one to 'Ali. 'Umar said: "Messenger of God, you sent me this suit and I had heard what you said about it!" The Prophet said: "I sent it to you so that you may sell it or meet some need with it".'

---

256. Related by Muslim.

The second *ḥadīth* is the same as *Numbers* 26 and 71, with slight variation in the wording. However, the two *ḥadīths* show that Islam does not disapprove of fine clothing; only silk and gold are forbidden for men to wear. Hence, the Prophet objected to wearing a silk suit, but he wore a garment with brocade borders.

352. Abu Hurayrah reports that the Prophet said: 'A man visited a brother of his in a village. God set an angel in wait for him on the road. The angel asked the man: "Where are you going?" The man replied: "[To visit] a brother of mine in this village". The angel asked him: "Has he done you a favour which you want to repay?" The man said: "No. I love him for God's sake".

The angel said: "I am sent by God to you: God loves you as you love him".'[257]

This *ḥadīth* expresses most effectively the importance Islam attaches to love within the Muslim community. The Prophet is speaking about two believers who belonged to an earlier Divine religion, but what applied to them also applies to Muslims in an equal, if not greater measure. The *ḥadīth* speaks about a man visiting his friend, whom he loves for God's sake. The bond between them is that of faith. God wanted to let him know the importance of such love. He, therefore, places an angel in wait for him. When he is close to the angel, the angel asks him about his purpose and he says that he is only motivated by his love for this brother in faith. The angel gives him the message he is entrusted to deliver to him: 'God loves him for loving his brother in faith'. Can anything be of greater value to a believer?

The shortest way to heaven

Muslims realise that to truly love the Prophet is the surest way leading to heaven. In support of this belief the following *ḥadīth* is quoted:

---

257. Related by Aḥmad, Muslim, Ibn Ḥibbān and Abu 'Awānah.

353. Abu Dharr reports: 'I said: "Messenger of God, what about a man who loves some people but cannot match their good deeds?" He said: "You, Abu Dharr, will be with those whom you love". I said: "I love God and His Messenger". He said: "You will be with those whom you love, Abu Dharr".'[258]

This is a perfectly sound argument in so far as it goes. The *ḥadīth* they quote enjoys a good degree of authenticity and the idea it expresses is correct. Moreover, when the Prophet said it, it was in the context of loving God and His messenger. We may wonder, then why scholars and others always tell us that we must do all sorts of things by way of worship and implement a strict code of conduct in order to stand a chance of being forgiven our sins and scrape through to heaven.

A careful look at the *ḥadīth* aimed at understanding the sort of love that ensures a high degree in heaven shows that its framework is one of action, not sentiment. Abu Dharr, the noble and conscientious companion of the Prophet, phrases his question in his typically modest way. He is not satisfied with what he does in the service of Islam. He believes that others are far ahead of him in this respect. His love of the Prophet is, however, genuine and sincere. He wonders what he should do in order to catch up with those who are recognised to be better servants of Islam. Hence, he specifies in his question that he is asking about catching up with their work; that is, their good deeds in the service of Islam. The question he puts to the Prophet is about 'a man who loves certain people but cannot match their good deeds'. So, an effort is made by him, but he views that effort as modest and unsatisfactory. Hence, he wonders what will happen to him. Will he have a chance to be with those whom he loves?

The Prophet, who knew everyone of his companions thoroughly, immediately recognised what was troubling Abu Dharr. He, therefore, reassures him that he will be with the ones he loves. Abu Dharr was a man of true faith and an always alert conscience. Moreover, ever since becoming a Muslim, he had showed that he was prepared to give any sacrifice that was required of him. In the Tabuk Expedition, which was meant as a test for all the Prophet's companions, the task the

---

258. Related by Aḥmad, Abū Dāwūd, Ibn Ḥibbān, al-Dārimi and Abu 'Awānah.

Prophet set was very difficult. The Muslim army traversed the desert from Madinah to Tabūk, a distance of 800 kilometres, in the blazing sun and heat of summer. Those who did not have camels to ride, had no hope of joining the army. Abu Dharr had but a weak camel. After having travelled some distance, his camel kept falling behind. When he realised that he ran the danger of not being able to catch up with the rest of the army, Abu Dharr carried his stuff on his back and walked as fast as he could until he caught up with the Muslim army when they encamped for rest. He did not do this for any reason other than his burning desire to always be with the Prophet in any effort to defend Islam and establish its state on solid foundations. Knowing him to be a man who understood that love must be expressed by action, the Prophet gave him the reassuring answer that he would be in the Hereafter with those whom he loved: Abu Dharr wanted to make absolutely sure that he understood the Prophet well. So he said that he loved God and His messenger and the Prophet repeated his earlier answer.

It is, then, within the context of action as an expression of love that we must understand this *ḥadīth*. Islam is a religion which requires action by its followers. It is for this reason that it has detailed legislation in every aspect of life. If action was of little value, it would have not been given the emphasis which we find throughout the Qur'an and the Sunnah. There is also a very similar *ḥadīth* which adds further clarification to this point:

354. Anas reports: 'A man asked the Prophet: "Prophet, when will the Last Hour come?" He said: "What preparations have you made for it?" The man said: "I have not prepared much, except that I love God and His Messenger". The Prophet said: "Everyone will be with those one loves".' Anas said: 'I have never seen the Muslims so pleased with anything after having embraced Islam more than they were pleased with this *ḥadīth*'.[259]

The context of this *ḥadīth* is set by the first question and the Prophet's answer. The man asks about the time when human life ends and people

259. Related by al-Nasā'ī, Abū Dāwūd, al-Tirmidhi and al-Ṭabārani.

are resurrected to face the reckoning and the judgement. It is a basic principle of Islam that everyone is judged on the basis of his deeds and actions. We go through this life preparing for the life to come by word and deed. We know that it is not enough to say that we have faith, unless our claim has proper practical effect. It is our deeds that we put forward in preparation for that reckoning in the hope that we will be judged favourably. Hence, the Prophet's answer is a question asking what the man has prepared for that hour. This is highly significant on more counts than one. First, it draws the attention of the questioner to the fact that he should not try to know the timing of the Hour, because he will not know it. That information God has kept to Himself. The Hour, however, is certain to come, and it always comes suddenly. Hence the need for conscientious preparation for its arrival. Secondly, there is an implicit reminder of the fact that for every person the Hour falls at the time when one dies. Preparations for it can only be made during one's life. When one dies, one no longer prepares anything for the life to come. There is, thirdly, the emphasis that it is action and good deeds which make all the difference when that Hour inevitably comes.

The man acknowledges that he has not prepared much, except to love God and His Messenger. The Prophet's answer is the one which gives his companions the greatest moment of happiness after they have become Muslims: 'Everyone will be with those one loves'. Again, we need to remember that the type of love the Prophet refers to is that which manifests itself in action and sacrifice.

We do not demonstrate our love of the Prophet by singing his praises. It is not enough for anyone to sing, recite, or even compose a poem to extol the Prophet beyond measure. Words count for very little. It is how conscientiously one follows the Prophet by conducting one's life according to his teachings that really proves that one loves the Prophet. Otherwise, it is extremely easy to spend a couple of hours every day repeating expressions of love. This does not require any effort. Heaven is earned only through great efforts. Martyrs are admitted into heaven because they make the greatest effort of all to demonstrate their love for God and the Prophet. We should follow their example if we truly love the Prophet and want to be with him in the Hereafter.

19

Young and Old

SOME *ḤADĪTHS* WERE reported by different companions of the Prophet and in different chains of transmission. This indicates that the Prophet might have said the *ḥadīth* on different occasions to different people, or that he might have said it on an occasion when he had a large audience.

355. Abu Hurayrah reports that the Prophet said: 'A person who is not compassionate to our young, and does not respect the rights of our old people does not belong to us'.[260]

356. 'Abdullāh ibn 'Amr reports the same *ḥadīth* in the same wording.[261]

260. Related by al-Ḥākim.
261. Related by Aḥmad, Abū Dāwūd, al-Tirmidhi and al-Ḥākim.

357. 'Abdullāh ibn 'Amr reports that the Prophet said: 'He does not belong to us who does not show due respect to our elderly and is not compassionate to our young'.

358. Abu Umāmah reports that the Prophet said: 'Whoever is unkind to our young and does not honour our elderly does not belong to us'.

359. (*Athar* 88) Al-Ash'ari said: 'It is a mark of glorifying God to honour Muslims who have grown grey; to respect a person who knows the Qur'an by heart, provided that he neither goes to excess nor is negligent of it, and to honour a ruler who maintains justice'.[262]

360. 'Abdullāh ibn 'Amr reports that the Prophet said: 'He does not belong to us who is not compassionate to our young and does not honour our elderly'.

In all these *ḥadīths* the Prophet mentions two groups for special treatment. The young who need compassion more than anything else in the way we treat them, and the old who need respect. People may love the young and instinctively be kind to them, but they may also feel them to be a burden, particularly when a child is rebellious, ill or unable to express its needs. Compassion eases any difficulty that a child may cause. It motivates the adult to try to understand the child and identify the causes of its happiness or irritation, enhancing the first and dealing with the second. Therefore, the Prophet stresses the need to be compassionate to children in all these *ḥadīths*.

On the other hand, these *ḥadīths* focus on the treatment that should be given to elderly people. It goes without saying that when one grows old, one's strength declines. Several faculties weaken, including memory, hearing and eyesight. Some elderly people may become unable to express themselves as well as they used to. The problem is that there is little hope of recovery; indeed, the reverse is true and the weakness is increased as time goes by. Hence, some people may treat an elderly person with condescension, which may hurt their feelings.

262. Related by Abū Dāwūd.

To be kind to an elderly person, showing respect and understanding, and overlooking that they may be slow in one thing or another, are all easy for anyone who has a clear sense of social values. We can learn much from the wisdom and experience of older people. To dismiss any elderly person as someone who is past usefulness is particularly cruel. Because it is easy to fall into this trap, the Prophet repeatedly stressed the importance of showing respect and kindness to our elderly; they are people we should honour.

Ḥadīth Number 359 provides a good example of how the Prophet combined the treatment of three different categories of people under one heading. The *ḥadīth* says: 'It is a mark of glorifying God to honour Muslims who have grown grey; to respect a person who knows the Qur'an by heart, provided that he neither goes to excess nor is negligent of it, and to honour a ruler who maintains justice'.

An elderly person who has grown grey may be only an ordinary person who never aspired to high position. He may be far removed from the person in power whom the *ḥadīth* tells us to honour if he maintains justice. Both may have little in common with a person who has learnt the Qur'an by heart. The latter may only be a youth in his teens. Nevertheless, the Prophet tells us that to honour all these people is a mark of proper glorification of God. It goes without saying that to glorify God is an act of worship which is required by a Muslim throughout his life. This is indeed the mark of true faith. Therefore, when the Prophet defines a certain type of behaviour in society, relating it to glorification of God, he emphasises its importance as a proper Islamic attitude. Consequently, Muslims acquire this as part of their social values.

This is the reason why the elderly have always enjoyed a position of respect in Muslim societies. Wherever we may go in the Muslim world, we find families taking care of their elders, even when providing such care involves putting in much effort and represents a heavy burden. Looking after a senile or invalid elderly person may be very hard and tiring. Muslim families undertake these tasks with patience, hoping to receive God's reward. In fact, old people's homes are scarce in Muslim countries, because society makes it shameful for a family to relinquish its duty of providing proper care for its elderly.

The Prophet mentions two other categories that need to be honoured. The first of these is that of those who learn the Qur'an by heart, without being pedantic or negligent of it. To learn the Qur'an by heart requires devoting much time to its study and memorisation, as well as a daily recitation of a long part of it. Thus a special relationship with the Qur'an ensues, one which always emphasises that Muslims must have a proper code of values and maintain proper standards of behaviour. Its injunctions must be implemented in one's life. A person who reads the Qur'an everyday will feel the need to mould his life in accordance with it. Therefore, he deserves to be honoured. However, the Prophet sets two provisos to deserve such honour: the memoriser of the Qur'an must not be pedantic, showing off his knowledge and emphasising his own importance; and he must not be negligent of the Qur'an. If he exhibits either characteristic, he forfeits his right to be honoured.

The third type of person who deserves to be honoured is the one in power who maintains justice. Scholars say that to deserve such honour, a ruler or governor must at least be closer to justice than to injustice. The more he exhibits of his justice, the greater is his claim to be honoured by all people. The fact that the Prophet includes honouring such a governor among the characteristics indicative of properly glorifying God serves to show the great importance Islam attaches to rulers and governors maintaining justice. This *ḥadīth* encourages everyone who is in a position of government to be just to his people and places a duty on the people to honour their just ruler. Thus, the proper relationship between the ruler and the ruled is established and nurtured.

One aspect of honouring elderly people is to give them the lead when they are in a group of people.

361. Rāfiʿ ibn Khadīj and Sahl ibn Abu Ḥathmah report: ''Abdullāh ibn Sahl and Muḥayyiṣah ibn Masʿūd went to Khaybar. They took separate ways amid the palm trees. 'Abdullāh ibn Sahl was murdered. 'Abd al-Raḥmān ibn Sahl, Ḥuwayyiṣah [ibn Masʿūd] and Muḥayyiṣah ibn Masʿūd went to the Prophet and spoke to him about their [killed] companion. 'Abd al-Raḥmān, the youngest of the group, started to speak, but the Prophet said to him: "Let the eldest among you

[speak first]". They explained the case of their companion. The Prophet asked them: "Will you prove [your claim] to the blood money of your murdered man – or he might have said your friend – by an oath taken by fifty of your men?" They said: "Messenger of God, this is something we have not seen". The Prophet said: "Then shall the Jews exonerate themselves by the oaths of fifty of their men?" They said: "Messenger of God, they are unbelievers". The Prophet himself paid the blood money'.

Sahl said: 'I chased one of those she-camels [given as part of the blood money] as she went into an enclosure of theirs and she kicked me'.[263]

The subject matter of this *ḥadīth* is the case of a murdered Muslim in a Jewish area, when there was no evidence pointing to the criminal. However, it is entered in this book, which focuses on morals and manners, because of the Prophet's order to let the eldest of the group speak first. This is the proper practice and it is beneficial in more than one way. Even if the eldest is not a good speaker, starting the discussion affords him the sort of respect to which he is entitled. His position of seniority is not overtaken by a younger man who may be a better speaker. When he has set the ball rolling, others may join in the discussion as the situation may require. If the elder is a wise man, he can draw on his experience to put the matter in a useful and beneficial way. If he is not a good speaker and he is not given his chance first, he may have to sit throughout the session without joining in, which may hurt his feelings.

The *ḥadīth* tells us of the murder of one of the Prophet's companions with no evidence or indication pointing to the murderer. He was killed at Khaibar, the main concentration of Jews in Arabia, and there was already much conflict between the Muslims and the Jews at the time. According to Ibn Mājah's report, his neck was broken and his body was thrown in a shallow well.

When the case was put to the Prophet, he could not impose any punishment without establishing guilt in the proper way. Since there was no chance of knowing the murderer, he suggested to the Anṣār

263. Related by al-Bukhari, Muslim, Abū Dāwūd, al-Tirmidhi, Ibn Majah and Abu 'Awānah.

that fifty of their men should take an oath testifying to the Jews as killers. They declined because they did not see the murder. The Prophet told them that the Jews could exonerate themselves by fifty of their men taking an oath denying the charge. The Anṣār refused this on account that an unbeliever may not find it hard to lie under oath in order to win a reprieve. The protestations of the Anṣār should not be misinterpreted. Sometimes, people who are at war do not hesitate to shed their scruples altogether when they deal with people from the opposite side. Since no trust could be established in the Jews' oaths, regardless of the number of those swearing, the process of testifying in this way could not ease consciences or pacify tempers.

The Prophet realised that he had to remove the tension or the Muslims would have had to go to war against the Jews in revenge for their murdered companion. He decided to pay the blood money, which means that the Muslim state footed the bill.

362. 'Abdullāh ibn 'Umar reported that the Prophet said: "Tell me of a tree that is like a Muslim: it gives its fruits at all times by the will of its Lord, and its leaves never fall". I felt that it was the palm date tree, but I did not want to speak as Abu Bakr and 'Umar (may God be pleased with them) were present. When neither of them spoke, the Prophet (peace be upon him) said: "It is the palm date tree". When I left with my father, I said: "Father, I thought that the tree was the palm date". He said: "What stopped you from saying so? Had you said it, it would have been more welcome to me than so and so". I said: "Nothing stopped me except that I saw that neither you nor Abu Bakr spoke. Therefore, I did not like to speak".'[264]

To honour an older person is a virtue, even when one may have to forego one's own rights or privileges. This is what we have been taught by our scholars, generation after generation, reaching back to the first Muslims whose manners, social conduct, values and mutual relations were moulded by the Prophet himself.

---

264. Related by al-Bukhari, Muslim and al-Tirmidhi.

The *ḥadīth* shows how well entrenched the respect of older people is in the minds of Muslims. Had 'Abdullāh ibn 'Umar answered the Prophet's question when he saw that neither his father nor Abu Bakr gave an answer, he would have violated no social norm. Islam does not encourage its young people to suppress their knowledge, simply because those who are older than them may not have the same knowledge. 'Abdullāh was simply honouring his father and the closest companion to the Prophet, Abu Bakr, who was older than his father. Had it been imperative that 'Abdullāh should not have spoken in their presence, his father would not have said to him that he would have dearly loved that he should say it, because that would have made him proud of his son.

363. Ḥakīm ibn Qays ibn 'Āṣim said: 'When death was approaching my father, he enjoined his sons, saying to them: "Fear God and give your leadership to your eldest. When people make their eldest their leader they succeed their father [in good practices], but if they make their young one their leader, they lower their own standing among their peers. Take care of your money and use it well. It increases respect for the generous and makes you in no need of mean people. Never beg from people, because begging gives the lowest acquisition a person may have. When I die, do not lament my death. There was no lamentation when God's Messenger died. When I die, bury me at a spot where the Bakr ibn Wā'il [tribe] will not know my grave. I used to stage surprise raids against them in pre-Islamic days".'[265]

This *ḥadīth* gives the advice of one of the Prophet's companions to his sons as he was about to depart this life. It is related to the present topic as Qays told his sons that they should give their leadership to their eldest, as this would continue their good traditions, while if they made their young ones their leaders, other people may discredit their elders. The rest of the advice is self explanatory, but the *ḥadīth* will come again in a much longer version, under Number 956, when it will be discussed further.

---

265. Related by Aḥmad, al-Nasā'ī and al-Ṭabārani.

Compassion for the young

The Prophet was the kindest of people to children. He always wanted to please them and to ensure that they were happy.

364. Abu Hurayrah said: 'When God's Messenger was brought the early date fruits, he would say: "Our Lord! Bless our city for us and bless our weight and volume measures (mudd and sāʿ), a blessing upon a blessing". He would then give it to the youngest child in attendance'.[266]

This *ḥadīth* gives us an image of life in Madinah during the Prophet's lifetime. Madinah was a city with plenty of agricultural produce, but its main fruit was dates. When the first dates begin to ripen and show early redness or yellowness, they begin to be sweet. It was then that the people of Madinah brought the Prophet such early fruit. Before he put a date in his mouth, the Prophet would pray for the city and its people, making his supplication, as usual, suitable to the occasion. Therefore, he prayed for a blessed harvest and plenty of produce. Rather than eat it himself, he would give it to the youngest child present. The phraseology of the *ḥadīth* suggests that on such occasions several children might be present. Therefore, the Prophet began with the youngest, as this was an occasion that promised a good harvest for the city and its population. Another report suggests that when the Prophet was brought early fruit, he would touch his eyes and lips with it, feeling very pleased and thanking God for it. He might or might not taste it. His supplication might include: 'Our Lord, as You have shown us this early fruit, let us see its last'.

365. ʿAbdullāh ibn ʿAmr reports that the Prophet said: 'He does not belong to us who is not compassionate to our young and does not recognise the rights due to our elderly'.[267]

---

266. Related by Muslim, al-Nasāʾī, al-Tirmidhi and Ibn Mājah.
267. Related by Aḥmad.

This *ḥadīth* is the same as Numbers 355-357, with slightly different wording.

366. Ya'la ibn Murrah said: 'We went out with the Prophet (peace be upon him) and we were invited for dinner. Ḥusayn [the Prophet's grandson] was playing in the street. The Prophet went faster, ahead of his companions and spread out his arms. The boy ran this way and that way, while the Prophet was making him laugh, then he held him. He put one hand under the boy's chin and the other on his head, then he hugged him. The Prophet then said: "Ḥusayn belongs to me and I belong to Ḥusayn. May God love whoever loves Ḥusayn. Al-Ḥusayn is a grandchild of mine".'[268]

To understand this *ḥadīth* we need to recall the general attitude of the Arabs at the time towards children. One day an Arab chief visited the Prophet and he saw him kissing one of his grandsons. The chief was shocked and said to the Prophet: 'Do you kiss young children? I have ten sons and I never kissed one of them'. The Prophet said to him: 'How can I help you if God has not placed compassion in your heart?'

The Prophet's behaviour, which is normal for any loving grandparent, seeing a young grandson playing in the street seems to be a clear departure from the prevalent social norms. The fact that the Prophet also prayed for everyone who loves Ḥusayn, makes us all love the Prophet's grandchild, so as to be included in the Prophet's prayer, which is definitely answered.

Against this background, which approved of burying young daughters alive for fear of poverty or fear that they might bring shame to the family, we appreciate the great change Islam accomplished when we look at the following two *ḥadīths*:

367. (*Athar* 89) Makhramah ibn Bukayr reports that his father saw 'Abdullāh ibn Ja'far kissing Zaynab bint 'Umar ibn Abu Salamah. She was about two years of age.

268. Related by Aḥmad, al-Tirmidhi and Ibn Mājah.

368. (*Athar* 90) Al-Ḥasan said: 'If you can avoid looking at the hair of anyone of your family, except your wife or a young girl, then do so'.

Ja'far, the father of the person mentioned in the first *ḥadīth*, was the Prophet's cousin and a brother of 'Ali ibn Abu Ṭālib. The girl he kissed was the daughter of the Prophet's stepson. It appears that they were not related.

369. Yūsuf ibn 'Abdullāh ibn Salām said: 'It was the Prophet who named me Yūsuf. He sat me on his lap and stroked my head'.[269]

This *ḥadīth* tells us how the Prophet lived with his companions. The father was formerly the chief Jewish rabbi in Madinah, but when the Prophet arrived there, he embraced Islam and became one of the Prophet's good companions. When his son was born he brought the child to the Prophet who named him. The *ḥadīth* does not say whether the stroking of the child's head was at the same time or at a later occasion. It is more probable that it refers to a later occasion, when the child was a few years old and the Prophet saw him. It was the Prophet's habit to be very friendly to young children.

370. 'Ā'ishah said: 'I used to play with dolls in the Prophet's home, and some of my friends would play with me. When God's Messenger came in, they might hide from him. He would call them to join me and we played together'.[270]

Here again we note that the Prophet was friendly with young people. 'Ā'ishah might have been referring to a time when she had only recently married the Prophet. Her friends were young women, and they might have been in awe of the Prophet, so they would hide when he came in. However, he would reassure them and call on them to join his wife. The *ḥadīth* also tells us that there is nothing wrong with

---

269. Related by Aḥmad and al-Tirmidhi.
270. Related by al-Bukhari, Muslim, Abū Dāwūd and Ibn Mājah.

playing with dolls as 'Ā'ishah, a married woman, played with them in the Prophet's own home and he was aware of this.

371. (*Athar* 91) Abu al-'Ajlān al-Muḥāribi said: 'I was in ['Abdullāh] Ibn al-Zubayr's army when a cousin of mine passed away. In his will, he mentioned that a camel of his should be given [in charity] for God's cause. I said to his son: "Give me this camel, for I am in Ibn al-Zubayr's army". He said: "Let us go to Ibn 'Umar and ask him". We did so and I said to him: "Abu 'Abd al-Raḥmān, my father died and bequeathed a camel to be used in God's cause. This is my cousin, and he is in Ibn al-Zubayr's army. May I give him the camel?" Ibn 'Umar said: "God's cause includes every good action. Since your father bequeathed his camel to be used for God's cause, then when you see a host of Muslims going to fight unbelievers, give them the camel. This man [Abu al-'Ajlān] and his friends are fighting others over the stamp of authority".'

Ibn al-Zubayr ruled Arabia and Iraq and tried to extend his authority over Syria so as to be the undisputed caliph. His brother Muṣ'ab was the commander of his army, and after winning some battles, he lost against 'Abd al-Malik ibn Marwān, the Umayyad Caliph. However, it appears that this *ḥadīth* relates to a later period, when the Umayyad army took over Arabia.

Ibn 'Umar did not see the fighting between Muslim armies as one that served God's cause. Therefore, he did not approve that the camel, consecrated to be used for God's cause, could be given to a soldier in Ibn al-Zubayr's army, although many scholars at the time considered him the legitimate ruler of the Muslim state. Ibn 'Umar felt that fighting between Muslims was totally unacceptable.

372. Jarīr reports that the Prophet said: 'God, the Mighty and Exalted, will not show mercy to a person who does not show mercy to people'.[271]

---

271. Related by al-Bukhari and Muslim.

373. (*Athar* 92) 'Umar said: 'Whoever does not show mercy will not be shown mercy; whoever does not forgive will not be forgiven; whoever does not pardon will not be pardoned; and whoever does not protect himself will not be protected'.[272]

374. (*Athar* 93) The same as *ḥadīth* Number 373, with a different chain of transmission.

The first *ḥadīth* is a direct quotation from the Prophet stating that a cruel person who does not show mercy to people when he has power over them can not hope to be shown mercy by God. This is not limited to rulers or people in government, but it applies equally to everyone who might have some sort of authority over others, whether they are servants, labourers working for him, employees of his company, staff serving under him, etc. In any situation where mercy is called for and is not shown puts the person who withholds it under the threat of this *ḥadīth* whereby they will be liable to be denied God's mercy.

Needless to say, all of us are in need of God's mercy, and we all are liable to commit sin, err and slip. We need God's forgiveness. Without it we will suffer His punishment. Islam teaches that God's forgiveness is available to all who seek it, but the two *ḥadīths* attributed to 'Umar make clear that a person who does not forgive and pardon his subordinates will not be forgiven or pardoned by God. Likewise, a person who does not try to protect himself from sin will not be protected from God's punishment.

The reporter of the last two *ḥadīths*, Qubayṣah ibn Jābir, was one of the best scholars of the generation that followed the Prophet's companions. Ibn Khuzaymah reports this *ḥadīth* in the same wording, but adds: 'Qubayṣah comments: "I have never seen anyone who has better insight in God's faith, or knows the Qur'an, or has better knowledge of God than 'Umar".'

375. Qurrah ibn Iyās reports that a man said: 'Messenger of God, when I slaughter a sheep, I feel compassion for it'. Or he might have said: 'I feel for the sheep [so as to be reluctant] to

272. Related by Ibn Khuzaymah.

slaughter it'. The Prophet said: 'If you are compassionate even to the sheep, God will be compassionate to you'. [He said this twice].

The man was soft hearted and felt for the sheep he wanted to slaughter for food. The Prophet approved of what he said and made it clear that compassion towards God's creatures will be rewarded by compassion from God Himself. Needless to say, all of us need God's mercy and compassion. Therefore, we need to nurture feelings of compassion towards people, animals and other creatures.

376. Abu Hurayrah said: 'I heard the truthful who never lies, Abu al-Qāsim, say: "Mercy is never removed from anyone except the most miserable".'[273]

As we have noted, many *ḥadīths* link God's mercy to man's being merciful and compassionate to people and other creatures. If mercy is removed from someone's heart, this means that this person shows no mercy to anyone else. As such, he or she will not be shown mercy by God Almighty. Thus, he is left to account for what he does, but he has nothing to present to God to solicit His mercy. As such, he is doomed and certainly most miserable.

377. Jarīr reports that the Prophet said: 'God, the Mighty and Exalted, will not show mercy to a person who does not show mercy to people'.

This is the same as *ḥadīth* Number 372, but with a different chain of transmission.

Parents are naturally compassionate towards their children. A loving, caring and compassionate relationship exists between parents and children. It has been given to us by God in order to ensure the continuity of human life. Islam stresses the importance of compassion in human society and promises generous reward for compassionate people. The necessity for compassion between parents and children

---

273. Related by Aḥmad, ʿAbdullāh, al-Tirmidhi and al-Ḥākim.

was stressed by the Prophet on many occasions. He himself showed much compassion towards children, particularly his own. We should remember that his three sons died in infancy, while three of his four daughters predeceased him.

378. Anas ibn Mālik said: 'The Prophet (peace be upon him) was most compassionate towards children. He had a son nursed in a place near the outskirts of Madinah. His wet nurse's husband was a blacksmith and we used to go to him. His house would be full of smoke from the forge. The Prophet would kiss the child and hold him close'.[274]

Ibrāhīm, the Prophet's son, was born to Maria, the slave woman sent to him as a gift by the ruler of Egypt. The Prophet frequently visited his son at his wet nurse's place, and he made sure that the boy was well looked after. However, the child died when he was less than eighteen months old.

379. Abu Hurayrah said: 'A man came to the Prophet holding a little boy. He cuddled the boy. The Prophet asked him: "Do you feel compassion towards him?" The man said: "Yes". The Prophet said: "God is more merciful to you than you to him. He is indeed the Most Merciful of all those who are merciful".'[275]

The Prophet used the fact that the father manifested his natural love and compassion towards his son in order to stress God's attribute of mercy. He tells the father that God is more merciful to him than he is to his son. In human relations, nothing can be stronger than parents' bond with their own offspring. Human beings disobey God all the time, yet He gives them all they need. When they use His gifts disobeying Him, He still forgives them, gives them more, and rewards them for the little good they do with admittance to heaven. God appreciates people's kindness even to animals and gives them rich reward for it:

---

274. Related by Muslim and Abū Dāwūd; and related in part by Aḥmad and al-Bukhari.

275. Related by al-Nasā'ī.

380. Abu Hurayrah reports that the Prophet said: 'While walking down a road, a man felt very thirsty. He then found a well, went down into it and drank. As he came up, he saw a dog panting, licking the dust because of his thirst. The man thought: "This dog must be as thirsty as I have just been". He went down into the well once more, filled his shoe with water, held it in his mouth [as he climbed up] and then gave it to the dog to drink. God was thankful to him and He forgave him [his sins]'. People asked: 'Messenger of God, are we rewarded for what we do to animals?' He replied: 'You are rewarded for any kindness you do to every living creature'.[276]

The image given by the Prophet in this *ḥadīth* is particularly effective. The feeling of thirst experienced by the man and the dog is well known to us that we almost reach out for a drink as we read the *ḥadīth*. However, what is especially effective here is that the man is forgiven his sins because of his kindness to a dog, an animal which is considered impure by Islam. Generally speaking, Muslims do not like dogs and they do not keep them for pets as people do in other countries. Muslims may use guard dogs, or blind people may have guide dogs, but unless they have a special purpose for keeping a dog, dogs are not allowed in their homes. Nevertheless, the Prophet stresses here that this man was forgiven for his kindness to a dog. This makes the image portrayed in this *ḥadīth* even more powerful.

A similarly effective image is given by the Prophet in the following *ḥadīth*:

381. 'Abdullāh ibn 'Umar reports that the Prophet said: 'A woman has been punished for what she did to a cat. She imprisoned the cat until it died of hunger. Because of this, the woman enters the Fire. It will be said [to her]; and God knows best: You have given the cat neither food nor drink when you imprisoned it; nor did you release it to let it eat of what the earth would give'.[277]

---

276. Related by al-Bukhari, Muslim, Abū Dāwūd and Ibn Ḥibbān.
277. Related by al-Bukhari and Muslim.

The last two *ḥadīths* are mutually complementary. In the one about the dog, the man is rewarded for his kindness to an animal, while in the second the woman is punished in hell for her cruelty to a cat. These two *ḥadīths* should always be in the minds of Muslims when they deal with animals. The kinder they are to animals, the better for them. Their motive for showing such kindness should be the principle stated by the Prophet in the *ḥadīth* on the man and the dog: 'You are rewarded for any kindness you do to every living creature'.

The way the Prophet shaped the Muslim mind makes mercy and compassion guiding values in the way every Muslim looks at life and the world around.

382. ʿAbdullāh ibn ʿAmr reports that the Prophet said: 'Be merciful and you will be shown mercy; forgive and you will be forgiven. Woe to people who are like funnels when they listen to words [of advice]. Woe to people who knowingly persist in doing [wrong]'.[278]

Again the image here is very powerful. The Prophet likens people who do not take good advice to a funnel in which liquid passes through and it retains nothing of it. These people learn what is good and what benefits them but they allow it all to slip through, continue with their erring ways and take no heed. Therefore, they will be doomed for their carelessness. The Prophet puts this image in the context of the need to show mercy to other people and to forgive their errors. Thus, a hard person who shows no mercy or forgiveness leaves himself exposed to God's punishment as God may not be merciful to him and may not forgive him his sins. Yet God's Mercy is available to anyone who shows mercy even to an animal. In fact, the Prophet even extends this to a feeling of compassion one may have towards an animal one is about to slaughter for food:

383. Abu Umāmah reports that the Prophet said: 'A man who shows mercy, even to an animal meant for slaughtering, will be shown mercy by God on the Day of Judgement'.[279]

278. Related by Aḥmad.
279. Related by al-Ṭabarāni.

384. ʿAbdullāh ibn Masʿūd said: ʿThe Prophet encamped at a place. A man took the eggs of a little bird and the bird came close to God's Messenger's head and clapped with its wings. The Prophet said: "Who of you has hurt this bird, taking away its eggs?" A man said: "Messenger of God, I took its eggs". The Prophet said: "Put the eggs back in mercy to the bird".'[280]

385. (*Athar* 94) Hishām ibn ʿUrwah said: ʿIbn al-Zubayr was in Makkah, and the Prophet's companions carried birds in cages'.

386. Anas said: ʿThe Prophet came in and saw a [young] son of Abu Ṭalḥah called Abu ʿUmayr who had a sparrow he used to play with. The Prophet said to him: "Abu ʿUmayr, what happened to – or where is – the little sparrow?"'

These four *ḥadīths* stress the concept of compassion and mercy and its applicability to all living creatures. The first *ḥadīth* speaks of compassion to an animal ready to be slaughtered for food. A feeling of compassion to such an animal along with certain practical steps, as mentioned in another *ḥadīth*, such as making sure that the slaughterer is using a very sharp knife, and making the animal comfortable at the point of slaughter, will ensure God's mercy to the slaughterer.

The second *ḥadīth* mentions a small bird that becomes worried when its eggs are taken away. The Prophet orders his companion who had taken the eggs to put them back, in compassion to the little bird. Compare this with the attitude of many people who treat animals and birds as having no feeling.

Islam does not forbid putting birds in cages, using them as pets, or for any beneficial purpose, provided that they are well treated, and given proper food and drink. This is the message of the third *ḥadīth*, while the fourth tells us that the Prophet was kind to the young boy who lost his bird, asking him about it and keeping his memory of the pleasant time he had with the bird fresh in his mind.

---

280. Related by Aḥmad and Abū Dāwūd.

20

True and False

THE PROPHET ALWAYS emphasised the need to be truthful. When he wanted to impress on his followers the importance of a certain virtue, he referred to it on several occasions, highlighting its importance. A very clear example is that of the need to always speak the truth. Islam does not approve of lying in any ordinary situation. The Prophet makes this clear in numerous *ḥadīths* and different situations. However, since there are situations when telling the truth may cause aggravation of a bad situation or may lead to harming other people, the Prophet outlines the situations when lying may be acceptable.

387. Umm Kulthum bint 'Uqbah reports that she heard the Prophet say: 'He is not a liar who brings about reconciliation between people, saying something good or promoting what is good'. She added: 'I have never heard him [meaning the Prophet] allowing any concession with regard to what lies people may tell, except in three situations: to achieve reconciliation between

people, and in a man's conversation with his wife and in a wife's conversation with her husband'.[281]

This *ḥadīth* outlines certain situations in which telling a lie seems to be permissible. The Prophet first describes a certain type of person as not a liar, although he may say or report an untruth. The purpose which he is trying to serve is to achieve reconciliation between people who would otherwise remain opposed or hostile to each other. Since Islam attaches great importance to maintaining good relations in society and does not countenance the possibility of a quarrel between two Muslims lasting over a long period, it allows a mediator between them to tell an untruth, if by doing so he believes that he can bring about reconciliation between them. The sort of lies which the mediator may tell are to assure one of the two quarrelling parties that the other wishes him well, or that despite the quarrel, he has spoken well of him. This may be untrue, but the mediator asserts this in order to make the very idea of reconciliation acceptable to his interlocutor. He then goes to the other party and assures him of the good intentions harboured by his opponent towards him. By doing so, he smoothes the way for reconciliation. That sort of untrue statement may be overlooked by God, since the purpose is to achieve peace between quarrelling Muslims.

The very statement made by the Prophet leads to the question whether telling an untruth is acceptable in any other situation. Hence, the comment by the lady companion of the Prophet who describes two other situations of this sort. These concern lying within the family, when either a husband or a wife feels that a white lie may maintain a good family atmosphere, without harming anyone. When a husband assures his wife, or she assures him, of their genuine love for each other, they do not commit a sin if their aim by such an assertion is to keep the family together and strengthen its internal relationships. However, if such assertions are made to cover up some wayward behaviour, the case is different. If, for example, a man tells his wife that he is going on duty travel required by his work and in fact his trip is with some friends and for pleasure, such a lie is forbidden. What one has to

281. Related by al-Bukhari, Muslim, Abū Dāwūd, al-Nasā'ī and al-Tirmidhi.

determine in such a situation is whether anyone is likely to suffer as a result of one's lie and what sort of benefit is realised out of it. If the benefit is assured and the harm is negligible, then telling such a lie is not a sin, although, strictly speaking, it is an untruth.

At the time of 'Umar ibn al-Khaṭṭāb, the second Caliph, a man said to his wife: 'I ask you in the name of God: Do you hate me?' She told him not to ask her in such a way. He insisted. She told him that she did. The Caliph called her in and asked her: 'Are you the one who tells her husband that she hates him?' She said: 'He appealed to me by God to tell him the truth and I felt it impossible for me to lie. Should I have lied?' The Caliph said: 'Yes, in such a situation you may lie. If any of you does not like her husband, she should not tell him so. Few are the houses which are built on love. Most people live together by doing their Islamic duties and being kind'.

In a family situation, one should consider how to maintain good relationships without causing any ill effects and with the minimum assertions which one knows to be untrue. When a husband promises his wife something which he knows he will not be able to fulfil, but he nevertheless makes that promise in order to assure her of his love and to maintain the proper family atmosphere, he commits no sin.

This point is perhaps best explained by Imam al-Ghazāli who says that words are only a means leading to certain objectives. When either telling the truth or telling a lie may result in the achievement of a certain good objective, then resorting to lies for its achievement is forbidden. If that good objective can only be attained by lying, then to tell a lie is not sinful, provided that the attainment of that particular objective is permissible. If that objective is essential, then lying in order to achieve it is required, particularly when failing to secure it will cause certain harm.

Take for example the case of an innocent person who goes into hiding in order to escape the soldiers of a tyrant. If one knows his hiding place and happens to be asked about it, he must lie in order not to give that person away. Similarly, if he has been given something by a neighbour for safekeeping and someone who wrongfully wants to take it away asks him about it, he should tell a lie in order to prevent its confiscation. If he is asked to swear that he does not know where it is, he should do so. Again, if one tells a lie in order to prevent a quarrel or to achieve peace between two quarrelling families or to persuade someone to forgo his right of retaliation, that sort of lie is not forbidden, especially when the purpose cannot be achieved otherwise.

Another case in which lying is permissible is when a governor asks a person whether he may have committed a grave sin, which is unknown except to himself and God and no one is harmed by it, then he should deny having committed it. The point here is that if it is left to God, the offender may be forgiven. If the ruler knows of it, he must punish him. Islam does not like to exact punishment. It prefers that people repent for their sins and be forgiven by God.

All these are good examples of situations in which telling a lie is acceptable, because it ensures that a worse situation is avoided. In other words, telling a lie is the lesser of two evils.

When the Prophet makes a direct reference to a particular quality, such reference signifies that the point at issue is of vital importance. However, the greatest importance given to a certain quality, or virtue, would be for the Prophet to speak highly of it, indicating that maintaining it will contribute to eventual entry into heaven. Needless to say, admission to heaven is the ultimate prize towards which all actions and practices of a believer are directed. So, when something is pointed out by the Prophet as leading to winning this ultimate prize, this indicates its particular importance to all Muslims in all times.

A highly authentic *ḥadīth* describes stating the truth as an action which sets a person on the road to heaven. It contrasts this with telling lies and shows it as leading to the opposite end, which we should guard against.

388. ʿAbdullāh ibn Masʿūd reports that the Prophet said: 'Always state the truth. Truthfulness leads to righteousness, and righteousness leads to heaven. A person will continue to tell the truth until he is recorded with God as truthful. Do not lie. Lying leads to transgression, and transgression leads to hell. A person will continue to lie until he is recorded with God as a liar'.[282]

282. Related by al-Bukhari, Muslim, Abū Dāwūd and al-Tirmidhi.

The *ḥadīth* shows a progression which is inevitable in either situation of telling the truth or lying. When a person speaks the truth, he is righteous. This term is an Islamic one which signifies all that is good and praiseworthy. This means that telling the truth will help a person to do every good thing. It will remind him that virtue requires that he should state the truth in every situation.

It is important to note here that the truthfulness to which the Prophet is referring is not limited only to a verbal statement that is true, but also includes true and genuine intentions. This means that when a person does something he must always do it for a good purpose and with clear intention seeking only God's pleasure by doing so. Thus when he stands up in prayer and states that he turns his face towards God, he must not be preoccupied with anything other than his prayer. If such a preoccupation is on his mind, he is then not stating the truth. His face is not really and completely turned towards God.

Similarly, if he intends to do something good, he should be genuinely and clearly willing to do it. Suppose that a person is looking up to be entrusted with a good position in government. He may resolve within himself that if he is given that position, he will not be unjust to anyone. He will maintain justice without fail. If he is actually given that position, his first action should be to strengthen that resolve and fulfil it. This would be an act of truthful intention. Again, his actions should confirm what he states. This would show him to be the same in public and in private. He does not allow himself ever to be two-faced.

When we look at truthfulness in this light, we realise that it certainly leads to righteousness, as the Prophet said. Under righteousness we may include every good quality and action. Thus when a person is true to his word, true in both intention and action, such truthfulness facilitates for him to do good in all situations. He will always opt for what is good although it may bring him less in the short run, or even cause him difficulty. He will in any case prefer what is ultimately good. This makes him a genuinely good person and leads him to being admitted to heaven.

The Prophet adds a quality which comes with maintaining truthfulness in all situations. When a person maintains truthfulness so that it becomes an essential quality of his, he earns an entry in God's records as a truthful person. This is a rank that is coveted by every believer. The Prophet uses here the term '*ṣiddīq*', which is superior to '*ṣādiq*', the normal term indicating 'truthful'. It means a habitually truthful person who, by nature, would prefer to tell the truth even if it is to his clear and immediate disadvantage. Earning this rank deserves every sacrifice of any short term advantage.

The Prophet also demarcates the opposite course of action. A person who tells lies clearly puts himself on the road to transgression. While telling a lie is in itself an act of transgression, it also facilitates further transgression. A person who lies does not find it difficult to indulge in other acts of disobedience to God. This is because by telling a lie in the first place, he is disobeying God. Indeed, God wants us to tell the truth in all situations, without exception, apart from the concessions we have already noted.

What is more, a liar always thinks that he can cover up his transgression with a lie. Thus he indulges in what is clearly a violation of God's commands and instructions. He thinks that he can maintain an appearance of obedience by telling lies. This takes him further and further away from the path leading to heaven. Rather, it sets him on the road to hell.

Again, the contrast is made complete in the *ḥadīth* with the final part which speaks of a habitual liar. Such a person will be entered in God's Book under that heading. Such a person is, in the Islamic sense, devoid of goodness. However, one can avoid such a horrible fate by making a strong resolve to maintain the truth in all situations. No person who maintains the truth will regret this. In fact, he will earn people's praise in this world and God's reward in the Hereafter, which is stated by the Prophet to be heaven.

The question may arise whether lying is permissible if it is only meant as a joke:

389. (*Athar* 95) 'Abdullāh ibn Mas'ūd said: 'Lying is inappropriate in earnest or in jest, not even when any of you promises his child something and does not fulfil his promise'.[283]

---

283. Related by Abū Dāwūd.

This puts the seal on the matter. No situation, serious or not, earnest or jest, allows lying. A Muslim must always tell the truth in all cases.

It may be suggested that this could mean that life is devoid of some of its pleasures, as people like to joke, and this may be more interesting if an element of lying which will not harm anyone is allowed. This, however, is untrue. The Prophet himself made some jokes but he always told the truth, even when he was joking. If people allow themselves to lie in order to laugh, the mere fact of lying in jest leads them to approve of lying in other situations, and this may lead to very serious lies. It is much better to close this door altogether and tell the truth in all situations.

The Prophet gives an example of situations in which people may accept lying, such as when one promises a child something without intending to fulfil that promise. This may happen when the child needs to be pacified, particularly if he is complaining of some pain or discomfort. A parent may promise the child something or another in order to keep the child quiet. When he does so, he should also be truthful, intending to fulfil that promise whenever he can. ʿAbdullāh ibn ʿĀmir reports: 'My mother once called me when the Prophet was with us in our home. She said, "Come here and I will give you something". The Prophet asked her, "What do you intend to give him?" She said, "I want to give him some dates". The Prophet said, "Good, because if you were not to give him something, this would have been counted against you as a lie".'

The next *ḥadīth* speaks about mixing and dealing with people. This is important because a Muslim should be an advocate of his faith.

390. ʿAbdullāh ibn ʿUmar reports that the Prophet said: 'A believer who mixes with people and puts up with their abuse is better than one who neither mixes with people nor puts up with their abuse'.[284]

The Prophet here is referring to mixing with people who are not good believers, because good believers do not abuse a believer. Islam inculcates feelings of brotherhood among its followers and believers feel

284. Related by Aḥmad, al-Nasāʾī, al-Tirmidhi and Ibn Mājah.

that this brotherhood is real and genuine. Therefore, even when they differ, they treat one another with mutual love and respect. Those who abuse a believer do so because they dislike the message he calls on them to adopt. He mixes with them in order to have a chance to present the message to them. When he does, they may abuse him. It is such a person that the Prophet describes as better than the one who prefers to isolate himself from people in order to avoid their abuse. However, if one feels unable to tolerate any ill treatment one may receive, and that one's attempt to repel such treatment may lead to more trouble, one may adopt an attitude of aloofness, provided that one continues to be with the Muslim community, attend congregational prayers, exchange greetings with believers and fulfil one's duties towards them, such as visiting those who are ill and maintaining proper social ties.

When the Prophet speaks of tolerating abuse, he does not mean that a Muslim should always accept any abuse which other people may hurl on him. What he means is the sort of abuse that those who oppose the message of Islam may level at him because of his stand in support of God's message and his attempt to persuade people to accept it. He tolerates this because he does not consider the message to be his personal one. It is God's message and he is simply a believer entrusted with the task of conveying it. If the fulfilment of this duty involves some sort of adversity, he shows himself to be patient. If he is to repel abuse with similar measures, he may aggravate tension within the community and such tension may rebound on the message itself. Muslims should never allow this to happen.

Tolerating abuse does not come easy to anyone. Therefore, the Prophet gives us great examples, including practical ones:

391. Abu Mūsa al-Ash'ari reports that the Prophet said: 'No one – or [he might have said 'no being'] tolerates offensive remarks which he hears more than God, the Mighty and Exalted. They allege that He has a son, yet He cures them and provides them with sustenance'.[285]

---

285. Related by al-Bukhari, Muslim, al-Nasā'ī, Ibn Mājah and Abu 'Awānah.

Indeed people give every affront to God, without even thinking that they are in need of His grace and mercy at every moment in their lives. Still they give Him the most offensive of actions and remarks but He nevertheless grants them what they need to have a comfortable life. There is nothing more offensive to God than the false allegation that He has taken a son to Himself. People still claim this and expect that God sends them rain and cures their illnesses and provides for them. He certainly does all this and gives them a chance to correct their attitude. If they do, He bestows more of His Grace upon them.

The Prophet himself gave us great examples of tolerating abuse and offensive remarks:

> 392. 'Abdullāh ibn Mas'ūd reports: 'The Prophet (peace be upon him) shared out something among people, as he usually did. A man from the Anṣār said: "By God, this is a division that does not seek to please God, the Mighty and Exalted". I thought that I should tell the Prophet. I went to him and he was sitting with some of his companions. I whispered my report to him. He took it very hard and it showed in his face. He was so angry that I wished I had not told him. He then said: "Moses suffered even greater abuse, but he tolerated it with patience".'[286]

This incident took place after the Battle of Ḥunayn when the Muslims scored a total victory after an initial setback. As the enemies brought with them all their women, children, cattle and money, all these were taken over by the Muslims who subsequently released all women and children on the Prophet's recommendation. The cattle and money were war gains and were distributed on the basis outlined in the Qur'an: one-fifth goes to the state and four-fifths are divided among the army. The Prophet gave generous gifts out of the one-fifth at his disposal to a number of the Quraysh chiefs and other tribes who were newcomers to Islam, so as to strengthen their commitment to their new faith. This is what upset some people as no similar gifts were given to the Anṣār. However, this man's remark was particularly offensive. Yet, when the

---

286. Related by Aḥmad and al-Bukhari.

Prophet's anger subsided, he declared that he would follow Moses' example, and endure what might upset him.

Better than prayer, fasting and charity

Can there be anything better or more important than these? These are the most essential Islamic duties, as they provide three of the five pillars upon which the structure of Islam is built. No one can state this other than the Prophet:

393. Abu al-Dardā' reports that the Prophet said: 'Shall I tell you of a grade which is higher than prayer, fasting and ṣadaqah [i.e. charity]?' His companions said: 'Yes, please'. He said: 'To set the relationship between yourselves to right. For, to allow your internal relations to go bad is the eraser'.[287]

394. (*Athar* 96) Ibn 'Abbās said [concerning the Qur'anic verse that says] '*Remain God-fearing and set to rights the relationship between yourselves*' (8: 1): 'This is a clear injunction from God to the believers to fear Him and to set their internal relations on the right basis'.

As we have noted earlier, it is permissible for a Muslim to lie in order to bring about reconciliation between quarrelling people or to prevent relationships among families or members of the same family from going sour. In this *ḥadīth*, we are told by the Prophet that to work for the achievement of the right sort of relationship between Muslims has a superior grade to that of prayer, fasting and charitable offerings. The importance of maintaining such good relationships, therefore, cannot be over emphasised. As appears from the way the *ḥadīth* is phrased, setting the internal relationship within Muslim society on the right basis is superior to all these acts of worship put together.

287. Related by Aḥmad, Abū Dāwūd, al-Tirmidhi and Ibn Ḥibbān. Al-Tirmidhi's version adds: 'I do not say that it shaves off hair, but it oblitrates religion itself'.

Some scholars are of the opinion that it is better than offering the voluntary part of prayer, fasting and donations. But there is nothing in the *ḥadīth* to support such a narrowing of the meaning. Such scholars may argue that an obligatory act of worship is superior to all other actions, because it is done in fulfilment of what God has ordered us to do. This is certainly true, but God has also ordered us to set our internal relations on the right footing. This is clearly a duty.

Moreover, if we imagine a situation in which internal relations within the Muslim community, or within small sections of it, may lead to a bloody fight in which firearms may be used and people may be killed, or property destroyed or looted and houses ransacked, etc. then trying to remedy such a situation and achieve reconciliation should be given priority over all other actions, including obligatory prayers. If the matter is so urgent and there is absolutely no time to lose, then one should delay offering obligatory prayer in order to prevent a fight between Muslims. Acts of worship are primarily something between a person and God. Therefore, they may be offered, even when their time has lapsed. One can pray to God for forgiveness if one has delayed such obligatory worship for such a purpose, and God is certain to forgive this. He knows that the delay is not caused by negligence but by attending to something urgent and immediate.

Furthermore, the Prophet describes the deterioration of relations between Muslims as the razor. He further says that it erases faith altogether. That is because in a community where relations have gone so sour that people no longer have any trust in each other, Islamic principles and values cannot be firmly rooted. How can one imagine that good neighbourliness or kindness to relatives can flourish in such a community? Yet these are basic values in any Muslim community. What we have to remember is that Islam builds a closely knit community in which the interests of the individual and the community as a whole are well balanced and closely interlinked. Every Muslim feels himself to be a brother to every other Muslim. That bond is very real because it is established by faith.

Moreover, everyone in the Muslim community shares in the individual and collective task of delivering God's message to mankind. Unless the Muslim society is well built, it does not provide a model for other communities to emulate. In other words, when relations within the Muslim community are allowed to deteriorate, Islam does not have a chance to flourish within the community which is supposed to present it to mankind. Islamic values are thus allowed to be neglected and forgotten. Feelings within the community are allowed to go sour. Everyone will be looking after their own selfish interests. Thus, Islam is weakened and its enemies have a chance to overcome it. Therefore, the Prophet's description is apt: to allow internal relations within the Muslim community to go sour erases faith itself.

It is perhaps useful to remember here that the order to the Muslim community to set relations among them on the right footing is given by God Himself. The first verse in Surah 8, entitled *al-Anfāl*, or The Spoils of War, uses these very words to state a Divine order. This surah comments on the events of the Battle of Badr in which the Muslims under the leadership of the Prophet achieved their first major victory against the non-believers, inflicting a heavy defeat on a far superior force. The Muslims gained much in that battle but they soon disagreed on how the spoils should be shared out. God then revealed in the Qur'an: '*They ask you about the spoils of war. Say: All spoils of war belong to God and His Messenger. Remain, then, God-fearing and set to rights the relationship between yourselves, and pay heed to God and His Messenger, if you are truly believers*'. (8: 1) 'Abdullāh ibn 'Abbās states that in view of this order, there can be no choice for believers except to always remain conscious of their Islamic duties to be God-fearing and to maintain the bond of brotherhood between themselves. This bond must be felt by all of them to be both real and practical.

Worse than lies

We mentioned earlier that Islam does not approve of lying, even ones intended as jokes or ones of the sort people call 'white lies':

395. Sufyān ibn Usayd al-Ḥadrami reports that the Prophet said: 'It is grave treachery to say something to your brother and he believes you when you are lying to him'.[288]

---

288. Related by Abū Dāwūd.

This *ḥadīth* refers to a common situation. Some people do not hesitate to make use of the trust of others and tell them something which they know to be untrue. They realise that their interlocutors believe them and take what they say on trust. Nevertheless, they show no indication whatsoever to suggest that the truth is different from what they say. They may have some reason for this, but generally speaking their reason is a very selfish one. They may stand to gain as a result of this talk or they may lead the person who believes them to do certain actions which will serve a particular interest of their own. Surely, this is extremely selfish. The Prophet describes it as grave treason, and this is a very apt description. Perhaps nothing in social relations is worse than to exploit the trust of others in order to tell them an untruth. Whatever the reason, it is totally unacceptable. Furthermore, it destroys mutual respect within the Muslim community.

It is well known that most lies are discovered after some time. When a person who believes another later discovers that his trust was misplaced and that the person was telling him lies, he feels very much aggrieved. When the speaker is aware that what he is saying is a plain lie, his action is much worse than lying, because it involves fooling a brother or playing a trick on him. No one does this in idle jest, if he has any shred of faith. People do it in order to achieve something. When they do it deliberately, the dignity of their Muslim brothers seems not to be of any importance to them. They are indeed being treacherous towards them. Hence, the Prophet denounces such action in the clearest of terms.

Because Islam attaches great importance to the need to keep relations within the Muslim community on a proper footing, the Prophet consistently advised against practices that may lead to strained relations within the Muslim community:

396. Ibn ʿAbbās reports that the Prophet said: 'Do not be too argumentative with your brother; do not make fun of him; and do not promise him something without fulfilling your promise'.[289]

---

289. Related by al-Tirmidhi.

This *ḥadīth* gives a general instruction to believers to refrain from certain practices that are bound to have adverse effects on relationships within the community. On different occasions, the Prophet spoke against being too argumentative. Indeed, such an attitude does not bring about any proper understanding of the opposite view. What the Prophet is warning against is argument for argument's sake. He does not tell us not to have different views on matters which admit such differences, but he tells us not to try to defend our views as if proving ourselves to be right is an end in itself. The goal should always be to try to arrive at the proper view through enlightened discussion. This is what Muslim scholars have understood and practised. One of the most eminent of our scholars, Imam al-Shāfi'i, is reported to have said: 'To us, our view is right but we do not exclude the possibility that we may be mistaken, and the opposing view is wrong, but we do not exclude the possibility that it may be right'. This is indeed the attitude of a truth-seeker.

The second practice the Prophet warns against is what many people sometimes do by way of taking jesting and joking to excess, trying to play tricks on others or making fun of them, in order to make those who are present have a good laugh. This may be at the expense of one person among a group who then takes it hard given he is treated as the cause of laughter. Indeed, any type of joking which generates ill feeling is shunned by the Prophet. As we have repeatedly emphasised, to establish good and close relationships within the community is a paramount consideration to which the Prophet attached great importance. Hence, his instructions that we should not carry our jokes with others to excess or make fun of them.

To fulfil one's promises and to be true to one's word is a characteristic of every good Muslim. Hence, the Prophet emphasises it in this *ḥadīth* as well as in many others. It should be noted that the last two types of action which the Prophet shuns are closely related to lying, since they may involve a falsehood which may be deliberate or incidental.

397. Abu Hurayrah reports that the Prophet said: 'Two practices will not be abandoned by my community: lamenting the dead and abuse of lineage'.[290]

290. Related by Muslim and al-Tirmidhi.

This *ḥadīth* highlights two practices that Islam forbids but Muslims continue to do. Needless to say, not every Muslim will be guilty of these, but the majority of people find abandoning them very difficult. The first is lamenting the dead. A Muslim believes that death occurs when the time of life God allows a person comes to an end. It is God's decision and every believer should accept it with resignation and submission to God's will. No doubt, parting with loved ones is very difficult, and feeling sad at the death of a dear and close relative is natural. Islam does not forbid this. What it forbids is lamentation and outcries that border on protesting against God's will.

The other practice is abuse of lineage. This may take the form of claims that a certain person is not the son of the family to which he belongs, or ridiculing the ancestors of people and alleging that they were guilty of such and such an offence or crime. This is an easy form of attacking people, particularly those who are too powerful to be faced in an open challenge. Islam forbids this practice because it creates enmities within the community.

398. Fusaylah bint Wāthilah said: 'I heard my father say that he asked God's Messenger: is it blind tribalism to help one's people in a situation of injustice [to others]?' He said: 'Yes'.

Islam does not approve of injustice in any type or form. It makes it a duty of every Muslim to stand up against injustice. Therefore, helping one's tribe or community to carry on with injustice to others is totally unacceptable. It was the practice of tribal Arabia, prior to Islam, that loyalty to one's tribe meant that people would support their tribe in every situation, including that of gross injustice to others. The Prophet makes clear that this cannot be sanctioned by Islam. The Prophet described such blind loyalty to one's tribe as decadent and foul.

21

A Pledge that must not be Fulfilled

IT IS WELL known that Muslims may not boycott one another. If they quarrel or disagree, they should always keep their relationships alive and strong. It is not right that they should allow the relationship that exists between them by God's blessing to deteriorate to the extent that they turn their backs on each other. Such an attitude does not fit at all with the bond of brotherhood that Islam establishes between its followers. The Prophet often emphasised that Muslims may not boycott each other for more than three days.

However, it is possible that a situation may develop which makes one person particularly upset or offended by another. In a moment of anger, he may swear never to speak to the other person again. Islam requires us to maintain as true anything to which we swear. If it is our intention to boycott someone who has offended us, then after three days, we should end that boycott. Three days are normally sufficient to allow tempers to cool down and to cast a fresh look on the whole relationship. If we harbour no ill will to one another, it is always possible to restore good relations after they may have worsened. Yet sometimes it is very difficult to mend worsening relations within three days, particularly when one swears to boycott the other for a much longer period.

The following *ḥadīth* is reported by ʿĀ'ishah's nephew whose father is ʿĀ'ishah's brother by her mother:

399. ʿAwf ibn al-Ḥārith reports: 'ʿĀ'ishah was informed that ʿAbdullāh ibn al-Zubayr commented on something ʿĀ'ishah was selling or giving away as a gift: "By God, ʿĀ'ishah shall stop doing this, or else I will impose an order of restriction on her". She said: "Has he really said this?" They said: "Yes". ʿĀ'ishah said: "I am hereby making a vow before God: I shall not speak a single word to [ʿAbdullāh] ibn al-Zubayr ever again".

As her boycott was prolonged Ibn al-Zubayr tried to get some people from the Muhājirīn to intercede with her on his behalf. She said: "By God, I will never accept any intercession on his behalf and I shall not go back on my oath".

Time passed and ʿAbdullāh felt very keenly that the boycott had gone on for too long. He spoke to al-Miswar ibn Makhramah and ʿAbd al-Raḥmān ibn al-Aswad, both of whom were of the Zuhrah clan.[291] He said to them: "I appeal to you by God to go to ʿĀ'ishah. It is not lawful for her to make a pledge to boycott me".

Al-Miswar and ʿAbd al-Raḥmān covered him under their robes and all three went together. They both sought permission to enter ʿĀ'ishah's rooms, saying: "Peace be to the Prophet along with God's mercy and blessings. Can we come in?" ʿĀ'ishah said: "Enter". They asked: "All of us, Mother of the Believers?" She said: "Yes, all of you". She was not aware that Ibn al-Zubayr was with them.

When they entered, ʿAbdullāh ibn al-Zubayr went into the screened off section and hugged her and entreated her and wept. Al-Miswar and ʿAbd al-Raḥmān also entreated ʿĀ'ishah to speak to ʿAbdullāh and to forgive him. They said: "You know that

---

291. ʿĀ'ishah was very close and compassionate to the Zuhrah clan because they were related to the Prophet through his mother.

> the Prophet (peace be on him) has prohibited boycott between Muslims, and that it is not lawful for a Muslim to boycott his brother for more than three days. They continued to remind and press her. She also reminded them [of her pledge] and cried out saying: "I have made a vow and it is hard for me". They continued to entreat her until she spoke to Ibn al-Zubayr. She set free in atonement 40 slaves. Afterwards, she used to remember this and cry until her scarf became wet'.[292]

'Ā'ishah was known to be very generous. She always spent in charitable purposes whatever money she could lay her hands on. If she received a share from the Caliph, which was due to her by right, she would spend it the same day, distributing it to poor people, leaving pretty much nothing for herself. She might even do more and sell a piece of property in order to spend its price for charitable purposes. The reporters of this *ḥadīth* are not sure which of these cases made her nephew, 'Abdullāh ibn al-Zubayr, feel that she was doing what was unnecessary. Hence he declared that she must stop or he would make her.

'Ā'ishah's generosity was at a level that could not be emulated. Many stories are reported of her exceptional generosity. Once she received a gift amounting to 80,000 *dirhams*, [a *dirham* was the silver currency at the time]. She started dividing it and sending it to people as gifts and charity. She was fasting on that day. As sunset approached and she was due to complete her fast, she told her servant to have her meal ready. The servant her nothing but bread and oil. A woman in the house said to her: 'Of all the money you have distributed today, could you not have spared us one *dirham* to buy some meat for our meal?' 'Ā'ishah said: 'Do not reproach me. Had you reminded me, I would have done so'.

When her nephew, a great companion of the Prophet, made his threat, he exceeded his limits. To start with, 'Ā'ishah was not only his mother's sister to whom he should show respect, but she was the Prophet's wife, and as such, she was mother to him and to all believers. Hence, she was so terribly offended when she heard his remarks. In her anger, she made her vow to teach him a lesson.

---

292. Related by Aḥmad, al-Bukhari, Muslim and Abū Dāwūd.

It was very hard for him to be so boycotted by his aunt whom he loved so dearly. He might have done well not to utter such remarks, but then he did not mean to offend his aunt. Nor did he expect such a reaction from her.

When all mediation efforts failed, he had no option but to send some people who were sure to have a sympathetic ear from ʿĀ'ishah. They preferred to take him to her in such a way that she could not refuse him admission. When he was in, he went straight to her and entreated her as hard as he could.

ʿĀ'ishah's attitude shows how seriously Muslims took their pledges and oaths. She had sworn that she would not talk to her nephew, and she meant to fulfil her oath. He, on the other hand, had a very valid point. A believer must not pledge to God to do something which God does not like; boycott between Muslims is unacceptable. When we pledge something for God's sake, it should be of the type which He wants us to do, such as a pledge to offer night worship, or to fast for a certain number of days, or to spend so much money for charitable purposes and so on. But to pledge a boycott with another Muslim is not right. Hence, ʿĀ'ishah yielded to the entreaties of ʿAbdullāh and the two men who interceded on his behalf.

In atonement for her oath and pledge, she set free forty slaves. It is reported that ʿAbdullāh himself sent her ten slaves and she set them all free. Then she bought more until she had freed forty slaves. Nevertheless, she was so sorry that she did not fulfil her oath, despite knowing that she had broken it for a better purpose, which was permissible. When she freed them, she repeatedly said: 'I wish I had specified something I would do, because I might have done it and fulfilled my vow'. This would certainly have been better and much easier.

The Prophet emphasises this fact in a number of *ḥadīths* which make it absolutely clear that Muslims must always maintain good and close relationships within their community:

400. Anas ibn Mālik reports that the Prophet said: 'Do not hate each other; and do not envy one another; and do not turn your back on one another. Servants of God, be always brothers.

> It is not lawful for a Muslim to boycott his brother for longer than three nights'.[293]

This *ḥadīth* makes it clear that any actions which tends to weaken the bond of brotherhood is not admissible in the internal relations between Muslims. Hate, envy and arrogance are qualities which should have no trace within the Muslim community. It is not lawful for a Muslim to hate, envy or turn his back on any other Muslim. Indeed, the opposite qualities are encouraged. Muslims always love, help and are friendly towards one another. This is emphasised in the overall order the Prophet issued to all servants of God i.e. to be brothers.

The Prophet categorically states that it is not lawful for a Muslim to boycott any of his Muslim brothers for a period longer than three days. This means that it is permissible, although by no means encouraged, for two Muslims not to be on speaking terms for a shorter period. This should be understood as a concession given in view of quarrels that may take place between people who are otherwise good Muslims. It is only natural for a human being to get angry at times and to allow his anger to get the better of him. If he quarrels with someone, his anger may cause him to use abusive or insulting words which make the situation between the two of them much worse. This may lead to an estrangement or a boycott between them. Muslims who find themselves in such a situation are allowed three days to let their tempers cool down and to reconsider their relationship with their brothers. In the overwhelming majority of cases, three days are sufficient to mend the relationship. This applies when the quarrel results from a temporary disagreement. Quarrels which result from long-harboured hate or envy will take much longer to mend. However, we are commanded by the Prophet not to entertain such feelings for any length of time against fellow Muslims. When the estrangement or quarrel is the result of a temporary lapse which makes a person neglect his duties towards his brother or allows him to backbite his brother or speak ill of him on some occasion, steps can be quickly taken to remove the effects of that lapse and renew the bond of brotherhood.

---

293. Related by Mālik, al-Bukhari, Muslim, Abū Dāwūd and al-Tirmidhi.

Perhaps it should be added here that when a person fears that his continued relationship with a particular person is bound to cause him harm, whether in respect of his worldly interests or in respect of his fulfilment of Islamic duties, he is right not to maintain a very close relationship with that person. He need not boycott him altogether, but he may keep him at arm's length.

Sometimes when a quarrel takes place between two people, they regret it and both of them are eager to mend the relationship, but they cannot bring themselves to start the process of reconciliation. Each feels that he will be compromising his dignity if he goes to the other and greets him warmly as if there had been no quarrel. The Prophet encourages us not to allow such considerations to stop us from doing what is right:

401. Abu Ayyūb reports that the Prophet said: 'It is not lawful for anyone to boycott his brother for over three nights. They may meet and each of them turns his face away. The one who is first to greet the other is the better one of the two'.

It is not easy for people to overcome their egos and bring themselves to greet a person with whom they have quarrelled, especially when they genuinely feel hurt because the other person was totally in the wrong. But it is this particular attitude which the Prophet wants to play down so that it does not prevent Muslims from making up after they have quarrelled.

A Muslim always tries to excel. He wants to earn more reward so that he makes sure of being forgiven his sins on the Day of Judgement and admitted into heaven. So, the overriding criterion for a Muslim is what to do in order to earn God's pleasure and receive more reward from Him. When the Prophet points out a method or an action which makes a person better, his very statement provides a motive for every Muslim to follow that message or to perform that action. In this particular instance, it makes it easier for a Muslim to overcome his pride and to start the process of making up, even though he may feel that he was hard done by.

402. Abu Hurayrah reports that the Prophet said: 'Do not hate each other; and do not contend with one another. Servants of God, be always brothers'.

This *ḥadīth* is similar to Number 400.

403. Anas reports that the Prophet said: 'When two people establish a close relationship based on love of God, the Mighty and Exalted, or Islam, they cannot allow estrangement to exist between them at the first sin committed by either of them'.[294]

In this *ḥadīth*, the Prophet teaches us to take it easy when we quarrel with our Muslim brothers. The first disagreement should never be allowed to cause a prolonged estrangement between us. Forgiveness and forbearance should be our first reaction. When your brother is at fault, your immediate attitude should be one of forbearance. Even when this is repeated once or twice, you should always be ready to overlook his faults. Later, you may point out to him that you are upset that he finds it easy to commit what is sinful, but such discussion should be geared towards keeping your relations close and healthy. In this sort of atmosphere, brotherhood flourishes. This is why Islam is keen to make such brotherly atmosphere always prevalent in Muslim society.

404. Hishām ibn 'Āmir al-Anṣāri, Anas ibn Mālik's cousin whose father was a martyr in the Battle of Uḥud, reports that the Prophet said: 'It is not permissible for a Muslim to boycott another Muslim for more than three days. Both are away from the Truth as long as they continue their boycott of each other. The first of them to move back [to proper relations] makes amends for his earlier attitude. Should they die boycotting each other, neither of them will ever be admitted into heaven. If one of them greets the other but the latter refuses to return or accept

294. Related by Aḥmad in a longer version, starting with: 'Every Muslim is a brother of every Muslim. He neither deals unjustly with him nor does he let him down'.

his greeting, then an angel returns the greeting to him, while the other will have his answer from Satan'.[295]

This *ḥadīth* describes most vividly and clearly how Islam views quarrels and boycotts between Muslims. We are told by the Prophet that regardless of which party is in the right and which is at fault, both are in the wrong as long as they boycott each other. Should they continue with their boycott for the rest of their lives, this is sufficient grounds to deny them admission into heaven. Of course, this presupposes that they have deliberately continued with their boycott despite having a chance, or indeed repeated chances, for bringing about reconciliation. It also suggests that people who allow a quarrel to continue throughout their lives do not have the sort of character which encourages them to do what they should in order to earn adequate reward from God to qualify for admission into heaven. They cannot bring themselves to attach the proper Islamic value to their bond of brotherhood. They allow their egos to have the better of them.

Yet this may not apply to both of them. Either one may try to achieve reconciliation and start greeting the other. The very fact that he has started is sufficient to ensure his forgiveness for his part of the boycott. If his overture is not answered, God makes sure that an angel answers him. The other has the worst of all answers, because his reply comes from the devil.

Like every household, there were some disagreements in the Prophet's own home. It may be pertinent to ask here how the Prophet or his wives conducted themselves when such disagreements took place.

405. 'Ā'ishah reports that the Prophet once said to her: 'I know when you are angry and when you are happy'. She asked: 'How do you know that, Messenger of God?' He said: 'When you are happy you answer: "Yes indeed, by the Lord of Muhammad". When you are angry you would say: "No, by the Lord of Abraham". She said: "This is true. I only stop using your name".'[296]

---

295. Related by Aḥmad.

296. Related by al-Bukhari and Muslim.

This shows how the Prophet's wife was keen to observe Islamic values even when she was angry. Obviously, the only reason which made her unhappy with the Prophet at any particular moment could be attributed to jealousy. Since she was one of several wives, and since the Prophet was always keen to maintain absolute justice between his wives, she might have felt on occasions that something was not to her liking. She might be dissatisfied. Her dissatisfaction, however, did not manifest itself in any way other than swearing by the Lord of Abraham instead of her habitual usage of the Lord of Muhammad. This is exactly the sort of moderate expression of dissatisfaction that we should emulate when we are unhappy with our Muslim brothers or sisters.

As we have noted, when two people boycott each other for life, they are not granted admittance into heaven. Some people may find it difficult to understand why the Prophet states such severe punishment.

406. Abu Kharāsh al-Aslami reports that the Prophet said: 'Whoever boycotts his brother for a year is like one who sheds his brother's blood'.[297]

407. A man from the Aslam clan who was a companion of the Prophet reports that the Prophet said: 'To boycott a believer for a year is like shedding his blood'.[298]

Commenting on these two *ḥadīths*, scholars say that a person who boycotts his Muslim brother for a year goes beyond all limits in insisting on taking such a wrong attitude. For one thing, a person who does this demonstrates his total disregard for the principle of Islamic brotherhood. When God describes the believers as brothers, Muslims must demonstrate that this bond of brotherhood is real. They have to nurture and foster it at all times. Nothing negates such brotherhood more than a total boycott between two Muslims. It is inconceivable that two people who claim to be believers demonstrate the total collapse of a quality which God describes as essential to believers. When they do so, they automatically disqualify themselves

---

297. Related by Aḥmad, Abū Dāwūd and al-Ḥākim.
298. Related by Aḥmad, Abū Dāwūd and al-Ḥākim.

from admission to heaven. Moreover, a prolonged boycott not only kills Islamic ties; it kills something else. In both these *ḥadīths* the Prophet says that boycotting a believer for a year means killing him, using the sword of boycott. When we have such a description by the Prophet, there is nothing more to add.

It is understandable, nevertheless, that things may happen between any two people that strain their relations. This happens between brothers, sisters and between husbands and wives. Islam teaches us that when we get angry with someone who is close to us, or with any Muslim brother or sister, we should not carry our anger any further than is absolutely necessary. Moreover, we must not forget that what exists between us cannot be easily washed away. Islamic ties are much too important to be trampled over casually.

To emphasise the importance of maintaining good relations within the Muslim community, al-Bukhari enters similar *ḥadīths*:

408. Abu Ayyūb reports that the Prophet said: 'It is not lawful for anyone to boycott his brother for over three nights. They may meet and each of them turns his face away. The one who is first to greet the other is the better one of the two'.

This is the same as *ḥadīth* Number 401, with a difference in the transmission chain.

409. Hishām ibn 'Āmir reports that the Prophet said: 'It is not permissible for a Muslim to boycott another Muslim for more than three days. Both are away from the Truth as long as they continue their boycott of each other. The first of them to move back [to proper relations] makes amends for his earlier attitude. Should they die boycotting each other, neither of them will ever be admitted into heaven'.

This is the same as *ḥadīth* Number 404, but is a shorter version.

410. Abu Hurayrah reports that the Prophet said: 'Do not hate each other; and do not envy one another. Servants of God, be always brothers'.

This is the same as *ḥadīth* Number 400, but this is a shorter version and has a different chain of transmission. It will come up again in a longer version in Number 412.

411. Abu Hurayrah reports that the Prophet said: 'You shall find that among the worst of people in God's sight on the Day of Judgement is the one who is double-faced: he meets one group of people with one face and meets others with another face'.[299]

Needless to say, to be double-faced is one of the worst characteristics a person may have. It betrays cowardice, hypocrisy and a strong element of selfishness. Such a person wants to be in all people's good books, but he ends in none. He tries to please one group of people, hoping to get some benefit from them. If they are in conflict with another group, he assures them that he is on their side, but when he goes to the other group, he does the same, giving them his every assertion that he is, heart and soul, on their side. He may be able to get away with this for some time, but his reality is more likely to be discovered by one or both sides, and he will be discarded by them both. He does not only suffer exposure in this present life, but he is to receive God's punishment on the Day of Judgement, and he is considered by God to be among the worst of people.

Acting on suspicion

412. Abu Hurayrah reports that the Prophet said: 'Beware of suspicion, for suspicion is the worst form of lying. Do not help to trick others [in trade]; and do not envy one another; and do not hate each other; and do not contend with one another; and do not turn your back on one another. Servants of God, be always brothers'.

This *ḥadīth* is a fuller version of Numbers 400, 402 and 410. This suggests that the Prophet warned against these qualities on different

299. Related by al-Bukhari, Muslim, Abū Dāwūd and al-Tirmidhi.

occasions, highlighting each time the relevant qualities Muslims should guard against. The first one in this *ḥadīth* is suspicion that is not based on real evidence. The Prophet describes this as the worst type of lying, because it tends to generate enmity between people for no real reason. It may be suggested that suspicion may be involuntary, and as such cannot be avoided. What is necessary is to refrain from what leads to suspicion and this is perfectly possible.

The Prophet makes this strong warning against suspicion, because he wants the Muslim community to be a closely knit community, where all believers feel their brotherhood to be real and genuine. Therefore, action must always be based on fact and reality, not on suspicion. Needless to say, one must always be cautious. Therefore, when we entertain any suspicion, we should take the necessary measures to establish the truth of the matter.

The Prophet then warns against helping to trick others in sales. This includes showing a desire to buy something at a high price, without really intending to buy it, and doing so merely to get someone else to buy at that high price. It also includes cooperation between shopkeepers and business people to raise prices.

The Prophet also warns against envy and hate. Both qualities tend to weaken society and allow discord within the community to grow and spread. Islam builds a community that is based on trust and mutual love. As such, envy and hate should have no place within the Muslim community. Therefore, in this *ḥadīth*, the Prophet mentions various qualities that weaken ties within the community, including contention between Muslims and turning one's back on one's Muslim brothers. To counter all these, the Prophet urges Muslims to be true brothers to one another, feeling that their brotherhood is generated by their belief in God and His oneness.

Forgiveness withheld

As we have noted, the Prophet often warned against strained relations between Muslims. The worst form of such strained relations is a total boycott between Muslims. When this takes place, the parties concerned immediately remove themselves from among believers whom God favours with His immediate forgiveness. To a Muslim, the process of forgiveness of sins is continuous. One who commits a sin or makes a serious slip is always eager to have it quickly forgiven. Islam has several ways of ensuring forgiveness. A Muslim may resort to any one of these and couple it with sincere repentance and a resolve not to commit that sin again. He is then more or less certain of being forgiven. The Prophet tells us that this continuous process of forgiveness also has its peak times.

413. Abu Hurayrah reports that the Prophet said: 'The gates of heaven are opened on Mondays and Thursdays. Every servant of God who associates no partner with Him whomsoever will have his sins forgiven, except for a person who sustains hostility towards a Muslim brother of his. It is said: "Delay these two until they have worked out a reconciliation between them".'[300]

This *ḥadīth* encourages us to always make the best of the special times of forgiveness. We should try, therefore, to improve our position with God for the time of forgiveness on Monday and Thursday of every week. When the time arrives and a Muslim is found to be doing something good and useful, he proves his merit. This is one reason for the Prophet's recommendation that Muslims may fast on Mondays and Thursdays. Fasting is one of the actions for which God rewards very generously. Therefore, voluntary fasting on these days earns great merit. Moreover, fasting teaches patience and forbearance. Therefore, a Muslim who is fasting is less likely to enter into quarrels or harbour grudges. It is easier for him to recognise that he needs to improve his situation, especially if he has done something wrong over the past few days.

The Prophet then tells us of the criterion on which forgiveness is granted to people. When we hear this, we are bound to recognise that God's bounty is limitless. Everyone without a trace of associating partners with God is sure to be forgiven. What we are required to do, then, in order to ensure our forgiveness, is to make sure of what believing in God's oneness entails and that our faith remains pure.

---

300. Related by Mālik, Muslim, al-Tirmidhi, Ibn Mājah, Ibn Ḥibbān, Abu 'Awānah and Ibn Khuzaymah.

The Prophet adds a very clear warning, however. He makes an exception in the case of people who harbour hostility towards each other. They may be otherwise good believers, but their forgiveness will not be forthcoming. God tells His angels who are in charge of recording people's actions and what reward or punishment He may determine in the case of each one of them to withhold His forgiveness until they have purged their hearts of hostility and worked out their reconciliation.

414. (*Athar* 97) Abu al-Dardā' said: 'Shall I tell you of a grade which is higher than prayer, fasting and *ṣadaqah* [i.e. charity]?' 'It is to set the relationship between yourselves to rights. For, to allow your internal relations to go bad is the eraser'.

This *ḥadīth* has already been discussed in its slightly different versions, entered as Numbers 260 and 393. Al-Bukhari enters it here again, with a different chain of transmission, to emphasise the importance of maintaining good relations between believers in the Muslim community. The same notion is emphasised in other *ḥadīths*:

415. Ibn 'Abbās reports that the Prophet said: 'Three qualities, the absence of which in any person ensures the forgiveness of everything else (that is to whom He may wish): a person who dies having associated no partners with God, and having been no magician practising what magicians do and having harboured no grudges against his brother'.

We note that the Prophet includes a proviso so as to make the forgiveness of any person dependent on God's will. The Prophet always included such provisos in his statements in order to emphasise all the time that God's will is free. Although God commits Himself to do certain things or forgive certain people, He does so by His own free choice. God maintains absolute justice among His servants and when the Prophet points out a certain way which ensures forgiveness, God is certain to operate it. After all, the Prophet never said anything relevant to the religion of Islam which was his own opinion. Everything he said was revelation from God.

The Prophet tells us here of the importance of always staying alert so as to take appropriate action to ensure that we have none of the three qualities that block forgiveness. The first is allowing traces of polytheism to linger in our minds. The second is to have nothing to do with magic or magicians. There are numerous warnings in the Qur'an and in the *Ḥadīth* which make it clear to Muslims that magic is unacceptable in Islam. Indeed, to learn magic is absolutely forbidden; to practise it is tantamount to disbelief in God. In this *ḥadīth*, the Prophet mentions magic as one of three qualities which block forgiveness.

The third one is harbouring grudges against Muslims. Indeed, it is sufficient to appreciate the seriousness with which Islam views the existence of hostility or grudges among Muslims to include it in such a *ḥadīth* which speaks of forgiveness after death, when man no longer has any chance of correcting past mistakes. For this reason, the Prophet teaches us to take positive action in order to mend our relations with our fellow Muslims.

416. Abu Hurayrah reports that the Prophet said: 'It is not lawful for a man to boycott a believer for more than three days. When three days have passed, he should meet and greet him. If the other answers his greeting, both of them share in the reward. If he does not answer, the one who started with the greeting absolves himself of the sin of boycott'.[301]

As noted in earlier *ḥadīths*, three days are the maximum period of estrangement which is allowed between Muslims. In this *ḥadīth*, the Prophet tells every Muslim who has boycotted a fellow Muslim for that length of time to make sure of meeting and greeting him. This is the simple way of ending such a boycott. When the greeting is returned by the other person, the way is paved for an honest discussion of their differences and a proper reconciliation to be worked out. Needless to say, the one who starts by greeting his boycotted brother makes sure of his own forgiveness.

---

301. Related by Abū Dāwūd.

Miscellaneous

417. (*Athar* 98) ʿAbdullāh ibn ʿUmar said: ʻʻUmar used to say to his sons: "Separate in the morning and do not gather in the same house. I fear that you will quarrel or that discord may occur between you".ʼ

This reported advice by ʿUmar to his children aims at maintaining a good atmosphere between young people. He realised that differences can easily occur between them and the best way to keep good relations between youths who are closely related is that they should separate and have their own friends with whom they may be more relaxed.

418. Wahb ibn Kaysān said: ʻAbdullāh ibn ʿUmar saw a shepherd having sheep that were grazing in a place with little water. He also saw a better place [for grazing]. He said to him: "You, shepherd! Move them. I heard God's Messenger say: ʻEvery shepherd is accountable for his flock'."ʼ[302]

Al-Bukhari enters this *ḥadīth* under the subheading: ʻGiving advice without being asked'. In it we learn that Ibn ʿUmar advised the shepherd to take his sheep to a better place for grazing, because he did not want the shepherd to be held to account for not seeking the best place for the sheep to graze.

419. Ibn ʿAbbās reports that the Prophet said: ʻIt is not for us to set a bad example. The one who takes back a gift is like a dog who swallows his own vomit'.[303]

The Prophet is talking here about good believers and that they must always conduct themselves in a way that avoids blame. They must always show that they choose best conduct. He gives an example of something that invites universal disapproval, which is taking back one's gift after having given it to someone. The Prophet likens this behaviour to one of the worst traits of some animals, which is that of a dog who

---

302. Related by Aḥmad.
303. Related by al-Bukhari, al-Tirmidhi and al-Nasāʾī.

goes back to his own vomit to eat it. It is disgusting behaviour and going back on one's gift is similar to this.

420. Abu Hurayrah reports that the Prophet said: 'A believer is guileless and generous, but the unbeliever is a swindler and miserly'.[304]

This *ḥadīth* contrasts the essential characteristics of believers and unbelievers. A good believer naturally steers away from evil, and this often makes him unaware of those who perpetrate evil. Moreover, he is not one to put up pretences. What people see of him is consistent with his feelings and intentions. He does not try to look into people's hearts because he knows that whatever is related to matters of this present life is easily dealt with. With regard to the Hereafter, he is diligent and wants to be foremost in what earns God's pleasure and reward. By contrast, an unbeliever tries to gain whatever he can, even though he may have no legitimate right to it. He is keen to increase his money and property, resorting to whatever means is available.

421. Ibn 'Abbās reports: 'Two men verbally abused each other during the Prophet's lifetime. One of them reviled the other who remained silent. The Prophet remained seated. After a while the other man answered back and the Prophet got up [to leave]. He was asked: "You have got up?" He said: "The angels left and so I left with them. While this man remained silent, the angels were answering the man who was reviling him. When he answered, the angels left".'[305]

This *ḥadīth* makes clear that it is better not to reply to verbal abuse because replying to it will inevitably lead to more abuse and this hardens the feelings of those engaged in it. If one of the two parties remains silent and does not reply to abuse, he will earn the angels' support. The version related by Abu Dāwūd gives more details of what happened on this occasion. It mentions that the person who remained silent at first

---

304. Related by Abū Dāwūd, al-Tirmidhi and al-Ḥākim.
305. Related by Abū Dāwūd.

was Abu Bakr. It adds that the other person offended Abu Bakr twice without reply. However, when the man went on the offence the third time, Abu Bakr answered him back. The report also mentions that Abu Bakr asked the Prophet whether he was upset by his behaviour. The Prophet said to him: 'An angel came down from heaven to counter what the man said. When you defended yourself, the angel left while Satan stayed behind. I would not remain where Satan is'.

422. (*Athar* 99) Umm al-Dardā' reported that a man came to her and said that a man spoke ill of you in the presence of 'Abd al-Malik [the Caliph]. She said: 'We may be criticised for something we have not done. We have long been praised for things which we have not done'.

This shows the manners Islam cultivates in its followers. Umm al-Dardā' was a companion of the Prophet and her husband was a companion and a scholar. Both are graded as highly reliable in their reporting of *ḥadīths* they heard directly from the Prophet. When she is told that someone spoke ill of her at the Caliph's when others were present, she could not verify whether the report was true. She did not wish to retaliate against that person, who is not named. She simply suggested that whatever was said did not truly apply to her. However, she did not say this outright. She said that this is the way people talk: when they criticise they may exaggerate, and when they praise they also exaggerate. If her praises were exaggerated, then she could easily take an exaggerated criticism. She left the matter at that.

423. (*Athar* 100) Qays reports that 'Abdullāh ibn Mas'ūd said: 'If a man says to his fellow, "You are my enemy", then one of them is out of the fold of Islam or has disowned the other'. Qays added: 'Abu Juḥayfah mentioned to me later that 'Abdullāh said: "Except the one who repents".'

A Muslim cannot be an enemy to another Muslim. Therefore, if a Muslim tells another person that he is his enemy then he believes that that person is not a Muslim, or he may himself be a non-Muslim. However, repentance is sure to resolve the dispute between them.

22

No End to Charitable Work

ṢADAQAH REFERS TO all charitable donations, whether obligatory or voluntary. It is, however, more frequently used to refer to voluntary charitable donations. The meaning which immediately springs to mind when the term *ṣadaqah* is used is financial help given to a poor person, without any obligation on the part of the giver or any condition imposed on the recipient. Anyone who is familiar with Islamic philosophy can easily appreciate the great value Islam attaches to *ṣadaqah*. This is further emphasised by the fact that Islam does not confine it to financial help, for kindly actions and good turns done by one person to another are considered in the same light. The term has acquired great significance and it has come to be used in ordinary speech by all people, whether educated or not, to refer to any good and kindly action.

In *Ḥadīth*, it is often mentioned in this light, especially with the repeated encouragement by the Prophet to his followers to do what is good and helpful to others. But the Prophet does not confine his teachings to encouragement to be good to others. He makes it clear that a good deed benefits the one who does it as well. By doing it, he does himself a good turn. It is his duty to give, and the benefit is his for having done so.

> 424. (*Athar* 101) 'Abdullāh ibn 'Abbās said: 'A human being has 360 joints [or bones], and every one of them owes a *ṣadaqah* every single day. Every word of kindness is a *ṣadaqah*; help rendered by a man to his brother is a *ṣadaqah*; a drink of water given [to another person] is a *ṣadaqah*; and the removal of a harmful object from [people's] way is a *ṣadaqah*'.[306]

The examples given in this *ḥadīth* of charitable work refer to physical actions, rather than financial help. He first speaks of a kindly word. This is something strongly encouraged by Islam. What people say affects their relations and their standing in society. When a person learns to use good words all the time and to refrain from using bad ones, he is loved by his companions and by all those who come into contact with him.

Ibn 'Abbās does not specify any particular sort of help that qualifies as charity, or *ṣadaqah*. Therefore, every type of help, whatever it may be, if given voluntarily and freely is an act of charity. The recipient may not be in need of such charity or help. He may be able to pay for and obtain any help he needs, but when you come forward to help him you earn the reward of having been charitable.

A drink of water is considered a charity. This is highly significant because, according to Islam, water is one of three things in which all people share. Indeed, they can claim their shares at any time. If someone asks you for some water, you have to give him some because it cannot be your exclusive property. Nevertheless, when you see a thirsty person and give him a drink, that is charity.

The last example tells us something about the sort of social cooperation Islam promotes. When you see a harmful object in people's way and you remove it, you are charitable. That harmful object may be no more than the skin of a banana thrown on the road by someone who is careless. It could be harmful, because it may cause a pedestrian

---

306. Related by al-Bazzār and Ibn Ḥibbān.

to slip if he is unaware of it. If you take it away so that it can no longer cause any harm, you are charitable. It counts as a charity although it is not given to a particular person.

There are further examples of such charitable actions. The same *ḥadīth* is rendered in a different and more authentic version, reported by Abu Hurayrah, who quotes the Prophet as saying: 'A charity is due for every joint in each person on every day the sun comes up: to act justly between two people is a charity; to help a man with his mount, lifting him onto it or hoisting up his belongings onto it, is a charity; a good word is a charity; every step you take to prayers is a charity; and removing a harmful thing from the road is a charity'.[307]

The order in which examples are given in a *ḥadīth* or in the Qur'an may be significant. Keeping this in mind, the importance of maintaining justice between people becomes readily apparent. A Muslim is supposed to be just all the time; that is his duty. By its fulfilment he earns the reward of doing something for charity. If he has to struggle in order to maintain justice, then that charity becomes great. His reward for it is also proportionately greater.

In the second example the Prophet specifies one form of help. It is of the type that people may turn away from, because they may appear to be serving another person. But the Prophet makes it clear that carrying someone else's belongings and putting them on his mount is an act of charity. By citing this example, the Prophet implies that one must never hesitate to render help, regardless of the situation or how one may appear to others when rendering such help.

Again, a kindly word is mentioned in this version of the *ḥadīth* as an act of charity. What is then added is attending congregational prayers in the mosque. Every step counts as an act of charity.

In another version of this *ḥadīth*, the Prophet is quoted as mentioning a different example of action which counts as charity, 'to smile at your brother is a charity'. Needless to say, a friendly smile works wonders in maintaining and strengthening good relations within the community. When you meet your brother with a cheerful face, you actually promote love, compassion and kindness within the community. These are values which Islam always encourages.

---

307. Related by al-Bukhari and Muslim.

23

No Room for Abuse

PEOPLE OFTEN ENGAGE in verbal abuse of each other. In Islam, however, this practice is unacceptable, a fact repeatedly emphasised by the Prophet, even though he was aware that sometimes it is not easy to control oneself. It may be that one easily finds oneself answering another who has started being abusive. In this scenario, the one who starts first bears the responsibility. However, the Prophet reminds us that when we answer back we must never be excessive:

425. Abu Hurayrah reports that the Prophet said: 'When two people revile each other, the responsibility for what they say rests on the one who starts, as long as the one who is wronged does not become excessive'.[308]

308. Related by Muslim, Abū Dāwūd, al-Tirmidhi, Abu 'Awanah and Ibn Ḥibbān.

426. Anas reports the same as *ḥadīth* Number 425.[309]

This is in line with Islamic teachings making clear that when two people exchange wrongful abuse, whether by word or action, the one who started it bears all the responsibility for what ensues from his words or actions. This is only fair because, had he been able to control himself and say only what is right, he would have spared the community the unbecoming incident of two Muslims abusing each other. The whole community suffers as a result because when two of its members enter into a slanging match, relations between them are strained. Whatever detracts from the unity of the Muslim community is unwelcome. Hence, the Prophet drove home to us that restraint is always a virtue, especially when lack of it leads to wronging one another.

Indeed, the Prophet warned against every type of action that leads to strained relations between members of the Muslim community:

427. The Prophet asked [his companions]: 'Do you know what calumny is?' They said: 'God and His Messenger know best'. He said: 'Telling people what others have said in order to sow discord between them'.

Needless to say, this practice is universally viewed as despicable. It tells of the wickedness of the person who does it; he is seeking to spoil relations between people.

Islam means submission to God. A true Muslim submits himself totally to God. Submission to God is demonstrated by carrying out His orders. Whatever God commands people to do is a duty which they must fulfil. Some of them may decide not to fulfil a particular duty or indeed all duties assigned to them by God. They turn their backs on God's messenger and message. By so doing, they not only demonstrate their disbelief in God, but also that they are conceited and proud. Such pride is misled, because it reverberates in their relations with God Himself.

A true believer, on the other hand, shows his humility by implementing God's orders to the best of his ability. When God

---

309. Related by Ibn Mājah.

forbids something, he refrains from it. He knows that God bids us nothing but what is useful and beneficial to us, and He forbids us only what is evil and harmful. Yet this is not a believer's prime motive in obeying God's orders and refraining from what is forbidden. Rather, his prime motive is his submission to God, which he declares when he makes up his mind to be a Muslim and states that he believes in God's oneness and the message of Muhammad, the last of all prophets and messengers.

428. The Prophet said: 'God, the Mighty and Exalted, has revealed to me that you must show humility and that you must not wrong one another'.

This *ḥadīth* comes in a fuller version shortly and we will comment on it then.

429. 'Iyāḍ ibn Ḥimār reports: 'I said: "Messenger of God, [suppose that] someone reviles me". He said: "The two people who revile each other are two satans slandering and denouncing each other as liars".'[310]

430. 'Iyāḍ ibn Ḥimār reports that the Prophet said: 'God has revealed to me that you must show humility and that you must not wrong one another or stress one's own merits'. I said: 'Messenger of God, suppose that someone reviles me in front of people who are lower in status than me and I answer him back. Do I commit any wrong [by doing so]?' He said: 'The two people who revile each other are two satans slandering and denouncing each other as liars'.

431. 'Iyāḍ added: 'I was still opposed to God's Messenger, but I offered him a she-camel as a gift before I became Muslim. He refused to accept it and said: "I dislike the gifts of idolaters".'[311]

310. Related by Aḥmad, Muslim and Ibn Ḥibbān.

311. Related by Abū Dāwūd, al-Tirmidhi and Ibn Mājah.

Needless to say, something which God instructs the Prophet to convey to us through revelation and which the Prophet makes sure of explaining to us must be very serious. Here, we have one such example which is expressed by the Prophet in one word and explained very clearly in a few more. The key word is humility. Here, it means that we should show humility to God by obeying His orders and refraining from what He has forbidden. We must also demonstrate our humility in front of God by always remembering His greatness and that He is the Lord of the universe. Conceit is, in effect, a false claim of greatness made by human beings. A conceited person incurs God's displeasure by his mere attitude. Therefore, a true believer only belittles himself in order to guard against conceit.

Humility is also a virtue in dealing with other people. It prevents injustice and wrongdoing. When a person maintains humility in dealing with others, he earns their love. Nothing is more hateful to people than someone who tries to demonstrate to them that he is higher or better or nobler than them.

The way the Prophet phrased this order is very significant. He tells us to show humility and elaborates by pointing out the result that must come out of this humility: no one deals unjustly with another and no one treats another with disdain. All are equal. No distinction can be achieved by any person except through the fulfilment of God's commandments and abstention from what He has forbidden.

The Prophet's questioner puts to him a situation that happens often. A person may find himself being abused by another in front of people who may be inferior to him or may be his subordinates. He instinctively wants to answer back, but this may lead to mutual aggravation and exaggeration. People answer a word of abuse with one which is worse. Thus, they start a slanging match which may include much of what is false. It takes much more power for a person to refrain from answering his own defamation. The Prophet, however, describes the two people who enter into such a slanging match as two satans who accuse each other of lying. When we remember that the Prophet has singled out lying as something which a believer never does, we are in a better position to understand what he is saying in this *ḥadīth*.

In the last of these three *ḥadīths* the Prophet is stated to have returned 'Iyāḍ's gift when he was an idolater, stating that he disliked idolaters' gifts. Perhaps the Prophet felt that by so doing, the man might reconsider his position towards Islam, as we know he subsequently became a Muslim and reported a number of *ḥadīths*. The Prophet accepted gifts from al-Muqawqis, the ruler of Egypt and from Ukaydar Doomah, both of whom were Christians.

432. Sa'd ibn Mālik reports that the Prophet said: 'To revile a Muslim is wicked'.[312]

433. Anas reports: 'God's Messenger (peace be upon him) was not given to using abusive, cursing or reviling language. If he took offence, he said [in reference to the one who caused it]: "What is wrong with him? May his forehead be dusty".[313]

434. 'Abdullāh ibn Mas'ūd reports that the Prophet said: 'To revile a Muslim is wicked, and to fight him is tantamount to disbelief'.[314]

The Prophet provided a practical example of what Islam means in actual life. When his wife, 'Ā'ishah, was asked to describe his manners, she said: 'His manners were the Qur'an in practice'. (*Ḥadīth* Number 309) It is for this reason that God has made it a requirement of our faith that we should follow the example of the Prophet in everything we do. Very often we deduce the Islamic rule on a particular situation on the basis of what the Prophet did in similar situations. The second of these three *ḥadīths* shows his guidance in restraining oneself from abusing others.

Perhaps it is important to explain that the expression, 'may his forehead be dusty', is one of those expressions which every language contains and which are used so frequently as to lose their literal meaning. Literally, it is a supplication that the person concerned fall on his face to the ground. The Prophet did not, however, mean this literally. It is simply an expression denoting disapproval. God answered

---

312. Related by al-Nasā'ī and Ibn Mājah.
313. Related by al-Bukhari.
314. Related by Aḥmad, al-Bukhari, Muslim, al-Nasā'ī, al-Tirmidhi and Ibn Mājah.

the Prophet's every single prayer. Had he meant this prayer literally, people would have seen that person actually falling to the ground on his face. But the Prophet did not pray that someone should come to any harm, except in the case of a sworn enemy of Islam. Indeed, he did not use any evil language.

Anas was one man who knew all the Prophet's habits and how he reacted in all situations. He tells us categorically that the Prophet was not one who used abusive, cursing or reviling language. He always said what was good. Furthermore, the Prophet taught by example. His companions noticed that he did not use such language and so they too refrained from using it. Moreover, they have told us about this so that we may do likewise. You will always find believers refraining from such language, as they find its use repugnant.

The other two *ḥadīths* clearly illustrate this. Perhaps it is important to explain that the Prophet is referring here to the worst type of reviling as in the case when a person is totally unscrupulous when he speaks ill of another. He does not confine himself to pointing out the other person's bad qualities, but rather says about him what he knows to be false. There is no doubt that this is wicked.

So what about fighting a Muslim which the Prophet describes here as tantamount to disbelief? He certainly does not mean a rejection of the Islamic faith altogether, because a person may actually believe in God and the message of Islam and yet still fight another Muslim. Some scholars explain that this applies to a person who thinks that fighting a Muslim is permissible. If he does, then he is actually an unbeliever. Other scholars argue that a Muslim is entitled to be helped by all other Muslims and he is entitled to be spared all harm by them. Therefore, when one of them fights another, he is actually denying the other these rights to which he is entitled. Perhaps the Prophet only means here to give a stern warning against indulging in a fight with another Muslim, whether by word or action, using one's hands or a weapon. All this is unacceptable. Relations between Muslims must always remain friendly, intimate and based on mutual care. In such a relationship, there is no room for using vile language or for any fighting.

Using abusive language does not achieve any purpose. Indeed, it can only bring the user something he dislikes. The Prophet tells us that all abusive language rebounds on the one who uses it.

435. Abu Dharr reports that the Prophet said: 'Anyone who accuses another of transgression or disbelief, his accusation will rebound on him if the accused is not as he said'.[315]

The warning implied in this *ḥadīth* is very grave. One should be careful how one describes others, because if the description is false, it attaches to the person so attributing it. If one falsely accuses another of being a disbeliever, this description becomes true of the accuser. This is God's punishment for false accusation, and it is grave indeed.

But what if the accusation is true? The answer is that the accuser is spared the rebound, but his action could still be considered highly objectionable. It certainly depends on his purpose. If he is giving a testimony, whether in court, in private or in social dealings, then he must say what he knows to be the truth. If, on the other hand, he wants to harm the other and defame him, then he incurs a sin. This is because he actually disregards what he is required to do.

A Muslim must always overlook the faults of others and try to keep them secret. When he identifies a fault in someone else, he should admonish him privately and gently. He should try to teach him how to get rid of his fault and replace it with something good. As long as this can be achieved gently, a Muslim should not resort to force in order to achieve it. Force can easily cause the person who is on the receiving end to persist with his fault and consider that changing his way detracts from his dignity. If he is approached in a gentle, friendly way, he may very easily correct his fault. It is in order to spare the Muslim community the evil effects of force that the Prophet emphasises in the strongest manner that this is the wrong approach to adopt in dealings with other Muslims.

A case of deliberate forgery

Adoption has been an age-long practice in many parts of the world. It was practised in pre-Islamic Arabia, with people joining into their families children or youths they knew not to belong to them. Islam

315. Related by Aḥmad, al-Bukhari and Muslim.

dislikes adoption, since it is, in effect, a form of forgery based on false claims. God revealed in the Qur'an instructions to the Muslim community never to claim as their own children those whom they know to belong to others. A verbal or written claim of parenthood does not change the facts. It is for this reason that adoption is totally forbidden in Islam. God says: '*He never made your adopted sons truly your sons. These are but figures of speech you utter by your mouths, whereas God speaks the truth. It is He alone Who can show [people] the right path*'. (33: 4) The Prophet also very strongly stated the sinful nature of adoption:

> 436. Abu Dharr reports that the Prophet said: 'He who knowingly claims to be the son of someone other than his father is an unbeliever. A person who claims to belong to a certain community when he is not one of them is sure to have his position in hell. He who describes someone as an unbeliever, or calls him, 'enemy of God,' when he is not so, will have that description rebounding on him'.[316]

This *ḥadīth* shows how important truthfulness is with respect to family and community relations. Islam does not merely forbid child adoption by a couple, but it also forbids very strictly that anyone should claim to be the son of another when he knows this is false. It goes without saying that all false claims, whatever they are, can only be described as forbidden. The truth is something so important that Islam does not countenance any falsehood. Of all false claims a person may make about his position, education, attitudes, marriage, etc. the false claim of belonging to a family which is not his own is the most unacceptable. The Prophet describes as an unbeliever anyone who knowingly makes such a claim.

This is further emphasised by the second part of this *ḥadīth* which makes it clear that to falsely claim a relationship with a certain community ensures for the claimant a position in hell. It goes without saying that a person who is condemned to hell is the most miserable of people. If this is the result of falsely claiming to belong to a certain

---

316. Related by Aḥmad, al-Bukhari and Muslim.

community, then this is a very serious affair. As we all know, Islam does not make any distinction between people on the basis of lineage or family relations. The only criterion of distinction is that of being a God-fearing believer. Therefore, the only motivation to claim attachment to certain people must be the benefits which accrue to the claimant as a result of his claim. Since the claim is false, the benefits received as a result of it must deprive other people of their rights. Otherwise, they would not have belonged to the claimant. This is, in effect, a method leading to injustice. Islam views injustice with total repugnance. It does not allow it in any shape or form. Therefore, anything that leads to injustice is forbidden.

The last part of the *ḥadīth* teaches us not to describe anyone as an unbeliever or as an enemy of God, when we know him not to be so. The result of such an abuse is that the description becomes applicable to the one who makes it. What a prize one earns for describing someone who believes in God as an unbeliever!

Diffusing anger

Every believer must abide by any advice given by the Prophet, because Prophet Muhammad taught nothing but good. He never suggested something that could bring harm to anyone. God commands us in these words: '*Whatever the Messenger gives you, take it; and whatever he forbids you, abstain from it*'. (59: 7) This verse states a fundamental principle that applies to all situations. Failure to follow the Prophet's advice will deprive the person concerned from a certain benefit.

437. Sulaymān ibn Ṣurad said: 'Two men reviled each other in the presence of the Prophet (peace be upon him). One of them was very angry to the extent that his face swelled and changed colour. The Prophet said: "I know a word which will make what [this man] feels disappear if he will only say it". A man went up to him and told him what the Prophet said. He also said to him: "Seek refuge with God against the accursed Satan".

The man said: "Is there anything wrong with me? Am I insane? Go away".'[317]

It is clear that this man was in a fit of anger. The Prophet wanted to indicate to his companions that when a man is overwhelmed by anger he only needs to remember God and to seek refuge with Him against Satan and his instigation. However, the angry man was not prepared to listen to advice. Hence his violent retort when the Prophet's companion communicated to him the Prophet's advice. His failure to follow it, however, meant that his anger got the better of him. He could not think clearly. He did not earn any reward which a believer would surely earn by following the Prophet's advice. He must have regretted all this when he cooled down, but then regret would have been to no avail.

438. (*Athar* 102) 'Abdullāh ibn Mas'ūd said: 'Between every two Muslims there is a veil from God, the Mighty and Exalted. If either of them says some ugly words to the other, he rents God's veil. Should either of them say to the other, "You are an unbeliever", one of them is so'.

The second part of this *ḥadīth* repeats what we have commented on earlier, that when one person accuses another of being an unbeliever, the accusation applies to one of them. In the first part the Prophet tells us that hurling abusive words on another Muslim causes the veil that God places between every two Muslims to be torn into shreds. To a believer, this is very serious, because everyone is keen to have such a veil, covering their privacy. Therefore, Muslims in all generations attach great importance to verbal and practical decorum, using only decent words when they speak to each other.

When the Prophet recommends a certain thing to us, we should follow his instructions. He only teaches us what is beneficial to us. God makes sure that we prosper when we follow the Prophet's example and He rewards us for this. Whether the recommendation by the Prophet relates to something of this world or to a matter of worship, we are certain to achieve the best results by following his advice. Those who

---

317. Related by al-Bukhari, Muslim, Abū Dāwūd and al-Nasā'ī.

do not wish to follow the Prophet can only blame themselves for the outcome accruing from their attitude.

439. 'Ā'ishah reports: 'The Prophet (peace be upon him) did something with a view to giving people a concession [i.e. indicating that it is permissible]. Some people, however, felt that they should not do it. This was communicated to the Prophet. He addressed the people, praised God, then said: "What is the matter with some people that they refrain from doing something which I have done? By God, I know God better than them and I fear Him most".'[318]

In this report we are told of some of the Prophet's companions, who, in their eagerness to maintain a high standard of devotion, felt that they should not do something which the Prophet did. In this particular report the thing which the Prophet indicated as permissible, but these people refrained from doing, is not specified. Some commentators indicate that this relates to a particular action of one sort or another. It is perhaps more accurate to say that it refers in particular to three companions of the Prophet and their action.

Those three men went to the Prophet's wives, asking them about his worship, how often he prayed at night, how often he fasted voluntarily and how his life at home with his wives was. When they were given these details, they felt that such a standard of worship was not sufficient for them, although it might have been sufficient for the Prophet. After all, he was already forgiven by God any slip or error he might have made. They wanted to adopt a harder course of action. One of them pledged himself to fast every day of his life; the second indicated that he would be standing up in worship all night every night. The third pledged never to marry.

When the Prophet was told of this, he realised the danger it involved to the community of believers and to future generations. This is the sort of danger always associated with going to extremes. The Prophet always indicated that Islam is an easy religion, with easy to follow instructions. Therefore, he wanted to make it absolutely clear that a

---

318. Related by al-Bukhari, Muslim and al-Nasā'ī.

middle course is the best one to follow and that his example must be followed by all Muslims. When he spoke to his companions, he put the issue succinctly. He stated that he knew God better than all others and that he feared Him most. To know God is to fear Him. For no one has true knowledge of God and still continues to disobey Him. The better a person knows God, the easier it is for him to do what he is bidden and to refrain from what he is forbidden.

Thus, the Prophet's actions and example show us our best course of action. When we follow his example, we are certain to earn God's pleasure. By contrast, those who thought little of the Prophet's example could only think of ways that did not take into account all factors that might influence people. They wanted to impose on themselves a very strict course. This is why the Prophet, according to other versions of this *ḥadīth*, was very angry when he heard what they said. He told them that they must not impose their own restrictive view. They should follow his example. If he were to do something when he knows God best and fears Him most, then that which he does is certainly permissible and useful.

The Prophet was always keen not to hurt anyone's feelings. He did not criticise people's actions in a direct or blunt manner:

> 440. Anas reports: 'The Prophet (peace be upon him) rarely said to anyone something that one might dislike. One day a man came to him who apparently had some make-up on. When the man left, the Prophet said to his companions: "Perhaps he should have changed or removed this colouring".'[319]

The Prophet felt that it was unbecoming for a man to appear in such a light. However, he did not criticise the man openly, while he was with him. He only mentioned to his companions that the man should have removed or changed his make-up. The Prophet knew that what he said would be conveyed to the man. His companions also benefited by his remark, so that they would not do the same.

---

319. Related by Aḥmad, Abū Dāwūd, al-Nasā'ī and al-Tirmidhi.

Forgiveness in advance

Is it possible that God will forgive people their future sins, even before they have committed them? The following *ḥadīth* gives us an idea:

441. 'Ali ibn Abu Ṭālib said: 'God's Messenger (peace be upon him) sent me with Al-Zubayr ibn al-'Awwām, both of us on horseback. He said: "Go to such and such meadow, where you will find a woman who has a letter with her from Ḥāṭib to the idolaters. Bring her to me". We found the woman travelling on a camel at the place the Prophet described. We said to her: "Give us the letter you have". She said: "I do not have any letter". We searched her and her camel. My companion said: "I do not find it". I said: "The Prophet (peace be upon him) does not lie". [I turned to the woman and said: "By Him Who holds my soul in His hand, I will strip you unless you produce the letter". She put her hand in the knot of her shawl – as she was wearing a woollen shawl – and got it out. We took it to the Prophet (peace be upon him). 'Umar said: "He [i.e. Ḥāṭib] has betrayed God, His Messenger and the believers. Let me strike his head off". The Prophet asked Ḥāṭib: "Why have you done this?" He said: "I am certainly a believer. I only wanted to do those people some favour". The Prophet (peace be upon him) said: "He tells the truth, 'Umar. Has he not fought in the Battle of Badr? Perhaps God has looked at the people who fought in Badr and said, 'Do what you like, for I have forgiven you'." 'Umar was in tears and said: "God and His Messenger know best".'[320]

This incident took place at a time when the Prophet was preparing to launch an attack on the unbelievers in Makkah after they had violated the provisions of the peace treaty which the two sides had signed two years earlier. The people of Makkah took part in an attack launched by a tribe allied to them against a tribe allied to the Prophet.

---

320. Related by al-Bukhari, Muslim and Abū Dāwūd. In Muslim's version, 'Ali was accompanied on this mission by al-Zubayr and al-Miqdād, and it is given in more detail.

The Prophet was keen to give the Quraysh, the major tribe in Arabia, a lesson on how to respect its treaties. However, he was also keen to achieve his purpose with minimum bloodshed. He took all precautions to make sure that the Quraysh would be taken by total surprise. All mobilisation efforts were completed in total secrecy. People were prevented from coming into Madinah and leaving it. However, it was one of the Prophet's companions who thought of breaking the news to the people of Makkah, hoping that he would be able to hold this as a favour ensuring the safety of his immediate family there.

That his action was sinful is beyond doubt. The Prophet had issued express orders to all his companions to maintain total secrecy. Moreover, it was a time when war could easily break out. It would have meant a great difference in both the conduct of the battle and its outcome if the Quraysh knew in advance of the Muslim army marching towards Makkah instead of being taken completely by surprise. Yet Ḥāṭib ibn Abu Baltaʿah did not consider any of these aspects. He was only concerned with his own affairs and feared for his immediate family.

In view of his very serious action, ʿUmar, who was known not to mince words about the importance of abiding by the Prophet's instructions, suggested that the man should be executed. He volunteered to do this if the Prophet so approved. The Prophet reminded him that Ḥāṭib was one of the soldiers who fought in the Battle of Badr, the first major battle between the Muslims and the Quraysh. The Prophet further suggested that those who fought in Badr might have been forgiven any subsequent sin by God.

The normal situation is that when a believer commits a sinful action, he regrets what he has done and prays to God to forgive him. If his repentance is genuine, then God grants him forgiveness. Moreover, forgiveness is hastened by doing a good deed of equal or more importance than the sin committed. Those who fought in Badr were true soldiers of Islam. They faced an enemy with much greater forces than their own. Furthermore, they were ill-equipped for battle. Nevertheless, they fought hard and remained steadfast until they achieved victory. What this meant in practice was that those who fought in Badr achieved a degree of distinction that ensured the forgiveness of their past sins, and made them worthy of forgiveness of whatever sin they might commit in the future. Yet the fact that they were worthy of forgiveness does not necessarily mean that they would inevitably be forgiven, unless God so wills to forgive them.

It is this to which the Prophet is referring. They were people who had strong faith to ensure that they would sincerely repent any sin or future mistake. In the case of Ḥāṭib who had committed a clear and serious mistake, his repentance would be on the same level. It is for this reason that the Prophet stopped ʿUmar from harming or killing Ḥāṭib.

The Prophet was keen that any of his followers who slipped would go on to correct his error. This does not mean an automatic forgiveness of all future sins, but it is an indication that those particular people would have what it takes to be forgiven: i.e. genuine faith and the willingness to own upto mistakes and rectify them. The Prophet did not mean that none of them would ever commit a mistake or a sin. Indeed, if any had committed any punishable sin, the Prophet would have inflicted the punishment prescribed by Islam on them. But the Prophet who always told the truth was also speaking the truth in this instance. Every single one of those who fought in Badr and continued to perform their Islamic duties with diligence and give whatever sacrifice was required of them until they died. This was sufficient to ensure God's forgiveness for them, which is always the best guarantee for admission into heaven.

It is important to realise that what Ḥāṭib did was really serious, for he took practical action to inform the enemies of Islam that a Muslim army was about to attack them. What this meant was that the element of surprise giving the Muslims great advantage would have been lost. Moreover, the Prophet wanted to minimise the chances of fighting by confronting the unbelievers with a large army which they could not hope to overpower. So it was natural that the other companions should view Ḥāṭib's action very seriously.

Scholars argue that it is open to an Islamic court to sentence to death a spy who works for the enemies of Islam, even though he may be a Muslim. The Prophet did not disagree with ʿUmar's suggestion on the grounds of Ḥāṭib being a Muslim, but rather because he was one of those who fought at Badr. If it was sufficient that he be a Muslim to prevent his killing, the Prophet would have highlighted this, because this would be the grounds for judgement in any similar case that might take place in the future. He would not have needed to mention the fact that he was a Muslim soldier at the Battle of Badr, a special distinction that applied to a little over 300 Muslims in the first generation of Islam.

We note that ʿAli threatened the woman who carried the letter that they would undress her, unless she produced the letter voluntarily. The threat to undress a woman appears to be particularly serious when we remember that Muslim women must always dress properly when they go out in public, covering their bodies, with the exception of their faces and hands.

The question arises whether it was right for ʿAli and his companion to make such a threat. Would they have carried it out if the woman continued to deny having the letter? In this case, taking the letter from her was a matter of huge importance. It affected the security of the whole Muslim community. It was indeed a matter of public interest. Therefore, an individual's rights and privileges may be suspended when they represent the much lesser interest. Moreover, ʿAli and his companion were absolutely certain that the woman was lying. ʿAli stated his grounds for delivering such a threat, namely, that the Prophet does not tell an untruth. She must have had the letter and must produce it. He was acting on the basis of absolutely correct information.

The question remains whether Ḥāṭib's action would have benefited him, or whether the unbelievers would have viewed his position so leniently. He certainly misjudged the consequences of his action; he thought it would do the Muslim community no harm. But even then, what was the purpose? He simply hoped that the unbelievers would return his favour by protecting his immediate relatives.

This is the sort of patronage that Islam does not allow to exist between Muslims and the enemies of Islam. Indeed, it is in connection with this particular incident that the first verses of Surah *al-Mumtaḥanah*, or The Examined Woman, were revealed. The surah starts with this express order by God: '*Believers, do not take My enemies, who are also your enemies, for your intimate friends, showing them affection when they have rejected the truth you have received*'. (60: 1)

Perhaps it should be explained that friendship between a Muslim and a non-Muslim person who is not hostile to Islam is not forbidden. It is friendship with the enemies of God and the Muslim community that is clearly forbidden here. It is this sort of relationship Ḥāṭib wanted to establish with the people in Makkah, but this would not have availed him any benefit. He should have trusted his relatives to God's care. This would have spared him the trouble of violating the Prophet's express orders.

442. ʿAbdullāh ibn ʿUmar reports that the Prophet said: 'If a person says to his Muslim brother, "You are an unbeliever", then this applies to one of them'.[321]

443. ʿAbdullāh ibn ʿUmar reports that the Prophet said: 'When someone says to another, "You are an unbeliever", then one of them is an unbeliever. If the one to whom it is said is an unbeliever, then the one who said it has spoken the truth, but if this is not the case, then the one who said it has brought down disbelief on himself'.[322]

These two *ḥadīths* warn against labelling any Muslim an unbeliever, because this will rebound on the one who says it, if the other person is a believer. It is a very serious matter because the person who says it claims to know the inner thoughts of the other person, when this is known only to God Himself. The Prophet makes clear that there can only be one of two situations: either the one addressed by this description is truly an unbeliever, and the speaker is telling the truth, or he is a believer which means that the description will rebound on to the speaker.

444. Abu Hurayrah reports that 'the Prophet used to seek refuge [with God] from evil results and the gloating of enemies'.[323]

When people meet misfortune, they often attribute this to fate. No doubt we often have to face situations over which we have no control. When these appear to work to our disadvantage, we say that it is ill

321. Related by Mālik, al-Bukhari, Muslim and al-Tirmidhi.

322. Related by Aḥmad and al-Bukhari.

323. Related by Aḥmad and Muslim.

fate. If such a situation is very serious, it gives us much pain. This is what the Prophet used to seek refuge from. It should be understood that every event or outcome is known to God long before it takes place. Time does not apply to God's knowledge which is perfect and complete. However, we often confuse His knowledge with predetermination. What we need to understand is that God does not wish to bring anything evil to mankind. It is their own action that brings them evil outcomes. What comes from God is always good: it can either be an act of justice or an act of grace. Human actions can bring about much misery for large numbers of people. Hence, the Prophet used to seek God's shelter against the evil outcome of people's actions.

He also sought God's refuge against the enemy gloating over our misfortune. To see an enemy pleased with an evil outcome befalling us can hurt very badly. Hence, the Prophet's seeking refuge with God against it.

24

Wasting Money

445. Abu Hurayrah reports that the Prophet said: 'God is pleased for you to have three qualities and displeased if you have three others. He is pleased when you worship Him alone, associating no partners with Him; when you hold fast together to your bond with God; and when you give good counsel to those God puts in authority over you. He is displeased if you engage in idle talk, ask too many questions and squander your property'.[324]

When the Prophet mentions that a certain quality pleases God, every Muslim should ensure it becomes part of his nature, and when the Prophet mentions that another quality displeases God, every believer should refrain from it. The Prophet often contrasted things he recommended with others he discouraged. Such contrast may be in

324. Related by Mālik, Ibn Khuzaymah, Abu 'Awānah and Ibn Ḥibbān.

number only, as in the case of this *ḥadīth*. The two sets of qualities mentioned in this *ḥadīth* are not opposites. However, when we learn that a certain quality pleases God, we should realise that its opposite displeases Him. The same applies in the reverse situation.

What pleases God most of all is that our relationship with Him is set on the fundamental principle of His oneness. Thus, people should worship Him alone, associating no partners with Him. This is the central theme of Islamic faith, as it is the central theme of all Divine religions. It was advocated by all prophets and messengers, from Adam to Muhammad (peace be upon them all).

The other two qualities that please God relate to the community of believers. They should be united in holding fast to their bond with God and never allow disunity to creep into their ranks. They should also give sound advice to those in authority. Sincere and honest advice to a ruler is bound to bring good results to the whole community when the ruler acts on it. He will only do so when he feels that it is meant sincerely and for the good of both the ruler and the ruled.

People often engage in idle talk, repeating what they have heard without establishing whether it is true or false. Their conversation is often based on: 'It is said..., people claim..., they say...'. This is something that God dislikes and the Prophet warns against it because it wastes time and may bring about bad results. The second quality that displeases God is asking too many questions that do not aim to seek knowledge or learn what is useful. This is another aspect of idle talk. As these two qualities relate to what people may say, they imply that we should always be careful of what we say, so as to ensure that we say what is useful and pleasing.

The last quality God dislikes for His people is their squandering of property. Money should always be used properly and for the benefit of the owner, his family and community. When money is used for unproductive things, it is wasted. Many people tend to squander their money when they have plenty. They may be extravagant or may even gamble. Such actions put money to uses that displease God and a Muslim must never do this.

446. (*Athar* 103) Commenting on the Qur'anic verse that says: '*Whatever you give for His sake He will replace it for you, for He is*

the best of providers' (34: 39), Ibn 'Abbās said: 'Provided that it is spent neither in extravagance nor in a niggardly way'.

God gives a general promise that He will replace whatever we spend for His sake. This applies to what we spend in looking after our families and dependants, and whatever we give to the poor or to charitable causes. Ibn 'Abbās makes clear that spending in such good causes should be neither extravagant, nor niggardly. It should always maintain a middle course.

447. (*Athar* 104) Abu al-'Ubaydayn said: 'I asked 'Abdullāh [ibn Mas'ūd] about those who squander. He said: "They are those who spend for no right purpose".'

448. (*Athar* 105) 'Ikrimah reports that Ibn 'Abbās said that the squanderers are those who spend for no right purpose.

These two *ḥadīths* are the same, except that they have different chains of transmissions. Ibn 'Abbās explains the squander of money as spending it for wrongful purposes. A person who uses his money to fulfil the duties God has assigned to him, looking after his family and dependants, being hospitable to his guest, helping those in need, etc. is not a squanderer. This is using one's money for the right purposes. When money is used for forbidden purposes then it is squandered.

449. (*Athar* 106) Aslam said: ''Umar used to say on the platform (i.e. *minbar*): "People, keep your homes well maintained and scare these snakes before they can frighten you. The Muslims among the jinn [living in your houses in the form of small snakes] will never appear to you. We have not lived in peace with them since we have been hostile to them".'

In this *ḥadīth,* 'Umar advises Muslims to keep their dwellings secure and well maintained so that snakes do not find their way to abide within them. A snake moves in a slithering way and people may be unaware of them even when they are very close. Some of the jinn may also take the form of snakes. As is well known, the jinn are creatures that have been given freedom of choice, and they are required to believe in God's oneness like human beings. Prophet Muhammad (peace be upon him) was sent as God's last messenger to humans and the jinn. Hence, some of them are Muslims, even though the majority are not. This is what ʿUmar is warning against. If a jin takes the form of a snake and takes its abode in someone's home, it will not be known if it is a believer who will not harm people. It is better to take the precaution to keep human dwellings secure against all snakes, so as to protect our children, families and ourselves.

450. (*Athar* 107) Khabbāb said: 'A person is rewarded for whatever he spends except on buildings'.

Khabbāb ibn al-Aratt was one of the earliest people to accept Islam. As he was one of the weaker members of Makkan society, he was subjected to immense torture by the unbelievers, yet still he remained steadfast. This *ḥadīth* is understood to refer to high buildings that people do not need; it does not apply to people's homes. Moreover, it is important to make mosques and public buildings secure and safe. Islam does not like high-rise buildings and spending much money on their design and beauty.

451. (*Athar* 108) Nāfiʿ ibn ʿĀṣim said: 'ʿAbdullāh ibn ʿAmr asked a nephew of his who had come from al-Waht [i.e. Taif]: "Are your workers attending to their work?" He replied: "I do not know". ʿAbdullāh said: "Had you been from Thaqīf, you would have known what your workers are doing". He then turned to us and said: "When a person works with his workers in his house [or in his business], he is one of the workers of God, the Mighty and Exalted".'

ʿAbdullāh ibn ʿAmr was one of the young and early companions of the Prophet and he was a scholar who reported more than 700 *ḥadīths*. Here, he is giving advice to his nephew, telling him to be directly involved in his work, and not to leave his workers without supervision. He tells his nephew, who apparently lived in Taif, the town that was inhabited at the time by the major Arabian tribe, the Thaqīf, that the people of Thaqīf worked with their workers, and as such ensured that their work was properly done. 'Abdullāh then tells those who were present that a person who is involved with his workers is considered one of God's workers. This is a special grade to which everyone should aspire.

Raising buildings high

452. Abu Hurayrah reports that the Prophet said: 'The Last Hour will not come before people have competed with each other in constructing high buildings'.[325]

453. Al-Ḥasan said: 'I used to go into the homes of the Prophet's wives during 'Uthmān ibn 'Affān's reign. I could reach their ceilings with my hand'.[326]

454. Dāwūd ibn Qays said: 'I saw the apartments [of the Prophet's wives] with stumps of palm trees used in their building, which were covered with skins on the outside. I think that the width of the hall from the door of the apartment to the door of the inner room was about six or seven arm lengths, and I guess that the inner room was ten arm lengths and the roof was seven or eight arm lengths high, or thereabouts. I stood at 'Ā'ishah's door and discovered that it faced west'.[327]

455. (*Athar* 109) 'Abdullāh al-Rūmi said: 'I visited Umm Ṭalq. I said to her: "How low the roof of your home is!" She said: "The Caliph, 'Umar ibn al-Khaṭṭāb, wrote to his officials that they must not make their buildings tall, as this will come about in the worst of your days".'

All these *ḥadīths* make clear that people must not build their homes tall. The first *ḥadīth* makes the construction of high rise-buildings,

325. Related by al-Bukhari.
326. Related by Abū Dāwūd.
327. Related by Abū Dāwūd.

with people competing to make their buildings higher and higher, one of the signs of the Day of Judgement's approach. The second and third *ḥadīths* tell us how humble the Prophet's wives' homes were. Each one consisted of an entrance hall and one bedsitter of moderate size and the roof was so low that a young man like al-Ḥasan could reach the ceiling with his hand, using no chair or step ladder to stand on.

The Prophet's guidance was followed by his companions and successors. As we see in the last of these *ḥadīths* that 'Umar wrote to his officials that to construct high-rise buildings and making them a source of pride signalled the worst days. What shall we say about what we see in our cities across the world today?

456. Sallām ibn Shuraḥbīl said: 'Ḥabbah ibn Khālid and Sawā' ibn Khālid came to see the Prophet. They found him repairing a wall – or a building – and they helped him'.[328]

Apparently, the Prophet was attending to some damage that affected a building or a wall so as to repair it. When these two brothers saw him doing this, they volunteered their assistance. This was always the way of the Prophet's companions; delighting in any chance to help the Prophet in whatever he was doing.

457. Qays ibn Abu Ḥāzim said: 'We visited Khabbāb as he was ill after he had been cauterised seven times. He said: "Our companions who passed away have departed without letting this present life cause them any loss. Today we have so much that we can find no way of spending it except in buildings. Had it not been for the fact that God's Messenger has forbidden us to pray for death, I would have prayed for it".'[329]

458. 'We visited him another time when he was building a wall of his. He said: "A Muslim is rewarded for whatever he spends except for what he spends on buildings".'

---

328. Related by Aḥmad, Ibn Ḥibbān and Ibn Mājah.
329. Related by al-Bukhari, Muslim, al-Nasā'ī, al-Tirmidhi, and Ibn Mājah.

Khabbāb's illness was apparently aggravated by the torture he suffered in Makkah at the hands of the unbelievers. He once said: 'I do not know of any one of the Prophet's companions who suffered as much torture as I'. Yet he was lamenting the fact that he lived longer and became rich, feeling that this might have been part of his reward for his earlier sacrifices. He would have preferred that his reward was stored in full for him to receive such in the life to come, as was the case of those companions of the Prophet who died earlier. This explains his remark that he would have prayed to God to cause his death. However, he did not do so because the Prophet had prohibited it; such could be construed as a form of objecting to God's will and the bounty He grants to His servants in this life.

The second *ḥadīth* is the same as Number 450 and they both apply to buildings that a person does not need for his family residence. It should not be taken as meaning Khabbāb himself was building something he did not need. It is more likely that he was repairing some damage to his wall.

459. ʿAbdullāh ibn ʿAmr reports: 'The Prophet passed by when I was repairing a hut of ours. He asked: "What is this?" I said: "I am mending our hut, Messenger of God." He said: "The matter is sooner than that".'[330]

The Prophet's comment must not be understood as objecting to what ʿAbdullāh was doing, repairing his family's hut. He only meant that people may build houses and other constructions thinking that they will enjoy their use for many years to come. This diverts their attention from the need to prepare for the future life of the Hereafter.

460. Nāfiʿ ibn ʿAbd al-Ḥārith reports that the Prophet said: 'Aspects of man's happiness include a spacious dwelling, a good neighbour and a comfortable means of transport'.[331]

---

330. Related by Aḥmad, Abū Dāwūd, al-Tirmidhi, Ibn Mājah and Ibn Ḥibbān.
331. Related by Aḥmad.

This *ḥadīth* is the same as Number 116, and we have already explained it.

461. Thābit reports: 'I was with Anas at al-Zāwiyah in the upper storey of his house. He heard the call to prayer and he came down. I came down with him. As he walked, he took short steps and he explained: "I was with Zayd ibn Thābit and he walked with me in the same fashion. He said to me: 'Do you know why I am doing this before you? I was with the Prophet when he walked with me in this manner. He said to me: "Do you know the reason I am walking with you in this way?" I said: God and His Messenger know best. He said: "So that we will take a greater number of steps as we are walking to join the prayer".'[332]

Both Anas and Zayd ibn Thābit were companions of the Prophet, and this *ḥadīth* tells us that when they wished to join the congregational prayer, and had someone walking with them to the mosque, they walked in a certain fashion, taking short steps. Each of them asked his companion whether they realised why they were walking in this fashion. We then learn that it was the Prophet who started it, explaining that he wanted to increase the number of his steps as he walked to the mosque. Thus, the Prophet's companions were keen to pass the information on to others so that they could benefit by it. Increasing the number of steps means an increase in God's reward, as He gives the reward of a good deed for every step a person takes towards the mosque to join congregational prayer. Thus the *ḥadīth* gives us two points: the increased reward as we increase our steps walking to prayer, and passing on this information to others so that they can act on it.

462. Abu Hurayrah reports that the Prophet said: 'The Last Hour will not come before people build houses [they adorn] like coloured garments'. Ibrāhīm explained: 'He meant striped garments'.

---

332. Related by Ibn Abi Shaybah.

The Prophet has given us a number of signs that indicate the approach of the Day of Judgement. In this *ḥadīth* he talks about people becoming so affluent that they will decorate their houses as they design their garments. This is a scenario people realise when their standards of living rise and as a result, they begin to think of new ways of adornment and comfort.

463. Warrād, al-Mughīrah's scribe, said: 'Mu'āwiyah wrote to al-Mughīrah asking him to write down for him something he heard from God's Messenger (peace be upon him). Al-Mughirah wrote back: "The Prophet used to say after every [obligatory] prayer:

La ilāha illa Allah waḥdahu la sharīk lah. Lahu al-Mulk wa lahu al-ḥamd, wa huwa 'ala kulli shay'in qadir. Allahumma la māni'a lima a'ṭayt wala Mu'ṭiya lima mana't. Wala yanfa'u dhal jadd minka al-jadd."

Al-Mughīrha also wrote to him that the Prophet 'forbade idle talk, asking too many questions and squandering wealth. He also forbade undutifulness to mothers, burying daughters, withholding things and asking [others to give]".'[333]

The first thing to note about this *ḥadīth* is that Mu'āwiyah, the fifth of the Prophet's companions to be a caliph and who ruled the Muslim state for twenty years, would write to another companion asking him to write something he heard from the Prophet. He was asking him for something that he could do to earn reward from God. The Caliph was a late comer to Islam; his father led the Quraysh in its fight against Islam for a very long time, before finally accepting Islam. Mu'āwiyah accepted Islam before his father, but he kept this secret. When he joined the Prophet, he was one of the scribes to whom the Prophet dictated the Qur'anic revelations when he received them. He was keen to learn from other companions of the Prophet what the Prophet did or said.

---

333. Related by Aḥmad, al-Bukhari, Ibn Khuzaymah, Ibn Ḥibbān, Abu 'Awānah and al-Dārimi.

The first part al-Mughīrah wrote consisted of glorifications of God the Prophet used to say after each obligatory prayer. The meaning of these is as follows:

La ilāha illa Allah waḥdahu la sharīk lah means 'There is no deity other than God, the One Who has no partners'. *Lahu al-Mulk wa lahu al-ḥamd* means 'To Him belongs all dominion and to Him all praise is due'. *Wa huwa ʿala kulli shay'in qadīr* means 'He has power over all things'. *Allahumma la māniʿa lima aʿṭayt wala Muʿṭiya lima manaʿt* means 'My Lord, no one can withhold what You give, and no one can give what You withhold'. *Wala yanfaʿu dhal jadd minka al-jadd* means 'The efforts exerted by any hard worker can be of no avail against Your will'. This last sentence may also be interpreted as 'The possessions of any wealthy person can avail him nothing against You'. The only thing that is useful to a person is his or her obedience to God and doing His bidding. We will do well to follow the Prophet's example and say these glorifications after we finish every obligatory prayer.

Al-Mughīrah then gives the Caliph an aspect of the Prophet's guidance that is most relevant to his status. He tells him that the Prophet 'forbade idle talk, asking too many questions and squandering wealth'. All these we have explained in commenting on *ḥadīth* Number 445, but we may add that these may be particularly relevant to the Caliph as those who may attend him may engage in these.

Al-Mughīrah adds three other practices the Prophet made clear to his community that they are forbidden. The first is undutifulness to mothers. It is well known that Islam requires its followers to be dutiful to their parents, but the Prophet stressed that a Muslim must not be undutiful to his mother. This is because it is easier to be undutiful to one's mother, as this is unlikely to be known in the community, and also because women are more vulnerable to abuse than men.

Prior to Islam, parents used to bury their young daughters alive for fear of poverty or shame. A girl did not earn her living and did not participate in fighting. If she was guilty of illegitimate sex, she could bring shame to her family and her clan. To guard against such eventualities, some Arabs buried their daughters alive when they were very young. Islam makes clear that this practice is strictly forbidden.

The last practice the Prophet mentions is miserliness and greed. This is expressed in the *ḥadīth* as withholding things while asking for what others have. Needless to say, people look up to their rulers for what they want and rulers can withhold what is due to their subjects. Hence, al-Mughīrah felt such instructions by the Prophet should be conveyed to the Caliph.

Requirement to enter heaven

464. Abu Hurayrah reports that the Prophet said: 'None of you will be saved by his actions [alone]'. People asked: 'Not even you, Messenger of God?' He replied: 'Not even me, unless God bestows His mercy on me. Therefore, act correctly and wisely, and worship in the morning and evening and during part of the night. Keep to a middle path and you will arrive'.[334]

This is a clear statement by the Prophet that one's own actions will never be sufficient to save one. How is it, then, that we insist that everyone must strive hard to do what pleases God? How is it that we always say that only through good actions can one ever hope to achieve admission into heaven? Scholars maintain that admission into heaven is not the reward equivalent to what any one may do in this life. All good actions that a person may do throughout his life, when done in the best shape and form, free from hypocrisy and self-indulgence, are not equivalent to express one's gratitude to God for even a fraction of the great favours He bestows on man. When this is the case, how can his good actions suffice to admit him into heaven? When we consider that man must show enough gratitude to God for the grace He has bestowed on him and all the blessings with which He has favoured him, then we realise that no matter how well a man does throughout his life, he continues to fall short of what is required of him.

However, there are plenty of Qur'anic verses and *ḥadīths* which emphasise that man must always do well and that his actions will determine whether he is admitted into heaven or not. One Qur'anic verse tells us that on the Day of Judgement believers will be addressed in the following words: '*Enter into heaven as a result of what you*

334. Related by al-Bukhari, Muslim and Ibn Mājah.

have done [in your life]'. (16: 32) What we have to remember is that there can be no conflict between an authentic *ḥadīth* and a Qur'anic statement. This *ḥadīth* enjoys a high degree of authenticity. How can we, then, reconcile its message with that of the Qur'anic verses like the one we have quoted?

Scholars speak at length on this, advancing several opinions which are perfectly valid and logical. For example, Imam Ibn Ḥajar, a leading authority on *ḥadīth* makes it clear that actions by themselves do not make a person merit heaven. They must first be accepted by God. Such acceptance is God's own prerogative. He determines which actions to accept and which to reject. No one can decide for Him and no one can be certain that his own actions will be accepted by God. When God accepts someone's actions, He does so by His Grace. He bestows that grace on whomever He wills. If we understand this, we know that the Qur'anic verse means that the believers will be admitted to heaven as a result of those of their actions which God accepts.

What this means in a nutshell is that good actions require something extra to ensure admission to heaven; they cannot give that result by themselves. The extra factor is that they must be accepted by God. His acceptance is an act of grace with which He favours only those of His servants who show an exemplary degree of dedication to His cause.

In explaining this *ḥadīth*, Imam al-Nawawi mentions that it is only through God's grace that a person is guided to do what pleases God and to make his actions solely dedicated to the service of His cause. Similarly, acceptance of people's actions is a sign of God's grace. Developing his idea, al-Nawawi says that the net sum of all this is that a person is not admitted to heaven on account of his actions only, since he has been guided to do these actions by God's grace. At the same time, his actions are the cause of his admission to heaven and this in itself, is part of God's grace.

Indeed, God's grace is bestowed on us from the moment we see the light of this world until we depart from it. It is manifested in a great many ways. We cannot be as we are, and cannot think, evaluate matters or act in any situation as we actually do without God's grace. Again, it is God's grace that has given us the guidance contained in the message which He revealed to His messenger, Prophet Muhammad (peace be upon him). When we follow it, we do so only through His grace. Therefore, when we do what pleases God, we benefit by what He has bestowed on us. Therefore, we cannot consider our actions in isolation of His grace. When He accepts our actions, He shows us even greater favour by accepting that which we could only do through His favour. His acceptance means admission to heaven and that is the greatest act of grace He bestows on us.

It must have surprised the Prophet's companions to hear him state that none can be saved by his own actions. After all, they were striving hard to please God. Therefore, they asked him whether the same ruling applied to him. The question is certainly pertinent because we know that the Prophet is sure to have the highest position in heaven which will be given to any human being. If the same rule applied to him, then it applied to every human being. Sure enough, the Prophet stressed that the rule applies to him, but he also mentioned something which gives us all clear hope: 'Not even me, unless God bestows His mercy on me.' It goes without saying that if the Prophet needs God's mercy for getting the position assured him on the Day of Judgement, then every one of us stands in much greater need of God's mercy. We know that God is always merciful and that He grants His mercy to everyone who asks for it, provided that he supports his request with actions that please God.

This conversation between the Prophet and his companions may make some despair that no matter how hard they try, they will not rise to a level which even remotely compares with that of the Prophet. So, should one dedicate oneself totally to worship, excluding all other activities and concerns? Should we abandon all the comforts of life and concentrate on worship during the day and the night, allowing ourselves only little rest before we start again? Should we fast every day and stand in prayer every night? Even if we do this, how sure are we of being accepted and saved?

The Prophet realised that such thoughts might have been in the back of his companions' minds, or may be entertained by Muslims in subsequent generations. Therefore, he went on to make it clear that this is not required. He stated: 'Therefore, act correctly and wisely, and worship in the morning and evening, and during part of the night. Keep to a middle path and you will arrive'.

The first point about what we should do is to act correctly. This means following the Prophet's example. God has given us in the Qur'an, and the Prophet has explained to us in the Sunnah, what actions are correct and likely to be accepted by God. But we should also act wisely, which means that we are not supposed to tire ourselves out in worship, in order to avoid reaching a point of saturation and boredom that leads us to slacken. There are numerous *ḥadīths* which stress the need to maintain moderation in worship. The *ḥadīth* we are discussing goes further to explain that worship, when done wisely, means that one allocates a part of one's time in the morning and a part in the afternoon to worship, as well as some time in the night.

The total sum of the Prophet's advice is to 'keep to a middle path'. This stresses moderation in all aspects, including worship. If we do this, without going to extremes in either direction we 'will arrive'. This means arriving at being saved, as this is the message we understand from the way the beginning of this *ḥadīth* is phrased. It speaks about salvation from the fire of hell. We arrive in heaven, which means the most complete salvation. No one who arrives there needs anything else because he has achieved the prize to which all people aspire and which ensures his everlasting happiness.

25

A Gentle Approach All the Time

SOME TIMES PEOPLE deliberately twist words so that they mean something totally different from what they are supposed to mean. Some of the Jews in Madinah tried to do this when they met the Prophet. It is worth remembering that the standard Islamic greeting is '*al-salamu 'alaykum*', which means 'peace be to you'. The standard answer is to return the same greeting, saying, '*wa 'alaykum al-salam*,' which means, 'and to you be peace'. One can add to this in order to make the answer a better greeting. However, the operative word is '*salam*'; but if one omits the letter, 'l', to make it sound like *saam*, it acquires a totally different meaning, for '*sām*' means 'death'. At times, some of the Jews in Madinah tried to vent their hostility against Islam by saying to Muslims, '*al-sāmu 'alaykum*', omitting the 'l' in the first word. On one particular occasion, the Jews tried to do this to the Prophet himself.

465. ʿĀ'ishah, the Prophet's wife, reports: 'A group of Jews came in to see God's Messenger (peace be upon him), but they said, "*al-sāmu ʿalaykum*". I understood what they said and answered them: "And to you be *sām* and God's curse". God's Messenger said to me: "Gently, ʿĀ'ishah. God loves gentleness in all matters". I said, Messenger of God! Have you not heard what they said?" He replied, "I said to them, 'and to you!'"'[335]

It is easy to understand ʿĀ'ishah's reaction to such an abominable method of twisting words in order to abuse instead of greet. She was a young wife who loved her husband dearly and was infuriated by the fact that the Jews who had come to see him, pretending to be friendly were actually wishing him death. What concerns us most here is the way the Prophet tried to calm her. He reminds her that God does not like Muslims to react violently in returning insults. He prefers that they take a gentler approach. When she protested that she was only answering them back, the Prophet said to her that he had returned what they said to him by saying, 'And to you'. Indeed, he instructs us in a different *ḥadīth* to return the greetings of non-Muslims in this manner because they may twist their words in order to conceal their hostility.

It is most significant that the Prophet uses this particular occasion in order to drive home to us the fact that God prefers that we take a gentle, caring approach. One may ask: why do we have to care about people who wish us death? The answer is that we should not try to deliberately escalate hostility. Moreover, a gentle attitude is perhaps the most effective way of reducing their hostility to us, when we cannot win them over to a position of friendship. If we are in the business of conveying God's message to mankind, we should try to ensure a favourable reception to it by others. We cannot achieve this without overcoming initial grudges and hostility. A kind, caring and compassionate approach is the surest way to achieve this result.

In his own behaviour, the Prophet gives a perfect example of the caring and compassionate approach he advocates. Knowing that the

335. Related by al-Bukhari.

Prophet never preaches something without being himself the first to put it in practice, we can easily say without any fear of being contradicted that he was the most gentle, caring and compassionate of people. You need only cast a glance at the *ḥadīths* which encourage such an attitude to realise this.

466. Jarīr ibn 'Abdullāh reports that the Prophet said: 'Whoever is denied gentleness has been denied goodness'.[336]

467. Abu al-Dardā' reports that the Prophet said: 'He who has been given his portion of gentleness has been given his full share of goodness. He who is denied his portion of gentleness has been deprived of his share of goodness. Good manners are the weightiest element in a believer's balance on the Day of Resurrection. God dislikes a person who is coarse and foul-mouthed'.[337]

468. 'Ā'ishah reports that the Prophet said: 'Overlook the slips of virtuous people'.[338]

All people slip and make mistakes. To overlook the slips and errors of people who are known to be virtuous is to help them to be more cautious so that they do not make further errors. This applies to a judge or ruler who looks at the errors of others, and it also applies to others who should acknowledge the status of such people and treat them accordingly.

469. Anas reports that the Prophet said: 'If there is roughness in any thing, it mars it. God is gentle and He loves gentleness'.[339]

---

336. Related by Aḥmad, Muslim, Abū Dāwūd, Ibn Mājah, Abu 'Awānah and Ibn Khuzaymah.

337. Related in part by al-Tirmidhi and Abū Dāwūd, and in full by Ibn Ḥibbān and Ibn Khuzaymah.

338. Related by Abū Dāwūd and al-Nasā'ī in Al-Sunan al-Kubra.

339. Related by al-Tirmidhi and Ibn Mājah.

470. Abu Sa'īd al-Khudri said: 'God's Messenger (peace be upon him) was more modest than a virgin in her private room. When he disliked something, we recognised this in his face'.[340]

This *ḥadīth* is entered in the context of ease and gentleness on account of the Prophet's reaction to what he disliked. He did not confront people with what he felt; he was too modest for this. He let them do what they wanted, as long as it was permissible, but they recognised his feelings by changes in his facial expression. How polite and considerate!

471. Ibn 'Abbās reports that the Prophet said: 'Right guidance, good behaviour and a moderate way of life are one of seventy parts of prophethood'.[341]

472. 'Ā'ishah said: 'I was on a camel that was somewhat troublesome. The Prophet (peace be upon him) said [to me]: "Be gentle. When gentleness is in something, it adorns it, and when it is removed from it, it mars it".'[342]

Even in dealing with animals, the Prophet urged gentleness. Roughness brings no good results. The *ḥadīth* mentions that his wife was finding her camel troublesome and difficult. She was apparently irritated. Another version of this *ḥadīth*, which will be stated under Number 478, mentions that she beat the camel. However, the Prophet told her that her action would not bring about the desired result. It is only gentleness and an easy approach that makes things right and enjoyable. Even in dealing with a difficult animal, gentleness is more likely to succeed. Needless to say, beating a camel, a horse, or a donkey too hard may lead to the opposite result of what the rider intends.

---

340. Related by al-Bukhari and Muslim.

341. Related by Abū Dāwūd.

342. Related by Muslim

Greed and injustice

One quality which the Prophet was always keen to emphasise, warning his companions and followers against its consequences, was greed and its related aspects of miserliness and avarice.

473. Abu Hurayrah reports that the Prophet said: 'Beware of avarice. It destroyed those before you. They shed each other's blood and cut off their relatives. Injustice will become piles of darkness on the Day of Resurrection'.[343]

This *ḥadīth* is very similar to Number 486, and we note that in both the Prophet combines injustice with avarice even though they most probably were stated on different occasions. Perhaps we do not need to speak about injustice on this occasion, because no one denies that injustice is a great evil. The fact that there is so much injustice in the world serves only to emphasise that the misery which results from it is widespread. Its description as 'piles of darkness on the Day of Judgement' is very significant. The believers will have light all around them, wherever they go; their faces will be beaming with it. Since injustice is associated with so much darkness, it is described in terms of disbelief.

In Arabic, injustice and darkness are thought of as very close, especially because, linguistically, they are derived from the same root, *ẓalama*. In this particular *ḥadīth*, the Prophet uses the feminine form of the word injustice to denote darkness. This is perfectly acceptable from a linguistic point of view, but darkness is denoted in other forms, also derived from the same root as injustice. Indeed this usage is more emphatic than using any other word with similar derivation, because the Prophet uses the feminine form in its plural, while other derivations cannot be so used.

The Prophet tells us about the effects on social life of avarice when it is wide spread. It leads people to ruin. An avaricious person will do all he can in order to hold on to his property and deny it to others.

343. Related by Aḥmad and Ibn Ḥibbān.

In this *ḥadīth*, the Prophet tells us that an avaricious person can kill in order to deny others a share of his wealth. But this is not the only way that avarice can lead to bloodshed. Indeed, it can lead to civil strife.

When the rich in society do all they can to hold on to their privileges, much of which may be unjustly preserved, this leads to the fermentation of hatred in society. The poor, who have endured long term poverty and deprivation, while looking at the rich enjoying their luxuries without allowing them to have any part of this great surplus, may rise up in revolt. The rich may want to protect their privileges and this may lead to a civil war as has happened throughout history. It is to this that the Prophet refers when he says that avarice has destroyed communities before us.

Equally important in the eyes of the Prophet (peace be upon him) is the fact that avarice leads to the boycotting of one's relatives, especially the poor among them. An avaricious person will not want his poor relatives to come to him, because he may feel obliged to help those who are badly in need. He prefers instead to bury his head in the sand, pretending that the difficulty of having to help a relative will just disappear. This is nothing less than shutting one's relatives out. Islam attaches great importance to furthering ties of kinship. Anything that militates against the strengthening of these ties is condemned by Islam. Avarice is such a trait. Therefore, it receives such strong condemnation from the Prophet.

474. (*Athar* 110) Kathīr ibn 'Ubayd said: 'I called on 'Ā'ishah, the Mother of the Believers. She said: "Wait until I mend my garment". I waited. [When I entered] I said: "Mother of the Believers, if I were to go out and tell people about this, they would consider what you did as a sign of miserliness". She said: "Mind your own business. A person who does not wear his old garments will have no new clothes".'

'Ā'ishah was very generous. She might receive a great amount as her own share from the state, but she would give all this away, leaving very little for herself. The Prophet encouraged her to do so, and he told her not to get new clothes until she had worn her old ones until they were patched. She acted on his advice until the end of her life.

In this *ḥadīth* we are told that Kathīr, who was her brother through breastfeeding, felt that her action might be seen as an act of miserliness. She cared little for this because people were aware of her generosity.

475. ʿAbdullāh ibn Mughaffal reports that the Prophet said: 'God is gentle and He loves gentleness. He gives for it what He does not give for harshness'.[344]

476. Anas ibn Mālik reports that the Prophet said: 'Make things easy and do not make them difficult. Calm people down and do not cause them to be alarmed'.[345]

477. (*Athhar* 111) ʿAbdullāh ibn ʿAmr said: 'A guest was with a family of the Children of Israel. They had a bitch in the house. They said to her: "Bitch, do not bark at our guest". The puppies under her barked. They mentioned this to a prophet of theirs. He said: "This is like a community that will come after you, in which idiots will prevail over its men of knowledge".'[346]

478. ʿĀ'ishah said: 'I was on a camel that was somewhat troublesome. I beat the camel, but the Prophet (peace be upon him) said [to me]: "Be gentle. When gentleness is in something, it adorns it, and when it is removed from it, it mars it".'[347]

All these *ḥadīths* stress the importance of gentleness in all aspects and all spheres of life. The Prophet makes his advice general so that it applies to all situations. In the first *ḥadīth* he encourages gentleness, showing that it is the attitude God loves people to maintain. He rewards them for it far more than harshness that aims to achieve the same result. Harshness may be employed to deter people from doing wrong, but if one can achieve this by adopting a gentle approach, one stands to earn greater reward from God.

---

344. Related by Muslim and Abū Dāwūd.
345. Related by al-Bukhari, Muslim and al-Nasā'ī.
346. Related by Aḥmad.
347. Related by Muslim.

The second *ḥadīth* gives general advice to make things easy and facilitate their doing. The Prophet emphasises his point by advising one thing and following it up with advice against its opposite.

The fourth *ḥadīth* is the same as Number 472, but in this instance, it adds that 'Ā'ishah beat the camel when it was troublesome. Yet the Prophet advised her that gentleness to the animal was more likely to get her what she wanted. It is more becoming of her because gentleness adorns everything it is associated with.

A proper look at life

479. (*Athar* 112) Abu Naḍrah reports that one of their men called Jābir or Juwaybir said: 'I went to 'Umar when he was Caliph to request something I needed. I arrived in Madinah during the night, so I went to see him in the morning. I was a man of intelligence and clear expression – or he said eloquence. I spoke, condemning the life of this world, belittling it so as to show it worth nothing. There was by 'Umar's side a man with grey hair wearing white clothes. When I had finished, he said: "All that you said was almost correct, except for your belittling of the life of this world. Do you know what this present life is? It is through this life that we reach our goal in the life to come, or perhaps it is here that we have what we need to get to the life to come. It is in this life that we do our deeds that earn our reward in the life to come". Thus it was described by someone who knew it better than me. I asked the Caliph: "Who is this man sitting next to you?" He said: "He is the best of Muslims, Ubay ibn Ka'b".'

Who was Ubay ibn Ka'b, the man described by no lesser an authority than 'Umar ibn al-Khaṭṭāb as the Muslims' master, or the best of Muslims? He belonged to the Anṣār and was among the earliest people in Madinah to accept Islam. He was one of four Anṣāri men who learnt the Qur'an, in full, by heart during the Prophet's lifetime. One day the Prophet went to him and said: 'God has commanded me to recite to you this surah'. Ubay asked: 'And God has mentioned me by name?' The Prophet said: 'Yes'. Overwhelmed, Ubay wept and said: 'Then recite, Messenger of God'.[348] The Prophet recited as instructed by God. Needless to say, a man named by God in this way is very special indeed. Ubay was so special that recitation of the Qur'an was learnt from him by so many in the early days of Islam.

The *ḥadīth* is reported by an intelligent person who could put an argument across and express his thoughts very clearly. In conversation with the Caliph, he started to belittle our present life in this world. This is very common among Muslims. They often criticise this present life, stating that it is worthless and of little consequence. Ubay gave the counter argument. It is this life that is a bridge leading to the life to come. If we want to arrive at the right abode, heaven, in the life to come then we must do what it takes to ensure our comfortable passage. It is through our actions in this life that we receive God's reward that enables us to be admitted into heaven.

480. Al-Barā' ibn 'Āzib reports that the Prophet said: 'Ingratitude is evil'.

This *ḥadīth* needs no comment. It is certainly evil to show no gratitude when anyone does us a favour. Needless to say, God has bestowed great favours on everyone of us, and to be ungrateful to God does not bring any good thing to the one who is so ungrateful.

481. (*Athar* 113) Al-Ḥārith ibn Laqīṭ said: 'Anyone of us might have his mare giving birth to a colt, and he would slaughter it, saying: "I do not think that I will live to ride this horse?" We then received 'Umar's letter telling us to make good use of what God has given us for there is plenty of time'.

The Qur'an often mentions that the Last Hour that signals the arrival of the Day of Judgement is close at hand. The early Muslims accepted this as so real that they felt that it could come at any time. This *ḥadīth* describes the attitude of some of them as one may look at a newborn colt feeling that one might not live long enough for the colt to become

348. Related by al-Bukhari.

a rideable horse. Therefore, one might consider slaughtering it. This, however, was the wrong attitude. When 'Umar heard of it, he wrote to these people saying that there would be plenty of time.

Today, most Muslims do not take the arrival of the Day of Judgement as close at hand, because they realise that fourteen centuries have passed since the Qur'an's revelation and life continues. They, thus, put the description of its being close in its proper perspective, in relation to the age of the earth and the length of human life. They realise that we need to understand the Last Hour in its two different senses: the individual and the general. As related to individuals, the Last Hour may come at any moment, as it signifies death. When a person dies, he can no longer do anything to affect his destiny. The general sense relates to the Day of Judgement.

The idea of effort and reward is central to Islamic thinking. Every action can earn reward from God if it is intended for the right purpose. Since it is the amount of reward a person earns in this life that ensures his destiny in the Hereafter, then everything that may increase his reward is very appealing to a Muslim.

The Prophet was always keen to point out what action or attitude could earn reward and he encouraged his companions to do as many as possible of such actions. He often emphasised the importance of certain types of work by pointing out that they were bound to earn reward.

482. Anas ibn Mālik reports that the Prophet said: 'If the Last Hour is highly imminent and any one of you has a palm-cutting in his hand, and he can manage to plant it before the Hour strikes, then he should plant it'.[349]

Another version of this *ḥadīth* makes its ending clause as follows: 'Then he should plant it, for he will be rewarded for this'.

What is particularly significant here is not merely the fact that a purely worldly action is given a heavenly reward, but the action itself is of no particular use either to the person who does it or to anyone else. The cutting that is likely to grow into a tree, which the Prophet

349. Related by Aḥmad.

encourages us to plant, even at the point when the Last Hour is about to strike, is a date tree, which does not start to yield its fruit for several years. However, this is very consistent with Islamic philosophy which gives reward for every constructive action. When one has a choice between planting a small tree and leaving it to die, one should not hesitate for a single moment. Planting it is a constructive action, so it must be done. Moreover, that action signifies an attitude which promotes life. Therefore, it is rewarded by God.

The Prophet expresses his message in a particularly vivid manner. The *ḥadīth* shows a person who is trying hard to push back the Last Hour until he has finished planting the young tree. But why should he bother in the first place? After all, the end of human life on earth is very close. Who will benefit by that tree? The answer is that most probably no one will ever benefit by it. But the Prophet's message serves to emphasise that one must do good work at every moment in one's life. Work stops when life has stopped, not a moment earlier. Such an approach builds civilisations. And it is this particular attitude that has made the Islamic civilisation unique. It always looks at what is constructive and takes every measure to fulfil it. This is not to say that Islam does not allow its followers to enjoy their spare time, rather that the best enjoyment is a constructive one.

Although the *ḥadīth* speaks of the Last Hour, which signals the end of human life, and indeed all life on earth, it has a particular significance to everyone. Human beings always tend to think that life will continue forever. After all, so many generations have passed and there is nothing peculiar to make our own generation unique. Therefore, it should not be expected that the Day of Judgement comes at the end of our lifetime.

Death, then, is the hour for every single one of us. At the point of death, if any of us has the time or the ability to do a good action, even though it may be of no benefit to oneself or to one's offspring, one should do it because then one will be earning a reward from God for it. This improves one's lot in the life to come. For a Muslim, this is something worth working for, right to the last breath of one's life.

This *ḥadīth* is echoed by another attributed to one of the Prophet's companions:

483. (*Athar* 114) 'Abdullāh ibn Salām said: 'If you hear that the Impostor (*al-Dajjāl*) has come out and you are planting a date sapling, do not give up on planting it properly. For people still have life after that'.

This *ḥadīth* speaks about the Impostor (*al-Dajjāl*) whose appearance is one of the signs of the approaching Day of Judgement, but it does not signify that it is highly imminent. Hence, it mentions that life will still continue.

484. Abu Hurayrah reports that the Prophet said: 'Three supplications are definitely answered: a supplication by one who suffers injustice; a supplication by one who is travelling; and a supplication by a parent against his own child'.

To start with, we may say that all supplications said in earnest are answered. God says in the Qur'an: 'Your Lord says: "*Call on Me, and I shall answer you*". (40: 60) However, the answer to the prayer may take one of three forms: God may give the supplicant what he has prayed for, or He may give him something better because He knows that what he prayed for is not good enough for him, or He may defer the answer until the Day of Judgement. When the supplicant realises what he is getting instead of what he missed out on in this present life, he will wish that God had deferred answering all his supplications.

This *ḥadīth* tells us that these three are certain to have their prayers answered. The first is the supplication of one who suffers injustice. God dislikes injustice, as we will see presently. He knows what the sufferer of injustice feels and He answers his prayer. In our world today we see much injustice, and we wonder why God allows it. This life is human life, and God lets people do what they want. He will settle all accounts and give justice to everyone who suffers injustice. There is no doubt about this.

When a person is travelling, he misses his family and is eager to make sure that they are all right. He longs to return so as to feel settled. His prayers are answered as they mostly concentrate on the welfare of his family and community.

The last one is a prayer by a parent against his own child. This must be due to the child doing something really bad, hurting his parents and making them feel miserable. A parent does not pray against his child unless he is immensely hurt. Hence, his prayer is definitely answered.

485. Jābir reports that he heard the Prophet saying on the platform (i.e. *minbar*): 'He looked towards the Yemen and said: "My Lord, let their hearts come forward". He looked towards Iraq and said the same. He looked in every direction and said the same. He then said: "Our Lord, provide for us out of what the earth produces and bless our measures for us".'[350]

This *ḥadīth* shows that the Prophet was keen that people everywhere were enabled to see the truth of God's message and believe in it. Hence, his supplication that their hearts should come forward and respond to the call of truth. He then prayed for plentiful provisions and a blessing in what people buy and sell by measure.

486. Jābir reports that the Prophet said: 'Guard against injustice, for injustice will become piles of darkness on the Day of Resurrection. Beware of avarice. It destroyed those before you. It led them to shed each other's blood and to indulge in what they were forbidden'.[351]

This *ḥadīth* is very similar to Number 473, with only a slight variation in wording and a different chain of transmission. We explained it earlier. It will come again in part under Number 488, in a different arrangement in 490 and with similar wording in 491.

487. Jābir reports that the Prophet said: 'In the late generations of my community there will be punishment by deformation, missiles and a sinking earth. It will begin with people who commit injustice'.

350. Related by Aḥmad.
351. Related by Aḥmad, Muslim and Abu 'Awānah.

This *ḥadīth* speaks about types of punishment which God may inflict on some people in later generations. The *ḥadīth* does not specify what will bring about such punishment or the sins that the people to suffer such punishments will have committed. Yet we should always remember that God is always fair to all people. The Prophet specifies that the first to be punished are those who commit injustice.

488. ʿAbdullāh ibn ʿUmar reports that the Prophet said: 'Injustice will be piles of darkness on the Day of Resurrection'.[352]

489. Abu Saʿīd al-Khudri reports that the Prophet said: 'When believers are saved from the Fire they will be halted on a bridge in between heaven and hell. They will set off wrongs they have done each other in the life of this world. After they have been cleansed and disciplined, they will be given permission to enter heaven. By Him Who holds Muhammad's soul in His hand, every one of them will know his place there better than his dwelling in this world'.[353]

490. Abu Hurayrah reports that the Prophet said: 'Guard against injustice, for injustice will become piles of darkness on the Day of Resurrection. Beware of vulgar language, as God does not like a person who is given to utter vulgarities and obscenities. Beware of avarice. It led those before you to shed each other's blood and to indulge in what they were forbidden'.[354]

491. Jābir reports that the Prophet said: 'Guard against injustice, for injustice will become piles of darkness on the Day of Resurrection. Beware of avarice. It destroyed those before you. It led them to shed each other's blood and to indulge in what they were forbidden'.[355]

---

352. Related by Aḥmad, al-Bukhari, Muslim, al-Tirmidhi and Abu ʿAwānah.
353. Related by Aḥmad, al-Bukhari, and al-Tirmidhi.
354. Related by Aḥmad and Ibn Ḥibbān.
355. Related by Muslim with slightly different wording.

The first, third and fourth of these *ḥadīths* are similar to Number 473 which has been fully explained.

Ḥadīth Number 489 speaks about a situation in the life to come, when the believers will have safely crossed the narrow passage over hell. Now they are safe from hell and are being prepared for admission into heaven. Yet they have done one another some injustice and committed wrongs against one another. Justice needs to be restored between them. They are required to set off their wrongs against each other. This is done by taking away some of the good deeds of one person and giving these to the one he wronged. Both may be guilty of doing some wrong to each other and these are set off against each other. Some scholars suggest that these wrongs must be trivial, because serious ones are only purged through the fire. However, God's mercy may erase even the worst of sins. The set off process is to cleanse them and prepare them for admission into heaven. When they are permitted to enter, they aim to get to their places, and each will know his or her place there.

492. (*Athar* 115) Abu al-Ḍuḥa said: 'Masrūq and Shutayr ibn Shakal were together in the mosque. The people in different circles in the mosque moved towards them. Masrūq said [to Shutayr]: "I can only think that these people have gathered around us in order to listen to something useful from us. So either you relate some things you heard from 'Abdullāh [ibn Mas'ūd] and I will confirm you, or I will relate some things from 'Abdullāh and you confirm me". He said: "You relate, Abu 'Ā'ishah".

'[Masrūq] said: "Did you hear 'Abdullāh say: 'The eyes commit fornication, the hands commit fornication and the legs commit fornication, and then the genitals either confirm this or deny it'?" [Shutayr] said: "Yes, I heard it". Masrūq said: "And I heard him say it. Did you hear 'Abdullāh say: 'No verse in the Qur'an is more comprehensive in stating the permissible and the forbidden, commands and prohibitions than "*God enjoins justice, kindness [to all], and generosity to one's kindred; and He forbids all that is shameful, all reprehensible conduct and aggression?*" (16: 90) Shutayr said: "Yes, I heard it". Masruq said: "And I heard him say it. Did you hear 'Abdullāh say: 'No verse in the Qur'an brings relief faster than '*For everyone who fears God, He will grant a way out?*" (65: 2) Shutayr said: "Yes". Masrūq said: "And I heard him say it. Did you hear 'Abdullāh say: 'No verse in the Qur'an is stronger in entrusting everything to God than "*You servants of Mine who have transgressed against their own souls! Do not despair of God's Mercy: God forgives all sins; He alone is much forgiving, ever merciful?*"" (39:53) Shutayr said: "Yes". Masrūq said: "And I heard him say it".'[356]

Both Masrūq and Shutayr belonged to the generation of al-tabi'īn, which succeeded the Prophet's companions. They were both disciples of 'Abdullāh ibn Mas'ūd, one of the most learned scholars among the Prophet's companions. Therefore, when people in different circles in the mosque saw them together, they gathered around them, hoping to listen to something that was very useful and having the authority of the Prophet's companion. This they gave them, with both confirming the source.

The first part speaks of different organs committing fornication. This is mentioned in other *ḥadīths* as well. When someone casts lustful looks at a woman other than his wife, this is an act of fornication even though only his eyes are involved. If a person goes to a place where he wants to commit fornication, the very act of walking there is an act of fornication, although only his legs are involved. Hence, the statement adds that the genitals either confirm such fornication, by going the full distance or not. If the man stops short of committing actual fornication, then looks, steps and other actions are considered minor offences that God may forgive when the person concerned declares his repentance and seeks God's forgiveness.

The rest of the *ḥadīth* is self explanatory. It highlights the message given in each of the verses quoted.

356. Related by al-Ḥākim.

26

No Room for Injustice

493. Abu Dharr reports that the Prophet said that God [limitless is He in His Glory] said: 'My servants, I have forbidden oppression for Myself and have made it forbidden among you, so do not oppress one another. My servants, you sin by night and by day, and I forgive all sins and do so freely, so seek forgiveness of Me and I shall forgive you.

'My servants, all of you are hungry except for those I have fed, so seek food of Me and I shall feed you. My servants, all of you are naked except for those I have clothed, so seek clothing of Me and I shall clothe you.

'My servants, were the first of you and the last of you, the human of you and the jinn of you to be as pious as the most pious heart of any one man of you, that would not increase My kingdom in anything. My servants, were they all to be as wicked as the most wicked heart of any one man of you, that would not decrease My kingdom in anything. My servants, were they all to

> rise up in one place and make a request of Me, and were I to give everyone what they have requested, that would not decrease what I have any more than a needle decreases the ocean if put into it.
>
> 'My servants, it is but your deeds that I reckon up for you and then recompense you for, so let him who finds good praise God and let him who finds other than that blame no one but himself'.[357]

This *ḥadīth* is very important because it defines certain aspects of the relationship between God and ourselves. When we consider it in its details, we are bound to come to the conclusion that it is absolutely correct in every word. However, what is significant in this *qudsi ḥadīth* is that it gives a preamble for every instruction it contains.

We are clearly told by God that we must not oppress one another. The reasons He gives for this are the fact that He has forbidden oppression for Himself and that He has forbidden oppression among us. There is no doubt that when God forbids something we must refrain from doing it. The authority to forbid anything belongs solely to God. This is a primary concept of Islam. God has created man and put him in charge of the earth, making everything on it subservient to him. This authority which God has given to man can only be restricted by the One Who has given it, namely, God Himself. The statement of prohibition here is one of the clearest. It leaves no doubt that injustice and oppression are absolutely forbidden. Since the ultimate goal of man in this life, as Islam defines it, is to earn God's pleasure through obeying His commandments, then committing oppression and injustice is bound to make the attainment of that goal unlikely.

Yet there is an even stronger reason for refraining from oppression. This is the one outlined in the first statement which tells us that God has forbidden Himself injustice. We all know that God has full power to do what He likes in this universe. There is neither authority nor power to stand up to Him or to prevent His purpose. His will is done in the heavens and on earth. Yet it is He Who has chosen to restrict that power by forbidding Himself oppression and injustice.

---

357. Related by Aḥmad, Muslim, Ibn Mājah, al-Hakim, Ibn Ḥibbān and Abu 'Awānah.

When we appreciate this, we are bound to realise how hateful oppression is. Indeed, it is the most hateful practice a human being may follow. It is degrading to the one who purports injustice and to the one at the receiving end of it. Whatever we do, we must not allow ourselves to be guilty of injustice or oppression. It is for this reason that Islam stresses in a variety of ways the importance of justice.

God then directs our attentions to the fact that we are in need of His favours at every turn of our lives. God tells us next that we are so prone to sin to the extent that we indulge in it at all times, by night and day, and we are liable to bear the consequences of what we do. This is a fact that no one can dispute. We need only to look at what we do, what thoughts we may entertain and how we try to accomplish our ends. If God were to punish us as we deserve for all this, our punishment would be very severe indeed. However, God reminds us here that He forgives all sins and mistakes. No sin is unforgivable with the exception of associating partners with God and claiming that Godhead and Lordship in the universe are not His alone. Short of this, even the most grievous of sins may be forgiven if we turn to God with sincere repentance and pray to Him to forgive us.

It may be asked, why is forgiveness dependant on our praying to God for it? Why does He not forgive us our sins of His own accord? The answer is that He certainly does. When we follow a bad deed which we may have committed with a good one, the latter is sufficient to ensure the forgiveness of the former. However, when we pray to God to forgive us, we are actually acknowledging His Lordship and this puts us in a better position towards Him. This makes our forgiveness all the more certain.

The *ḥadīth* then tells us that even the most basic of our needs are only satisfied by the grace of God. Without His provisions, we remain hungry; without the clothing He makes available to us, we remain naked. In order to understand these statements, we have to remember that it is God Who opens up ways for us to earn our living. It is He Who has made human beings mutually dependent on one another so as to give everyone a chance of doing something useful for which he or she earns what may be sufficient to meet their basic needs. This is indeed a manifestation of God's grace, because it ensures that no one remains in want, unless a community suffers from a great imbalance in the distribution of its resources. Nevertheless, the very basic means of earning a living have been provided by God. It is He Who has given the earth the quality of producing food for man and animal. It is He Who has made man able to make use of what is available in this world to make useful advances and to build civilisation.

Moreover, when we pray to God for our basic needs, He may answer our prayers by giving us abundance to meet them generously. Since it is in human nature to seek a comfortable and luxurious life, God is telling us here that prayer can be a way to achieve this.

Some people may look at the great advancements achieved by scientists over the last fifty or sixty years and compare human life before these advancements with what has been achieved through them. The thought may occur to some people that with such a great rate of progress, man may move into wider horizons which he could not even have thought to exist a few years ago. With such progress, could not man achieve a much higher position than he has so far occupied in the universe? Well, man may attain any great height he is capable of attaining. No matter how great his achievements are, he will never be able to cause harm or bring benefit to God.

The *ḥadīth* gives further details of this inability in a most conclusive manner. Were all beings, human and jinn, in all generations to demonstrate the greatest standard of piety, righteousness and proper behaviour, they will give God nothing. Conversely, if they were as wicked as the most wicked person that has ever existed, they will cause no decrease in God's kingdom. In other words, neither our piety, worship and model behaviour are of any benefit to God, nor are our sins and wickedness of any harm to Him. Indeed, it is we who benefit by our piety and suffer harm as a result of our sins. And it is we who will always be in need of God.

This thought is carried even further. An image is drawn which can easily be perceived by us: imagine that all human beings together with all the jinn who lived ever since the beginning of life and who are living now and will live in the future till the end of life were brought together and each one of them was told that he or she was free to pray to God to give them anything they wished. Everyone will start making their lists of comforts and luxuries they wish to enjoy. Imagine then that each single person was given all their requests, how much would this constitute? If we were to evaluate all this in our monetary terms, the value is bound to reach astronomical proportions. After all, we see so much misery in the world and yet individual countries estimate their annual budgets in billions of pounds and dollars. We need only to imagine that if all people were to live comfortably, these budgets would have to be multiplied several times. That is the need of one generation. When we think that human life has seen perhaps thousands of generations and may see thousands more, what sort of figure should we imagine would be sufficient to meet all basic needs of all humanity throughout all generations? Nevertheless, if every single one of them, and of other beings as well, were to ask God for everything they could desire or imagine, and if they were all to be granted all their requests, what would the cost of all this be to God?

In this sacred *ḥadīth*, God gives us an idea. He compares all that to what He has and says that it is in the same proportion as a needle will decrease the water of the ocean when it is dipped into it just once. Indeed this comparison is given for our benefit in order to imagine God's greatness and the vastness of His kingdom. Indeed, if He were to grant everyone their requests, this would not decrease what He has in any way. A needle dipped into the ocean would decrease its water by a fraction of a single drop. To our minds, the ocean remains the same, because of the great difference between what is taken out of it and what is left. Nevertheless, that tiny little drop of water costs much more than what granting the requests of all human beings and jinn would cost God.

The *ḥadīth* concludes with an important reminder to all human beings that they can influence their outcome on the Day of Judgement. It is on that day that their deeds are reckoned up. The result will determine whether they will receive reward or punishment. But then, the reward comes by God's Grace, because it is He Who has guided us and Who has given us everything to enable us to do well. If we do not do well, the fault is with us and we are responsible for this. Hence, on the Day of Judgement, if we find the result to be good, then we should praise God for His bounty, provisions, guidance and forgiveness. Those who find their results otherwise – and we pray sincerely not to be included among them – have only themselves to blame. Everything has been given them to help them maintain a life which will bring them happiness in this life and ensure their happiness in the life to come, but they abandoned all this choosing a life which might bring momentary pleasures but certainly ends up in misery.

27

Illness and Forgiveness

THE PROPHET'S COMPANIONS were able to develop a keen insight into Islam, its constitution and method of dealing with human life. The best among them were even able to attain a highly refined understanding of the basic Islamic concepts which made their judgement both accurate and mature.

494. (*Athar* 116) Ghaṭīf ibn al-Ḥārith said: 'A man came to visit Abu 'Ubaydah ibn Al-Jarrāḥ when he was ill. He asked him: "How is the reward of the *Amīr* getting on?" In reply Abu 'Ubaydah asked him: "Do you know what earns you a reward?" The man said: "What befalls us of things which we dislike". Abu 'Ubaydah said: "You are rewarded for what you spend or get to be spent on you for God's cause". He then enumerated all articles of a horse's equipment, even including the horse's bridle.

"The physical weakness you feel is credited to you by God in the form of erasing some of your sins".'[358]

In this *ḥadīth*, Abu 'Ubaydah makes a clear distinction between what earns a reward and what erases past mistakes and sins. Abu 'Ubaydah was one of the very early companions of the Prophet. The Prophet sent him on several missions, some of which involved fighting or chasing unbelievers. His leadership qualities were manifest to the extent that Abu Bakr appointed him as one of the principal commanders of Muslim armies fighting in Syria and Palestine. During 'Umar's time, he was made commander-in-chief of all Muslim armies fighting in Syria and Palestine. The Prophet gave him the title of 'The Trusted Man of the Muslim Community'. Moreover, he was one of the ten companions of the Prophet who were given the happy news of assured admission into heaven.

It is not uncommon to confuse earning a reward with forgiveness of sins. Abu 'Ubaydah's visitor made this common error, and asked him about his illness in an indirect but comforting manner. He asked about his reward, meaning that if the illness was very severe, his reward would be greater. To a Muslim, this is most comforting. He is reminded that what he suffers does not go in vain.

However, Abu 'Ubaydah felt that he should correct his visitor. He pointed out to him that a handsome reward is earned by donating one's money to further the cause of God. He enumerated every article of equipment a horseman needs, no matter how cheap it might be. This example is only to be expected from an army commander. To him, the most important thing is to concentrate his soldiers' attention on their duty to sacrifice. On the other hand, physical complaints, pains and illness erase some of one's past sins.

One's reward is weighed up against one's sins so as to determine one's destiny in the Hereafter. The fewer one's sins are, the higher one's position in heaven is. Again, the greater one's reward, the better one's position. The two will be weighed against each other and the side which is preponderant determines the outcome.

358. Related by Aḥmad.

Nevertheless, the distinction between reward and forgiveness of sins is real. When we examine the Prophet's *ḥadīths* on this, we find that they concur in stressing the erasing of sins as a result of illnesses, calamities and reversals which one may have had to endure in life.

495. Abu Sa'īd Al-Khudri and Abu Hurayrah report that the Prophet said: 'Whatever befalls a Muslim of physical weakness, fatigue, worry, distress, harm or sorrow, even a thorn-pick, is used by God to erase some of his sins'.[359]

In this *ḥadīth*, the Prophet enumerates all aspects of misfortune, going down to a thorn in one's finger. All these will be used to forgive him some of his past sins. When he endures whatever happens to him with patience and perseverance, his reward is much greater. This is because he combines the misfortune with patience, which is, in itself, a virtue.

496. (*Athar* 117) Sa'īd ibn Wahb said: 'I was with Salmān when he visited a sick person from Kindah. When he entered, he said: "Good news! God makes a believer's illness a means of forgiveness of sins and granting favours, whereas the illness of an unbeliever is like a camel whose owner ties him then releases him. The camel does not know why he was tied and why he was then released".'

497. Abu Hurayrah reports that the Prophet said: 'Affliction may continue to befall believers, men and women, in their bodies, families or properties [thus earning them forgiveness of sins] until they meet God, the Mighty and Exalted, free of all sin'.[360]

The same *ḥadīth* is reported by Muhammad ibn 'Amr, adding the words 'or offspring' after 'properties'.

This is indeed an aspect of God's Grace which many people tend to overlook. We are told by the Prophet that when illness, affliction or

359. Related by Aḥmad, al-Bukhari, Muslim and al-Tirmidhi.

360. Related by Aḥmad and al-Tirmidhi.

misfortune continue for any length of time, the person who endures them may arrive on the Day of Judgement without a sin to account for. He will already have been forgiven.

Yet what about a person who goes through life without suffering illness or misfortune?

498. Abu Hurayrah reports: 'A bedouin came to the Prophet. The Prophet asked him: "Have you ever suffered from Umm Mildam [i.e. fever]?" The man asked: "What is Umm Mildam?" The Prophet said: "Heat between the skin and the flesh". The man said: "No". The Prophet asked: "Have you had a headache?" The bedouin said: "What is a headache?" The Prophet said: "An affliction in the head which beats one's veins". The man said: "No". When he left, the Prophet said: "Anyone who wishes to look at a man who will be a dweller in hell may look at that man".'[361]

The *ḥadīth* tells us of a man who does not even know the names of fever and headache. He never experienced any illness. As such, he missed out on what is certain to wipe away his sins. He will have to account for every sin he might have committed. Therefore, he is in great peril, as people may often do what is sinful without paying much attention to it.

Does this condemn that person to hell? Not on its own. If he was a pious and righteous person, he would still earn forgiveness. However, the Prophet must have been inspired by God on this occasion that the bedouin was certain to be in hell, perhaps because he was an unbeliever, or one who committed grave sins.

When we consider all these *ḥadīths*, we are no longer surprised at the patience and fortitude shown by the early Muslims in the face of calamities. They treated whatever befell them as part of life and were happy to earn forgiveness for their past sins. This continues to be the attitude of those of us who know what we stand to gain in return for enduring misfortune with patience. Again the companions of the Prophet provide us with good examples to follow.

---

361. Related by al-Ḥākim and Ibn Ḥibbān.

Ḥudhayfah ibn Al-Yamān was a companion of the Prophet from the Anṣār. He was appointed as a commander of a Muslim army fighting against the Persian Empire. He was at Al-Mada'in when he was taken ill.

499. (*Athar* 118) Khālid ibn al-Rabīʿ said: 'When Hudhayfah's people of the Anṣār learnt that his illness was very serious, they came to visit him during the night or just before dawn. He asked them: "What hour is it?" They said: "Late night or nearly dawn" [as the case might be]. He said: "I seek shelter with God against a morning of fire". He then asked them: "Have you brought a shroud for me to be wrapped in [for burial]?" They said: Yes. He said: "Do not spend over much on such a shroud. If I have favour with God, it will be replaced by something better. If my situation is the other one, I will be stripped very quickly".'[362]

500. ʿĀ'ishah reports that the Prophet said: 'When a believer suffers an illness, God purifies him as the bellows purify the dross of iron'.

501. ʿĀ'ishah reports that the Prophet said: 'For any Muslim who suffers affliction, whether pain or illness, it will be an expiation of sins, even if it be as little as a thorn-prick or a worry'.[363]

What we learn from all these *ḥadīths* and reports is that we should face up to any misfortune with courage and patience. When we do so, we earn forgiveness for much of our sin. Our position in the Hereafter is, thus, enhanced. We stand a better chance of being admitted into heaven.

362. Related by al-Ḥākim.

363. Related by Muslim and al-Nasā'ī.

Inheritance, will and illness

Islam has a detailed system of inheritance which defines heirs and their shares in a very elaborate manner. However, heirs take their shares only after the payment of any debts the deceased has left outstanding and the execution of any will he might have made. A will normally has two purposes: either as a charitable act, by which a person makes sure that one portion of his or her property goes to charity. He hopes that by so doing he will increase his reward from God. Some people provide for a continuous act of charity, such as using the money to finance some sort of public utility, for example a health centre, school, or an orphanage, or, as used to happen in the past, to provide drinking water on travellers' routes. By doing so, they ensure continuous reward for themselves after they have died.

The other purpose of a will is to provide for relatives who are not heirs but who may be in need of help. If a person has been looking after poor relatives and fears that they will not have enough to look after themselves after his death, he may make sure that they receive a portion of his property after his death through a will. The only condition in this case is that such relatives must not be among his heirs who have shares apportioned to them by God. A will may not be made in favour of an heir. The logic behind this restriction is simple. The shares of heirs have been determined by God. His division is based on perfect justice. Had a person been free to leave an additional portion to an heir by will, this may disturb the system God has laid down, which is fair and equitable. Such a disturbance of fairness can only lead to injustice.

The question may arise: how much can a person leave by will? Schools of thought are unanimous that the maximum is one third of one's property. This is based on the following authentic *ḥadīth*:

502. Sa'd ibn Abu Waqqāṣ related: 'I was seriously ill in Makkah and the Prophet came to visit me. I said: "Messenger of God, I will be leaving property and I only have one daughter. May I make bequests equal to two-thirds of my property and leave [her] a third?" He said: "No". I said: "May I bequeath one half and leave her one half?" He said: "No". I said: "May I then bequeath

one-third and leave her two-thirds?" He said: "A third, but one-third is plenty". He then placed his hand on my forehead, then wiped my face and my abdomen. He then said: "My Lord, cure Sa'd and complete his migration for him". I still imagine that I feel the coolness of his hand on my liver until now'.[364]

This took place in Makkah when it fell to Islam towards the end of the eighth year after the Prophet's migration. Other versions of this *ḥadīth* show that Sa'd was worried that he might die in Makkah while he wanted his migration to Madinah to be complete. Hence the Prophet's prayer for him in this respect.

Sa'd was among the the Prophet's rich companions. We note that he was keen to leave most of his property to charity. He had only one daughter and probably she was well provided for. To him, the best use of his money might have been to put it to charitable purposes. In this way he would ensure that his reward would continue to be credited to him by God after his death.

It may be felt that Sa'd's argument for leaving most of his wealth to charity was a sound one. He had only one daughter who might have been rich in her own right. She was also likely to get married and would be well looked after. If so, then Sa'd would not be doing her any great wrong by leaving his money to charity. Nevertheless, the Prophet gave a decidedly negative answer. Even when Sa'd dropped his suggestion to only one half of his wealth, the Prophet gave him a firm no for a reply. The Prophet only agreed to one-third, but he added that 'one-third is plenty'. This means that the third is the maximum, and it is probably better to go below one-third.

Another version of this *ḥadīth* adds that the Prophet also gave Sa'd the reason for his verdict. 'To leave your heirs self-sufficient is far better than to leave them poor, begging people for a portion of what they have'. It is much better for any person to leave enough for his heirs to spare them the need to ask for other people's help. It is useful to mention here that begging is forbidden in Islam, because Islam does not accept such a humiliating position for its followers.

---

364. Related by al-Bukhari, Muslim, Abū Dāwūd, al-Nasā'ī, al-Tirmidhi and Ibn Mājah.

One-third is a substantial portion to leave to charity, or even to relatives who are not heirs. If it is reward that one is after, to give to charity during one's life, when one is hoping to live for many years to come earns more reward than leaving a portion of one's money to charity after one has no further need for it. On the other hand, only when one's heirs are very few in number do any of them receive one-third or more.

The Prophet prayed for Sa'd's recovery and Sa'd recovered and lived for at least forty-five years after this conversation with the Prophet. His life was certainly very useful to the Muslims, because he led Muslim armies in great battles and achieved spectacular victories.

The unbelievers were certainly not pleased with Sa'd. Indeed they came to grief at his hands, suffering humiliating defeats. To the unbelievers of that period, Sa'd's name was one to put fear in their hearts. Whenever they went to fight an army led by Sa'd, they realised that they would soon come to grief. This is a very clear example of how the Prophet's prayers and wishes were always answered by God.

Illness and God's reward

Does illness deprive a person of the chance of increasing his reward? A person may be used to offering voluntary prayers, particularly night worship, or fasting for certain days of the week or month. He may not, however, be able to continue with such habits when he is ill.

503. 'Abdullāh ibn 'Amr reports that the Prophet said: 'Whoever falls ill will be credited with what he used to do when healthy'.[365]

504. Anas ibn Mālik reports that the Prophet said: 'Any Muslim who is tried with physical illness will be credited with what he used to do when healthy, as long as he is ill. If God grants him recovery, He gives him more comfort, and if he dies, He forgives him his sins'.[366]

---

365. Related by Aḥmad, 'Abd al-Razzāq and al-Ḥākim.
366. Related by Aḥmad

This is certainly an aspect of grace which only God can bestow. Human beings may be kind enough to understand that an ill person cannot fulfil his obligations and they may grant him a period of grace to catch up with what he has to do after recovery. To credit him with the reward of what he used to do before his illness is something much greater which only God, whose grace is limitless, will grant.

Yet God gives us much more for illness than this. When a Muslim falls ill and he accepts his ordeal with contentment, realising that illness is a test to which he is subjected by God, he is granted reward for his patience. Indeed, any sort of physical harm he may suffer could be a source of reward for him:

505. Abu Hurayrah reports: 'Fever came to the Prophet (peace be upon him) and said: "Send me to your favourite people". He sent it to the Anṣār. It thrust itself on them for six days and nights, causing much suffering. He went to visit them in their homes and they complained to him. The Prophet entered every single home of theirs and every room. He prayed for their good health. As he was going back, one of their women caught up with him and said: "By Him Who sent you with the Truth, I belong to the Anṣār and my father is one of the Anṣār. Pray for me as you have prayed for the Anṣār". The Prophet said: "As you wish. However, if you like, I will pray to God to give you good health. But if you wish to endure it with patience, you will be in heaven". The woman said: "I will endure it, because I do not wish to risk losing heaven".'

506. (*Athar* 119) Abu Hurayrah said: 'The illness I like best to befall me is fever, because it enters my every part and God, the Mighty and Exalted, will give every part of me its portion of the reward'.[367]

507. (*Athar* 120) Abu Wā'il said: 'Abu Nuhaylah, [a companion of the Prophet], was requested to pray to God. He said: "My Lord, decrease the illness but do not decrease the reward".

---

367. Related by Ibn Abi Shaybah.

> He was told: "Pray more; pray more". He said: "My Lord, place me among those brought near [to You] and make my mother one of the women of heaven".'[368]

Perhaps the first thing to point out is that we do not know how exactly fever came to the Prophet and spoke to him, but we accept this without question because God is able to make fever present itself to the Prophet in person, as it were. How His will works is not for us to discuss, having believed that God is able to do everything.

When fever asked the Prophet to send it to his favourite followers, she meant that as a means of earning reward. If they suffered an illness, they would earn reward from God. Indeed, the Prophet tells us that even when a person is pricked by a thorn, this gives him reward from God if he endures it patiently. The report also tells us that to pray to God for good health when ill does not contradict patient endurance or being contented with what God has given one. The Prophet prayed for his followers to have their illnesses removed.

The choice the Prophet gave to the woman is meant as offering one of two certainties. Had the Prophet prayed to God to remove her illness, she would certainly have recovered. God answered every supplication the Prophet made. However, the Prophet pointed out to the woman something greater than good health in this life. This was patient perseverance when tested because such perseverance earns the greatest reward of all, namely, heaven. The woman realised this and she wanted to have the certainty of being admitted into heaven.

Perhaps it should also be pointed out that if one complains to God of what befalls one, this does not detract from the fact that one endures the test with patience. Prophet Job was the one to suffer a very serious and painful illness. He complained to God and God described him as a patient and contented believer. Nor is it objectionable to explain one's situation to fellow human beings, provided that one does not believe that they can remove his suffering by themselves. He should only pray to God to grant him recovery. He may certainly seek the best medical treatment available. The Prophet tells us to seek medical treatment because God has created a cure for every illness.

---

368. Related by al-Nasā'ī.

508. ʿAṭāʾ ibn Abu Rabāḥ said: 'Ibn ʿAbbās once said to me: "Would you like me to point out to you a woman who will be in heaven?" ʿAṭāʾ said: "Yes". Ibn ʿAbbās said: "This black woman came once to the Prophet (peace be upon him) and said: "I suffer from severe epilepsy and parts of my body get exposed. Will you please pray to God for me?" The Prophet said to her: "You may wish to endure it with patience and you will be in heaven; or you may wish me to pray to God to cure you". She said: "I will endure it with patience". She added: "But parts of my body get exposed, so pray to God for me not to be exposed". The Prophet prayed for her'.[369]

509. (*Athar* 121) Ibn Jurayj said: 'ʿAṭāʾ mentioned to me that he saw that woman, Umm Zufar, tall and black, on the steps of the Kaʿbah'.

Ibn Jurayj said: 'ʿAbdullāh ibn Abu Mulaykah told me that al-Qāsim told him that ʿĀʾishah told him that the Prophet said: "Whatever afflicts a believer, a prick of a thorn or whatever more, will erase his sin".'[370]

The woman in this story was called Suʿayrah, an Abyssinian black woman, known as Umm Zufaṛ, who was attached either through slavery or alliance to the Azd tribe. She used to come to the Prophet after the death of his first wife, Khadījah, and he used to treat her with kindness and fitting hospitality. He knew that she was a firm believer. Therefore, when she asked him to pray for her recovery, he wanted to point out to her that enduring her hardship, which was serious, would lead her to heaven. Since this is the most coveted prize of all, he did not want her to miss the chance of making sure of earning it. She knew that had the Prophet prayed for her recovery, she would have been immediately cured. God answered every supplication the Prophet made at any time of his life on behalf of any of his companions. As a firm believer, she did not want to risk the greatest prize. Therefore, she immediately chose to endure her trouble with patience and perseverance.

---

369. Related by al-Bukhari, Muslim and al-Nasāʾī.
370. Related by al-Bukhari.

Anyone who suffers a fit of epilepsy becomes unconscious. People tend to think of an epilepsy sufferer as an inferior person. He cannot control his mental power. Even when he is not suffering a fit, he is looked upon with a mixture of condescending sympathy, pity and superiority. Nevertheless, the woman was willing to endure all this for the much greater reward of admission into heaven.

We can further appreciate that she was a woman of strong belief because she was worried about what may happen to her when she had a fit. Unconscious, she may expose some parts of her body which she was supposed to keep covered. As we all know, a Muslim woman may not expose in front of men who are unrelated to her any part of her body except her face and hands. As she might fall down she might leave her arm or her leg or her head, or any part of her body to be seen by any passer-by. She wanted to avoid this if she could. Nothing would guarantee this better than a prayer by the Prophet which he offered on her behalf without hesitation. We are also told that when the woman felt that a fit of epilepsy was about to overtake her, she went to the Kaʿbah where she held tight to its covers. Thus, she was actually appealing to God to protect her. Needless to say, no blame could be attached to her for exposing her body when she was unconscious. Nevertheless, she wanted to remain covered. Hence, her appeal to God and the Prophet. Recognising the significance of all this, Ibn ʿAbbās had no hesitation in describing her as a woman who is destined to go to heaven.

When a believer understands all this, he does not feel too depressed when he suffers a serious illness. No one suggests that a Muslim should wish for illness or try to catch it. Indeed health is a blessing which every one of us should work diligently to preserve. The Prophet points out that good health is the greatest blessing with which anyone may be favoured, next to being strong in faith. Moreover, we are accountable for how we use our good health. If we undermine it, we expose ourselves to suffering ill health in this world and also to punishment in the life to come. But if one is taken ill, one should accept the trial with patience, remembering that one will be rewarded for it.

510. Abu Hurayrah reports that the Prophet said: 'Any Muslim who is hurt in this world by even a thorn, and endures it with patience, shall have some of his sins erased on the Day of Judgement'.[371]

511. Jābir reports that the Prophet said: 'Any believer, man or woman, and any Muslim, man or woman, who suffers an illness shall have some of his sins wiped off in compensation'.[372]

These *ḥadīths* echo earlier ones which confirm that God rewards anyone who endures illness and physical affliction, however small, with patience by erasing some of their sins.

---

371. Related by Aḥmad.
372. Related by Aḥmad.

28

Visiting Sick People

512. (*Athar* 122) ʿUrwah ibn al-Zubayr said: 'ʿAbdullāh ibn al-Zubayr and I went to see Asmā', ten days before ʿAbdullāh was killed. She was in pain. ʿAbdullāh said: "How do you feel?" She said: "I am in pain". He said: "I am close to death". She said: "Perhaps you desire my death for that reason. Do not do so. By God, I do not wish to die until one of two things happen to you: either you win and I will be happy, or you will be killed and I will resign myself to that in hope for God's reward. Be careful: if you are offered a proposal that is unsuitable to you do not accept it out of fear of death".

Ibn al-Zubayr referred to his killing as something that would grieve his mother.

Al-Bukhari does not enter this *ḥadīth* in his book for any historical purpose. He merely enters it to explain that an ill person may complain and express what he or she feels. Asking how his mother was, ʿAbdullāh is informed that she was in pain. She would not have said this if there had been any question about making such a complaint.

'Abdullāh ibn al-Zubayr was the first child born to the Muhājirīn in Madinah, shortly after the Prophet's arrival there. The event the *ḥadīth* mentions occurred only ten days before his death, in year 73 AH. His mother, Asmā' bint Abu Bakr was 100 years of age at the time. 'Abdullāh ibn al-Zubayr claimed the caliphate and he ruled over Hijaz and Iraq for nine years before he was defeated by the Umayyad army and killed in battle.

513. Abu Sa'īd Al-Khudri reports that he visited the Prophet when he was unwell. He had covered himself with a piece of velvet. He put his hand on him and he felt his temperature through the velvet covering. Abu Sa'īd said: 'Messenger of God, how hot your fever is!' He replied: 'We are like this: our trials are very hard and our reward is multiplied'. Abu Sa'īd asked: 'Messenger of God, which people have the greatest affliction?' He answered: 'The Prophets and then the most pious and righteous. Any one of them may be tested with poverty until he can find nothing more than a robe to cover himself with and he will wear that. Another could be tested with fleas until they almost kill him. They were more pleased with their affliction than any of you may be pleased with gifts'.[373]

This *ḥadīth* confirms all the previous ones that mentioned that a believer is rewarded for any illness, hardship, affliction or pain he may suffer. The reward is given in the form of erasing his sins. The more frequent he suffers such affliction, the greater his reward is. Ultimately, he will walk away with no sin recorded against him. In this *ḥadīth*, the Prophet tells us that the people who suffered most were prophets, and then the righteous. The more pious and God-fearing a person is the greater his trials are. Thus, God increases his reward and he is assured of a high status in the life to come.

The Prophet showed by practical example that it is important to visit sick people, even if they are in a state where they cannot recognise

373. Related by Aḥmad and Ibn Mājah.

their visitors. An ill person is always pleased to find people enquiring after his health and coming and talk to him. His family realise that they are not alone in this hardship, but that they can rely on the good will of others. When you visit your brother who is ill, you also pray for his recovery and his hopes rise as he feels that your prayer may be answered. The Prophet set us the example of visiting his companions when any of them fell ill. When one of his companions received such a visit, he was so happy because he realised that God's Messenger cared for his well-being. When he prayed for his recovery, he was certain of speedily regaining his health, because a prayer by the Prophet was soon answered.

Moreover, if the Prophet felt that there was something he may do that could benefit his companion who was ill, he did not hesitate to do it.

> 514. Jābir ibn ʿAbdullāh reports: 'I was ill, and the Prophet (peace be upon him) came walking with Abu Bakr to visit me. They found me unconscious. The Prophet (peace be upon him) performed the ablution, then he threw water left from his ablution on my face. I regained consciousness and saw the Prophet (peace be upon him). I asked him: "Messenger of God, what shall I do with the money I have? How shall I determine the distribution of my property?" Ḥe ḍid not give me any answer until the Qur'anic verse giving the ruling of inheritance was revealed'.[374]

Here the Prophet used the water with which he performed ablution to throw over the face of his unconscious companion so as to help him regain consciousness. When the Prophet used something personally before giving it to any of his companions, it had more than its usual effect because it was blessed by the Prophet's usage. In this instance, Jābir immediately regained consciousness when the Prophet used his ablution water to awaken him.

Apparently Jābir was preoccupied with the division of his property should his illness end in death. At that time, Jābir did not have children

---

374. Related by al-Bukhari, Muslim and al-Nasā'ī.

of his own, nor were either of his parents alive, but he had several sisters. At that time, the verse (4:176) which outlines inheritance in such cases had not yet been revealed. It is to this fact that Jābir refers when he says that the Prophet did not answer him until that verse was revealed.

The Prophet did not hesitate to visit a patient even when he was a young child. People who were close to him realised this and requested him to visit their sick in the hope that they would recover when he prayed for them.

515. Usāmah ibn Zayd reports: 'A child of one of the Prophet's daughters [Zaynab] was seriously ill. His mother sent a word to the Prophet (peace be upon him) telling him, "My child is dying". He said to her messenger: "Go and tell her that to God belongs whatever He takes and whatever He gives. With Him, everything has a definite term. Let her, then, be patient and resign herself to God's will".

'The messenger went back and conveyed to her what the Prophet said. She sent again to him, asking him by God to come over and see the child. The Prophet went to her with a number of his companions including Sa'd ibn 'Ubādah. The Prophet (peace be upon him) picked up the child and put him on his chest. Internal noise in the child's chest was audible. The Prophet was in tears. Sa'd said to him: "Do you, Messenger of God, weep?" The Prophet answered: "I weep out of compassion for her. God does not bestow his mercy except on those of His servants who are compassionate".'[375]

Most probably the child was 'Ali ibn Abu al-'Āṣ, son of Zaynab, the Prophet's eldest daughter. Some reports suggest that it was one of Zaynab's daughters. The identity of the child is not a matter of great importance. What is important is that the Prophet responded to a call to come and see a child who was seriously ill. We must not understand the Prophet's answer to the messenger as hesitation to go and see the child. Indeed, it was not. The Prophet realised that his

375. Related by al-Bukhari, Muslim, Abū Dāwūd, al-Nasā'ī and Ibn Mājah.

daughter must be in great distress, seeing that her child was about to die. Therefore, he wanted to send to her words of encouragement. Moreover, he was with a number of his companions and he did not want to leave them immediately so that none would feel uneasy about his departure. Knowing what might have held her father from coming immediately, Zaynab sent the messenger again to ask him by God to come. This shows that it is permissible for anyone of us to entreat a superior person, asking him by God to do something for us, provided that by so doing, we do not put ourselves in a derogatory position.

The Prophet's words which he sent his daughter represent the attitude of every Muslim towards death. He may suffer the death of a very dear person and the dearest is one's own child, but he should soon resign himself to the fact that death is ordained by God. It is He Who gives life and it is He Who takes it away. Therefore, we must resign ourselves to our loss and accept it as we accept God's will in any matter. Indeed, to be overwhelmed by one's sense of loss to the extent that one speaks in bitter words about it or says what may be construed as a protest against God's will is alien to Islam.

The compassion shown by the Prophet towards the child whose chest infection must have been very serious to the extent that it produced an audible noise was the compassion of a parent and a Prophet who considered everyone in his community to be under his guardianship. His companions were surprised to see tears in his eyes. They had learnt from him that one must accept God's will with patience. Therefore, he explained that his tears were nothing of the sort which was unacceptable. They did not mean that he was complaining. They were only an expression of his grief and his compassion towards the mother and her child. He further explained that a person devoid of compassion is not worthy of God's mercy.

516. (*Athar* 123) Ibrāhīm ibn Abu 'Ablah said: 'My wife was ill and I went often to Umm al-Dardā'. She would ask me: "How is your wife?" I would say to her: "Ill". She would order some food for me and I would eat. I visited her again and she asked me: "How are they?" I said: "Nearly recovered". She said: "I ordered food for you when you told me that your wife was ill. Since she is now nearly recovered, I am not ordering anything for you".'

Umm al-Dardā' was a caring lady. When Ibrāhīm told her that his wife was ill, she gave him food to eat, so as to spare him and his wife the need to cook. When his wife was nearly recovered, Umm al-Dardā' told him that she would not give him food. This was her way of telling him that he should be with his wife, looking after her and helping her recovery.

Visiting people in distress

The Prophet visited his companions when they were ill, and visited people who were not Muslims when he came to know that they were in distress. Even when a patient is liable to offend his visitor enquiring after his health, visiting him is recommended. The Prophet did not hesitate to do so.

> 517. Ibn 'Abbās reports: 'The Prophet visited a bedouin who was ill. He said to him: "Do not worry. It is purification, God willing". The bedouin said: "No, indeed. It is fever that boils over an old man leading him to the grave". The Prophet said: "Then, it may be so".'[376]

What we have here is a typical example of a person who is totally uncouth, speaking roughly to a well-wisher who is none other than the Prophet. Had the bedouin known better, he would have been so pleased with the Prophet's words. What the Prophet said to him as he entered was a prayer that his illness would be the means of God's forgiveness. If so, then the patient had, as the Prophet said, nothing to worry about. If he recovered and regained his health, he would have profited on two counts: health and forgiveness. If his illness ended in death, then he would at least be forgiven his sins and that is a great profit indeed.

The Prophet's statement, "You have nothing to worry about. It is a source of purification", was followed by his saying, "God willing". This signifies that his words were meant as a prayer, not as a statement of

---

376. Related by al-Bukhari.

fact. It means that not everyone who has an illness receives forgiveness of past sins as a result. He has to accept what has befallen him as something that God has willed, proving his good, strong faith to earn God's forgiveness. Therefore, we are advised to follow the Prophet's example and pray for the forgiveness of patients when we visit them.

The possibility of encountering some hostility should not deter us from visiting those who are ill. Indeed, we are recommended to do so in all situations. Such action is counted among the best that cements social ties.

518. Abu Hurayrah reports that one day the Prophet asked his companions: 'Who of you has started the day fasting?' Abu Bakr said: 'I have' The Prophet said: 'Who of you has visited an ill person today?' Abu Bakr answered: 'I have'. The Prophet then asked: 'Who of you has today attended a funeral?' Abu Bakr said: 'I have'. The Prophet asked again: 'Who has fed a needy person today?' Abu Bakr said: 'I have'.

Marwān ibn Mu'āwiyah, a transmitter of this *ḥadīth*, adds that he learnt that the Prophet commented: 'Whoever combines all these actions on the same day will be admitted into heaven'.[377]

Needless to say, the Prophet asked his companions these questions on a day when fasting was not required by way of duty. Had it been a duty to fast, all his companions would have been fasting. Abu Bakr was then fasting voluntarily on that day. It is well known that voluntary fasting is richly rewarded by God in all cases. This is because fasting is an action that admits no hypocrisy. When a person abstains from eating and drinking, he does so in order to please God.

The Prophet then asks about three actions which cannot fail to cement social ties, namely, visiting patients, attending funerals and feeding needy people. Such actions are indicative of care towards others. If you go and visit a patient, you sacrifice your time and effort in order to cheer him up and help him face his misfortune with patience and fortitude. You also give moral support to his family. When you attend a funeral, you demonstrate to the family of the deceased that you share

377. Related by Muslim and al-Nasā'ī.

in their grief. Your ties with them are not of the sort that demonstrate themselves only in a situation of comfort and good health.

The last action the Prophet asks about is feeding a poor person. Again this demonstrates care for the community. It is true that God has made it an obligation on all of us to pay zakat, which is a contribution collected in order to alleviate poverty and other hardships. The Prophet is asking here about voluntary actions and when he asks about feeding a poor person, most probably he means that this is done on top of paying zakat.

The Prophet's comment that when all these actions are done by the same person on the same day, they qualify that person for admittance into heaven. These four actions can only be combined on the same day by a person who has strong faith and who is keen to earn reward at every possible moment. He allows no opportunity of earning reward to escape. He is keen to do voluntary worship as in the case of fasting, and he is keen to share other people's grief as in the case of visiting patients and attending funerals, and he is very generous when he realises that they are deserving of his generosity. Abu Bakr was such a person who combined strong faith with a strong desire to do good and a compassionate heart.

519. Jābir reports that the Prophet visited Umm al-Sā'ib and she was shivering. He said: 'What is wrong with you?' She said: 'It is the fever; may God disgrace it'. The Prophet said: 'Gently. Do not curse it. It removes a believer's sins like the bellows remove the dross from iron'.[378]

The Prophet was keen to teach his companions to accept whatever comes from God with patience. Everyone may curse the illness he or she suffers from. The Prophet points out to this patient that the illness is the cause of erasing one's sins.

520. Abu Hurayrah reports that the Prophet said that God will say [on the Day of Resurrection]: 'Son of Adam, I asked you for food, and you did not feed Me'. He will say: 'Lord, how should

---

378. Related by Muslim, Ibn Ḥibbān and Abu 'Awānah.

I feed You when You are the Lord of the worlds?' He will say: 'Did you not know that My servant so-and-so asked you for food and you did not feed him? Did you not know that had you fed him you would surely have found that with Me? Son of Adam, I asked you to give me drink and you did not give me drink'. He will say: 'Lord, how should I give You drink when You are the Lord of the worlds?' He will say: 'My servant so-and-so asked you to give him drink but you did not. Had you given him drink you would have surely found that with Me. Son of Adam, I fell ill and you did not visit Me'. He will say: 'Lord, how should I visit You when You are the Lord of the worlds?' He will say: 'Did you not know that My servant so and so had fallen ill and you did not visit him? Did you not know that had you visited him you would have found Me with him?'[379]

Perhaps the first thing to be pointed out in this sacred *ḥadīth* is that there is a special significance to the phrase used in all three examples about feeding the hungry, giving the thirsty something to drink and visiting patients. In all three cases, God tells every human being that if he responds to these requests, made verbally or not, he will find his action with God. The action will be credited to him in his record of good deeds. Finding it 'with God' means that it will certainly be rewarded most generously. Hence, the emphasis here is on actions that are calculated to strengthen social ties within the Muslim community. It makes everyone well contented, no one is left hungry or thirsty and no one is left to struggle with illness without feeling that the whole Muslim community wish him well and pray for his recovery.

The mode of expression God has chosen in this sacred *ḥadīth* is of particular importance. God owns the whole universe and He is the Lord of all the worlds. With His kingdom being so great, when we say that He is in no need of any man or anything, we are only stating the obvious. Nevertheless, in this sacred *ḥadīth*, He describes Himself as asking human beings for food and drink and as a patient who would have welcomed a visit. Surely, this could not be the case. How could it be that the Lord of all worlds needs to be given something to eat and

379. Related by Muslim and Abu 'Awānah.

drink by a creature of His. There is no doubt that God needs nothing of this sort. He only describes the need as His in order to elevate His servant needing them to a position of honour. He is telling us not to underrate or be contemptuous of anyone who may be poor, or in need of help, or in need of a visit to raise his spirits.

God also tells us that when we do something which has a social significance or when we visit a patient, we should make our actions solely dedicated to Him. It should not matter in the least whether the person we feed or give a drink to or the patient we visit repays our kindness with thanks. We should not expect that. Our action should be addressed to God alone. From Him we receive the reward for it. Indeed, this applies to all actions. When we make the purpose behind any action of ours the earning of God's pleasure, we have the satisfaction of being genuinely sincere in our desire to do something good. We will never feel disappointed because our good action is not reciprocated.

Note also the expression used in the *ḥadīth* in the example of visiting an ill person. God says: 'Had you visited him you would have found Me with him'. It tells us of the standard of care God takes of His servants which we cannot imagine or appreciate. It tells us that God is there, by the bedside of His ill servant, recording the names of his visitors in order to reward them. If someone is looked after by God, he needs nothing. The reward we expect from God cannot be matched by any thanks or expression of gratitude by the patient himself.

521. Abu Saʿīd al-Khudri reports that the Prophet said: 'Visit the sick and march with the funerals. They will remind you of the life to come'.[380]

522. Abu Hurayrah reports that the Prophet said: 'Three things are required of every Muslim: to visit the sick, to attend funerals and to bless a person who sneezes if that person praises God, the Mighty and Exalted'.[381]

---

380. Related by Aḥmad and Ibn Ḥibbān.
381. Related by Ibn Ḥibbān.

These two *ḥadīths* stress the importance of visiting the sick and attending funerals. As the Prophet says, they remind us of death and that we will be resurrected and have to account for our deeds in this life. Therefore, they provide motivation to keep us on the path of righteousness.

The second *ḥadīth* adds blessing the one who sneezes. The proper thing is that when someone sneezes he should say: 'All praise belongs to God'. If he says this aloud, then the one who hears it should say to him: 'May God bestow mercy on you'. He answers: 'May He give you guidance and peace of mind'. The main point is that the one who sneezes should be the first to begin, praising God and thanking Him.

These three are required of every Muslim, but the requirement is not by way of obligation, but recommendation, although scholars attach different degrees of requirement according to the status of the person concerned.

523. Three of Sa'd ibn Abu Waqqāṣ's sons related from their father: 'The Prophet visited Sa'd when he was ill in Makkah. He wept and the Prophet asked him: "Why are you weeping?" He said: "I fear that I will die in the land from which I have migrated, like Sa'd [ibn Khawlah]". The Prophet said: "My Lord, grant Sa'd recovery", [repeating his supplication three times]. Sa'd said: "I have plenty of property and I only have one daughter to inherit me. May I will away all my property?" The Prophet said: "No". Sa'd said: "Then two-thirds?" He said: "No". Sa'd said: "Then one half?" The Prophet said: "No". Sa'd said: "Then one-third?" The Prophet said: "A third, but one-third is plenty. What you give to charity out of your money is *ṣadaqah*, and what you spend on your dependants is *ṣadaqah*, and what your wife eats of your food is *ṣadaqah*. To leave your family in a state of prosperity is better than leaving them in a state where they beg people for help". He signaled with his hand'.[382]

382. Related by Muslim.

This relates to the same visit the Prophet made to Sa'd ibn Abu Waqqāṣ when he was ill in Makkah, mentioned in *ḥadīth* Number 502. We have here a fuller version, and we will discuss the added parts only.

In his illness, Sa'd felt sorry for himself that he might have to stay behind after the Prophet and his companions had returned to Madinah. He worried that he might die in Makkah, like another companion of the Prophet named Sa'd ibn Khawlah who returned to Makkah earlier and died there, thus losing the status of migration which applied to those of the Prophet's companions who left Makkah with him, in support of the cause of Islam, and those who joined him in Madinah from other places before Makkah fell to Islam. To be counted among the Muhājirīn, i.e. migrants to Madinah, was a great honour. Sa'd would have done anything not to lose that status. Hence, the Prophet prayed that all his companions who migrated with him be accepted by God and none of them would turn back on his heels.

The Prophet explains to Sa'd the wisdom behind the Islamic system of inheritance which does not give anyone sole discretion over how to dispense with his wealth after he dies. The words of the Prophet need no comment: 'To leave your family in a state of prosperity is better than leaving them in a state where they beg people for help'. There is no virtue in poverty. It is true that if one is poor, one should not grumble and complain much. One should accept what God has given him and work hard to improve one's situation. If he has to accept zakat money and charity, there is no harm in this, as the zakat system is meant to help the poor. However, if one is well off, paying his zakat regularly, and spending it in charity, he has the means to earn more reward from God. Furthermore, he ensures the future of his children. It is to this fact that the Prophet refers by this statement.

The Prophet's statement tells us a great deal about how to use our money in order to earn reward. Every small amount we spend can bring us reward, if it is spent in a way that pleases God. The Prophet gives the example of a bite placed by a man in his wife's mouth. In order to understand the significance of this statement, we have to remember that a man is required to support his wife and look after her by way of duty. Indeed, he is required to support her even when she is richer than him. Therefore, when he gives her food, he is only doing what he is bound to do. If he places a bite in her mouth, he does this only as a gesture of endearment. But even then, he can earn reward if his intention is to fulfil his duty and to make his wife happy. If this sort of gesture can earn reward, then every action and every little amount we spend can earn reward, provided that the purpose is sound.

524. Abu al-Ash'ath al-Ṣan'āni reports that Abu Asmā' said: 'Whoever visits his sick brother will be in the *khurfah* of Paradise'. 'Āṣim asked Abu Qilābah: 'What does *khurfah* mean?' He said: 'It means ripe fruits'. I asked him: 'From whom did Abu Asmā' relate this *ḥadīth*? He said: 'From Thawbān who heard it from God's Messenger (peace be upon him)'.

Commentators on *Ḥadīth* suggest that the metaphor means that a person who goes visiting the sick is like one who has climbed the date trees in heaven to collect their fruits. He ends up with something of the best reward God preserves for His servants.

525. Ja'far ibn 'Abdullāh ibn al-Ḥakam reported that 'Abu Bakr ibn Juz', Muhammad ibn al-Munkadir and a number of people who frequented the mosque visited 'Umar ibn al-Ḥakam ibn Rāfi' al-Anṣāri who was ill. They said to him: "Abu Ḥafṣ, relate [some *ḥadīth*] to us." He said: "I heard Jābir ibn 'Abdullāh say that the Prophet said: 'When someone visits an ill person, he dips into mercy and when he sits [with the sick person] he is well settled in it'."'

526. (*Athar* 124) 'Aṭā' said: 'Ibn 'Umar visited Ibn Ṣafwān when he was ill. When it was time for prayer, Ibn 'Umar led the prayer offering it in two rak'ahs. He explained: "We are travelling".'

These *ḥadīths* repeat what has been clearly stated in earlier *ḥadīths* about the encouragement of visiting people who are suffering an illness, to comfort them and dispel the gloom of illness. The first mentions the great reward God gives for such visits, describing it in a highly vivid image. The second *ḥadīth* mentions in particular the shortened prayer offered by Ibn 'Umar while he was travelling, using the concession God has given to travellers.

It is not only our close relatives and friends whom we should visit when they fall ill, but rather, visiting any Muslim whom we know, or even do not know, is an act of kindness. It is also permissible to visit ill people who follow other religions.

527. Anas reports: 'A young Jewish lad who used to serve the Prophet fell ill. The Prophet went to visit him and sat by the top end of his bed. As he talked to the lad, the Prophet said to him: "Embrace Islam". The lad looked up to his father who was standing by him. The father said to him: "Obey Abu al-Qāsim". The lad declared that he was a Muslim. When the Prophet left, he said: "Praise be to God Who saved him from the fire".

The father called the Prophet Abu al-Qāsim, as it was customary in Arabia to call a person as the father of his eldest son. Al-Qāsim was the first son to be born to the Prophet. He died at a very young age.

Scholars deduce from this *ḥadīth* that when a young child, below the age of puberty, embraces Islam, his or her action is valid. Such a young person is considered a Muslim. Some readers may wonder at the attitude of the boy's father. It may be that he was too embarrassed to say anything to his son that could offend the Prophet, as the Prophet was their visitor. Most probably, the father realised that Muhammad was genuinely the last Prophet and messenger to be sent by God. He personally might not have felt able to declare that he was a Muslim and break with his tribe and people. His son was still young and as he was approaching death, he would be saved by declaring his acceptance of Islam.

528. 'Ā'ishah reports: 'When God's Messenger (peace be upon him) migrated to Madinah, Abu Bakr and Bilāl came down with a fever. I visited them and asked: "Father, how do you feel?" and "How do you feel, Bilāl?" When Abu Bakr's fever was worse, he would say:

"Every man may be with his people in the morning, when death is closer to him than the strap of his sandal".

And when the fever gave Bilāl some relief, he would chant:

"Would that I knew whether I may spend a night in the valley of Makkah, surrounded by *idkhir* and *jalīl.*

Will I ever be at the waters of Majinnah; and will I ever see the mountains of Shāmah and Ṭafīl?"

'Ā'ishah said: "I went to the Prophet and told him. He said: 'My Lord, let us love Madinah as we love Makkah or more. Make it healthy for us, and bless our measures of its produce. Take away its fever and transfer it to al-Juḥfah'."'[383]

The story reported in this *ḥadīth* needs no explanation. Many of the Muslims who migrated to Madinah with the Prophet fell ill. It appears from the *ḥadīth* that the fever was severe and that those who contracted it might be unaware of what they said. However, it is clear that they missed Makkah. Bilāl mentions *idkhir* and *jalīl.* These are herbs that grew in the valley of Makkah. Majinnah was a place near Makkah where a seasonal bazaar was organised; and Shāmah and Ṭafīl were two mountains near Makkah.

The Prophet appealed to God to remove the fever from Madinah and place it at al-Juḥfah, which was mostly a desert area in enemy territory.

529. This *ḥadīth* is the same as Number 517, but with a different chain of transmission.

530. (*Athar* 125) Nāfi' reports: 'When Ibn 'Umar visited a sick person he would ask him how he felt. When he was about to leave, he would say: "May God give you what is best for you". He did not say anything more'.

'Abdullāh ibn 'Umar was always keen to follow the Prophet's example. Whatever he saw the Prophet doing, he would do the same, even when it was something unrelated to religion. His conduct in visiting ill people is seen in this light. He would ask the patient how he felt and understand what he was told. Before leaving, he would pray to God to choose for the patient what was best for him.

---

383. Related by Mālik, al-Bukhari, Muslim and al-Nasā'ī.

531. (*Athar* 126) Sa'īd ibn 'Amr reports: 'Al-Ḥajjāj came to visit Ibn 'Umar when I was with him. He asked how he felt. Ibn 'Umar said: "Fine". Al-Ḥajjāj asked: "Who harmed you?" He said: "The one who ordered people to carry arms on a day when it is unlawful to carry arms". He meant al-Ḥajjāj himself'.[384]

Al-Ḥajjāj was a governor and army commander during the Umayyad period. The incident referred to in this *ḥadīth* took place during the pilgrimage days and the Prophet had made it clear that arms must not be carried by soldiers on the Eid day. A stray spear hit Ibn 'Umar in his foot. When al-Ḥajjāj asked him who had hit him with a spear, Ibn 'Umar referred to him as the one who ordered soldiers to carry their weapons. This is clear. If a governor or a commander gives an order in violation of Islamic teachings, he is responsible for whatever occurs as a result of such violation. Although al-Ḥajjāj was not the one directly responsible for Ibn 'Umar's injury, responsibility attaches to him on account of his giving the orders.

532. (*Athar* 127) 'Abdullāh ibn 'Amr said: 'Do not visit wine drinkers when they are ill'.

This is due to the fact that visiting them may be construed as condoning their behaviour. A Muslim should not do anything that may be thought to approve an action that violates clear Islamic principles.

533. (*Athar* 128) Al-Ḥārith ibn 'Ubaydillāh al-Anṣāri said: 'I saw Umm al-Dardā' going to visit an Anṣāri man from the mosque and she was on her mount in an uncovered howdah'.

In *ḥadīth* Number 519 we learnt that the Prophet visited Umm al-Sā'ib when she was ill. In this *ḥadīth* Umm al-Dardā' visits a man from the Anṣār. These two *ḥadīths* make clear that it is perfectly permissible for men to visit sick women and for women to visit sick men, provided that all Islamic standards of propriety are observed. This proviso is clearly stated in the next *ḥadīth*.

---

384. Related by al-Bukhari.

534. (*Athar* 129) 'Abdullāh ibn Mas'ūd visited someone who was ill, and he was accompanied by some people. There was a woman in the room, and one of the men stared at her. 'Abdullāh said to him: 'It would have been better for you to have your eyes forced out'.

The man was guilty of something highly unbecoming. The woman must have been one of the patient's family, attending him or welcoming his visitors. To stare fixedly at her is very embarrassing for her and contrary to Islamic teachings. Hence, 'Abdullāh ibn Mas'ūd's comment, which is meant literally.

535. Zayd ibn Arqam said: 'My eyes were inflamed and the Prophet came to visit me. [When I recovered] he said to me: "Zayd, if the illness in your eyes persisted, what would you have done?" I said: "I would have endured with patience, hoping for God's reward". He said: "If the illness in your eyes persisted and you endured with patience and in hope for God's reward, your reward would be admittance into heaven".'[385]

536. Al-Qāsim ibn Muhammad reported: 'One of the Prophet's companions lost his eyesight. He said to his visitors: "I was keen to have my eyes in health so that I could look at the Prophet (peace be upon him). Now that the Prophet has passed away, it would not delight me that my complaint had befallen a gazelle in Tibālah".'

537. Anas reports that the Prophet said: 'God, the Mighty and Exalted, said: "When I test a servant of Mine taking away his two dearest ones [i.e. his eyes], and he endures with patience, I give him heaven in compensation".'

538. Abu Umāmah reports that the Prophet said: 'God says: Son of Adam, if I take your two precious ones and you bear the shock with patience, enduring it in the hope of My reward, I will not be happy with anything less than heaven for your reward'.

---

385. Related by Aḥmad, Abū Dāwūd and al-Ḥākim.

These *ḥadīths* give us the same message, making it clear that the reward God gives a believer who is tested by the loss of his eyesight is nothing less than admittance into heaven. The first *ḥadīth* is stated by the Prophet when he made this clear to one of his companions who suffered from conjunctivitis. In the last two *ḥadīths* the reward is promised directly by God. The second *ḥadīth* tells us of the attitude of one of the Prophet's companions who lost his eyesight. He was apparently aware of the reward God had promised. Hence, he would not exchange his situation. He wanted his eyesight to see the Prophet, but after the Prophet had passed away, everything else was unimportant.

The first two *ḥadīths* identify that we should visit a sick person even if the illness is not very serious or if it is unlikely to persist for long.

539. Ibn 'Abbās reports: 'When the Prophet (peace be upon him) visited a sick person, he would sit close to his head and say, seven times: "I appeal to God, the Great, Lord of the great Throne, to cure you". [i.e. *As'alu Allah al-Aẓīm, Rabb al-'Arsh al-'Aẓīm, an yashfik.*] If his time had not yet come, he was cured'.[386]

540. (*Athar* 130) Al-Rabī' ibn 'Abdullāh said: 'I went with al-Ḥasan to visit Qatādah when he was ill. Al-Ḥasan sat close to his head and asked him how he felt. He then prayed for him saying: "My Lord, cure his heart and give him full recovery". [i.e. *Allahumma ishfi qalbah; wa ishfi saqamah*]'.

These two *ḥadīths* focus on two points: where to sit when visiting a sick person and what to pray for. The best place to sit is close to the patient's head, so that if his speech is low one can hear him without difficulty. Prayers for the patient should concentrate on asking for full recovery.

386. Related by Aḥmad, Abū Dāwūd, al-Tirmidhi, al-Ḥākim and Ibn Ḥibbān.

What to do at home

From the early days of Islam, Muslims wanted to learn how the Prophet conducted himself at home:

541. Al-Aswad ibn Yazīd reports: 'I asked 'Ā'ishah (may God be pleased with her) what the Prophet did when he was at home with his family. She said: "He attended to what his family needed. When it was time for prayer, he left".'[387]

542. 'Urwah ibn al-Zubayr said: 'I asked 'Ā'ishah (may God be pleased with her) what the Prophet did at home? She said: "He mended his shoes and did what any man normally did at home".'[388]

543. 'Urwah ibn al-Zubayr said: 'I asked 'Ā'ishah (may God be pleased with her) what the Prophet did at home? She said: "He mended his shoes and patched clothes and stitched".'[389]

544. 'Amrah said: ''Ā'ishah (may God be pleased with her) was asked what God's Messenger (peace be upon him) used to do at home. She said: "He was a man like all men: he removed fleas from his garment and milked his sheep".'[390]

All these *ḥadīths* give the same answer, showing us that the Prophet was the most caring husband and father. He attended to his own and to his family's needs. He did not disdain doing anything that was needed, whether mending shoes, patching a garment or milking sheep. Yet many men would think that such tasks are beneath them, even when they themselves need them or when they are needed by their families.

---

387. Related by al-Bukhari and al-Tirmidhi.
388. Related by Aḥmad.
389. Related by Aḥmad and Ibn Ḥibbān.
390. Related by al-Tirmidhi and al-Bazzār.

To love your Muslim brother

The brotherhood of Islam is a very real bond. It applies to all Muslims, men and women. Every Muslim considers all other Muslims his brothers and sisters. Islam encourages this bond and attaches great reward to it. When two Muslims love one another genuinely and sincerely, without ulterior motives, but simply as two people united in their faith, they earn reward for their love. It is within this context that we should understand the Prophet's encouragement to his followers to make their feelings known to those of their brothers whom they truly loved.

545. Al-Miqdām ibn Ma'd Yakrib reports that the Prophet said: 'When any of you loves his brother, he should tell him that he loves him'.[391]

546. Mujāhid said: 'A companion of the Prophet met me and put his hand on my shoulders from behind and said to me: "I love you indeed". I said: "May you be loved by the One for whose sake you have loved me". He said: "I would not have told you this, had it not been for what God's Messenger (peace be upon him) has said: 'When one man loves another, he should tell him that he loves him'." He then spoke of a marriage offer, saying: "We have this young woman who is ill-mannered".'

When the Prophet speaks of love between Muslims, he wants to make it clear to them that when they cement their relations and set them on the right footing, the benefit is not merely that which accrues to them as individuals and to their community, but there is also a heavenly reward for this. It is for this reason that we find friendship between good Muslim believers to be much stronger than ordinary friendship between other people, or between Muslims and people who do not share their faith. This has served to strengthen the feeling of unity within the Muslim community throughout history. It is not surprising, therefore, that we find the Prophet encouraging it and also

391. Related by Abū Dāwūd, al-Tirmidhi, al-Nasā'ī, Ibn Ḥibbān and al-Ḥākim.

encouraging whatever can bring Muslims closer together and increase their love of each other.

The last point in this *ḥadīth* is the marriage offer. The Prophet's companion spoke about his relative whom he wanted Mujahid to marry. The *ḥadīth* does not give us the full details, but it tells us that the Prophet's companion did not extol her praises, rather he pointed out her faults. This is the proper attitude in business and indeed other dealings so that the parties involved are well aware of the situation.

547. Anas reports that the Prophet said: 'When two men have the bond of love, the better of the two is the one who loves his brother more'.[392]

In this *ḥadīth*, the Prophet seems to encourage his followers to nurture their love of one another so that it is pure and strong. It must be the sort of love that is not motivated by serving personal interests. The Prophet was also keen to teach us how to protect our social relations and what to avoid in order not to spoil good relations with a brother in Islam.

548. (*Athar* 131) Muʿādh ibn Jabal said: 'When you love a brother of yours, do not enter into any unnecessary argument with him nor treat him badly. Do not enquire about him, because you may be asking an enemy of his and he will tell you something false about him, and thereby cause a split between the two of you'.

When we consider the points against which we are warned about in this *ḥadīth*, we find that every one of them can spoil a close friendship. Futile arguments are always unnecessary. Between friends they are even more so. All such an argument achieves is wasting time over something useless instead of doing something that strengthens a sound relationship.

It is part of human nature that when someone is wronged, he wants to retaliate. To feel that one has been treated unfairly or deprived of

392. Related by al-Ḥākim and Ibn Ḥibbān.

something that is due to him by right is very unpleasant. If the wrong comes from a friend, it gives a feeling of deep hurt. It is only natural that you want to pay back in kind. This means the end of friendly relations.

Moreover, if you feel that a brother of yours is close to you and you do love him and your love is for God's sake, then you need not ask others about him. You have seen enough of him to put your relationship on a sound basis. Why do you need to go around asking about him? When you do, how can you tell that the person you are asking has the interests of that brother of yours at heart? Indeed, he may harbour a grudge against him. If he is dishonest, he will tell you something false about him and your relationship with him, which started on a sound basis, will be undermined. It could have earned the sort of reward which will benefit both of you in the Hereafter, but it is no longer so. Therefore, you should not allow that possibility in the first place by not asking others about your friend whom you have loved after having formed a very good opinion of him.

The Prophet stresses that brotherly love must be pure. A Muslim loves his brother because he is a believer and because he knows him to be dedicated to the service of God's cause. It is, in other words, love for God's sake, established on the basis of Islamic brotherhood.

549. ʿAbdullāh ibn ʿAmr reports that the Prophet said: 'Whoever loves a brother for the sake of God, and in the service of God's cause, should say to him: "I love you for God's sake". If both of them are admitted into heaven, the one whose love is purely for God's sake will have a higher rank than the one he loved, because of his love'.

This *ḥadīth* links the bond of Islamic brotherhood, which is the basis of Islamic love, with the sort of position a Muslim may have in heaven, in the life to come. The purer and stronger the love is, the higher the lover's position is. This is due to the fact that such pure love encourages good action which has no personal motive apart from earning God's pleasure. Such practical actions have a very important by-product by way of cementing social ties and strengthening the unity of the Muslim community.

The Prophet touches on a very important point in human nature. When you feel that you are loved for no reason other than your being a good Muslim, you have the satisfaction that your faith has made you a better person, one who is held in high esteem in his community. Moreover, you are bound to reciprocate such feelings. This works wonders for the strengthening of social relations.

550. (*Athar* 132) ʿIyāḍ ibn Khalīfah reports that he heard ʿAli ibn Abu Ṭālib say at Ṣiffīn: 'Intelligence is in the heart, mercy in the liver, compassion in the spleen and breathing in the lungs'.

This statement is attributed to ʿAli, without a reference to the Prophet. Normally, *ḥadīth* scholars consider statements by the Prophet's companions that are related to religion as *ḥadīths* because they know that none of the Prophet's companions would say anything about religion unless he or she had learnt it from the Prophet. Yet they might hesitate to attribute it to the Prophet for fear of forgetting or omitting something, or making an unintentional error. This statement does not seem to be in this category. Therefore, entering it here does not seem to have any strong basis. Emotions like mercy and compassion are not associated with particular organs of the human body, although in Arabic, the liver is often associated with tender emotions, particularly towards children. As for the heart being the location of intelligence, the Arabs used the word *qalb*, which means heart, but can be used interchangeably with mind.

29

Pride: The Quality to Avoid

Definition of pride

551. 'Abdullāh ibn 'Amr reports: 'We were sitting with God's Messenger (peace be upon him) when a bedouin approached, wearing a green robe with brocade edges. He came in until he stood before the Prophet and said: "Your friend here wants to put down every man of honour and elevate every shepherd". The Prophet took him by the collar of his robe and said: "I see that you are wearing the clothes of one who is devoid of sound mind". Then he went on to say: "When the Prophet Noah (peace be upon him) was close to death, he said to his son: 'I will give you some instructions. I command you to observe two things and forbid you two things. You must declare that "there is no deity except God". [i.e. *La ilāha illa Allah*]. If all the seven heavens and the seven earths were to be placed on the scales against "there is no deity except God", it would outweigh them. And if the

seven heavens and the seven earths were made into a solid ring, it would break that ring. [I also command you] to declare that "God's Glory is limitless and He is infinite in His praise, [i.e. *Subḥān Allah wa biḥamdih*]". This is the prayer of everything, and by it everything receives its provisions. I forbid you the association of partners with God and pride'."

'The Prophet was asked: "We know about associating partners with God, but what is meant by pride? Does pride mean that a person among us may have a fine suit to wear?" He answered, "No". They asked: "Does it mean that a person may have a good pair of sandals with two fine straps?" He answered, "No". They asked again: "Does it mean, then, that a person may have his own animal to ride?" Again he said, "No". Then he was asked: "Does it mean that he has companions who socialise with him?" But the Prophet again answered: "No". They said: "Messenger of God, what is pride, then?" He replied: "It is to ignore the truth and to treat people with contempt".'[393]

The story begins with the bedouin and the way he entered the mosque where the Prophet was sitting with his companions. His attitude must have betrayed that the man thought too highly of himself. His rich clothes must have added to the impression he left on the Prophet's companions. His first words are meant as an objection to the Islamic principles that people are all equal. Hence, he said that the Prophet wanted to shame every man of honour and elevate those who are not usually held in high esteem. He obviously considered himself of the first group, and perhaps said this in complaint about what he felt to be the threat represented by Islam to people enjoying positions of honour and influence. Perhaps this was also the purpose of his wearing such fine clothes.

The Prophet wanted him to understand that appearances count for little. He described the man's clothes as those of a person devoid of intelligence. That must have come as a shock to the man who thought that his dress gave him some advantage and that he was entitled to receive a good reception from the Prophet. The Prophet,

393. Related by Aḥmad, al-Nasā'ī, al-Bayhaqi and al-Ḥākim.

however, made it clear to him that the way he dressed meant nothing to him.

The Prophet then told the bedouin and his companions the story about Prophet Noah and his final words to his son. As is well known, Muslims believe in all the prophets who preceded Prophet Muhammad and acknowledge that they brought messages from God to mankind. Therefore, whatever agrees with Islam in the message of any earlier prophet is incorporated as part of our religion. Where any religion clashes with Islamic principles, the clash is due either to an abrogation of an earlier rule as in the case of punishments prescribed in the Torah for murder and causing bodily harm. The principle of retaliation and causing the perpetrator similar injury is established in the Torah. The Qur'an introduced an extra provision, allowing the injured party the chance to pardon his aggressor. Such a variation is understandable. When two Divine religions seem to be in opposition, we declare that the earlier one has been distorted, since God has guaranteed to preserve the message of the Qur'an intact for all times. Hence, when the Prophet mentions the last words of Prophet Noah, he does so to endorse them and to make it clear to his companions and his followers that they apply to them.

If we examine these words, we find that they are in full agreement with Islam. The two things Noah ordered his son to observe and maintain are his belief in God's oneness and glorifying and praising Him. This is the guiding principle in all Divine messages. On the other hand, the two things he forbade him were polytheism, or associating partners with God, and pride. This last part of Noah's words probably came as a surprise to the bedouin and indeed to the Prophet's companions. The reporter of the *ḥadīth*, 'Abdullāh ibn 'Amr, a learned companion of the Prophet speaks of long questioning of the Prophet by his companions about the exact meaning of pride. The line of questioning is easy to understand. Since the Prophet commented on the bedouin's dress, his companions started by asking him whether pride was demonstrated by wearing fine clothing.

The Prophet explains that appearances are not what matters. A person may wear fine clothes and fine shoes without being guilty of pride. The Qur'anic instructions in this regard are very clear. God states: "*Who is there to forbid the beauty which God has brought forth for His creatures, and the good things of life? Say: They are [lawful] in the life of this world to all believers, to be theirs alone on the Day of Judgement*". (7: 32)

The Prophet also explains that pride need not be the quality of a man who has friends who come to him on social visits; as long as he treats them well and does not ignore the rights of any of them, he has nothing to worry about.

When the Prophet's companions had put to him all these questions and he explained that none of these situations need be one of pride, they asked him directly to define pride for them. As usual, the Prophet's definition is most clear and to the point. 'Pride', he explains, 'is ignoring the truth and denying people their rights'. Ignoring the truth comes in a variety of ways. Some commentators on *Ḥadīth* give the following example: a man may owe you some money, but he denies it altogether. Another person who knows that he has borrowed money from you reminds him that he should fear God and pay you your money. Instead of accepting his admonition and acknowledging his debt, he takes a hostile attitude to the man and the truth. As for denying people their rights, this need not only be with respect to material rights. If he shows conceit and looks at other people with contempt, he denies them their rights. It is perhaps the latter attitude which is more important. When a man is contemptuous of his fellow human beings, treating them with arrogance, he is guilty of committing something which prophets have put alongside associating partners with God. This is a very grave matter indeed.

The Prophet often spoke about pride and the adoption of conceit, describing it in terms which made every one of his companions want to ensure that they could never be described as proud or conceited. Every Muslim who knows the essence of his religion must have a good understanding of what is lawful and what is unlawful. Therefore, it was necessary for the Prophet to explain on occasions that certain behaviour classified a person as conceited and certain actions were sufficient evidence for him not to be so described.

552. 'Abdullāh ibn 'Umar reports that the Prophet said: 'He who gives himself airs or walks with an arrogant gait will find

out when he meets God, the Mighty and Exalted, that He is displeased with him'.[394]

The first quality the Prophet mentions here is giving oneself airs. This is perhaps the most important element of conceit. A proud or conceited person claims to himself, and believes, that he is great. He does not recognise that whatever blessing he may enjoy has been bestowed on him by God. It is part of God's grace which He grants to people as a demonstration of His mercy. No human being can earn by his knowledge or his action all the favours God bestows on him. When a person claims that he has made himself what he is, his claim means that God has had no choice but to grant him His blessings. This is a very arrogant attitude that puts the person in a very unfavourable position with God.

In the Qur'an, we are told about Korah, or Qārūn, who belonged to the people of Moses, and who arrogantly exalted himself above them. He was a man of enormous wealth. When he was told that he must use his wealth to ensure a good position for himself in the life to come, he arrogantly said that he had been given his wealth by virtue of his own knowledge. God destroyed him, causing the earth to swallow him and his dwelling. Neither his wealth, his servants nor henchmen could avail him of anything against God's punishment. A detailed account of his attitude is given in Surah 28, verses 76–83.

In this Qur'anic account, it is clear that Korah showed both qualities that the Prophet mentions in this *ḥadīth* as a cause of God's displeasure. He gave himself airs by claiming that what he had was a result of his knowledge and he went about arrogantly, looking at ordinary people with contempt. God taught him a lesson and made of him an example to all mankind. If others adopt the same attitude, they may not necessarily suffer the same fate in this life. They will, however, certainly have the same position in the life to come. When, on the Day of Judgement, someone finds himself having incurred God's displeasure, he is certainly lost.

It is pertinent to ask, then, what a person should do in order not to appear proud or conceited.

---

394. Related by Aḥmad and al-Ḥākim.

553. Abu Hurayrah reports that the Prophet said: 'He is not conceited who allows his servant to eat with him, rides a donkey in the marketplace and ties up his sheep and milks it'.

These qualities indicate an attitude of readiness to do what one needs, regardless of what people may think. The first action is for a person to allow his servant to eat with him. This need not be something that is done all the time, especially with domestic servants. The point that Islam stresses is that servants should be given of the same food one eats. In this particular *ḥadīth*, this attitude is mentioned as evidence that a person is not proud or conceited. When the occasion arises, he does not disdain to have his servant share his food or sit with him at the table. There are occasions when leaving a servant to eat alone may cause the servant pain as he will be made to feel that he belongs to a lower class. This is the sort of feeling Islam wants to stamp out. Therefore, Muslims are encouraged not to allow any of their number to feel inferior.

The Prophet was of course talking of people in terms of what was familiar to them. It was the ordinary practice for most people to go to the market riding donkeys. The person who does so, when he can afford to go to the market riding a horse, is one who adopts the right approach on every occasion. He does not disdain to be seen riding a donkey. Today, this does not apply except perhaps in some rural areas of some countries. People nowadays go to the market by car. Therefore, we should take the essence in this *ḥadīth* to mean doing our things in the normal way other people do them. We do not try to show that we are superior in any way.

The same applies to the last action mentioned by the Prophet, namely, milking a sheep. It was normal for people in Arabia to have sheep from which they used to obtain their milk. A proud person would not milk a sheep himself, but would ask others to bring him milk. Therefore, the Prophet mentions the person who milks his own sheep as someone who is devoid of conceit.

This was understood well by the Prophet's companions. We have reports that even the most distinguished among them, those who ruled the Muslim state, were keen to do things themselves without asking others for help. The following *ḥadīth* speaks of 'Ali when he was Caliph, ruling the entire Muslim state:

554. (*Athar* 133) Ṣāliḥ quotes his grandmother: 'I saw 'Ali (may God be pleased with him) buying dates for a *dirham* and carrying them in his cloak. I said to him [or someone said to him]: "May I carry it for you, Amir al-Mu'minīn?" He said: "No. The head of the family is the one to carry it".'

Obviously, if someone has something heavy which he cannot carry himself, there is nothing wrong with asking someone else to help.

Pride: God's own cloak

Since Islam views pride in such a negative light, how do we explain the fact that it is mentioned in the Qur'an as one of God's attributes. To explain we may say that there are qualities and attributes belonging to God that no human being is allowed to have. Before we elaborate, let us look at the Qur'anic references which associate pride with God.

The final verses of Surah 59 enumerate several attributes of God, such as His being the Ever Merciful, the All-knowing, the Sovereign, the Supreme, etc. Together with His other attributes, God is also described as *al-Mutakabbir*, an adjective which in reference to human beings means, 'conceited'. But in this Qur'anic context, it has a different sense altogether. Its best translation is the 'One to whom all greatness belongs'.

Similarly, in Surah 45, the final two verses contain the richest and most inspiring and expressive praise of God. The second of these verses speaks of all 'pride' as belonging to God. But in this context, the term means much more than pride. Many translators of the Qur'an use the word 'majesty' to render its meaning. Thus, the two final verses of this surah may be rendered in translation as follows: '*All praise is due to God, the Lord of heavens, the Lord of the earth and the Lord of all the worlds. His alone is all supremacy in the heavens and the earth. He alone is the Almighty, the Wise*'. (45: 36-37)

In both instances, the context is that of greatness which belongs to God. In neither do we find commentators on the Qur'an or its translators feel that the term used refers to pride as the quality demonstrated by some people who are disliked in their community.

Indeed, God does not show such an attitude to any of His creatures. The reverse is correct. He shows compassion to all of them. He bestows His Grace on those who deserve it and those who do not. Even when some people who have lived their lives disbelieving in Him find themselves in distress and appeal to Him for help, His help is always forthcoming. Much exalted He is to show an air of arrogance to anyone. What need has He to do so, when all heavens and earth acknowledge their servitude to Him alone?

Strictly speaking, the word *kibriyā'*, meaning pride, is used in reference to God in the Qur'an and *Ḥadīth* makes clear that it belongs to God alone. The following is a sacred or *qudsi ḥadīth*, i.e. one which is reported by the Prophet as having been said by God:

555. Abu Sa'īd al-Khudri and Abu Hurayrah report that the Prophet said: 'God, the Mighty and Exalted, says: "Greatness is My robe and Pride is My cloak. I shall punish anyone who contends with Me in respect of either of them".'[395]

It is clear that this *ḥadīth* is meant figuratively. Otherwise, God does not need a cloak and a robe. Indeed, He is in need of nothing and no one. But the description of cloak and robe here indicates that pride and greatness belong to God. One's garments are the closest to one. Moreover, they are very personal. You cannot just take a part of your friend's jacket or dress. You may admire them on him or her, but that is as far as you can say or do, even if you would very much like to have a similar garment. But when something is described by God as belonging to Him alone, then that is where it belongs. Human beings should not try to have any portion of it for themselves.

In this *qudsi ḥadīth*, God speaks of a person who may contend with Him over His cloak, which is pride, or His robe, which is greatness. Such contention takes the form of attitude and behaviour. Obviously, a man does not contend with God in order to get more of something that God does not want him to get. Through one's own behaviour, however, and through one's attitude towards others, showing pride, insolence, arrogance and similar traits, one actually claims a station

395. Related by Aḥmad, Muslim, Ibn Mājah and al-Ḥākim.

above that of other human beings. This sort of superiority belongs to God alone. Hence, when a human being makes such a claim, he is actually competing with God, or trying to usurp His position. God does not condone anything of the sort. Therefore, He punishes the person who makes such a claim by throwing him in hell.

It is perhaps appropriate to stress once again that God's pride does not relate to arrogance or conceit. Far be such from God. The term is simply an emphasis of His greatness. This is how we should understand the Qur'anic verses and *ḥadīths* which speak of His pride.

When it comes to human behaviour, pride is the quality that sends people headlong into the fire:

556. (*Athar* 134) Al-Nu'mān ibn Bashīr said: 'Satan sets some snares and traps. His traps and snares include ingratitude for the grace God bestows, boasting about God's gifts, arrogant behaviour towards God's servants and following vain desires in what displeases God'.

The first three of these qualities are interrelated. A person who is ungrateful to God after enjoying His grace is one who is very likely to be proud and to behave insolently. Similarly, one who boasts that God has given him so much actually tries to show that he is being honoured by God for something special he has. This is a false claim to greatness. Instead, a good believer praises God and thanks Him for everything that He has given him. When he does so, he realises that God's gifts have been given to him not because of anything special that he has, but because God bestows unlimited gifts on His servants. These two qualities are closely related to conceit and behaving towards other people with arrogance. All three qualities are described by the Prophet's companion as traps which Satan sets to catch people and turn them away from the path which gains them God's pleasure and forgiveness. The last quality is following one's vain desires and caprice in preference to what God has ordered us to do. This is the surest way to go astray.

What destiny for mankind

God has told us about heaven and hell as the destiny of all mankind. In a future life, people will be judged on the basis of their actions. Those who believe in God and His messenger and do good deeds will earn the reward of heaven. While their actions, however beneficial, self-denying and good in intention and execution, may not be sufficient to thank God for all the blessings He has granted them, He nonetheless fulfils His promise to them, bestowing His grace on them and admitting them to heaven. On the other hand, those who stand in a position of challenge to His message, act with arrogance and tyrannise others, will invariably be thrown in hell.

In the Qur'an and the *Ḥadīth* we read vivid descriptions of both places and what their dwellers receive or endure. At times, the two places are described as talking and arguing. We are told in the Qur'an that hell is asked whether it has reached its full capacity and it replies: '*Can I have more?*' (50: 30) In the following *ḥadīth*, heaven and hell argue about the type of person assigned to each of them.

557. Abu Hurayrah reports that the Prophet said: 'Heaven and Hell fell in argument and hell said: "The tyrants and the conceited and arrogant will enter me". Heaven said: "The weak and the poor enter me". God, the Blessed and the Exalted, says to heaven: "You are My Grace which I bestow on whomever I will". He says to hell: "You are a place of suffering in which I punish whomever I will. Each of you will have its fill".'[396]

The first point to consider in this *ḥadīth* is that appearances in this life count for little in the life to come. At times, we tend to think that those who are favoured with power, influence and luxuries may also be favoured and since they have achieved excellence in this life then excellent is their position in the future life. This is a narrow way of thinking. The person who is given wealth and riches and does not thank God for His favours by sharing his privileges with others and

396. Related in a longer version by al-Bukhari. Also related by Aḥmad, Muslim, al-Tirmidhi, Ibn Khuzaymah, Abu 'Awānah and Ibn Ḥibbān.

paying the dues God has required him to pay and who behaves towards others as if he has earned his riches is a conceited and arrogant. Such a person can be sure that he will have his place in hell. A person who is placed by God in a position of power and who can have his orders obeyed by soldiers, policemen and the government machinery must obey God first and foremost in the way he uses his power. If he does not then he is a tyrant who oppresses others. He may enjoy his authority in this life and people may fear his might, but that is no insurance that he will have an easy passage in the life to come. Indeed, the reverse is true. Tyrants will most certainly be in hell.

In this *ḥadīth* hell is described as thinking that it is favoured with such people who have been given privileges in this world. They imagine that they are given such privileges because they are superior to others, but this is a naïve way of thinking. Since they have abused their privileges, they are the worst of people.

On the other hand, enduring suffering in this life and being in a position of weakness does not belittle the value of any person or his being worthy of the greatest honour. Hence, heaven need have no complaint about its dwellers. God explains to both of them that they are merely means for the execution of His will. Heaven is a manifestation of His grace which He bestows on those who earn it through their diligence in obeying His orders. Hell, on the other hand, is a manifestation of His displeasure and a punishment He inflicts on whoever deserves it.

That each place will have its fill ensures absolute justice. Whoever earns God's pleasure is sure to be well rewarded and whoever incurs His displeasure is sure to be punished. No one misses out on the first and no one escapes a deserved punishment. The capacity of each one is unlimited, in the sense that each one will accommodate those who deserve to be in it.

558. (*Athar* 135) Abu Salamah ibn ʿAbd al-Raḥmān said: 'The Prophet's companions were neither too meek nor apathetic. They used to recite poetry in their gatherings and mentioned their practices in pre-Islamic days. However, when any of them was

approached to accept a compromise concerning any aspect of faith, his eyes would turn round with rage'.[397]

This description of the Prophet's companions is very significant because the first point it makes is that those who understood Islam best, i.e. the first people to believe in Islam and to have constant access to God's messenger, did not feel that they had to demonstrate their lack of arrogance by adopting an opposite attitude and trying to appear meek or apathetic. There is certainly a difference between the absence of pride and trying to give such an impression by being too meek. We recognise the absence of pride in the ordinary person's behaviour. One need not go out of one's way to show that one is humble.

We have several reports to confirm this. One such example states that when 'Umar saw a man hanging down his head, he said to him: 'Raise your head; Islam is not ill'. He saw another man trying to appear weak and approaching death. He said to him: 'Do not give our faith an air of death, may God bring about your death'. 'Ā'ishah saw a man appearing too submissive and giving the impression that he was about to die. She asked what was wrong with him and she was told that he was a good reciter of the Qur'an. She said: 'Umar was the best of Qur'anic reciters, but he was fast when he walked, spoke aloud, and when he hit anyone, he caused him pain'.

The second point in the description of the Prophet's companions is that they used to recite poetry. It is well known that poetry flourished in the period that preceded Islam. People loved to listen to its recitation and every tribe felt very proud when one of its young men showed promise that he could be a poet and gain fame. Poetry in pre-Islamic days dealt mainly with love, passion and other feelings as well as mundane matters. Since Islam gave its followers a noble call to pursue, it was only to be expected that the early companions of the Prophet would have had no time for poetry. However, the fact is that the Prophet's companions continued to enjoy poetry and recite it in their gatherings. They went further than this and reminisced over their healthy and enjoyable practices in their pre-Islamic days. In other words, they lived a normal, ordinary life, having time for leisure and

397. Related by Ibn Abi Shaybah.

enjoying some of the pleasures of life. They did not try to suppress any of their ordinary human inclinations.

As we have mentioned earlier, what we normally do without showing arrogance is sufficient as evidence of not being proud. This applies even if we seem to enjoy the comforts and pleasures of this world.

559. Abu Hurayrah reports that 'a handsome man came to the Prophet and said: "I love what is beautiful and I have been given what you see. I do not like to see anyone superior to me, not even by the strap of a sandal or by a red sandal thong. Is that what pride is all about?" The Prophet answered: "No. Pride is to disdain the truth and be contemptuous of people".'[398]

Thus we come back to the same definition of pride the Prophet gives in *ḥadīth* Number 551. It is perfectly permissible to wear fine clothes and to show that God has bestowed His grace on one. But this must not be done in such a way that tells others that they are inferior. Arrogance means contempt of others. Therefore, arrogance smells of pride. On the other hand, when one enjoys God's grace, behaving as a Muslim should behave towards other Muslims, one is in no way guilty of pride.

560. 'Abdullāh ibn 'Amr reports that the Prophet said: 'Those who have been conceited and arrogant in this life will be raised on the Day of Judgement like tiny red ants in the shape of human beings. They are overwhelmed by humiliation and they are driven to a prison in hell called Bolus. A fiercely raging fire rises high over them and they are made to drink from the pus discharged by hell dwellers which makes their minds disturbed'.

The first part of the punishment to be inflicted on these arrogant people is that they find themselves in a position that is the opposite of the appearance they try to maintain in this life. While every one of them seeks to appear mighty and commanding respect, he is given on the Day of Judgement an infinitely small figure so that he is looked

---

398. Related by Abū Dāwūd.

down upon by all people and creatures. He is no bigger than a small red ant, although he has the shape and form of a man. Humiliation is poured over them from everywhere so that they suffer a fate which is the antithesis of the position they had coveted. Since a conceited person tries to appear able to do whatever he wishes, it is not sufficient that he is thrown in hell on the Day of Judgement but that he is driven to a prison therein. The name of that prison certifies despair, which is a feeling those conceited people will be made to experience. They have no hope that God will bestow His grace on them. They cannot expect any mercy from Him. Instead, the fire engulfs them and their minds are disturbed as they are made to taste their awful drink. To avoid such a situation a believer needs to behave in a way that does not give any impression of conceit.

30

Wives' Jealousy

561. 'Ā'ishah reports that the Prophet said to her: 'Go ahead; retaliate'.[399]

Although this *ḥadīth* is mentioned in this form, it suggests that it relates to a situation when the Prophet's wives were in dispute. This is a case that refers either to the incident mentioned in the next *ḥadīth* or to a similar one.

562. 'Ā'ishah reports: 'The Prophet's wives sent Fāṭimah to the Prophet. She sought permission to enter. The Prophet was with 'Ā'ishah, with both covered by her cloak. He gave her permission and she entered. She said: "Your wives have sent me to request you for justice regarding the daughter of Abu Quḥāfah [i.e. 'Ā'ishah]". The Prophet said: "Daughter, do you love what I

399. Related by al-Nasā'ī and Ibn Mājah.

love?" She said: "Yes, indeed". He said: "Then love this one". She rose and left, and she told them. They said: "You have not done much for us. Go back [and speak] to him". She said: "By God, I will never speak to him about her again".

'They sent Zaynab, the Prophet's wife, and she sought permission to enter and he gave her permission. She said the same thing to him, and then Zaynab spoke ill of me. I looked [at the Prophet] to see whether the Prophet would permit me. I continued to look until I realised that the Prophet was not averse to my retaliation. I attacked Zaynab and was soon able to inflict a severe defeat on her. The Prophet smiled and then said: "She is Abu Bakr's daughter".'[400]

Of all his wives that he married after Khadījah, the Prophet loved 'Ā'ishah best. This did not contradict the requirement of fairness that is essential for anyone who marries more than one wife. Fairness is required in treatment, not in feeling, because feelings cannot be controlled by people. The Prophet used to maintain absolute fairness in the treatment of his wives but he could not help loving 'Ā'ishah more. He used to pray to God for forgiveness, saying: 'My Lord, I am doing what I can to be fair in what I can control. Please do not hold me to account for what I cannot control'.[401]

The Prophet's preference for 'Ā'ishah was known to his companions. Many of the Anṣār were keen to send the Prophet gifts, which could be as simple as some food or fruit or other things. Needless to say, the Muhājirīn were too poor to be able to do the same. The ones who were distinguished for their frequent gifts included the two main figures of the Anṣār, Sa'd ibn 'Ubādah and Sa'd ibn Mu'adh, as well as 'Imārah ibn Ḥazm and Abu Ayyūb. Such people were eager to make their gifts more pleasing to the Prophet. Therefore, they chose the nights when the Prophet was with 'Ā'ishah to send their gifts. He used or ate of those gifts in 'Ā'ishah's home and he sent some of it to his other wives.

It is not unnatural that his other wives were not too happy about the situation. They felt that whatever gifts came to them were routed

400. Related by al-Bukhari, Muslim, al-Nasā'ī and Ibn Mājah.

401. Related by Aḥmad, al-Tirmidhi and al-Hakim

through 'Ā'ishah's home. It was not surprising that they talked to each other about the situation and wanted to remedy it. Since the Prophet's wives were living in a single room each, close to the mosque, it was only natural that some alliances or groupings should surface among them. One group included Umm Salamah, Zaynab bint Jaḥsh, Umm Ḥabībah, Juwairiyah bint Al-Ḥārith and Maymoonah. The others, Ḥafṣah, Ṣafiyyah and Sawdah were in a group with 'Ā'ishah.

Jealousies between the Prophet's wives were sometimes of an individual character, while at other times these groupings made them more pronounced. The question of gifts being sent to the Prophet while he was at 'Ā'ishah's home caused some unease with some of them. Hence they sought to remedy it, requesting that he should tell his companions not to favour 'Ā'ishah with their gifts, but to send them wherever he might happen to be. The request was made repeatedly, twice by Umm Salamah on behalf of the others, then they sent Fāṭimah, the Prophet's daughter and ultimately Zaynab spoke to him. The Prophet refused all these requests, because he felt that he could not speak to people about their gifts, as if he was expecting them. It was up to the people to determine what to send and when to send it. Had it been a matter which he himself could control, he would not have hesitated to please them, but he could not ask people to give them gifts.

31

In Times of Hardship

PEOPLE MAY GO through hard times, as a result of either natural causes such as drought and famine or man-made disasters such as wars and maldistribution of wealth. Islam places great value on helping sufferers:

> 563. (*Athar* 136) Abu Hurayrah said: 'There will be famine in the distant future. He who witnesses it should equate nothing with feeding the hungry'.

When people are starving and are in need of the smallest amount of food to survive and when there is nothing available to relieve their hunger, coming forward with supplies to feed such victims of famine is the greatest act of charity. It is the way to ensure the best reward from God.

Islam establishes a bond of brotherhood between its followers, so that when times are hard, people who are at a disadvantage will find help from their brethren who are better off. This was the case in the very first generation of Muslims. The Prophet established a close bond between his companions who migrated with him to Madinah, the Muhājirīn, and the Muslim population in the city, the Anṣār. The Anṣār welcomed the Muhājirīn and were very hospitable. Nothing the Muhājirīn needed was withheld from them.

564. Abu Hurayrah reports: 'The Anṣār said to the Prophet: "Divide the date trees between us and our brothers [i.e. the Muhājirīn]". He said: "No". Then they said to the Muhājirīn: "Then spare us the trouble of your upkeep and we will share the fruits with you". They said: "We listen and obey".'[402]

In this *ḥadīth* we find the whole community of the Anṣār coming with an offer to share their main assets with their brothers, the Muhājirīn. The Prophet, however, did not like that the Anṣār should part with half of their property in this way. He wanted to deepen the concept of sharing in the work and in the fruit. The Muhājirīn would be responsible for the necessary work in the date farms and, as such, they would be entitled to half the fruits yielded. The Prophet realised that things would change and he hoped for developments that would put the whole Muslim community in better conditions. The offer made by the Anṣār, however, remains as a good example of how Muslims should feel towards each other when they go through times of hardship.

These *ḥadīths* lay down a general principle applicable in all times of famine or emergency. When people cannot find enough to eat, or when things are so difficult that they are unable to cope, then providing food for the hungry is a good action which earns the best reward. In this connection, however, it is proper to ask how does the Muslim government react. The best example is given to us by 'Umar ibn al-Khaṭṭāb whose government provided the best example in finding practical solutions to practical problems. Such solutions have always been inspired by the Islamic system and remained within its framework.

During 'Umar's reign, Arabia went through a period of very severe drought. There was hardly any area in the whole of the Arabian

---

402. Related by al-Bukhari, Muslim and al-Nasā'ī.

Peninsula that escaped the hardship. People in Madinah suffered greatly. That year is known in Islamic history as 'the year of Ramādah', a term derived from a root that means ashes. This is because the winds blew sand over agricultural areas and considerably reduced their fertility. Even animals suffered a great deal, to the extent that those living in the wild came to town seeking food. All agricultural areas were dry and very little produce could be collected from them.

565. (*Athar* 137) 'Abdullāh ibn 'Umar said: ''Umar ibn al-Khaṭṭāb spoke in the Year of Ramādah, which was particularly severe, after he had taken every measure to help the bedouins with camels, wheat and oil from all the rural areas, until these rural areas were exhausted. 'Umar stood up supplicating: "Our Lord, provide them with help coming soon". God answered 'Umar's and the Muslims' prayers. When abundant rain fell, 'Umar said: "All praise be to God. By God if God had not given us relief, I would have placed with every well off Muslim family an equal number of poor people. Two people would not die from hunger if they shared the food sufficient for one only".'

When the drought was biting hard, 'Umar resorted to the well tried measure recommended by Islam. He called on all Muslims to offer the 'prayer for rain'. In this prayer, people go out of town wearing something plain and gather in an open area. They take their women and children with them and pray to God in all humility and sincerity to send them rain. They should couple this with showing repentance for their sins. It is recommended that one of them, well known for his devotion, should lead them in such a prayer.

'Umar called on the Muslims in Madinah to assemble outside for this prayer. He asked al-'Abbās, the Prophet's uncle to be the one who led the Muslims in their supplication. 'Umar was also praying earnestly. He prayed to God to let the rescue of the Muslim community be seen on the tops of the mountains. This was a reference to clouds which he prayed to be so near. God answered his prayers and those of the Muslim community. The sky was soon pouring with rain.

This was a clear case of emergency. The measure 'Umar suggested and would have implemented had the emergency lasted longer was to share equally the food available to rich families. This is certainly an exceptional measure. He would have been within his rights to impose such a measure, because it was his responsibility to ensure that people did not die of hunger. There is a principle in the Islamic system that allows the Muslim government to take an additional amount of the money of rich people when zakat funds are not sufficient to alleviate poverty. This principle empowers the ruler to levy such an addition on a gradual basis, until the purpose of alleviating poverty is accomplished. The principle goes as far as taking from the rich all the money that they have in excess of what is sufficient to meet their needs.

Special measures in times of hardship are taken for granted in the Muslim community:

566. Salamah ibn Al-Akwa' quotes the Prophet as saying to his companions when they were at the time of the Eid of Sacrifice, i.e. Eid al-Aḍḥa: 'Your sacrifices! Let no one of you leave in his home any amount of the sacrificial meat after three days'. The following year, the Prophet's companions asked him: 'Messenger of God, should we do like we did last year?' He answered: 'You may eat and store up. Last year, people were going through a kind of hardship and I wanted you to help'.[403]

This authentic *ḥadīth* shows that the Prophet put in force a special measure in a time of emergency. Although it is perfectly permissible for anyone to save a good portion of the meat of his sacrifice for cooking later, that year the Prophet instructed his companions not to have anything more than what was sufficient for them for three days. This meant that whatever they could not eat during those three days they had to give to the poor and needy. The Prophet wanted the whole community to share in the festive occasion of the Eid and enjoy a period of plenty at a time of hardship.

403. Related by al-Bukhari and Muslim.

32

Miscellaneous

567. (*Athar* 138) 'Urwah ibn al-Zubayr said: 'I was sitting at Mu'āwiyah's and he talked to himself. Then he was alert and said: "Forbearance comes from experience". He repeated this three times'.[404]

MU'ĀWIYAH WAS THE first Umayyad Caliph and he was renowned for his patience and forbearance. In this report he appears to have been in deep thought when he recovered and said that forbearance comes from experience. It appears that what he was thinking about called for some measures to be taken. His subsequent words and their repetition suggests that he might have been thinking of taking strong measures against some people but he thought the better of it and decided instead to show forbearance.

404. Related by Ibn Ḥibbān and Ibn Abi Shaybah.

568. (*Athar* 139) Abu Sa'īd al-Khudri said: 'No one acquires the quality of forbearance without having slipped into error; and no one acquires wisdom except through experience'.

Al-Bukhari adds the same report with a different chain of transmission, but this time Abu Sa'īd attributes the full statement to the Prophet.

This *ḥadīth* tells us that people may learn through their errors and from what they experience. If a person slips into error and feels shame, he may benefit from this and deal with forbearance when he sees someone else committing the same error. He prefers to overlook such errors, only giving advice in private to the errant person. Experience teaches a thinking person wisdom, so as to avoid what may bring trouble.

569. (*Athar* 140) Muhammad ibn al-Ḥanafiyyah quotes 'Ali as saying: 'To have a group of my brothers and serve them a good measure or two of food is preferable to me than to go down the marketplace and set a slave free'.

Muhammad ibn al-Ḥanafiyyah was 'Ali's own son, but he was affiliated to his mother so that people do not imagine that he belonged to Fāṭimah, the Prophet's daughter who was 'Ali's first wife. Here, he quotes his father stating this preference. To free a slave from bondage is an action that earns great reward from God. 'Ali definitely loved to earn such reward, but he gives an alternative that earns equal or greater reward, which is to serve some food to one's friends and brethren in Islam. This shows how Islam is keen to cement relations between Muslims.

570. 'Abd al-Raḥmān ibn 'Awf reports that the Prophet said: 'I attended with my uncles the alliance of *al-Muṭayyibīn*. I would not wish to break it for any worldly riches'.[405]

The Prophet is referring to an alliance he attended with his uncles, but in this *ḥadīth* the reference is to the *al-Muṭayyibīn* alliance that

---

405. Related by Aḥmad.

took place before the Prophet was born. The alliance he attended in ʿAbdullāh ibn Judʿān's home was the al-Fuḍūl alliance, which confirmed the earlier one. This alliance was between the Quraysh clans which agreed that they would stand together, and even go to war, in support of anyone suffering injustice in Makkah, whether the person belonged to its people or was just a visitor. The Prophet is reported to have said on different occasions that he would honour this alliance if he were to be appealed to under its terms. This is because supporting anyone, even an unbeliever, against injustice is a principle that Islam enshrines. Therefore, the Prophet would not break this alliance for anything.

571. Anas reports that, 'The Prophet established a bond of brotherhood between [ʿAbdullāh] ibn Masʿūd and al-Zubayr'.[406]

572. Anas ibn Mālik reports: 'God's Messenger established an alliance between the Quraysh and the Anṣār in my home in Madinah'.[407]

It is well known that one of the four major steps the Prophet took after migrating to Madinah was to establish a bond of brotherhood between the Muhājirīn and the Anṣār, making each one of the Muhājirīn a brother to one of the Anṣār. Anas mentions his home in Madinah, but he means his parents' home because he was only 10 or 12 years of age when the Prophet migrated to Madinah.

The first *ḥadīth* refers to an earlier bond of brotherhood the Prophet established between Muslims when he was still in Makkah. This *ḥadīth* specifies the brotherhood between these two companions of the Prophet who were among the very early Muslims. This brotherhood did not pay any attention to the social status of the two parties. Al-Zubayr belonged to one of the main Quraysh clans while ʿAbdullāh ibn Masʿūd was of a lesser status in Arabian tribal society. This did not, however, prevent their being brothers.

406. Related by Aḥmad.

407. Related by al-Bukhari, Muslim and Abū Dāwūd.

573. ʿAbdullāh ibn ʿAmr reports: 'The Prophet (peace be upon him) sat on the steps of the Kaʿbah in the year of the conquest of Makkah. He praised God and glorified Him. He then said: "Whoever is party to an alliance made in pre-Islamic days, Islam only increases its strength. There is no migration after the conquest of Makkah".'[408]

Al-Bukhari enters this *ḥadīth* in his anthology *Al-Adab al-Mufrad* under the subheading, 'No alliance in Islam', but other scholars report this to be the initial part of the *ḥadīth*. In other words, it is part of what the Prophet meant. When Makkah fell to Islam, mostly peacefully, there was no longer any need for an alliance between Muslims and other people. The bond of brotherhood Islam establishes between its followers is sufficient. They stand together against any enemy.

However, existing alliances are ḥonoured, and the Muslims would support anyone or any group of them that was bound by an alliance with others. As such, the alliance enjoys greater strength as it brings the entire Muslim community into it.

Moreover, the fact that Makkah came into the Islamic fold meant that there was no need for any Muslim to migrate to Madinah. Peace had been established in Arabia and Muslims assumed power there. Hence, the entire population of Arabia became one nation.

574. Anas reports: 'Rain fell on us when we were with the Prophet (peace be upon him). The Prophet pulled his garment to let rain fall on his body. We asked: "Why have you done that?" He said: "Because it has newly come from its Lord".'[409]

What the Prophet meant is that rain was newly created, and as such, it had the blessing of being a recent creation. He wanted such blessing to be in contact with him.

575. (*Athar* 141) Ḥumayd ibn Mālik ibn Khuthaym said: 'I was with Abu Hurayrah in his land at al-ʿAqiq when some

---

408. Related by Aḥmad, al-Tirmidhi, Abū Dāwūd and Ibn Khuzaymah.

409. Related by Muslim, al-Nasāʾī and Abū Dāwūd.

people from Madinah arrived on animals and dismounted. Abu Hurayrah said to me: "Go to my mother and say to her: 'Your son sends you his greetings and says: can you give us something to eat'." She brought out three barley loaves, some oil and salt on a platter. I placed it on my head and took it to them. I placed it before them. Abu Hurayrah said: "Allah Akbar God is great. All praise be to God who has given us our fill of this bread. There was a time when all that we had of food was only dates and water". The people ate nothing of the food. When they left, he said to me: "Nephew, take good care of your sheep. Brush the dust and mucous off them, and make their evening pasture good and pray near them. They are among the animals of heaven. By Him who holds my soul in His hand, there will soon be a time when a person would prefer to have a flock of sheep rather than Marwān's house".'[410]

576. 'Ali reports that the Prophet said: 'A sheep in the house is a blessing, and two are two blessings, and three sheep are all blessings'.

577. Abu Hurayrah reports that the Prophet said: 'The height of unbelief lies towards the East. Pride and arrogance lie with the bedouins who possess hundreds of horses and camels. Serenity is characteristic of the people who possess sheep'.[411]

578. (*Athar* 142) Ibn 'Abbās said: 'I wonder at dogs and sheep. Sheep are slaughtered in large numbers every year and many others are sacrificed'.

These *ḥadīths* need no comment. They speak of sheep as a blessing in the home and mention that sheep are associated with serenity and tranquillity. This is evident when we watch a shepherd. He has all the time in the world to reflect and think while his flock is grazing. Watching them feeding is a pleasure. Moreover, they tend to be plentiful

410. Related by Mālik.
411. Related by Aḥmad, al-Bukhari and Muslim.

in number. Although other animals may reproduce more, sheep keep on the increase, despite what people eat and sacrifice of them.

579. (*Athar* 143) Abu Ẓabyān said: ''Umar ibn al-Khaṭṭāb said to me: "Abu Ẓabyān, how much is your stipend?" I said: "2,500". He said: "Abu Ẓabyān, buy agricultural land and livestock before the lads of the Quraysh take over as rulers. To them such a stipend does not represent much money".'

This advice was given by 'Umar, the second Caliph, to a man who used to receive a stipend as a soldier in the Muslim army. 'Umar realised that his income was plentiful for his needs, and he told him to invest in productive land and livestock. He warned him against a time when such a stipend, large as it was, would count for nothing. This appears to be a warning against inflation. As such, the same advice applies across all ages. What is productive is a good investment.

580. 'Abdah ibn Ḥazn said: 'The people keeping camels and the people keeping sheep vied with each other. The Prophet said: "Moses was given his message when he was a shepherd, and David was given prophethood when he was a shepherd. I was given my message and I used to tend sheep for my people at Ajyād".'

A shepherd takes his flock of sheep to grazing grounds. As they graze, he feels the serenity of being with such docile creatures. If he is intelligent, he will reflect on the world around him. He will think of the sheep he is tending and of the open horizon before him. He will think of the heavens and the earth and inevitably he will look for what is beyond. Hence, to be a shepherd is good preparation for bearing the Divine message and delivering it to people. It is to this that the Prophet alludes in this *ḥadīth*.

It does not follow that the first revelation to all these prophets came at a time when they were tending sheep. We know that Prophet Muhammad worked as a shepherd in his youth, but he left it after a while, and he did not receive his first revelation until he was 40 years of age. The situation could have been the same for other prophets.

581. (*Athar* 144) Abu Hurayrah said: 'The major sins are seven in number: the first is to associate partners with God, then murder, false accusation of chaste women and going back to live as a bedouin after the migration'.

582. Thawbān said: 'God's Messenger said to me: "Do not live in remote areas, for the dweller of a remote area is like the dweller in a grave".'

These two *ḥadīths* warn against living in a remote area in the desert or in a rural location where other people are rarely seen. This leads to stagnation. One does not learn anything new, nor does one mix with people and interact socially. Moreover, strange ideas may be bred in such areas. Therefore, it is wrong to seek such a place for living after one has been accustomed to an urban area.

The only exception is when there is strife in the community and one does not wish to side with any party. Some of the Prophet's companions sought such refuge at the time of the troubles that led to the murder of the third Caliph.

583. Shurayḥ said: 'I asked 'Ā'ishah about going out into the desert and whether the Prophet used to do it. She said: "Yes, he used to go out to these hillside streams".'

584. (*Athar* 145) 'Amr ibn Wahb said: 'I saw Muhammad ibn 'Abdullāh ibn Usayd riding when he was in a state of consecration [i.e. *iḥrām*]. He took his garment off his shoulders and put it on his thighs. I asked him the reason and he said: "I saw 'Abdullāh doing this".'

What the Prophet warned against in the previous two *ḥadīths* is to go and live in a desert or remote area permanently. This does not exclude going there for a short time, such as a picnic or an outing with friends. This is what the Prophet used to do when he went to the hillside streams which were not far from Madinah.

Ḥadīth Number 584 is entered here under the same subheading as the one that precedes it, but the connection between the two is not readily apparent, unless the practice mentioned was something bedouins did. Hence, the question by the narrator. The answer he is given simply mentions that it was done by someone who is of better knowledge.

Keeping secrets

585. (*Athar* 146) 'Abdullāh ibn 'Abd al-Raḥmān of Qārah reported that 'Umar ibn al-Khaṭṭāb was with a man from the Anṣār when 'Abd al-Raḥmān ibn 'Abd came and sat with them. 'Umar said: 'We do not like that what we may say will be disclosed'. 'Abd al-Raḥmān said: 'I do not sit with such people, *Amīr al-Mu'minīn*'. 'Umar said: 'You may sit with this and that, but do not disclose what we may say'. Then 'Umar asked the Anṣāri man: 'Who do you think people say will be my successor?' The Anṣāri named several people from among the Muhājirīn, but did not mention 'Ali. 'Umar said: 'What do they have against Abu al-Ḥasan [i.e. 'Ali]? By God, he is the one who is most likely, when in charge, to set them on the path of the truth'.

'Umar apparently wanted this particular conversation not to be disclosed, because he realised that if circulated, people might misinterpret it or misquote what was said. This is generally the case when people do not take special care to report matters accurately.

We are not aware of the Anṣāri man who was in conversation with 'Umar, but apparently he was close to the people and could have had an informed view of what went on. 'Umar asked him who the people might choose to succeed him as Caliph after he died. His interlocutor only nominated figures from among the Muhājirīn, meaning that this aspect was settled and that the Anṣār did not consider that any of their number could be Caliph.

'Umar was surprised that the candidates mentioned in people's conversation did not include 'Ali, although he was the most qualified and could be the one to ensure the Muslim community followed the right course. This echoes a *ḥadīth* related by Aḥmad, with a sound chain of transmitters: 'The Prophet was asked: "Whom should we appoint as leader after you, Messenger of God?" He said: "If you choose Abu Bakr, you will find him trustworthy, caring little for this life and much for the life to come. If you choose 'Umar, you will find him strong, fearing no opposition in implementing God's law. If you choose 'Ali, and I do not think you will, you will find him a good guide and rightly guided, and he will keep you on the straight path".' Needless to say, the Prophet was absolutely right and each one he named proved his profound insight.

33

Caution and Forbearance

SCHOLARS THROUGHOUT ALL generations have always followed the Prophet's example in stressing the importance of good qualities, whenever the occasion arose. They might also relate a story in order to emphasise the importance of a certain quality:

586. (*Athar* 147) Al-Ḥasan said: 'A man died leaving behind a young son and a *mawla*.[412] Before he died, he asked his *mawla* to take care of his son. The *mawla* did all he could to ensure a good upbringing of the boy and in time he arranged his marriage. The youth then said to him: "Do the necessary preparation for me to take a trip of learning". He did so. The youth met a scholar and asked him to teach him. After some time, the scholar said to him: "Let me know when you intend to go back home, so that

412. A *mawla* is a former slave whose master has set him free but who chose to remain associated with his former master, serving him for remuneration.

I may teach you certain matters [of importance]". Later, the youth said to the scholar: "It is time for me to leave, so instruct me". The scholar said: "Remain always God-fearing; and be patient; and never act in haste". Al-Ḥasan comments that these three include all goodness.

'The young man went back home feeling that he could hardly ever forget these phrases. After all, they were only three. When he arrived home and dismounted, he saw as he entered a man sleeping away from his wife. His wife was also asleep. He thought to himself: what am I waiting for with this man? He went back to his camel intending to pick up his sword but he thought: "Remain God-fearing; be patient and never act in haste". He went back. When he stood over the man's head the second time, he thought: "I will not wait at all to deal with this man". He went to his camel and was about to draw his sword but he remembered the phrases. He went back to the man and stood there.

'Then the sleeping man woke up and saw the young man. He jumped up with joy, hugged and kissed him and asked him what he did after he left him. The young man said: "I have certainly learnt a great deal of good. What happened to me after I left you was that I walked between my sword and your head three times tonight, but the knowledge that I have acquired stopped me from killing you".'

Obviously the young man felt that his *mawla* who brought him up was not fulfilling his trust in looking after his wife. This is why he considered killing him. However, the phrases he learnt about the need to be patient and never act in haste and to be God-fearing stopped him from carrying out his evil intentions.

It should be noted that the scholar seems to have had an insight into the character of his pupil. Hence, he wanted him to address certain weaknesses. He told him that he would give him some important advice when he intended to depart. He wanted his words to remain present in his pupil's mind. He apparently realised that the pupil was prone to act hastily. Hence, his final advice addressed this very weakness.

Had the pupil acted on impulse when he arrived home, he would have broken all three points of his teacher's instruction. He would have shown no patience to investigate what was happening at home, and he would have acted in haste. He would have killed the man who brought him up and who had taken good care of him. He would have not abided by the requirement of being God-fearing.

The Prophet used a variety of methods in order to instill in his followers the notion that it is not sufficient to admire people with good manners; it is more important to try to amend one's inclinations so that they are in line with good manners. A person who studies the Prophet's Sunnah and tries to understand fully what Islam encourages and recommends will soon develop the motivation to adopt every good manner the Prophet praised.

587. Ashajj ʿAbd al-Qays said: 'The Prophet (peace be upon him) said to me: "You have two qualities that God loves". I asked: "What are they, Messenger of God?" He said: "Forbearance and modesty". I asked: "Have they been with me for a long time or are they new?" He said: "You have had them long". I said: "All praise be to God for having given me two qualities He loves".'[413]

588. Qatādah said: 'One of the people who met the delegation of the ʿAbd al-Qays tribe to meet the Prophet told us; and Qatādah also mentioned Abu Naḍrah reporting from Abu Saʿīd al-Khudri: "The Prophet (peace be upon him) said to the Ashajj of ʿAbd al-Qays: 'You have two qualities which God loves: forbearance and deliberation'."'[414]

589. Ibn ʿAbbās reports that the Prophet said to the Ashajj of ʿAbd al-Qays: 'You have two qualities which God loves: forbearance and deliberation'.[415]

590. Mazīdah al-ʿAbdi reports: 'Al-Ashajj came walking until he took the Prophet's hand and kissed it. The Prophet said to him: "You have two qualities which God and His Messenger

413. Related by al-Nasā'ī, Abu Yaʿla and others.
414. Related by Muslim in a longer version.
415. Related by Muslim, al-Tirmidhi, Ibn Majah, Abu ʿAwanah and Ibn Hibban.

love". He asked: "Are these part of my nature with which I was created or are they acquired qualities?" The Prophet said: "They are part of your nature". Al-Ashajj said: "Praise be to God Who has created me as God and His Messenger love".'[416]

These four *ḥadīths* focus on what the Prophet said to al-Ashajj regarding his own qualities. The visit by the 'Abd al-Qays delegation is reported at length in *ḥadīth* Number 1204, and we will comment on it then. For now, we will concentrate on what these four *ḥadīths* tell us.

One method used by the Prophet was to praise a particular person among his companions for a certain quality he might have. In this way, he generated within that particular person the motivation to preserve and enhance that quality. More importantly, other companions would be keen to follow that person's example in order to adopt the manner praised by the Prophet. Following generations of Muslims will also have a clear instruction that if they want to be good people, they should have the same qualities that merited the Prophet's praise.

Mundhir ibn Al-Ḥārith came to the Prophet at the head of his tribe's delegation, the 'Abd al-Qays, which used to live near the East coast of the Arabian Peninsula. He himself came to be known as the Ashajj of 'Abd Al-Qays. The term *ashajj* means a person who has a mark left by a deep cut on his forehead. When he was a baby, Mundhir ibn al-Ḥārith was hit by a donkey's hoof, leaving a mark in the shape of a crescent on his face. When the Prophet saw him, he called him the Ashajj and thereafter he was known by that name. He was a man of honour among his tribe.

In all its versions, this *ḥadīth* names three qualities which the Prophet describes as being loved by God and His Messenger. The first, which is mentioned in all four versions, is forbearance. This quality comes in for unqualified praise in Islam. It signifies readiness to overlook faults in others which may cause pain or distress. If someone has done some wrong to you and you know the person to be good at heart, you want to encourage his goodness by showing forbearance.

416. Related by al-Bukhari.

Some people are profoundly and positively affected when their faults are overlooked. They have as a result a very strong motivation to avoid any situation that makes them liable to be blamed. When a Muslim overlooks the faults of his brother, particularly when a fault manifests itself in something that has pained him, he stands to earn reward from God. Moreover, he is praised in his community because he shows himself to be a man of honour.

Another quality praised in this *ḥadīth* is modesty. It is true that modesty may sometimes put a person in a difficult position, but in most cases, modesty is a good quality. The Prophet himself was very modest. But this did not prevent him from taking a strong position in any situation where an Islamic principle was involved. His modesty never weakened his determination to stand out for God's cause. His modesty contrasted with the boldness that prompts people to take what belongs to others.

The other quality is that of caution and deliberation before taking action. This ensures that anything a person does is well considered. A person who has such a quality never rushes into action which he may later regret.

Unfairness

591. (*Athar* 148) Ibn 'Abbās said: 'If a mountain is unjust to another mountain, the aggressor will be levelled down'.

This report makes clear that Islam does not countenance any aspect of injustice. No matter how powerful a person is, if he commits injustice, he will be punished for it. This *ḥadīth* gives the comparison of a mountain being unfair to another mountain. God's punishment will be inflicted on the wrongdoer, no matter what status he enjoys.

592. Abu Hurayrah reports that the Prophet said: 'Heaven and Hell fell into argument and Hell said: "The tyrants and the conceited and arrogant will enter me". Heaven said: "The weak and the poor enter me". God, the Blessed and the Exalted, said to Heaven: "You are My Grace which I bestow on whomever I

will". He said to Hell: "You are a place of suffering in which I punish whomever I will. Each of you will have its fill".'[417]

This *ḥadīth* is the same as Number 557, but with a different chain of transmission. We have already explained its meaning.

593. Fuḍālah ibn 'Ubayd reports that the Prophet said: 'Three men are not to be asked about [i.e. they are condemned and doomed]: a man who parts company with the community and rebels against his *imām* and dies a rebel. He is not to be asked about. And a slave girl or a slave who runs away from their master; and a woman whose husband is away, having left her all she needs, but she displays her adornments to strangers and mixes freely. And three others are not to be enquired after: a man who contends with God in respect of His cloak; for His cloak is pride and His robe is might; and a man who entertains doubts about God Himself; and a man who despairs of God's mercy'.

When we look at the first three groups, we realise that in some way or another they have not been faithful to their trust. The one whose crime is the gravest of all is obviously the first one, because he rebels against the *imam* or the ruler, thus creating division within the community. Perhaps we should explain here that this has nothing to do with having a different opinion to that of the ruler, concerning the conduct of any particular community matter. Islam allows differences of opinion and finds nothing wrong in expressing different views on policy or on the implementation of laws or the conduct of state affairs. However, when the stage of discussion is over and the ruler has opted for a particular course of action, the Muslim community should obey his rule. In this way, the community continues to be coherent, united in purpose and close in rank. When this stage is reached, disobedience creates division. This is inadmissible from an Islamic point of view. It constitutes rebellion. If the rebel maintains his position until he dies, then we should not enquire about his destiny, because his is the worst

417. Related in a longer version by al-Bukhari. Also related by Aḥmad, Muslim, al-Tirmidhi, Ibn Khuzaymah, Abu 'Awānah and Ibn Ḥibbān.

fate. This applies particularly to rebels who carry arms against the Muslim state. If they do so without valid justification, then they are deemed at war against the Muslim state and this is a crime for which specific punishments have been prescribed by God.

It is useful to mention a brief word about the second type, although it no longer exists. Slaves who run away are actually in breach of their trust, because Islam regulates the relationship between slave and master and orders masters to be kind to their slaves. If such a slave runs away, he is returned to his master, unless his running away was caused by fear or being overworked. In other words, there should be no valid justification for running away for a slave to merit such a severe punishment.

The third type is a woman who is in breach of her trust with her husband. She takes the chance of his being away in order to exhibit her adornments and she mixes with men in a way which she cannot do when her husband is around. Although he has provided well for her for the period of his absence, she nevertheless violates his trust.

The three types in the second group adopt a wrong attitude towards God. The first type is that of a man who is too proud and conceited. He treats others with arrogance. In this way, he places himself above the rest of mankind, making himself a semi-god. He is to be thrown into hell and no one will enquire after him. The second type is that of a person who is not a true believer. He has doubts about the very nature of God and His authority over the whole universe. As such he is a confirmed unbeliever.

The last type of person is the one who despairs of God's mercy. Everyone should realise that God's mercy is certain to come. It encompasses all and stops at nothing. God forgives all sins and treats all his creatures with kindness. If we turn to Him praying for His mercy, it is sure to come. Entertaining despair is equivalent to doubting God's existence. Hence, such doubters are not to be enquired after in the world to come. They are lost and doomed. To enquire after them is of no avail.

594. Abu Bakrah reports that the Prophet said: 'God will defer the punishment of whatever He wills of people's sins until the Day of Resurrection, except for rebellion, undutifulness to parents

and unkindness to relatives. He will hasten [some] punishment for these in this world before [the offender's] death'.[418]

This *ḥadīth* is similar to Numbers 29 and 67. These offences are against people to whom one is required by God to be kind and dutiful. In order to make an example of them, God hastens some punishment for the offenders so that others will be deterred from committing the same. This does not, however, reduce the punishment for these offences in the life to come.

595. (*Athar* 149) Abu Hurayrah said: 'A person will see a particle of dirt in his brother's eye while he is oblivious to a stick in his own eye'.

This points out a characteristic that affects a large proportion of people. They criticise others for certain faults when they have the same faults in a much greater measure, or they may have other and more serious faults to which they remain oblivious.

596. Mu'āwiyah ibn Qurrah said: 'I was once [walking] with Ma'qil al-Muzani when he removed a harmful object that was in people's way. Later on, I saw a harmful object and I hurried to remove it. He said to me: "What made you do this, my nephew?" I said: "I saw you doing something and I wanted to do likewise". He said: "You have done well, my nephew. I heard the Prophet (peace be upon him) say: 'He who removes a harmful object from the passageway of Muslims will be credited with a good deed. Whoever has a good deed accepted from him will be admitted into heaven'."'

This *ḥadīth* shows someone who is quick to learn a commendable practice. When he saw a companion of the Prophet removing a harmful object from people's way, he immediately followed his suit. We also note that the Prophet's companion was keen to impart the knowledge he had heard from the Prophet and to put it in a most acceptable way

418. Related by Ibn Mājah.

that would ensure that the beneficiary would keep it in mind. He first asks his companion the reason for his action. When he learnt that he simply wanted to follow his example, as he was a companion of the Prophet, the latter explained the basis of his action. Thus, he added the religious element to something that is socially very useful.

The Prophet encouraged every aspect that strengthens the social cohesion of the Muslim community. One of these is to exchange gifts:

597. Abu Hurayrah reports that the Prophet said: 'Give gifts to one another so that you will love one another'.[419]

598. (*Athar* 150) Anas used to say to his children: 'My children, exchange gifts, for it will increase your mutual love'.

The Prophet encouraged the Muslim community to give and accept gifts, because such an exchange definitely strengthens bonds between people and makes them love one another. A gift is a mark of thoughtfulness and when one receives a gift, one knows that the person who has given it has been thinking about one in a positive way. Such a feeling will be reciprocated unless there is a strong reason to prevent it. When Sahb ibn Juthāmah gave the Prophet a gift in the form of a portion of an animal he had hunted, the Prophet could not take it. He was in a state of consecration, i.e. *iḥrām*, when hunting is forbidden. A person in this state may not even point out the place of an animal for another person to hunt it. The Prophet explained to Sahb why he could not accept his gift.

People may give presents to a generous person hoping to receive a more precious gift in return. If the return gift does not match the expectations of the first person, he may be upset. If he entertains such feelings, then he wastes much of the reward he would have received from God for his first gift if it was made freely, to strengthen the ties of brotherhood. In any case, no blame attaches to the other person for a return gift that may be more valuable than the one he received.

The Prophet was the most generous of all people. Indeed, his generosity knew no limits. During the month of Ramadan, in

419. Related by al-Nasā'ī and al-Bayhaqi in Shu'ab al-Īmān.

particular, he excelled himself in generosity. His hand is described as 'more generous with what is good than unrestrained wind'. He might buy something from a person and give him the price and then give him the goods he bought from him as a gift. He did this with Jābir ibn 'Abdullāh, from whom he bought a camel, as they were on their way back to Madinah. The sale was agreed on condition that Jābir would give him the camel when they arrived back in Madinah. Jābir did so and brought the camel to the Prophet leaving it outside the mosque. When the Prophet came out and saw the camel, he gave it back to Jābir after giving him the agreed price. Whenever the Prophet was given a gift, he made sure of giving something better in return. People realised this and although many of his companions were keen to bring him gifts, just to please him, some people kept an eye on the expected return gift.

599. Abu Hurayrah reports that 'a man from the Fazārah tribe gave a she-camel to the Prophet as a present. The Prophet gave him a gift in return, but the man was not very pleased. I heard the Prophet as he spoke on the platform [i.e. the *minbar*] and said: "One of you may give me a present and I give him something in return, within what I may have. He is nevertheless unhappy. By God, I shall not accept after this year a gift from Arabs, except from the people of the Quraysh, the Anṣār, Thaqīf or Daws".'[420]

It is authentically reported that the Prophet gave the bedouin six she-camels of a young age in return, yet the man was displeased. Here, we have a good example of someone who intends his gift as a means for easy gain. When he is handsomely compensated, he is unhappy because he expected more. His attitude is that of one who wants to dictate what he gets in return. This is a wrong attitude, especially if one is dealing with someone known for his generosity. It should be sufficient for reward that the Prophet was pleased with one's gift. This in itself would bring a rich reward from God.

---

420. Related by Aḥmad, Abū Dāwūd, al-Nasā'ī, al-Tirmidhi, Ibn Ḥibbān and al-Bayhaqi.

When the Prophet said these words on the platform in the mosque, he was actually praising the people of those four or five tribes he named, the Quraysh, the Anṣār who belonged to the two tribes of the Aws and the Khazraj, Thaqīf and Daws. When any person of those tribes gave a gift, he expected nothing in return. They were very generous and content with what they had. If they received nothing or a small gift in return, they would realise that the Prophet did not have a better one to give. They simply prayed to God to bless them and what they had, realising that such a blessing would be much more valuable than any material gain they might have had.

The Prophet must have been upset to say what he said, because he did not like to refuse a gift. But he decided not to accept any from the Bedouin Arabs in general with the exception of those five major tribes. He did not wish to upset anyone. But if the gift was given to him merely for the purpose of receiving a much bigger one, then it was simply a burden which might at times be inconvenient.

We should learn from this *ḥadīth* that we are recommended to exchange gifts, but we should not expect back something over and above what we have given. Let us look forward to the reward we stand to gain from God for making a gift with the pure intention of pleasing our brethren in faith.

34

Modesty: An Invaluable Virtue

ISLAM IS THE final and complete version of God's message to mankind. Therefore, it endorses earlier messages in their original form. It obviously rejects the distortion that might have crept into them, but when something is certain to have been part of the original message, Islam accepts and endorses it. Hence, we accept without question anything that God or His messenger confirms to have been included in earlier scriptures or revelations. We also accept those portions of the Old and New Testaments that are in full agreement with the Qur'an as such agreement is clear proof that it stands in its original, revealed form. Moreover, if the Prophet tells us that something in particular was revealed to earlier prophets, we accept it as part of our own religion. The following *ḥadīth* is phrased in an unusual fashion. However, its phraseology serves to give emphasis to its message.

600. Abu Mas'ūd 'Uqbah ibn 'Amr al-Anṣāri reports that the Prophet said: 'Among the words people have learned from early prophets are: "if you feel no shame, then do as you wish".'[421]

This *ḥadīth* admits more than one interpretation. The first is that if you feel you will not be ashamed of doing what you intend to do because you can justify it as correct and further that there is nothing in it to be ashamed of, then you may go ahead and do it without hesitation. It may be that what you are about to do is something right, although some people may prefer that you do not do it. Since you are sure that it is just and fair, then you have nothing to answer for as a result of doing it. You are perfectly entitled to do it. If we prefer this interpretation of the *ḥadīth*, then it is important to examine what we intend to do before embarking on it. If we find it to be perfectly acceptable and we are clear in our conscience that it is right for us to do it, then that is all we need to ascertain in order to proceed with it.

Secondly, the *ḥadīth* may be taken to mean that if a person is incapable of any feeling of shame, and could not care less whether he brought shame on himself, his family or his people, then there is nothing to stop him from doing what is censurable. If we take this interpretation of the *ḥadīth*, then we observe that although it is phrased in the imperative, it is meant as a reproach. It could also be said that the *ḥadīth* means that not to have any sense of shame is much worse than what one may actually do.

It is important to know what may be included in having a proper sense of shame. Some people suggest that a shy person is incapable of confronting others with the truth he knows. As a result, he does not fulfil his duty to enjoin what is right and to speak out against what is wrong. His shyness may even lead him to the non-fulfilment of certain rights or duties. Such an attitude is not what is meant in having a sense of shame in this *ḥadīth*. This is simply a manifestation of weakness. A proper sense of shame is that which causes a person to feel afraid of being blamed for something unbecoming. It may also lead a person to forgo what rightfully belongs to him because he

421. Related by Aḥmad, al-Bukhari, 'Abdullāh, Ibn Mājah and Ibn Ḥibbān.

is too shy to demand it. Hence the virtue Islam values highly is to feel ashamed as a result of a wrong that one may do, to be afraid of blame for committing something unbecoming, and to be too modest to demand something for oneself if people think that such a demand is made for personal gain. It is such modesty that the Prophet describes as being part of faith.

601. Abu Hurayrah reports that the Prophet said: 'Faith consists of more than sixty (or seventy) branches. The highest of these is *la ilāha illa Allah* [i.e. there is no deity other than God] and the lowest is to remove a harmful object from people's way. Modesty is a branch of faith'.[422]

The *ḥadīth* mentions that faith has more than seventy branches, even though it expresses doubt as to whether they are more than seventy or sixty. We should point out, however, that the Prophet did not say that faith is 'more than sixty or seventy branches', but rather mentioned one of the two figures. The doubt is on the part of the last narrator of this *ḥadīth* whose name was Suhayl. Although scholars have discussed these two figures, most agree that the accurate figure is 'more than seventy'.

Scholars have tried to identify all those branches or elements of faith. Only three are mentioned in the *ḥadīth*. However, the efforts made by a renowned scholar of *Ḥadīth*, Abu Ḥātim ibn Ḥibbān, are worthy of note. He says: 'I have tried to pinpoint the exact meaning of this *ḥadīth* for a period of time and I counted the actions that represent obedience to God only to find that they exceed this figure by far. Therefore, I referred to *ḥadīths* and counted every action of obedience mentioned by God's messenger as constituting part of faith, but the total figure was short of seventy. I then referred to God's Book and read it carefully, counting every action of obedience that God has described as part of faith and I again found that they fall short of seventy. Thereafter I counted what I found in the Qur'an and what I found in the Sunnah, without duplication when one is mentioned in

422. Related by al-Bukhari, Muslim, al-Nasā'ī, Abū Dāwūd, al-Tirmidhi and Ibn Mājah.

both. I found out the total number of what God and His Messenger mention as constituting part of faith to be seventy-nine. I realised that the Prophet (peace be upon him) has given us the number we can find in the Qur'an and the Sunnah together'. Ibn Ḥibbān mentions those seventy-nine branches in detail in his book to which he gives the title, Waṣf al-Īmān wa Shuʿabuh, [i.e. Description of faith and its branches]. Unfortunately, this work by Ibn Hibban is lost, but we have a massive work on this subject by Imam al-Bayhaqi, entitled Shuʿab al-Īmān which is in print.

The main element of faith mentioned in this *ḥadīth* is a declaration that there is no deity except God. This is only to be expected since belief in God's oneness is the cornerstone of faith. No good action is of any value unless it relies on this solid basis of faith. Everyone who wishes to be a believer must entertain no doubt whatsoever as to God's oneness and that there is no one and nothing like Him or having any resemblance of Him. Unless a person believes in God's oneness, he or she is an unbeliever, even though they may practise many of the elements of faith. Such practice is of little value since it does not rely on the only foundation of faith.

Last in the elements of faith is the removal of harmful objects from people's path. This is a very simple quality that many people do naturally because they are good at heart. If this is part of faith, then we can imagine what its other elements are like.

The *ḥadīth* makes clear that faith consists of mental and practical aspects. The mental ones include belief, intention, sincerity, honesty, etc. and the practical ones include the fulfilment of duties and attending to what the Prophet has recommended.

We note that the Prophet has singled out the quality of modesty, mentioning it as a branch of faith. By doing so, the Prophet has drawn attention to its importance. Although modesty may be an inherent quality, it can be refined and enhanced by one's own action. Being modest and having a sense of shame deter a person from doing what he or she may be blamed for. As such, modesty works in-line with faith, restraining believers from slipping into error.

The Prophet himself was a very modest person. His shyness was apparent to any observer who might be looking at him:

602. Abu Sa'īd al-Khudri reports: 'The Prophet (peace be upon him) was more modest than a virgin girl in her private room. When he disliked something, we recognised it in his face'.[423]

This means that the Prophet's modesty prevented him from making his feelings known to the person whose action he disliked. He simply showed his feeling involuntarily, reflected as it was on his face. It is quite natural, then, for a good Muslim to be modest.

603. 'Uthman and 'Ā'ishah related: 'Abu Bakr requested permission to come in when the Prophet was at home, lying on 'Ā'ishah's bed, wearing her cloak. The Prophet gave Abu Bakr permission without changing his position and Abu Bakr told him what he came for' Abu Bakr then left. Then 'Umar requested permission to come in and the Prophet gave him permission, again without changing his position. 'Umar told him what he came for then left.

'Uthmān said: 'Then I requested permission to come in, and he sat up. He said to 'Ā'ishah: "Arrange your clothes properly". I told him what I came for then I left'.

'Ā'ishah said: "Messenger of God, I did not see you showing Abu Bakr and 'Umar the same consideration you showed to 'Uthmān". God's Messenger said: "'Uthmān is a very shy person and I feared that if I gave him permission to come in while I was in that state, he would not express well what he came for".'[424]

The *ḥadīth* shows the Prophet's consideration for his companions. He realised that 'Uthmān was a very shy person. To come into a friend's house when that friend is on his wife's bed and wearing her cloak might make him feel embarrassed and his shyness would become an impediment preventing him from putting to the Prophet whatever he came to see him about. Therefore, the Prophet sat up and told his wife to appear in a more appropriate way. This must have taken place before Muslim women were commanded to wear the hijab when they

423. Related by al-Bukhari, Muslim and Ibn Mājah.

424. Related by Muslim.

are in mixed company. It was certainly before the Prophet's wives were ordered not to be seen by strangers.

The *ḥadīth* makes clear that consideration should be made to people's feelings when we meet them, even in our own homes, as the Prophet showed such consideration for 'Uthmān whom he knew to be very shy. It also tells us that the Prophet's companions sought his advice about all matters at all times, They would come to him at home even though they were certain to see him at the time of every prayer.

604. Anas ibn Mālik reports that the Prophet said: 'When modesty is present in any matter, it adorns it; and when vulgarity is in any matter, it detracts from it'.[425]

To be modest or to have a sense of shame is to fear people's reproach or rebuke should one's unbecoming action come to light. Thus, modesty acts as a deterrent from unbecoming behaviour, while vulgarity leads to carelessness about other people's reaction. Therefore, it gives a foul image.

605. 'Abdullāh ibn 'Umar reports: 'God's Messenger passed by a man who was admonishing his brother about his modesty. The Prophet said to him: "Leave him alone; modesty is part of faith".'

[In another version], Ibn 'Umar reports: 'God's Messenger passed by a man who was reproaching his brother for being too modest, even to the point of saying , "It has brought you much trouble". The Prophet said to him: "Leave him alone; modesty is part of faith".'[426]

Apparently the man who was being blamed was too modest to claim what rightfully belonged to him. It might have been very difficult for him to change his attitude. Many a person lends money to another for a specific period of time. When the term of the loan is over, the borrower may take his time before settling his debt. The lender may be in need of the money, but his modesty prevents him from demanding

425. Related by Aḥmad, al-Tirmidhi and Ibn Mājah.

426. Related by Mālik, al-Bukhari, Muslim, al-Nasā'ī, Abū Dāwūd, al-Tirmidhi and Ibn Mājah.

repayment. His difficulty in requesting repayment is greater than that of the borrower in asking for the loan in the first place.

We notice that the Prophet counselled the man to leave his brother alone making it clear to him that such modesty and having a sense of shame is indicative of strong faith. The Prophet's statement makes it clear that although modesty may prevent a person from demanding his rights, it remains a virtue for which no one should be blamed. It is true that a modest person may not get his rights, but by foregoing them, he is sure to receive a much greater reward from God. It should be added here that the Prophet himself was a very modest person. As expressed in an earlier *ḥadīth*, he is described as being more modest than a virgin in her private room.

606. 'Ā'ishah related: 'the Prophet was lying down in my home, with his thigh or his shins uncovered when Abu Bakr requested permission to come in. The Prophet gave Abu Bakr permission without changing his position and he came in and talked to him. Then 'Umar requested permission to come in and the Prophet gave him permission again without changing his position and he came in and talked. Then 'Uthmān requested permission to come in. The Prophet sat up and arranged his clothes. (Muhammad, the last narrator said: I do not say that it was all on the same day.) 'Uthmān came in and talked to him. When he left, I said: "Messenger of God, Abu Bakr came in but you did not show much concern, then 'Umar came in and you did not show much concern. When 'Uthmān came, you sat up and arranged your clothes". He said: "Should I not be shy before a man when the angels are shy before him?"'[427]

This *ḥadīth* is very similar to Number 603, and perhaps they both talk about the same occasion. In this version 'Ā'ishah mentions that the Prophet's thigh or shins were uncovered when both Abu Bakr and 'Umar entered, but the Prophet did not take any action. Yet he did when 'Uthmān came in, saying that even the angels themselves are shy before 'Uthmān, who is described in the earlier *ḥadīth* as very retiring.

---

427. Related by al-Bukhari and Muslim.

35

On Supplication

607. Abu Hurayrah said: 'In the morning, the Prophet said [in his supplication]: "We have reached the morning and dominion belongs to God. All praise be to God who has no partner. There is no deity other than God and to Him all shall be resurrected". [*Aṣbaḥna wa aṣbaḥ al-mulk lillāh; wal-ḥamd kulluhu lillāh la sharīka lah. La ilāh illa Allah wa ilayh al-nushūr.*] In the evening, he said: "We have reached the evening and dominion belongs to God. All praise be to God who has no partner. There is no deity other than God and to Him all shall be resurrected". [*Amsayna wa amsa al-mulk lillāh; wal-ḥamd kulluhu lillāh la sharīka lah. La ilāh illa Allah wa ilayh al-nushūr.*]'

The Prophet praised and glorified God all the time and at every juncture. His companions reported many of his supplications, and he taught them much of what he said in private so that people might learn and do as he did. This *ḥadīth* tells us one of his supplications which the Prophet said early in the morning and in the evening. It praises God, acknowledges His dominion of the universe and that He has no partners. It also declares belief in resurrection. As such, it is a short supplication that reiterates the major principles of the Islamic faith: God's oneness, dominion and life after death.

608. Abu Hurayrah reports that the Prophet said: 'The nobleman, son of the nobleman, son of the nobleman, son of the nobleman: Joseph son of Jacob, son of Isaac, son of Abraham, the friend of God, the Lord of Grace, the Blessed and Exalted'.

God's Messenger said: 'Had I remained in prison as long as Joseph and the call had come to me, I would have accepted it. [Joseph], however, said [to the messenger bringing the invitation]: "*Go back to your lord and ask him about the women who cut their hands*". (12: 50) May God bestow mercy on Lot. He certainly had strong support when he said to his people: "*Would that I had the strength to defeat you, or that I could lean on mighty support*". (11: 80) God sent every prophet after him with good support from among his people'.[428]

The Prophet refers first to the most noble lineage of four prophets in the same line, ending with Joseph. He then refers to Joseph's attitude as given in the story detailed in *Surah* 12 of the Qur'an. Joseph was imprisoned as a result of a false accusation made against him by his master's wife. She had tried to seduce him but he resisted her advances. When the matter became publicly known and she feared a scandal, it was deemed that the best course was to throw Joseph in prison. He came to know two prisoners who related their dreams to him. Joseph was given the ability to interpret dreams and his interpretation was always right. One of those prisoners was released. Several years later, he was in the king's service when the king recalled a significant dream. It was referred to Joseph and he gave the right interpretation. At that point, with the king fully convinced, he ordered that Joseph should attend him. Joseph, however, refused to leave the prison and told the king's messenger to go back and ask the king about the women who

428. Related by Aḥmad, al-Tirmidhi and Ibn Mājah.

had cut their hands with their own knives when they saw him; they could not take their eyes off him. These women had heard the master's wife admit to them that she was the one who had tried to seduce him and she had threatened to have him imprisoned if he did not yield. Therefore, Joseph was keen to establish his innocence before he was prepared to leave prison.

The Prophet's statement is one of praise for Joseph, but it also implies a degree of humility on the part of Prophet Muhammad. Had he been in the same position as Joseph, most probably he would have done the same, but he says that he would not have bothered to establish his innocence. This should be understood as a gesture of humility, describing oneself as being unable to reach others' high standards.

In the same *ḥadīth* the Prophet refers to the difficult time Prophet Lot faced when he had to confront his people who were trying to assault his guests. He tried hard to pacify them and to offer them what he could in order to save his guests, not knowing that they were angels. He offered them his daughters in marriage, if they would leave his guests alone. They would not, however, listen to his entreaties. At that moment, he cried out: 'Would that I have the strength to defeat you, or that I could lean on mighty support'. Lot did not have any great influence among the people to whom he was sent. He came from Iraq to live with the people of Sodom in Palestine. He was aware of his vulnerability as an outsider. Hence, he wished he had the support of others against the rest of his people who wanted to assault his guests.

The Prophet refers to the mighty support Lot enjoyed. This is a reference to God Himself, who supports His servants when they face trouble from unbelievers. We have no doubt in our minds that Lot realised that he could rely on God's support. At that particular moment, however, he felt that his people's aggression should be repelled by another group who could defend him and his guests. Hence, his exclamation and the wish he expressed for some support. He should have added something to indicate his reliance on God. This would easily have been done by qualifying his statement with a sentence referring to his total reliance on God. The Prophet prayed for Lot's forgiveness of his mistake, done unwittingly.

The Prophet adds that subsequently God gave strong support to every prophet among his people. This indicates that God has chosen to give the prophets support because of the genuine feelings which led to Lot's exclamation. At a moment of great distress, anyone would wish to have visible support from those who are prepared to defend one. Prophet Muhammad enjoyed the protection of his uncle Abu Ṭālib for ten years at the beginning of his mission. Abu Ṭālib never failed to give support to his nephew, Prophet Muhammad, whenever he needed it.

It is worth noting how Prophet Muhammad refers in a very polite and humble manner to the omission on the part of an earlier prophet. He simply prays to God to forgive him and points out that support was there for him, making an implicit suggestion that Lot should have indicated his acknowledgement of that support and relied on it.

Which prayer is answered?

As supplication constitutes a significant portion of what we do to accomplish a specific purpose, it is appropriate to ask which prayer or supplication God answers. What is required by the person who prays to God so that his prayers may be accepted? Are there any particular points which should be remembered when we perform our supplication so that it will not be rejected outright?

Al-Rabīʿ ibn Khuthaym was a scholar who belonged to the generation that succeeded the Prophet's companions, i.e. the *tabiʿīn*. He used to attend the circle of another highly renowned scholar of the same generation, ʿAlqamah. Al-Rabīʿwas famous for his devotion and wisdom.

609. (*Athar* 151) ʿAbd al-Raḥmān ibn Yazīd said: ʿAl-Rabīʿ [ibn Khuthaym] used to go to ʿAlqamah every Friday. If I was not there, they would send for me. Once he went there when I was not. ʿAlqamah met me [sometime later] and said: "Have you heard what al-Rabīʿ said? He said: Do you wonder how often people pray and how little of their prayers are answered. This is due to the fact that God, the Mighty and Exalted, does not answer except the purest of supplication". I [ʿAbd al-Raḥmān] replied that ʿAbdullāh [ibn Masʿūd] himself said something to

that effect. He ['Alqamah] said: "What did he [Ibn Mas'ūd] say?" I ['Abd al-Raḥmān] told him that he said: "God does not listen to someone who prays to Him so that people should hear him, nor someone who shows off, nor one who plays [i.e. is not serious]. He only responds to the one whose supplication is earnest, coming from his heart". ['Abd al-Raḥmān] was asked whether 'Alqamah remembered it. He said: "Yes".

We note that all these three scholars checked with one another what they had heard and whether it related to religious principles or practices. They had a scholarly approach to information. When this is backed by someone who is in a position of authority, they accepted it without hesitation. We see here 'Alqamah asking 'Abd al-Raḥmān about something he had heard from al-Rabī'. When the answer confirmed that 'Abdullāh ibn Mas'ūd, the Prophet's companion, said something to the same effect, 'Alqamah accepted it willingly.

The observation which al-Rabī' makes is that people pray to God so much, but very little of their prayers are answered. This applies to all generations. Indeed, we wonder how this could have been true in those very early days of Islam, when people were supposed to be totally devoted in their worship. The fact is that many people tend to make their supplication in a very casual manner. If we remember that we will be happier to have this or that purpose fulfilled, then we make a casual prayer to God to fulfil it for us. Such a casual approach to supplication renders it unacceptable. This is the reason al-Rabī' gives for this state of affairs. He states that God does not answer except the most sincere of all supplications.

It may be asked why 'Alqamah wondered at al-Rabī''s statement. 'Alqamah might have felt that the statement was in conflict with the Qur'anic verse: '*Your Lord says: pray to Me and I will answer you*'. (40: 60) The Qur'anic statement is general and does not specify any conditions for answering people's prayers. How then can a scholar assert that God accepts only the most sincere of prayers?

There is certainly no conflict between the two statements. The Qur'anic verse should be understood to mean that when we pray to God, as He likes us to pray to Him, fulfilling all conditions of such prayer or supplication, then He will certainly answer our prayers whatever we ask of Him. The first prerequisite of answerable supplication is that it should be sincere. It should come from the heart and be combined with a feeling that without God's help we cannot accomplish any purpose.

It occurs to some people that they should not be asking God to grant them anything relating to this world. They say that God has bestowed on us His grace in abundance. He has given us everything we have. He has made life possible for us and He has made available to us everything necessary to support life. He has given us provisions and endowed us with faculties that will ensure our progress. It is up to us to make use of what He has given us in order to improve the situation in which we find ourselves. They point out that if someone has been granted a great deal, it will only show him in a bad light if he asks for more. A child whose parents ensure that nothing he needs is lacking will appear to be a spoiled child if he continues to ask for more. Therefore, such people add the phrase, "if You wish", when they make their supplication.

610. Abu Hurayrah reports that the Prophet said: 'When anyone of you makes a supplication, he should not say, "if You wish". Let him be firm and decisive in the asking. He should show his keenness to have what he is asking for. Nothing is too great for God to grant'.[429]

611. Anas reports that the Prophet said: 'When any of you makes a supplication, he should be forthright in his supplication. Let him not say, "my Lord, grant me this if You will". God cannot be forced to do something against His will'.[430]

These two *ḥadīths* include a very clear instruction by the Prophet that we must not make what we request from God as conditional. Such a statement indicates that we are not really eager to have our prayer answered and it gives the impression that we do not really feel that

429. Related by al-Bukhari, Muslim, Abū Dāwūd, al-Tirmidhi, Ibn Mājah, Ibn Ḥibbān and Abu ʿAwānah.

430. Related by Aḥmad, al-Bukhari, Muslim and al-Nasāʾī.

we are in need of His grace and bounty. Instead, we should show our keenness to have our prayer answered by praying earnestly for it. We should not hesitate to ask God for whatever we are keen to have. There is nothing too great for God to give and there is nothing that He cannot accomplish. Indeed, God likes that people should pray to Him to help them achieve their purposes. When they do, they acknowledge their need of His help and that without such help, they see little prospect of achieving their purposes. He certainly grants earnest supplication.

What these *ḥadīths* mean is that we need not be ashamed in requesting of God that He grant us anything we hope for, even though it may seem that we are asking for too much for ourselves. There is nothing wrong with asking for what seems to us to be a great honour or great wealth. God can accomplish this for us without any decrease in what He has. In a sacred, or *qudsi ḥadīth*, the Prophet quotes God as saying: 'My servants, were the first of you and the last of you, the human of you and the jinn of you to rise up in one place and make requests of Me and were I to give everyone what he requested, that would not decrease what I have, anymore than a needle decreases the sea if dipped once into it'.[431]

One little point still needs some clarification. Some people may say that they have prayed most sincerely and with all the earnestness they can muster, but still their prayers have not been answered. We are told by the Prophet that God answers all prayers, when they are made with sincerity. Sometimes He gives us what He knows to be better for us. However, He may fulfil what we ask Him in this life or He may defer such fulfilment to the life to come, when He will reward us for praying to Him. The Prophet makes it clear that when we see what God has in store for us in compensation for deferring the fulfilment of our prayers, we will wish that He had not fulfilled any prayers we made to Him in this life, but had rather deferred all to the Day of Judgement. Hence, we should not worry if the answer to our prayers should not be forthcoming. If we are patient we will see all our prayers answered.

---

431. Related by Muslim, al-Tirmidhi and Ibn Mājah.

612. (*Athar* 152) Abu Nu'aym Wahb said: 'I saw Ibn 'Umar and Ibn al-Zubayr supplicating then wiping their faces with their palms'.

This is a normal practice when supplicating. The Prophet instructed his companions to lift their hands with their palms facing up, hoping that their prayers would be answered. God does not like to let His servant go empty-handed. Wiping one's face with one's palms at the end is a gesture expressing happiness that one's prayers are fully answered, God willing.

613. 'Ā'ishah said: 'I saw the Prophet having raised his hands and supplicating. He said: "I am only human. If I ever harm or curse any believer, please do not punish me for this".'[432]

The Prophet always stressed his own humanity, pointing out that sometimes his feelings and reactions may be too quick. Hence, he prays to God to forgive him for any failing. In this *ḥadīth* he prays for forgiveness if he harms or curses any believer. We all do this at times, when we are particularly angered by someone else's action. We need to make amends for this, either by apologising in a way that is acceptable to the other party, or seeking God's forgiveness for what we have done or said.

We know that God has forgiven the Prophet any mistake or error he might have committed. We also know that the Prophet had the keenest sense of fairness. Once he was marshalling his troops for a battle, having a stick in his hand. He poked someone in his abdomen to get him in line. The man said to him: 'You have caused me pain, Messenger of God'. He handed him the stick and lifted his robe and said: 'Come on, avenge yourself'. The man went down on his knees and kissed the Prophet's abdomen'. When the Prophet asked him why he did so, he said that he wished the last thing which he touched before he died in battle would be the Prophet's body.[433]

Sometimes people pray against others who might have offended them. This is unacceptable. However, the Prophet himself did at times

---

432. Related by Aḥmad, al-Bukhari, Muslim and al-Nasā'ī.
433. Ibn Hisham, Al-Sīrah al-Nabawiyyah, vol. 2, p. 266.

pray against some people. How can we, then, reconcile his action with the unacceptability of prayer to cause harm? The answer is that the Prophet had no personal grudge against people. Those he prayed against were confirmed enemies of Islam who treated Muslims very badly, persecuting those under their control. He also prayed against a few individuals who spared no effort in scheming against Islam. Such supplications against Islam's opponents is perfectly legitimate. Moreover, the Prophet never made a supplication against a community of unbelievers. When he went to Taif seeking support for his cause, he was given a very hostile reception. The chiefs of the Thaqīf tribe that lived there induced their boys, servants and slaves to chase him out, stoning him as he walked, until both his feet bled. As he sat down to rest after walking some distance out of the city, God sent him the angel in control of mountains who told him that he would do whatever he commanded him. If he wished, the angel would crush their city between two mountains. The Prophet refused any such suggestion, saying: 'I hope that God will bring out of their offspring people who worship Him alone'.

The same applied in the case of the Daws tribe when they rejected his message. The story of the efforts to bring the Daws around so as to accept Islam is very interesting. A man from the Daws called al-Ṭufayl ibn 'Amr once came to Makkah to visit the Ka'bah. This was at a time when the Prophet had only recently begun preaching the message of Islam in public. Al-Ṭufayl met the Prophet and listened to the Qur'an and the principles of Islam. He became a Muslim and went back to his tribe, advocating Islam there, but most of his people took a negative attitude.

614. Abu Hurayrah reports: 'Al-Ṭufayl ibn 'Amr al-Dawsi came to God's Messenger and said: "Messenger of God, the [tribe of] Daws have disobeyed and rejected, so pray to God against them". God's Messenger faced the qiblah and lifted his hands. People thought he was about to pray against them, but he said: "My Lord, guide the Daws and bring them [into Islam]".'[434]

---

434. Related by al-Bukhari and Muslim.

The Prophet's prayers were always answered in the best and fullest way. Therefore, if he prayed against some people, they were certain to suffer. Hence, he never prayed against any community. He only prayed against certain individuals who were sworn enemies of Islam.

Al-Ṭufayl continued his efforts with his tribe and was able to make better headway after the Prophet's supplication. At the time of the Battle of Khaibar against the Jews, al-Ṭufayl brought eighty of his tribe to join the Muslim army. When Makkah fell to the Prophet two years later, al-Ṭufayl suggested to him that he, i.e. al-Ṭufayl, be sent to the idol named Dhul-Kaffayn which was installed by ʿAmr ibn Ḥumamah, to burn it. The Prophet sanctioned this and al-Ṭufayl burnt this symbolic idol of paganism in Arabia.

615. Anas reports: 'One year, rain was so scarce. Some Muslims went to the Prophet (peace be upon him) on a Friday and said to him: "Messenger of God, rain has not been forthcoming; the land is hard and dry; and cattle are dying". The Prophet raised his hands to pray. No cloud could be seen anywhere in the sky. He stretched his arms in front of him, raising them high, and I could see the whiteness of his armpits. He made a supplication praying for rain. When we had finished Friday Prayers [the rain was pouring so heavily that] even a young man living close by felt that going back home would be troublesome. It continued to rain for a week. On the following Friday, people said: "Messenger of God, homes have collapsed and travellers have been stranded". The Prophet smiled at how quickly human beings change moods. He made a new supplication pointing with his hand saying: "My Lord, let it fall around us, not over us". It was soon falling over the area surrounding Madīnah'.

When the Prophet said a prayer in front of some of his companions, everyone could clearly see these immediate results. This *ḥadīth* shows how God honoured the Prophet, answering his supplication instantly and with all around to see. The Prophet's supplication could not have been made much earlier than Friday Prayer. The Prophet did not take long in his sermon on Friday, as some imams do these days. Generally speaking, his sermons took around 10–15 minutes. With prayers to follow, it is reasonable to assume that the period of time between the Prophet's supplication, which was made with no cloud visible in the sky, and the end of prayer when people wanted to leave could not have been more than one hour. It must have been torrential rain. Roads were fast impassable, to the extent that people living nearby worried about their return home. When on the following Friday the Prophet made a new supplication, requesting that God take the rain away from the centre of Madinah, again the supplication was answered without delay. This sort of honour God reserved for the Prophet because it strengthened people's faith in his message.

Moreover, the Prophet was a perfect example of humility. He never entertained any desire to press a personal advantage or to give himself a position which enabled him to do whatever he liked with people. It is true that God says in the Qur'an that the Prophet has a higher claim over the souls of the believers than their own claims, but the Prophet never took personal advantage of his position. Indeed, he was always ready to acknowledge his humanity which meant that he could make a mistake in worldly matters. He also prayed to God to protect him against being unjust to others. He further prayed to be forgiven anything wrong he might have done to other people.

616. This is the same *ḥadīth* as Number 613, but with a different chain of transmission.

The Prophet never hesitated to say a prayer for any individual who requested him to do so or whom he felt needed such a prayer:

617. Jābir ibn 'Abdullāh reports: 'Al-Ṭufayl ibn 'Amr said to the Prophet (peace be upon him): "Would you like [to move to] a fortress and a secure place?" The Prophet declined because of what God had in store for the Anṣār. Al-Ṭufayl migrated together with another man from his tribe. The man soon fell ill and he was so worried because of his illness. He crawled to his luggage and picked up an arrow with a wide head and cut his own jugular veins and died. Al-Ṭufayl saw him in his dream and asked what happened to him. The man said: "God has forgiven me because of my trip to join the Prophet (peace be on him.)

Al-Ṭufayl asked him about his hands? He answered that he was told: "We will not put right your hands with which you did very badly". Al-Ṭufayl reported this to the Prophet who, on hearing it, lifted his hands and prayed: "My Lord, forgive his hands as well".'[435]

This *ḥadīth* confirms the Qur'anic statements: '*God forgives all sins*'. (39: 53) '*For a certainty, God does not forgive that partners are associated with Him. He forgives any lesser sin to whomever He wills.*' (4: 48) The *ḥadīth* mentions the case of one who committed suicide, a sin which most people think to be unforgiveable. Yet it tells us that God forgave on account of the person who committed it having migrated to join the Prophet in Madinah. Moreover, the Prophet prayed for his total forgiveness. It is important, therefore, that no one should ever despair of God's forgiveness. The essential requirement is to believe, without any doubt, in God's oneness and to repent for any sin one may have done.

The Prophet often included in his supplication a prayer to God to grant him certain qualities or to rid him of others that were undesirable, unbecoming or improper. His appeal to God to rid him of these was made frequently and on different occasions. Some of his companions recorded these and their versions may differ according to what the Prophet said on a particular occasion. If the Prophet appealed against a certain quality on various occasions, his appeal serves to emphasise that it is most undesirable. Every Muslim, should, therefore, try to rid himself of it and pray to God to help him do so.

If we look at some of the *ḥadīths* which report such supplications, we soon recognise that a quality which is mentioned on several occasions by the Prophet is highly important because it profoundly affects the individual's personality. Its presence in a certain person lowers his standing in society and in God's eyes. It is, therefore, important to know what sort of qualities the Prophet highlighted in his supplication as most undesirable.

We find that the Prophet often used the form 'My Lord, I seek shelter with You against ...', to highlight the undesirability of a certain

---

435. Related by Aḥmad, Muslim, al-Ḥākim, Ibn Ḥibbān and Abu 'Awānah.

quality. Seeking shelter with God is the best form of guarding against the effects of that quality, because God's shelter is most extensive and effective.

618. Anas ibn Mālik said that the Prophet sought God's protection and said: 'My Lord, I seek shelter with you against laziness; I seek shelter with You against cowardliness, I seek shelter with You against weakness in old age and I seek shelter with You against miserliness'. [*Allāhumma inni aʿūdh bik min al-kasal; wa aʿūdh bik min al-jubn; wa aʿūdh bik min al-haram; wa aʿūdh bik min al-bukhl.*][436]

The first quality in this list is laziness which, in this context, refers to an attitude that prefers ease and comfort to doing one's duty or what is necessary. God denounces the hypocrites in the Qur'an for their unwillingness to do what is good despite being able to do so. Needless to say, one who is too tired, too weak or too ill to do something cannot be described as lazy. He is not included among those who are denounced for their laziness.

Cowardliness is a quality which prevents a person from fighting an enemy or compels him to accept an enemy's dictates. A cowardly person allows his mind to be overpowered by fear. Hence, he does not fulfil his duty. At times, cowardliness puts a man in a position where he loses the respect of his community, his friends, his family and even himself.

What the Prophet prays for when he seeks refuge with God against old age is good health, since old age is associated with partial or total loss of certain powers or abilities.

Since miserliness causes a person to neglect some of his duties, particularly financial ones, such as zakat and hospitality, the Prophet appeals for protection against it. It should be mentioned here that miserliness could also apply to verbal matters since the Prophet defines a miserly person as 'one who is unwilling to pray to God to grant peace to the Prophet'. A scholar who refuses to impart knowledge to those who seek it is also miserly.

---

436. Related by al-Bukhari.

How does God receive our prayers and supplications. This is defined in a sacred, or *qudsi ḥadīth*:

619. Abu Hurayrah reports that the Prophet said: 'God, the Mighty and Exalted, says: "I am as My servant expects me to be. I am with him when he prays to Me".'[437]

This is a great *ḥadīth* which tells us that God treats His servants as they hope He will. If a person expects God to grant him success, recovery from illness and the achievement of his noble purposes, then God will make his expectations come true. On the other hand, if a person feels that God will aggravate his illness, or let him die, this will be done. Moreover, God grants him better than he expects and forgives him much of his ill-conceived thoughts. Sometimes people feel that God has abandoned them but He nevertheless responds to their prayers and grants them their wishes. It is essential, therefore, that a believer should work hard to fulfil the duties God has imposed on him, trusting that God will accept his efforts and respond to him. The Prophet instructs us: 'Pray to God and be sure that your prayers will be answered'.

How do we reconcile this with the concept of fearing God which is essential to faith? The answer is simple because we must always fear God's punishment because it is severe, particularly to hardened sinners. Nevertheless we hope that God will forgive us whatever sins or mistakes we make. The key to forgiveness is faith and repentance. The latter means that we are really sorry when we yield to temptation and commit a sin. We sincerely regret this and hope that in future we will not repeat it. Because of man's nature, however, a second slip is always possible. Man often yields to the lure of immediate and easy pleasure.

We must, therefore, strike the right balance between fearing God's punishment and expecting His forgiveness and reward. We should always include in our supplication a prayer that God forgives us our sins, even the smallest among them, and accept our good deeds and render them pure and dedicated to His cause. If we do this and balance our hopes against our fears, then God will surely forgive us, if He so

437. Related by al-Bukhari, Muslim, al-Tirmidhi and Ibn Mājah.

wills. It may be noted that here we attach God's forgiveness to His will, while we reported *ḥadīths* that make clear that we must not say in our supplication something like 'My Lord, grant me this or that if You will.' To add it in our supplication is to show that we are not eager in our supplication, but when we refer to God and His answering our supplication, we acknowledge that His will is free.

Some people tend to think little of their chances of being forgiven. They imagine that their sins are too great to be forgiven by God. They are always in fear of His punishment. When you tell them that God is most merciful, most gracious, they retort saying that their sins are too great. When people so believe, God abandons them to their beliefs, which are erroneous in the sense that they do not recognise that His mercy is always available. It can wipe away the sins of even the most hardened of sinners. There is only one thing that God will never forgive, namely, ascribing divinity to other beings and associating partners with Him. He forgives any lesser sins to whom He wills.

A believer should always balance his hope of forgiveness against his fear of God's punishment. The two should always be almost equal but should make hope slightly stronger. Such a balance helps a person to return to the fold if he slips and commits a cardinal sin. He realises that forgiveness is possible with the right approach and the right effort. He worries that his repentance might not be totally sincere, so he always tries to purge it of any traces of insincerity. When he feels that death is approaching, however, a believer should trust to God's forgiveness. His fear of punishment should dwindle and his hope of being accepted and pardoned by God should increase. This ensures for him the treatment God extends to good believers. During his life, he should neither despair of receiving God's mercy, nor allow complacency to creep into his life, trusting that God will forgive him whatever he does. Only hypocrites follow the latter approach, claiming that they will always be forgiven whatever they may do. At the point of death, however, a believer feels that he has done whatever he can, and there is no chance of doing any more. He looks at what he has done in life and feels that it is too little to save him from punishment. Therefore, it is God's mercy which guarantees his salvation. He trusts that he will receive it because God tells us that He responds to our good thinking of Him.

620. Shaddād ibn Qays reports that the Prophet said: 'The best formula of seeking forgiveness is: "Oh God, You are my Lord. There is no deity except You. You have created me and I am Your servant. I honour my covenant with You and my promise to You as much as I can. I seek refuge with You from the evil of what I have committed. I acknowledge Your Grace and I confess to my sinful actions, so forgive me. Only You forgive sinful actions. I seek refuge with You from the evil of what I have done'.

'If a person says this in the evening then dies, he is admitted into heaven – or he will be one of the people of heaven – and if he says it in the morning and dies on the same day, it is the same.'[438]

[*Allāhumma anta rabbi, la ilāha illa ant. Khalaqtani wa ana ʿabduk; wa ana ʿala ʿahdlika wa waʿdika mastaṭʿt. Abū' laka biniʿmatika ʿalay, wa abū' bidhanbi, faghfir li, fa innahu la yaghfiru aldhunūb illa ant. Aʿudhu bika min sharr ma ṣanaʿt.*]

We will presently discuss some of the best known formulae of the Prophet's supplications in order to have a full grasp of what is required in supplication to make it answerable by God. It should be mentioned here that such supplication may be said in Arabic, or in any language. Most people prefer to use the Arabic formula since it is the one used by the Prophet. This is fair enough. However, if we use our own words and our own language, conforming to the lines the Prophet has demarcated, we certainly do well. It is useful, however, to provide the Arabic text with every supplication we discuss.

The Prophet describes this formula as the best one to seek forgiveness. It is not difficult to understand why. It starts with an acknowledgement of God's Lordship and Godhead. It then states that He is the only god in the universe and moves on to define the relationship between the supplicant and the One to whom the supplication is addressed. It is a creature addressing his Creator. The supplicant then reiterates his commitment to his pledges which he has already made making clear that he tries to fulfil as best he can. However, knowing that he

438. Related by al-Bukhari, al-Nasā'ī and al-Tirmidhi.

has committed some sinful actions, he seeks refuge with God from them. This is followed by an acknowledgement of God's grace and that he himself is a sinner who seeks forgiveness from the only One Who can give it.

The comment added by the Prophet explains why this is the best formula for seeking forgiveness. If it is properly understood and sincerely made, forgiveness is assured. This is the reason for classifying the supplicant who uses it and dies that day as a person assured of admission into heaven.

621. 'Abdullāh ibn 'Umar reports: 'We used to count in the assembly of the Prophet that he would say 100 times: "My Lord, forgive me and accept my repentance. You are the One Who accepts repentance, the Ever-Merciful".'[439]

622. 'Ā'ishah said: 'God's Messenger prayed al-Ḍuḥa [the voluntary prayer offered in mid-morning] then said 100 times: "My Lord, forgive me and accept my repentance. You are the One Who accepts repentance, the Ever-Merciful".'[440]
["*Rabbi, ighfir li wa tub 'alay. Innaka anta al-Tawwāb al-Raḥīm.*"]

We have something to learn here since we often commit wrongful or sinful actions and, if we are true believers, we soon repent having committed them. Repentance must be sincere in order to be accepted by God. Hence, a prayer to God to accept our repentance is perfectly in order. When we use this formula, we ask God first to forgive what we have done and then pray to Him to accept our repentance. This means that we are requesting Him to make our repentance sincere, so that it is acceptable to Him. The formula also includes praising God and acknowledging His attributes which are particularly suitable to the request we are making of Him. Hence, the attributes made prominent here are His mercy and acceptance of repentance.

439. Related by Aḥmad, Abu Dawud, al-Nasā'ī, al-Tirmidhi and Ibn Hibban.
440. Related by Aḥmad and al-Nasā'ī

623. This is the same *ḥadīth* as Number 620, but with a little variation of the order of some phrases and a different chain of transmission. There is also emphasis in the second part on the need to believe in what is being said and to say it with total sincerity.

624. 'Abdullāh ibn 'Umar reports that the Prophet said: 'Turn to God in repentance: I turn to Him in repentance 100 times every day'.[441]

Some people may wonder why the Prophet turned to God in repentance so often. The answer is that it is mainly to teach us what we should do. The fact is that when we say certain words or sentences very often, it becomes habitual. We may repeat them without paying much attention to what we say. However, in some cases a repeat may be more honest and sincere than the first statement.

Moreover, we may commit sins and offences at any time, even while sitting in the same position where we express our repentance of past sins. These offences may be very small, but still we need to have them forgiven by God. Hence, the need to repeat our repentance. We only need to remember that if the Prophet used to turn to God in repentance one hundred times a day, the least we should do is follow his example.

625. (*Athar* 153) Ka'b ibn 'Ujrah said: 'A person who repeats what comes after [prayer] shall not be disappointed. These phrases are: "All glory be to God, i.e. *Subḥān Allah*; Praise be to God, i.e. *al-Ḥamd lillāh*; There is no deity other than God, i.e. *La ilāha illa Allah*; God is supreme, *Allah akbar*". One hundred times'.[442]

These phrases are said after prayers and before going to sleep. The one hundred times may be divided equally, saying each phrase 25 times, or saying the first three 33 times each and finishing with the fourth

---

441. Related by Muslim, Abū Dāwūd, al-Nasā'ī and Abu 'Awānah.
442. Related by Muslim, al-Tirmidhi and al-Nasā'ī.

phrase once only. A different version is to say the first two 33 times and the third 34 times, dropping the fourth phrase.

It is inherent in Islamic culture that Muslims request of each other that they pray for them, particularly when parting:

626. 'Abdullāh ibn 'Amr reports that the Prophet said: 'The quickest supplication to be answered is the one made by one person for another in his absence'.[443]

627. (*Athar* 154) Abu Bakr al-Ṣiddīq said: 'The supplication of a brother [for another brother] is answered'.

The main point about such supplication is the fact that the two people are not together. It is certainly commendable that one person prays for another when they are together, as when one says to his Muslim brother, 'May God reward you, or give you honour, or may He enhance your position in the Hereafter, etc'. Yet, it cannot be absolutely certain that this supplication is totally free of personal elements. One may pray for another to assure him that he cares for him and harbours no ill intentions towards him. Or he may try to assert his friendship by showing how keen he is that the other receives God's grace. When the two are not together, such a prayer aquires special significance. No one prays for another when the latter is absent unless he is sincere and he cares for his wellbeing. It is because of this sincerity that God answers such a supplication and rewards the supplicant as well.

Abu al-Dardā' was one of the scholars among the Prophet's companions and he was well known for his thoughtfulness, asceticism and indifference to worldly matters. His wife was similarly devout. Their son-in-law, Ṣafwān, gives us the following *ḥadīth*:

628. Ṣafwān ibn 'Abd al-Malik, who was married to al-Dardā' bint Abu al-Dardā' said: 'I visited them in Syria and I found Umm al-Dardā' at home, but not Abu al-Dardā'. She asked me: "Are you intending to perform the pilgrimage this year?" I said: "Yes". She said: "Pray to God to grant us what is good.

---

443. Related by al-Tirmidhi and Abū Dāwūd.

The Prophet said: 'The supplication by a Muslim for his brother in his absence is answered. An angel stands at his head and every time he prays to God to grant something good to his brother, the angel says, "Amen, and may you have the same".'" I met Abu al-Dardā' in the market after that and he said something similar, relating it from the Prophet'.[444]

This *ḥadīth* encourages us to pray for our relatives and friends and other Muslims. We are certain that our supplication on their behalf will be answered and a similar prayer is granted by God to us. Hence, if we act on this *ḥadīth*, we are bound to cement brotherly relations within Muslim society. We know that God can answer every prayer and give everyone of His creation all that they may request of Him.

This point may not be very clear to some people. They may imagine God in the same light as a king or emperor. They seek the maximum they can from Him before anybody else can secure a share, as if they fear that what God has to give away to His servants may be exhausted. They do not realise that it is inexhaustible.

629. 'Abdullāh ibn 'Amr reports: 'A man said: "My Lord, forgive me and Muhammad alone". The Prophet said to him: "You have excluded from it a great many people".'[445]

This is certainly a very narrow view. God's mercy is sufficient to wipe away every sin committed by mankind. He may bestow it on whomever He wills. To fear that it may be exhausted is contrary to Islamic teachings, because we are required to always think well of God. With regards to this particular point of God's mercy, we have to remember the *ḥadīth* which tells us that when God created mercy, He divided it into one hundred portions. He kept ninety-nine portions for Himself and distributed the last portion among His creation. All the mercy and compassion we see in this world and all the mercy that is exercised by every species of creatures anywhere in the universe is part

444. Related by Muslim, Abū Dāwūd, Ibn Mājah, Ibn Ḥibbān and Abu 'Awānah.
445. Related by al-Bukhari, Muslim and Ibn Ḥibbān.

of that last portion. The Prophet says that 'Even when an animal lifts its leg to allow its youngsters to pass', does so as a result of having a share of that last portion of mercy which God has distributed among all His creatures.

Someone may ask: What does God do with those other ninety-nine portions? The answer is that He may bestow His Mercy on His creatures in this world, but He certainly withholds much of it for the Day of Judgement when He forgives His servants and bestows His mercy on them then. This should give us an idea of how much mercy and forgiveness God will exercise on that Day. We pray that we will all be among those whom God chooses to be recipients of His mercy on that Day.

630. Ibn 'Umar reports: 'I heard the Prophet requesting God's forgiveness 100 times in a single session, saying these words: "My Lord, forgive me, accept my repentance and bestow mercy on me. You are the One Who accepts repentance, the Ever-Merciful".' [*Rabbi ighfir li, wa tub 'Alay wa-rḥamni. Innak anta al-Tawwāb al-Raḥīm.*]

This *ḥadīth* is similar to Numbers 621 and 622, but adds a supplication for God's Mercy.

631. (*Athar* 155) 'Abdullāh ibn 'Umar said: 'I supplicate for everything I do, even that God may make the stride of my mount wider, so that I may enjoy that'.

This statement by one of the Prophet's companions, who was a leading scholar, keen to emulate the Prophet in all aspects of daily life, is meant to educate us. There is nothing that we may not pray to God for to make it better or more comfortable for us.

632. (*Athar* 156) 'Amr ibn Maymūn al-Awdi said: ''Umar used to say in his supplication: "My Lord, gather me to You with the righteous and do not leave me among the evil ones. Join me to the best people".'

'Umar's supplication shows us that he wanted to be in the company of the righteous both in life and death. He did not want to live after the best of people whom he knew had died. The last part of his supplication means that he hoped to be helped in doing good deeds, and that his deeds be accepted by God, so that he would be grouped among the best of people.

633. (*Athar* 157) Shaqīq reports that 'Abdullāh [ibn Mas'ūd] often said the following supplication: 'Our Lord, let peace prevail between us; Guide us along the path of Islam; Save us from the darkness [and bring us] into the light; Remove from us all lewd actions whether visible or concealed; Bless us in our hearing, sight, hearts, spouses and offspring; Accept our repentance, for You are the One Who accepts repentance, the Ever-Merciful; let us be thankful for Your Grace, ready to proclaim it and show gratitude for it, and perfect it for us'.[446]

[*Rabbana aṣliḥ baynana; ihdina sabīl al-Islam; najjina min al-ẓulumāt ila al-nūr; iṣrif 'anna al-fawāḥish ma ẓahara minha wa ma baṭan; bārik lana fi asmā'ina wa Abṣārina wa qulūbina wa azwājina wadhurriyātina; tub 'alayna; innaka anta al-Tawwāb al-Raḥīm; ij'lna shākirin li ni'matik, muthnīn biha, qā'ilīn biha, wa atmimha 'alayna.*]

This is a comprehensive supplication by one of the Prophet's most learned companions. It first prays for a peaceful and serene atmosphere within the Muslim community. Then it requests guidance along the path of Islam. Next is a supplication for salvation from the darkness of unbelief, hypocrisy and sin and guidance into the light of belief and obedience of God. The supplication seeks God's help to steer away from all lewd practices whether done in public or private. It seeks God's blessing of one's senses and feelings, along with spouses and offspring. It concludes with an appeal for forgiveness and acceptance of repentance and for being grateful for God's favours.

446. Related by Abū Dāwūd and Ibn Ḥibbān.

634. (*Athar* 158) Thābit said: 'When Anas prayed for his brother, he would say: "My Lord, include him in the prayers of pious people, who are neither unjust nor corrupt, and who stand up in prayer at night and fast during the day".'

[*Ja'al Allah 'alayhi ṣalāt qawmin abrār, laysū bi-ẓalamatin wala fujjār; yaqumūn billayl wa yaṣūmūn bil-nahār.*]

The prayers that are certainly answered are those of the devout who steer away from sin and injustice. Therefore, Anas prayed for his brethren to be included in the supplication of such people.

635. 'Amr ibn Ḥurayth said: 'My mother took me to the Prophet (peace be upon him) and he stroked my head and prayed for my provisions to be plentiful'.

'Amr was a young child when his mother took him to the Prophet to bless him. When the Prophet passed away, he was only 12 years of age. Another *ḥadīth* mentions that the Prophet prayed that God blesses his transactions. He earned great wealth and was deputy governor of Kufah where he resided for a long time.

636. (*Athar* 159) Some people said to Anas ibn Mālik: 'Your brethren have come from Basrah to visit you. He was at al-Zāwiyah at the time. They wish that you supplicate for them. He said: "Our Lord, forgive us and bestow mercy on us. Grant us what is good in this world and what is good in the life to come and protect us from the torment of the fire". They asked him for more and he said the same thing, adding: "If you are given this, you have been given the best of this world and the best of the life to come". [*Allāhumm ighfir lana warḥamna wa ātina fi al-dunyā ḥasanah, wa fi al-ākhirati ḥasanah, wa qina 'adhāb al-nār.*]

Anas knew what was best, as he served the Prophet throughout his stay in Madinah and was very close to him. His supplication included everything a person should wish for. He prayed for forgiveness, mercy, the best of this world and the best of the life to come together with protection from punishment in hell. Therefore, when he was asked for more, he said the same thing, giving his explanation.

637. Anas ibn Mālik reports: 'The Prophet took a [small] branch of a tree and shook it, but no leaves fell off. He shook it again but nothing fell off. He shook it a third time and nothing fell off. He then said: "Limitless is God in His Glory [i.e. *Subḥān Allah*]; All praise be to God [i.e. *al-ḥamd lillāh*]; and there is no deity other than God [i.e. *La ilāha illa Allah*]. [These phrases] will shake off errors just like a tree drops its leaves".'[447]

The small branch was dry and apparently it had no leaves. Therefore, when the Prophet shook it, it dropped nothing. He indicated to those who were with him that before the branch fell off the tree, it had dropped all its leaves. He then explained that these glorifications, when said frequently, erase slips and sinful actions, leaving nothing of them, just like a tree becoming bare of leaves in winter.

638. Anas said: 'A woman came to the Prophet complaining that she was a needy person. He said to her: "Shall I point out to you what is better than that? When you go to bed, say: 'There is no deity other than God' 33 times, 'Limitless is God in His Glory' 33 times and 'All praise be to God' 34 times. This makes up 100 and it is better than this world and all that it contains".' [*la ilāha illa Allah; subḥān Allah; al-ḥamd lillāh*]

Anas does not mention who the lady was, but we have identified a *ḥadīth* that relates that Fāṭimah, the Prophet's daughter, asked him for a servant. He went to her when she and her husband were in bed and sat between them. He told them to do this glorification when they went to bed, and that it would be better for them than having a servant. This *ḥadīth* by Anas may be a reference to Fāṭimah, the first lady of mankind, or it may be a similar situation and the Prophet gave the same advice in both cases.

---

447. Related by Aḥmad.

639. The Prophet said: 'If a person says "There is no deity other than God" 100 times, "Limitless is God in His Glory" 100 times, and "God is supreme" 100 times, it will be better for him than freeing ten slaves and sacrificing seven camels'.

A Muslim may set one slave or more free, seeking to please God and having reward from Him only, and he may sacrifice animals to distribute their meat to the poor. Such actions will bring him rich reward from God. However, the Prophet says that when one habitually, or after obligatory prayers, says these glorifications this will be better. This is because such glorifications lead to the person being forgiven his sins. To have such forgiveness is better than making such sacrifices and setting slaves free, rich as the reward for such actions may be.

640. A man came to the Prophet and asked: 'Messenger of God, what is the best supplication?' The Prophet replied: 'Ask God for forgiveness and wellbeing in this world and in the life to come'. The man came again the following day and asked: 'Prophet, which is the best supplication?' The Prophet replied: 'Ask God for forgiveness and wellbeing in this world and in the life to come. If you are granted wellbeing in this world and the life to come, you have achieved success'.

When we study the Prophet's supplication, we find that comprehensiveness is one of its basic characteristics. The likelihood to fall into sin applies to all human beings. Indeed, every one of us often slips and exposes himself to God's punishment. Hence, it is essential to pray for forgiveness. On many occasions, the Prophet highlighted the importance of this prayer. In this *ḥadīth* he answers the question about the best of supplications by first stating an appeal for forgiveness. This should always be our first prayer, because we are all likely to make mistakes and commit sins. When God grants forgiveness, this keeps our record of good deeds intact and facilitates our admission into heaven. The Prophet also recommends his questioner to pray for wellbeing in this life and in the life to come. Wellbeing should be understood to be both general and comprehensive, encompassing everything in life. Therefore, the

theirs or their basic rights, all have been warned that their deeds will condemn them to God's punishment.

Punishment may come sooner, with torment in the grave being a foretaste. Hence, the Prophet advises us to seek God's shelter against it.

The Impostor (*al-Dajjāl*) is an unbeliever who makes his appearance close to the end of time. He will claim that he is the Messiah and will kill good believers. They will recognise him as an impostor and stick to their faith in God's oneness. He will kill many believers, but his term is short. The Prophet mentions that he rules for forty days, but one of his days is as long as a week and one as a month and one is equal to a year. His time will be very hard for believers and the temptation to try to be safe by following him will be great. This aspect is the one which the Prophet highlights, as this is the essence of the trial faced by believers.

The trials of life are plenty. They include every test a person goes through, but the worst of them is the temptation to indulge in sin. The trials of death include the examination by angels and the torment that afflicts unbelievers.

652. Jābir reports that the Prophet used to say in his supplication: 'My Lord, keep my hearing and my eyesight sound for me until I die, and help me against anyone who wrongs me, and show me my revenge on him'. [*Allāhumma aṣliḥ li samʿi wa baṣari, wa ijʿalhuma al-wārithayn minni, wa-nṣurni ʿala man ẓalamani, wa arini minhu tha'ri.*]

653. The same *ḥadīth* but with a different chain of transmission, and the narrator is Abu Hurayrah.[455]

Sometimes the Prophet included in his supplication prayers which related only to this life. However, these were mainly requests to God to grant him a good life and ward off catastrophe, whether caused by natural events or by other people. In this instance, the Prophet prays first for the protection of his hearing and eyesight. Needless to say, these are the most important of human senses. God often

455. Related by al-Tirmidhi and al-Ḥākim.

describes Himself in the Qur'an as the One who hears all and sees all. A person who loses either one of these two senses is severely handicapped. If one retains both in his old age, he can cope with most of the difficulties that may befall him. We should follow the Prophet's example and pray to God to keep these two senses sound throughout our lives.

The Prophet also teaches us to pray for support against oppression and help against anyone who treats us with injustice. Perhaps nothing is more demoralising or takes a greater toll on our physical and mental wellbeing than injustice. When we are the victims of injustice, we certainly need support and God provides the best and most effective support for us. The last part of the Prophet's supplication leaves it up to Him to exact retribution against the perpetrators of injustice against us. This stresses the fact that we need God's support while He needs nothing from us.

Working hard in order to ensure happiness in the life to come does not necessarily mean denying oneself the pleasures of this world. It only means refraining from what is forbidden, enjoyable and tempting as it may seem. God tells us in the Qur'an that we should make use of what He has given us in such ways as draw us nearer to Him and secure for us admission into heaven. We should not, however, deny ourselves a share of the pleasures of this world. He says: '*Seek, by means of what God has granted you, the good of the life to come, without forgetting your rightful share in this world*'. (28:77) Hence, when the Prophet was asked by his companions what they should say in their supplication, he taught them short prayers which sought happiness in this life as well as in the life to come.

654. Ṭāriq ibn Ashyam said: 'We used to go in the morning to the Prophet (peace be upon him). A man or a woman may come to him and say: "Messenger of God what should I say when I pray?" He would answer: "Say: My Lord, forgive me and have mercy on me; guide me, and provide for me. These words combine for you what you need in this life and in the life to come".'[456] [*Allahumma ighfir li, wa-rḥamni, wa-hdini, wa-rzuqni.*]

456. Related by Muslim and Ibn Mājah.

Here the Prophet teaches his followers to include four things in their supplications. The first relates purely to the Hereafter, since it requests forgiveness which ensures easy reckoning on the Day of Judgement. The last relates only to this world as it seeks plenty of provision. The middle two are prayers for mercy and guidance, which relate to both this world and the next. A person who enjoys God's mercy and guidance in this life is happy, and without God's mercy on the Day of Judgement no one can hope to be granted admission into heaven.

The Prophet's companions who had the privilege of requesting that he pray for them stood witness to what it meant when God answered a prayer in full.

655. Umm Qays reported that the Prophet said to her: 'Whatever she said, may she be granted long life'.

[The narrator said:] We do not know of any woman who lived as long as she did.

Umm Qays Āminah bint Miḥṣan had the misfortune of losing a young son. Her grief was so overwhelming that she could not concentrate properly during the initial period of her loss. She said to the man who was about to give the dead child the ritual bath before burial: 'Do not wash my son with cold water, lest you kill him'. Her brother, 'Ukkāshah went to the Prophet and told him what she had said. The Prophet smiled and said this *ḥadīth*.

The *ḥadīth* included this little prayer said by way of comment on an interesting description of the woman's grief at losing her son. Yet the Prophet's prayers were never said casually. He always meant what he said because of his sense of God's presence and provision of everything that goes on throughout the universe. It has been authentically reported to us that every time the Prophet uttered a prayer, whether for a person or for the Muslim community in general, that prayer was fulfilled in the clearest and most vivid of manners. The narrator of this *ḥadīth* comments that no woman was known to have lived as long as Umm Qays Āminah bint Miḥṣan.

Anas ibn Mālik was in his early teens when his mother, Umm Sulaym, told him to stay with the Prophet and serve him all the time. Anas learned a great deal from the Prophet and reported a large number of *ḥadīths*. Umm Sulaym and her family were so close to the Prophet that visitors to Madinah might have thought them to belong to the Prophet's household.

656. Anas reports: 'The Prophet (peace be upon him) used to come in frequently to see us. One day he came in and prayed for us. Umm Sulaym said to him: "This, your little servant: would you pray for him?" He said: "My Lord, give him plenty of money and children, prolong his life and forgive him". He said three supplications for me. I have buried 103 of my offspring. My fruits are harvested twice a year. I have lived so long that I feel embarrassed and I hope for God's forgiveness'.[457]

If we look at the gist of the Prophet's prayer for Anas, we find that it combines happiness in this life with happiness in the Hereafter. The birth of a child is always a pleasure. Watching children as they grow up spreads a feeling of happiness in the family. When this is combined with a life of plenty, there is no worry about feeding one's children. A large, well-to-do family is bound to exercise influence within its community. As the young generation grow up, they are bound to expand the family's area of interest, and each one of them begins to chart up his career. A prayer by the Prophet for forgiveness ensures a happy end for the person concerned. This leads to heaven, the place in which every dweller enjoys happiness unblemished by any worry.

Anas speaks about his life after the Prophet's supplication. He became very rich and his fruit trees yielded twice every year. Much of his wealth was in real property, not in cash. As for burying so many of his offspring, this was due to the great plague that occurred in year 96 AH/715CE, which claimed an estimated 75,000 lives. We have different reports about how long Anas lived. The minimum number given in these reports puts his age at the time of his death at ninety-nine, while other reports say that he lived 107 years. Anas was also hopeful of forgiveness in the Hereafter. He is reported by Muslim to have said: 'The Prophet said three prayers for me. I have seen the results of two of them in this life and I hope to see the third in the Hereafter'.

---

457. Related by al-Bukhari, Muslim and al-Tirmidhi.

When we make our supplication, we should not hesitate to pray to God to grant us our wishes in this world. Nor should we forget to pray for happiness in the Hereafter. Miserable indeed is the person who enjoys a life of plenty in this world, but has nothing to show in the Hereafter.

Unanswered supplication

We wonder at times whether our prayers will ever be answered. We may face a problem, endure an illness, contend with difficulty or suffer an injustice. We feel that we need help which often cannot be given by any human being. Such help can only come from God. Hence, we turn to Him with our supplication, hoping that our wishes are soon fulfilled. At times, we experience the fulfilment of our prayers straightaway; often though we feel the response is slow in coming. This makes us wonder whether God has accepted our prayer and whether or not it will be answered.

657. Abu Hurayrah reports that the Prophet said: 'The supplication of any one of you is answered as long as he does not get impatient, saying: I have prayed to God and my prayers have not been answered'.[458]

658. Abu Hurayrah reports that the Prophet said: 'The supplication of any servant of God continues to be answered unless he prays for something sinful, or for the severance of a tie of kinship, and unless he is hasty, saying: I have prayed but I do not see my prayers answered. He then stops his supplication'.[459]

There is a simple formula for supplications to be answered. A person who puts a request to God should first of all be sincere in his attitude. He should purify himself physically and mentally which means that he should repent of his sins. It is unthinkable that a person indulges

458. Related by al-Bukhari, Muslim, Abū Dāwūd, al-Tirmidhi and Ibn Mājah.
459. Related by al-Bukhari, Muslim, Abū Dāwūd, al-Tirmidhi and Ibn Mājah.

in sin and at the same time requests that God grant his wishes, some of which are purely materialistic. He simply does not show any regret that he has exceeded the limits set by God. How does such a person expect that God will answer his prayers, when he does not expect the same treatment from his fellow human beings? If he has offended someone, he knows that he cannot ask that person a favour. Yet he expects favours from God when he persists in offending Him! The first prerequisite for God to answer our supplication is sincere repentance and seeking His forgiveness.

The second requirement is that one should not be hasty and impatient. We should not precipitate God's actions. He answers our prayers in His Own good time, but always in the way and at the time which is best for us. Indeed, we must not entertain any thought that our prayers may not be answered.

In these two *ḥadīths*, the Prophet advises us against giving up or thinking that our prayers may remain unanswered. A person may become disenchanted and stop praying to God. If he does so, his attitude is interpreted as one who considers his supplication as a favour or he may imply that he has done enough supplication to warrant being answered. This suggests that he considers God's favours unforthcoming, while he should realise that God can answer all supplications and can easily grant every single one of His servants everything they ask for.

There are, however, certain reasons which may make a particular prayer or supplication unanswerable. The second *ḥadīth* outlines some reasons for supplications not being answered. It explains that God does not answer any prayer for something sinful or one which leads to the worsening of ties of kinship.

659. 'Abdullāh ibn 'Amr reports that he heard the Prophet supplicating: 'My Lord, I seek shelter with You from laziness and debt. I seek shelter with You from the trial of the Impostor (*al-Dajjāl*), and I seek shelter with You from the punishment of the Fire'.[460]

---

460. Related by Aḥmad and al-Nasā'ī.

660. Abu Hurayrah reports: 'The Prophet (peace be upon him) used to seek shelter with God from the evils of life and death, and from the torment in the grave and from the evil of the Impostor'.[461]

These two *ḥadīths* are similar to Number 651, but the first of them adds a supplication for shelter from laziness and debt. Everyone knows that these are two terrible conditions. A lazy person leaves so much undone, and one encumbered with debt may feel life very tight, even suffocating. Therefore, the Prophet included this supplication with others that sound terrible.

The Prophet describes supplication as 'the core of worship'. As such, it is hugely important. There is no set quantity, time or manner for supplication which has to be observed. Each time a person addresses God with his requests, God rewards him for his supplication. If he does not make any request of God and does not address any prayer to Him, then he betrays arrogance. He suggests that he is in no need of God's help. Hence, his attitude is an affront to God.

661. Abu Hurayrah reports that the Prophet said: 'A person who does not make requests from God incurs His displeasure'.[462]

It is therefore right to conclude that supplication is one of the most important duties a believer owes to God. To avoid what incurs God's anger is certainly obligatory. A person who often prays to God does well because he makes his requests of the One who is able and willing to answer.

662. The same as 611 with a different chain of transmission.

An important area for supplication is to pray to God to repel harm from us. The Prophet taught us a short supplication and recommended that we say it three times each morning and three times each evening in order to be spared all harm:

---

461. Related by Aḥmad and Ibn Ḥibbān.
462. Related by Aḥmad, al-Tirmidhi and Ibn Mājah.

663. 'Uthmān reports that the Prophet said: 'Whoever says three times every morning and three times every evening: "[I appeal] by the name of God, through whose name nothing in the earth or in the heavens can cause harm. He is the One who hears all and knows all", will not be harmed by anything.'[463]

[*Bismi Allah alladhi la yaḍurru ma'a ismihi shay'un fi al arḍ wa la fi al-samā', wa huwa al-samī' al-'alīm.*]

It is sufficient to say that this *ḥadīth* tells us of a form of supplication which ensures that nothing can inflict any harm on us when we say it three times early in the morning after dawn has broken and three times after sunset. I have heard many people confirming that they have acted on the Prophet's advice repeating this prayer as he instructed and found that it works as the Prophet said. I can add further confirmation from my own experience. The one who transmitted this *ḥadīth* from 'Uthmān was his son, Abān ibn 'Uthmān. He himself suffered partial paralysis. One of his visitors during his illness looked at him with surprise. Abān realised that he wanted to ask him about his illness. He said to him: 'The *ḥadīth* by the Prophet is as I have told you. I did not attribute a lie to 'Uthmān and 'Uthmān did not attribute a lie to the Prophet. It so happened that on the day this happened to me, I had not said it. Thus, God's will was done'. The version related by Abu Dāwūd, quotes Abān's explanation as follows: 'But on the day on which I suffered this, I had been angry and I forgot to say the supplication'. It tells a great deal of Abān's firm faith in the truth of everything the Prophet said to continue to teach this *ḥadīth* despite his paralysis and to explain it the way he did.

Certain times are recommended for supplications as it is then more likely that they will be answered:

664. (*Athar* 160) Sahl ibn Sa'd said: 'The gates of heaven are opened at two times. Rarely is a supplication made at these times rejected: when the call to prayer is made and when an army stands ready for a battle in God's cause'.

---

463. Related by Abū Dāwūd, al-Nasā'ī, al-Tirmidhi, Ibn Mājah and Ibn Ḥibbān.

The time when a prayer is called is most suitable for supplication, because it is the time when believers get ready to respond to the call. God is pleased with them for their response and He gives them generously.

When soldiers stand ready to fight for God's cause and to ensure that His word is supreme, they are ready to fight to the finish. Therefore, anyone who says a supplication at this time, requesting that God grant him whatever he wishes, God is certain to answer his supplication.

665. Abu Ṣirmah Mālik ibn Qays al-Anṣāri reports that the Prophet said: 'My Lord, I appeal to you to grant me prosperity and to grant it to my dependants'.[464]

In this *ḥadīth* the Prophet prays for prosperity for himself and his dependants. This shows that there is nothing wrong with requesting that God grant us what we aspire to have of the good things of this life, in addition to appealing to Him for forgiveness, mercy and admittance into heaven.

666. Shakl ibn Ḥumayd reports that he said to the Prophet: 'Messenger of God, teach me a supplication that will benefit me'. He said: 'Say: My Lord, protect me from the evil of my hearing, sight, tongue, heart and sperm'.[465]
[*Allāhumma ʿāfini min sharri samʿi, wa baṣari, wa lisāni, wa qalbi, wa sharri maniyy.*]

In this supplication, the Prophet teaches us to request God's protection against what sins we may do with our senses and other organs. The evil of hearing is to listen to backbiting, obscenities, falsehood, perjury, etc. If we deliberately sit with people who engage in such foul talk, we share with them their sins. This is the evil of our hearing. Needless to say, if we hear such things by coincidence, without taking part in them, or seeking to hear them, we are not accountable for that.

---

464. Related by Aḥmad.
465. Related by al-Nasāʾī, Abū Dāwūd, al-Tirmidhi and al-Ḥākim.

The evil of eyesight is to look deliberately at what is forbidden or to look at sins being committed by others, condoning them or finding pleasure in them. It is also evil to look stealthily at what we should turn our eyes away from. The evil of our tongues is to utter falsehood of any sort. That of our hearts is to entertain evil thoughts.

The last type of evil we request God's protection from is that of our sexual desires, whether it be fornication or its preliminaries.

667. 'Abdullāh ibn 'Abbās reports that the Prophet used to say: 'My Lord, help me and do not help anyone against me. Support me and do not support anyone against me. Facilitate for me the [following of] right guidance'.[466]

668. 'Abdullāh ibn 'Abbās reports that the Prophet used to say: 'My Lord, help me and do not help anyone against me. Support me and do not support anyone against me. Scheme for me and do not scheme against me. Facilitate for me the [following of] right guidance. Grant me Your aid against anyone who unjustly attacks me. My Lord, make me grateful to You, always mindful of you, fearful of You, obedient to You and humble before You and make me tender hearted, penitent. Accept my repentance, wash away my wrong actions and answer my supplication. Substantiate my plea and guide my heart. Let my tongue always say the truth and purge my heart of all rancour'.[467]

[*Rabbi a'inni wala tu'in 'alay, wanṣurni wa la tanṣur 'alay, wamkur li wa la tamkur 'alay, wa yassir li al-huda, wanṣurni 'ala man bagha 'alay. Rabbi ij'alni shakkāran lak, thakkāran rāhiban lak, mitwā'an, mukhbitan lak, awwāhan munīban. Taqabbal tawbati waghsil ḥawbati, wa ajib da'wati, wathbbit ḥujjati, wahdi qalbi, wa sadded lisāni, waslul sakhīmata qalbi.*]

The first of these two *ḥadīths* is a short version of the second which is a comprehensive supplication that needs no explanation. It appeals to God to grant us everything that we may desire in this life and to

466. Related by 'Abdullāh, al-Tirmidhi, Ibn Mājah, Ibn Ḥibbān and al-Ḥākim.
467. Related by 'Abdullāh, al-Tirmidhi, Ibn Mājah.

protect us against all evil. It also requests that He facilitate for us the following of right guidance that will ultimately lead to heaven.

669. Mu'āwiyah ibn Abu Sufyān said, [speaking in the mosque] on the platform: 'I heard these words from the Prophet in this very place: "None can withhold what You give, nor give what God withholds. No one's endeavour will be of benefit to him against Him. When God wills good for a person, He gives him insight into the religion".'[468]

The narrator of this *ḥadīth* was the sixth Caliph and the last of the Prophet's companions to be ruler of the Muslim state. He ruled for twenty years and was renowned for his intelligence, forbearance and justice. It tells much about the nature of a state ruled according to Islamic principles, that the Caliph reports to the public what he heard from the Prophet.

We explained earlier the meaning of the first part of this *ḥadīth*. The last part tells us that a person who acquires insight into the Islamic faith is someone to whom God wants to give what is definitely good. And when God gives good things, they are the best that any person can have.

670. Abu Hurayrah reports that the Prophet said: 'The supplication most likely to be answered is to say: You are my Lord and I am your servant. I have wronged myself and I admit my sin. None but You forgive sins. My Lord, forgive me'.[469]

[*Allahumma anta rabbi wa ana 'abduk, ẓalamtu nafsi wa' taraftu bi dhanbi, la yaghfiru al-dhunūb illa ant. Rabbi ighfir li.*]

The first thing to note about this supplication is the acknowledgement of God's Lordship and the reiteration of the relationship between Him and His servants. This is always the right approach. Once we acknowledge this relationship and we are fully aware of its implications, we put ourselves on the right course to receive God's grace. It is He

---

468. Related by Mālik.
469. Related by Aḥmad.

Who has promised to answer our supplication as He says in the Qur'an: '*Your Lord says: Pray to Me and I will answer you*'. (40: 60)

The second point is the acknowledgement of the fact that when we commit sins we wrong ourselves, because we incur God's displeasure and expose ourselves to His punishment. This can only be avoided by seeking His forgiveness. This acknowledgement of our sins is made in a private address we make to God. Hence, it is acceptable. It must be distinguished from the sort of boasting some hardened sinners may indulge in when they tell others about what they have committed. A person of this type may speak of his, say, drinking and participation in an orgy, or he may boast about robbing other people and making away with their property in order to show his strength. This is an added sin he commits, which makes forgiveness even more difficult for him to obtain. When we acknowledge our sins before God, we are actually blaming ourselves and expressing our repentance. The final point is the acknowledgement that only God forgives sins and wrongs. As such, we pray to Him to forgive us.

671. Abu Hurayrah reports that the Prophet used to say in his supplication: 'My Lord, keep my faith, which is my life's mainstay, on the right course; and set on the right course my life in this world where I have my livelihood. Make death a mercy and escape for me from every evil'.[470]

[*Allahumma aṣliḥ li dīni alladhi huwa ʿiṣmatu amri; wa aṣliḥ li dunyāy allati fīha maʿāshi; wa ijʿal al-mawt rāḥatan li min kulli sūʾ.*]

Short as it is, this supplication is comprehensive, requesting all that a person needs for his life in this world and the life to come. It starts with an appeal to keep one safe on the right course, pure of any misguided ideas, erroneous beliefs, rigidity and narrow-mindedness. This is the best that any person can have, because proper faith and freedom from error makes him better in his principles, values and practices.

The supplication then requests that one's life be set on the right course. This means that one is appealing for a good livelihood that

---

470. Related by Muslim and Abu ʿAwānah.

does not involve committing any sin or indulging in any improper conduct. Yet it is pleasant as one's efforts are successful.

The last part appeals to God to make death an escape from evil. Thus, one is free from any slip into what undermines one's prospects in the life to come. This is not a prayer for death *per se.* It is a prayer for a life that is free of evil, but if evil is going to engulf one's life, then death is better.

672. Abu Hurayrah reports: 'The Prophet (peace be upon him) used to seek God's shelter from a burdensome trial, ending up in wretchedness, evil results and the gloating of enemies'.[471]

Sufyān, the last in the chain of transmission, said: 'There were three matters in the *ḥadīth* and I added one, but I do not remember which one'.

The present life is a test and trial for everyone. Aspects of the test differ from one person to another, and the trials one goes through are varied, but they all constitute a test which determines one's destiny in the life to come. Hence, when the trial is too hard and the burden heavy, it is something in which we should seek God's help so that we may pass through it successfully.

The most important thing to appeal for is a good end both in this life and in the Hereafter. Whatever effort we undertake in this life, we would like to see it successful. Therefore, a wretched end may be greatly depressing. To have a wretched end in the life to come is much worse. Hence, the Prophet's appeal for a successful end.

The other two, namely, evil results and the gloating of enemies, have been explained under *ḥadīth* Number 444.

We may well ask about Sufyān, the narrator's statement that he added one quality and how he could do so. Sufyān is classified by *ḥadīth* scholars as reliable. It appears that when he was old, his memory might have failed him in some ways. He therefore alerted his listeners to the fact that he added a quality as he did not remember well. However, the *ḥadīth* is authentic as al-Bukhari enters it twice in his *Ṣaḥīḥ* anthology.

471. Related by al-Bukhari, Muslim and al-Nasā'ī.

The Prophet often included in his supplication a prayer to God to grant him certain qualities or rid him of other qualities which were undesirable, unbecoming or improper. His appeal to God to rid him of these was made frequently and on different occasions. Some of his companions recorded these and their versions may differ according to what the Prophet said on a particular occasion when they heard him make his supplication. If the Prophet appealed against a certain quality on various occasions, then that serves to emphasise that it is most undesirable. Every Muslim, should, therefore, try to rid himself of it and pray to God to help him do so.

673. ʿUmar reports: 'The Prophet (peace be upon him) used to seek refuge from five qualities: laziness, miserliness, feebleness in old age, the trial of what is in the breast and torment in the grave'.[472]

The last two mentioned in this prayer by the Prophet refer to matters which affect one's future life. The reference to the trial of what is in the breast denotes every quality, desire or idea which is unacceptable in Islam and entertained by a person, such as injustice, envy, unwillingness to accept the truth and erroneous beliefs.

674. Anas ibn Mālik reports: 'The Prophet (peace be upon him) used to say: "My Lord, I seek shelter with You from incapacity, laziness, cowardice and old age. I seek shelter with You from the trials of life and death; and I seek refuge with You from torment in the grave'.[473]

675. Anas reports that he heard the Prophet say: 'My Lord, I seek refuge with You from worry and sorrow; incapacity and laziness; cowardice and miserliness; the heavy weight of indebtedness and being overpowered by men'.[474] [*Allāhumma inni ʿaūdhu bika min*

472. Related by al-Nasā'ī, Abū Dāwūd and Ibn Mājah.
473. Related by al-Bukhari, Muslim and al-Nasā'ī, Abū Dāwūd and al-Tirmidhi.
474. Related by al-Bukhari, Abū Dāwūd, al-Nasā'ī and al-Tirmidhi.

al-hamm wal-ḥazan; wal-ʿajz wal-kasal; wal-jubn wal-bukhl; wa ẓalaʿ al-dayn wa ghalabat al-rijāl.]

These two *ḥadīths* speak of several qualities that affect one's life. Some are repeated and we will explain each briefly, but we have already explained what is meant by the trials of life and death and the torment in the grave.

The second *ḥadīth* lists the qualities in pairs. The first pair of qualities are closely related since they refer to depression either in expectation of what may happen or as a result of what has happened. If either state is too strong or prolonged, it is bound to have a profound effect on the person concerned. Laziness causes a person to miss out on good things that may brighten his life, but it is possible for a person to do something about that quality and force himself to do his duty despite his preference for easy living. Incapacity, however, is something involuntary. When a person feels that he is unable to achieve his purpose or secure his needs or the needs of his family, he feels terribly depressed.

Cowardliness is a quality which prevents a person from fighting an enemy or compels him to accept that enemy's dictates. A cowardly person allows his mind to be overpowered by his fear. Hence, he does not fulfil his duty. At times, cowardliness puts a man in a position where he loses the respect of his community, his friends, his family and even himself.

What the Prophet prays for when he seeks refuge with God against old age is good health, since old age is associated with partial or total loss of certain powers or abilities.

Since miserliness causes a person to neglect some of his duties, particularly financial ones, such as zakat and hospitality, the Prophet appeals for protection against it. It should be mentioned here that miserliness could also apply to verbal matters since the Prophet defines a miserly person as 'one who is unwilling to pray to God to grant peace to the Prophet'.[475] A scholar who refuses to impart knowledge to those who seek it is also miserly.

When a person is deeply in debt and cannot find the means to repay creditors, his whole personality may change. He may feel humiliated

475. Related by al-Tirmidhi.

since he cannot repay those who have done him a favour by advancing money when needed. On the other hand, being overpowered by people, particularly when they use their power unjustly may degrade a person and cause him no end of trouble. This is particularly so in communities which suffer from the tyranny of despotic governments. Over the last hundred years some Musilm countries succumbed to the rule of dictators who humiliated their people, imprisoned many thousands of their citizens and inflicted on them untold torture. When the Prophet appealed to God for refuge from being overpowered by men, his prayer includes such situations.

It is always useful to follow the Prophet's example by making the same supplication to God as often as we can.

676. Abu Hurayrah reports that the Prophet included in his supplication: 'My Lord, forgive me whatever sin I did in the past or may do in the future, what I might have concealed or done in the open, and what You know of me better than I know myself. You are the One Who brings forward and sets back. There is no deity other than You'.[476] [*Allāhumma ighfir li ma qaddamt wama akhkhart, wama asrart wama aʿlant, wama anta aʿlamu bihi minni. Innaka ant al-muqaddim wal-mu'akhkhir. La ilāha illa ant.*]

This is a supplication for forgiveness of all sins, major and minor, whenever and however they are done. It includes sins that one may not be aware of, but God certainly knows. It concludes with acknowledging God's attributes of knowledge and oneness.

677. ʿAbdullāh ibn Masʿūd reports that the Prophet used to say in his supplication: 'My Lord, I request You grant me guidance, virtue and wealth'.[477] [*Allāhumma inni as'aluk al-huda wal-ʿafāf wal-ghina.*]

Al-Bukhari said: Our companions report this *ḥadīth* from ʿAmr with the addition of 'and God-fearingness', i.e. al-tuqa.

---

476. Related by Aḥmad and al-Ḥākim.

477. Related by Muslim, al-Tirmidhi and Ibn Mājah.

The Prophet supplicated for wealth along with three qualities that are primarily associated with character. There is nothing wrong with wealth when it is in the hands of a pious, God-fearing person. Wealth that corrupts values and moral standards is bad. Moreover, one's wealth need not only be in money. A contented person is wealthy regardless of the amount of luxuries he owns, or otherwise.

678. (*Athar* 161) Thumāmah ibn Ḥazn said: 'I heard an old man calling out very loudly: "My Lord, I seek shelter with You from total evil". I asked who the old man was, and I was told that he was Abu al-Dardā'.

679. 'Abdullāh ibn Abu Awfa reports that the Prophet used to say: 'My Lord, cleanse me with snow, hail and cold water as a dirty garment is cleansed of dirt. My Lord, praise is due to You as would fill the earth and the skies and whatever else You wish beyond them'.[478] [*Allāhumma Ṭahhirni bil-thalj wal-barad wal-mā' al-bārid, kama yuṭahhar al-thawb al-danis min al-wasakh. Allāhumma rabbana lak al-ḥamd mil'a al-samā' wa mil'a al-arḍ, wa mil'a ma shi'ta min shay'in ba'd.*]

It is said that sins and disobedience of God give the heart, or the spirit, heat, impurity and weakness, just like fuel added to a fire. The more sins a person commits, the more fiercely his heart's fire rages. As we know, water washes off dirt and puts fire out. When the water is cold, it gives us strength and solidity. Hence, the Prophet's supplication for cleansing with water that is cold or frozen.

Praises of God cannot be measured with the fill of anything, but the Prophet uses this metaphor to indicate boundless praise of God, as the human mind cannot imagine anything greater or larger.

680. Anas reports that the Prophet often used the following supplication: 'Our Lord, grant us what is good in this world and what is good in the life to come and protect us from the

478. Related by Muslim and Abū Dāwūd.

torment of the fire'.[479] [*Rabbana ātina fi al-dunya ḥasanah, wa fi al-ākhirati ḥasanah, wa qina 'adhāb al-nār.*]

What is good in the life to come is paradise, but in the present life the supplication refers to everything that makes us happier and more satisfied. A believer is always happier when he is attending to his religious duties. Some scholars, however, say that the best thing in this world is a good spouse. There is much to be said for that.

681. Abu Hurayrah reports that the Prophet used to say: 'My Lord, I seek shelter with You from poverty, deprivation and humiliation; and I seek shelter with You from being unjust and from being unjustly done by'.[480] [*Allāhumma inni a'ūdhu bika min al-faqr wal-qillah wal-dhillah; wa a'ūdhu bika an aẓlim aw uẓlam.*]

This supplication needs no comment. The five scenarios the Prophet sought God's shelter from all lead to humiliation, whether it be an internal feeling or treatment by others. The Prophet, however, also sought God's shelter against dealing unjustly with others. Although a person who is unjust to others may feel powerful, he nonetheless ends up with humiliation, often in this life but certainly in the life to come.

682. Abu Umāmah said: 'We were with the Prophet (peace be upon him) and he made a long supplication that we could not memorise. We said: "You have made a long supplication and we cannot remember it". He said: "I will say something that puts it all together for you. Say: Our Lord, we ask You the same as Your Prophet Muhammad asked You, and we seek shelter with You from whatever Your Prophet Muhammad sought shelter with You from. Our Lord, You are the One to whom we turn for help, and You are the One who brings it about. No power operates except by Your will", or words to this effect.'[481]

---

479. Related by al-Bukhari, Muslim and Abū Dāwūd.

480. Related by Abū Dāwūd, al-Nasā'ī, Ibn Majah and al-Ḥākim.

481. Related by al-Tirmidhi.

[Allāhumma inna nas'aluka mimma sa'alaka nabiyyuka Muhammad, wa nasta'īdhuka mimma ista'ādhaka minhu nabiyyuka Muhammad. Allāhumma ant al-musta'ān wa 'alayk al-balāgh, wa la ḥawla wala quwwata illa billāh.]

No supplication is more comprehensive than this one. Prophet Muhammad (peace be upon him) supplicated for every good thing in both this life and the life to come, and sought God's shelter from every evil that anyone can imagine in this world or the world Hereafter. Therefore, saying this supplication includes every good thing and seeks God's help against every evil thing. It concludes by asserting that help is sought only from God and that all power in the universe operates only by His will.

683. 'Abdullāh ibn 'Amr reports: 'I heard the Prophet (peace be upon him) say: "My Lord, I seek shelter with You from the trial of the Impostor (*al-Dajjāl*), and I seek shelter with You from the trial of the Fire".'

This is a shorter version of the supplication included in *ḥadīth* Number 659.

684. (*Athar* 162) Sa'īd said: 'Ibn 'Abbās used to say: "My Lord, make me content with the provisions You have granted me and bless them for me, and compensate me well for whatever I do not have".'[482] [*Allāhumma qanni'ni bima razaqtani, wa bārik li fīh; wa-khluf 'alayya kulla ghā'ibatin bikhayr.*]

To be contented with what one has is a tremendous blessing, as it makes one self-sufficient, happy and free of grudges and envy. God has placed in the earth resources that can easily provide good sustenance for all creatures. When we see people dying of hunger, this is not due to lack of resources, but to the maldistribution of wealth, which is unfortunately common in all countries, including the very rich ones.

482. Related by Ibn Khuzaymah and al-Ḥākim.

685. This is the same as *ḥadīth* Number 680 with a different chain of transmission.

686. Anas reports: 'The Prophet used to say frequently: "My Lord, You control hearts. Make my heart firm in Your religion".'[483] [*Allāhumma ya muqallib al-qulūb thabbit qalbi 'ala dīnik.*]

The heart is often used in Arabic to refer to mind and soul. People may change their ideas, views and beliefs. This supplication aims to seek God's help in staying firm in one's belief in His oneness and the religion He wants mankind to adopt, which is Islam, based on self-surrender to God.

687. 'Abdullāh ibn Abu Awfa reports that the Prophet used to say: 'My Lord, praise is due to You as would fill the earth and the skies and whatever else You wish beyond them. My Lord, cleanse me with hail, snow and cold water; purify me of all sins and cleanse me as a white garment is cleansed of dirt'.[484] [*Allāhumma rabbana lak al-ḥamd mil'a al-samā' wa mil'a al-arḍ, wa mil'a ma shi't min shay'in ba'd. Allāhumma Ṭahhirni bil-barad wal-thalj wal-mā' al-bārid. Allāhumma ṭahhirni min al-dhunūb, wa naqqini kama yunaqqa al-thawb al-abyaḍ min al-danas.]*

This *ḥadīth* is the same as Number 679, but with a change of order and slight difference in wording. It also has a different chain of transmission.

688. 'Abdullāh ibn 'Umar said: 'God's Messenger (peace be upon him) used to say in his supplication: "My Lord, I seek shelter with You from the withdrawal of Your bounty, the loss of wellbeing, the suddenness of Your revenge and all causes of Your displeasure".'[485] [*Allāhumma inni 'aūdhu bika min zawāl ni'matic, wa taḥawwul 'āfiyatik, wa faj'at niqmatik, wa jamī' sakhaṭik.*]

---

483. Related by Aḥmad, al-Tirmidhi, Ibn Mājah and al-Ḥākim.
484. Related by Aḥmad, Muslim and al-Nasā'ī, al-Tirmidhi, Ibn Ḥibbān and Abu 'Awānah.
485. Related by Muslim, Abū Dāwūd, al-Nasā'ī and Abu 'Awānah.

God's bounty is so extensive, regardless of the situation a person finds himself in. Even when one is contending with great adversity, one still enjoys much of God's bounty. The fact that one is alive and able to think of what to do in such adversity means that one still has a great measure of God's bounty. If God were to withdraw his bounty, one would be wretched.

To be in a state of wellbeing is a great favour, and if this is withdrawn one would suffer greatly. Imagine that a person's immune system is functioning at a low pace. This could lead to various types of illness, and if one contends with more than one illness at the same time, one's suffering becomes intolerable.

God's punishment comes suddenly. Anyone who deserves such punishment rarely thinks of it. Therefore, when it comes, one is totally unaware, and this makes it even more painful and distressing. Therefore, the Prophet prayed for shelter from everything that may lead to God's displeasure.

689. 'A'ishah reports: 'When God's Messenger (peace be upon him) saw a cloud rising over the horizon, he would leave what he was doing, even though he was in prayer, and face towards it. If God dispersed it, he would praise God and if it rained, he would say: "My Lord, make it a beneficial rainfall".'[486]

The Prophet was worried when he saw anything similar to what befell earlier people who were punished by God. As some people were punished by storm winds and others by rain, he worried that the same might befall the Arabs who rejected Islam. Therefore, when he saw clouds gathering on the horizon, his worry was apparent. As his wife tells us in this *ḥadīth*, he would leave whatever he was doing. If he was praying, he would conclude his prayer quickly and face the clouds. He would supplicate, saying: 'My Lord, we seek shelter with You from any evil it has been sent with'. If it rained, he would pray for its benefit. His compassion was always overflowing. He would not have his people punished by God, hoping that in time they would realise the truth of his message and believe in it.

---

486. Related by Abū Dāwūd, al-Nasā'ī and Ibn Mājah.

690. Qays said: 'I visited Khabbab when he had been cauterised seven times. He said: "Had it not been for the fact that God's Messenger (peace be upon him) prohibited us to pray for death, I would have done so".'

Khabbāb was one of the very early Muslims. He was tortured most painfully by the unbelievers in Makkah. In later life, he suffered from a long abdominal illness. In this *ḥadīth* he mentions that the Prophet prohibited praying for death. This applies if one is suffering from physical illness or misfortune. However, in a situation where a person is facing oppression and he fears that he might be forced to renounce his faith, he may pray for death if he sees no other way out of his affliction.

691. Abu Mūsa al-Ash'ari reports that the Prophet used to say this supplication: 'My Lord, forgive me my errors, my ignorance, my excesses in all my affairs and what You know better than me. My Lord, forgive me all my slips and what I do out of ignorance or in jest, as all this applies to me. My Lord, forgive me what I did in the past and what I may do in future, what I do in secret and in the open. You are the One Who brings matters forward and sets them back. You have power over all things'.[487] [*Rabbi ighfir li khaṭī'ati wa jahli, wa isrāfi fi amri kullih, wa ma ant a'lam bihi minni. Allāhumma ighfir li khaṭa'i kullah, wa 'amdi wa jahli wa hazli; wa kullu dhālika 'indi. Allāhumma ighfir li ma qaddamtu wa ma akhkhart, wa ma asrartu wa ma a'lant. Anta al-muqaddim wa anta al-mu'akhkhir, wa anta 'ala kulli shay'in qadīr.*]

692. This *ḥadīth* states part of the one preceding it, but with a different chain of transmission.

This supplication concentrates on seeking forgiveness for whatever slip, error or sin a person falls into, whether deliberately, in ignorance, in jest or seriously, secretly or in the open, admitting that all this may occur at one time or another. It may appear that one is asking too

487. Related by al-Bukhari, Muslim and Ibn Abi Shaybah.

much, particularly as one acknowledges all this. We should remember that '*God forgives all sins. He is the All-Forgiving, the Ever Merciful*'. (39:53)

693. Mu'ādh ibn Jabal reports: 'The Prophet (peace be upon him) held my hand and said: "Mu'ādh!" I said: "At your service". He said: "I love you". I said: "And by God, I love you too". He said: "Shall I teach you some words to say at the end of all your prayers". I said: "Yes, please". He said: "Say: my Lord, help me to remember You, be grateful to You and to worship You well".'[488] [*Allāhumma a'inni 'ala dhikrika wa shukrika wa ḥusn 'ibādatik.*]

This is a prayer to be mindful of God in all situations, remembering what God commands and doing it, and to refrain from what He forbids. It also seeks God's help in being thankful and grateful for all His favours. God's help is also sought to worship Him well, attending particularly to what is obligatory and doing this in the best way.

As we have noted, the Prophet taught his companions many things to say after obligatory prayers. The question arises whether we are required to say all these every time. The answer is that we may say what we can of them, and alternate between them. The more we say, the better. A few each time is sufficient. As we have seen, most of them are short and a few will not take more than a couple of minutes.

694. Abu Ayyūb al-Anṣāri reports: 'A man said during prayer: "Praise be to God: abundant, pure and blessed praise". [When the prayer finished] the Prophet asked: "Who said that word?" The man kept silent thinking that he might have done wrong and the Prophet disliked it. The Prophet said: "Who is he? He said nothing incorrect". A man said: "I did, hoping that it is good". The Prophet said: "By Him Who holds my soul in His hand, I saw 13 angels racing in competition for the privilege of submitting it to God, the Mighty and Exalted".'[489]

---

488. Related by Aḥmad, Abū Dāwūd, al-Nasā'ī, Ibn Ḥibbān, al-Ḥākim and Ibn Khuzaymah.

489. Related by al-Ṭabārani

The man in this case was Rifā'ah ibn Rāfi' al-Zuraqi, who was one of the Anṣār who gave the pledge of loyalty to the Prophet at Aqabah, requesting that he and his companions migrate to Madinah. He was offering the Maghrib Prayer with the congregation in the Prophet's Mosque. As the Prophet lifted from bowing, he said as required, *sami'a Allah liman ḥamidah*, i.e. 'may God answer the prayer of anyone who praises Him'. Rifā'ah said this praise, which in Arabic is, *al-ḥamd lillāh ḥamdan kathīran ṭayyiban mubārakan fih*. However, when the Prophet asked who said these words, he feared that he might have been wrong, and so he kept quiet. The Prophet only wanted to reassure him that he had done well. The fact that thirteen angels raced for the privilege of submitting it to God speaks volumes about its good reception. It is recommended for us all to say it in our prayers.

695. Anas reports that when the Prophet wanted to go to the toilet, he said: 'My Lord, I seek shelter with You from the shayṭāns, male and female'.[490] [*Allahumma inni a'ūdhu bika min al-khubth wal-khabā'ith.*]

696. 'Ā'ishah reports that when the Prophet came out of the toilet, he said: 'I seek Your forgiveness'.[491] [*Ghufrānak.*]

These two *ḥadīths* show that the Prophet sought God's help and forgiveness at every moment and in all situations. Even going to the toilet and coming out were occasions when he did so, in simple and short supplications. Before entering the toilet he sought refuge from Satan, because one does not mention God there, and one's thoughts might go in the wrong direction. When coming out, we seek God's forgiveness of entertaining any thought of sin.

697. Ibn 'Abbās said: 'The Prophet (peace be upon him) taught us this supplication just as he taught us a surah of the Qur'an:

---

490. Related by al-Bukhari, Muslim, Abū Dāwūd, al-Nasā'ī, al-Tirmidhi and Ibn Mājah.

491. Related by Abū Dāwūd, al-Nasā'ī, al-Tirmidhi, Ibn Mājah, Ibn Ḥibbān and Ibn Khuzaymah.

"I seek shelter with You from punishment in hell; I seek shelter with You from the torment in the grave; I seek shelter with You from the trial of the Impostor (*al-Dajjāl*); I seek shelter with You from the trials of life and death; I seek shelter with You from the trial of the grave".'[492]

This *ḥadīth* groups together certain supplications that have been mentioned in Numbers 659, 660, 673 and 674.

698. Ibn ʿAbbās said: 'I spent a night at my aunt Maymūnah's home. The Prophet (peace be upon him) got up and answered a call of nature. He then washed his face and hands then went to sleep. He later got up and took the water-skin and loosened its strap. He performed the ablution in a moderate way, not using much water but doing it properly. Then he prayed. I stood up and stretched my body, as I disliked that he should see that I was watching him. I performed the ablution and stood to his left side. He took my hand and moved me to his right. His complete night prayer consisted of 13 rakʿahs. Then he lay down and went to sleep until his breathing was audible. When he slept, he breathed soundly. Then Bilāl came over to announce the prayer. He prayed without doing a fresh ablution. In his supplication, he said: "My Lord, give me light in my heart, light in my hearing, light to my right, light to my left, light above me, light under me, light in front of me, light behind me and make my light great".' [*Allāhumma ijʿal fi qalbi nūran, wa fi samʿi nūran, wa ʿan yamīni nūran, wa ʿan yasāri nūran, wa fawqi nūran, wa taḥti nūran, wa amāmi nūran, wa khalfi nūran, wa aʿẓim li nūran.*]

ʿAbdullāh ibn ʿAbbās was a cousin of the Prophet and Maymūnah, the last of the Prophet's wives, was his maternal aunt. He was a boy of 12 or 13 when this story took place. He had aspired to know what the Prophet's night worship was like. Therefore, one evening when his father sent him with an errand to the Prophet's home,

492. Related by Mālik, Aḥmad, Muslim, Abū Dāwūd, al-Nasāʾī and Ibn Mājah.

he was delighted when the Prophet told him to stay the night. He, therefore, pretended to sleep, watching for the time when the Prophet woke up. More detailed versions of this *ḥadīth* mention that the Prophet started with two short *rakʿahs* followed by eight long ones and three for Witr.

We learn from other *ḥadīths* mentioning the Prophet's night worship, i.e. *tahajjud*, that he never did more than eleven or thirteen *rakʿahs* after the Isha obligatory prayer. Thus, his regular prayer consisted of forty *rakʿahs* every day: seventeen obligatory, or *farḍ*, and twelve recommended, or Sunnah: (two before Fajr, four before Ẓuhr and two after it, two after Maghrib and two after Isha), eight *tahajjud* and three Witr. This is the best daily prayer routine and it is recommended people do it on a regular basis.

One may well ask how the Prophet got up again for prayer without performing a fresh ablution, or *wuḍūʾ*, after he had slept. The answer is one of two possibilities: either the Prophet did not sleep soundly but remained aware of what was happening, so as to know if he had invalidated his ablution or not, or that he was given the necessary information by God.

699. Ibn ʿAbbās said: 'When the Prophet (peace be upon him) finished his night prayer, he glorified God as He deserves. He said at the end: "My Lord, give me light in my heart, light in my hearing, light in my eyesight, light to my right, light to my left, light above me, light under me, light in front of me, light behind me and give me more light, give me more light, give me more light".' [*Allāhumma ijʿal li nūran fi qalbi, wa ijʿal li nūran fi samʿi, wa ijʿal li nūran fi baṣari, wa ijʿal li nūran ʿan yamīni, wa ijʿal li nūran ʿan shimāli, wa ijʿal li nūran min bayn yaday, wa nūran min khalfi, wa zidni nūran, wa zidni nūran, wa zidni nūran.*]

In the last two *ḥadīths*, the Prophet prayed for light, making a detailed request, mentioning light with different parts of his body and different directions. One may ask why he did not mention light once and request that it should be given everywhere around him. Scholars say that in the form the Prophet used, his prayer gives him far more light in both quantity and quality.

The Prophet first asks for light in his heart, hearing and eyesight. The heart in Arabic denotes also the mind, and when the mind is enlightened, it can better contemplate the signs all around us pointing to God and His creation. Thus this light makes us better believers. The same applies in a sense to light in one's sight and hearing. Eyesight shows us God's creation in which we can contemplate His greatness and the perfection of what He creates. With hearing we learn God's revelations and if we have light in our hearing, we are better able to understand Divine revelations and strengthen our faith.

When the Prophet makes further requests for light, he changes the form of expression so as to seek light to his left and right, not in both hands. This means that he wanted light to spread in both directions so as to benefit those who were close to him on both sides. The light ahead of him gives him a clear view of how to move on. This is guidance in every step he takes. The light from behind provides enlightenment for all those who follow him, both his companions and his followers in succeeding generations, for as long as human life on earth continues.

The Prophet also requests light from above and beneath. This is to complete all directions so as to have light in every situation, and not to be deprived of it under any circumstances. Such light can only be given by God, in the form of guidance which enlightens our way and directs our actions to ensure beneficial results for us and our community.

The Prophet completes his supplication by a request for increased light. This last prayer is made in recognition of the fact that without enlightenment granted by God, we are liable to err. Therefore, the Prophet's request teaches us that we simply cannot have too much of God's enlightenment and guidance. The more we have, the better for us, as God's light ensures that we know what to do and what measures to take in whatever problem we may face. Therefore, we should always remember the Prophet's supplication and pray to God for light in our hearts, eyesight and hearing, light to our right, left, front and back, light from above and below, and add a prayer for increased light at all times.

700. 'Abdullāh ibn 'Abbās said: 'When the Prophet (peace be upon him) woke up to pray in the middle of the night, he used to say: "All praise is due to You, my Lord. You are the light of the heavens and the earth and all in them. To You praise is due, for You are the Master of the heavens and the earth. Praise belongs to You, for You are the Lord of the heavens and the earth and all in them. You are the truth; Your promise is true; the meeting with You is true; heaven is true; hell is true; and the Last Hour is true. My Lord, to You I surrender myself, and in You I believe and place my trust. To You I turn, and Your case I plead, and to You I turn for judgement. Forgive me what I did in the past and what I may do in future; what I have done in secret or in the open. You are my Lord. There is no deity other than You".'[493]

[*Allāhumma lak al-ḥamd; anta nūr al-samāwāt wal-arḍ wa man fīhinn; wa lak al-ḥamd; anta qayyām al-samāwāt wal-arḍ; wa lak al-ḥamd; anta rabb al-samāwāt wal-arḍ wa man fīhinn. Anta al-ḥaqq; wa wa'duk al-ḥaqq; wal-jannatu ḥaqq; wal-nār ḥaqq; wal-sā'at ḥaqq. Allāhumma laka aslamt, wa bika āmant, wa 'alayka tawakkalt, wa ilayka anabt, wa bika khāṣamt, wa ilayka ḥākamt, fa ighfir li ma qaddamt wama akhkhart, wama asrart wama a'lant. Anta ilāhi, la ilāha illa ant.*]

The first thing we note in this supplication by the Prophet is that it starts with praising God for His favours. This is repeated several times in the *ḥadīth*, confirming the expression of gratitude for all that one is given. The first praise is followed by the statement that God is the light of the heavens and the earth and all creatures in them. This means that He provides all the light for the whole universe, and with Him every thing is seen clearly. Indeed, without God's light, the whole universe would be plunged into total darkness.

The praise and thanks are then repeated twice, asserting that God is the Master and Lord of the universe. These three statements in quick succession, separated by a repetition of thanksgiving praise, establish the sort of relationship a Muslim has with God. It is a relationship that symbolises the Islamic concept of God, whose authority over the

493. Related by al-Bukhari.

universe cannot be challenged, as He is the Lord, Master and light of the whole universe and all creatures in it.

This is followed by a submission defining the truth of the basic concepts of the relationship between God and man. Thus, God is the truth, and His promise is definitely true. It acknowledges that all mankind will come before God, then they will know their destinies. They go to either heaven or hell, both of which are acknowledged to be true. Moreover, the Last Hour, i.e. the resurrection, is stated to be true.

With God's greatness and position clearly stated, and man's responsibility, accountability and destiny confirmed, it only follows that man's appropriate role in this life should be outlined. This is stated most succinctly, with short expressive phrases, denoting total submission to God, complete belief and total trust in Him. Not only so, but a Muslim should always turn to God, acknowledging any slip he may make and seeking God's forgiveness. Moreover, his relations with other people are defined by their attitude to God. Thus, a Muslim aligns himself on God's side, and he is in dispute with other people only on the basis of their attitude to God. He refers any dispute to God for judgement. He is ready to give others whatever belongs to them according to God's law.

With all this clearly stated, the Prophet makes his request, which should be the one all believers make at all times. What he wants is God's forgiveness, total and complete. The request for forgiveness is made on the basis of the submission to God being already acknowledged. Moreover, the forgiveness requested should include past and future sins. This is an admission that, as human beings, we may weaken in the face of temptation and commit sins in the future. Therefore, our request for forgiveness should include what has already been committed and what may be committed later. Furthermore, we make mistakes and manage to keep them hidden from others. We may also make mistakes that people see clearly. The request for forgiveness includes both types, so that one may come on the Day of Judgement with a slate already wiped clean. This is the best position from which to appeal for God's mercy and admission to heaven.

The Prophet's supplication is wound up with a short recap: 'You are my Lord. There is no deity other than You'. This is the sum of Islamic belief: God's oneness and man's submission to His will.

701. Ibn ʿUmar said: 'The Prophet (peace be upon him) used to say the following supplication: "My Lord, I appeal to You for forgiveness and wellbeing in this life and in the life to come. My Lord, I appeal to You for a state of soundness in my faith and family. Veil my faults and assuage my fear. Protect me from before and behind me, on my right and left and from above me. I seek shelter with You from sudden destruction from beneath me".'[494] [*Allāhumma inni as'aluk al-ʿafwa wal-ʿāfiyah fi al-dunya wal-ākhirah. Allāhumma inni as'aluk al-ʿāfiyata fi dini wa ahli; wasṭur ʿawrati wa āmin rawʿati; waḥfaẓni min bayn yadayy wa min khalfi, wa ʿan yamīni, wa ʿan yasāri, wa min fawqi; wa aʿūdhu bika an ughtāl min taḥti.*]

This supplication is similar to earlier ones which suggest that the Prophet did not stick to one formula in his supplication. It was all instantaneous. Therefore, if one learns his supplication and uses it, one does fine, and if one supplicates in one's own words but in line with the Prophet's supplications, one also does fine.

702. Rifāʿah al-Zuraqi reports: 'On the Day of Uḥud after the unbelievers retreated, God's Messenger (peace be upon him) said: "Stand in line and let me praise my Lord". They formed ranks behind him. He said: "Our Lord, all praise is due to You. Our Lord, what You extend none can contract; what You put far away none can bring near; what You bring near none can put far away; what You withhold none can give and what You give none can withhold. Our Lord, bestow on us of Your blessings, grace, favour and provisions. My Lord, I appeal to You to grant us the abiding bliss that neither changes nor comes to an end. My Lord, I appeal to You to grant us happiness on the day of poverty, and security on the day of fear. My Lord, I seek shelter with You from the evil of what You have given us and the evil of what You have withheld from us. Our Lord, cause Your faith to be dear to us and give it beauty in our hearts, and make unbelief, wrongdoing and disobedience to You hateful to us. Place us among the rightly-

494. Related by al-Bazzār.

guided. Our Lord, let us die as Muslims and live as Muslims, and join us to the righteous. Let us be neither disgraced nor afflicted. Our Lord, fight the unbelievers who bar people from Your path and deny Your messengers. Set on them humiliation and Your punishment. Our Lord, fight the unbelievers who were granted revelations; You are the Lord of the Truth".'[495]

[*Allāhumma lak al-ḥamd kulluh. Allāhumma la qābiḍa lima basaṭt, wa la muqarriba lima bāʿadt, wa la mubāʿida lima qarrabt, wa la muʿṭiya lima manaʿt, wa la māniʿa lima aʿṭayt. Allāhumma ibsiṭ ʿalayna min barakātik wa raḥmatik wa faḍlik wa rizqik. Allāhumma inni as'aluk al-naʿīm al-muqīm alldhi la yaḥūl wa la yazūl. Allāhumma inni as'aluk al-naʿīm yawm al-ʿaylah, wal-amn yawm al-khawf. Allāhumma ʿā'idhan bik min sū' ma aʿṭaytana wa sharri ma manaʿt minna. Allāhumma ḥabbib ilayna al-īmān wa zayyinhu fi qulūbina, wa karrih ilayna al-kufr wal-fusūq wal-ʿiṣyān, wa ijʿalna min al-rāshidīn. Allāhumma tawaffana muslimīn wa aḥyina muslimīn, wa alḥiqna bi-ṣṣāliḥīn, ghayra khazāya wala maftūnīn. Allāhumma qātil al-kafarata alladhīn yaṣuddūn ʿan sabīlik wa yukadhdhibūn rusūlak, wajʿal ʿalayhim rijzak wa ʿadhābak. Allāhumma qātil al-kafarata alladhīn ʿūtu al-kitāb. Ilāh al-ḥaqq.*]

This long supplication took place shortly after the Battle of Uḥud. The battle started with the Muslims gaining the upper hand against an enemy that heavily outnumbered them. They forced the enemy to retreat, but then their rearguard unit abandoned its position on the hill overlooking the battlefield. This enabled the unbelievers to launch a counter attack and score a military victory before they withdrew. It was after the Muslims buried their dead and attended to the seriously wounded that the Prophet said this supplication, in which his six hundred surviving fighters shared.

The supplication starts with praising God for His grace. It confirms the belief that everything occurs according to God's will, and appeals to Him for His blessings and favours, particularly security and peace. The Prophet and his companions also prayed for firm belief and to remain

495. Related by al-Nasā'ī, al-Ḥākim and Ibn Ḥibbān.

Muslims throughout their lives and to die as Muslims. It concludes with an appeal for God's help in fighting the unbelievers.

703. Ibn ʿAbbās reports: 'In times of distress, the Prophet used to say this supplication: "There is no deity other than God, the Supreme, the Clement. There is no deity other than God, the Lord of the heavens and the earth and the Lord of the magnificent Throne".'[496] [*La ilāha illa Allah, al-ʿaẓīm al-ḥalīm. La ilāha illa Allah rabbu al-samāwāt wal-arḍ wa rabbu al-ʿarsh al-ʿaẓīm.*]

Every one of us may go through times of distress, which can result from natural causes, as in the case of illness, or can result from other people's hostility, or it may even be self-inflicted. At such times, a believer turns to God for help and the removal of the causes that have brought about his or her distress.

This *ḥadīth* is described as the Prophet's prayer at a time of distress, yet it contains no supplication, prayer or request. It is simply a form of glorification of God. This point may be answered in two ways: the first is that it may be an opening for prayer, which may take any form. As it starts with this glorification of God, it is certain to be answered. The other interpretation is that a supplication may be stated clearly or implicitly. To glorify God or praise Him is to put one's request to Him, because He is aware of our needs and He responds to our glorification with grace and compassion.

Besides, God has told us in the Qur'an about the Prophet Jonah who was swallowed alive by the whale. In his distress, Jonah turned to God with an appeal for help. However, in his appeal, Jonah said no more than a heartfelt glorification, recognizing his position in relation to God: '*Indeed, there is no deity other than You; limitless are You in Your glory. Certainly, I have done wrong*'. (21:87) God follows this by saying that He responded to Jonah's appeal, relieved his distress and helped him come out of the whale safely.

Numerous stories speak of believers appealing to God by glorifying Him when they are faced with difficult situations, and that their appeals work wonders as God relieves their distress by the most unexpected

---

496. Related by Aḥmad, al-Bukhari, Muslim, al-Tirmidhi, Ibn Majah and

means. Al-Ḥajjāj was a governor of Iraq for many years towards the end of the first century of the Islamic era. He was famous for his strong measures against those suspected of opposition to Umayyad rule. One day, he sent for al-Ḥasan ibn Abu al-Ḥasan. Al-Ḥasan realised that this call bore no good will towards him, as he was known for being against Umayyad rule. He, therefore, feared for his life. However, he had no option but to go. Just before setting out, he prayed glorifying God: 'There is no deity other than God, the Compassionate, the Benevolent. All glory belongs to God. Blessed is God, the Lord of the Great Throne. All praise is due to God, the Lord of all the worlds'. When he was admitted before al-Ḥajjāj, the latter looked at him silently, then said: 'I have sent for you intending to order your execution. Now I feel inclined towards you, and I love you dearly'.

Although one may offer such appeals with all sincerity, one's distress may still not be removed immediately, as in the two cases of Prophet Jonah and al-Ḥasan. In such an eventuality, one should trust that God has allowed the distress to continue because He wants only what is good for the believer. It may well be that He knows that by allowing the distress to continue for a while, He will open a better prospect for His servant. The best example is the fact that God causes even His best servants to die. Death involves distress, at least for those who love the dying person. Yet death is necessary for a much better prospect, namely admitting the dying person into heaven.

704. 'Abd al-Raḥmān ibn Abu Bakrah reported that he said to his father: 'Father, I have heard you saying this supplication every day: "My Lord, keep me healthy in my body; my Lord, keep me healthy in my hearing; my Lord, keep me healthy in my sight. There is no God other than You". You repeat it three times every evening and every morning. And you say: "My Lord, I seek refuge with You from disbelief and poverty; My Lord, I seek shelter with You from the torment in the grave. There is no deity other than You". You also repeat this three times every evening and every morning'. He replied: 'Yes, son. I have heard the Prophet saying these words and I like to follow his example'. [The first supplication in Arabic: *Allāhumma 'āfini fi badani, allāhumma 'āfini fi sami'ī, allāhumma 'āfini fi baṣari.*

La ilāha illa ant. The second: *Allāhumma inni a'ūdh bika min al-kufr wal-faqr, allāhumma inni a'ūdh bika min 'adhāb al-qabr. La ilāha illa ant.*]

He also said: God's Messenger (peace be upon him) said: 'The supplication of the person in distress: My Lord, I plead for Your grace. Do not leave me to myself for the blink of an eye. Set all my affairs aright. There is no deity other than You'.[497] [*Allāhumma raḥmatak arju, wa la takilni ila nafsi ṭarfata 'ayn, wa aṣliḥ li sh'ni kullah. La ilāha illa ant.*]

It is highly significant that the Prophet combined in one supplication an appeal for protection against disbelief and against poverty. The two may seem to be widely apart, but the fact is that poverty often leads a person to disbelief. He may feel that he is hard done by when he sees others, who may be less talented than him, enjoying a life of riches while he lives in poverty. This may cause him to doubt God's justice. If he allows such feelings to linger in his mind, he may find himself moving along the way to denying first God's justice, then denying God Himself. On the other hand, a person may find poverty a very hard burden. So, he tries to relieve it by every means. If he cannot, he may resort to crime or sinful actions. These may jeopardise his position in the Hereafter. In this sense, poverty brings him close to the position of an unbeliever. Hence, the Prophet appeals to God to spare him both unbelief and poverty.

The other prayer appeals for sound health in body, hearing and sight. Although the latter form part of the body, and sound body includes sound sight and hearing, yet they are singled out because they are the most important faculties a person has. If one loses either of them, one may suffer much difficulty. Sound faculties and sound health mean a great deal to every one of us. Hence, the Prophet's prayer which we do well to repeat three times every morning and every evening.

The last supplication is for God's abundant grace. Every one of us knows that we will not be able to cope with the problems of life on our own. We need God's help and grace at all times. Hence we need to

497. Related by Aḥmad.

pray that God sets to right every one of our affairs. When we say such supplications, we will do well to repeat our belief in God's oneness.

705. Ibn ʿAbbās reports: 'In times of distress, the Prophet used to say this supplication: "There is no deity other than God, the Supreme, the Clement. There is no deity other than God, the Lord of the heavens, the Lord of the earth and the Lord of the noble Throne. My Lord, avert its evil".'[498] [*La ilāha illa Allah, al-ʿaẓīm al-ḥalīm. La ilāha illa Allah rabbu al-samāwāt wa rabbu al-arḍ wa rabbu al-ʿarsh al-karīm. Allahumma iṣrif sharrah.*]

This is the same as *ḥadīth* Number 703, with a different chain of transmission, slight difference in words, and with the addition of the last part, praying for evil to be removed.

706. Jābir reports: 'The Prophet (peace be upon him) used to teach us the *istikhārah* (i.e. seeking guidance) in all matters just as he would teach us a surah of the Qur'an. "When a person is about to decide something, let him pray two rakʿahs then say: 'My Lord, I seek the help of Your knowledge in making a choice and seek Your assistance based on Your power, and appeal to You to bestow on me some of Your limitless favour, for You are powerful and I am not, and You know all, while I do not know. You are the One Who knows all that cannot be perceived. My Lord, if You know this matter [the supplicant should specify the matter] is beneficial to me in my faith, my livelihood and in the outcome of my affair – (or he said: in my short-term) and long-term affairs, then facilitate it for me. But if You know this matter [the supplicant should specify it again] is disadvantageous for me in my faith, my livelihood, and in the outcome of my affair – (or he said: in my short-term) and long-term affairs, then keep it away from me and keep me away from it. Give me what is good for me whatever it may be and make me happy with it'.[499]

498. Related by Aḥmad, al-Bukhari, Muslim, al-Tirmidhi and Ibn Majah.
499. Related by al-Bukhari, al-Nasāʾī, Abū Dāwūd, al-Tirmidhi and Ibn Mājah.

[*Allāhumma inni astakhīruka bi-ʿilmik, wa astaqdiruka bi-qudratik, wa asʾaluka min faḍlik al-ʿaẓīm; fa innaka taqdir wa la aqdir, wa taʿlam wa la aʿlam, wa anta ʿallām al-ghuyūb. Allāhumma in kunta taʿlam anna hādha al-amr khayrun li fi dīni wa maʿāshi wa ʿāqibati amri wa ājilih faqdurhu li. Wa in kunta taʿlam anna hādha al-amr sharrun li fi dīni wa maʿāshi wa ʿāqibati amri wa ājilih faṣrifhu ʿanni waṣrifni ʿanh, waqdur li al-khayr ḥaythu kān wa raḍḍinin bih.*]

Please note: the phrase wa ʿāqibati may be replaced by wa ʿājili in both instances. Also instead of hādha al-amr one should specify the matter one is making the supplication about.

It is important to highlight the following points:

1. *Istikhārah* does not mean a request to know what is stored for us in the future. It is merely a prayer that seeks God's help in making the right choice.
2. Seeking God's help in making a choice applies only to permissible matters. We may not resort to *istikhārah* over anything Islam requires of its followers as a duty, or anything forbidden.
3. When the *istikhārah* is done, we accept what comes up in the matter concerned, trusting that God has made the right choice for us. This means that if things do not turn out in the way one expects, one should realise that the alternative would have been even worse.
4. The Prophet taught his companions and followers in all generations to resort to *istikhārah* in practically everything of importance.

The first thing to note about this supplication is that we begin with the admission of our lack of knowledge, and therefore we request God to choose for us because His knowledge is absolute. He knows what is beneficial for us and we are seeking His help to give us that. Moreover, we seek God's help in making what is good and beneficial within our reach, because we may get to know what it is but we may not have the power to attain it. Therefore, we appeal to God to make it, by His power, easy for us to obtain. We also acknowledge God's abundant grace, His power over all things and His knowledge of every secret.

Having established this basis, we then concentrate on the specific matter in hand. If God knows it to be good and beneficial for us in our present life and in the life to come, then we appeal to Him to make it easy for us to obtain and to give us His blessings to enjoy it. If He knows it to be otherwise, then our appeal trusts to His wisdom and seeks to be spared that totally. We further seek God's help to forget all about it. We also appeal to Him to give us what is good and beneficial whatever it may be.

All this supplication, made at a time when one is fully aware of one's own inability and lack of knowledge, consciously and deliberately seeking God's help, is a sign of strong belief in God, and a complete trust in His choice. It also shows a well satisfied heart. Hence, whatever result takes place, the believer accepts it, knowing it to be the choice God has made, which means that it is certain to be good.

707. Jābir ibn 'Abdullāh said: 'God's Messenger (peace be upon him) supplicated in the mosque, the Fatḥ mosque, on Monday, Tuesday and Wednesday, and his supplication was answered in between the two prayers on Wednesday'.

Jābir said: 'Whenever I encountered something serious, I would make sure of the time and I prayed to God at that time, between the two prayers on Wednesday, and I would soon see the answer [to my supplication]'[500].

Answering a supplication is something God will always do, because when we pray to Him, we actually acknowledge His Lordship, power and kindness. He returns this acknowledgement with a positive response. This is what He has promised us in the Qur'an: '*Your Lord says: Pray to Me and I will answer you*'. (40:60) This is a very clear promise, and God's promise always comes true. However, it is important to add whatever confirms that we are sincere and will consciously accept God's will. This will increase the chances of seeing our wishes fulfilled by God.

What ensures such a response even more is to make our supplication at a time that is designated by God as one when He answers

500. Related by Aḥmad.

supplications, as made clear in this *ḥadīth*. We note that Jābir does not mention here the nature of the Prophet's supplication on that occasion. In Aḥmad's version, it is clear that the prayer was to defeat the army raised by the two tribes, the Quraysh and the Ghatafan, together with the Jews in and outside Madinah. This was the time when these forces combined in an attack aiming at eradicating Islam and the Muslims altogether. Aḥmad also mentions that after the Prophet made his supplication on Wednesday, his companions saw him with his face beaming with pleasant expectation. He must have been assured of God's positive answer to his prayer.

What happened in the case of those forces was that God subjected them to a fierce wind of hurricane power which sent a sense of fear, frustration and total helplessness into their hearts. They decided to withdraw and marched away that night, after having besieged Madinah for nearly a month. Thus God foiled their purpose, gave the believers victory without having to engage in a fight, and made their city safe and secure. This was a turning point ensuring a permanent switch in the balance of power in favour of the Muslims.

We also note Jābir's keenness to pray for the resolution of grave matters at the same time the Prophet said his supplication. This was on Wednesday between the Ẓuhr and Asr Prayers. This is an opportunity we can all take, particularly as it demonstrates following the Prophet's example to the letter. This is something God loves as it demonstrates total belief.

The mosque where the Prophet prayed is the one on Sal'ma mountain, just outside Madinah, where the Muslims took their positions to face the besieging unbeliever army.

708. Anas reports: 'I was with the Prophet (peace be upon him) and a man said in his supplication: "You are certainly the Originator of the heavens, the Ever-Living, the Master of all. I beseech You". The Prophet said: "Do you know by what he has supplicated? By Him Who holds my soul in His hand, he has prayed to God by the name which, whenever He is prayed by, He is certain to answer".'

[*Ya badīʿ al-samāwāt; ya ḥayy, ya qayyūm; inni as'aluk.*]

The important thing about this *ḥadīth* is that it teaches us something that ensures the answering of our prayers. It all depends on adopting the proper attitude, which inevitably involves recognising one's own weakness and God's power over all things. When we pray to God, we should realise that only through God's help can we achieve our purpose. If one says a supplication feeling that one has a right for it to be answered by God, then this displays an arrogance God dislikes. Such arrogance is unacceptable even when a person asks something of his subordinate. So how can it be accepted when we address God?

The best attitude to adopt when supplicating is one of humility, all the time recognising God's oneness and greatness. The more praise of God we include in our prayer, indicating our firm belief in His Almightiness, the better are our chances of having our prayers answered.

709. ʿAbdullāh ibn ʿAmr reports: 'Abu Bakr said to the Prophet (peace be upon him): "Teach me a supplication which I may say in my prayer". He said: "Say: My Lord, I have greatly wronged myself, and none forgives sins except You. Grant me [complete] forgiveness from Yourself. You are Much-Forgiving, Ever-Merciful".'[501] [*Allāhumma inni ẓalamtu nafsi ẓulman kathīran, wa la yaghfir al-dhunūba illa ant, faghfir li min ʿindik maghfirah. Innaka ant al-ghafūr al-raḥīm.*]

This supplication combines all requirements to ensure its being answered: 1) acknowledgement of one's errors and sins, which is reflected in the supplicant saying that he has wronged himself; 2) showing humility in addressing God; 3) praising God confirming His great attributes of Forgiveness and Mercy, and 4) a genuine resolve to mend one's ways.

An important situation in which a person thinks an appeal to God for protection is his only resort is when he is afraid of ruling authorities. Dictatorial rulers often treat their subjects as insignificant. When dictators do not fear to be held accountable for what they do, people suffer a great deal of injustice. Should one fear to be wrongly punished for something one has not done, or to be subject to persecution by

---

501. Related by Aḥmad, al-Bukhari, Muslim, al-Nasāʾī, al-Tirmidhi and Ibn Mājah.

ruling authorities, one can always appeal for God's help. The Prophet taught us some supplications to say in such situations.

710. (*Athar* 163) 'Abdullāh ibn Mas'ūd said: 'If any of you fears the arrogance or injustice of a ruler, let him say: "My Lord, the Lord of the seven heavens and the magnificent Throne, protect me against so-and-so the son of so-and-so and his henchmen among Your creatures. Spare me that any one of them should exceed the limit. The one You protect is safe and secure. Great indeed is Your praise. There is no deity other than You".'

711. (*Athar* 164) Ibn 'Abbās said: 'If you come into the presence of a ruler who is held in awe and you fear that he may ill-treat you, then say: "God is Supreme. God is more powerful than all His creatures. God is mightier than what I fear and all that I am wary of. I seek shelter with God, other than whom there is no deity, the One Who holds the seven heavens from falling over the earth except by His will. [I seek shelter with You] against any evil that may be done by Your servant so-and-so, his soldiers, followers or henchmen, both human and jinn. My Lord, protect me from their evil. Great indeed is Your praise, and the one You protect is safe and secure. Your name is glorified and there is no deity other than You". He should repeat these words three times'.

[*Allah akbar. Allah a'azzu min khalqihi jamī'a. Allah a'azzu mimma akhāf wa ahdhar. Wa a'ūdhu billāh alladhi la ilāha illa hū, al-mumsik al-samāwāt al-sab' an yaqa'na 'ala al-arḍ illa bi'idhnih, min sharri 'abdik fulān wa junūdih wa atbā'ih wa ashyā'ih min al-jinn wal-ins. Allāhumma kun li jāran min sharrihim. Jalla thanā'uk wa tabārak ismuk, wa la ilāha ghayruk.*]

712. (*Athar* 165) Ibn 'Abbās said: 'Whoever experiences worry, sorrow or distress, or fears a ruler and says the following supplications will be answered. I appeal to You by [the fact that] there is no deity other than You, the Lord of the seven heavens and the Lord of the magnificent Throne. I appeal to You by [the fact that] there is no deity other than You, the Lord of the seven

heavens and the Lord of the noble Throne. I appeal to You by [the fact that] there is no deity other than You, the Lord of the seven heavens and the seven earths and all who are in them. You have power over all things. Then name your request'.

[*As'aluk bi la ilāha ill ant rabb al-samāwāt al-sab' wa rabb al-'arsh al-'aẓīm. As'aluk bi la ilāha ill ant rabb al-samāwāt al-sab' wa rabb al-'arsh al-karīm. As'aluk bi la ilāha ill ant rabb al-samāwāt al-sab' wal-arḍīn al-sab' wa ma fīhinn. Innaka 'ala kull shay'in qadīr.*]

In all three *ḥadīths* the emphasis is on glorifying God, remembering His power and that He is the Almighty who subjects everything to His power. This is only natural since one is only afraid of a ruler or a person in authority because of the power that person wields and the feeling that he can use such power with impunity. Hence, it is important to remember that he, and all his might, soldiers, henchmen, police and security apparatus, are subject to God's power and cannot escape anything God may wish to inflict on them.

Moreover, by glorifying God and remembering His power we initiate a feeling of security because we entrust our safety to Him. Moreover, we are able to put the whole situation in proper perspective. This means that we remember that nothing takes place unless God wills it to happen. Therefore, whatever the unjust ruler might wish to do will only happen if God allows it to happen. If He does, then that must be for a definite purpose of His. If He allows the injustice to take place, He will reward us handsomely for suffering it patiently, and He will bring about some other good results by it. Therefore, we will gain a handsome reward and the tyrant will reap the evil consequences of his injustice.

It should be remembered that this applies not only in the case of unjust rulers, but also in the case of anyone who deals unjustly with people. In modern times, it could be a low ranking official who exploits his position to harm people or deny them their rights unless they bribe him, or someone who could use some other authority. Whatever the situation, a supplication in the terms indicated by the Prophet will bring certain results, if God so wills.

The answer to supplication

People often wonder why they are not granted what they ask for. Since God has promised to answer prayers, and we pray to Him often, why is it that we do not see the fulfilment of our prayers as quickly as we would like?

713. Abu Saʿīd al-Khudri reports that the Prophet said: 'Any Muslim who addresses a supplication to God that is free of injustice or severing ties of kinship will be given one of three alternatives: either God will answer his prayer straightaway, or save it for him to the Hereafter, or spare him evil in a measure equal to it'. Someone said: 'Then we may pray much'. He answered: 'God's response is much more'.[502]

714. Abu Hurayrah reports that the Prophet said: 'Whenever a believer turns his face to God, making a request, He will grant it, either by fulfilling it in this life or keeping it for him in the Hereafter, as long as he does not hasten fulfilment'. The Prophet was asked how one hastens it? He said: 'By saying, I have prayed and prayed and I do not see that my prayer has been answered'.[503]

The first *ḥadīth* outlines what happens to our prayers when we address them to God. The first condition for answering a prayer is that it should not seek God's help to inflict injustice or aggravate relations between Muslims. If it does, then God turns it down unanswered. How can anyone appeal to God to inflict injustice on another, when God is just and fair to all His servants? Moreover, God does not like severing ties with relatives. Hence, He does not aid in any matter that leads to it.

When prayers are free of these two ills, they are certainly answered. But the answer may come in one of three ways. The first is that it is answered in this life. However, God will choose the time for answering it, and that is the time when it gives us its best advantage. This does

---

502. Related by Aḥmad and al-Ḥākim.
503. Related by Aḥmad, al-Ḥākim, Ibn Ḥibbān and Abu ʿAwānah.

not necessarily fit with what we hope for, because our judgement is restricted to what we perceive. But God determines our interest according to His own knowledge, which is perfect, absolute, taking every factor into consideration.

The second possibility is that God will keep that prayer till the Day of Judgement, which means that He will not answer it in this life, because He knows that deferring it is infinitely better for us. The Prophet tells us that when, on the Day of Judgement, we see what God will reward us with for such prayers He chooses to keep, we will wish that He had kept all our prayers unanswered in this life, so that we then have their reward.

The third alternative is that God will spare us some harm or evil which is certain to afflict us, but He removes it in response to our prayer. What this means is that although our prayer is not meant to avoid that particular harm or evil, God decides to spare us it because He knows that it is better for us than answering our prayer in the way we want.

When the Prophet's companions realised that each one of these alternatives works to our own benefit, they suggested that they pray more often. The Prophet encouraged this by saying that God's response and generosity are much greater than what we may ever ask for in our prayers.

The second *ḥadīth* illustrates an important factor in answering prayers. It warns against being impatient for their fulfilment. One must always realise that when one's prayer is sincere, acknowledging one's need for God's help, it will be answered, but God will choose for us in answering it what He knows to be better for us. This definitely puts the supplicant on a winning course. He either receives his response at the best time in this life, or receives something infinitely better in the Hereafter, or has some evil that was going to befall him diverted. Any of these is a net gain. Hence, there should be no despair or thought of inattention.

715. Abu Hurayrah reports that the Prophet said: 'Nothing is given a higher position by God than supplication'.[504]

716. Abu Hurayrah reports that the Prophet said: 'The most noble form of worship is supplication'.

717. Al-Nuʿmān ibn Bashīr reports that the Prophet said: 'Supplication is worship'. He then recited: 'Pray to Me and I will answer you'.[505] (40: 60)

That supplication is given the status of worship is due to the fact that when we address our supplication to God, we acknowledge Him as the Lord of the universe and we acknowledge our need for His help and assistance. The answer to this particular type of worship is that God accepts it and rewards the supplicant for addressing it to Him. This means that the reward is not confined to the fulfilment of what the supplicant asks for. Its reward may be much greater than that. When God fulfils what we pray to Him for, He will store the rest of the reward of our supplication for us. Nothing is lost for the supplicant. God often grants much more than the worth of our supplication, and this comes as an act of grace.

Sometimes, a person asks for something which he is not qualified for. For example, a person who does not attend properly to his worship duties, may pray to God to rank him among those who are exemplary in their diligence and devotion. In this case, God rewards the supplicant for his prayer and worship, but does not give him the rank he requests because this is only earned through effort and he has not made the necessary input.

It may also happen that God knows that what we are asking for is not good for us, or that it will turn to our disadvantage. In this case, He does not give us what we pray for, because He is kinder to us than ourselves. This is fitting with His grace and kindness, because if He were to give us what works to our disadvantage, this would be

504. Related by Aḥmad, al-Bukhari, al-Tirmidhi, Ibn Mājah, al-Ḥākim and Ibn Ḥibbān.

505. Related by Abū Dāwūd, al-Nasā'ī, al-Tirmidhi, Ibn Mājah and al-Ḥākim.

tantamount to a punishment rather than a reward. Such a situation is similar to that of a sick child asking his father to give him some food which the doctor has specified would have an adverse effect on him. Here, the father should never grant the child's request. It is kinder to the child to deny him what he asks for and to try to divert his attention elsewhere. Moreover, when we pray to God we feel the reassurance generated by knowing that He is on our side, forthcoming with His help.

Certain conditions will ensure that our supplication is answered. These are:

1. Presence of mind; because every aspect of worship must be intended as such. Supplication should be addressed as worship, not merely uttered by word of mouth when our mind is distracted by other things;
2. It should be addressed purely to God, when we are fully aware that He is the only one to answer supplication;
3. The supplicant must be a believer who does not associate any partners with God, in supplication, worship or belief;
4. The supplication must conform to the Prophet's guidance with regard to all aspects and appearances; without raising one's voice, seeking a particular time or place, except as directed by the Prophet;
5. It must include nothing that is unjust or unkind to relatives or the like;
6. One must never despair of having one's prayers answered, even though one might have prayed repeatedly, and
7. The supplicant must not neglect to take all the necessary measures within his or her ability to achieve what they are asking for. A person must not pray to God to give him water to drink, knowing that he only has to turn the tap on for water to come through. To neglect taking such measures is to fall short of one's duty. In this regard, one may cite the example of a person who lends another some money without having the necessary acknowledgement or witnesses to it, and who then prays to God to ensure that his loan is acknowledged and repaid by the borrower.

This last point merits further explanation. We are required to take every precaution to ensure that our interests are safeguarded. It is reported that a man claimed that he had lent another some money, without having any evidence to support his claim. When he explained the situation, the Prophet directed him to ask the debtor to make an oath in support of what he claimed. When the man was about to make the oath, the claimant said: 'God is sufficient for me'. The Prophet did not like this. He said to the man: 'Seek God's help but do not give up, feeling powerless. Should things turn out in a way that you cannot help, then you may say that God is sufficient for you'.

This is the main point made by the Prophet here, which requires that a person does all that he or she can themselves, and only then seeks God's help. In this regard, the Prophet directed his followers to shut the doors of their homes at night, mentioning God's name, and also to cover their food utensils and containers at night. It is not sufficient that one mentions God's name or says that one places one's trust in God, leaving the door open, or the food containers uncovered. One must take all precautions first then place one's trust in God. If a burglar comes in when one has left the door open, that is the homeowner's fault. But should he close the door and trust to God, God will protect him, if He so pleases.

When a person takes all precautions and prays to God for whatever purpose he wishes, then God will answer his prayers in the way we have explained. However, he must remember that all matters are left to God to determine as He pleases. Thus, if the supplicant's wishes are granted, then this is by God's grace. If they are not, then this is God's choice, and it is better than his own choice for himself. One must never attach too high importance to destiny so as to neglect taking necessary measures and precautions. One must remember that taking such measures is part of what is required by God. One has to follow the way shown by God's messenger (peace be upon him). He was exemplary in putting all his trust in God, yet he never neglected to take all necessary measures and precautions. This is the proper way for a believer in God.

718. 'Ā'ishah reports that the Prophet was asked: 'Which type of worship is best?' He said: 'A prayer for oneself'.[506]

This *ḥadīth* reflects the Prophet's insight into human feelings. It is only natural that when a human being addresses a supplication to God that he or she should start with themselves, and that they should first seek God's help in matters relating to their immediate needs in this present world. When a prayer is so concerned, it expresses a felt need. This ensures that the supplicant is earnest in appealing for God's help. When this is followed by a prayer for happiness in the Hereafter, it is also sincere and likely to be answered.

It is in this light that we should understand the Prophet's practice reported in the following *ḥadīth*: 'Whenever the Prophet mentioned someone else in his prayers, he would start by praying for himself'.[507] These two *ḥadīths* provide a perfect reply to those who claim that a supplication is better and more rewarding when it is confined to glorification of God and a prayer for the Muslim community as a whole, and that it is better not to pray for oneself. This is contrary to human nature, and Islam is a religion that always takes into account natural feelings, desires and aspirations.

In any situation where something good or harmful is expected, one thinks of oneself, trying to get a share of what is good and seeking to ensure that one is spared what is harmful. When we address our prayers to God, believing that He is able to accomplish anything He wants, we will always harbour a desire to be granted something of the good things He bestows. A supplication for ourselves will answer that aspiration. Starting with such a prayer for ourselves ensures that the next prayer we address on behalf of others is also made with the most sincere of feelings.

However, whatever prayer we address to God, we must always ensure that our faith in God is pure, untainted by any feelings of hypocrisy, pride or high reputation. The Prophet tells us that such feelings constitute a subtle form of idolatry.

---

506. Related by al-Ḥākim.
507. Related by Muslim and al-Tirmidhi.

719. Ma'qil ibn Yasār reports: 'I went with Abu Bakr al-Ṣiddīq to the Prophet (peace be upon him). He said: "Abu Bakr, idolatry in your minds is more subtle than the sound of an ant as it walks". Abu Bakr said: "Does not idolatry mean only the association of partners with God?" The Prophet said: "By Him Who holds my soul in His hand, idolatry in your minds is more subtle than the sound of an ant as it walks. Shall I tell you something to say so as to remove its great and small forms? Say: My Lord, I seek refuge with You against knowingly associating partners with You and appeal for Your forgiveness of what I may unknowingly do".' [*Allāhumma inni a'ūdh bika an ushrika bika wa ana a'lam, wa astaghfiruka lima la a'lam.*]

Subtle idolatry includes hypocrisy, seeking high reputation, arrogance, pride, etc. Such characteristics set in the front of one's mind certain considerations to which one attaches great importance. One hopes to gain through them something that is so dear that one is prepared to disregard God's orders in order to achieve it. This is akin to worshipping such goals. The only way to eradicate these vices from oneself is by knowing one's real position. Such knowledge tells us that whatever goodness we have comes from God. Without God's grace we could not have refined our good characteristics, and without His guidance, we could not have trodden a virtuous path, or acquired wealth, etc. This is what we need to realise in order to be good believers.

When we attribute some causes of our success or failure to people, forgetting that all matters belong to God and happen only by His will, we risk having something of idolatry in our attitude. Such action may be one of *shirk* [i.e. associating partners with God], but the person so doing it is genuinely ignorant of this. If he refrains from it immediately, i.e. as soon as he realises the fact, then he has done all he must do and no blame is attached to him. If he is told that his action is highly censurable and he does not take the necessary steps to learn the fact and correct his behaviour, he is at fault and may incur God's punishment.

Our Lord, we appeal to You to guide us to the right path so that we may entertain no thoughts of anything that is contrary to pure belief in Your oneness and Your sovereignty over the whole universe.

We seek refuge with You against knowingly associating partners with You, and we seek your forgiveness of what we may do unknowingly. You are our only Lord.

Supplication in different climatic conditions

The Prophet's supplication encompassed every pleasant or unpleasant situation. This is an indication of total faith in God, linking every event in the universe and in our own world, as well as all our feelings and thinking to God, the Creator and controller of man and the universe. This shows the degree of faith the Prophet had; the thought of God's control of the universe and that everything takes place only by His will was never away from his mind. Hence, he prayed for anything that brings benefit and for protection from anything that causes harm to himself or his community. The Prophet's behaviour is a model for us to emulate. God tells us in the Qur'an that we should take the Prophet as the example to follow, whether this relates to religious practice or not. By following such an example we are sure to benefit in both our present life in this world and in our life to come.

An important aspect of such connection is the change in weather patterns. Such changes occur every day and at different times. Whether sunshine gives way to cloudy and rainy weather, or the day brightens up after a gloomy start, changes are frequent and most people pay little attention to what they mean. But the Prophet teaches us that they are signs of God's power and control over the universe. Hence, we find the Prophet addressing a prayer at every dramatic change of weather, to link in the Muslims' minds the operation of natural forces to the overall power of God and His will.

720. Anas reports: 'When strong winds started to blow, the Prophet would say: "My Lord, I request You to give me of the best that this wind has been sent for, and I seek shelter with You from the worst it has been sent for".'

[*Allāhumma inni as'aluk min khayr ma ursilat bih, wa a'ūdh bika min sharri ma ursilat bih.*]

In this supplication the Prophet reminds us that wind may produce very beneficial results but may also wreak havoc and destruction. Therefore, he prays for the best and seeks protection against the worst.

721. Salamah reports that when wind became very strong, the Prophet used to say: 'My Lord, let it bring fertility and not be a barren wind'.[508]

[*Allāhumma lāqiḥan la ʿaqīma.*]

The Prophet mentions a particular aspect of what wind does, and he prays to God to make the blowing wind one that drives clouds bearing rain, not one that carries no water or benefit for mankind or other creatures. Apparently the Prophet said this prayer several times in different versions. Al-Shāfiʿi relates on Ibn ʿAbbās's authority that whenever wind blew, the Prophet sat on his knees and prayed: 'My Lord, make it a wind of mercy, not a wind of punishment'. This refers to the fact that some past communities were destroyed by wind when they adamantly refused the guidance given them by their prophets.

Because wind can be highly destructive, people often harbour fears of it, particularly when it becomes of gale or hurricane force. Hence, some people speak of it in abusive terms. The Prophet warned against this:

722. (*Athar* 166) Ubay said: 'Do not curse wind. Should you see of it what you dislike, say: Our Lord, we request You to give us the good things of this wind and the good that it brings about and we seek shelter with You from the evil of this wind and the evil it has been sent for'.[509]

[*Allāhumma nas'aluk khayr hādhihi al-rīḥ wa khayr ma fiha wa naʿūdh bika min sharri hādhihi al-rīḥ wa sharri ma ursilat bih.*]

723. Abu Hurayrah reports that the Prophet said: 'Wind is an aspect of God's mercy: it may bring mercy and it may bring

508. Related by Ibn Ḥibbān.

509. Related by Aḥmad, al-Tirmidhi and al-Ḥākim.

punishment. Do not curse it, but ask God for the good it brings and seek shelter with Him from its evil'.[510]

Other weather phenomena inviting supplication include thunder and thunderbolts:

724. 'Abdullāh ibn 'Umar reports that whenever the Prophet heard thunder or a thunderbolt he said: 'Our Lord, do not kill us by Your thunderbolt, and do not destroy us by Your punishment. Save us from all that'.

[*Allāhumma la taqtulna bi ṣa'qik, wa la tuhlikna bi 'adhābik, wa 'āfina qabl dhālik.*]

In this supplication, the Prophet makes clear that a thunderbolt carries a danger and he teaches us to appeal to God for protection from such.

In the Qur'an, thunder is described as glorifying God and praising Him. This is reflected in the prayers the Prophet's companions are known to have said. It should be mentioned here that when such a prayer is said by one of the Prophet's companions, it is assumed that they learnt it from the Prophet himself.

725. (*Athar* 167) 'Ikrimah said: 'When Ibn 'Abbās heard thunder, he used to say: "All glory belongs to the One Whom you glorify. Thunder is an angel who calls for rain just like a shepherd calling for his sheep".'

726. (*Athar* 168) 'Āmir ibn 'Abdullāh ibn al-Zubayr said: 'When 'Abdullāh ibn al-Zubayr heard thunder, he would stop speaking, but he would say: "All glory belongs to the God: '*The thunder and the angles extol His limitless glory and praises; all are in awe of Him.*'" (13: 13) He would then say: "This is a very strong warning to the people of the earth".'[511]

---

510. Related by Aḥmad, al-Nasā'ī, Abū Dāwūd, Ibn Mājah, al-Ḥākim Ibn Ḥibbān and Abu 'Awānah.

511. Related by Mālik.

The Prophet used to teach his companions what to say in their supplication and what different prayers meant. For example, the Prophet taught his companions to pray for good health and safety from affliction in all its physical and non-physical aspects:

727. Abu Bakr said after the Prophet had passed away: 'Last year the Prophet (peace be upon him) was standing where I am standing now...' Abu Bakr wept; then he continued [quoting the Prophet]: 'Always be truthful: it goes hand in hand with piety and they are together in heaven. Beware of lying, as it goes hand in hand with sinful behaviour, and they are together in hell. Pray for good health, because, second to faith, no one has ever been given anything better than good health. Do not sever your ties, work against one another, envy or hate one another. Maintain your ties of brotherhood, servants of God'.[512]

Today, with our increased knowledge of disease and the importance of taking protective action to ensure good health, we can better appreciate the importance of this great favour granted by God. Therefore, it is not surprising that we find the Prophet placing strong emphasis on praying for good health and safety from all difficulties.

But the Prophet's teachings also included how to pray and how we should understand what we pray for:

728. Muʿādh ibn Jabal reports: 'The Prophet (peace be upon him) passed by a man who said [in his supplication]: "My Lord, I request You to grant me perfect bounty". The Prophet said: "Do you know what the perfect bounty is? Perfect bounty is to be admitted into heaven and to be saved from the Fire". He then passed by a man who said: "My Lord, grant me patient perseverance". He said to him: "You have prayed to Your Lord for affliction; now pray to Him for wellbeing". He also passed by a man who said: "My Lord, the Lord of majesty and generosity". He said to him: "Now, put your request".'[513]

---

512. Related by Aḥmad, al-Tirmidhi, Ibn Mājah and Ibn Ḥibbān.
513. Related by Aḥmad and al-Tirmidhi.

To the first person the Prophet gave the exact meaning of his prayer for perfect bounty, telling him that only when one is admitted to heaven is one given such perfection of favours. This is the ultimate goal of every believer. Hence, it signifies the true meaning of perfect favours. To the second man, the Prophet gave a lesson in what to ask for. When he requested that God give him perseverance, his request implied that he should have difficult tests requiring patience and perseverance so as to endure and pass. Hence, the Prophet told the man to add a prayer for wellbeing. This would ensure that he passeed successfully. When the third man appealed to God by His majesty and generosity, the Prophet told him that such an appeal is always accepted and he should make a specific request. In some versions of this *ḥadīth* an addition is given, quoting the Prophet as saying to this third man: 'Now put your request, for your prayer has been accepted'.

It should be made clear that when we pray to God, we should always be clear in our minds that God does not shut the door in anyone's face. Indeed, He accepts and answers every sincere prayer. Blessed is His name and abundant is His grace.

729. Al-ʿAbbās ibn ʿAbd al-Muṭṭalib reports: 'I said: "Messenger of God, teach me something to pray to God for." He said: "'Abbās, pray to God to grant you wellbeing." I tarried a short while then came and said: "Messenger of God, teach me something to pray to God for". He said: "'Abbās, God's Messenger's uncle, pray to God to grant you wellbeing in this life and in the life to come".'[514]

Perhaps nothing combines the best of both worlds better than wellbeing in this life and in the life to come, as the teacher of all goodness, Prophet Muhammad (peace be upon him) taught his uncle.

---

514. Related by al-Tirmidhi.

Praying for hardship

Some people think that they do not do well enough to earn God's pleasure or that they do not deserve to be treated with compassion on the Day of Judgement. If they happen to find it difficult to do some good deeds which earn rich reward from God, then they think themselves really unfortunate. They want to have what they think to be a sure way of securing a place in heaven. They examine the areas of actions and attitudes praised in the Qur'an and the Sunnah as exemplary and sure to bring rich reward from God, and they find among them the quality of perseverance. They think that this is something which they can try to attain. So, they pray to God to put them through difficulties so that they persevere and earn His reward.

730. Anas reports: 'A man said in the Prophet's presence: "My Lord, You have not given me plenty of money to give away in *ṣadaqah* [i.e. charity], so test me with an affliction that brings me reward". The Prophet said to him: "Limitless is God in His glory. You cannot endure that. You better say: *My Lord, grant us what is good in this world and what is good in the life to come and protect us from the torment of the Fire*" (2:201).'

731. Anas reports: 'The Prophet visited a man who was very ill, looking like a chick whose feathering had been plucked. The Prophet said to him: "Pray to God for something, or make a request of Him". The man said: "My Lord, whatever punishment You will inflict on me in the Hereafter, hasten it and inflict it on me in this present life". The Prophet said to him: "Limitless is God in His glory. You cannot endure that. You better say: My Lord, grant us what is good in this world and what is good in the life to come and protect us from the torment of the Fire". He prayed for him and God, the Mighty and Exalted, cured him'.[515]

These two *ḥadīths* speak of two of the Prophet's companions having the same thought of going through some trial in this world in order

515. Related by Muslim and al-Tirmidhi.

to enhance their position in the Hereafter. The first wanted to increase his reward for good deeds, but he had no money to donate to charity, and he thought that the best way for him was to endure some hard difficulties with patience. The other thought of enduring God's punishment in this life so as to be clean and pure of sin when he meets his Lord in the Hereafter. The Prophet pointed out to them that this is a wrong way of thinking.

First of all, such a test is bound to be very hard. The man in the second *ḥadīth* looked very poorly, suffering great pain. Since human beings have little patience, the possibility of showing lack of patience or protesting against God's trial is always there. It is wrong to imagine ourselves able to maintain the same degree of contentment when we are facing a hard trial. When the Prophet realised what the two men prayed for, he told them that they would not be able to endure what they prayed for. And when a trial is unendurable, it can easily lead a person to do wrong. This would put the person concerned in a position that may incur God's punishment in the Hereafter. This would be the worst result of all, because misery would be his lot in both this life and in the life to come.

Hence the Prophet instructed both men to say the same prayer, appealing to God to grant them what is good in this life, and what is good in the life to come. Praying in this way indicates one's trust in God's generosity and kindness. It is only He that may grant us what brings us happiness and a goodly life in this world as well as enabling us to use these to enhance our position in the Hereafter. The person who complained of not having money to give away in charity may be given such money if he prayed in the way the Prophet taught. Then he would be able to enjoy the comforts that wealth brings and earn better reward when he spends some of it helping the poor and financing useful projects.

The man in the second *ḥadīth* prayed for hastening his punishment. He would have been better advised to pray for God's forgiveness. In fact, his prayer tells of his fear of God's punishment in the Hereafter, but shows how little trust he has in God's forgiveness, when God repeatedly mentions that He is Forgiving, Merciful and Compassionate. It is far better for us to pray to Him for His mercy, rather than seek His punishment. The proper Islamic attitude is that one should never wish for hardship, but when hardship comes one's way, one should endure it with patience.

The Prophet, who taught us every good thing, also teaches us to seek God's protection from hard trials.

732. (*Athar* 169) 'Abdullāh ibn 'Amr said: 'A man may say, "My Lord, I seek shelter with You from severe affliction", and stop. If he says this, he should add, "except an affliction that brings elevation".'

733. Abu Hurayrah reports: 'The Prophet (peace be upon him) used to seek God's shelter from a burdensome trial, ending up in wretchedness, evil results and the gloating of enemies'.[516]

The Prophet teaches us to pray to be spared a trial that saps one's strength. This is a very apt description, because when a trial lasts long or seems unending, it often leads to depression, which takes away one's strength. Distress can also be very oppressive, particularly when it continues for a long time. It smothers one's faculties, blurs one's vision causing one to make mistakes, and makes life truly miserable. However, the first of these two *ḥadīths* makes an exception if the hardship brings the one afflicted by it elevated status which ensures that he gets a higher position in heaven due to his patient perseverance in adversity.

The other two situations the Prophet includes in his prayer for God's protection are from misfortune that may befall us, giving pleasure and gratification to our enemies and exercising wrong judgement. These have been explained under *ḥadīth* Number 444.

734. Abu Nawfal ibn Abu 'Aqrab Khuwaylid ibn Bujayr said that his father asked the Prophet (peace be upon him) about [voluntary] fasting. The Prophet said: 'Fast one day every month'. I said: 'May my parents be sacrificed for you. Give me more'. He said: 'Give me more! Give me more! Fast two days every month'. I said: 'May my parents be sacrificed for you. Give me

516. Related by al-Bukhari and Muslim.

more. I feel strong.' He said: 'I feel strong! I feel strong!' He was then silent for a while and I thought he would not give any more. He then said: 'Fast three days every month'.[517]

Some people insist on doing much of voluntary worship, hoping that it will enhance their position on the Day of Judgement. No doubt voluntary worship which is done purely for God's sake, not to show off or to boast about, will be generously rewarded by God. However, the Prophet always advised a moderate approach so that we do not find it too hard when our circumstances change.

Fasting is a hard task, because it involves refraining from what a person needs most. Therefore, the Prophet advised an easy approach. In this *ḥadīth*, the Prophet advised his questioner to fast no more than three days a month, despite his insistence. The Prophet repeated his words to check the man's enthusiasm. In effect, he made three days a month a high standard because God rewards a good deed by at least ten times its value. Therefore, three days are given the reward of fasting a whole month.

Any three days a person may choose are good enough, although the three middle days, 13, 14 and 15 of a lunar month are preferred because their nights are bright with the full moon.

517. Related by al-Nasā'ī.

36

On Backbiting

735. Jābir ibn 'Abdullāh reports: 'We were with God's Messenger (peace be upon him) when a terrible, foul stench was sensed. The Prophet said: "Do you know what stench is this? It is the smell of people who backbite believers".'[518]

736. Jābir said: 'A foul-smelling wind was blowing during God's Messenger's lifetime. He said: "Some hypocrites have been backbiting some Muslims, and this smell has spread as a result".'[519]

THESE TWO *ḤADĪTHS* paint a vivid picture as they describe wind as having a repulsive smell. When everyone is nauseated and disgusted, the Prophet tells them the nature of this wind. It is nothing like going

---

518. Related by Aḥmad.
519. Related by Aḥmad and Abu 'Awānah.

over any foul smelling stuff or passing an area where sewage is collected for treatment. Nor does it pass over factories that produce foul smelling gases or discharge nasty effluent. It is caused by the words uttered by certain people.

We are all aware words do not carry any smell given they lack physical substance. Yet the Prophet clearly says, in authentic *ḥadīths*, that the foul smell people experienced was as a result of backbiting. The second *ḥadīth* specifies that the offenders were hypocrites backbiting Muslim believers.

This picture fills us with disgust at those who find no better pastime than speaking ill of others in their absence, and for no other reason than that they have declared their belief in God and His messenger. It is universally agreed that backbiting is a vice, because it makes fun at others' expense in their absence, when they cannot defend themselves. Yet many people so indulge in backbiting, giving little heed to what religion or moral values say about such behaviour. People describe their conversation when they mention others in an unpleasant way as gossip, making little of its effect. They think that since the person concerned is absent, he or she will not know what was said, and will not be hurt. How wrong! For their action has a very negative effect on themselves, those who are listening to them, and the person about whom they are speaking.

The backbiter himself thinks little of what he does, becomes accustomed to the same, and so allows this noxious habit to develop. Furthermore, when it is known that a person is a habitual backbiter, people try to dissociate themselves from him, realizing that just as he speaks ill of other people to them, so will he speak ill of them to others. Those who listen to a habitual backbiter, laughing at his jokes about others, will also be adversely affected. They will incur God's displeasure by so listening, and they will think little of the seriousness of their action. They will feel that associating with such a person has no negative effect even though it impairs their vision, tending to make such action acceptable. The effect on the person being spoken of in his or her absence is too clear to need discussion.

Moreover, backbiting is a type of treachery and deception, because neither the backbiter nor his audience cherish the prospect of the person who is being talked about making a sudden appearance. They will immediately stop the conversation, feeling embarrassed, and worried lest that person has overheard them speaking or laughing.

Scholars define backbiting as someone saying something unpleasant about someone else in their absence, whether it relates to their physical appearance, faith, career, personal traits, property, parents, children, spouses, servants, clothes, movements, facial expressions, and the like. Backbiting may take the form of verbal speech, writing, movement, indication, a wink or other ways of communicating something that is readily understood by others. It also includes imitating someone, such as the way he or she talks, walks, eats or does other things. In fact some scholars consider this type of imitation as one of the worse types of backbiting because it exaggerates faults, making them identifiable. Thus, if the subject of backbiting is lame and someone imitates his walk to make others laugh, the next time they see that person they look more attentively at his gait to make sure of what was shown them by way of imitation. They may laugh in private, remembering the imitation.

If one refers vaguely to another when speaking ill of him and listeners identify that person easily, the reference is one of backbiting, despite the fact that the person concerned has not been mentioned by name. The point here is that all those present understand to whom the reference is made. On the other hand, if one makes remarks generally, without specifying a person or a group, and listeners understand that what is being criticised is a certain behaviour or action, not a person or a group, then this is not backbiting. Similarly, if the behaviour is mentioned in general terms, but the speaker means only to advise his listeners to refrain from it, then this is a case of giving advice, not backbiting.

It should be pointed out that in certain situations it is appropriate to point out some of a person's faults. One such situation might be when you are asked about the character of a friend of yours by the family of a woman to whom he has proposed. They want to know his character before they agree to the proposal. In this situation, it is perfectly permissible to give them an honest assessment of his character, pointing out faults that may significantly influence their decision for or against such a marriage. The same applies when testimony is required for financial or commercial transactions. If your friend has proposed to someone that they should form a business partnership, and you are asked what you know of your friend's honesty and integrity, you should give an honest assessment, whether this happens to be favourable or not.

Other situations where backbiting is permissible include explaining a situation which is the subject of complaint, so as to ensure that wrongdoing is removed. The same applies to warning someone against a source of evil or foul play, warning against any type of wrongdoing, pointing out the faults of reporters and witnesses so that their reports and testimonies may be properly examined and evaluated. Similarly, it is permissible to mention injustice perpetrated by someone to those in authority so that the latter may be able to remove that injustice. In short, any proper objective that aims to do something right may be a cause of exemption from backbiting.

The Prophet not only teaches us what actions or faults to avoid; he also teaches us what to do when such actions or faults are done in our presence. Hence the question: what should we do when a person sitting with us starts to backbite others?

737. (*Athar* 170) 'Abdullāh ibn Mas'ūd said: 'Whoever speaks in defence of a believer when he is being backbitten in his presence will be well rewarded for his action in this life and in the life to come; and whoever refrains from defending a believer being backbitten in his presence will have a foul recompense in this life and in the life to come. No one eats anything worse than backbiting a believer: if he says something he knows to be true, that is backbiting and if he says something which he does not know to be true, that is malice'.

This *ḥadīth* makes it clear that a believer should support his brother believer when he is being spoken ill of in his absence. The same applies to women believers. So, when any of us hears a fellow Muslim being the subject of backbiting, he or she should support that believer, and speak out in his or her defence. This is the only attitude acceptable to God, and it is the one which earns reward from Him. To keep quiet, or to share in the enormity being committed by tacit approval or by laughing at the expense of the absent person is something that incurs

God's displeasure and subjects the perpetrator to an evil recompense in this life and in the life to come.

Describing the ghastliness of backbiting, the *ḥadīth* makes it clear that whether the fault being mentioned is true or not, mentioning it to others in a person's absence is indeed bad. If it is true, then that is backbiting, and if it is not true, it is malice. Neither is a quality that a believer should have.

738. Jābir ibn ʿAbdullāh reports: 'We were with God's Messenger (peace be upon him) when he came upon two graves whose dwellers were suffering torment. He said: "They are punished for something that is not very serious; rather, it is. One of them was given to backbiting and the other did not cleanse himself from urine". He then asked for one or two fresh palm-stalks, and he broke them. He ordered that each be planted on a grave. God's Messenger then said: "This will lessen their punishment as long as the palm-stalk remains moist – or he said, as long as they have not become dry".'[520]

The Prophet first said that the sins which these dead people were suffering torment for were not very serious, but then immediately added that they were. Such offences do not rank in the same degree as associating partners with God, denying His message, murder or undutifulness to parents. Yet they are nonetheless serious because of their consequences. Purification is the first requirement for the validity of prayer, and it starts with cleansing oneself from discharges through one's private parts. If a person does not cleanse himself from urine, his prayer – if he prays – is invalid. Hence, it is very serious.

Backbiting may not be that serious when one indulges in it once in a while, but if it becomes a habit, it becomes very serious; it ruins social relations and creates hatred within the community.

Compassionate as he always was, the Prophet made this gesture of planting two moist palm-stalks on the graves of these two people, saying that this would lessen their torment as long as they did not

---

520. Related by Aḥmad and al-Tabarani with a different chain of transmission that gives Abu Bakrah as the Prophet's companion relating this *ḥadīth*.

become dry. There is nothing special about palm-stalks or other plants that lessens torment. Rather, it is that the Prophet planted these with his blessed hand that served as an appeal to God to reduce their trouble.

Other *ḥadīths* speak of the Prophet performing this gesture, and scholars give different views on whether they are all related to one incident or two similar incidents. Whatever is the case, the Prophet's action speaks of his compassion, and his words should serve as warning against these two sins.

As already mentioned, people often think lightly of backbiting, yet the offence is portrayed in the Qur'an and the *ḥadīth* above in a most foul way. God says: '*Do not backbite one another. Would any of you like to eat the flesh of his dead brother? Surely you would loathe it*'. (49: 12) However, the image is delineated more horribly in the following *ḥadīths*:

739. (*Athar* 171) 'Abdullāh ibn 'Amr was walking with some of his friends when they passed by a swollen dead mule. He said to them: 'By God, it is better for anyone to eat this, filling his belly, than to eat the flesh of a Muslim [i.e. backbite him]'.

740. Abu Hurayrah reports: 'Mā'iz ibn Mālik al-Aslami came to the Prophet [repeatedly confessing adultery] and the Prophet ordered him to be stoned after the fourth confession. The Prophet and a number of his companions later passed by his grave, and one of them said [to his friend], "This dead person came to the Prophet several times, and he told him to go away, [but he continued] until he was killed like a dog". The Prophet did not say anything until he passed by a dead donkey whose leg was hanging. He said to them: "Eat of this!" They said: "[Are we to eat] of the corpse of a dead donkey, Messenger of God?" He said: "What you have said about your brother a short while ago is worse than this. By Him Who holds Muhammad's soul in His hand, he swims in a river in heaven".'[521]

---

521. Related by al-Bukhari and al-Nasā'ī.

In both *ḥadīths* backbiting, particularly of a dead person, is given an image drawn on its description in the Qur'anic verse quoted. In the first *ḥadīth*, 'Abdullāh ibn 'Amr uses the occasion to give clear advice to his companions. In the second, the Prophet waits until something offers itself to drive a point home. When he saw the dead donkey, he called the person backbiting a dead man and the one who was listening to him over and told them both to eat of it. No one would eat such foul stuff, particularly when the donkey had been dead for some time that its corpse had swollen to the extent that its leg was hoisted high. When they expressed their abhorrence, he told them that the way they had spoken about a dead believer was worse than eating such foul meat. This was sufficient to tell both people and all Muslims how abhorrent backbiting is, even when the subject is a dead man.

This *ḥadīth* tells us that even when the dead person has committed a cardinal sin, adultery in this case, he may be pardoned. In fact, Māʿiz insisted on the punishment being inflicted on him, after he had repented of his deed. When he was punished, he was absolved of his sin. This is an important principle in Islamic teachings. Therefore, his sin is not counted against him. In fact, his repentance is credited to him and he is rewarded for it. His other actions are also rewarded. Hence, the Prophet mentions that he is certain to be in heaven. In Islam, every sin may be forgiven, except associating partners with God.

We also note from this *ḥadīth* that the man who talked did not say anything untrue, except perhaps the way he described his death, saying that he was killed like a dog. Moreover, the man about whom he was speaking was dead and he would not be affected by anything said about him. Yet the Prophet made it absolutely clear that his death did not mean that he may be spoken ill of without being defended. If we compare this with Western laws which punish for libel against living people but not against those who are dead, we realise how superior Islamic law is.

It is also worthwhile reminding ourselves of Māʿiz's story, a companion of the Prophet who admitted adultery. This was a voluntary confession. The Prophet gave him chance after chance to recant his admission, pointing out that he might have done only what is preliminary to sexual intercourse, such as kissing or cuddling, but he insisted time after time that he had committed adultery. The Prophet then made sure that he was of sound mind, and that he had no mental condition. When it was clear that the man's confession was absolutely true, the Prophet had no option but to inflict punishment. This, as already pointed out, absolved him of his sin. The way was, then, open for him to go to heaven, and indeed he was going there as the Prophet clearly indicated.

741. ʿUbādah ibn al-Walīd ibn ʿUbādah ibn al-Ṣāmit said: 'My father and I went out when I was a young man. We met an old man wearing one striped robe and a Yemeni robe [called maʿāfiri], and his slave was likewise wearing a striped robe and a Yemeni robe. I said to him: "Uncle, why do you not take your servant's striped robe and give him your Yemeni robe? You would be wearing a suit and he a suit". He asked my father: "Is this your son?" My father said: "Yes". He wiped my head and said: "My Lord, bless him. Nephew, I heard the Prophet as he said: 'Feed them from the food you eat and clothe them from what you wear. I prefer to lose some of the comfort of this world than that he should take away some of my good actions on the Day of Judgement". I asked my father who the man was and he said: "Abu al-Yasar, Kaʿb ibn ʿAmr".'[522]

This *ḥadīth* is very similar to Numbers 187 and 194, and it is discussed under the latter.

---

522. Related by Muslim and Ibn Mājah.

37

Exemplary Hospitality

WHEN WE DISCUSS a social value that is encouraged by Islam, we look to how it was implemented by the first Muslim community of the Prophet's companions. That community was moulded under the direct supervision of the Prophet. He was keen to strengthen and consolidate every social aspect that tended to bring the Muslim community together. His companions understood this, and were able to mould their community into a unit with strong brotherly ties. They also passed this closely-knit relationship on to the following generations.

742. (*Athar* 172) Muhammad ibn Ziyād reports: 'I witnessed the early generations [of Muslims] when they lived with their families in the same house. It may have happened that a guest was received by one of them. Another resident might have had his saucepan on the stove, [cooking his meal]. The guest's host would take it to serve the food to his guest. The owner of the food came back to find his saucepan gone. He would ask who

had taken the saucepan? The host would tell him: "We have taken it for our guest". He would say: "May God bless it for you", or something to that effect. They would do the same if they were baking bread. They lived with only walls made of canes and reeds separating them'.

Such neighbourly cooperation is something that any community may dream about without being able to fulfil except in small measure. Yet it was the daily practice in that early Muslim community. The host did not hesitate to serve his neighbour's food to his guest, knowing that his neighbour would be very happy to help, even if that were the only food he had for the day. He and his family would have to make do with whatever else they might have had. With such cooperation everyone felt reassured that should anything happen to them, his family and children would be well looked after by his neighbours.

Preferring a guest to oneself was normal habit among Muslims. In fact, it is mentioned in the Qur'an, but the statement is left more general than kindness to a guest. Thus the Qur'anic reference speaks of a quality that is inherent in true Muslims. They are ready with their kindly help whenever it is needed: '*They rather give others preference over themselves, even though poverty be their own lot*'. (59: 9) The verse speaks of the Anṣār, the Prophet's companions from Madinah who received their Makkan brethren and shared all their resources with them. But their action, and the Qur'anic praise it earned, became the model to follow by succeeding Muslim generations.

743. Abu Hurayrah reports: 'A man came to the Prophet and the Prophet sent to his wives [checking what they had]. They said that they had nothing but water. The Prophet said to his companions: "Who will be this man's host tonight?" A man from the Anṣār said: "I will". He took the man home and said to his wife: "Be hospitable to God's Messenger's guest". She said: "We have nothing other than our children's supper". He said: "Prepare your food and get your lantern ready, and put your children to sleep if they want their supper". She did as he said, then she stood up as if to move the lantern, but she put it out [leaving the place in darkness]. Both man and wife pretended that they

were eating with their guest, but they did not touch the food and slept that night without eating. In the morning the Anṣāri man went to the Prophet who said to him: "God is pleased with what you two have done". Then God revealed the verse that says: "*They give them preference over themselves, even though they are in want. Those who are saved from their own greed are truly successful*".'[523] (59: 9)

We note that the Anṣāri man, Abu Ṭalḥah, volunteered to take the Prophet's guest knowing that he had very little food at home, but he also realised that nothing much was expected. It is clear that the whole community was going through hard times. The man himself was starving, and the Prophet's homes were without food. Hence, anyone who had what was sufficient for his family was considered as being in a good situation. However, on arrival at home, Abu Ṭalḥah discovered that his position was not very rosy. His wife told him that they had nothing other than what would serve to give their children their supper. He dealt with the situation in a most generous way, telling his wife to prepare the food and put the children to sleep. She was as hospitable as her husband. We see her putting the light out so that the guest would eat while she and her husband would not. Thus, the whole family slept hungry that night in order to be hospitable to their guest.

The man received his reward immediately when the Prophet told him that God was pleased with what he and his wife did. Nothing is more precious to a true believer than knowing that his action was pleasing to God. Such action is certain to bring rich reward, because God will definitely reward anything done for His sake.

We might wonder here at depriving children of their supper so as to serve it to a guest. The Prophet tells us that the first claim is that of one's dependents. The children in this case would not suffer anything if they slept without having their supper. They would have something to eat in the morning. Moreover, hospitality to a starving guest is a duty, while giving food to the children in this case was not a duty, because they were less in need of food. They had eaten their lunch and might have had something afterwards.

---

523. Related by al-Bukhari.

Duration of hospitality

744. Abu Shurayḥ al-Khuzāʿi said: 'I was listening with my ears and looking with my eyes when the Prophet spoke and said: "Whoever believes in God and the Last Day should be generous towards his neighbour. Whoever believes in God and the Last Day should be generous in his gift to his guest". [People] asked: "What is his gift, Messenger of God?" He said: "One night and one day. Hospitality is for three days. After that, it is an act of charity for the guest. Whoever believes in God and the Last Day should speak well or remain silent".'[524]

745. Abu Hurayrah reports that the Prophet said: 'Hospitality is for three days. What is offered after that is an act of charity'.[525]

The first of these two *ḥadīths* is highly authentic while the second states only a part of the first. The first *ḥadīth* sets out certain principles of social ties, linking them all to the basic principles of faith, which are the beliefs in God's oneness and in the Day of Judgement. This means that people who pay no heed to these principles of kindness to neighbours and guests, and saying only what is good and beneficial, demonstrate that their belief is questionable.

The first principle is to be generous towards one's neighbours. Islam stresses the importance of such kind treatment in a number of *ḥadīths* that we have fully discussed earlier.

The second area of proper Islamic social ties is that of hospitality to one's guests. It makes such hospitality an essential trait intertwined with belief in God and the Day of Judgement. Relating it to faith in this way indicates that such hospitality will be rewarded by God. The Prophet begins by speaking about generosity by the host towards his guest when he is at the point of departure to continue his journey or to return home. This is something that modern societies have forgotten about, but here the Prophet mentions it clearly and his audience ask him for clarification of this gift. He says that it should be sufficient for

524. Related in all six authentic anthologies.
525. Related by Aḥmad and Ibn Ḥibbān.

a day and a night. We understand that he means that the host should give the departing guest some food and drink to meet his needs for twenty-four hours, so that he may continue his travels without worry of hunger and thirst. Any traveller, even in the desert, should be able to find a place to get what he needs within a day of starting out. Thus, the gift ensures his wellbeing until his next stop.

The Prophet then states the duration of hospitality extended to one's guest. It is for three days, during which time the guest will have relaxed and rested sufficiently to continue his journey or attend to his business. If the guest stays longer and the host continues to be hospitable, this becomes an act of charity, or *ṣadaqah* that earns good reward from God.

Putting the matter in this way, the Prophet gives a clear hint to guests that they must not make themselves a burden on their hosts. People do not like to be given charity if they have the means to look after themselves. Hence, by saying that after three days what the guest receives is charity, the indication is that he should not stay longer than three days.

746. Abu Shurayḥ al-Kaʿbi reports that the Prophet said: 'Whoever believes in God and the Last Day should speak well or remain silent. Whoever believes in God and the Last Day should be generous in his gift to his guest: one night and one day. It is not permissible for the guest to stay with his host to the point when it causes embarrassment'.[526]

This is a different version of *ḥadīth* Number 744 adding an important point that clearly defines the guest's responsibility. When a guest stays a long time with his hosts he may cause them trouble. They may have to take on extra duties in order to accommodate him and look after him. Or they may not find it easy to go to the extra expense to meet his needs. All this may mean that the host feels that his guest has become a burden and that it is embarrassing for him in one way or another. Alternatively, it may cause him to talk about his guest in an unpleasant way, which may become backbiting. A host may, for example, need to

---

526. Related by Aḥmad and al-Bukhari.

tell his wife to prepare new things for a guest that has overstayed his welcome. She might ask him whether the guest has indicated how long he intends to stay. This may trigger an expression of feeling troubled, which may be a criticism of the guest. Thus, the whole thing becomes a sour point. Hence, the Prophet made it clear that a guest should not stay on for long as he then becomes an embarrassment to his host.

Scholars agree that during the first night, a host should give his guest extra kindness, to make him feel that he is really welcome. This is natural, as most people and most cultures consider it highly commendable to provide one's guest on the first day with special, kindly treatment. On the next two days, scholars agree, the host need not go to any extra trouble. It is good hospitality to treat a guest as a member of one's family and serve him the same type of food and drink one normally provides for the family. This is proper hospitality. If one does more, willingly and without embarrassment, one earns God's reward for this. But when the three days of hospitality are over, and the guest stays on, anything given to the guest becomes an act of charity.

This distinction is important because people need to know what they are supposed to provide so that they do not fail to do what is expected of them and what they hope to earn God's reward for. Some people would be hard put to look after a guest for an extended period. Hence, the Prophet defines the limits when hospitality ends and charity begins.

So what about a situation where the people are inhospitable and travellers are in need of help? Can one expect a minimum amount of hospitality? This is very reasonable, particularly in small villages and desert areas where it is difficult to find anything to eat after the fall of darkness. It is to meet people's needs in such situations that the Prophet makes it clear that a minimum of hospitality is a duty.

747. Al-Miqdām Abu Karīmah al-Sāmi reports that the Prophet said: 'A guest's night is a duty incumbent on every Muslim. Should a person find [a guest] at his doorstep, hospitality becomes a debt he owes to him. He [i.e. the guest] may demand it if he wishes, or may forego it if he so prefers'.[527]

527. Related by Aḥmad, Abū Dāwūd, Ibn Majah, al-Darimi and al-Ḥākim.

Perhaps this *ḥadīth* is the clearest statement by the Prophet making hospitality an Islamic duty. Some scholars limit this duty to areas where a traveller cannot buy food for the night. Yet the Prophet's statement is general and does not call for such limitation. This is more appropriate because a traveller may not find it easy to look after himself on his first arrival in a town or a city. He may be too tired or may not have ready money to buy what he needs. Rather than allow a traveller to suffer lack of hospitality when he has had to contend with the hardship of travelling, the Prophet makes it clear that hospitality for the first night is a duty incumbent on all Muslims. Not only so, but he makes it a debt owed by the host to his guest. Needless to say, a debt must be settled, and the creditor can demand it when it falls due. Hence the Prophet gives further details stating that when a guest arrives at somebody's door, hospitality for one night is a duty on that person. The guest may demand it like a creditor demands the repayment of a loan. It is up to him to forego it, if he so wishes.

Now how does a guest demand his right to hospitality? In our modern world, this seems totally impractical. There is a hotel or a guest house in almost every locality, where people can pay for their food and lodging. Even if one has run out of cash, there are bank cheques and credit cards. So, things are easy for a traveller. But this is not the case everywhere. There are vast areas of populated land where such facilities are still in their very early days or even non-existent. If one can look after oneself in a place where one does not know anybody, all well and good. If one cannot, because the facilities are not there, or because one might have had a misfortune on the way, then one has to rely on people's hospitality. Thus, the Prophet's teachings provide a code which should be applied in order to ensure that nobody starves in a place where they are a stranger.

748. ʿUqbah ibn ʿĀmir reports that he said to the Prophet: 'Messenger of God, you send us on missions and we may stop at some people's quarters but they do not extend any hospitality to us. What do you advise in such a situation?' He said: 'If you stop at some people's quarters and you are offered the sort of

hospitality due to a guest, you should accept it. If they do not, then take from them what a guest is entitled to have by right.'[528]

This is a remarkable *ḥadīth* giving a guest who has not been shown any hospitality the right to take, even without permission, what is reasonably due to him as a guest. He does not start with that. He waits until he finds out whether his host is about to give him something to eat. If he does, then the guest should accept this without complaint or hesitation. In this case, he simply takes what he is given. But when the host is not so forthcoming, then he takes what he needs.

We note in the phraseology of this *ḥadīth* some important points. The Prophet does not refer to what may be taken by a guest who has been denied hospitality as 'a duty on the host'. Nor does he say to us, 'take what you are entitled to'. He puts it in a milder way, referring to it as 'what they ought to give'. Hospitality remains a kindness and every one ought to be hospitable. But people differ in nature and what a person is ready to give without being asked, another will deny even when asked. Hence the Prophet tells a denied guest to take what he thinks ought to be given to him. The Prophet does not tell him that this is his right or that he may take it by force. He puts him in the host's place so that he does not take more than the minimum needed.

Perhaps nothing makes a guest feel more welcome than for the host to be warm in his reception, and to ask his guest about his general welfare, and about his family. Moreover, when the host himself takes part in serving his guests, this adds to the warmth of his welcome.

749. Sahl ibn Saʿd said: 'Abu Usayd al-Sāʿidi invited the Prophet to attend his wedding. His wife, the bride, was the one who served them that day. She [later] said: 'Do you know what [drink] I prepared for the Prophet? I prepared some dates and put them overnight in a metal pot of water'[529].

528. Related by al-Bukhari, Muslim, Abu Dāwūd and al-Tirmidhi.
529. Related by al-Bukhari.

This *ḥadīth* suggests that the bride herself was the one to prepare what she intended to serve her guest, the Prophet. Needless to say, she would not have troubled herself if the guest was anyone other than the Prophet. She wanted to show how she loved having him attend her wedding. Not only so, but she was proud to have done, speaking about it later when the occasion arose. The fact that she prepared the date juice the night before tells of her excitement at having the Prophet present with other guests.

In al-Bukhari's *Ṣaḥīḥ* version of this *ḥadīth*, it is stated that 'no one prepared any food or served it to them except his wife', i.e. the bride herself. This shows that she was so keen on making the Prophet more than welcome, taking upon herself a task no bride takes on the night of her wedding. This is exemplary hospitality which people will be stretched to match.

750. Nu'aym ibn Qa'nab reports: I went to visit Abu Dharr, but I did not find him at home. I asked his wife: 'Where is Abu Dharr?' She said: 'He is attending to some household duties and he will not be long'. I sat down waiting. He came leading two camels, one tied to the back of the other, and each having a waterskin hanging from his neck. He took these off and came to me. I said to him: 'Abu Dharr, there is no one I love to meet more than you, yet none I dislike to meet more than you'. He said: 'Bless you. How can this be?' I said: 'I had buried a girl alive in the pre-Islamic days of ignorance, and I feared that you would say to me that my repentance would not be accepted and that there is no way out. Yet I hoped that you would say that my repentance would be accepted'. He said: 'Did you do that in pre-Islamic days?' I said: 'Yes'. He said: 'God has pardoned what was in the past'. Then he said to his wife to bring us some food, but she refused, and he asked her again but she refused. He kept asking her until they were shouting. Then he said to her: 'Well, women are just like what God's Messenger has said'. I asked him: 'What did God's Messenger say about them?' He said: 'A woman is like a rib; if you try to straighten it, you will break it, and if you try to appease her, there will remain in her some crookedness and what will help you through life'.

She went away and then brought a plate of food that looked like pigeons. He said to me: 'Have some food but do not worry about me, because I am fasting'. He then started praying, but he made his prayer in quick succession, and then turned to me and started eating. I said: 'Well, I never entertained any fear that you might lie to me'. He said: 'Bless you. I have not said a lie since I first saw you'. I said: 'Have you not said that you were fasting?' He replied: 'Yes, I have fasted three days this month, and I earned the month's reward, and now eating is permissible for me'.[530]

The reporter, Nuʿaym ibn Qaʿnab, was a well respected person in pre-Islamic days. When he came to see the Prophet for the first time, he brought with him the zakat due from him and his household. The Prophet was pleased with this and rubbed his face with his hand in a friendly gesture.

This report gives us several points. The first is that a person's sins committed prior to his becoming a Muslim are effaced by God once he declares his faith in God's oneness and in Muhammad's message, i.e. acceptance of Islam. This is so even when the sin is grave like killing one's own daughter, burying her alive, as used to be the practice in many parts of Arabia prior to Islam. Then we have the guest's puzzling statement that he both loved and hated to meet his host, hoping to receive reassurance that his sin would be forgiven and fearing the opposite. This is an indication of the sensitivity Islam cultivates in people's minds. They hope for reassurance that the wickedness of the past is erased. Abu Dharr gives his guest that reassurance, but then he is met with the woman's refusal to serve him. We are not told why she was so unwilling to extend hospitality, but we assume that it was because of what he said about burying his daughter alive. It is only to be expected that when a woman hears of such a crime against a helpless girl that she would not want to serve the perpetrator, even though what occurred was in his pre-Islamic days, and even though his repentance is evident from the way he talked to her husband. Eventually, however, she relents and serves him.

530. Related by Aḥmad, al-Nasāʾī and al-Dārimi.

Then we have Abu Dharr's strange behaviour. First he told his guest that he was fasting, and that he should eat as he pleased, without worrying about him. He then starts praying. Then he makes his prayer short and starts eating. In a way, this mirrors his guest's contradictory statement at the beginning. Apparently Abu Dharr wanted to give him something similar. Hence, he told him that he was fasting and then ate with him. Abu Dharr's explanation is very useful. He had fasted three days that month, which meant that he had earned the reward of fasting 30 days, or the whole month, on the basis of the rule that a good action is rewarded ten times its worth. So, in a sense, he was fasting because he had the reward of fasting, and he would eat because he did not fast on that particular day.

38

Miscellaneous

Supporting one's dependants

ISLAM OFTEN SETS a perspective which is totally different from what people have been used to. This enables Muslims to look from different angles and in different light at issues that have been well established in people's thinking. With the new light Islam sheds on them, they acquire new dimensions. When the matter is one of relationships and duties, the Islamic view may re-shape people's attitudes. Thus, what might have seemed a burden may become a task bringing pleasure, closer relations and stronger motivation.

751. Thawbān reports that the Prophet said: 'The best *dinār* a man spends is the one he spends on his family, the one he spends

on his companions for God's cause, and the one he spends on his mount [when using it] for God's cause'.[531]

Abu Qilābah, a narrator in the chain of transmission, said: 'He started with the family. None earns greater reward than a man spending on young children until God, the Mighty and Exalted, enables them to be independents'.

At face value, the *ḥadīth* makes all three purposes equal. Thus, the pursuit of jihad, which requires money, either to keep oneself in good shape or to buy one's equipment, or to donate to the war effort, or to get one's transport in good shape will earn generous reward from God, if He so wills. Similarly, spending one's money to support one's own family is a means to earn rich reward. However, the fact that the Prophet started with support for one's family suggests that this is the more rewarding expenditure.

This view is supported by a number of *ḥadīths*, all of which make support for one's family a highly rewarding action. Here, we are not speaking of the immediate reward one receives in having a happy family and loving wife and children, which is a very gratifying reward. We are speaking of the reward one receives from God on the Day of Resurrection. This is the best reward, because it is given when one needs it most to ensure safety from hell and admission into heaven.

752. Abu Mas'ūd al-Badri reports that the Prophet said: 'When anyone spends something on his family, dedicating his action to God, it counts as a *ṣadaqah*'.[532]

We need to explain here that the meaning which immediately springs to mind when using the term *ṣadaqah* is charity. Charity is rewarded to great extent by God. Hence the Prophet uses this term to indicate that the reward generated by such action is great. However, the term *ṣadaqah* is derived from a root that indicates truth and speaking the truth. In one *ḥadīth* the Prophet defines *ṣadaqah* as 'evidence of the

531. Related by Aḥmad, Muslim, al-Tirmidhi, Ibn Mājah, Ibn Ḥibbān and Abu 'Awānah. The *dinār* was the unit of gold currency, equivalent to ten silver *dirhams*.

532. Related by al-Bukhari, Muslim, al-Nasā'ī and al-Tirmidhi.

truth'. This is indeed true, because when one spends money to support others, seeking no return other than God's reward, he proves his faith in God. Similarly, when one supports his wife and children, intending his action purely for God's sake, he proves a willingness to fulfil the responsibility God has placed on him. Therefore, God, most generous and gracious as He is, will reward him for it.

Another *ḥadīth* gives us an order of priority for our spending.

753. Jābir reports: 'A man said: "Messenger of God, I have a *dinār*". The Prophet said: "Spend it on yourself". The man said: "I have another". The Prophet said to him: "Spend it on your servant; or he might have said 'on your children'." The man again said: "I have another. The Prophet told him: "Donate it for God's cause. This is the least of the three".'[533]

This order of priority takes human nature into account. The most important thing for any person is to ensure one's own safety and wellbeing. Hence, the first purpose for which money is dedicated is to look after oneself. The second purpose given in this *ḥadīth* is to look after one's servant, or one's children. The reporter of the *ḥadīth* is unsure. However, if the Prophet told the man to spend his second *dinār* on his servant, then spending on one's children and family is included in the first purpose, which indicates that responsibility for one's family is part of one's own welfare. This fits with the Islamic view that considers a man's wife and children to be partners in his earnings.

As the *ḥadīth* mentions supporting one's servant ahead of spending to further God's cause, we realise the importance Islam places on extending kindness to the weaker and more vulnerable groups of the community. A servant takes his or her wages, but if one supports them with a little extra, one stands to be well rewarded by God.

The Prophet mentions that the least of the three purposes is to spend the money for furthering God's cause, a highly worthy purpose. Indeed, many verses in the Qur'an and statements by the Prophet encourage supporting God's cause with one's effort and money, promising rich reward for this. This *ḥadīth* does not run contrary to

---

533. Related by Aḥmad, Muslim and Abū Dāwūd.

them; it simply indicates the greater reward one receives for proper usage of one's money looking after oneself and one's family.

754. Abu Hurayrah reports that the Prophet said: 'Four *dinārs*: one you give to a poor person; one you give to free a slave; one you spend in God's cause and one you spend to support your family. The best is the one you spend on your family'.[534]

Scholars have commented in detail on this *ḥadīth*, outlining who is meant by one's family. Some of them come out in favour of one's wife, while others give preference to one's children. Imam Ibn Ḥazm mentions this difference and expresses his view that both wife and children are in the same position. A man must not prefer one over the other but should treat both equally, so that they receive his support at the same level of priority. He mentions that the Prophet used to repeat a *ḥadīth* three times to ensure that his listeners understand his purpose very clearly. Ibn Ḥazm suggests that the Prophet might have mentioned one's wife first and then started with one's children the second time. This variation indicates that both wife and children are of the same degree and supporting them is equally required of every Muslim man.

In this *ḥadīth* the Prophet mentions three of the best rewarding purposes for which one may donate money: helping poor people, helping to free slaves, and aiding God's cause. All these are well engraved in a Muslim's subconscious so as to be ready to give generously to any of these purposes, for God's sake and in the hope of receiving His reward. But the Prophet tells us that what a man spends in looking after his family earns greater reward than any of the three.

This must never be construed as an invitation to give everything to one's family and to neglect all other purposes. Indeed, this is not the Prophet's intention. What he means is that one should always begin by looking after oneself and family. When he has done so, he may attend to other purposes. But if his means are limited and he barely earns what is sufficient for his family's living, he is not required to deprive himself, his wife or children of their right. He looks after them first, and then helps in other good purposes.

---

534. Related by Aḥmad, Muslim, al-Nasā'ī, Abū Dāwūd, al-Ḥākim and Abu 'Awānah.

Here, we might legitimately ask if it is so that we receive reward from God for providing our families with what is essential for their living. The answer is that reward is earned for everything one spends on one's family, provided that one always has the intention of doing what pleases God.

755. Sa'd ibn Abu Waqqāṣ said: 'The Prophet said to me: "You will be rewarded for everything you spend, as long as you intend your spending for God's sake, even for the food you put in your wife's mouth".'[535]

Here, the Prophet is referring literally to putting a bite in the mouth of one's wife, even when it is a gesture of love and play. A man may do this to emphasise to his wife how dearly he loves her, and he hopes that she will return his love. Even then, with all his self-interest in the matter, he will be rewarded for it. The important proviso is that he should intend it for God's sake. In this case, his intention may be merely to acknowledge and fulfil his duty, as imposed on him by God. God certainly rewards us for fulfilling every duty He has placed on us. The clearest example is prayer, which earns most reward. It is a duty God has imposed on us, and He rewards us for fulfilling it. Similarly, when we look after our families, we earn His reward.

But the Prophet goes further than this, pointing out that when we have an interest in fulfilling a duty in a certain way, we still receive a reward for fulfilling it. In this case, a man gets a reward for giving his wife one bite, when she does not need it, because she is well provided for. He puts the food in her mouth as a loving gesture, which she will return and they have a better family atmosphere and better satisfaction of their desires. Nevertheless, they both earn reward.

This explains God's generosity which is beyond limit. It is He Who has given us everything, and yet He rewards us for using what He has given us for a purpose that brings us benefit. How generous and how gracious. This is how we Muslims know God to be. Limitless is God in His Glory, and limitless indeed is His Grace.

---

535. Related by al-Bukhari.

A time for answering prayers

We always have a prayer to address to God. Life is so hard and difficult, even when we are in the best of situations, that we feel we need God's help at every juncture. We realise that without God's help life could become so suffocatingly oppressive that we may not be able to cope with its demands. Addressing our prayers to God is the way to ensure that we receive His help. This will certainly add to our strength and make us better able and more firmly resolved to face whatever difficulties we face. Should we feel that our prayers are definitely answered, then the difficulties we are dealing with begin to dwindle and we experience a gradually increasing resolve to manage these trusting that God's help will see us through even the worst of times and the hardest of problems.

756. Abu Hurayrah reports that the Prophet said: 'Our Lord, the Glorious, the Exalted, descends to the lowest heaven every night when one third of the night remains, and He says: Who is praying to Me so that I will answer his prayer? Who is requesting me so that I will grant his request? Who is seeking My forgiveness so that I will forgive him?'[536]

This *ḥadīth* states an invitation to every human being to put any type of request to God at the particular time mentioned. The Prophet specified three types of prayer. The first is general, which means that it could be a request for good health by a person suffering illness, or for overcoming a particular difficulty, or for help in achieving a particular goal, or for certain things in one's life to be set on a better footing. Whatever one may pray to God for under this heading is answered. The wording the Prophet has chosen to express his meaning makes the answering of prayer a certainty. This is confirmed in more than one Qur'anic verse, such as the one stating: '*Your Lord says: Pray Me, and I will answer you*'. (40:60).

---

536. Related in all six authentic anthologies. Also related by al-Dārimi and Ibn Khuzaymah. This *ḥadīth* is narrated by no less than twelve of the Prophet's companions, which makes it one of the most authentic *ḥadīths*.

The second is more specific: it concerns requests for God's favours. Here, the door is being opened for any request, whether it relates to this present life or the life to come. So we may ask God to increase our income, to make our life more comfortable, to facilitate our purposes, to give us wisdom, or indeed whatever we may think of. Perhaps it is pertinent to recall here the prayer of the Prophet Solomon who requested that God give him what no one else would ever have, and God granted his request. There is simply no limit on what God may grant to any one of His servants, man, woman or child. And the Prophet tells us that the opportunity to make such requests is available every night.

The third is specifically for God's forgiveness. This means that whatever sin we may commit, the door for forgiveness is open. All that it needs is sincere repentance, a resolve to steer away from sin and an honest appeal for His forgiveness.

All this reaffirms what every Muslim knows of the fact that there is simply no limit to what God may grant people. Whatever God may give us does not decrease His kingdom. What is important though is to know how and when to make our requests. In this *ḥadīth* the Prophet mentions a particular time, which is the last third of the night. This is a time when most people are asleep. It is not easy to get up, because we will not have had sufficient sleep, even though we may go to bed early. Thus, to wrench oneself out of bed, particularly on a cold night, or in summer when the night is very short, requires good effort which only a person feeling real need for God's help will make. Therefore, a person who makes such effort indicates that he or she seriously desires what God may give, and realises that what God gives cannot be given by anyone else. Moreover, such a person knows that he or she needs to make an honest and sincere appeal to God, free of any element of showing off or hypocrisy. Nothing demonstrates this better than forcing oneself out of bed to stand up in prayer, read the Qur'an, glorify God and appeal to Him to grant us whatever we need.

If we understand this *ḥadīth* as highlighting the importance of night worship, we should also realise that it speaks even more emphatically about purging our minds and thoughts of anything other than pure dedication to God. When we wake up at that time of night, perform our ablutions and start our prayer, we should feel that we are in direct communication with God. Hence, our preoccupation should be that we are really fit to make such a direct appeal. This is achieved by purity of thought, and recognition that when we receive God's help we are in need of no one else. Therefore, our prayers should start with seeking God's forgiveness for whatever errors we might have committed, and an expression of our total faith before we put our requests to Him, trusting that He will answer them all, or give us what is even better for us than what we think is best.

A word needs to be said about the way this *ḥadīth* begins, describing God as descending to the lowest heaven. What is important to know is that the very concept of place and space does not apply to God, which means that it is wrong to say that He is present in one place and not present in another. Nor is it right to say that God is everywhere, although He is with us wherever we may be. So, what does this descending mean?

The answer is that we do not know what it actually signifies in real terms. The nature of God and most of His attributes belong to the world that lies beyond the reach of our perception. Therefore, we will not make any attempt to explain this in terms of our world. What we say is that all description of God and His actions are given in terms that make them easy for us to understand. This cannot be done except by what is familiar to us. What is significant here is that God is so near to us at that time of night that a response to our prayers is given immediately. This is not to say that He is far from us at other times, or that He does not answer our prayers. It simply means that prayers are more readily and quickly answered than at other times. Otherwise, the door for repentance is open at any time, and God's answering of our prayers is easy for Him at any moment. He listens to our prayers and responds to them. The *ḥadīth* simply specifies an occasion which makes our prayers more sincere and more serious so as to make God's answer immediate and comprehensive.

Not backbiting

Abu Ruhm Kulthūm ibn al-Ḥuṣayn al-Ghifāri was one of the Prophet's companions who gave him the Pledge of al-Riḍwān at al-Ḥudaybiyah, which required the believers to fight the Quraysh to the end. This was shortly before a delegation from the Quraysh arrived and the Treaty of al-Ḥudaybiyah was concluded.

757. Abu Ruhm reports: 'I joined God's Messenger (peace be upon him) on the Tabuk expedition. I was close to the Prophet one night near al-Akhḍar,[537] and we were very drowsy. I kept waking up to find my camel drawing closer to the Prophet's. I was worried at this, fearing that my camel might hit his leg in the stirrup. I was repeatedly trying to get my she-camel behind, until I was overtaken by sleep for a part of the night. It was then that my camel jostled against the Prophet's, hitting his leg as it was in the stirrup. I woke up only when I heard him giving a sound of pain. I said, "Messenger of God, pray for my forgiveness". The Prophet said to me: "Move on". He began asking me about the people who did not join the expedition from the Ghifār tribe. Then he said: "What about the tall, red-faced people with thin beards?" I told him that they stayed behind. He asked, "And what about the short, black, curly-haired people who have cattle at Shabakat Shadkh?" I tried to remember these as belonging to Ghifār, but I could not. Then I remembered that they belonged to the tribe of Aslam, and I said, "Messenger of God, these are from Aslam". He said: "What prevents any of these, should he stay behind, from providing a camel for a strong man to join a campaign for God's cause? My people for whom I feel most saddened should they stay behind are the Muhājirīn from the Quraysh, and the Anṣār, Ghifār and Aslam".'[538]

In this *ḥadīth* we have an insight into the Prophet's treatment of his companions and the way they tried to spare him any trouble. Here, we find one of his companions resisting sleep and moving his she-camel away from the Prophet's camel, for fear that it might give him a knock. Anyone of the Prophet's companions would have loved to be travelling with him side by side, but Abu Ruhm tries to move away, fearing to

537. Al-Akhdar is a mountain near Taif.

538. Related by Aḥmad.

give him pain, should sleep overtake him and the camel move closer to the Prophet's camel.

Yet all that Abu Ruhm feared came true, and the Prophet was in pain as his companion's camel hit his leg. But instead of shouting at him, or rebuking him for his carelessness, the Prophet simply uttered a small cry of pain, which woke the man up. He immediately realised what had happened and sought the Prophet's pardon, requesting him to pray for his forgiveness. The Prophet then told him to ride by his side and speaks to him about his people. By doing so, the Prophet wanted his companion to forget that little mishap and divert his attention to something more serious. Hence, he questions him about the people that stayed behind on that momentous expedition.

We should remember that this expedition was a hard test for the believers aimed at identifying the hypocrites in their midst. The task set for the expedition was very hard, a distance over 700 km undertaken in the middle of the summer in the blazing heat of the Arabian desert. No one without a camel could join the army. Yet the Prophet required all his companions to join.

The Prophet mentions in particular two groups of the tribes of Ghifār and Aslam who had not joined the expedition. He then expresses his particular sadness at their staying behind, describing them as his own people. These together with the Anṣār and the Muhajirīn, were the best of the Prophet's companions who defended Islam most courageously when it faced determined opposition.

The Prophet also suggests that when a believer finds it difficult to join a particular expedition, then he should provide assistance to the army, by giving a fighter the necessary equipment to join that army. At this particular time, this could easily have been achieved by providing a horse or a camel to a fighter who had no mount. At other times, financial help given to the war effort might have been a suitable contribution and compensation.

We need to look a little closer at Abu Ruhm's attitude when he realised that he had hurt the Prophet physically. Another, more detailed version of this *ḥadīth* mentions that Abu Ruhm hurt the Prophet's leg with the edge of his shoes. He adds that the Prophet 'said to me, "You have hurt me! Move your leg", and he hit my leg with a whip. I was so worried that I could think of nothing else. I feared that new

Qur'anic verses would be revealed concerning this, because it was very grave. When we were at al-Jiʿirrānah, I went to graze the cattle we had, although it was not my turn, because I feared that the Prophet would ask for me. When I took the cattle back, I enquired and was told that the Prophet asked for me. I went to him feeling very apprehensive. But he said: "You hurt me with your leg and I hit you with a whip. Take these sheep in compensation". My happiness with his forgiveness was greater than this world and all that it contained'.

In this detailed version we see another aspect of the Prophet's compassion. He realised that his use of the whip was an instinctive reaction to the pain he suffered. Therefore, he wanted to compensate his companion, and he gave him a number of sheep. In another version, the gift is mentioned to have been eighty sheep. Yet his companion loved the fact that the Prophet was not displeased with him far more than this very generous gift.

It is with such mutual feelings of love and compassion that Islam builds the closest of communities.

758. 'Ā'ishah reports: 'A man sought permission to see the Prophet, and the Prophet said: "This is a bad brother of his tribe". Yet when the man was admitted, the Prophet welcomed him well. I took it up with [the Prophet]. He said: "God does not love the obscene and ill-mannered among people".'

This *ḥadīth* is a shorter version of Number 339, which we discussed in detail. However, we need to reiterate here that the Prophet's words were a mere statement of facts. It is meant to alert the people present to a certain characteristic in the person concerned.

759. 'Ā'ishah reports: 'Sawdah, who was a heavy, sluggish woman, sought and obtained the Prophet's permission to move on early on the night of Muzdalifah'.

Here 'Ā'ishah is describing Sawdah, another of the Prophet's wives, as heavy and sluggish. She simply remarked on her being overweight and on her slow walking. It is clear that she did not mean this in any derogatory sense, because the description relates to the situation they were in. This was during the pilgrimage when all pilgrims, having spent the day at Arafat, move on after sunset to Muzdalifah where they are required to spend the night till just before sunrise and then move on to Mina. It is a tiresome journey and an overweight person who finds walking or moving difficult is bound to be doubly tired.

The Prophet had given permission to those who were ill and weak, and to women generally, to spend only a short time at Muzdalifah and then move on to Mina after midnight, rather than stay till they had prayed Fajr, or dawn prayer. This makes things easier for them, particularly because in Arabia's very hot weather, it is always easier to walk at night. Moreover, those who proceed early have more time to make the journey and more time to rest after it. Hence, an overweight, slow-moving person would be well advised to move early. The Prophet's wife, Sawdah, realised all this when she sought his permission to move on. It is perhaps useful to mention here an addition that some *ḥadīth* scholars have quoted 'Ā'ishah as saying: 'I wish I sought a similar permission from the Prophet. I would then have prayed Fajr at Mina and done my stoning at the Jamrah before the bulk of people had arrived'.

Keeping people's faults secret

Sometimes we are faced with a situation where quoting an incident or a person's behaviour may serve a good purpose. Is it acceptable, from an Islamic point of view, to give such a report, or does this fall under backbiting which is forbidden in Islam?

760. 'Abdullāh ibn Mas'ūd reports: 'When God's Messenger (peace be upon him) was at al-Ji'irranah, he divided the spoils of war gained at the Battle of Ḥunayn. People crowded up around him. He said: "Once God sent one of His servants to a certain community but they rejected him, accused him of lying and injured him in his head. He wiped the blood off his forehead and said, 'My Lord, forgive my community for they do not know [the truth]'." Ibn Mas'ūd adds: "I can almost see God's Messenger doing the same as the man and wiping his forehead".'[539]

---

539. Related by Aḥmad, Ibn Mājah, Ibn Ḥibbān and Abu 'Awānah.

This is a simple report which the Prophet felt useful to quote in that particular situation when people did not pay attention to the fact that they were hurting the Prophet in their scrambling for shares of the booty. He reports to them that earlier prophets suffered ill-treatment at the hands of their people, to the extent that a prophet might be physically assaulted and injured. This was a subtle hint by the Prophet to those who hurt him, so that they might desist.

What the Prophet told his companions was that it was often the lot of a messenger of God to be hurt. Like this prophet he mentioned, he himself was subjected to much abuse, both mental and physical, on several occasions. When he went to Taif to call on its people to accept Islam, he was chased by slaves and boys who threw stones at him and he suffered injuries. Enduring such hostility is a common occurrence among those who call on people to believe in God.

761. Abu al-Haytham reports: 'Some people visited 'Uqbah ibn 'Āmir and said: "We have neighbours who drink and do other deeds: should we report them to the ruler?" He said: "No. I heard God's Messenger say: 'Whoever sees a fault in a Muslim and overlooks it is like one who saves a young girl who has been buried alive'."'[540]

This is an important *ḥadīth* which defines the attitude a Muslim should take when he sees something wrong done or practised by a fellow Muslim. What we are talking about here is a practice that constitutes disobedience of God, but does not injure or constitute an injustice to anyone else. In this case, the best thing to do is to keep the matter secret and not to publicise it. The reason for so doing is twofold:

For one thing, publicity of people's faults puts them in a defensive position. Some people may think that such publicity gives them a chance to boast about what they do, even though it is unworthy of a Muslim. The fact that it has become known encourages them to boast about it in defiance of accepted Islamic norms. Thus, instead of encouraging them to mend their ways, publicity hardens their attitude.

---

540. Related by Aḥmad.

On the other hand, publicity may encourage others to follow such people's example, particularly if the practice involved is associated with pleasure, desire gratification, material gain or the like. Thus, publicity tends to help make forbidden practices commonplace in a Muslim community. For this reason, Islam wants its community to refrain from indulgence in gossip.

From another point of view, keeping someone else's faults secret allows us a chance to talk to them, counselling them to mend their ways, or giving them advice on how to get rid of such faults. We will be able to help them in this way. We must not forget that a person who commits an error is always likely to receive God's forgiveness once he repents and resolves not to repeat it. To encourage someone to repent and seek God's forgiveness requires that we keep secret what that person has done.

The encouragement the Prophet provides to keep other people's faults secret is such that he likens it to saving a poor girl from certain death. The Arabs in pre-Islamic days used to bury young girls alive, for fear of poverty or shame. Islam put an end to this abhorrent practice. Saving such a girl is highly commendable. Hence the Prophet likens this to overlooking other people's faults.

We should add here that Abu Ayyūb, a companion of the Prophet, used to travel to meet other companions to ask them about a *ḥadīth* they might have heard from the Prophet. It is reported that Abu Ayyūb travelled to Egypt to meet 'Uqbah ibn 'Āmir, the first narrator of this *ḥadīth*. When he arrived at the home of Maslamah ibn Makhlad, the Governor of Egypt, Maslamah came out to receive him and hugged him assuring him of a warm welcome. He then asked him about his business in Egypt so that he might facilitate it for him. Abu Ayyūb said, 'I have come to meet 'Uqbah ibn 'Āmir and ask him about a *ḥadīth* he and I heard the Prophet saying and we are the only survivors to do so. Could you please send someone with me to guide me to his home'.

The governor did so, and when 'Uqbah heard of Abu Ayyūb's arrival, he came out to give him a very warm welcome. Abu Ayyūb said: 'I have come to ask you about a *ḥadīth* concerning keeping secret other people's errors. You and I are the only survivors of those who heard it'. 'Uqbah said: 'Indeed, I heard the Prophet as he said,

'Whoever keeps secret a shameful deed done by a Muslim, God will grant him His cover on the Day of Judgement'." Abu Ayyūb said, 'This is true'.

Abu Ayyūb thus finished his business in Egypt and started on his return journey to Madinah. The governor inquired after him, but he was told that he had already left. He sent some of his men with a gift, but they did not catch up with him until he reached al-Arish. This gives us an idea about the care early Muslims took to ascertain the reporting of every *ḥadīth*.

Taking care with what to say

The Prophet took particular care to make his companions mindful of what they said. He told them frequently that a wrong word may lead to serious results. He also chose certain phrases and statements that people frequently said to enlighten his companions on their desirability or otherwise.

> 762. Abu Hurayrah reports that the Prophet said: 'When you hear a man saying, "Mankind are ruined", then [know that] he is the most ruined of them all'.

This *ḥadīth* alerts us to a common fault to which people rarely pay any attention. It is that of finding fault with people and remaining oblivious of one's own fault. When this becomes habitual, the person then becomes preoccupied with the faults of others, making a simple fault far more serious than it actually is and a single error a common one. He may add to this an expression of sorrow at the degeneration of moral values among Muslims generally, showing eagerness to reform them and admitting inability to do anything in that regard. This begins to give this person a sense of self satisfaction that may develop into a feeling of moral superiority. He may even tend to despise people.

All this makes such a person, as the Prophet says, the most ruined among them. This is because such a person's remarks are recorded against him as backbiting, which is both sinful and earns grievous punishment. Moreover, the fact that such people overlook their own faults leads them to be arrogant and arrogance is an attitude that incurs God's displeasure.

The net result of such an attitude is that this person will have his normal faults as well as the sins of backbiting and arrogance taken into account, while other people only have their normal faults. Hence, he is in a far worse position, or, to use the Prophet's expression, he is the most ruined of them all.

The foregoing applies to the person who sees himself as superior to others. However, the one who means his remark only by way of a sort of diagnosis of society's ills , considering that what he says is also applicable to him, is in a different situation. This person may be keen to do something to help his community get rid of its faults, and he may seek the cooperation of others in such an endeavour. The Prophet's statement does not apply to this person. On the contrary, he may earn reward from God for his words and actions because he only seeks to improve his community's situation.

Another *ḥadīth* alerts us to be careful about what to say to others, particularly those whom we know to be suspect in their beliefs.

763. Buraydah reports that the Prophet said: 'Do not call a hypocrite, "Master", because if he is then he is master over you and you incur your Lord's displeasure'.[541]

The Prophet's instruction makes it clear that honesty must always be observed in how we address people. Thus, if we know that someone is a hypocrite, because of his behaviour or because we see him saying something to people's faces and something different behind their backs, then we must not call him master. A hypocrite has too many faults to deserve to be master over others. Hence, when he is called master, he is placed in a position to which he has no claim and in which God has not placed him. This may incur God's displeasure with those who give him such appellation.

Moreover, if such a person is really a master, then he deserves to be obeyed. And when the person to be obeyed is a hypocrite, then

541. Related by Abū Dāwūd and al-Ḥākim.

those over whom he is a master are also hypocrites. He would then be leading them to what is evil. In this case, all of them deserve God's punishment.

On the other hand, if such a person is not master in his community and they call him master despite knowing his hypocrisy, then they are acting like him. Again, their behaviour incurs God's displeasure. In all such cases, they put themselves in a position where God's punishment may be inflicted on them. This shows the importance of not extending any civility to a hypocrite.

764. (*Athar* 173) 'Adiy ibn Arṭa'ah said: 'When any of the Prophet's companions were praised, he would say, "My Lord, do not hold me responsible for what they say, and forgive me what they do not know".'[542]

This is exemplary behaviour by the Prophet's companions. No one can control other people's behaviour. Nor can we control another person should he be wont to praise us in front of others. Hence, when a companion of the Prophet found himself in such a position, he would turn to God with a short supplication that was certain to prevent any feeling of self satisfaction creeping into him. First, he prayed not to be held responsible for what was being said about him. This prayer ensured that nothing he had done or said encouraged others to praise him. In essence, if our behaviour invites praise, we ourselves should not be seeking it.

The second prayer is, 'forgive me what they do not know'. It is an acknowledgement that one is rarely as good as one appears to be. We all commit some sort of sin, and many of our sins may be private, unknown to others. Hence, this prayer puts that side against the praise given by others, so as to produce a feeling of humility, thereby countering any satisfaction generated by praise.

The version related by al-Bayhaqi adds a third prayer: 'and make me better than what they think'. This prayer seeks God's help to achieve an even better position than what those who praise us describe. This acknowledges that there remains a great distance between anyone and

542. Related by al-Bayhaqi in Shu'ab al-Īmān.

the degree of perfection people can attain. Therefore, God's help is sought for the achievement of this goal.

765. Abu Qilābah said: 'Abu 'Abdullāh said to Abu Mas'ūd; or perhaps Abu Mas'ūd said to Abu 'Abdullāh: "What did you hear the Prophet say about the [use of the phrase], 'It is claimed'? He answered: "It is a bad mount for anyone".'[543]

766. 'Abdullāh ibn 'Āmir said: 'Abu Mas'ūd, what did you hear God's Messenger (peace be upon him) say about the phrase, "people claim"?' He answered: 'I heard him say that it is a bad mount for anyone. I also heard him say: "To curse a believer is like killing him".'[544]

These two *ḥadīths* refer to the frequent practice of some people when they want to report something of which they are unsure, or they want to disclaim responsibility for what they want to say. Hence, they begin by this phrase, 'it is claimed', or 'people say', or 'it is alleged', etc. so as to appear to be uncommitted to what follows. People often do this when they realise that what they are communicating is untrue. Thus, they use the phrase as a cover up for their lies.

When a person uses such phrases, he seeks to have something to fall back on, should his lies be discovered. In this case, when he is questioned about what he alleged, he will say that he only reported what he had heard from someone else and that he did not even report it with any assertion, but had left the matter subject to questioning by only saying that it was claimed. Thus, he finds his defence easy and escapes any charge of lying, while he knows full well the falsehood he is trying to spread.

This is different from using the phrase when one is certain of what one is stating, attributing the statement to someone else. This person starts by naming his source and says that that person claims. This is merely a way of reporting. It tells us that there is nothing wrong with

543. Related by Aḥmad and Abū Dāwūd.
544. Related by al-Bukhari.

the phrase making a claim. However, it is the way people use it that may land them in trouble as they would be spreading rumours or repeating what is untrue.

We may note how the Prophet compares the phrase, 'it is claimed', to a person's mount. He prepares his mount and rides it when he wants to go somewhere. Such preparation takes place before he starts his journey. Similarly, 'it is claimed' serves as preparation for making a false claim. Hence, the Prophet describes it as a foul mount.

The second point in the second *ḥadīth* refers to cursing a believer, and the Prophet likens this to killing him. A believer is someone that has set his relationship with God on the right footing. To curse him, or her, is to condemn him as someone undeserving of God's mercy. This is very serious, similar to killing him, as the Prophet says.

767. (*Athar* 174) Ibn 'Abbās says: 'Let none of you say in reference to something that he does not know, "God knows this", when God knows different. He would thus be attributing to God's knowledge what He does not know. This, in God's sight, is very serious indeed'.

This is a reference to what many people do when they want to assert something of which they are unsure. They hesitate to swear to its truth, because they are worried lest their oath be false or they may have too much respect for God to drag His blessed name into that of which they are uncertain. Hence, they say in a form of assertion, 'God knows this'. This is described by scholars as highly unbecoming, because the person who resorts to it actually states that God knows something when he himself is unsure of it.

Moreover, if the person making such assertion knows the matter to be different to what he says and still claims that God knows it, this is extremely serious. His statement claims that God knows the matter in question as being different to what it actually is. Should he be aware of this difference, his statement is tantamount to disbelief in God.

When a person is unsure of something, he should make this clear before speaking of God's knowledge. Thus, he may say: 'This is how I think the matter is like, but God knows best'. In this way, he does not assert the matter to be in a particular form. Rather, he states his view of the matter without calling God as a witness to his own view; he simply attributes to God perfect knowledge, leaving his listener aware that he himself may be wrong.

Another subtle difference may be noticed in the perfectly legitimate statement: 'I have done this for God's sake, and God knows that'. Here the person concerned is stating his own intention, which he or she knows to be true. When they confirm it with God's knowledge, they are certain of it. Hence, there is nothing wrong with such an expression. Reference to God's knowledge is wrong when we are uncertain of the matter we are referring to and what it may really be. 'Umar ibn al-Khaṭṭāb asked someone about something, and the man said, 'God knows better'. 'Umar said, 'We are in a sorry state indeed if we say this when we do not know what we are being asked about. If any of you is asked about something he does not know, his reply should indicate his lack of knowledge'.

Yet it may be pointed out that the Prophet's companions replied to his questions on several occasions by saying, 'God knows best'. This is true, but in their case, the statement was intended as an admission that they had no knowledge of the matter. In this way, their reply indicated their belief in God's perfect knowledge in addition to their lack of information on that particular subject. Therefore, when it is clear that the person's intention is to indicate the same and the listener realises that it is so, such a reply is in order. But when it is merely stated to add weight to one's uncertain statement, it is unacceptable.

768. (*Athar* 175) Ibn 'Abbās said: 'The galaxy is one of the gates of heaven. The rainbow is security from drowning after the people of Noah (peace be upon him)'.

769. (*Athar* 176) Ibn al-Kawwā' asked 'Ali about the galaxy, and he replied: 'It is the water-trough from which the heavens opened up with flowing water'.

770. (*Athar* 177) Ibn 'Abbās said: 'The rainbow is security from drowning for the people of the earth. The galaxy is the door of the heavens where it will be cleft asunder'.

I am unable to comment on these three statements by two of the Prophet's learned companions. Nor am I certain whether the reference to 'the galaxy' in all three statements points to the Milky Way, or to galaxies in general. In the second statement, the phraseology of the heavens opening up with flowing water echoes the Qur'anic description of the great floods that drowned Noah's people.

Where God's Mercy abides

Some people wonder whether God's Grace has an abode? If so, where is it?

> 771. (*Athar* 178) Abu al-Ḥārith al-Karmāni said: 'A man said to Abu Rajā': "I extend my greetings to you and I pray to God that He will join us together where His mercy abides". Abu Rajā' said: "Can anyone bear that? Where do you think God's mercy abides?" The man said: "In heaven". Abu Rajā' said: "You are not right". The man asked: "Then where does it abide?" Abu Rajā' replied: "With God, the Lord of all worlds".'

Abu Rajā' 'Imrān ibn Milḥān was a young boy during the last years of the Prophet but did not see him. This means that he belonged to the generation that followed, i.e. the *tabi'īn*.

People speak of the abode of God's mercy as the place where He bestows His grace in full. This is where people may enjoy His highest blessings. Hence they may pray to God to place them in heaven, describing it as the abode of His mercy. But the fact is that God's mercy is not limited to heaven. It is bestowed at all times in all places and on all creatures. Even unbelievers enjoy much of God's mercy in this life. Had God willed to punish people in this world for the sins they commit, He would not have left any creature on the face of the earth.

'Imrān ibn Milḥān, who met many of the Prophet's companions and learnt much from them, corrects his interlocutor when he defines God's mercy's abode as heaven. He tells him that it abides with God Himself. This is perfectly understandable, because it is an essential attribute of God: He bestows it at will. Heaven is the place in which we end up should God be pleased to bestow His mercy on us. Hence, we must pray to Him to grant us His mercy and bestow on us His grace, forgiving our sins and rewarding us generously for our good deeds.

Another fault people often commit when they meet misfortune, whether affecting their property, health or relatives is that they curse life or time. This is very serious. Therefore, the Prophet gives us a clear warning against it.

772. Abu Hurayrah reports that the Prophet said: 'Let none of you say: foul is time, because God is time'.[545]

773. Abu Hurayrah reports that the Prophet said: 'Let none of you say: foul is time, because God is time. God, the Mighty and Exalted, says: "I am time. I send the night and the day, and I can take them away if I so will". Do not describe grapes as *karm*, because *karm* is the Muslim individual'.[546]

What a Muslim must realise is that whatever misfortune befalls anyone, it happens by God's will. Hence, when he curses life or time for a misfortune, he is actually cursing the cause of that misfortune. Thus, the curse is directed at God Himself. This is a very grave sin. We only need to consider how and when people curse time to realise the truth of the Prophet's statement. They often do so when they incur a financial loss, particularly when it is due to something unforeseen, like a slump in prices, or a natural calamity that destroys some of their property. They also curse time when they feel that things are not going in their favour. Thus, if one loses one's job, or suffers the loss of a close and beloved relative, or fails to realise something he dearly wants, he curses time. But in all this, the hand of God is the one that directs matters, according to the laws He has set in operation for our world. Therefore, the curse rebounds to God, and this is very serious.

This is what is clear in the added portion in the second *ḥadīth*. This addition forms a sacred, or *qudsi ḥadīth* as the Prophet attributes

545. Related by al-Bukhari, Muslim, al-Nasā'ī and Abū Dāwūd.
546. Related by Aḥmad, al-Bukhari, Muslim, al-Dārimi and Abu 'Awānah.

to God the statement, 'I am time. I send the night and the day, and I can take them away if I so will'. This explains that God is not the actual passage of day and night, which indicates time. He is the One who creates night and day and their cycle of succession. He is also able to stop this, because He can stop the earth from moving in its orbit round the sun and from revolving in its position. This would hold day and night, and we would no longer have time. Since all this happens only by God's will, then cursing time is a curse directed at God and His will. This is not acceptable from anyone, let alone a Muslim who believes in God and His oneness.

Sometimes, indeed often, the misfortune we suffer is the result of our own doings, negligence, or deliberate omission. To attribute any such fault or its result to God is absolutely wrong.

The last statement in the second *ḥadīth* does not allow describing grapes as *karm*. We should explain that this word is derived from *karam*, which means generosity. It is used in some parts of the Arab world to denote a vineyard. But the Prophet's prohibition really attaches to using the word *karm* to describe wine. The Arabs of old called it by this name as they valued generosity very highly and considered it a source of pride. They realised that they were more generous when they were under the influence of intoxicants. Therefore, they derived this name for wine which encouraged them to be more generous. The Prophet, however, did not wish to mention wine in this connection. He only mentions the fruit from which it is made.

As *karm* is a noble name, denoting purity and generosity, the Prophet says it is better used for a Muslim. In fact, a different version of this *ḥadīth*, also related by al-Bukhari, says: '*Karm* is a believer's heart'. This refers to the fact that a believer's heart is full of faith and its light. It benefits by the right guidance embodied in Islam. Hence it is far more deserving of this noble name than wine, which is evil, casting a cloud over man's thinking and leading him to more sin.

Refining brotherly relations

The Prophet was keen to establish relations between individual Muslims on the right footing, which is a brotherhood that unites them all in faith and in their service of the Divine cause. But to him, this was a first step. He was also keen to refine this relationship so that it is strengthened by all sorts of good manners that are brought into play.

774. (*Athar* 179) Mujāhid reports: 'It is discouraged for a person to stare pointedly at his brother, or to follow him with his eye when he leaves, or ask him: Where have you come from and where are you going?'

What we have here is an indication of certain things that may cause a person some embarrassment, particularly if he is of a shy disposition. When one gazes pointedly at a brother, or a woman does this with another woman, or when they keep looking at them after they have departed, this may be a source of embarrassment. It is as if one is questioning the other, or indicating that there is something wrong either with his appearance, behaviour or attitude. Hence, anything that is exaggerated and could cause embarrassment should not be done so as to keep the brotherly relation free of any blemish.

This *ḥadīth* suggests that one should not ask his brother where he has been or where he is going. The context of the *ḥadīth* suggests that it is a sort of interfering in another person's private business. Otherwise we are commanded by the Prophet to enquire after our brethren and make sure that they are all right. When the questions asked show our care for them, then these are perfectly appropriate. But when they sound as an attempt to pry into someone else's affairs, then they are certainly discouraged. An important factor of distinction between the two types is how the one being asked such questions perceives them. It is he who may feel embarrassed or irritated, and it is to spare him such irritation or embarrassment that the *ḥadīth* is intended.

We can imagine that this *ḥadīth* is intended to protect a rather sensitive person from what causes him something that is not particularly welcome. However, sometimes we need to express our own irritation or point out the singularity of some idea or behaviour. A threatening word may be acceptable on such occasions.

775. Anas reports that the Prophet saw a man leading a she-camel [intended for sacrifice] and told him: 'Ride it'. The man

said: 'It is a sacrificial she-camel'. The Prophet said: 'Ride it'. The man said: 'It is sacrificial'. [Again] the Prophet said: 'Ride it'. [Once more] the man said it was for sacrifice. The Prophet said: 'Ride it, or else'.[547]

In pre-Islamic days, the Arabs used to pledge animals for their idols or for other purposes. These animals would then be left unused for any purpose, such as riding, carrying or farm work. Islam put an end to all such idolatrous practices. This makes it clear that the Prophet's order was meant to counter this unwarranted practice. This is best done by using the animal for the purpose the pagans did not intend it to be used for. Hence, the Prophet told the man to ride the camel. When the man was not ready to comply, the Prophet warned him. In the Arabic original, the warning word the Prophet uses is stronger than 'or else', but a literal translation would make it too strong. It would give the wrong impression about the Prophet's language. Needless to say, if the camel was one of those pledged for idolatrous practices, then observing such practices would have placed the man in a position that is unacceptable to Islam. Thus, he might incur God's displeasure and that would be very serious indeed.

A different explanation is that the Prophet was merely giving the man a piece of advice. It is very important to act on the Prophet's advice in any situation. Hence, the man should not have repeated the same objection three times. Having done so, he was risking disobedience of the Prophet. Again, that is very serious.

776. (*Athar* 180) Al-Miswar ibn Rifā'ah al-Quraẓi said: 'I heard Ibn 'Abbās as a man asked him: "I have eaten bread and meat; should I perform ablution?" Ibn 'Abbās said: "How singular! Do you need to have a fresh ablution for eating wholesome food?"'

Ibn 'Abbās was a highly learned companion and cousin of the Prophet. As such, he was well placed to express disapproval, particularly when the matter concerned religious practice. Ablutions are preformed in

547. Related by Aḥmad, al-Bukhari, Muslim, al-Tirmidhi, al-Nasā'ī, Ibn Mājah, al-Dārimi and Ibn Khuzaymah.

preparation for prayer and other religious practices. But when one has performed ablution, he remains in a state of purity, ready to pray, until he has invalidated his ablution by urination, wind discharge or defecation. But this man had done nothing of that. He had only eaten some wholesome food. Hence, Ibn 'Abbās was amazed that he was asking whether he should renew his ablution. This he expresses in a rhetorical question: 'How singular! Do you need to have a fresh ablution for eating wholesome food?' The very thought is strange.

A most fair division

The Prophet was always very fair in all his dealings with his companions and with his enemies. Injustice, of any type or form, was very hateful to him. Never did he wish to have something that belonged to another person. On the contrary, he was very generous giving away what he had, without any thought that he might need it at a later time. Hence, if he was accused of injustice or of trying to favour himself or his close companions with something, this would certainly hurt him.

> 777. Jābir reports: 'After the Battle of Ḥunayn, God's Messenger (peace be upon him) was at al-Ji'irranah, and Bilāl had gold in his lap, and the Prophet was dividing it. A man came to him and said: "Be fair, for you have been unfair". The Prophet said: "Confound you! Who maintains fairness if I am unfair?" 'Umar said: "Messenger of God! Allow me to strike off this hypocrite's head". The Prophet said: "This one has friends who read the Qur'an but it does not go beyond their throats. They take themselves away from religion in the same way as an arrow goes through the body of its target".'

The Battle of Ḥuanyn yielded great war gains for the Muslims. The enemy leader did not stop at mobilising the most numerous fighting force he could muster. He also brought their women, children and property and placed these behind his army, thinking that his men would fight hard to protect them. He was certainly misguided. Practically all their wealth was taken as war gains and it was divided according to

Islamic rules: four-fifths for the soldiers and one-fifth for the Prophet as the head of state to use according to Qur'anic guidance.

The man who is at the centre of this incident is known by name and description but scholars of *Ḥadīth* prefer not to mention him so that the action itself rather than the man is highlighted. Obviously he was a bedouin, which accounts for his rough manner, and a newcomer to Islam, unaware of the Prophet's exemplary conduct and his absolute fairness in all situations.

The Prophet was deeply hurt by the man's remark. Hence, his rhetorical question. Other versions of this *ḥadīth* add different expressions by the Prophet, such as: 'And who would obey God if I would not?' and: 'With whom will you find justice if you do not find it with me?' All these expressions give us the clear impression of how hurt the Prophet was by the man's remark. It touched on a value to which the Prophet attached great importance. Hence, it was only natural that 'Umar was ready to kill the man, had the Prophet given him permission to do so.

However, the Prophet did not wish his personal feeling to be the dominant subject. Therefore, he turned the conversation to something else. He explained to 'Umar a phenomenon which remains with us even today. He tells him that the man and his friends will read the Qur'an but that it will hardly go beyond their throats. This description means that such people will not let the Qur'an influence their behaviour or values. It will be a mere verbal recitation that neither improves their behaviour nor gives them a better relation with God. If they were true Muslims, they would reflect on what they recite, try to understand it well and implement it in their lives. But they do nothing of the sort. Hence, their recitation is of no benefit to them. Their adoption of Islam is no different from their abandoning it. Their situation is similar to that of an arrow which hits an animal and goes through it so fast that no trace of blood is seen on it.

This description applies to al-Khawārij, who rebelled against 'Ali ibn Abu Ṭālib, the fourth Caliph and the Prophet's cousin and son-in-law. 'Ali was one of the most learned of the Prophet's companions. When he was questioned about al-Khawārij, he described their situation accurately. He was asked whether they were unbelievers. He answered: 'They have run away from disbelief'. Thus, he credited them with the good intention and proper desire to be away from disbelief. He was then asked whether they were hypocrites. He answered: 'Hypocrites remember God but little, while these people remember and praise Him morning and evening'. He then stated their condition, saying: 'They have been afflicted by confusion and thus become blind and deaf'.

This *ḥadīth* and 'Ali's accurate description of al-Khawārij should keep us always on the alert. A person may be full of desire to hold on to faith and to be a good believer. He may read the Qur'an, attend to his worship and remember God in all times and situations, but none of these actions influences his behaviour or makes him a better person. They remain a mechanical exercise. This situation is far removed from true faith, in which a person seeks to understand Islamic values and principles so as to put them into practice. A belief which is not reflected in the believer's behaviour, values and principles is not worth anything, because it neither refines a rough nature nor rectifies deviant behaviour.

This idea is highlighted in a well-known *ḥadīth* in which the Prophet defines true belief as 'What is firmly held as conviction and to which credit is given by actions'. This is indeed true faith. Otherwise, everyone may claim to believe without showing in practice any sign to confirm his claim. When faith stops at the mere verbal statement, it is of little value to the individual or the community. We pray to God to enable us to be good believers and to make our actions a credit to our faith.

Positive response bringing great benefit

The Prophet always liked a good name, one which delivers a pleasant impression the moment it is said. Prior to Islam, the Arabs did not care what name they gave to their children. They might call a son after the first animal they saw after the child was born. When someone with such a name, or with a name that indicated a different belief, declared his acceptance of Islam, the Prophet changed his name.

778. Bashīr ibn Ma'bad al-Sadūsi (whose original name was Zah ibn Ma'bad migrated to join the Prophet. The Prophet asked him: 'What is your name?' He said: 'Zaḥm'. The Prophet

said: 'No. You are Bashīr'.) Bashīr said: 'I was walking with the Prophet when he passed by the graves of some unbelievers. He said: "These have missed much good". He repeated this three times. He then passed by the graves of some Muslims and said: "These received much good". He also repeated this three times. The Prophet then looked around suddenly and he saw a man walking in the graveyard, wearing sandals. He said to him: "You, the man wearing fine sandals, remove your sandals". The man looked up and when he saw the Prophet, he took off his sandals and threw them away".'

The first thing to say in comment on this *ḥadīth* is that the Prophet gave the man a much better name than his original one which was derived from a root that meant 'overcrowding'. Bashīr means 'the bearer of good news'.

In this *ḥadīth*, the Prophet repeatedly comments on those who accepted Islam and those who rejected it. In both cases he comments on the good one group received and the other missed out on. There is no doubt that faith in God's oneness and Muhammad's message brings a person much good. Anyone who knows the truth of Islam realises this. On the other hand, a person who rejects the faith deprives himself of the good that permeates life and gives him happiness both in this life and in the life to come.

Secondly, the Prophet asks the man wearing fine sandals in the cemetery to take them off. Scholars say that this is out of respect to the dead, or may be because the man was walking in a somewhat arrogant way. Alternatively, the Prophet might have spotted some filth on the man's shoes and of which he was unaware. There is no question that wearing fine shoes is permissible.

Thirdly, we note the man's immediate compliance with the Prophet's directive. This is the attitude of true believers. Whenever they realise that the Prophet orders something, they immediately move to fulfil it.

779. Muhammad ibn Abu Fudayk reports that Muhammad ibn Hilāl said that he saw the compartments of the Prophet's wives built up with palm trunks, and covered with sheets made of animal hair. 'I asked him about 'Ā'ishah's home and he

answered: "Its door faced the direction to Syria". I asked whether it had one door or twin doors. He said: "It had a single door". I asked what the door was made of. He said: "It was made of cypress or teak wood".'

Life in the Prophet's home was far from luxurious, although he could have had whatever he wanted of luxury. Had he wished, he could have provided his wives with the sort of comforts and luxuries that were only available in the palaces of the emperors of Persia and Byzantium. But the Prophet did not care for any such luxury. Indeed, he preferred a simple life in which his household got what they wanted without having any special privileges that placed them above the standard of others in Madinah.

This is not surprising, for the Prophet showed in every aspect of his life that the material refinements of this world meant little or nothing to him. He also educated his wives to such a sublime standard that gives value to everything that elevates human life, but does not respect fleeting comforts and imagined luxuries. We appreciate that the Prophet actually practised what he preached. His life was a manifest reflection of the great value embodied in his statement: 'Had this whole world been worth, in God's sight, anything similar to the span of the wing of a single mosquito, He would not have given a single unbeliever a drink of water'.[548] If this is how the Prophet viewed life on earth, what do little comforts count for in such a standard of values?

The Prophet was keen to warn his followers against anything that might prejudice their fate in the life to come, even if it was not forbidden.

780. Abu Hurayrah reports that the Prophet said: 'The Last Hour will not fall due until people build houses and adorn them like they adorn painted garments'.

Ibrāhīm, the last in the chain of transmission said: 'He meant striped clothes'.

548. Related by al-Tirmidhi.

This *ḥadīth* is a reference to aspects of luxury people are very keen to have. Needless to say, comfort in one's home is provided by the inside amenities the home provides. People may spend much on improving these amenities so that they find in their homes all that gives them comfort and happiness. However, when they start to paint the outside of their homes in a way that is considered luxurious, then they are placing too much emphasis on material values. Such action tells of competition in apparent luxuries which take up much of their resources. These resources could have been used to improve the lot of the community as a whole instead of wasting them over something that brings no benefit other than hollow satisfaction for homeowners.

Which charity is best?

When we study the Prophet's *Ḥadīth* in depth we realise that sometimes he may not give a straightforward answer to a question put to him. He might choose to highlight an area that was better suited to the occasion or to some factor of importance for his questioner. This shows that the Prophet was always aware of the needs not only of his community but also of the needs of his individual companions and their general situations. In this he was a model leader who never underrated any one of his companions. To him, even the least privileged among them was as important as anyone else. He took care of everyone and tried to help each with whatever they needed.

781. Abu Hurayrah reports: 'A man came to the Prophet and asked him: "Messenger of God, which charity is rewarded best?" The Prophet replied, "Well, by your father! I will give you a full answer: to give away money in charity when you are in good health, holding on to what you have, fearing to become poor and hoping to achieve riches. Do not wait until you are at the point of death and then say: I leave so much to this person and so much to that, while the other has such and such".'[549]

549. Related by Aḥmad, al-Bukhari, Muslim, Ibn Mājah, Ibn Khuzaymah and Ibn Ḥibbān.

The question the man put to the Prophet sought information about the type of charity that earns best reward. He might have expected an answer outlining the best purposes for which charity may be given, such as helping those who are very poor or donating to jihad to repel an attack on a Muslim state , or looking after orphans. But the Prophet did not mention any purpose whatsoever. He merely spoke about situations.

What we understand from the *ḥadīth* is that the charity that earns the best reward is the one for which one has to overcome all sorts of restraining factors. A person who is in the prime of life and enjoying good health is always thinking of the future. He has great ambitions, any of which requires money to fulfil. Besides, with young age and ambition there is always the fear that things might not go so well, and one ends in poverty. At the same time one entertains hopes of becoming rich. Needless to say, anyone who hopes to be rich is careful about his money, holding on to it, feeling that with proper usage, he will be able to get more and set himself on the road to affluence.

It is at such times of high hopes and corresponding fears, when one is healthy and feels that life stretches far in front of him that charity is hard. Hence, it is precisely at this time that charity gives the highest reward.

The Prophet gives the opposite situation of one who is on his deathbed, realizing that he has only very little time left. He knows that no amount of wealth will make any difference. He cannot buy additional time in life. No matter what his ambitions were, he has had his time and now the end beckons. No riches are of use. Hence, he can easily afford to give here and there. At this time charity is easy. It does not have to resist any force pulling in the opposite direction. Needless to say, charity in the first situation deserves a much higher reward from God than in the second situation, even though the latter may be much greater in amount.

Perhaps it should be explained that the Prophet's statement about the man on his bed giving away sums here and there refers to making bequests which are given after his death. As such, they do not affect what he has in life. Yet there is also a subtle reference in this statement. The first two sums are bequests by will, while the third one is an inheritance that is determined by God in the elaborate Islamic system of inheritance.

We should also explain that the opening of the Prophet's statement says: 'Well, by your father'. This is not an oath, because in Islam it is forbidden to swear by anyone other than God. It is merely a commonly used phrase which is not intended as an oath and never understood as such. What is forbidden is an intended oath by anyone other than God. Here, no such intention is made. Hence, it is permissible to say such a phrase.

Another *ḥadīth* takes up a different point, highlighting an important issue. The Prophet advises us on how to behave when we need others to give us something.

782. (*Athar* 181) ʿAbdullāh ibn Masʿūd said: 'When any of you requests something, let him do so gently, because he will only get what has been decreed for him. None of you should come to his fellow man and start flattering him and thus break his back'.

Everyone of us goes through situations where he can do with some help, service, kindness or advice from someone else. When you are in need of someone else, the proper Islamic way is not to request it with much persistence. If it is denied, then one should try to do without it. It is not good that one makes his request with very strong emphasis so as to embarrass the other person to the extent that he gives against his own wishes. It is always better to make one's request gently, without persistence, so that people either respond with kindness or excuse themselves without embarrassment.

Moreover, the *ḥadīth* advises us against heaping praise on the one from whom we request something. Some people resort to this, speaking very highly about the person concerned, seeking to ensure that their request is granted. This is akin to 'breaking his back'. Indeed, such praise could easily be a mark of hypocrisy. If the other person listens to his own praise, he is encouraging such hypocrisy. If he grants the request put to him after such praise, his motive may not be pure. He may, as a result of such heaped praise, give that person an unfair advantage. If he does so, he works to his own disadvantage, and the Prophet describes this as breaking his back.

An alternative reading of this last statement suggests that the person making such praise breaks his own back. If the praise is undeserved, then he is a hypocrite. If it is deserved, then by stating it to his face he is using the praise to gain advantage with that person. If it is undeserved, it is open hypocrisy. A hypocrite will not be successful. It is by hypocrisy that he breaks his own back.

783. Yasār ibn 'Abdullāh al-Hudhali reports that the Prophet said: 'If God wants to gather someone's soul in a particular place, He will place there something he needs'.[550]

The Prophet often spoke to his companions, and indeed to all generations of Muslims, pointing out the basic facts of life and faith. One of these is that death comes to us at all times and places. Sometimes a person lives in one place, but God has willed that he should die in a faraway place, perhaps in the other hemisphere. If he is unlikely to go there, then God will make it necessary for him to travel there. He will go and then meet his death. Nothing can frustrate God's will. Whatever He determines is and will be accomplished as He decides.

784. (*Athar* 182) 'Abd al-'Azīz said: 'Abu Hurayrah was with us one evening when he looked at a star facing him and said: "By Him who holds Abu Hurayrah's soul in His hand, some people to whom positions of government have been assigned would one day wish that they had been hanging to that star and not having taken up such positions". He then turned to me and said: "May your hater perish! Does all this seem fair to the people of the East in their provinces?" I said: "Yes, indeed". He said: "May God make them rue what they have done. By Him who holds Abu Hurayrah's soul in His hand, He will drive them like mutilated asses, with their heads hanging down, until they send back farmers to their fields and shepherds to their herds".'[551]

---

550. Related by Aḥmad, al-Tirmidhi and al-Ḥākim.
551. Related by Aḥmad and Ibn Ḥibbān.

The first point in this *ḥadīth* is that people who assume high positions in government may regret so doing. This is because a position of power may tempt that person to exceed the limits of what is right. A ruler may give orders and impose certain things to preserve his power. His orders may represent some injustice to others. If this is the case, he will be punished for such injustice. God's punishment is so severe that all the authority that position of government imparts will disappear and whatever a person enjoyed as a result of it will seem very trivial, when compared to the punishment he is made to suffer. Hence, he will wish any calamity could have happened to him if only he could be released from what he did.

The picture given here is so vivid that the wish to disown everything one has done is very clear to us. It is a picture of a person holding on to a star, fearing to fall, but sensing the inevitability of such a fall. What happens to a person when he falls from an aeroplane is so fearful that we can hardly imagine it, although, compared to the distance between the earth and a planet or a star, the height at which an aeroplane flies is insignificant.

The *ḥadīth* then wonders at the deeds people of the east did, and if they thought they were fair. The reporter answers in the affirmative. The people of the east included at the Prophet's time all areas beginning with Iraq. The Prophet said that trouble would come from that direction. It was from these provinces that the internal conflicts within the Muslim state leading to the assassination of the third and fourth Caliphs started. Later troubles came from areas further east, until the Tartars marched against the Muslim state and destroyed its capital Baghdad. There were other problems in between which also started in eastern provinces. All this may be taken as confirmation of the Prophet's statement.

The *ḥadīth* then mentions that God has made the consequences of their deeds turn badly against them. The destruction they caused might have seemed, at the time when it was wreaked, to spell out total victory against one of the most powerful states at the time. But it was soon to be checked. The tide was turned against them, particularly the Tartars who suffered a resounding defeat at the hands of the Egyptian army in the Battle of ʿAyn Jālūt in Palestine. They could not imagine that such an army, much smaller than their own, could stand up to their might. Their defeat was total and their power collapsed.

The end result is spelled out very clearly showing that they would be driven back like mutilated asses. The *ḥadīth* does not mention how mutilated they would be, but the important reference here is that their defeat would be total, that they would suffer a multitude of injuries. They would hang their heads down in total humiliation. Their endeavours which promised so much, as they scored victory after victory, came to nothing. Thus, they came to rue what they had done. It was like those people taking up positions in government wishing that they were hanging from faraway planets and stars, if only they could be freed from the burden of their power. In the same way, the Tartars were driven back, ruing the day they started their destructive mission. It all came to nothing and they would only wish to return to their fields and cattle.

We have related the *ḥadīth* to certain historical events, but it may not be limited to these particular events. It may also be a reference to similar ones that may take place in the future.

39

Forms of Speech

SOMETIMES WE SAY things without paying much attention to their significance. We may be used to saying them, or we may have heard others saying them time after time. This familiarity tends to make us overlook their subtle meanings. As we need to observe certain values in the way we talk, it is important to know what the real significance is of whatever we say.

> 785. (*Athar* 183) Mughīth claimed that 'Abdullāh ibn 'Umar asked him who his master was. He said: 'God and so-and-so', [naming a certain person]. Ibn 'Umar said to him: 'Do not say it like that. You must not join anyone with God. You should say: 'so-and-so after God".'

Needless to say, Mughīth had not thought of his master as a partner with God. However, the fact that he mentioned him with God, separated by the conjunction, 'and', suggests such partnership. It is the same when we refer to a company of two partners, mentioning the two names with 'and' in between. Hence Ibn 'Umar, a scholar with a keen sensitivity to what is contrary to Islamic practices and behaviour, drew his attention to the irregularity in the way he spoke. He also told him how to phrase his answer. He should mention his master's name, but he should add that he comes after God. Thus, he assigns to God the fact that He is the overall master of all situations.

The same applies to any form in which we mention someone's name second to God. We should make it clear that God's position is that of overall superiority to everyone and everything.

> 786. Ibn 'Abbās reports: 'A man said to the Prophet: "Whatever God wills and you will". The Prophet said to him: "You have set up an equal to God. It is what God alone wills".'[552]

The Prophet is clearly teaching us to place the will of any person as completely secondary to God's will. This is the proper Islamic attitude. The Prophet wanted to inculcate this point in the minds of his companions and followers. Thus, he points to the fact that the conjunction 'and' signifies partnership without ranking; thus it makes whatever it joins together as equals. In this it is different from the word, 'then', which signifies a secondary position. Thus, then makes the wish of a person subservient to God's will.

All this obviously applies to things in which people's wishes or actions play an actual part. Needless to say, there are things no one other than God can influence. These may not be attributed to anyone other than God, even if we use the conjunction, 'then'. To attribute them to anyone in addition to God signifies that God cannot accomplish them on His Own. This detracts from God's ability. Hence, we should be very careful. In fact, it is always better to speak of God's will as being the ultimate, without adding anyone as involved.

---

552. Related by Aḥmad, Ibn Majah, al-Nasā'ī in Al-Sunan al-Kubra and al-Darimi.

On singing and idle play

787. (*Athar* 184) ʿAbdullāh ibn Dinār reports: 'I went to the marketplace with ʿAbdullāh ibn ʿUmar where we passed by a young girl who was singing. He said, "Had Satan left anyone alone, he would have left this girl alone".'

This is not a *ḥadīth* attributed to the Prophet. It simply quotes a scholar of high repute who was one of the Prophet's companions. Scholars of *Ḥadīth* consider that the Prophet's companions would not have said something directly related to religion unless they were absolutely certain of their grounds, relying on guidance from the Prophet. Hence, they treat their statements as if they were attributed to the Prophet.

Some people quote this *ḥadīth* in support of the view that singing is forbidden, but this *ḥadīth* does not signify prohibition. It is well known that to pronounce anything as forbidden, we need very clear evidence, because the authority to prohibit anything belongs to God alone. All that this statement by ʿAbdullāh ibn ʿUmar signifies is that the girl's action had been encouraged by Satan. This may refer to what the girl was singing, which means that the lyric she was singing was not appropriate, or to the fact that she was singing in the marketplace.

As for singing itself, it is subject to different rules according to the words, the person singing and the way the singing is performed. If the singing is of the chanting type, like one does when repeating a poem or saying poetry with an affected voice, to indicate one's pleasure or to give pleasure to an audience, all this is permissible. If, on the other hand, one is singing something that describes a certain woman's beauty, or a lyric describing wine and its effect on one's mind so as to encourage drinking or to associate it with pleasure and happiness, or to arouse other evil thoughts, then such singing is forbidden.

All this shows that singing may be permissible in certain situations and forbidden in others. What influences the verdict is the type of song, its words, the aim of the singer and the way it is sung.

When singing is only a pastime, then the ruling differs according to the situation. If we are listening to singing for relaxation purposes, after which we go back to our serious work, then this is perfectly legitimate. If we are just killing time by listening to singing, we may be close to committing something forbidden, because killing time aimlessly and without benefit is close to prohibition. It is in this framework that we should understand the next *ḥadīth*:

788. Anas ibn Mālik reports that the Prophet said: 'I do not belong to idle play and idle play does not belong to me in any way'. He meant that he does not do any worthless thing.

This *ḥadīth* makes it clear that the Prophet did not approve of killing time in any profitless pursuit. Islam is serious and it wants people to benefit by their time so that they improve their situation in this life and in the life to come.

789. (*Athar* 185) Commenting on the verse that says: '*Among people there are some who would pay for idle talk*,' (31: 6) Ibn 'Abbās said: 'It is singing and similar things'.

790. Al-Barā' ibn 'Āzib reports that the Prophet said: 'Spread the greeting of peace and you will attain to safety. Idle play is evil'.

791. (*Athar* 186) Fuḍālah ibn 'Ubayd was with a group of people when he was informed that some people were playing with dice, or backgammon. He got up in anger and spoke against it in the strongest of terms. He said: 'A person who plays it to devour what it brings him is like one who eats the flesh of swine or performs his ablution with blood".

In the first of these three *ḥadīths* Ibn 'Abbās refers to singing as an aspect of 'idle talk'. Scholars agree that the verse has a much broader significance. It is anything that people use to divert others from following God's guidance and to lead them astray. This applies to any temptation or seduction that encourages people to abandon God's guidance in preference to something that draws them away from the right path. Some singing falls into this category and some does not. If it does, it is forbidden.

The second *ḥadīth* encourages us to spread the greeting of peace, which is characteristic of Muslims. It encourages friendly relations, since we tell people that we wish them peace and happiness the first moment we see them. It is a much better greeting than what other communities have, such as 'good morning' and its equivalents. The second sentence in this *ḥadīth* refers to wasting time which the Prophet describes as evil.

The third *ḥadīth* is more specific than the other two, but it relates merely to playing games with dice. Scholars say that games that rely merely on chance, like those decided with the throw of a dice, such as backgammon, cards and the like, are forbidden. They are not only a way to pass time in useless pursuits; they often lead to friction between friends. However, when such a game is used as a means of gambling, as when the two players or parties to the game pledge a wager which the winner of the game receives, while the loser gets nothing, then they are doubly forbidden. This is what Fuḍālah spoke about very strongly, likening the taking of such winnings to eating pork or using blood for ablution. Both are obviously forbidden.

792. (*Athar* 187) Zayd ibn Wahb reports that 'Abdullāh ibn Mas'ūd said: 'You are living at a time when there are many people of understanding and few orators. There are few who ask and many who give. In this time action directs desire. In future, there will be a time when few are the people of understanding and orators are in plenty. There will be many who ask and few who give. Desire will direct action. Know that at the end of time good behaviour is better than some actions'.[553]

'Abdullāh ibn Mas'ūd was one of the earliest of the Prophet's companions and he acquired great insight into Islam and reported numerous *ḥadīths*. He is speaking about his own time, when people dedicated themselves to do the best that could earn God's pleasure and increase their reward. Hence, there were among them many who sought to have insight into faith, while they were sparing in what they said. They preferred that their deeds should speak for them, and their deeds were guided by what they learnt directly from the Prophet.

---

553. Related by Mālik.

He is warning against a time when the reverse situation will prevail, with many people ready to speak out while only few are true scholars of good insight. Such people are often guided by their desire and their eagerness to have the best in this life, caring little for the life to come. Even good behaviour will be better than some actions, as these will not be dedicated to earn God's pleasure.

793. Al-Jurayri said: 'I asked Abu al-Ṭufayl: "Did you see the Prophet?" He said: "Yes, and I do not know of any man left alive on earth who saw the Prophet other than myself. He was white with a handsome face".'

Yazīd ibn Hārūn quotes al-Jurayri as saying: 'Abu al-Ṭufayl (ʿĀmir ibn Wāthilah al-Kināni) and I were performing the *ṭawāf* around the Kaʿbah when he said: "No one who saw the Prophet remains alive except myself". I asked: "And you saw him?" He said: "Yes". I asked: "What did he look like?" He said: "He was white, handsome and of medium stature".'[554]

This *ḥadīth* is given twice, each time with a different chain of transmission, both ending with al-Jurayri quoting Abu al-Ṭufayl. He gives a simple description of the Prophet, stating that he was perhaps the last of the Prophet's companions alive.

794. Ibn ʿAbbās reports that the Prophet said: 'Right guidance, good behaviour and a moderate way of life are one of twenty-five parts of prophethood'.[555]

Ibn ʿAbbās reports that the Prophet said: 'Right guidance, good behaviour and a moderate way of life are one of seventy parts of prophethood'.

This *ḥadīth* is entered in this way, given twice with a different chain of transmission in each. It groups three components as a portion or feature of prophethood. In the first version they are one of twenty-five parts, while in the second they constitute one of seventy parts of

554. Related by Muslim and Abū Dāwūd.

555. Related by Abū Dāwūd.

prophethood. This does not mean that anyone can acquire the other parts to become a prophet. The line of prophethood has ended with the final Prophet, Muhammad (peace be upon him). What it means is that these are good features which are certain to earn God's pleasure and give a person good standing with God. The second version is the same as *ḥadīth* Number 471.

795. 'Ikrimah said: 'I asked 'Ā'ishah: "Have you ever heard God's Messenger (peace be upon him) quoting poetry?" She said: "When he came home, he sometimes said: News may be brought to you by someone whom you have not commissioned [for the task]".'[556]

769. Ibn 'Abbās said: 'This is a Prophet's word: "News may be brought to you by someone whom you have not commissioned [for the task]".'

These two *ḥadīths* are very similar. The Prophet was the most eloquent of all Arabs, at a time when they stored much by good speech, and poetry flourished among them. When they realised that a young man could compose poetry, they celebrated the news and gave him every encouragement. Poetry played the role of the media in our own time. However, the Prophet did not compose any poem, or even a line of poetry, although he appreciated it and commented on what was of high standard. God says in reference to the Prophet: '*We have not taught him poetry; nor is it fitting for him [to be a poet]*'. (36: 69) Hence, 'Ikrimah's question was whether the Prophet might have quoted some lines of poetry. She told him that he sometimes said this sentence, which is the second half of a line from a poem by Ṭarafah ibn al-'Abd, a fine pre-Islamic poet. We have no report by any of the Prophet's companions that he ever quoted a single full line of poetry, although we have a *ḥadīth* when he asked one of his companions to recite to him some poetry, as stated in Number 802.

The second *ḥadīth* quotes Ibn 'Abbās saying that his half line of poetry was the word of a Prophet. He either meant that the Prophet said

556. Related by al-Nasā'ī and al-Tirmidhi.

it, or that it was said by an earlier prophet. That Prophet Muhammad said it is clear from the first *ḥadīth*, but it might have been said by an earlier prophet and Ṭarafah knew it, using it in his poem after phrasing it in what suited his purpose.

797. Abu Hurayrah reports that the Prophet said: 'If any of you expresses a wish, he should consider what he is hoping to have. He does not know what he will be granted'.[557]

The Prophet's instruction merely alerts us to being careful so that we know for certain what we are requesting God to grant us. It may be that we wish for something and pray for it. Then when we are granted that very thing, we may regret it because it turns out to be disadvantageous. A good practice to make sure that we are only given what is good is to pray to God to grant us our wish if He knows that it will bring us benefit.

Some people, however, think that we should not be praying for too much, so that we do not show ourselves to be greedy. This may be true if we are seeking a gift from a human being like ourselves. But when we pray to God for a favour, we know that we are asking the One who owns the whole universe. He will not be any poorer for granting us whatever we ask Him. It is to this aspect that the Prophet points in the *ḥadīth* reported by his wife, 'Ā'ishah: 'When anyone expresses his wish, he should ask for plenty. He is only asking his Lord, the Mighty and Exalted'.[558] So if we are seeking riches or benefits from God, we need not feel shy to seek much, because we are asking the Most Generous.

798. Wā'il ibn Ḥujr reports that the Prophet said: 'Do not call grapes karm, but call them *ḥabalah*'.[559]

In certain parts of the Arab world, a vineyard is called *karm*, and grapes are also called by this name, while *ḥabalah* refers to certain

557. Related by Aḥmad and al-Bayhaqi in Shu'ab al-Īmān.
558. Related by al-Ṭabārani in Al-Mu'jam al-Awsaṭ.
559. Related by Muslim, al-Dārimi, Ibn Ḥibbān and Abu 'Awānah.

types of grapes. *Karm* is derived from a root that signifies generosity. Perhaps the Prophet was thinking of this when he said this *ḥadīth*, considering that wine is made of grapes. Hence, he did not wish wine to be associated with generosity, even in a very implicit way. Needless to say, in some communities where wines and intoxicants are part of the social habit, certain manners are observed, including a drinking hospitality.

799. This is the same as Number 775, with a different chain of transmission.

800. Ḥamnah bint Jaḥsh reports that the Prophet said: 'What is it? O person!'

801. (*Athar* 188) Ḥabib ibn Ṣahbān al-Asadi said: 'I saw 'Ammār praying an obligatory prayer. When he finished, he said to a man next to him: 'O person!' Then he got up.

These last two *ḥadīths* do not tell us the context in which the Prophet and his companion, 'Ammār ibn Yāsir, used this phrase. They tell us, however, that the Prophet's companions were keen to report everything they heard from the Prophet and to do as he did. Ḥamnah was the Prophet's sister-in-law, as he married her sister Zaynab. Ḥamnah was married to Ṭalḥah ibn 'Ubaydillāh, one of the Prophet's earliest companions and one of the ten to whom the Prophet gave the happy news of being in heaven. 'Ammār was also one of the earliest people to accept Islam, and he endured much torture by the idolaters who tried to force him to renounce his new faith. Although he saw both his parents killed by the unbelievers, he remained steadfast. He lived to old age and was killed fighting in the Battle of Ṣiffīn, alongside 'Ali ibn Abu Ṭālib. The second *ḥadīth* suggests that he might have seen something that reminded him of what the Prophet said on a similar occasion, and he said the same thing.

802. Al-Sharīd ibn Suwayd said: 'The Prophet took me behind him on his mount and said: "Do you memorise some of the poetry of Umayyah ibn Abi al-Ṣalt?" I said: "Yes", and I recited

one line. He said: "Go on". [I continued] until I recited 100 lines'.[560]

Umayyah ibn Abi al-Ṣalt was a fine poet from Taif who prayed for a prophet to save the Arabs from the absurdity of idolatry. He met the Prophet and listened to his recitation of Surah 36 of the Qur'an, commenting afterwards that the Prophet said the truth. However, it is said that he had hoped to be the one to be chosen by God for prophethood. He hesitated long about Islam, and is said to have decided to accept it. However, some idolaters reminded him of his relatives who were killed by the Muslims in the Battle of Badr and this stopped him from accepting the faith. His poetry was full of wisdom. Hence, the Prophet wanted to listen to it. In this instance, no less than a hundred lines were recited to him.

803. 'Abdullāh ibn Abu Mūsa reports that 'Ā'ishah said: 'Do not stop standing up at night to pray. The Prophet never omitted to do so. If he was ill or felt lack of vitality, he would pray seated'.[561]

Night worship is strongly recommended. It was made obligatory for the Prophet at the beginning of Islam, but one year later, the obligation was relaxed to make it voluntary. However, the Prophet continued to do it practically every day of his life. He is quoted to have said that the best type was that practised by Prophet David who slept the first half of the night, then woke up for prayer and continued in worship for one-third of the night, going to sleep for the last one-sixth part of the night. Thus, he would start the day refreshed after having spent a long portion of the night in worship.

Night worship can take any form: prayer, recitation of the Qur'an, glorification of God and praising Him, supplication, etc. It is highly effective in sharpening one's sense of faith and strengthening one's resolve to steer away from sin.

---

560. Related by Muslim.

561. Related by Abū Dāwūd.

The *ḥadīth* tells us that the Prophet might do his night worship, or part of it, in a sitting position if he was ill or tired. This option is open to us in similar situations.

804. This *ḥadīth* is the same as Number 675, with a different chain of transmission.

805. Anas ibn Mālik reports: 'Abu Ṭalḥah knelt before God's Messenger, emptied his quiver and chanted: "May my face be protection for your face, and may I perish to save you".'

The Prophet's companions realised the great blessing God had given them as they were the first to believe in Islam and support His messenger (peace be upon him). They recognised that being in the Prophet's company gave them the best life in this present world and ensured for them a happy state in his company in the life to come. Their recognition was manifest in the way they addressed him, expressing their love and readiness to do their best to ensure that he was safe and could deliver his message without trouble or impediment.

In the Battle of Uḥud, the Muslims were on the losing side and the unbelievers launched a determined attack aiming at killing the Prophet. Most of the Muslim army were in retreat. Only a few of his companions remained steadfast by him, determined to defend him to the last drop of their blood. One of these was Abu Ṭalḥah, who was a good marksman. He had his quiver with him and placed his arrows in front of the Prophet. He took them one by one and aimed them at the unbelievers, trying to stop their attack. Every time he took an arrow, he looked at the Prophet and said: 'May my face be protection for your face, and may I perish to save you'. Some reports suggest that he might have added: 'Peace be to you, without saying farewell'. The fact that one of the Prophet's companion said, 'may I perish to save you', to the Prophet and he approved it suggests that it is perfectly permissible.

806. Abu Darr said: 'The Prophet was heading towards al-Baqīʿ, and I followed him. As he turned his head back, he saw me and called out: "Abu Dharr". I said: "At your service, Messenger of

God, and may I be a sacrifice for you". He said: "Those who enjoy riches in this life will be the ones with very little on the Day of Judgement, except for those who spend freely, in the right ways". I said: "God and His Messenger know best". He repeated this three times. We then came close to Mount Uḥud. He called out: "Abu Dharr". I said: "At your service, Messenger of God, and may I be a sacrifice for you". He said: "I would not like that Muhammad's family should have the equal of Uḥud in gold and they hold on by nightfall to a single *dinār*, or he might have said a little weight". Sometime later we passed by a valley, and he moved away from me. I thought he wanted to relieve himself, so I sat down at an edge waiting for him, but he took so long that I started to worry about him. Then I heard him as if he were talking to someone, but then he came alone. I asked: "Messenger of God, who was the man you were talking to?" He asked me: "Did you hear him?" I said: "Yes". He said: "It was Gabriel who came to give me the happy news that anyone of my followers who dies associating no partners with God will be in heaven". I said: "Even if he commits adultery and theft?" He answered: "Yes".'[562]

The first thing to be said about this highly authentic *ḥadīth* is that the Prophet used to speak to his companions about things that he knew would appeal to them. Abu Dharr was a man to whom riches represented no temptation. His life showed that he cared very little for worldly pleasures and riches. Hence, the Prophet wanted to strengthen this trait in his character. Thus, he spoke to him about the worthlessness of life's comforts and pleasures. Money, which is essential for any material comfort, means very little.

The first comment the Prophet makes is that those who have riches will be the poor relatives on the Day of Judgement unless, in this life, they spend their money for good purposes. He then confirms this when he sees Mount Uḥud, stating that even if he had a similar mountain of gold in his family's possession, he would not be very happy unless he could spend it all the same day for charitable purposes. This is a highly graphic description, because no one could ever own a gold mountain,

562. Related by al-Bukhari under several headings.

but even if the Prophet could have had it, he would have spent it all, leaving nothing for his family. Life would not be any poorer for that. Indeed this is the usage of wealth that earns rich rewards.

The third point concerns the happy news given to him by the Angel Gabriel. It is indeed a happy news for every believer in God. It is made clear to us all that we need to ensure the purity of our faith to be guaranteed admission into heaven. This means that we must not entertain any thought of there being any deity in any shape or form, other than God, the Mighty and Exalted. He is the only God in the universe with no partners of any sort. We need to understand fully what God says in a sacred *ḥadīth*, as quoted by the Prophet: 'I am the least in need of partners: anyone who associates with me anyone or anything, I abandon him to that partner'.[563]

Thus, if one believes in God's oneness, and does not allow this belief to be marred by any thought of any partner with God, then he or she will be in heaven. We need to make it clear here that sometimes people who would not countenance any suggestion of there being any God or deity other than God, still may attribute some of God's essential qualities, which apply to Him alone, to other beings. This is a form of associating partners with God which we must guard against. For example, sovereignty in the universe belongs solely to God, and it is manifested most clearly in the exercise of the authority to legislate. If we assign such authority to anyone or any collective body, giving that person the right to enact legislation that contravenes God's law, then we are making that person a partner with God, since we have given him one of the most essential qualities that belong to God alone.

When the Prophet mentions this happy news to his companion, Abu Dharr, the latter is so delighted. However, he wanted to make sure. Hence, his question whether this applied to a person who might commit some of the more serious offences, such as theft and adultery. The Prophet confirms that this is the case. What this boils down to is the very basic principle that believing in God's oneness is the key to heaven. No sin is too great to be pardoned if one believes in God's oneness. Conversely, no good action is of any value if one is guilty of associating partners with God.

---

563. Related by Muslim and Ibn Mājah.

Reciprocated love

Perhaps there were no ties of love in the history of mankind stronger than those which existed between the Prophet and his companions. They disowned their old family and tribal ties to replace them with a new tie of faith that united them with their brethren. Furthermore, their relationship with the Prophet was of a very special type. They knew that to be true believers they should love God's messenger more than they loved anyone and anything. The Prophet himself loved his companions dearly and looked after them. He took interest in every one of them. None was unimportant. None was dispensable.

807. ʿAli said: 'I never heard the Prophet (peace be upon him) offering sacrifice for anyone after he said this to Saʿd [ibn Abu Waqqāṣ]. I heard him say: "Shoot; may my parents be sacrificed for your sake".'[564]

We need first to mention that the phrase, 'May I, or may my father or parents, be sacrificed for you', was never meant literally by the Arabs. It was an expression of genuine love, often coupled with approval of what the person addressed was doing. Thus, we should understand the Prophet's words as he spoke to Saʿd as encouragement for a fighter when a battle was raging. Saʿd was one of the early Muslims. His life showed complete devotion to the cause of Islam, and readiness to sacrifice his life at any time for his faith. In this instance, the Muslims were engaged in one of their first major battles when they were heavily outnumbered by the unbelievers. They needed every little extra effort to ensure their success. A good marksman like Saʿd needed no reminder of the critical situation, but the Prophet's words were sure to make him exert all his efforts in the battle.

The Prophet is also quoted to have said to his other companions, referring to Saʿd: 'This is my maternal uncle. Let everyone of you bring his uncle to us'. This is again a gesture intended to raise morale. Saʿd was much younger than the Prophet. At the time, he was perhaps just about 30 years of age, while the Prophet was nearly 55. Moreover,

---

564. Related by Aḥmad, al-Bukhari, Muslim and al-Tirmidhi.

Sa'd was not a close relation of the Prophet. He only belonged to the tribe of the Prophet's mother. So, by describing him as his uncle, the Prophet gave Sa'd additional determination to fight hard, which he duly demonstrated. He was one of the most courageous fighters, and he later commanded the Muslim army that fought the Battle of al-Qadisiyyah, which signalled the collapse of the Persian Empire at the hands of the Muslims.

The fact that the Prophet made this expression about parental sacrifice means that it is perfectly permissible to use it and similar expressions, even though one does not mean them literally. The fact that neither speaker nor addressee understands this expression literally makes it reasonable to use. Many of the Prophet's companions used it when they addressed him.

808. Buraydah said: 'The Prophet (peace be upon him) went out to the mosque where Abu Mūsa al-Ash'ari was reciting [the Qur'an]. He asked: "Who is this?" I said: "I am Buraydah, may I be sacrificed for you". The Prophet said: "This one has been given one of David's flutes".'[565]

Abu Mūsa was one of the finest reciters among the Prophet's companions. Apparently he had a melodious voice and he could recite in a highly inspiring way. When the Prophet heard him reciting, he was touched. Hence, his inquiry. When the narrator of the *ḥadīth* identified himself, the Prophet made his admiration of Abu Mūsa's recitation clear. He compared him to the Prophet David as he chanted his Psalms. When the Prophet David did so in praise of God, the mountains and the birds echoed his praises, as the Qur'an says. This is perhaps the most inspiring way of chanting God's praises.

The fact that the Prophet compares Abu Mūsa's recitation to the Prophet David's chanting of the Psalms speaks very highly of the inspiration Abu Mūsa's recitation generated.

We also note that Buraydah immediately indicated readiness to do whatever the Prophet ordered. This was a mark of his love for the Prophet.

---

565. Related by Muslim and al-Ḥākim.

Mutual love was also the mark of relations between the Prophet's companions. When a young man spoke to a senior companion of the Prophet, the latter would respond with endearing phrases.

809. (*Athar* 189) Sharīk ibn Namlah reports: 'I visited 'Umar ibn al-Khaṭṭāb. [He called me] "Nephew". He then asked me [about myself] and I told him my lineage. He realised that my father died before Islam. He, therefore, called me, "Son!"'[566]

810. Anas said: 'I was a servant of the Prophet, and I used to enter without asking permission. One day I came and he said to me: "Son, hold on. Something has changed. You may not come in unless you are given permission".'[567]

811. (*Athar* 190) Abu Ṣa'ṣa'ah said: 'Abu Sa'īd al-Khudri said to me: "My son."'[568]

These *ḥadīths* are grouped together because of the use of the appellation, 'my son', by the Prophet and his companions when addressing young men. They tell us how the Prophet's companions were keenly aware of their close ties as brethren belonging to the Muslim community. However, when any of them belonged to a father who had died without becoming a Muslim, then the ties are with that person alone. Hence, 'Umar's change of mode in his address. His ties were with Sharīk, not with his father. Therefore, he could call Sharīk his son, but he could not describe his father as his brother.

The second *ḥadīth* refers to the command given to the Prophet's wives to be veiled. Therefore, Anas could no longer just enter the Prophet's home without first requesting permission.

---

566. Related by Ibn Abu Shaybah.
567. Related by al-Tirmidhi.
568. Related by al-Bukhari.

On feelings

The Prophet was keen to show his companions and all Muslims that it is important to give a good impression, or to impart a good feeling to other people. Hence, he instructed his companions to choose good names for their children. Similarly, the Prophet taught his companions not to say things about themselves that may give a bad or a wrong impression.

812. ʿĀ'ishah reports that the Prophet said: 'Let none of you say, "I am foul"; rather, he should say, "I do not feel well".'[569]

813. Sahl ibn Ḥunayf reports that the Prophet said: 'Let none of you say, "I am foul"; rather, he should say, "I do not feel well".'[570]

What the Prophet points out here is that we should not attribute any foul status or feeling to ourselves, even if this only means that we are complaining of some illness, pain or discomfort. The Arabic word the Prophet uses for 'foul', which is *khabuthat*, is derived from the same root as 'evil'. Hence, he wanted Muslims never to attribute evil to themselves, because evil is Satan's work. When one wants to express a certain condition, he should make clear that he is only talking about what he feels at that particular moment, and he should simply say that he is not in the best of feelings or spirits.

Similarly, our names are like marks attached to us. Hence, we should not give the wrong marking to our children or ourselves. Arabs often use the formula 'Abū', which means 'father of' in speech, and this indicates respect. They use it in reference to each other, whether the person concerned is present or absent. This is an age old tradition. It could be attached to a man's eldest son, or to a particular quality of his, or to something special to him.

---

569. Related by al-Bukhari, Muslim and al-Nasā'ī.
570. Related by al-Bukhari, Muslim and Abū Dāwūd.

40

On Names and Appellations

814. Hānī' ibn Yazīd said: 'I came with my people to meet the Prophet (peace be upon him). He heard them calling me Abu al-Ḥakam. The Prophet called me and said: "It is God who is the arbiter, and to Him all rule belongs. Why have you called yourself Abu al-Ḥakam?" I said: "It is not so. But when my people are in dispute over something, they come to me and I arbitrate between them. Both parties are happy with my ruling". The Prophet said: "How excellent!" He then asked me: "How many children do you have?", I said: "I have Shurayḥ, 'Abdullāh and Muslim, all the sons of Hānī'". He asked "Who is the eldest?" I said: "Shurayḥ". The Prophet said: "Then you are Abu Shurayḥ". The Prophet prayed for me and my children'.

The Prophet heard the same group calling one of them 'Abd al-Ḥajar. The Prophet asked him: "What is your name?" He said: "'Abd al-Ḥajar". The Prophet said: "No. You are 'Abdullāh".

Shurayḥ said: "When it was time for Hānī' to return home, he went to the Prophet and said: "Tell me what would ensure admission into heaven for me?" The Prophet said: "Make sure to say what is good and offer food".[571]

THE FIRST THING to note about this *ḥadīth* is that the Prophet took names seriously and wanted his companions to have only what is good and acceptable appellation. Here we see him changing two people's names or titles. In the first case, the man was given a nickname on the basis of his sound judgement and fairness. But since al-Ḥakam is an attribute of God, giving such a name to a man is discouraged. There was nothing wrong with the name or the nickname itself. Indeed, it imparted a sense that the person concerned was wise and highly respected. However, it is better not to use it on account of the uneasy feeling it may generate given it is associated with God.

When the man explained to the Prophet the reason for having been given this nickname, the Prophet commended him. The Prophet replaced his title by the more normal one of calling him as the father of his eldest son. He further added a prayer for him and his children.

In the second case, the man was called 'Abd al-Ḥajar. 'Abd' means 'servant or slave', and this is acceptable only when one of God's names or attributes is added to it. In this case, however, what was added was al-Ḥajar, meaning 'the stone or rock'. This was perhaps a reference to an idol made of stone, or to a particular stone his people honoured. Such a name could not be accepted in an Islamic community. Hence, the Prophet changed it immediately, calling the man 'Abdullāh, which is an amalgamation of the two words: 'Abd and Allah. So there can be no confusion, he would admit to serve only God.

We note that in both cases, there was very good reason for changing the two men's names. Indeed the Prophet did not change the name of any of his companions, unless there was valid reason for so doing. When a name is in breach of an Islamic value, or when it has a bad meaning, the Prophet changed it. Otherwise, his companions retained their original names.

---

571. Related by al-Nasā'ī, Abū Dāwūd, al-Tirmidhi, al-Ḥākim and Ibn Ḥibbān.

The last portion of the *ḥadīth* indicates that the first man, Hāni', who used to be called Abu al-Ḥakam, was of strong faith and sound mind. He asked the Prophet a direct question, wanting to know the shortest way to heaven. The Prophet told him of two qualities, which such a wise person could readily appreciate: good speech and generosity. Both demonstrate kindness and care for others. When people are well received and offered food and hospitality, they are grateful. Offering these when one is able to do so not only earns people's gratitude, it earns reward from God. When these become a person's normal characteristics, they ensure admission to heaven.

Pleasant names

A good name imparts a good feeling. It is well received by people. When a name suits a particular occasion, it makes for optimism and expectation of success. The Prophet always preferred good names. If he wanted to assign a job to someone and found out that his name carried a good meaning, he felt pleased. If the man's name indicated the opposite, displeasure would clearly be seen on the Prophet's face.

815. Abu Ḥadrad reports that the Prophet said: 'Who will drive these camels of ours?' or he might have said: 'Who will deliver these camels of ours?' A man said: 'I will'. The Prophet said: 'What is your name?' The man mentioned his name, but the Prophet said to him: 'Sit down'. Another man stood up and the Prophet said: 'What is your name?' The man mentioned his name, but the Prophet said to him: 'Sit down'. Then another man stood up and the Prophet asked him: 'What is your name?' He said: 'Nājiyah'. He said: 'You are the man for this task. Drive them'.[572]

To start with we should mention that the name Nājiyah has connotations of fast travelling and going through a difficult mission safely. His name made him the right choice as it indicated successful completion of the

572. Related by al-Ḥākim.

task in hand. Apparently, this was at a time when the Prophet and his companions were prevented by the Quraysh from entering Makkah for their first umrah. They were in a state of consecration, and they had driven with them most of their animals which they intended to sacrifice at the end of their religious duty. Because they were physically prevented from getting into Makkah for umrah, they could not release themselves from consecration until after they had slaughtered their sacrificial animals. As the Prophet and his companions were so close to Makkah, he wanted the sacrifice to be offered within the Ḥaram area. Hence, his request for someone to drive them there.

Another version of this *ḥadīth* quotes Nājiyah ibn Jundub as saying: 'I went to the Prophet when he was prevented from visiting Makkah and said: "Messenger of God, send me with the sacrificial animals to slaughter inside the Ḥaram area". He asked: "How will you do it?" I said: "I will take a route through difficult valleys which they [i.e. the Makkans] cannot traverse". So he gave me the sacrificial animals and I slaughtered them in the Ḥaram'.

816. Ibn 'Abbās reports: 'The Prophet came towards us at speed when we were sitting down. We were alarmed by his speed as he walked towards us. When he reached us, he greeted us and said: "I have come speedily to inform you about the Night of Power, but I forgot which night it is as I was coming to you. Therefore, seek it in the last ten nights [of Ramadan]".'[573]

This *ḥadīth* is entered at this point, in between *ḥadīths* speaking about names. However, its subject matter is clear, and it is concerned with the identification of the Night of Power, or *Laylat al-Qadr*, which is described in the Qur'an as '*better than one thousand months*'. We are strongly recommended to spend this night, or the larger part of it in devotion, prayer, glorification of God and recitation of the Qur'an, etc. However, the Prophet did not define it exactly, mentioning that it is one of the last ten nights of Ramadan.

---

573. Related by Aḥmad.

817. Abu Wahb, a companion of the Prophet, reports that the Prophet said: 'Call your [children] by the names of the prophets. The names God loves best are 'Abdullāh and 'Abd al-Raḥmān. The most truthful names are Ḥārith and Hammām, and the most abhorrent are Ḥarb and Murrah'.[574]

Here, the Prophet gives us clear guidance on names, indicating which are liked by God and which are not so sound. First of all he encourages Muslims to call their children after earlier prophets. This is because the prophets were the best human beings. Anyone called after them derives honour from that fact. Hence, Muslims have always used these blessed names. Thus, names like Ibrāhīm, Isma'īl, Yūsuf, Yūnus, Mūsa, and the like are used by Muslims, generation after generation.

The Prophet then mentions that God loves the names of 'Abdullāh and 'Abd al-Raḥmān best. As we have already noted, 'Abd means servant or slave. When it precedes a name or an attribute of God, the name then acknowledges such servitude by the bearer to God. But even then the best of God's names and attributes to attach to it are Allah and al-Raḥmān. The first is God's own name which refers to none other than God. Al-Raḥmān attributes to God all mercy and power together. Again this is a name that may not be used, on its own, by anyone. Raḥīm, which also means merciful, may be used by us independently, but Raḥmān indicates absolute mercy by the One Who commands all power, which is the preserve of God alone. Hence, God loves these two names best.

Then, the Prophet tells us that Ḥārith and Hammām are the most truthful names. Literally, Ḥārith means a person who tills the earth for planting. We all strive in this life, and our striving is preparation for what we get in the life to come. As such we are in the same position as one who prepares his land and sows his seeds, hoping for a good harvest. We work in this life as much as we can, hoping that we arrive in the end with good results to ensure our happiness in the life to come. Hammām means a person who intends to do something or embarks on doing it. Needless to say, we all do this all the time.

---

574. Related by Aḥmad, al-Nasa'i and Abū Dāwūd.

Next, the Prophet mentions the most abhorrent names, Harb, which means 'war', and Murrah, which means 'bitter'. These were names used by the Arabs at the time. Why anyone would call his son by either name may be beyond our comprehension, but they did. The Prophet here expresses his disapproval of such names.

818. Jābir reports: 'One of us had a son born to him, and he called him al-Qāsim. We said to him, "We will not call you Abu al-Qāsim, and no position of honour may you have [on this account]". He mentioned this to the Prophet who told him: "Call your son 'Abd al-Raḥmān".'[575]

It should be explained that the Prophet was called Abu al-Qāsim, because his first son was named al-Qāsim. Although all three of the Prophet's sons died in infancy, he was known by that title. When this Anṣāri man named his son al-Qāsim, he would naturally be called Abu al-Qāsim, but then he would share a distinctive name with the Prophet. The Prophet's companions felt that they could not allow this. They made it clear to him that he could not gain easy honour in this way. Hence, his complaint to the Prophet. Hence, the Prophet chose the name God loves best, 'Abd al-Raḥmān to give to his son.

Changing names

When the Prophet saw a newborn, he would pray for the child and ask about his or her name. If he did not like it, he would change it. This was the case with boys and girls alike.

819. Sahl reports: 'Al-Mundhir ibn Abu Usayd was brought to the Prophet shortly after he was born. The Prophet placed him on his thigh and Abu Usayd was sitting near him. Then the Prophet was distracted by something. Abu Usayd told someone to take his son away, and he was lifted from the Prophet's thigh. Then the Prophet was alert and asked: "Where is the boy?"

575. Related by al-Bukhari.

Abu Usayd said: "We sent him home, Messenger of God". The Prophet asked: "What is he named?" The father told him, but the Prophet said: "No! His name is al-Mundhir".'[576]

In this instance, we note that the name given originally to the child is not mentioned. We realise that the Prophet disliked it for some reason. He gave him a new name, which means 'the warner', and the child was known by that name thereafter. His original name was forgotten. Needless to say, the Prophet would not have changed the child's name without reason. His practice was to change only those names which either gave a bad impression, or were unacceptable from an Islamic point of view.

820. Abu Hurayrah reports that the Prophet said: 'The worst name in God's view is that of a man who calls himself "king of kings".'[577]

The case here is very clear. This title belongs to God alone. No one may call himself by such a title, even though he may be an emperor who rules over a vast kingdom, in which many regions enjoy some autonomy and each of which has its king or president who defers to that emperor. This used to be the case in old empires, but even then, the overall lord of such an empire could not call himself king of kings, or by any similar title in any language. Anyone who rules over a kingdom or a state of any size must realise that being in such a position is an honour given to him by God and a great responsibility, as he will be accountable to God for his conduct. He should be grateful to God for the honour and privilege he has been given, and must do his best to ensure justice to all his people. If he calls himself 'king of kings', he only betrays his arrogance, and arrogant people are disliked by God.

821. Ṭalq ibn Ḥabīb reports: 'I was the most stubborn of people in denying intercession. I questioned Jābir and he said: "Ṭulayq, I heard the Prophet (peace be upon him) say: 'They

---

576. Related by al-Bukhari, Muslim and Ibn Mājah.

577. Related by al-Bukhari, Muslim, Abū Dāwūd and al-Tirmidhi.

will come out of the Fire after having entered it.' We recite [the Qur'an] as you recite".'[578]

This *ḥadīth* is entered here on account of Jābir calling his questioner Ṭulayq, a form that signifies reduction of the meaning of the original name. This form is used as an endearment or to signify a lower status. Jābir, who was close to the Prophet and reported more than 1,500 *ḥadīths*, knew Ṭalq's name, but he opted to reduce it to Ṭulayq to imply that he should defer to the Prophet's companions who had greater knowledge of both the Qur'an and the Sunnah.

Ṭalq ibn Ḥabīb belonged to the *tabi'īn* generation and he was known to be devout and truthful. However, he rejected the concept of the Prophet's intercession with God on the Day of Judgement on behalf of believers whose sins condemn them to hell. Yet, the reality is that God accepts the Prophet's intercession and orders their discharge. They are then admitted into heaven. This concept is confirmed in a number of authentic *ḥadīths*. However, people who deny the intercession rely on a couple of Qur'anic verses that state that the people of hell will not benefit by any intercession. Yet these verses clearly refer to unbelievers who either denied God altogether or associated partners with Him. To such people, no intercession will be of any benefit. Intercession will benefit people who committed many sins while believing in God's oneness and the message of Prophet Muhammad (peace be upon him).

Aḥmad's version of this *ḥadīth* is longer and quotes Ṭalq ibn Ḥabīb: 'I met Jābir ibn 'Abdullāh and recited to him every verse of the Qur'an in which God mentions that the dwellers of hell remain in it forever. He said to me: "Ṭalq, do you think that you know God's book and the Prophet's Sunnah better than me?" I said: "No, by God. You know God's book and the Prophet's Sunnah better than me". He said: "The verses you have recited concern the idolaters. As for people who commit sins, these are punished in hell before they are taken out of it". He then lifted his hands to his ears and said: "Have I not heard God's Messenger say: 'They will come out of the Fire after having entered it'."

578. Related by Aḥmad, al-Bukhari and Muslim.

822. Ḥanẓalah ibn Ḥidhyam said: 'The Prophet (peace be upon him) used to like that a person was called by the name he liked best and his favourite nickname'.

Everyone likes to be called by the name he prefers. The Prophet wanted this to be the normal practice in the Muslim community. As for nicknames, this refers to the formula Abū, which means 'father of' and it remains very common among Arabs. The preference applies to other nicknames, if people like to be called by them.

823. Ibn 'Umar reports: 'The Prophet (peace be upon him) changed the name 'Āṣiyah. He said to her: "You are Jamīlah".'[579]

As we have noted, the Prophet changed names only when necessary, and he did this with both boys and girls, men and women. In this case, the need for the change was very obvious. 'Āṣiyah is the female version of 'Āṣi and it means 'disobedient, rebellious, sinner, etc'. The Prophet points out here that such a name is unacceptable because it stresses a quality which is associated with rejecting the faith or being rebellious. The Prophet gave her the name Jamīlah, which means 'pretty'.

One girl name the Prophet consistently changed was Barrah, which apparently was very common among the Arabs. The name means 'righteous or dutiful'. There is nothing intrinsically bad about the name, but what the Prophet seemed to dislike is that it asserts something that no one can confirm. It is a sort of unsubstantiated claim.

824. Muhammad ibn 'Amr ibn 'Aṭā' reports: 'I visited Zaynab bint Abu Salamah. She asked me about the name of my sister. I said: "Her name is Barrah". Zaynab said: "Change her name. The Prophet married Zaynab bint Jahsh whose original name was Barrah and he changed it to Zaynab. He also came into Umm Salamah's room when he married her and he heard her calling me by my name, Barrah. He said [to my mother]: "Do not

---

579. Related by Muslim, Abū Dāwūd, al-Tirmidhi, Ibn Mājah, Ibn Ḥibbān and Abu 'Awānah.

commend yourselves. God knows best who of you is righteous and who is a sinner. Call her Zaynab". [My mother] said: "She is Zaynab". I said to her: "You then give her a new name". She said: "You replace it as God's Messenger (peace be upon him) did. Call her Zaynab".'[580]

In this story we have the reason for the change of name stated by the Prophet. He disliked a girl's or a woman's name asserting that she was righteous. In fact, the Prophet consistently highlighted the fact that a Muslim must not praise himself. If a woman is asked her name, and she says, 'I am Barrah', this may be construed as a pretence to purity or righteousness, when God states clearly in the Qur'an: '*Do not pretend to purity. He knows best who is truly God-fearing*'. (53:32)

In this story, the Prophet is said to have changed the name of one of his wives and the name of his step-daughter, both of whom were called Barrah. In each case, he called the woman or the girl concerned Zaynab, which is made up of two words Zayn and Abb, which respectively mean, adornment or beauty and father. This makes the name Zaynab akin to 'her father's darling'.

When the Prophet's stepdaughter heard the name Barrah given to a young girl, she told her brother to change her name. She gave her reasons and recommended very strongly that the girl be given the name the Prophet used in her own case. This is an exemplary case of following the Prophet's lead.

825. Ibn 'Abd al-Raḥmān ibn Sa'īd al-Makhzūmi said: 'My grandfather, whose name was al-Ṣarm, but which the Prophet changed to Sa'īd, told me: "I saw 'Uthmān reclining in the mosque".'[581]

Apparently the man was quite old when he accepted Islam at the time Makkah fell to Islam, or shortly before that. He fought with the Prophet in the Battle of Ḥunayn. It is reported that the Prophet asked him: 'Which of us is older: you or I?' His answer shows a great

---

580. Related by Aḥmad, al-Dārimi, Ibn Ḥibbān and Abu 'Awānah.
581. Related in part by al-Ḥākim.

degree of refinement, because the word *akbar* which means 'older' also means 'greater'. In answer, he said to the Prophet: 'You are greater than me, but I am more in years than you'. He is said to have lived until he was 120.

It is consistent with the Prophet's attitude to change this man's name, which meant 'cutting off', because the Prophet always encouraged kindness to others and maintaining good relations, particularly with relatives. However, in pre-Islamic Arabia, a tribal warring society, such a name was considered good, because it implied toughness.

As we noted in *ḥadīth* Number 817, the Prophet described the name Ḥarb, which means war, as most abhorrent. Yet such names sounded appropriate to the Arabs who were always at war with each other. Islam thus introduced radical changes into every aspect of the Arabs' lives:

826. 'Ali ibn Abu Ṭālib said: 'When al-Ḥasan was born, I named him Ḥarb. The Prophet came to us and said: "Show me my son. What have you named him?" We said: "Ḥarb". He said: "No, he is Ḥasan". Then when al-Ḥusayn was born, I named him Ḥarb. The Prophet came to us and said: "Show me my son. What have you named him?" We said: "Ḥarb". He said: "No, he is Ḥusayn". Then we had our third son and I named him Ḥarb. The Prophet came to us and said: "Show me my son. What have you named him?" We said: "Ḥarb". He said: "No, he is Muḥassin. I have given them the names of Aaron's children: Shabar, Shubayr and Mushabbir".'[582]

We should note first of all that 'Ali's third son mentioned in this *ḥadīth* was born to Fāṭimah, but apparently he died in infancy because nothing further is reported of him. The three names the Prophet chose for his grandchildren are derived from a root that means 'handsome, fine, acceptable, pleasing, etc.' While it was not surprising that 'Ali should wish to call his son Ḥarb, considering that he was one of the most heroic fighters for the cause of Islam, it was in line with the Prophet's attitude that he should change the name.

---

582. Related by Aḥmad and al-Ḥākim.

The *ḥadīth* does not mention why the Prophet changed the name on any of those three occasions. Hence, it may not be taken against 'Ali that he should call his second son by the name Ḥarb, which the Prophet changed the first time. However, what is amazing is that he should use it once more in naming his third son. It is very much unlike 'Ali to overlook the fact that the Prophet did not like such a name. Yet it is still difficult to see how he could use it the third time. Hence some *Ḥadīth* scholars have questioned the authenticity of this *ḥadīth*, or at least the part of it concerning the third child.

The Prophet's reference to the Prophet Aaron and the names of his three sons should be taken as it is. We do not know those names as they are apparently Hebrew names, but they have the same meanings as Ḥasan, Ḥusayn and Muḥassin.

827. Rā'iṭah bint Muslim reports that her father said: 'I fought with the Prophet in the Battle of Ḥunayn. He asked me : "What is your name". I said: "Ghurāb". He said, "No. Your name is Muslim".'[583]

Ghurāb is the Arabic word for the two birds, raven and crow. It is associated in Arabic culture with long separation between relatives and loved ones. As such, these birds are said to be harbingers of bad omens. In Islam, it is forbidden to attach a bad omen to anything. All events, good or bad, bringing good fortune or misfortune, are attributed to God alone. Yet still, the concept of bad omens is deeply rooted in human nature. Hence, the Prophet disliked any of his companions being so associated and hence, he changed the man's name to Muslim.

828. 'Ā'ishah reports: 'A man called Shihāb was mentioned in the presence of God's Messenger, and he said to him: "No. You are Hishām".'

Shihāb is another name the Prophet changed. It means a luminous meteor or a shooting star, but it also means 'flame, blaze, fire'. It is further said that it is the name of a place in hell. Hence the

---

583. Related by al-Bukhari.

Prophet did not wish that his companion be associated with such connotations. He, thus, changed his name to Hishām, which was a well liked Arabic name.

As noted in *ḥadīth* Number 823, the Prophet changed a woman's name from 'Āṣiyah to Jamīlah. The Prophet also changed the masculine form of this name, which is 'Āṣi.

829. Muṭī' said: 'I heard the Prophet say on the day of the liberation of Makkah: "No Qurayshi will be killed in punishment [for apostasy] from today until the Day of Resurrection". None of the Quraysh people named al-'Āṣ became a Muslim other than Muṭī'. He was called al-'Āṣ but the Prophet named him Muṭī''.[584]

This man is reported to have entered the mosque when the Prophet was seated on the platform. As he was entering, he heard the Prophet saying to the people to sit down. He immediately sat down where he was. When the Prophet finished, he went to the Prophet who asked him: 'How come I did not see you in the prayer?' He said: 'As I was coming in, I heard you saying to the people to sit down and I sat on hearing you'. The Prophet said to him: 'Then you are not al-'Āṣ, but rather you are Muṭī''. The two words have the opposite meanings. His original name meant 'rebellious' and the name given to him by the Prophet meant 'obedient'.

830. 'Ā'ishah reports: 'God's Messenger (peace be upon him) said to me: "'Ā'ish, this is Gabriel, giving you his greetings of salam". I said: "And I pay my greetings to him with God's mercy". The Prophet could see what I could not'.[585]

What is significant about this *ḥadīth* is that 'Ā'ishah is given a special greeting by the Angel Gabriel. She must have felt very happy at this, because angels could only act with God's permission. For the angel to offer his greetings to her means that she enjoys a special position,

584. Related by al-Dārimi.
585. Related in all six authentic anthologies.

which she certainly did. She returned the greeting with a better one, adding a wish for God's mercy. She also stated that she could not see the angel herself. It was only the Prophet who saw him.

In this *ḥadīth* the Prophet addresses his wife whom he loved dearly deleting the last letter of her name. This is a well known form of address, which expresses friendliness and endearment. In fact, such shortening of names is common in many cultures. English people use it very frequently. But when the Prophet used it, it signified that the person he was addressing had a special position in his esteem. The Prophet used this form with some of his very close companions, as is clear in the next *ḥadīth*:

831. Umm Kulthūm bint Thammāmah said: 'I went on pilgrimage. My brother, al-Mukhāriq ibn Thammāmah said to me: "Visit 'Ā'ishah and ask her about 'Uthmān ibn 'Affān. People have been saying all sorts of things about him here". I visited her and said: "One of your sons sends you his greetings and wishes to ask you about 'Uthmān ibn 'Affān". She answered: "And peace be to him with God's mercy. As for myself, I testify that I saw 'Uthmān in this house on a particularly hot night, when God's Messenger received revelations from Gabriel. The Prophet patted Ibn 'Affān's hand, or his shoulder and said: "Write down, 'Utham!" God would not have given such a close position to His Messenger except to one who is honoured by Him. God's curse be on anyone who abuses Ibn 'Affān".'[586]

In this *ḥadīth* the Prophet uses the name 'Uthmān in its reduced form, 'Utham, indicating close friendship. We note also the details given by 'Ā'ishah which confirm that she had full memory of the incident. She mentions the time and place where it happened. It was in her own room, on a very hot night. 'Uthmān was visiting the Prophet, and apparently he was the only one with the Prophet, apart from his wife and the Angel Gabriel. He was witnessing Qur'anic revelations being given to the Prophet. When the Prophet had received these new

---

586. Related by Aḥmad.

revelations, he asked 'Uthmān to commit them to writing, which he did frequently being one of the Prophet's scribes.

On this occasion, the Prophet did not merely ask him to write down the revelations he received. Instead, he patted him on the hand or shoulder, and used a very familiar form of address, expressing close friendship. 'Ā'ishah describes all these details and follows them with a comment which is in line with her profound understanding of Islam. God would not have allowed just an ordinary person to have such a close position with the Prophet unless he were genuinely good, and unless God Himself was pleased with him.

'Ā'ishah's final comment, damning anyone who abuses 'Uthmān is also appropriate. If God is so pleased with someone as to allow him closeness with His messenger, and if the Prophet trusts that man, speaks to him in a very friendly manner, and pats him as he speaks to him cordially, then what sort of man would heap abuse on such a person? Indeed he can only be a person to be cursed, and this is what 'Ā'ishah did. We disassociate ourselves from any such an attitude towards 'Uthmān and say without hesitation that 'Uthmān was one of the great personalities in the history of Islam. May God be pleased with him.

832. Bashīr ibn Ma'bad al-Sadūsi reports: 'I went to the Prophet and he asked me: "What is your name?" I said: "Zaḥm". The Prophet said: "No. You are Bashīr". I was walking with the Prophet and he said to me: "Ibn al-Khaṣāṣiyyah! What complaint do you still have against God? You are now walking side by side with God's Messenger". I said: "May my parents be sacrificed for you. I have no complaint against God. I have partaken of every good thing". He then passed by the graves of some unbelievers. He said: "These have missed much good". He repeated this three times. He then passed by the graves of some Muslims and said: "These received much good". He also repeated this three times. The Prophet then looked around suddenly and he saw a man walking in the graveyard, wearing sandals. He said to him: "You the man wearing fine sandals, remove your sandals". The man looked up and when he saw the Prophet, he took off his sandals and threw them away".'

833. Iyād ibn Laqīṭ said: 'I heard Layla, Bashīr's wife, narrating from Bashīr ibn al-Khaṣāṣiyyah. His name was Zaḥm, but the Prophet renamed him Bashīr'.

The first of these two *ḥadīths* is the same as Number 778, but adds here a question and answer: 'Ibn al-Khaṣāṣiyyah! What complaint do you still have against God? You are now walking side by side with God's messenger'. I said: 'May my parents be sacrificed for you. I have no complaint against God. I have partaken of every good thing'. In deviant beliefs, like those of the Arabian idolaters, people may have grievances or complaints against God when they feel that they are at some sort of disadvantage. Perhaps Bashīr might have voiced such a complaint in his pre-Islamic days. After he accepted Islam he banished any such thought and realised that he received God's grace.

834. Ibn ʿAbbās reports: 'Juwayriyyah's name was Barrah, but the Prophet (peace be upon him) renamed her Juwayriyyah'.[587]

835. Abu Hurayrah reports: 'Maymūnah's name was Barrah, but the Prophet (peace be upon him) renamed her Maymūnah'.

These two *ḥadīths* mean that three of the Prophet's wives were originally called Barrah, but each time he changed the name. The other one was Zaynab bint Jahsh. As noted earlier, his stepdaughter was also named Barrah and he renamed her Zaynab.

Good names, but not so good

836. Jābir reports that the Prophet said: 'If I live I will, God willing prohibit my community from giving [their children] the name of Barakah, Nāfiʿ, or Aflaḥ. (I am not sure that he also said Rāfiʿ.) It would be asked: "Is Barakah here?" and it would

587. Related by Aḥmad, Muslim, Abū Dāwūd, Ibn Ḥibbān and Abu ʿAwānah.

be answered, "No, not here". The Prophet died without having given such an order'.[588]

837. Jābir ibn ʿAbdullāh said: 'The Prophet wanted to prohibit giving children the names of Yaʿla, Barakah, Nāfiʿ, Yasār, Aflaḥ and similar names. However, he left the matter and said nothing about it'.[589]

Let us first of all look at the meaning of these names. Barakah means 'blessing'. Nāfiʿ means a person who brings benefit to others, while Aflaḥ means successful. The other two names added in the second *ḥadīth* are Yaʿla, which means to attain a higher position, and Yasār which means affluence. Yasār also has connotations of ease and dealing easily with people and problems.

Thus, all these names have good meanings and would give a good impression when mentioned. The Prophet, however, clarified why he disliked giving such names to children. He pointed out an everyday situation when people come to a person's home or workplace asking whether he is in. So, if the man, or the woman, are called Barakah, and someone asks for that person who happens to be absent, the answer could be taken to mean, 'there is no blessing in this place'. This applies to all these names. Thus, people may be told by a member of the person's family, 'there is no blessing, benefit, success, ease or going up in our place'. This is something that no one should say about their place, but it would be said in that situation. Hence, the Prophet wished to give his followers this advice.

We are told in both *ḥadīths* that the Prophet did not carry out his intention, which he had expressed in words. This is very significant. The Prophet delivered his message complete, leaving out nothing. It was not his practice to omit anything. Nor could it be said that he had forgotten, because God granted him the blessing of not forgetting anything related to his task of delivering His message to us. What the two *ḥadīths* mean in effect is that such names are discouraged, because of the Prophet's reasoning. Had the Prophet carried out his

---

588. Related by Abū Dāwūd.
589. Related by Muslim.

intention and issued this order, giving children such names would be totally forbidden. The fact that he only expressed an intention and did not carry it out signifies that the matter is less than forbidden, which means that it is discouraged.

Not only so, but if we can think of a situation where the point mentioned by the Prophet is not operative, then there would be no harm in giving such names. This is supported by the fact that some people had names of similar import, but the Prophet did not change them:

838. 'Umar ibn al-Khaṭṭāb reports: 'When the Prophet stayed away from his wives, I came across Rabāḥ, the Prophet's servant. I called out to him: "Rabāḥ! Ask permission for me to come in and see the Prophet".'

This is only a part of a *ḥadīth* al-Bukhari includes here because of its relevance to the theme of the chapter dealing with names. He wishes to make clear that such names are not forbidden. Rabāḥ means 'gain, profit and good fortune'. The same reason the Prophet disliked a name like Barakah applies to Rabāḥ, but the Prophet did not change his servant's name.

The Prophet encouraged calling children by the names of the prophets, including Muhammad. He himself named his only son born to him after prophethood, Ibrāhīm, which is the Islamic version of Abraham.

839. Abu Hurayrah reports that the Prophet said: 'Give yourselves my name, but not my appellation [i.e. kunyah]. I am Abu al-Qāsim'.[590]

840. Anas ibn Mālik reports: 'The Prophet was once in the market place when someone called out, 'Abu al-Qāsim!' The Prophet turned towards the man, but he said: "Messenger of

590. Related by al-Bukhari.

God, I am only calling this person'. The Prophet said: "Give yourselves my name, but not my appellation [i.e. *kunyah*]".'[591]

841. Yūsuf ibn 'Abdullāh ibn Salām reports: 'The Prophet (peace be upon him) named me Yūsuf, and he put me on his lap and wiped my head with his hand'.[592]

842. Jābir ibn 'Abdullāh reports: 'A man from us, the Anṣār, had a son born to him and he wanted to name him Muhammad'.
In the version narrated by Manṣūr: 'The Anṣāri man said: I carried him on my shoulder and took him to the Prophet...'
In the version narrated by Sylaymān: 'He had a son born to him and they wanted to name him Muhammad'.
'The Prophet said: "Give yourselves my name, but not my appellation [i.e. *kunyah*]. I am made the distributor [i.e. *qāsim*] so as to divide things among you".'[593]

843. Abu Mūsa said: 'I had a newborn son and I took him to the Prophet. He named him Ibrāhīm. He chewed up a date and gave it to him and prayed for him to be blessed. He then gave the child back to me'. This was Abu Mūsa's[594] eldest son.

All five *ḥadīths* are highly authentic. They confirm that Prophet Muhammad's practical guidance makes clear that all the names of the prophets may be used. Some of his companions called their children by earlier prophet's names and he approved of this. This is perfectly understandable, because it confirms the notion that Islam is only the final version of the faith preached by all prophets, ever since the beginning of human life.

The Prophet's own name may be used as well. This was the case even in his own time. It confirms that we are encouraged to use the Prophet's own name for our children. Muslims in all generations have acted on this and the name Muhammad is the most common name

591. Related by al-Bukhari.
592. Related by Aḥmad and al-Tirmidhi.
593. Related by al-Bukhari and Muslim.
594. Related by al-Bukhari and Muslim.

in all Muslim countries. It has been so throughout Islamic history. Today, it is also common in many countries with Muslim minorities. However, the Prophet made it clear that we may not use his other appellation, or *kunyah*, which is calling a man as the father of his eldest son. The Prophet's *kunyah* is Abu al-Qāsim, after his eldest son who died in early childhood. The Prophet says that he himself is a *qāsim*, using the name in its linguistic meaning, which is 'a person who shares out something among different people'.

Does this mean that we should not give our children the name Qāsim, so that we are not given the *kunyah* Abu al-Qāsim? The answer is that it is preferable that a Muslim should not call his first son by that name, in order not to disobey the Prophet's order. If one already has a different *kunyah*, then there is no harm in giving his first son this name. It is good to remember that Abu al-Qāsim is an appellation the Prophet wished to retain for himself only. We respect his wish and abide by his order.

844. Saʿīd ibn al-Musayyib related from his father that his grandfather 'came to the Prophet (peace be upon him). The Prophet asked him: "What is your name?" He said: "Ḥazn". The Prophet said: "You are Sahl". He said: "I will not change a name given to me by my father".'[595]

(Ibn al-Musayyib said: 'Roughness remained with us ever since'.)

Saʿīd ibn al-Musayyib was a famous scholar who belonged to the generation of *tabiʿīn*, the successors to the Prophet's companions. He lived in Madinah and his fame travelled far and wide. His father was one of the Prophet's companions.

Ḥazn, his grandfather's name, means 'rough ground', and Sahl means the opposite, or easy and lenient. The Arabs would use a name like Ḥazn to denote strength and a solid stand against enemies. But the Prophet wanted the man's name to indicate ease and kindness. The man decided that he preferred whatever name was given to him by his father. This was clearly a rough and unrefined attitude to adopt. It

595. Related by al-Bukhari, Muslim, Abū Dāwūd, al-Tirmidhi and Ibn Mājah.

could not have pleased the Prophet. Sa'īd ibn al-Musayyib, the man's grandson, gave an apt comment stating that roughness remained in his family.

What happens if the Prophet wanted to change someone's name, but that person refused? Obviously, this is something that does not touch on faith. That man did not contravene any fundamental Islamic principle, but he showed lack of respect for and obedience of the Prophet. Indeed, the best thing any person can do is to follow the Prophet and his guidance. If a man has a name which is not particularly pleasant, and the Prophet changes it, then he would be well advised to accept the change. It would be a source of honour for him that the Prophet himself gave him his name. Some of us may find it impossible to believe that anyone would reject such a name, but nonetheless, it happened.

845. Jābir reports: 'One of our men had a son and he named him al-Qāsim. The Anṣār said to him: "We shall not give you the appellation, Abu al-Qāsim, and will not give you that pleasure". He went to the Prophet and told him what the Anṣār said. The Prophet said: "The Anṣār have done well. Name yourselves after me but do not use my appellation. I am Qāsim [i.e. the distributor]".'[596]

This *ḥadīth* is akin to Number 818, but with some omission and addition. We have commented on this earlier.

846. Muhammad ibn al-Ḥanafiyyah said: 'A special allowance was given to 'Ali. He said: "Messenger of God, if I have a son after you, may I call him by your name and appellation?" The Prophet said: "Yes".'[597]

Muhammad ibn al-Ḥanafiyyah was 'Ali's son, but his mother was not Fāṭimah, the Prophet's daughter. He is called after her, al-Ḥanafiyyah, to distinguish him from his two half brothers al-Ḥasan and al-Ḥusayn.

---

596. Related by al-Bukhari, Muslim, Abū Dāwūd, al-Tirmidhi and Ibn Mājah.
597. Related by Aḥmad, Abū Dāwūd, al-Tirmidhi, Ibn Mājah and al-Ḥākim.

The *ḥadīth* simply speaks about a concession given specifically to ʿAli. The special concession is that the boy would have the Prophet's name and appellation together. Otherwise people are permitted to call their sons Muhammad but not to add the appellation Abu al-Qāsim.

It is clear that the appellation Abu al-Qāsim was the distinctive *kunyah* of the Prophet which was not to be shared with anyone else. The following *ḥadīth* adds another point:

847. Abu Hurayrah reports: 'God's Messenger has prohibited that anyone may have both his name and *kunyah*. He said: "I am Abu al-Qāsim. God gives and I share out [His gift among people]".'[598]

The question arises whether it is forbidden for anyone to be called, Abu al-Qāsim. The answer is that there is no strict prohibition. Although this *ḥadīth* and several ones of similar import make it clear that this is an appellation belonging only to the Prophet, we have a *ḥadīth* which quotes the Prophet as saying: 'Whoever has my name should not call himself by my *kunyah*, and whoever has my *kunyah* should not give himself my name'.[599] Since it is customary to use the traditional appellation, or *kunyah*, in Arab countries, it is observed that people give anyone called Muhammad a *kunyah* which uses a corruption of the name Qāsim. Thus, he would be called Abu Jāsim in some Arab countries, and Abu Gāsim in others.

It should also be pointed out that the Arabs at the Prophet's time used to give their children, or at least some of them, a *kunyah*, which would in this case be a form of endearment. In fact this is still the case in several Arab countries.

848. This is the same as *ḥadīth* 840, with a different chain of transmission.

849. Usāmah ibn Zayd reports: 'God's Messenger passed by a group of people which included ʿAbdullāh ibn Ubay ibn Salūl.

598. Related by al-Tirmidhi and Ibn Ḥibbān.
599. Related by Aḥmad, ʿAbdullāh, al-Tirmidhi and Ibn Ḥibbān.

This was before 'Abdullāh ibn Ubay claimed to be a Muslim. He said to the Prophet: "Do not disturb us in our gathering". The Prophet went to Sa'd ibn 'Ubādah and said: "Sa'd, have you heard what Abu Ḥubāb said?" [He meant 'Abdullāh ibn Ubay.]'[600]

This *ḥadīth* is entered at this point to make clear that there is nothing wrong with referring to an unbeliever, or addressing him, by an appellation of respect, such as the *kunyah*. 'Abdullāh ibn Ubay ibn Salūl was the chief hypocrite and he did his best to harm the Prophet, but the Prophet continued to address him as Abu Ḥubāb, even when his hypocrisy was flagrant.

850. Anas reports: 'The Prophet used to visit us. I had a young brother whose appellation was Abu 'Umayr. He had a small bird for a pet, but his bird died. The Prophet visited us shortly after this and he noticed that my brother was sad. He asked: "What is wrong?" He was told that his bird died. He said to him: "Abu 'Umayr! What happened to the little bird?"'

This *ḥadīth* is the same as Number 269 and it was explained then, but it is reproduced here for its relevance to the point under discussion, showing that the *kunyah*, could be given to a young child.

The Arabs might also give a *kunyah* to a man or a woman who is childless. This is perfectly appropriate.

851. (*Athar* 191) Ibrāhīm said: ''Abdullāh [ibn Mas'ūd] gave 'Alqamah the appellation Abu Shibl before he ['Alqamah] had a child'.

852. (*Athar* 192) 'Alqamah said: ''Abdullāh gave me a *kunyah* before I had any children'.

600. Related by Aḥmad, al-Bukhari and Muslim.

'Abdullāh himself was called Abu 'Abd al-Raḥmān by the Prophet before he had any children. The Prophet also gave his companion Ṣuhayb the appellation Abu Yaḥya, and he was known by this *kunyah* for the rest of his life, although he never had a son.

Similarly, the Prophet gave his wives who had no children appellations or *kunyah*.

853. 'Ā'ishah reports: 'I went to the Prophet and said: "You have given some of your wives a *kunyah*. Give me a kunyah". He said, "Give yourself an appellation after your nephew 'Abdullāh".'[601]

854. 'Ā'ishah reports: 'I said: "Prophet, will you not give me a *kunyah*?" He said: "Use your son's name for your *kunyah*".' He meant 'Abdullāh ibn al-Zubayr. She was then called Umm 'Abdullāh.[602]

It is well known that 'Ā'ishah remained childless. However, the Prophet referred to her nephew as her son, which was common practice among the Arabs at the time. Her nephew was the son of her sister Asmā' by her husband al-Zubayr ibn al-'Awwām.

A *kunyah* may be given to someone for a particular reason or situation, which has nothing to do with their children. Thus, they would be called as the father of something or some situation.

855. Sahl ibn Sa'd reports: 'Of all his names, 'Ali loved Abu Turāb best, and he was pleased to be called by it. No one gave him this name except the Prophet. One day he was angry with Fāṭimah [his wife and the Prophet's daughter]. He left home and sat reclining against the wall in the mosque. The Prophet followed him and was told that he was reclining against the wall. The Prophet went to him and found his back covered with dust. The Prophet began to wipe the dust off his back and said to him, "Sit up, Abu Turāb!"'[603]

---

601. Related by Abū Dāwūd.
602. Related by Abū Dāwūd and 'Abd al-Razzāq.
603. Related by al-Bukhari.

Turāb means dust. Thus, the Prophet called his son-in-law, who was also his own cousin, by this name in a friendly way, to ease the tension between 'Ali and his wife. His friendliness took all the tension away. 'Ali loved to be called by this name because when it was used, it showed that the Prophet was not angry with him on account of his having an argument with his wife, the Prophet's daughter. It thus expressed that 'Ali himself enjoyed a close position with the Prophet. This is why he loved to be called Abu Turāb.

41

Deference to Superiors

856. Anas reports: 'The Prophet was in a palm grove of ours – the palm grove belonged to Abu Ṭalḥah – he went out for something. Bilāl was walking behind the Prophet, (feeling uneasy to walk by the Prophet's side). The Prophet passed by a grave and stopped there until Bilāl caught up with him. He said: "Bilāl, do you hear what I am hearing?" Bilāl said: "I hear nothing". The Prophet said: "Torment is being inflicted on the man in the grave". He found out that the dead person in the grave was a Jew'.[604]

AL-BUKHARI ENTERS THIS *ḥadīth* under a subheading, 'Walking with superiors and virtuous people'. The Prophet's companions showed great respect to the Prophet and this was an expression of genuine feeling. Hence, we see that Bilāl walked a few steps behind the Prophet

604. Related by Aḥmad.

knowing that if the Prophet wanted to say anything to him, he would signal this to him and Bilāl would immediately be by his side. In the event, this took place when the Prophet heard something coming from a grave.

Torment in the grave is advance punishment for sinners. We do not know how this is administered, as it belongs to the realm of what is beyond our perception. Some people question it, arguing that it is not mentioned in the Qur'an. The fact, however, is that there is a subtle reference to it in the Qur'an. God says: '*Grievous suffering was to encompass Pharaoh's folk: before the fire they are brought, morning and evening, and then on the Day when the Last Hour comes, it will be said: "Cast Pharaoh's people into the worst suffering".*' (40: 45-46) It is clear that Pharaoh's people endure this suffering of being brought before the fire morning and evening. It happens before the Last Hour which signals the Day of Judgement when they will be cast into hell.

Numerous references in the Qur'an and *Ḥadīth* make clear that the intervening period between death and the Day of Judgement is a stage of life separating the two: our present life in this world and the life to come. This stage can be one of torment or one of happiness, depending on whether a person was a believer, a sinner or an unbeliever.

857. (*Athar* 193) Qays ibn Ḥāzim said: 'I heard Mu'āwiyah say to a young brother of his: "Let your servant ride on your mount behind you". The boy refused. Mu'āwiyah said to him: "How badly you have been taught". I heard Abu Sufyān say to him: "Leave your brother alone".'

This dates back to the time when Mu'āwiyah was a governor of Syria, a post he occupied for twenty years before he became Caliph. Abu Sufyān, his father, died many years before he became Caliph. The story mentions something that may occur at any time between elder and younger brothers, when the younger one will not listen to an order or request by his elder. However, the elder brother in this case was a governor of a vast area. Nevertheless, the younger brother disobeyed him and earned this remark from Mu'āwiyah. However, their father tells Mu'āwiyah to leave the young one alone. Mu'āwiyah acted with due respect to his father and did not respond to his brother's disobedience.

858. (*Athar* 194) 'Amr ibn al-'Āṣ said: 'When you have many close friends, you have many creditors'. Yaḥya said: 'I said to Mūsa: "What are creditors?" He replied: "Rights owed".'
Yaḥya is one of the narrators in the chain. He put the question to Mūsa ibn 'Ali, the narrator before him.

This is a statement attributed to one of the Prophet's companions, but scholars of *Ḥadīth* include it in their anthologies in acknowledgement that the Prophet's companions hesitated to attribute such statements to the Prophet fearing that they might not have remembered his words correctly. It suggests that every friend has certain rights and we must always be ready to fulfil their rights. Therefore, when a person is very popular and his circle of friends is large, he owes much to many people. He may not be able to fulfil their rights all the time. As such, he owes them what he fails to attend to. They become like creditors whose dues are not paid on time. Hence, close friends are described as creditors.

42

Fine Words, Fine Meanings

EVER SINCE THE start of human life, people have loved fine style and the ability to express one's thoughts and ideas clearly in fine words. In all cultures, poets and men of eloquence have been highly respected. In the past, a fine orator could make the difference between winning and losing a battle. William Shakespeare has attained unrivalled fame, lasting over centuries, on account of his exceptional dexterity with words and expressions, in addition to his several other literary gifts. Yet the highest position given to language excellence is that God has put his final message to mankind in the most superb literary style ever known in any human language, which we find in the Qur'an.

Gifted poets are likely to use their talent to express fine meanings just as much as they are able to use it to express profane feelings and thoughts. In every language poets harp on desire and passion more than they dwell on other themes. This is normal because a poet is a sensitive person to whom feeling and passion are very important. He gives them vivid expression, painting images that aim to generate the same feelings in his listeners. If his feelings give rise to fine and sound thoughts, his poetry will be of the good type that Islam approves of. On the other hand, if a poet's feelings are generated by profane and carnal passions, his poetry will try to arouse similar feelings that encourage people to resort to actions that may be forbidden in Islam.

Scholars have considered the most common purposes poets have. They say that when poetry is devoted to the expression of wisdom and it encourages people to remain committed to good values and proper behaviour, and when it praises God for His blessings, then it is fine. If it dwells on events, describes places and scenery, paints sound feelings, then it is permissible. On the other hand, if it defames opponents or expresses carnal desires, it is forbidden. When descriptions of beauty and human form is the purpose, without any clear or implicit encouragement of forbidden actions, it is discouraged, and may even be prohibited, depending on the poem itself. This applies to all human speech, whether poetry or prose. It is the meaning and the ideas that make certain speech worthy of God's reward or otherwise.

This was clearly understood by the Prophet's companions who encouraged only the type of poetry that is consistent with Islamic values.

> 859. (*Athar* 195) Khālid ibn Kaysān reports: 'I was with Ibn 'Umar when Iyās ibn Khaythamah visited him. He said: "Shall I recite to you some of my poetry, Ibn al-Fārūq?" He said: "Yes, but only recite to me what is good". He recited some poems, but when he included something that Ibn 'Umar disliked, he said to him: "Stop".'

It is clear in this report that Ibn 'Umar was only referring to what is acceptable or prohibited by Islamic standards. Otherwise, his responses would not be clear. What is good poetry to one man may be not so good to another. A literary critic may appreciate a poem which ordinary listeners may find average, simply because the critic finds it reflecting clear insight into human feeling. This may not be readily apparent to ordinary listeners. Hence they give the poem a lower rating than the literary critic who has appreciated its merits.

860. (*Athar* 196) Muṭarrif said: 'I travelled with 'Imrān ibn Huṣayn from Kufah to Basrah. Rarely did he stop at a place without reciting some poetry to me. He said: "Ambiguity provides a way of avoiding lies."'[605]

'Imrān ibn Huṣayn was a companion of the Prophet well known for his sincere devotion. Although he does not attribute his statement about ambiguity to the Prophet, he was most probably quoting him. This *ḥadīth* identifies a way that eliminates the need for telling a lie. This by use of an ambiguous statement that may direct the listener away from what the speaker does not want to tell him, and yet the statement is true. This is often used by poets, literary figures, politicians and ordinary people in every day speech. The statement would be true, but its relevance to the situation in hand is not readily apparent. Thus, the truth, which is meant to be avoided, can only be understood after reflection and deep thought. Rather, the listener's attention is deflected away from it by the apparent meaning of the statement, which is also true. Thus, the speaker does not say a lie, but rather avoids saying what he is keen not to say in order to avoid worsening the situation.

The Prophet himself resorted to this method on one occasion, when he answered a question put to him by a bedouin: 'Who are you from?' The bedouin was asking him about his tribe and people. This was shortly before the Battle of Badr and the Prophet was with his companions who were to fight that battle. Giving the bedouin a straight answer could have meant that the enemy would gather intelligence about the location of the Muslim forces. Hence the Prophet's answer was covered with ambiguity. He said: 'We are from water'. He meant that they, like all human beings, were created from semen. The bedouin understood the Prophet's answer as meaning that they belonged to the marshlands of Iraq where water was so plentiful that the area itself might be called water. There is nothing wrong in resorting to such ambiguity in order to avoid a straightforward answer that may land the speaker in trouble.

605. Related by al-Ṭabari and al-Ṭabarāni in Al-Mu'jam al-Kabīr.

861. Ubay ibn Ka'b reports that the Prophet said: 'Some poetry is pure wisdom'.[606]

This short *ḥadīth* states what people have always known about fine poetry, but expresses it in the clearest way. Furthermore, it distinctly implies a directive to anyone with fine poetic gifts to use such talent in an appropriate manner. All people praise wisdom and esteem a wise person. Therefore, when a poet expresses wisdom in his poetry, people are bound to appreciate his meaning and put it into practice. This helps to improve values in society. Indeed, many a poet has influenced practical behaviour in his community and encouraged it to aspire to a higher standard of values. It is this type of help the Prophet is implying in this *ḥadīth*.

Muslim poets have also devoted much of their poetry to God's praises and to pointing out the Prophet's fine character.

862. Al-Aswad ibn Suray' reports: 'I said: "Messenger of God, I have praised my Lord, the Mighty and Exalted, in some poems of mine". He said: "Your Lord loves to be praised". He did not say anything more.'

We all know that glorifying and praising God is one of the acts of worship Islam recommends. The Prophet also clarified that God gains nothing by our glorification or worship. It is we who benefit by it, because such praise gives us a clear sense that whatever blessing we have and enjoy is granted us by God. It is not the result of our own endeavour. It is what God bestows on us of His grace. God has also promised us that He will give us an increase of His blessings if we show gratitude to Him for what He has given us. A longer version of this *ḥadīth* is entered under Number 343.

863. Abu Hurayrah reports ...[607]

This *ḥadīth* is the same as 873, and we will discuss it there together with Number 874.

---

606. Related by al-Bukhari, 'Abdullāh and Ibn Mājah.

607. Related by al-Bukhari, Muslim, Abū Dāwūd, al-Tirmidhi and Ibn Mājah.

864. This is the same as 862, with a different chain of transmission.

In Islam poets can have a very prominent role. We know about Ḥassān ibn Thābit, who is often described as the Prophet's poet. Ḥassān was a fine poet and belonged to the Anṣār. As Islam was fighting the onslaught of the unbelievers who tried hard to suppress its message, the information battle was no less important than the military fight. Unbelieving poets were engaged in a determined attack on the Prophet and his companions. Poetry played the same role the media plays in our modern times. It travelled easily in Arabia and was appreciated by all Arabs. Hence, it was necessary for Muslim poets to rise to the occasion and defend Islam in poetry to reply to the abuse of pagan poets.

865. 'Ā'ishah reports: 'Ḥassān ibn Thābit asked the Prophet's permission to attack the unbelievers in his poetry. The Prophet asked him: "How about my relation to them?" He replied: "I will extricate you from them like a hair is pulled out from the dough".'[608]

This promise Ḥassān honoured with great dexterity. He was able to write poetry of the highest quality in praise of the Prophet, defence of Islam and criticism of the Quraysh and its attitude to both the Prophet and God's message. When he attacked the Quraysh, he made sure that none of his criticism applied to the Prophet who also belonged to the Quraysh. Thus, he attained high distinction as the main media fighter for the cause of Islam during the Prophet's lifetime and for many years thereafter.

His position was acknowledged by 'Ā'ishah, the Prophet's wife. It so happened that, on a certain occasion, Ḥassān took the wrong approach in a question involving 'Ā'ishah. Given she was innocent and free of blame surrounding the issue, this fact is expressly stated in the Qur'an. It was prior to her innocence being so confirmed in

---

608. Related by al-Bukhari and Muslim.

the Qur'an that Ḥassān said erroneous words about her. He came to regret this and the matter was thus settled.

866. 'Urwah ibn al-Zubayr said: 'I started to abuse Ḥassān in 'Ā'ishah's presence. She said to me: "Do not abuse him. He used to defend God's Messenger (peace be upon him)".'

This *ḥadīth* makes clear that 'Ā'ishah no longer thought about Hassan's wrong words. Rather, she valued his role in the advocacy of Islam. Her magnanimous attitude speaks volumes for her integrity and commitment to Islam. She forgot her personal grievance against the man and remembered only his virtue in defending Islam and the Prophet. Her attitude provides an example that should be followed by Muslims throughout all generations. It is an attitude that puts the cause of the Muslim community above the personal interests or grievances of individuals, regardless of their position in society.

876. This is the same as Number 861, with a different chain of transmission.

868. 'Abdullāh ibn 'Amr reports that the Prophet said: 'Poetry is the same as speech: the good of it is like good speech and the bad of it is bad'.[609]

869. (Athar 197) 'Ā'ishah said: 'Some poetry is good and some bad. Take the good and leave the bad. I have recited some poems by Ka'b ibn Mālik, including poems of 40 lines and some less than that'.

The Prophet listened to fine poetry and he distinguished between that which was frivolous and serious. He said: 'Poetry is like ordinary speech: fine poetry is like fine speech, and objectionable poetry is like objectionable speech'.[610]

---

609. Related by al-Dāraquṭni.
610. Related by al-Dāraquṭni.

These *ḥadīths* make clear the distinction between frivolous and serious poetry. This is absolutely fair, because it judges poetry on the basis of the meaning the poet wants to convey, and the way such meaning is expressed in the poem. It does not slam a blanket judgement condemning all poetry or all forms of art. It allows freedom of expression, provided that its principles are not violated. This is both fair and appropriate. Islamic principles include all that is good and beneficial for mankind, and preclude all that is bad and harmful. Therefore, commitment to Islamic principles is bound to heighten one's sense of propriety and fine speech. It also positively affects one's judgement of what constitutes fine poetry.

'Ā'ishah confirms the distinction between different standards of poetry on the basis of the meanings expressed. Thus, what is virtuous, or advocating proper values, or encouraging good action, is fine and may be used, quoted or recited as one feels fit. What is contrary to Islamic values should be abandoned, whether it is frivolous, obscene or mere exaggeration.

'Ā'ishah tells us of her own action, which may be taken as an example to be followed. She was the Prophet's wife who had fine insight into what is permissible in Islam and what is forbidden. Thus, when she spoke of reciting or memorising some poetry, this indicates the permissibility of doing so, particularly when she had already stated a criterion for distinguishing quotable poetry. She tells us that the poetry she recited was composed by Ka'b ibn Mālik, an Anṣāri companion of the Prophet. He was one of the very early people of Madinah to embrace Islam, and he was chosen among twelve of the people who pledged their loyalty and support to the Prophet to be given responsibility for their respective clans and tribes. His poetry was always used in the service of the Islamic cause. Hence, it was fine poetry, committed to the observance of Islamic values. It was no surprise that 'Ā'ishah, a highly intelligent and well educated lady, should choose his poetry to recite.

870. Shurayḥ said: 'I asked 'Ā'ishah: "Did God's Messenger quote any poetry?" She said: "He used to quote some of the poetry of 'Abdullāh ibn Rawāḥah. [Also] News may be brought

to you by someone whom you have not commissioned for the task".'[611]

'Abdullāh ibn Rawāḥah was another fine poet from the Anṣār and died in the Battle of Mu'tah, the first military engagement between the Islamic state and the Byzantine Empire. 'Abdullāh was a model believer who showed total commitment to the cause *of Islam and perfect obedience to God and His* Messenger. It is reported that he was going into the mosque whilst the Prophet was addressing his companions. He heard the Prophet saying, 'Sit down'. The Prophet said this to the whole congregation, but not as an order. In fact most of them were already seated. The Prophet was merely using the word in his speech. Nevertheless, it was in the form of an order, and although it was not addressed to any one in particular, 'Abdullāh ibn Rawāḥah immediately fulfilled it and immediately sat down. The Prophet noticed his action and said to him: 'May God increase your keenness to obey Him and His messenger'.

This *ḥadīth* tells us that the Prophet used to like poetry, although he himself never said a line of poetry. Indeed, he is not known to ever having recited a poem. He is described in the Qur'an as not being taught poetry by God, and that such education is not befitting of him. This is very true, because, as God's Messenger, his task is to deliver God's message embodied in the Qur'an, which is a much higher form of literary style than poetry. Had he been a poet, he would have been accused of inventing a new form. Indeed, when his opponents increased their level of hostility, they compared the Qur'an to poetry, although they were ready to concede that it was unlike any they knew. The Prophet nevertheless loved fine speech, including poetry.

The last part of the *ḥadīth* quotes the second half of a line from a famous poem by Ṭarafah ibn al-'Abd, a fine pre-Islamic poet.

871. This is the same as *ḥadīth* Numbers 862 and 864, with a different chain of transmission.

---

611. Related by al-Nasā'ī and al-Tirmidhi.

872. Al-Sharīd ibn Suwayd said: 'The Prophet asked me to recite some of the poetry of Umayyah ibn Abi al-Ṣalt?" I did and he repeatedly told me to say more. [I continued] until I recited 100 lines. He said: "He almost became a Muslim".'[612]

Umayyah was a very wise poet. Prior to Islam he sought to learn about Divine religions and he read the Bible and other scriptures. He mentions in his poetry the early prophets, particularly Abraham and Ishmael. He refused to worship his people's idols, and he forbade himself wines, urging others not to drink any intoxicants. When he learnt that a prophet would be sent to mankind and that he would be from the Hijaz in Arabia, he hoped that he would be this prophet. But when God's messenger, Muhammad, declared his message and Umayyah realised that he would not be the one, he felt envious and stopped short of embracing Islam. It is also reported that at one stage he was on his way to join the Prophet and declare his acceptance of Islam, but some unbelievers pointed out to him that a number of his relatives had been killed at the Battle of Badr. He was in great grief and he interrupted his journey without joining the ranks of the Muslims. He died later without ever becoming a Muslim. His poetry includes much of his ideas about God's oneness, the falsehood of pagan beliefs, as well as the importance of sound moral values. Hence the Prophet's comment in this *ḥadīth*. The Prophet is also reported to have said about him: 'His poetry is that of a believer, but his heart is that of an unbeliever'.

873. 'Abdullāh ibn 'Umar reports that the Prophet said: 'It is better for any person to have his inside full of pus than to fill it with poetry'.[613]

874. (*Athar* 198) Ibn 'Abbās quoted the Qur'anic verses: '*As for the poets, only those who are lost in error follow them. Are you not aware that they roam confusedly through all valleys, and that they say what they do not do?*' (26: 224-6) He said: '[God] makes an allowance and an exception, stating: "*Excepted are those who*

---

612. Related by Aḥmad, Muslim, Ibn Majah, al-Dārimi and Ibn Khuzaymah.
613. Related by Aḥmad and al-Dārimi.

believe, and do righteous deeds, and remember God often, and strive to be triumphant after they have been wronged. Those who are bent on wrongdoing will in time know what an evil turn their destiny will surely take".'(26: 227)[614]

It is often said that Islam does not encourage poetry. But such a general statement is far from accurate. The verses quoted in the second *ḥadīth* are the last of a medium length surah in the Qur'an, Al-Shu'arā', or The Poets. This is not a condemnation of all poetry or all poets. It distinguishes between exaggerated statements often used by poets and poetry and that which observes the moral values stressed by Islam, particularly commitment to the truth and resisting oppression. When poets indulge in unrestrained hyperbolic feeling, emotion or action, or extol their own virtues in an exercise of self-gratification, or assure their audience of great things which they know to be unreal, then Islam censures them strongly. But poets who use their talent to serve the cause of the truth, stressing good moral values, propagating true principles, and advocating Islam will have a double reward. They will achieve a good standing among people in their own generation and in later generations. This is a valuable reward in this life, and they stand to earn reward from God on the Day of Judgement.

It is to the first type of poetry that the first of these *ḥadīths* refers. The *ḥadīth* gives a horrid picture of the type of person who allows such pursuits to pervade his poetry, throwing to the wall all moral values that restrain people's speech, and encourages them to say only what is right and proper.

It must be stressed that Islam adopts a balanced view of poetry, praising what is good of it and condemning what is false, vile and exaggeration. This is clear in the following *ḥadīth*:

875. Ibn 'Abbās reports: 'A man, or a bedouin, came to the Prophet and spoke most eloquently. The Prophet commented: "Some fine speech is pure magic and some poetry is pure wisdom".'[615]

---

614. Related by Abū Dāwūd.

615. Related by Aḥmad, Abu Dawud, al-Tirmidhi Ibn Majah, and Ibn Hibban.

Here the Prophet compares the effect of fine speech to magic in the sense that both may captivate an audience. That speech may be captivating is a well known experience. The speaker may be an orator, or someone speaking at leisure when a group of people are listening, and he or she provides some especially interesting talk. His listeners may be all attentive as he expounds his ideas to them. Similarly, poets can use their talent and their understanding of human nature and their life experience to highlight some very useful meaning. This is particularly noticeable in the poetry of al-Mutanabbi, a famous Arab who lived around 800 years ago. Some of his wise sayings are still treated as very relevant to human society today.

876. (*Athar* 199) 'Umar ibn Sallām reports: ''Abd al-Malik ibn Marwān entrusted [some of] his children to al-Sha'bi to educate them. He said: "Teach them poetry so that they acquire dignity and vigour. Feed them meat so that they will have strength. Cut off their hair so that their necks will be stiffer. Take them to sit with men of distinction to argue with them".'

'Abd al-Malik ibn Marwān was an Umayyad Caliph who ruled the Muslim state for twenty years. He belonged to the generation that followed the Prophet's companions. Four of his sons became caliphs after his death. He took care of their education. His statement is included here because of its relevance to learning poetry.

877. 'Ā'ishah reports that the Prophet said: 'The ones guilty of the greatest type of crimes are a poet who indiscriminately abuses an entire tribe and a man who disclaims his father'.[616]

Poets may resort to this type of objectionable speech when they try to degrade their opponents. This used to be done frequently in Arabic poetry when a poet would use his talents to abuse an opponent, or a tribe that might have had a quarrel with his own tribe. Such abuse was sometimes highly effective. A tribe could be elevated or downgraded in Arabian ranking, on the basis of the

616. Related by Ibn Mājah and Ibn Ḥibbān.

poetry that mentions it. In this *ḥadīth* the Prophet highlights a poet's responsibility in this regard.

When a poet speaks disparagingly of an entire tribe or community, he is certainly including in his abuse some good people who are free of blame. He might have good reason to abuse some individuals of that tribe, as in the case of suffering an unjustifiable attack by a group belonging to it. They might have made away with his property, or abused him in some other way. If he has such a grievance, he may be justified in denouncing such people. However, when he abuses the whole tribe to which his attackers belong, he would be including in his abuse some God-fearing people who might have come to his aid had they known of the wrong he suffered. Thus, his poetry does not avenge the attack against him, but rather wrongs some who were innocent. This is a grave offence.

What applies to a poet in olden times also applies today to journalists and broadcasters who use the means available to them to unjustifiably abuse people who may be free of blame. This is particularly true when such journalists target an entire community. This is now recognised as a serious offence in contemporary society. Some countries include it in offences that can lead to community trouble. Some have constituted authorities that look into race relations, and an attack of this type is dealt with and punished by such authorities. Here, we see the Prophet describing such abuse as one of the worst offences a human being can commit.

The other crime the Prophet refers to is that of a man disclaiming his father. Perhaps nothing aggrieves a father more than seeing his son declaring that he does not belong to him, or claiming that he is born to a different father. If this is done because of the father's low rank in society and the son aspires to a higher level, it is especially injurious to the father. Thus, the father is paid back for all the kindness and love he has shown his son, and for the trouble he took in his upbringing. The father is bound to take such an insult to heart and to feel its pain for the rest of his life. We all know the emphasis Islam puts on being kind and dutiful to one's parents. Disclaiming one's father or mother is the ultimate insult that anyone can level at them. Hence, the Prophet says that it is one of the worst offences a human being can commit.

878. ʿAbdullāh ibn ʿUmar reports: ʿTwo orators from the Eastern parts visited Madinah during the Prophet's lifetime. They stood up and made their speeches and then sat down. Thābit ibn Qays, the Prophet's spokesman, stood up and spoke. People admired the two men's speech. Then, God's Messenger stood up and gave a speech. He said: "People! Say what you want to say. Giving excessive attention to words and phrases is prompted by Satan". God's Messenger then said: "Some fine speech is pure magic".'

What the Prophet warns against in this instance is using one's talent for expression to invite people's admiration. This may easily lead to arrogance as the speaker begins with a determined effort to solicit admiration. As he so enchants people with his speech, he begins to give himself airs. Needless to say, such arrogance is a vice encouraged by Satan. Hence the Prophet's statement that 'giving excessive attention to words and phrases is prompted by Satan'. However, the Prophet does not belittle the value of fine words and wise statements, and this is reflected in his last statement, which we have commented on earlier.

This *ḥadīth* does not mention the names of these two men or what they said in the Prophet's presence. We have reports giving these details and it may be useful to explain the *ḥadīth* on the basis of such reports. The two men are said to be al-Zibriqān ibn Badr and ʿAmr ibn al-Ahtam, who belonged to the tribe of Tamīm. They arrived in Madinah in the ninth year after Makkah had fallen to Islam. When al-Zibriqān spoke, he indulged in self praise, saying: 'Messenger of God, I am the master of the Tamīm tribe. In my tribe, my orders are obeyed and requests granted. I prevent my people from committing injustice and I limit them to what is rightfully theirs. This fellow [pointing to ʿAmr ibn al-Ahtam] will testify to that'.

Feeling that he was called upon to speak, ʿAmr ibn al-Ahtam said: 'Messenger of God, he is a man of real power; able to protect his immediate relatives and property, and obeyed by his kin'. Apparently, al-Zibriqān felt that ʿAmr's statement fell short of what he expected him to say and he therefore castigated him saying: 'Messenger of God, he knows of me what is far more than what he said; but it is envy that prevents him from stating what is true'. ʿAmr rejoined: 'Am I envious of you? Messenger of God, by God his maternal uncles are of low status, and he has only recently come into his money. His children are imbecile and he is disliked by his clan. By God, I only spoke the truth in my first statement and I told no lie in my second, but it is a trait of mine that when I am pleased with someone, I say the best I know of him, and if I am displeased, I highlight his worst qualities'.[617] It was in reply to this that the Prophet said: 'Some fine speech is pure magic'.

879. (*Athar* 200) Anas reports: 'A man made a speech in 'Umar's presence, making it long. 'Umar said: "Making speeches too long is motivated by Satan".'

Here I am deviating from strict translation to give the intended meaning because 'Umar provides an image likening ranting on by a speaker to a piece of red skin a camel may put out to the side of his mouth. Thus, he gives an image in which we see a fluent speaker like a strong camel, and his oratory is seen like what the camel brings forth from its mouth. Linking such speech to Satan is right because it is likely to include some falsehood.

880. Abu Yazīd, or Ma'n ibn Yazīd, reports: 'The Prophet said: "Gather in your mosques. When a community have gathered, let me know". He came first to us. One of us started to speak. He said: "All praise be to God. Praise directed to anyone but Him is aimless, and from Him there is no escape". The Prophet was angry and he left. We blamed one another and said: "We were the first to whom he came and now he went to another mosque". We went to him and spoke to him. He came back with us and sat where he had been sitting or near it. He then said: "All praise be to God Who places whatever He wishes in front of Him and whatever He wishes behind Him. Some fine speech is pure magic". He then instructed us and taught us'.[618]

617. Al-Bayhaqi, Dalā'il al-Nubuwwah, vol. 5, pp. 316-7.
618. Related by Aḥmad.

The Prophet simply showed his displeasure when the speaker used pompous words in praising God. Although no praise of God can be exaggerated, the speaker wanted to show off his linguistic dexterity. The Prophet objected to such pedantry in front of people. Therefore, he left the meeting without saying anything to the man, and moved on to attend to another group. The people who saw this realised why he had left them and went to apologise. He did not take this against them, but rather went back and gave them appropriate advice.

43

Types of Speech

881. ʿĀmir ibn Rabīʿah reports: 'ʿĀ'ishah said: "The Prophet was sleepless one night, and he said: "I wish that one of my righteous companions would come and guard me tonight". We then heard the sound of weapons, and the Prophet said: "Who is that?" Someone said: "It is Saʿd". Saʿd said: "Messenger of God, I have come to stand guard for you". The Prophet slept soundly'.[619]

THIS *ḤADĪTH* IS entered under the subheading of 'expressing a wish'. It does not tell us the time when this took place, but there must have been some indication of imminent danger. The *ḥadīth* mentions that the sound of weapons was heard, but this did not emante from the enemy. The unbelievers could not have reached so close to the Prophet's home without being detected. It was Saʿd's own weaponry

619. Related by al-Bukhari, Muslim, Abū Dāwūd and al-Tirmidhi.

that the Prophet and his wife heard. The question and answer clearly indicate this. Moreover, this was before the revelation of the verse that promised the Prophet protection against people's threats. God says: '*Messenger, proclaim what has been revealed to you by your Lord. For, unless you do it fully, you will not have delivered His message. God will protect you from all men. God does not guide those who reject faith*'. (5:67) When the Prophet received this verse, he ordered his companions who stood guard for him to go home. He told them that he no longer needed their protection. It is practically inconceivable that the Prophet could subsequently express a wish that some of his companions keep watch over him. If any of them were worried about him and stood in watch, they did so on their own initiative.

The fact that Sa'd came to guard the Prophet of his own accord confirms that this verse had not been revealed by then, and that there was some imminent danger to prompt a companion of the Prophet to stand guard at the Prophet's door. Most probably this was just before the Battle of Uḥud. The *ḥadīth* shows how devoted the Prophet's companions were to him.

It should be remembered that the Prophet was the most courageous of people. Even before the revelation of this verse the Prophet was the first to rush out and determine if there was any impending danger.

882. Anas ibn Mālik reports: There was some alarm in Madinah. The Prophet borrowed a horse belonging to Abu Ṭalḥah, which was named al-Mandūb. He mounted the horse and went. When he returned, he said: 'We have found nothing [to worry about], and we have found this horse to be like a sea'.[620]

This highly authentic *ḥadīth* shows how alert the Prophet was to any danger that threatened his community. Here we see him rushing to its source, not waiting for anyone to join him, borrowing a horse in order to be able to move speedily, and returning to reassure his people once he had established that there was nothing to worry about. What local leader would do this today, let alone the leader of any state? More likely, present-day leaders would go in the opposite direction.

620. Related by al-Bukhari, Muslim, Abū Dāwūd and Ibn Mājah.

The safety of the leader is considered as far superior to the safety of the community. Even in the most caring systems, the safety of the leader is given paramount importance, although he may take measures to ensure the safety of his people. The Prophet, however, was the one to move first thereby demonstrating to his successors that it is their duty to ensure that the people are safe.

When the Prophet reassured his companions that there was no danger, he immediately moved on to divert their attentions from the cause of alarm, so as to bring them back to normality. He thus spoke of the horse he had borrowed, describing him as highly useful and likening him to a sea, in so far as it flowed smoothly.

883. (*Athar* 201) Nāfiʿ said: 'Ibn 'Umar used to discipline his children when they made a language mistake'.[621]

884. (*Athar* 202) 'Abd al-Raḥmān ibn 'Ajlān said: ''Umar ibn al-Khaṭṭāb passed by two men shooting arrows. One of them said to the other *asabt.* 'Umar commented: "A language mistake is worse than a wild shot".

These two reports speak about mistakes in language, whether in pronunciation or grammar. The first tells us that 'Abdullāh ibn 'Umar was very keen that his children should attain a good standard in language, so much so that he would punish a child for any mistake in grammar. The second report is specifically about a pronunciation mistake. The man said *asabt*, meaning 'you have hit the mark', but he used the sound 's' instead of 'ṣ', which is a velarised sound. 'Umar was known to be especially eloquent. Hence, his comment that he would have preferred that the man mishit the target rather than his friend make this mistake in pronouncing an Arabic word'.

885. 'Ā'ishah reports: 'Some people asked the Prophet about soothsayers. He said: "They have nothing of substance". They said: "Messenger of God, they say a thing and it turns out to be true". The Prophet said: "This is a word a jinnee might

---

621. Related by Abū Dāwūd.

have snatched and mumbled in his human friend's ear, like the clucking of a hen. They mix it with more than one hundred lies".'[622]

The Prophet was also keen to develop in his companions a proper measure of things and situations. In pre-Islamic days people sought soothsayers and fortune tellers to put to them their problems and disputes and to seek their judgement and advice. Some of these used to foretell the future. All this was stopped when the Prophet Muhammad was sent with his message. It is forbidden to seek advice from a monk or a fortune teller in any situation. If one receives information that a certain person is telling something about future events, he should not believe him, even though there may be indications that what such fortune teller says might be true.

The Prophet's first answer made clear that such people have nothing of substance. What he meant was that they had no real basis for whatever they claimed of knowledge of the future, or knowledge of what other people may not know. All their claims are false, because they have no communication with the source of true knowledge, i.e. God. They do not receive revelation from God.

The jinn are creatures of God about whom we know only what God has told us in the Qur'an. We know that prior to Islam, they used to climb up into the sky trying to eavesdrop on angels as they communicated with each other concerning the fulfilment of God's commands. This is no longer possible. It was in such an attempt at eavesdropping that the jinn might have heard something here or there and they might reiterate what they heard. This might only be partial information, or it might be taken out of context. They might also convey this to their human friends. If it did not sound coherent, the soothsayer or fortune teller would mix it with some other information in order to make it plausible. In this way, they mix it with falsehood. In fact the falsehood might be much greater than the substance of what they heard. Hence, the Prophet's description: 'They mix it with one hundred lies'.

622. Related by al-Bukhari.

886. Anas ibn Mālik reports: 'God's Messenger was on one of his journeys and the camel-driver was chanting. The Prophet said to him: "Gently, Anjushah. Careful with the gentle creatures".'[623]

The Prophet was always considerate of women. He always wanted his companions to take good care of them, and not to burden them with what they might not be able to handle. There are numerous *ḥadīths* stressing our duty to take good care of women, in all situations. This *ḥadīth* refers specifically to this during a journey which was most probably when the Prophet performed pilgrimage. On that occasion he would have had thousands of companions travelling with him, many of them accompanied by female relatives.

When a caravan or a procession travelled in the desert and people were on camel back, the pace was dictated by the front camel. Each caravan would have a driver and a chanter whose melodious voice would make the camels go faster. The chanter might be singing for a while when the camels would go fast, then he would stop to allow a period of more leisurely pace. On this occasion, the Prophet told the chanter to take it easy and not to drive the camels too fast. It is to be noted that the Prophet did not mention women as such, but used a metaphor describing them as 'bottles'. All this was because he feared that the pace would be too tiring for women. The metaphor he used confirms this, because a bottle can break easily and a weak woman may be in discomfort if she is on the back of a camel travelling at speed. This also shows how the Prophet referred to women in a kindly manner.

Avoiding telling a lie

It is well known that telling lies is totally unacceptable in Islam. No matter what the situation is, and how one stands to be adversely affected by telling the truth, one must not tell a falsehood. This is the standard attitude of Islam. Exceptions are permitted in three situations: in war, when one may tell a lie to protect oneself and one's colleagues;

623. Related by al-Bukhari.

to achieve reconciliation between two people who have fallen out; and between man and wife in the interests of a good family life. However, no lies are permitted in order to gain unfair advantage, or to cover up deception.

If these are the only exceptions, and telling lies is a grave sin, how can one avoid an embarrassing situation? It is argued that someone may need to tell a lie in a very innocent situation, simply because stating the truth could cause some difficulty or put a person in an untenable position. In such circumstances, we may resort to ambiguity in what we say.

An ambiguous statement carries more than one meaning, and the listener may very well take the meaning the speaker wants him to understand. This meaning may be untrue, but the statement itself is correct. This is achieved by making the wrong meaning more obvious, so that the listener is diverted from the true situation.

887. (*Athar* 203) Abu 'Uthman reports that 'Umar said:[624] 'It is sufficient lying that one should report everything one hears'. Abu 'Uthmān added that he thought that 'Umar said: 'Does not ambiguity provide a Muslim with a way out of lying'.[625]

888. This is the same as Number 860, with a different chain of transmission.

The first part of this *ḥadīth* draws our attention to a fact of life which shows that if we were to report everything we hear, we would be telling lies. This is because some people do lie, and if we take their words and relay them to others without checking whether they are true or not, we will be sharing their guilt. Moreover, sometimes people do not deliberately tell lies, but may nonetheless be confused about something, or unaware of the full facts. They may be only stating what they heard without checking its truth. It is well known that when

---

624. The final transmitter in the chain mentions some doubt about the identity of the first transmitter, i.e. 'Umar, which makes the authenticity of this *ḥadīth* questionable.

625. Related by Abū Dāwūd and al-Ḥākim. The latter also relating it as a quotation from the Prophet.

people do this, they are likely to miss a point here or there, or to misunderstand something and report it wrongly. If we relay what we hear, we may, in turn, do the same. This means that what we report will be even further from the truth, and we may inadvertently tell a lie. Therefore the *ḥadīth* warns us against reporting everything we hear.

889. (*Athar* 204) ʿAmr ibn al-ʿĀṣ said: 'I wonder at a man who tries to escape from what God has willed when it will inevitably come to pass; and at one who sees a mote in his brother's eye while overlooking a stick in his own eye; and at one who uncovers rancour in his brother but leaves it within him. I have never trusted anyone with a secret of mine and blamed him for disclosing it. How could I blame him when I myself could not keep it'.[626]

These matters may at first sight seem unrelated, but they in fact share a quality of overlooking something that should be immediately apparent, while attention is given to a lesser aspect. Thus, everyone should know that God's will is certain to come to pass. In no way can we avoid it. No method of escape is of any use. Therefore, it is far wiser to be ready for it when it comes.

The second and third scenarios the *ḥadīth* wonders at are very common. We see a fault in others while overlooking our own larger fault. A mote in someone else's eye may not be visible to us, while the one who has it is bound to feel it because of the irritation it causes. Nevertheless a person may see such a particle in someone else's eye but not the much bigger object in his own eye, regardless of how irritating or painful it may be. This is a very vivid image the *ḥadīth* paints, because every one of us has experienced the irritation of a foreign object in one's eye. To imagine a little stick getting there is to feel the pain. The contrast the *ḥadīth* highlights makes us keenly aware of the irony.

The same applies to rancour which should be removed so that our hearts are purged of it. Here we are talking about a feeling, but the feeling is no less irritating than the physical discomfort or pain caused

626. Related by Ibn Ḥibbān.

by something in one's eye. Hence, the first image which refers to tangible objects is followed by a reference to feelings. Here the *ḥadīth* speaks of a person who harbours ill feelings while he is keen that others should bring such feelings out and remove them. He wants them not to harbour any wrong feelings against him, yet he does not start by purging his own heart of such ill feelings towards them.

The last situation is that of one who trusts someone else with his secret and expects him to keep it. He forgets that by entrusting another person with his own secret he has already revealed it to him. If this is the case, then that person may feel the same about it and reveal it to others. How can he be blamed for so doing when the one who is most concerned, or the owner of that secret, could not keep it to himself? This is a very wise statement which implies that if we want our secret to be kept, we better keep it to ourselves.

890. (*Athar* 205) 'Ā'ishah said: 'A man suffering from an illness passed by some women, and they made fun of him. Some of them then contracted that same illness'.

There are countless *ḥadīths* that advise us to watch what we say. Indeed, the Prophet warned against every type of unacceptable behaviour, even when it is limited to words. One type is to make fun of others, particularly if the person being made fun of has some affliction, illness or unsightly appearance. Some *ḥadīths* warn that God may inflict immediate punishment on people who are guilty of such unacceptable practice.

This *ḥadīth* does not state what our attitude should be when we see someone suffering an affliction or having a defect, deformity or handicap. The right behaviour is detailed in other *ḥadīths* which make clear that a Muslim must always be ready with help and must look at anyone with such a disorder or handicap with respect and kindness. We must in no way impart to such a person an impression that he loses some of our esteem because of his difficulties. This *ḥadīth* simply warns that God's punishment may be near at hand. It could be that we will become subject to the same ridicule we levelled at that person by contracting the same illness or suffering the same physical defect. We do well to heed the warning.

Keeping one's cool

891. A young companion of the Prophet from the Baliy tribe reports: 'I visited God's Messenger (peace be upon him) with my father, and he spoke to my father on his own, without me hearing. I [later] asked my father: "What did he say to you?" He answered: "If you are set on doing something, you proceed with a measured pace until God shows you the way out of it, or until God has provided you with a way out".'

Staying calm and keeping one's cool is the only way to guarantee proper thinking and well considered action. In every situation, we need to look at the positive and the negative aspects of the measures we want to take. If we happen to be upset, angry, worried, complacent, careless, hasty, etc. we may overlook factors that are too important to lose sight of. Similarly, if we are keen to have or to avoid something, we may be blinded to the effect of having or avoiding it. Staying cool and maintaining a measured pace is the only course of action that reduces to a minimum the chances of taking wrong measures or steering the wrong way. Hence the Prophet's advice.

But we also detect a subtle element in the Prophet's advice. This is implied in the last part of the *ḥadīth*: 'until God shows you the way out of it, or until God has provided you with a way out it'. This refers to the need to rely on God in all our affairs. With such reliance, we are able to handle matters in a better and well considered way, trusting that God's help will not fail to come. Thus, if we are in a tight situation or a difficulty, He will provide a way out for us.

The early Muslims understood well such teachings by the Prophet. They communicated the same message to others, quoting the Prophet, but they might either quote him directly without attributing the quote to him, which makes it an *athar*, or they might make it clear that the statement they were making is his, which means that it is a *ḥadīth*. However, both cases are treated by *Ḥadīth* scholars in the same way with regard to verification and authentication. An *athar* is considered as a *ḥadīth* because scholars make clear that none of the Prophet's companions said anything related to religion unless he heard it from the Prophet.

892. (*Athar* 206) Muhammad ibn al-Ḥanafiyyah said: 'He is not a wise person who does not deal in a reasonable manner with someone whom he cannot avoid dealing with, until God has provided him with a release or a way out'.

This is a reference to a variety of situations where any one of us might find himself having to deal with someone who adopts an unreasonable attitude. The latter may be a boss at work, or a colleague with whom we have to work on a long task, or an unreasonable spouse, or an unfriendly neighbour whom we cannot get rid of, or a fellow road traveller with whom we have very little in common. In any such situation, particularly one which does not seem to offer any opening for a change, wisdom requires that we resort to a very calm and reasonable approach, always praying to God to provide us with a way out.

In a different vein of social relations, the Prophet encourages kindness to others in every way. He shows us that such kindness is always richly rewarded by God. Whatever we do in this life affects our standing on that Day. Hence, we should always seek and do what improves our position and refrain from what is likely to have a negative effect.

893. Al-Barā' ibn 'Āzib reports that the Prophet said: 'Whoever lends another something to use, or guides another down a lane – or he said a path - will have a reward similar to that of freeing a slave'.

Sometimes the Prophet tells us that God promises very rich reward for an action that does not appear, in our estimation, to deserve such treatment. This is not for us to question, because God rewards a good action with at least ten times its value. He may increase that reward up to 700 times as much, and even more, if He so wishes. Besides, when the action is likely to cement social relations within the Muslim community, then God rewards it very richly. Hence we need not be surprised at the reward promised in this *ḥadīth*.

The rich reward promised is for lending something to be returned after use, but the *ḥadīth* phraseology refers mostly to a cow, a she-camel, a sheep, etc. or to a useful article. Such animals used to be given to a family to use for a while, making use of their milk, or for riding in the case of a camel or a horse, and for them to return after a while. Thus the benefit given by such an offer is stretched over a period of time. Hence, it is so richly rewarded. On the other hand, a person who shows the way to someone in unfamiliar surroundings gives badly needed assistance. Hence, it deserves rich reward.

Charity without money

The word 'charity' is too limited as a translation of the Islamic term *ṣadaqah*, because the latter combines all the full meaning of charity and kindness to others with connotations of 'truth, right, etc.' The term is derived from the root *ṣidq* which means truth. In its Islamic usage, *ṣadaqah* retains the connotations of its root. This is the reason the Prophet says '*Ṣadaqah* is a proof'.[627] What he alludes to in this *ḥadīth* is that it proves a person's claim of belonging to his community by being charitable and kind to others.

The Prophet was keen to ensure his companions understand the full extent of charity, or *ṣadaqah*, in its broad Islamic perspective. Therefore, he pointed out on many occasions the different forms of kindness that count as a charity.

> 894. Abu Dharr said quoting the Prophet: 'To pour water out of your bucket into your brother's is a *ṣadaqah*; to enjoin what is right and forbid what is wrong is a *ṣadaqah*; to meet your brother with a smile on your face is a *ṣadaqah*; to remove a stone, thorn or bone from people's passage is credited to you as a *ṣadaqah*; and to guide a person in an area where he fears to be lost is a *ṣadaqah*'.

This *ḥadīth* mentions several things that a good and kind person might do as a matter of course on any day, without hesitation. If someone asks for directions after losing his way, people normally try to help him, without thinking that they are performing a special kindness. It is, after all, the thing to expect from people when one approaches them

---

627. Related by Muslim.

for directions. Yet the Prophet describes this as a charity, because it is indicative of the right attitude to fellow human beings. We note here that the Prophet speaks of guiding a person, which means guiding anyone, including non-Muslims. Just the fact that he is lost, or fears to be lost, means that we should help him and give him directions, and such help is described by the Prophet as a charity.

The Prophet goes further than this and cites other simple actions as charity. The one with which he begins is a very simple thing. It mentions a situation where people are taking water from a well or a stream, and one of them pours out of his bucket into that of his brother. This is a simple action meant to show care or friendliness, sparing the other the trouble of drawing the water out. It simplifies the recipient's task and spares him some effort. Yet this too counts as a charity.

The next example is a more serious one which takes courage and commitment. It involves advising people to do what is right and proper, and to refrain from what is wrong or forbidden. This is a duty Islam requires of all Muslims, and of the community as a whole. In fact it is a main characteristic of the Muslim community for which God describes it as '*the best community ever raised for mankind*'. (3: 110) In order to encourage us to fulfil this duty, the Prophet describes it here as a charity. This means that we receive a double reward for it: one for discharging a duty and the other for charity.

The Prophet then mentions a very simple act and describes it as a charity: to smile at one's brother. This does not cost anything, either in effort or money. Yet it counts as a charity because of its social effect. We all love to be greeted with warmth. In most cultures stress is placed on meeting people with an air of welcome. Nothing shows such welcome better than meeting others with a smile. Although the friendly feeling such a smile generates is itself a reward, God adds to this by counting it as a charity and rewarding us for it as such.

The fourth type of charity the Prophet mentions is a communal action which again shows commitment to the larger welfare. It is the removal of harmful objects from people's way, so that they do not fall or hurt themselves. What is more is that it keeps clean the environment, which we may appreciate more these days as we become more aware of the hazards of pollution and uncleanliness.

When we look at these five aspects of charity, none of which involves money, we note that some of them are very simple, while others are of far-reaching effect. The combination serves to highlight the Islamic concept that every good action, no matter how small, is a kindness that earns God's reward.

The Prophet stresses this in another *ḥadīth* reported by Jābir ibn Sulaym who says: 'I went to Madinah where I saw a man who was obeyed by people. Whatever he said, people immediately acted upon. I asked about him and I was told: "This is God's messenger, peace be upon him". I spoke to him and said: "To you, messenger of God, I say peace twice". He said: "Do not say, 'to you peace', because it is the greeting of the dead. Say instead, 'peace be to you'." I said: "Are you God's messenger?" He replied: "Yes, I am the messenger of God to whom you pray whenever you meet an adversity and He removes it for you; and if you go through a period of drought you pray to Him and He causes the earth to be fertile again; and if you are in the middle of the desert and you lose your mount, you pray to Him and He brings it back to you". I said: "Messenger of God, teach me". He said: "Be always God-fearing. Do not belittle any kindness, not even pouring some water out of your bucket into someone else's container, or to speak to your brother with smiling face. Avoid dropping your robes low, because that is a sign of arrogance which God dislikes. If a man shames you on account of something he knows about you, do not try to shame him for what you know about him. Let it be that he reaps its consequences and you get its reward. And do not abuse anything". I never abused an animal or a human being after that'.[628]

The lessons given in this *ḥadīth* are very clear and require no comment. We note however how the Prophet answers the man when he asks him whether he was really God's messenger. He does not speak about himself, but about God and in a way the man would recognise. He gives several attributes of God which everyone is certain to acknowledge.

The man seeks to be taught, and the Prophet gives him a number of qualities which are certain to steer him away from conceit and to encourage him to be kind in every way. The most important thing

---

628. Related by Aḥmad, 'Abdullāh and al-Tirmidhi.

is that we must never look down on any act of kindness, however simple. Moreover, any gesture of arrogance is to be shunned, even if it is wearing long clothes. This, however, is subject to social custom. If it is normal in a community that people wear their clothes long, covering their ankles, and if this applies to rich and poor, as is the case today in communities where trousers are part of people's normal dress code then there is nothing wrong with this because no one associates wearing ankle-covering trousers with arrogance. We note also how the Prophet teaches the man not to publicise other people's faults even though they start by publicising his faults. He wants him to prefer the reward that is bound to be given to him if he bears their abuse without replying to it.

What is also noteworthy is the man's implementation of the Prophet's advice. He mentions specifically that he never used abusive words after hearing what the Prophet said, not even to an animal. This is the sort of compliance with the Prophet's teachings that takes people to heaven.

895. Ibn ʿAbbās reports that the Prophet said: 'May God curse the one who deliberately misguides a blind man'.[629]

This *ḥadīth* gives us the opposite situation to the one described in *ḥadīth* Number 893 where a very rich reward is promised to a person guiding another down a lane or a path. Here we see a person who withholds such assistance betraying a very mean character. He goes further than denying guidance along the road to someone who is in bad need of it. Is there a clearer indication of meanness of character than to see a blind man walking along his way and to deliberately lead him astray. Such a mean person deserves the curse the Prophet invokes.

The sum of all goodness

896. ʿAbdullāh ibn ʿAbbās reports: 'The Prophet was sitting at the front of his house in Makkah when ʿUthmān ibn Maẓʿūn

629. Related by al-Ḥākim and Ibn Ḥibbān.

passed by and smiled at the Prophet. The Prophet said to him: "Would you like to sit with me?" He said: "Yes". The Prophet sat facing him. As they were in conversation, the Prophet stared fixedly at the sky. He then said: "A messenger from God came to me now while you were sitting with me". He asked: "What did he say to you?" He replied: "*God enjoins justice, kindness [to all], and generosity to one's kindred; and He forbids all that is shameful, all reprehensible conduct, and aggression. He admonishes you so that you may take heed*". (16: 90) 'Uthmān said: "It was then that I felt faith taking hold of my heart and I loved Muhammad".'[630]

Perhaps we should say a word about the man at the centre of this *ḥadīth*, 'Uthmān ibn Maẓ'ūn. Apparently this occurred during the very early days of Islam, because 'Uthmān was the fourteenth person to accept Islam. He says that he only accepted Islam because he was too shy to refuse, after the Prophet had spoken to him about it several times. But only when this verse was revealed did he feel a strong desire to become a Muslim. He also says that he recited this verse to al-Walīd ibn al-Mughīrah, one of the Quraysh elders, and he commented on the Qur'an, saying: 'It is certainly beautiful; it flows so easily. It is like a tree with fruit at the top and goodness at the bottom, and it is in no way the speech of human beings'. Abu Jahl also said: 'God certainly enjoins the best of principles'.

There is no doubt that 'Uthmān ibn Maẓ'ūun was a man of fine character and good qualities. This is why the Prophet was keen that he should accept Islam. The fact that this verse was the immediate cause of his belief testifies to his good character. Let us now look at this verse and the message it gives. Commenting on it, Sayyid Qutb writes:

This book, the Qur'an, has been revealed in order to bring a nation into existence, and to regulate a community; to establish a different world and initiate a new social order. It represents a world message for the whole of mankind, which does not allow any special allegiance to a tribe, nation or race. Faith is the only bond that unites a community and a nation. It puts

---

630. Related by Aḥmad.

forward the principles that ensure unity within the community, security and reassurance for individuals, groups and nations, as well as complete trust that governs all transactions, pledges and promises.

It requires that justice should be established and maintained, because justice ensures a solid and constant basis for all transactions and dealings between individuals and communities; a basis subject to no prejudice, preference or favouritism; a basis influenced by no family relationship, wealth or strength; a basis that ensures equal treatment for all and subjects all to the same standards and laws.

Along with justice, the Qur'an urges kindness, which relaxes the strictness of absolute justice. It lays the door open for anyone who wishes to win the heart of an opponent to forgo part of what is rightfully his. This means that the chance is available to all to go beyond strict justice, which is both a right and a duty, to show kindness in order to allow wounds to heal or to win favour.

Kindness has an even broader sense. Every good action is a kindness. The command enjoining kindness includes every type of action and transaction. It thus covers every aspect of life, including a person's relationships with his Lord, family, community and with the rest of mankind.

Perhaps we should add here that some commentators on the Qur'an say that 'justice' is the obligatory part, while 'kindness' is voluntary, but highly encouraged, particularly in as far as matters of worship are concerned. They say that this verse is part of the revelations received by the Prophet in Makkah, when the legal provisions had not yet been outlined. But the way the verse is phrased uses both justice and kindness in their broadest sense. Moreover, from a purely ethical point of view, both are generally applicable principles, not mere legal provisions.

One aspect of kindness is 'generosity to one's kindred', but it is specially highlighted here in order to emphasise its importance. From the Islamic point of view, this is not based on narrow family loyalty, but on the Islamic principle of common solidarity which moves from the smaller, local circle to the larger, social context. The principle is central to the implementation of the Islamic social system.

The verse proceeds to outline three prohibitions in contrast with the three orders with which it begins, stating that God '*forbids all that is shameful, and reprehensible conduct, and all transgression*'. Under shameful conduct everything that goes beyond the limits of propriety is included, but the term is often used to denote dishonourable assault and indecency. Thus it combines both aggression and transgression. Hence it has become synonymous with shamefulness.

'Reprehensible conduct' refers to any action of which pure, undistorted human nature disapproves. Islam also disapproves of any such conduct because it is the religion of pure human nature. Yet human nature may become distorted, but Islamic law remains constant, pointing to what human nature was like before distortion creeps into it.

'Aggression' in this context denotes injustice as well as any excess that goes beyond what is right and fair.

No community may survive when it is based on the spread of shameful, reprehensible conduct and transgression. No community allows shameful conduct in all its connotations, and reprehensible actions of all sorts, and transgression with all its consequences and then hopes to flourish. Hence human nature is bound to rebel against these whenever they are allowed to spread in society.[631]

897. Anas reports that the Prophet said: 'Whoever brings up two girls until they attain puberty, will enter heaven with me like these two, (pointing with his index and middle fingers)'.

When the Prophet began to receive God's message, he was living in a society that was extremely unfair to women. The birth of a girl was greeted with gloom to the extent that her father would hide away for days on end in order not to show his face in public. Fathers buried their daughters alive, either for fear of poverty or fear of shame. The

631. Sayyid Qutb, In the Shade of the Qur'an, 2005, Vol. 11, pp. 86-88.

Prophet set out to change this attitude so that women would be treated equally with men. In all Islamic teachings women are addressed on an equal footing as men. They are assigned the same religious duties and they receive the same reward. Thus, the two sexes are perfectly equal.

Moreover, the Prophet wanted a daughter to receive all the love and compassion that is given to her brother. Hence, the Prophet encouraged his followers to be very kind to their daughters as is clearly apparent in this *ḥadīth*.

To a Muslim, the great prize that he or she wants to have in the Hereafter is to be admitted into heaven. However, to be with the Prophet in heaven is the ultimate prize, because the highest position there is reserved for him. So, if something can guarantee that prize, Muslims are definitely keen to do it. Here, the Prophet says that what guarantees this ultimate prize is kindness to one's daughters. Yet people continue to claim that Islam is unfair to women. How misguided and unfair they are!

898. And: 'Two punishments are advanced in this world: rebellion and severance of ties of kinship'.

This *ḥadīth* is entered in this form in al-Bukhari's book, but it occurs with its full chain of transmission in *ḥadīth* Number 29.

Good ancestry and noble character

The Prophet highlights that when nobility of character based on piety and God-fearingness is combined with nobility of descent, then this is the noblest lineage:

899. Abu Hurayrah reports that the Prophet said: 'A noble man, son of a noble man, son of a noble man, son of a noble man is Joseph ibn Jacob ibn Isaac ibn Abraham'.

This is a lineage of four generations, and each one is a prophet. In this version only this part of the *ḥadīth* is mentioned. Another version we saw earlier gives a fuller statement in which the Prophet refers to

Joseph's attitude when the king ordered that he should be brought to him after he had interpreted the king's dream. At the time Joseph was in prison, where he had spent several years, on false charges. He refused to leave until the case was verified and his innocence established. The Prophet referred to his attitude, describing it as most admirable. Anyone would have seized the opportunity to have an audience with the king, when he might have been reprieved. But Joseph wanted his innocence to be established and this was what he received.

900. Abu Hurayrah reports that the Prophet said: 'The people who will be close to me on the Day of Resurrection are the God-fearing, even though a certain lineage may be nearer of kin than another. Let not other people come to me with their good deeds and you come carrying stuff of this world on your necks. You will appeal to me, saying: "O, Muhammad!" and I will say: "No, this way and that way", (turning away both left and right)'.

Islam emphasises that all human beings are equal. They are equal at the point of birth and equal on the Day of Judgement. They are given the same duties and promised the same reward. Thus, their equality in God's sight is complete. People, however, create all sorts of standards to raise some people high and keep others down. Islam does not recognise any such standards. The only criterion that raises some people above others is their being pious and God-fearing, provided always that they maintain this throughout their lives. This is stated clearly in the Qur'an. The Prophet further emphasised it in a number of statements and traditions.

This *ḥadīth* describes the Prophet's attitude to people's situations on the Day of Judgement. Those whose life is characterised by fearing God and piety will be the ones who bring forward their deeds hoping for a rich reward from God. They are certain to have the Prophet's support and God's reward. They are the ones to be given a position close to the Prophet, because their actions in this life confirm what they profess of accepting the Islamic faith and implementing it.

The Prophet acknowledges that kin relationships may bring some people closer to others. Thus some people might be closer to the Prophet by virtue of blood relations, but he warns here that it is actions that count on the Day of Judgement. He further paints a very vivid picture of those who rely on being related to him for their salvation on the Day of Judgement while not doing enough to save themselves. They come carrying stuff of this world on their shoulders. This is a reference to anything, material or not, that people gain unfairly in this life. As they have to account for it, they carry it on their necks. In another *ḥadīth* the Prophet says that people may come on the Day of Judgement carrying a lamb, a sheep or a camel on their shoulders. They will do so if in this life they took such animals unfairly from others. Thus, even if a person gains a position or an honour unfairly, when it should have been given to another person, he or she will come on the Day of Judgement carrying it on his back, until they have accounted for it before God Almighty.

The Prophet further warns that those who profess to follow him will appeal to him for help, but he will not be in a position to help them. He will simply turn away because he cannot help anyone except those who, in this present life, truly follow him. They might commit some sins, but they always seek God's forgiveness and try to rectify their deeds. It is such people that hope to benefit by his intercession on their behalf. As for those who deliberately wronged others and got away with things to which they had no rightful claim, persisting in their misdeeds and showing no sign of repentance, they will carry their heavy burdens and they will have no one to support them as they face God's reckoning.

901. (*Athar* 207) Ibn ʿAbbās said: 'I do not see anyone implementing the Qur'anic verse that says: "*Mankind! We have created you all out of a male and a female, and have made you into nations and tribes, so that you might come to know one another. Indeed, the noblest of you in the sight of God is the one who is most God-fearing. God is All-Knowing, All-Aware*". (49:13) Nevertheless, one man would say to another, "I am more noble than you". Be sure that no one is nobler than another except through being God-fearing'.

902. (*Athar* 208) Ibn ʿAbbās said: 'What would you consider nobility? God has clearly stated what nobility is: the noblest of you are those who are most God-fearing. Whom do you consider to have good lineage? The best lineage belongs to the ones who are the best in character'.

In the first report ʿAbdullāh ibn ʿAbbās, who benefited by the Prophet's prayer to God to give him sound knowledge in religion and sound understanding of the Qur'an, speaks of the Islamic criterion of nobility. He highlights the fact that people may seek to press their advantage based on whatever consideration might be acceptable in their community. But the one criterion which specifies real nobility is the one outlined in the verse he quotes. He laments the fact that people tend to overlook this.

In the second *ḥadīth (*we find definitions of two terms which people often use, in reference to good descent and honourable personality. But it is clearly stated that none of these is acquired through descent. They cannot be inherited. The basis is one's own deeds and one's own qualities and manners. Thus, if a person is God-fearing and is kind to others, considerate and benevolent, he is the one God considers noble and who deserves to be honoured.

Friendship of souls

Sometimes the Prophet gives us a glimpse of insight into the realm of the soul, which we know very little about. The important thing to remember in this connection is that God has chosen not to give us a detailed knowledge of the soul. We should also remember that whatever He has chosen to withhold from us will not affect our role on earth and the fulfilment of the task assigned to us in this life. Therefore, we limit ourselves to what is outlined in the Qur'an and to what the Prophet has given us in authentic *ḥadīths*. However, people continue to try to explore the realm of the soul and come up with all sorts of ideas to show that they have special knowledge that is denied to others. All such claims are false, because they do not rely on any confirmed knowledge imparted to us by God through His messenger.

903. ʿĀʾishah reports that the Prophet said: 'Souls are like soldiers standing in ranks: those of them with similar qualities will be friends, and those which are dissimilar in their qualities will be in conflict'.[632]

904. The same as Number 903, but reported by Abu Hurayrah with a different chain of transmission.[633]

This *ḥadīth* has several versions with different chains of transmission, all of which are authentic. This makes it highly authentic. One version which throws some light on its meaning mentions that a Makkan woman who was known to have a sense of humour and to love to play tricks travelled to Madinah where she was a guest of a woman of similar qualities. When ʿĀʾishah heard of this, she said: 'My beloved husband always told the truth… [and she quoted this *ḥadīth*]'.

What this *ḥadīth* means is that God created souls and gave them their qualities. Those of similar qualities will easily be friends when they meet in this life, while those who have different natures are likely to be in conflict. This accounts for endless cases of people getting along together when their apparent circumstances should have kept them well apart. Moreover, it tells us something about what brings good people together and what allows evil ones to flock together and even trust each other, when they know that they are evil at heart.

If this sounds difficult to understand, it is because we know very little about the nature of the soul. However, some *ḥadīths* tell us of things that may sound extremely strange, such as the following very authentic *ḥadīth*:

905. Abu Hurayrah reports that the Prophet said: 'A shepherd was tending his sheep when a wolf attacked and took away one sheep. The shepherd chased him, but the wolf turned round and said: "Who will protect her on the day of the lion, when I will be its only shepherd". The people attending the Prophet said:

---

632. Related by al-Bukhari, Muslim and Abū Dāwūd.
633. Related by Muslim and Abū Dāwūd.

> Limitless is God in His Glory, [i.e. *subḥān Allah*]". The Prophet rejoined, 'I do believe it, and so do Abu Bakr and 'Umar'.[634]

The first thing that attracts our attention in this *ḥadīth* is the wolf speaking to the shepherd in human language. To start with, this is not difficult for God to bring about. He made infants talk in adult language, such as Jesus Christ, and the child witness testifying to Joseph's innocence when the Egyptian minister's wife said to her husband. God is able to do whatever He wishes, and He accomplishes His purpose, no matter how impossible it may appear to human eyes. For the wolf to talk in human language is, to God, as easy as making human beings speak. If we look into how human children learn to speak we are bound to conclude that they would have never done so of their own accord, unless God instils in them the ability to so learn.

When the Prophet's audience expressed their amazement, he confirmed his belief in the truth of the story, and he also asserted that Abu Bakr and 'Umar also believed in it. He mentions his closest companions who showed the most profound insight into the Islamic faith. They would not hesitate to believe in the story, amazing as it may sound to us. In fact, we should have no difficulty in accepting the story, because it merely tells us about one aspect demonstrating God's power. When we assert our belief in God, we also make clear that we believe that God is able to do everything. Making a wolf speak in human language is very simple to Him, and He can make this happen at any time.

Apparently, this *ḥadīth* speaks about an incident that took place long before the Prophet's time. In his *Ṣaḥīḥ* anthology, al-Bukhari enters it in the chapter he devotes to *ḥadīths* concerning the Children of Israel. But the same thing happened to one of the Prophet's companions called Ahbān ibn Aws. The relevant *ḥadīth* is related in connection with his acceptance of Islam. The report says: 'A wolf attacked his flock of sheep and pursued one of them. Ahbān shouted at the wolf, trying to drive him away. The wolf turned to him and said: "Who will protect her when you are preoccupied with other things? Do you prevent me provisions that God has given me?" Ahbān clapped with his hands

---

634. Related by al-Bukhari.

in amazement and said: "By God, I have never seen a more amazing thing!" The wolf said: "But there is a more amazing thing. Here is God's messenger sitting under these date trees, calling on people to believe in God". Ahbān went to the Prophet and told him the story and declared that he believed in Islam'.[635]

I do not find it amazing that a wolf speaks to a man in his language. God is able to accomplish this at any time. What I find amazing is that the same story should happen twice, the first time with a person from the Children of Israel, and then during the Prophet's own time, with the addition that the wolf directs the man to the place where God's messenger was speaking to people calling on them to believe in God. Glory be to God; He is able to do whatever He wills.

---

635. Related by Ibn Ḥajar in *Fatḥ al-Bāri*, his voluminous commentary on al-Bukhari's *Ṣaḥīḥ*, vol. 7, p. 20.

44

Man and Destiny

PEOPLE OFTEN SPEAK about predestination, suggesting that no matter what a person does in this life, there is no escape from what has been predetermined.

906. 'Ali reports: 'The Prophet was in a funeral procession and he picked up something with which he scratched the ground. He then said: "Every one of you has been assigned his place in hell and his place in heaven". People said: "Messenger of God, would it then be right to rely on what has been assigned and exert no effort?" He said: "Do what you can. Everyone's way is made easy to accomplish what one is created for". He added: "The one who is with the happy people will find it easy to do the actions leading to happiness, and the one who is with the wretched people will find it easy to do the actions leading to wretchedness". He then recited: "*As for him who gives and is God-fearing and believes in the truth of the ultimate good, We shall smooth the way to perfect*

> *ease. But as for him who is a miser and deems himself self-sufficient, and rejects the truth of the ultimate good, We shall smooth the way to affliction*".' (92: 5-10)

People who lack faith always take such statements to support their claims that religion puts man in a strait jacket, making his end a foregone conclusion because God has already determined it, even before a person is born. They make such claims to justify their sinful actions and negligence of duties. Such people say that they would have done better, had God guided them to the right way. Thus, they put the blame on God for their erring ways, and the inevitable outcome of such ways. The fact is that it is man who determines his own fate in the life to come through his action in this present life. The *ḥadīth* makes it clear that the two possibilities are open to man. Everyone has a place assigned to him in both heaven and hell, and it is he who chooses where to go. It is when a person makes his or her choice that his path is made easy to the end that his or her choice leads to. We need only to read the verses the Prophet quoted in explanation to realise that what determines man's fate is his own choice, decision and action. Here is what Sayyid Qutb says in comment on the verses the Prophet quotes in this *ḥadīth*:

> These are the two positions at which disparate souls line up where all diverse striving and divergent ways of life end. Each group has its way in this life smoothed, with all obstructions removed: '*As for him who gives and is God-fearing and believes in the truth of the ultimate good, We shall smooth the way to perfect ease*'. He who is charitable, God-fearing and believes in an ideology which is synonymous with ultimate good has indeed done his best to purify himself, seeking right guidance. Hence, he deserves the help and grace which God has, by His own will, committed Himself to provide. For without this grace man finds himself absolutely helpless. He whose path to perfect ease and comfort is made smooth by God achieves something great. What is more, such a person achieves this great goal in this life without difficulty. He lives in ease. Indeed, ease flows from him to all around him. Ease becomes characteristic of his movement,

action and handling of all things and situations. Success and quiet contentedness become the distinctive mark of his life in all its details and general aspects. He attains the highest grade of all, in the sense that he joins the Prophet as a recipient of God's promise to His Messenger: '*We shall smooth your way to perfect ease*'. (87: 8)

'*But as for him who is a miser and deems himself self-sufficient, and rejects the truth of the ultimate good, We shall smooth the way to affliction. What will his wealth avail him when he goes down [to his grave].*'

He who sacrifices nothing of himself or his wealth, professes that he is in no need of His Lord or His guidance and disbelieves in His message and religion, makes himself vulnerable to evil. For so doing he deserves that everything should be made hard for him. Hence, God makes easy his path to affliction, and withholds from him all kinds of help. God makes every stride he takes really hard, drives him away from the path of right guidance, and leaves him to traverse the valleys of misery, although he may imagine himself to be taking the road to success. How greatly mistaken he is! He loses balance: thus he tries to avoid falling only to go down heavily, and finds himself further away from the path set by God, deprived of His pleasure. When he eventually goes down to his grave, he can make no use of the wealth he has hoarded. It is that very wealth that has caused him to imagine himself in no need of God or His guidance. '*What will his wealth avail him when he goes down [to his grave]*'. Facilitating evil and sin is the same as facilitating the way to affliction, even though the sinful may be successful and prosperous in this life. For is there any affliction worse than hell? Indeed, hell is affliction itself![636]

636. Sayyid Qutb, In the Shade of the Qur'an, Vol. 18, pp. 238-9.

45

Prohibitions, Weather Change, Omen etc.

SOME OF THE Prophet's companions who were very close to him did not report many *ḥadīths*. One of these was Abu Qatādah al-Ḥārith ibn Rib'i of the Anṣār who only reported 170 *ḥadīths*.

907. Usayd's mother said: 'I said to Abu Qatādah: "Why do you not narrate the Prophet's *ḥadīths* as other people do?" He said: "I heard God's Messenger (peace be upon him) say: 'Whoever attributes something false to me prepares for himself a position in hell to recline upon'. As the Prophet said this, he smoothed the ground with his hand".'

This *ḥadīth* states why many of the Prophet's companions were especially reluctant to quote him, fearing that they might replace a word here or there, or misquote him in some other way. If they were to attribute it to the Prophet and state that he said this, they feared that it might be counted as a lie. This would, then, put them in the position the Prophet warned against. Needless to say, God knows that they intended no such a thing, and if they erred, it would have been a genuine mistake. We know that God would not punish anyone for a genuine mistake, as the Prophet himself made clear. Nevertheless, these companions remained reluctant to quote the Prophet for fear of making a mistake. Some of them would quote him only very sparingly, as in the case of Abu Qatādah, who would have reported several times as many *ḥadīths* as are related through him. Others would qualify any quotation they made from the Prophet by adding the phrase, 'or he might have said something similar to this'.

It is often the case that the Prophet's companions might say a *ḥadīth* which they heard the Prophet say, but without attributing it to him. This means that the *ḥadīth* would be reported as if it was said by the companion reporting it, but scholars of *Ḥadīth* would know that no one of the Prophet's companions would ever have said anything relevant to the religion of Islam unless he had heard it from the Prophet. This is one of the reasons why *Ḥadīth* scholars include such reports, calling them *athar*, particularly when a report involves a prohibition. No one would dare describe anything as forbidden without clear evidence from the Qur'an or the Sunnah, because the authority to forbid anything belongs only to God.

908. ʿAbdullāh ibn Mughaffal al-Muzani reports: 'The Prophet warned against *khadhf*, and said: "It neither kills game nor hurts an enemy, but it may gouge an eye or break a tooth".'[637]

Khadhf is a form of throwing little pebbles, by placing the pebble between one's index and middle fingers, or between one's thumb and index finger, or between the back of the middle finger and the inside of the thumb and shooting it. The *ḥadīth* is reported in other ways, one of which suggests that ʿAbdullāh ibn Mughaffal saw someone doing it, and he told him not to. He then reported the *ḥadīth* to him.

The Prophet gives a clear explanation for his prohibition of this method of shooting pebbles. It certainly gives the pebble more speed than a normal throw, thereby making it more effective. But the Prophet

637. Related by al-Bukhari, Muslim and al-Nasāʾī.

explains that although it delivers a more powerful shot, it nonetheless does not achieve either of the two legitimate purposes for which it may be done, namely killing game and hurting an enemy. It might be suggested that it could help a hunter by injuring game, or even killing it, but even then it is not acceptable, since this is only possible in a very narrow sense. Normally, people would not resort to hunting by shooting little stones at game. Nor does it hurt the enemy, although it may be more painful than when one is hit by a pebble thrown normally.

The main problem in so misusing pebbles is that if they hit a person or animal, it might blind or break a tooth. This, then, is sufficient reason for discouraging it, even to the point of prohibition.

909. Abu Hurayrah reports: 'A strong wind blew on people on the road to Makkah when 'Umar was [leading the people] on the way for pilgrimage. 'Umar said to those around him: "What is wind?" They did not give an answer. I urged my camel forward and I caught up with him. I said: "I am told that you have asked about the wind. I heard God's Messenger (peace be upon him) say: 'The wind is [a phenomenon] of God's mercy: it may bring mercy and it may bring suffering. Do not curse it, but ask God to grant you the good in it and seek His shelter from its evil'."'[638]

Needless to say, 'Umar was not asking about the making of the wind. His question was about its role in the system of God's creation. Abu Hurayrah understood this and was keen to impart what he had heard the Prophet say in this respect. His information places wind among various other natural phenomena which God may use to grant mercy to some people or administer punishment to others. Therefore, even when it causes damage and devastation, it should not be cursed. Rather, what we should do when a storm blows hard is to pray to God to grant us the good it brings and to avert from us any evil it causes.

---

638. Related by Aḥmad, Abū Dāwūd, al-Nasā'ī and Ibn Mājah.

A sum of all goodness

910. Zayd ibn Khālid al-Juhani reports: 'God's Messenger led the congregational Fajr [i.e. dawn] prayer one day at al-Ḥudaibiyah after it had been raining at night. When he finished his prayers, he turned to people and said: "Do you know what your Lord says?" They replied: "God and His Messenger know best". He said: "God says: 'Some of My servants are believers this morning and some are unbelievers. A person who says, "We have been sent rain by God's grace and mercy", believes in Me and disbelieves in the planet. As for the one who says, "We have had rain because this planet", disbelieves in Me and believes in the planet'."'[639]

This *ḥadīth* refers to a belief that a set of planets which are paired in the sense that when one of them goes down in the west, the other rises in the east. These are believed to complete their turn of ascent and descent once a year. People used to associate rain with the going down of the wintry ones. Even today, people in some countries, particularly in coastal cities, attribute rainfalls to certain cyclic climatic phenomena. This is the concept to which the Prophet refers in this *ḥadīth* in which he quotes God's word. When the text of a *ḥadīth* attributes a statement to God, it becomes a sacred, or *qudsi ḥadīth*.

When we look at the text of the *ḥadīth*, we realise that the way people look at things and how they happen makes a fundamental difference to their status as believers or unbelievers. Here, the Prophet refers to a particular habit, in which people attribute rainfall to the ascent or descent of a certain planet. Thus they make the movement of the planet, or the planet itself, the cause of the rainfall. If so, then the planet has a will of its own which determines the movement of clouds and the fall of rain. Since a believer attributes all that happens in the universe to God alone, to attribute something like rainfall to a planet, or to any cause, is an act of associating partners with God.

We have to make a fine distinction here. The *ḥadīth* speaks of a person saying the rain took place 'because this planet is on the

---

639. Related by al-Bukhari, Muslim, al-Nasā'ī and Abū Dāwūd.

ascendance'. If a person says instead, 'we had rainfall when this planet was on the ascendance', there is nothing wrong with this. He is simply referring to the time of the rainfall, not attributing its cause to the planet and its movement.

What all this means is to stress the Islamic principle of attributing everything that takes place in the universe to God and His will. When we have rainfall, we say that it takes place by God's will and grace. When rain is scarce, we pray to God to send us rain. We do not look to any cause or factor, because we know that they all operate by His will.

When we speak of God's will, we should always remember that it is free, unrestricted by anything. God may will whatever He likes at any time, and He brings it about as He wishes. The laws of nature are all subject to His will. He operates them as He pleases and He suspends or replaces them as He wishes. Nothing influences His decision. He has power over all things, and He always accomplishes His purpose as He pleases.

This means that we must never take anything for granted. We do not say that since this or that has taken place, then we expect the following consequences. Although such a statement may rely on what we have experienced of cause and effect, we must not attribute any result or event to any factor other than God's will. This was how the Prophet looked at all events.

911. 'Ā'ishah reports: 'When the Prophet saw a rain cloud, he would be uneasy, going in and out, walking to and fro, and his face would change colour. When rain began to fall, he would relax'. 'Ā'ishah pointed this out to him once. He said: 'How can I tell? It may be like what God, the Mighty and Exalted, said: "*When they saw a cloud approaching their valleys, they said: 'This cloud will bring us rain'. No, indeed. It is the very thing you wanted to hasten: a stormwind bearing painful suffering which will destroy everything by the command of its Lord*".'[640] (46:24-25)

---

640. Related by al-Bukhari, al-Nasā'ī and al-Tirmidhi.

Here, the Prophet is referring to the punishment God inflicted on the 'Ād, an early community to whom the Prophet Hūd was sent but who rejected his message, despite the clear evidence that God gave them to prove that he preached the message of truth. Thus, they earned their punishment, which began by sending clouds that they mistook for an indication of rain.

The fact that the Prophet looked uneasy, or troubled when he saw clouds and his explanation that he could not tell whether the clouds brought in the prospect of rain or something totally different confirms his firm belief that God's will is free. No one can tell for certain what may come in the wake of any event, not even a natural phenomenon which we see every day. Therefore, we must always be on our guard, lest we incur God's displeasure and deserve His punishment. We must always pray to Him to forgive us our sins, and not to hold our shortcomings against us. If the Prophet worried at a natural development, because he could not tell what it heralded, then we have much less reason to be confident that it would bring only what is good and beneficial. We should trust to God's grace and mercy, but we should try to earn this by being always mindful of our duties and keen to do what He has ordered.

Good and bad omen

People often associate certain things, or events, or signs with good or bad omen. These differ from one culture to another. In the old Arabian culture, when people went out on some business, they tried to determine whether their task would be successful. They usually looked for any bird they might see. If the bird flew to the right, they considered this to be a good omen and they continued with their task. If the bird flew left, they thought this was a bad omen and they would desist with whatever they had embarked upon. In fact, this was so entrenched in their culture that the Arabic name for sensing bad omens is derived from the word *ṭayr*, which means bird. It is used even when the object, action or event that causes a bad omen has nothing to do with birds. Apparently this was not limited to Arabs. Even in other cultures, people looked to birds for sensing what may come about. The English word 'auspice' is defined in the Oxford Dictionary as 'an observation of birds for omens'.

Needless to say, all this is forbidden in Islam. It is contrary to the very concept that knowledge of the future is the preserve of God alone. It is also against the principle of putting our trust in God.

912. 'Abdullāh ibn Mas'ūd reports that the Prophet said: '[Believing in] a bad omen is a form of idolatry. It may occur to anyone of us, but God clears it away when we rely totally on Him'.[641]

913. Abu Hurayrah reports that the Prophet said: '[Do not entertain] bad omens. The best of it is the good one'. People asked: 'Which is the good one?' He answered: 'A good word any of you may hear'.[642]

This *ḥadīth* is very clear in its import. It describes bad omens as a form of idolatry, or polytheism, but it recognises that thoughts of such a nature may be quick to our minds. The way to rid ourselves of them is therefore identified. The first sentence is very definitive. That it was associated in old Arabian society with the direction a bird flies is indicative of its absurdity. How can a bird know future events? What does the direction of its flight signify anything in human language? How can it relate its knowledge to the actions of human beings, or to the people around? If the bird were to know all this, it would be much superior to man in knowledge, when not even the people who attached their omen to its direction of flight would have credited it with this.

In the second *ḥadīth*, the Prophet gives a clear order that finding a bad omen in any sign is unacceptable in Islam. In fact it is forbidden, unless one tries to dispel its effects by placing one's trust in God. Next, the Prophet speaks about good omens as being the best. The comparative here is not between two good things with one being better than the other, because there is nothing good in allowing bad omens to dictate our course of action. The comparative is merely in what we

641. Related by Abū Dāwūd, al-Tirmidhi and Ibn Mājah.
642. Related by Aḥmad, al-Bukhari, Ibn Ḥibbān, Ibn Khuzaymah and Abu 'Awānah.

feel when something causes us to be optimistic or pessimistic about something we are embarking upon.

Besides, the Prophet explains that people normally find good omen in a good word they hear. It is not a sign from a bird, animal or inanimate object. A good word may affect a person because it expresses some favourable feeling, or describes a positive situation. It is in human nature that we like fine expressions, beautiful scenery, peaceful surroundings, even when none of it belongs to us. Similarly, words that speak of a good thing happening to us soon are bound to have a good effect on us. We note here that such words may be without foundation, but the fact that they give us a sense of optimism is beneficial, provided that we attribute all future events to God's will.

To give an example, a mother says to her daughter on the morning she is taking her exams, 'I feel in my heart that you will do well'. The daughter feels optimistic and approaches her exam in good spirits. There is nothing wrong with this, as long as the daughter does not attribute her fine results to her mother's words or feelings.

Yet people often experience thoughts of bad omens when they hear something or see something taking place. Should this happen, a believer must not entertain such thoughts for long. He should be quick to place his trust in God and rely on Him in all life's situations. When a believer does so, all thoughts of bad omens are dispelled because a believer knows that whatever befalls us comes from God. When we place our trust in Him, He is sure to enable us to overcome difficulties and to reward us for our patience when we meet adversity. In this respect, we may recall the *ḥadīth* in which the Prophet wonders at a believer's lot: 'I wonder at a believer's affairs, as they all end up into what is good. This applies to none other than a believer. If something good comes his way, he expresses his gratitude to God, and it will be good for him; and if he experiences adversity, he remains patient, and that will again be good for him'.[643]

So, we have to differentiate between a temporary thought which we try to dispel by placing our trust in God, and giving in to a bad omen. In the latter situation, people change their plans, restrict their

643. Related by Muslim.

movements and do different things to avoid what they think bodes ill for them. This is the sort of thing the Prophet warns against. A man called Muʿāwiyah ibn Ḥakam said to the Prophet: 'I have only recently abandoned ignorant beliefs, and now God has favoured us with Islam. Some of our people visit fortune tellers'. The Prophet said: 'Do not visit them'. The man added: 'And some of us associate bad omens with certain things'. The Prophet replied: 'This is something that people may occasionally entertain. Let them not be deterred from their purpose'.[644]

This *ḥadīth* clearly distinguishes temporary pessimistic thoughts from giving in to bad omens. The distinction is at its clearest when one goes ahead with whatever one is planning or what one is about to do, disregarding all negative thoughts and relying totally on God, and, on the other hand, giving in to such thoughts, changing one's plans and purposes.

Qualities of the best

914. ʿAbdullāh ibn Masʿūd reports that the Prophet said: 'Communities were shown to me during the pilgrimage days, and I was pleased with the large numbers of my community: they filled the plains and the mountains. I was asked: "Muhammad, are you happy?" I said: "Yes, my Lord". He said: "Along with these there are seventy thousand who will be admitted into heaven without reckoning. These are the ones who neither ask others to pray for them when they are ill, nor sear themselves, nor believe in bad omens, but place their trust in God". A man called ʿUkkāshah said: "Pray to God to make me one of these". The Prophet prayed: "My Lord, make him one of them". Another man said: "Pray to God for me to be one of them". The Prophet said: "ʿUkkāshah has been ahead of you in this".'[645]

---

644. Related by Muslim.
645. Related by Aḥmad, al-Bukhari and Muslim.

The first point the *ḥadīth* makes is that the Prophet was reassured by the large multitude of his followers who filled up a great expanse. Every advocate of a good cause feels extremely happy when his advocacy earns good response. In this *ḥadīth* the Prophet is asked by none other than God if he was happy with the response to his call. When he sees the numbers he is certainly pleased. However, it should be pointed out that there is an element of symbolism here, as the Prophet is shown a panoramic view, with his followers filling up the planes and the mountains. It does not necessarily mean that he was shown every one of his followers throughout all generations. Yet this is not beyond God's ability to do if He so pleases.

When the Prophet expressed his happiness with what he saw, he was told that added to them are seventy thousand who attain a higher status, for which they are admitted to heaven without being questioned about their deeds in this life. Before we discuss the qualities of this special group, we should mention that in Arabic generally, and in such statements in particular, the number is often symbolic. Arabs often use the number seven and its multiples to indicate plenty, rather than the exact number. In some reports, we are told that with every thousand of these there are seventy thousand and plenty more. But these have the distinction that their admission to heaven is made much easier, as they are spared the difficult task of having to account for their deeds. This means that their sins and bad deeds are forgiven without question, and their good deeds are generously rewarded. So it is very important to know what qualifies them for this distinction.

The first quality is that they do not ask others to pray for their recovery when they are ill. What is wrong with such a request? To start with, there is nothing wrong with a person who visits a friend or a relative who is ill and prays to God to speed that person's recovery. The Prophet did so on some occasions, but he chose to do it, and was not asked by the patient. It is also open to the patient to pray for recovery. As he is the one suffering from the illness, his prayers are likely to express more urgency and sincerity, knowing that it is God alone Who can ensure his full recovery. Sincere prayers are certain to be answered when coupled with complete trust in God. Requesting others to pray for one may indicate impatience, or doubt that one's own prayers are being answered. Besides, one never knows what another person may include in his prayers. If he includes something unacceptable, such as attributing any power of recovery to any being other than God, then such prayer is counterproductive.

The second quality is that they do not sear themselves as a method of healing. This was a practice in olden times, that people may burn their skin with a hot iron, believing that such searing would remove an illness. Searing one's skin is strongly discouraged because it involves permanent physical scarring and may have serious side effects. It is different from cauterisation, which is done under good medical care. It is applied to a particular spot which may be very tiny, but causing much discomfort or pain.

These people do not allow bad omens to dictate their actions. As we already noted, it is forbidden to allow omens to decide what we may or may not do. In this *ḥadīth* the Prophet makes it clear that people who deserve to be in heaven without having to account for their deeds do not entertain any thought of bad omens. Thus, they negate it at source.

The fourth quality is a positive action that counters all three negative ones. People who do so are described here as those who place their trust in their Lord. This trust is complete, unhesitating and unquestioning. Such trust adds an important element, namely a complete and reassuring relationship with God. One feels that whatever happens, it will eventually have good results, because God will always reward His good servants who place their trust in Him.

We also have to remember here that by speaking against these practices, the Prophet does not in any way encourage adopting a negative attitude towards illness, as done by some people who do not seek medical treatment and refuse to take any medication. Such people claim that seeking such treatment is contrary to complete reliance on God. This is a totally mistaken notion. The Prophet encouraged medical treatment and made it clear that God has provided a cure for every illness, whether such a cure be known to people or not. Moreover, seeking medical treatment should be construed as part of the process of reliance on God, as it means that we do our part, and use all the means available to us. Such measures are required. When we have done this, we couple it with placing our full trust in God alone. This combination of doing what we can and relying on God is the best means to achieve any purpose.

Needless to say, when the Prophet described such people to his companions, everyone hoped to be among them. Hence, 'Ukkāshah asks the Prophet to pray that God may count him as one of them. The Prophet prayed for him and there is no doubt that any prayer by the Prophet is answered in the most perfect way. However, the Prophet did not say a similar prayer for the next man making the same request. He told him that that honour had been taken by the first to make the request.

There are several explanations why the Prophet did not pray for the second man. Some say that he was not of the calibre to be included with such elite, but we do not know for certain the man's identity. Some reports suggest that he was a distinguished figure among the Prophet's companions. Therefore, we take the view that the Prophet was not allowed to make that prayer for more than one person on that particular occasion.

The man who benefited by the Prophet's prayer, 'Ukkāshah ibn Miḥṣan, was one of the early Muslims, and a good fighter for God's cause. During the Battle of Badr, his sword was broken in his hand. The Prophet gave him a small stick from a tree and it was transformed in his hand into a long, solid sword which he used in subsequent battles, until his death as a martyr against rebellious apostates during Abu Bakr's reign.

More on omens

915. 'Alqamah quoted his mother who said: 'Children used to be brought to 'Ā'ishah and she prayed to God to bless them. A baby boy was once brought to her. As she was arranging the baby's pillow, she saw a razor under his head. On enquiring about it, she was told: "We put it there for protection against the jinn". She took the razor, threw it away and forbade them to use it for that purpose. She said that God's messenger disliked bad omens he hated them?. 'Ā'ishah also ordered people not to believe in them.'

This *ḥadīth* tells us about an objectionable practice that people resorted to in Arabia before Islam. We have mentioned the way Arabs used to make a bird fly in order to decide whether to go ahead or abandon an important action. This *ḥadīth* tells us of an absurd practice, that of placing a knife or razor under a newborn's pillow to prevent jinn harming the child. 'Ā'ishah threw the razor away and told the people that the Prophet prohibited such practices.

916. Anas reports that the Prophet said: 'Do not cause disease transmission, nor entertain bad omens. I like hopeful optimism based on good words'.[646]

917. Ḥābis ibn Rabī'ah reports that the Prophet said: 'There is nothing true about the owl's cry. The omen that comes near to reality is a good optimistic word. An envious eye is real'.[647]

The first of these two *ḥadīths* prohibits the intentional transmission of disease. This is perhaps concerned with the individual level, when someone tries to infect a healthy person with the disease he is already suffering from. Several reports were circulated in recent years about AIDS sufferers deliberately giving the disease to others, as a way of taking revenge against society, because they felt that they were wronged by others. This is a case of taking revenge against people who were not involved in their suffering. Other reports suggested deliberate infection for political reasons. Nothing of this can be ascertained. Yet the idea of deliberate transmission of disease is possible. The *ḥadīth* makes clear that this is forbidden in Islam. As for spreading a disease among the population of a large area, as in germ warfare, this is a crime against humanity.

Over the centuries, certain things have been associated with good or bad omens in different communities. In pre-Islamic Arabia, people attached bad omens to owls, weaving certain legends around this nocturnal bird. As Arabian society was tribal and largely lawless, when it came to individual and vengeance killings, Arabs considered taking

---

646. Related by al-Bukhari, Muslim, Abū Dāwūd, al-Tirmidhi and Ibn Mājah.
647. Related by al-Tirmidhi.

revenge for any wrongful killing to be of paramount importance. They believed that if a person was killed and his tribe or family did not manage to avenge his killing, his soul turned into an owl which would cry at night: 'I am thirsty; give me a drink'. Should they manage to kill someone in revenge, it flew away.

All this was stopped by Islam. In the second of these two *ḥadīths* the Prophet tells us about three things that are more or less related. He first makes clear that all beliefs about the owl and the bad omen it brings are without foundation. However, he confirms that an envious eye may bring some harm. This refers to a person who looks admiringly at something that belongs to another, but who is at the same time full of envy, wishing that the thing he is admiring were his own. If he feels that it is beyond him, then he wishes that the owner be deprived of it. Such ill thoughts may bring harmful effects to the person viewed with such envy.

The other thing the Prophet refers to in this *ḥadīth* is what we mentioned earlier about feeling optimistic when hearing a good word or a piece of good news. Here, the Prophet describes it as the nearest thing to reality when people have some expectations about the immediate future. An example of this is to feel good when we hear a person's name and it bodes well for our purpose:

918. 'Abdullāh ibn al-Sa'ib reports: 'In the year of al-Ḥudaybiyah, 'Uthmān ibn 'Affān mentioned that Suhayl [ibn 'Amr] had been sent by his people to arrange a peace agreement, requiring the Prophet to return home that year in return for them leaving Makkah empty for him for three days the following year. When [Suhayl] arrived people said: "Here is Suhayl", and the Prophet said: "God has facilitated your business".'

'Abdullāh ibn al-Sā'ib met the Prophet.

When the Prophet and his companions tried to visit Makkah in the sixth year after their migration to Madinah, the Quraysh tried to prevent them from entering the city, even though their intent was only to worship at the Ka'bah. Long and protracted negotiations ensued, and the two parties were close to war, despite the Prophet's attempts to prevent it. 'Uthmān was sent by the Prophet to Makkah to persuade its people that the Prophet's mission was peaceful, with no aim other than offering worship at the Ka'bah. On his return 'Uthmān informed the Prophet that Suhayl would be coming to negotiate a peace agreement. Suhayl was one of the Quraysh's distinguished figures and he laid down their terms for a peace agreement, which the Prophet accepted in full and the agreement came to be known as the al-Ḥudaybiyah Peace Treaty. When the Prophet was told that the Quraysh delegate was Suhayl ibn 'Amr, he said to his companions: 'God has facilitated your business'. The Prophet said this because the man's name is derived from the root word *sahala* which means ease and facility. Thus, he associated the name with the hope of an easy resolution for the dispute.

We need to clarify a point about associating bad omens with three matters: a woman, a horse or a home. These are even acknowledged in some *ḥadīths*:

919. 'Abdullāh Ibn 'Umar reports that the Prophet said: 'Bad omens may be in a house, a woman and a horse'.[648]

920. Sahl ibn Sa'd reports that the Prophet said: 'If a bad omen may be associated with anything, then with a woman, a horse or a house'.[649]

The second *ḥadīth* is conditional in phraseology, implying that this need not be the case. In both *ḥadīths* the Prophet was referring to what actually happens in life. People tended to associate misfortune with the three matters mentioned in the *ḥadīth* more than with anything else. This is only natural because these three were closely related to people's lives. Therefore, if one experiences such thoughts, then the best thing is to change them because God has allowed divorce and it is perfectly legitimate to sell a horse or a home and to buy another. Why, then, keep any of them when one feels so uncomfortable. However, when one embarks on changing any of these three, one must always believe that it is God who determines all affairs. None of these is responsible for any misfortune in themselves. We may point out that as times

648. Related by al-Bukhari, Muslim, al-Nasā'ī, Abū Dāwūd and al-Tirmidhi.
649. Related by al-Bukhari, Muslim, Ibn Mājah.

change, people may associate bad omens with other things that are commonly used or needed, such as replacing a horse in the *ḥadīth* with a car. Thus, if one buys a new car and gets involved in an accident a few days later, he may feel that the new car boded ill for him.

921. Anas ibn Mālik reports: 'A man said: "Messenger of God, we were in a home where we had an increase in our family numbers and in our wealth. We then moved to another home, and we suffered decrease in numbers and property". The Prophet said: "Leave that home, for it is not good".'[650]

This *ḥadīth* simply suggests a measure to deal with a situation that arose with this family. It does not confirm that a bad omen is associated with that particular house. The family that moved into it had felt that misfortune had subsequently taken place. Therefore, it was best that they should leave it so that they did not continue to entertain such thoughts. We should read the Prophet's suggestion as a remedial one, not as a confirmation that the house itself brought misfortune to its dwellers. It may well happen that another family would move in and no misfortune occur to them.

It should be noted that al-Bukhari writes under this *ḥadīth* that its chain of transmission is questionable, suggesting that it is less than authentic.

650. Related by Abū Dāwūd.

46

Good Manners in All Situations

THE PROPHET WAS keen to instil into the Muslim community a keenness to elevate all occurrences and social interactions so that they earn reward from God and strengthen relations in Muslim society. When a Muslim realises that whatever happens in life occurs by God's will, then he expresses his gratitude for whatever is good and accepts what may be adverse, showing patience and resignation. Both attitudes earn reward from God. Even in ordinary matters such as sneezing and yawning, which happen as a result of what we feel at a certain point in time, the Prophet has given us guidance on how to behave in order to earn God's reward and strengthen relations with others. Sometimes the Prophet gives descriptions that are bound to capture the interest of the listener, but they are not meant literally. The following *ḥadīth* is a case in point:

922. Abu Hurayrah reports that the Prophet said: 'God likes sneezing and dislikes yawning. If a person sneezes and praises

God, every Muslim who hears him is bound to pray to God to grant him mercy. Yawning, on the other hand, is from Satan, so one should repress it as much as possible. When one says 'Hah!', Satan laughs at him'.

What God likes and dislikes are not the actions themselves, but what they lead to. Sneezing is bound to make the person more alert. It should be followed, as the Prophet recommends, with praising God, and with a prayer by other people. All this is good and merits reward. Hence God likes it. On the other hand, yawning reflects boredom or tiredness. The yawning person's image is distorted and this makes Satan laugh at him. Hence, the Prophet recommends that we try to dispel yawning as far as possible, and when we cannot avoid it, we should cover our mouths with our hands.

The question that arises here is whether the Prophet's statement about the reactions of others indicates a duty or a recommendation. A number of scholars consider this to be a duty, because the *ḥadīth* states it in an emphatic way. Other scholars consider it a collective duty, which means that it is sufficient that some of those around, or even one, should do it for this duty to be considered fulfilled. If no one does it, then all are at fault and may have to account to God for their failure.

923. (*Athar* 209) Ibn 'Abbās said: 'If any of you sneezes and says: "Praise be to God", the angel will say: "the Lord of all worlds". If the person adds the phrase, "Lord of all worlds", to his initial praise, the angel says to him: "May God have mercy on you".'[651]

The first statement by the angel is intended to complement the praise the person himself says after sneezing. It is to prompt the person to make his praise in full, acknowledging God's Lordship over the whole universe. If he so says, then the angel prays to God to grant him mercy.

---

651. Related by al-Ṭabarānī.

924. Abu Hurayrah reports that the Prophet said: 'When any of you sneezes, he should say, "*Alḥamd lillāh*, i.e. Praise be to God". If he says it, his brother or friend should say to him, "*yarḥamuk Allah*, i.e. May God have mercy on you". If his brother says it, he should reply, "*yahdīk wa yuṣliḥ bālak*', i.e. And may He give you guidance and reassurance".'[652]

Al-Bukhari comments that this *ḥadīth* is the most authentic on this subject, related by Abu Ṣāliḥ al-Sammān. The Prophet tells us what sort of reaction we should have when one of us sneezes. It is the best wish that expresses a very friendly and caring attitude, because God's mercy ensures the best that one may have in this life and in the life to come. The same may be said about the reply. If one receives God's guidance in this life, one is sure to avoid error and to feel contentment and reassurance. When such an exchange is made as a result of a natural and physiological occurrence such as sneezing, it can only enhance good relations within the community. The Prophet also tells us that this may be done if the person sneezes three times with short intervals in between. If he still sneezes, then he has a cold or some other condition. In this case, we pray for that person's recovery, saying *shafāk Allah*, or 'may God give you good health'.

It is to be noted that the statements recommended by the Prophet in this instance are made in the singular form, which is the more familiar between people. In other *ḥadīths*, it is given in the plural, which is more formal. It may be said that when the plural form is used, it can be taken to include the angels who watch over us. Thus, when one says to a person who sneezes, 'May God have mercy on you', he means that person and the angels around him or her, and the reply would be in the plural involving the angels with the other interlocutor.

What the Prophet has taught in such common and everyday occurrences was taken up by Muslims and became part of their tradition. People who receive religious education or upbringing learn to praise God after they sneeze and to pray to Him to grant mercy to other people who do so. This has been the tradition started with the early Muslim generations.

---

652. Related by al-Bukhari and Abū Dāwūd.

925. ʿAbd al-Raḥmān ibn Ziyād ibn Anʿum reports: 'My father told me that he was on a maritime expedition during the reign of Muʿāwiyah, [the fifth Caliph]. [He said]: "[As the boats came to shore at some stage], our boat was next to the boat of Abu Ayyūb al-Anṣāri. When it was time for our dinner, we invited him and he came over. He said: 'You have invited me and I am fasting. However, I have to accept your invitation because I heard God's Messenger say: "A Muslim is duty bound to respond to his brother in six matters. If he omits any of them, he omits a duty that is due to his brother. [These are]: to greet him when they meet; to accept if he invites him; to pray to God to grant him mercy when he sneezes; to visit him if he is ill; to attend his funeral when he dies; and to give him sincere good counsel if he asks his advice".'

He adds: 'Among us was a man with a good sense of humour. He turned to another person who shared our meal and said to him, "May God give you a good and handsome reward". However, the man was angry with him when he said it too many times. So, the humorous man asked Abu Ayyūb: "What should I do with a man who, when I pray for him to be rewarded well, gets angry and reviles me?" Abu Ayyūb said: "We used to say that a person who is not served well with a good thing may be better served with its opposite. So, you may try the opposite". When the man came back, the humorous man said to him: "May God give you a foul and awful reward". He smiled and said, "You will not give up your tricks". He said: "May God give handsome reward to Abu Ayyūb al-Anṣāri".'

This *ḥadīth* is included here because it outlines six duties that Muslims should observe in their social relations. These will be stated again, in part, in full or with an addition, in some of the *ḥadīths* that follow.

926. ʿAbdullāh ibn Masʿūd reports that the Prophet said: 'Four things one Muslim owes to another: to visit him when he is ill;

to attend his funeral if he dies; to accept his invitation; and to pray to God to grant him mercy if he sneezes'.[653]

If we look at these practices, we find that they are all conducive to close social relations. The first is to visit people when they are ill. This is important because nothing cheers up the one who is ill more than feeling that his friends and relatives are thinking of him, and praying for his recovery. Spending some time with a person who is ill is also good for the visitor, because he realises that his good health is a blessing from God for which he needs to be thankful. Needless to say, visiting is not required when a person is suffering an infectious disease. In this case, it is sufficient to make the ill person aware that they are thinking of him and praying for his recovery.

Attending the funeral of a deceased person is the last expression of good will we can do for the departed one. As we walk or move to the cemetery we pray for the deceased, and appeal to God to forgive him or her their sins and to admit them into heaven. Moreover, we offer our condolences to their family and show them that we share their sorrow. We also remember that we are bound to arrive at the same end and this should motivate us to prepare for this eventuality.

The third aspect the Prophet mentions is to accept one's brother's invitation. This is also important, because when a friend invites us, he has certainly shown us good will which we have to return. This can only be by accepting the invitation. We must not make a decision on whether to accept or decline an invitation on the basis of personal or social considerations, as though our presence would impart honour to our host. The rule is that if we do not have a valid reason to prevent us from responding, we should accept the invitation, because this improves relations within the Muslim community.

The last of these four is to pray to God to grant His mercy to a person who sneezes and to follow this by saying a word of praise of God. As we noted earlier, sneezing is a refreshing action, except when it is caused by a cold or some other illness.

---

653. Related with different chains of transmission by Aḥmad, Ibn Mājah, al-Ḥākim and Ibn Ḥibbān.

927. Al-Barā' ibn 'Āzib reports: 'God's Messenger has ordered us to do seven things and prohibited seven others. He ordered us to visit the ill, attend funerals, pray for one who sneezes, honour the vow of a person who pledges something under oath, support the wronged, spread the greeting of peace, and accept invitations. He forbade us to wear gold rings, use silver utensils, fine saddles, garments with silk stripes, thick brocade, embroidered silk and pure silk'.[654]

This *ḥadīth* adds three things to the four mentioned in the previous one. The first is honouring another person's vow. If we can help someone in honouring his oath, we should do so. People often make oaths or vows the honouring of which may depend on others as much as on themselves. In this case, we are duty bound to help them honour their vows. Otherwise they may find themselves in a very difficult position.

Another practice the Prophet was keen to make a part of Muslim's standard values is support to a person who is subjected to oppression or injustice. God hates oppression and describes it as worse than murder. Hence, it is only natural that the Prophet frequently repeats the duty of every Muslim to support anyone subjected to oppression. We note here that the Prophet does not specify a Muslim under oppression as deserving our help. Muslims are required to support anyone, Muslim or non-Muslim, who is subjected to oppression, whether by an individual or a group or a state. Removing injustice and oppression is a great virtue, one that Muslims should always seek to do.

Spreading the greeting of peace is also helpful in consolidating ties of brotherhood in the community. Hence the Prophet urged his followers to offer this greeting to all people, whether they knew them or not. When a greeting is offered to us, we must return it with at least its equivalent, if we cannot offer a better greeting.

The things the Prophet forbade pertain to all aspects of ostentatious luxury. The Prophet was keen to ensure that in the Muslim community those who are well off do not hurt the feelings of their less fortunate brethren by showing off their wealth in their appearance. Yes, people may enjoy their luxury, but they do not have to press the point in

654. Related by al-Bukhari, Muslim, al-Tirmidhi, al-Nasā'ī and Ibn Mājah.

what they wear. Besides, gold and silk are mentioned by the Prophet on several occasions as being forbidden to Muslim men, but they are permissible for Muslim women.

The Prophet mentioned these good practices in several *ḥadīths*, depending on the occasion and the people attending him.

928. Abu Hurayrah reports that the Prophet said: 'Every Muslim owes other Muslims six duties'. He was asked: 'What are they?' He said: 'If you meet [your Muslim brother] greet him; if he invites you, accept his invitation; if he seeks your advice, give him good counsel; if he sneezes, pray to God to grant him mercy; if he falls ill, visit him; and if he dies, take part in his funeral'.[655]

These are the same as mentioned by Abu Ayyūb al-Anṣāri in *ḥadīth* Number 925.

929. (*Athar* 210) 'Ali said: 'When a person hears a sneeze and says: "All praise be to God, the Lord of all the worlds, in all situations", he will never complain of tooth or ear ache'.

930. This is the same as *ḥadīth* Number 924, with a different chain of transmission which uses the plural form instead of the singular.

931. This is the same as *ḥadīth* Number 922, with a different chain of transmission.

932. (*Athar* 211) 'When Ibn 'Abbās sneezed and someone prayed to God to bestow mercy on him, I heard him respond by saying: "May God protect us and you from the Fire. May God bestow mercy on you".'

This gives us a different response to the supplication offered to the one who sneezes, suggesting that a good response, in similar terms to the one mentioned in earlier *ḥadīths* is perfectly in order. It is to

---

655. Related by Ibn Ḥibbān and Abu 'Awānah.

be noted that Ibn ʿAbbās used the same supplication he was offered, but preceded it by another, praying for protection from the Fire for all present.

933. Abu Hurayrah reports: 'We were sitting with God's Messenger (peace be upon him) when a man sneezed and praised God. The Prophet said to him: "May God bestow mercy on you". Another man sneezed but the Prophet did not say anything to him. He said: "Messenger of God, you answered the other man but you did not say anything to me?" The Prophet said: "He praised God, but you remained silent".'

934. Anas reports: "Two men sneezed in the Prophet's presence. He said to one of them, "May God bestow mercy on you", but said nothing to the other. The man said: "You have prayed for this one but not for me". The Prophet replied: "He praised God and you did not".'[656]

935. Abu Hurayrah reports: 'Two men were sitting with the Prophet (peace be upon him), one of them was of a better social status than the other. The higher-ranking person sneezed but did not praise God. The Prophet did not say the usual prayer for him, "may God bestow mercy on you". Then the other person sneezed and praised God, so the Prophet prayed for him. The higher-ranking person said to the Prophet: "I sneezed while I am sitting with you and you did not pray for me; but when this man sneezed you prayed for him". The Prophet said: "This man remembered God, so I remembered him; and you forgot to praise God, so I omitted to pray for you".'[657]

These *ḥadīths* may refer to the same incident, or to different but similar incidents. They make the prayer to the person who sneezes conditional

---

656. Related by al-Bukhari, Muslim, Abū Dāwūd, al-Nasā'ī, al-Tirmidhi and Ibn Mājah.

657. Related by Aḥmad, Muslim, Abū Dāwūd, al-Tirmidhi, Ibn Mājah, al-Ḥākim and Ibn Ḥibbān.

on him or her praising God after sneezing. The identity of the two men is not mentioned in the third *ḥadīth* which speaks about their social ranking. However, al-Ṭabarāni mentions that they were ʿĀmir ibn al-Ṭufayl and his nephew. According to Arabian tradition, a nephew could not be given a higher rank than his uncle. Moreover, the uncle in this case was held in high respect by his tribe in the Najd area. Therefore, it was only natural that the uncle should remark on the Prophet's behaviour in identical situations. Hence the Prophet explains that when a person omits to praise God after sneezing, we do not pray for mercy for him.

936. (*Athar* 212) Nāfiʿ said: 'When ʿAbdullāh ibn ʿUmar sneezed and it was said to him, "May God bestow mercy on you", he would reply saying, "May He have mercy on us and you, and may He forgive us and you".'[658]

937. (*Athar* 213) ʿAbdullāh ibn Masʿūd said: 'When one of you sneezes, he should say: "Praise be to God, the Lord of all the worlds". Anyone who responds should say, "May God bestow mercy on you". He should reply: "May God forgive me and you".'[659]

These two reports make clear that a sneeze calls for praising God by the person who sneezes and a response with a supplication for mercy by anyone present. This is rejoined by a prayer by the first person.

A sneeze is a frequent involuntary symptom made by a person with a cold. So does it require the same pattern of prayer every time?

938. Salamah ibn al-Akwaʿ reports.... This *ḥadīth* will be repeated under 941 and we will discuss it then.

939. (*Athar* 214) Makḥūl al-Azdi said: 'I was next to Ibn ʿUmar when a man on one side of the mosque sneezed. Ibn ʿUmar said: "May God bestow mercy on you, if you have praised God".'

---

658. Related by al-Ḥākim and al-Bazzār.

659. Related by al-Ḥākim and al-Ṭabarāni.

940. (*Athar* 215) Mujāhid said: 'A son of 'Abdullāh ibn 'Umar – either Abu Bakr or 'Umar – sneezed and said "Āb!" Ibn 'Umar said to him: "What is this Āb. Āb is a name of a devil which is in between a sneeze and a praise".'[660]

The fact that so many *ḥadīths* stress that one should follow a sneeze with praising God suggests that the Prophet's companions were very diligent in following his guidance even in very small matters. The fact that God is praised at such situations gives an impression that in social relations in the Muslim community, everything is attributed to God or related to Him in some way.

941. Iyās ibn Salamah said: 'My father told me that a man sneezed in the Prophet's presence and the Prophet said to him: "May God bestow mercy on you". The man sneezed again, and the Prophet (peace be upon him) said: "This man has a cold".'[661]

942. (*Athar* 216) Abu Hurayrah said: 'Pray [for the person who sneezes] once, twice and three times. Anything more than that is due to his having a cold'.[662]

The approved guidance in such a case, when we realise that a person is sneezing because of having a cold, is to say: 'May God grant you recovery'. The Prophet realised that the sneeze was due to a cold after the second bodily function, but this may not be so readily apparent in all cases. Therefore, the second *ḥadīth* suggests that after the third sneeze, it is clear that the person has a cold or an allergy. Therefore, we pray for his or her recovery.

943. Abu Mūsa al-Ash'ari reports: 'The Jews used to try to bring about a sneeze when they were with God's Messenger, hoping that he would say to them "May God bestow mercy on

---

660. Related by Ibn Abu Shaybah, replacing Ab with Ash.

661. Related by Aḥmad, Muslim, al-Nasā'ī, Abū Dāwūd, al-Tirmidhi, Ibn Mājah and al-Dārimi with slightly different wording.

662. Related by Abū Dāwūd.

you". However, he used to say to them: "May God grant you guidance and reassurance".'[663]

Even those who were most opposed to the Prophet and his message realised that when he prayed for someone, that person would see the answer to the prayer in the most perfect and complete way. There are many instances confirming this. The Jews living in Madinah during the Prophet's time saw this with their own eyes. Hence, they would induce a sneeze in his presence hoping that he would pray to God to bestow mercy on them. Instead, however, he prayed to God to give them guidance. This was the best he could pray for them at the time.

944. Abu Burdah [son of Abu Mūsa al-Ash'ari] said: 'I entered when Abu Mūsa was visiting Umm al-Faḍl ibn al-'Abbās. I sneezed, but he did not say to me, "May God bestow mercy on you". She then sneezed and he prayed for her. I reported this to my mother. When he came home, she blamed him, saying: "My son sneezed and you did not pray for mercy for him, but when she sneezed, you did". He said to her: "I heard the Prophet (peace be upon him) say: 'When one of you praises God after he sneezes, then pray for mercy for him, but if he does not praise God then do not pray for him'. My son sneezed but did not praise God, and I did not pray for him. When she sneezed and praised God, I prayed to God to grant her mercy". She said: "You did well".'[664]

Even when the person concerned is one's closest relative, the same standard applies. Apparently Abu Burdah was still young when this took place. This is the only way to explain his being upset and his complaint to his mother. But when the mother realised that her husband did only what the Prophet had said, she was fully in agreement with him.

945. Abu Hurayrah reports that the Prophet said: 'When any of you yawns, he should try to repress it as much as possible'.

---

663. Related by Aḥmad, Abū Dāwūd, al-Tirmidhi and al-Ḥākim.

664. Related by Muslim, Abū Dāwūd and al-Tirmidhi.

This is because yawning is uncomfortable for both the person concerned and those around him. They feel that he is bored and may be they also feel unwelcome, or that he cannot wait to be alone. It also contorts his face and makes him look unsightly.

Unique relationship

> **946.** Mu'ādh ibn Jabal reports: 'I was behind the Prophet on his mount when he called me, "Mu'ādh!" I said: "I am at your service". He repeated this address three times [and I replied in the same manner]. He then said: "Do you know what right mankind owe to God? That they worship Him alone, associating no partners with Him". He rode on for a while and then said to me: "Mu'ādh!" I said: "I am at your service". He said: "Do you know what people earn by right from God if they do that? That He will not put them to any suffering".'

This *ḥadīth* outlines in a most precise manner the essence of faith and what people are entitled to have if they truly believe. The fact that the Prophet addressed Mu'ādh, who was one of his most learned companions, three times before saying anything about what he wanted to say served to make the addressee especially attentive. It was clear that the Prophet was preoccupied with something of great importance. Other versions of the *ḥadīth* mention that there was a time gap separating the Prophet's call to Mu'ādh by name. This was to alert Mu'ādh to the fact that he was about to give him special information. Hence, his companion was awaiting his communication with much interest. When the Prophet spoke, he certainly delivered a hugely important message, putting it in the clearest of terms. He stated something owed by all people to God, and described it as a right belonging to God Almighty. Moreover, the Prophet did not wait for his companion to say whether he knew the answer to his question; instead, he gave the answer immediately. 'People must worship God alone, associating no partners with Him'.

This is the basic and most fundamental principle of faith, which admits of no compromise whatsoever. A person may either believe in God's oneness, or he may not. If he believes that all Godhead belongs to God alone, he must guard against any trace of polytheism, of whatever shape or form. The Prophet's statement suggests that when people fulfil this condition, they meet the basic requirement of faith.

The Prophet left his companion to contemplate his statement for a while before putting another question to him. This time he asked whether he knew the result that people could expect. Again the Prophet described this as a right which is owing to people for their fulfilment of their basic requirement. This right is such that God will not punish them.

It is a very clear and straightforward bargain, establishing mutual rights: God's right to be worshipped alone, without any claim assigning partners to Him, whether in people's minds or actions; and people's right to suffer no punishment. This means that when people truly believe in God's oneness and worship Him alone, they spare themselves punishment in the Hereafter. This is a great prize which all people should try to achieve. The way is facilitated for them by this outline given by the Prophet.

But what does this actually mean in practice? Is it sufficient that people recognise God's oneness? The Prophet's statement is precise. It gives two qualities as owing to God: worshipping Him and believing in His oneness. This statement does not stop at mere intellectual and theoretical ideas. Rather, recognition of God's oneness has a practical manifestation in worship. Proper worship is offered in the manner which God considers satisfactory and which He has made clear to us through His messenger. His oneness means that we allow no trace of associating partners with Him, in worship, legislation or daily action. It requires an acknowledgement of His sovereignty over both the universe and human life.

Thus, people must couple this belief with diligent worship, addressed to God and making it clear that they associate no partner with Him. This must continue throughout their lives. Thus, there is no room for complacency or laziness. In return, they earn the right not to suffer any punishment.

947. ʿAbdullāh ibn Kaʿb ibn Mālik said: 'I heard Kaʿb ibn Mālik telling his story when he stayed behind, not joining God's

Messenger on the Expedition of Tabuk, then God accepted his repentance. "After God's Messenger had finished the Fajr Prayer, he announced that God had accepted our repentance. People came to me in groups to congratulate me on the acceptance of my repentance. They said: 'Congratulations for God's forgiveness'. I then entered the mosque: there was God's Messenger surrounded by people. Ṭalḥah ibn 'Ubaydillāh got up and came hurriedly towards me, shook hands with me and congratulated me. By God, he was the only one of the Muhājirīn to get up for me. I will never forget Ṭalḥah's gesture".'[665]

Al-Bukhari enters this *ḥadīth* and the next three *ḥadīths* under the subheading 'Standing up for One's Brother'. Hence he includes only a short version of the story, concerned mainly with Ṭalḥah's gesture and its effect on Ka'b. His story merits telling in full detail.

Joining the expedition was obligatory for all Muslim men. This was a test to expose the hypocrites, none of whom joined. However, Ka'b and a few other true believers stayed behind with no excuse. It was merely a case of laziness and negligence of duty. When the Prophet and his army returned, without having to engage in battle against the Byzantines as originally had been feared, the hypocrites came to the Prophet with their flimsy excuses. Ka'b and two others offered no such excuse. Instead, he said to the Prophet:

Messenger of God, had I been speaking to anyone on the face of the earth other than you, I would have been able to avoid his anger by giving some sort of an excuse. I can make a case for myself. But I know for certain that if I were to tell you lies in order to win your pleasure, God would soon make the truth known to you and I would incur your displeasure. If, on the other hand, I tell you the truth and you are not happy with me because of it, I would hope for a better result from God. By God, I have no excuse whatsoever. I have never been more physically able or in better circumstances than I was when I

665. Related in greater detail by al-Bukhari, Muslim, Abū Dāwūd, al-Nasā'ī and al-Tirmidhi.

stayed behind. The Prophet said to me: "You have certainly told the truth. You await God's judgement".[666]

This started a period of hardship for Ka'b and his two companions, which he describes in detail:

The Prophet ordered all his companions not to speak to us three. He made no similar instruction concerning anybody else of those who stayed behind. All people were now evading us. Their attitude was changed. It was very hard for me to the point that I did not even know myself or the place I was in. This was no longer the town I lived in. My world had changed. We continued in this condition for fifty days.

My two companions, Murārah ibn al-Rabīʿ and Hilāl ibn Umayyah, stayed at home. I was the youngest of the three. I continued to go out and attend the congregational prayers with other Muslims. I frequented all the markets, but nobody would speak to me. I would also go to the Prophet and greet him as he sat down after prayers. I would always think to myself: 'Have I detected any movement on his lips suggesting that he has answered my greeting?' I would pray close to him and look at him stealthily. When I was preoccupied with my prayers he would look at me, but when I looked towards him, he would turn his face away.

When this boycott by all the Muslim community seemed to have lasted too long, I climbed the wall of an orchard which belonged to a cousin of mine named Abu Qatādah, who was very close to me. I greeted him, but he did not answer. I said to him: 'Abu Qatādah, I beseech you by God to answer me: do you know that I love God and His Messenger?' He did not answer. I repeated my question three times, but he still did not answer.

I then beseeched him again, and his answer came: 'God and His Messenger know better'. Tears sprang to my eyes and I came down. I went to the market and as I was walking I saw a strange man, apparently from Syria, enquiring about me. People

---

666. A. Salahi, Muhammad: Man and Prophet, p. 713.

pointed me out to him. He came to me and handed me a letter from the King of Ghassān, the Arab tribe in Syria. The letter was written on a piece of silk and read: 'We have learnt that your friend has imposed a boycott on you. God has not placed you in a position of humiliation. If you join us, we will endeavour to alleviate all your troubles'. When I read it, I thought it to be yet another test of my sincerity. I have reached so low that an unbeliever hopes that I would willingly join him. I put the letter in an oven and burnt it. When we had spent forty nights in that situation, a Messenger from the Prophet came to me and said: 'God's Messenger (peace be upon him) commands you to stay away from your wife'. I asked whether that meant that I should divorce her and he answered in the negative. He told me only to stay away from her. My two companions also received the same instruction. I told my wife to go to her people's home and stay there until God had given his judgement in this matter.

Hilāl ibn Umayyah was an old man. His wife went to the Prophet and said: 'Messenger of God, Hilāl ibn Umayyah is very old and has no servant. Do you mind if I continue to look after him?' He said: 'That is all right, but do not let him come near you'. She said: 'By God, these things are far from his mind. He has not stopped crying ever since this has happened to him. I indeed fear for his eyesight'. Some people in my family suggested that I should seek the Prophet's permission to let my wife look after me. I said: 'I am not going to ask him that. I do not know what his answer would be, considering that I am a young man'.

Another ten nights passed, to complete fifty nights since the Prophet instructed the Muslims not to talk to us. At dawn after the fiftieth night I prayed at the top of one of our houses. I was still in that condition which I have described: the world seemed to me suffocatingly small and I did not recognize myself any more. As I sat down after dawn prayers, however, I heard a voice from the direction of Mount Silʿ saying: 'Kaʿb ibn Mālik! Rejoice!' I realised that my hardship was over, and I prostrated myself in gratitude to God.

What happened was that the Prophet informed the congregation after finishing the dawn prayer that God had pardoned us. People moved fast to give us that happy news. A man came at speed on horseback to tell me, while another from the tribe of Aslam went on top of the mountain to shout the news to me. His voice was quicker than the horse. When I heard that man's voice giving me the happiest piece of news I ever received, I gave him my two garments as a gesture of gratitude. By God, they were the only clothes I had at that time. I borrowed two garments and went quickly to the Prophet. People were meeting me in groups, saying: 'Congratulations on being forgiven by God'. I entered the mosque and saw the Prophet sitting with a group of people around him. Ṭalḥah ibn 'Ubaydillāh came quickly towards me, shook my hand and congratulated me. He was the only one from the Muhajirīn to do that. I will never forget Ṭalḥah's kindness.

When I greeted the Prophet, he said to me, with his face beaming with pleasure: 'Rejoice, for this is your happiest day since you were born!' I asked him: 'Is my pardon from you, Messenger of God, or is it from God?' He said: 'It is from God'. When the Prophet was pleased at something, his face would light up and look like the moon. We always recognised that.

When I sat down facing him, I said to him: 'Messenger of God, I will make my repentance complete by giving away all my property in charity'. The Prophet said: 'Keep some of your wealth, for that is better for you'. I answered that I would keep my share in Khaibar. I then added that I was forgiven only because I told the truth, and I would make my repentance complete by never telling a lie at any time in my life.

I feel that the greatest grace God has bestowed on me ever since He guided me to accept Islam is my telling the truth to the Prophet on that day. Had I invented some false excuse, I would have perished like all those who told him lies. God has described those people in the worst description ever. He says in the Qur'an: '*They will swear by God to you when you return to them so that you may leave them alone. Turn away from them, for they are an impurity. Hell is their abode as a punishment for what they used to do. They swear to you so that you may be pleased with them. If you are pleased with them, know then that God will never be pleased with the evildoers*'. (9: 95-96) I have never knowingly or deliberately told a lie ever since I said that to the Prophet. I pray to God to help me keep my word for the rest of my life.[667]

948. Abu Sa'īd al-Khudri reports: 'Certain people declared that they would accept Sa'd ibn Mu'ādh's judgement in their case. He was sent for and he came on a donkey. When he approached the mosque, the Prophet said: "Come forward to [meet] the best of you, or to your master". He then said: "Sa'd! These people declared their acceptance of your judgement". Sa'd said: "My judgement is that their fighters shall be executed and their children shall be enslaved". The Prophet said: "You have given God's judgement", or he said: "You have given the judgement of the Sovereign".'

This *ḥadīth* refers to the Jewish tribe of Qurayẓah. On migrating to Madinah, the Prophet made a covenant with the Jews and the Arab unbelievers living there. This is known as the Madinah Document, establishing the first written constitution in human history. It established a pluralist society that joined all three groups in a covenant requiring them to defend Madinah against any outside force that sought to attack it.

When the forces of the confederate tribes sought to attack Madinah with the declared aim of exterminating Islam and Muslims, the Prophet ordered the digging of a dry moat to prevent the attacking army's penetration. A siege of the city by the unbelievers ensued and during which the Muslims endured much hardship. The covenant had made it a duty of the Qurayẓah Jews to defend Madinah alongside the Muslims. Instead, they joined forces with the attackers and prepared to launch a pincer attack on the besieged Muslim community. God foiled their plans and the unbelievers withdrew. The Prophet laid siege to the Qurayẓah and eventually they surrendered. Their case was judged by Sa'd ibn Mu'adh, who was their ally in pre-Islamic days. The

667. bid, pp. 714-7.

ḥadīth gives Sa'd's judgement which was carried out against a small number of people who were considered 'fighters' as they were the perpetrators of the Qurayẓah treachery. Some historians consider that the judgement applied to all their men, women and children. This is based on a single report stated by Muhammad ibn Ishaq, but the report suffers serious flaws that make it unreliable, in addition to the fact that its chain of transmission is clearly suspect. Moreover, this is contrary to Islamic principles that do not permit collective punishment. Islam does not allow meting out punishment to a whole community or to the population of a city, town or even a small village because it upholds the principle of individual responsibility. It may punish a group of people for a single crime, but such punishment must be based on the involvement of each one of the group in that crime. Punishment in such cases is determined according to the role of each one. There can be no blankment judgement on a group or community.

For a full treatment of the case of the Qurayẓah Jews and the punishment they received for their treachery, reference may be made to Chapter eighteen of my book *Muhammad: His Character and Conduct.*

949. Anas reports: 'They [meaning the Prophet's companions] did not love to see anyone more than they loved to see the Prophet. When they saw him, they did not stand up to greet him, because they were well aware that he disliked it'.

The Prophet lived with his companions as one of them. He did not like that they should treat him like a king. Here we are told that he did not even like them standing up when he arrived. We note, however, that in Sa'd's case, he ordered them to rise and greet him. This was a special occasion when Sa'd was asked to judge in the case of the Qurayẓah whose actions had threatened the existence of the Muslim community in Madinah. The Prophet's companions loved him more than they loved their own families, and when they realised that he disliked them standing when he entered, they did not do so. Thus, the mark of their love was to do what he liked.

950. ʿĀ'ishah reports: I never saw anyone who more resembled the Prophet in conversation, speech or the way he sat than Fāṭimah. When the Prophet saw her coming, he welcomed her, then stood up to greet her and kissed her. He would then take her hand in his and lead her to sit in his place. When the Prophet went to visit her, she would welcome him, then stand up to greet him and kissed him. Once she came to him when he was in his last illness. He welcomed her and kissed her and whispered something in her ear. She cried. Then he whispered to her again and she laughed. I said to other women, 'I used to think that this woman is superior to other women, but I see that she is just like them. She laughs just as she is crying'. I asked her: 'What did he say to you?' She said: 'If I tell, I would be unworthy [of a secret]'. After the Prophet's death she said: 'He whispered to me: "I am dying", and I cried. Then he told me in a whisper: "You will be the first of my household to join me", and I was pleased with that'.[668]

This *ḥadīth* highlights the close relationship between the Prophet and his youngest daughter, Fāṭimah. We find in his behaviour towards her something that is rare. He was apparently very pleased to see her at any time. He would welcome her at a distance, and then would stand to greet her and then kiss her. Fathers may have a very close relation with their sons or daughters, and they may spoil their daughters, but it is rarely the case that a father will stand to greet his daughter and kiss her in public. Fāṭimah would also do the same every time her father, the Prophet, visited her.

The particular occasion this *ḥadīth* deals with occurred during the last days of his illness, shortly before his death. Fāṭimah's presence gave him pleasure which is indicated in his greeting and whispering to her, giving her first the sad news of his approaching death, and then the happier news that she would be the first to join him. Again this reiterates their close relationship.

---

668. Related by Abū Dāwūd, al-Nasā'ī, al-Tirmidhi, al-Ḥākim and Ibn Ḥibbān.

In this *ḥadīth* we have ʿĀ'ishah's statement remarking on the close similarity between the Prophet's manner in his speech and movement and his daughter's Fāṭimah, the youngest of his children. She makes a further comment, stating that she used to think very highly of Fāṭimah, but when she saw her crying then laughing in quick succession, she felt that she did not have such a status, as her feelings could swing so easily. Yet the change of mood filled ʿĀ'ishah, and probably others, with curiosity and she asked Fāṭimah what her father, the Prophet, had said to her. The answer shows that Fāṭimah was fully aware of the Islamic moral standard, revealing nothing of what was told her in secret. However, when the Prophet had passed away, she was free to disclose what he had said to her, since it had become partly known. The Prophet told her that he was dying, and after he had actually passed away, that part of the conversation was no longer a secret. The other part concerned Fāṭimah herself and she was free to tell it.

This *ḥadīth* speaks again about standing up to meet someone as he or she arrives. The *ḥadīth* mentions that the Prophet used to stand to greet his daughter, and she did likewise. Here we note that the two people involved are father and daughter. It is normal, and well in line with Islamic manners, that a son or a daughter stands up when their parents come in. It is a gesture of genuine respect. But the Prophet's standing when his daughter arrived is a gesture of genuine love and kindness. In neither case, can there be any confusion of feelings or actions.

951. Jābir reports: 'The Prophet was ill and we prayed behind him while he was praying seated. Abu Bakr relayed his *takbir* so that the congregation could hear. The Prophet turned [slightly] to us and saw that we were standing. He signaled to us and we all sat down to pray with him sitting down. When he finished his prayer, he said: "You were about to do the same as the Persians and the Byzantines: they would stand in the presence of their kings who would be seated. Do not do that; rather, do as your prayer leaders do. If the imam prays standing, you stand up; and if he prays seated, then pray seated".'[669]

---

669. Related by Muslim.

In this *ḥadīth* the Prophet makes it clear that the congregation should do like the imam. If the imam can only pray in a seated position because of an illness, injury or disability, the congregation should do likewise. According to Imam Mālik and Muhammad ibn al-Ḥasan of the Ḥanafi School of *Fiqh*, this is obligatory, to the extent that if the congregation stands when the imam is seated, then the prayer is invalid. However, other schools of *fiqh* consider this permissible, relying on other equally strong evidence.

As for standing up to meet respected people, we have noted that there are *ḥadīths* which show that this is permissible when there is no question of confusing this with glorifying the person concerned

952. Abu Sa'īd al-Khudri reports that the Prophet said: 'When a person yawns, he should put his hand over his mouth. Satan will enter it otherwise'.

953. (*Athar* 217) Ibn 'Abbās said: 'If one yawns, he should cover his mouth with his hand. Yawning is from Satan'.

954. The same as Number 952, with a different chain of transmission.

This is just another instruction of the social behaviour that prevails in Muslim societies. When a person yawns in public, he is frowned upon if he does not cover his mouth with his hand. The idea of Satan entering one's mouth is figurative, because yawning makes one's face rather unpleasant. The image of Satan serves to make yawning with an open, uncovered mouth very unpleasant.

955. Anas ibn Mālik said: 'The Prophet (peace be upon him) used to visit Umm Ḥarām bint Milḥān and he would eat at her place. She was married to 'Ubādah ibn al-Ṣāmit. She served him food and stroked his head. The Prophet then slept. He then woke up smiling'.[670]

---

670. Related by Mālik, Aḥmad and in all six authentic *Ḥadīth* anthologies.

This is a short version of a highly authentic *ḥadīth*. The full version of the *ḥadīth* adds the following: 'She asked him the reason for his smile, and he said: "I was shown in my dream a group of my community travelling by sea, looking like kings on their couches". She said: "Messenger of God, pray to God to make me one of them". He said: "You are one of them". He then dozed off again, and woke up smiling. Again she asked him why he was smiling, and he said the same thing. Once more, she said, "Pray God to make me one of them". The Prophet said to her: "You are in the first group". She subsequently married 'Ubādah ibn al-Ṣāmit who joined an expedition by sea and he took her with him. As she was about to ride a mule, she fell off, broke her neck and died'.[671] Ibn al-Athīr said that this expedition was the Cyprus expedition where she was buried.

This is an authentic *ḥadīth* from which we may deduce several rulings, such as the desirability of visiting a female relative, even when the relationship is distant. Umm Ḥarām was the Prophet's maternal aunt. Scholars mention several alternatives of this relationship, dating back to the Prophet's father or grandfather, but it is clear that she and her sister, Umm Sulaym, were related to him. Hence, he visited her, ate at her place and slept. She waited upon him and asked him why he was smiling, as any relative would do.

We also find in this *ḥadīth* a basis for women going out with a Muslim army to fight or to give support, even though the expedition requires extraordinary bravery. For the Arabs in Madinah, travelling by sea was felt to be very hazardous, because they lived in a city in the midst of a vast desert, far from any coastal area. When the woman felt that the Prophet was very pleased with those who would be undertaking such a task, she requested that he pray so that she would be among them. He did so, assuring her of the same. When she repeated the request after the second nap the Prophet had with the same dream, he told her that she would be with the first group.

What the Prophet said to her came true. She travelled with her husband, whom she married after this particular visit. Their expedition was by sea during the reign of the third Caliph, 'Uthmān ibn 'Affān. The commander of that expedition was none other than Mu'āwiyah

671. Related by al-Tirmidhi.

ibn Abu Sufyān, a companion of the Prophet who was later to become the fifth Caliph.

956. Qays ibn ʿĀṣim al-Saʿdi reports: 'I went to see God's Messenger and he said: "This is the master of the people of the desert". I said: "Messenger of God, how much may I own without owning any claim to one who comes with a request or as a guest?" He said: "Forty is good property; sixty is plentiful; and woe to those who have hundreds, except for one who gives away of the best, lends the animal with abundant milk, and sacrifices a fat animal to eat and feed the poor who beg or do not beg". I said: "Messenger of God, noble indeed are these qualities. The valley where I live is full of my cattle". He asked: "What do you give as a gift?" I said: "I give the virgin camel and the elder she-camel". He asked: "What do you give in animal loan?" I said: "I lend a hundred". He said: "What do you do about she-camels that are ready to mate?" I said: "People come with their ropes [to use as halters for the male camels] and no one is prevented from taking a camel on which he puts a halter. He keeps it until he himself returns it". The Prophet (peace be upon him) asked me: "Which do you love better: your property or that of your heirs?" I said: "Mine". He said: "Yours is that which you eat or consume, or what you spend and give away. The rest belongs to your heirs". I said: "Absolutely true. When I go back, I shall reduce their number [by giving many away]".'

When he was near death, Qays gathered his children and said: 'My children, learn this from me. You will not have an advice from anyone who gives you a more sincere counsel. Do not lament my death. No one wailed for God's Messenger (peace be upon him) and I hear the Prophet forbid lamentation. Wrap me for my burial in the clothes I used to pray in. Make your eldest your leader. If you do, you will continue to have a successor from your father. If you make your young one your leader, then your elders will be lowered in people's eyes. People will then think little of you. Conduct your livelihood well so as to be free of the need to ask others for help. Never resort to begging, as it is the worst of anyone's earnings. When you bury me, flatten my grave.

There was some ill feeling between me and the tribe of Bakr ibn Wā'il leading to some injuries. I fear that some fool of them might do something to cause you disgrace'.

The *ḥadīth* is clear and needs no explanation. However, when we look at Qays's conversation with the Prophet we need to remember that he was a chief among his bedouin people. When he speaks of property, his was in cattle. Hence, when he asked the Prophet about property that places no claim for others on his generosity, the Prophet answered in numbers. These referred to camels. Thus 40 camels meant that their owner is in comfortable means, while 60 are plentiful. People who have hundreds should be very generous and help others.

Qays appeared very generous and looked after his people. He lent female cattle so that the people who borrowed them could benefit by their milk and wool from sheep. He would lend male camels to others in the mating season, without asking the borrower to return them, until they did so of their own will. He realised from his talk with the Prophet that it was better for him to give away more, so he promised to do so and to reduce the numbers of his cattle. His advice to his children is sound in every respect.

The Prophet made use of every opportunity to teach his companions, and later generations of Muslims, what is important to them in their life, both in relation to faith and in ordinary matters. If he wanted to stress a point, he often alerted his companions by making a gesture or using a particular expression. When his companions were on the alert, he would give them precise and short advice, or an admonition.

957. Abu Dharr al-Ghifāri said: 'I brought the Prophet water for his ablution. The Prophet shook his head and bit his lips. I said: "May my parents be sacrificed for your sake! Have I hurt you?" He said: "No. But you will see rulers – or imams – who delay offering their prayers beyond its time". I said: "What do you command me to do?" He said: "Offer your prayers on time. Then, if you find yourself with them [when they pray] then pray with them also. Do not say, 'I have already prayed, so I will not pray now'."[672]

672. Related by Muslim, Abū Dāwūd and al-Tirmidhi.

We note first how the Prophet made a gesture to capture his companion's attention and alert him to what he would be telling him. We know that when the Prophet's companions were with him, they were always eager to learn from him. So they would always be fully alert and attentive. We note this with Abu Dharr's response. He immediately noticed the Prophet's gesture and was worried that he might have inadvertently hurt him. When the Prophet realised that his companion was fully attentive, he gave him a very important piece of advice.

The first point the Prophet makes is that some people in high position offer their prayers later than its preferred time. As we know, each prayer has a time range, with the earlier part preferred over the later one, even though the prayer is still valid. A ruler, or an imam, should maintain exemplary conduct. Therefore, he should always be keen to offer prayers at their preferred time. When delaying prayers becomes a habit, as it is understood from the wording of the *ḥadīth*, a factor of carelessness begins to creep in, albeit very discreetly. This is the reason for the Prophet's expression of amazement. Rulers and imams are in full control of their time. No matter what duties they have to attend to, they can manage their time well, so as to offer their prayers at the preferred time, thus earning greater reward.

The Prophet then informs his companion what to do in such cases. As an individual, he should remain keen to offer his prayers early in their time range. Thus, he fulfils his duty as best as he can. He is not supposed to do more than this, apart from offering advice when this is possible.

This might create a difficult situation, when an individual has prayed early and finds himself with a congregation who have not yet offered the same prayer. The Prophet makes it clear that in such a situation, the individual should repeat his prayer. He should not step aside and say that he will not join the prayer on account of having already prayed. To do so is inadvisable on two counts: the first is that it gives an impression that Muslims are not totally united when it comes to prayer, and the second is that it could allow for a feeling of superiority to creep into the thinking of the person concerned. He would be seen in a different light from the person who takes the lead in offering prayers. If he joins the congregational prayer, he would then be offering voluntary prayers, which earns him additional reward.

Situations of amazement

Every statement by the Prophet has its value, because the Prophet taught only what is good and beneficial to mankind.

958. ʿAli said: ʿGod's Messenger (peace be upon him) came to me and Fāṭimah one night and said: "Would you not pray?" I said: "Messenger of God, our souls are with God. If it is His will that we wake up, we will wake up". The Prophet left without saying anything to me. Then as he went away, I heard him striking his thigh and quoting: ʿ*Man is, above all else, always given to contention*".ʾ[673] (18:54)

The Prophet went to wake up his daughter and son-in-law, who was also his cousin, so that they might perform some night worship, which is voluntary. By so doing, the Prophet was keen that these two people, whom he loved dearly, should avail themselves of the great benefit that is certain to attend those who offer voluntary night worship. Scholars of *Ḥadīth* take the Prophet's words as he woke them up as an expression of encouragement that carries an element of love. This is only to be expected when the Prophet addressed his young daughter and her husband.

ʿAli's response only mentions a fact made clear by Islam. In the Qur'an we read: ʿ*God takes away people's souls upon their death, and the souls of those who are not dead during their sleep*ʾ. (39: 42) It is clear that the Prophet did not like ʿAli's response, but ʿAli only wanted to apologise for his sleep. He had just been woken, and at such a time a person may not be very attentive. Had ʿAli been fully awake, then most probably his reply would have been different, because he would have immediately realised that the Prophet was only encouraging him to do something that was certain to bring him immense reward.

The Prophet was, nevertheless, amazed at ʿAli's rejoinder, and his amazement is reflected in his gesture and quotation from the Qur'an as he went away. Had he been offended, he would not have hesitated to tell ʿAli that his reply was unacceptable. The Prophet did not, however, do this. He merely went away, amazed.

---

673. Related by Aḥmad, al-Bukhari, Muslim and al-Nasāʾī.

959. Abu Razīn reports: 'I saw him [Abu Hurayrah] striking his forehead with his hand and saying: "People of Iraq! You have been saying that I fabricate lies and attribute them to the Prophet? Will you thus have the pleasure and I bear the sin? I testify that I heard God's Messenger when he said: 'If the strap of your sandal breaks, do not walk with one sandal until you have repaired the other'."'[674]

Abu Hurayrah's gesture of smacking his own forehead is meant to express not only his extreme amazement at the way those people thought, but also signifies his extreme irritation at their accusation. Since Abu Hurayrah was only teaching people what would benefit them in the Hereafter, learning from him how to follow the Prophet's guidance, they would have the pleasure of being in the right. If he was inventing something which the Prophet did not say and attributing it to the Prophet, then he would be in manifest error. Furthermore, he would be liable to God's punishment as the Prophet warns: 'Whoever knowingly attributes to me something I have not said will have his place in hell'.[675]

Abu Hurayrah heard this *ḥadīth* from the Prophet and he knew exactly what it would mean for him if he attributed to the Prophet something that he did not say. Hence, he said to the people that they would be well off if they followed his admonition, but he would end up with God's punishment. This is not something anyone should look forward to.

Abu Hurayrah then mentions a *ḥadīth* to confirm that what he had heard was directly from the Prophet. This *ḥadīth* tackles something simple, and by reporting it, Abu Hurayrah makes clear that the Prophet even taught his companions things that are of little significance. The Prophet gave guidance even in a situation where the strap on one's sandal is broken. Here, he tells his companions not to walk with only one sandal on. This is to avoid an unsightly situation, where a person walks in a lame way. He should repair his sandals first. Needless to say, this is recommended, not a duty.

---

674. Related by Aḥmad, Muslim, Ibn Mājah, al-Nasā'ī and Abu 'Awānah.

675. Related by al-Bukhari and Muslim.

960. Abu al-ʿĀliyah al-Barāʾ said: "ʿAbdullāh ibn al-Ṣāmit passed by me. I gave him a chair and he sat down. I said to him: "Ibn Ziyād has delayed the prayer, what should we do?" He struck my thigh once[676] then said: "I asked Abu Dharr the same question, and he struck my thigh as I struck yours and said: 'Offer your prayer at the proper time, and then if you are with them when they pray, join them in prayer. Do not say: I have already prayed and I am not praying again'.""[677]

The main point in this *ḥadīth* is the same as Number 957. We should always be keen to offer our prayers early, so that we receive the reward of attending to prayer at its most preferred time. If it happens that we find ourselves with a group who have not yet offered their prayer and are about to start congregational prayer, we should repeat the prayer, so that we are part of the congregation and receive additional reward for our voluntary prayer.

However, this *ḥadīth* also shows that what the Prophet foretold came true, not long after his death. Ibn Ziyād was a governor of Iraq during the second half of the first century of the Islamic era, and he apparently delayed the congregational prayer. At the time, it was customary that a ruler or a governor would be the one who led the prayers. People who were used to praying early found this highly questionable. Hence, they asked each other about it.

We note that everyone who was asked about this made the same gesture first, which was to strike the person putting the question on his thigh. They did this because the Prophet did it with the first one who put the question to him, Abu Dharr. The Prophet did so in order to make his companion fully attentive to his advice. As later transmitters reported the *ḥadīth*, they did the same for a dual purpose: the first to report the Prophet's statement and action so as to put the listener in the same frame of mind, and second to achieve maximum attention. Needless to say, when you ask someone a question and he strikes you on your thigh before answering, you

---

676. The narrator adds here: 'I think he said that the strike was 'so hard that it left a mark on it'.

677. Related by Muslim and al-Nasāʾī.

are amazed and want to know why he has done so. Thus, you are doubly attentive.

Some scholars rely on this authentic *ḥadīth* to give a ruling that a man's thigh is not part of what he must always cover, i.e. the *'awrah*. It is true that Abu Dharr and all latter transmitters had their clothes on, and the striking was done over the clothes, but the action indicates that touching someone else's thigh is permissible. These scholars conclude that had it been obligatory to cover one's thighs, the Prophet would not have made this gesture, and he would also have clearly indicated that it must be kept covered.

961. 'Umar ibn al-Khaṭṭāb went with God's Messenger and a number of his companions to find Ibn Ṣayyād. They found him playing with other boys at a fort of Maghālah [the Anṣāri clan]. Ibn Ṣayyād was then close to puberty. He was not aware [of their approach] until the Prophet patted him on his back. He then said to him: 'Do you declare that I am God's Messenger?' Ibn Ṣayyād looked at him and said: 'I declare that you are the messenger to the unlettered people'. He added: 'Do you believe that I am God's Messenger?' The Prophet squeezed him and said: 'I believe in God and His Messenger'. He then said: 'What [dreams] do you see?' Ibn Ṣayyād said: 'Some come true and some are false'. The Prophet said: 'You are confused'. The Prophet then said to him: 'I have withheld something from you'. He said: 'It is Dukh'. The Prophet said: 'Shun it! You will not go above your rank'. 'Umar said: 'Messenger of God, will you permit me to strike off his head?' The Prophet said: 'If it is him [i.e. the Impostor (*al-Dajjāl*)], then you shall not be the one to kill him. If not, then you gain nothing good by killing him'.

Sālim said that he heard 'Abdullāh ibn 'Umar say: 'Some time later, the Prophet went with Ubay ibn Ka'b al-Anṣāri to the palm trees where Ibn Ṣayyād was. When the Prophet entered he shielded himself behind the trees, trying to hear something Ibn Ṣayyād was saying before he saw him. Ibn Ṣayyād was lying on his bed and covered with a sheet. Some murmur was heard from there. Ibn Ṣayyād's mother saw the Prophet as he was behind the trees, and she said to him: "Ṣāf (which was his name)! Here is

Muhammad". Ibn Ṣayyād stopped. The Prophet said: "Had she left him alone, the business would have been clear".'

Ṣālim said that 'Abdullāh said: 'The Prophet stood up and addressed the people. He praised God as He should be praised. He then mentioned the Impostor and said: "I am warning you about him. Every Prophet warned his people about him. [Prophet] Noah warned his people. However, I will tell something no Prophet ever said to his people. You know that the Impostor (*al-Dajjāl*) is one-eyed, and God is not one-eyed'.[678]

Ibn Ṣayyād was a Jewish boy known as Ṣāf, living in Madinah and he had pretensions to be a prophet. Prophet Muhammad wanted to establish his status. Hence, his two visits. The first was open and he talked to him directly. The Prophet did not have any doubt that he could not be a prophet, but he wanted to know if he was the Impostor, or *al-Dajjāl*. Ibn Ṣayyād described the Prophet as messenger for the unlettered people, meaning the Arabs. This was what the Jews said about the Prophet.

When 'Umar suggested that he kill him, if given permission, the Prophet told him that if he was the Impostor, then his killer would be Prophet Jesus, on his second coming. If he was not, then killing him was of no use. The Prophet's second visit and his attempt to learn what Ibn Ṣayyād said was only to try to determine whether he was the Impostor.

The whole situation pertaining to Ibn Ṣayyād is of little importance. We learn about it from this *ḥadīth* but we need not give it much concern. He lived to adulthood and he used to express his anger at being described as an imposter. Some reports suggest that he died in Madinah, but others suggest that he died somewhere else, without specifying the place.

---

678. Related by al-Bukhari, Muslim, Abū Dāwūd and al-Tirmidhi.

Following the Prophet's practice

In any religious matter, the Prophet's practice should be the guide for us, because he gave us the full model of Islamic life:

962. Jābir ibn 'Abdullāh reports: 'When the Prophet wanted to clean himself from a state of *janābah*, or ceremonial impurity, he poured over his heads three handfuls of water". Al-Ḥasan ibn Muhammad said to Jābir: "My hair is too thick". He answered: "The Prophet's hair was more plentiful and beautiful".'[679]

It is well known that removing the state of *janābah*, or ceremonial impurity, requires washing one's whole body, from head to foot, with water. In our present time and modern living, taking a shower is the best way. A dip in a pool, river or the sea is also good enough for this purpose. However, in situations where water is not available in plenty, it is better to economise with water. Hence, the report that using one's hands to take three handfuls of water and pour them over one's head is sufficient for washing one's head. This should be followed by pouring water over the rest of one's body.

Some people, however, impose on themselves a more rigid approach, or they may suffer from a kind of obsession with cleanliness. Therefore, guidance is provided for them in the Prophet's own action. It is clearly stated in this *ḥadīth* that a small amount of water, such as a bucket, should be sufficient. This is symbolised by how the Prophet washed his head.

The man who pointed out to Jābir his own difficulty, having thick hair, was the grandson of 'Ali ibn Abu Ṭālib, the Prophet's cousin, but his grandmother was Ali's second wife whom he married after the death of Fāṭimah, the Prophet's daughter. Jābir, a companion of the Prophet, replied that the Prophet's own hair was more plentiful. If three handfuls were sufficient for him, then they are sufficient for anyone.

---

679. Related by al-Bukhari, Muslim and al-Nasā'ī.

963. Jābir reports: 'The Prophet fell off a horse in Madinah and landed on the trunk of a felled date tree. His foot was dislocated. We used to visit him in 'Ā'ishah's room. We came once when he was praying seated, and we joined him in his prayer but we stood up. We came another time and he was offering obligatory prayer, also seated. We joined him in congregation, standing, but he signaled to us to sit down. When the prayer was over, he said to us: "If the imam prays seated, then pray seated, and if he stands up, then pray standing up. Do not stand when the imam is seated as the Persians do, glorifying their leaders".'

This *ḥadīth* relates to the same incident given in *Ḥadīth* 951, but gives us more details about the Prophet's complaint. The first point to note is the Prophet's companions' action on both occasions that they visited him. When they saw him praying, they immediately joined him in congregation. This shows how keen they were to join him in prayer on every occasion, whether he was offering voluntary or obligatory prayer. It is well known that a prayer in congregation is granted twenty-seven times the reward of a prayer one offers on his own.

However, on this point we may add that the Prophet's illness was at the end of the fifth year after his migration to Madinah. Several years later, shortly before his death, the Prophet offered obligatory prayer in the mosque when he was seated and the whole congregation were standing up. He did not order them to sit down. It is a general rule of Islamic law that a later practice supersedes an earlier one. As the permissibility of taking a different position is given later, then this is the final ruling. Moreover, the Prophet makes the reason for his earlier teaching very clear. The important thing is not to give leaders of the Muslim community a position of glorification. A leader should certainly be treated with respect, and his orders should be obeyed, but he is not to be glorified or exalted to a position where people make themselves inferior to him. There is no superiority or inferiority on account of position, but there are duties on both the ruler and the ruled. When these duties are fulfilled, then that is all that should be said and done.

News of things to come

Given resurrection and the Day of Judgement are so strongly emphasised in Islam, the Prophet's companions were keen to ask him about it whenever occasion arose.

964. Jābir reports: 'A young man from the Anṣār had a son born to him, and he called him Muhammad. The Anṣār said to him, "We will not call you with the Prophet's appellation [i.e. the *kunyah*]". We then sat by the roadside and asked the Prophet about the Last Hour. He said to us: "You have come to ask me about the Last Hour". We said: "Yes". He said: "No one alive today will complete one hundred years". We said: "A young man from the Anṣār had a son whom he called Muhammad, but the Anṣār said to him, we will not call you after the Prophet". He said, "The Anṣār have done well. You may call your children by my name, but do not use my appellation [or *kunyah*]".'[680]

When the man referred to in this *ḥadīth* called his son Muhammad, the Anṣār objected because, according to the Arab tradition that remains in force, they would have had to call him Abu Muhammad, and they felt uneasy about this when the Prophet was still among them.

It should be added that this took place only a few weeks before the Prophet's death. According to some reports, it was a month before the Prophet's death. Therefore, we take the last statement of the *ḥadīth* as permitting use of the Prophet's name for our sons, but not his parental appellation, Abu al-Qāsim. Throughout history countless numbers of Muslims have been called Muhammad, but no one other than the Prophet has called himself Abu al-Qāsim.

The central point in this *ḥadīth* is the question about the Last Hour, which is another name for the Day of Judgement. The Prophet was asked about this many times. In the Qur'an, he is instructed to say that only God knows its time: '*They ask you about the Last Hour: When will it come to pass? Say: Knowledge of it rests with my Lord alone. None but He will reveal it at its appointed time. It will weigh heavily*

---

680. Related by Abū Dāwūd, Ibn Ḥibbān, Ibn Khuzaymah and Abu 'Awānah.

on the heavens and the earth; and it will not fall on you except suddenly. They will ask you further as if you yourself persistently enquire about it. Say: Knowledge of it rests with God alone, though most people remain unaware'. (7:187)

Yet people will always ask, and the answer will remain the same. This is something that God has chosen not to reveal to us. Hence, we need not ask about it. Therefore, the Prophet always diverted the question to alert us to something closely related to it. To us, what is important is the time of death, because after we die, we cannot alter what we have done in this life, or earn further reward, except in the three specified ways of a continuous charity, a useful contribution to knowledge and prayer by our children. The Prophet's answers when he was asked about the Last Hour were always in this vein: reminding his interlocutors of their approaching death. On one occasion, he said to a man asking him about the Last Hour: 'What have you prepared for it'. Here, in this *ḥadīth*, he tells his companions that no one alive that day would live more than one hundred years. This does not preclude the possibility of people born after that day living more than a hundred years. The Prophet's answer alerts them to the fact that after death, it does not matter to anyone when human life is brought to an end, because their own hour has already come.

The other point is that this *ḥadīth* tells of a future happening. The Prophet did mention future events in a number of *ḥadīths*, and everything he mentioned came to pass. Never did he mention anything and it failed to take place in exactly the same way he described. Had there been a register of death at the time, we can be sure that everyone alive that day, anywhere on earth, would not have lived longer than a hundred years.

965. Jābir ibn 'Abdullāh reports: 'God's Messenger passed through the market, coming from its upper side. People were with him walking on both his sides. As he walked, he saw a dead goat with its two ears cut off. He held it by the remaining part of one ear. He then said: "Who of you would like to have this for one *dirham*?" They said: "We do not like to have it for anything whatsoever. What shall we do with it?" He asked again: "Would you like to have it anyway?" They said: "No". He repeated this

last question three times. They added in answer: "We would not like to have it at all! Had it been alive, it would have the defect of having no ears. How could it be worth anything when it is dead?" The Prophet said: "By God, the whole of this world is, in God's sight, of lesser value than this is to you".'[681]

In his dialogue with his companions, the Prophet made sure that everyone of them was clear in his mind that he would not take the dead goat for the smallest amount of money. When this was clear to all, he told them that, to God, the entire world we live in is even more worthless. The description here is so graphic that the intended message is clearly understood.

Anyone who contemplates the message of this *ḥadīth* is filled with wonder when he looks at how people strive hard to get what they cherish and think most valuable in this life. Yet, what they can get is only a fraction of what this world offers. The entire wealth of the richest person on earth is only a fraction of what this world contains, and the most powerful ruler enjoys only a small portion of the authority and power that our world exhibits. The same applies to everything that people covet and desire. But if we put this whole world together with all the wealth, power, beauty and happiness it can provide to all its inhabitants, it is worth practically nothing in God's sight. This is what we should remember when we wonder why unbelievers may have power, riches, and life's comforts. We should not be surprised because we know that God may give whatever people may desire in this life to both believers and unbelievers, but He gives the happiness of the Hereafter to believers only.

It has to be said, however, that Islam does not advocate a total rejection of life's comforts. On the contrary, a Muslim may enjoy these, provided that he acquires them in a legitimate way. He must not seek to acquire a position of arrogance as a result of having such comforts. On the contrary, he should use them to show kindness to his neighbours and to the poor in the community. If he does, then these luxuries become a means of earning reward from God.

---

681. Related by Aḥmad, Muslim and Abū Dāwūd.

966. ʿUtayy ibn Ḍamurah said: 'I saw at Ubay's place a man who appealed for support in the fashion of pre-Islamic days and Ubay immediately rebuked him in clear terms and did not call him by his parental appellation, or *kunyah*. The people present looked at him [with disapproval]. He said to them: "It seems that you disapprove of what I said. I do not fear anyone at all. I heard the Prophet say: 'Whoever appeals on the basis of ignorant bonds should be rebuked in clear terms and not called by his parental appellation'."'[682]

What is significant in this *ḥadīth* is that it recommends the use of clear abusive language, not merely indirect disapproval. Such language may be thought contrary to the values Islam advocates, which disapprove of vulgar language. There is no contradiction between the two, because the warning against the use of such language is made in the case of people who do not deserve such abuse. The situation to which this *ḥadīth* applies merits such usage as part of the punishment for those who resort to ignorance. Indeed, the Prophet disapproved even when some people made an appeal for support invoking ties much closer to Islam than tribal loyalties. In a dispute between two Muslims, one called out to the Muhājirīn and the other to the Anṣār for support. But the Prophet told them: 'Abandon such blind loyalty, for it stinks'.[683] Although the two men were invoking an Islamic loyalty, it was akin to what the people of ignorance in pre-Islamic days used to make. Hence, the Prophet's censure.

967. (*Athar* 219) ʿAbd al-Raḥmān ibn Saʿd said: 'Ibn ʿUmar felt that his foot became numb. A man said to him: "Mention the name of the person you love most". He said: "Muhammad".'

As there is nothing in this report that is attributed to the Prophet, the man's suggestion has no religious support. However, we note Ibn ʿUmar's response when he was told to name the person he loved most.

---

682. Related by Aḥmad and Ibn Ḥibbān.
683. Related by al-Bukhari and Muslim.

This should be the case with every Muslim.

968. Abu Mūsa al-Ash'ari mentioned that he was with the Prophet inside a farm in Madinah, when the Prophet had a twig in his hand with which he stroked the water and mud. A man was by the gate seeking admission, and the Prophet said [to Abu Mūsa]: "Open it for him and give him the news that he will be in heaven". Abu Mūsa said: "I went [to open the gate] and there I found Abu Bakr. I opened it for him and gave him the happy news". Another man sought admission, and the Prophet said: "Open it for him and give him the news that he will be in heaven". It was 'Umar, and I opened it for him and gave him the happy news. Then another man sought admission, and the Prophet was reclining. He sat up and said to me: "Open it for him and give him the news that he will be in heaven, but only after he has gone through some affliction [in this world]". I went to do so, and it was 'Uthmān. I opened it for him and told him what the Prophet had said. He only said: "I seek only God's help".'[684]

This *ḥadīth* gives us a very clear message. The Prophet's three companions were given this happy news as they were the most deserving. They were his closest companions, trusted by him and giving their utmost in the service of God's cause. We note however that although both 'Umar and 'Uthmān were assassinated, the Prophet's mentions only the hardship to be endured by 'Uthmān. This is a reference to the last period of his life when rebels surrounded Madinah and then stormed his home to kill him. At the time, he showed total faith in God, and he decided not to resist the rebels. He could certainly have defended himself and Madinah, but he decided to sacrifice his life in order to spare Muslim blood. Thus, he gave one of the shiniest examples of total devotion to Islam's cause. May God be pleased with all three of the Prophet's companions mentioned, and with Abu Mūsa, the reporter of this *ḥadīth*.

---

684. Related by al-Bukhari, Muslim and al-Tirmidhi.

969. (*Athar* 220) Salamah ibn Wardān said: 'I saw Anas ibn Mālik shaking hands with people. He asked me: "Who are you?" I replied: "I am a servant of the Layth clan". He stroked my head three times and said: "May God bless you".'

970. Anas ibn Mālik reports: 'When the people of Yemen came, the Prophet (peace be upon him) said: "The people of Yemen have come, and they are more soft-hearted than you". They were the first to introduce shaking hands'.[685]

971. (*Athar* 221) Al-Barā' ibn 'Āzib said: 'To shake hands with your brother makes your greeting complete'.[686]

Apparently shaking hands was not a standard greeting in Makkah or Madinah prior to Islam. It is also apparent that the reporter was still a young boy at the time. He was keen to shake hands with Anas, because of his standing as a companion of the Prophet. We are not told whether he shook hands with him, but probably he did. Anas was interested in him and asked him about his people. If they did not shake hands, Anas would have told him why he did not shake hands with him, or Salamah would have mentioned it. The fact that neither is made clear supports the conclusion that the pattern was maintained, and since Anas was shaking hands with people, he shook hands with Salamah, and added the inquiry which the reporter mentions.

The second *ḥadīth* tells us that the people of Yemen were the first to introduce shaking hands in Hijaz. Another version of this *ḥadīth* states: 'They were the first to greet us with the shaking of hands'. Yet another version says: 'They were the first to shake hands publicly'.

The people of Yemen, whom the Prophet describes as more soft-hearted than his companions who belonged to the Quraysh and the Madinah tribes of Aws and Khazraj, were the first to use this gesture of greeting. However, Islam encouraged this practice, as clearly mentioned in the third *ḥadīth*. A similar version of the third *ḥadīth* related by al-Tirmidhi attributes its statement to the Prophet himself.

---

685. Related by Abū Dāwūd.
686. Related by Abū Dāwūd, al-Tirmidhi and Ibn Mājah.

It should be pointed out that such shaking of hands is a part of greeting when people meet. However, some people have extended this so as to shake hands after prayer. This is wrong, because practices of religion are those which the Prophet ordered, encouraged or approved. At no time did he relate shaking hands to finishing a congregational prayer. Moreover, we have reports that when the Prophet shook hands, he used his two hands. Although using the right hand is sufficient, using both hands is better, because it indicates greater warmth and a closer relationship.

Another gesture of greeting is that mentioned in the first of these *ḥadīths*, i.e. rubbing a child's head. This applies as long as the child has not attained puberty, and it could be by either by a man or a woman.

972. (*Athar* 222) Marzūq al-Thaqafi reports: ''Abdullāh ibn al-Zubayr sent me to his mother, Asmā' bint Abu Bakr, to tell her how al-Ḥajjāj was treating them and so that she would pray for me and stroke my head. I was still a young lad at the time.'

The woman mentioned in this *ḥadīth*, Asmā', was the Prophet's companion and sister-in-law. She was a woman of strong character and great knowledge. She would not do anything that might be thought of as inappropriate, let alone forbidden. Indeed, the way she treated the young lad who brought her the news was the proper way, because it combined endearment with a prayer to God to protect the child and take good care of him.

Perhaps it is useful to add a word of explanation about the events to which this *ḥadīth* refers. 'Abdullāh ibn al-Zubayr was a young companion of the Prophet, with a strong and ambitious character. His father was one of the earliest of the Prophet's companions and one of the ten the Prophet assured of being in heaven in the life to come. 'Abdullāh strove to become Caliph, and he saw his chance when the Umayyad rule seemed to be faltering. He was chosen Caliph by the people of Hijaz and Iraq, but the Umayyad ruler fought several battles against his forces, the last of which was in Makkah itself. Al-Ḥajjāj was the Umayyad commander who fought and defeated him in that battle and in which 'Abdullāh was killed.

973. Jābir ibn ʿAbdullāh said: 'I heard that one of the Prophet's companions was relating a *ḥadīth.* Therefore, I bought a camel and travelled for a month until I reached Syria where I met ʿAbdullāh ibn Unays. I sent him word that I was outside. The messenger came back and asked: "Are you Jābir ibn ʿAbdullāh?" I said: "Yes". He came out and hugged me. I said: "[I have come] for a *ḥadīth* which I did not hear [from the Prophet] and I feared that you or I would die [before we meet]". He said: "I heard the Prophet (peace be upon him) say: 'God will resurrect people and they will gather naked, uncircumcised, having nothing with them. He will call out to them in a voice heard by the furthest away [I think he added, 'just like it is heard by the one who is very near.']: I am the King. None of the people of heaven may enter heaven while one of the people of hell is seeking him for some injustice done to him. Nor may anyone of the people of hell enter it while one of the people of heaven is seeking him for some injustice done to him'. I asked: "But how, when we will be naked and have nothing". He [ʿAbdullāh ibn Unays] said: "By trading good deeds and bad deeds".'[687]

This *ḥadīth* confirms that God does not erase people's claims against one another but gets them to settle what is due to others. This they do with their own good deeds, or by bearing some of the bad deeds of the one they treated unfairly.

The *ḥadīth* shows how keen the Prophet's companions were to learn *ḥadīths* from other companions who heard them directly from the Prophet. Jābir travels for a month on camel back to meet another companion and ask him about this *ḥadīth,* seeking explanation when needed.

One interesting point is that al-Bukhari enters this *ḥadīth* under a subheading on Muslims hugging each other when they meet after some absence.

974. ʿĀ'ishah reports: 'I never saw anyone who more resembled the Prophet in conversation, speech or the way he sat than

---

687. Related by Aḥmad, al-Bukhari, al-Ḥākim and al-Ṭabarāni.

Fāṭimah. When the Prophet saw her coming, he stood up to welcome and greet her and kissed her. He would then seat her in his place. When the Prophet went to visit her, she would stand up to welcome and greet him, kissed him and seated him in her place. Once she came to him when he was in his last illness. He welcomed her and kissed her'.[688]

This is a shorter version of *ḥadīth* Number 950, with slight variation in wording.

975. 'Abdullāh ibn 'Umar said: 'We were on a military expedition, and the people had to abandon the battlefield. We thought: "How can we meet the Prophet when we have fled?" Qur'anic verses had been revealed stating: '*Except when manoeuvring for battle*'. We thought that We should rather not go to Madinah so that none would see us. Then we thought: It may be better that we should go". As the Prophet came out of the dawn prayer, we said to him: "We are the ones who ran away!" He said: "No, you are the ones who will return". We kissed his hand, and he said to us: "I am your supporting troop".'[689]

This *ḥadīth* refers to the first military encounter between the Muslims and the Byzantine Empire in the Battle of Mu'tah, when a small Muslim army, about 3,000 strong faced a huge Byzantine force more than sixty times its number. The Prophet nominated three of his companions to take command, one after the other, in case the commander was killed. He also told them that if all three were killed in battle, then the army should choose its commander. As it happened, the three commanders, Zayd ibn Ḥārithah, Ja'far ibn Abu Ṭālib and 'Abdullāh ibn Rawāḥah, fought hard and fell in battle. The command was then taken by Khālid ibn al-Walīd, a shrewd military strategist who realised that his forces could not hold their own against such a mighty army. Hence, his plan, which he successfully implemented, was to withdraw with minimum casualties. As they approached Madinah, the men in the army, who

688. Related by Abū Dāwūd and al-Tirmidhi.

689. Related by Aḥmad, Abū Dāwūd, Ibn Mājah and al-Tirmidhi.

were all companions of the Prophet, felt ashamed of meeting him, because they could easily be accused of fleeing from battle.

The Prophet's statement describing those who were on this expedition refers directly to Qur'anic verses from which the quotation in the *ḥadīth* is taken. They explain the two situations in which withdrawing from battle is permissible. The verses mean: '*Believers, when you meet in battle those who disbelieve, do not turn your backs to them in flight. Anyone who turns his back to them on that day, except when manoeuvring for battle or in an endeavour to join another troop, shall incur God's wrath, and hell shall be his abode: how vile a journey's end*'. (8: 15-16) The two possibilities, then, are: doing a manoeuvre, perhaps to regroup or to attack a certain weakness in the enemy lines, or to join supporting forces. In both cases, the withdrawal becomes a step towards a new engagement. Hence, the Prophet describes this army as 'the ones who will return'. He then makes the point even clearer by telling them that their returning to Madinah was to join him, and he acts as their support. Thus, they are totally exempt from responsibility.

Those companions of the Prophet were overwhelmed when the Prophet told them that they were not deserters; rather, they were a reliable unit in a future battle. They express their gratitude by kissing his hand. This is a gesture of utmost love and gratitude.

Although this *ḥadīth* sums up an event of much significance at the time of the Prophet, it is included by al-Bukhari under a subheading that represents only a side issue in the *ḥadīth*, namely, kissing another person's hand indicating its permissibility to express gratitude for a favour done. Other *ḥadīths* under this heading show that it is also permissible as a sign of respect.

976. ʿAbd al-Raḥmān ibn Ruzayn reports: 'We were passing through al-Rabadhah when we were told that Salamah ibn al-Akwaʿ was present there. We went to see him, and when we greeted him, he put out his two hands and said: "With these two hands of mine I pledged allegiance to the Prophet." He put out his hand – as massive as a camel's hoof. We stood up and kissed his hand'.

In this *ḥadīth*, it is clear that the people kissed Salamah's hand because he had shaken hands with the Prophet. This was common with people who met the Prophet's companions, as is clear from the following *ḥadīth*:

977. Thābit said to Anas: 'Did you touch the Prophet with your hand?' Anas answered: 'Yes'. Thābit kissed his hand.

Indeed, in some cases it is permissible to kiss a person's hands and feet, as when a son or daughter kisses the feet of their parents, provided that this does not take a form similar to worship in any way. A *ḥadīth* reported by al-Wāziʿ ibn ʿĀmir, a man who belonged to the Ṣabāḥ clan from the ʿAbd al-Qays tribe was a member of the tribe's delegation to meet the Prophet.

978. Al-Wāziʿ ibn ʿĀmir reports: 'When we arrived, people said: "That man is God's Messenger". We kissed his hands and feet'.

979. (*Athar* 223) Ṣuhayb said: 'I saw ʿAli kissing al-ʿAbbās's hand and his two feet'.

It is clear from the context of these *ḥadīths* that the action was only a gesture of profound respect. The delegation of the ʿAbd al-Qays included some very devout people and they were eager to meet the Prophet. When they saw him, they expressed their love in the most telling gestures. The second *ḥadīth* confirms this, because al-ʿAbbās was ʿAli's uncle and the Prophet loved him dearly.

In the same vein we may also mention standing up to greet a person, indicating respect.

980. Abu Mijlaz reports: 'As Muʿāwiyah started to leave, ʿAbdullāh ibn ʿĀmir and ʿAbdullāh ibn al-Zubayr were seated. Ibn ʿĀmir stood up while Ibn al-Zubayr – who was the more sagacious of the two men – remained seated. Muʿāwiyah [told Ibn ʿĀmir to sit], adding: "The Prophet said: 'Anyone who loves

to see people standing in his presence will have his place in the Fire'."'

What we should know is that standing up to honour a man of good conduct who occupies a position of authority, or one's teacher or friend is acceptable, or may even be desirable, provided that it is done of one's own accord and without being expected by the other person. What is not acceptable is that a person in a higher position should sit down, leaving subordinates standing up around him, to indicate that they are inferior to him.

47

The Greeting of Peace and Love

981. Abu Hurayrah reports that the Prophet said: 'God created Adam and he was sixty arms in height. He said to him: "Go and greet those over there (pointing to a group of angels sitting together) and listen to how they reply to you. This will be your own greeting and that of your descendants". Adam said to them: "Peace be to you, or *assalām 'alaykum*". They replied: "And to you be peace and God's mercy, or *'alaykum assalām wa raḥmatullāh*". Thus, they added "God's mercy" to his greeting. Every one who is admitted to heaven will be in his image. Creation continued to shrink up till now".'[690]

THIS HIGHLY AUTHENTIC *ḥadīth* tells us how people's greeting started. It was part of the training Adam received in heaven, prior to his fall to earth. We note the careful hand of God in his training. He is

---

690. Related by al-Bukhari and Muslim.

told to greet angels, who return his greeting with a better one, wishing that he will receive God's mercy. Prior to this, God makes it clear to him that the greeting he exchanges with the angels will be the one to be used by him and future human generations. It is a greeting of peace, which is returned with an addition of mercy bestowed by God.

The *ḥadīth* includes a number of points which we will briefly explain. The first is that Adam was of a much larger stature than people today, but human stature continued to gradually shrink over many generations up to the time of Prophet Muhammad when it reached its ultimate size. This is clearly understood from the last sentence. But when people are admitted into heaven they will be in their perfect shape. It seems that Adam was of a gigantic size, which may be the size suitable for heaven, but after the fall, his size was to be made more suitable for life on earth. Hence, his shrinking, and the indication that human beings will shrink no more.

The Islamic greeting took humanity back to the greeting Adam used in heaven with the angels, and it is returned in the same way the angels used. It is the greeting of peace, or *salām* in Arabic. This word, *salām,* which means peace, is also one of God's names. Thus, when we offer this greeting to anyone, we do not merely indicate that we are happy to be in peace with them, but we wish them God's help and protection. Hence, the return greeting also adds a wish of mercy from God. Bearing in mind all these connotations, the Prophet taught us to use this greeting extensively.

982. Al-Barā' reports that the Prophet said: 'Spread widely the greeting of peace, so that you will be in peace'.[691]

It goes without saying that when we offer people the greeting of peace, we remove any initial misunderstanding that may exist. If this is used extensively, peace will be the guiding principle in social relations. Indeed, the Prophet made this greeting the gateway to the spread of love in the Muslim community:

---

691. Related by Ibn Ḥibbān.

983. Abu Hurayrah reports that the Prophet said: 'You shall not be admitted into heaven unless you [truly] believe; and you will not believe unless you love one another. Shall I point out to you something that generates love between you?' People said: 'Yes, please, Messenger of God'. He said: 'Spread the greeting of peace widely among you'.[692]

This *ḥadīth* states a main condition which must be met in order for people to be admitted to heaven. From this condition we know that people must be true believers before they can gain a status that ensures the reward of heaven. To be true believers, they must have an essential quality of mutual love in their community. This tells us that people cannot combine mutual hatred in their community with being true believers. The two qualities of faith and hatred are mutually exclusive. A true believer loves others and is always keen for their welfare, both in this life and in the life to come.

The Prophet then points out the way to ensure mutual love within the Muslim community, and this is to greet others, whether we know them or not, with the greeting of peace. We see evidence of this in our daily lives. In Muslim countries, this quality has become part of local culture. As you walk down the street, you hear people offering this greeting to those they do not know, as they pass by. The greeting is always returned with a better one. Thus, an air of peace and love is generated in society. This is a truly valuable quality achieved by a small gesture used widely.

The Prophet encouraged such extensive use of this greeting on numerous occasions, using different forms.

984. 'Abdullāh ibn 'Amr reports that the Prophet said: 'Worship the Lord of Grace, give food to people and spread the greeting of peace, and you will be in heaven'.

This *ḥadīth* maps an easy way to be certain of admittance into heaven. We must worship God alone, who is referred to here in His main attribute of mercy. The other two actions are to be hospitable to other

---

692. Related by Muslim.

people, giving them of our food, particularly those who are poor, and to use the greeting of peace extensively, saying it even to those we do not know.

So, when two or more people meet, who should start the greeting? We note this from the practice of some of the best learned of the Prophet's companions. Besides, the Prophet did not leave the question unanswered himself.

985. (*Athar* 224) Bashīr ibn Yasār said: 'No one started or was ahead of Ibn 'Umar in offering the greeting of peace'.[693]

986. (*Athar* 225) Jābir said: 'The one who is riding should greet the one who is walking; and a walking person greets the one who is seated. When two people meet as they walk, the one who offers the greeting first is more commendable'.

We note here a consistent approach, placing the onus on the one who is able to see the other first, or who takes fuller view, to start. If it was left to the one who is sitting to greet the one who is walking, or the latter to greet the one who is riding, there could be some misunderstanding. If a person sitting at the doorstep of his shop is to greet the one who is walking by, he may not be heard, particularly if the latter has already begun to walk away. There is little chance of this happening in the other situation, because the walking person offers his greeting as he is approaching the one who is seated. The same can be said in the case of a riding and a walking person: the rider is moving faster so he is better able to deal with the situation. Hence, he is the one to start. But when people meet as they walk in opposite directions, then the one who starts receives a greater reward.

The first of these two *ḥadīths* shows how diligent the Prophet's companions were in implementing his advice. Perhaps one of the most diligent of all was 'Abdullāh ibn 'Umar. Convinced beyond any shred of doubt that whatever the Prophet did or said was only good and for the benefit of both individual and community, Ibn 'Umar was keen to

---

693. Related by al-Bukhari and Muslim with different chains of transmission, as also Ibn Ḥibbān and Abu 'Awānah.

implement it fully. Hence he was always the first to greet others. This is the proper attitude the Prophet taught, and Ibn 'Umar implemented it, encouraging others to do likewise.

987. Ibn 'Umar reports: 'Al-Agharr (a companion of the Prophet from the Muzaynah tribe) had a large quantity of dates owed to him by a man from the clan of 'Amr ibn 'Awf, and he went to him several times [requesting settlement]. [Al-Agharr] said: "I went to the Prophet [requesting his help] and he sent Abu Bakr with me. As we walked, everyone whom we met offered us the greeting of peace. Abu Bakr said to me: 'Do you not see how people are the first to greet you so as to earn more reward?'".' 'Abdullāh ibn 'Umar adds encouraging his audience: 'Be the one who starts in order to gain the greater reward'.[694]

Al-Agharr went to the Prophet to complain when another person was slow in settling his debt. This was the last resort for the Prophet's companions, and the Prophet was always ready to help whoever was demanding his rights. In this instance, he sent Abu Bakr as support and to emphasise to the debtor that the case was now with the Prophet. In other words, he had no option but to settle.

It was natural that people should greet Abu Bakr as he passed by them, because they were aware of his close association with the Prophet and they held him in high esteem. Abu Bakr tried to point out to his companion that he should be keen to get the greater reward. He put it in a most gentle manner, reminding his companion of an easy way to earn reward.

What happens when people are in dispute or quarrel with each other? They may not be on speaking terms. If offering a greeting is obligatory, then they are in trouble for not fulfilling an obligation. In order not to overburden people, God has made offering a greeting when people meet a recommended practice, but answering a greeting offered to us is obligatory. A Muslim simply may not ignore a greeting offered to him, even by one whom he is boycotting.

---

694. Related by al-Ṭabarāni.

988. Abu Ayyūb reports that the Prophet said: 'It is not lawful for any Muslim to boycott his brother for more than three days. They may meet and each of them turns away from the other. The better one of the two is the one who offers the greeting of peace to the other'.[695]

This *ḥadīth* states a principle and provides a graphic description of a case for acting on it. The principle is that of not allowing a dispute that leads to a boycott of one Muslim by another to last more than three days or three nights. The three-day period is allowed in order to give a chance for tempers to cool down and grievances to be aired. The boycott must, however, end after three nights. This applies to all Muslims, but it applies with greater vigour to members of the same family.

The graphic description is that of two people who are in dispute. When they meet, each of them turns away from the other. If they are to apply the principle, one of them has to start by greeting the other. The one who starts is recognised by the Prophet as being the better of the two.

Although all these *ḥadīths* use the masculine form, they apply equally to men and women. This is standard in Arabic, and in Islam. The Qur'anic address applies to men and women, unless it is specifically only applicable to women.

989. Abu Hurayrah reports: 'As the Prophet was sitting with a group of people a man passed by and said: "Peace be to you, or *al-salām 'alaykum*". The Prophet said: "Ten good deeds". Another man then passed by and said: "Peace and God's mercy be to you, or *al-salām 'alaykum wa raḥmatullāh*". The Prophet said: "Twenty good deeds". A third man said as he passed by: "Peace, God's mercy and blessings be to you, or *al-salām 'alaykum wa raḥmatullāh wa barakātuh*". The Prophet said: "Thirty good deeds". Then a man stood up and left the group without saying any greeting. The Prophet said: "How quickly your friend has forgotten! If one of you comes to a group, he should begin with

695. Related by al-Bukhari, Muslim, Abū Dāwūd and al-Tirmidhi.

a greeting. Then if he likes to sit with them, he may do so. When he stands up to leave, he should also say a greeting. The first greeting is no more important than the second".'[696]

As people may not be fully aware of what reward they miss by not greeting others, the Prophet used this occasion to spell it out so that we are certain of the reward we get for greeting others. To start with, when each of the three men offered a greeting, the Prophet and his companions replied to the greeting. This goes without saying because, as we have noted earlier, offering a greeting is recommended but replying to it is obligatory. The Prophet would not have left out an obligatory duty in any situation. The reporter of the *ḥadīth* does not mention the Prophet's reply because it is taken for granted. He wanted to emphasise the two points made clear in this *ḥadīth.* The first one is that of the reward. The better the greeting, the greater the reward. Since, a good deed is rewarded by at least ten times its worth, the first man earned the reward of ten good deeds, while the second earned double that because his greeting was a better one as he had added a wish for God's mercy to be granted to the people he was greeting. The third man added more, and so earned more.

The other point in this *ḥadīth* is that another greeting is due on departure. Thus, when two people part they should greet each other, and if one is leaving a group, he should say a greeting of peace before he leaves. The Prophet makes it clear that this greeting at the point of departure is no less important than the first one offered on meeting others.

990. (*Athar* 226) ''Umar reports: I was riding behind Abu Bakr on his mount. When he passed by people, Abu Bakr said: "*al-salām 'alaykum*", and they replied: "*wa 'alaykum al-salām wa raḥmatullāh*". Or he may greet them saying: "*al-salām 'alaykum wa raḥmatullāh*", and they would reply: "*wa 'alaykum al-salām wa raḥmatllāh wa barakātuh*". Abu Bakr commented: "Today, people have gained much more than us".'

696. Related by al-Nasā'ī and Ibn Ḥibbān.

We note that every time Abu Bakr offered a greeting, its reply was the same with an addition. The first one was the short form of the greeting of peace. The reply meant: 'And to you be peace together with God's mercy'. Thus, the reply adds a prayer that the person who offered the greeting should be blessed with God's mercy, both in this life and in the life to come. When the person who starts the greeting includes in it this same prayer for mercy to the one being hailed, the latter replies with yet another addition which adds a wish for God's blessing to the one who took advantage and offered us a friendly greeting. Abu Bakr's comment at the end of the *ḥadīth* shows that he was pleased with the fact that people always replied to his greeting with a better one.

Another *ḥadīth* speaks of the importance of the wording of the Islamic greeting:

991. 'Ā'ishah reports that the Prophet said: 'The Jews do not envy you for anything more than they do for the greeting of peace and saying *Āmīn*'.[697]

This *ḥadīth* stresses the special distinction given to the Islamic greeting. The Jews the Prophet refers to here are the ones with profound knowledge, such as well versed rabbis. They are the ones to appreciate the significance of the Islamic greeting of peace. *Āmīn* is a word which we say when someone addresses a prayer to God. It signifies a request made to God to answer his prayer. This makes the prayer a collective one, with all those who are present joining their fellow Muslim in an appeal to God on behalf of the one who is saying the prayer. But why would the Jews be envious of our greeting? The word *salām*, which means peace, is also a name of God. Using it in our greeting is a constant reminder of the special relation between a believer and God.

992. Anas reports that the Prophet said: '*Salām* is one of the names of God, the Most High, which He has placed on earth. Therefore, spread the *salām* [i.e. the peace greeting] among yourselves'.[698]

---

697. Related by Ibn Mājah and Ibn Khuzaymah.
698. Related by al-Ṭabarāni and al-Bazzār.

This means that peace is the state of affairs God wants to see on earth. Within the Muslim community God has made the best greeting the one which uses His name, in the form of *al-salām ʿalaykum*, or peace be to you. When one person says it to another, it immediately generates an air of peace and tranquillity between them, even though they may be at odds with each other.

To emphasise this feeling, and the significance of this one of God's names, the Prophet taught us the following formula to say in our supplication and after we finish an obligatory prayer: 'Our Lord, You are peace, and peace emanates from You, and to You all peace returns, so greet us, our Lord, with the greeting of peace'. This form of prayer begins with praising God by His attribute of Peace, and ends with an appeal to Him to give us a greeting that spreads peace within and among us. Indeed, people and communities greatly value a state of peace, because it gives them a sense of security and reassurance. Nevertheless, when states and politicians feel themselves to be powerful and immune from retaliation, they disturb peace and engineer a state of war. No ruler who led his country into an unnecessary war is considered truly great. He might have been considered so at the time of his triumph. He may also be remembered as brave or a man of great determination, but people do not associate human greatness with war, not even with winning it. It is always the leader who ends war and ensures peace that is considered great.

993. ʿAbdullāh ibn Masʿūd reports: 'People were praying with the Prophet when he heard one of the worshippers saying, "Salām to Allah", or "Peace to God". When he finished his prayer, the Prophet said to the congregation: "Who is the one who said, 'peace to God'? It is God Who is peace. You better say: 'Greetings are offered to God, together with blessings and all good things. Peace be to you, Prophet, with God's mercy and blessings. Peace be to us and to all righteous servants of God. I bear witness that there is no deity other than God, and I bear witness that Muhammad is God's servant and Messenger'." They used to learn this form in the same way as they learned the Qur'an'.[699]

---

699. Related in all six authentic anthologies of *Ḥadīth*.

These are the words we say every day at least nine times in our five obligatory prayers. We say them many more times if we offer voluntary, or Sunnah prayers as we are strongly recommended to do.

The Prophet first points out that it is wrong to offer a greeting to God in the same way as we offer greetings to one another, particularly the one using His name, *Salām*. Instead the Prophet teaches us that greeting God is done by grouping all greetings used by human beings in all cultures, and also adding blessings and all good things. Needless to say, this is for our benefit, because it is a fact that all good things belong to God. We are only reiterating these in acknowledgement of our position in relation to Him.

Secondly, we address our greeting to the Prophet, using the form of the second person, as though he is with us. Moreover, we say this in private, in all situations, even when we are alone in the depth of the night, or in broad daylight in the middle of the desert. This gives our greeting an element of intimacy, because we know that our greeting to the Prophet is delivered to him by God, although we do not know how. It also emphasises the Prophet's position and the way all Muslims love him, remembering him always in their prayer and requesting God to grant him His blessings and grace.

The next part stresses the community feeling among all Muslims. But we note here that we first offer the greeting to ourselves and then include all God's righteous servants. This is the proper way, that the Prophet used, because it reflects man's true feelings. Every human being thinks first of himself, praying for his own happiness. We include others only after we have sought what we need from God: forgiveness, mercy, happiness, ample provision, etc. But then we should remember all those with whom we are bound by ties of faith. In this respect, we should remember all prophets, angels and true believers who abide by God's law and follow His guidance.

Next, we declare our belief in God's oneness and the message of Prophet Muhammad (peace be upon him). This comes in the form which is used to declare one's acceptance of the Islamic faith, bearing witness to the two most fundamental principles: all Godhead belongs to God alone with no partners, and Muhammad's role as God's servant and messenger who conveys to us God's message and guidance. Thus, we accept nothing from any other source, because this is the only source through which God explains His guidance. It is not merely through verbal teachings that the Prophet instructs us how to offer our worship and how to serve God, but he also gives us a practical example. He was the perfect example which we will do well to follow in order to achieve happiness both in this life and in the life to come.

994. Abu Hurayrah reports that the Prophet said: 'Every Muslim owes other Muslims five duties'. He was asked: 'What are they?' He said: 'If you meet [your Muslim brother] greet him; if he invites you, accept his invitation; if he seeks your advice, give him good counsel; if he sneezes, pray to God to grant him mercy; if he falls ill, visit him; and if he dies, take part in his funeral'.[700]

This *ḥadīth* is the same as *ḥadīth* Number 928, but here the number of duties is mentioned as five, while the details show that they are six as mentioned in Number 928 and also in 925, where the narrator is Abu Ayyūb. These duties have already been explained.

995. 'Abd al-Raḥmān ibn Shibl reports that the Prophet said: 'Let the one who is riding greet the one who is walking; the one who is walking greet the one who is sitting; and the few greet the many. Whoever answers the greeting, it is for him and whoever does not gets nothing'.[701]

996. The same as the one before it, but without the last sentence.

997. (*Athar* 228[702]) Jābir said: 'When two pedestrians meet, the one who offers the greeting first is the better one'.

998. The same as 995, but without the last sentence.[703]

---

700. Related by al-Bukhari and Muslim.

701. Related by Aḥmad, Muslim, al-Nasā'ī, Abū Dāwūd, Ibn Mājah.

702. *Athar* No. 228 has not been included because it is part of *Ḥadīth* No. 990, which bears *Athar* No. 227, and repeats it with a different chain of transmission giving it the number we have omitted.

703. Related by al-Bukhari, Muslim, Abū Dāwūd and al-Tirmidhi.

999. Fuḍālah reports that the Prophet said: 'Let the one who is riding greet the one who is walking and the few greet the many'.[704]

1000. (*Athar* 229) Huṣayn ibn 'Abd al-Raḥmān said: 'Al-Sha'bi met a man on a horse and al-Sha'bi was the first to offer the greeting. I asked: "Is it right that you start and offer the greeting?" He said: "I saw Shurayḥ walking and taking the initiative in offering the greeting".'

1001-3. All three *ḥadīths* are the same as 995, but without the last sentence with different narrators.

All these *ḥadīths* confirm certain teachings about the proper way to exchange greetings in different situations. As we have already noted, the point that they repeat means that the party who is in a better position to see the other or to make himself heard is the one who should start the greeting. We may reiterate that offering a greeting is strongly recommended, but replying with at least a similar greeting is obligatory.

The fact that we have so many *ḥadīths* stressing these points suggests that the Prophet used different occasions and spoke to different audiences so that this social practice should be known to all within a short period of time.

1004. Abu Hurayrah reports that the Prophet said: 'A young person should offer the greeting of peace to the older one; the one who is walking to the one sitting and the few to the many'.[705]

The first point emphasises the consistent value Islam attaches to seniority. Although the question here is seniority of age, scholars extend this to seniority of Islamic standing. Thus, at the time of the Prophet, a newcomer to Islam would be the one to offer greetings to one who embraced Islam earlier. Similarly, one who was known to be

704. Related by Aḥmad, al-Nasā'ī, al-Tirmidhi, al-Dārimi and Ibn Ḥibbān.
705. Related by al-Bukhari and al-Tirmidhi.

dedicated to serving the Islamic cause is shown respect by people when they are the ones to start greeting him.

The other two points are perfectly natural. The one who is walking is more alert to what is around him. Thus, when he sees someone sitting and he is about to reach him, he begins the exchange of greetings. Similarly, if two people are walking together and they are met by a group of three or four people, the smaller group should be the one to start.

1005. (*Athar* 230) Abu al-Zinād reports: 'Khārijah [ibn Zayd ibn Thābit] used to write on Zayd's letter when he wrote the greeting: "Peace be to you, Amīr al-Mu'minīn, with God's mercy, blessings, forgiveness and His best blessings".'

The normal form of greetings mostly used in Muslim communities is *al-salām 'alaykum*. The full greeting is '*al-salām 'alaykum wa raḥmatullāh wa barakātuh*'. Rarely does a greeting go beyond this. It is reported that a man from the Yemen visited 'Abdullāh ibn 'Abbās and greeted him with the full greeting, but added something extra. Ibn 'Abbās told him: 'A greeting of peace ends with the wish for God's blessings'. This means that Ibn 'Abbās thought that such addition was unnecessary. However, Khārijah ibn Zayd, a scholar of very high standing who belonged to the generation that followed the Prophet's companions, i.e. the *tabi'īn*, used to write the greeting in full when he addressed the Caliph, but he also added: '*wa maghfiratuh wa ṭayyib ṣalawātih*'.

The added phrases express a prayer that the addressee will also have God's forgiveness and special blessings. Khārijah would not have added these phrases if he had the slightest doubt about such addition being inappropriate. His father was distinguished among the Prophet's companions for his scholarship. When we have two reputable scholars expressing opposite views, we say that one of them was aware of something the other did not know. Perhaps Khārijah was aware that when addressing a person of eminence, the use of additional phrases would be in order.

Should greetings always be verbal when people meet? This is the standard form. However, sometimes, a signal greeting may be sufficient.

1006. (*Athar* 231) Abu Qurrah al-Khurāsāni said: 'I saw Anas when he passed by and signalled his greeting to us with his hand. He had some white spots. I also saw al-Ḥasan using yellow dye and wearing a black turban. And Asmā' said that the Prophet waved with his hand to the women indicating his greeting'.[706]

1007. (*Athar* 232) Sa'd said: 'I went out with 'Abdullāh ibn 'Umar and al-Qāsim ibn Muhammad. They stopped at Sarf. Then 'Abdullāh ibn al-Zubayr passed by and he made a gesture of greeting to them and they answered him'.

1008. (*Athar* 233) 'Aṭā' ibn Abu Rabāḥ said: 'They used to dislike making a signal with one's hand as a form of greeting'.

The pronoun 'they' in the last *ḥadīth* refers to the Prophet's companions. However, the other two suggest that it was acceptable. It may be that when there is some distance between the people that a gesture with the hand is acceptable as a greeting. Alternatively, if one is making the gesture to a large group of people, it is well understood. The first *ḥadīth* suggests that the Prophet greeted women with a gesture of his hand. Again, this is most probably because he was at a distance from them. Otherwise, he would have greeted them verbally. Moreover, the fact that he sometimes used a signal greeting was to indicate its permissibility. The general rule is to make one's greeting verbal, because it serves the purpose better.

1009. (*Athar* 234) Thābit ibn 'Ubayd reports: 'I came to a group of people which included 'Abdullāh ibn 'Umar. He said to me: "If you offer a greeting, make it clearly audible. A greeting of peace is from God, blessed and goodly".'

Two important points are made here. The first is that the one offering the greeting should say it clearly and loud enough to be heard by those to whom it is offered. Some people are too shy, particularly when they

706. Related by Aḥmad, al-Dārimi and Abu 'Awānah with a different chain of transmission.

are young. They whisper their greeting, particularly when they see people who command general respect in society. ʿAbdullāh ibn ʿUmar, a highly learned companion of the Prophet, urged such people to say their greetings loud enough. Nothing is perhaps more encouraging to a shy person than knowing that when he says *al-salām ʿalaykum*, he is actually offering a blessed and goodly greeting. Moreover, it is the greeting enjoined by God and taught to us by the Prophet.

As we have noted, the Islamic greeting, which means 'peace be to you', actually uses one of God's names, *salām*, which also means peace. Thus, it generates a generally peaceful atmosphere in society. The more frequently it is used, the more people feel closer to one another. This is a point the Prophet clearly emphasised and his companions acted upon.

> 1010. (*Athar* 235) Al-Ṭufayl ibn Ubay ibn Kaʿb mentions that he used to visit ʿAbdullāh ibn ʿUmar and they both would go to the marketplace. 'When we went to the market, ʿAbdullāh ibn ʿUmar would offer the greeting of peace, *al-salām ʿalaykum*, to everyone including a junk seller, a man with a small stall, a poor person or anyone at all'. Al-Ṭufayl reports: 'I once went to ʿAbdullāh ibn ʿUmar and he asked me to accompany him to the marketplace. I said: "What business do you have in the market when you never stop at a shop, ask about any merchandise, offer to buy anything or sit with anyone? Would it not be better to sit and have our conversation here?" He said to me: "You fat man! We only go to the marketplace so that we offer the greeting of peace to people we find there".'[707]

It should be remembered that ʿAbdullāh ibn ʿUmar was distinguished as a scholar by his diligence in following the Prophet's Sunnah in all situations. The fact that he made a point of frequently going to the market to greet people and have them returning his greeting reflects his strong desire to act on the Prophet's advice. Since the Prophet urged his companions to spread the greeting of peace, ʿAbdullāh ibn ʿUmar took his advice literally and frequently went to the marketplace

707. Related by Mālik and al-Bayhaqi in Shuʿab al-Īmān.

to greet people. In this *ḥadīth*, the reporter, Al-Ṭufayl who was born before the Prophet's death and his father was perhaps the best reciter of the Qur'an among the Prophet's companions, questions him about his frequent visits to the market. He points out that 'Abdullāh really had nothing of the normal reasons that people have to go to the market. He was not after buying anything. He did not even stop to look for anything that he might be in need of. Yet he would go to the market and greet everyone there.

Ibn 'Umar's answer was friendly and educative. He refers to the fact that al-Ṭufayl was fat, but only in a friendly way, and makes his purpose clear. He had no need to go to the market other than greeting people. This implements the Prophet's advice and allows a friendly social atmosphere to spread. Besides, it earns a dual reward from God: one for following the Prophet's advice and the other for the greetings offered.

1011. Abu Hurayrah reports that the Prophet said: 'When any of you comes to join a group of people, he should offer his greeting. If he then departs, he should again offer a greeting. The second greeting is in no way less needed than the first'.[708]

1012. Abu Hurayrah reports that the Prophet said: 'When any of you comes to join a group of people, he should offer a greeting. If he sits down then wishes to leave before the group is ready to disperse, he should again offer a greeting. The first greeting is in no way more required than the second'.[709]

These two *ḥadīths* describe the same situation, giving clear instructions to a person joining a group or leaving them. He should be the one to offer the greeting of peace, *al-salām 'alaykum*. Both are the right thing to do, because they are indicative of good manners and friendliness towards one's community. Sometimes, a person wants to leave silently, either because he does not wish to disrupt the discussion, or because he wants his departure not to be noticed. While circumstances like

---

708. Related by Aḥmad, al-Nasā'ī and Ibn Ḥibbān.

709. Related by Abū Dāwūd, al-Nasā'ī and al-Tirmidhi.

these may be considered according to the particular situation, the normal practice that follows the Prophet's guidance is to indicate one's departure by offering a greeting of peace.

Besides, when a person is noticed to leave quietly, without offering a greeting, his behaviour may raise questions or doubts, particularly if the people he is leaving have been discussing a private matter. The greeting of peace is significant in such respect. It tells the people so greeted that they are in peace with the person as he arrives and as he leaves. So, it is reassuring. Hence, the Prophet makes it clear that the second greeting, i.e. at the point of departure, is equally as important as the first, which people normally expect by all.

The second *ḥadīth* gives a clearer description of the situation when an individual joins a group, sits with them, then departs before them. This excludes a person who passes by a group, greets them and leaves. In this case, one greeting is all that is required. But when a person joins the group and sits with them for a while and then wants to depart, he should offer another greeting.

In the second *ḥadīth* the order in the concluding sentence is changed. It says that the first greeting is equal to the second in the fact that both are required. People feel that the first greeting is more important. As the man is joining a group, he should be the one to greet them so that his arrival is felt in a friendly way. Hence, the Prophet makes it clear that the second greeting, at the point of departure, is not to be taken lightly. It is equally required.

1013. (*Athar* 236) Mu'āwiyah ibn Qurrah said: 'My father said to me: "Son, if you are with a group of people and hope to gain the benefit of their meeting, but you have to leave early for something, then say *al-salām 'alaykum* to the people. You will then share in the reward they gain in that meeting. A group who meet and then depart without remembering God in their talk leave as though they were meeting around the carcass of a dead donkey".'[710]

---

710. Related by al-Ṭabarāni.

Al-Ṭabarāni's version is slightly different, as it quotes Qurrah as saying: 'When we were with God's Messenger, and hoped to gain...' In other words, the statement is not a direct advice, but a report which explains the practice to be followed. It provides an aspect of God's grace as He rewards the person who departs and greets his fellows on departing for whatever good takes place in their meeting even after his departure.

The *ḥadīth* also adds a different point, which shows that Muslims should always take the opportunity of meeting together in order to help each other maintain the path that earns God's reward. If they were to limit themselves to gossip and idle talk in their meeting, then that meeting is not much better than sitting next to a dead donkey's corpse. The description is very vivid, as is the case in all *ḥadīths*. Mentioning God's name and remembering Him happens when people exchange greetings as they meet. A newcomer may only say *al-salām 'alaykum*, but the greeting includes God's name *Salām*. The reply is likely to be even better adding a wish for God's grace to be given to the one who offered the greeting.

The Islamic greeting is encouraged in all situations. Indeed, the proper practice includes situations where other people might not even think of offering a greeting.

1014. (*Athar* 237) Abu Hurayrah said: 'Whoever meets his brother should greet him. If [they are walking together and] a tree or a wall separates them, then they are back together, he should greet him anew'.[711]

1015. Anas ibn Mālik reports: 'The Prophet's companions might be walking together and a tree happened to be along their way. As they walked past it some of them walked to the right and some to the left. When they rejoined each other again, they offered a greeting to one another'.[712]

We can easily imagine the situation, with two friends walking together and at one point a tree or some sort of barrier makes them part so

711. Related by Abū Dāwūd.
712. Related by al-Ṭabarāni.

as to walk on either side. This is a momentary separation. Indeed they may continue to talk without thinking of stopping while they walk past the tree. Yet it is recommended for both of them to renew their greeting by saying it again. The second *ḥadīth* suggests that this was common practice among the Prophet's companions. Today, our practice is different, because we have lost our sense of what a greeting of peace means in terms of strengthening social relations. The sooner we revive such practices, the more closely knit our community will be.

1016. (*Athar* 238) Thābit al-Bunāni reports that Anas ibn Mālik used to apply in the morning fine smelling ointment to his hand in readiness to shake hands with his brethren.

It is normal practice in Muslim society to shake hands when people meet. This has been the case right from the time of the Prophet. Therefore, some scholars encourage using perfume on one's hands so that the smell should rub onto others as hands are shaken.

1017. 'Abdullāh ibn 'Amr ibn al-'Āṣ reports: 'A man said: "Messenger of God! Which [aspects of] Islam are best?" The Prophet answered: "You feed others, and offer greetings to people you know and people you do not know".'[713]

This is perhaps the clearest example of how Islam wants its followers to be friendly with others. The man was asking about the best qualities or aspects of Islamic behaviour. The Prophet does not mention any acts of worship that are obligatory to all Muslims, although offering these in the proper manner is certain to earn great reward from God. Instead, he emphasises social qualities. The first is to feed others. The Prophet does not specify whether the feeding should be limited to poor people, or people who do not have the means to feed themselves because of extreme poverty. Although these are the ones most in need of care, and feeding them is certainly encouraged at all times, the *ḥadīth* is general here. Hence, it includes all feeding of other people,

713. Related by al-Bukhari, Muslim, al-Nasā'ī, Abū Dāwūd, Ibn Mājah, Ibn Ḥibbān and Abu 'Awānah.

including relatives, neighbours and friends; rich and poor. It is an important way of strengthening social ties. Hence, the Prophet gives it particular emphasis.

The second quality he mentions is to offer greetings to all, whether we know them or not. The Prophet's teaching here is very specific. It attaches an added value to the bond of brotherhood that exists between all Muslims. Other *ḥadīths* make it clear that unbelievers and hypocrites are excluded from this teaching. This means that when we know someone to be a total unbeliever or a confirmed hypocrite, we do not offer our greetings to him. In all other situations, we try to take the opportunity of being the first to greet them.

1018. Abu Hurayrah reports: 'God's Messenger (peace be upon him) prohibited sitting in front of houses and on the road. Muslims said: "We cannot do it; it is very hard to avoid". He said: "If you would not, then give the road its due". They asked what its due was. The Prophet said: "That you lower your gaze, give guidance to people asking for directions, bless a person who praises God after he sneezes and reply to greetings".'[714]

What the Prophet sought when he ordered that sitting by the roadside should be stopped was that people should learn how to behave towards their fellow Muslims if they have to sit nearby. In this way, the Prophet gave added emphasis to what he then specified. Thus, people sitting near the road must not stare fixedly at others. They should be helpful to people who are unsure which direction to follow. They should also bless a person if he sneezes and praises God, and they must reply to greetings.

1019. (*Athar* 239) Abu Hurayrah said: 'The most miserly person is one who is stingy with his greetings. The one who does not reply to a greeting does himself an injustice. If a tree separates you from your brother, try to be the one who greets the other. Let him not beat you to it'.

---

714. Related by Abū Dāwūd.

This *ḥadīth* emphasises the point mentioned earlier and makes it clear that everyone should be keen to offer a new greeting when we meet again after passing an impediment that may separate us for a moment. This is a competition for greater reward from God. It is also instrumental in providing a relaxed atmosphere.

We also note how this *ḥadīth* begins. It defines the most miserly of people as the one who is stingy with his greetings. It is very difficult to relate miserliness to the normal practice of offering greetings to others. Yet some people begrudge others the very simple gesture of a greeting. Hence, the *ḥadīth* describes these as the most stingy of people.

When a greeting is offered, it must be returned. The Islamic rule requires that it should be returned with a better greeting, or at least the same one. Yet some people do not bother to reply, particularly if the one who is offering the greeting is felt to be below them. This *ḥadīth* describes a person who does not reply to a greeting as one who injures himself. It is a self-inflicted injustice. Hence, he is hard done by, although the injustice he suffers is of his own doing.

Because of all this emphasis on greeting, Muslims developed an extremely friendly way of greeting one another. They do not confine their greeting to the verbal form; they also shake hands and make other gestures, particularly with close relatives and intimate friends. This is the case in most situations.

1020. (*Athar* 240) Sālim, ʿAbdullāh ibn ʿAmr's servant, said: 'When Ibn ʿAmr was greeted, he returned the greeting adding to it. I came to him once and said, *al-salām ʿalaykum*, or 'peace be to you'. He replied, '*wa ʿalaykum al-salām wa raḥmatullāh*'. I came to him another time and said, '*al-salām ʿalaykum wa raḥmatullāh*'. He replied, '*wa ʿalaykum al-salām wa raḥmatullāh wa barakātuh*'. I came to him a third time and said, '*al-salām ʿalaykum wa raḥmatullāh wa barākatuh*'. He replied, '*wa ʿalaykum al-salām wa raḥmatullāh wa barakātuh wa ṭayyib ṣalawātih*'.

It is a clear Qur'anic injunction that says: '*When a greeting is offered you, answer it with an even better greeting, or [at least] with its like. God keeps count of all things*'. (4: 86) In this *ḥadīth* we note that ʿAbdullāh ibn ʿAmr implements the instruction fully, opting for a better reply each time. The first time, his servant merely offered the greeting of peace. In his reply, 'Abdullāh added God's mercy. When the servant added this in his greeting, 'Abdullāh mentioned the same and added God's blessings. The servant wanted to see his response when he offered the full greeting. 'Abdullāh returned it fully and added God's special blessings.

People not to be greeted

In our discussion of greetings and their importance in Islamic social behaviour, we emphasised that it is good to offer greetings to all people, whether we know them or not. So does this include everyone regardless of their behaviour, habits, attitude to Islam, etc?

1021. (*Athar* 241) 'Abdullah ibn 'Amr ibn al-'Āṣ said: 'Do not offer greetings to those who regularly drink'.[715]

Although this *ḥadīth* is reported in a way which infers that the statement is made by 'Abdullāh ibn 'Amr, it is agreed by all scholars that no companion of the Prophet would make such a statement, which is specifically related to religious injunctions, unless he had directly heard it from the Prophet. The Prophet's companions' reluctance to attribute such statements to the Prophet is due to their fear that they might replace one word with another of similar import, or even with a synonym. They were worried lest this might fall under telling an untruth. The fact that al-Bukhari includes it in his *Ṣaḥīḥ* anthology confirms that it comes from the Prophet.

This *ḥadīth* provides a clear order not to offer a greeting of peace, i.e. *al-salām 'alaykum,* to a person who habitually drinks alcohol. The reason is clear. Drinking is one of the grave sins under Islamic law. A person who habitually violates this rule is not worthy of a greeting that uses one of God's names, *Salām*. Besides, a drunken person may not appreciate what is being said to him. He may take a serious statement in a frivolous manner. If such a statement uses a name of God, his frivolity may become very offensive.

---

715. Related by al-Bukhari.

1022. (*Athar* 242) Al-Ḥasan said: 'There should be no gesture of respect between you and a transgressor'.

1023. (*Athar* 243) Abu Zurayq said: 'I heard 'Ali ibn 'Abdullāh [ibn al-'Abbās] expressing dislike for *ishtranj* and ṣaying: "Do not greet the one who plays it. It is a kind of gambling".'

These two reports suggest that greetings should not be offered to people who habitually violate Islamic rules, resorting to what is forbidden. However, the word *ishtranj* used in the second report is a Persian word which normally refers to chess. Chess is considered permissible by major schools of Islamic law, including al-Shāfi'i School, because it is a game of skill and talent. Hence, the report is understood by scholars to refer to backgammon as it is a game of chance, and games of chance are not permissible.

1024. 'Ali ibn Abu Ṭālib reports: 'The Prophet passed by a group of people among whom there was one who had used some feminine makeup. The Prophet looked at them and greeted them with *salām*, but he turned away from that man. The man asked him: "Why have you turned away from me?" The Prophet said: "You have a brand of fire in between your eyes".'

It is clear that the man had something that was totally unbecoming according to Islamic social standards. The makeup he had used was visible on his face and it was specifically feminine. The Prophet wanted to show him his disapproval, and to teach others so that they might realise that such behaviour is unacceptable from an Islamic point of view. Rather than tell him in a direct manner, the Prophet wanted him to realise that there was something unacceptable about him. When the Prophet turned away from him, the man realised that there was something wrong and enquired. The Prophet pointed out his mistake and gave it a highly graphic description so that the man would not do it again. His description serves as a warning to Muslims in following generations.

1025. ʿAbdullāh ibn ʿAmr reports: 'A man came to the Prophet wearing a gold ring. The Prophet turned away from him. When the man noticed that the Prophet disliked it, he went away and threw the ring away, wearing instead a ring made of iron. He came to the Prophet again, but the Prophet told him: "This is worse. This is the adornment of the people of hell". The man went away again and threw the ring away and put on a silver ring. The Prophet did not comment'.

This *ḥadīth* shows what we always say about Islam steering a middle road in all aspects. It leans neither towards excess nor towards stringency. It does not approve of gold and silk for men, but it does not advocate a harsh attitude that shuns comfort, good appearance and enjoyment. The Prophet did not approve of the man wearing an iron ring, but approved a silver one.

We also note that in both *ḥadīths*, we see the Prophet turning away from a man to indicate his disapproval of something in his appearance. This is an aspect of the Prophet's delicate approach in order not to cause his companion much embarrassment. He simply shows his disapproval by a gesture to invite the man to enquire about the cause. A similar *ḥadīth* provides even more detailed information about what is unacceptable for a man to wear.

1026. Abu Saʿīd al-Khudri reports: 'A man from the Bahrain[716] came to the Prophet and offered him the greeting of peace, but the Prophet did not reply to his greeting. The man was wearing a gold ring and a silk coat. The man left feeling very sad. He told his wife what happened, and she said: "It may be that the Prophet did not like your coat and ring. Take them off and go back to him". He acted on his wife's advice, and the Prophet returned his greeting this time. The man said to the Prophet: "I came to you earlier but you turned away from me". The Prophet said: "You had a brand of fire in your hand". He said:

716. In its early usage around the time of the Prophet, Bahrain referred to the entire area between Basra in Southern Iraq and Oman. It should not be understood that the man came from what is now the Kingdom of Bahrain.

"Then I have brought with me too many brands of fire". The Prophet said: "What you have brought with you does not do anyone much better than the stones of the Harrah [the area of volcanic rock near Madinah], but it is, nevertheless, part of the enjoyment of the life of this world". The man asked what he should use for a ring. The Prophet said: "Silver, or brass or metal".'[717]

In this case the man was wearing the two things that are forbidden for Muslim men: silk and gold. Hence, the Prophet's attitude to him. He did not reply to his greeting; but turned away from him. Apparently the man was a sensitive person who wished to do what is proper. His complaint to his wife shows that he was distressed over the Prophet's reaction. When he realised the strong disapproval of wearing gold, he remarked that the jewellery he had with him was to be treated like fire brands. The Prophet takes this opportunity to explain that gold is in no way superior to volcanic stones, which are of little use to anyone. However, people may use it in their business in this life. It is an ornament and a means to complete transactions. When we treat it in this way, it is fine to use, but if we consider that it gives its owner a higher position, we are wrong.

The last part of this *ḥadīth* makes it appropriate to wear a ring made of metals of lesser value. However, other *ḥadīths* are clear in disapproving of iron or brass rings. To reconcile these *ḥadīths*, scholars say that an iron or brass ring with some silver lines is appropriate, but one with nothing extra is discouraged.

Greeting rulers

1027. (*Athar* 244) 'Umar ibn 'Abd al-'Azīz asked Abu Bakr ibn Sulaymān: 'Why did Abu Bakr write [starting his letters]: "From Abu Bakr, God's Messenger's *Khalīfah* [i.e. successor]..." and then 'Umar wrote "From 'Umar ibn al-Khaṭṭāb, Abu Bakr's *Khalīfah*?

717. Related by Aḥmad and al-Nasā'ī.

Who was the first to write *Amīr al-Mu'minīn*?"[718] He replied: "My grandmother, al-Shifā' (who was one of the first migrant women. When 'Umar ibn al-Khaṭṭāb came into the market, he used to visit her.) related this to me:

'Umar ibn al-Khaṭṭāb wrote to the Governor of Kufah and Basrah to send him two strong men of high calibre to give him information about Iraq and its people. The governor sent to him Labīd ibn Rabī'ah and 'Adiy ibn Ḥātim. When they arrived in Madinah, they sat their camels outside the mosque and entered the mosque where they saw 'Amr ibn al-'Āṣ. They said to him: ''Amr, request permission for us to see Amīr al-Mu'minīn, 'Umar'. 'Amr immediately entered 'Umar's room and said: '*al-salām 'alayk ya Amīr al-Mu'minīn,* [i.e. peace be to you]'. 'Umar said: 'What has given you, Ibn al-'Āṣ, the idea to address me with this name? You have to give me an explanation?' He said: 'Yes, Labīd in Rabī'ah and 'Adiy ibn Ḥātim have just arrived and said to me: Request permission for us to see Amīr al-Mu'minīn'. I said: 'You have certainly got the right title for him: he is the ruler [i.e. Amīr] and we are the believers, [i.e. al-Mu'minīn]'. The title was used ever since".'[719]

This *ḥadīth* is self-explanatory. However, we may point out that neither of the first two Caliphs sought any of the titles that magnify the role of ruler. Both used the word, khalīfah, or caliph, which means 'successor', and each used it in its linguistic sense. Abu Bakr described himself as successor to God's messenger in his position as a ruler, and 'Umar as Abu Bakr's successor. However, the term was felt to be unsuitable as the succession would continue. May be some of the Prophet's companions were thinking on these lines, and considering what title should be given to the ruler of the Muslim state. Hence, 'Amr ibn al-'Āṣ's reaction to the title used by the two men: Amīr al-Mu'minīn. 'Amīr' means 'prince, commander or ruler'.

718. Amīr al-Mu'minīn was the official title of the caliph, starting with 'Umar ibn al-Khaṭṭāb. It means 'the leader or governor of the believers'. It is still used by the King of Morocco. Other rulers of Muslim states may at times resort to it to indicate that they are religious.

719. Related by Ibn 'Abd al-Barr in Al-Istī'āb.

A person in that post is honoured to be the head of a community of believers.

We may refer briefly to the people mentioned in this *ḥadīth*, six of whom were companions of the Prophet. The three best known ones are Abu Bakr, ʿUmar and ʿAmr. The reporter of the *ḥadīth* is quoting his grandmother, al-Shifā' bint ʿAbdullāh ibn ʿAbd Shams. She belonged to the ʿAdiy clan of the Quraysh, Umar's own clan. She embraced Islam in its early days in Makkah, and migrated with her son Sulaymān to Madinah when the Muslims were instructed by the Prophet to leave Makkah. She was a very wise and respectable woman. The Prophet used to visit her at home, and he would at times have his afternoon nap at her place. Therefore, she had a special mattress for him to use. ʿUmar appointed her as controller of the market in Madinah, which was a highly significant position. She was also well informed in medicine. ʿUmar also assigned some aspects of supervision in the market to her son, Sulaymān, who was also a wise man whom ʿUmar often asked for advice.

Prior to Islam, Labīd ibn Rabīʿah was a fine and renowned poet. In fact, he was one of seven poets who acquired greater fame than the rest, when they placed their masterpieces on the walls of the Kaʿbah in pre-Islamic days. He then embraced Islam, but did not write much poetry in his Islamic days, because he devoted himself to the Qur'an. He was a strong man and a good fighter. When this event took place, he must have been over 60 years of age, but he lived to very old age. It is said that when he died, during or after Muʿāwiyah's reign, he was around 120 years old.

ʿAdiy ibn Ḥātim was the son of the man who is known in Arabian history as the most generous and hospitable. This in a land that valued generosity and hospitality among the main virtues honourable people should have. In his pre-Islamic days, ʿAdiy was a Christian and the chief of his tribe, the Ṭayyi'. He tried hard not to meet the Prophet or listen to his message. However, his sister was taken captive by the Muslims, and the Prophet was very kind to her. When a group of her people arrived in Madinah, he sent her with them so that she could return safely to her people. She advised her brother to go and see the Prophet, which he did and recognised him as God's last messenger. He then became one of the most committed among the Prophet's companions. He fought in many battles during the reigns of Abu Bakr, 'Umar and 'Uthmān, and also fought alongside 'Ali in his main battles of Ṣiffīn and al-Nahrawān. He too lived to a very old age, having lived more than sixty years after becoming a Muslim. Although he was the chief of his people, he was a modest man. When he became very old and could not sit comfortably on the floor, he requested his people's permission to use a chair. He feared that if he did not explain, they might have thought that he wanted to be seen above them. The thought was far from his mind.

When we look at this *ḥadīth*, we have a glimpse of life in the early Islamic period. 'Umar ibn 'Abd al-Azīz asks a scholar about the title with which he is addressed as the ruler of the Muslim world. The scholar quotes his grandmother, a companion of the Prophet. On the other hand, 'Amr uses the title he feels best suited to the Muslim ruler, but credits it to the ones who were the first to use it. 'Umar, the Caliph, wants to know about the people of the area that has come under his rule. His governor meets his request, sending him two of the wisest and most intelligent people to give him a clear picture.

Some people who have high position in government are sensitive about the way they are addressed. More often their subordinates take issue on this particular point. They may feel that a person who does not address the ruler, governor or president properly may do so deliberately, to imply lack of recognition, respect or loyalty.

1028. (*Athar* 245) 'Ubaydillāh ibn 'Abdullāh reports: 'When Mu'āwiyah came [to Madinah] on his first pilgrimage after becoming the Caliph, he was visited by 'Uthmān ibn Ḥunayf al-Anṣāri. 'Uthmān offered his greeting, saying: "*al-salāmu 'alayk ayyuha al-Amīr wa raḥmatullāh*", which means: "Peace be to you, Amīr, together with God's mercy". The people from Syria who were present objected, saying: "Who is this hypocrite whose greeting falls short of what is due to Amīr al-Mu'minīn?" 'Uthmān sat on his knees and said: "Amīr al-Mu'minīn! These people are taking issue with me over something that you know better than them. By God, I have used the same greeting to address Abu Bakr, 'Umar and 'Uthmān. None of them raised any objection". Mu'āwiyah said to the Syrians who made the objection: "Cool down! What he says is largely true". He also said to 'Uthmān: "When these troubles took place, the people from Syria made it clear that the address to the Caliph should never be shortened. I think that you, the people of Madinah, use the same word, Amīr, even to an employee collecting zakat".'[720]

The first point to be said here is that there was nothing wrong with 'Uthmān's greeting of the Caliph, because he acknowledged him as the ruler or commander. He, however, used the word *amīr* on its own, without qualifying it by adding '*al-Mu'minīn*'. Thus, it can be taken in its more general sense as a person who is in a position of command. But this could be a command over a couple of people, or a limited area, as well as a command over the whole state. Thus, it could be taken as implying non-recognition of Mu'āwiyah as the overall ruler of the Muslim state. The sensitivity of the Syrian people in Mu'āwiyah's company immediately surfaced in their impulsive reaction. Yet the man at the centre of this was one of the Prophet's companions, the most honourable people in Islamic history.

'Uthmān protests that he used the same greeting with the first three Caliphs, without encountering any objection. Those were the rulers who least cared for the paraphernalia associated with the post. They wanted to be addressed as men of their people. Mu'āwiyah acknowledges this, and explains to 'Uthmān the sensitivity. He also points out to him that the word he used is often mentioned by the people of Madinah when they speak to practically any government official.

Such sensitivity of rulers and people in their company is well known. However, sometimes, it is positive, when the ruler sees himself only as one of the people. He does not want to be distinguished by exaggerated address.

We find this in the following *ḥadīth*, concerning al-Mughīrah ibn Shu'bah, a companion of the Prophet, when he was governor of Kufah in Iraq.

---

720. Related by 'Abd al-Razzāq in Al-Muṣannaf.

1029. (*Athar* 246) Jābir reports: 'I entered al-Ḥajjāj's place but I did not greet him'.[721]

Al-Ḥajjāj played an important role in consolidating the Umayyad rule after a period of trouble. He fought fierce battles in Iraq and Hijaz, including Makkah itself, to crush opponents. He then became the governor of Iraq.

Jābir ibn 'Abdullāh was a companion of the Prophet belonging to the Anṣār and he was close to the Prophet, reporting a large number of *ḥadīths*. He died in 74 AH at the age of 94. He lost his eyesight when he was very old. We cannot determine the time when he visited al-Ḥajjāj, or why he did this. Most probably this occurred after al-Ḥajjāj fought 'Abdullāh ibn al-Zubayr in Makkah in year 73 AH and killed him. Jābir was much displeased with al-Ḥajjāj's action of fighting in Makkah. This explains the reason for not greeting him. We surmise that he did not visit al-Ḥajjāj at his own initiative; rather, the latter sent for him and he attended him, hoping to restrain his harsh action.

1030. (*Athar* 247) Tamīm ibn Hidhlam says: 'I well remember the first one to be addressed as Amīr in Kufah. Al-Mughīrah ibn Shu'bah once went out through Bab al-Raḥbah when a man from Kindah, probably Abu Qurrah, came to him and greeted him saying: "Peace be to you, Amīr, and God's mercy. Peace be to you all". Al-Mughīrah was not pleased. He, therefore, repeated the same words: "Peace be to you, Amīr, and God's mercy. Peace be to you all! Am I one of them or not?"'

The point at issue here is the usage of pronouns in the greeting offered to the governor. The man addresses him in the singular 'you' to make the greeting personal to him. He follows this with a greeting to the people present, using a plural form of 'you'. Al-Mughīrah did not like this, because he wanted to be treated as one of the group, without distinction. Hence, his words as he repeated the form in disapproval: 'Am I one of them or not?' This means that a greeting in the plural

---

721. Related by al-Ḥākim.

form, addressed to the group, was sufficient. The one addressed to him personally was unnecessary.

A different aspect of sensitivity is shown by Ruwayfi' ibn Thābit, an Anṣāri companion of the Prophet, who was a governor of Antablus, a city between Alexandria in Egypt and Barqah in today's Libya.

1031. (*Athar* 248) Ziyād ibn 'Ubayd reports: 'We visited to Ruwayfi' when he was a governor of Antablus. A man came in and offered a greeting saying, "Peace be to the Amīr." ('Abdah – another reporter – puts the greeting offerd as "Peace be to you, Amīr".) Ruwayfi' said to him: "Had you offered a greeting to us, we would have certainly returned your greeting. You are only greeting Maslamah ibn Makhlad [the ruler of Egypt]. Go to him and he will reply to your greeting".' Ziyad adds: 'When we came to visit him in his council room, we would only say: "Peace be to you", using the plural form.'

This companion of the Prophet was a local governor of an area affiliated to the governor of Egypt. He felt that the title Amīr was too large for his office. Hence, he objected to the man using this form of address. He told him in a polite manner that it was a title more suited to the governor of Egypt, who was his superior, rather than to him. This is yet another example of how the Prophet's companions looked at positions of authority. They did not feel that it gave them any particular distinction. They showed this in both word and deed.

1032. Al-Miqdād ibn al-Aswad reports: 'The Prophet used to come in at night, when he would offer a greeting in a voice that would not disturb anyone asleep, but would be heard by whoever was awake.'[722]

This *ḥadīth* shows how caring the Prophet was. He made sure that he did not wake up anyone sleeping. Yet at the same time, he greeted those who were awake. In so doing, he showed by practical example that the one sleeping should be given time to so rest by others in close

722. Related by Muslim.

proximity. They were to do this by speaking in low voices and avoiding all noise. It is well known that the Prophet's companions were always keen to emulate him, knowing that he provided the best example, even in matters where no religious edict was necessary.

1033. (*Athar* 249) Al-Sha'bi reports that 'Umar said to 'Adiy ibn Ḥātim: 'May God greet you, as you are a splendid person to know.'

As noted earlier, 'Adiy ibn Ḥātim was the tribal chief of Ṭayy'. As a Christian Arab, he was able to ascertain that Prophet Muhammad was God's final messenger and he believed in Islam. Thereafter, he was exemplary in his service to the Islamic cause. Therefore, it was natural that 'Umar should welcome him warmly. This is a practice he learnt from the Prophet who greeted certain people in a way that indicated how highly he valued them.

1034. 'Ā'ishah reports: 'Fāṭimah came along; she walked just like the Prophet used to walk. He said: "Welcome to my daughter", then he sat her to his right or perhaps to his left'.[723]

1035. 'Ali reports: ''Ammār sought admission to see the Prophet. The Prophet recognised his voice and said: "Welcome to the goodly person, enhanced in goodness".'[724]

The first *ḥadīth* is given in longer versions in Numbers 950 and 974. The second *ḥadīth* refers to 'Ammār who was one of the earliest people to embrace Islam. As he did not belong to the Quraysh tribe, but was only an ally, he was vulnerable to the Quraysh's terror campaign against weaker Muslims. In fact, his parents were the first two martyrs in Islamic history, both tortured to death as Abu Jahl directed the campaign of persecution. 'Ammār suffered much torture but survived, and he was one of the best servants of the Islamic cause. Hence, the Prophet's welcome, which indicated that the Prophet valued 'Ammār and loved him.

723. Related by al-Bukhari and Muslim.
724. Related by al-Tirmidhi and Ibn Majah.

An important point one should know about greeting is how best to reply. The essential rule is that given in the Qur'an: '*When a greeting is offered you, answer it with an even better greeting, or [at least] with its like. God keeps count of all things.*' (4: 86)

1036. 'Abdullāh ibn 'Amr reports: 'As we were sitting with the Prophet in the shade of a tree in between Makkah and Madinah, a very rough and uncouth bedouin came over and said: *al-salām 'alaykum*. They replied: "And to you".'

There was something wrong with the attitude of the bedouin to make the reporter of this *ḥadīth*, a learned scholar among the Prophet's companions, describe him as very rough and uncouth. This accounts for the way his greeting was returned, just the same as it was offered. Otherwise, it is well known to all Muslims that the normal return Islamic greeting adds a prayer to the offered greeting.

1037. (*Athar* 250) Abu Jamrah reports: 'I heard Ibn 'Abbās when he replied to greetings offered to him by saying: "*Wa 'alayk; wa raḥmatullāh*".'

1038. Qaylah bint Makhramah, a lady companion of the Prophet, reports: 'A man said: "*Al-salām 'alayk*, Messenger of God." The Prophet answered: "*Wa 'alayk al-salām wa raḥmatullāh*".'[725]

1039. Abu Dharr reports: 'I came to the Prophet when he had just finished his prayer, and I was the first one to offer him the Islamic greeting. He said: "And to you; together with God's mercy. From which tribe are you?" I said: "From Ghifār".'[726]

1040. 'Ā'ishah reports: 'God's Messenger (peace be upon him) said to me: "'Ā'ish, this is Gabriel, giving you his greetings of salām". I said: "And to him I wish peace together with God's

725. Related by al-Tirmidhi.

726. Related by in a longer version stating how Abu Dharr came to embrace Islam.

mercy and blessings. You, [Messenger of God], see what I do not".'[727]

1041. (*Athar* 251) Mu'āwiyah ibn Qurrah says that his father, a companion of the Prophet, said to him: 'Son, if a man passes by you and says *Al-salām 'alaykum,* do not reply saying, *wa 'alayk,* as though you are greeting him on his own. Rather, say: *al-salām 'alaykum.*'

From these *ḥadīths* we learn that the form we use now is the final one while earlier the Prophet used other forms. The singular form, *'alayk,* was used by the Prophet and his companions, but we note that whenever the Prophet used this form he always added a prayer for mercy to be granted to the one who offered the greeting. We also note that 'Ā'ishah returned Gabriel's greeting with the full form adding a prayer for God's mercy and blessings. Indeed, the Prophet's companions instructed their children in the proper manner of replying to a greeting. When it is offered in the singular, the reply should be in the plural.

Therefore, we need always to refer to the Qur'anic instruction, replying to a greeting with a better one, or at least with its like. Hence, if one is offered a greeting in the plural form and replies in the singular without adding a prayer, then he has not complied with Qur'anic instructions. Moreover, the singular form suggests that the reply is given to the person on his own. Islamic manners require that one uses the plural form even when the person offering the greeting is alone. The Prophet's habitual practice was to use the plural form and to reply with a better greeting at the same time.

Grudging a greeting

It is not unknown in human behaviour that some people do not reply to a greeting when one is offered to them. What should our attitude be when we experience such an un-Islamic and uncivilised attitude?

---

727. Related in all six authentic anthologies.

1042. ʿAbdullāh ibn al-Ṣāmit reports: 'I said to Abu Dharr: "I passed by ʿAbd al-Raḥmān ibn Umm al-Ḥakam and offered him the greeting of peace, but he did not reply to me." He said: "My nephew, how does that affect you? Someone better than him has replied to you: an angel to his right".'

ʿAbd al-Raḥmān ibn Umm al-Ḥakam bint Abu Sufyān was the son of Muʿāwiyah's sister and his father was a man from the Thaqīf tribe called ʿAbdullāh ibn ʿUthmān. His uncle, Muʿāwiyah gave him several posts, including the governorship of Kufah, but people were displeased with him. Therefore, Muʿāwiyah sacked him saying: 'Son, I have tried to promote you, but you insist on being hard to sell.' There are other reports which suggest that he was self-centred. Perhaps he felt it beneath his position to be accosted by ordinary people. Hence, he did not reply to greetings. Abu Dharr consoles the man who greeted him, because he was hurt. He told him that his greeting was certainly returned by an angel, even though he himself did not hear it.

Abu Dharr would not have made such an assertion unless he had heard it from the Prophet. This is confirmed by the following report:

1043. ʿAbdullah ibn Masʿūd said: 'Salām is one of God's names, but He has chosen to place it on earth. Therefore, spread it among you. A man who offers a greeting of peace to others and who then reply to him earns a step over them, because he reminded them of the greeting of peace, or salām. If his addressee does not return his greeting, it is returned by someone better than him'.[728]

This *ḥadīth* again confirms that the Islamic greeting uses one of God's names, Salam, which means peace. Thus, it is intended to generate an atmosphere of peace within the Muslim community. Moreover, it earns a reward for the person offering it and the one returning the greeting, because both mention God. If some people grudge returning a greeting, this should not be disheartening or cause any of us to

---

728. Related by al-Bayhaqi, Ibn Abu Shaybah, al-Bazzar and al-Tabarani, with some giving a direct quotation from the Prophet.

abandon the highly recommended practice of offering greetings to others. We should know that a greeting is always returned, either by the greeted person or by an angel close to him. Moreover, the one who starts earns a better position because of using God's name and reminding others to use it. The one who does not return a greeting puts himself in the wrong position:

1044. (*Athar* 252) Al-Ḥasan said: 'To offer a greeting is highly recommended, and to return a greeting is obligatory'.

Thus, a person who does not reply to a greeting fails to perform a clear duty. As a result, he makes himself open to God's punishment. Furthermore, such a person is very miserly.

1045. (*Athar* 253) 'Abdullāh ibn 'Amr said: 'A confirmed liar is a person who lies against his oath; a miser is the one who is stingy with his greetings; and a thieving person is one who knocks off his prayers very quickly'.

1046. (*Athar* 254) Abu Hurayrah reports: 'The most miserly person is the one who begrudges greetings, and the most lacking in ability is one who is unable to pray to God'.

This *ḥadīth* uses an adjectival form that implies a higher degree of the three qualities it describes. Thus, it speaks of a confirmed liar who does not hesitate to lie. This is when a person lies despite having taken an oath to the contrary. Thus, his assertion flies in his face to condemn him as a confirmed liar. Similarly, a person who knocks off his prayer, without allowing himself time to properly fulfil its requirements, aiming to finish it very quickly is described as a thieving person. He actually steals from himself, because in his hurry, he does not give proper attention to the various actions, recitation, glorification and praise of God, which are required in prayer. Hence, he deprives himself of much of the reward he would have earned. Thus, he steals from himself, and who is a worse loser than that? In the middle of these two qualities the Prophet places the one who begrudges others a greeting of peace, either by not replying to their greetings or not offering a greeting when he should have. Such a person is on a higher degree of miserliness.

The second *ḥadīth* speaks in the superlative degree, condemning one who does not greet others, or who does not reply to their greetings, as the most miserly of people. Such a person is placed on a par with one who is unable to pray to God for what he wants. God listens to our prayer, no matter in what language or how clearly stated they are. He knows what we think, say or do. Thus, we only need to appeal to Him, putting our request in such a way as we would to a person we are most familiar with. It is a matter of articulating what we feel and need. This is a simple thing that all people, regardless of their degree of education, eloquence or intellectual ability, can easily do. To feel unable to pray to God is certainly a mark of the worst disability.

1047. Thābit al-Bunāni reports: 'Anas ibn Mālik passed by young boys and offered the greeting of peace to them. He then said: "The Prophet (peace be upon him) used to do this".'[729]

1048. (*Athar* 255) 'Anbasah reports: 'I saw Ibn 'Umar greeting young boys in their elementary school'.

The Prophet has taught us in every possible way that greeting others is to be praised and rewarded. He used to greet all people including young children. When we follow his example, we not only follow the right path, but also earn reward from God. Hence, we should know that greeting children is a commendable action that earns reward for us, in addition to the fact that it teaches these children to be sociable.

Greeting men and women

One thing that troubles people in certain societies is exchanging greetings with members of the opposite sex. Yet there is no problem in this, as long as the values of propriety are observed.

729. Related by al-Bukhari, Muslim, Abu Dāwūd and Ibn Mājah.

1049. Umm Hānī' bint Abu Ṭālib, the Prophet's cousin, said: 'I went to visit the Prophet and found him taking a bath. I greeted him, and he asked: "Who is the lady?" I said: Umm Hānī'. He said: "Welcome".'[730]

1050. Al-Ḥasan reports: 'Women used to greet men'.

The first *ḥadīth* is highly authentic and it tells us the fact that even though the Prophet was taking a bath, this did not stop his cousin from greeting him. Of course, they did not see each other as they exchanged the greeting. This is made even clearer by the fact that on hearing the greeting, the Prophet asked who the woman greeting him was. We also note that the Prophet did not use the normal form of greeting, which mentions the word Salam. This is because this word, which means peace, is also one of God's names. Hence, it should not be mentioned in the bathroom. Therefore, the Prophet replied to his cousin's greeting by telling her that she was welcome.

The second report is simply a statement making it clear that for women to greet men when they met them was normal practice. This is only to be expected in a Muslim society. However, a greeting can be offered verbally or by gesture.

1051. Asmā' bint Yazīd reports: 'The Prophet passed through the mosque when a group of women were seated. He signalled a greeting to them with his hand. Then he said: "Be careful not to deny other people's favours. Be careful not to deny other people's favours". One of them said: "Prophet, we seek shelter with God against denying God's favours". He said: "Indeed, a woman may stay unmarried for a long while. Then [after she marries] she may be upset [with her husband] and she may say: By God I never experienced an hour of goodness from him. This is a denial of God's favours and people's favours".'

1052. Asmā' bint Yazīd of the Anṣār reports: 'The Prophet passed by me when I was with some friends. He greeted us and

730. Related by in all six anthologies.

said: "Be careful not to deny people's favours". I was among the most forward in putting questions to him. I said: "Messenger of God! What is meant by denying favours?" He said: "Any of you may stay long unmarried in her parents' home. God then favours her with a husband and she begets a child. She may be angry one day and she denies [his kindness] and says [to him]: I have never seen anything good from you".'[731]

These two *ḥadīths* refer to the same occasion. Al-Bukhari enters them here because of the part concerning the Prophet's greeting to women. Whatever the Prophet did is certainly permissible. Hence, for a man to offer a greeting as he passes by a group of women is perfectly permissible. However, we need to say a word about the rest of the *ḥadīth*, which warns against a woman allowing her anger to make her deny her husband's past kindness. This is a terrible situation which leads to destroying a family in addition to its being a lie. Thus, it gives the woman concerned a very poor return both in this life and in the life to come. The proper attitude is to control one's anger and not to allow it to get the better of oneself. When a woman brings her anger under control, she is much less likely to deny the kindness shown to her by her husband. Needless to say, the same applies in reverse. In fact, anger management is highly important for everyone so that one does not say or do during a fit of anger what one may regret for a long time, or even for the rest of one's life.

Sometimes a person passes a group of people and offers a greeting mentioning some of them by name. This is objectionable because it ignores the presence of other people who are also entitled to be greeted.

1053. Ṭāriq ibn Shihāb who belonged to the *tābi'īn* generation, reports: 'We were sitting at 'Abdullāh ibn Mas'ūd's place when his servant came and said: "The prayer is called". He rose and we rose with him until we arrived at the mosque. He saw that those in the front of the mosque were bowing [i.e. in *rukū'*], so he started praying and bowed as well. We walked on and did like he did. A man walking fast passed by us and said: "Peace be to you,

731. Related by Abu Dāwūd, al-Tirmidhi, Ibn Mājah and al-Dārimi.

Abu 'Abd al-Raḥmān". He commented: "God certainly tells the truth and His messenger has delivered His message". After the prayers, he returned and entered his home. We remained outside waiting for him to come out again. Some of us were saying: "Who will ask him?" Ṭāriq said: "I will". He asked him [to explain his reply to the greeting by the man walking fast]. 'Abdullāh quoted the Prophet as saying: "As the Last Hour draws near, people will offer greetings specifying certain people; business will flourish to the extent that a woman would help her husband in business; ties of kinship will be severed; knowledge will be widely available; and perjury will emerge while honest testimony for the truth will be suppressed".'[732]

The first thing to note in this *ḥadīth* is that when a companion of the Prophet sees something to which the Prophet had referred, he immediately confirms that what is happening endorses the Prophet's statement. Here 'Abdullāh ibn Mas'ūd immediately refers to this *ḥadīth* because of hearing someone offering his greeting to a particular person among the group. This is objectionable, because a Muslim should offer his greeting to the group as a whole. The point of objection is very clear. When a greeting is offered to a particular person among a group, it signifies that the one offering the greeting does not care about the rest.

Perhaps it should be clarified that when the man passed by and offered the greeting, the group had finished their prayers. It is unlikely that he would offer a greeting to people engaged in prayer, even though the one he was addressing might have finished his own prayer.

We also note that 'Abdullāh's friends were eager to ask him about his comment, but they waited for him to give them the information. When they felt that it may not be forthcoming, they selected one of them to put the question to him. This is part of the good manners which people at the time felt they must observe with scholars and with the Prophet's companions. When the question was put to him, 'Abdullāh gave them the full statement by the Prophet, which mentions some of the indications of the closeness of the Day of Judgement. Some of the

---

732. Related by Aḥmad, al-Ḥākim, al-Bayhaqi and al-Ṭabarāni.

other indications relate to people's social lives, while some relate to the weakness of faith among them to the extent that perjury, a very grave sin, and suppression of the truth are practised in society.

1054. ʿAbdullāh ibn ʿAmr ibn al-ʿĀṣ reports: 'A man said: "Messenger of God! Which [aspects of] Islam are best?" The Prophet answered: "You feed others, and offer greetings to people you know and people you do not know".'[733]

This is the same as Number 1017.

733. Related by al-Bukhari, Muslim, al-Nasāʾi, Abu Dāwūd, Ibn Mājah, Ibn Ḥibbān and Abu ʿAwānah.

48

A Special Ruling for the Prophet's Wives

1055. Anas reports: 'I was ten years of age when God's Messenger arrived in Madinah. My mothers [meaning his mother and women related to her like her mother and sisters] were encouraging me to serve him. I indeed served him for ten years and he passed away when I was twenty. I am better aware than all people of the question of screening. It first started with the Prophet's marriage to Zaynab bint Jaḥsh. The day after he was wedded to her, he invited people for dinner. After they had eaten they left, except for a group of people who stayed long. Then the Prophet went out and I went out with him so that they might leave. He walked and I walked with him until he stopped at the threshold of 'Ā'ishah's room, when he thought they might have left. He returned and I returned with him and went into Zaynab's place. He found that they were still sitting there. So he returned, and I returned with him. He walked again until he reached the threshold of 'Ā'ishah's room. Again, thinking that they might have left, he returned and I returned with him. When he got there, they had already left. The Prophet put up a screen between him and me, and then the verse concerning the screening was revealed'.[734]

THE FIRST THING to mention here is that this event took place at the dinner the Prophet gave to his companions shortly after his marriage to Zaynab. This is normal practice, and a highly recommended Sunnah. It is part of the publicity given to marriage so that the new relationship, establishing a new family, becomes widely known. The Prophet gave such a dinner after every one of his marriages. At the time of the Prophet's marriage to Zaynab, which took place in the fifth year after his migration to Madinah, Muslims had not been instructed to speak to the Prophet's wives only from behind a screen. Therefore, the Prophet's wives appeared in public in the same way as other women. It is well known that the Prophet's wives held special status, which imposed on them certain restrictions that do not apply to other Muslim women. One of these was that they could only speak to men who are not their closest relatives from behind a screen. This is what is meant by the *ḥijāb* in Arabic. Muslims nowadays use this same word to indicate women's head covering when they appear in public. However, the linguistic and Islamic meaning of the word is a screen or a barrier that conceals what is behind it.

In this event, when the Prophet's guests had finished their dinner, it was time to go, but they stayed to talk. Then, when most guests had left, some stayed behind, absorbed by their conversation. The Prophet wanted them to leave because he wanted to be left alone with his new wife, but those guests were oblivious to the fact. The Prophet felt that he could not say anything if they wanted to stay. He was too shy even to politely indicate this. Therefore, he felt that if he left them there and disappeared for a short while they would notice. Hence, he walked out. He did not go away for long, because if his absence was prolonged and people noticed, they might feel offended, as it would indicate that they were not welcome in his place. Therefore, he walked only the short

734. Related by al-Bukhari, Muslim, al-Nasā'ī and al-Tirmidhi.

distance to 'Ā'ishah's room, but did not enter, and returned, feeling that they might have noticed and left.

It should be realised that the Prophet assigned rooms to each one of his wives, and these were next to each other, close to the mosque. So, his absence was short. This explains why his guests, absorbed as they were in their conversation, did not notice his absence on his first walk. They stayed behind. The Prophet felt that he could not do more than he did the first time. Therefore, he went out again, with his absence not lasting more than a few minutes each time, until the lingering guests decided to leave.

Anyone of us today facing a similar situation, finding his guests would rather stay while he is busy, will find a way to hasten their departure. There are different methods, and people resort to one or the other, according to their relationship with their guests. In the case of the Prophet, his companions were keen to do whatever pleased him once it was indicated. None of them would have stayed long, had they realised that the Prophet wanted to be alone. He could not indicate this to them in any pointed way because of his shyness. In fact, he is described by one of his companions as more shy than a maiden girl.

This event is mentioned in the Qur'an, in Verse 53 of *Surah* 33, which instructs the Prophet's companions that when they are invited to a meal at the Prophet's home, they should depart after they have had their dinner. They should not stay behind engaged in social conversation, because it is inconvenient for the Prophet. The verse mentions the Prophet's shyness and that he could not do anything in the circumstances. Therefore, the instruction comes from God.

The same verse mentions some of the restrictions imposed on the Prophet's wives. These included that the Prophet's wives could not marry anyone else after his death. The fact that these restrictions are specific to the Prophet's wives means that they may not be observed by other people. There is no encouragement for Muslim women to conduct their affairs on the same lines.

49

Privacy at Home

A VERSE IN the Qur'an mentions three times during the day and night when even children below the age of puberty should knock on the door before entering any room in the house where someone may be present. The verse says: '*Believers! Let those whom you rightfully possess, and those of you who have not yet attained to puberty, ask leave of you at three times of day: before the prayer of daybreak, and whenever you lay aside your garments in the middle of the day, and after the prayer of nightfall. These are three occasions on which you may happen to be undressed. Beyond these occasions, neither you nor they will incur any sin if they move freely about you, attending to one another*'. (24: 58)

1056. (*Athar* 256) Tha'labah ibn Abu Mālik al-Quraẓi mentioned that he rode to 'Abdullāh ibn Suwayd of the Ḥārithah ibn al-Ḥārith clan to ask him about the three times of undress. 'Abdullāh used to observe these three times.

Tha'labah said: 'He asked me: "What is your purpose?" I said: "I want to observe them". He said: "When I take off my garment at noon, none of my family who has reached puberty may enter my room without my permission, unless I call them, when my call is their permission. Nor do they come at dawnbreak when people are aware of it, until the [dawn] prayer has started. Nor do they come in after I have prayed Isha and taken off my garment in order to go to bed".'

This *ḥadīth* explains how the Qur'anic verse is put into practice. It applies to all societies. According to the Qur'anic verse, even young children should not see their parents undressed. Therefore, they are required to request permission to enter a room at these times when the likelihood of seeing someone undressed is greater than at other times. As for those who have attained puberty and adults, they should seek permission before entering any room at all times.

1057. 'Ā'ishah reports: 'I was eating *ḥays* [a mixture of dates, butter and flour] with the Prophet when 'Umar passed by. The Prophet invited him and he ate [with us]. 'Umar's hand touched my fingers and he said: "Oh! If I have my way about you [women], no eye would ever see you". Thereafter the command about the *ḥijāb* was revealed'.[735]

1058. Umm Ṣubayyah bint Qays said: 'My hand and the Prophet's hand were put in turn into one vessel'.[736]

These two *ḥadīths* indicate that the Muslim society in Madinah did not enforce strict segregation of men and women. It is clear that the first of these two *ḥadīths* took place before the Prophet's wives were required to remain behind a screen when they talked to people. However, the second *ḥadīth* shows that men and women could use the same vessel to perform their ablution. A *ḥadīth* quotes Ibn 'Umar: 'During the Prophet's lifetime, men and women used to perform their ablution

735. Related by al-Nasā'ī.

736. Related by Aḥmad, Abū Dāwūd, Ibn Mājah, Ibn Abu Shaybah and al-Ṭabarāni.

[i.e. *wuḍū*] together'.[737] Ibn Mājah's version of this *ḥadīth* adds: 'from the same vessel'. However, when the rules were established concerning women's garments, requiring them to cover their bodies except their faces and hands, this no longer applied except within the same family and with relatives that cannot get married, i.e. *maḥrams*.

1059. (*Athar* 257) 'Abdullāh ibn 'Umar said: 'When a person enters a house with no inhabitants, he should say: Peace be to us and to God's righteous servants'.[738]

1060. (*Athar* 258) Ibn 'Abbās said: 'God says: "*Believers! Do not enter houses other than your own unless you have obtained permission and greeted their people*". (24: 27) However, an exception is made: "*You will incur no sin if you enter uninhabited houses wherein there are things of use for you*".' (24: 29)

1061. (*Athar* 259) Ibn 'Umar referred to the verse that begins with '*Believers! Let those whom you rightfully possess*', and said: 'It applies to men but not to women'.

This *ḥadīth* explains a verse which requires us to offer a greeting on entering a home. God says: '*Whenever you enter houses, greet yourselves with a blessed, goodly greeting, as enjoined by God*'. (24: 61)

This Qur'anic statement is meant to greet the people in the house we enter, but it is phrased in this way to indicate the strong ties that bind people together in the Muslim community. Thus, when we greet our relatives or friends as we come into their homes, we are actually greeting ourselves, because we all belong to the same community. However, the statement is expressed in the indefinite form which applies on entering any house. So how do we carry this out if there is nobody in the house? It is this question that is answered by the *ḥadīth* we have just mentioned. In this case we should say a greeting to ourselves and include with us all goodly servants of God. This gives

---

737. Related by al-Bukhari, *Ḥadīth* No. 193.
738. Related by Ibn Abu Shaybah.

us a relaxed feeling on entering an empty home, instead of one that might be associated with loneliness.

Another aspect of good manners encouraged by Islam is given in the second *ḥadīth* which refers to the same *surah*, as it says: '*Believers! Do not enter houses other than your own unless you have obtained permission and greeted their people*'. (24: 27) Ibn 'Abbās explains that an exception is made in the case of entering certain houses: '*You will incur no sin if you enter uninhabited houses wherein there are things of use for you*'. (24: 29) This instruction relates only to premises of more or less a public nature, like shops, rest houses, administrative offices, etc. One does not need prior permission to enter such premises. As for private houses, the fact that they may be uninhabited does not give a right of entry to anyone. They still belong to their owners and cannot be entered without their permission.

Furthermore, when one's children attain puberty they should seek permission before entering their parents' rooms. This is clear in the Qur'anic verse: '*When the children among you attain to puberty, they should ask leave of you like those before them have been enjoined to ask it*'. (24: 59) This is a question of upbringing. When a child attains puberty, he or she is no longer a child. Therefore, they should not intrude on their parents' privacy without first seeking permission. We can easily think of different situations when parents would be embarrassed if their teenage children burst into their rooms without first knocking and are being given leave to enter. A father may be changing his clothes when his daughter enters, or a mother may have part of her body exposed when her son comes in. In order not to cause any such embarrassment, the instruction is given in this verse that such children should seek permission before entering their parents' rooms. This is reflected in the following *ḥadīth*:

1062. (*Athar* 260) Nāfi' said: 'Ibn 'Umar used to separate any of his children when they attained puberty. He required them to seek permission before entering his room'.

Some people may find this unnecessary. They wonder whether this puts a sort of barrier between parents and children. The fact is that it does not. It leads to more respect and kindness.

1063. (*Athar* 261) 'Alqamah said: 'A man came to 'Abdullāh [ibn Mas'Ūd] and said: "Should I ask permission before entering my mother's room?" 'Abdullāh said: "She does not like you to see her in all her positions".'

1064. (*Athar* 262) Muslim ibn Nadhīr said: 'A man asked Hudhayfah: "Should I ask permission before entering my mother's room?" He answered: "If you do not obtain her permission, you will see what she does not like [you to see]".'

1065. (*Athar* 263) Mūsa ibn Ṭalḥah said: 'I entered with my father my mother's room. He went in and I followed him. He turned and pushed me hard and I fell back on my bottom. He then said: "Would you enter without permission?"'

These *ḥadīths* put in a nutshell the case for seeking one's parents' permission before entering their rooms. The Prophet's companions were always keen to implement his guidance and to teach their children to do as he advised.

All this shows that even with one's parents, privacy should be respected by everyone who has attained puberty. This emphasises the importance of decency which should be observed even in one's own home. So, what about other close relatives, including siblings and grandparents? We say that what applies to parents also applies to grandparents.

1066. (*Athar* 264) Jābir said: 'A man should seek permission to enter the room of his son, daughter, mother – even though she may be elderly – brother, sister and father'.

These are the closest relatives who may be living in the same house and are in frequent contact every day. Nevertheless, they have to knock on the door and wait for permission before entry. Such are the proper Islamic manners. Islam sets high standards of decency which it requires its followers to observe. Other communities and cultures may not have the same standards and may find it difficult that such a requirement applies to all close relatives, even when they are living in the same home.

1067. (*Athar* 265) 'Aṭā' ibn Abu Rabāḥ said: 'I asked 'Abdullāh ibn 'Abbās: "Should I seek permission from my sister?" He said: "Yes". I repeated the question adding: "I have two sisters whom I support and provide for. Should I seek permission when entering their place?" Ibn 'Abbās answered: "Yes. Would it be appropriate for you to see them naked?" He then recited the verse that says: "*Believers! Let those whom you rightfully possess, and those of you who have not yet attained to puberty, ask leave of you at three times of day: before the prayer of daybreak, and whenever you lay aside your garments in the middle of the day, and after the prayer of nightfall. These are three occasions on which you may happen to be undressed*". (24: 58) Ibn 'Abbās added: "These are ordered to seek permission only during these three times". Ibn 'Abbās then read the verse that says: "*Yet when your children attain to puberty, let them ask leave of you, as do those senior to them [in age]*". (24: 59) He then said: "Seeking permission is obligatory". Ibn Jurayj adds: "It is obligatory for all people".'

The man who put the question to Ibn 'Abbās was 'Aṭā' ibn Abu Rabāḥ, a learned scholar in his own right who belonged to the generation succeeding that of the Prophet's companions. Hence, the questioning should be seen as that of a student wanting to understand the details of the issue. This is why he puts one question after another to cover all aspects. The first question was general, and the answer established that a brother should seek his sister's permission before entering a room in which she is on her own. The second question makes a special case when the brother is actually the breadwinner and he is supporting his sisters, providing them with their living. It is as if some people might think that because they support their children or their sisters, then this entitles them to a greater privilege including, perhaps, intruding on their privacy. Ibn 'Abbās explains to him in very clear terms the point about respecting privacy: "Would it be appropriate for you to see them naked?"

The verse Ibn 'Abbās quotes establishes the requirement that children who are not yet teenagers should seek permission before entering their parents' rooms at three different times during the day, when people normally have their rest, or are in bed. As they may be in a position of relaxation, when they are alone or with their spouses only, such young children should ask leave before they enter. When Aṭā' points out the three periods, Ibn 'Abbās quotes another verse to emphasise that seeking permission is required of all people.

All this is supported by a *ḥadīth* in which the same points are raised about looking after a close relative who lives with one in the same home. Neither point provides grounds for waiving the requirement to seek permission before entry. 'A man asked the Prophet: "Should I seek permission for entering my mother's place?" The Prophet said: "Yes". The man said: "I am living with her in the same house". The Prophet said: "Obtain permission before entry". The man said: "I am serving her". The Prophet asked him: "Would it be appropriate for you to see them naked?" The man said: "No". The Prophet said: "Then, ask permission before entry".'[739]

We see how the man was pointing to aspects that may be taken as grounds for relaxing the requirement. Apparently, the man's mother was unable to look after her needs and her son served her in different ways to help her. Even then, the Prophet makes it clear that permission is necessary before entry. He identifies the reason for which such a step is necessary. It is to avoid any embarrassment that may occur when one enters a room where a relative might be undressed, feeling that his or her privacy is compromised.

Indeed, the requirement to seek permission before entry applies in all cases.

1068. (*Athar* 266) Ibn 'Abbās said: 'A man should seek permission of entry from his father, mother, brother and sister'.

This is similar to *ḥadīth* Number 1066 which also included one's son and daughter. Privacy should be respected in all cases, even when a father or a mother wants to enter their adult son's or adult daughter's rooms. The point is to avoid any embarrassment for the one who enters and the one who is in the room. In privacy, a person may be in any situation. As people take care to be seen only in a decent situation, then respecting other people's privacy is essential to save embarrassment and to maintain relations on a sound footing.

---

739. Related by Mālik in Al-Muwaṭṭa'.

When permission is not given

As we have seen, Islamic manners make it clear that privacy must be respected. No one should intrude on another. However, when Islam makes a certain requirement, it looks at all aspects and provides guidance for different situations. Hence, we need to look at this guidance so that we know what to do in any circumstance. One important point is that seeking permission to enter a place may only be done three times. If one does not obtain permission after three requests, one should go back. Thus, if you are visiting a friend or a relative and you knock on the door three times, you have done all that you may do to obtain permission. If the people inside do not open for you, then you should leave.

1069. ʿUbayd ibn ʿUmayr said: ʿAbu Mūsa al-Ashʿari requested permission to see ʿUmar ibn al-Khaṭṭāb but permission was not given. It appears that ʿUmar was busy. Abu Mūsa left. When ʿUmar was free, he said: "Did I not hear the voice of ʿAbdullāh ibn Qays [i.e. Abu Mūsa]? Let him in". He was told that he had left. He sent for him, and Abu Mūsa explained, saying: "We were told to do this". ʿUmar said: "You shall bring me proof of this". Abu Mūsa went to a group of the Anṣār and requested them [for help]. They said: "Only the youngest of us, Abu Saʿīd al-Khudri, will testify to this. Abu Mūsa went with Abu Saʿīd [to clear the issue]. ʿUmar then said: "Has much of God's Messenger's commandments been unknown to me? I must have been too busy in the markets".ʾ[740]

This *ḥadīth* will be discussed in greater detail in Number 1077.

As already noted, it is important to announce oneself when visiting relatives, friends or other people. One must seek permission before entry. While this may be taken for granted in urban areas and contemporary houses which have doors and locks, the case is not so in some rural areas and other communities. In Arabia at the time of the Prophet most homes did not have doors, and people could enter

740. Related by al-Bukhari, Muslim, Abū Dāwūd, al-Tirmidhi and Ibn Mājah.

at will. The Prophet emphasised that everyone must seek permission before entering the home of even the closest relative. This is because in their homes people must have their privacy; they may be in a position which they do not want to be seen by anyone. To enter unannounced may cause much embarrassment, leading to hard feelings.

The Prophet needed to teach his companions not only to seek permission before entry, but also what to say and how to seek permission. His companions carried this to other communities and to later generations.

1070. (*Athar* 267) ʿAṭāʾ ibn Abu Rabāḥ reports that Abu Hurayrah said concerning a person who seeks permission to enter before he has offered the greeting: 'He is not given permission unless he starts with the greeting'.

1071. (*Athar* 268) Abu Hurayrah said: 'If someone comes in without first saying "Peace be to you", then say: "No", until he produces the key, which is the greeting of peace'.

Thus, the greeting of peace, which is the normal Islamic greeting of *al-salām ʿalaykum*, is the key that a visitor needs to use before gaining entry into the home of any other than his own. Indeed, even when one enters one's own home and finds no one in, one should offer oneself the greeting of peace, and consider it as a greeting by God in one's own place. This shows that the greeting should be offered before one asks permission to enter. In fact, this is what the Prophet taught.

When we realise how often the Prophet impressed on his companions the need to seek permission before entry, the question that may be asked is whether sparing someone the odd embarrassment requires such emphasis. The point at issue here is that in one's own home, one should feel absolutely secure, with privacy properly respected. Until one has properly announced oneself, the people inside may be totally unaware of your presence. They certainly do not wish to be seen or heard. Hence, privacy should be given its due importance.

So, what if people look and see their relatives and friends inside their homes? Is this an offence? If so, how serious?

1072. Abu Hurayrah reports that the Prophet said: 'If a man looks at the inside of your home, and you throw a pebble at him and gouge his eye, you have nothing to answer for'.[741]

This is a very clear answer to our question. One may take any action to stop a person looking at the inside of one's home without permission, to the extent of causing them a serious eye injury. This is supported by other *ḥadīths*:

1073. Anas reports: 'The Prophet was standing up in prayer when a man looked at the inside of his home. The Prophet took an arrow out of his quiver and aimed it at the man's eyes'.[742]

We note here that the Prophet did this while he was engaged in prayer. So, even if one is praying and discovers someone looking at one's family in one's home, when the people inside are unaware of such presence, one may take action to stop the man, without interrupting one's prayer. It is clear that the Prophet only threatened the man in this way, but we understand that if the man had not stopped immediately, the Prophet would then have aimed the arrow at him. This was within his right.

1074. Sahl ibn Sa'd al-Anṣāri said: 'A man looked at the Prophet's home from a hole in the door. The Prophet was scratching his head with a comb. When the Prophet saw the man, he said to him: "Had I known that you were looking at me, I would have hit you in your eyes with this [meaning the comb".'[743]

The Prophet explained on several occasions that seeking permission to enter is required so that people realise that they may not look into other people's homes when they are unaware.

---

741. Related by Aḥmad, al-Bukhari, Muslim, Abū Dāwūd and al-Nasā'ī.

742. Related by al-Bukhari, Muslim, al-Nasā'ī and Abū Dāwūd.

743. Related by al-Bukhari, Muslim, al-Nasā'ī and al-Tirmidhi.

1075. The Prophet said: 'Seeking permission is required because people look'.

1076. Anas reports: 'A man looked through a hole to see the inside of the Prophet's rooms. The Prophet aimed a blade at him, and the man withdrew his head'.[744]

All these *ḥadīths* are highly authentic. They confirm that any injury caused to a man peeping into somebody's home without permission will have no compensation, because the man is the offender, and the homeowner has the right to look after his family and property.

1077. Abu Mūsa al-Ash'ari said: 'I sought permission three times to see 'Umar but I did not have permission; so I left. He called me and said: "'Abdullāh, have you found it hard to wait at my door? You better know that people may find it hard to wait at your door". I said: "No. I have sought permission three times and I did not obtain it; so I left, as we have been commanded to do so". He said: "Whom have you heard this from?" I said: "From the Prophet". 'Umar said: "Have you heard from the Prophet what we have not heard? You will either provide me with proof or I will certainly punish you".

'I left him and went to the mosque where I found a number of the Anṣār sitting there. I asked them [about the case], and they said: "Does anyone doubt this?" I told them what 'Umar said to me. They said: "Then the youngest among us should go with you". Abu Sa'īd al-Khudri came with me to 'Umar and told him: "We accompanied the Prophet as he wanted to visit Sa'd ibn 'Ubādah. When he arrived, he offered the greeting of peace, but no permission was given him. He repeated his greeting a second time and a third, but no permission was given. He then said: 'We have done what we can'. Then he left. Sa'd came fast after him, and said: 'Messenger of God! By Him who has sent you with the message of the truth, every time you said the greeting I heard it

744. Related by al-Bukhari, Muslim, Abū Dāwūd, al-Nasā'ī and al-Tirmidhi.

and replied. But I only wanted that you offer more greetings to me and to my household'."

Abu Mūsa then said [to 'Umar]: "By God I am worthy of trust when it comes to reporting the Prophet's *Ḥadīth*". 'Umar said: "Certainly. I only wanted to ascertain the matter".'

The first point to make about this *ḥadīth* is the teaching that one may seek permission to enter someone else's home three times. If one does not gain such permission one should not try a fourth. This is easily understandable because if you are at a friend's or relative's door, you should get an answer with the first or second request. The request here may be the mere knocking at the door. If no one opens after you have knocked three times, it follows that either there is no one inside, or if they are, they must be very busy. In this case, it is better to leave and try again some other time. Needless to say, this is better all round. The visitor does not wait too long, or try to knock too hard. The people inside can attend to their business without embarrassment.

The other point is 'Umar's attitude which sounds strange. He knew that Abu Mūsa was a learned companion of the Prophet. He would not have doubted his knowledge. Nevertheless, he asked him to support his statement. In some reports of this *ḥadīth*, 'Umar tells him later that he did not doubt his knowledge, but only wanted that people should not attribute things casually to the Prophet. It might have been that there were with him some new Muslims who had not learnt how to treat the *Ḥadīth*. Therefore, 'Umar wanted to demonstrate to them that when anything is attributed to the Prophet, the person making the quotation should be absolutely certain of his knowledge.

Another point is that the people who learnt of what 'Umar asked Abu Mūsa decided to send the youngest among them. Abu Saʿīd al-Khudri was one of the most learned companions of the Prophet, who reported a large number of *ḥadīths*. In sending the youngest, they wanted to say to 'Umar that the matter in question is common knowledge.

Finally, the report given by Abu Saʿīd refers to one of the closest companions of the Prophet, Saʿd ibn 'Ubādah, a leading figure among the Anṣār. When the Prophet visited him, he delayed his permission, because he wanted the Prophet to say more greetings to him and his household. He felt that such a greeting of peace was a blessing for him and his family. Who would not try to obtain more of such a blessing when the Prophet himself is its source? Yet the Prophet taught his companions the right attitude in such a situation: seek permission three times, and if you do not obtain it, leave.

A different point about seeking permission concerns a visit paid when one has been invited:

1078. (*Athar* 269) ʿAbdullāh ibn Masʿūd said: 'If a man is invited, then he has already been given permission'.

1079. Abu Hurayrah reports that the Prophet said: 'If any of you is invited and he comes with the messenger, this is his permission'.

1080. Abu Hurayrah reports that the Prophet said: 'A man's messenger to another is the latter's permission'.

All these three *ḥadīths* stress the same point. If a person is requested to attend, then the request is all the permission he needs. He should come in straightaway. However, he needs to make his presence known because although he is expected, the people of the house may not be aware of him. Therefore, he should offer a greeting to the people inside before entering their home. Although the permission is there in the fact that he was sent for, rather than coming on his own accord, he should still be considerate and allow people a chance to be ready to receive him.

1081. (*Athar* 270) Abu al-ʿAlāniyah reports: 'I went to visit Abu Saʿīd al-Khudri and I offered the greeting of peace but I was not granted permission to enter. I said the greeting again but no permission was given. I said it the third time raising my voice, and saying: "Peace be to you, the people of this house". Still no permission was granted. I stepped aside and sat down. A boy came out and said to me: "Come in". I entered and Abu Saʿīd said to me: "Had you asked permission more [than three times] no permission would have been given". I asked him about the vessels [which were used for brewing wine] and whichever I named, he said that it was forbidden. I even asked him about al-Jaff, and he said that it is forbidden. Muhammad [ibn Sīrīn] said: [al-Jaff] is a pot with a skin placed at the top to tighten it'.[745]

In this *ḥadīth* we note that Abu Sa'īd al-Khudri informs his visitor, who apparently was eager to meet him, that he should not seek permission to come in more than three times. His impatience was apparent in the fact that he raised his voice the third time. As such, he did all he could. Therefore, if no permission to enter is given, he should leave because it means either the people are not in or are not ready to receive him.

He wanted to know about the vessels which were used to brew wine. These were of different types and had different names. They were not forbidden to have at home, or to use in an ordinary way, but when used to make intoxicating drinks, their use is forbidden. The rule that applies here is that 'Whatever intoxicates when taken in large quantity, even a small sip is forbidden'.[746]

How to seek permission

When a person visits friends or relatives, he normally knocks on the door and waits until someone opens. This is how we seek permission to enter other people's houses. This is part of our contemporary urban life. The situation may be different in other places, particularly in rural areas, remote villages, or indeed in shanty towns. In a safe neighbourhood, people may leave their doors open because they frequently come in and out, treating their neighbours' homes as their own. At the time of the Prophet, people generally did not have doors for their homes. This meant that it was easy for anyone to come into a house unannounced. Thus, people might find someone entering when they were not ready to receive a visitor. Hence, the Prophet was keen to teach his companions how to seek permission to enter.

745. Related by al-Nasā'ī.

746. Related by Aḥmad, Abu Dāwūd, al-Nasā'i, al-Tirmidhi and Ibn Ḥibbān.

His guidance was detailed and repeated on numerous occasions, with different companions, so that his purpose would be known to all, and to subsequent generations.

> 1082. ʿAbdullāh ibn Busr said: 'When the Prophet approached the entrance of a house where he wanted to request permission to enter, he did not face it directly. He would be either to the right or to the left. If he was invited, he would go in. Otherwise, he would leave'.

This *ḥadīth* shows how the Prophet respected the privacy of his companions. Although it was normal that people entered each other's houses freely, he would not even approach a house directly facing the entrance, so that he did not accidentally see what he was not supposed to see. Preferring to approach on either side of the entrance leaves no chance for this. He would then seek permission to enter, by offering the people in that house his greeting. He would wait for permission. If it were not forthcoming, he would leave, not feeling any irritation, because people are free to admit or otherwise anyone into their homes.

Sometimes a person is not ready to receive someone in his home. He prefers to meet his visitor outside. This is perfectly understandable, and should be no cause for upset.

> 1083. (*Athar* 271) Muʿāwiyah ibn Khadij reports: 'I visited ʿUmar ibn al-Khaṭṭāb and sought permission to enter. I was told: "Stay there and he will come out to see you". I sat close to his door. He came out and then asked for water to be brought to him. He performed his ablutions, wiping over his shoes. I asked him whether he needed to have a fresh ablution because he had urinated. He said: "May be because of passing urine or because of something else".'[747]

It is clearly understood that when the reporter of this *ḥadīth* wished to see the Caliph, he caught him at a time when he was not ready to receive him in his home. Hence, he was told that the Caliph would

---

747. Related by Aḥmad and Abū Dāwūd.

come out to see him. The Caliph did not wish his guest to wait long, so he did not perform his ablution before so meeting him. Rather, he went out to welcome his guest first. It is assumed, even though not indicated in the *ḥadīth*, that he welcomed his guest and had asked him if he wanted something in particular, or whether his visit was merely a social one.

When 'Umar had been talking to his guest for a while, he wanted to perform a fresh ablution. Perhaps the time for prayer was drawing near, and he wanted to be ready. He then performed his ablutions while his guest was watching. Perhaps the guest was at a loss for a topic of conversation. Hence, his question about the reason for 'Umar's new ablution. This is a very private matter. Hence, 'Umar politely indicated that it is so, and he did not answer further.

1084. Anas ibn Mālik reports: 'The Prophet's doors were knocked with people's nails'.

We learn from this *ḥadīth* that the Prophet had doors fixed to his wives' homes, because they opened to the mosque and were small homes. Hence, he needed to ensure privacy by having these doors. Moreover, at one stage, the instruction was given to the Prophet's companions that they might not speak to the Prophet's wives except from behind a screen. Thus, people who wished to speak to the Prophet had to knock at his door when he was in. However, they feared to disturb him if he was resting or busy. Therefore, they only knocked very softly, so that if he was asleep, they would not wake him. This manifested itself in using their fingernails for knocking. It was all a gesture of respect to the Prophet.

This need not be emulated when people knock on each others doors, particularly when the house they are visiting is large and a soft knock might not be heard in a remoter part of the house. A knock at a door is a request for permission to enter. Hence, the people inside should be able to hear it. Otherwise, it is meaningless.

1085. Kaldah ibn Ḥanbal said: 'Ṣafwān ibn Umayyah sent me to the Prophet at the time when Makkah fell to Islam with a gift of some milk, a young gazelle and some *daghābīs* [vegetables].

The Prophet was at the time at the top of the valley. I neither offered the greeting nor sought permission to enter. The Prophet said: "Go back and say, 'Peace be to you. May I enter?'" This was after Ṣafwān accepted Islam'.[748]

This *ḥadīth* mentions the behaviour of someone who was not a Muslim at the time. He just went to the Prophet and expected to see him without offering the greeting or seeking permission. The Prophet instructed him in good manners, telling him to go back and do what is necessary. It should be noted that the reporter, who was Ṣafwān's half brother, mentioned that the event he referred to was after Ṣafwān accepted Islam. This is doubtful. Probably it was before this, because the Prophet gave Ṣafwān a four month period of grace to learn about Islam and decide whether he wanted to be a Muslim and the Prophet did not stay long in Makkah after the Battle of Ḥunayn.

1086. Abu Hurayrah reports that the Prophet said: 'If a person looks inside a home, he should not be given permission to enter'.[749]

This *ḥadīth* ties up with similar ones that we have discussed earlier, stating that a person looking inside a home without permission has no rights, even if the people inside cause him a serious eye injury. This *ḥadīth* adds that such a person should not be given permission to enter. His action forfeits any claim he had.

1087. (*Athar* 272) Abu Hurayrah said: 'If someone comes in without first saying "Peace be to you", then say: "No", until he produces the key. I asked him: Is the key the greeting of peace. He said: "Yes".'

This is the same as *Ḥadīth* Number 1071, but the earlier *ḥadīth* does not mention the narrator's question about the key.

748. Related by Abū Dāwūd and al-Tirmidhi.
749. Related by Abū Dāwūd.

1088. Rib‘i ibn Ḥarāsh said: ‘A man from the ‘Āmir tribe told me that he went to the Prophet and said: “May I enter”. The Prophet said to a servant: “Go out and tell this man to say: ‘Peace be to you; may I come in’. He has not sought permission properly”. The man said: “I heard this before the servant could come out to give me this message. So I said: “Peace be to you; may I come in”. The Prophet said: “And to you. Yes, come in”. I went in and asked him: “With what message have you been sent?” He said: “I have come to you with nothing but good. I have come to you so that you will worship none other than God who has no partners. You must abandon the worship of idols like Al-Lāt and Al-‘Uzza. You must pray five times each night and day, fast a month in each year, and perform the pilgrimage to the House [i.e. the Ka‘bah], and take a portion of the money of the rich among you so as to give it to your poor”. I asked him: “Is there any part of knowledge unknown to you?” He replied: “God certainly knows what is good. Some knowledge is known only to God alone. There are five things that are unknown to anyone other than God: ‘*With God alone rests the knowledge of when the Last Hour will come; and He [it is who] sends down rain; and He knows what is in the wombs; whereas no one knows what he will reap tomorrow; and no one knows in what land he will die*’.’ (31: 34)

The first part of this *ḥadīth* has already been explained in connection with other *ḥadīths*. When the man asked the Prophet about his message, the Prophet outlined it for him in clear and concise terms. The first thing the Prophet said was the main essence of faith, which is God’s oneness. We note how the Prophet made his statement so emphatic, asserting the need to worship God alone and to ensure that no partners are associated with Him. But he went on to add the important practical shape this faith should take. To an Arab at the time, this could not be illustrated in a better form than abandoning the worship of the main idols he had been used to glorify. Thus the Prophet gave his interlocutor both the belief and its practical manifestation in both what needs to be done and what must be abandoned.

The Prophet then outlined for his interlocutor the four main acts of Islamic worship, namely prayer, fasting, pilgrimage and zakat. These cover all areas of life. Prayer is a bond between a human being and his Lord, God Almighty. It is renewed five times every day because a human being needs to be constantly aware of this bond. Such awareness is the best support anyone can have against temptation. During the day, every day, a Muslim is either approaching a prayer or having just finished a prayer. In either case, prayer serves as a reminder putting a Muslim on his guard.

Fasting, on the other hand, is a worship that signifies complete and pure devotion, because it involves abstaining from food and drink, the two things closely connected with our survival. When we withstand hunger and thirst for God's sake, resisting the temptation of food and drink, we are better able to resist all temptation and sin. The pilgrimage is an act of worship that symbolises the unity of the Muslim community all over the world, not only in the present generation, but also throughout history. Zakat is a financial act of worship that aims to ensure complete social security for all people. We note here how the Prophet makes it clear that it should work within the community: You 'take a portion of the money of the rich among you so as to give it to your poor'. This strengthens bonds within the community, because both giver and taker are fulfilling an act of worship.

The next question the man asks is about knowledge. The Prophet attributes all to God Who knows all goodness. He then quotes a verse from the Qur'an that outlines five areas which are known to God alone: '*With God alone rests the knowledge of when the Last Hour will come; and He [it is Who] sends down rain; and He knows what is in the wombs; whereas no one knows what he will reap tomorrow; and no one knows in what land he will die*'. (31: 34)

The first is that of the Last Hour, when all creation will be gathered before God on the Day of Resurrection. No one, not even a prophet or an angel, is ever given such knowledge. But it is not merely the timing of the Last Hour that is withheld from our knowledge. What comes next is also known to God alone. This applies to both heaven and hell and whatever God has chosen to create for that life, of which we have no doubt is coming.

Secondly, the verse the Prophet quotes mentions that it is God alone who sends down rain. When we relate this to knowledge, we may think of the quantity of rain that is sent down each time a cloud sheds its contents. This is definitely an area which scientists have not even tried to explore. Even if they do, they can only hazard a guess with regard to the volume of rain, or its duration and the area where it falls. They may develop technology to give them better results. But God knows every drop of rain and where it falls, long before a cloud is formed. Not only so, but He knows the effects of such rain, and whether it will seep through the earth strata into an underground reservoir or pour into a river. He also knows which of His creation will benefit by each rainfall, and how much it contributes to the life of plants and animals.

Thirdly, God knows 'what is in the wombs'. In his translation of the Qur'an, Muhammad Asad adds the following comment:

> This relates not merely to the problem of the sex of the as yet unborn embryo, but also to the question of whether it will be born at all, and if so, what its natural endowments and its character will be, as well as what role it will be able to play in life; and life itself is symbolised by the preceding mention of rain, and the end of all life in this world, by the mention of the Last Hour.[750]

We may add that God's knowledge does not apply to human embryos only, but to the unborn young of all species.

The fourth aspect of knowledge known only to God is that of the future, expressed in the Qur'anic verse in these words: '*Whereas no one knows what he will reap tomorrow*'. It is indeed knowledge of the next moment that is kept from us. No one can ever claim to have clear and certain knowledge of what will happen beyond the present moment, or indeed whether he or she will survive to take another breath. But everything that will happen to the end of time is known to God in every minute detail.

---

750. M. Asad, The Message of the Qur'an, p. 632.

The final aspect also relates to the future, but it is more closely related to a person's life and its end: 'No one knows in what land he will die'. It is not merely the place of death that is unknown to us. Its timing and causes are also withheld. We realise this as we see in life that death cannot be predicted for any person, whether he suffers from ill health or he enjoys robust and good health. It may come through the least expected of causes and in the most unusual of ways. The only thing that is certain about it is that it occurs in every case, at the time God has chosen.

1089. Ibn 'Abbās reports: ''Umar requested permission to visit the Prophet and said: "Peace be upon God's Messenger; peace be to you. May 'Umar come in?"'

This is the perfect example of seeking permission to enter a place. 'Umar, a very close companion of the Prophet, was always highly respectful of God's Messenger. To him, no one including himself could be of equal status to the Prophet. Hence, when he greeted the people inside, after knocking at the door, he offered the first greeting to the Prophet personally, before extending a similar greeting to whoever was inside the Prophet's home. He then announced himself by name seeking entry. Thus, he did not leave the people inside in any doubt about their visitor's identity. This enabled them to decide immediately what to say. If the visitor could be admitted without difficulty or embarrassment, then they would say so. Otherwise, they would let him know that the timing of the visit was inconvenient.

Today this sort of guidance is particularly relevant. If someone is visiting a friend and rings the bell, it is important to announce oneself properly. Suppose the building has an intercom system. When we ring the bell, the hosts want to establish the identity of the person at the door. It is important that we begin by offering the greeting of peace, or *salām*. The host is certain to reply, returning our greeting. We should then identify ourselves. We may also state the purpose of our visit if this is suitable, particularly if we are visiting someone with whom we do not have a close relationship. The Prophet did not like a visitor not identifying himself properly.

1090. Jābir ibn ʿAbdullāh reports: 'I went to see the Prophet concerning a debt that my father left outstanding. When I knocked at the door, he said: "Who is it?" I said: "It is I". He said: "It is I. It is I". He sounded as though he disliked my reply'.[751]

In this instance, Jābir does not mention his name, trusting that the Prophet will recognise his voice. This is not easy all the time. A person may think that his voice is easily recognisable, but the other person may be busy, attended by some people or there may be some background noise around him. All these situations, and others too, may interfere with his attention and he may not recognise the person on the other side of the door. Hence, the Prophet's answer was to repeat Jābir's reply, implying that he did not like that answer. It is far better to announce oneself by name.

Jābir's purpose was to seek the Prophet's help in settling his father's debt. His father died in the Battle of Uḥud, leaving behind one son and seven daughters. He apparently left an outstanding debt. Jābir did not have the means to repay his father's debt. Therefore, he went to the Prophet seeking either advice or assistance in settling this debt. Assistance could be either by seeking some arrangement with creditors to make settlement easier, or by direct help in repayment. When any of his companions died, the Prophet used to ask whether he had left behind any outstanding debt. If he was told that this was the case, the Prophet would instruct his companions to offer the *Janāzah* Prayer for the deceased, but he would indicate that he would not be leading the prayer. This worked well, because some relatives of the deceased, or a rich person among his companions, would undertake settlement of that debt. Needless to say, the deceased's family, relatives and friends were eager that the Prophet should offer the prayer, because a considerable part of it was supplication for the deceased and prayer for God's mercy. The Prophet's prayer was always answered in full. Thus, the Prophet's attitude of staying away from the prayer ensured that someone would volunteer to repay the debt, and the Prophet would thus lead the prayer. Later on, when the Muslim state was richer, if the Prophet was told that a deceased person had left some outstanding debt, he would undertake

751. Related by al-Bukhari and Muslim.

to pay it himself. He took this action as the head of state, indicating that this is the proper thing to do in a Muslim state, so that people are not reluctant to help each other in their hour of need.

Personal identification is required in any situation when a person is requested to give this.

1091. Buraydah reports: 'The Prophet (peace be upon him) went out to the mosque where Abu Mūsa al-Ash'ari was reciting [the Qur'an]. He asked: "Who is this?" I said: "I am Buraydah, may I be sacrificed for you". The Prophet said: "This one has been given one of David's flutes".'[752]

This *ḥadīth* is the same as Number 808, but it is related in this section because of the point concerning identifying oneself properly when asked.

1092. (*Athar* 273) 'Abd al-Raḥmān ibn Jud'ān said: 'I was with 'Abdullāh ibn 'Umar when he sought permission to enter a house. Someone said: "Enter in peace". He refused to enter'.

In the Qur'an we read: '*The God-fearing shall dwell amidst gardens and fountains. [They are received with the greeting]: "Enter here in peace and security*".' (9: 45-46) The fact that whoever in that house used the same greeting as the angels welcoming the people of heaven made Ibn 'Umar refuse to enter. He might have felt that it was presumptuous on the part of these people to use this welcome. Or the words might suggest uncertainty about the visitor.

Ḥadīths 1072, 1073 and 1074 mention that it is a grave offence to look through the door at the inside of a house or a room without first seeking permission to enter. We commented briefly on these *ḥadīths*, but here are some more.

1093. Abu Hurayrah reports that the Prophet said: 'If one's eye enters a place, then no permission to enter may be given'.[753]

---

752. Related by Muslim and al-Ḥākim.
753. Related by Aḥmad, Abū Dāwūd and al-Tirmidhi.

This is clearly a statement of disapproval of such an action, where a person is looking at the inside of a house or a room before seeking permission to enter. This applies even within the home, when one member of a family wants to enter another member's room, even that of his mother or daughter. Privacy should always be respected. The Prophet's companions understood this well and were keen to impress it on others.

1094. (*Athar* 274) Muslim ibn Nadhīr said: 'A man sought permission to enter Hudhayfah's home, but he first looked inside and said: "May I enter". Hudhyfah said to him: "Your eye has entered, but not your backside".'

Hudhayfah ibn al-Yamān was a companion of the Prophet. If it is suggested that his reply was rude, certainly the man's action was much more so.

1095. (*Athar* 275) This is the same as *ḥadīth* Number 1064.

Sometimes the Prophet emphasised his point in different ways, choosing what best suited the occasion or the people he was speaking to.

1096. Anas ibn Mālik reports: 'A bedouin came to the Prophet's house and put his eye at a hole in the door. The Prophet took up an arrow or a stick with a sharp end and aimed it at the bedouin as if to stab his eye. The bedouin moved away. The Prophet said to him: "Had you remained in your position, I would have certainly gouged your eye".'

Perhaps the Prophet was certain that the bedouin would move away once he realised that he was serious when he aimed the stick at his eye. The Prophet's action, however, indicates that he considered the bedouin's action to be so serious as to merit such strong action. It also tells us that if one finds oneself in a similar position and one hurts the offender, one will not be taken to task for so doing. It is the person who looks into another person's place that commits the offence, and what we do in retaliation is right.

1097. (*Athar* 276) 'Umar ibn al-Khaṭṭāb said: 'He who deliberately looks at the yard of a house, before he is given permission, commits a serious offence'.

The same principle is stated clearly at the beginning of a *ḥadīth* in which the Prophet points out several aspects of Islamic manners.

1098. Thawban, the Prophet's servant, reports that the Prophet told him: 'It is not permissible for any Muslim to look at the inside of a house until he has been given permission. Should he do so, he has actually entered. No Muslim who leads others in prayer may single himself with a supplication, to the exclusion of his congregation until he has finished his prayers. No one may pray when he feels the urge to urinate until he has relieved himself'.[754]

The first part of this *ḥadīth*, which al-Bukhari describes as the most authentic of whatever relates to this topic, confirms what we have been saying about seeking permission not only for entry into someone else's house or room, but also before looking inside. Here, we have a clear prohibition of deliberate looking inside without first obtaining permission to enter. Such a look is clearly equated with actual entry, because such a person would be looking at what the people of the house or those inside the room are doing, or what they are wearing. This is not right.

Secondly, the Prophet tells anyone who leads a congregational prayer to look after his congregation. If he supplicates, he should include his congregation in every prayer. Scholars say that if an imam uses some of the supplication used by the Prophet in the singular form, he should do so intending that all his congregation are included with him, or he should use the same words in the plural form. This is again an aspect of Islamic manners, because when the imam says a supplication, the congregation could only confirm what he says. If he is using the singular form, they may feel that he is only praying for himself and their role is to endorse his prayer. On the other hand,

---

754. Related by Aḥmad, Abū Dāwūd and al-Tirmidhi.

when he uses the plural form, everyone feels that the supplication is for them all. Their endorsement is thus more heart-felt.

The last point concerns someone who wants to pray but he feels the urge to go to the toilet. It is imperative that he should do so before he prays. If he prays in this condition, he is unlikely to be able to concentrate on his prayer. He would be preoccupied with self control so that he does not discharge a drop of urine on his clothes. Indeed, he would find attending to prayer very difficult. Hence, he should not put himself in such a situation. The proper procedure is to relieve himself first, renew his ablutions and then offer his prayers.

God's Own guarantee

Many Qur'anic and *Ḥadīth* statements include promises given by God. Every such promise is certain to be fulfilled because God's promises always come true.

> 1099. Abu Umāmah reports that the Prophet said: 'Three people have a guarantee from God: each one of them has the assurance that if he lives, he is spared evil, and if he dies he is admitted into heaven. Whoever enters his home saying a greeting of peace has a guarantee from God, the Mighty and Exalted, and whoever goes out to the mosque has a guarantee from God, and whoever goes out striving for God's cause has a guarantee from God.'

The *ḥadīth* is self-explanatory. It gives a guarantee to a person who says a greeting on entering his or her own home. If there are people inside, then the greeting is offered to them, and this spreads a pleasant and welcoming feeling inside the home, with one's own family. If nobody is in, then the greeting is to oneself. This is also encouraged, because when we go into an empty home, there is always a feeling of apprehension, until one is certain that nothing wrong has taken place in one's absence.

The *ḥadīth* gives a similar guarantee from God to the one who goes out to the mosque where he has no business other than offering obligatory prayers with the congregation and benefiting by any useful thing he finds in the mosque. Going on a mission striving for God's cause, whether in peace or in war, also provides such a guarantee. The Prophet says that these three types of people will be spared evil while they are attending to their different tasks. It does not preclude that any of them may die at that time, but should such a person die then, the guarantee means admission into heaven. This is the best that anyone can achieve.

There are people who think too highly of themselves, or treat their own families as subordinates. A man of this type wants his wife and children to come up to him and greet him as he enters. He is reluctant to be the first to offer a greeting. This is not the proper Islamic practice.

1100. (*Athar* 277) Jābir said: 'When you enter your home, offer a greeting to your family, for it is a blessed, goodly greeting from God'.

Al-Bukhari adds under this *ḥadīth*: 'He said: "I think that this is a part of the meaning of the Qur'anic verse that says: '*When a greeting is offered you, answer it with an even better greeting, or [at least] with its like*', (4: 86)"'. He does not specify who said this, but most probably he is referring to one of the narrators in the chain of transmission of this *ḥadīth*.

A similar *ḥadīth* is reported by Anas who quotes the Prophet as saying: 'Son, when you enter your own home, offer a greeting of peace for it is a blessing to you and to your family'.[755] Needless to say, this is part of the good manners Islam teaches. It is aimed at generating the right atmosphere of love and compassion within the family. However, there is another aspect to greeting when one enters one's own home.

1101. Jābir reports that the Prophet said: 'When a man enters his own home and mentions the name of God, the Mighty and Exalted, as he enters and when he has his meal, Satan says [to his offspring]: "Tonight, you have neither a place to stay nor food here". If the man enters without mentioning God's name, Satan

755. Related by al-Tirmidhi.

says: "You have a place to stay tonight". Then if the man does not mention God's name when he eats, Satan says: "You have both a place to stay and food tonight".'[756]

This is obviously a figurative statement. It is not a matter where Satan is looking for a place where he can lodge his offspring, or provide food for them. They do not eat the same type of food we eat. But it is a question of their being able to find a place where they can do their evil work of seduction, tempting people to do what is forbidden, and stirring trouble between people. When one is used to mentioning God's name before embarking on any action, including entering one's own home and eating, then Satan has little room to play. Every time a person mentions God's name, he reminds himself of God, and is on his guard, trying to bring his actions and his thoughts in line with what pleases God. In this way, he leaves no room for Satan to influence him in thought or action.

A question arises as to whether seeking permission is required for all places, or only when one wishes to enter a home.

1102. (*Athar* 278) Aʿyan al-Khuwārizmi said: 'We visited Anas ibn Mālik and he was sitting alone in his front corridor. My friend greeted him and asked: "May I come in?" Anas said: "Come in. This is a place where no one is required to seek permission". He then put some food before us and we ate. And he brought a large goblet with a sweet soft drink. He drank of it and gave us to drink'.

It is clear from this *ḥadīth* that when a person is at the entrance of his own home, or in the front corridor, where he can see anyone coming near, there is no need to seek permission. It is not a place where one has privacy which needs to be respected. Rather, it is a place where one is almost in the street. Hence, seeking permission is not required. The same applies to shops and the market place.

---

756. Related by al-Ḥākim, Ibn Ḥibbān and Abu ʿAwānah.

1103. (*Athar* 279) Mujāhid reports: ''Abdullāh ibn 'Umar used not to seek permission before entering shops in the market'.

1104. (*Athar* 280) 'Aṭā' reports: 'Ibn 'Umar used not to ask permission to enter the stalls of clothes sellers'.

This is only natural because if we were required to seek permission before entering a shop, then this means that a shopkeeper, or an assistant should always be near the door to give such permission. This may be hard for them to maintain. When a person opens his shop in the morning, he is seeking business, which means that people should come in and look for what they need. He is ready to receive whoever calls. It is unlike a home or a private room where one maintains one's privacy. Here neither the shopkeeper nor his customers expect privacy. It is a business place where people are welcome to enter and look for what they need.

1105. (*Athar* 281) Abu 'Abd al-Malik said: 'My mistress sent me to Abu Hurayrah and he came with me. When he was at the door, he said in Persian *andarāyīm*? [meaning: may we come in?] She said in Persian: *andarūn* [meaning: come in]. Then she said: "Abu Hurayrah, visitors come to see me after Isha, may I have conversations with them?" He said: "You may have conversations as long as you have not prayed *Witr*. If you have prayed the *Witr* then stop all conversation".'

This *ḥadīth* is entered here in order to make clear that a request for permission to enter may be stated in any language understood by the one who offers it and the one to whom it is addressed. However, it addresses a different subject, which is how long a person may have conversation with his visitors after Isha. Abu Hurayrah tells his lady questioner that she may have her social function and talk to her visitors until she has offered her witr prayer.

Witr is a 3-*rak'ah* prayer which is offered after Isha, at night. It is a highly desirable Sunnah prayer, and some scholars even consider it a duty, but not obligatory. Most scholars recommend that it should be offered just before one goes to bed, so that one concludes the day with a good, reward-earning action. This is so, unless one intends to wake up for night worship, before dawn. In this case, the witr is offered after the night worship.

Offering greetings to non-Muslims

Some people suggest that non-Muslims should not be offered the same greetings as Muslims. It is well known that the Islamic greeting is one of peace. It uses the word *Salām*, which is one of God's names. Hence, it should not be offered to a non-Muslim. However, when we look at *ḥadīths* that refer to this subject, several points become apparent.

1106. Abu Mūsa wrote to a Persian village chief and offered him the greeting in his letter. He was asked: 'Do you greet him when he is an unbeliever?' He said: 'He wrote to me and offered me a greeting, so I am returning his greeting'.

Abu Mūsa explained his action by stating that he was merely returning a greeting, because we are required to return a greeting with at least a similarly good one. God says: '*When a greeting is offered you, answer it with an even better greeting, or [at least] with its like*'. (4: 86) However, when people read this *ḥadīth* they may ask: are we not to offer a greeting to an unbeliever?

1107. Abu Baṣrah al-Ghifāri reports that the Prophet said to his companions: 'I will ride to visit the Jews tomorrow. Do not begin by offering them the greeting of peace. Should they offer it to you, then say: "And to you".'[757]

1108. Abu Hurayrah reports that the Prophet said: 'Do not offer the people of earlier revelations the greeting of peace. Constrain them to a narrow part of the road'.[758]

---

757. Related by Aḥmad.

758. Related by Muslim, al-Tirmidhi, Abū Dāwūd, Ibn Ḥibbān and Abu 'Awānah.

1109. (*Athar* 283) ʿAlqamah said: ''Abdullāh [ibn Masʿūd] greeted the Persian village chiefs with a gesture'.

1110. Anas reports: ' A Jew passed by the Prophet and said: *as-sām ʿalaykum*, and the Prophet's companions returned the greeting [as though he said correctly, wishing them peace]. The Prophet said to them: "He only said *as-sām ʿalaykum*". The Jew was held and, [on being questioned], he admitted [that what the Prophet said was true]. The Prophet said to them: "Return his wish to him".'[759]

1111. ʿAbdullāh ibn ʿUmar reports that the Prophet said: 'When a Jew offers you a greeting of peace, he actually says: *as-sām ʿalayk*. Therefore, answer by saying "and to you".'[760]

In the first of these *ḥadīths* the Prophet's companions who would be travelling with him were instructed not to start by offering the Jews the greeting of peace. They were to reply when offered a greeting by giving a reduced form which returns the same greeting to the speakers. Thus, we have here clear instructions to adopt what may be described in modern terms as a strictly formal attitude. The question that may be asked here is whether this applies in all situations or on that particular occasion?

There is nothing in Islam that prevents us from developing and maintaining good and friendly relations with non-Muslims, particularly those who are citizens in an Islamic state, or those who enter into a peaceful agreement with the Muslim community. The Prophet says that harming such a non-Muslim is like causing harm to the Prophet himself. The Prophet's companions were keen to follow his teachings and they maintained very good relations with their non-Muslim neighbours. However, the Islamic greeting is a very special one because it uses a name of God, and it should always be answered in the same form or in an even better one. Hence it should be offered only to those who are certain to answer it properly. Those who do not may be greeted in a different way, such as we wish them good morning, or good day.

---

759. Related by in a longer version by Muslim, al-Nasāʾī and Abū Dāwūd.
760. Related by al-Bukhari, Muslim, Abū Dāwūd and al-Nasāʾī.

From another point of view, the Jews of Madinah used to twist their tongues giving the Islamic greeting a different meaning. The last *ḥadīth* makes this clear. The correct form of the Islamic greeting is *al-salām ʿalayk*, when offered in the singular, and adding the plural marker to make it *ʿalaykum*, when offered to more than one person. The Prophet points out that the Jews used to omit the letter 'l', so as to make the first word sound as *sām*, which is an Arabic word that means death. Thus, they wished death to the addressee while giving him the impression that they were wishing him peace. Hence, the Prophet tells his companions to return their wish to them.

Apparently some of the Jews in Madinah thought that this was a way to ridicule the Muslims, laughing at them privately. The fourth *ḥadīth* reports a special case when a Jew tried to get away with wishing death to the Muslims. They thought that he greeted them and they were returning his greeting but the Prophet informed them of the facts. The Jew admitted his guilt, and the Prophet only told them to return his wish to him.

In other reports of this incident, some Muslims were really angry at the Jew who thought that he could fool so many Muslims as they sat with the Prophet. Therefore one or two of them suggested that they should kill the Jew. However, the Prophet put the matter into the right perspective and told them to return his wish to him. It should be said that the reaction of those companions of the Prophet was a natural one, but the Prophet stressed that they should deal with others according to Islamic standards. He assured his companions that the wish of such devious people will not be answered because God does not answer a wish for harm against an innocent person. However, the reply is answered because it is from the aggrieved party. It was the Jews who started this, trying to fool and ridicule the Muslims. Hence, they are totally in the wrong. On the other hand, if one is to carry this too far and repay the offender in an unjust way, he would then be in the wrong.

Some Muslims feel that these *ḥadīths* mean that we should not offer the Islamic greeting to non-Muslims. There is no strict rule to suggest so. The rule that applies to Muslims and non-Muslims alike is that if a non-Muslim offers us the Islamic greeting of peace, we return it at least in equal measure, but it is always preferable to return a greeting with a better one. In the first *ḥadīth* Abu Mūsa al-Ash'ari wrote to a Persian offering him the greeting of peace because it was the Persian who started with such a greeting . A Muslim does not fail to reply to a greeting with a better one, or at least a similar one. Moreover, there is nothing sacred about the Islamic greeting of peace. We offer it to all, if they are willing to offer it to us.

Moreover, it is authentically reported that some of the Prophet's companions and their successors used to say *al-salam 'alaykum* to non-Muslims when they met them. This is a clear indication that they understood the Prophet's *ḥadīth* as applicable only to that particular occasion, when he had some problems with the Jews that he needed to sort out. On that occasion, the Muslims needed to show a very serious attitude towards the Jews who had no good-will towards the Muslim community.

1112. (*Athar* 284) Ibn 'Abbās said: 'Return the greeting of peace to a Jew, a Christian or a Magian. God says: "*When a greeting is offered you, answer it with an even better greeting, or [at least] with its like*".' (4: 86)

Thus, he makes clear that the Qur'anic verse applies to all people, regardless of their faith or lack of it. Indeed, the quoted verse provides a maxim that applies in all situations. We should never hesitate to reply to a kind greeting with a better one, no matter who the person offering it may be. We do not question the motives of that person, because we cannot determine them for certain. We only take people's words at face value, giving them the benefit of the doubt, as it were.

1113. Usāmah ibn Zayd reports: 'The Prophet rode on a donkey with a straw saddle covered by a rug from Fadak, and he took Usāmah ibn Zayd behind him, going to visit Sa'd ibn 'Ubādah [who was sick]. He passed by a group of people including 'Abdullāh ibn Ubay, before the latter claimed to embrace Islam. The group included some Muslims and others who were unbelievers and idolaters. The Prophet greeted them with the greeting of peace'.[761]

---

761. Related by al-Bukhari, Muslim and al-Tirmidhi.

This *ḥadīth* shows that Islam does not hold back from extending kind treatment to non-Muslims, even though this may be in the form of a greeting. The Prophet could have singled out the Muslims with his greeting of peace and offered a different greeting to the others. But he did not do so, because he wished the others to know that Islam extends the hand of peace to all.

1114. 'Abdullāh ibn 'Abbās said: 'Heraclius, the Byzantine Emperor sent for Abu Sufyān ibn Ḥarb. He then had the Prophet's letter sent with Diḥyah al-Kalbi to the governor of Busra. The letter was handed to Heraclius and he read. It said: 'In the name of God, the Lord of Grace, the Ever-Merciful. From Muhammad, God's Messenger to Heraclius, the Byzantine ruler. Peace be to those who follow right guidance. I call on you to believe in Islam. Adopt Islam and you will be safe, and God will give you a double reward. If you decline, you shall bear responsibility for the Arians.[762] "*Say: People of earlier revelations. Let us come to an agreement which is equitable between you and us: that we shall worship none but God, that we shall associate no partners with Him, and that we shall not take one another for lords beside God. And if they turn away, then say: Bear witness that we have surrendered ourselves to God*".'[763] (3: 64)

This was one of several letters the Prophet sent to the rulers of the two great empires at the time, the Byzantine and Persian, and also to the rulers of neighbouring countries, calling on them to accept the message of Islam. Some of them, like Negus of Abyssinia, responded well and accepted Islam. Some, like the Emperor of Persia and the ruler of Busra, took a very hostile attitude. Others, such as Heraclius and the ruler of Egypt, sent a friendly reply but did not accept Islam.

Before Heraclius made up his mind, he ordered that anyone from Arabia who was present in the surrounding area should be brought to

762. The Arians were the followers of Arius, the Egyptian who believed in the Oneness of God and denied that the father and the son were two manifestations of the Lord.

763. This is a short version of this *ḥadīth*. It is related in full by al-Bukhari and Abū Dāwūd.

him. It happened that Abu Sufyān and a few other unbelievers from Makkah were in Palestine and they were taken to him. He questioned Abu Sufyān thoroughly about the Prophet, and recognised that he was truly God's Messenger, but he did not act on his conviction. His dialogue with Abu Sufyan reveals his thorough knowledge of what a messenger of God should be like.

1115. Jābir reports: 'Some Jewish people greeted the Prophet but said: *al-sām 'alaykum*. He said: "And to you". Feeling very angry, 'Ā'ishah said to him: "Have you not heard what they said?" He said: "I did, and I replied to them. Our prayer will be answered, but theirs will not".'[764]

This refers to the same occasion mentioned in *ḥadīth* 312, which gives it in greater detail. The Jews in Madinah used to resort to this way of speaking so as to wish death upon the Prophet and Muslims. The Prophet ordered his companions to simply reply saying 'and to you', which meant that if a Jew wished peace, i.e. *salām,* to Muslims, they were to reply with a similar wish, but if he wished them death, i.e. *sām*, they again wished him the same. The Prophet advised 'Ā'ishah to calm down and told her that their prayer would not be answered, because it represents aggression, while the Muslims' prayer would be because they were only responding to an offence.

1116. Abu Hurayrah reports that the Prophet said: 'If you meet the idolaters in the street, do not be the first to offer them the greeting of peace. Constrain them to a narrow part of the road.'[765]

This *ḥadīth* relates to a particular occasion and is not meant for general application. A number of the Prophet's companions and their successors used to offer the Islamic greeting to non-Muslims, as we have explained earlier.

---

764. Related by Muslim.
765. Related by Muslim and al-Tirmidhi.

Constraining them to a narrow part of the road means that a Muslim should have priority and take the main part of the road. However, if the road is narrow and just about sufficient for the two to pass each other easily, it is not permissible to try to take a major part of it and cause harm to the idolater or unbeliever. It is not permissible to cause harm to an unbeliever, regardless of his or her faith, if they behave peacefully towards us. Indeed we may pray for them wishing them all good things:

1117. (*Athar* 285) Abu ʿAmr al-Shaybāni reports: ʻʻUqbah ibn ʿĀmir al-Juhani passed by a man who looked like a Muslim who offered him the greeting of peace. He replied saying: "And to you be peace, together with God's mercy and blessings". A boy who was close to him said: "The man is a Christian". ʿUqbah followed the man and caught up with him. He then said: "God's mercy and blessings are wished to believers only, but I say to you: May God give you a long life and an increase in wealth and children".'

This is a delicate matter for Muslims, because God's mercy is granted in this life, but its great manifestation is on the Day of Judgement when everyone's destiny is determined by Him. It is not for any human being to say a prayer concerning the destiny of any unbeliever. Prophet Abraham prayed for his father who refused to believe in God's oneness, but this was in fulfilment of a promise he had made without knowing that it was not permissible for him to pray for his father's forgiveness. God says: '*It is not for the Prophet and the believers to pray for the forgiveness of those who associate partners with God, even though they may be their close relatives, after it has become clear that they are destined for the blazing fire. Abraham prayed for the forgiveness of his father only because of a promise he had made him. But when it became clear to him that he was God's enemy, he disowned him; Abraham was most tender-hearted, clement.*' (9: 113-114)

We note that the Prophet's companion wanted to clarify an issue to a Christian who offered him a greeting of peace. The normal addition in reply, when such a greeting is offered to us by a Muslim, is to pray to God to bestow mercy and blessings on the man or woman offering it.

When 'Uqbah was informed that his interlocutor was a non-Muslim, he wanted him to know that this type of returned greeting is normally given to believers. Since he was not a Muslim, 'Uqbah prayed for him in a different way, asking God to prolong his life and give him wealth and children. This is a very good prayer, and the man must have felt very happy to hear it.

1118. (*Athar* 286) Ibn 'Abbās said: 'If Pharaoh said to me, 'May God bless you', I would have said to him, 'And you'. Yet Pharaoh is dead.

This is to confirm that no matter who gives us a good wish or a pleasant greeting, we should respond in kind. We cannot be less forthcoming than others. If they wish us well, we should wish them well. In fact we wish all people well, regardless of their faith, race, or attitude. The Prophet was exemplary in this respect. His people, the Quraysh, continued to treat him and his companions in every possible bad way, yet he was kind to them, wishing them the best, and fearing that they would condemn themselves to God's ultimate punishment.

1119. Abu Mūsa al-Ash'ari reports: 'The Jews used to try to bring about a sneeze when they were with God's Messenger, hoping that he would say to them "May God bestow mercy on you". However, he used to say to them: "May God grant you guidance and reassurance".'[766]

This *ḥadīth* is the same as Number 943, and we have already commented on it.

1120. (*Athar* 287) ''Abd al-Raḥmān said: 'Ibn 'Umar passed by a Christian and he offered him the greeting of peace. He was then told that the man was a Christian. Ibn 'Umar returned to him and said: "Give me back my greeting".'

---

766. Related by Aḥmad, Abū Dāwūd, al-Tirmidhi and al-Ḥākim.

Ibn 'Umar was keen to implement Islamic teachings very strictly. He realised that the greeting of peace should not be offered to a non-Muslim, because it includes a name of God, but it may be returned to a non-Muslim who offers it to us. However, it is surprising that he should go to the man and demand that he give him back what he had said. He might have said something else akin to what we read in *Ḥadīth* Number 1117, offering him a different greeting with a prayer for good health, or something similar. Probably this *athar* is reported in a short version here, as many *ḥadīths* are.

1121. Abu Salamah ibn 'Abd al-Raḥmān reports that 'Ā'ishah told him: 'The Prophet said to me: "Gabriel offers you the greeting of peace". She said: "And to him peace and God's mercy".'

This is a shorter version of *Ḥadīth* Number 830, and we have already commented on it.

1122. (*Athar* 288) Ibn 'Abbās said: 'I think that answering a letter is a duty, just like returning a greeting'.

This statement is self explanatory. Ibn 'Abbās's understanding of Islamic teachings and values is second to none. His view on this point is based on Islamic principles.

1123. 'Ā'ishah bint Ṭalḥah said: 'I spoke to 'Ā'ishah [the Prophet's wife] when I was in her care. People used to come from everywhere to visit her. Older people used to come to me because of my relation to her. Younger men treated me as a sister, gave me presents and sent me letters from their different places. I would say to 'Ā'ishah: "Aunt, this letter and this gift are from so-and-so". She would say to me: "Daughter, answer him and reward him. If you do not have something to send him as a reward, let me know and I will give you". She would certainly give me'.

'Ā'ishah bint Ṭalḥah was 'Ā'ishah's niece. Her mother was Umm Kulthum bint Abu Bakr and her father was Ṭalḥah ibn 'Ubaydillāh, one of the ten to whom the Prophet gave the happy news of being in heaven. He was among the very early Muslims. ʿĀ'ishah bint Ṭalḥah was well known for her beauty, and she was visited by dignitaries, men of letters and poets from all over the Muslim world.

She was highly educated by her aunt, ʿĀ'ishah, the Prophet's wife. In this *ḥadīth*, she mentions that people sought her and sent her presents, hoping that she would facilitate for them attending ʿĀ'ishah, the Mother of Believers, and ask her about the Prophet and learn some *ḥadīths* directly from her. The *ḥadīth* is entered here by al-Bukhari because of ʿĀ'ishah's instruction to her niece to answer people's letters and send them gifts in return for their gifts. ʿĀ'ishah would even pay for her gifts if she did not have something to send back. We should remember that she did not know these people, yet the Prophet's wife would not allow that their letters and gifts remained unanswered.

1124. (*Athar* 289) ʿAbdullāh ibn Dīnār said: 'ʿAbdullāh ibn ʿUmar wrote to ʿAbd al-Malik ibn Marwān pledging his allegiance to him: "To ʿAbd al-Malik, *Amīr al-Mu'minīn*, from ʿAbdullāh ibn ʿUmar. Peace be to you. I praise God, other than whom there is no deity, to you and I acknowledge that I owe you obedience according to the practice enjoined by God and His Messenger, in as much as I can".'[767]

ʿAbd al-Malik was the fifth Caliph of the Umayyad dynasty. He ruled for twenty years but the first few years of his reign were fraught with trouble and he had to fight battles in Iraq and Hijaz. Ibn ʿUmar's letter must have been written when ʿAbd al-Malik managed to overcome his rivals and the entire Muslim world came under his rule. Ibn ʿUmar then felt that he should pledge his allegiance to him.

It should be noted that such allegiance was always conditional on the Caliph implementing Islamic law, and within one's ability. In the letter, Ibn ʿUmar addresses ʿAbd al-Malik as *Amīr al-Mu'minīn*, which was the Caliph's official title. It means 'ruler or commander of the believers'. We will be speaking presently about the form of address used by Ibn ʿUmar in this letter, as we need to look at it together with other *ḥadīths*.

767. Related by Mālik and al-Bukhari.

1125. (*Athar* 290) Zayd ibn Aslam reports: 'My father sent me to Ibn 'Umar and I saw him writing: *Bismillāh al-Raḥmān al-Raḥīm. Amma ba'd...*' [i.e. In the name of God, the Lord of Grace, the Ever-Merciful. Following this...]'.[768]

1126. Hishām ibn 'Urwah said: 'I have seen some of the Prophet's letters. At the end of every topic, he said: "Following this..." '.

The first of these two *ḥadīths* relates how Ibn 'Umar started his letter. It is well known that he was very strict in literally following the Prophet's example. If he did something in a particular way, it was certain that he was only following the Prophet's guidance. Thus starting a letter with this formula is the right one. The phrase *amma ba'd* is usually written after the opening of the letter with God's name. It means: 'following this', 'to start with', or even 'meanwhile'. If it occurs after the opening greeting, it means 'to start with'. If it occurs in the middle, it signifies a shift to a new point. This means that the Prophet's letters were to the point, and well structured. They always started with 'In the name of God, the Lord of Grace, the Ever Merciful'.

The Prophet's letters always started with an identification of the sender. He would thus write: 'From Muhammad, God's servant and Messenger, to ... (and he mentioned the addressee's name)'. The Prophet wrote to a number of kings and heads of state always using this formula. This angered the Persian emperor who was used to having his name mentioned at the beginning before anyone else. Needless to say, the Prophet occupied the highest position of all mankind, since he was chosen by God to deliver His last message to mankind.

The Prophet's companions and other Muslims who followed his example would normally identify themselves first in the same way. However, when one of them wrote to someone in a higher position, the question arose about how to begin.

---

768. Related by Mālik and al-Bukhari.

1127. (*Athar* 291) Khārijah ibn Zayd said: 'Zayd ibn Thābit wrote this letter: "In the name of God, the Lord of Grace, the Ever Merciful. To God's servant Mu'āwiyah, *Amīr al-Mu'minīn*, from Zayd ibn Thābit. Peace be to you, *Amīr al-Mu'minīn*, with God's mercy. I praise God, other than whom there is no deity, to you. Following this..."'[769]

Here we note that Zayd put the name of the addressee first, as he was the Caliph, giving him his title of *Amīr al-Mu'minīn*,. He followed this with the greeting of peace, and praising God for His grace. The opening of letters with 'in the name of God...' was normal practice:

1128. (*Athar* 292) Abu Mas'ūd al-Jurayri said: 'A man asked al-Ḥasan about reciting In the Name of God, the Lord of Grace, the Ever Merciful [in prayer]. He said to him: "This is at the opening of letters".'

This is related to reciting the opening verse aloud in prayer. Many scholars are of the view that it should be vocalised but not aloud. It should not be heard by other worshippers. Al-Ḥasan does not give a straightforward answer. He refers to the fact that the phrase is used at the beginning of letters which are not normally read aloud.

The Prophet's companions followed his example and identified themselves first in their letters before they mentioned the name of the addressee. However, when Zayd ibn Thābit wrote to Mu'āwiyah, the Caliph, he opened with the Caliph's name before identifying himself, as a sign of respect. However, this was not readily acceptable to all the Prophet's companions.

1129. (*Athar* 293) Nāfi' reports: 'Ibn 'Umar needed something from Mu'āwiyah and he wanted to write to him. People said to him: "Write his name first". They continued to impress this on him until he wrote: "In the Name of God, the Lord of Grace, the Ever Merciful. To Mu'āwiyah".'

---

769. Related by al-Bayhaqi.

ʿAbdullāh ibn ʿUmar wanted to maintain the same form the Prophet used, identifying himself first. To him, this was the right way, whether he wrote to the Caliph or an ordinary person. However, other companions of the Prophet insisted that he should mention the Caliph's name first. He relented and then realised that this is the right way. He did the same in his letter to a later Caliph, ʿAbd al-Malik, as mentioned in *ḥadīth* 1124.

There is no doubt that ʿAbdullāh ibn ʿUmar commanded a much higher position in the Muslim community than that of the Caliph. Ibn ʿUmar was a companion of the Prophet and a scholar of the highest standing. ʿAbd al-Malik belonged to the second generation of *tabiʿīn*, but he was the Caliph. As such, he had the right to be obeyed by all Muslims as long as he implemented God's law and the Prophet's Sunnah.

1130. (*Athar* 294) Anas ibn Sīrīn said: 'I used to write for [ʿAbdullāh] ibn ʿUmar and he would say to me: "Write: In the Name of God, the Lord of Grace, the Ever Merciful. Following this, to so-and-so".'

1131. (*Athar* 295) Anas ibn Sīrīn said: 'A man wrote in the presence of Ibn ʿUmar: In the Name of God, the Lord of Grace, the Ever Merciful. To so-and-so. Ibn ʿUmar objected and told him to write: In the Name of God. This is to...'

The first of these *ḥadīths* suggests that Ibn ʿUmar accepted that it is perfectly appropriate to mention the addressee first.

The second *athar* is rather vague. There is hardly any difference between what was objected to and what was acceptable. However, I may only suggest that there should be a separating phrase after the opening name of God and His attributes. I cannot determine what Ibn ʿUmar objected to exactly. Shaikh al-Albani said that he could not determine the difference.

1132. (*Athar* 296) This is the same as Number 1127 (*Athar* 291).

1133. Abu Hurayrah reports that the Prophet said: 'A man from the Children of Israel – and he mentions the *ḥadīth* in full – and his friend wrote to him: "From so-and-so to such-and-such".'

This is how the *ḥadīth* is entered here. It is obvious that al-Bukhari enters it merely for the relevance of how letters were started. However, in order to have the full significance of the *ḥadīth*, we will now quote it in full, since it is authentic.

Quoting God's Messenger, Abu Hurayrah said: 'A man from the Children of Israel requested another from the Children of Israel to lend him 1,000 *dinars*.[770] The man said: "Bring me witnesses." He said: "God is sufficient as a witness". He said: "Then bring me a guarantor". He said: "God is sufficient as a guarantor". The man said: "You are right". He gave him the money for a specified term. The borrower travelled by sea and attended to his business. As he sought a boat to go back and repay his debt at the specified date, no boat was to be found. He took a [large] piece of wood and made a hole in it. He placed in the hole 1,000 *dinars* and a letter from him to his friend,[771] and he sealed the wood. He then stood by the seaside and said: "My Lord, You know that I borrowed from such-and-such 1,000 *dinars*, and he asked me for a guarantor and I said: 'God is sufficient as a guarantor'. He accepted You. I have tried my best to find a boat to send him what I owe him but I cannot find one. I am entrusting the money to You". He then threw the wood into the sea and made sure that it was well into it. He then left, but continued to look for a boat to take him home.

'The lender went to the port hoping to find a coming boat bringing him his money. He found the wood that contained the money. He took it home to use as firewood. When he sawed it he found the money and the letter.

'Then the lender arrived and went to the borrower with 1,000 *dinars*. He said to him: "By God, I tried hard to find a boat to

770. The dinar was the gold currency unit.

771. Another version of the *ḥadīth* mentions that he wrote in his letter: 'I am giving your money to my guarantor who gave you the guarantee'.

bring you your money, but I could not find one before the one that brought me. The lender asked him: "Have you sent me anything". He answered: "I am telling you that I could not find a boat before the one on which I travelled". The lender said: "God has given me on your behalf what you sent in the piece of wood. Keep your 1,000 *dinars* and take care".'[772]

1134. Maḥmūd ibn Labīd reports: 'When Sa'd [ibn Mu'ādh] was seriously wounded during the clashes around the Moat, he was placed [in a tent] to be nursed by a woman called Rufaydah who was a nurse treating the wounded. When the Prophet passed by him in the evening, he would ask him: "How are you this evening?" and when he passed by him in the morning, he asked him: "How are you this morning?" Sa'd would tell him'.[773]

Sa'd ibn Mu'ādh was one of the earliest Muslims in Madinah and he was the chief of the clan of 'Abd al-Ashhal that belonged to the Aws tribe. On the day he converted to Islam, all his clan followed suit. He was very close to the Prophet, dedicated to the service of Islam. His wound was very serious, as it had cut the main artery in his arm. He was being nursed during the siege of the Jewish tribe of Qurayẓah after they had violated their treaty with the Muslims and sided with the attacking forces. The Prophet ordered that he should be nursed close to Muslim forces so that he could visit him while he was treated. This *ḥadīth* tells us that the Prophet visited him every day, in the morning and evening.

1135. Ibn 'Abbās reports: 'When 'Ali came out of the Prophet's home, during the Prophet's final illness, people asked him: "Abu al-Ḥasan, how is God's Messenger this morning?" He replied: "All praise be to God; he is recovering". Al-'Abbās ibn 'Abd al-Muṭṭalib took 'Ali by the hand and said to him: "Look here! By God, you shall be under someone else's authority in three days. By God, I think that God's Messenger (peace be upon him) will

772. Related by al-Bukhari in his Ṣaḥīḥ anthology, Number 2291.
773. Related by al-Bukhari.

die as a result of his present illness. I can recognise the approach of death on the face of any of 'Abd al-Muṭṭalib's descendants. Let us go back to God's Messenger (peace be upon him) and ask him who will be the ruler? If it will be one of us, we will know that. If it will be someone else, we will also know it and he may put in a good word with him for us". Ali replied: "By God, if we ask God's Messenger (peace be upon him) to give us such authority and he refuses, people will never give it to us. I shall never request that of God's Messenger (peace be upon him)".'[774]

This *ḥadīth*, which is highly authentic, provides the ultimate argument that the Prophet did not, at any time, appoint a successor to be the head of the Muslim state after him. Had he made such an appointment, it would have been known and the whole suggestion by al-'Abbās, the Prophet's uncle, to his nephew, 'Ali, would have been pointless and 'Ali would have reminded him that such an appointment was already made and known. The Prophet only made an indication when he appointed Abu Bakr to lead the prayer during his illness. Abu Bakr led the congregational prayer in the Prophet's Mosque for seventeen consecutive obligatory prayers. When the Prophet passed away, the leading figures of the Muhājirīn and the Anṣār met and chose Abu Bakr to be their head of state. Their argument was that since the Prophet appointed him to lead the community in their matters of faith, he should be their leader in life affairs. Had there been an appointment by the Prophet of his successor, the meeting would have been unnecessary.

1136. (*Athar* 297) Abu al-Zinād reports that he took this letter from Khārijah ibn Zayd [ibn Thābit] and from the senior members of Zayd's family: 'In the name of God, the Lord of Grace, the Ever Merciful. To God's servant Mu'āwiyah, *Amīr al-Mu'minīn*, from Zayd ibn Thābit. Peace be to you, *Amīr al-Mu'minīn*, with God's Mercy. I praise God, other than whom there is no deity, to you. Following this: you have asked me about the division of the estate of a deceased person who leaves behind

774. Related by Aḥmad and al-Bukhari.

his grandfather and his siblings. [Abu al-Zinād mentions the contents of the letter before stating its final part]: We pray to God for guidance, preservation and certainty in all our affairs. We seek His shelter against error, ignorance or assuming what we do not know. Peace be to you, *Amīr al-Mu'minīn*, with His mercy, blessings and forgiveness. This is written by Wuhayb on Thursday, 18 Ramadan, 42 AH'.

The opening of this *ḥadīth* has already been mentioned in Numbers 1127 and 1132, but even here, it does not include all its details. This is a long *ḥadīth* referring to a letter written by Zayd ibn Thābit in reply to a letter from the Caliph, Mu'āwiyah, asking Zayd about the division of inheritance where the deceased is survived by neither of his parents nor any children. His closest relatives who survive him are his grandfather and his siblings. Zayd was the best authority among the Prophet's companions on the subject of inheritance. The case the Caliph was asking about was a rare one, but it is possible. The Islamic system of inheritance, detailed in the Qur'an, does not mention it. Nor is it mentioned in a *ḥadīth* since it did not occur during the Prophet's lifetime. Hence, the Prophet's companions addressed it. Their views differed on how the deceased's estate should be divided. Apparently, Mu'āwiyah wanted to know the basis of these differences. Zayd wrote back to him explaining this. We note that the letter is dated at the end, mentioning the day, month and year, as well as the name of the scribe who wrote it as Zaid dictated it.

This *ḥadīth* shows that a letter is treated like a normal meeting, with a greeting of peace at the beginning and another at the end. Zayd ibn Thābit addresses the Caliph with all the respect due to him, although Zayd was senior to Mu'āwiyah as a companion of the Prophet, as he belonged to the Anṣār and was the man entrusted, by Abu Bakr first and later by 'Uthmān, with the task of collating the Qur'an in reference copies. He was the head of the committee handling this very important task. The fact that he was chosen by the two Caliphs reflects his acknowledged eminence as a scholar. However, since Mu'āwiyah was now the Caliph, Zayd addressed him with all the respect due to him. His letter shows that it is the proper way to add another greeting at the end. It does not have to be a letter to a person of high position in order to contain the two greetings. This could be done in any letter to any addressee.

Good manners are observed in the Muslim community all the time. While other communities may have their own high standards of good manners, Islamic manners are characterised by the fact that Muslims praise God all the time, thanking Him for every good thing they have in their lives. Muslims acknowledge that whatever they enjoy in life is given to them by God. Hence, they praise Him and acknowledge their gratitude to Him. If a person does not do so, his conduct is seen as strange.

1137. (*Athar* 298) Anas ibn Mālik reports: 'I heard 'Umar ibn al-Khaṭṭāb as he was greeted by someone. 'Umar replied to his greeting, and then asked him: "How are you?" The man said: "I praise God to you". 'Umar said: "This is what I wanted to hear from you".'[775]

Perhaps 'Umar was testing the man, or making sure that he would give the proper answer. It may be that 'Umar was aware of something that put him in doubt as to the man's knowledge of Islamic manners. Hence, he was pleased to hear the man praising God for His blessings, when asked about his condition. This is the proper way Muslims should answer. They remember the many favours granted to them by God. Even when a Muslim is suffering from an illness or a disability, he always praises God, knowing that he is in a better condition than many other people. It is sufficient of a blessing that we have faith and we believe in God. This puts us in a better situation than that of any person who lacks such faith, even though such a person may be extremely wealthy, enjoying good health and high position. No blessing or favour is equal to the blessing of being a person of strong faith.

The Prophet has taught his community the best of manners. Foremost among these is to praise God and express gratitude to Him in all situations. The Prophet also taught us to remember situations that could bring grief or sadness:

775. Related by Mālik.

1138. Jābir ibn ʿAbdullāh reports: 'The Prophet was asked: "How are you this morning?" He said: "I am well, belonging to a community that has not seen a funeral or visited an ill person".'

This means that a community that does not have a death or an illness in its midst one day is in a good situation indeed. God is to be praised for this. The Prophet's companions followed his example and related their good situations to their faith.

1139. (*Athar* 299) Muhājir, the jeweller, said: 'I used to sit with one of the Prophet's companions, who was of large stature and belonged to Hadramout. When he was asked: "How are you this morning?" he would answer: "Well. We do not associate partners with God".'

This companion of the Prophet realises that the fact that he believed in God's oneness and did not associate partners with Him is a great blessing. Hence, it did not matter what his physical condition was. An illness or physical disability is of far less importance compared to believing in none other than God. This is what he was keen to stress in his answer to the question about the way he felt on the day.

1140. (*Athar* 300) Sayf ibn Wahb said: 'Abu al-Ṭufayl asked me how old I was. I said: "I am 33". He said: "Shall I tell you something I heard from Hudhayfah ibn al-Yamān? A man from the Muḥārib ibn Khaṣafah [clan] called ʿAmr ibn Ṣulayʿ was a companion of the Prophet and was of my age on that day and I was of your age today. We went to Hudhayfah in a mosque and I sat at the end behind the people. ʿAmr went over until he stood in front of him. He asked him: 'How are you this morning (or this evening), servant of God?' Hudhayfah said: 'I praise God'. ʿAmr said: 'What are these reports we have been receiving concerning you?' Hudhayfah asked: 'What have you heard of me, ʿAmr?' He said: '*Ḥadīths* that I have never heard'. Hudhayfah said: 'By God, were I to relate to you all I have heard, you would not leave me till the middle of this night. However, ʿAmr ibn Ṣulayʿ, if you see the Qays [tribe] taking power in Syria, then beware and again beware. By God, the Qays will leave no believer but they will either put him in a state of fear or kill him. By God, there will come upon them a time when they will be powerless'. 'Amr said: 'What helps you against your own people, may God have mercy on you'. Hudhayfah said: 'This I keep to myself.' He then sat down".'[776]

In this *ḥadīth* Hudhayfah, who was a close companion of the Prophet and belonged to the Anṣār tells his questioner that he heard much from the Prophet that people would need to sit a long time before he could exhaust the subject. It is natural that he should have heard from the Prophet much more than 'Amr who belonged to southern Arabia, a very long distance from Madinah. Therefore, he explained to 'Amr that his lack of knowledge is justified. He tells him about future events the Prophet had foretold. Some of these have already happened. I do not think that we need to delve deeply into these, because their timing is always withheld. Hence, it is of little benefit to us to ask questions about them since we do not know whether we will see such events or not. If they occur in our time, we should hold tight to our faith and not compromise.

The Prophet's companions realised that Islam provided them with the best manners. They were aware of the wide gulf that separated their social manners before and after Islam. They realised that Islam approved every good thing in their customs, amended what needed to be amended and discarded what was wrong or unsocial. Hence they were keen to demonstrate the proper Islamic manners, pointing out the Prophet's teaching wherever needed, so that the following generations could consolidate what they learnt from them.

776. Related by al-Ḥākim.

50

Courteous Behaviour

ABU SA'ĪD AL-KHUDRI was a young companion of the Prophet and lived long after him. He was received everywhere with the respect due to one of the Prophet's companions who was at the same time a fine scholar.

1141. 'Abd al-Raḥmān ibn Abu 'Amrah al-Anṣāri reports: 'One day Abu Sa'īd al-Khudri was informed of a funeral. Apparently he was delayed and came only when people had already taken their places. When he came and people saw him they hastened to make room for him. Some of them stood up to give him their places. He said to them: "Do not do that. I heard the Prophet say: 'The best meeting place is the one most accommodating'." He moved aside to sit in a place where there was plenty of room'.

We see in this *ḥadīth* that many people were keen to show their respect for one of the Prophet's companions, giving up their places so that he could sit in a better position. But we see also that he would not accept this, explaining that it is not right for a latecomer to displace some of those who arrived before him. In our societies we see this happening all the time, with young people moving towards the end of a large room, because of the arrival of someone who is highly placed in society. While this is a good sign of respect, the proper manner is that shown by Abu Saʿīd al-Khudri, where the latecomer sits at the end so as to give the least disturbance to others. In this instance, Abu Saʿīd had plenty of room and he was able to sit comfortably. It is also preferable to sit facing the *qiblah* if possible.

1142. (*Athar* 301) Munqidh ibn Qays reports: ''Abdullāh ibn ʿUmar would mostly sit facing the *qiblah*. Once as he was sitting, Yazīd ibn ʿAbdullāh ibn Qusayṭ recited a verse of the Qur'an containing a prostration [i.e. *sajdah*] when the sun had just been rising. When he read the prostration verse, he and everyone else prostrated themselves except ʿAbdullāh ibn ʿUmar. Later when the sun had risen well in the sky, ʿAbdullāh ibn ʿUmar untied his top robe and prostrated himself. He then said to the reciter: "Have you not seen how your friends prostrated themselves at a time when prayer may not be offered".'

The first point in this *ḥadīth* is the desirability of facing the *qiblah* wherever we sit. This is to be encouraged, but it is by no means obligatory. Had it been so, it would cause people much inconvenience. Hence, when it is feasible, without causing any inconvenience, it is preferable. If it causes inconvenience to oneself or to others, then it need not be done. The reporter of this *ḥadīth* makes clear that ʿAbdullāh ibn ʿUmar mostly sat facing the *qiblah;* he did not insist on doing so, but did it wherever possible.

Secondly, we learn that if a group of people are listening to someone reciting the Qur'an and he reads a verse where it is recommended to offer a prostration, the reciter and the audience should prostrate themselves. There are fourteen or fifteen verses in the Qur'an in this category, each of them containing a reference to prostration as a mark of true submission to God alone. Hence, offering a prostration when such a verse is recited indicates compliance with this universal requirement. The Prophet made it clear that this is to be done, even when we are reading these verses in prayer. Hence, everyone listening to the recitation in this instance prostrated themselves.

The last point to make is that concerning ʿAbdullāh ibn ʿUmar's delayed prostration. This has to do with the times when prayer is discouraged. There are certain times in the day when we should not offer any prayer, and this includes the prostration offered at reciting, or listening to, any of the verses containing a prostration. These times are: 1) after we have offered Fajr Prayer until the sun has risen well into the sky; 2) at the time when the sun is at its highest point in the sky at midday until it starts to move down; and 3) after we have prayed Asr until the sun has completely set. The reason for discouraging prayer in these times is that Islamic worship should never be thought of as associated with the sun and its position in the sky. This is due to the fact that in certain communities, the sun was worshipped as a deity. Hence, it is important that our worship should not be confused with the worship of those communities.

In the case described in this *ḥadīth*, ʿAbdullāh ibn ʿUmar was the only one who noted the time when the reciter read the relevant verse. It was just when the sun had appeared. As such, it was the wrong time for prayer. Therefore, he delayed his prostration for something like twenty minutes or half an hour and offered it then. This is the proper practice.

1143. Abu Hurayrah reports that the Prophet said: 'If any of you leaves his place and then comes back to it, he is more entitled to it'.[777]

It is apparent from the way this *ḥadīth* is phrased that the person who leaves makes it clear that he will be absent only for a short while. If he does not make this clear and then on his return finds his position occupied, he has no claim to it.

The point here is that a person who comes early to a public place, such as a mosque or a study circle, may sit wherever he wishes. If he sits in the front, no one who comes later can ask him to leave.

---

777. Related by Muslim, Abū Dāwūd, and Ibn Mājah.

He has more right to it than anyone who comes later. Therefore, if anyone else claims it, his claim has no basis. This applies on a wider scale. For example, if a scholar habitually sits in a certain place in the mosque where he teaches or answers people's queries and issues rulings, the place should be kept for him. The same applies to small traders who sit in the open market. When such a trader habitually sits at a particular spot, he has more right to it than anyone else. This does not mean that the place should be reserved for him as though he owns it. It only means that he has a claim to it until he finishes his purpose. Suppose such a trader normally finishes his work by midday and leaves, the place may be used by anyone else for the rest of the day. The following morning the place should be kept free for the trader to conduct his business.

1144. Anas reports: 'God's Messenger (peace be upon him) came to us, a group of young boys, and he greeted us. He then sent me on an errand and sat by the roadside waiting for me until I returned. As a result, I was late arriving at Umm Sulaym's [Anas's mother]. She said: "What kept you?" I said: "The Prophet sent me on an errand". She asked: "What was it?" I said: "It is a secret". She said: "Keep the Prophet's secret (peace be upon him)".'[778]

The most important point in this *ḥadīth* is the way Anas spoke to Umm Sulaym and her reaction. Umm Sulaym was his mother and she was very close to the Prophet. When her son told her that he was on an errand for the Prophet, she naturally wanted to know what sort of errand. However, her son, who clearly was still young, told her that he could not give her that information, because it was a private matter. The mother immediately confirmed this and directed her son to keep the Prophet's secret. This is the proper manner of upbringing. A child should learn how to keep other people's secrets, even from his closest relatives.

---

778. Related by Aḥmad, al-Bukhari, Muslim, Abū Dāwūd, al-Tirmidhi, Ibn Mājah, al-Dārimi and Ibn Khuzaymah.

Al-Bukhari lists this *ḥadīth* under the heading 'sitting by the roadside'. In this way he highlights the Prophet's action as he sat waiting for Anas until he returned. What all Muslims know is that if the Prophet did something, without any explanation of its status, then that thing is permissible, i.e. *ḥalāl*. People may do it if they wish. Hence, the *ḥadīth* indicates that there is nothing wrong with sitting by the roadside; it is perfectly permissible. Otherwise, the Prophet would not have done so.

The same *ḥadīth* is reported differently by other scholars. Indeed, al-Bukhari himself lists it differently in his main anthology, the *Ṣaḥīḥ*, where we find it under the heading, 'seeking permission'. This refers to the fine point mentioned in the *ḥadīth* stating that the Prophet greeted the boys before taking Anas aside to tell him of the errand he wanted him to run. It is as though the greeting served as a permission to take one of the group aside. The Prophet would not have spoken to Anas on his own without greeting the group of boys who were with him. That they were only boys and he was God's Messenger and the head of the Muslim state was not contrary to giving the group their rights.

Approaching a group of people

An important aspect of social manners that Islam encourages is how to approach a meeting where a group of people are present. The Prophet has taught us everything we need to promote good relations within the Muslim community. His guidance is such that he neglects no aspect of fine manners without informing us of it. He looks at what pleases everyone involved.

1145. 'Abdullāh ibn 'Umar reports that the Prophet said: 'Let none of you make another rise from his place in order to sit there. Instead, readjust to make room for others'.[779]

This is a very fine point the Prophet is highlighting. When a group of people are sitting somewhere and the place is full, then someone of

779. Related by al-Bukhari, Muslim, Ibn Ḥibbān, al-Dārimi and Abu 'Awānah.

high status in the community comes in, there will be one or more who will try to leave their places so that the newcomer may feel included. What these people do is fine because they are preferring the newcomer to themselves. The Prophet wants such a person to be equally polite and to refuse sitting in anyone else's position. This means that he appreciates their gestures but he makes an equally fine gesture by declining. The proper thing then is for the whole group to adjust themselves so as to allow more room and give the newcomer a proper position. This is not normally possible when each person is sitting in a separate seat. In this case, the seating arrangement should be modified so as to allow room for more chairs.

1146. Jābir ibn Samurah reports: 'When we went to the Prophet (peace be upon him), everyone of us used to sit at the end'.[780]

What this means is that when the Prophet's companions joined him, no one would disturb the group. Each sat at the empty place at the end. The Prophet emphasises this in more than one *ḥadīth*, and here we learn that the Prophet's companions put this into effect, so that it became the standard practice. Moreover, the Prophet makes clear that where there are only two people, one should not cause their separation.

1147. 'Abdullāh ibn 'Amr reports that the Prophet said: 'It is not permissible for anyone to separate two people, unless they permit this'.[781]

This *ḥadīth* applies to situations where there are two people sitting or walking together. If another person joins them he disrupts their business or conversation. Hence, he should ask permission to join them. If the group is larger, seeking permission is also preferable, but it is normally easier to join a larger group than a smaller one. At least with a large group, the question of disruption does not apply.

---

780. Related by al-Nasā'ī, Abū Dāwūd and al-Tirmidhi.
781. Related by Aḥmad, Abū Dāwūd and al-Tirmidhi.

A different aspect of joining a group is that whereby there are many people attending a scholar or person of high position, such as a ruler, a governor, etc. If the newcomer has some urgent business with the head of the meeting, should he seek to approach him, even though this means moving in between people? In former times, people used to sit on the floor, and moving forward meant that one would literally walk over them. The same is the case today when people attend a scholar's circle in a mosque. The following *ḥadīth* gives us the answer.

1148. (*Athar* 302) Ibn ʿAbbās reports: 'When ʿUmar was stabbed, I was one of those who carried him into his home. He said to me: "Nephew! Go and find out who stabbed me and whom he wounded alongside me". I did as he said and came back to tell him, but the house was full of people. I was still young, and I disliked to walk over people's necks. Therefore I sat down, although it was ʿUmar's rule that when he sent anyone on an errand to tell him alone straight away. He was lying and covered when Kaʿb al-Aḥbār came in. He said: "By God, if *Amīr al-Muʾminīn* would pray to God, He will let him be and will keep him for this community until he does this and that". He mentioned some of the hypocrites by name and others by inference. I said to Kaʿb: "Shall I tell him what you have just said?" He replied: "I have said it only so that you will tell him". This encouraged me, and I stood up and moved forward, stepping over people's shoulders until I sat close to his head. I said: "You have sent me on this errand. The man wounded alongside you thirteen men, and he also wounded Kulayb al-Jazzār when he was performing his ablution at the rock with a water-containing cavity. Kaʿb is swearing to this and that". ʿUmar said: "Call in Kaʿb". He was summoned, and ʿUmar asked him about what he said. He confirmed it all. ʿUmar said: "By God, no. I will not say this prayer. But ʿUmar will certainly be in great misery if God will not forgive him".'

There are several reports by different companions of the Prophet about ʿUmar's assassination, each one mentioning one or more points. Together they provide a complete picture of what happened that morning, when he was stabbed as he led the dawn prayer. We will not discuss that event here, but we will concentrate on the points mentioned in the *ḥadīth*. The main point related to our subject is that it is permissible for someone to walk across a circle of people, even though this means that he will walk over them, if he needs to speak to the head of the meeting. At first Ibn ʿAbbās was reluctant to do so because he recognised that more senior companions of the Prophet were ahead of him. But when he had important information to give the Caliph, he did so. He had judged that the information he had at first was not so urgent, but when he heard what Kaʿb had to say, Ibn ʿAbbās felt that he must pass on the information immediately.

ʿUmar asked Kaʿb, who was a rabbi before becoming a Muslim, to come forward, and when he confirmed that the Caliph would live if he prayed for this, ʿUmar said he would not. Needless to say, ʿUmar realised that he would be a martyr if he died as a result of his wounds. He dearly loved to gain a martyr's reward. But even at this late stage in his life, he never lost sight of the need to earn God's forgiveness. May God bless him, for he was the perfect example for all Muslim rulers.

Who qualifies as a Muslim?

1149. ʿĀmir al-Shaʿbi reports: 'A man came to see ʿAbdullāh ibn ʿAmr when he had visitors sitting with him. He tried to walk through in order to reach him but they tried to prevent him doing so. ʿAbdullāh told them to let him come over. As he sat close to him, he said: "Tell me something that you heard from God's Messenger (peace be upon him)". ʿAbdullāh said: "I heard God's Messenger (peace be upon him) say: 'A Muslim is the one from whose tongue and hand Muslims are safe; and a migrant is the one who abandons what God has forbidden'."'[782]

This highly authentic *ḥadīth* provides two definitions for a Muslim and a migrant. We note that it does not touch on the essential qualities necessary for a person to be a Muslim, such as the declaration of

782. Related by Aḥmad, al-Bukhari, Muslim, Abū Dāwūd, al-Nasāʾī, Ibn Ḥibbān and al-Dārimi.

believing in God's oneness and in Muhammad as God's messenger. It speaks of an attitude that respects other Muslims, causing them no harm. Thus it does not define the essential requirements that bring a person into the fold of Islam; rather, it tells us of the nature of the best Muslim people. In this sense it highlights a quality that every Muslim should try to acquire, so that he may be a loved member of the Muslim community. This quality is to cause no harm, physically or mentally, to any other Muslim. When this becomes characteristic of a person to the extent that others feel safe from any abuse that he may cause, he attains the standard that fits this definition by the Prophet of the best and true Muslims.

We note here that the Prophet spoke of harm by mouth first, before adding physical harm caused by hand. This is because most abuse is caused verbally. In other words, people cause more harm by what they say than what is caused by action. Furthermore, we note that the Prophet used the word 'tongue' rather than 'mouth'. This is significant because sometimes abuse is caused by the movement of one's tongue, as when a person puts out his tongue to indicate displeasure, or to make faces at another. This may result in the latter feeling abused. Thus, the Prophet's usage includes all actions in which the tongue is involved, whether by gesture or speech.

Similarly, the Prophet refers to all physical, harm-causing action using the word 'hand', which is the organ used in most physical actions. Moreover, in Arabic, as in most other languages, the word 'hand' is used figuratively, as in 'lay his hand on something' which may not belong to him. This may signify wrongful acquisition of what belongs to others. We also say, 'take the law into one's own hands', signifying unauthorised action that may cause harm. Hence, the *ḥadīth* means that a good Muslim is a person who does not cause harm to other Muslims, either physically or mentally, by hand, word or gesture.

Secondly the Prophet says that 'a migrant is one who abandons what God has forbidden'. This is a reference to migrating for God's cause, which is considered one of the most important actions a person can take in serving the cause of the Islamic faith. Those early Muslims who migrated with the Prophet from Makkah to Madinah provided the role model for Muslims in following generations. The fact that they abandoned their own homes and town for no reason other than to be with the Prophet and to serve the Islamic cause is noted in the Qur'an as a mark of true faith. The Prophet gives us here a different definition of migration, which is to abandon what God has forbidden. The Prophet uses a word derived from the same root, so as to link leaving one's home to abandoning God's prohibitions.

We also note in this *ḥadīth* that the visitor wanted to get close to ʿAbdullāh ibn ʿAmr before he put his request to him. He moved forward causing inconvenience to the people present. Yet ʿAbdullāh asked them to let him come forward, because he felt that the man was eager to learn. As his visitor, he did not wish to embarrass him. Hence, he requested his other visitors to bear with him. Treating a guest so cordially is characteristic of the Muslim community, particularly in Arabia where hospitality to one's guests was long recognised as a most important trait. The Prophet's companions highlight this:

1150. (*Athar* 303) Ibn ʿAbbās said: 'The most honoured person to me is the one sitting by me'.

1151. (*Athar* 304) Ibn ʿAbbās said: 'The most honoured person to me is the one sitting by me. He may move over people's shoulders in order to sit by me'.[783]

Al-Nawawi adds: 'If I could prevent flies from landing on his face, I would certainly do so'.

Because this is a value of great importance, the Prophet's companion provides a description of what he would do to ensure his neighbour's comfort. Moreover, people normally try to show their respect for others by bringing them near to where they are sitting.

1152. (*Athar* 305) Kuthayyr ibn Murrah reports: 'I went into the mosque on a Friday and found ʿAwf ibn Mālik al-Ashjaʿi sitting with a circle of people, with his legs stretched out. When he saw me, he drew up his legs and said to me: "Do you know why I stretched my legs out like that? It is so that a good man might come and find a place to sit near".'

---

783. Both these *ḥadīths* are related by Ibn Ḥibbān.

It is a case of reserving some space for a worthy person. This also shows that there is nothing wrong with stretching out one's legs when sitting with people, if they are clear that the person doing so is merely ensuring that he is comfortably seated.

The Prophet was a most considerate person. He did not like to inconvenience people in any way. He was keen that he always had a pleasant smell, so that people did not feel displeased when they came near him. He was also very kind to all people. He would respond to any one's request, unless the request was not in line with Islamic values and principles. Moreover, he would remove any inconvenience from people's way.

1153. Al-Ḥārith ibn 'Amr al-Sahmi reports: 'I went to the Prophet when he was in Mina, or probably in Arafat, and people were gathered around him. When bedouins saw his face, they would say: "This is a blessed face". I said to him: "Messenger of God! Pray for my forgiveness". He said: "My Lord! Forgive us". I turned round and said again: "Pray for my forgiveness". He said: "My Lord! Forgive us". I turned again and said once more: "Pray for my forgiveness". He said: "My Lord! Forgive us". He went aside, carrying his spit in his hand, and rubbed it on his shoes so that it would not fall on anyone around'.

We note in this *ḥadīth* that the Prophet did what is very inconvenient for any person, which is to spit on his hand and deal with it so that he does not cause irritation to anyone else. He ensured that it was properly removed. When something like this happens, the person concerned is preoccupied with it, trying to find a way to get rid of the irritant before attending to anything else. The reporter of this *ḥadīth* requested the Prophet to pray for his forgiveness, three times in succession. The Prophet was not fed up with the repeated request. Every time the man repeated his request, the Prophet prayed for him and those around, thus teaching him, and us, to include others when we address a prayer to God. When the Prophet said in response to the repeated request: 'My Lord! Forgive us', he actually did as the man requested, but he also included those who were around in his prayer for forgiveness.

But we also note the reporter's observation that those who saw the Prophet for the first time always commented on how pleasant the Prophet looked. Bedouins, who were known to have a keen eye when it came to assessing people at first sight, always commented that the Prophet had a 'blessed face'. The same comment was echoed by many people, because people recognised him to be a man whom they could trust and be safe with.

The road has rights

Another aspect of social behaviour the Prophet taught his companions, and all Muslims, relates to what may be done when one sits by the roadside.

1154. Abu Hurayrah reports: 'The Prophet ordered his companions not to sit by the roadside. They said: "Messenger of God! It is very hard for us to sit at home". He said: "If you sit by the roadside, you must fulfil the rights due from you". They asked: "What are these rights, Messenger of God?" He said: "To guide whoever asks for directions, return people's greetings, lower your gaze, and to enjoin what is right and forbid what is wrong".'[784]

1155. Abu Sa'īd al-Khudri reports that the Prophet said: 'Beware of sitting by the roadside'. They said: 'Messenger of God! We cannot dispense with our sitting places, as we sit to talk together'. He said: 'Since you refuse, you must give the road its due right'. They asked: 'What is the right of the road, Messenger of God?' He said: 'To lower one's gaze, refrain from what causes harm to anyone, enjoin what is right and forbid what is wrong'.[785]

The first thing to note about this *ḥadīth*, in both its versions, is that the Prophet begins with a warning against a social practice. He was

---

784. Related by Abū Dāwūd and Ibn Ḥibbān.
785. Related by al-Bukhari, Muslim and Abū Dāwūd.

fully aware that his audience would find it very difficult to comply with the warning, since the practice was interwoven with their social relations. People used to sit by the road, because it was close to their homes, gave them a pleasant atmosphere and provided them with a chance to sit with neighbours and friends. They least expected that such a practice would be forbidden. Hence their reply that they would find this very difficult. The Prophet's rejoinder tells us that he wanted to ensure that they were attentive to what was coming later, which is an explanation of the right behaviour if one has to occupy a position by the roadside. The Prophet describes this as a right 'due to the road'. This means that we are duty bound to fulfil it.

What is this right, then? It consists of a number of practices that ensure better social relations within the community. The first is to provide guidance for people who enquire about something or other. People may ask about the way or someone's residence. To provide such guidance is very important.

Secondly, if someone greets you when you are sitting by the roadside, you must return the greeting. This is required in all situations, but the Prophet re-emphasises it here because when someone is sitting by the roadside, he is likely to be offered greetings by many passers by. He must always be ready with a civil return to their greetings.

'Lowering one's gaze' refers to the way we look at others. People may have something or an other which they would not like to be deliberately stared at, or they may prefer to be unnoticed. If one does not look very attentively at people as they pass by, this may be appreciated.

Lastly, the Prophet re-emphasises a very essential duty of every Muslim, namely to encourage or enjoin what is right and to speak out against what is wrong or unjust. This requirement is repeatedly stated in the Qur'an and *Ḥadīth*. It ensures that the moral standards of the Muslim community remain high. When people sit outside, they are bound to notice other people's behaviour. Hence, they should try to help and encourage what is good and right, and speak out against what is wrong.

A promise unlike any other

1156. Abu Mūsa al-Ash'ari reports: 'One day the Prophet went into a farm where he had some private matter. I followed him. When he entered the farm, I sat at the door and thought that I would be the Prophet's doorman for the day. He did not order me to do so. He went deep into the farm to answer a call of nature, then returned and sat at the mouth of a well, baring his legs up to the knees and lowering them into the well. Abu Bakr came and told me that he wanted to go in. I said to him: "Stay here until I ask permission for you to go in". He did while I went to the Prophet and said: "Messenger of God! Abu Bakr requests permission to enter". He said: "Admit him and give him the happy news that he will be in heaven". He came in until he was to the Prophet's right and bared his legs and lowered them into the well. Then 'Umar came. I said to him: "Stand here while I ask permission for you to come in". The Prophet said to me: "Admit him and give him the happy news that he will be in heaven". He went in until he was to the Prophet's left and bared his legs and lowered them into the well. That side of the well was thus fully taken and no one else could sit there. 'Uthmān then came, and I said: "Wait here while I ask permission for you to enter". The Prophet said: "Admit him and give him the happy news that he will be in heaven, but that he will have to endure some affliction". He went in and found that he could not sit on their side. So he moved around until he was facing them, by the mouth of the well, and he bared his legs and lowered them into the well. I hoped and prayed that my brother should come in, but he did not until they had left'.

Sa'īd ibn al-Musayyib, who narrated this *ḥadīth* from Abu Mūsa said: 'I interpreted this as indicating their graves with the three being together while 'Uthmān is buried away from them'.

This *ḥadīth* is reported in several versions, with the one we have just quoted being of middle length. It tells us how the Prophet's companions used to behave when they were with the Prophet. They showed him all the respect and love he deserved. Abu Mūsa sees the

Prophet walking alone, and he walks behind him so that he could give him any help he required. When he enters the farm, he decides to be the Prophet's doorman so that he can enjoy his privacy if he wanted. It so happened that this was a special occasion, because the Prophet received there three of his closest companions. Apparently, the Prophet received special revelations on this occasion concerning the destiny of his three companions. Hence, every time one of them arrived, the Prophet told Abu Mūsa not only to let him in, but also to give him the happiest news any believer could receive from the Prophet himself, namely the promise of entry into heaven.

In the case of ʿUthmān, however, the good news is coupled with a reference to the trouble he endured at the end of his reign as the third Caliph, when he faced rebellion engineered by hostile elements who falsely accused him of abusing power. Thus, this *ḥadīth* provides a clear indication to all Muslims that ʿUthmān was right and his accusers were in the wrong.

We also note how Abu Mūsa would have dearly loved that his brother should arrive next, hoping that if he did, the Prophet would give him the same happy news, but this was not to be. It is also interesting to read how Saʿīd ibn al-Musayyib, a renowned early scholar who met many of the Prophet's companions, sees the way the four sat at the well as mirroring their graves, because the Prophet, Abu Bakr and ʿUmar were buried in ʿĀ'ishah's room, with Abu Bakr to the Prophet's right and ʿUmar to his left. Meanwhile, ʿUthmān was buried at al-Baqīʿ the Madinah graveyard where most of the Prophet's companions were buried.

1157. Abu Hurayrah reports: 'The Prophet went out on a hot day. He did not speak to me and I did not speak to him. He went up to the Qaynuqāʿ market. He then went to Fāṭimah's place and sat outside, and asked: "Is the little one there? Is the little one there?" She kept him a little while and I thought she was either changing his clothes or washing him. He then came running and the Prophet took him close, hugging him and kissing him. He then said: "My Lord! Love him and love anyone who loves him".'[786]

786. Related by Aḥmad, al-Bukhari, Muslim, Ibn Ḥibbān and Abu ʿAwānah.

When Abu Hurayrah mentions that he did not speak to the Prophet as he walked by his side he only indicates the attitude of the Prophet's companions when they were with him. They always were in awe, speaking to him only when they realised that they had his permission to say what they wanted. The Prophet would normally have spoken to his companion, but on this occasion he might have been preoccupied with something. Hence, Abu Hurayrah did not venture to speak to him.

The reporter does not tell us what the Prophet did at the market place, perhaps because it was so ordinary a matter. He is more interested in telling us about the Prophet's action at his daughter's home. He sits at the entrance and enquires whether her young son, al-Ḥasan, is there. He then describes the meeting of the little boy with his grandfather, the Prophet. He is a loving grandfather who takes the little boy to himself, carries and kisses him. He then says a most caring prayer, appealing to God to love the little one and to love everyone who loves him. Needless to say, al-Ḥasan was loved by everyone who knew him, and loved by countless millions of Muslims throughout all following generations.

1158. Ibn 'Umar said: 'The Prophet forbade that anyone should make a man rise when he is sitting with a group of people in order to sit in his place'.

(*Athar* 306) 'If a man rose from his place for Ibn 'Umar, he would not sit in his place'.

This *ḥadīth* is similar to Number 1145, but with the added *athar* describing Ibn 'Umar's practice. Even if someone tried to give him his place, he would not take it, fearing that the man did it out of embarrassment.

1159. Anas reports: 'I served God's Messenger one day, until I thought that I had finished what I had to do. I thought that the Prophet would then have his midday nap. So I left him, and I saw some boys playing. I stopped to watch their game. The Prophet came out until he reached them, and he greeted them. He sent me on an errand and stopped in the shade until I came back. I was late for my mother. She asked me: "What delayed you?"

I said: "The Prophet sent me on an errand". She asked what it was. I said: "It is a secret of the Prophet". She said: "Keep God's Messenger's secret". I never mentioned that errand to anyone. Had I told it, I would have told it to you'.[787]

This is similar to Number 1144 with a few more details.

Description of the Prophet

Several *ḥadīths* describe the Prophet, some of which are more detailed than others. The following *ḥadīth* describes him in reasonable detail:

1160. Sa'īd ibn al-Musayyib quotes Abu Hurayrah as he described the Prophet: 'He was of medium height, but nearer to being tall; very white, with a black beard. He had fine front teeth, long eyelashes, broad shoulders and full, flat cheeks. When he walked, he stepped with all his feet which did not have a hollow. When he turned towards someone or turned away, he turned fully. I have never seen the like of him'.

From the *ḥadīths* that describe the Prophet we have a picture of a very handsome and pleasant looking man. The Arabs used to say that a person's most important features are his eyes and mouth: if these are pleasant, he is altogether pleasant. Here the Prophet's companion tells us something about both these features. We learn that his eyelashes were long, which most people consider to be an aspect of beauty, and when his lips parted, fine teeth were revealed.

The *ḥadīth* describes the Prophet's movement, telling us that the curve on his foot was neither too deep nor too shallow, which allowed him to step with all his feet. But he also tells us about the way he turned towards people. The Prophet did not make a slight turn, but rather turned with all his body so as to face a person or go away from him. It is as if his turning reflected his attitude of

---

787. Related by al-Bukhari in a shorter version, Muslim, as well as Aḥmad and Abu 'Awānah, with some variations.

honesty, straightforwardness, and openness. He had nothing to hide. Moreover, the Prophet's companion appears to tell us that the Prophet had a presence which was keenly felt by anyone who saw him, and his presence was felt with every step, whether he was coming or going.

This is confirmed by the heading al-Bukhari gives to the theme under which this *ḥadīth* is entered in this anthology: 'Turning with one's whole body'. There is no other entry under this heading. This is an aspect of al-Bukhari's method, making his headings part of the full picture a chapter is meant to convey. He borrows this heading from another *ḥadīth* giving further description of the Prophet, stating that 'when he turned, he turned with his whole body'.

1161. (*Athar* 307) Aslam said: ''Umar said to me: "If I send you to someone [to find out something], do not tell him why I sent you to him. If you do, Satan will prompt him to say a lie".'

1162. (*Athar* 308) Mujāhid said: 'It is disliked for a man to look sharply at his brother, or to follow him with his eyes when he leaves, or to ask him: "Where have you come from and where are you going".'

These two *ḥadīths* point out some fine manners. The first one relates instructions by 'Umar to one of his assistants, making clear that when he wanted to find out something about someone, the information should be gathered without telling that person, because when he is told he might try to appear in a false light, or to conceal what he does not wish to be known. In all this, he may be guilty of falsehood.

The second *ḥadīth* is about sparing people embarrassment and respecting their privacy. Looking sharply or staring fixedly at a person may make that person feel uncomfortable, while following him with one's eyes when he leaves makes him uneasy if he notices it. It also gives the wrong impression to anyone present. Being inquisitive about people's affairs suggests disrespect for their privacy. All these are contrary to good manners. Hence, the early Muslim society shunned such actions.

1163. (*Athar* 309) Mālik ibn Zubayd reports: 'We passed by Abu Dharr at al-Rabadhah and he asked us: "Where are you coming from?" We said: "From Makkah", or "from the Ancient House [i.e. the Kaʿbah]". He asked: "Is this all you went for?" We said: "Yes". He again asked: "Have you done some trading or business with it?" We said: "No". He said: "Now resume your action".'[788]

Abu Dharr was one of the best known of the Prophet's companions, and he moved to al-Rabadhah, which is a short distance from Madinah, during ʿUthmān's reign in fulfilment of the Prophet's advice to him. When these people visited him, he welcomed them and established that their pilgrimage was intended purely for worship. This is what he meant by his question, 'Is this all you went for?' In other words, he was asking them whether their trip was an action they wished to put to their credit when they account to God on the Day of Judgement. This is clearly understood from his follow-up question of whether it was a pilgrimage that was not coupled with trade or business. It should be mentioned that there is no prohibition against doing some trading or business when one travels for pilgrimage or umrah, but this could sometimes be the main purpose of one's journey while the pilgrimage becomes a secondary one. Hence, Abu Dharr sought to establish that his visitors had no other purpose behind their pilgrimage. When they assured him of this, he told them to resume their action.

Abu Dharr was, in effect, referring to the fact that the pilgrimage earns a great reward from God that includes forgiveness of all past sins. Thus, he reassured them that the purity of their purpose meant that their forgiveness was certain, God willing. The proper line to follow in this case is to show gratitude to God by maintaining a good way of life that seeks to earn more reward in the Hereafter. This is the action Abu Dharr advised his visitors to resume. He himself was one who sought greater reward in the Hereafter in every aspect of his life. His dedication was exemplary. He cared nothing for the comforts of this present world. All he cared for was success in the Hereafter, and he was assured of this by God's grace.

---

788. Related by Mālik.

It may appear that Abu Dharr's attitude goes contrary to the previous *ḥadīth*, which advised against asking people where they have come from or where they are going. We need to say that the advice against such questioning applies generally, but when one is with close friends or with someone from whom one is looking to learn, such questions are not intended to invade another's privacy. Rather they may be an expression of care and friendliness, or they may be leading to good advice. These people went to Abu Dharr, knowing his long companionship with the Prophet. They looked to learn from him and obtain some good advice, which was certainly forthcoming.

1164. Ibn ʿAbbās reports that the Prophet said: 'Whoever makes an image will be required to blow spirit into it, and will be punished as he will never be able to blow spirit. Whoever claims to have seen a vision in a dream will be required to string two pieces of hair together, and will be punished as he will never be able to string them together. And whoever eavesdrops on people who try to be away from him will have molten lead poured into his ears'.

When the Prophet advised his companions, and all Muslims, to avoid certain actions, he always made his advice short and precise. He neither dwelt too long over descriptions, nor used two sentences where one was sufficient. However, he might link two or three pieces of advice together, seeking to establish such a link by different means, even though the points he tackled might be widely diverse. However, his description was always very clear, graphic and life-like.

The first point the Prophet warns against in this *ḥadīth* is making an image. This is a reference to making images of living things, such as people or animals. This is clearly understood from the reference to breathing spirit into an image one has made, so as to make it living. Obviously, no one can do this, because the spirit is breathed into the living by God alone.

But what sort of image is the Prophet speaking about here? The Arabic words used in the *ḥadīth* are the same we use today for photography and photocopying. Needless to say, the Prophet was not talking about these, because they were not known during his lifetime, and for many centuries later. Some people say that this *ḥadīth*, and others prohibiting likeness making, applies to photography, but such a view is mistaken, because the Prophet could not speak about something that was not known by mankind during his lifetime. Even if God told him about it, his audience would not understand his meaning. God describes both the Qur'an and the Messenger to whom it was revealed, i.e. Prophet Muhammad, as 'making things clear'. He could not make things clear if he were to speak of things unknown to his audience. Therefore, we have to look at the usage of the word during the Prophet's lifetime so as to associate it with what the Prophet's companions could associate it with. When we do so, we discover that the term used here means "to shape, mould, fashion, etc".

Moreover, when we take this *ḥadīth* with others addressing the same topic, we conclude that the Prophet speaks about making something so much life-like that people may think it real. In a sacred, or *qudsi*, *ḥadīth*, the Prophet quotes God as saying: 'Who can do more wrong than one who tries to create something like my creation! Let such people create a speck, or a seed, or a seed of barley'.[789] The wording of this *ḥadīth* is so strong, leaving us in no doubt as to the strict prohibition of making anything with the intention of leading people to think that it is comparable to what God creates.

It is particularly this sort of image that is strongly forbidden, whether it comes in the form of a statue, or in any other form. As for photography, it does not come into this category, because a photograph is nothing more than a print of a reflection in a lens. As such it is no different from a reflection in a mirror, which is indeed truer than a printed photo.

Because the attempt to produce a likeness of this sort seeks to imitate God's creation, the person who tries it will be required to breathe life into it. Needless to say, no person can do so. Hence, he will be punished for his deed.

The second point the Prophet warns against is to make a false claim of a dream a person did not see. Why should this be so serious? First of all, it is a lie, and telling lies is viewed very seriously by Islam. Islam simply makes no allowance for what people term as a 'white lie,' or a 'lie of convenience'. All lies are false and falsehood is strongly shunned.

---

789. Related by Muslim.

Secondly, a dream is an aspect of God's creation. It may have no substance as far as we are concerned, but it takes place by God's will. Any dream seen by any of us occurs by God's will and as He determines. Therefore, a false claim of having seen a particular dream, and relating such a false dream to others, means that one is lying to God Himself. As such, this action links with the previous one of creating a likeness of a living thing. Both are false and lies, but one in words and the other in action. Both are required to do something akin to their claims. The one who lies about his dream is required to string together two small hairs so as to make them look like one, which is practically impossible. As he fails, he is punished for his sin.

Thirdly, the Prophet warns against eavesdropping on people. He provides a graphic picture of such a person who tries to hear others talking, but they are trying to hide from him. Such a person would raise his hand to his ear in order to hear people's whispers. This is totally unacceptable from an Islamic point of view and earns severe punishment.

We have to realise that this punishment is earned for trying to overhear others, even though the attempt to do so fails. It is, then, the intention that earns such a person his or her punishment. A similar case is that of one who spies on people through a hole in the door or in a wall, or through a window, etc. If we are in our homes and realise that we are being spied on in this way, we may use a stick to hit the spy in his eye. If that person loses his eyesight as a result, he has no claim to make against us, because the initial fault is his own.

Similarly, the punishment for an eavesdropper is incurred by his very attempt to eavesdrop, even though he does not manage to hear anything being said. The Prophet describes the punishment graphically, as he tells us that molten lead is poured into such a person's ears. Needless to say, he would lose his hearing faculty as a result, but such a loss is only one aspect of his punishment.

1165. (*Athar* 310) 'Al-'Uryan ibn al-Haytham reports: 'My father visited Mu'āwiyah when I was still a young boy. When my father entered, [Mu'āwiyah] said: "Welcome! Welcome!" A man who was sitting with him on his couch asked him: "*Amīr al-Mu'minīn*, who is this man you are welcoming?" He said: "This is the master of the people of the east; this is al-Haytham ibn al-Aswad". [My father] asked: "Who is this?" He was told: "This is 'Abdullāh ibn 'Amr ibn al-'Āṣ". [My father] asked him: "Abu so-and-so, from where will the Impostor (*al-Dajjāl*) appear?" He said: "I have never seen the people of any land asking about what is distant and overlooking what is near at hand, more than the people to whom you belong". He then said: "He will appear in Iraq, in a land full of trees and dates".'

Some people may consider the important point in this *ḥadīth* to be the place where the Impostor, or the *Dajjāl*, will come from. However, scholars highlight other points. 'Abdullāh ibn 'Amr mentions that the Impostor's appearance will be in Iraq, a country defined in the *ḥadīth* as distinguished by its trees and dates. Indeed, Iraq is very rich in both.

'Abdullāh's reply carries a gentle objection to his interlocutor's interest in the Impostor. He describes it as inquiring about what is distant, in preference to that which is near at hand. What he means is that people should be more careful about their own end, which is near, as death can occur at any time. As death means an end of what people can do to improve their lot in the Hereafter, it should be their most important concern. This concern should be translated into good actions so as to ensure a better position with God in the Hereafter. An event in this world can be very distant, if it occurs after one's death.

We note in this *ḥadīth* how Mu'āwiyah, the Caliph, honours his guests. 'Abdullāh ibn 'Amr is honoured and invited to sit on the Caliph's own couch in recognition of his standing as a scholar and a senior companion of the Prophet who adopted Islam much earlier than the Caliph himself. Al-Haytham, a man belonging to the second generation of Muslims, i.e. the *tābi'īn*, is also warmly welcomed because of his standing with his people, and an introduction is made by the Caliph to establish a cordial feeling between his guests.

When a person invites his guest to sit on his couch, the gesture is intended to make the guest feel very welcome. If it is made by a person in a higher position, it is a gesture of honour:

1166. (*Athar* 311) Abu al-'Āliyah reports: 'I sat with Ibn 'Abbās on a couch'.

(*Athar* 312) Abu Jamrah, Naṣr ibn 'Imrān, reports: 'I used to sit with Ibn 'Abbās and he would seat me with him on his couch. He once said to me: "Stay with me and I will give you an allowance from my own money. I stayed with him for two months".'[790]

The gesture made by Ibn 'Abbās had a scholarly aspect. Abu Jamrah mentions that he offered the pilgrimage and the umrah in the *tamattu'* method, which is that recommended by the Prophet, although some people prefer different ones. Abu Jamrah says that some people told him that he would have done better following a different method. However, he mentioned the fact to Ibn Abbas and he approved of his action. He then saw in his dream a man saying to him: 'May your pilgrimage be accepted as pure and may your umrah be acceptable'. He mentioned this to Ibn 'Abbās who commented: 'Your method is the one the Prophet recommended'. He then invited him to stay so as to corroborate this view by mentioning his dream.

1167. Khālid ibn Dinār Abu Khaldah said: 'I heard Anas ibn Mālik say as he was sitting on a couch with al-Ḥakam [ibn Abi 'Aqīl], the governor of Basrah: "The Prophet used to delay the congregational prayer when the weather was hot, but when it was cold, he started the prayer early".'[791]

This *ḥadīth* is entered under the heading of honouring people by inviting them to sit on one's couch. Here Anas ibn Mālik is given this treatment by the governor of Basrah. The *ḥadīth* is very significant as it shows how the Prophet used to delay prayer or start it early depending on the weather. In doing so, the Prophet wanted to ensure that his companions would not endure undue hardship in order to offer the prayer with him. Therefore, if either of the two prayers offered in the middle of the day, i.e. Ẓuhr and Asr, could be more comfortable if delayed in hot weather, he would do so. When there was no need for this in winter time, he would start the prayer early in its time range.

790. his is part of a *ḥadīth* related by al-Bukhari and Muslim.
791. Related by al-Bukhari, al-Nasā'ī and al-Bayhaqi.

Seeking to make prayer more comfortable was a permanent consideration with the Prophet. ʿAbdullāh ibn Masʿūd reports that the Prophet made prayer shorter in summer than in winter. Of course prayers continued to be offered in the same number of *rakʿahs* throughout, but in the summer the Prophet would read shorter passages of the Qur'an, and make his prostration shorter so that the whole prayer would take less time when the weather was very hot. In winter, which is normally mild in Arabia, the Prophet would make his prayer longer, but not too long. Needless to say this flexibility ensures that people are always more attentive when they pray, and they can concentrate on the meaning of what they read or hear of Qur'anic verses during their prayers.

No worldly comforts for the Prophet

1168. Anas ibn Mālik reports: 'I entered the Prophet's room when he was reclining on a couch with a band woven on it. Under his head was a pillow made of hide and stuffed with bast, with no shirt to separate his body from the couch. ʿUmar came in and tears sprang to his eyes. The Prophet asked him: "What makes you weep, ʿUmar?" ʿUmar said: "What makes me weep is that I know for certain, Messenger of God, that you are more honoured by God than the Emperors of Persia and Byzantium, and they are enjoying all the comforts of this world and you are in this state I see". The Prophet said to him: "ʿUmar! Are you not content that they have what this life offers and we have the Hereafter?" ʿUmar said: "Yes, indeed, Messenger of God!" He said: "That is the way it is".'[792]

This *ḥadīth* tells us that life in the Prophet's home was not one of comfort and luxury. Yet he could have had all the comforts he wanted. He was loved by his companions as no leader was ever loved. They would have given him whatever he wished to take of their money and property, but he never took anything from anyone, other than what

792. Related by Aḥmad and Ibn Ḥibbān.

he ate as a guest in their homes or what they sometimes sent him of small gifts. As we learn from other reports about this particular visit from 'Umar, the Prophet was ill with a high temperature. This explains why he was not wearing a shirt or a robe to cover the upper part of his body. Yet he was lying on a couch made of fibre and woven with a band, while his pillow was filled with bast. That is a very rough place for someone who is ill to lie on, providing very little comfort. Hence, 'Umar, who dearly loved the Prophet, was in tears.

This was a natural reaction by a man who realised that the patient he was visiting was the noblest and most honoured human being that ever lived. 'Umar thought of the leaders of the two superpowers of the time, the Byzantine and Persian Empires. They had all the comforts of this life. Had either of them suffered a rise in temperature, he would have been in a most comfortable bed, receiving the best medical attention available. Servants would be at hand waving their fans to cool down his body. 'Umar also thought of the Prophet's standing with God, and could not control his emotion. He expressed his thoughts to the Prophet.

The Prophet reassured 'Umar, reminding him of the life to come. That is a life of permanent bliss, comfort and happiness granted as a reward to those who believe in God and do good deeds in this present life. Those who are not in this category are deprived of such comfort and bliss. The emperors 'Umar mentioned had perpetrated much injustice. Hence, their lot in the Hereafter would be totally different from that of good believers who were keen to do only what God ordered and to refrain from what He had forbidden. The Prophet's answer also alludes to the fact that whatever we enjoy or suffer in this life is of a momentary nature. It soon changes and what remains is only what affects our position in the Hereafter.

Yet Islam does not prescribe a life of self-denial, depriving oneself of comforts that may be available. On the contrary, such comforts may be enjoyed as one pleases, provided that they are earned in a legitimate way. God says in the Qur'an: '*Say: Who is there to forbid the beauty which God has produced for His servants, and the wholesome means of sustenance? Say: They are [lawful] in the life of this world to all who believe – to be theirs alone on the Day of Resurrection*'. (7: 32)

Interrupting the Prophet's sermon

1169. Abu Rifā'ah Tamīm ibn Asad al-'Adawi said: 'I arrived when the Prophet was giving his speech. I said: "Messenger of God! Here is a stranger who has come to enquire about his religion, and he does not know what religion to follow". The Prophet turned to me and stopped his speech. He was brought a chair and I thought its legs to be made of iron. He sat on it and taught me something of what God had taught him. He then resumed his speech until he finished'.[793]

The first thing we note about this *ḥadīth* is the manner with which the question is put and the Prophet's response. The Prophet was in the mosque giving a speech, which was most probably for Friday Prayer. The man comes in and immediately puts his question to the Prophet interrupting his speech. In most societies today, this is unacceptable behaviour which could earn censure, particularly if the speaker commands a high position. No position was higher than that of the Prophet in that community. Yet the man interrupts him, which indicates either that the man was so eager to learn something, or that he was uncouth.

We are not told what the question was, but it appears from the Prophet's reaction and the man's manner that it was about the basics of faith. The man describes himself as one who does not know which faith to follow. Hence, the Prophet loses no time in teaching him the basics of faith. There is simply no time to lose. Everyone was entitled to learn from the Prophet about the essentials of faith whenever they saw him, and the Prophet did not give priority to anything over delivering his message. Every individual is important. Hence, the Prophet did not tell the man to wait until he had finished. He interrupted his speech and sat with the man to teach him the basics of faith. He was also keen that all those present were able to listen. Hence, he sat on a chair so that he could be heard better.

If the occasion was not the Friday *khutbah*, then there is no harm in interrupting the speech, even if it is a long interruption, since the

793. Related by Muslim and al-Nasā'ī.

interruption was with something that was of benefit to his audience. If the speech was that of Friday Prayer, then we learn from this *ḥadīth* that it can be interrupted, if the interruption is not long, and the speaker intends to resume it. Or perhaps the interruption was long, but the Prophet judged that what he said to the man could be incorporated in it, as it tackled the basics of faith. Whatever the case might have been, the *ḥadīth* tells us that every individual is entitled to learn from the highest authority in Islam about God's message. This is a task that applies to all scholars in all generations and communities. A scholar cannot refuse to teach anyone seeking to know about Islam, or the Qur'an. If a person says that he does not know which faith to follow, then scholars have to teach him the basics of the Islamic faith without delay.

1170. (*Athar* 313) Mūsa ibn Dihqān said: 'I saw Ibn 'Umar sitting on a bridal seat and wearing a red garment'.

1171. 'Imrān ibn Muslim said: 'I saw Anas ibn Mālik seated on a couch placing one leg over the other'.

The Prophet's companions endured hardship patiently and did not deprive themselves of the comfort when it was granted. We have to remember that life in Madinah was mostly hard during the Prophet's lifetime. Although Madinah had its farms and date trees, yet things were not easy, considering the frequent military expeditions that had to be sent out, with unbelievers mounting attack after attack on the Muslims, threatening to annihilate them. Besides, the Muslims were only that group of believers in Madinah, and a handful of small groups and individuals from other tribes who could not migrate to Madinah. The Muslims had to endure that sort of life, sacrificing everything for their faith and proving that they were equal to the numerous challenges thrown at them. Hence, God later gave them provisions in plenty, and they were able to carry God's message to other communities in neighbouring areas and states.

The Prophet shared in the hardship when things were hard, and he shared in the comforts when things were plentiful. It is reported that at times, no cooking was done in the Prophet's homes for longer than a month. Later, when the Muslims enjoyed their share of the produce of Khaibar, the Prophet used to give his family imperishable provisions that sufficed for a year.

While these two reports do not speak of any luxurious lifestyle, they mention two of the Prophet's companions availing themselves of comforts which *ḥadīth* 1168 suggests were not available to the Prophet. This is the proper attitude Islam recommends: patience in adversity, and enjoying comforts when they are legitimately available.

1172. (*Athar* 314) Saʿīd al-Muqbiri said: 'I passed by Ibn ʿUmar when he was speaking with a man. I went up to them. He hit me on my chest and said: "If you see two people in a discussion, do not join them until you have sought their permission". I said: "May God keep you on the right path, Abu ʿAbd al-Raḥmān. I only hoped to listen to some useful thing from you two".'

1173. (*Athar* 315) Ibn ʿAbbās said: 'Whoever eavesdrops on people when they dislike that he should do so will have molten lead poured into his ears and whoever claims to have seen a vision in a dream will be required to string two pieces of hair together'.

These *ḥadīths* speak about the same actions the Prophet censures in *ḥadīth* 1164, and we have fully discussed these already. The additional point here is that Ibn ʿUmar uses his hand to bring the point home to the person who hoped to listen to some good advice or something concerning Islamic law and values.

1174. ʿAbdullāh ibn ʿUmar reports that the Prophet said: 'If there are three people, two should not engage in conversation to the exclusion of the third'.[794]

1175. ʿAbdullāh ibn Masʿūd reports that the Prophet said: 'If there are three of you, let not two of them be in conversation to the exclusion of the third, because this will hurt him'.[795]

---

794. Related by al-Bukhari, Muslim, Abū Dāwūd, Ibn Mājah and Abu ʿAwānah.
795. Related by al-Bukhari, Muslim, Abū Dāwūd and Ibn Mājah.

1176. Ibn 'Umar reports that the Prophet said: [quoting the same as in 1174]. We asked: 'What if there are four people'. He said: 'There is no harm then'.[796]

1177. 'Abdullāh ibn Mas'ūd reports that the Prophet said: 'If there are three of you, let not two of them be in conversation to the exclusion of the third until they have mixed with other people, because this will hurt him'.[797]

1178. (*Athar* 16) Ibn 'Umar said: 'If there are four people, there is no harm'.

These authentic *ḥadīths* are very similar, suggesting that the Prophet gave this advice on different occasions and with different wordings, so that it would be known and people would act on it. The Prophet is concerned here for the third person who is left out of the conversation between the other two. We do not have any qualification to limit this instruction to any situation, which means that whoever the third person happens to be, he or she must not be so obviously excluded. The Prophet clarifies that such an action is bound to hurt the excluded person. Hence, it must not be done, and the order he gives represents a very clear prohibition.

Thus, if they are three brothers, or three classmates, or colleagues, or indeed any three, the restriction applies. The Prophet mentions the figure three because it is the least number where exclusion may occur. But it also applies to any larger number of people where such an exclusion could take place.

The question is all about exclusion. Therefore, when there are four people, it is not inappropriate for two of them to have some private conversation. The restriction does not apply here because the other two could talk to each other, and so the feeling of exclusion does not apply. However, if three of them talk together and exclude the fourth, the same prohibition applies.

---

796. Related by Abū Dāwūd and Ibn Ḥibbān.
797. Related by al-Bukhari.

The Prophet also taught his companions to seek permission from their guest if they wish to leave.

1179. (*Athar* 317) Abu Burdah ibn Abu Mūsa said: 'I sat with 'Abdullāh ibn Salām. [After a while] he said: "You are sitting with us but now it is time for us to leave". I said: "As you wish". He rose and I walked with him to the door'.

This means that there is nothing wrong if one wishes to leave, provided one so explains to one's guest, or host, before departing.

1180. Ḥuṣayn ibn 'Awf reports: 'I came in when God's Messenger (peace be upon him) was giving a speech. I stood in the sun and he commanded me and I moved to the shade'.[798]

The Prophet cared for every individual in his community, and part of his care was that even when he addressed them in the mosque or anywhere else, he was aware of what was happening. This *ḥadīth* tells us that he noticed his companion as he stood in the sun. He interrupted his speech to tell him to move where he would be in the shade. There is no advantage in doing what is hard when a more comfortable situation is available. Hence, the Prophet pointed this out to his companions and instructed the man to move.

1181. Abu Sa'īd al-Khudri reports: 'God's Messenger (peace be upon him) forbade two types of garment and two sale transactions. He forbade in sale the *mulāmasah* and *munābadhah* (*mulāmasah* means that a man touches the other person's garment, and *munābadhah* means that a person throws his garment to the other) and this concludes the sale between them without inspection. The two types of dress are *al-ṣammā'* (meaning that a person puts the edge of his robe on his shoulder which leaves one side of his body uncovered). The other is to wrap oneself up in

798. Related by Aḥmad, al-Ṭayālisi, al-Ḥākim, Ibn Ḥibbān and Ibn Khuzaymah.

a garment when sitting down, leaving one's private parts totally uncovered'.[799]

The prohibition in dress is to show one's nakedness, even when there are only a few people around, or even one. The Prophet mentions two situations of carelessness, which probably were not infrequent in pre-Islamic Arabia, but Islam changed people's outlook and practices. To show one's nakedness is totally forbidden in any situation.

The two types of sale transactions the *ḥadīth* mentions involve buying something without inspecting it to make sure that it has no defect. These show a person buying a garment at night or during the day, without looking at it properly. He merely touches it or feels it casually. The point is that if he later discovers that there is something wrong with the garment and wants a refund, this may cause friction between the buyer and seller. Therefore, the Prophet advises proper inspection before concluding the sale.

The Prophet was very easy in his manners. He cared for everyone and never despised any form of hospitality given to him, or showed that he expected something better. If he visited a poor person, he would sit wherever was suitable and show no dissatisfaction. People welcomed him and gave him the best they had, but their best might be not very comfortable. He would pay no attention to poor conditions. He was more concerned with the people themselves, and every one of them was important to him.

1182. Abu Qilābah reports: 'Abu al-Malīḥ said to me that he and my father visited ʿAbdullāh ibn ʿAmr and he told them: "The Prophet (peace be upon him) was informed of my fasting and he visited me. I gave him a cushion made of hide and stuffed with bast. He sat on the floor and the cushion was between the two of us. He said to me: "Is it not sufficient for you to fast three days every month?" I said: "Oh, Messenger of God!" He said: "Five". I said: "Oh, Messenger of God!" He said: "Seven".

799. Related by al-Bukhari and al-Nasā'ī.

I said: "Oh, Messenger of God!" He said: "Nine". I said: "Oh, Messenger of God!" He said: "Eleven". I said: "Oh, Messenger of God!" He said: "The maximum is the practice of David: Half the time: fasting one day and a break one day".'[800]

In this *ḥadīth*, we see the Prophet doing what is very simple to put his host at ease. He leaves the cushion between the two of them, so that both could use it for support. When we hear or read such *ḥadīths*, with such detailed description, we realise that the Prophet's companions could not have left anything unreported.

This *ḥadīth* speaks about the Prophet's advice to 'Abdullāh about his voluntary fasting. He apparently fasted very frequently. The Prophet wanted him to take things easy, but he felt that he could do more. There are several versions of this discussion, but they all agree that the Prophet suggested to him to fast only three days every month, but he kept asking to be allowed more. Thus the Prophet suggested five days, then seven, nine, and eleven but 'Abdullāh wanted to fast more. The Prophet then told him that no one could do better than the Prophet David who used to fast on alternate days. 'Abdullāh ibn 'Amr did this, and continued to do so until he became an old man, when he regretted not acting on the Prophet's advice. He still, however, observed what he committed himself to do in the presence of the Prophet.

We learn from the Prophet's manners described in numerous *ḥadīths*, related by a large number of his companions that it was very easy to get along with him, and he respected everyone.

1183. 'Abdullāh ibn Busr reports that the Prophet stopped at his father's place and he gave him a rug. The Prophet sat on it.

This *ḥadīth* does not tell us anything about what went on between the Prophet and his host. The reporter merely mentions how the Prophet was received. Apparently, there was nothing special on this occasion to comment on. It shows that the Prophet's companions reported his every movement, action, and word. In this instance, nothing of

---

800. Related by al-Bukhari.

importance took place. Therefore, the reporter merely mentions that the Prophet sat on the offered rug.

Muslims never tire of stressing that the Prophet was a human being in every sense of the word. His feelings and manners were what is normal with all men, except that he had a greater share of every good thing, and was without fault in his morality and manners. He behaved naturally. He sat the way that was most comfortable at the time and place. Hence, his companions report what they saw of him, giving us a detailed picture of his character.

1184. Qaylah said: 'I saw the Prophet sitting in a squatting position, and when I saw him the Prophet (peace be upon him) sitting in such a humble way, I trembled with fear'.[801]

1185. Dhayyāl ibn 'Ubayd reports: 'I went to the Prophet and I found him seated cross-legged'.

1186. (*Athar* 318) Ma'n al-Qazzāz said: 'Abu Ruzayq said that he saw 'Ali ibn 'Abdullāh ibn 'Abbās seated cross-legged, with one leg over the other, the right over the left'.

1187. (*Athar* 319) 'Imrān ibn Muslim said: 'I saw Anas ibn Mālik sitting like this, cross-legged, with one foot over the other'.

The reporter of the first *ḥadīth* does not mention why she felt terrified, but we can deduce that the Prophet was in deep thought and he might have looked exceedingly serious. With him sitting in the unusual squatting position, the girl was scared. Al-Ṭabarāni, who also relates this *ḥadīth*, provides more details: 'The man sitting with the Prophet said to him: "Messenger of God, the poor girl is scared". Without looking at me, he said: "Poor girl, have peace". All the fear that I felt went away'.

Here, we see how the Prophet was very kind to young people. When he realised that the girl was scared, he did not try to speak to

801. Related by Abū Dāwūd and al-Tirmidhi.

her or calm her by direct speech, because with children this could easily be counterproductive. Instead, he prayed for her to have inner peace, and soon enough she shed her fear. Whenever the Prophet prayed for anyone, his prayer was answered in the most perfect manner.

The second *ḥadīth* simply describes the way the Prophet sat on this particular occasion. Apparently he sat on the floor, because the way he sat could only be done on the floor or on a flat surface with a large area. His legs were double crossed, which is a comfortable form of sitting, with each foot placed under the other thigh. If a person is used to this way of sitting, he can sit for hours without needing to change his position. The last two *ḥadīths* refer to one of the Prophet's companions and one of their successors sitting in the same way, which suggests that they were very comfortable.

1188. Sulaym ibn Jabir al-Hujaymi said: 'I visited the Prophet and he was wrapped in a cloak with its edges over his feet. I said: "Messenger of God, advise me". He said: "Make sure to be God-fearing. Do not scorn any small kindness, not even pouring water out of your bucket into that of someone who needs it, or talking to your brother with a cheerful face. Beware of dragging your lower garment, because it is an act of arrogance which God dislikes. If a man tries to shame you for something he knows about you, do not try to shame him for something you know of him. Let him face the consequences of what he does while you have the reward for it. Do not abuse anything". After this, I never abused anything, neither an animal nor a human being'.[802]

We have discussed some of these points the Prophet mentioned as they were also stated in other *ḥadīths*, such as Numbers 305, 427 and 894. In this *ḥadīth,* the Prophet refers to dragging one's robe or garment. In fact, this is mentioned in other *ḥadīths* and they are authentic, but every time the Prophet mentions this, he points out that it is an aspect of arrogance. Thus, he does not censure it for its own sake, but for the fact that it was in his time and place a mark of arrogance, done by the rich to stress that they were privileged. Some people nowadays

802. Related by Aḥmad, 'Abdullāh, al-Ḥākim and Ibn Ḥibbān.

make an important issue about the length of one's garment, without referring to any point of arrogance. The fact is that Islam does not disapprove of a particular type of dress, but it lays down principles. Whatever can be associated with arrogance is condemned. When a type of clothing is not so associated, it is acceptable, even if it covers the ankles, as trousers do.

The Prophet also makes it clear that one should not retaliate to an evil action with a similar one. The Prophet tells his interlocutor that he should not shame a person in retaliation for being shamed. Let the other person bear the consequences, and receive God's punishment, while the one accepting the situation with forbearance receives the reward.

We also note how the man accepted all the Prophet's advice. He says that he never abused an animal or a human being after this occasion. The Prophet simply told him not to abuse anything and he applied this to animals in addition to humans.

1189. Abu Hurayrah reports: 'Whenever I see Ḥasan, my eyes are filled with tears because the Prophet went out one day and found me in the mosque. He took me by the hand and I walked with him. He did not speak to me until we reached the Qaynuqāʿ market. He walked there and looked around then he left and I went with him until we returned to the mosque He sat and wrapped himself in his garment. He asked: "Where is the little one? Call me the little one". Ḥasan came running until he fell in the Prophet's lap, and put his hand in the Prophet's beard. The Prophet opened his mouth and Ḥasan's mouth touched the Prophet's mouth. The Prophet then said: "My Lord! Love him and love anyone who loves him".'[803]

This *ḥadīth* describes the same event as Number 1157. Here the reporter, Abu Hurayrah, says that his eyes were tearful whenever he saw Ḥasan, the Prophet's grandson, because he would remember this event.

---

803. Related by al-Bukhari, Muslim, Ibn Mājah and al-Ḥākim.

The *ḥadīth* draws a very normal picture of a grandfather wanting to play with his little grandson. He allows the child to play with his beard and he lovingly puts his mouth over the child's mouth. But the prayer he says is exceptionally moving. He prayed to God not only to love the child but to love those who love him as well. And history records that all Muslims loved the Prophet's grandsons. He not only merited this love on account of his relation to the Prophet, but he was a man people liked and wished to associate with. Moreover, when he became Caliph, he stepped down after six months, to ensure the unity of the Muslim state.

1190. Anas ibn Mālik reports: 'One day the Prophet led the Ẓuhr Prayer. When he finished he stood on the platform [i.e. the *minbar*] and spoke about the Last Hour. He said that it involves great things. He then said: "Whoever wishes to ask about something, let him put his question. By God, whatever you may ask me, I will answer you, as long as I am in this position of mine".

Anas said: 'People cried much when they heard the Prophet saying this. The Prophet invited people several times to ask. Then 'Umar sat on his knees and said: "We are happy to believe in God as our Lord, in Islam as our religion, and in Muhammad as God's Messenger". When 'Umar said this, the Prophet stopped inviting questions. Then the Prophet said: "By Him who holds Muhammad's soul in His hand, I have been shown heaven and hell in the centre of this wall, as I was praying. I have never witnessed a day like this, both in what is good and what is evil".'[804]

We note first that the reporter is keen to indicate the timing when this incident took place. It was after the Prophet and his companions finished their obligatory Ẓuhr Prayer. In al-Bukhari's *Ṣaḥīḥ* anthology, it is 'after the sun had moved a little after midday'. Both times are very close, but the *Ṣaḥīḥ* version does not mention that the Ẓuhr Prayer was offered first.

---

804. Related by al-Bukhari, Muslim and al-Tirmidhi.

An additional, but important point, is found in the version related by Muslim, which starts as: 'The Prophet heard something about his companions, and he spoke to them ...' This explains why the atmosphere was so tense on this occasion, with the Prophet inviting questions and few of them putting forward any. We have no idea what the Prophet heard about his companions, but it seems something that did not particularly please him. It may be deduced that it could have been something about the extent of his knowledge, but this is by no means certain. Since we are not told, we should not speculate about it. Anyway, there is sufficient material in the *ḥadīth* for us to learn from.

As the Prophet started his speech, he mentioned the Last Hour, when all life on earth will come to an end, the Day of Judgement arrives and people are resurrected to be given their rewards. Apparently, the Prophet wanted his companions to think of this, because by doing so they would be able to rise above the concerns of this life. Moreover, both the Qur'an and the *Ḥadīth* stress that it is certain to come.

The Prophet then invites questions, promising to answer any question put to him at that time while he was in his position. This indicates that the Prophet was given complete information about everything, but his knowledge was limited to that particular session. Or he might have been promised by God to have the information he would need when a question was put to him. Both situations indicate a special favour granted to him by God. The Prophet was a human being to whom all the limitations of human beings apply, except for what God grants him as a special favour.

His audience were apparently preoccupied with thoughts about the Hereafter, since the Prophet reminded them of this and mentioned some details which sounded very serious.

Then 'Umar came forward and made his statement: 'We are happy to believe in God as our Lord, in Islam as our religion, and in Muhammad as God's messenger'. Kneeling on his knees and making this statement, 'Umar wanted to dispel the Prophet's displeasure. Nothing would have pleased the Prophet more than to find that people believed in God and in him as God's messenger. Thus, 'Umar reassured the Prophet of the fact that they all believed in him and his message. 'Umar also indicated that as believers, they did not need to trouble the Prophet with their questions. They simply accepted whatever came their way because as believers, they trusted that God would bestow His grace on them, as He bestowed His grace when he sent them Muhammad as His messenger to explain to them the truth and what benefits them in this life and in the Hereafter.

Moreover, we see that the Prophet's displeasure was indicative of his care for his companions. He was made to see heaven and hell during his prayer. If he had heard something unpleasant about his companions, he wanted them to do what they needed to do in order to ensure that they would go to heaven. Hence, he wanted them to be reassured. This is why he invited their questions, hoping that what they would ask would help them to be firmer in their belief. Thus, 'Umar's statement was on the same wavelength. He reassured the Prophet that they all believed and were firm in their faith. This was sufficient to calm the Prophet.

As we have noted, the Prophet always behaved normally, reflecting easy manners and showing that he was one of his community:

1191. 'Abdullāh ibn Zayd ibn 'Āṣim al-Māzini said: 'I saw him [meaning the Prophet] lying down, with one of his legs over the other'.[805]

1192. (*Athar* 320) Al-Miswar ibn Makhramah said: 'I saw 'Abd al-Raḥmān ibn 'Awf lying down with one of his legs over the other'.

According to Abū Dāwūd's version, this was in the mosque, which makes it clear that it is perfectly permissible to lie down in a mosque. Some people suggest that the Prophet warned against lying down with one leg over the other. This *ḥadīth*, which is definitely authentic, makes clear that there is nothing wrong with this. The problem arises only if it is thought that by doing so one exposes that part of one's body which should remain covered. If this is the case, then it is strongly urged that one should not do so. If, on the other hand, one is certain that there is no chance of this happening, then one may do so, since the Prophet is reported to have done it. The second *ḥadīth* shows that the Prophet's close companions were aware of this.

---

805. Related by Mālik, al-Bukhari, al-Nasā'ī and Abū Dāwūd.

Guidance in all situations

The Prophet was keen to give us guidance in all situations, even in the way we sit, stand or lie down. Some people today may wonder why the Prophet would concern himself with such things, when they are subject to either social manners or personal choice. The fact is that the Prophet was keen to establish a code of social and personal behaviour that would bring good results to both individual and society. Moreover, the Prophet might alert us to something that is good for our health, or want us to avoid something because it is harmful. Sometimes he would tell us the reason for a particular order, but he might also give an order without explanation. At times his order might be obligatory, which means that we commit an offence if we do not comply, but at other times, his order might be only a recommendation. This distinction is either expressly stated or easily deduced.

1193. Ṭikhfah ibn Qays al-Ghifāri, who was one of the people of al-Ṣuffah said: 'I was one night sleeping in the mosque when, towards the end of the night, someone came while I was lying on my stomach, and he alerted me with his foot. He said: "Wake up, This position is disliked by God'. I lifted my head and I saw the Prophet standing over my head".[806]

1194. Abu Umāmah said: 'God's Messenger (peace be upon him) passed by a man in the mosque who was lying on his front. He kicked him gently with his foot and said: "Get up. This is the way of sleeping in hell".'[807]

The people of al-Ṣuffah were a group of the Prophet's companions who were very poor and homeless. They came to Madinah from different parts of Arabia to join the Muslim community. The Prophet placed them in the mosque and looked after them. Abū Dāwūd's version of this *ḥadīth* is longer, starting with the Prophet coming to them and saying: 'Let us go to 'Ā'ishah's place. We all went with him. He said

---

806. Related by Aḥmad, al-Nasā'ī, Abū Dāwūd and Ibn Mājah.
807. Related by Ibn Mājah.

to 'Ā'ishah: "Bring us some food", and she brought us a Jashīshah [a dish made of wheat, meat and dates] which we ate. He again said to her: "Give us some food to eat". This time, walking in short steps, she brought Ḥaysah [a sweet dish made of dates and fat]. He then said: "Give us something to drink", and she brought us a large jug of milk which we drank. He then said again: "Give us more to drink", and she brought us a small jug, and we drank. He then said: "You may sleep if you wish, and you may go back to the mosque if you prefer".'

This version of the *ḥadīth* speaks of the Prophet's generosity. It is clear that his wife served all the food, sweet and drink she had. It was later in the night, when the Prophet was preparing for Fajr Prayer that he saw the man lying down on his stomach and told him to change position.

We need to know that there is no special preference of how one should lie down, except these *ḥadīths* which make it clear that lying on one's stomach is disliked by God. It does not mean that this position is forbidden, but rather that it is discouraged or reprehensible. The Prophet does not explain here why it is so, and we do not add anything without guidance. In the second *ḥadīth* the Prophet mentions that it is a position the people of hell take. However, we may add that if someone is uncomfortable in other positions, or if he is ill and needs to lie in this position, then his case is a special one and so may override the ruling.

It is well known that Muslims generally prefer to use their right hand, particularly for eating and drinking. This is taught by the Prophet:

1195. 'Abdullāh ibn 'Umar reports that the Prophet said: 'Let no one eat or drink with his left hand, for Satan eats and drinks with his left hand'.[808]

This is a general recommendation that is extended to other activities. One version of this *ḥadīth* adds that we should not take or give anything with our left hands. In the Islamic sense, the right hand is always associated with goodness and happiness. Those who will go to

808. Related by Mālik, Muslim, Abū Dāwūd and al-Tirmidhi.

heaven in the Hereafter are described in the Qur'an as 'the people of the right', or 'those on the right hand side', while the ones who go to hell are called 'the people of the left', or 'those on the left hand side'. Moreover, the Arabic term *yamīn*, which means the right hand, is derived from a root that signifies goodness and goodly expectations.

It should be pointed out that this is a general recommendation. If one is left-handed and finds it difficult to use one's right hand for ordinary tasks, there is no harm for such a person to use his or her left hand. As for Satan, we only know that which we are told in the Qur'an and *Ḥadīth*. Apparently he eats and drinks, but he uses his left hand. This is enough reason for us to use our right hands in order to show that we always want to take a different path to his.

1196. Ibn 'Abbās reports: 'It is part of the Sunnah that when a person sits down, he should remove his sandals and put them to his side'.[809]

This is another recommendation relating to manners. The *ḥadīth* describes a situation where people sit on the floor. If they keep their sandals or shoes on, they will be obtrusive and ugly. It is courteous to put them aside so that people are not offended by their sight or smell. In a different situation, where people sit on chairs and feet and shoes are hardly seen, there is no harm in keeping them on.

1197. (*Athar* 321) Abu Umāmah said: 'Satan may come to someone's bed after his wife had prepared it and throw a stick or a stone or something on it, so that he will stir trouble between the man and his wife. If you find something of the sort, do not get angry with your wife, because it is done by Satan'.

We are told in the Qur'an that when Satan was expelled from heaven, he vowed to do everything in his power to dislodge Adam and his progeny from the right path. So, he tempts us to violate every rule in God's message, and to indulge our pleasures in every way. If we do so, we please him and displease God. Similarly, Satan tries to sow discord

---

809. Related by Abū Dāwūd.

among us, creating trouble within the same family or between friends, brothers and sisters. If we fall into his trap, we end up losing either a reward or something that we really care for. Here, we are told that he might stir trouble between man and wife by spoiling her work. We should know that when we have cordial and caring relations with our friends and family, we leave little room for Satan to trouble us. It is when we are angry that he can tempt us into doing what is wrong. Therefore, if we are always ready to overlook mistakes and pardon those who are close to us, we end up in better relations with them and receive more reward from God.

This *ḥadīth* may be taken literally or figuratively. In both cases its message is true.

Taking normal precautions

The Prophet impresses on his companions, and indeed all Muslims, that they should take normal precautions against what causes them harm. Thus a Muslim should take any measure that enhances his safety, or the safety of his family and dependants. If someone fails to take such measures, he forfeits any rights he might have been entitled to have, from other people or from God, because of his failure.

1198. 'Ali ibn Shaybān reports that the Prophet said: 'Whoever sleeps on a rooftop with no barriers forfeits all claims'.[810]

1199. (*Athar* 322) 'Ali ibn 'Imārah reports: 'Abu Ayyūb al-Anṣāri came over and I went up with him on a flat roof. He came down and said: "I was about to spend a night with no claim [for God's protection]".'

In our modern days when we have air conditioning and comfortable beds we may wonder who wants to sleep on a rooftop. We need only to go back a little bit in time and imagine a place with a very hot climate, and with no air conditioning. Many people preferred to sleep

---

810. Related by Abū Dāwūd.

on the roofs of their homes because it felt far more comfortable than sleeping in their bedrooms which were much hotter. In this *ḥadīth*, the Prophet tells us very clearly that we must take reasonable precautions against a fall. To start with, he points out that if the rooftop is without a reasonable barrier, then sleeping there is wrong. A sleeping person may be exposed to certain risks. If he turns over and happens to be near the edge, he might fall down. A fall is also possible if he wakes up and starts to walk before he is completely alert. He might step over something he cannot see and fall as a result, causing himself a serious injury. Or he may be disoriented if he has not yet recovered all his senses; so he starts walking in the wrong direction. If it is still dark, he might fall down. In all these situations, a fall is possible. Therefore, one must not expose oneself to the risks.

God has been generous and compassionate to us, assigning angels to watch over us. We see this clearly in situations of imminent danger which we have overlooked. We suddenly are alert to the danger and take a reflex action to avoid trouble. We wonder how we saw the danger in the nick of time, when all factors should have prevented us from so seeing it. Take the example of someone driving alone and getting tired. He may be about to fall asleep when something suddenly alerts him. God says in the Qur'an: '*There are guardians watching over you, noble recorders, who know all your actions*'. (82: 10-12)

But in order to be in the safest position, we need to take all reasonable precautions in every situation. Thus, we should not drive for a long distance when we are tired and feel that we could easily fall asleep. Instead, we should have some sleep before we start our journey. In the same way, a person who sleeps on a rooftop without an edge or a barrier to prevent a fall should take reasonable precautions. If he does not, and falls causing his own death, no claim can be made against anyone. Moreover, he may have forfeited any reward from God he would otherwise have received. If someone takes proper precautions and prays to God for his own safety, but nevertheless meets his destiny by a fall, he is considered a martyr and receives good reward.

This was perfectly understood by the Prophet's companions as it is clear from Abu Ayyūb's remark in the second *ḥadīth*.

1200. One of the Prophet's companions reports that he said: 'A person who sleeps on a rooftop without edges and falls and dies has no claim. And a person who sails in the sea when it is rough and dies forfeits all claims'.[811]

This *ḥadīth* mentions two types of exposure to danger. In both situations the person concerned does something careless. As a result he forfeits all his rights. There is first the right to be helped by the guardian angels, and then the right of reward that results from such danger.

Although the Prophet mentions only these two types, the import of the *ḥadīth* is clear in its applicability to all types of danger. One of these is exposure to illness. Some diseases are contracted through careless behaviour, while others are caused through a failure to take preventative measures. Nowadays, we have vaccinations against a variety of diseases, including some of the worst diseases that affect children, such as tuberculosis, measles, whooping cough and meningitis. If we fail to vaccinate our children at the right time, we are not giving them the immunity that spares them much trouble. Some of these diseases are killers. If parents fail to immunise their children through vaccination, they are exposing them to these killer diseases. They risk coming under the Qur'anic verse that states: '*Losers indeed are those who, in their ignorance, foolishly kill their children*'. (6: 140) Failure to immunise children when the means are available could be through either negligence or ignorance. Neither is a valid justification. So, if parents neglect to vaccinate their children, and as a result, a child contracts a disease which ends in his death, the parents have to answer to God for a very serious failure.

1201. Abu Mūsa al-Ashʿari reports that 'the Prophet was sitting in a farm at the edge of a well, with his legs lowered into the well'.

This is a portion of *ḥadīth* Number 1156, which we have discussed fully.

---

811. Related by Aḥmad and al-Bayhaqi.

1202. (*Athar* 323) Muslim ibn Abu Maryam said: 'When Ibn 'Umar left home he would say: "My Lord, keep me safe and keep others safe from me".'

1203. Abu Hurayrah reports: 'When the Prophet left his home, he would say: "In the name of God; on Him I do rely; no power operates except by His will".' [*Bismillah; al-tuklan 'ala Allah; wa la ḥawl wala quwwata illa billāh.*]

These two *ḥadīths* are part of the overall perspective a Muslim should have. He is in a constant relationship with God and he trusts all his affairs to Him. When a person goes out, he does not know what he will encounter. There may be some dangers of which he is unaware, or he may be in a situation where he could deliberately or unintentionally cause harm to others. Hence, Ibn 'Umar's supplication as he went out, praying to God to keep him safe and ensure he caused no harm to others.

The Prophet started with God's name, as this was customary for him. He used to say that any action of importance should start with God's name. Otherwise, it remains disconnected. He made it clear that he relies on God and entrusts himself to Him, acknowledging that no power can operate except by His will. We will do well to emulate the Prophet in every respect. If we say this simple supplication as we go out, we feel much more relaxed.

Highlighting the best characteristics

The 'Abd al-Qays tribe lived in the eastern provinces of today's Saudi Arabia, and the Prophet had some correspondence with them, starting when one of their number, Munqidh ibn Ḥayyān, who visited Madinah on a trade trip. The Prophet explained the message of Islam to him and he accepted the faith. He took the Prophet's letter which was the start of their acceptance of Islam.

1204. Some of the 'Abd al-Qays delegation reported: 'When we decided on visiting the Prophet (peace be upon him), we set out on our trip. Shortly before our arrival, we met a man riding fast on a young camel. He greeted us and we replied to him. He stopped and asked us to which tribe we belonged. We said: "We are the delegation of the 'Abd al-Qays". He said: "You are welcome here. I have come on purpose to see you and to give you happy news. The Prophet said to us yesterday as he looked to the east: "You will receive tomorrow the best Arab delegation, coming from this direction (meaning the east)". I was restless through the night. So, early in the morning I prepared my camel and set out fast until the day was well advanced. Then I thought that I should start on my journey back home, but I saw the heads of your camels.

'He then turned his camel back and sped on his way home, until he arrived and met the Prophet who was sitting with some of his companions from both the Muhājirīn and the Anṣār around him. Addressing the Prophet, he said: "May my parents be sacrificed for your sake! I have come to give you the news of the arrival of the 'Abd al-Qays delegation". He said: "How do you know about them, 'Umar?" He answered: "They are following me fast. They will be here in no time". He mentioned how he saw them. The Prophet said to him: "May God give you happy news". The people with the Prophet began to prepare themselves [to receive the newcomers]. The Prophet was seated, and he put the end of his robe under his hand as support, stretching his legs.

'The delegation arrived and both the Muhājirīn and the Anṣār were delighted to see them. When the new arrivals saw the Prophet and his companions, they let their mounts free and came forward speedily. The seated people moved to give them space to sit while the Prophet remained reclining. A man from among them, nicknamed al-Ashajj, but known as Mundhir ibn 'Ā'idh ibn Mundhir stayed behind. He collected their camels, sat them down and relieved them of their loads gathering it all together. He then took out a box of his luggage, took off his travelling clothes and put on a suit [of his best garments]. He came towards the Prophet walking calmly. The Prophet asked them: "Who is your chief and the one whose lead you follow?" They all pointed to al-Ashajj. The Prophet asked: "Is he the descendant of your chiefs?" They said: "In pre-Islamic days, his forefathers were our chiefs, and it was he who has led us to Islam". When the man drew near, he wanted to sit in a corner, but the Prophet sat up and said to him: "Come and sit here, Ashajj". This was the first time he was nicknamed al-Ashajj, which means 'one with a cut in his forehead'. When he was an infant, a donkey hit him with its hoof, making a moon-like mark on his face. The Prophet sat him next to him and recognised his higher status.

'The people asked the Prophet many questions and he answered them all. As they were about to finish, the Prophet asked whether they still had some of the food they had carried with them. They answered in the affirmative, each of them going quickly to his luggage and bringing some dates in their hands. They were all placed on a mat before him. He had with him a date branch stripped of its leaves which was between one and two arm-spans long and which he used to lean against. It was almost always with him. He pointed with it to a pile of dates and said: "Do you call this kind al-Taʿḍūḍ?" They answered: "Yes". He said: "And do you call this one al-Ṣarafān?" They said: "Indeed". He again asked: "Do you call this kind al-Burni?" They again answered: "Yes". He said: "This is the best of your dates and the freshest".

'Some of the tribe's elders said: "This is the most blessed. It used to be plentiful and we used it as fodder for our camels and donkeys. But when we returned after this trip, we were keen to grow more of it until it became our main dates and we found out that it yielded blessed harvests".'

We see how the Prophet spoke with these people asking them about matters of their own concern. This was customary with the Prophet, so that his guests would feel at ease. We also see how the Prophet's companions took his word seriously, even when it did not refer to something related to religion. When the Prophet described a particular type of date as the best and most beneficial, they concentrated on farming it, and soon began to yield its benefits.

Another authentic version of this *ḥadīth* mentions that al-Ashajj said to the Prophet: 'Messenger of God! Our land is heavy and polluted.

Unless we have our wine drinks, we change colour and our tummies bulge out'. The Prophet said: 'Do not drink al-Dubbā', al-Ḥantam or al-Naqīr. On the contrary, drink in a container whose mouth can be sealed'. Al-Ashajj said: 'May my parents be sacrificed for your sake! Give us a concession for this [pointing with his hands to indicate a small amount]'. The Prophet said: 'If I were to give you such a concession, you would drink it in something similar to this [pointing with his hands wide to indicate a large amount]. Then when one of you gets drunk, he would stand up to his cousin and hit his leg with his sword'.

This was a reference to an incident that happened sometime previously when a group of them were drinking in a house. One of the group, called al-Ḥārith, said a line of poetry mentioning a woman of that same household. Qutham ibn Jahm, a relative of hers, was angry and he hit him on his leg with his sword, injuring him. Al-Ḥārith was present with the delegation when this conversation took place between the Prophet and al-Ashajj. He said: 'When I heard the Prophet mentioning this incident, I tried to hide the mark of the strike on my leg with my robes, but God had revealed it all to His messenger'.[812]

By referring to an incident that took place in their midst and of which they were all aware, the Prophet highlighted some of the terrible effects of drinking alcohol. There could have been no compromise or concession on such drinking. But the Prophet wanted to make the strict prohibition more graphic by highlighting the evil consequences of alcohol.

---

812. Ibn al-Qayyim, Zad al-Ma'ād, vol. 3, p. 606.

51

Supplication at all Times

WHEN WE STUDY the Prophet's daily actions, we wonder at the extent of his supplication at different times of the day and night. He practically said a prayer at every point during the day.

1205. Abu Hurayrah reports: 'In the morning, the Prophet would say: "My Lord! With Your power we see this morning, as we see the evening. With Your power we live, and with it we die, and to You we will be resurrected". In the evening, he would say the same prayer, putting the evening before the morning, and replacing the last phrase with: 'to You we will return'.[813] [*"Allāhumma bika aṣbaḥna, wa bika amsayna, wa bika naḥya, wa bika namūt, wa ilayka al-nushūr"*. And in the evening: *"Allāhumma bika amsayna, wa bika aṣbaḥna wa bika naḥya, wa bika namūt, wa ilayka al-maṣīr"*.]

813. Related by Aḥmad, Abū Dāwūd, al-Nasā'ī, al-Tirmidhi, Ibn Mājah, Ibn Ḥibbān and Abu 'Awānah.

In this supplication, the Prophet stresses that all situations of the day and night, including people's life and death, are determined by God alone. Hence, the fact that we live in the morning is brought about by God's power, just as is our life in the evening. If we die, it is by God's will, just as is our life. After death, we are resurrected at a point in time determined by God, when we all return to Him. Thus, the Prophet's supplication, which we do well to say every morning and evening, is an acknowledgement that we are under God's care all the time, and His will applies to us in all situations.

1206. Ibn 'Umar said: 'God's Messenger used always to say the following words, morning and evening: "My Lord, I pray to You for wellbeing in this life and in the life to come. My Lord, I pray to You for forgiveness and wellbeing in my faith and my life, with my family and in my property. My Lord, cover my defects and give me reassurance in time of fear. Grant me protection, my Lord, from the front and the rear, from the right and the left, and from above. I seek shelter with You against any evil that may overwhelm me from under me". [*Allāhumma inni as'aluk al-'āfiyah fi al-dunya wal-ākhirah. Allāhumma inni as'aluk al-'afwa wal-'āfiyah fi dini wa dunyāy, wa ahli wa māli. Allāhumma stur 'awrāti, wa āmin raw'āti. Allāhumma iḥfaẓni min bayn yadayya wa min khalfi, wa 'an yamīni wa 'an shimāli wa min fawqi, wa a'ūzu bi'aẓamatik an ughtāla min taḥti.*]

In this supplication, the Prophet is appealing to God for wellbeing in all situations and all aspects of one's life. This is clear at the beginning where wellbeing in faith, which means having only sound beliefs and following the Divine guidance in worship and other practices, is stressed ahead of safety in life which indicates physical and psychological health. The Prophet also teaches us to pray for the wellbeing of one's family and property. This prayer addresses practically all the main concerns of everyone. Having sound faith, feeling healthy, and taking proper care of family and property are the total sum of what everyone would like to have at any moment in time.

But the Prophet's supplication also addresses what may unexpectedly happen. To start with he prays for the covering of his defects and to be granted reassurance in time of fear. Needless to say, the Prophet had no defect in character, action or feelings towards others. He never entertained any feeling of hatred. He loved all people and cared for them. Even those who opposed him and did him much harm would have enjoyed his love had they, at any time, acknowledged the truth of his message and believed in God.

As a human being, the Prophet experienced times of fear, but he always placed his trust in God, and prayed to Him for wellbeing, safety and security. Hence, in this supplication, he prays for reassurance in times of fear, and for God's protection all round. He expresses this in a very tangible way, since human beings have to think within their limited world. Besides, his supplication is meant as guidance for us so that we know how to pray to God for our own protection from all evil. We cannot do better than follow the Prophet's example and repeat his supplication.

The Prophet varied his supplication, using different formulae so that his supplication did not become too stereotyped. Moreover, the variation meant that different people heard different prayers and supplications, and reported them. We have, as a result, a good variety, and whatever we learn is sufficient as such supplication is recommended, not obligatory.

1207. Anas ibn Mālik reports that the Prophet said: 'Whoever says in the morning: "Our Lord! We appeal to You this morning to bear witness, You and the bearers of Your throne and all angels and all Your creation, that [we believe that] You are God. There is no deity other than You and there is no partner with You, and that Muhammad is Your servant and Messenger": whoever says this God will spare one quarter of him from the fire. If he says it twice, God saves one half of him from the fire, and if he says it four times, God saves him from the fire that day'.[814] [*Allāhumma inna aṣbaḥna nushhiduk wa nushhidu ḥamalata ʿarshik wa malāʾikatak wa jamīʿ khalqik annak anta Allah, la ilāha illa ant, waḥdak la sharīka lak; wa anna Muhammadan ʿabduk wa rasūluk.*]

814. Related by Abū Dāwūd, al-Nasāʾī and al-Tirmidhi.

This supplication is fascinating, because it calls on God and the angels to bear witness to His oneness. Of course God knows that He is one, and that He has no partners. But invoking Him as a witness provides here a most emphatic statement by the supplicant of his or her unshakable belief in God's oneness. You do not call on God to witness, in support of your own statement, unless you are absolutely certain that what you say is true. Otherwise you risk incurring God's wrath, and this is not a good prospect for anyone.

At times, one of the Prophet's companions asked him to teach him something to say at a particular time, and he would teach him that. The teaching is never meant for that particular person alone. Unless clearly indicated to be otherwise, it is meant for all of us. Hence, we do well to learn it and use it as the Prophet advises.

1208. Abu Hurayrah reports: 'Abu Bakr said to the Prophet: "Messenger of God! Teach me something to say, morning and evening". The Prophet replied: "Say: 'My Lord, You know all that lies beyond the reach of human perception and all that is witnessed. You are the Creator of the heavens and the earth. Everything is in Your hand. I bear witness that there is no deity other than You. I seek Your shelter against the evil that is in my soul and the evil of Satan and his tricks'. Say this prayer morning and evening, and also when you lie down to sleep".'[815] [*Allāhumma ʿālim al-ghayb wal-shahādah, fāṭir al-samāwāt wal-arḍ, kullu shay'in bikaffik. Ashhad an la ilāh illa ant. Aʿūdhu bika min sharr nafsi, wa min sharr al-Shaytan wa sharakih.*]

1209. Abu Hurayrah reports the same *ḥadīth* but adds in the glorification the words: 'You are the Lord of everything and its Master'.

We note that whenever the Prophet wanted to pray to God for something, he started with praising and glorifying Him in clear terms,

815. Related by Aḥmad, al-Bukhari, al-Nasāʾī, Abū Dāwūd, al-Tirmidhi, al-Ḥākim, al-Dārimi and Ibn Ḥibbān.

acknowledging His oneness as well as His creation and control of the universe. This is strongly recommended, because it establishes the true and correct relationship between God and the supplicant. We are all God's creatures and servants who need His help, protection and forgiveness. Our acknowledgement of this makes our supplication more sincere. Here, when the Prophet teaches Abu Bakr what to say, he begins with such acknowledgement of God's position. When we say that God knows everything in our world and beyond, we remember that He knows our thoughts. Hence, we try to make our supplication sincere, free of any thoughts that may not please Him. When we say that He is the Creator of the heavens and the earth, we acknowledge His supreme Godhead over the entire universe. We realise our position as small creatures on a tiny planet in the solar system. But then we reiterate our belief in God's oneness before asking Him for protection against evil that may come from within ourselves or from Satan. These are the two sources of evil thoughts and actions. It is either personal greed and desire, or Satan and his continuous attempts to trick us into doing what displeases God.

This *ḥadīth* is reported in more than one version. It is useful to add here another version.

1210. Abu Rāshid al-Ḥubrāni said: 'I visited 'Abdullāh ibn 'Amr and said to him: "Tell us something you heard from God's Messenger (peace be upon him)". He gave me a sheet and said: "This is what the Prophet dictated to me". I looked at it and read that Abu Bakr asked the Prophet to teach him something to say in the morning and evening. The Prophet said: "Abu Bakr, Say: 'My Lord, You are the Creator of the heavens and the earth. You know all that lies beyond the reach of human perception and all that is witnessed. You are the Lord of everything and its Master. I seek Your shelter against the evil that is in my soul and the evil of Satan and his tricks, and against perpetrating harm to myself or causing it to another Muslim'."

[In Arabic, this addition goes as follows: *wa an aqtarifa 'ala nafsi sū'an aw ajurrahu ila Muslim*.]

The Prophet was keen to say some supplication when he went to bed and when he woke up. There are many *ḥadīths* mentioning several such formulae at these times.

1211. Hudhayfah reports: 'When the Prophet wanted to sleep, he would say: "It is in Your name, my Lord, that I die and live". When he woke up from sleep, he would say: "Praise be to God Who has given us life after he has caused us to die, and to Him we all return'."[816] [The Arabic wording of the first part is: "*Bismik allāhumma amūtu wa aḥya*". The wording of the second part: "*Al-ḥamd lillāh alladhi aḥyana ba'da ma amātana wa ilayhi al-nushūr*".]

We note here that the Prophet compares sleep to death and waking up to coming back to life. This is a point the Prophet stressed many times. It is indeed accurate, because when we go to sleep, we lose consciousness of everything around us, in the same way a dead person is unconscious of what goes on next to him. Waking up is a return to activity and full control of one's senses. This comparison is also stated in the Qur'an, when God says that He gathers people's souls when they die, but those who are not dead, He gathers their souls when they sleep. He then keeps with Him those who died and releases the others for a specified time. (39: 42) To acknowledge this, as the Prophet teaches us in this supplication, is to acknowledge God's control of our lives and that death is as near to us as the next time we go to sleep.

1212. Anas reports: 'When the Prophet went to bed, he used to say: "Praise be to God Who has fed us and given us drink, giving us all that we need and provided us with shelter. Many are those who neither get what they need nor are provided with shelter".'[817] [*Alḥamd lillāh alladhi aṭ'amana wa saqāna, wa kafāna wa āwāna. Kam mimman la kāfya lah wa la mu'wiy.*]

---

816. Related by al-Bukhari, Abū Dāwūd, al-Nasā'ī, al-Tirmidhi and Ibn Mājah.
817. Related by Muslim, Abū Dāwūd, al-Nasā'ī and al-Tirmidhi.

In this *ḥadīth* the Prophet does not pray to be given anything. He simply acknowledges God's favours and praises Him for them. Thus, food, drink, home and everything we have come from God, and He is to be thanked for them. The praise is made by way of thanksgiving, which ensures continuity of the blessings. God has promised that when we thank Him for His favours, He gives us more of them and even better ones besides.

Before going to sleep

1213. Jābir says: 'The Prophet used not to go to sleep before reading the two surahs, al-Sajdah and al-Mulk'.[818]

Abu al-Zubayr, who reports this *ḥadīth* from Jābir, mentions that 'these two surahs earn seventy good deeds more than any other surah in the Qur'an. Whoever recites them earns seventy good deeds, is given a rise of seventy steps; and seventy bad deeds are erased from his record'.

All types of worship earn rich reward from God. This applies to prayer, fasting, zakat, reciting the Qur'an, glorifying God and remembering Him. However the Prophet was keen to recite certain surahs or verses at particular times because of the meanings they stress. In this *ḥadīth* we are told that he used to read these two surahs, which together run into five and a half pages of the Qur'an. There is strong emphasis in both surahs on the life to come, the resurrection as well as the reckoning and reward. Since sleep is a kind of death, as we lose consciousness of everything around us in both situations, the reminder of the Hereafter is most apt at this particular time.

It is important to clarify how some surahs are said to be better than others. A number of scholars do not approve of the notion that certain parts of the Qur'an can be described as better than the rest. They say that this is contrary to the fact that all of the Qur'an is God's Word and should be viewed as a complete whole, with every part of it equal to the rest. Other scholars agree that the Qur'an should be viewed

---

818. Related by al-Nasā'ī, al-Ḥākim and Ibn Abu Shaybah.

in the same light, with no preference given to any part over the rest. However, they maintain that this does not contradict that God may give greater reward for reciting certain surahs. They also say that on certain occasions, or at certain times, reciting a particular surah may be better. They cite the example of reciting Surahs 32 and 76 in the two *rak'ahs* of Fajr Prayer on Fridays, or reciting Surahs 87, 109 and 112 in the three *rak'ahs* of witr Prayer every day.

This is a valid point, but other scholars also mention that the result of reciting a particular surah at a certain time is what may give it preference at that time. In this case, reciting these two surahs before going to sleep is stated to ensure that one does not suffer torment in the grave after one's death. While a supplication to be spared such suffering after reciting any part of the Qur'an may be certainly answered, it is hoped that reciting these two surahs gives a greater chance of this, if God so wills.

Moreover, reciting the Qur'an, or glorifying God and repeating some supplication and prayer before going to bed makes it easier for a person to get to sleep.

1214. (*Athar* 324) 'Abdullāh ibn Mas'ūd said: 'Being overtaken by sleep when glorifying God is brought about by Satan. You may try this if you wish. When you go to bed and you want to get to sleep straightaway, glorify God and praise Him'.[819]

This is something we can try ourselves. Indeed scholars encourage people who complain of insomnia to recite the Qur'an or engage in God's glorification, and then they do not take long to get to sleep. What the Prophet's companion refers to in his statement is that Satan will help to get to sleep a person who is reciting the Qur'an or praising God and glorifying Him, so that he does not earn more reward for his glorification and remembrance of God. Whether we can attach such influence to Satan is rather debatable, because he is stated in the Qur'an as not having any control over us, unless we give in to his promptings. However, when we recite the Qur'an or glorify God,

819. Related by al-Nasā'ī, Abū Dāwūd, and al-Tirmidhi.

Satan feels depressed and he cannot come near us. As such, he would not be prompting us or keeping us awake. By leaving us alone, we feel the pleasure and relaxation of what we are reciting or saying, and such relaxation helps us to get to sleep faster.

1215. This is the same as *Ḥadīth* Number 1213, without the addition of what Abu al-Zubayr said about the two surahs.

1216. Abu Hurayrah reports that the Prophet said: 'When any of you wishes to go to bed, he should undo the edge of his robe and strike his bed with it. He does not know what has been on his bed since he left it. He then lies on his right side and says: 'In Your name I lay myself on my side. If You gather my soul, bestow on it Your mercy; and if You release it, then protect it with what You protect the righteous among Your servants'. [*Bismika waḍa'tu janbi. Fa'in iḥtabasta nafsi farḥamha, wa in arsaltaha faḥfaẓha bima taḥfaẓu bihi 'ibādak al-ṣāliḥīn.*]'

The point about striking the bed with one's garment is simply to shake off anything that has crept onto it and to ensure that no crawling or harmful creature is hidden in it. Perhaps this is unnecessary in modern homes and apartments, but following the Prophet's example and doing his actions earns reward from God. In country homes, villages and in desert areas, the risk of something like a scorpion or a snake crawling into a bed where it finds warmth is very real. In European countries, a spider may find its way into our beds. Striking the bed with one's garment is bound to disturb such a creature and drive it away. Or at least the person will see it moving and take the necessary action to ensure a comfortable sleep.

1217. Al-Barā' ibn 'Āzib said: 'When the Prophet went to bed, he slept on his right side and said: "My Lord, to You I turn my face, and to You I surrender my soul, and to You I turn for protection, in fear and hope of You. There is no place of refuge and safety from You except with You. I believe in Your Book which You have bestowed from on High, and I believe in Your Prophet whom You sent as Your Messenger". Whoever says this supplication and dies that night is sure to die holding to the true faith'.[820] [*Allāhumma wajjahtu wajhi ilayk, wa aslamtu nafsi ilayk, wa alja'tu ẓahri ilayk, rahbatan wa raghbatan ilayk. La manja wa la malja mink illa ilayk. Āmant bikitābik alladhi anzalt, wa binabiyyaka alladhi arsalt.*]

This is a highly authentic *ḥadīth*, which is reported in different versions with some change in the order of its phrases. But the supplication it includes is one of the most expressive of self surrender to God in all situations. Hence the comment that if one dies after having said this supplication, one is deemed to have died as a believer in the true faith. Needless to say, nothing ensures forgiveness of sins and admission to heaven more than sound and pure faith. To say this supplication before going to sleep is one way of ensuring that one finishes the day holding to the right faith.

Indeed the Prophet used to say several prayers and supplications before going to bed. He might change and say some of them on certain days and other prayers on other days. But the central point in them all is the same: total self surrender to God in all situations.

1218. Abu Hurayrah said that God's Messenger used to say the following supplication when he went to bed: 'My Lord, the Lord of the heavens, the earth and everything, who causes the grain and the fruit-stone to split, and who revealed the Torah, the Gospel and the Qur'an! I seek refuge with You from every evil-monger You hold by the forelock. You are the First before whom there was none, and You are the Last after Whom there will be none. You are the Outward above whom there is none, and You are the Inward under whom there is none. Repay my debts and let me not suffer poverty'.[821] [*Allāhumma rabb al-samāwāt wal-arḍ, wa rabba kulli shay', fāliq al-ḥabb wal-nawa, munzil al-Tawrāh wal-Injīl wal-Qur'an! A'ūdhu bika min kulli dhi sharr anta ākhidhun bināṣiyatih. Anta al-awwal falaysa qablak shay', wa*

820. Related by al-Bukhari, Muslim, Abū Dāwūd and al-Tirmidhi.

821. Related by Muslim, Abū Dāwūd, al-Nasā'ī, Ibn Mājah, Ibn Abu Shaybah, Ibn Ḥibbān and Abu 'Awānah.

anta al-ākhir falyasa ba'dak shay', wa anta al-ẓāhir falaysa fawqak shay', wa anta al-bāṭin falaysa dūnak shay'. Iqḍi 'anni al-dayn wa aghnini min al-faqr.]

This highly authentic *ḥadīth* is very inspiring. Like other supplications by the Prophet, it starts with statements of God's glory, stressing first that God is the Lord of the universe and all it contains. It then highlights an important aspect of creation, which is the splitting of grains, seeds and fruit-stones to bring about new shoots and trees. It also mentions Divine guidance to mankind throughout history, represented in the revelation of the three main books of His guidance, the Torah, the Gospel and the Qur'an. When all this has been acknowledged, the supplicant appeals to God, the Creator of all and the provider of guidance, for protection from the evil caused by anyone, re-stating that all are within God's control. Again the Prophet stresses some of the most important attributes of God before requesting Him to help him with his debt and to relieve him from poverty.

1219. This is the same as *Ḥadīth* Number 1217, with a different chain of transmission and a slight variation of wording.

1220. (*Athar* 325) Jābir said: 'When a person enters his home or goes to bed an angel and a devil come straight to him. The angel says to him: "Finish with something good", while the devil says: "Finish with something evil". If the man praises God and glorifies Him [the devil] is driven away and the angel stays to watch over him. When he wakes up an angel and a devil come quickly to him and say something similar. If he glorifies God and says: "Praise be to God who has returned my soul after it was gathered and has not caused it to die while asleep. Praise be to God who upholds the celestial bodies and the earth, lest they deviate. For if they should ever deviate, there is none that can uphold them after He will have ceased to do so. He is ever-forbearing, much forgiving. Praise be to God who holds the celestial bodies, so that they may not fall upon the earth except by His leave. Most compassionate is God, and ever merciful to mankind". If he should die, he is a martyr, and if he lives and rises to pray, he prays in an excellent way'.[822] [*Al-ḥamd lillāh alladhi radda ilyya nafsi ba'da mawtiha, wa lam yumitha fi manāmiha. Al-ḥamd lillāh alladhi yumsik al-samāwāt wal-arḍ an tazūla, wa la'in zālata in amsakahuma min aḥadin min ba'dih. Innahu kana halīman ghafūra. Al-ḥamd lillāh alladhi yumsiku al-samā' an taqa'a 'ala al-arḍ illa bi'idhnih. Inna Allaha binnās lara'ufūn raḥīm.*]

Having discussed the other *ḥadīths* and explained why the Prophet was keen to say such a supplication in the morning and evening, and before going to bed, I think this *ḥadīth* does not need further explanation, except to say that the one who says this and dies during the night receives the reward of one who sacrifices his life for the cause. That is a rich reward, because martyrs are certain to be admitted to heaven.

1221. Al-Barā' said: 'When the Prophet wanted to sleep, he placed his hand under his right cheek and said: "My Lord, protect me against Your punishment on the day You bring Your servants back to life".'[823] [*Allāhumma qini 'adhābak yawm tab'athu 'Ibādak.*]

This *ḥadīth* mentions an action and a supplication by the Prophet at the time when he went to bed, which is a natural thing we do every day. Since he did not indicate that putting his hand under his right cheek was obligatory or recommended or would achieve a desirable result, it is not a Sunnah. However, if one does it with the intention of emulating the Prophet, believing that whatever the Prophet did was good, one receives a reward for intention, but the act itself does not count as a Sunnah. The supplication, on the other hand, is a Sunnah because it is an appeal to God, and in whatever concerns man's relations with God we should follow the Prophet's lead. It would be obligatory only if the Prophet said so. Since he did not, it remains a Sunnah, although it is not strictly emphasised.

---

822. Related by al-Nasā'ī and Ibn Ḥibbān.

823. Related by al-Nasā'ī, who said that the Prophet said this supplication three times. It is also related by al-Tirmidhi and Ibn Mājah in a longer version.

What we should be even more keen to do is outlined in the following *ḥadīth* where the Prophet makes his recommendation clear, encouraging his followers to observe certain things at certain times.

> 1222. 'Abdullāh ibn 'Amr reports that the Prophet said: 'Two practices, if maintained by a Muslim, will ensure his admission into heaven. Although easy, they are maintained only by a few'. People asked: 'What are these, Messenger of God?' The Prophet replied: 'After each prayer, a person should say *Allahu akbar* ten times; *al-ḥamdu lillāh* ten times; *subḥān Allah* ten times. That makes up one hundred and fifty phrases he says with his tongue, but they are counted as one thousand five hundred in the balance [of good deeds]'. I saw the Prophet counting them on his fingers. [The Prophet then added]: 'And when one goes to bed, one says the same three phrases to make up a total of one hundred times, which will be counted as one thousand in the balance. Who of you commits two thousand five hundred bad deeds in one day and one night?' People asked: 'Messenger of God! How is it that a person might not maintain them?' He said: 'Satan comes to him during his prayer reminding him of this and that, and so he will not remember to say them'.

The Prophet's encouragement to say these phrases is very clear. First of all he tells us that they will get us into heaven if we practise them regularly. Then he explains how, adding them up and multiplying their reward ten times on the basis of the rule that God rewards every good action at least ten times its worth. He then compares this abundant reward with possible bad deeds one may commit. It is highly unlikely that anyone should commit 2,500 bad deeds a day. Hence the reward he gets for such glorification of God is certain to wipe out any punishment he might incur for his bad deeds. Indeed, he will be left with a balance of reward, which accumulates and ensures his admission to heaven.

The Prophet then points out what happens with most people to make them negligent of such an easy reward-earning practice. Distraction and thinking about worldly matters get the better of us so that when we finish our prayers we immediately rush to attend to our business, while a minute spent in glorifying and praising God is much better for us.

What do these phrases mean? *Allahu akbar* means 'God is supreme'. It is an acknowledgement of His supremacy over all beings anywhere in the universe. *Al-ḥamdu lillāh* is a form of thanksgiving which means 'praise be to God', while *subaḥān Allah* means 'limitless is God in His Glory'. Together they represent the form of glorifying God prescribed in Islam. They are the glorifications used by the angels and other creatures of God.

1223. This is the same as *Ḥadīth* Number 1216 with a slight difference in wording and a different chain of transmission.

1224. Rabīʿah ibn Kaʿb reports: 'I used to stay the night near the Prophet's door and I would give him water for his ablutions. I would hear him at some point in the night saying "May God answer a person who praises Him", and I would hear him at another point in the night saying "All praise is due to God the Lord of all worlds".'[824]

Here, a companion of the Prophet speaks of his experience at a time when he used to stay close to the Prophet's home. A number of the Prophet's companions used to do this serving as a bodyguard, protecting him against any danger or attack. They did this until the verse was revealed which told the Prophet that God would take care of him against anyone who sought him harm. The Prophet then dispensed with the services of these people and told them to stay in their own homes, for he would need no protection. Rabīʿah was his servant and he stayed at his door until he ensured that the Prophet went to sleep.

The Prophet's companion tells us here that the Prophet spent part of the night, each night, in prayers. He would wake up, perform his ablution and pray. His prayer is indicated by what his companion mentions he heard the Prophet say. The two sentences are used at certain points in prayer. At different times of the night he would hear him either reciting the Qur'an or indicating a movement in prayer.

---

824. Related by Aḥmad, Muslim, Abū Dāwūd, al-Nasā'ī, al-Tirmidhi and Ibn Mājah.

It is well known that night worship was obligatory for the Prophet and all Muslims in the early days of Islam. Then this requirement was relaxed and made voluntary, promising very rich reward for those who do it. The Prophet continued to perform it on most nights for the rest of his life.

52

Miscellaneous

1225. Ibn 'Abbās reports that the Prophet said: 'Anyone who goes to bed with grease on his hand without washing it off, and something happens to him, should blame none other than himself'.

1226. This is the same as Number 1225, but reported by Abu Hurayrah with a different chain of transmission.

THIS *ḤADĪTH* WARNS against a simple hazard to which people may not be aware. Traces of fat or grease may be on one's hand as a result of doing some tasks around the home or eating fried food. If one goes to sleep, the smell may attract some crawling or flying insect whose bite may be very painful, or may cause some disease. This is particularly relevant in hot climates when people may not use a cover when they sleep, or may leave a window open all night. The Prophet alerts us to the need to wash our hands carefully before going to sleep.

Indeed, the Prophet emphasised the need to take precautions against various hazards that may be ignored when people go to sleep.

1227. Jābir ibn ʿAbdullāh reports that the Prophet said: 'Secure your doors, tie up your waterskins, turn over your vessels, cover up your dishes, and put off your lights. Satan does not open a secured door, untie a knot, or uncover a dish. However, a mouse could set a house on fire'.[825]

This *ḥadīth* provides very useful instructions which remain valid for most people. The first instruction is to secure our doors before going to sleep. Today, in most places, this goes without saying because burglary is very common. But it need not be so. There are places in many parts of the world where people are safe from burglars, either because they live in a small community where everyone knows everyone else, or where social conditions provide enough security. Yet one may not be safe from other creatures finding their way into homes causing people some harm when they are asleep. Hence, securing our doors provides the necessary standard of safety.

Today, people have water supplied into their homes by pipes and tanks, where it is safe from ordinary contamination. However, in times past, people had to make sure that they had sufficient water for their drinking and home use. Hence, they stored it in containers, some types of which were made of hide or some other material. It is such containers, and indeed any other type, that the Prophet wanted to make sure were tightened so as to prevent any harmful object or insect from falling into them. The same applies to any plate, pot or saucepan where food is kept. While today we leave much of our food in fridges, there remains around the house much food that may be left exposed. The important thing in this *ḥadīth* is not to leave food exposed overnight. Some insect might get into it or dust and harmful particles might drop on it, making it a cause of harm instead of a source of nourishment.

Putting off the light is the next injunction in this *ḥadīth*, particularly when we talk about oil lamps and similar lights. Such a lamp may be blown over by wind, or by a cat, and it could then cause a fire. This

825. Related by al-Bukhari and al-Tirmidhi.

is what the Prophet warns against when he mentions that a mouse could set a house on fire. What attracts a mouse is the wick of a lamp, and it could pull it and cause the lamp to fall over, spilling its oil and causing a fire. Hence, the Prophet repeatedly warned against leaving lamps on at night, or in a position where a mouse could pull at it. Here are some of the *ḥadīths* pointing to this risk.

1228. Ibn ʿAbbās reports: 'A mouse once began to drag the wick of a lamp, and a maid tried to frighten it away. The Prophet said to her: "Leave it". The mouse pulled the lamp until it dropped it on the mat he was sitting on, burning an area as small as a coin. The Prophet said: "When you go to bed, put out your lamps. Satan points them to such as this and it may burn you".'[826]

1229. Abu Saʿīd al-Khudri reports: 'The Prophet woke up one night to find that a mouse had dragged the wick of the lamp and climbed with it up to the roof, and was about to set fire to the house. The Prophet cursed it and made it permissible to kill, even by a person in a state of consecration, or iḥrām'.[827]

1230. ʿAbdullāh ibn ʿUmar reports that the Prophet said: 'Do not leave a fire burning at home when you go to sleep'.[828]

1231. (*Athar* 326) ʿUmar said: 'Fire is an enemy of yours: guard against it'. ʿAbdullāh ibn ʿUmar used to go round the house to put out any burning fire before he went to sleep.

ʿAbdullāh ibn ʿUmar reports that the Prophet said: 'Do not leave an open fire in your homes; for it is an enemy to you'.

Abu Mūsa al-Ashʿari reports that a house in Madinah was burnt one night while its people were asleep. This was reported to the Prophet who said: 'Fire is an enemy to you. When you go to sleep, put it out'.[829]

---

826. Related by Abū Dāwūd, al-Ḥākim and Ibn Ḥibbān.
827. Related by al-Ḥākim.
828. Related by Aḥmad, al-Bukhari, Muslim, Abū Dāwūd, al-Tirmidhi, Ibn Mājah and Abu ʿAwānah.
829. Related by al-Bukhari, Muslim and Ibn Mājah.

The fact that the Prophet warned against leaving a fire unattended, or keeping it burning and going to sleep in several *ḥadīths* means that he said this several times, to different audiences, so that his instruction was well known to all. The Prophet also included a warning against a danger that may be caused by a mouse which could drag or upturn an oil lamp which people may think that they have left secure. The *ḥadīth* remains valid today. An electric or gas stove should not be left burning when we go to sleep, as something may go wrong making it a fire hazard. Moreover, leaving electric wiring exposed may represent a fire risk.

The Prophet made the killing of a mouse permissible. It should be pointed out here that when one is in a state of consecration he may not kill any animal except one that poses serious danger to man, such as snakes, scorpions and very aggressive dogs. A mouse is also included because it may cause some serious risk.

1234. (*Athar* 327) Abu Mulaykah said: 'When it rained, Ibn 'Abbās told his servant: "Bring out my saddle; bring out my garments". He would recite the verse that says: "*We have sent down blessed water from the sky*".' (50:9)

This reflects the Prophet's companions genuine and firm faith. They took whatever is mentioned in the Qur'an as absolutely true and understood it in its simple and direct meaning. The Qur'an describes rain water as blessed. Hence, Ibn 'Abbās wanted his garments and saddle to be washed with rain water because it is blessed, and its blessing might rub onto them.

1135. Ibn 'Abbās reported that the Prophet instructed people to hang up a whip in their homes.

This *ḥadīth*, which is poor in authenticity, does not specify the purpose of hanging up a whip, unless it is meant to be a threat that punishment would be forthcoming for any misbehaviour. However, Islam does not encourage such punishment for one's family or servants. On the contrary, it encourages proper education and kind treatment of all. That the whip is hung up may only serve as a reminder that it is there, but it certainly must not be used except to repel danger from an aggressor or a dangerous animal.

1136. Jābir ibn 'Abdullāh reports that the Prophet said: 'Do not stay up in conversation deep into the stillness of the night. You do not know what creatures God sends about. Secure your doors, tie up your waterskins, turn over your vessels and put out your lamps'.[830]

The first part of this *ḥadīth* warns against staying up in conversation deep into the night because it is time when people feel that they are safe from prying eyes or eavesdroppers. Yet this is a false sense of security because there may be other creatures nearby and we may not be aware of them, while our conversation gives them advantage as it indicates our presence and determines our position. The second part is similar to *ḥadīth* 1227 and gives the same instructions which we have already discussed.

1237. Jābir reports that the Prophet said: 'Restrain your children until the early darkness of the night has gone, for it is a time when satans are most active'.

This advice relates to a particular time. People realise that as the night starts and darkness begins to gather, children feel uneasy and they may be up to some mischief. The Prophet advises that this is a time when satans are very active. So, the need is there to restrain children and make sure that they are quiet until such a time when they are back at their ease.

1238. (*Athar* 328) Mujāhid reports that 'Ibn 'Umar disapproved of inciting animals against each other'.[831]

This is another aspect of the fine manners Islam inculcates in its followers. Some animals can be easily excited to fight each other, and

830. Related by Aḥmad.
831. Related by al-Tirmidhi as reported by Ibn 'Abbās and attributed to the Prophet.

their fight may be fierce causing serious injury or even death, as in cock fighting which used to be considered as a pastime for spectators and a gambling occasion in some European and American countries. This is not permissible in Islam, regardless of whether the animals are of the same kind or not.

1239. Jābir ibn ʿAbdullāh reports that the Prophet said: 'Make going out after the night has come scarce. God sends out some creatures of His at that time. Whoever hears the barking of a dog or the braying of a donkey should seek shelter with God against Satan, the accursed. These creatures see what you do not see'.[832]

1240. Jābir ibn ʿAbdullāh reports that the Prophet said: 'If you hear the barking of dogs or braying of donkeys at night, seek shelter with God against Satan, the accursed. They see what you do not see. Shut your doors and mention God's name when you do. Satan does not open a door that has been shut and God's name is mentioned on it. Cover your pots, tie up your waterskins and turn over your vessels'.

1241. This is the same as Number 1239, with slight variation and a different chain of transmission.

The Prophet does not specify what sort of creatures God sends out in the stillness of the night, but the Prophet's advice is sound, because when one is out in the depth of the night, one cannot be aware of all that is around, even when we are in cities where the streets are lit. These *ḥadīths* mention the barking and braying of dogs and donkeys, suggesting that they might be caused by something they see but we cannot. It is well known that some animals feel things ahead of man. Some of them, such as birds and dogs have sharp senses of sight and/or hearing. A house dog barks when someone approaches, while the inhabitants of the house are totally unaware that anyone is close by.

---

832. Related by Aḥmad and Abū Dāwūd.

The rest of the second *ḥadīth* outlines certain precautions that we should take as part of normal daily practice. These have been mentioned in earlier *ḥadīths* which we have discussed.

1242. Abu Hurayrah reports that the Prophet said: 'If you hear the crowing of a cock at night, this indicates that he has seen an angel. So, request God to grant you of His favours. If you hear the braying of a donkey at night, this indicates that he has seen a satan. Seek God's refuge from Satan'.[833]

This is something that we only learn through the Prophet. We do not know how cocks see angels or how donkeys see devils. Yet what the Prophet tells us is certainly true. He tells us that a supplication in each case is the right thing to do, requesting God's favours when a cock crows at night, and seeking His shelter when a donkey brays at night.

1243. Anas ibn Mālik reports: 'A man cursed a flea in the Prophet's presence. The Prophet said to him: "Do not curse it, because it woke up one of the prophets for his prayer".'[834]

We may put this in a broader perspective, because it was not the same flea that woke up a prophet, but the same type of insect. Everything God has created has a role and a purpose. Some are readily apparent to us, but most others are not. Therefore, we respect God's creation and accept that they fulfil their roles which may have some positive or negative aspects.

1244. (*Athar* 329) al-Sā'ib relates from 'Umar: 'Sometimes a few men from the Quraysh would sit by Ibn Mas'ūd's door. When the sun had turned and shadows began to take shape, he would say to them: "Get up. Any time spent here after this is for Satan". He made everyone he saw sitting there get up and leave. As he was doing so, someone said: "Here is the ally of Bani

833. Related by al-Bukhari, Muslim, Abū Dāwūd, al-Nasā'ī, al-Tirmidhi, Ibn Ḥibbān and Abu 'Awānah.

834. Related by Aḥmad, al-Ṭabarāni and al-Bazzār.

al-Hashās chanting poetry". He called him and said: "What have you been saying?" The man said: "Bid farewell to Sulayma when you are getting ready to join a campaign. Sufficient as warners [against sin] are grey hair and Islam". Ibn Mas'ūd said to him: "This is enough. You have spoken the truth".'

1245. (*Athar* 330) al-Sā'ib ibn Yazīd said: ''Umar used to pass by us in the middle of the day, or near to it, and say: "Get up and take a nap. Any time spent here after this is for Satan".'

1246. (*Athar* 331) Anas said: 'They used to take a midday nap after they had prayed Friday Prayers'.[835]

To explain, Ibn Mas'ūd would tell those people to leave after the midday prayer had been offered, so that they could have some rest at home. He did not encourage them to stay and chat, because they might indulge in frivolous talk, which would please Satan. We also see how he appreciated the man's poetry. Growing grey should serve as a warner against sin, because it indicates that the person concerned has attained maturity and his activity will begin to decline. This is a first reminder that death is approaching.

The other point of warning emphasises the need to maintain the right path so as to save oneself punishment in the Hereafter. It reminds people of the Day of Judgement when they will meet God and have all their deeds done in this present life reckoned and when they will be rewarded or punished on the basis of that reckoning.

Taking an afternoon nap is very useful, particularly in hot climates, as it is refreshing and invigorating. After a short nap, one can start a fresh period of activity. By contrast, when people sit to talk for a long period after they have had lunch, this may lead to some undesirable action. Hence, he told them that staying to chat is for Satan, meaning that it gives an opportunity for Satan to try to tempt people to indulge in what displeases God. If they are tired, they may have less resistance to temptation.

---

835. Related by Aḥmad, Ibn Ḥibbān and Ibn Khuzaymah.

Prompt compliance

An indication of the Prophet's companions' practice is seen in the following *ḥadīth* which speaks mainly about something different, but mentions an occasion when some of the Prophet's companions took a nap in the afternoon:

> 1247. Anas reports: 'At the time when wines were made unlawful, no drink was liked better by the people of Madinah than wine made from dates mixed with unripe dates. Once I was serving some of the Prophet's companions who gathered at Abu Ṭalḥah's place when a man passed by and said: "Wine has been forbidden". They neither asked when, nor suggested waiting until they made sure. They simply said to me: "Anas, spill it off". They then had a nap at Umm Sulaym's until the day was a little cooler, and they washed. Umm Sulaym gave them some perfume and they went to see the Prophet where they learnt that the news they had heard was true. They never tasted wine again'.

The relevance of this *ḥadīth* to the subject we are discussing is that the Prophet's companions had their nap after midday, when the temperature was at its highest. But then we have the main point of the *ḥadīth*, which is the readiness of the Prophet's companions to comply with Divine orders the moment they hear them. Here we find some of them relaxing with a drink of the best wine they used to enjoy, when a man tells them that a new injunction has been given prohibiting wines and spirits. They do not question him, or try to check, or go on drinking until they have confirmed the report. They immediately tell the young man serving them to spill all the wine over, for they no longer have any use for it. This is the proper attitude of a Muslim.

When they have had their nap and washed, their hostess, Umm Sulaym who was Abu Ṭalḥah's wife, gave them some perfume to remove any lingering trace of the smell of wine they might have had and they proceeded to see the Prophet. When the report of the prohibition of intoxicants was confirmed, they never tasted it again. There can be no better attitude of such prompt compliance with Divine orders.

A nap is most beneficial in the afternoon. If it is taken towards the end of the day, it becomes counterproductive.

1248. (*Athar* 332) Khuwāt ibn Jubayr said: 'Sleeping early in the day betrays ignorance, in the middle of the day is right, and at the end of the day is stupid'.

Human experience confirms all this, as a person who spends the early part of the day asleep seems not to know what he needs to do in his day, while sleeping in the early afternoon is healthy and beneficial, but at the end of the day and before nightfall causes inactivity instead of refreshment.

Nāfiʿ was a servant of ʿAbdullāh ibn ʿUmar and he learnt and reported everything from him.

1249. (*Athar* 333) Maymūn ibn Mahrān said: 'I asked Nāfiʿ whether Ibn ʿUmar invited people to a banquet? He tells us that he was once asked whether ʿAbdullāh ibn ʿUmar used to invite people to dinner. He answered: "Once a camel of his broke his leg and we slaughtered it. He then said to me: 'Invite all the people of Madinah'. I said: 'Abu ʿAbd al-Raḥmān, what shall we invite them to eat when we have no bread?' He said: 'My Lord, all praise and thanks are due to You! Here we have meat and sauce. Whoever wishes to eat will eat, and whoever does not will bid us goodbye and leave'."'

ʿAbdullāh ibn ʿUmar learnt much from the Prophet and whatever he learnt, he implemented. His attitude here is the one encouraged by the Prophet who was keen to instil in his companions the notion that they should not despise even the smallest act of kindness. If one has only some humble food to eat, he should not hesitate to invite a friend, a poor person or a neighbour to share it with him. Such kindness is rewarded by God even if some people do not appreciate it. Needless to say this applies to very poor people. Those who are not so poor, will not appreciate it unless they are true believers.

On circumcision

1250. Abu Hurayrah reports that the Prophet said: 'Abraham was circumcised when he was 80 years of age. He was circumcised at Qadūm'.[836]

This is an authentic *ḥadīth* which establishes the practice of circumcision for boys. God says in the Qur'an: '*Follow the creed of Abraham, who was true in faith*'. (16:123) What has been established of earlier revelations to God's messengers applies to Muslims unless it is modified or abrogated in the Qur'an or *Ḥadīth*. Although Abraham was at this advanced age when he was told to circumcise himself, the Prophet makes it clear that circumcision should be performed seven days after the boy's birth or shortly thereafter; then, it is healthier and quicker to heal.

1251. (*Athar* 334) Umm al-Muhājir said to me: 'I was taken captive with some girls from the Byzantines. 'Uthmān invited us to accept Islam, but only one other girl beside me accepted Islam. 'Uthmān said: "Take them away to circumcise and purify them".'

Like all reports on female circumcision, this report is poor in authenticity. It appears that some circumcision of girls was practised in Arabia in pre-Islamic days, and perhaps it continued for a while but then died down. There is no authentic report to suggest that it is recommended for girls.

1252. (*Athar* 335) Sālim said: 'Ibn 'Umar circumcised me and Nu'aym and he sacrificed a ram for us. We showed our delight to other boys for the fact that he sacrificed a ram for us'.[837]

Although it is agreed that circumcision is best when it is performed in the early days after birth, this report suggests that it is not a confirmed

---

836. Related by al-Bukhari and Muslim.
837. Related by Ibn Abu Shaybah.

Sunnah. Otherwise, Ibn ʿUmar would not have delayed circumcising his son for a few years. The fact that Sālim was expressing delight to other boys for the sacrifice suggests that he was at least four years of age.

1253. (*Athar* 336) Umm ʿAlqamah reports: ʿWhen ʿĀʾishah's nieces were circumcised, she was asked: "Shall we call someone to amuse them?" She replied: "Yes". She sent for ʿAdiy and he came. ʿĀʾishah passed by the room and saw him singing and moving his head in rapture. He had much hair on his head. She said: "Ugh! A satan! Get him out! Get him out!"'

This report is very poor in authenticity. It is very unlikely that ʿĀʾishah would have invited a man to come and sing in her room to amuse adolescent girls who were in pain as a result of a practice that she knew not to be a Sunnah. Besides, the singer was unknown. In a different version he is mentioned as a bedouin and in a third merely as a singer.

1254. (*Athar* 337) Aslam, ʿUmar's servant said: ʿWhen we came to Syria with ʿUmar ibn al-Khaṭṭāb, a certain dignitary came to him and said: "*Amīr al-Muʾminīn*, I have prepared some food for you and I would like you to bring a number of your noblemen with you. This will strengthen me in my duties and be a great honour for me". ʿUmar said to him: "We cannot enter your churches because of the images which are there".'

ʿUmar's objection to entering the church was due to the statues inside representing prophets or angels. He would have accepted the invitation had it been somewhere else.

1255. (*Athar* 338) This is the same as Number 1251, with the same chain of transmission.

1256. (*Athar* 339) Saʿīd ibn al-Musayyib reports that Abu Hurayrah said: ʿAbraham was circumcised at the age of 120 and he lived 80 years after that'.[838]

---

838. Related by al-Bukhari, Muslim, al-Ḥākim and Ibn Ḥibbān.

Saʿīd added: 'Abraham was the first to be circumcised, the first to give hospitality, the first to trim his moustache, the first to cut his nails and the first to grow grey. He said: "My Lord, what is this?" He said: "An aspect of dignity". Abraham said: "My Lord, give me more dignity".'

1257. (*Athar* 340) Al-Ḥasan said: 'Are you not surprised at this man [Mālik ibn al-Mundhir]? He checked some elders of Kaskar who accepted Islam and ordered that they should be circumcised, although it was winter. I heard that some of them died [as a result]. Greeks and Abyssinians became Muslims during God's Messenger's time, but none of them was checked'.

1258. (*Athar* 341) Ibn Shihāb said: 'When a man accepted Islam, he was ordered to be circumcised, even if he was old'.

All these reports are not attributed to the Prophet. Therefore, they are considered lacking in authenticity, unless they have something to corroborate them, as in the case of Number 1256. Even then, the figures it gives about Abraham's age are not particularly reliable, because we do not have further evidence to corroborate them. In Number 1250, Abraham is said to have been 80 when he was circumcised. Here we have his age at the time to be 120. There is a huge difference which is inexplicable. Moreover, to imagine that he was the first to trim his moustache and clip his nails appears unlikely. On the other hand, circumcision is only a Sunnah, so it should not be given this great importance as to order grown or old men to be circumcised when they accept Islam. The matter should be left to them to decide, because if they opt not to do it, they incur no sin.

A high standard of piety

Some of the Prophet's companions are well known. Their names are often mentioned, and their service to Islam is cited as an example for new generations. Others are not well known, but they might have been exemplary in their strength of faith, conduct, piety and commitment to Islam. We get to know these from one or two *ḥadīths* or reports that reveal particular aspects of their characters. One of this latter type was better known by his nickname Abu Qurṣāfah, following the Arab custom of calling a man as the father of his eldest son. He is rarely mentioned by his own name, which is Jandarah ibn Khayshanah. We learn something of Abu Qurṣāfah's piety from the following report:

1259. (*Athar* 342) Bilāl ibn Ka'b al-'Akki reports: 'Ibrāhīm ibn Adham, 'Abd al-'Azīz ibn Qurayr, Mūsa ibn Yasār and I visited Yaḥya ibn Ḥassān (al-Bakri al-Filisṭīni) in his village. He served us with food, but Mūsa did not eat because he was fasting. Yaḥya said: "A companion of the Prophet from the Kinānah called Abu Qurṣāfah led us in prayer in this mosque for 40 years, and he always fasted on alternate days. A son was born to my father, and he invited him to a meal on his day of fasting. He came and broke his fast". Ibrāhīm stood up and covered him with his own coat. Mūsa then ate and broke his fast'.

This report shows that it is not only appropriate, but also desirable that a person who is fasting voluntarily should end his fast if he is invited for a function, or indeed if he is with a group of people and their host offers them food. It is wrong to continue fasting when others are eating. This means that acknowledging one's host's kindness and returning it by eating takes precedence over continuing one's voluntary fast. There is no doubt that the person concerned will gain a reward from God for his intention to fast, and will also be rewarded for his friendly manner towards his host. This is why Abu Qurṣāfah, a companion of the Prophet who used to fast on alternate days, shared in the meal when he was invited to a dinner on his fasting day.

His granddaughter, 'Azzah bint 'Iyāḍ ibn Abu Qurṣāfah, reports that one of her grandfather's sons was taken prisoner by the Byzantines. At every prayer time, Abu Qurṣāfah would stand on top of the wall of the city of Asqalan and shout to his son by name saying that it was time for prayer. His son would hear him every time although they were separated by hundreds of miles. This report is related by al-Ṭabarāni, with a chain of transmission that gives it an authentic grade. We are not surprised that this should be the case because God is able to accomplish His purpose. Since Abu Qurṣāfah was aware that his voice would not be heard at such a distance, he trusted to God to communicate his message to his son. God responded by granting his wish, which was expressed with complete trust and faith.

It is not surprising to learn of Abu Qurṣāfah's unshakable faith. He was a firm believer since embracing Islam as a young lad. His granddaughter reports that she heard her grandfather telling his story of accepting Islam: 'I was an orphan[839] child living with my mother and my maternal aunt, and I had a few sheep which I took to graze. My aunt often told me not to go near the Prophet so that he would not lead me astray. But when I reached the grazing area, I often left my sheep and went to the Prophet listening to him. In the evening I would go home, but my sheep would have no milk. My aunt questioned me about my dry sheep and I protested that I did not know the reason for their having no milk. One day I heard the Prophet (peace be upon him) saying: "My people! Migrate for God's cause and hold fast to Islam. Migration does not stop as long as jihad continues". I continued to frequent his place and listen to him until I embraced Islam, pledged my allegiance to him and shook hands with him. I told him about my aunt and my sheep. The Prophet told me to bring my sheep to him. When I brought them, he wiped their backs and their breasts, praying to God to bless them. They soon were full of fat and milk. When I went home to my aunt and she looked at them, she said: "Always graze like this, son". I said to her: "I simply went to the same place I have been going every day. But I will tell you my news. I went to the Prophet (peace be upon him) and embraced Islam". I told her about him and what he taught. Both my mother and my aunt asked me to take them to him. All three of us went to see him together, and my mother and aunt embraced Islam, pledged their allegiance to the Prophet and shook hands'.[840]

This report indicates how people were afraid of going near the Prophet because they heard the unbelievers' propaganda accusing him of leading people astray. Yet when they realised what he taught, they

---

839. In Arabic and Islamic culture an orphan is a child whose father has died.
840. Related by al-Ṭabarāni with a sound chain of transmission.

were impressed and were soon ready to accept Islam. This happened with many different people at different times.

It also tells us how the Prophet was kind to everyone. He did not put pressure on anyone to accept the faith until that person was ready. Abu Qurṣāfah, a young lad at the time, went to listen to him time after time, abandoning his sheep, and the Prophet gave him time to think and make up his mind. When he was ready, he declared his belief and pledged himself to the Prophet as one of his followers.

The *ḥadīth* also tells us that Muslims used to put their personal problems to the Prophet hoping for help. Abu Qurṣāfah complained to him about his aunt and the problem he was having as a result of abandoning his sheep so as to listen to him. The Prophet took action, and prayed to God to bless the sheep and their produce. Every prayer the Prophet said was answered in the most perfect way, which was a sign serving to reassure his companions. As the lad went home, his sheep were full of milk, and he used the occasion to tell his mother and his aunt about Islam. Soon, they too followed his suit and embraced Islam.

Naming a newborn

1260. Anas reports: 'I took 'Abdullāh ibn Abu Ṭalḥah to the Prophet the day he was born. The Prophet was wearing his robe and marking his camel with tar. The Prophet asked me; "Do you have any dates?" I answered: "Yes". And I gave him a few. He chewed them a little, opened the baby's mouth and put the chewed date in his mouth. The baby sucked it and licked his lips. The Prophet said: "How the Anṣār love dates!" He named the child 'Abdullāh'.[841]

We see here how the Prophet's companions' love for their children prompted them to send a newborn to the Prophet so that he would bless and pray for the child. They knew that every prayer the Prophet said for anyone would be answered in the broadest and most complete way.

---

841. Related by al-Bukhari, Muslim, Abū Dāwūd and Ibn Mājah.

We also see the Prophet very pleased with the child, responding to the parents' wish. The version of this *ḥadīth* quoted by al-Bukhari in his *Ṣaḥīḥ* anthology mentions that Anas was told to take the baby to the Prophet 'so that he gives him his finger to suck', hoping that this would be a blessing for the child. This version mentions that 'the first thing the child swallowed was the Prophet's saliva'. In our version, the child sucked the dates the Prophet had chewed a little, giving the same effect. The Prophet also blessed the child and named him.

It is interesting to ask what sort of man the child grew up to be. We have several reports, such as the one by Anas, his half brother, who says: 'He was one of the best people in his time'. Al-Aṣbahāni says: 'He died a martyr in Persia'. Others, however, mention that he died in Madinah in 84 AH. *Ḥadīth* scholars grade him as reliable but he reported only a few *ḥadīths*.

Following such examples, it is only natural that people should request the most God-fearing people they know to bless their newly born children.

1261. (*Athar* 343) Muʿāwiyah ibn Qurrah reports: 'When my son Iyās was born, I invited some of the Prophet's companions and served them a meal. They prayed for us. I said: "You have prayed for me, and may God bless you for doing so. Now I am saying a supplication and hope that you will join me and say *Amen*". I prayed long for my son, so that he would be a man of faith, and would have a sound mind, etc. I certainly see in him that God has answered our supplication on that day'.

It is a good practice to ask some of the most pious people one knows to pray for one's newborn, and it is also recommended that the parents themselves pray for the child. Their supplication is bound to be sincere and will be answered as God always answers sincere prayers.

1262. (*Athar* 344) Kathīr ibn 'Ubayd said: 'When a child was born to anyone in 'Ā'ishah's family, she did not ask whether it was a boy or a girl. She only asked: "Is the child created well and sound?" If the answer was: "Yes", she would say: "All praise be to God, the Lord of all the worlds".'

This is the proper attitude. In Arabian culture, boys were far more welcome than girls. It appeared that no Arab wanted ever to have a daughter! Islam changed their perspective to impress on them that boys and girls are equal. 'Ā'ishah did not bother to ask about the sex of the newborn. She only cared that the child was well and sound.

Natural practices

1263. Abu Hurayrah reports that the Prophet said: 'Five practices are naturally sound: trimming one's moustache, clipping one's nails, shaving the pubic area, plucking armpit hair, and brushing one's teeth'.[842]

Scholars differ on whether it is preferable to shave a moustache or only to trim it. Many of them prefer that it should be shaved or trimmed very short, so as one's upper lip is clear. What is certainly unacceptable from an Islamic point of view is to leave one's moustache to grow over one's lips, covering them. It would thus become unhygienic, gathering germs and falling into one's drink. Not so is the beard which is more desirable to grow. However, the Prophet makes it clear that we should take care of our hair, not leaving it to grow wild. This applies to facial hair as much as it applies to hair over one's head. Hence, if one has a beard, one should keep it tidy, and not allow it to grow huge as some people do.

As for the other practices, they are all part of normal hygiene. If one left one's nails too long, they would gather dust and dirt, and if pubic hair is not shaved, the area becomes too smelly. Armpit hair also smells badly if left for long, without being periodically removed or shaved. Although the *ḥadīth* mentions plucking, removing such hair by shaving or using some modern product is appropriate. As for brushing one's teeth, this is a very important part of hygiene. The Prophet used to brush his teeth often, several times a day. He used a *miswāk*, which is a tooth stick, similar to a toothbrush. Today, we can use a toothbrush and toothpaste.

---

842. Related by Aḥmad, al-Bukhari, Muslim, Abū Dāwūd, al-Nasā'ī, al-Tirmidhi, Ibn Mājah and Ibn Ḥibbān.

1264. (*Athar* 345) Nāfiʿ reports: 'Ibn ʿUmar used to clip his nails every 15 days and remove his pubic hair every month'.

This report gives us an idea of how often we should attend to these practices. ʿAbdullāh ibn ʿUmar always followed the Prophet's guidance wherever possible. Armpit and pubic hair should be done as necessary, but not left longer than forty days. As for trimming one's moustache, it should be done as necessary so as to ensure that it does not grow long. The Prophet brushed his teeth several times every day.

Prohibition of all gambling

All societies have different forms of gambling, in accordance with the prevailing customs, resources and useful articles they have. These are all grouped together in Islam under the heading *maysir*, which we translate as 'games of chance', where the result depends on chance, luck, the throw of dice, the card drawn, etc. rather than any skill the players have. The types that the Arabs practised before Islam are clearly mentioned so that they serve as examples for others practised by other communities, which naturally carry the same Islamic verdict of prohibition.

1265. (*Athar* 346) Saʿīd ibn Jubayr said 'Ibn ʿAbbās explained to me [one form of gambling that prevailed in pre-Islamic days]. He said: "It used to be asked, 'Where are those who would join in gambling for a camel?' Ten people would enrol, and they would buy a camel for ten newborn camels to be handed over at the time when they are weaned. They will then shuffle their arrows, and one would lose, leaving the newborn camels to nine. They go on shuffling the arrows until they are all left on one person, while the rest would lose one newborn camel each, to be given at the time of weaning. This is indeed maysir".'

1266. (*Athar* 347) Ibn ʿUmar said: 'Maysir is gambling'.

This sort of game provided entertainment and excitement as the participants went about excluding one of their number at a time. It could have dragged on for sometime, so as to generate public participation and support for one or other of the players. The winner at the end would have had a very exciting time. But here the number of losers is limited to nine, while in modern games of chance the number goes significantly higher. Besides, to the Arabs in pre-Islamic days, this sort of game was a source of pride, as the winner did not use the camel he won for any purpose. He would slaughter it and leave all its meat to the poor and penniless.

In a sense, this was similar to national lotteries which we see in many countries. Very large prizes are given to winners who choose those winning numbers. These are normally selected at random and entered in accordance with the rules of the game. If they are drawn at the time when the result is declared, then the person who chose them is given a substantial prize. The rest of the money is used by the government in support of good causes. Many are the charities, museums and research establishments which benefit from a share of such lottery money. Yet Islam does not permit this. It is totally forbidden.

The point about lottery and similar games that give the proceeds or a portion of them to good causes is that people are motivated only by the desire to win a large sum of money for themselves. They are not thinking of the good causes when they buy their lottery tickets. They only think of the great prospect that would open before them if they win. Moreover, when the government runs a lottery to support 'good causes' it assumes that society is devoid of goodness and that people will not donate to such causes unless they dangle before them the prospect of winning a large amount of money. Islam prefers instead to enhance the motives to do good among its followers, so that they seek to win God's pleasure, rather than an amount of money, however large it may be.

The Qur'an describes all games of chance as an '*abomination devised by Satan*' (5:90) to highlight its effect on participants and society. Hence, its prohibition is not in doubt. We also note that the view of early Muslims, such as the rightly-guided Caliphs, was very strict on this.

1267. (*Athar* 348) Rabī'ah ibn 'Abdullāh ibn al-Hadīr reports: 'Two men gambled over two cocks during 'Umar's reign. 'Umar ordered that the cocks be killed. A man from the Anṣār said to him: "Would you kill a community of God's creation which glorifies Him?" 'Umar did not proceed with his order'.

This is an example of the seriousness with which all gambling was viewed in the early period of Islam. When two people wanted to engage in a game of cockfighting 'Umar wanted to prevent this ever happening again by killing the birds used for such a purpose. Needless to say, the birds have no say in organising the fight or what people gamble with. They are indeed the victims, as in a cockfight both birds suffer a great deal, and one or both may die as a result.

Yet people are always willing to risk their money in the hope of winning a larger sum. The Prophet shows a good way to overcome this temptation.

1268. Abu Hurayrah reports that the Prophet said: 'Whoever of you swears and [unwittingly] includes in his oath al-Lāt and al-'Uzza should say, "There is no deity other than God", and whoever says to a friend, "Let us bet", should give something to charity'.[843]

The first point in this *ḥadīth* mentions a mistake that new Muslims could unwittingly make. They might, by force of habit, include in their oaths the two main idols that the Arabs used to worship before Islam. The Prophet tells them that anyone who says this unwittingly should follow it by confirming his belief in God's oneness, repeating the first part of the main declaration we say to state that we are Muslims, i.e. *La ilāha illa Allah*. Thus, the person concerned confirms his belief in God's oneness and renders the inclusion of those idols in his oath as meaningless words.

The Prophet also gives us an order that anyone who suggests a bet, risking some money for any reason, should give that money in charity. This atones for his mistake and earns him some reward for his money.

843. Related in all six authentic anthologies.

Thus, he ensures that he wins, because the reward he gains for his charity is certainly greater than any amount he could win as a result of betting or gambling.

1269. (*Athar* 349) Ḥuṣayn ibn Mus'ab reports: 'A man said to Abu Hurayrah: "We wager two pigeons and we do not want there to be a third unwagered pigeon between them so as not to take the winnings". Abu Hurayrah said to him: "This is childish and you better abandon it".'

This needs no explanation. It is childish play as the people involved have no real control over their pigeons. They realise this as they do not wish to have a third pigeon involved, because both of them might lose.

1270. Anas reports: al-Barā' ibn Mālik used to do the camel-chant for the men and Anjushah for the women. The Prophet said: "Easy, Anjushah, as you are driving gentle creatures".'[844]

This *ḥadīth* is the same as Number 264, and it shows that the Prophet took care of all his community.

1271. (*Athar* 350) Sa'īd ibn Jubayr quotes Ibn 'Abbās as he commented on the verse that says: '*Among people there are some who would pay for idle talk, so as to lead people astray from the path of God*'. (31: 6) He said: 'This applies to singing and similar things'.

The Qur'anic verse speaks of a general situation and a definite purpose, namely, leading people astray from God's path. As such it applies to whatever is used for leading people astray. To relate it to singing in particular does not provide any explanation, as singing is not prohibited in Islam. The Prophet once went into 'Ā'ishah's home where there were two servants singing. He lay on his bed while they continued to sing. A short while later Abu Bakr came in and tried to stop them, but the Prophet disapproved and told him: 'Leave them. We are in Eid days'.

844. Related by al-Ṭayālisi and al-Nasā'ī.

If singing is geared to lead people astray from God's path, it is definitely forbidden, as is anything used for such purpose.

1272. Al-Barāʾ ibn ʿĀzib reports that the Prophet said: 'Spread the greeting of peace and you will attain to safety. Idle play is evil'.

This *ḥadīth* is the same as Number 790. It encourages us to spread the greeting of peace, which is characteristic of Muslims. It encourages friendly relations, since we tell people that we wish them peace and happiness the first moment we see them. It is a much better greeting than what other communities have, such as 'good morning' and its equivalents. The second sentence in this *ḥadīth* refers to wasting time which the Prophet describes as evil. Time should always be spent in what is useful and beneficial. When it is wasted in idle play, it is lost and cannot be recovered. Some very important tasks may be unattended to as one indulges in idle play. Hence, scholars have always urged people to make the maximum and best use of their time.

1273. (*Athar* 351) Fuḍālah ibn ʿUbayd was with a group of people when he learnt that some people played with dice, or backgammon. He stood up in anger and made clear that it is strictly forbidden. He then said: 'Whoever plays it to devour its winnings is like one who eats the flesh of swine or one who performs his ablution with blood'.

This *ḥadīth* is the same as Number 791, and we have already explained it. Any game played with dice is a game of chance and it falls within the area of gambling which is strictly forbidden.

1274. (*Athar* 352) Muslim reports: 'When ʿAli went out of the al-Qaṣr gate and saw people playing backgammon, he would take them and lock them up from morning till night. Some of them he would lock up till midday. Those locked up till night were the ones that played for silver money, and those whom he locked up till half the day were the ones who played for amusement only. He ordered that they should not be greeted'.

There is no mandatory punishment for playing a game of chance or gambling. The matter is left to the ruler or any law enacted by a Muslim government. Probably such people were not Muslims. At the time when ʿAli was the Caliph, some areas of the Muslim state were still new to Islam, and many of its people retained their old religions. In that period, a Muslim would not play such a game in public. It is obvious that the punishment enforced by ʿAli was very mild. It was meant to tell such people that their practice was unacceptable. He differentiated between those who played for money and those who played for mere amusement. The former were gambling while the others were merely playing a forbidden game. He wanted them to feel that they were defying society, and this was demonstrated by people refusing to greet them.

1275. Abu Mūsa al-Ashʿari reports that the Prophet said: 'Whoever plays backgammon disobeys God and His Messenger'.[845]

This *ḥadīth* is very clear in its import. It describes playing backgammon as an act of disobedience of God and His Messenger. Needless to say, when something is described as constituting disobedience to God or the Prophet then it is forbidden.

1276. (*Athar* 353) ʿAbdullāh ibn Masʿūd said: 'Refrain from these two marked cubes that are associated with omens, for they are a form of gambling'.

1277. Buraydah reports that the Prophet said: 'Whoever plays backgammon is like one who stains his hand with the flesh and blood of a pig'.[846]

1278. This is the same as Number 1275 with a longer chain of transmission.

---

845. Related by Aḥmad, Ibn Mājah, al-Ḥākim, Ibn Ḥibbān and al-Dāraquṭni.
846. Related by Mālik, Muslim, Abū Dāwūd and Ibn Mājah.

1279. (*Athar* 354) Nāfiʿ reports: 'When ʿAbdullāh ibn ʿUmar saw any of his family playing backgammon, he chastised them and broke the board'.[847]

1280. (*Athar* 355) ʿĀ'ishah was informed that some people living in a room in her house [as tenants] had a backgammon board. She sent to them a message saying: 'If you do not remove it, I will evict you from my house'. She rebuked them for it.

1281. (*Athar* 356) Kulthūm ibn Jabr said: ''Abdullāh ibn al-Zubayr addressed us and said: "People of Makkah, I have heard that some men from the Quraysh play a game called backgammon. God says "*Believers! Intoxicants, games of chance, idolatrous practices and divining arrows are abominations devised by Satan. Therefore, turn away from them so that you may be successful*". (5: 90) I swear by God that anyone who is brought to me for having played it will be punished physically in his hair and body, and I will give his personal effects to the person who brings him to me".'

1282. (*Athar* 357) Yaʿla ibn Murrah said: 'I heard Abu Hurayrah say: "Whoever plays backgammon in a betting game is like one who eats pig meat, and the one who plays it without betting is like one who dips his hand in a pig's blood, and the one who sits there watching a game is like one looking at pig meat".'

1283. (*Athar* 358) ʿAbdullāh ibn ʿAmr ibn al-ʿĀṣ said: 'The one who plays the two cubes [of dice] for a bet is like one eating pig meat, and the one who plays them without betting is like one dipping his hand in pig's blood'.

The first of these *ḥadīths* makes a clear reference to backgammon which relies on two cubes of dice with a number given to every side of the cube. It is not the dice itself that is a form of gambling, but the purpose for which it is used in a game. Since the throw of a dice

847. Related by Mālik.

is unpredictable, the whole game becomes a game of chance and such games are gambling. Hence, they are forbidden.

We note the frequency of condemnation of backgammon by the Prophet and his companions. Several of these *ḥadīths* give very graphic descriptions of the status of a person who plays it, as we see in the last two *ḥadīths*. The fact that two of the Prophet's companions who are among the top narrators of *ḥadīths* give the same description clearly suggest that this description quotes the Prophet himself. 'Ā'ishah's attitude to her tenants who had the game at home is clear evidence that she considered the game to be strictly forbidden. It should be noted that they were not living with her in the same home, as her home was a single room. This must have been a house that she acquired, most likely through inheritance.

Ḥadīth 1281 quotes 'Abdullāh ibn al-Zubayr warning that he would enforce severe punishment on anyone playing it. Ibn al-Zubayr was a companion of the Prophet and he ruled Hijaz and Iraq for nine years, and endeavoured to be the recognised Caliph throughout the Muslim state. His was no vain threat.

All these *ḥadīths* and reports confirm the strict prohibition of backgammon as an example of games of chance that are associated with gambling. Some of us may wonder about the reason for such strict prohibition that extends even to playing games without betting on the result. The answer is that such games of chance, like backgammon, always tempt to add a little bet 'to make the game more exciting'. They also have the same characteristics of gambling in making a person hooked on them, wasting too much time playing them.

When gambling is involved, it means that the winner takes the money of the loser without having earned it. Islam teaches us to follow the proper practice in earning money through our work and effort, not relying on chance. Moreover, property has its own sanctity. It cannot be taken by another person except in exchange for something else, i.e. goods for money, or as a gift or charity. To take it through gambling is to take it forcibly, without any returns.

It is not surprising that those who gamble often harbour grudges against each other, even though they put up appearances of friendship and acceptance. This is due to the fact that they are always divided into winners and losers. If the loser does not speak out against the winner, it is because he cannot do anything about his loss. Moreover, failure in one game prompts the loser to seek another game in order to have a chance to regain his lost money. The winner also wants another game, feeling that if his luck holds he stands a chance to double his winnings. If the roles are changed, each would experience moments of success and failure. They want to play more and more. This leads to compulsive gambling, which is a serious condition. The gambler ends up gambling away everything he has, including his family, honour and integrity.

No repeated deception

Some *ḥadīths* specify certain characteristics or qualities of believers. Such *ḥadīths* either express the normal state of things or a state to which a believer should aspire to because it indicates how a believer should handle matters, or how he should conduct himself in different situations.

1284. Abu Hurayrah reports that the Prophet said: 'A believer is not bitten from the same hole twice'.[848]

The Prophet uses a word here for biting that is associated primarily with biting by reptiles or other poisonous creatures. This *ḥadīth* means that while it is possible for a believer to suffer a bite by a snake or a similar creature because he is taken unawares, the same thing should not be allowed to happen twice. He should always be careful so that he does not commit the same mistake twice, or be in the same situation of overlooking real danger.

While this *ḥadīth* speaks of a real life situation that requires paying full attention to one's surroundings at all times, it is also meant figuratively. Indeed, the circumstances leading to this statement provide a clear indication that it is so. During the Battle of Badr, one of the unbelievers taken prisoner by the Muslims was Abu ʿAzzah, a poet who often attacked Islam and the Prophet. When the Prophet

---

848. Related by Aḥmad, al-Bukhari, Muslim, Abū Dāwūd and Ibn Mājah.

decided that the prisoners could be freed in return for ransom, Abu ʿAzzah spoke to the Prophet and appealed to him to grant his release without a ransom, because he was poor and had a family to support. The Prophet granted his request after the man pledged that he would never criticise the Prophet or attack Islam again. However, soon after he was granted his freedom, Abu ʿAzzah reverted to insulting the Prophet and satirising Islam in his poetry. Some time later, he was again taken prisoner by the Muslims. Again he appealed to the Prophet for his release, protesting that he had a poor family to support. In reply to his appeals, the Prophet made this statement: 'A believer is not bitten from the same hole twice'.

Thus, the *ḥadīth* means that a believer should never be so gullible that he is deceived by the same trick more than once, in the same way one who is bitten by a snake is very careful not to be bitten again.

The Prophet also highlighted certain actions and made it clear that a person who resorts to them does not belong to the Muslim community. These are actions that are treacherous, hostile or unbecoming. One such action that is universally known by all Muslims is cheating, because the Prophet says: 'Whoever cheats us does not belong to us'.[849]

1285. Abu Hurayrah reports that the Prophet said: 'Whoever shoots at us at night does not belong to us'.[850]

Al-Bukhari writes under this *ḥadīth* that its chain of transmission is questionable, implying that there is doubt about its authenticity. Moreover, Aḥmad's version reads differently: 'Whoever shoots us with arrows does not belong to us'. In Arabic writing the two versions look very similar with only a difference in two letters of one word. Regardless of how we read it, the Prophet makes it clear that a person whose attitude is such as to try to cause injury to a group of believers does not belong to that community of believers.

1286. Abu Hurayrah reports that the Prophet said: 'Whoever bears arms against us does not belong to us'.

---

849. Related by Muslim.
850. Related by Aḥmad and Ibn Ḥibbān.

1287. Abu Mūsa ak-Ash'ari reports.... This is the same as the *ḥadīth* before it, with a different chain of transmission.

This is easily understood because a person who carries arms against a group of people certainly has no love for them and does not consider himself as belonging to them even though he may be related to them by blood. This applies in a wider context, to one who carries arms against a group of Muslims, in his own community or in a different community, and is thus pronounced as not belonging to the community of Muslims, i.e. he is not a Muslim. How could he belong to them when he is ready to fight them with arms? Commenting on this *ḥadīth*, Imam al-Nawawi says: 'Such a person does not benefit by our guidance, follow our example and implement our ways. It is like a father who says to his son, "you do not belong to me", when the son's behaviour is unacceptable to the father'.

All these *ḥadīths* that place certain individuals outside the Muslim community point out certain odious, contemptible or evil practices which cannot be associated with the Prophet, his message, or Divine faith. Hence, the Prophet always described them as not belonging to him or to his community. Only what is good, respectable and beautiful belongs to him. Hence people who do the former type of practices do not belong to the Prophet's community, and those who do the latter type belong to him.

1288. Yasār ibn 'Abdullāh reports that the Prophet said: 'If God wants to gather someone's soul in a particular area, He will place there something he needs'.[851]

This *ḥadīth* (which is the same as Number 783) provides a hint of how God's will is accomplished. God does not determine only the time when every living thing dies, but He also determines how and where that person or animal meets their death. The Prophet tells us in this *ḥadīth* that if a person is scheduled by God to die at a particular place, God makes it necessary for him to go there. It may be something that

851. Related by Aḥmad, al-Tirmidhi, al-Ḥākim and Ibn Ḥibbān.

attracts him to the land in question, or he may need to go there for business or to attend to some other need. Whatever it may be, if he lives somewhere else, or happens to be somewhere else and his time of death approaches, but it is scheduled to happen at a distant place, he will find it necessary to go to the place where he is to spend his last moments. When he is there, death occurs at the time appointed by God and by the cause He has determined. The important thing for every one of us is to be ready to meet one's end at anytime, because we cannot be sure when this happens. Since we will all meet God, it is important to be prepared at all times, doing what earns His pleasure and refraining from what incurs His anger.

> 1289. (*Athar* 359) Ibn Sīrīn said: 'Abu Hurayrah blew his nose using his garment and then said: "Well, well! Abu Hurayrah blows his nose in linen. In the past, I could faint between 'Ā'ishah's room and the platform [i.e. *minbar*] in the mosque. People would call me, "Mad", when there was nothing wrong with me except that I was starving".'

Abu Hurayrah compares his present situation when he said this to what he used to suffer a few years earlier. The earlier situation was shortly after he joined the Prophet and accepted Islam, while the second was when the Muslim state defeated the Persian and Byzantine Empires and took large parts of their land. The state revenue was such that 'Umar and 'Uthmān used to give people regular benefits. There was vast improvement in their living conditions. Hence, Abu Hurayrah's remarks about his clothes and the fact that he could blow his nose using his fine garment. In his earlier condition, perhaps he would not have believed that he would be wearing such a robe.

Thoughts and actions

People often find themselves thinking of doing or saying something which they know to be forbidden in Islam. If such thoughts are often repeated, they are troubled by them. They know that what they are thinking of is sinful, but the thought often occurs. Do such thoughts constitute a sin? Are people liable to be punished for them? How are they to overcome them?

1290. Abu Hurayrah reports that the Prophet said: 'People said to the Prophet: "We entertain thoughts which we would not like to put in words even though we could have everything under the sun". The Prophet said: "Do you really feel that?" They answered in the affirmative. He said: "This is a clear sign of firm faith".'[852]

This *ḥadīth* tells of the Prophet's companions' reluctance to express in words the thoughts that occurred to them. They would not do so for anything this world has to offer. This indicates that their thoughts are bad, evil or forbidden, and they abhor the fact that they occur to them. They know that they cannot stop these thoughts, but they are troubled by them and steer away from acting on them, or even putting them in words. Hence, the Prophet reassures them that their abhorrence, which sums up their reaction to such thoughts, indicates true and clear faith. This is indeed the case, because it is their strong faith that generates their reaction to their thoughts. Had they not been strong in faith, they would not have hated them so much.

1291. Shahr ibn Ḥawshab reports: 'I visited 'Āishah with my maternal uncle, and he said to her: "Any one of us may entertain thoughts which, if he would put in words, would ruin him in the Hereafter. If he were to act on them, he would be sentenced to death". She said *Allah-u akbar* [i.e. God is supreme] three times, then she said: "The Prophet was asked about this and he answered: 'If this happens to anyone of you, let him say *Allah-u akbar* three times. None but a true believer feels this way'."'

Again this is perfectly true, because only a believer can judge his thoughts in the way expressed by the man putting the question. He knows that such thoughts could lead him to disbelieve or to committing a sin that earns capital punishment. Hence he tries to suppress these thoughts.

852. Related by Muslim, Abū Dāwūd and Ibn Ḥibbān.

It should be clarified that such thoughts are not punishable in this life or on the Day of Judgement, as long as they remain within the realm of thought and whim. If they are not acted upon or stated verbally [should they relate to creeds and beliefs], then they are overlooked by God. Thoughts may vary in grade. Some are merely fleeting that leave no impression on a person's way of thinking, beliefs or actions. Others are stronger, or longer lasting, but they do not provoke any action. Others still get a person to make a decision, but when the chance offers itself to act on his thought, he refrains from doing so. Even though these grades differ, they all remain unpunishable. Even if the action is prevented by circumstance, no sin is recorded against the person concerned, because the sinful action has not materialised. This is part of God's grace, because if we were to be held accountable for our thoughts, along with our actions, we would be in a very difficult position on the Day of Judgement.

Consider the case of a young man who is troubled by his sexual urges. In today's world, with satellite television available everywhere, and channels devoted to sexual obscenities and horrid perversions, thoughts of committing a sin to satisfy one's desire may regularly occur to such a young man. If he takes action to suppress such thoughts, as the Prophet taught, then he is rewarded for not so acting. His self control is an act that testifies to his faith.

By contrast, when action is taken, then punishment for the sin intended or committed is incurred, even though the action did not achieve the end in mind. Suppose a man thought of killing another and lay in ambush. When the intended victim draws near, he aims his gun and shoots. Suppose that the target was not hit and the man not killed, yet the one who fired the gun incurs the punishment for his action, which is attempted murder. Fadlullah al-Jaylani gives the following example: Five people aim their guns at an intended victim: one hits him in his leg, injuring him, while another hits him in his head and the man dies. The third misses him altogether, while the fourth's gun is stuck and does not fire. The fifth had no bullet in his gun but he thought that it did. All five incur punishment, although the first two may have a greater punishment than the other three. But all of them are party to a murder.

Sometimes thoughts are centred on questions of belief. The Prophet gives an example of the most common ones.

> 1292. Anas ibn Mālik reports that the Prophet said: 'People will continue to ask questions about what has no reality until they say: "God has created everything, but who created God?"'[853]

This *ḥadīth* is related by al-Bukhari in his *Ṣaḥīḥ* anthology with the following addition: 'If a person gets to this point, he should seek refuge with God and put an end to such questions'. A similar version is related by Muslim, in which the ending is different: 'If a person gets to this point, he should say: "I believe in God and His messengers".' Another version related by Abū Dāwūd and al-Nassā'ī gives yet a different ending with the Prophet recommending reading Surah 112, Purity of Faith, making a gesture like spitting to the left and seeking refuge with God.

All such versions are authentic, which suggest that the Prophet was asked about this more than once and every time he gave an answer that suited the person putting the question. This question will continue to occur to people at all times. Some put it to believers to try to turn them away from their faith. The Prophet's answer makes it clear that we must not pursue this line of questioning because it leads us nowhere. It is not possible for the human mind to pursue it to a logical end. Hence, the best thing to settle the problem is to declare one's belief in God. This may be in words, or in reading the surah that sums up in four very short verses the Islamic concept of God. '*Say: He is God, the One and only God, the Eternal, the Absolute. He begets none, nor is He begotten, and there is nothing that could be compared to Him.*' (112: 1-4)

Clearing suspicion

Suspicion can ruin relations between people, particularly when it is based on flimsy evidence, or hearsay. The Prophet spoke in very clear

---

853. Related by al-Bukhari.

terms about misplaced suspicion, giving clear orders to refrain from it. The following authentic *ḥadīth* groups together some of the actions that cause discord within the community and make people dislike one another

1293. Abu Hurayrah reports that the Prophet said: 'Beware of suspicion, for suspicion is the worst form of lying. Do not spy against one another, or compete with one another. Do not turn your back on one another, nor envy nor hate one another, but remain – you servants of God – brothers and sisters'.[854]

This *ḥadīth*, which is similar to Numbers 400, 402, 410 and 412, stresses the importance of maintaining good relations within the Muslim community. The Prophet highlights certain things that would undermine such relations, and he tells us not to allow ourselves to indulge in them. Boycott, envy and hate should never be allowed to exist, let alone flourish in any Muslim community. Relations between Muslims should always be close. All members of the Muslim community should look at one another as brothers and sisters. They must value this tie of brotherhood, because it is established on the best basis, which is servitude to God and pure faith.

However, the *ḥadīth* begins with a warning against suspicion describing it as the most untrue of speech. This is an apt description because whatever is said on the basis of suspicion has no basis in reality. It is all conjecture, leading to false accusations and ideas. It poisons relations and leads to discord and hostility. It also encourages what the Prophet mentions next, which is spying on one another. People do not spy on their neighbours or competitors unless they have some sort of suspicion they want to explore. Hence, they try to gather information secretly, perhaps through spying. This is again forbidden.

The Prophet teaches us that we should help one another not to entertain any doubt leading to suspicion.

---

854. Related by Aḥmad, al-Bukhari, Muslim, Abū Dāwūd, al-Tirmidhi, Ibn Mājah and Ibn Ḥibbān.

1294. Anas reports: 'As the Prophet was with one of his wives, a man passed by. The Prophet called him and said: "This is my wife so-and-so". The man said: "Whoever I might suspect, I would not suspect you". The Prophet said: "Satan goes through man like his blood".'[855]

This *ḥadīth* is reported in different versions and it is useful to look at the most detailed one which quotes Ṣafiyyah, the Prophet's wife. She mentions that one day, as the Prophet was spending the last ten days of Ramadan in the mosque, devoting his time to worship, she came to visit him. She sat with him for sometime before she left. The Prophet walked with her towards her home. As they were close to the door of the mosque, passing close to Umm Salamah's [another of his wives] door, two men from the Anṣār passed by and greeted the Prophet. The Prophet said to them: 'Wait a moment. This is Ṣafiyyah'. They said: 'Limitless is God in His glory'. They felt very bad, but the Prophet said to them: 'Satan goes as close to man as his own blood, and I feared that he might put something into your minds'.[856]

All versions of this *ḥadīth* agree that the Prophet sought to clear any doubts that might have occurred to the two passers by, even before they occurred. They were upset that the Prophet thought they might suspect him. One of them said to the Prophet: 'Whoever I might suspect, I would not suspect you'. This is clearly the attitude of believers towards the Prophet whom they loved and trusted. How could they suspect him when they believed that he received revelations from on High? But the Prophet was clear on this point. Yet he wanted to teach his companions something that benefits them in their social relations. This he explains by the closeness of Satan to man and his thoughts. He can creep into one's mind so as to be as close to him as his own blood. This means that at any time suspicion might arise at the slightest indication, or the smallest gesture. This is what the Prophet expresses in a most graphic description: 'Satan goes through man like his blood'. Hence, a wrong thought can very easily be planted in someone's mind.

---

855. Related by Muslim and Abū Dāwūd.
856. Related by al-Bukhari, Muslim and Abū Dāwūd.

Therefore, when we feel that a particular situation we are in might give rise to some thought or doubt, we should clarify it, as the Prophet did when he told his two companions that the woman walking with him was his wife, Ṣafiyyah.

> 1295. (*Athar* 360) 'Abdullāh ibn Mas'ūd said: 'A person who has been the victim of theft continues to suspect until he becomes worse than the thief'.

This is clearly true. When we suffer a misfortune like theft, we are so aggrieved that we begin to suspect people, thinking that they were the perpetrators. But when we entertain such doubts on no firm basis, we soon become guilty of a worse offence, which is suspicion without evidence. The Prophet's companions, particularly the scholars among them, understood this well and acted on it:

> 1296. (*Athar* 361) Bilāl ibn Sa'd al-Ash'ari said: 'Mu'āwiyah wrote to Abu al-Dardā': "Write down for me the names of all transgressors in Damascus". Abu al-Dardā' said: "What business would I have with transgressors in Damascus? How would I know them?" His own son, Bilāl said: "I will write their names". He did so. His father said to him: "How do you know them? You cannot know that they are transgressors unless you are one of them. Begin with yourself". He did not send their names [to Mu'āwiyah]'.

We note here that Abu al-Dardā' refused the Caliph's request on grounds that he could not for certain judge anyone unless he had clear information. How could he when he did not have firm first-hand information? How could he have such information unless he was there and spoke to them? Hence, when his son wrote down their names, he told him that his action was not acceptable, because having the necessary information required associating with such transgressors. Hence, he told his son to start with reforming himself. We should note that Abu al-Dardā' refused to accept his son's information as correct because it did not rely on first-hand knowledge. His son was later to become the chief justice in Damascus, during the time of Yazīd ibn Mu'āwiyah.

1297. (*Athar* 362) 'Abd al-'Azīz ibn Qays said: 'I visited 'Abdullāh ibn 'Umar and I saw his servant shaving his hair. He said: "The lime depilatory makes the skin supple".'[857]

Ibn 'Umar's words simply speak about the agent that was used at his time to remove hair. He mentions something about its properties.

The Prophet addressed all situations and indicated the best guidance in all respects. One aspect which he addressed was personal cleanliness and hygiene.

1298. Abu Hurayrah reports that the Prophet said: 'Five practices are based on sound human nature: circumcision, shaving pubic hair, plucking armpit hair, trimming the moustache and clipping one's nails'.[858]

1299. This is the same as Number 1298, placing the five practices in a different order and with a different chain of transmission.

1300. (*Athar* 363). This is the same again, with a different order and different transmission.

These three *ḥadīths* are the same as Number 1263, but they include circumcision instead of brushing one's teeth which occurs in the earlier *ḥadīth*. They emphasise that these are part of uncorrupted human nature. Other *ḥadīths* indicate a time range for some of these practices, such as shaving pubic hair and plucking armpit hair, which are recommended to be done at intervals of no more than forty days. Needless to say, these two areas have strong body odour and if they are left without removing the hair, the smell becomes strong and offensive.

Clipping one's nails is a mark of cleanliness. If nails are left to grow long they attract dirt and germs, which could fall in one's food. Keeping them short is the best precaution against that.

---

857. Related by al-Ṭabarāni.

858. Related by al-Bukhari, al-Nasā'ī and al-Tirmidhi.

Similarly, if one leaves one's moustache untrimmed, it grows long and covers one's upper lip. The hair then dips into one's drink and particles of food may be trapped in it. This is not merely unsightly, but could also be injurious to one's health.

The case is similar with regard to circumcision. Unless the piece of foreskin is cut, it attracts dirt which becomes trapped under its folds. It could represent a health risk. Islam takes care of all these as a measure of health protection and personal hygiene.

For old time's sake

The Prophet was very loyal to everyone who had something to do with his upbringing, or had some good relation with him or his family. There are several *ḥadīths* that speak of him demonstrating such loyalty and care. While this is a highly commendable quality which all people appreciate, the Prophet was the perfect example in truly caring for his old acquaintances, particularly those who looked after him as a youngster.

> 1301. Abu al-Ṭufayl reports: 'I saw the Prophet distributing meat at al-Ji'rānah [a place between Makkah and Taif, which is also pronounced as al-Ji'irrānah]. At the time I was a young lad and could carry a camel's bone. A woman came to him, and he laid his own robe for her to sit on. I asked who the woman was, and I was told that she was the one who suckled him when young'.

This is the impression of a young lad who saw the Prophet honouring and welcoming an old woman who was not known to the people around. The gesture he performed indicated that he honoured her and gave her the position suited to a mother. Her visit to him is recorded in other *ḥadīths* as well. One such *ḥadīth* mentions that the woman's husband, who is considered his father through breast-feeding came first, and the Prophet honoured him, placing part of his robe for him to sit on. Then came Ḥalīmah, his suckling mother, and he placed the rest of his robe out for her to sit on. Then came her son, i.e. his breast-feeding brother, and the Prophet stood up to greet him and sat him next to himself.[859] Other *ḥadīths* mention that when Ḥalīmah approached, the Prophet stood up to welcome her, shouting with delight: 'My mother, my mother!'

The Prophet's action on such occasions impressed on his companions the need to honour old friends and acquaintances. While this is natural, some people may show reluctance to extend any warm feeling towards old acquaintances, thinking that they belonged to days gone by. But the Islamic practice is that old friendships and old relations should be honoured and welcomed warmly.

Once, a woman was taken captive by a Muslim army. She said to the soldiers that she was the Prophet's sister through breast-feeding. They took her to him and he asked her for evidence. She mentioned a mark on her arm, and he recognised this. He extended the best treatment to her, although her relationship with him was no more than that she was the daughter of his wet nurse. He then offered her the choice of staying with him or returning to her people. When she chose the latter, he gave her gifts and ensured her safe return journey.

Al-Mughīrah ibn Shuʿbah was a companion of the Prophet who was appointed governor of Kufah and other areas by different caliphs, such as ʿUmar, ʿUthmān and Muʿāwiyah.

1302. (*Athar* 364) Al-Mughīrah ibn Shuʿbah said: 'A man said [to me]: "May God make you thrive. Your doorkeeper knows certain people and he gives them preference with permission to enter to see you". Al-Mughīrah said: "May God excuse him. Old friendship is useful even with a biting dog or with an aggressive camel".'

This is a true word of approval by one of the Prophet's companions. If old acquaintances are not given their due, then man would not be as faithful to friendship as a dog or camel. Al-Mughīrah indicated to the man who objected to the preferential treatment that he would not take it against his doorkeeper that he was kind to his old friends.

859. Related by Abū Dāwūd.

Good manners in all situations

The Prophet always emphasised the importance of good manners, alerting his companions, and his followers, to the need to show good manners in all situations. According to the Prophet, good manners include every good thing that is likely to make people happy and strengthen good relations between them, removing causes of doubt and friction. The Prophet recognised the needs of different people and allowed whatever was lawful. With children and young people, he understood their need to play and allowed them this, provided that whatever they played at did not contravene any Islamic teachings. Some people look at child play as unbecoming and try to impose on their children a very serious outlook. This is contrary to human nature, because children need their play, particularly its make-belief aspect. The Prophet did not object to this. We understand this from different *ḥadīths*.

Ibn Abbas reports: 'I was playing with other boys when the Prophet passed by. I tried to hide behind a door. He came to me and with his open hand, he patted me once on my back between my shoulders, and said: "Go and tell Mu'āwiyah to come to me". I did, and when I returned I said: "He is eating"…'.[860] The *ḥadīth* is a little longer, but we need to emphasise the message of only this portion, which shows that the Prophet did not object to play. Ibn 'Abbās was a young lad playing with boys of his age. When the Prophet passed, he hid, perhaps because he was a little ashamed that the Prophet should see him playing. The Prophet went to him and told him to call one of his companions to come over to him. He does not reproach him for playing or wasting time. On the contrary, he gave him a friendly gesture to remove his embarrassment, before he asked him to call one of his companions whom he needed to speak to. This was understood by his companion and they followed his practice:

1303. (*Athar* 365) Ibrāhīm said: 'Our elders used to allow us all sorts of playthings except dogs'. [Al-Bukhari said: He meant for young boys.]

---

860. Related by Muslim.

1304. (*Athar* 366) Abu 'Uqbah reports: 'I was once walking along the road with Ibn 'Umar when we passed by some Abyssinian boys playing. He took out two *dirhams* and gave them to them'.

Nothing could be a better gesture of approval than giving the playing children some money. They may use the money to buy some refreshment to renew their energy. When Ibrāhīm refers to his elders he means the Prophet's companions, as he belonged to the generation that followed them.

1305. 'Ā'ishah reports: 'The Prophet used to let my friends come to me to play with dolls'.[861]

This *ḥadīth* shows that the Prophet was aware of the needs of his young wife, and took action so that her friends would come to her to play together. This should not be understood that they were children, because the Prophet did not marry 'Ā'ishah as a child, but as a young woman. Yet it is normal for teenage girls to play with dolls, sew dresses for them and care for them as if they were real children. This is an expression of the motherly instinct women have.

In these *ḥadīths* we see that the Prophet and his companions encouraged, or at least accepted, children and teenagers play. Yet some of us look disapprovingly on it, which we should not do. However, when play leads to something forbidden, the Prophet made his disapproval clear, as fits the type of play.

1306. Abu Hurayrah reports: 'God's Messenger once saw a man chasing a pigeon. He said: "It is one devil chasing another".'[862]

1307. (*Athar* 367) Al-Ḥasan said: 'Every time 'Uthmān gave the speech before Friday Prayer, he urged that [stray] dogs be killed and that pigeons be slaughtered'.

---

861. Related by al-Bukhari.

862. Related by Aḥmad, Abū Dāwūd and Ibn Mājah.

(*Athar* 368) Al-Ḥasan said: 'I heard 'Uthmān giving a speech and ordering the killing of dogs and slaughtering of pigeons'.[863]

Some thoughtless people, particularly teenagers, may chase pigeons, take their eggs or their young to play with. This is totally unacceptable. Moreover, playing with pigeons is often a cover for some unacceptable behaviour. A person may keep pigeons on the roof of his home, and fly them in the neighbourhood, but his real purpose is to look at his neighbours when they are unaware of his presence. He may cause some damage, such as breaking glass or dropping some dirt in their homes. Hence, Islam looks at such pastimes in a very unfavourable light. 'Uthmān, the third Caliph, often encouraged the killing of stray dogs and slaughtering of pigeons because of the harm they caused.

A different aspect of Islamic manners is clearly demonstrated by 'Umar, the second Caliph. Zayd ibn Thābit was a close companion of the Prophet who learnt much from him, becoming a scholar. He was the one employed by both Abu Bakr and 'Uthmān to supervise the task of putting together the complete copies of the Qur'an that would serve as reference for people in different parts of the Muslim state. He was also well known for his scholarship, particularly his insight into the Islamic inheritance system.

1308. (*Athar* 369) Zayd ibn Thābit reports that ''Umar ibn al-Khaṭṭāb came to visit him and sought permission to enter. Zayd duly gave him permission. As 'Umar entered, Zayd was having his head combed by a slave girl of his. He lifted his head [to welcome the Caliph], but 'Umar told him to continue. Zayd said: "Had you sent for me, I would have come to you". 'Umar said: "It is I that have a need to see you for".'[864]

This report shows the respect the Prophet's companions had for one another. 'Umar, the Caliph who was the overall ruler of a vast and expanding Muslim state, goes to visit someone who was very much his junior because he needed something from him. He could certainly

863. Related by 'Abd al-Razzāq.

864. Related by al-Bayhaqi.

have summoned him, and Zayd would have willingly gone to him, but 'Umar shows the respect due to his fellow companions of the Prophet. Since he had something to ask Zayd, he went to him, and sought admittance. He did not want to disturb anything Zayd was doing. So, he told him to continue with having his hair combed while asking him about the problem he was considering. Other versions of this *ḥadīth* give the details of the problem 'Umar needed Zayd's advice on. It was the inheritance due to the deceased's grandfather, when the deceased is survived only by his grandfather and siblings. In other words, the deceased had neither parents nor offspring.

1309. (*Athar* 370) Abu Hurayrah said: 'If a person needs to spit when he is with other people, he should shade his mouth with his palm so that his spit falls to the ground. When he fasts, he should apply some oil so that no one may realise that he is fasting'.

These are aspects of good manners encouraged by Islam. If one must spit, one should cover this so as not to cause disgust, and if one is fasting voluntarily, one should keep this between oneself and God. People need not know that one is fasting.

1310. (*Athar* 371) Ḥabīb ibn Thābit said: 'When a person speaks to a group, his turning towards a particular person was disliked. He should instead make his address to them all'.

While this *ḥadīth* does not quote the Prophet, it refers to the first generation of Muslims, i.e. the Prophet's companions, who were the ones who transformed their lives in accordance with Islamic values and standards. If one was with a group of people, making some point in the discussion, then one should direct one's address to the group, rather than a single person among them, as some people do, particularly if that person has a distinguished position. To address such a person in particular may cause the others to feel uneasy. Hence, to remove any ill feelings, the recommendation is to make the address general.

1311. (*Athar* 372) Ibn Abu al-Hudhayl said: '‘Abdullāh [ibn Mas‘ūd] visited one of his companions when he was ill. He was accompanied by one of his friends. When they entered the house, his friend stared about. ‘Abdullāh said to him: "Had your eyes been gouged, it would have been better for you".'

1312. (*Athar* 373) Nāfi‘ said: 'A group of people from Iraq visited Ibn ‘Umar, and they saw a gold neck-band on one of his servants. They looked at each other. He said to them: "How quick you are to think of evil".'

When visiting people, one should always make sure to behave properly and to be mindful that one is only a visitor while the hosts are in their own home. Therefore, one should not stare about as if one wants to learn about them what one does not know, or to look at what they do not like to be seen by others. The visitor should particularly make sure that he is not looking at members of the family who might not be aware that they are seen. Hence, ‘Abdullāh ibn Mas‘ūd's comment to the man who was staring about in the home they visited, telling him that the sin he was committing was more detrimental to him than having his two eyes gouged. The sin is looking at people in their privacy when they are unaware.

Ibn ‘Umar's comment to those who were looking at his servant wearing a gold neck-band is similar. They might not have uttered any words, but their looks said much. Perhaps they were wondering why a servant or slave girl had a gold article of jewellery. This is not their concern. They should respect their host and give all attention to him.

1313. (*Athar* 374) Abu Hurayrah said: 'No good comes about from excessive talk'.

1314. Abu Hurayrah reports that the Prophet said: 'The worst of my community are those who talk too much, resorting to pedantry and insolence; while the best of my people are those who have the best manners'.[865]

865. Related by Aḥmad.

In the first *ḥadīth* Abu Hurayrah clearly states that speaking too much is of little or no use. People should be precise and limit themselves to making their meaning clear without unnecessarily harping on about what is already clear. This is not surprising. Abu Hurayrah was very close to the Prophet and reported a very large number of *ḥadīths* and we know that the Prophet included rich meanings in few words.

In the second *ḥadīth* the Prophet mentions three qualities that make a person join the worst type of people. These are the chatterers who almost speak non-stop. They admire their own speech and feel that they have a claim to being listened to. They love to hear themselves speaking. This is an attitude of arrogance that some people often exhibit. If such a chatterer adds pedantry and insolence to his speech then he is really a pain in the neck. What is worse is that he merits the Prophet's description as being one of the worst in the Muslim community. By contrast, the best people are those whose manners are fine and who are kindly to people. They listen to others and accept what is right, without claiming any monopoly of speech or knowledge.

Hypocrisy: pure evil

One of the worst characteristics that Islam abhors is hypocrisy. The Prophet spoke about it several times, and every time he used some graphic description that showed how ugly and unbecoming all types of hypocrisy are.

1315. Abu Hurayrah reports that the Prophet said: 'One of the worst people is a double-faced man, who comes to one group with one face and to another group with a different face'.[866]

The Prophet describes a hypocrite person as double-faced, and then he explains why he has described him as such, showing him as though he actually has two faces. If there are two groups with some differences, or involved in a dispute, he will speak to each one in a way that pleases them, saying to one group the opposite of what he says to the other.

---

866. Related by al-Bukhari, Ibn Ḥibbān and Abu 'Awānah.

Hence, the Prophet says that such a person is one of the worst types of people. This is certainly true, because such a person cannot be a man of faith who fears God. As such, he always seeks what he thinks to serve his immediate interests, knowing that this will mean that he lies to both groups, or at least one of them.

1316. ʿAmmār ibn Yāsir reports that the Prophet said: 'Whoever is double-faced in this life will on the Day of Resurrection have two tongues of fire'. A big man then passed by and the Prophet said: 'This is one of them'.[867]

Here, the Prophet gives a more graphic description of hypocrites. The description concentrates on the hypocrite's tongue, because it is with his words that he tries to cheat and get the better of people. He always says to his interlocutors what pleases them, so that he is included in their good books. He does not care if what he says is untrue, because all that he cares about is his own interest.

Because a hypocrite relies on lying, thinking that he can manipulate his way out of any difficulty, God gives him two tongues on the Day of Judgement, but both are made of fire. This is a horrid picture, but very apt for such a person.

One thing every hypocrite lacks is a sense of shame. When he does something against societal morality, he does not feel ashamed because he thinks that he can still get away with it, saying a few words to please this person and a few others to please someone else. That his words are lies does not trouble him. He has no sense of shame. But this sense is one that all Divine messages try to promote. The Prophet says: 'Among the words people received from early prophets are: if you feel no shame, then do as you wish'. This *ḥadīth* is reported and explained under Number 600.

1317. This *ḥadīth* is the same as Number 339, and we have already explained it.

---

867. Related by Abū Dāwūd, Ibn Ḥibbān and al-Dārimi.

1318. ʿImrān ibn Ḥuṣayn reports that the Prophet said: 'Modesty brings nothing but good'. Bashīr ibn Kaʿb said to him: 'It is written in al-Ḥikmah: Modesty brings propriety; modesty gives inner serenity'. ʿImran said to him: 'I am reporting to you what God's Messenger said and you speak to me of what is written in your scroll!'.[868]

We need to explain two things here. First is the Prophet's statement that modesty brings only what is good. This obviously applies in any situation that does not necessitate asserting the Islamic point of view or the Islamic rule. Where these need to be stated and clarified, refraining from doing so under the pretext of modesty is not to be condoned. Similarly, choosing not to speak out against some evil action is closer to cowardice than modesty, and the two are different. While cowardice is unacceptable by any standard, modesty is praised in most societies and by all Divine religions.

The other point is the objection the *ḥadīth* reporter made when someone in the audience tried to confirm his statement by quoting from al-Ḥikmah, or the Book of Wisdom. The objection was not to what was stated. There is no doubt that it was correct and in line with Islam. But the person making the statement appeared to be making a counter statement, rather than quoting something in support. It is as though he was saying: 'Oh, yes! This has been said before by others'. While this may be acceptable when we have a discussion with colleagues, or between equals, it is not acceptable when it is in a rejoinder to a Qur'anic or *Ḥadīth* text, because this would be putting people's own statements on a par with the Qur'an or with the Prophet's *Ḥadīth*, when *Ḥadīth* is a form of revelation. This is what is clear from ʿImrān's, the Prophet's companion's, rejoinder: 'I am reporting to you what God's messenger has said and you speak to me of what is written in your scroll'.

1319. (*Athar* 375) Ibn ʿUmar said: 'Modesty and belief are joined together: if one of them is removed, the other is removed'.[869]

868. Related by al-Bukhari, Muslim and al-Tabarāni.

869. Related by al-Ḥākim.

1320. Abu Bakrah reports that the Prophet said: 'Modesty is part of faith, and faith leads to heaven. Vulgarity is part of unkindness, and unkindness leads to hell.'[870]

Several *ḥadīths* describe modesty as part of faith. This means that it is an essential quality of believers. A true believer refrains from claiming anything that does not belong to him. In fact, he is hesitant to claim all that is due to him for fear that he might be thought of as ill-mannered or presumptive. He is always ready to forgo something of what is due to him as an act of good will or generosity, or when he feels that forgoing it serves a better purpose, or pleases others or brings them happiness. All these qualities are encouraged by faith, which teaches all virtues and as such leads the faithful to the right destination in the life to come, i.e. heaven.

The opposite quality, which is rendered in the *ḥadīth* as vulgarity, includes a range of bad manners, including vulgar language that demonstrates lack of propriety and decorum. Needless to say, such a quality encourages contravening Islamic values and standards. As such it leads its people to disobey God and His messenger. When this becomes a habit, it certainly leads the perpetrator to hell where he suffers God's punishment.

Modesty is a virtue the Prophet was keen to stress. Indeed, it is a universally acclaimed virtue, with most religions and traditions praising it. However, Western societies sometimes try to cast an air of disapproval on modesty, picturing it as a weakness that inhibits a person from claiming what is due to him. Instead, they emphasise the need to be assertive so that others do not take advantage of our modesty.

This is the wrong way of looking at things. Being modest in social dealings does not mean that a person should abandon what is rightfully his or hers. Modesty is the opposite of boasting and asserting what one does not have. It is thus the opposite of presumption, temerity or cheek. Assertiveness, on the other hand, is often associated with being aggressive or domineering. As such, it may be a virtue where people generally do not give due consideration to others, but it is far

870. Related by Ibn Majah, al-Ḥākim and Ibn Ḥibbān.

from being so where people are very considerate and willing to allow others not only what is rightfully theirs, but a little more in addition.

In a Muslim community people are always encouraged to be kind and generous, morally and materially. The Prophet makes it a condition of faith that one considers others in the same way as one considers oneself. He says: 'By God! A person is not a believer unless he loves for his brother what he loves for himself'.[871] This applies to all situations. Where a person finds something that he loves to have or enjoy, he should love that all his brothers and sisters should have or enjoy the same thing. Thus, selfishness is reduced within the Muslim community as everyone is considerate of others.

This is why Islam stresses the virtue of modesty as it helps us to keep the selfish tendency down and to stresses instead the brotherhood of all believers. One does not seek to stress one's own position, but rather considers oneself as part of a greater entity, the Muslim community. The Prophet even says that modesty is highlighted by earlier prophets as a virtue to be sought.

1321. 'Ali said: 'God's Messenger (peace be upon him) had a large head and big eyes. When he walked he leant forward as if he was walking downhill. When he turned, he turned with all his body.'[872]

Al-Bukhari enters this *ḥadīth* here because it describes how the Prophet turned, particularly when he was speaking to someone. He would turn with all his body so as to face him. He thus makes his interlocutor feel his closeness. It, thus, relates to the previous *ḥadīth*, giving the opposite image of a vulgar person who does not care for others.

1322. Abu Mas'ūd reports: 'Among the words people received from early prophets are: if you feel no shame, then do as you wish'.[873]

---

871. Related by al-Bukhari and Muslim.

872. Related by Aḥmad and by al-Tirmidhi in a more detailed description.

873. Ri Aḥmad, al-Bukhari, Ibn Mājah and Ibn Ḥibbān.

This *ḥadīth* is the same as Number 600 where we have already given it a full explanation.

Anger and self restraint

The Prophet, who highlighted for us every aspect of good behaviour, repeatedly spoke about anger and the need to control it. We all know that people often do things when angry, which they regret afterwards. When one is in a fit of anger, one may abuse, verbally if not physically, those who are very close to one. An angry young man often speaks ill to his parents, or to his elders. When some people lose their temper, they commit crimes which they would never contemplate when they are in possession of their senses. We also know that many people divorce their wives when they are in a fit of temper, then they regret what they have said and try to find a way out of their dilemma. Because of the great harm anger often causes, the Prophet spoke repeatedly, and in a variety of ways, about the importance of self restraint:

> 1323. Abu Hurayrah reports that the Prophet said: 'It is not the one who physically overpowers others that is strong. A strong man is one who controls himself when angry'.

In this *ḥadīth*, the Prophet redefines strength, making clear that it is totally different from what people think. A person may be physically powerful, and he may be able to wrestle with anyone and beat them. He may be able to physically beat two or three people when he fights them single-handed. Yet he is not truly strong, according to the Prophet's definition of strength. The one who is truly powerful is the person who, being very angry, is able to exercise self-restraint, controlling his temper and not allowing his anger to get the better of him. We all know this to be true, because we all experience anger and we know that unless we tame it with self control, it can easily make us do what we will soon regret.

The Prophet puts this thought in a different way. Anas reports that the Prophet passed by some people who were wrestling. He asked about the occasion, and he was told that one of them was too strong for the others, able to beat every challenger. The Prophet said to them: 'Shall I tell you about someone who is more powerful than him? A man who is verbally abused by another, but he exercises self restraint. He thus beat the other person, his own satan and the other man's satan'.[874] Thus we see how the Prophet uses the occasion of a wrestling match in which people admire physical strength in order to highlight what is more important, which is the need to remain in control even when anger is likely to get the better of us.

The fact that several *ḥadīths* speak about the same thing means that the Prophet attached importance to the subject matter because of its relevance to people's lives. In the two *ḥadīths* we quoted the Prophet related self restraint to strength. In another *ḥadīth*, he shows that such self restraint can earn good reward from God.

1324. (*Athar* 376) 'Abdullāh ibn 'Umar said: 'No bitter gulp earns greater reward than that of a person who controls his anger only for God's sake'.[875]

In this *ḥadīth*, which is also related as a direct quote from the Prophet, controlling one's temper is described as something bitter which one has to swallow. It is much easier to give vent to one's anger, hurling verbal abuse on the person who has been the cause of such anger, or even resorting to physical action. But when self restraint is exercised for no reason other than to please God, then it earns great reward indeed. This applies in a situation where the angry person can easily avenge himself on the one who caused his anger, but refrains from doing so, controlling himself in order not to worsen the situation, or to ensure some other benefit. Yet people do not like to be reminded of this great virtue, particularly when they are angry.

1325. Sulaymān ibn Ṣurad reports: 'Two men abused each other in the Prophet's presence. One of them was so angry that his face was red. The Prophet looked at him and said: "I know a word which would dispel this man's trouble if he would only say

---

874. Related by al-Bazzār.

875. Related by Aḥmad as directly quoting the Prophet and by Ibn Mājah.

it: I seek shelter with God from the accursed Satan, or *A'ūdhu billāh min al-shayṭān al-rajīm*". A man went up to that man and said: "Do you know what he [i.e. the Prophet] said? You should say: 'I seek shelter with God from the accursed Satan'." The man retorted: "Do you think I am mad".'[876]

1326. This is the same as the *ḥadīth* before it, with slightly different wording.

This example illustrates the sort of reaction angry people may give when they are reminded of the need to control themselves. When the man was told to seek refuge with God against his satan, he retorted that he was not crazy. No one described him as such, and no one would think that seeking God's protection is a sign of madness, but in his anger the man could not judge things properly. Hence, his angry reaction. Therefore, it is important to study such *ḥadīths* and learn the importance of controlling our tempers so that when we get angry we can make use of what we have learnt and accept advice when we are reminded of the way to control our anger. The *ḥadīth* is the same as Number 437, and we included further explanation of it there.

Another *ḥadīth* tells of a different way to prevent temper from flying high. It is simply to remain silent and to say nothing when one is angry.

1327. Ibn 'Abbās reports that the Prophet said: 'Teach and make things easy; teach and make things easy'. He repeated this three times, then went on saying: 'When you are angry, remain silent'. He repeated it twice.[877]

This *ḥadīth* is the same as Number 245, and we have given it full explanation there. We may add here that the two parts of the *ḥadīth* are not unrelated. Making things easy to learn and to practise is very important. When things are made difficult, people will simply not learn or do them. One thing the Prophet teaches us in this *ḥadīth* is self restraint, and this can be achieved by something that is by no

---

876. Related by al-Bukhari, Muslim, Abū Dāwūd and al-Nasā'ī.

877. Related by Aḥmad and al-Ṭayālisi.

means difficult, which is to remain silent. By doing so, we not only control our own temper, but it also gives the other person no cause to get angry or to reply to anything.

Sentimental and reasonable

Islam encourages Muslims to adopt certain qualities and characteristics so that they are able to cope with the problems of life and conduct their social relations in the best way. This helps to cement relations within the Muslim community and maintain strong ties between its members. Moreover, Islam stresses the need to tame one's feelings of love and hate.

> 1328. (*Athar* 377) 'Ali ibn Abi Ṭālib said to Ibn al-Kawwā: 'Do you know the old statement: Love your beloved one moderately, for he may be the one you hate in future; and hate whomever you hate moderately, for he may be the one you love in future'.[878]

This is very sound advice because when feelings of love and hate are too strong, they blur a person's vision and he or she is then unable to put things in the proper perspective. It is universal wisdom that tells us that when we love we tend to overlook the faults of the person we love. Should that person make mistakes, we try to find justification for them. If others criticise him for his mistakes, we are ready to defend him. Sometimes we go to great lengths in order to show that what is a clear mistake or flaw of character is not what it appears to be. Such an attitude always leads to problems, because it expects perfection where it is not possible. Hence, when a mistake is repeated once too many, or a flaw consistently appears to be visible, facts stare us in the face and we have to admit that what we valued too high is far from meeting our expectations. If this happens over something of importance, then it could lead to love giving way to hate. The stronger our love used to be, the greater our disappointment and the more likely that it will be replaced by hate that could again be too strong.

---

878. Related by al-Tirmidhi and al-Ṭabarāni.

The same thing can be said in reverse. Should we hate someone for their misdeeds, unacceptable conduct or some other cause, our hate should be tampered with reason. If it is exaggerated, it will blind us to that person's positive points. It should be remembered that no one is without some goodness that reflects in his or her actions or character. To ignore such good points and think only of the hate we feel towards such a person is wrong, because it can lead to further complications. On the other hand, some people whom we may not like may prove us wrong and allow their good side to prevail in their dealings with us. This puts us in a bad light, because we will be ignoring what is universally approved as good.

On the other hand, our hate might be due to a mistake or some failing on our own part, and the person concerned may take some positive action to clear a misunderstanding or remedy a bad situation. When we allow this to take place and give a positive response to a good initiative we may set in a complete transformation in our relationship. In time, the old hate may change into love. If our initial hate is too strong, it could hamper such a process and deprive us of a chance to win over a good friend.

1329. (*Athar* 378) Aslam reports that 'Umar ibn al-Khaṭṭāb said: 'Do not allow your love to be too passionate, or your dislike to be ruinous'. I asked him: 'How is that?' He said: 'When you love, you become like an infatuated child and when you hate you feel you want to ruin the one you hate'.

Indeed, strong love or hate should never be the feelings entertained by adults. This is stressed by Islamic values. This *ḥadīth* sums up the point about allowing passions to be too strong and the need to tamper them with moderation and reason. Unless we do so, we would be like children when we love or wish ruin on the ones we do not. This is not a proper attitude for a Muslim.

***

May God accept my humble contribution to explaining Islamic manners and morality. May He grant peace and blessings to Prophet Muhammad who taught goodness to mankind.

Index

B

G

H

O

P